# Lecture Notes in Computer Science 11621

*Commenced Publication in 1973*
Founding and Former Series Editors:
Gerhard Goos, Juris Hartmanis, and Jan van Leeuwen

More information about this series at http://www.springer.com/series/7407

Sanjay Misra · Osvaldo Gervasi ·
Beniamino Murgante · Elena Stankova ·
Vladimir Korkhov · Carmelo Torre ·
Ana Maria A. C. Rocha ·
David Taniar · Bernady O. Apduhan ·
Eufemia Tarantino (Eds.)

# Computational Science and Its Applications – ICCSA 2019

19th International Conference
Saint Petersburg, Russia, July 1–4, 2019
Proceedings, Part III

 Springer

*Editors*
Sanjay Misra 
Covenant University
Ota, Nigeria

Beniamino Murgante 
University of Basilicata
Potenza, Italy

Vladimir Korkhov 
Saint Petersburg State University
Saint Petersburg, Russia

Ana Maria A. C. Rocha 
University of Minho
Braga, Portugal

Bernady O. Apduhan
Kyushu Sangyo University
Fukuoka, Japan

Osvaldo Gervasi 
University of Perugia
Perugia, Italy

Elena Stankova 
Saint Petersburg State University
Saint Petersburg, Russia

Carmelo Torre 
Polytechnic University of Bari
Bari, Italy

David Taniar 
Monash University
Clayton, VIC, Australia

Eufemia Tarantino 
Polytechnic University of Bari
Bari, Italy

ISSN 0302-9743 ISSN 1611-3349 (electronic)
Lecture Notes in Computer Science
ISBN 978-3-030-24301-2 ISBN 978-3-030-24302-9 (eBook)
https://doi.org/10.1007/978-3-030-24302-9

LNCS Sublibrary: SL1 – Theoretical Computer Science and General Issues

This Springer imprint is published by the registered company Springer Nature Switzerland AG
The registered company address is: Gewerbestrasse 11, 6330 Cham, Switzerland

# Preface

These six volumes (LNCS volumes 11619–11624) consist of the peer-reviewed papers from the 2019 International Conference on Computational Science and Its Applications (ICCSA 2019) held in St. Petersburg, Russia during July 1–4, 2019, in collaboration with the St. Petersburg University, St. Petersburg, Russia.

ICCSA 2019 was a successful event in the International Conferences on Computational Science and Its Applications (ICCSA) series, previously held in Melbourne, Australia (2018), Trieste, Italy (2017), Beijing, China (2016), Banff, Canada (2015), Guimaraes, Portugal (2014), Ho Chi Minh City, Vietnam (2013), Salvador, Brazil (2012), Santander, Spain (2011), Fukuoka, Japan (2010), Suwon, South Korea (2009), Perugia, Italy (2008), Kuala Lumpur, Malaysia (2007), Glasgow, UK (2006), Singapore (2005), Assisi, Italy (2004), Montreal, Canada (2003), and (as ICCS) Amsterdam, The Netherlands (2002) and San Francisco, USA (2001).

Computational science is a main pillar of most of the current research, industrial and commercial activities, and plays a unique role in exploiting ICT innovative technologies. The ICCSA conference series have been providing a venue to researchers and industry practitioners to discuss new ideas, to share complex problems and their solutions, and to shape new trends in computational science.

Apart from the general track, ICCSA 2019 also included 33 workshops, in various areas of computational sciences, ranging from computational science technologies, to specific areas of computational sciences, such as software engineering, security, artificial intelligence, and blockchain technologies. We accepted 64 papers distributed in the five general tracks, 259 in workshops and ten short papers. We would like to show our appreciations to the workshop chairs and co-chairs.

The success of the ICCSA conference series, in general, and ICCSA 2019, in particular, is due to the support of many people: authors, presenters, participants, keynote speakers, workshop chairs, Organizing Committee members, student volunteers, Program Committee members, Advisory Committee members, international liaison chairs, reviewers and people in other various roles. We would like to thank them all.

We also thank our publisher, Springer, for accepting to publish the proceedings, for sponsoring part of the best papers awards and for their kind assistance and cooperation during the editing process.

We cordially invite you to visit the ICCSA website http://www.iccsa.org where you can find all relevant information about this interesting and exciting event.

July 2019

Osvaldo Gervasi
Beniamino Murgante
Sanjay Misra

# Welcome to St. Petersburg

Welcome to St. Petersburg, the Venice of the North, the city of three revolutions, creation of czar Peter the Great, the most European city in Russia. ICCSA 2019 was hosted by St. Petersburg State University, during July 1–4, 2019.

St. Petersburg is the second largest city in Russia after Moscow. It is the former capital of Russia and has a lot of attractions related to this role in the past: imperial palaces and parks both in the city center and suburbs, respectable buildings of nobles and state institutions, multitude of rivers and canals with more than 300 bridges of various forms and sizes. Extraordinary history and rich cultural traditions of both imperial Russia and the Soviet Union attracted and inspired many examples of world's greatest architecture, literature, music, and visual art, some of which can be found in the famous Hermitage and State Russian Museum located in the heart of the city. Late June and early July is the season of white nights where the sun sets only for a few hours, and the nighttime is covered with mysterious twilight.

What to do in the city:

- Enjoy the white nights, see the open bridges during the night and cargo ships passing by from Ladoga Lake to the Gulf of Finland and back. Dvortsovy bridge is open at about 1am. Be sure to stay on the correct side of the river when the bridges open!
- Visit Hermitage (Winter palace) and State Russian Museum to see great examples of international and Russian art, and the Kunstkammer, the oldest museum of St. Petersburg founded by Peter the Great.
- Travel to St. Petersburg suburbs Peterhof and Tsarskoe Selo to see imperial palaces and splendid parks, famous Peterhof fountains.
- Eat Russian food: borsch (beetroot soup), pelmeni and vareniki (meat and sweet dumplings), bliny (pancakes), vinegret (beetroot salad), drink kvas and maybe some vodka.
- Walk around and inside the Peter and Paul Fortress, the place where the city began in 1703.
- Visit the Mariinsky Theater for famous Russian ballet and opera.
- Have a boat tour along the Neva River and canals to look at the city from the water.
- Walk along Nevsky Prospect, the main street of the city.
- Climb St. Isaac's Cathedral colonnade to enjoy great city views.
- Go down to the Metro, the city's underground train network with some Soviet-style museum-like stations.
- Pay a visit to the recently renovated Summer Garden, the oldest park of St. Petersburg.
- Visit a new modern open space on the New Holland Island to see modern art exhibitions, performances and just to relax and enjoy sitting on the grass with an ice cream or lemonade during a hot summer day.

St. Petersburg State University is the oldest university in Russia, an actively developing, world-class center of research and education. The university dates back to 1724, when Peter the Great founded the Academy of Sciences and Arts as well as the first Academic University and the university preparatory school in Russia. At present there are over 5,000 academic staff members and more than 30,000 students, receiving education in more than 400 educational programs at 25 faculties and institutes.

The venue of ICCSA is the Faculty of Economics located on Tavricheskaya Street, other faculties and university buildings are distributed all over the city with the main campus located on Vasilievsky Island and the natural science faculties (Mathematics and Mechanics, Applied Mathematics and Control Processes, Physics, Chemistry) located on the campus about 40 kilometers away from the city center in Peterhof.

Elena Stankova
Vladimir Korkhov
Nataliia Kulabukhova

# Organization

ICCSA 2019 was organized by St. Petersburg University (Russia), University of Perugia (Italy), University of Basilicata (Italy), Monash University (Australia), Kyushu Sangyo University (Japan), University of Minho, (Portugal).

## Honorary General Chairs

| | |
|---|---|
| Antonio Laganà | University of Perugia, Italy |
| Norio Shiratori | Tohoku University, Japan |
| Kenneth C. J. Tan | Sardina Systems, Estonia |

## General Chairs

| | |
|---|---|
| Osvaldo Gervasi | University of Perugia, Italy |
| Elena Stankova | St. Petersburg University, Russia |
| Bernady O. Apduhan | Kyushu Sangyo University, Japan |

## Program Committee Chairs

| | |
|---|---|
| Beniamino Murgante | University of Basilicata, Italy |
| David Taniar | Monash University, Australia |
| Vladimir Korkov | St. Petersburg University, Russia |
| Ana Maria A. C. Rocha | University of Minho, Portugal |

## International Advisory Committee

| | |
|---|---|
| Jemal Abawajy | Deakin University, Australia |
| Dharma P. Agarwal | University of Cincinnati, USA |
| Rajkumar Buyya | Melbourne University, Australia |
| Claudia Bauzer Medeiros | University of Campinas, Brazil |
| Manfred M. Fisher | Vienna University of Economics and Business, Austria |
| Marina L. Gavrilova | University of Calgary, Canada |
| Yee Leung | Chinese University of Hong Kong, SAR China |

## International Liaison Chairs

| | |
|---|---|
| Ana Carla P. Bitencourt | Universidade Federal do Reconcavo da Bahia, Brazil |
| Giuseppe Borruso | University of Trieste, Italy |
| Alfredo Cuzzocrea | ICAR-CNR and University of Calabria, Italy |
| Maria Irene Falcão | University of Minho, Portugal |
| Robert C. H. Hsu | Chung Hua University, Taiwan |
| Tai-Hoon Kim | Hannam University, South Korea |
| Sanjay Misra | Covenant University, Nigeria |

| | |
|---|---|
| Takashi Naka | Kyushu Sangyo University, Japan |
| Rafael D. C. Santos | National Institute for Space Research, Brazil |
| Maribel Yasmina Santos | University of Minho, Portugal |

## Workshop and Session Organizing Chairs

| | |
|---|---|
| Beniamino Murgante | University of Basilicata, Italy |
| Sanjay Misra | Covenant University, Nigeria |
| Jorge Gustavo Rocha | University of Minho, Portugal |

## Award Chair

| | |
|---|---|
| Wenny Rahayu | La Trobe University, Australia |

## Publicity Committee Chairs

| | |
|---|---|
| Elmer Dadios | De La Salle University, Philippines |
| Hong Quang Nguyen | International University (VNU-HCM), Vietnam |
| Daisuke Takahashi | Tsukuba University, Japan |
| Shangwang Wang | Beijing University of Posts and Telecommunications, China |

## Workshop Organizers

### Advanced Transport Tools and Methods (A2TM 2019)

| | |
|---|---|
| Massimiliano Petri | University of Pisa, Italy |
| Antonio Pratelli | University of Pisa, Italy |

### Advanced Computational Approaches in Fractals, Wavelet, Entropy and Data Mining Applications (AAFTWTETDT 2019)

| | |
|---|---|
| Yeliz Karaca | University of Massachusetts Medical School, USA |
| Yu-Dong Zhang | University of Leicester, UK |
| Majaz Moonis | University of Massachusettes Medical School, USA |

### Advances in Artificial Intelligence Learning Technologies: Blended Learning, STEM, Computational Thinking and Coding (AAILT 2019)

| | |
|---|---|
| Alfredo Milani | University of Perugia, Italy |
| Sergio Tasso | University of Perugia, Italy |
| Valentina Poggioni | University of Perugia, Italy |

### Affective Computing and Emotion Recognition (ACER-EMORE 2019)

| | |
|---|---|
| Alfredo Milani | University of Perugia, Italy |
| Valentina Franzoni | University of Perugia, Italy |
| Giulio Biondi | University of Florence, Itay |

**Advances in Information Systems and Technologies for Emergency Management, Risk Assessment and Mitigation Based on the Resilience Concepts (ASTER 2019)**

| | |
|---|---|
| Maurizio Pollino | ENEA, Italy |
| Marco Vona | University of Basilicata, Italy |
| Beniamino Murgante | University of Basilicata, Italy |

**Blockchain and Distributed Ledgers: Technologies and Application (BDLTA 2019)**

| | |
|---|---|
| Vladimir Korkhov | St. Petersburg State University, Russia |
| Elena Stankova | St. Petersburg State University, Russia |

**Bio and Neuro-inspired Computing and Applications (BIONCA 2019)**

| | |
|---|---|
| Nadia Nedjah | State University of Rio de Janeiro, Brazil |
| Luiza de Macedo Mourell | State University of Rio de Janeiro, Brazil |

**Computer Aided Modeling, Simulation, and Analysis (CAMSA 2018)**

| | |
|---|---|
| Jie Shen | University of Michigan, USA |
| Hao Chen | Shanghai University of Engineering Science, China |
| Youguo He | Jiangsu University, China |

**Computational and Applied Statistics (CAS 2019)**

| | |
|---|---|
| Ana Cristina Braga | University of Minho, Portugal |

**Computational Mathematics, Statistics, and Information Management (CMSIM 2019)**

| | |
|---|---|
| M. Filomena Teodoro | Portuguese Naval Academy and Lisbon University, Portugal |

**Computational Optimization and Applications (COA 2019)**

| | |
|---|---|
| Ana Maria Rocha | University of Minho, Portugal |
| Humberto Rocha | University of Coimbra, Portugal |

**Computational Astrochemistry (CompAstro 2019)**

| | |
|---|---|
| Marzio Rosi | University of Perugia, Italy |
| Dimitrios Skouteris | Master-up, Perugia, Italy |
| Fanny Vazart | Université Grenoble Alpes, France |
| Albert Rimola | Universitat Autònoma de Barcelona, Spain |

**Cities, Technologies, and Planning (CTP 2019)**

| | |
|---|---|
| Beniamino Murgante | University of Basilicata, Italy |
| Giuseppe Borruso | University of Trieste, Italy |

## Econometrics and Multidimensional Evaluation in the Urban Environment (EMEUE 2019)

| | |
|---|---|
| Carmelo M. Torre | Polytechnic of Bari, Italy |
| Pierluigi Morano | Polytechnic of Bari, Italy |
| Maria Cerreta | University of Naples Federico II, Italy |
| Paola Perchinunno | University of Bari, Italy |
| Francesco Tajani | University of Rome La Sapienza, Italy |

## Future Computing System Technologies and Applications (FISTA 2019)

| | |
|---|---|
| Bernady O. Apduhan | Kyushu Sangyo University, Japan |
| Rafael Santos | National Institute for Space Research, Brazil |

## Geographical Analysis, Urban Modeling, Spatial Statistics (GEO-AND-MOD 2019)

| | |
|---|---|
| Beniamino Murgante | University of Basilicata, Italy |
| Giuseppe Borruso | University of Trieste, Italy |
| Hartmut Asche | University of Potsdam, Germany |

## Geomatics for Resource Monitoring and Control (GRMC 2019)

| | |
|---|---|
| Eufemia Tarantino | Polytechnic of Bari, Italy |
| Rosa Lasaponara | Italian Research Council, IMAA-CNR, Italy |
| Benedetto Figorito | ARPA Puglia, Italy |
| Umberto Fratino | Polytechnic of Bari, Italy |

## International Symposium on Software Quality (ISSQ 2019)

| | |
|---|---|
| Sanjay Misra | Covenant University, Nigeria |

## Land Use Monitoring for Sustainability (LUMS 2019)

| | |
|---|---|
| Carmelo M. Torre | Polytechnic of Bari, Italy |
| Alessandro Bonifazi | Polytechnic of Bari, Italy |
| Pasquale Balena | Polytechnic of Bari, Italy |
| Beniamino Murgante | University of Basilicata, Italy |
| Eric Gielen | Polytechnic University of Valencia, Spain |

## Machine Learning for Space and Earth Observation Data (ML-SEOD 2019)

| | |
|---|---|
| Rafael Santos | Brazilian National Institute for Space Research, Brazil |
| Karine Reis Ferreira | National Institute for Space Research, Brazil |

## Mobile-Computing, Sensing, and Actuation in Cyber Physical Systems (MSA4CPS 2019)

| | |
|---|---|
| Saad Qaisar | National University of Sciences and Technology, Pakistan |
| Moonseong Kim | Seoul Theological University, South Korea |

**Quantum Chemical Modeling of Solids with Computers: From Plane Waves to Local Structures (QuaCheSol 2019)**

Andrei Tchougréeff           Russia Academy of Sciences, Russia
Richard Dronskowski         RWTH Aachen University, Germany
Taku Onishi                 Mie University and Tromsoe University, Japan

**Scientific Computing Infrastructure (SCI 2019)**

Vladimir Korkhov            St. Petersburg State University, Russia
Elena Stankova              St. Petersburg State University, Russia
Nataliia Kulabukhova        St. Petersburg State University, Russia

**Computational Studies for Energy and Comfort in Building (SECoB 2019)**

Senhorinha Teixeira         University of Minho, Portugal
Angela Silva                Viana do Castelo Polytechnic Institute, Portugal
Ana Maria Rocha             University of Minho, Portugal

**Software Engineering Processes and Applications (SEPA 2019)**

Sanjay Misra                Covenant University, Nigeria

**Smart Factory Convergence (SFC 2019)**

Jongpil Jeong               Sungkyunkwan University, South Korea

**Smart City and Water. Resource and Risk (Smart_Water 2019)**

Giuseppe Borruso            University of Trieste, Italy
Ginevra Balletto            University of Cagliari, Italy
Gianfranco Becciu           Polytechnic University of Milan, Italy
Chiara Garau                University of Cagliari, Italy
Beniamino Murgante          University of Basilicata, Italy
Francesco Viola             University of Cagliari, Italy

**Sustainability Performance Assessment: Models, Approaches, and Applications Toward Interdisciplinary and Integrated Solutions (SPA 2019)**

Francesco Scorza            University of Basilicata, Italy
Valentin Grecu              Lucia Blaga University on Sibiu, Romania
Jolanta Dvarioniene         Kaunas University, Lithuania
Sabrina Lai                 University of Cagliari, Italy

**Theoretical and Computational Chemistry and Its Applications (TCCMA 2019)**

Noelia Faginas Lago         University of Perugia, Italy
Andrea Lombardi             University of Perugia, Italy

**Tools and Techniques in Software Development Processes (TTSDP 2019)**

Sanjay Misra                Covenant University, Nigeria

### Virtual Reality and Applications (VRA 2019)

| | |
|---|---|
| Osvaldo Gervasi | University of Perugia, Italy |
| Sergio Tasso | University of Perugia, Italy |

### Collective, Massive and Evolutionary Systems (WCES 2019)

| | |
|---|---|
| Alfredo Milani | University of Perugia, Italy |
| Valentina Franzoni | University of Rome La Sapienza, Italy |
| Rajdeep Niyogi | Indian Institute of Technology at Roorkee, India |
| Stefano Marcugini | University of Perugia, Italy |

### Parallel and Distributed Data Mining (WPDM 2019)

| | |
|---|---|
| Massimo Cafaro | University of Salento, Italy |
| Italo Epicoco | University of Salento, Italy |
| Marco Pulimeno | University of Salento, Italy |
| Giovanni Aloisio | University of Salento, Italy |

## Program Committee

| | |
|---|---|
| Kenneth Adamson | University of Ulster, UK |
| Vera Afreixo | University of Aveiro, Portugal |
| Filipe Alvelos | University of Minho, Portugal |
| Remadevi Arjun | National Institute of Technology Karnataka, India |
| Hartmut Asche | University of Potsdam, Germany |
| Ginevra Balletto | University of Cagliari, Italy |
| Michela Bertolotto | University College Dublin, Ireland |
| Sandro Bimonte | CEMAGREF, TSCF, France |
| Rod Blais | University of Calgary, Canada |
| Ivan Blečić | University of Sassari, Italy |
| Giuseppe Borruso | University of Trieste, Italy |
| Ana Cristina Braga | University of Minho, Portugal |
| Massimo Cafaro | University of Salento, Italy |
| Yves Caniou | Lyon University, France |
| José A. Cardoso e Cunha | Universidade Nova de Lisboa, Portugal |
| Leocadio G. Casado | University of Almeria, Spain |
| Carlo Cattani | University of Salerno, Italy |
| Mete Celik | Erciyes University, Turkey |
| Hyunseung Choo | Sungkyunkwan University, South Korea |
| Min Young Chung | Sungkyunkwan University, South Korea |
| Florbela Maria da Cruz Domingues Correia | Polytechnic Institute of Viana do Castelo, Portugal |
| Gilberto Corso Pereira | Federal University of Bahia, Brazil |
| Alessandro Costantini | INFN, Italy |
| Carla Dal Sasso Freitas | Universidade Federal do Rio Grande do Sul, Brazil |
| Pradesh Debba | The Council for Scientific and Industrial Research (CSIR), South Africa |
| Hendrik Decker | Instituto Tecnológico de Informática, Spain |

| | |
|---|---|
| Frank Devai | London South Bank University, UK |
| Rodolphe Devillers | Memorial University of Newfoundland, Canada |
| Joana Matos Dias | University of Coimbra, Portugal |
| Paolino Di Felice | University of L'Aquila, Italy |
| Prabu Dorairaj | NetApp, India/USA |
| M. Irene Falcao | University of Minho, Portugal |
| Cherry Liu Fang | U.S. DOE Ames Laboratory, USA |
| Florbela P. Fernandes | Polytechnic Institute of Bragança, Portugal |
| Jose-Jesus Fernandez | National Centre for Biotechnology, CSIS, Spain |
| Paula Odete Fernandes | Polytechnic Institute of Bragança, Portugal |
| Adelaide de Fátima Baptista Valente Freitas | University of Aveiro, Portugal |
| Manuel Carlos Figueiredo | University of Minho, Portugal |
| Valentina Franzoni | University of Rome La Sapienza, Italy |
| Maria Celia Furtado Rocha | PRODEB–PósCultura/UFBA, Brazil |
| Chiara Garau | University of Cagliari, Italy |
| Paulino Jose Garcia Nieto | University of Oviedo, Spain |
| Jerome Gensel | LSR-IMAG, France |
| Maria Giaoutzi | National Technical University, Athens, Greece |
| Arminda Manuela Andrade Pereira Gonçalves | University of Minho, Portugal |
| Andrzej M. Goscinski | Deakin University, Australia |
| Sevin Gümgüm | Izmir University of Economics, Turkey |
| Alex Hagen-Zanker | University of Cambridge, UK |
| Shanmugasundaram Hariharan | B.S. Abdur Rahman University, India |
| Eligius M. T. Hendrix | University of Malaga/Wageningen University, Spain/The Netherlands |
| Hisamoto Hiyoshi | Gunma University, Japan |
| Mustafa Inceoglu | EGE University, Turkey |
| Jongpil Jeong | Sungkyunkwan University, South Korea |
| Peter Jimack | University of Leeds, UK |
| Qun Jin | Waseda University, Japan |
| A. S. M. Kayes | La Trobe University, Australia |
| Farid Karimipour | Vienna University of Technology, Austria |
| Baris Kazar | Oracle Corp., USA |
| Maulana Adhinugraha Kiki | Telkom University, Indonesia |
| DongSeong Kim | University of Canterbury, New Zealand |
| Taihoon Kim | Hannam University, South Korea |
| Ivana Kolingerova | University of West Bohemia, Czech Republic |
| Nataliia Kulabukhova | St. Petersburg University, Russia |
| Vladimir Korkhov | St. Petersburg University, Russia |
| Rosa Lasaponara | National Research Council, Italy |
| Maurizio Lazzari | National Research Council, Italy |
| Cheng Siong Lee | Monash University, Australia |
| Sangyoun Lee | Yonsei University, South Korea |

| | |
|---|---|
| Jongchan Lee | Kunsan National University, South Korea |
| Chendong Li | University of Connecticut, USA |
| Gang Li | Deakin University, Australia |
| Fang Liu | AMES Laboratories, USA |
| Xin Liu | University of Calgary, Canada |
| Andrea Lombardi | University of Perugia, Italy |
| Savino Longo | University of Bari, Italy |
| Tinghuai Ma | NanJing University of Information Science and Technology, China |
| Ernesto Marcheggiani | Katholieke Universiteit Leuven, Belgium |
| Antonino Marvuglia | Research Centre Henri Tudor, Luxembourg |
| Nicola Masini | National Research Council, Italy |
| Eric Medvet | University of Trieste, Italy |
| Nirvana Meratnia | University of Twente, The Netherlands |
| Noelia Faginas Lago | University of Perugia, Italy |
| Giuseppe Modica | University of Reggio Calabria, Italy |
| Josè Luis Montaña | University of Cantabria, Spain |
| Maria Filipa Mourão | IP from Viana do Castelo, Portugal |
| Louiza de Macedo Mourelle | State University of Rio de Janeiro, Brazil |
| Nadia Nedjah | State University of Rio de Janeiro, Brazil |
| Laszlo Neumann | University of Girona, Spain |
| Kok-Leong Ong | Deakin University, Australia |
| Belen Palop | Universidad de Valladolid, Spain |
| Marcin Paprzycki | Polish Academy of Sciences, Poland |
| Eric Pardede | La Trobe University, Australia |
| Kwangjin Park | Wonkwang University, South Korea |
| Ana Isabel Pereira | Polytechnic Institute of Bragança, Portugal |
| Massimiliano Petri | University of Pisa, Italy |
| Maurizio Pollino | Italian National Agency for New Technologies, Energy and Sustainable Economic Development, Italy |
| Alenka Poplin | University of Hamburg, Germany |
| Vidyasagar Potdar | Curtin University of Technology, Australia |
| David C. Prosperi | Florida Atlantic University, USA |
| Wenny Rahayu | La Trobe University, Australia |
| Jerzy Respondek | Silesian University of Technology Poland |
| Humberto Rocha | INESC-Coimbra, Portugal |
| Jon Rokne | University of Calgary, Canada |
| Octavio Roncero | CSIC, Spain |
| Maytham Safar | Kuwait University, Kuwait |
| Chiara Saracino | A.O. Ospedale Niguarda Ca' Granda - Milano, Italy |
| Haiduke Sarafian | The Pennsylvania State University, USA |
| Francesco Scorza | University of Basilicata, Italy |
| Marco Paulo Seabra dos Reis | University of Coimbra, Portugal |
| Jie Shen | University of Michigan, USA |

| | |
|---|---|
| Qi Shi | Liverpool John Moores University, UK |
| Dale Shires | U.S. Army Research Laboratory, USA |
| Inês Soares | University of Coimbra, Portugal |
| Elena Stankova | St. Petersburg University, Russia |
| Takuo Suganuma | Tohoku University, Japan |
| Eufemia Tarantino | Polytechnic of Bari, Italy |
| Sergio Tasso | University of Perugia, Italy |
| Ana Paula Teixeira | University of Trás-os-Montes and Alto Douro, Portugal |
| Senhorinha Teixeira | University of Minho, Portugal |
| M. Filomena Teodoro | Portuguese Naval Academy and University of Lisbon, Portugal |
| Parimala Thulasiraman | University of Manitoba, Canada |
| Carmelo Torre | Polytechnic of Bari, Italy |
| Javier Martinez Torres | Centro Universitario de la Defensa Zaragoza, Spain |
| Giuseppe A. Trunfio | University of Sassari, Italy |
| Pablo Vanegas | University of Cuenca, Equador |
| Marco Vizzari | University of Perugia, Italy |
| Varun Vohra | Merck Inc., USA |
| Koichi Wada | University of Tsukuba, Japan |
| Krzysztof Walkowiak | Wroclaw University of Technology, Poland |
| Zequn Wang | Intelligent Automation Inc., USA |
| Robert Weibel | University of Zurich, Switzerland |
| Frank Westad | Norwegian University of Science and Technology, Norway |
| Roland Wismüller | Universität Siegen, Germany |
| Mudasser Wyne | SOET National University, USA |
| Chung-Huang Yang | National Kaohsiung Normal University, Taiwan |
| Xin-She Yang | National Physical Laboratory, UK |
| Salim Zabir | France Telecom Japan Co., Japan |
| Haifeng Zhao | University of California, Davis, USA |
| Fabiana Zollo | University of Venice Cà Foscari, Italy |
| Albert Y. Zomaya | University of Sydney, Australia |

## Additional Reviewers

| | |
|---|---|
| Adewumi Oluwasegun | Covenant University, Nigeria |
| Afreixo Vera | University of Aveiro, Portugal |
| Agrawal Akshat | International Institute of Information Technology Bangalore, India |
| Aguilar Antonio | University of Barcelona, Spain |
| Ahmad Rashid | Microwave and Antenna Lab, School of Engineering, South Korea |
| Ahmed Waseem | Federal University of Technology, Nigeria |
| Alamri Sultan | Taibah University, Medina, Saudi Arabia |
| Alfa Abraham | Kogi State College of Education, Nigeria |
| Alvelos Filipe | University of Minho, Portugal |

| | |
|---|---|
| Dereli Dursun Ahu | UNSW Sydney, Australia |
| Devai Frank | London South Bank University, UK |
| Di Bari Gabriele | University of Florence, Italy |
| Dias Joana | University of Coimbra, Portugal |
| Diaz Diana | National University of Colombia, Colombia |
| Elfadaly Abdelaziz | University of Basilicata, Italy |
| Enriquez Palma Pedro Alberto | Universidad de la Rioja, Spain |
| Epicoco Italo | University of Salento, Italy |
| Esposito Giuseppina | Sapienza University of Rome, Italy |
| Faginas-Lago M. Noelia | University of Perugia, Italy |
| Fajardo Jorge | Universidad Politécnica Salesiana (UPS), Ecuador |
| Falcinelli Stefano | University of Perugia, Italy |
| Farina Alessandro | University of Pisa, Italy |
| Fattoruso Grazia | ENEA, Italy |
| Fernandes Florbela | Escola Superior de Tecnologia e Gestão de Bragancca, Portugal |
| Fernandes Paula | Escola Superior de Tecnologia e Gestão, Portugal |
| Fernández Ledesma Javier Darío | Universidad Pontificia Bolivariana, Bolivia |
| Ferreira Ana C. | University of Lisbon, Portugal |
| Ferrão Maria | Universidade da Beira Interior, Portugal |
| Figueiredo Manuel Carlos | Universidade do Minho, Portugal |
| Florez Hector | Universidad Distrital Francisco Jose de Caldas, Colombia |
| Franzoni Valentina | University of Perugia, Italy |
| Freitau Adelaide de Fátima Baptista Valente | University of Aveiro, Portugal |
| Friday Agbo | University of Eastern Finland, Finland |
| Frunzete Madalin | Polytechnic University of Bucharest, Romania |
| Fusco Giovanni | Laboratoire ESPACE, CNRS, France |
| Gabrani Goldie | Bml Munjal University, India |
| Gankevich Ivan | St. Petersburg State University, Russia |
| Garau Chiara | University of Cagliari, Italy |
| Garcia Ernesto | University of the Basque Country, Spain |
| Gavrilova Marina | University of Calgary, Canada |
| Gervasi Osvaldo | University of Perugia, Italy |
| Gilner Ewa | Silesian University of Technology, Poland |
| Gioia Andrea | University of Bari, Italy |
| Giorgi Giacomo | University of Perugia, Italy |
| Gonçalves Arminda Manuela | University of Minho, Portugal |
| Gorbachev Yuriy | Geolink Technologies, Russia |
| Gotoh Yusuke | Kyoto University, Japan |
| Goyal Rinkaj | Guru Gobind Singh Indraprastha University, India |
| Gümgüm Sevin | Izmir Economy University, Turkey |

| | |
|---|---|
| Gülen Kemal Güven | Istanbul Ticaret University, Turkey |
| Hegedus Peter | University of Szeged, Hungary |
| Hendrix Eligius M. T. | University of Malaga, Spain |
| Iacobellis Vito | Polytechnic of Bari, Italy |
| Iakushkin Oleg | St. Petersburg State University, Russia |
| Kadry Seifedine | Beirut Arab University, Lebanon |
| Kim JeongAh | George Fox University, USA |
| Kim Moonseong | Korean Intellectual Property Office, South Korea |
| Kolingerova Ivana | University of West Bohemia, Czech Republic |
| Koo Jahwan | Sungkyunkwan University, South Korea |
| Korkhov Vladimir | St. Petersburg State University, Russia |
| Kulabukhova Nataliia | St. Peterburg State University, Russia |
| Ladu Mara | University of Cagliari, Italy |
| Laganà Antonio | Master-up srl, Italy |
| Leon Marcelo | Universidad Estatal Peninsula de Santa Elena – UPSE, Ecuador |
| Lima Rui | University of Minho, Portugal |
| Lombardi Andrea | University of Perugia, Italy |
| Longo Savino | University of Bari, Italy |
| Maciel de Castro Jessica | Universidade Federal da Paraíba, Brazil |
| Magni Riccardo | Pragma Engineering S.r.L., Italy |
| Mandanici Emanuele | University of Bologna, Italy |
| Mangiameli Michele | University of Catania, Italy |
| Marcellini Moreno | Ecole normale supérieure de Lyon, France |
| Marghany Maged | Universiti Teknologi Malaysia, Malaysia |
| Marques Jorge | Universidade de Coimbra, Portugal |
| Martellozzo Federico | University of Florence, Italy |
| Mengoni Paolo | University of Florence, Italy |
| Migliore Marco | University of Cassino e del Lazio Meridionale, Italy |
| Milani Alfredo | University of Perugia, Italy |
| Milesi Alessandra | Istituto Auxologico Italiano, Italy |
| Mishra Biswajeeban | University of Szeged, Hungary |
| Molaei Qelichi Mohamad | University of Tehran, Iran |
| Monteiro Vitor | University of Minho, Portugal |
| Moraes João Luís Cardoso | University of Porto, Portugal |
| Moura Ricardo | Universidade Nova de Lisboa, Portugal |
| Mourao Maria | Universidade do Minho, Portugal |
| Murgante Beniamino | University of Basilicata, Italy |
| Natário Isabel Cristina Maciel | Universidade Nova de Lisboa, Portugal |
| Nedjah Nadia | Rio de Janeiro State University, Brazil |
| Nocera Silvio | University of Naples Federico II, Italy |
| Odun-Ayo Isaac | Covenant University, Nigeria |
| Okewu Emmanuel | University of Lagos, Nigeria |
| Oliveira Irene | University of Trás-Os-Montes e Alto Douro, Portugal |
| Oluranti Jonathan | Covenant University, Nigeria |

| | |
|---|---|
| Osho Oluwafemi | Federal University of Technology Minna, Nigeria |
| Ozturk Savas | The Scientific and Technological Research Council of Turkey, Turkey |
| Panetta J. B. | University of Georgia, USA |
| Pardede Eric | La Trobe University, Australia |
| Perchinunno Paola | University of Bari, Italy |
| Pereira Ana | Instituto Politécnico de Bragança, Portugal |
| Peschechera Giuseppe | University of Bari, Italy |
| Petri Massimiliano | University of Pisa, Italy |
| Petrovic Marjana | University of Zagreb, Croatia |
| Pham Quoc Trung | Ho Chi Minh City University of Technology, Vietnam |
| Pinto Telmo | University of Minho, Portugal |
| Plekhanov Evgeny | Russian Academy of Economics, Russia |
| Poggioni Valentina | University of Perugia, Italy |
| Polidoro Maria João | University of Lisbon, Portugal |
| Pollino Maurizio | ENEA, Italy |
| Popoola Segun | Covenant University, Nigeria |
| Pratelli Antonio | University of Pisa, Italy |
| Pulimeno Marco | University of Salento, Italy |
| Rasool Hamid | National University of Sciences and Technology, Pakistan |
| Reis Marco | Universidade de Coimbra, Portugal |
| Respondek Jerzy | Silesian University of Technology, Poland |
| Riaz Nida | National University of Sciences and Technology, Pakistan |
| Rimola Albert | Autonomous University of Barcelona, Spain |
| Rocha Ana Maria | University of Minho, Portugal |
| Rocha Humberto | University of Coimbra, Portugal |
| Rosi Marzio | University of Perugia, Italy |
| Santos Rafael | National Institute for Space Research, Brazil |
| Santucci Valentino | University Stranieri of Perugia, Italy |
| Saponaro Mirko | Polytechnic of Bari, Italy |
| Sarafian Haiduke | Pennsylvania State University, USA |
| Scorza Francesco | University of Basilicata, Italy |
| Sedova Olya | St. Petersburg State University, Russia |
| Semanjski Ivana | Ghent University, Belgium |
| Sharma Jeetu | Mody University of Science and Technology, India |
| Sharma Purnima | University of Lucknow, India |
| Shchegoleva Nadezhda | Petersburg State Electrotechnical University, Russia |
| Shen Jie | University of Michigan, USA |
| Shoaib Muhammad | Sungkyunkwan University, South Korea |
| Shou Huahao | Zhejiang University of Technology, China |
| Silva-Fortes Carina | ESTeSL-IPL, Portugal |
| Silva Ângela Maria | Escola Superior de Ciências Empresariais, Portugal |
| Singh Upasana | The University of Manchester, UK |
| Singh V. B. | University of Delhi, India |

| Skouteris Dimitrios | Master-up, Perugia, Italy |
|---|---|
| Soares Inês | INESCC and IPATIMUP, Portugal |
| Soares Michel | Universidade Federal de Sergipe, Brazil |
| Sosnin Petr | Ulyanovsk State Technical University, Russia |
| Sousa Ines | University of Minho, Portugal |
| Stankova Elena | St. Petersburg State University, Russia |
| Stritih Uros | University of Ljubljana, Slovenia |
| Tanaka Kazuaki | Kyushu Institute of Technology, Japan |
| Tarantino Eufemia | Polytechnic of Bari, Italy |
| Tasso Sergio | University of Perugia, Italy |
| Teixeira Senhorinha | University of Minho, Portugal |
| Tengku Adil | La Trobe University, Australia |
| Teodoro M. Filomena | Lisbon University, Portugal |
| Torre Carmelo Maria | Polytechnic of Bari, Italy |
| Totaro Vincenzo | Polytechnic of Bari, Italy |
| Tripathi Aprna | GLA University, India |
| Vancsics Béla | University of Szeged, Hungary |
| Vasyunin Dmitry | University of Amsterdam, The Netherlands |
| Vig Rekha | The Northcap University, India |
| Walkowiak Krzysztof | Wroclaw University of Technology, Poland |
| Wanderley Fernando | New University of Lisbon, Portugal |
| Wang Chao | University of Science and Technology of China, China |
| Westad Frank | CAMO Software AS, USA |
| Yamazaki Takeshi | University of Tokyo, Japan |
| Zahra Noore | University of Guilan, India |
| Zollo Fabiana | University of Venice Ca' Foscari, Italy |
| Zullo Francesco | University of L'Aquila, Italy |
| Žemlička Michal | Charles University in Prague, Czech Republic |
| Živković Ljiljana | Republic Agency for Spatial Planning, Serbia |

# Sponsoring Organizations

ICCSA 2019 would not have been possible without tremendous support of many organizations and institutions, for which all organizers and participants of ICCSA 2019 express their sincere gratitude:

Springer Nature Switzerland AG, Germany
(http://www.springer.com)

St. Petersburg University, Russia
(http://english.spbu.ru/)

University of Perugia, Italy
(http://www.unipg.it)

University of Basilicata, Italy
(http://www.unibas.it)

Monash University, Australia
(http://monash.edu)

Kyushu Sangyo University, Japan
(www.kyusan-u.ac.jp)

Universidade do Minho, Portugal
(http://www.uminho.pt)

# Contents – Part III

## Computational Optimization and Applications (COA 2019)

## Computational Astrochemistry (CompAstro 2019)

## Cities, Technologies and Planning (CTP 2019)

## Future Computing System Technologies and Applications (FISTA 2019)

## Geographical Analysis, Urban Modeling, Spatial Statistics (GEO-AND-MOD 2019)

# Computational and Applied Statistics
## (CAS 2019)

# Application of DOE for the Study of a Multiple Jet Impingement System

Flávia V. Barbosa[1][✉], Sérgio D. T. Sousa[2],
Senhorinha F. C. F. Teixeira[2], and José C. F. Teixeira[1]

[1] MEtRICs I&D Centre, School of Engineering, University of Minho,
Guimarães, Portugal
flaviab@dem.uminho.pt
[2] ALGORITMI I&D Centre, School of Engineering, University of Minho,
Guimarães, Portugal

**Abstract.** Jet impingement is widely implemented in a variety of engineering applications and industrial processes where high average heat transfer coefficients and the uniformity of the heat transfer over the impinging surface are required to enhance the process and to avoid local hot (or cold) spots. Multiple jet impingement involves several parameters that interfere with the performance of the process, and there are no universal optimal solutions. To ensure the optimization of the process, it is important to understand the influence of these parameters in the heat transfer over the target surface. To perform this study an experimental research will be performed on a purpose-built test facility which has been commissioned, using a Particle Image Velocimetry system. However, to reduce time and costs associated to the experimental tests, it is important to perform a Design of Experiments, that allows to reduce the number of trials, focusing on the parameters that have a greater influence on the process performance. Taguchi's method allows the optimization of the process through the selection of the most suitable parameters values. This work presents the method that must be followed before the development of experiments related to the multiple jet impingement over a complex surface, from the design of the experimental setup to the design of the matrix of experiments.

**Keywords:** DOE · Jet impingement · Heat transfer

## 1 Introduction

Multiple jet impingement is a technology widely implemented in several applications since it provides high average heat transfer coefficients and enhance the uniformity of the heat transfer over the target surface [1]. To enhance this process, studies have been performed to increase the heat transfer over the impinging surface. The analysis of the influence of the process variables on jet impingement efficiency have been focused on: jets pattern [2], jet-to-jet spacing [3], nozzle-to-plate distance [4], nozzle shape [5–7], jet inclination [8], Reynolds number [2], [9–12], jet temperature [7] and target surface geometry [13, 14].

© Springer Nature Switzerland AG 2019
S. Misra et al. (Eds.): ICCSA 2019, LNCS 11621, pp. 3–11, 2019.
https://doi.org/10.1007/978-3-030-24302-9_1

As the multiple jet impingement process involves several variables, the study of all of them, each one with different levels, would result in a great number of combinations to be analyzed (for example 7 factors each one with three levels result in $3^7 = 2187$ different combinations). However, some of them are more relevant than others depending on the application. To reduce the number of experiments, it is fundamental to select the ones that have a higher influence on the heat transfer performance. In that sense, a Design of Experiment (DoE) methodology will be applied in this study. DoE has been used in several industries to improve the process performance, enhancing the process yield and to decrease the process variability [15]. One of the techniques widely applied in engineering design is the Taguchi's method. According to Karna and Sahai [16], the engineers adhered to this method since it applies parameter design, an engineering technique for product or process design which focuses on the determination of parameters (factors) producing the best levels of a quality characteristic (performance measure) with minimum variation. To determine the best design, Taguchi's method applies a DoE that expose the process to various levels of design parameters previously defined, without testing all the combinations, and thus reducing the total number of experiments [16]. In jet impingement studies, this DoE method was implemented by Lau et al. [17] as a tool to perform an optimization of the thermal stress of a solder joint and cooling rate of a ball grid array package. Other works [18–20] also applied Taguchi techniques to study specific problems of heat transfer in jet impinging a surface.

Considering the advantages of the application of Taguchi's method in DoE, it will be applied in this study. The aim of this paper is to develop the methodology for the study of multiple jet impingement over a non-flat plate. This work presents the design and construction of a purposed-build setup for the analysis of the influence of the target surface geometry and jet flow dynamic parameters on the heat transfer performance. Taguchi's method will be applied as a tool to identify the parameters that enhance the multiple jet impingement to optimize the process. It is not the aim of this paper to present experimental results regarding the heat transfer, in contrast, it is expected to be relevant for researchers that intend to start studies in this field.

## 2  Experimental Apparatus

### 2.1  Experimental Setup

The experimental apparatus was specially designed and constructed for the study of the flow field of multiple jets impinging on a target surface. The 3D-model performed using the *SolidWorks*™ software is presented in Fig. 1. The aim of this apparatus is to reproduce with accuracy the reflow soldering process. This setup is flexible to allow to change the test conditions and process variables easily and to ensure the measurement of the flow field through Particle Image Velocimetry (PIV) technique. PIV method consist on the illumination of the measurement zone through a laser and the capture of the images through a camera positioned perpendicularly to the laser. These images allow the velocity field measurement of the airflow. In that sense, the walls of the test chamber (1) must have two transparent surfaces positioned perpendicularly, represented in Fig. 1, by the numbers (2) and (3). The air is blown by a centrifugal fan (4) and flows through a nozzle plate (5), generating jets. Since the study will focus on the heating process, the air is heated by heaters positioned at the bottom of the oven (6). One of the critical aspects related to the jet impingement process is the uniformity of the heating, being extremely difficult to achieve. In order to stabilize the flow, ensuring a uniform heating over the target surface (7), a plenum (8) was created before the test chamber and a honeycomb structure (10) was applied in order to distribute the flow. To minimize the turbulence, a metallic mesh was introduced before the honeycomb structure (11). After impinging the surface, the air flows through another mesh (12) and re-enters inside the fan, since the setup is a closed loop. This oven has several characteristics which make it suitable for the development of different experimental tests. It is equipped by a frequency controller which is connected to the fan to increase or decrease the air velocity. The nozzle plate can be easily changed by another plate with different configuration and nozzle diameter, and the support base of the target surface can be positioned at different distance from the nozzle plate.

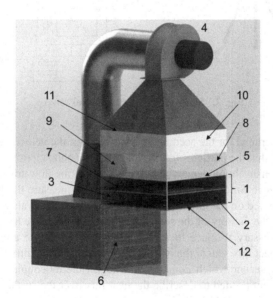

**Fig. 1.** Oven for experimental tests.

## 2.2   Procedure

The study of the flow field behaviour and its complex interaction with the target surface will be performed using a 2D-PIV system allowing the measurement of instantaneous velocity fields of a fluid flow through the image analysis of marker particles [21]. A double pulse laser illuminates a two dimensional plan across a seeded flow in two short pulses and a CCD camera records the images of the flow field [22]. In this study, the laser applied is a DualPower laser which emits two independently controlled beams with a pulse energy of 145 mJ at a wavelength of 532 nm, positioned at an angle of 90°

with the CCD camera, as shown by Fig. 2. The camera has a pixel size of 6.5 µm and a pixel resolution of 2560 × 2160 (5.5 Megapixel). The data acquisition and processing of the images is performed by the software Dynamic Studio.

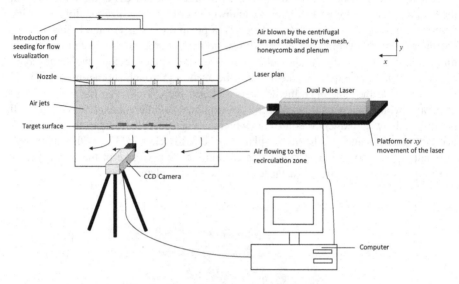

**Fig. 2.** Scheme of the experimental setup.

The seeding is crucial for the accurate measurement of the velocity field of the flow, being fundamental that the particles follows the instantaneous motion of the air [23]. In this study, high density homogeneous smoke was used for flow tracking, being generated by an Aerotech Smoke Generator. In addition, to measure the heat flow, a flux sensor will be mounted on the target surface. Thermocouples will also be placed on the impinging plate in the vicinity of the sensor to measure the surface temperature locally. It will also be necessary to place thermocouples near the nozzle exit to monitor the temperature. The heat flux sensor that will be applied for the heat flux measurement is a thin-film heat flux sensor which contains an integral thermocouple for discrete temperature measurement needed to describe the heat flux over the surface. The difference in temperature across thermal barrier is proportional to the heat flow through the sensor.

Before starting the experiments, it is important to identify the variables and to choose the ones that have a higher impact on the heat transfer over the target surface to develop a plan of the experimental tests that must be performed. After the selection of the process variables, a DoE must be implemented to focus the experiments on the most relevant variables, discarding the ones that have a low effect. To perform a simple and low-cost DoE, the Taguchi's method is implemented in this study.

# 3 Design of Experiments

The analysis of the influence of each variable in the heat transfer, as well as the interaction between them, is a great challenge. Proceeding to a careful analysis, the following 14 variables were identified in the literature review: jet pattern; jet-to-jet spacing; nozzle shape; nozzle-to-plate distance; jet inclination; target surface geometry; target surface inclination; target surface motion; nozzle plate motion; crossflow; jet temperature; Reynolds number; Prandtl number; Mach number. If for each variable, 2 values (or levels) are tested, the number of possible different combinations rises up to $2^{14} = 16384$ experiments (if a full factorial method is applied). Considering that, conclusions should not be drawn based on a single evidence, each experiment should be repeated increasing the total number of experiments. This is impracticable in laboratory, or in industry, which could be considered an unjustified waste of time and resources.

The Taguchi's method consists of three main stages: system design, parameter design and tolerance design [24]. Considering the aim of this work, it seems that the parameter design approach is the most suitable to perform the DoE, since it is intended to select the best combination of control factors in order to optimize the process and increase its robustness towards the noise factors [25]. While control factors are employed to select the best conditions for stability in design of manufacturing process, the noise factors are related to the factors that cause variations in the process [20]. The use of this approach requires the application of a fractional factorial [26], which are displayed in standard tables known as orthogonal arrays (OA).

To perform a DoE based on Taguchi's approach, the following steps need to be conducted [25]: (1) Determination of the quality characteristic to be optimized; (2) Identification of the noise factors and test conditions; (3) Identification of the control factors and their levels; (4) Design of the matrix experiment and definition of the data analysis procedure; (5) Conduct the matrix experiment; (6) Data analysis and determination of the optimum levels for control factors; (7) Prediction of the performance at these levels. This work focuses on the steps (1) to (4).

## 3.1 Quality Characteristic, Noise Factor and Test Conditions

The aim of this study consists on the analysis of the influence of several process parameters on the heat transfer over a complex target surface. In that sense, according to Taguchi's method, heat transfer is the quality characteristic to be optimized. To calculate the deviation between the experimental values and the desired ones, Taguchi used a loss function which is transformed into a signal-to-noise ratio (SN) [20]. Considering the jet impingement process the "larger the better" [27] was selected since it is expected to obtain the maximum heat transfer over the target surface, being evaluated by Eq. (1).

$$SN = -10 \log \left( \frac{1}{n} \sum\nolimits_{i=1}^{n} \frac{1}{Y_i^2} \right) \tag{1}$$

Where SN indicates the signal to noise ratio (for each test or combination given by a matrix row), $n$ is the number of repetitions of each combination, $Y_i$ is the quality characteristic measured in each test [28].

The experiments will be conducted at an air temperature of 150 °C and a velocity of 10 m/s at the exit of the nozzles. The target surface will be introduced inside the oven at an ambient temperature which can vary in function of the day of the year. This is a noise factor, since it is an uncontrollable parameter that can interfere with the performance of the system. Thus, half of the repetitions of each test should be made with the target surface at low temperature and the other half with higher temperature.

## 3.2   Control Factors and Levels

The factors selected need to be the ones that influence the process, and for each one the number of levels (values that a factor assumes when applied in an experiment) need to be defined. Considering the number of variables registered in multiple jet impingement, traduced as factors in DoE method, it is important to limit the number of levels, in order to analyze the effect of the parameters with the minimum number of experiments.

Considering the information presented in the state of the art, and to reduce the number of experiments, it is possible to exclude the variables that, in one hand, have minimal effects in heat transfer and, on the other hand, the ones that present just one significant value/configuration. This is the case of the nozzle shape factor, since the circular shape was considered the one that enhance the heat transfer over the target surface. Due to the limitations of the experimental setup, the Prandtl and Mach numbers, target surface inclination and motion, nozzle plate motion, crossflow and jet temperature will also be discarded, reducing the study to 6 parameters. The variables relevant to the process are defined by Taguchi's as control factors, and the values that need to be tested (levels), are summarized in Table 1. These values were selected based on literature review and expert's opinions. If Taguchi's method was not applied, the total amount of experiments would rise to up to $2^4 \times 4^2 = 256$ experiments. In addition, Table 1 also includes the degrees of freedom (DoF) of each factor, which is equal to the number of levels minus one, being relevant to select the appropriate OA.

**Table 1.** Selected factors and their levels.

| Control factor | Level | | | | DoF |
|---|---|---|---|---|---|
| | 1 | 2 | 3 | 4 | |
| Jet-to-jet spacing, $S_x = S_y$ (A) | 2D | 3D | 5D | 6D | 3 |
| Nozzle-to-plate distance (B) | 2D | 3D | 5D | 7D | 3 |
| Jet pattern (C) | Inline | Staggered | | | 1 |
| Jet inclination (D) | 20° | 0° | - | - | 1 |
| Plate geometry (E) | Flat | Non-Flat | - | - | 1 |
| Reynolds number (F) | 2000 | 1000 | - | - | 1 |

### 3.3  Selection of the Orthogonal Array

According to Table 1, ten degrees of freedom are identified. Proceeding to the analysis of the OA presented by the Taguchi's model, the $L_{16}$ seems to be the most appropriate OA, since it allows a mix between 2 and 4 levels. In that sense, the array was generated by Minitab™ [19]. As it can be observed through Table 2, a total of 16 experiments need to be performed. As mentioned by [28], trials should be repeated. Considering that the analysis of the influence of the noise factor must also be analyzed, three repetitions will be performed in each test, one with the target plate at cold ($\approx$10°C), medium ($\approx$20 °C) and hot temperature ($\approx$30 °C). The design of the experiments is presented by the OA (Table 2). To obtain the optimal process parameters configuration, the results obtained must be analyzed using the signal-to-noise ratio (*SN*) presented above, which represents the ratio between the mean (signal) and the standard deviation (noise) [25]. The *SN* of each parameter are compared and the parameter value that influence the most the quality characteristic is determined. From this analysis, an optimization of the quality characteristic must be performed.

**Table 2.**  Design orthogonal array generated using Minitab.

| Trials n° | A | B | C | D | E | F |
|-----------|-----|-----|--------|------|----------|------|
| 1 | 2D | 2D | Inline | 0° | Flat | 1500 |
| 2 | 2D | 3D | Inline | 0° | Flat | 5000 |
| 3 | 2D | 5D | Stag. | 20° | Non-Flat | 1500 |
| 4 | 2D | 7D | Stag. | 20° | Non-Flat | 5000 |
| 5 | 3D | 2D | Inline | 20° | Non-Flat | 1500 |
| 6 | 3D | 3D | Inline | 20° | Non-Flat | 5000 |
| 7 | 3D | 5D | Stag. | 0° | Flat | 1500 |
| 8 | 3D | 7D | Stag. | 0° | Flat | 5000 |
| 9 | 5D | 2D | Stag. | 0° | Non-Flat | 5000 |
| 10 | 5D | 3D | Stag. | 0° | Non-Flat | 1500 |
| 11 | 5D | 5D | Inline | 20° | Flat | 5000 |
| 12 | 5D | 7D | Inline | 20° | Flat | 1500 |
| 13 | 6D | 2D | Stag. | 20° | Flat | 5000 |
| 14 | 6D | 3D | Stag. | 20° | Flat | 1500 |
| 15 | 6D | 5D | Inline | 0° | Non-Flat | 5000 |
| 16 | 6D | 7D | Inline | 0° | Non-Flat | 1500 |

## 4  Conclusions

This work presents an experimental setup that will be used for the development of experiments that aim to study the heat transfer of multiple jets impinging over a target surface. Through this study, it is expected to fully understand the influence of the process variables on the heat transfer performance of a multiple jet impingement process. This work presents the variables that interfere with the process and the values, cited in the literature, that enhance the heat transfer. Through this state of the art, it was easier to understand which are the process variables that have more influence on the quality characteristic and which are the range of values that improve the performance of the system. This information was used to develop a design of experiment using the Taguchi's method. The construction of an OA was fundamental to define the experiments that must be conducted throughout the study. This work summarizes the steps that will be conducted before the development of experiments, focusing on the most relevant parameters, minimizing the time and costs. In that sense, it can be an added value for all the researchers that pretends to start their studies in the multiple jet impingement field.

**Acknowledgments.** The first author would like to express her gratitude for the support given by the Portuguese Foundation for Science and Technology (FCT) and the MIT Portugal Program. This work has been supported by FCT within the Project Scope UID/CEC/00319/2019 (ALGORITMI Center) and Project Scope UID/EMS/04077/2019 (METRICS Center).

# References

1. Can, M., Etemoglu, A.B., Avci, A.: Experimental study of convective heat transfer under arrays of impinging air jets from slots and circular holes. Heat Mass Transf. und Stoffuebertragung **38**(3), 251–259 (2002)
2. Florschuetz, L.W., Metzger, D.E., Truman, C.R.: Streamwise flow and heat transfer distributions for jet array impingement with crossflow. ASME Gas Turbine Div. **3**(Jan), 1–10 (1981)
3. Yong, S., Zhang, J.Z., Xie, G.N.: Convective heat transfer for multiple rows of impinging air jets with small jet-to-jet spacing in a semi-confined channel. Int. J. Heat Mass Transf. **86**, 832–842 (2015)
4. Lee, J., Lee, S.J.: The effect of nozzle configuration on stagnation region heat transfer enhancement of axisymmetric jet impingement. Int. J. Heat Mass Transf. **43**(18), 3497–3509 (2000)
5. Dano, B.P.E., Liburdy, J.A., Kanokjaruvijit, K.: Flow characteristics and heat transfer performances of a semi-confined impinging array of jets: effect of nozzle geometry. Int. J. Heat Mass Transf. **48**, 691–701 (2005)
6. Reodikar, S.A., Meena, H.C., Vinze, R., Prabhu, S.V.: Influence of the orifice shape on the local heat transfer distribution and axis switching by compressible jets impinging on flat surface. Int. J. Therm. Sci. **104**, 208–224 (2016)
7. Vinze, R., Chandel, S., Limaye, M.D., Prabhu, S.V.: Influence of jet temperature and nozzle shape on the heat transfer distribution between a smooth plate and impinging air jets. Int. J. Therm. Sci. **99**, 136–151 (2016)
8. Attalla, M., Maghrabie, H.M., Specht, E.: Effect of inclination angle of a pair of air jets on heat transfer into the flat surface. Exp. Therm. Fluid Sci. **85**, 85–94 (2017)
9. Caliskan, S., Baskaya, S., Calisir, T.: Experimental and numerical investigation of geometry effects on multiple impinging air jets. Int. J. Heat Mass Transf. **75**, 685–703 (2014)
10. Metzger, D.E., Florschuetz, L.W., Takeuchi, D.I., Behee, R.D., Berry, R.A.: Heat transfer characteristics for inline and staggered arrays of circular jets with crossflow of spent air. J. Heat Transf. **101**, 526–531 (1979)

11. Xing, Y., Spring, S., Weigand, B.: Experimental and numerical investigation of heat transfer characteristics of inline and staggered arrays of impinging jets. J. Heat Transf. **132**(9), 092201 (2010)
12. Li, W., Li, X., Ren, J., Jiang, H., Yang, L.: Effect of reynolds number, hole patterns, target plate thickness on cooling performance of an impinging jet array: part II—Conjugate heat transfer results and optimization. Vol. 5B Heat Transf. **139**(April), V05BT16A009 (2016)
13. Andrews, G.E., Abdul Hussain, R., Mkpadi, M.C.: Enhanced impingement heat transfer : Comparison of co-flow and cross-flow with rib turbulators. In: Proceedings of International Gas Turbine Congress, Tokyo, Japan, IGTC 2003, Tokyo TS-075 (2003)
14. Caliskan, S., Baskaya, S.: Experimental investigation of impinging jet array heat transfer from a surface with V-shaped and convergent-divergent ribs. Int. J. Therm. Sci. **59**, 234–246 (2012)
15. Zahraee, S.M.: Teaching the Design of Experiment and Response Surface Methodology Using Paper Helicopter Experiment, no. April (2013)
16. Karna, S.K., Sahai, R.: An overview on Taguchi method. J. Eng. Math. Sci. **1**, 11–18 (2012)
17. Lau, C.S., Abdullah, M.Z., Ani, F.C.: Optimization modeling of the cooling stage of reflow soldering process for ball grid array package using the gray-based Taguchi method. Microelectron. Reliab. **52**(6), 1143–1152 (2012)
18. Chandramohan, P., Murugesan, S.N., Arivazhagan, S.: Heat transfer analysis of flat plate subjected to multi-jet air impingement using principal component analysis and computational technique. J. Appl. Fluid Mech. **10**(1), 293–306 (2017)
19. Caliskan, S., Nasiri Khalaji, M., Baskaya, S., Kotcioglu, I.: Design analysis of impinging jet array heat transfer from a surface with V-shaped and convergent-divergent ribs by the Taguchi method. Heat Transf. Eng. **37**(15), 1252–1266 (2016)
20. Celik, N., Turgut, E.: Design analysis of an experimental jet impingement study by using Taguchi method. Heat Mass Transf. **48**(8), 1407–1413 (2012)
21. Keane, R.D., Adrian, R.J.: Theory of cross-correlation analysis of PIV images. Appl. Sci. Res. **49**(3), 191–215 (1992)
22. O'Donovan, T.: Fluid Flow and Heat Transfer of an Impinging Air Jet, University of Dublin (2005)
23. Melling, A.: Tracer particles and seeding for particle image velocimetry. Meas. Sci. Technol. **8**, 1406–1416 (1997)
24. Chamoli, S.: A Taguchi approach for optimization of flow and geometrical parameters in a rectangular channel roughened with V down perforated baffles. Case Stud. Therm. Eng. **5**, 59–69 (2015)
25. Dean, E.B., Unal, R.: Taguchi approach to design optimization for quality and cost: an overview. In: 1991 Annual Conference of the International Society of Parametric Analysts, pp. 1–10 (1991)
26. Athreya, S., Venkatesh, Y.D.: Application of Taguchi method for optimization of process parameters in improving the surface roughness of lathe facing operation. Int. Ref. J. Eng. Sci. **1**(3), 13–19 (2012)
27. Semioshkina, N., Voigt, G.: An overview on Taguchi method. J. Radiat. Res. **47**(Suppl. A, 2), A95–A100 (2006)
28. Roy, R.K.: A Primer on the Taguchi Method. Society of Manufacturing Engineers, USA (2010)

# Computing Topics on Multiple Imputation in Big Identifiable Data Using R: An Application to Educational Research

Maria Eugénia Ferrão[1,2(✉)] ⓘ and Paula Prata[1,3] ⓘ

[1] University of Beira Interior, Covilha, Portugal
meferrao@ubi.pt, pprata@di.ubi.pt
[2] Centre for Applied Mathematics and Economics (CEMAPRE),
Lisbon, Portugal
[3] Instituto de Telecomunicações (IT), Covilha, Portugal

**Abstract.** This article shows how to conduct multiple imputation in big identifiable data for educational research purposes. The R statistical package and procedures to handle missing data applied for the purpose of this study were "BaylorEdPsych" and "mi". Firstly, we checked that every dataset rejected the null hypothesis for Missing Completely At Random (MCAR), using the function "LittleMCAR". Simulated and real data analyses were conducted. Results suggest that the improvement of the quality of imputation requires alternative methods to be developed.

**Keywords:** Multiple imputation · R programming · Big data · Education research

## 1 Introduction

Several authors mention having written on the use of big data for research purposes, which may be simultaneously an opportunity or a threat (Diggle 2015). If the research purposes include inferences from big data statistical modelling and the big data does not cover the entire target population or there is a selective mechanism that produces missing data that are not completely at random, the research itself may be compromised.

The concept of missing data is defined as "the difference between the data we planned to collect and what we have managed to collect" (Longford 2005, p. 13). In several educational research studies, missing data are due to item nonresponse, i.e. participants in a survey or test who do not give responses for every item or question administered (item missing). In some situations the expected participants in the survey or test do not appear (subject missing).

According to Schafer (1999, p. 1), when the incomplete cases comprise only a small fraction of all cases (say, five percent or less) then case deletion may be a perfectly reasonable solution to the missing-data problem. In multivariate settings where missing values occur on more than one variable, however, the incomplete cases

© Springer Nature Switzerland AG 2019
S. Misra et al. (Eds.): ICCSA 2019, LNCS 11621, pp. 12–24, 2019.
https://doi.org/10.1007/978-3-030-24302-9_2

are often a substantial portion of the entire dataset. If so, deleting them may be inefficient, causing large amounts of information to be discarded. Moreover, omitting them from the analysis will tend to introduce bias, to the extent that the incompletely observed cases differ systematically from the completely observed ones.

Schaffer (1999) proposed 5% as the cutoff, but other authors suggested 10% or even 20%. Moreover, research papers in education often do not mention the occurrence of missing data despite best practice recommendations in reporting and handling missing data (Pampaka et al. 2016; Schlomer et al. 2010) in quantitative based research.

In addition, the use of quantitative methods in the field of education and other related disciplines such as economics, sociology, political science, has been strongly conditioned either by the availability of data or by their quality (c.f. Bratti et al. 2004; Foley and Goldstein 2012). For example, an increasing number of researchers use large and complex data surveys, such as TIMSS (Trends in International Mathematics and Science Study), PIRLS (Progress in International Reading Literacy Study), TALIS (Teaching and Learning International Survey), or PISA (Programme for International Student Assessment) collected in more than 60 countries, or assessment and evaluation data collected within each country, for innovative contributions in the field of economics of education, sociology of education, psychology, etc. For certain research purposes, however, omit the occurrence of missing data or assume naïve solutions for missing imputation, could undermine the scientific innovative contribution.

Three main contributions arise from this paper: (1) What should the researcher do with incomplete data? (2) How to identify the pattern of missing data? (3) How to conduct multiple imputation with big identifiable data? The remainder of this paper consists of five parts. Section 2 presents concepts and definitions on missing data classification, and the explanation of a statistical test to identify the pattern of item missingness. Section 3 describes the R statistical package and procedures to handle item missing data. Section 4 deals with multiple imputation procedures applied to simulated and real data. The "Prova Brasil" 2017 (INEP 2018) was used as an example of educational research where identifiable big data (Shlomo and Goldstein 2015) does not cover the entire target population and, thus, the missing items may not be completely at random. The section includes data description, the simulation study and performance evaluation. Finally, the conclusion constitutes the Sect. 5.

## 2 Concepts and Definitions on Missing Data

Regarding data quality for statistical modelling purposes, the kind of missing data randomness matters (Little 1988; Little and Rubin 2002), i.e., it may occur as Missing Completely At Random (MCAR), as Missing At Random (MAR) or as Not Missing At Random (NMAR). "One way of assessing this is to compare the means of recorded values of each variable between groups defined by whether other variables in the dataset are missing or not" (Little 1988, p. 1198). The respective definitions and examples in education research are as follows (Little 1988). Consider $\mathbf{y}$ as the $n \times p$

data matrix where n is the number of subjects and p the number of variables; and **r** as the respective n × p missingness indicator matrix, such that,

$$\text{if } y_{ij} \text{ is missing then } r_{ij} = 1 \text{ else } r_{ij} = 0.$$

Consider also the set of unknown parameters $\Theta$, $\Psi$ such as the data and missing mechanism are specified by the following distributions:

$$f(y|\Theta) \text{ for y and } f(r|y, \Psi) \text{ for r.}$$

Following the author, we write $y = (y_{obs}, y_{mis})$, where $y_{obs}$ denotes the observed values of y, and $y_{mis}$ denotes the missing values of **y**.

Rubin (1976) (cited by Little 1988) defined the missing occurrence as completely at random (MCAR) if

$$f(r|y_{obs}, y_{mis}, \Psi) = f(r|\Psi), \forall_{y_{obs}, y_{mis}},$$

which is the highest level of randomness, i.e., missingness does not depend on the observed nor on the missing values of y. The probability of an instance ij having a missing value for an attribute does not depend on either the known values or the missing data. In this level of randomness, any missing data treatment method may be used without risk of introducing bias on the analysis and inferences conducted.

Rubin (1976) (cited by Little, 1988) also defined MAR as

$$f(r|y_{obs}, y_{mis}, \Psi) = f(r|y_{obs}, \Psi), \forall_{y_{mis}},$$

meaning that missingness does not depend on $y_{mis}$ but may depend on $y_{obs}$. Under such conditions, the author called the missing data mechanism as ignorable for likelihood-based inferences. The same is to say that the probability of an instance ij having a missing value for an attribute may depend on the known values, but not on the missing value itself. The remaining situation is classified as NMAR that occurs when the probability of an instance ij having a missing value for a variable that could depend on the value of such variable.

Big data is characterized by large volume of data available at high velocity and in varying formats. The review by Wamba et al. (2015), citing many other authors, adds veracity and value to the general principles of big data. The report of the American Association for Public Opinion Research (Japec et al. 2015) includes administrative data in the sources of big data. A definition for big identifiable data is presented in the special issue by Shlomo and Goldstein (2015), "If the elements in a data set can be meaningfully associated with a unit at a given place and time, such as an individual, institution, product or geographical location, then big data can be made fit for purpose for statistical inference." (p. 787). This is the conceptual and methodological frame-work we adopt in this study to investigate the topic of missing data imputation on the Brazilian open access big identifiable data.

# 3  Statistical Packages and Procedures

The R statistical package and procedures to handle missing data applied for the purpose of this study were "BaylorEdPsych" and "mi". Firstly, we checked that every dataset rejected the null hypothesis for MCAR, using the function "LittleMCAR" (Beaujean 2015). That function belongs to the "BaylorEdPsych" package (R Package for Baylor University Educational Psychology Quantitative Courses). Then, a process composed of four main steps was conducted, in order to get the respective complete data,

1. Missing values imputation;
2. Testing convergence;
3. If it does not converge then go to step (1);
4. Collecting results;
5. In the simulation study, assessing the error (root mean square error and the mean absolute error);
6. Adjusting the linear regression models;
7. Evaluating the results obtained.

To do multiple imputation, the "mi" package (Missing Data Imputation and Model Checking) was used. That package imputes missing values in an approximate Bayesian framework (Su et al. 2015). After converting the initial data into a missing_data.frame object, the main features of each "missing variable" can be observed. For instance, each "missing variable" is classified with a type (continuous, binary, etc.) and a family (Gaussian, binomial, etc.). That initial classification done by the "missing_data.frame" function can be modified by the user accordingly to his knowledge, using the "change" function. At that moment the "mi" function can be called to perform the imputation. An iterative algorithm is used to model each "missing variable" as a function of all the other "missing variables" and their missing patterns. Multiple chains are run and convergence is assessed after a pre-specified number of iterations. The number of chains used should be related with the number of cores available so they can be run in parallel. In this work both approaches, sequential and parallel, were tested. As the study was done in windows operating system, parallel processing is achieved via sockets. A cluster of $n$ nodes was created, being $n$ the number of available logical cores. Using sockets has higher overhead than parallelism via forking, but that can just be used in POSIX systems (Errickson 2017). After the conclusion of a number of iterations (30 by default) the convergence was tested with the "mipply" and "Rhats" functions. With "mipply", a function can be applied to an object of class "mi", that is, the object returned by the imputation process. That object contains for each chain the data evolution throughout all the iterations. Computing the "mean" of each complete variable in each chain, the user can stop the iterative process when the "means" are approximately the same. The "Rhats" function will monitor the "mean" and "standard deviation" of each variable over the iterations, across the chains. Values close to 1 mean convergence.

Both the root mean square error (RMSE) and the mean absolute error (MAE) are usually employed in performance evaluation studies. Some authors argue in favor of MAE (Willmott and Matsuura 2005), suggesting that the RMSE is not a good indicator of average model performance and might be a misleading indicator of average error, others (Chai and Draxler 2014) contend that the proposed avoidance of RMSE and the use of MAE is not the solution to the problem, demonstrating that the RMSE is not ambiguous in its meaning, and that the RMSE is more appropriate to represent model performance than the MAE when the error distribution is expected to be Gaussian, which is the case in our study. We decided to use both metrics. To simplify, we assume that we already have $n$ samples of model errors $\varepsilon$ representing the error between the complete and the imputed data, calculated as $e_i, i = 1, 2, \ldots, n$. The RMSE and MAE statistics are calculated for each data set as

$$\text{MAE} = \frac{1}{n} \sum_{i=1}^{n} |e_i|$$

$$RMSE = \sqrt{\frac{1}{n} \sum_{i=1}^{n} e_i^2}$$

In addition, a linear regression model was considered with Y as the response variable and X1, X2 as the covariates, in order to assess the impact of multiple imputation on the estimates of coefficients. A regression equation of the form

$$y_i = \beta_0 + \beta_1 x1_i + \beta_2 x2_i + \tau_i$$

explains the value of a dependent variable $y_i$ in terms of a set a two observable variables $x1_i$, $x2_i$ and an unobservable random variable $\tau_i$. According to the assumptions, the elements $\tau_i$ are distributed independently and identically with expected values zero and a common variance of $\sigma^2$. More details can be found in Greene (2011) for example.

## 4  Big Identifiable Data with Multiple Imputation

### 4.1  "Prova Brazil" 2017 Data

The education data used in this study is the "Avaliação Nacional do Rendimento Escolar" (INEP - Instituto Nacional de Estudos e Pesquisas Educacionais Anísio Teixeira 2015), well known as "Prova Brasil". The "Prova Brasil" was created in 2005 under the scope of the Basic Education Evaluation System (SAEB) with the aim of assessing students learning at Brazilian public schools. It is a quasi census type applied to students at the 5th and 9th grades of primary education in schools with 20 or more students enrolled in these grades. It covers all Brazilian territory and is carried out every two years by the INEP, which is responsible for developing and applying educational assessments, and also the census of education. The "Prova Brasil" comprises standardized tests on Portuguese Language (reading) and Mathematics, as well as questionnaires targeting students, teachers, principals and schools. Tests are prepared following SAEB's Reference Matrix, which contains the description of competencies and abilities that guide the production of test items. The scores of student proficiency are obtained by item response models, allowing the use of Balanced Incomplete Block

Design (BIBD) and equating. SAEB's proficiency scales range from 0 to 500 with mean 250 and standard deviation 50 to 9th grade students.

For the purpose of this paper, we consider the 5th year data collected in 2017. The finite population is, then, a large identifiable sample of size N = 2.594 million students of its super population of the 5th grade. The performance scores in Maths and Reading are available for 2.170 (84%) million students and the socioeconomic status for 2.132 (82%) students (Alves and Ferrão 2018; Ferrão and Alves 2019).

## 4.2    A Simulation Study

In this section we carry out simulation studies to assess the impact of multiple imputation on estimates of linear regression given a non-ignorable pattern of missingness. The simulation study is based on samples drawn from "Prova Brazil 2017" using the Rondónia Federation Unit (FU = 11), involving 27874 students. For the purpose of simulations the complete data was generated by applying listwise to the real data. We considered three relevant variables for research in educational evaluation or educational equity: Student's performance in reading (Y), Student' socioeconomic status (X1) and Student's trajectory without grade repetition (X2).

Based on the complete data (n = 20408), we carried out four samples Y, X1, X2 with 5% (Miss5), 10% (Miss10), 15% (Miss15), and 20% (Miss20) of missing occurring randomly in the variables Y and X1, respectively for the group of low-performing students and poorer students. Descriptive statistics for complete and missing data are presented in Tables 1 and 2, respectively. We can observe that, as expected, the mean and median increase as the percentage of missing increases due to the generator process of missing values.

**Table 1.**  Descriptive statistics of complete data.

|          | Y      | X1    | X2     |
|----------|--------|-------|--------|
| Mean     | 0.073  | 5.082 | 0.775  |
| Median   | 0.040  | 4.960 | 1.000  |
| Variance | 0.822  | 1.105 | 0.175  |
| Skewness | 0.172  | 0.525 | −1.315 |
| Kurtose  | −0.313 | 0.510 | −0.271 |

**Table 2.**  Descriptive statistics of missing data.

|          | Y Miss5 | X1 Miss5 | Y Miss10 | X1 Miss10 | Y Miss15 | X1 Miss15 | Y Miss20 | X1 Miss20 |
|----------|---------|----------|----------|-----------|----------|-----------|----------|-----------|
| Mean     | 0.166   | 5.166    | 0.232    | 5.230     | 0.295    | 5.289     | 0.340    | 5.327     |
| Median   | 0.100   | 5.000    | 0.200    | 5.100     | 0.300    | 5.200     | 0.300    | 5.200     |
| Variance | 0.747   | 1.022    | 0.723    | 0.995     | 0.721    | 1.003     | 0.742    | 1.028     |
| Skewness | 0.238   | 0.612    | 0.175    | 0.591     | 0.066    | 0.495     | −0.027   | 0.425     |
| Kurtose  | −0.241  | 0.638    | −0.134   | 0.689     | −0.050   | 0.682     | −0.079   | 0.551     |

**Checking the Missing Pattern.** As said before we started to assess each multivariate dataset for missing completely at random with the "LittleMCAR" function that uses Little's test. We tested the datasets Miss5, Miss10, Miss15 and Miss20 described above and four additional cases where the generated missing values are MCAR. MCAR10X1 represents a dataset with 10% of missing values randomly occurring in variable X1, MCAR10X1Y has 10% of missing randomly values occurring in variables X1 and Y. MCAR20X1 and MCAR20X1Y have the same structure but with 20% of missing values. Table 3 contains the results obtained.

**Table 3.** Results of Little's test.

|  | Chi-square | Degrees of freedom | p-value | Missing patterns | X1, number of missing values | Y, number of missing values |
|---|---|---|---|---|---|---|
| Miss5 | 594.50 | 5 | <0.001 | 4 | 969 (4.75%) | 983 (4.82%) |
| Miss10 | 733.52 | 5 | <0.001 | 4 | 1979 (9.70%) | 1970 (9.65%) |
| Miss15 | 929.28 | 5 | <0.001 | 4 | 3115 (15.26%) | 3083 (15.11%) |
| Miss20 | 911.31 | 5 | <0.001 | 4 | 4036 (19.78%) | 4078 (19.98%) |
| MCAR10X1 | 0.82 | 2 | 0.66 | 2 | 2107 (10.32%) | 0 |
| MCAR10X1Y | 7.79 | 5 | 0.17 | 4 | 2107 (10.32%) | 2115 (10.36%) |
| MCAR20X1 | 2.91 | 2 | 0.23 | 2 | 4096 (20.07%) | 0 |
| MCAR20X1Y | 3.53 | 5 | 0.62 | 4 | 4096 (20.07%) | 4065 (19.92%) |

No matter the percentage of missing data, the results show that the Little's test rightly identifies the pattern of non-ignorable missing data at the level of significance of 5%, since p value <0.001, as can be observed in Table 3. In addition, the test pro-vides p values greater than 0.05 for datasets where missing were generated as completely at random.

**Results of Simulation Study.** Table 4 contains descriptive statistics of imputed data. It can be observed that the values of mean and median tend to increase as the multiple imputation was applied to larger percentage of missing values, and the dispersion tends to be reduced.

**Table 4.** Descriptive statistics of imputed data.

|  | Y MI5 | X1 MI5 | Y MI10 | X1 MI10 | Y MI15 | X1 MI15 | Y MI20 | X1 MI20 |
|---|---|---|---|---|---|---|---|---|
| Mean | 0.143 | 5.162 | 0.186 | 5.224 | 0.238 | 5.280 | 0.266 | 5.317 |
| Median | 0.100 | 5.000 | 0.100 | 5.100 | 0.200 | 5.200 | 0.300 | 5.200 |
| Variance | 0.751 | 1.020 | 0.732 | 0.997 | 0.728 | 1.010 | 0.748 | 1.030 |
| Skewness | 0.228 | 0.590 | 0.154 | 0.532 | 0.053 | 0.421 | −0.030 | 0.335 |
| Kurtose | −0.199 | 0.611 | −0.088 | 0.625 | −0.029 | 0.588 | −0.040 | 0.489 |

The Figs. 1 and 2 illustrate the RMSE and MAE for different values of missing percentage. The effect of increasing the percentage of missing data does not change substantively the relationship between the variables, but the magnitude is lower than it should be. It can be observed that the error is higher in X1 than in Y.

The Table 5 includes the correlation between Y and the linear predictor (R), the coefficients estimates (B1, B2) and the respective standard errors (SE(B1), SE(B2)), for regression models applied to the complete data (1st row), to the datasets resulting from multiple imputation (2nd to 5th rows) and to the respective data considering the missing values (6th to 9th rows).

Considering the results of the model applied to complete data (with R = 0.369) and comparing them with those obtained from multiple imputation, it can be observed that the maximum absolute difference on correlation is 0.015 (MI5 data, R = 0.354). However, differences on parameter estimates are larger in MI15 for B1. Concerning the standard errors, the results are always lower or equal than those obtained for complete data. Regarding the B1 estimates obtained either by multiple imputation or with the assumption of MCAR, the results are generally biased towards zero. It should be noted that the correlation is lower when MCAR assumption is used no matter the percentage of missing data. Since X2 is a complete data variable, a clear pattern for B2 estimates was not found.

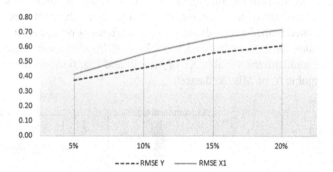

**Fig. 1.** Root square mean error.

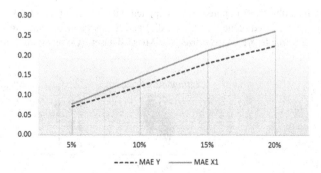

**Fig. 2.** Mean absolute error.

**Table 5.** Estimates of the linear regression models.

|  | R | B1 | SE (B1) | B2 | SE (B2) |
|---|---|---|---|---|---|
| Complete data | 0.369 | 0.135 | 0.006 | 0.688 | 0.014 |
| MI5 | 0.354 | 0.126 | 0.006 | 0.638 | 0.014 |
| MI10 | 0.359 | 0.121 | 0.006 | 0.649 | 0.013 |
| MI15 | 0.359 | 0.113 | 0.006 | 0.656 | 0.013 |
| MI20 | 0.365 | 0.114 | 0.006 | 0.679 | 0.014 |
| Miss5 | 0.347 | 0.127 | 0.006 | 0.639 | 0.015 |
| Miss10 | 0.350 | 0.122 | 0.006 | 0.658 | 0.016 |
| Miss15 | 0.340 | 0.122 | 0.007 | 0.651 | 0.017 |
| Miss20 | 0.350 | 0.121 | 0.007 | 0.696 | 0.018 |

Figures 3, 4, 5 and 6 show the plots of the imputation process for datasets Miss5 and Miss20. Figure 3 shows on the left the histogram of completed data (in grey), the histogram of observed data (blue line) and the histogram of imputed data (red line) for the standardized variable X1 of Miss5 dataset. The plot in the middle of the same Figure shows a comparison of completed data (in blue) to the fitted values (in red). Colours just can be observed in the online version. Finally on the right hand side of the Figure the associated binned residuals are presented. Figure 4 represents with the same structure the values for the standardized variable Y of Miss5 dataset. Figure 5 shows the plots for the standardized variable X1 of Miss20 and Fig. 6 shows the plots for the standardized variable Y of Miss20 dataset.

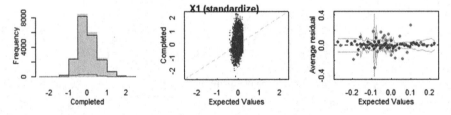

**Fig. 3.** Histogram of observed, imputed and completed data (at the left hand side), comparison of completed data to the fitted values (at the middle) and the associated binned residuals (at the right hand side) for variable X1 (standardized) of Miss5 dataset. (Color figure online)

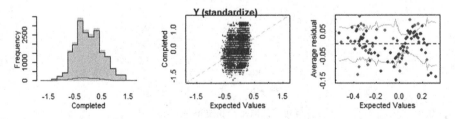

**Fig. 4.** Histogram of observed, inputted and completed data (left hand side), comparison of completed data to the fitted values (at the middle) and the associated binned residuals (left hand side) for variable Y (standardized) of Miss5 dataset. (Color figure online)

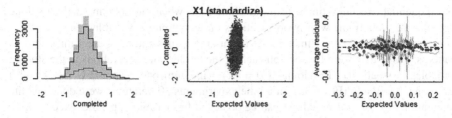

**Fig. 5.** Histogram of observed, inputted and completed data (left hand side), comparison of completed data to the fitted values (middle) and the associated binned residuals (right hand side) for variable X1 (standardized) of Miss20 dataset. (Color figure online)

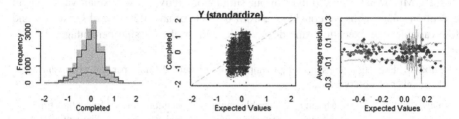

**Fig. 6.** Histogram of observed, inputted and completed data (left hand side), comparison of completed data to the fitted values (middle) and the associated binned residuals (right hand side) for variable Y (standardized) of Miss20 dataset. (Color figure online)

The graphs of Figs. 3, 4, 5 and 6 confirm that the imputation on Y presents a smaller error than on X1. Despite the impact of the error on regression model estimates being always lower than 0.02, the multiple imputation can be improved by increasing the number of variables included in the joint distribution.

## 4.3  Execution Time and Performance

This section describes the limitations imposed to this study by using a common laptop. We analyze the execution times needed to run multiple imputations when varying the number of records present in the data files, the number of variables and the type of variables.

The execution times were obtained in two computers. A laptop that will be referred as LT1, with an I7-4600U processor (speed from 2.1 GHz up to 2.7 GHz) with 2 physical cores (four threads) and 8 GB of RAM. A second laptop referred as LT2, is a machine with an I7-8550U processor (speed from 1.8 GHz up to 4.0 GHz, with 4 physical cores (8 threads) and 16 GB of RAM. Both computers run a Windows 10 operating system (64 bits version). Besides the processing speed, the biggest difference between the two machines is the available memory. We got the time at the start and at the end of the block of code in study with the function Sys.time() and estimated the time after running 3 times the same code.

Starting by studying the impact of using the "mi" function in parallel in a Windows system we got the results presented in Table 6. It shows the approximations for parallel and sequential execution times, using machine LP1, when multiple imputation is done in a missing_data.frame with N observations on 3 continuous variables. In all cases, 2 of the variables have approximately 5% of missing values and there are 4 missing data patterns. Three FUs were chosen considering the number of observations in the studied variables: a small one, Rondônia (FU = 11) a medium one, Ceará (FU = 23) and a large one, São Paulo (FU = 35). In all the experiments 30 iterations were done and the imputation process converged. As can be observed from Table 6, parallel execution, in cases with a small number of missing patterns, just has advantage for data with more than 20 000 observations. For smaller cases the overhead of creating a cluster surpasses the gain of running the different chains in parallel.

The experiments on datasets with different percentages of missing values, as Miss5, Miss10, Miss15 and Miss20 used in our simulation study, showed small variations in execution times. Thus we conclude that for datasets of about 20 000 observations and few variables the execution time does not depend on the missing percentage.

**Table 6.** Execution times of multiple imputation, sequential versus parallel when varying the number of observations.

| Observations | Missing patterns | Variables with missing values | Execution time (Parallel) | Execution time (Sequential) |
|---|---|---|---|---|
| 20408 (FU – 11) | 4 | 2 | 30 to 40 s | 40 to 50 s |
| 86628 (FU – 23) | 4 | 2 | 2 to 3 min | 3 to 4 min |
| 376325 (FU – 35) | 4 | 2 | 4 to 5 min | 14 to 15 min |

Next, we increased the number of observations, increased the number of variables with missing values and included binary variables. All studied cases have more than half a million observations (N = 513304). The execution times obtained in both machines, LT1 (8 GB of RAM) and LT2 (16 GB of RAM) are shown in Table 7.

**Table 7.** Execution times of multiple imputation for datasets with 513304 observations varying the number and type of missing variables in a computer with 8 GB of RAM versus a computer with 16 GB of RAM.

| Missing patterns | No. of variables (with missing) | Class of variables with missing | Execution time (8 GB of RAM) | Execution time (16 GB of RAM) |
|---|---|---|---|---|
| 8 | 6 (4) | Continuous | 29.9 min | 9.3 min |
| 8 | 6 (4) | 2 continuous 2 binary | 33.0 min | 9.6 min |
| 18 | 10 (8) | Continuous | 116.4 min | 30.8 min |

The case presented in the first row, has 6 continuous variables being 4 with missing values. For that case the execution times vary from about 10 min in LP2 to almost 30 min with LP1. In the second case two of the variables with missing values are binary. As can be seen in that case the execution time is slightly larger in both machines but the difference is inconclusive. In all cases the computer memory is fundamental to the performance of the imputation routine; this is especially visible in the last case when we double the number of variables with missing values. With 18 data patterns the limit of memory in LT1 machine is almost reached. Finally, it should be noted that those three cases were executed running 4 chains in parallel, with a limit of 35 iterations, but some variables did not converge. It would be necessary to continue iterating.

## 5 Conclusion

In this article we showed how to use R packages to conduct multiple imputation in big identifiable data for the purpose of educational research. As long as the number of cases and the number of variables increase, the time also increases. Preliminary results suggest that the improvement of multiple imputation via the inclusion of additional variables is limited to execution time and the machine processor and memory available. Thus, as future work we intend to explore the use of a distributed computing engine like Apache Spark either in machines with more memory and cores or in cloud platforms. Further research to include categorical variables in the process of multiple imputation is going on, and in order to validate the conclusions a Monte Carlo study is planned to be conducted.

**Acknowledgements.** This work was partially funded by FCT- Fundação para a Ciência e a Tecnologia through project number CEMAPRE - UID/MULTI/00491/2019 and by FCT/MEC through national funds and when applicable co-funded by FEDER – PT2020 partnership agreement under the project UID/EEA/50008/2019.

## References

Alves, M.T.G., Ferrão, M.E.: Uma década de Prova Brasil: Evolução do desempenho e da aprovação (2018, submitted)

Beaujean, A.A.: Package "BaylorEdPsych" (2015). https://cran.r-project.org/web/packages/BaylorEdPsych/BaylorEdPsych.pdf. Accessed 11 Feb 2019

Bratti, M., McKnight, A., Naylor, R., Smith, J.: Higher education outcomes, graduate employment and university performance indicators. J. R. Statist. Soc. A **167**(3), 475–496 (2004). http://www.jstor.org/stable/3559775

Chai, T., Draxler, R.R.: Root mean square error (RMSE) or mean absolute error (MAE)? Geosci. Model. Dev. Discuss. **7**(1), 1525–1534 (2014)

Diggle, P.J.: Statistics: a data science for the 21st century. J. R. Stat. Soc. A **178**, 793–813 (2015)

Errickson, J.: Parallel processing in R (2017). http://dept.stat.lsa.umich.edu/~jerrick/courses/stat701/notes/parallel.html. Accessed 10 Feb 2019

Ferrão, M.E., Alves, M.T.G.: Grade repetition in Brazilian primary education: 2007–2017 cross-sectional data modelling (2019, submitted)

Foley, B., Goldstein, H.: Measuring Success: League Tables in the Public Sector. British Academy, London (2012)

Greene, W.H.: Econometric Analysis. Prentice Hall, New York (2011)

INEP - Instituto Nacional de Estudos e Pesquisas Educacionais Anísio Teixeira, ANRESC (Prova Brasil) (2015). http://portal.inep.gov.br/educacao-basica/saeb/sobre-a-anresc

Japec, L., Kreuter, F., Berg, M., Biemer, P., Decker, P., Lampe, C.: AAPOR Report on Big Data (2015). https://www.aapor.org/getattachment/Education-Resources/Reports/BigDataTaskForce Report_FINAL_2_12_15_b.pdf.aspx

Little, R.J.A.: A test of missing completely at random for multivariate data with missing values. J. Am. Stat. Assoc. **83**(404), 1198–1202 (1988)

Little, R.J.A., Rubin, D.B.: Statistical Analysis with Missing Data, 2nd edn. Wiley, Hoboken (2002)

Longford, N.T.: Missing Data and Small-Area Estimation. Springer, New York (2005). https://doi.org/10.1007/1-84628-195-4

Pampaka, M., Hutcheson, G., Williams, J.: Handling missing data: analysis of a challenging data set using multiple imputation. Int. J. Res. Method Educ. **39**(1), 19–37 (2016). https://doi.org/10.1080/1743727X.2014.979146

Schafer, J.L.: Analysis of Incomplete Multivariate Data. Chapman & Hall/CRC, Boca Raton (1999)

Schlomer, G.L., Bauman, S., Card, N.A.: Best practices for missing data management in counseling psychology. J. Couns. Psychol. **57**(1), 1–10 (2010). https://doi.org/10.1037/a0018082

Shlomo, N., Goldstein, H.: Editorial: big data in social research. J. R. Stat. Soc. A **178**, 787–790 (2015)

Su, Y.-S., Goodrich, B., Kropko, J.: Package "mi" (2015). https://cran.r-project.org/web/packages/mi/mi.pdf. Accessed 11 Feb 2019

Wamba, S.F., Akter, S., Edwards, A., Chopin, G., Gnanzou, D.: How "big data" can make big impact: findings from a systematic review and a longitudinal case study. Int. J. Prod. Econ. **165**, 234–246 (2015). https://doi.org/10.1016/j.ijpe.2014.12.031

Willmott, C., Matsuura, K.: Advantages of the mean absolute error (MAE) over the root mean square error (RMSE) in assessing average model performance. Clim. Res. **30**, 79–82 (2005)

# Comparing Empirical ROC Curves Using a Java Application: CERCUS

Daniel Moreira[1] and Ana C. Braga[2]

[1] Department of Informatics, School of Engineering,
University of Minho, Braga, Portugal
a.daniel.t.moreira@gmail.com
[2] ALGORITMI Centre, University of Minho,
4710-057 Braga, Portugal
acb@dps.uminho.pt

**Abstract.** Receiver Operating Characteristic (ROC) analysis is a methodology that has gained much popularity in our days, especially in Medicine, since through the ROC curves, it provides a useful tool to evaluate and specify problems in the performance of a diagnostic indicator.

The area under empirical ROC curve (AUC) it's an indicator that can be used to compare two or more ROC curves.

This work arose from the necessity of the existence of software that allows the calculation of the necessary measures to compare systems based on ROC curves.

Several software, commercial and non-commercial, are available to perform the calculation of the measures associated to the ROC analysis. However, they present some flaws, especially when there is a need to compare independent samples with different dimensions, or also to compare two ROC curves that intersect.

In this paper is presented a new application called **CERCUS** (Comparison of Empirical ROC Curves). This was developed using a programming language (Java) and stands out for the possibility of comparing two or more ROC curves that cross each other.

The main objective of **CERCUS** is the calculation of several ROC estimates using different methods and make the ROC curves comparison, even if there is an intersection, either for independent or paired samples. It also allows the graph representation of the ROC curve in a unitary plan as well the graph of the area between curves in comparison.

This paper presents the program's versatility in data entry, test menus and visualization of graphs and results.

**Keywords:** ROC curve · CERCUS · Java · R

## 1 Introduction

The ROC analysis was developed between 1950 and 1960 that emerged from the decision theory more concretely in the theory of signal detection [3,6]. This

© Springer Nature Switzerland AG 2019
S. Misra et al. (Eds.): ICCSA 2019, LNCS 11621, pp. 25–37, 2019.
https://doi.org/10.1007/978-3-030-24302-9_3

emerged as a need to identify and differentiate in a radar operator, a reliable signal (allies, enemies) of a noise (clouds, birds, etc.). Since this time the ROC analysis has gained a lot of popularity because although it is a useful tool to evaluate the performance of an indicator, it is able to compare different indicators and to select in a practical way an optimal threshold [4].

This methodology has been applied to several scientific areas and in the field of medicine has been an important factor in medical decisions making, as well as in the areas of epidemiology, diagnostic tests, radiology and bioinformatics [9].

The graph of the ROC curve in the unit plane is a technique that can be used to organize and select classifiers by evaluating their performance. This technique consists of a two-dimensional graphical representation that has as $x$ axis, "1-specificity" and in the ordinate $y$, "sensitivity", that vary from 0 to 1 [6]. In terms of data in medicine, the sensitivity corresponds to the probability of an illness being present, when in reality the individual is sick and the specificity corresponds to the probability to exclude the disease, when in reality it is absent [3].

For comparison of two ROC curves, there is a method that obtains from the ROC graph, a scalar value that represents its performance, the area under the curve, AUC. Since AUC is a portion of the unit plane, its values vary from 0 to 1.

If you draw a line diagonally from the origin in this plane, it represents a value of AUC of 0.5, so no realistic classifier should have a AUC less than 0.5 [6], and in practice the value of AUC ranges from 0.5 to 1.0. Hanley and McNeil [10] can compare two ROC curves, through a $Z$ statistic, which uses this estimate as indicator for the two systems to be compared. Empirical estimation of the AUC can be obtained by the trapezoid rule, to compute the area below the curve, or by the Wilcoxon statistic, where the statistical properties of this can be used to predict the properties of the AUC of the ROC curve.

When comparing ROC curves when they intersect, [1] present a methodology that allows the comparison of ROC curves in different regions of the space, by the determination of partial areas. Using a methodology based on the comparison of Pareto curves in multi-objective optimization, the `Comp2ROC` package, developed in R [2], is the result of this methodology.

The analysis through the ROC curves is important in different fields of applicability, however there are few applications available to systematize this analysis, namely with regard to graphical representation and comparison of two systems. The growing use of this methodology in different areas, such as in the medical field, requires the existence of a unique tool that encompasses the most important methodologies of the study of ROC curves. The development of simple and intuitive software capable of analysing ROC curves using the `Comp2ROC` functionalities is the great motivation of this work.

The main objective of this work is to present an application developed in Java which is a high-level language, for comparing two systems based on ROC curves that cross or not.

The **CERCUS** (Comparison of Empirical ROC Curves) application is a software developed in Java that facilitates analysis through ROC curves, providing the results of the curves and their graphs. The **CERCUS** name, was obtained using key words ("Comparison", "Empirical", "ROC", "Curves" and "Cross"), in an acronym generator available at: http://acronymcreator.net/. The logo is original and was inspired by the representation of ROC curves in the unitary ROC space. The application allows the incorporation and edition of data, being possible to compare two or more ROC curves.

## 2   Methodology

The methodology of the ROC curves is used for the evaluation of the performance of systems and their comparison, for independent and paired samples. For the development of the application, it is used the technique of algorithm (programming by objects), making use of libraries already developed and available in Java.

### 2.1   Programming in Java

Java is an object-oriented computer programming language that was originally released in 1995 by Sun Microsystems (which was acquired by Oracle Corporation).

The code is compiled to byte code, which can be run on any Java virtual machine, regardless of the operating system [8].

Unlike other programming languages, Java is not just a language that consists only of object programming. This is based on an attractive and appropriate programming and application development environment, especially from the Java Development Kit (JDK) system [8].

The main feature of the Java language is that it includes a simple language that can be programmed without extensive programmer training, where key concepts are learned quickly. The robustness and security of this type of language is to have an extensive compilation-time check, followed by a second level of run-time verification. That is, in the development of Java code the system will find errors quickly, where the main problems will not be suspended until there is an update of the code. On the other hand, Java allows to include cryptographic keys in the code itself, thus enabling the identification of the origin of the code [8].

Basically the development of applications using this type of language originates a software of high security and performance that includes multiple architectures, operating systems and graphical interface.

Additionally, developers have access to existing libraries of tested objects that provide additional functionality to the new program.

## 2.2   Rserve Library

Programming languages, such as Java, are widely used for application development, but are not very efficient when it comes to statistical and/or mathematical modelling. To compensate for this gap, there are languages like R, which has a wide range of statistical libraries. By integrating these two technologies, we can create applications based on high quality statistical modelling. The `Rserve` is a library available in Java, which enables communication between Java and R, making it possible to obtain statistical results using functions and libraries available in R.

The interpolation of the application with the `Rserve` is accomplished by incorporating the program R into the project. With this operation, in the application it is possible to open the R, run the algorithm and then close it. Figure 1 illustrates a scheme, explaining superficially the operation of `Rserve` with Java.

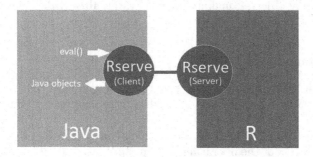

**Fig. 1.** `Rserve` schema interconnecting Java with R.

## 2.3   Requirements

Although there are some programs that perform ROC analysis, there are none that can match the graphical presentation with the comparison of two or more ROC systems when the samples are independent. To facilitate the information process regarding ROC estimates, the **CERCUS** application contemplates the different ROC methodologies for comparison. The requirements for the construction of the application were:

1. the user must be able to create, open and save data files;
2. the tool should allow the user to edit data files;
3. it should be possible to import/export EXCEL (.xls) files;
4. the tool should have basic commands like copy, cut and paste;
5. it should present the results of ROC estimates in a simple and intuitive way;
6. it should be able to make a graphical representation, which the user can write to image file (.jpeg);
7. it should have a help button to make it easier to use the new program.

## 2.4  Methodological Approach

The approach chosen was the development of Java software that implements ROC methodologies.

Figure 2 represents a simplified scheme for the development of the CERCUS. The interface class is primarily responsible for the structure of the program and to get results or graphics you will need to use classes like DataFrame and Table. These classes allow you to collect values that the user provides to the program and to calculate the various ROC estimates using specific methods present within them. If there is an intersection of the ROC curves, another class (Comp2Roc) is used, which makes use of the `Rserve` library and the alternative method proposed by Braga et al. [1] to calculate the respective metrics for comparison through empirical ROC curves that whether they cross, or not.

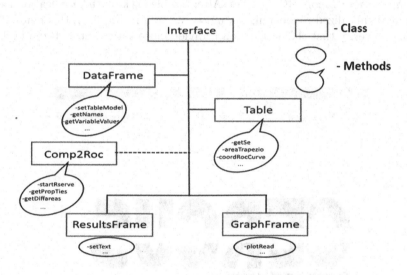

**Fig. 2.** Schematic of the workflow.

The **CERCUS** application follows the scheme exemplified in Fig. 2 and all the requirements listed above.

# 3  CERCUS Application

## 3.1  Operating Systems

**CERCUS** is available for Windows and for its use only needs to open the application available to download on https://cercus9.webnode.pt/. This first version is available to download in a `.zip` file which includes the `.jar` application, a folder called **fun** that contains additional functions and a folder with examples files.

For the UNIX system, **CERCUS** is also available, to download in a .zip file with the same folder but for this system.

To work with this application, in both systems, the user needs to install the R program from CRAN: https://cran.r-project.org/ choosing the correspondent system, Windows or UNIX, and also install the Comp2ROC and Rserve packages by using the code instruction install.packages("Comp2ROC") and install.packages("Rserve") in R.

For any doubt in the zip file the user has a readme.txt with instructions for the requirements of the systems.

## 3.2   Running CERCUS

The application enables the incorporation and editing of data, making it possible to compare two or more ROC curves. After double click on the application icon, software is initialized by opening a window, as seen in Fig. 3. In this figure it is possible to verify that the application is divided into three sectors listed by 1, 2 and 3.

**Fig. 3.** CERCUS presented in 3 different sectors: 1. Menu bar; 2. Toolbar and 3. Background panel.

**Menu Bar.** The Menu Bar is divided into five groups:

– *File* is a menu for opening, creating and saving data.
– *Edit* is a menu that consists of editing data and windows. This is shown in the toolbar.
– *Analyze* is a menu that is based on calculating ROC estimates.
– *Graphs* is a menu that shows the illustration of the respective graphs.
– *WindowGraph* is a menu that consists of editing the graphics window.

**Toolbar.** The toolbar is divided in two sectors, these is the data editing sector (located in the left side of the Fig. 4) and the window editing sector (located in the right side of the Fig. 4), except for the **help** button.

**Fig. 4.** Toolbar image.

In the data edit group, the three buttons are respectively for copying, cutting and pasting values in the data window. These will only work after the input and subsequent selection of the data window.

In the window editing group, two buttons are available to minimize and close all available windows in the application background.

## 3.3   Data Entry

The introduction of data in the application can be done in three different ways:

– by creating a new data file that can be saved for editing;
– from a file previously saved in the application;
– from an Excel (.xls) file.

Figure 5 serves to better understand the **File** menu presented in CERCUS. This menu was inspired in ROCNPA program [12].

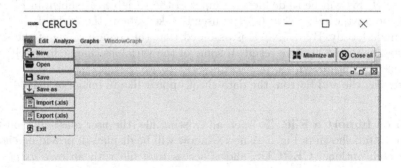

**Fig. 5.** Window of **File** menu. (Color figure online)

The red boxes in Fig. 5 correspond to the different choices to introduce data.

There is a prerequisite for data entry that is associated with the operating conditions of the Comp2ROC package. In the data files, in the result variable must be listed first all values of the distribution of negative cases (0), followed by the positive ones (1).

**Creating a New File.** To create a new data file, it is necessary to press the **New** button of the **File** menu where the program will present three dialogues for complete the definition of variables as shown in Fig. 6.

The first one, is used to characterize the sample, that is, it questions how many variables are being studied and identifies the type of data (paired or independent samples) (Fig. 6a).

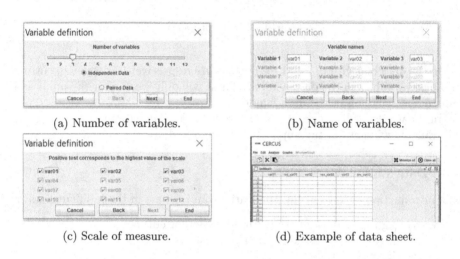

(a) Number of variables.    (b) Name of variables.

(c) Scale of measure.    (d) Example of data sheet.

**Fig. 6.** Example of new data creation for 3 independent samples.

After pressing the **Next** button, a second window will be displayed. The purpose of this will be to define the names of the variables as shown in Fig. 6b.

In the next window (Fig. 6c) the user is asked about the scale of the variables under study. By default it is assumed that the highest value of the scale corresponds to the positive result. If some of the variables change inversely, the visa must be withdrawn.

Pressing the end button, the data sheet appear like in image of Fig. 6d.

**Open or Import a File.** To open an existing file, the user must click on the **Open** button shown in Fig. 5. A new window will be displayed, providing choice and search options. **CERCUS** allows access to a file with an own extension `.cer`.

To import an EXCEL file it is necessary to click the **Import (.xls)** button located in the **File** menu, shown in Fig. 5. The window in Fig. 7a will be displayed so that clicking on the **Open File** button will allow selection of the file, in this case limited by the `.xls` extension. Still in this window is the selection of data type. If the user presses the **Next** button without characterizing the sample, an error message will appear.

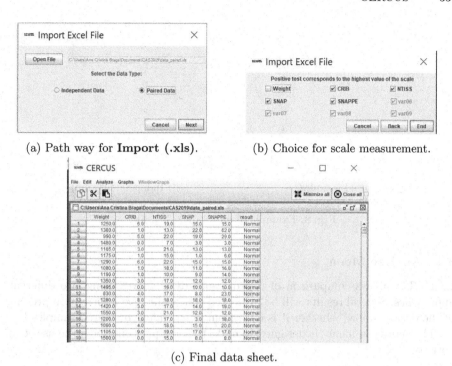

(a) Path way for **Import (.xls)**.

(b) Choice for scale measurement.

(c) Final data sheet.

**Fig. 7.** Example of import EXCEL file for paired samples.

In Fig. 7b, in the case of the Weight variable, it is verified that the smallest value of the scale corresponds to the positive test (result that corresponds to the death of the newborn).

For the EXCEL file to be imported correctly, it must be in `.xls` (Excell 97-2003) and also be filled in from the first row and column. That is, there can be no white-space between columns in the first row. If this happens the reading of the file will not be correctly processed. Also note that variable names must be in the first row only. If the file encounters non-numeric characters after the first line, importing the file will be impossible. On the other hand, in files for paired samples, the last column should be (0 = negative result or 1 = positive result), and in the files for independent samples the variables and the respective response (0 or 1) should be merged side by side. The Fig. 8 illustrates an example of how data should be distributed in Excel.

It is important to note that in the data structure the response variable (0 and 1) must be ordered according to the data procedure to be processed in Comp2ROC in the R, that is, the negative cases (0) must first be placed and then the positive ones (1), either whether they are paired or independent samples.

To save the data files we can press the **Save** or **Save As** buttons, where the `.cer` file is automatically associated. In case we want to export to the EXCEL format, we can proceed to **Export As**, where the `.xls` extension is associated.

| H1 | | | fx | | |
|---|---|---|---|---|---|
| A | B | C | D | E | F |
| Weight | CRIB | NTISS | SNAP | SNAPPE | Result |
| 1250 | 6 | 19 | 15 | 15 | 0 |
| 1380 | 1 | 13 | 22 | 62 | 0 |
| 990 | 5 | 22 | 19 | 29 | 0 |
| 1480 | 0 | 7 | 3 | 3 | 0 |
| 1165 | 3 | 21 | 13 | 13 | 0 |
| 1175 | 1 | 15 | 1 | 6 | 0 |
| 1290 | 6 | 22 | 15 | 15 | 0 |
| 1080 | 1 | 18 | 11 | 16 | 0 |
| 1190 | 1 | 10 | 9 | 14 | 0 |
| 1350 | 3 | 17 | 12 | 12 | 0 |
| 1495 | 0 | 16 | 10 | 10 | 0 |
| 830 | 4 | 17 | 8 | 23 | 0 |

(a) Paired samples.

| I1 | | | fx | | |
|---|---|---|---|---|---|
| A | B | C | D | E | F |
| Hospital1 | Res1 | Hospital2 | Res2 | Hospital3 | Res3 |
| 2 | 0 | 2 | 0 | 1 | 0 |
| 4 | 0 | 12 | 0 | 8 | 0 |
| 1 | 0 | 2 | 0 | 0 | 0 |
| 2 | 0 | 3 | 0 | 1 | 0 |
| 2 | 0 | 0 | 0 | 1 | 0 |
| 14 | 0 | 4 | 0 | 8 | 0 |
| 1 | 0 | 0 | 0 | 3 | 0 |
| 3 | 0 | 1 | 0 | 2 | 0 |
| 2 | 0 | 8 | 0 | 0 | 0 |
| 3 | 0 | 7 | 0 | 1 | 0 |
| 0 | 0 | 14 | 0 | 7 | 0 |
| 4 | 0 | 3 | 0 | 2 | 0 |

(b) Independent samples.

**Fig. 8.** Example of data in EXCEL file.

### 3.4 Analyze Menu

**CERCUS** allows comparison of two or more ROC curves using two different approaches. Several results will be presented concerning the information present in the data window, whether it is data from independent or paired samples.

The **Analyze** menu, is designed to make this comparison giving the user two options:

- **Traditional Multiple Comparison Test**, provide the user with a series of ROC estimates, that are used when the ROC curves do not cross each other. Statistical computations according the methodology proposed by Hanley and McNeil [11] and Delong et al. [5].
- **Roc Sampling Results**, gives the user the analytical results of comparing two ROC curves. This option is used when ROC curves cross each other resulting in more detailed ROC estimates according the methodology developed by Braga et al. [1] and implemented in Comp2ROC in R [7].

Intrinsic to the **CERCUS** program, the Rserve library is used in the option **Roc Sampling Results** to calculate the respective ROC comparison results using the **Comp2ROC** library [2].

Basically, after selecting **Roc Sampling Results** the dialogue box, shown in Fig. 9a, allows the selection of the variables that the user wants to compare. Internally after selecting the data window, it removes the information about the two variables selected in the dialogue window (see Fig. 9a), calculates the results using the connection with R (Rserve) and consequently presents the results in a new window as presented in Fig. 9b that could export to .HTML format.

### 3.5 Graphs Menu

The **Graphs** menu is intended for presentation of the graphs associated with the analysis through empirical ROC curves. This representation is divided into three parts and the user can subsequently save the produced graphics to a .jpeg file:

(a) **Roc Sampling Results** dialogue box.          (b) Output window.

**Fig. 9.** Example of **Roc Sampling Results** menu.

- Empirical ROC curve(s);
- Empirical ROC curves (2 by 2);
- Area between curves ROC.

Figure 10 illustrates the **Graphs** menu presented in **CERCUS**.

**Fig. 10.** Menu graphs.

The empirical ROC curves are produced by joining the coordinate points, which correspond to the pairs (1 - specificity, sensitivity), calculated for each case. For the option **Empirical ROC curves (2 by 2)** will first be asked to select the variables and then the union of the coordinate points.

For the areas between ROC curves, after the selection of the variables to be compared, the application once again uses the **Rserve** to obtain the values of *Lower Bound*, *Upper Bound* and *Degrees* using the method proposed by Braga et al. [1] implemented in **Comp2ROC**.

Figure 11 shows the set of result windows produced by the introduction of five paired samples (Fig. 10).

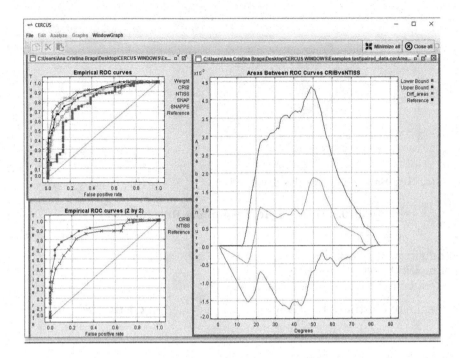

**Fig. 11.** Output graphs.

## 4    Final Remarks

The main focus of this work was the development of an application for personal computers that can integrate the different methodologies of comparison based on empirical ROC curves, allowing the comparison of two systems based on empirical ROC curves that intersect or not.

In the case of the methodology in which the ROC curves that intersect, the **CERCUS** application, in spite of visually identifying the regions of the space where there is better performance of one system in relation to the other, it was not possible to implement a metric conversion algorithm to identify in the unit ROC space which pairs (1-specificity and sensitivity) correspond to this region.

This work allows to answer to the lack of software capable of systematizing the analysis through the ROC curves, particularly with regard to graphical representation and comparison of two or more systems, either for independent data or for paired data.

The elaboration of the algorithm was based on the structure of the ROCNPA program, trying to simplify its functionality to the maximum. Although there are still many improvements to be made to the **CERCUS** interface, it is versatile and robust for analysing samples of any type.

The application was tested on both operating systems, Windows and UNIX, using the R version 3.4.4.

We are aware that the work presented here can be improved and supplemented. For example, implementing a button that can translate the results into a text file will help the user make a more detailed comparison of the ROC curves. On the other hand, since windows are not intuitively available, creating a menu that makes windows open will assist the user in making the selection.

Finally, we believe that the implementation of new ROC analysis methodologies, such as curve fitting and presentation of confidence intervals, will improve the future development of **CERCUS**.

**Acknowledgments.** This work has been supported by FCT – Fundação para a Ciência e Tecnologia within the Project Scope: UID/CEC/00319/2019.

# References

1. Braga, A.C., Costa, L., Oliveira, P.: An alternative method for global and partial comparison of two diagnostic systems based on ROC curves. J. Stat. Comput. Simul. **83**(2), 307–325 (2013)
2. Braga, A.C., Frade, H., Carvalho, S., Santiago, A.M.: Package 'Comp2ROC' (2014). https://cran.r-project.org/web/packages/Comp2ROC/Comp2ROC.pdf
3. Braga, A.C., Oliveira, P.: Diagnostic analysis based on ROC curves: theory and applications in medicine. Int. J. Health Care Qual. Assur. **16**(4), 191–198 (2003)
4. Cheam, A., McNicholas, P.D.: Modelling receiver operating characteristic curves using gaussian mixtures, pp. 1–15 (2014)
5. Delong, E.R., Delong, D.M., Clarke-pearson, D.L., Carolina, N.: Comparing the areas under two or more correlated receiver operating characteristic curves: a nonparametric approach. Biometrics **44**(3), 837–845 (1988)
6. Fawcett, T.: An introduction to ROC analysis. Pattern Recogn. Lett. **27**(8), 861–874 (2006)
7. Frade, H., Braga, A.C.: Comp2roc. In: Mohamad, M.S., Nanni, L., Rocha, M.P., Fdez-Riverola, F. (eds.) 7th International Conference on Practical Applications of Computational Biology & Bioinformatics. AISC, vol. 222, pp. 127–135. Springer, Heidelberg (2013). https://doi.org/10.1007/978-3-319-00578-2_17
8. Greenberg, I., Xu, D., Kumar, D.: Processing Creative Coding and Generative Art in Processing 2. Apress, Berkeley (2013). https://doi.org/10.1007/978-1-4302-4465-3
9. Hajian-Tilaki, K.: Receiver operating characteristic (ROC) curve analysis for medical diagnostic test evaluation (2013)
10. Hanley, A., McNeil, J.: The meaning and use of the area under a receiver operating characteristic (ROC) curve. Radiology **143**, 29–36 (1982)
11. Hanley, J.A., McNeil, B.J.: A method of comparing the areas under receiver operating characteristic curves derived from the same cases. Radiology **148**(3), 839–843 (1983)
12. Mourão, M.F., Braga, A.C.: Evaluation of the CRIB as an indicator of the performance of neonatal intensive care units using the software ROCNPA. In: 2012 12th International Conference on Computational Science and Its Applications, pp. 151–154, June 2012. https://doi.org/10.1109/ICCSA.2012.37

# A Nonlinear Dynamical System Perspective on Team Learning: The Role of Team Culture and Social Cohesion

Isabel Dórdio Dimas[1,2]([✉]) [iD], Teresa Rebelo[3,4] [iD], Paulo Renato Lourenço[3,4] [iD], and Humberto Rocha[5,6] [iD]

[1] ESTGA, Universidade de Aveiro, 3750-127 Águeda, Portugal
idimas@ua.pt
[2] GOVCOPP, Universidade de Aveiro, 3810-193 Aveiro, Portugal
[3] FPCEUC, Universidade de Coimbra, 3000-115 Coimbra, Portugal
{terebelo,prenato}@fpce.uc.pt
[4] IPCDVS, Universidade de Coimbra, 3001-802 Coimbra, Portugal
[5] CeBER and FEUC, Universidade de Coimbra, 3004-512 Coimbra, Portugal
hrocha@mat.uc.pt
[6] INESC-Coimbra, 3030-290 Coimbra, Portugal

**Abstract.** This paper examines team learning within a nonlinear dynamical system (NDS) perspective. Research has successfully identified various conditions that promote learning behaviors in teams. In the present study, our focus is on the role played by team culture and by social cohesion as supporting conditions of team learning. Previous studies revealed that a culture oriented to learning tends to promote the adoption of team learning behaviors in the group. Results concerning the role played by social cohesion in team learning is, however, less clear. Indeed, while social cohesion might promote learning behaviors because it increases the willingness to work together and to help each other, high levels of social cohesion could also lead to uncritical acceptance of solutions. The complex relationship between social cohesion and team learning behaviors led us to study it under the NDS framework. Using the dynamic difference equation model, the present research proposes a cusp catastrophe model for explaining team learning, implementing the team culture as the asymmetry variable and social cohesion as bifurcation variable. The sample of the present research is constituted by 44 project workgroups, and data were collected at two moments of the life cycle (half-time and end) of teams, with single-item visual analogue scales. Results reveal that the cusp models are superior to the pre-post linear models by explaining a larger portion of the variance. In addition, the cubic term, the bifurcation effect and the asymmetry term are statistically significant. Social cohesion acts as a bifurcation factor, that is to say, beyond a certain threshold of social cohesion, groups that have the same cultural orientation might oscillate between two attractors, the modes of high and low learning behaviors respectively. These results suggest that a small variation of social cohesion causes the system to enter an area of unpredictability in terms of team learning, where sudden shifts

© Springer Nature Switzerland AG 2019
S. Misra et al. (Eds.): ICCSA 2019, LNCS 11621, pp. 38–49, 2019.
https://doi.org/10.1007/978-3-030-24302-9_4

in the outcomes might be expected. Leaders and members need to monitor the levels of social cohesion of the team, to avoid phenomena like groupthink, which jeopardizes the implementation of learning behaviors, such as the exploration of different opinions or error discussion.

**Keywords:** Cusp model · Nonlinear analysis · Team learning · Team cohesion · Team culture

# 1    Introduction

Organizations worldwide face, more than ever, the need to continually rethinking their practices in order to succeed and to be sustainable over time. The ability to reflect, to experiment with new ways, rejecting old models and adopting more appropriate strategies, i.e., the capacity to learn, emerges as a fundamental process for individuals, teams and organizations [1]. As teams are the cornerstone of modern organizations [2], team learning has a central role in the team and organizational success [3–5].

According to Edmondson, Dillon, and Roloff [6], team learning might be conceptualized as performance improvement (i.e., as an increase in knowledge), as task mastery (i.e., the ability to coordinate team members' knowledge to accomplish tasks) or as a process of collectively sharing, discussing and reflecting on experience. In the present study, team learning is conceptualized as a process that involves different behaviors: seeking internal and external feedback in order to evaluate the group functioning and results; exploring new approaches and sharing and debating ideas; testing new paths to achieve the teams' aims; reflecting on the team behavior and results; analyzing errors and discussing ways to prevent them [7].

Due to the key role that team learning has in organizations, studying the conditions that enable teams to learn is of crucial importance for both research and practice. In the present study, our aim is contributing to the body of knowledge of team learning, by analyzing the antecedents of this team process adopting a nonlinear dynamical system (NDS) perspective. The NDS approach is the "study of how complex processes unfold over time and is sometimes known as chaos theory or complexity theory" [8]. It is not simply a group of methods for nonlinear data analysis, rather it is a set of concepts that describe ways by which a system can change over time [9]. The theoretical concepts and methodological tools of the NDS approach have been applied in several fields of social and behavioral sciences, namely in the study of group dynamics (e.g., [10–13]). Indeed, in order to acknowledge the complexity of teams, one should adopt perspectives and methods that recognize the nonlinear nature of the relationships that take place in the team context [14].

Research has successfully identified various conditions that promote the learning process in teams. It has been shown that, among other variables, team culture, that is, team members' beliefs about "the way things are done" in the group could have this kind of influence [5,15]. Team culture is an emergent set of norms, values and actions that team members develop and share [16] and is characterized by a certain stability over time. Indeed, when a hint, a value or a rule is implemented and works repeatedly and successfully [17] becomes a guide for action, influencing the way team members behave and interact with each other. Since team learning is a set of behaviors that involve sharing, reflecting and discussing, it is expected that different team cultures will have distinct impacts on the learning behaviors that are adopted by the team. Therefore, in teams where the shared values are oriented to learning, learning behaviors will be more frequent than in teams with a team culture less oriented to learning [15]. Accordingly, a positive linear relationship is expected between team learning orientation and team learning behaviors.

Team cohesion, which can be defined as the result of all the forces acting on members to remain in the team [18], has been also identified as a supporting condition for team learning [19]. Team cohesion has been conceptualized as a multidimensional concept, being the two-dimensional model, which distinguishes between task and social cohesion, widely accepted [20,21]. Previous studies found that task cohesion, i.e., the shared commitment among members to achieve goals that requires collective efforts, is a supporting condition of team learning behaviors (e.g., [22]). Results for the role of social cohesion, which concerns emotional bonds, such as liking, sense of belonging, caring, and closeness among group members, are, however, less clear (e.g., [3,19,23]). By promoting the desire of being part of the group, social cohesion might increase the levels of resources (e.g., cognitive, temporal) that team members invest in the team, increasing team learning behaviors. At the same time, social cohesion may lead to uncritical acceptance of solutions, namely due to team members' fear of being rejected. The studies reviewed by Bell *et al.* [19] pointed to this direction, suggesting that cohesion enhances team learning processes, but at the same time learning may be impeded when teams are characterized by excessive social integration or when cohesion is not supplemented with processes that facilitate the critical processing of information.

Thus, the ambiguous findings regarding the relationship between social cohesion and team learning behaviors that emerged from previous studies using linear models led us to study it under the NDS framework, in order to analyze social cohesion as a bifurcation variable, using cusp catastrophe modeling. Catastrophe models enables the analysis of discontinuous, abrupt changes in dependent variables resulting from small and continuous changes in independent variables [24]. In particular, cusp catastrophe models describe change between two stable states of the dependent variable (i.e., order parameter) and two independent variables (i.e., control parameters). The possibility of modeling discontinuous changes is one advantage of this technique that can contribute to the knowledge about the complex relationships between either team processes or emergent states with team outcomes [25].

Thus, under the scope of the NDS approach, the purpose of this study is to test a cusp model, summarized in Fig. 1. Team learning is considered the dependent variable or the order parameter, which is influenced by team culture

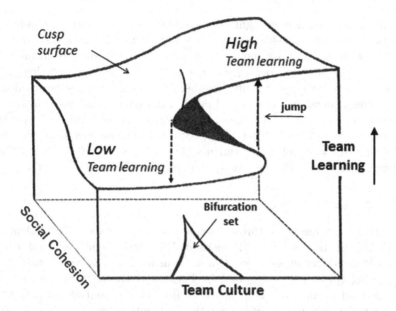

**Fig. 1.** A three-dimensional display of the cusp catastrophe response surface of team learning as a function of team culture (asymmetry) and social cohesion (bifurcation).

and social cohesion (independent variables or control parameters). Based on the literature presented above, it is expected that team culture will maintain a linear relationship with team learning over time. However, it might be positive or negative, depending on the characteristics of the culture that is developed by the teams. Hence, team culture will be considered the asymmetry variable in the cusp model since this type of control parameter is related to the order parameter in a consistent pattern [25]. Since the inconsistency of results concerning the relationship between social cohesion and team learning might be a clue for the existence of a nonlinear and complex relationship, social cohesion is a candidate for the role of bifurcation parameter.

## 2 Materials and Methods

### 2.1 Procedure and Participants

Data were collected on 44 teams made up of undergraduate students of engineering and technology courses of one Portuguese university. These courses are organized according to the Problem Based Learning (PBL) model. The teams (randomly constituted) have a semester to develop their work, which consists of a project that gives an answer to a current organizational need. Each group has a tutor that acts as a facilitator, guiding the group when needed. Data were collected at the middle (T1) and at the end (T2) of the academic semester. In T1, team members were asked about what had occurred since the beginning of the group till that moment (roughly in the half of its allotted time). Similarly, in T2, participants were asked to respond based on what had happened since the last data collection. At both moments of data collection, data regarding team culture and team learning behaviors were collected in a team meeting, where members answered a questionnaire together by reaching a consensus. Information concerning social cohesion was obtained from team members individually.

Teams were composed of 4 members on average (SD = 0.9; min = 3, max = 6). The mean age was 24 years (SD = 6.5), 88% of the team members were male and the majority were full time students (78%). Finally, 31% of students were attending the first year, 7% the second year and 55% the third year of the degree.

## 2.2   Measures

All constructs were measured through single-item measures and Visual Analogue Scales (VAS). In the case of multidimensional constructs (such as, team culture and team learning behaviors) a single-item measure was created for each dimension following the criteria suggested by Fuchs and Diamantopoulos [26]. The use of this kind of measures is in line with Roe, Gockel and Meyer [27], which state that multi-item measures are not the best option for capturing change in groups over time and that single-item measures and graphic scales are suitable alternatives in longitudinal studies.

These single-item measures were submitted to a set of experts and to three pilot studies for estimating content and face validities, respectively, and no problems have been identified, as reported in Santos, Costa, Rebelo, Lourenço, and Dimas [28]. To overcome some psychometric shortcomings of single-item measures and raise the confidence in their use in this study, convergent validity studies with the original instruments on which these measures were based [26], were carried out.

**Team Learning.** To measure the occurrence of team learning behaviors, five single-item measures were developed based on the multi-item Team Learning Behaviors' Instrument [29], which in turn is based on Edmondson's [7] types of learning behaviors. Thus, our five single-item measures correspond to five team learning behaviors: exploring and co-construction of meaning, collective reflection, error management, feedback seeking, and experimenting. An example of this single-items is the item developed for assessing error management behavior: "we discussed collectively our errors and the best way to avoid them". In the five single-items, teams had to mark on a VAS, from 0 (*never*) to 10 (*always*), the occurrence of the respective learning behavior. Concerning validity studies, a sample of 212 Portuguese higher education students was used. The correlations between each single-item measure and the respective multi-item dimension of the Team Learning Behaviors' Instrument ranged from .48 to .68. These results offer satisfactory confidence in these single-item measures.

**Team Culture.** Four single-item measures were developed based on the FOCUS questionnaire [30], an international questionnaire that measures organizational culture according to Quinn's [31] competing values model. Thus, four cultural orientations were assessed in each group: support (emphasizes the establishment of cohesion and commitment in the group), innovation (highlights flexibility, change, and creativity), rules (values internal stability through efficiency and coordination), and goals (is oriented towards performance and goals achievement). An example of these single-items is the one developed to assess support orientation "our team was characterized by: mutual understanding, acceptance of failure, mutual trust, mutual support when carrying out tasks, good interpersonal relationships, good working atmosphere, mutual support in issues not related to work". Each group had to mark on a VAS, from 0 (*not at all*) to 10 (*absolutely*) the presence of each of the four cultural orientations. The sample used for the validity studies was made up of 250 Portuguese higher education students. Regarding convergent validity, the correlations between the single-item measure and the respective multi-item dimension of the FOCUS questionnaire (adapted for the group level) ranged from .53 to .67. All in all, and similarly to the single-item measures for team learning behaviors, these results are satisfactory.

**Social Cohesion.** One single-item was developed ("to what extent I felt part of this team?"), where team members' were asked to mark on a VAS, from 0 (*not at all*) to 10 (*absolutely*) their feeling. The choice of this single-item was based on the multi-item social cohesion scale of Sargent and Sue-Chan [32] and on the items that measure social cohesion of the Group Environment Questionnaire (GEQ), originally developed by Carron, Widmeyer, and Brawley [33] and adapted by Chang and Bordia [34] for use with work teams.

In terms of convergent validity, the sample of 212 Portuguese higher education students (previously mentioned for team learning single-items validation) was used. The correlation with our single-item measure with the GEQ social cohesion items was .43, offering sufficient confidence in its subsequent use.

## 2.3   Data Analysis Procedures

Mathematically, the cusp model is expressed by a potential function $f(y)$:

$$f(y/a, b) = ay + \frac{1}{2}by^2 - \frac{1}{4}y^4. \tag{1}$$

Equation (1) represents a dynamical system, which is seeking to optimize some function [35,36]. Setting the first derivative of the Eq. (1) to zero, it results in the Eq. (2), which represents the three-dimensional equilibrium response surface of the cusp model:

$$\frac{df(y)}{dy} = 0 \Leftrightarrow -y^3 + by + a = 0, \tag{2}$$

where $a$ is the asymmetry factor and $b$ is the bifurcation factor.

In the present research design, two measurements of team learning behaviors were carried out at the middle of teams' life (T1) and at the end of the teams' life (T2). These two measures in time facilitate the application of the dynamic difference equation modeling approach, which implements least squares regression techniques [37].

The specific equation to be tested in this study for a cusp catastrophe model is:

$$\Delta z = z_2 - z_1 = b_1 z_1^3 + b_2 z_1 SC + b_3 C + b_4 \tag{3}$$

where $z$ is the normalized order parameter, while $SC$ and $C$ are the normalized bifurcation (Social Cohesion) and the asymmetry (Culture) at T1, respectively. The nonlinear model is tested against its linear alternatives, from which the most antagonistic is the pre/post model:

$$z_2 = b_1 SC + b_2 C + b_3 z_1 + b_4. \tag{4}$$

In order to test the nonlinear hypothesis that a cusp catastrophe is an appropriate model to describe teams' learning, the regression Eq. (3) should account for a larger percent of the variance in the dependent variable than the linear alternatives. In addition, the coefficients of both the cubic and the product terms in Eq. (3) must be statistically significant.

The sum of the five team learning behaviors was used as order parameter, since this sum shows how much learning behaviors each team engaged, independently of each form of learning. As aforesaid, social cohesion was implemented as bifurcation variable, while the four types of cultural orientation were implemented as asymmetry variables.

The unit of analysis in the present study is the group thus members' answers to social cohesion single-item were aggregated to the team level. In order to justify this aggregation, the $AD_M$ index [38] was used. The average $AD_M$ value obtained was 1.23 (SD $= 1.22$), which is below the upper-limit criterion of 2.0, allowing the aggregation of team members' scores to the team level.

## 3   Results

Table 1 presents the means, standard deviations and the correlation matrix for all variables under study.

Tables 2, 3, 4 and 5 show the regression slopes and standard errors for four cusp catastrophe models and their pre/post linear counterparts (one for each cultural orientation).

As can be observed, the four cusp models are superior to the respective pre-post linear models by explaining a larger portion of the variance (The $R^2$ values obtained for the cusp models are .43 for support culture, .42 for rules culture, .52 for innovation culture and .42 for goals orientation as asymmetry variables, against .19, .08, .18, and .19, respectively). Additionally, in all four cusp models, the cubic term, the bifurcation and the asymmetry are statistically significant, although support and rules orientations emerged as marginally significant asymmetry variables.

Overall, the results reveal the existence of a cusp structure in our data. The role of social cohesion as bifurcation variable is supported, revealing a nonlinear and discontinuous effect in the process of team learning.

**Table 1.** Means, standard deviations, and intercorrelations of study variables.

| | Mean | SD | 1 | 2 | 3 | 4 | 5 | 6 | 7 |
|---|---|---|---|---|---|---|---|---|---|
| 1. Social cohesion T1 | 7.87 | 1.54 | – | – | – | – | – | – | – |
| 2. Support T1 | 7.71 | 1.93 | .13 | – | – | – | – | – | – |
| 3. Innovation T1 | 7.31 | 2.14 | .23 | $.46^{***}$ | – | – | – | – | – |
| 4. Rules T1 | 6.69 | 1.97 | .20 | $.55^{***}$ | $.48^{***}$ | – | – | – | – |
| 5. Goal T1 | 6.79 | 2.24 | .08 | $.62^{***}$ | $.40^{**}$ | $.54^{***}$ | – | – | – |
| 6. Team learning T1 | 39.58 | 7.62 | .04 | $.72^{***}$ | $.33^{*}$ | $.35^{*}$ | $.52^{***}$ | – | – |
| 7. Team learning T2 | 40.64 | 6.59 | .15 | .28 | .17 | .05 | .05 | $.31^{*}$ | – |

Note: $^{***}$ $p < .001$, $^{**}$ $p < .01$, $^{*}$ $p < .05$.

**Table 2.** The difference model estimated by least squares regression: Model Fit for Cusp and the Linear Control. Support culture as asymmetry variable.

| Model | Variable name | $R^2$ | B | SE B | $\beta$ |
|---|---|---|---|---|---|
| **Pre/Post** | | $.19^{*}$ | | | |
| $z_1$ | Team learning | | 0.43 | 0.15 | $.47^{***}$ |
| b | Social cohesion | | 0.11 | 0.14 | .12 |
| a | Support | | 0.31 | 0.16 | .31 |
| **Cusp 1** | | $.43^{***}$ | | | |
| $z_1^3$ | Team learning | | −0.13 | 0.04 | $−.50^{***}$ |
| b | Social cohesion × $z_1$ | | 0.38 | 0.15 | $.33^{*}$ |
| a | Support | | 0.34 | 0.17 | $.29^{\dagger}$ |

Note: $^{***}$ $p < .001$, $^{**}$ $p < .01$, $^{*}$ $p < .05$, $^{\dagger}$ $p < .10$.

**Table 3.** The difference model estimated by least squares regression: Model Fit for Cusp and the Linear Control. Rules culture as asymmetry variable.

| Model | Variable name | $R^2$ | B | SE B | $\beta$ |
|---|---|---|---|---|---|
| **Pre/Post** | | .08 | | | |
| $z_1$ | Team learning | | 0.26 | 0.15 | .26 |
| b | Social cohesion | | 0.07 | 0.15 | .07 |
| a | Rules | | 0.09 | 0.15 | .10 |
| **Cusp 1** | | $.42^{***}$ | | | |
| $z_1^3$ | Team learning | | −0.18 | 0.04 | $−.67^{***}$ |
| b | Social cohesion × $z_1$ | | 0.35 | 0.16 | $.29^{*}$ |
| a | Rules | | 0.26 | 0.15 | $.22^{\dagger}$ |

Note: $^{***}$ $p < .001$, $^{**}$ $p < .01$, $^{*}$ $p < .05$, $^{\dagger}$ $p < .10$.

**Table 4.** The difference model estimated by least squares regression: Model Fit for Cusp and the Linear Control. Innovation culture as asymmetry variable.

| Model | Variable name | $R^2$ | B | SE B | $\beta$ |
|---|---|---|---|---|---|
| **Pre/Post** | | .18* | | | |
| $z_1$ | Team learning | | 0.30 | 0.14 | .30* |
| b | Social cohesion | | 0.16 | 0.14 | .16 |
| a | Innovation | | 0.25 | 0.14 | .25 |
| **Cusp 1** | | .52*** | | | |
| $z_1^3$ | Team learning | | −0.21 | 0.03 | −.78*** |
| b | Social cohesion × $z_1$ | | 0.32 | 1.35 | .28* |
| a | Innovation | | 0.48 | 0.14 | .42*** |

Note: *** p < .001, ** p < .01, * p < .05, † p < .10.

**Table 5.** The difference model estimated by least squares regression: Model Fit for Cusp and the Linear Control. Goal culture as asymmetry variable.

| Model | Variable name | $R^2$ | B | SE B | $\beta$ |
|---|---|---|---|---|---|
| **Pre/Post** | | .19* | | | |
| $z_1$ | Team learning | | 0.36 | 0.15 | .37* |
| b | Social cohesion | | 0.10 | 0.14 | .10 |
| a | Goals | | 0.32 | 0.15 | .33* |
| **Cusp 1** | | .42*** | | | |
| $z_1^3$ | Team learning | | −0.15 | 0.04 | −.57*** |
| b | Social cohesion × $z_1$ | | 0.32 | 0.15 | .27* |
| a | Goals | | 0.32 | 0.15 | .28* |

Note: *** p < .001, ** p < .01, * p < .05, † p < .10.

## 4 Discussion and Conclusions

The findings of this study suggest that both team culture and social cohesion play a significant role in the team learning process, but that their contributions are different. The emergence of cusp structures with social cohesion acting as a bifurcation factor suggests that beyond a certain threshold of social cohesion, groups that have the same cultural orientation might oscillate between two attractors, the modes of high and low learning behaviors respectively. That is to say, a small variation of social cohesion could cause the system to enter an area of unpredictability in terms of team learning, where sudden shifts in the occurrence of learning behaviors might be expected.

Thus, this study supports the nonlinear dynamics of the learning process in groups, adding to the growing body of research that considers teams as complex, adaptive and dynamic social systems [39]. It also contributes to the small group research literature by presenting the role for social cohesion as bifurcation, which might explain the discrepancies between various findings related to the effect of social cohesion on team learning behaviors (e.g., [19]). The idea that beyond a certain threshold, social cohesion might induce a bifurcation effect in team learning behaviors suggests that team supervisors and members should be aware that high social cohesion may lead to some phenomena, such as groupthink [40], which in turn, can lead members to avoid team learning behaviors, such as the exploration of different opinions or error discussion.

Regarding the asymmetry variable (group culture), the four cultural orientations analyzed (support, innovation, rules and goals) are positively related to the learning process in teams. Therefore, our results highlight that the presence of all the four orientations is important to the adoption of team learning behaviors, although the innovation and the goals culture assume a more prominent role in promoting learning in teams. This finding is in line with the operationalization of learning culture proposed by Škerlavaj, Štemberger, Škrinjar, and Dimovsky [41], who suggest that a learning culture predominantly covers support and innovation orientations, while it has aspects of goals and rules orientations.

Despite the contributions of this study, it also has limitations. Two of them are the sample size and the type of groups of the sample (project groups of students). Therefore, future studies should replicate the present findings with different teams, such as organizational workgroups, and with larger samples.

# References

1. Wilson, J.P.: Human Resource Development: Learning for individuals & organizations. Kogan Page, London (2001)
2. Mathieu, J.E., Tannenbaum, S.I., Donsbach, J.S., Alliger, G.M.: A review and Integration of team composition models moving toward a dynamic and temporal framework. J. Manag. **40**, 130–160 (2014)
3. Decuyper, S., Dochy, F., Van Den Bossche, P.: Grasping the dynamic complexity of team learning: an integrative model for effective team learning in organisations. Educ. Res. Rev. **5**, 111–133 (2010)
4. Koeslag-Kreunen, M., Van den Bossche, P., Hoven, M., Van der Klink, M., Gijselaers, W.: When leadership powers team learning: a meta-analysis. Small Gr. Res. **49**, 475–513 (2018)
5. Sessa, V., London, M.: Group learning: an introduction. In: Sessa, V., London, M. (eds.) Work Group Learning. Understanding, Improving and Assessing How Groups Learn in Organizations, pp. 1–14. Lawrence Erlbaum, Mahwah (2008)
6. Edmondson, A.C., Dillon, J.R., Roloff, K.S.: Three perspectives on team learning. Acad. Manag. Ann. **1**, 269–314 (2007)
7. Edmondson, A.C.: Psychological safety and learning behavior in work teams. Admin. Sci. Quart. **44**, 350–383 (1999)
8. Guastello, S.J., Liebovitch, L.S.: Introduction to nonlinear dynamics and complexity. In: Guastello, S.J., Koopmans, M., Pincus, D. (eds.) Chaos and Complexity in Psychology: Theory of Nonlinear Dynamical Systems. The Cambridge University Press, Cambridge (2009)
9. Guastello, S.J.: Catastrophe modeling of equity in organizations. Behav. Sci. **26**, 63–74 (2007)

10. Dimas, I.D., Rebelo, T., Lourenço, P.R., Rocha, H.: A cusp catastrophe model for satisfaction, conflict, and conflict management in teams. In: Gervasi, O., et al. (eds.) ICCSA 2018. LNCS, vol. 10961, pp. 335–350. Springer, Cham (2018). https://doi.org/10.1007/978-3-319-95165-2_24
11. Gorman, J.C., Amazeen, P.G., Cooke, N.J.: Team coordination dynamics. Nonlinear Dyn. Psychol. Life Sci. **14**, 265–289 (2010)
12. Guastello, S.J., Correro, A.N., Marra, D.E.: Cusp catastrophe models for cognitive workload and fatigue in teams. Appl. Ergon (2018)
13. Ramos-Villagrasa, P.J., Marques-Quinteiro, P., Navarro, J., Rico, R.: Teams as complex adaptive systems: reviewing 17 years of research. Small Gr. Res. **49**, 135–176 (2018)
14. Mathieu, J.E., Hollenbeck, J.R., van Knippenberg, D., Ilgen, D.R.: A century of work teams in the journal of applied psychology. J. Appl. Psychol. **102**, 452–467 (2017)
15. Rebelo, T., Stamovlasis, D., Lourenço, P.R., Dimas, I., Pinheiro, M.: A Cusp catastrophe model for team learning, team potency and team culture. Nonlinear Dyn. Psychol. Life Sci. **20**, 537–563 (2016)
16. Earley, P.C., Mosakowski, E.: Creating hybrid team cultures: an empirical test of transnational team functioning. Acad. Manag. J. **43**, 26–49 (2000)
17. Schein, E.: Organizational Culture and Leadership, 2nd edn. Jossey-Bass, San Francisco (1992)
18. Festinger, L.: Informal social communication. Psych. Rev. **57**, 271–282 (1950)
19. Bell, B.S., Kozlowski, S.W.J., Blawath, S.: Team learning: a theoretical integration and review. In: Kozlowski, S.W.J. (ed.) The Oxford Handbook of Organizational Psychology, vol. 2, pp. 859–909. Oxford University Press, Oxford (2012)
20. Mullen, B., Copper, C.: The relation between group cohesiveness and performance: an integration. Psychol. Bull. **115**, 210–227 (1994)
21. Vanhove, A.J., Herian, M.N.: Team cohesion and individual well-being: a conceptual analysis and relational framework. In: Salas, E., Vessey, W.B., Estrada, A.X. (eds.) Team Cohesion: Advances in Psychological Theory, Methods and Practice. Research on Managing Groups and Teams, vol. 17, pp. 53–82. Emerald Group Publishing Limited, Bingley (2015)
22. Van Den Bossche, P., Gijselaers, W.H., Segers, M., Kirschner, P.: Social and cognitive factors driving teamwork in collaborative learning environments. Small Gr. Res. **37**, 490–521 (2006)
23. Wong, S.: Distal and local group learning: performance trade-offs and tensions. Organ. Sci. **15**, 645–656 (2004)
24. Thom, R.: Structural Stability and Morphogenesis: An Outline of a General Theory of Models. W. A. Benjamim, Reading (1975)
25. Escartin, J., Ceja, L., Navarro, J., Zapf, D.: Modeling workplace bullying using catastrophe theory. Nonlinear Dyn. Psychol. Life Sci. **17**, 493–515 (2013)
26. Fuchs, C., Diamantopoulos, A.: Using single-item measures for construct measurement in management research: conceptual issues and application guidelines. Die Betriebswirtschaft **69**, 197–212 (2009)
27. Roe, R.A., Gockel, C., Meyer, B.: Time and change in teams: where we are and where we are moving. Eur. J. Work Organ. Psychol. **21**, 629–656 (2012)
28. Santos, G., Costa, T., Rebelo, T., Lourenço, P.R., Dimas, I.: Desenvolvimento Grupal: uma abordagem com base na teoria dos sistemas dinâmicos não lineares - Construção/adaptação e validação de instrumento de medida [Group development: A nonlinear dynamical system approach - development/adaptation and validation of a measure]. In: Actas do VIII SNIP, Aveiro, Portugal (2013)

29. Savelsbergh, C.M.J.H., van der Heijden, B.I.J.M., Poell, R.F.: The development and empirical validation of a multidimensional measurement instrument for team learning behaviors. Small Gr. Res. **40**, 578–607 (2009)
30. Van Muijen, J., Koopman, P., De Witte, K., De Cock, G., Turnipseed, D.: Organizational culture: the focus questionnaire. Eur. J. Work Organ. Psychol. **8**, 551–568 (1999)
31. Quinn, R.E.: Beyond Rational Management: Mastering the Paradoxes and Competing Demands of High Performance. Jossey-Bass, San Francisco (1988)
32. Sargent, L.D., Sue-Chan, C.: Does diversity affect group efficacy?: the intervening role of cohesion and task interdependence. Small Gr. Res. **32**, 426–450 (2001)
33. Carron, A.V., Widmeyer, W.N., Brawley, L.R.: The development of an instrument to assess cohesion in sport teams: the group environment questionnaire. J. Sport Psychol. **7**, 244–266 (1985)
34. Chang, A., Bordia, P.: A multidimensional approach to the group cohesion group performance relationship. Small Gr. Res. **32**, 379–405 (2001)
35. Gilmore, R.: Catastrophe Theory for Scientists and Engineers. Wiley, New York (1981)
36. Poston, T., Stewart, I.: Catastrophe Theory and its Applications. Dover Publications, New York (1978)
37. Guastello, S.J.: Managing Emergent Phenomena: Non-Linear Dynamics in Work Organizations. Erlbaum, Mahwah (2002)
38. Burke, M.J., Finkelstein, L.M., Dusig, M.S.: On average deviation indices for estimating interrater agreement. Organ. Res. Methods **2**, 49–68 (1999)
39. Sundstrom, E., De Meuse, K.P., Futrell, D.: Work teams: applications and effectiveness. Am. Psychol. **45**, 120–133 (1990)
40. Janis, I.L.: Victims of Groupthink. Houghton Mifflin, Boston (1972)
41. Škerlavaj, M., Štemberger, M.I., Škrinjar, R., Dimovski, V.: Organizational learning culture - the missing link between business process change and organizational performance. Int. J. Prod. Econ. **106**, 346–367 (2007)

# Demand Forecasting: A Case Study in the Food Industry

Juliana C. Silva[1] , Manuel C. Figueiredo[2]([⊠]) , and Ana C. Braga[2]

[1] DPS, School of Engineering, University of Minho, Braga, Portugal
ju_silva21@hotmail.com
[2] ALGORITMI Centre, University of Minho, 4710-057 Braga, Portugal
{mcf,acb}@dps.uminho.pt

**Abstract.** The use of forecasting methods is nowadays regarded as a business ally since it supports both the operational and the strategic decision-making processes.

This paper is based on a research project aiming the development of demand forecasting models for a company (designated here by PR) that operates in the food business, more specifically in the delicatessen segment.

In particular, we focused on demand forecasting models that can serve as a tool to support production planning and inventory management at the company.

The analysis of the company's operations led to the development of a new demand forecasting tool based on a combination of forecasts, which is now being used and tested by the company.

**Keywords:** Forecasting demand · Exponential smoothing · ARIMA · Combining forecasts

## 1 Introduction

### 1.1 The Company

PR Company already has more than half a century of history, presenting itself today as a reference company in the production and distribution of delicatessen.

From its foundation to the present, PR has specialized and transformed itself into a modern organization, with a professional management and equipped with the latest technologies, thus managing to anticipate the challenges and specificities of competitiveness and globalization without never losing its roots in Portugal.

It should also be mentioned that PR is a highly certified company by several standards that attest Quality Management Systems (ISO 9001: 2008), Environmental Management System (ISO 14001: 2004) and Food Safety Management Systems (ISO 22000: 2005). It is also internationally recognized by specific standards by the food industry, such as IFS - International Featured Standard, which strengthens its competitiveness in the global market.

© Springer Nature Switzerland AG 2019
S. Misra et al. (Eds.): ICCSA 2019, LNCS 11621, pp. 50–63, 2019.
https://doi.org/10.1007/978-3-030-24302-9_5

The company's strategy is essentially a sustained business growth, always guaranteeing a quality of excellence to the consumer, assuming quality and safety as a business priority. In order to respond to market demand, PR presents a diverse portfolio of products, which can be grouped into six different product families as shown in Fig. 1.

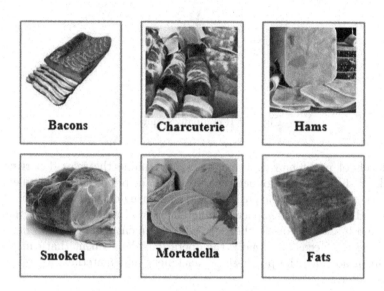

**Fig. 1.** Product families.

Currently, PR is present in the most diverse sectors of the national distribution: retail, cash & carry, modern distribution and professional channels.

In addition to the domestic market, where it has been gaining strength and holding leading positions, PR has already achieved strong internationalization of its brand in countries such as: Angola, Brazil, France, Germany, Holland, Luxembourg, Mozambique, United Kingdom, Russia, South Africa and Sweden (Fig. 2).

## 1.2   The Importance of Demand Forecasting in the Food Industry

Due to the increasing level of competitiveness among companies, forecasting plays an important role in supply chain management, and the viability of a company is often dependent on the efficiency and accuracy of forecasts [14]. Demand forecasts are behind all strategic and planning decisions in any retail business as they directly affect the company's profitability and competitive position.

For these reasons, the use of demand forecasting techniques is a fundamental support in planning and managing a company's supply chain [7].

Its importance becomes patent, since its outcome is used for many functions within the organization: they allow the financial department to estimate

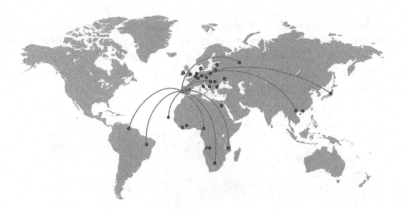

**Fig. 2.** PR company's markets.

costs, levels of profit and capital needs; they enable the sales department to obtain know-how of each product's sales volume; the purchasing department may plan short- and long-term acquisitions; the marketing department can plan their actions and evaluate the impact of different marketing strategies on the sales volume and brand awareness; the logistics department will be able to define the specific logistics needs and finally, the operations department that can manage and plan in advance the purchase of machinery and materials, as well as the hiring of labor.

It is therefore consensual that forecasts are very useful, and even essential for most companies. Accurate demand forecasts have the potential to increase profitability, improving the chain's efficiency and reducing waste.

This paper describes various demand forecasting models for products made by a food company. In the food business, a proper management of inventories involves numerous articles whose particular characteristics, namely perishability, are relevant. Bad decisions in this area can lead to large losses related to excess stock.

## 2   Demand Forecasting

### 2.1   Demand Forecasting Methods

Predicting demand is a fundamental activity as it can reveal market trends and contribute to the strategic planning of the company. According to [1], demand forecasting is an essential tool for a faster and safer decision-making process.

There are several techniques available to support analysts in forecasting demand. Although these techniques have substantial differences, there are common characteristics:

- They generally assume that the causes that have influenced demand in the past will continue to act in the future;

- Forecast accuracy decreases as the forecasting horizon increases;
- Aggregated forecasts for product groups are more accurate than individual product forecasts.

Forecasting methods may be divided into quantitative and qualitative methods. Quantitative methods require the construction of mathematical models, using historical data, that describe demand variation over time. These methods include decomposition, moving averages, exponential smoothing, ARIMA, etc.

In general, qualitative methods result from the opinion of process specialists to predict demand. They are frequently questioned as the systematic approach provided by quantitative techniques presents a better performance concerning future estimates. However, in cases of information scarcity, for example in the launching of new products, the experience and know-how of managers may be useful.

## 2.2   Demand Forecasting Process at PR

The data available consisted of weekly sales from the first week of 2013 through week 17 of 2016 (Fig. 3).

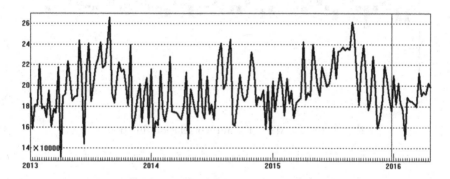

**Fig. 3.** Sales from week 1 of 2013 to week 17 of 2016.

We start by analysing how the company predicts its sales in order to optimize processes and reduce unnecessary stocks or avoid lost sales.

The demand forecast performed by PR is based on a 4-week moving average. Thus in week $t$, a demand forecast for week $t + 2$ is made for each product based on the actual sales concerning weeks $t - 4$, $t - 3$, $t - 2$ and $t - 1$.

Fig. 4 shows the actual sales (black) and the forecasts obtained with the 4-week moving average model (red).

The error autocorrelation function for this model is illustrated in Fig. 5.

We evaluated the normality of the errors using Kolmogorov-Smirnov test, which reveals that the errors could be considered normally distributed ($p = .200$). This result is illustrated in Fig. 6 (a and b).

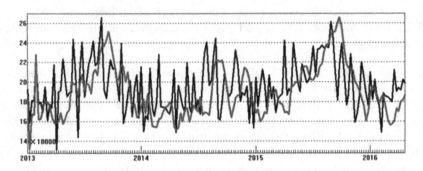

**Fig. 4.** Actual sales vs Forecasts using the 4-week MA model. (Color figure online)

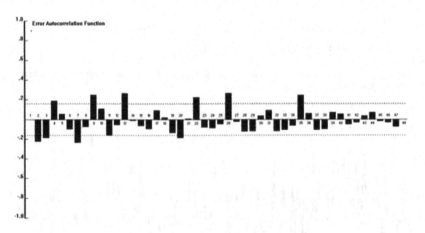

**Fig. 5.** 4-week MA error autocorrelation function.

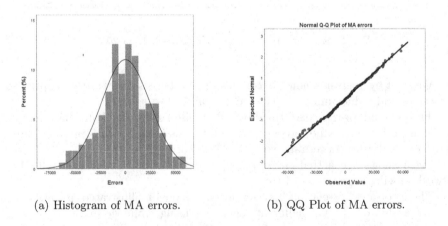

(a) Histogram of MA errors.           (b) QQ Plot of MA errors.

**Fig. 6.** Normality assumption for MA errors.

Currently, and as a form of support, the company has a file in Excel format, which is updated weekly with the actual sales.

These base forecasts may be adjusted according to qualitative information obtained from its sales force. Salespeople play a key role in obtaining information for forecasts as they work very closely to customers and to the market. It is up to the task manager to generate forecasts, informally collect information from the sales team in order to adjust the base forecasts, obtained from the method above described.

The inputs collected from the commercial team can be of various nature. For example, a sales campaign for a particular product for a particular customer, or the exit from the market of a competing product. In this case, the sensitivity and experience of the task manager comes into play, which can increase or decrease orders to a reasonably weighted value.

Accordingly, the value of expected sales (in kg), calculated on the basis of the 4-week moving average, is adjusted by the person responsible for the forecasts, which includes the inputs that he collects from both past sales and future sales. The aim is mainly to try to decode the demand peaks of certain products and/or their low demand in certain weeks.

In summary, after the calculation of the base forecasts based on the 4-week moving averages (MA), in order to include all the relevant information it becomes necessary to receive inputs from the marketing area (promotion of new products and promotional plans), the commercial area (customer and market data) and operational planning (capacity constraints, logistics, etc.) in order to adjust the values against these inputs.

After collection, processing and analysis phases, the final values obtained are validated once more and communicated to the production planning department.

## 3   Exponential Smoothing Models

In the moving average method described in the previous section, the forecast is determined by assigning the same weight to each of the last 4 observations available ($t - 1$, $t - 2$, $t - 3$ and $t - 4$) and ignoring all the older observations (prior to week $(t - 4)$).

However, it is reasonable to assume that the most recent observations contain more relevant information about what might happen in the future and therefore should have a greater weight in forecasting than the older observations. Exponential smoothing methods are based on this principle.

Exponential smoothing is one of the most popular forecasting methods. This method applies a weighted average to the observations of a time series, with greater weights being given to the most recent information.

Single exponential smoothing is based on the Eq. 1

$$F_{t+1} = \alpha X_t + (1 - \alpha)F_t \qquad (1)$$

where $F_{t+1}$ is the forecast for period $t + 1$, $\alpha$ is the smoothing constant and $X_t$ is the observed value for period $t$.

Since the smoothing constant varies between 0 and 1, more weight is given to the most recent observations in determining forecasts. Its application in forecasting appears to have been pioneered in 1956 by Robert Brown. In 1957, Holt described double exponential smoothing and, in 1960, Peter R. Winters improved the algorithm by adding seasonality. This algorithm became known as triple exponential smoothing or the Holt-Winters method [10, 13].

Using data from 2013, 2014 and 2015 and the Forecast Pro software, we developed exponential smoothing models to forecast the first 17 weeks of 2016. The model selection criterion was the Mean Absolute Deviation (MAD), defined in Eq. 2.

$$MAD = \frac{\sum_{i=1}^{n} |X_i - F_i|}{n} \tag{2}$$

where $X_i$ and $F_i$ represent, respectively, the actual sales in week $i$ and sales forecast for week $i$.

The model that minimized within sample MAD is described in Table 1.

Table 1. Exponential smoothing model selected.

| Forecast model | Exponential smoothing: No trend, Multiplicative seasonality |
|---|---|
| Smoothing weights | |
| Level | $\alpha = 0.05227$ |
| Seasonal | $\gamma = 0.3294$ |
| Mean Absolute Deviation: | $MAD = 14100$ |

Figure 7 shows the actual sales (black) and the forecasts obtained with the selected model (red).

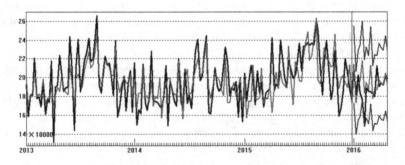

Fig. 7. Actual sales vs Forecasts using Exponential smoothing model. (Color figure online)

The error autocorrelation function for this exponential smoothing model is illustrated in Fig. 8.

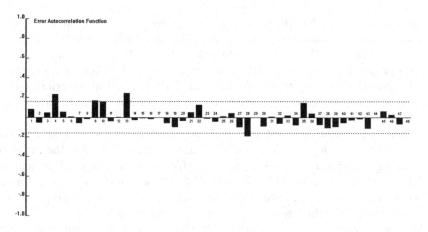

**Fig. 8.** Exponential smoothing error autocorrelation function.

In addition, we evaluated the normality of the errors using Kolmogorov-Smirnov test, which reveals that the errors could be considered normally distributed ($p = .058$). This result is illustrated in Fig. 9 (a and b).

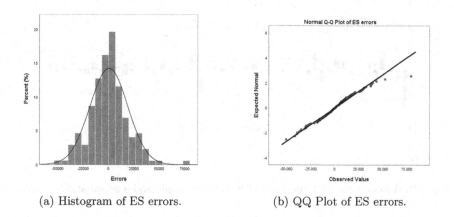

(a) Histogram of ES errors.                    (b) QQ Plot of ES errors.

**Fig. 9.** Normality assumption for ES errors.

## 4   ARIMA Models

In 1970 George Box and Gwilym Jenkins popularized ARIMA (Autoregressive Integrated Moving Average) models in their seminal textbook, *Time Series Analysis: Forecasting and Control*. ARIMA models generated a lot of interest in the academic community, due mostly to their theoretical foundations, which proved that, under certain assumptions, the models would produce optimal forecasts.

However, the Box-Jenkins methodology apparently hasn't been widespread adopted among the business community. This was mostly due to the difficult, time-consuming and subjective procedure described by Box and Jenkins to identify the proper form of the model for a given dataset. Furthermore, empirical studies showed that despite the ARIMA model's theoretical superiority over other forecasting methods, in practice the models did not regularly outperform other time series methods.

Generically, a non-seasonal Box-Jenkins model is represented as ARIMA $(p, d, q)$, where $p$ indicates the number of AR terms, $d$ indicates the order of differencing, and $q$ indicates the number of MA terms. A seasonal Box-Jenkins model is symbolized as ARIMA $(p, d, q) * (P, D, Q)$, where the $p,d,q$ indicate the model orders for the short-term components of the model, and $P,D,Q$ indicate the model orders for the seasonal components of the model.

We used Forecast Pro to build the ARIMA models. After transforming data in order to remove trend (using a simple difference) and seasonality (using a seasonal difference) we analysed the Autocorrelation function (ACF) and the Partial Autocorrelation function (PACF), presented in Figs. 10 and 11.

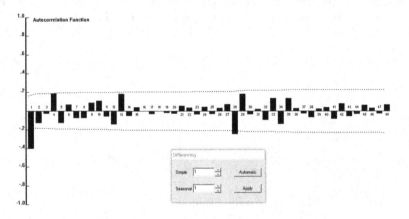

**Fig. 10.** Autocorrelation Function (ACF) after a simple and a seasonal difference.

This analysis led to an ARIMA$(0, 1, 1) * (0, 1, 1)^{52}$ that minimized within sample $MAD = 9772$ and is summarized in Table 2.

**Table 2.** ARIMA model selected.

| Term | Coefficient | Std. error | t-statistic |
|------|-------------|------------|-------------|
| $q[1[$ | 0.8878 | 0.0447 | 19.84 |
| $Q[52[$ | 0.7160 | 0.0465 | 15.38 |

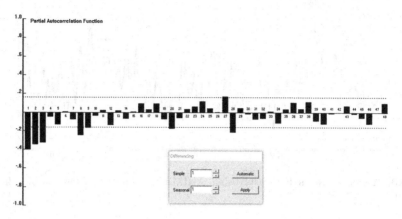

**Fig. 11.** Partial Autocorrelation Function (PACF) after a simple and a seasonal difference.

Model coefficients are significant and the Error Autocorrelation function (Fig. 12) shows that errors are random. Figure 13 shows the actual sales (black) and the forecasts obtained with the selected model (red).

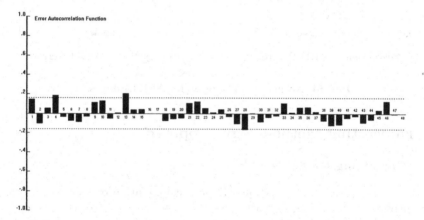

**Fig. 12.** Error Autocorrelation Function (ACF) for $ARIMA(0,1,1) \times (0,1,1)^{52}$.

Normality evaluation of errors for ARIMA model, using Kolmogorov-Smirnov test, reveals that the errors could be considered normally distributed ($p = .063$). This result is illustrated in Fig. 14 (a and b).

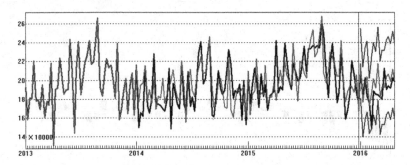

**Fig. 13.** Actual sales vs Forecasts using ARIMA$(0,1,1) \times (0,1,1)^{52}$. (Color figure online)

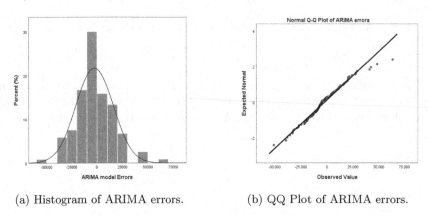

(a) Histogram of ARIMA errors.          (b) QQ Plot of ARIMA errors.

**Fig. 14.** Normality assumption for ARIMA errors.

## 5    Forecasting Methodology Proposed

### 5.1    Combining Forecasts

There are many reported situations where a combination of different forecasts can outperform individual forecasts.

The development of research on combining forecasts was largely documented by Clemen [5], who pointed out that "the primary conclusion of this line of research is that forecast accuracy can be substantially improved through the combination of multiple individual forecasts. Furthermore, simple combination methods often work reasonably well relative to more complex combinations."

The value of combining forecasts in an inventory management context has been reported by Chan et al. [4], in a case study where "the results show that combining different forecasts will lead to significant improvements in demand forecasting performance and savings of around 10% in the amount of safety stock that will need to be carried."

## 5.2    Combining Methods

Although a significant amount of research has been published on combining forecasts, the choice of which method should be used in a particular situation is not always clear. Over the last forty years, many combining methods have been proposed, ranging from the simple average to much more sophisticated approaches to determine optimal combinations.

The simple average is reported to perform well in many published studies. The simple average has the advantage of being uncomplicated and robust, which is a very attractive feature in a context where hundreds or thousands of items have to be periodically forecast.

Another approach, known as outperformance, Bunn [3], gives different weights to individual forecasts. Each weight is made proportional to the probability that the respective forecasting method will have the best individual performance. Each probability may be estimated on the basis of past performance of the alternative forecast methods, and can be revised using a Bayesian analysis. It has the advantage of being robust and having an intuitive meaning. Bates and Granger [2] proposed an approach where weights are calculated in order to minimise the error variance of the combination, assuming that each individual forecast is unbiased. Granger and Ramanathan [9] showed that this method is equivalent to a least squares regression, in which the constant is suppressed and the weights are constrained to sum to one. They proposed a regression method where individual forecasts are used as regressors, and the combining weights are not restricted, arguing that this has the advantage of producing an unbiased combined forecast even when individual forecasts are biased.

However, this has been questioned by a number of researchers. The theoretical work by Diebold [6] implies that using unrestricted least squares regression to combine forecasts will lead to serially correlated errors. His recommendation was to restrict the coefficients to sum to one. The same conclusion was made by de Menezes and Bunn [12] in a study to investigate the issue of serial correlation in combining methods.

## 5.3    Combining Results

It seems that there is still considerable disagreement concerning the best choice of combining rule. However, the M-Competition, a large scale forecasting competition with 1001 time-series, Makridakis et al. [11] and many other applications, Clemen [5] and Genre et al. [8], gave strong support for the simple average. This strong performance of the simple average may be due, as suggested by some authors, to the instability of "optimal" weights, resulting from changes in the individual forecast methods' performance over time. This may explain why a simple average, although having sub-optimal weights, may produce consistently good results.

We used a simple average to combine the three different sets of forecasts available (the 4-week moving average used by the company, the exponential smoothing and the ARIMA models developed), and compared the performance

**Table 3.** Model performance comparison.

| 2016 | Observed values | Company forecasts | Exp. smooth forecasts | ARIMA | Combined forecasts |
|------|-----------------|-------------------|-----------------------|-------|--------------------|
| 1 | 210170 | 195563 | 213706 | 217858 | 209042 |
| 2 | 182101 | 200109 | 173385 | 177080 | 183525 |
| 3 | 202687 | 197375 | 191788 | 196982 | 195382 |
| 4 | 183538 | 194809 | 196571 | 203926 | 198435 |
| 5 | 176603 | 188812 | 217957 | 172769 | 193179 |
| 6 | 148692 | 192680 | 183446 | 186774 | 187633 |
| 7 | 188945 | 194624 | 194643 | 201630 | 196966 |
| 8 | 185514 | 186232 | 186930 | 191736 | 188299 |
| 9 | 184927 | 177880 | 212852 | 217607 | 202780 |
| 10 | 182538 | 174445 | 177823 | 181638 | 177969 |
| 11 | 179680 | 174939 | 187624 | 192807 | 185123 |
| 12 | 212595 | 177020 | 186711 | 192316 | 185349 |
| 13 | 190533 | 185481 | 197910 | 203552 | 195648 |
| 14 | 194113 | 183165 | 193957 | 206776 | 194633 |
| 15 | 191991 | 189935 | 191605 | 198666 | 193402 |
| 16 | 202631 | 191337 | 204498 | 211532 | 202456 |
| 17 | 198675 | 194230 | 191943 | 199927 | 195367 |
| $MAD$ | 11826 | 11905 | | 12301 | 9219 |
| $MAPE$ | 6.49% | 6.60% | | 6.77% | 5.16% |
| $MSE \times 10^8$ | 2.65 | 2.92 | | 2.53 | 1.94 |

of these combined forecast with forecasts obtained with the model used by the company (described in Sect. 2.2). The combined forecasts reduced the MAD by 22% (from 11 826 to 9219), the MAPE by 21% and the MSE by 27%. These results are shown in Table 3.

# 6   Conclusions

In an increasingly competitive market where companies are fighting for market shares that are hard to achieve, the pursuit of operational efficiency as a competitive advantage is essential. The volatility of the markets makes planning and replanning an endless task, in order to respond to more demanding customers. As a result, the pursuit of process optimization as a way to ensure better results is a major focus of attention.

This study allowed the formulation of some conclusions about the demand forecasting process in the company under study.

The exponential smoothing and the ARIMA models developed using Forecast Pro software demonstrated their applicability, and the results are considered satisfactory and able to serve as the basis for the company to predict demand.

It has been shown that combining these forecasts significantly improves accuracy. Simple approaches to combining provide adequate results and combining methods can be used with little increase in cost. Therefore, on the basis of simplicity and efficiency, we believe that the simple average of the forecasts produced by the three different models(4-week moving average, exponential smoothing and ARIMA) may provide a good solution for this forecasting problem.

In addition to the model performance against the current methodology applied by the company, other advantages can be pointed out, such as the fact that this is a more robust methodology, able in a timely manner to generate demand forecasts, and thus releasing the managers of this task, so that they can provide more time for the analysis of scenarios and to improve the decisions taken in this area.

**Acknowledgments.** This work has been supported by FCT – Fundação para a Ciência e Tecnologia within the Project Scope: UID/CEC/00319/2019.

# References

1. Acar, Y., Gardner, E.S.: Forecasting method selection in a global supply chain. Int. J. Forecast. **28**(4), 842–848 (2012). https://doi.org/10.1016/j.ijforecast.2011
2. Bates, J.M., Granger, C.W.J.: The combination of forecasts. OR **20**(4), 451–468 (1969)
3. Bunn, D.W.: A Bayesian approach to the linear combination of forecasts. Oper. Res. Q. **26**(2), 325–329 (1975). (1970–1977)
4. Chan, C.K., Kingsman, B.G., Wong, H.: The value of combining forecasts in inventory management - a case study in banking. Eur. J. Oper. Res. **117**(2), 199–210 (1999). https://doi.org/10.1016/S0377-2217(98)00277-X
5. Clemen, R.T.: Combining forecasts: a review and annotated bibliography. Int. J. Forecast. **5**(4), 559–583 (1989). https://doi.org/10.1016/0169-2070(89)90012-5
6. Diebold, F.X.: Serial correlation and the combination of forecasts. J. Bus. Econ. Stat. **6**(1), 105–111 (1988). https://doi.org/10.1080/07350015.1988.10509642
7. Gaither, N., Frazier, G.: Administração da Produção e Operações. Thomson Learning (2007)
8. Genre, V., Kenny, G., Meyler, A., Timmermann, A.: Combining expert forecasts: can anything beat the simple average? Int. J. Forecast. **29**(1), 108–121 (2013). https://doi.org/10.1016/j.ijforecast.2012
9. Granger, C.W.J., Ramanathan, R.: Improved methods of combining forecasts. J. Forecast. **3**(2), 197–204 (1984). https://doi.org/10.1002/for.3980030207
10. Holt, C.C., Modigliani, F., Muth, J.F., Simon, H.A., Bonini, C.P., Winters, P.R.: Planning Production, Inventories, and Work Force. Prentice-Hall, Upper Saddle River (1960)
11. Makridakis, S., et al.: The accuracy of extrapolation (time series) methods: results of a forecasting competition. J. Forecast. **1**(2), 111–153 (1982). https://doi.org/10.1002/for.3980010202
12. de Menezes, L.M., Bunn, D.W.: The persistence of specification problems in the distribution of combined forecast errors. Int. J. Forecast. **14**(3), 415–426 (1998)
13. Winters, P.R.: Forecasting sales by exponentially weighted moving averages. Manag. Sci. **6**(3), 324–342 (1960). https://doi.org/10.1287/mnsc.6.3.324
14. Wong, W., Guo, Z.: A hybrid intelligent model for medium-term sales forecasting in fashion retail supply chains using extreme learning machine and harmony search algorithm. Int. J. Prod. Econ. **128**(2), 614–624 (2010)

# Periodic INAR(1) Models with Skellam-Distributed Innovations

Cláudia Santos[1,2(✉)] ⓘ, Isabel Pereira[2] ⓘ, and Manuel Scotto[3] ⓘ

[1] Coimbra College of Agriculture, Polytechnic Institute of Coimbra,
Coimbra, Portugal
[2] CIDMA, University of Aveiro, Aveiro, Portugal
{csps,isabel.pereira}@ua.pt
[3] CEMAT and IST, University of Lisbon, Lisbon, Portugal
manuel.scotto@tecnico.ulisboa.pt

**Abstract.** In this paper, an integer-valued autoregressive model of order one (INAR(1)) with time-varying parameters and driven by a periodic sequence of innovations is introduced. The proposed INAR(1) model is based on the signed thinning operator defined by Kachour and Truquet (2011) and conveniently adapted to the periodic case. Basic notations and definitions concerning the periodic signed thinning operator are provided. Based on this thinning operator, Chesneau and Kachour (2012) established a signed INAR(1) model. Motivated by the work of Chesneau and Kachour (2012), we introduce a periodic model, denoted by S-PINAR(1), with period $s$. In contrast to conventional INAR(1) models, these models are defined in $\mathbb{Z}$ allowing for negative values both for the series and its autocorrelation function. For a proper $\mathbb{Z}$-valued time series, a distribution for the innovation term defined on $\mathbb{Z}$ is required. The S-PINAR(1) model assumes a specific innovation distribution, the Skellam distribution. Regarding parameter estimation, two methods are considered: conditional least squares and conditional maximum likelihood. The performance of the S-PINAR(1) model is assessed through a simulation study.

**Keywords:** Integer-valued autoregressive models ·
Signed thinning operator · Skellam distribution

## 1 Introduction

The class of INAR models, based on the binomial thinning operator introduced by Steutel and van Harn (1979), can only be applied to count variables, i.e., to non-negative integer-valued r.v.'s as their range, therefore, cannot account for negative integers. Whilst models for non-negative integer-valued time series are now abundant, there is a shortage of similar models when the time series refer to

Supported by Fundação para a Ciência e a Tecnologia (FCT), within projects UID/MAT/04106/2019 (CIDMA) and UID/Multi/04621/2019 (CEMAT/IST-ID).

data defined on $\mathbb{Z}$, i.e., in both the positive and negative integers. The need for such models can also appear when taking differences of positive integer-valued count time series.

The binomial thinning operator has been generalized in a number of different ways. The first model for data with range in $\mathbb{Z}$ was introduced by Kim and Park (2008). Their model was based on the signed binomial thinning operator, allowing time series with negative values. A particular case of this model can be found in Andersson and Karlis (2014).

Using a slightly different version of the signed thinning operator defined by Kim and Park (2008), Kachour and Truquet (2011) focused on a more general class of $\mathbb{Z}$-valued processes denoted by SINAR (Signed INAR). This modified version of the thinning operator, called the signed thinning operator, allows for negative values both for the series and its autocorrelation function. Kachour and Truquet (2011) point out that the signed thinning operator is the natural extension of the Steutel and van Harn operator to $\mathbb{Z}$-valued random variables. The authors avoid, however, a parametric assumption for the innovation term. Based on the signed thinning operator and under a parametric assumption on the common distribution of the counting sequence of the model, Chesneau and Kachour (2012) focus on the simple SINAR(1) model.

For an adequate time series on $\mathbb{Z}$ we also need to consider a distribution for the innovation term defined on $\mathbb{Z}$. The literature is limited on this subject. However, discrete distributions defined on the set of integers has attracted the attention of several researchers. Two ways to define distributions on $\mathbb{Z}$ are: the differences between two non-negative discrete r.v.'s and the discrete version of continuous distributions on $\mathbb{R}$. The main distributions on the set $\mathbb{Z}$ are Poisson difference, discrete normal and discrete Laplace. The Poisson difference distribution, also known as the Skellam distribution, is traditionally linked to Skellam (1946) and has found applications in areas such as sports (Karlis and Ntzoufras 2009) and finance (Alzaid and Omair 2010). The extended binomial distribution was introduced as an alternative to the Skellam distribution by Alzaid and Omair (2012). A natural $\mathbb{Z}$-extension of the INAR model, originally defined on $\mathbb{N}$, was presented by Alzaid and Omair (2014). We also mention the extended Poisson distribution introduced by Bakouch et al. (2016), the first version of the Poisson distribution over the set of all integers.

In this paper, a new first-order integer-valued autoregressive model with time-varying parameters and sequences of innovations with periodic structure is established. Motivated by the work of Chesneau and Kachour (2012), we extended their model based on the signed thinning operator to the periodic case. A signed periodic INAR(1) process (S-PINAR(1) for short) with period $s$ is introduced. In contrast to traditional INAR(1) models, these models are defined in $\mathbb{Z}$ allowing for negative integer values and negative correlation. The properties of the S-PINAR(1) model are discussed. Focus is placed upon a specific parametric case which arises under the assumption of periodic Skellam-distributed innovations. Two methods are considered for parameter estimation: conditional least squares and conditional maximum likelihood. A modification of the traditional conditional least squares method was made through a two step procedure in order to provide estimators for all parameters involved in the periodic univariate model. The performance of the proposed estimation methods for the S-PINAR(1) model with period $s$ is accomplished and compared through a simulation study, contemplating six different combinations of the parameters.

In this section, basic notations and definitions concerning the periodic signed thinning operator are presented. A brief description of the periodic Skellam distribution defined on the whole set of integers is also provided.

## 1.1   Periodic Signed Thinning Operator

The definition of the signed thinning operator introduced by Kachour and Truquet (2011), adapted to the periodic case, is defined by

$$F_t \odot X = \begin{cases} sign(X) \sum_{i=1}^{|X|} U_{i,t}(\phi_t), & X \neq 0 \\ 0 & , \ otherwise \end{cases} \tag{1}$$

with $sign(X) = 1, x \geq 0$ and $-1$ otherwise and where $F_t$ represents the common distribution of the periodic sequence of i.i.d. counting sequences $(U_{i,t}(\phi_t))_{i \in \mathbb{N}}$. All counting sequences associated to the operator $F_t \odot$ are mutually independent.

We consider that $F_t$, the distribution of the periodic sequence of i.i.d. random variables $(U_{i,t}(\phi_t))_{i \in \mathbb{N}}$, has probability mass function given by

$$P(U_{1,t}(\phi_t) = a) = \begin{cases} (1 - \phi_t)^2, & a = -1 \\ 2\phi_t(1 - \phi_t), & a = 0 \\ \phi_t^2, & a = 1 \end{cases},$$

with $\phi_t = \alpha_v \in (0,1)$ for $t = v + ns; v = 1, \ldots, s$ and $n \in \mathbb{N}_0$. Chesneau and Kachour (2012) have also made use of this common distribution but without the periodic structure. Note that, for a fixed $v$, the random variable

$$U_{i,t}(\phi_t) = U_t(\phi_t) \overset{d}{=} R_t(\phi_t) - 1, \qquad R_t(\phi_t) \sim Bin(2, \phi_t) \tag{2}$$

and

$$P\left(\sum_{i=1}^{k} U_{i,t}(\phi_t) = l\right) = P\left(R_t^{(k)}(\phi_t) = k + l\right), \qquad l \in \{-k, \ldots, k\},$$

where

$$R_t^{(k)}(\phi_t) = \sum_{i=1}^{k} R_{i,t}(\phi_t), \qquad R_t^{(k)}(\phi_t) \sim Bin(2k, \phi_t), \ k \in \mathbb{N}. \tag{3}$$

Then, for $x \in \mathbb{Z} \backslash \{0\}$ and $y \in \mathbb{Z}$, the conditional probability function of the periodic signed thinning operator $F_t \odot$ defined in (1) is

$$P\left(F_t \odot X = y | X = x\right) = P\left(sign(x) \sum_{i=1}^{|x|} U_{i,t}(\phi_t) = y\right)$$

$$= P\left(R_t^{|x|}(\phi_t) - |x| = sign(x) \cdot y\right) = P\left(R_t^{|x|}(\phi_t) = |x| + sign(x) \cdot y\right)$$

$$= C_{|x|+sign(x) \cdot y}^{2|x|} \alpha_v^{|x|+sign(x) \cdot y} (1 - \alpha_v)^{|x|-sign(x) \cdot y}, \qquad y \in \{-|x|, \ldots, |x|\}$$

with mean value

$$E[F_t \odot X | X] = (2\alpha_v - 1)X \tag{4}$$

and variance

$$Var[F_t \odot X | X] = 2\alpha_v(1 - \alpha_v)|X| \tag{5}$$

for $t = v + ns$, $v = 1, \ldots, s$ and $n \in \mathbb{N}_0$.

## 1.2   Periodic Skellam Distribution

Let $\{Z_t\}$, $t = v + ns$; $v = 1, \ldots, s$ and $n \in \mathbb{N}_0$ be a periodic sequence of random variables. For a fixed $v$ ($v = 1, \ldots, s$), let $\lambda_v > 0$ and $\tau_v > 0$. The periodic $s$-dimensional r.v. $Z_t$ follows a periodic Skellam distribution, denoted by $Skellam(\lambda_v, \tau_v)$, if and only if

$$Z_{v+ns} \stackrel{d}{=} Y_{v+ns} - W_{v+ns},$$

where $Y_{v+ns}$ and $W_{v+ns}$ are two independent r.v.'s such that $Y_{v+ns} \sim Poisson(\lambda_v)$ and $W_{v+ns} \sim Poisson(\tau_v)$.

Thus, the probability mass function is given by

$$P(Z_{v+ns} = z) = e^{-(\lambda_v + \tau_v)} \lambda_v^z \sum_{i=max(0,-z)}^{\infty} \frac{(\lambda_v \tau_v)^i}{i!(i+z)!}, \ z \in \mathbb{Z}. \tag{6}$$

The random vector $Z_t$ has finite first and second-order moments. The mean of $Z_t$, $t = v + ns$ for a fixed $v$ ($v = 1, \ldots, s$), is

$$\xi_v = E[Z_{v+ns}] = E[Y_{v+ns} - W_{v+ns}] = \lambda_v - \tau_v. \tag{7}$$

Due to the independence of the r.v.'s $Y_{v+ns}$ and $W_{v+ns}$, the variance of $Z_t$ for $t = v + ns$ with a fixed $v$ is

$$\sigma_v^2 = Var[Z_{v+ns}] = Var[Y_{v+ns} - W_{v+ns}] = \lambda_v + \tau_v. \tag{8}$$

The probability generating function of $Z_{v+ns}$ is

$$G_{Z_{v+ns}}(r) = exp\{-(\lambda_v + \tau_v) + \lambda_v r + \tau_v / r\}, \ v = 1, \ldots, s.$$

## 2   The Univariate Periodic Model: S-PINAR(1)

Let $\{X_t\}$ be a periodic integer-valued autoregressive process of first-order defined by the recursion

$$X_t = F_t \odot X_{t-1} + Z_t, \ t \in \mathbb{Z}, \tag{9}$$

where $X_t$, $X_{t-1}$ and $Z_t$ are random $s$-vectors for $t = v+ns$ with $v = 1, \ldots, s$ and $n \in \mathbb{N}_0$. The random vector $Z_t = [Z_{1+ns} \ Z_{2+ns} \cdots \ Z_{s+ns}]^T$ represents a periodic sequence of independent random variables. The model defined in Eq. (9) will be referred to as S-PINAR(1) for Signed Periodic INteger-valued AutoRegressive model of order one with period $s \in \mathbb{N}$. For each $t$, the innovation term $Z_t$ in recursion (9) is assumed to be independent of $X_{t-1}$ and $F_t \odot X_{t-1}$. Writing the periodic signed thinning operator in (1) as

$$F_t \odot = \begin{cases} f_1 \odot, t = 1 + ns \\ f_2 \odot, t = 2 + ns \\ \vdots \\ f_s \odot, t = s + ns \end{cases},$$

the periodic model in (9) can have the form $X_{v+ns} = f_v \odot X_{v-1+ns} + Z_{v+ns}$ where $f_v \odot X_{v-1+ns} = sign(X_{v-1+ns}) \sum\limits_{i=1}^{|X_{v-1+ns}|} U_{i,t}(\phi_t)$ with $U_{i,t}(\phi_t)$ as in (2).

We assume the innovation term $Z_t$ in the S-PINAR(1) model proposed in (9) follows the periodic Skellam distribution with parameters $\lambda_v$ and $\tau_v$ established in Subsect. 1.2 with probability mass function given by Eq. (6). Therefore, for a fixed $v$ with $v = 1, \ldots, s$, the first and second-order moments of $Z_{v+ns}$ are defined in (7) and (8), respectively.

Some distributional properties of the S-PINAR(1) process in recursion (9) with Skellam-distributed innovation are derived, namely the conditional moments of first and second-order of the model. Hence, from (4) and (7)

$$E[X_{v+ns}|X_{v-1+ns}] = E[f_v \odot X_{v-1+ns} + Z_{v+ns}|X_{v-1+ns}]$$
$$= (2\alpha_v - 1)X_{v-1+ns} + \lambda_v - \tau_v \tag{10}$$

and from Eqs. (5) and (8),

$$Var[X_{v+ns}|X_{v-1+ns}] = Var[f_v \odot X_{v-1+ns} + Z_{v+ns}|X_{v-1+ns}]$$
$$= 2\alpha_v(1 - \alpha_v)|X_{v-1+ns}| + \lambda_v + \tau_v. \tag{11}$$

For a fixed value of $v = 1, \ldots, s$, the process $\{X_t\}$ with $t = v+ns$ is a Markov chain with transition probability function

$$p_v(b|a) = P(X_{v+ns} = b|X_{v-1+ns} = a)$$
$$= \sum_{l=-|a|}^{|a|} P\left(sign(a) \sum_{i=1}^{|a|} U_{i,t}(\phi_t) = l\right) \times P(Z_{v+ns} = b - l)$$

$$= \sum_{l=-|a|}^{|a|} P\left(R_t^{(|a|)}(\phi_t) = |a| + sign(a) \cdot l\right) \times P(Z_{v+ns} = b - l)$$

$$= \sum_{l=-|a|}^{|a|} \left\{ C_{|a|+sign(a)\cdot l}^{2|a|} \alpha_v^{|a|+sign(a)\cdot l}(1 - \alpha_v)^{|a|-sign(a)\cdot l} \right.$$

$$\left. \times e^{-(\lambda_v + \tau_v)} \lambda_v^{b-l} \sum_{i=max(0,-(b-l))}^{\infty} \frac{(\lambda_v \tau_v)^i}{i!(i + b - l)!} \right\}, \tag{12}$$

where the probability mass function of $R_t^{(|a|)}$ and $Z_{v+ns}$ can be found in (3) and (6), respectively.

## 3  Parameter Estimation

This section is devoted to parameter estimation of the S-PINAR(1) process with period $s$ under the parametric assumption previously mentioned. Lets us assume we have $(X_0, X_1, \ldots, X_{Ns})$ observations from the S-PINAR(1) process with Skellam-distributed innovations. Two estimation methods are proposed to estimate the parameters of the model: conditional least squares and conditional maximum likelihood. For the S-PINAR(1) model with period $s$, the vector of unknown parameters $\boldsymbol{\theta}$ has $3s$ parameters, i.e.,

$$\boldsymbol{\theta} := (\boldsymbol{\alpha}, \boldsymbol{\lambda}, \boldsymbol{\tau}) \tag{13}$$

with $\boldsymbol{\alpha} = (\alpha_1, \ldots, \alpha_s)$, $\boldsymbol{\lambda} = (\lambda_1, \ldots, \lambda_s)$ and $\boldsymbol{\tau} = (\tau_1, \ldots, \tau_s)$.

### 3.1  Conditional Least Squares Estimation

The conditional least squares (CLS) estimator of the vector of the unknown parameters in (13) is $\widehat{\boldsymbol{\theta}}_{CLS} := (\widehat{\boldsymbol{\alpha}}^{CLS}, \widehat{\boldsymbol{\lambda}}^{CLS}, \widehat{\boldsymbol{\tau}}^{CLS})$. The estimation procedure that follows was proposed by Klimko and Nelson (1978). The CLS estimators of $\boldsymbol{\theta}$ are obtained by minimizing the criterion function $S_1(\boldsymbol{\theta})$ given by

$$S_1(\boldsymbol{\theta}) = \sum_{n=0}^{N-1} \sum_{v=1}^{s} (X_{v+ns} - (2\alpha_v - 1)X_{v-1+ns} - \lambda_v + \tau_v)^2.$$

It is clear that differentiating $S_1(\boldsymbol{\theta})$ with respect to $\lambda_v$ and $\tau_v$ and equating the resulting expressions to zero, the same equation is obtained. For these parameters, direct CLS estimators are not available. The conditional least squares method was adapted by Alzaid and Omair (2014) with some modifications in order to be able to estimate all parameters integrating the model. Hence, in order to estimate $\lambda_v$ and $\tau_v$ using the CLS method, the following reparametrization is needed

$$\begin{cases} \xi_v = \lambda_v - \tau_v \\ \sigma_v^2 = \lambda_v + \tau_v \end{cases}, v = 1, \ldots, s. \tag{14}$$

Estimators for all parameters of the S-PINAR(1) process, i.e., $\alpha_v$, $\xi_v$ and $\sigma_v^2$ are obtained in a two step procedure as described below.

**First Step - Estimates for $\alpha_v$ and $\xi_v$ ($v = 1, \ldots, s$).** Consider the conditional mean prediction error

$$\begin{aligned} e_{1,v+ns} &= X_{v+ns} - E[X_{v+ns}|X_{v-1+ns}] \\ &= X_{v+ns} - (2\alpha_v - 1)X_{v-1+ns} - \xi_v, \end{aligned} \tag{15}$$

where conditional first-order moment $E[X_{v+ns}|X_{v-1+ns}]$ is defined in (10). The CLS estimators of $\alpha_v$ and $\xi_v$ are derived by minimizing the criterion function

$$S_2(\boldsymbol{\theta}) = \sum_{n=0}^{N-1} \sum_{v=1}^{s} e_{1,v+ns}^2 = \sum_{n=0}^{N-1} \sum_{v=1}^{s} (X_{v+ns} - (2\alpha_v - 1)X_{v-1+ns} - \xi_v)^2.$$

After differentiating $S_2(\boldsymbol{\theta})$ with respect to parameters $\alpha_v$ and $\xi_v$, the following system of equations arises

$$\begin{cases} \dfrac{\partial S_2(\boldsymbol{\theta})}{\partial \alpha_v} = \displaystyle\sum_{n=0}^{N-1} (X_{v+ns} - (2\alpha_v - 1)X_{v-1+ns} - \xi_v)\, X_{v-1+ns} = 0 \\[2ex] \dfrac{\partial S_2(\boldsymbol{\theta})}{\partial \xi_v} = \displaystyle\sum_{n=0}^{N-1} (X_{v+ns} - (2\alpha_v - 1)X_{v-1+ns} - \xi_v) = 0 \end{cases}$$

and consequently, for $v = 1, \ldots, s$, the CLS estimators are

$$\begin{cases} \widehat{\alpha}_v^{CLS} = \dfrac{1}{2}\left( \dfrac{N\displaystyle\sum_{n=0}^{N-1} X_{v+ns}X_{v-1+ns} - \displaystyle\sum_{n=0}^{N-1} X_{v+ns}\displaystyle\sum_{n=0}^{N-1} X_{v-1+ns}}{N\displaystyle\sum_{n=0}^{N-1} X_{v-1+ns}^2 - \left(\displaystyle\sum_{n=0}^{N-1} X_{v-1+ns}\right)^2} + 1 \right). \\[4ex] \widehat{\xi}_v^{CLS} = \dfrac{1}{N}\left( \displaystyle\sum_{n=0}^{N-1} X_{v+ns} - (2\widehat{\alpha}_v^{CLS} - 1)\displaystyle\sum_{n=0}^{N-1} X_{v-1+ns} \right) \end{cases} \tag{16}$$

**Second Step - Estimate for $\sigma_v^2$ ($v = 1, \ldots, s$).** The conditional variance prediction error has been used by Alzaid and Omair (2014) to obtain the CLS estimator for the variance parameter. Thus in the periodic case, the conditional variance prediction error is defined by

$$e_{2,v+ns} = (X_{v+ns} - E[X_{v+ns}|X_{v-1+ns}])^2 - Var[X_{v+ns}|X_{v-1+ns}]$$
$$= e_{1,v+ns}^2 - 2\alpha_v(1-\alpha_v)|X_{v-1+ns}| - \sigma_v^2$$

with conditional moments $E[X_{v+ns}|X_{v-1+ns}]$ and $Var[X_{v+ns}|X_{v-1+ns}]$ in Eqs. (10) and (11), respectively. The conditional mean prediction error ($e_{1,v+ns}$) is derived in the first step of the estimation procedure from (15). The equation $\sum_{n=0}^{N-1} e_{2,v+ns} = 0$ yields a direct estimator for $\sigma_v^2$ by solving the nonlinear equation

$$\sum_{n=0}^{N-1} \left(\hat{e}_{1,v+ns}^2 - 2\hat{\alpha}_v^{CLS}(1-\hat{\alpha}_v^{CLS})|X_{v-1+ns}| - \sigma_v^2\right) = 0,$$

i.e.,

$$\hat{\sigma}_v^2 = \frac{1}{N}\sum_{n=0}^{N-1} \left(\hat{e}_{1,v+ns}^2 - 2\hat{\alpha}_v^{CLS}(1-\hat{\alpha}_v^{CLS})|X_{v-1+ns}|\right), \tag{17}$$

where $\hat{e}_{1,v+ns} = X_{v+ns} - (2\hat{\alpha}_v^{CLS}-1)X_{v-1+ns} - \hat{\xi}_v^{CLS}$ with CLS estimators $\hat{\alpha}_v^{CLS}$ and $\hat{\xi}_v^{CLS}$ in (16). After estimating $\sigma_v^2$ through (17), the CLS estimators of $\lambda_v$ and $\tau_v$ from reparametrization (14) take the form

$$\begin{cases} \hat{\lambda}_v^{CLS} = \dfrac{1}{2}\left(\hat{\sigma}_v^{2,CLS} + \hat{\xi}_v^{CLS}\right) \\[2mm] \hat{\tau}_v^{CLS} = \dfrac{1}{2}\left(\hat{\sigma}_v^{2,CLS} - \hat{\xi}_v^{CLS}\right) \end{cases}, \quad v = 1,\ldots,s.$$

## 3.2   Conditional Maximum Likelihood Estimation

The conditional maximum likelihood (CML) estimator of the vector of the unknown parameters in (13) is $\hat{\boldsymbol{\theta}}_{CML} := (\hat{\boldsymbol{\alpha}}^{CML}, \hat{\boldsymbol{\lambda}}^{CML}, \hat{\boldsymbol{\tau}}^{CML})$. The conditional log-likelihood function is given by

$$C(\boldsymbol{\theta}) = ln(L(\boldsymbol{\theta}|\mathbf{x})) = \sum_{n=0}^{N-1}\sum_{v=1}^{s} ln\left(p_v(x_{v+ns}|x_{v-1+ns})\right), \tag{18}$$

where $p_v(b|a)$ has the expression given in (12) by replacing $a = x_{v-1+ns}$ and $b = x_{v+ns}$. Differentiating the conditional log-likelihood function in Eq. (18) with respect to the parameters $\alpha_v$, $\lambda_v$ and $\tau_v$ ($v = 1,\ldots,s$) in (13), the system of first-order partial derivatives follows

$$
\begin{cases}
\dfrac{\partial C(\boldsymbol{\theta})}{\partial \alpha_v} = 0 \\[3mm]
\dfrac{\partial C(\boldsymbol{\theta})}{\partial \lambda_v} = 0 \\[3mm]
\dfrac{\partial C(\boldsymbol{\theta})}{\partial \tau_v} = 0
\end{cases}
\Leftrightarrow
\begin{cases}
\displaystyle\sum_{n=0}^{N-1} \dfrac{\dfrac{\partial}{\partial \alpha_v} p_v(x_{v+ns}|x_{v-1+ns})}{p_v(x_{v+ns}|x_{v-1+ns})} = 0 \\[5mm]
\displaystyle\sum_{n=0}^{N-1} \dfrac{\dfrac{\partial}{\partial \lambda_v} p_v(x_{v+ns}|x_{v-1+ns})}{p_v(x_{v+ns}|x_{v-1+ns})} = 0 \\[5mm]
\displaystyle\sum_{n=0}^{N-1} \dfrac{\dfrac{\partial}{\partial \tau_v} p_v(x_{v+ns}|x_{v-1+ns})}{p_v(x_{v+ns}|x_{v-1+ns})} = 0
\end{cases}
, \; v = 1, \ldots, s,
$$

i.e.,

$$
\begin{cases}
\displaystyle\sum_{n=0}^{N-1} \dfrac{2|x_{v-1+ns}|}{1 - \alpha_v} \left( \dfrac{p_v(x_{v+ns} - 1|x_{v-1+ns} - 1)}{p_v(x_{v+ns}|x_{v-1+ns})} - 1 \right) = 0 \\[5mm]
\displaystyle\sum_{n=0}^{N-1} \dfrac{p_v(x_{v+ns} - 1|x_{v-1+ns})}{p_v(x_{v+ns}|x_{v-1+ns})} = N \\[5mm]
\displaystyle\sum_{n=0}^{N-1} \dfrac{p_v(x_{v+ns} + 1|x_{v-1+ns})}{p_v(x_{v+ns}|x_{v-1+ns})} = N
\end{cases}
, \; v = 1, \ldots, s.
$$

Calculus for first-order partial derivatives of transition probability function $p_v(x_{v+ns}|x_{v-1+ns})$ are omitted here. Numerical maximization can be obtained through standard statistical packages in R.

## 4   Simulation Study

In order to provide an idea about the relative merits of each method (CLS and CML) used in parameter estimation of the S-PINAR(1) model with period $s$ and Skellam-distributed innovation term, a simulation study is conducted. To generate count data from the periodic univariate model proposed in (9), we have set period $s = 4$, thus the vector of unknown parameters in (13) is $\boldsymbol{\theta} = (\boldsymbol{\alpha}, \boldsymbol{\lambda}, \boldsymbol{\tau}) = (\alpha_1, \alpha_2, \alpha_3, \alpha_4, \lambda_1, \lambda_2, \lambda_3, \lambda_4, \tau_1, \tau_2, \tau_3\tau_4)$. Several combinations of values for parameters $\boldsymbol{\alpha}, \boldsymbol{\lambda}$ and $\boldsymbol{\tau}$ are available in Table 1. Three sets, namely, Set 1, Set 2 and Set 3 are displayed. Each set has been subdivided into settings A and B, where parameter $\boldsymbol{\alpha} = (\alpha_1, \alpha_2, \alpha_3, \alpha_4)$ is fixed. Hence in Table 1, the different scenarios will be referred to as Set 1A, Set 1B, Set 2A, Set 2B, Set 3 A and Set 3B. For Set 1, values for $\alpha_v$ ($v = 1, 2, 3, 4$) are above and below 0.5. For both settings, A and B, different values for $\boldsymbol{\lambda}$ are considered while parameter $\boldsymbol{\tau}$ remains the same. Regarding Set 2, values for $\alpha_v$ are all below 0.5 and both parameters $\boldsymbol{\lambda}$ and $\boldsymbol{\tau}$ take different values. For Set 3, values for $\alpha_v$ are all above 0.5, parameter $\boldsymbol{\lambda}$ is fixed but parameter $\boldsymbol{\tau}$ assumes different values. The choice for certain values of parameters $\boldsymbol{\lambda}$ and $\boldsymbol{\tau}$ arise from the fact that $\lambda_v - \tau_v$ represents the mean of $Z_{v+ns}$ given in (7).

**Table 1.** Parameters: $\boldsymbol{\alpha} = (\alpha_1, \alpha_2, \alpha_3, \alpha_4)$, $\boldsymbol{\lambda} = (\lambda_1, \lambda_2, \lambda_3, \lambda_4)$ and $\boldsymbol{\tau} = (\tau_1, \tau_2, \tau_3, \tau_4)$.

| | | |
|---|---|---|
| Set 1 A: | $\boldsymbol{\alpha} = (0.60, 0.40, 0.75, 0.30)$; | $\boldsymbol{\lambda} = (2, 1, 6, 5)$; $\boldsymbol{\tau} = (4, 5, 3, 1)$ |
| B: | $\boldsymbol{\alpha} = (0.60, 0.40, 0.75, 0.30)$; | $\boldsymbol{\lambda} = (5, 2, 1, 6)$; $\boldsymbol{\tau} = (4, 5, 3, 1)$ |
| Set 2 A: | $\boldsymbol{\alpha} = (0.20, 0.45, 0.10, 0.30)$; | $\boldsymbol{\lambda} = (2, 1, 6, 5)$; $\boldsymbol{\tau} = (4, 5, 3, 1)$ |
| B: | $\boldsymbol{\alpha} = (0.20, 0.45, 0.10, 0.30)$; | $\boldsymbol{\lambda} = (5, 2, 1, 6)$; $\boldsymbol{\tau} = (2, 1, 4, 3)$ |
| Set 3 A: | $\boldsymbol{\alpha} = (0.75, 0.62, 0.51, 0.86)$; | $\boldsymbol{\lambda} = (4, 5, 3, 1)$; $\boldsymbol{\tau} = (1, 3, 2, 4)$ |
| B: | $\boldsymbol{\alpha} = (0.75, 0.62, 0.51, 0.86)$; | $\boldsymbol{\lambda} = (4, 5, 3, 1)$; $\boldsymbol{\tau} = (2, 1, 4, 3)$ |

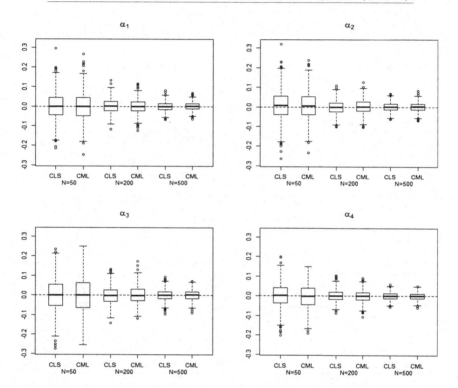

**Fig. 1.** Boxplots for the biases of the CLS and CML estimates of parameter $\boldsymbol{\alpha}$ in Set 1 A for $n = 4N = 200, 800, 2000$.

Three sample sizes are contemplated in this simulation study. For cycles $N = 50, 200, 500$, $n = 4N = 200, 800, 2000$. For a fixed set of parameters in Table 1, 1000 independent replications of the S-PINAR(1) process have been generated. All simulation and estimation procedures were realized through functions written in R. Table 2 reports the average parameter estimates for Set 1A. To facilitate comparison between the CLS and CML methods and the aforementioned sample sizes, the mean square error (MSE) was computed and included in parenthesis below each estimate. According to Table 2, parameter estimates in both cases are very close, because both methods give consistent estimates of

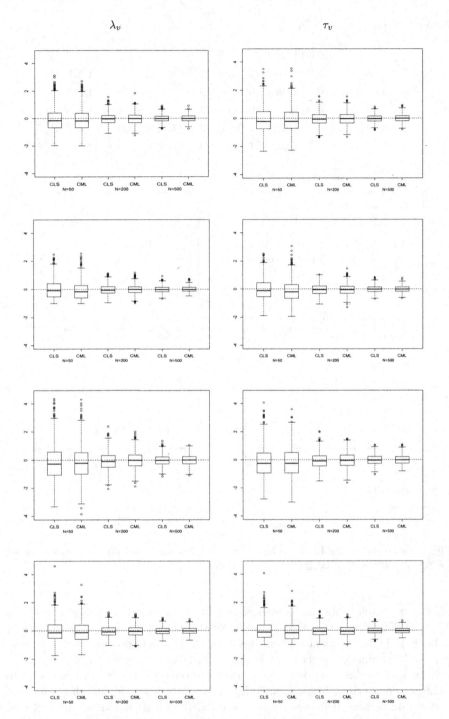

**Fig. 2.** Boxplots for the biases of the CLS and CML estimates of parameters $\lambda$ and $\tau$ in Set 1 A for $n = 4N = 200, 800, 2000$.

**Table 2.** CLS and CML estimates for $\theta = (\alpha, \lambda, \tau)$ in Set 1A. MSE in parenthesis.

| | $N = 50$ | | $N = 200$ | | $N = 500$ | |
|---|---|---|---|---|---|---|
| | CLS | CML | CLS | CML | CLS | CML |
| $\alpha = (0.60, 0.40, 0.75, 0.30)$ | | | | | | |
| $\hat{\alpha}_1$ | 0.599 | 0.600 | 0.601 | 0.600 | 0.600 | 0.601 |
| | (0.0003) | (0.0006) | (0.0002) | (0.0015) | (0.0006) | (0.0004) |
| $\hat{\alpha}_2$ | 0.407 | 0.406 | 0.399 | 0.402 | 0.401 | 0.402 |
| | (0.0113) | (0.0001) | (0.0007) | (0.0036) | (0.0002) | (0.0001) |
| $\hat{\alpha}_3$ | 0.749 | 0.750 | 0.747 | 0.751 | 0.751 | 0.750 |
| | (0.0160) | (0.0116) | (0.0001) | (0.0028) | (0.0007) | (0.0001) |
| $\hat{\alpha}_4$ | 0.302 | 0.297 | 0.301 | 0.300 | 0.300 | 0.299 |
| | (0.0003) | (0.0095) | (0.0010) | (0.0002) | (0.0001) | (0.0002) |
| $\lambda = (2, 1, 6, 5)$ | | | | | | |
| $\hat{\lambda}_1$ | 1.915 | 1.880 | 1.963 | 1.982 | 1.994 | 2.000 |
| | (0.1013) | (0.8744) | (0.0048) | (0.0774) | (0.0001) | (0.0319) |
| $\hat{\lambda}_2$ | 1.001 | 0.895 | 0.963 | 0.975 | 0.989 | 0.998 |
| | (0.6518) | (0.5694) | (0.0099) | (0.0357) | (0.0358) | (0.0542) |
| $\hat{\lambda}_3$ | 5.806 | 5.810 | 5.910 | 5.987 | 5.985 | 5.999 |
| | (0.0948) | (0.1168) | (0.1250) | (0.0944) | (0.1330) | (0.1804) |
| $\hat{\lambda}_4$ | 4.964 | 4.936 | 4.952 | 4.960 | 4.975 | 4.977 |
| | (0.4467) | (0.3806) | (0.0203) | (0.2504) | (0.0012) | (0.0220) |
| $\tau = (4, 5, 3, 1)$ | | | | | | |
| $\hat{\tau}_1$ | 3.893 | 3.880 | 3.965 | 3.970 | 3.991 | 3.998 |
| | (1.0386) | (0.9610) | (0.0930) | (0.0106) | (0.1715) | (0.0027) |
| $\hat{\tau}_2$ | 4.977 | 4.868 | 4.967 | 4.968 | 4.987 | 4.995 |
| | (0.7353) | (1.2057) | (0.0203) | (0.1526) | (0.0397) | (0.0037) |
| $\hat{\tau}_3$ | 2.812 | 2.834 | 2.937 | 2.970 | 2.984 | 2.987 |
| | (1.0748) | (0.3680) | (0.0517) | (0.0001) | (0.0200) | (0.0295) |
| $\hat{\tau}_4$ | 1.002 | 0.915 | 0.959 | 0.961 | 0.981 | 0.977 |
| | (0.4951) | (0.6673) | (0.0111) | (0.2119) | (0.0225) | (0.0019) |

the parameters. Nevertheless, the autoregressive parameters $\alpha$ appear to be less biased. For smaller samples, the CLS method seems to have a better performance in estimating the parameters. Computationally, there is extra work with the CML method. The accuracy of all estimation improves as the length of the time series increases. When length increases from $N = 50$ to 200, the improvement of accuracy is more obvious than when length increases from $N = 200$ to 500.

The bias of the produced estimates were used to quantify their quality. The boxplots of the bias for CLS and CML estimates of parameters $\alpha$, $\lambda$ and $\tau$ in Sets 1 A and 3 A are displayed in Figs. 1, 2, 3 and 4. These figures also show the effect of sample size on the behavior of CLS and CML estimators. No matter the

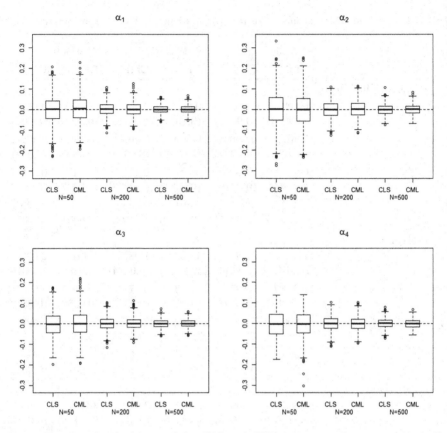

**Fig. 3.** Boxplots for the biases of the CLS and CML estimates of parameter $\alpha$ in Set 3 A for $n = 4N = 200, 800, 2000$.

sample size, the difference between CLS and CML is small and becomes even smaller when the length of time series increases. The estimates for parameter $\lambda$ seem slightly worse when parameter $\alpha$ has all values above 0.5 (Set 3A). The results for the remaining scenarios (Sets 1B, 2A, 2B and 3B) are not presented here due to lack of space. Furthermore, Figs. 1, 2, 3 and 4 reveal that estimates of $\lambda$ and $\tau$ componentwise tend to be biased to the left which implies that both estimation methods have a tendency to underestimate $\lambda$ and $\tau$, mainly in the case of small sample sizes. As expected, both bias and skewness approach zero as sample size increases. Overall, the difference between the two approaches will vanish when the length of time series increases.

$\lambda_v$                           $\tau_v$

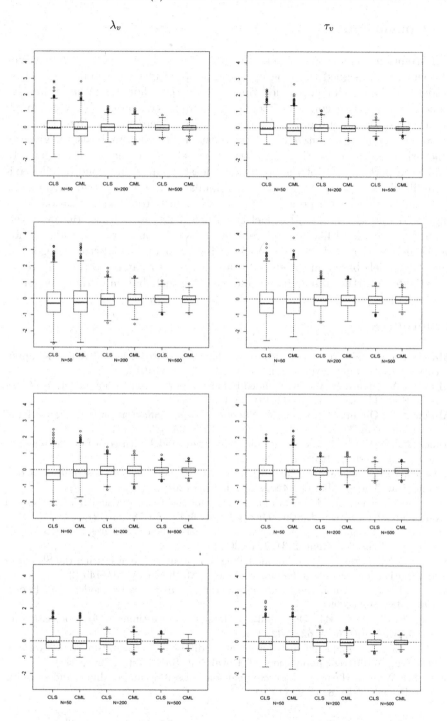

**Fig. 4.** Boxplots for the biases of the CLS and CML estimates of parameters $\lambda$ and $\tau$ in Set 3 A for $n = 4N = 200, 800, 2000$.

# 5   Conclusions

Our attention was focused on periodic INAR(1) models based on a different type of operator, the signed thinning operator, adapted to the periodic case. These models can handle integer-valued time series which allow for negative integer-valued and negative correlated count data unlike conventional INAR(1) models, that are only appropriate for non-negative integer-valued time series and could only deal with positive autocorrelations. Particular emphasis was given to innovations modeled by Skellam distribution defined on the set of integers. To study the performance of the conditional least squares and conditional maximum likelihood estimators, an extended simulation study was conducted for the S-PINAR(1) model with period $s$. Numerical results from the simulation study suggested that the proposed model is suitable for practical use. However, this is an issue we would like to explore in future work considering the application of the model to real data time series exhibiting periodic structure. Regarding periodic models based on the signed thinning operator, an important subject to investigate in further research, is the forecasting distribution of these models.

# References

Alzaid, A.A., Omair, M.A.: On the poisson difference distribution inference and applications. Bull. Malays. Math. Sci. Soc. **8**(33), 17–45 (2010)

Alzaid, A.A., Omair, M.A.: An extended binomial distribution with applications. Commun. Stat.-Theory Methods **41**(19), 3511–3527 (2012)

Alzaid, A.A., Omair, M.A.: Poisson difference integer-valued autoregressive model of order one. Bull. Malays. Math. Sci. Soc. **2**(37), 465–485 (2014)

Andersson, J., Karlis, D.: A parametric time series model with covariates for integers in $Z$. Stat. Model. **14**(2), 135–156 (2014)

Bakouch, H.S., Kachour, M., Nadarajah, S.: An extended poisson distribution. Commun. Stat.-Theory Methods **45**(22), 6746–6764 (2016)

Chesneau, C., Kachour, M.: A parametric study for the first-order signed integer-valued autoregressive process. J. Stat. Theory Pract. **6**(4), 760–782 (2012)

Kachour, M., Truquet, L.: A $p$-order signed integer-valued autoregressive (SINAR($p$)) model. J. Time Ser. Anal. **2**(3), 223–236 (2011)

Karlis, D., Ntzoufras, I.: Bayesian modelling of football outcomes: using the Skellam's distribution for the goal difference. J. Manag. Math. **20**(2), 133–145 (2009)

Kim, H., Park, Y.: A non-stationary integer-valued autoregressive model. Stat. Papers **49**(3), 485–502 (2008)

Klimko, L.A., Nelson, P.I.: On conditional least squares estimation for stochastic processes. Ann. Stat. **6**(3), 629–642 (1978)

Skellam, J.G.: The frequency distribution of the difference between two poisson variates belonging to different populations. J. Royal Stat. Soc. **109**(3), 296 (1946)

Steutel, F.W., van Harn, K.: Discrete analogues of self-decomposability and stability. Ann. Probab. **7**(5), 893–899 (1979)

# Computational Mathematics, Statistics and Information Management (CMSIM 2019)

# A Spatio-Temporal Auto-regressive Model for Generating Savings Calls to a Health Line

Paula Simões[1,3]([✉])(iD), M. Lucília Carvalho[4](iD), Sandra Aleixo[3,4](iD),
Sérgio Gomes[5](iD), and Isabel Natário[1,2](iD)

[1] Centro de Matemática e Aplicações (CMA), Faculdade de Ciências e Tecnologia,
Universidade Nova de Lisboa, Lisbon, Portugal
[2] Departamento de Matemática, Faculdade de Ciências e Tecnologia, Universidade
Nova de Lisboa, Lisbon, Portugal
[3] ISEL - Instituto Superior de Engenharia de Lisboa, Instituto Politécnico de Lisboa,
Lisbon, Portugal
paulasimoes@adm.isel.pt
[4] Centro de Estatística e Aplicações (CEAUL), Faculdade de Ciências da
Universidade de Lisboa, Lisbon, Portugal
[5] Direção Geral de Saúde, Lisbon, Portugal

**Abstract.** Urgency admission is one of the most important factors regarding hospital costs, which can possibly be mitigated by the use of national health lines such as the Portuguese Saúde24 line (S24). Aiming future development of decision support indicators in a hospital savings context, based on the economic impact of the use of S24 rather than hospital urgency services, this study investigates spatio-temporal dependencies of the number of S24 calls generating savings in each Portuguese municipality, over the period 2010–2016, under an autoregressive approach. An econometric analysis of the savings obtained by the use of S24 is also carried out considering a savings index.

Combining insights from classical spatial econometrics and from the analysis of spatio-temporal data, novel Bayesian Poisson spatio-temporal lag models are presented and applied in this paper. This extends to time the ideas of a Bayesian Poisson spatial lag model, considering both a parametric and a non-parametic structure for time and space-time effects.

The results obtained for the savings index reveal that, over the last seven years, there has been a more comprehensive spatial effectiveness of the S24 line in solving the non-urgent emergency situations, that could be handled by primary health care services or in a self care basis.

**Keywords:** Bayesian analysis · Spatial econometrics ·
Autoregressive models · Space-time correlation · Poisson

Supported by national funds through FCT - Foundation for Science and Technology - under the projects UID/MAT/00297/2019 and UID/MAT/00006/2013.

S. Misra et al. (Eds.): ICCSA 2019, LNCS 11621, pp. 81–96, 2019.
https://doi.org/10.1007/978-3-030-24302-9_7

# 1 Introduction

The use of national health lines can possibly mitigate the effects of one of the most important factors responsible for a considerable part of hospital costs, urgency admissions [1]. It is possible that a considerable part of the admissions corresponds to non-urgent cases that could be handled by primary health care services. This helps to understand why, in Portugal, hospital urgency service has become one of the most important worries of the Health Ministry over the last years.

Within this context in April 2007 a Portuguese National Health Line, Saúde24 line (S24), was created in order to improve accessibility to health care and to racionalize the use of existing resources [2]. The S24 service directs users to the most appropriate institutions of the public health service or offers counsels on self-care measures.

The S24 offers various services, including Triage, Couseling and Routing (TCR) in disease situations, which represents approximately 90% of the calls to the health line. This study focuses on these calls at a municipality level, in Continental Portugal, annually over the period 2010–2016. In order to evaluate the economic impact of the use of S24 rather than hospital urgency services, in terms of the reached savings by avoiding unnecessary urgent care in hospitals, the main interest is on the TCR calls whose initial intention of the user was to go to hospital urgency but, after using the health line the final disposal is a non-emergent situation, that does not require hospital emergency care. Taking into account that the savings achieved with S24 are proportional to the number of savings calls, considering the price of a simple medical appointment in the urgency, these are the calls analysed in this study, described as S24 savings calls.

Spatio-temporal dependencies might be expected on the number of S24 savings calls in each Portuguese municipality, during the study period, and should be accounted for in the modelling process [3], since observations from geographically close spatial units and temporally close time periods tend to have more similar values. This requires the selection of a neighbourhood structure that specifies the relations between regions to identify spatial association among them [4].

An autoregressive spatio-temporal Bayesian econometric approach for processing count data [5] can be implemented allowing, for example, to describe and evaluate in which municipalities the use of S24 must be potentiated and highlight those regions that most contribute to the economic success of the use of the health line. This resorts to Integrated Nested Laplace Approximation (INLA) methodology [6,7] for implementing the Bayesian paradigm.

The spatio-temporal modelling formulation proposed here extends the spatial autoregressive approach for count data in [5], allowing for temporal and spatio-temporal components. The essence of this methodology was driven based on the main idea that is plausible to consider that the risk of what is being counted in one area is related to the risk of what is being counted in the areas of its neighbourhoods. Within a Poisson response setting, a spatial lag term is included on the log relative risks accommodating the magnitude of the spatial influences while preserving other important factors. Additionally, temporal and spatio-temporal effects are allowed, considering both a parametric and a nonparametric structure for these components. When the purpose of the analysis is to estimate which areas are exhibiting linear trends in the response over time a parametric structure is considered with the model proposed by Bernardelli *et al.* [8]; however if time trends and spatial patterns are to be estimated considering interaction, a dynamic nonparametric formulation is more adequate and the propose of Knorr-Held is considered [9]. The lag model with temporal and space-temporal effects is now implemented for the first time in a Poisson response Bayesian setting. This contribution may also be important for other spatio-temporal econometric practitioners.

An econometric analysis of the savings obtained by the use of S24 is carried out considering a savings index, in order to reach a more detailed health econometric analysis, developing an economic understanding of the advantages for the health system. The main reason for the support of public health research is the common understanding that new knowledge leads to more effective health care, expecting that the upper mentioned econometrics analysis contributes, in general, to an improvement by helping to reduce the per capita costs of the health care, through management policies [10].

This work organises as follows: first, Sect. 2 presents an overview of the considered approaches and describes the new proposals of spatio-temporal autoregressive models for Poisson count data; then Sect. 3 describes and details the application of the econometric analysis of S24 calls to assess hospital savings; finally Sect. 4 discusses some of the main conclusions as well as some possibilities for future work.

## 2 Modelling Spatial and Temporal Variability on Count Data

Traditional spatial econometric models, such as the spatial autoregressive model (slm) and the spatial error model (sem), rely on the Gaussian assumption of the response variable [11], which does not hold for count data in areas or spatial units - *lattice data* [4, 12]. Consequently their usage for count data, such as the number of calls, demands data transformation to meet the assumptions of the models. In order to avoid that, this work investigates new possible spatio-temporal modelling strategies for handling count data following a Poisson distribution.

In the scope of these spatial autoregressive models there are alternatives for modelling counts that we have explored in a previous work [5]. More specifically, considering a standard spatial lag model developed within a new class of latent models defined in Integrated Nested Laplace Approximations (INLA) [13], by Gómez-Rubio, Bivand and Rue in 2015 [6]; considering a spatial autoregressive lag model of counts developed by Lambert, Brown and Florax in 2010 [14], under a classical perspective; a spatial lag autoregressive component was incorporated in the model for counts, under a Bayesian paradigm and using INLA methodology. This resulted in a spatial lag Poisson model for count data.

In this paper, this alternative is further elaborated into a more complex spatio-temporal autoregressive model where time and spatio-time effects are incorporated, eventually capturing dynamic evolutions [3,7]. The Bayesian estimation can be considered under INLA methodology, being implemented with R-INLA. The lag model with temporal and spatio-temporal interaction effects has not yet been implemented in a Poisson response Bayesian setting.

This section describes and explains different Bayesian spatio-temporal models for Poisson count data, that resort to random effects to account for spatial and temporal correlation. For spatial correlation, the models presented here take an autoregressive approach in space [15]. They further consider time effects modelled simply through a parametric linear trend model [8] or through a nonparametric dynamic trend model [9], implemented, respectively, within a Bayesian Poisson spatio-temporal lag linear model and a Bayesian Poisson spatio-temporal lag dynamic model.

## 2.1 General Log-Poisson Regression Model

Considering the study region divided into a set of $n$ spatial units let $y_t = (y_{1t}, \ldots, y_{nt})$ and $e_t = (e_{1t}, \ldots, e_{nt})$ represent, respectively, the number of observed and expected cases of what is being measured in each spatial unit $i = 1, \ldots, n$ and recorded for $t = 1, \ldots, T$ consecutive time periods. The counts $y_{it}$ are assumed to be Poisson distributed with expected value $E(y_{it}) = \mu_{it} = e_{it}\theta_{it}$, where $\theta_{it}$ is the relative risk in area $i$ and time $t$.

The general log-Poisson regression model is defined as:

$$y_{it}|\eta_{it} \sim \text{Poisson}\,(e_{it}\theta_{it}), \tag{1}$$

where $\eta_{it} = \log(\theta_{it})$, $i = 1, \ldots, n$, $t = 1, \ldots, T$, are the log relative risks. Note that $\log(e_{it})$ enter as known offsets in the model.

The log relative risks are decomposed into the effects of covariates $\mathbf{X}_{it}^T = (X_{it1}, \ldots, X_{itk})$ measured for spatial unit $i$ and time period $t$, corresponding $X_{it1}$ to the intercept term and being $\beta = (\beta_1, \ldots, \beta_k)$ the associated regression parameters, plus some random effects that are able to account for possible overdispersion:

$$\eta_{it} = \log(\theta_{it}) = \mathbf{X}_{it}^T\beta + u_{it}. \tag{2}$$

The $u_{it}$ term is a latent component for spatial unit $i$ and time period $t$ which may capture remaining space, time and spatio-temporal effects or trends in the data, after accounting for the covariates. Different configurations of $u_{it}$ correspond to different models.

For the regression coefficients $\beta_j$ weak informative Normal$(0, 1000)$ prior distributions are considered.

## 2.2 Spatio-Temporal Bayesian Autoregressive Log-Poisson Models

This subsection details spatio-temporal Bayesian autoregressive log-Poisson models as members of the general log-Poisson regression model.

**Spatial Component.** Under formulation (2), we get an autoregressive lag Poisson model if $u_{it}$ includes a spatial lag term $\varepsilon_{it}$ on the log relative risks.

In the formulation of the Bayesian Poisson spatial lag model [5], spatial dependencies are accounted in the observed responses through a spatial lag term $\varepsilon_{it}$ on the log relative risks, to be included in $u_{it}$ and given by:

$$\varepsilon_{it} = \rho \sum_{j \neq i} w_{ij} \eta_{jt}, \tag{3}$$

where $\eta_{jt}$ is the log relative risk for unit area $j$ and time $t$, $w_{ij}$ are the elements of an adjacency matrix $W$ defined by a contiguity criterion between areas [4], for establishing the neighbouring structure, and $\rho$ is the spatial autoregressive parameter. For the logit transformation of parameter $\rho$, $logit(\rho)$, a Normal(0,10) weak informative prior distribution is considered. The log-risks $\eta_{jt}$ are modelled also with temporal and spatio-temporal effects, justifying the dependency of the quantities $\varepsilon_{it}$ on time.

**Temporal and Spatio-Temporal Components.** Temporal effects may also be added into the $u_{it}$ component. These effects are going to be considered in two different ways, under a simplicity argument. Firstly we adopt a parametric trend for the temporal component as proposed by Bernardelli *et al.* [8], that includes in $u_{it}$ a separate linear trend for each area. Secondly we consider a nonparametric dynamic trend as proposed by Knorr-Held [9] for the temporal component, that includes in $u_{it}$ a temporally structured temporal effect and an unstructured space-time interaction effect.

*Linear Trend Model.* This model incorporates the spatio-temporal variation additively in $u_{it}$ in (2) as a separate linear trend in time for each area:

$$(\alpha + \delta_i)t^*, \tag{4}$$

where $t^*$ corresponds to the time normalized to belong to an unit interval. The spatial unit $i$ has then its own linear time trend with a spatially varying intercept $(\beta_1 + \varepsilon_{it})$ and a spatially varying slope $(\alpha + \delta_i)$. The differential trend $\delta_i$ represents the difference between the global trend $\alpha$ and the spatial unit specific trend. If $\delta_i > 0$ the trend for the corresponding spatial unit is steeper than the mean trend while it $\delta_i < 0$ is the other way around.

This specification is similar to the spatially varying linear time trend model proposed by Bernardinelli *et al.* [8] for spatio-temporal hierarchical models. It considers spatio-temporal interactions $\delta_i$ differentiated for each spatial unit.

It is assumed for each element of $\delta = (\delta_1, \ldots, \delta_n)$ and for the overall slope parameter $\alpha$ independent Gaussian prior distributions,

$$\begin{aligned} \delta_i &\sim \text{Normal}\,(0, \sigma_{slo}^2) \\ \alpha &\sim \text{Normal}\,(\mu_\alpha, \sigma_\alpha^2) \end{aligned} \tag{5}$$

For $\sigma_{slo}^2$ an inverse-gamma prior distribution is considered [7]. The corresponding hyperparameters $(a, b, \mu_\alpha, \sigma_\alpha^2)$ are chosen in this work such that the resulting prior distributions are weakly informative. It is assumed that $a = 1, b = 0.01$, $\mu_\alpha = 0$ and $\sigma_\alpha^2 = 1000$.

The assumption of linearity of the $\delta_i$ component can be relaxed, using instead a dynamic nonparametric formulation of the temporal component as follows.

*Dynamic Trend Model.* This model is similar to the simplest form of the one proposed by Knorr-Held [9] for spatio-temporal hierarchical models, although there are other more complex alternatives that could also have been explored. It incorporates additively in $u_{it}$ in (2), specific year spatial effects $\varepsilon_{it}$, an overall temporal trend common to all spatial units $\delta_t$ as well as space-time interactions $\gamma_{it}$:

$$\varepsilon_{it} + \delta_t + \gamma_{it}, \tag{6}$$

where $\delta_t$ are modelled dynamically by a random walk of order 1 and unstructured space-time random effect are considered [7]. Denoting $\delta = (\delta_1, \ldots, \delta_t)$ the set of temporal random effects, they are modelled through a random walk of order 1:

$$\delta_t - \delta_{t+1} \sim \text{Normal} \left(0, \sigma_T^2\right) \tag{7}$$

For the independent space-time interactions $\gamma = (\gamma_{11}, \ldots, \gamma_{nT})$ Gaussian prior distributions are specified,

$$\gamma_{it} \sim \text{Normal} \left(0, \sigma_I^2\right) \tag{8}$$

For $\sigma_I^2$ a weak informative inverse-gamma prior distribution is considered ($a = 1, b = 0.01$) and for $\log(\sigma_T^{-2})$ a weak informative log-gamma prior distribution is considered ($a = 1, b = 0.00005$).

The Bayesian Poisson spatial lag model [5] is now extended to allow the inclusion of a temporal and spatio-temporal components in $u_{it}$ in (2) through (4) or (6).

Analogously to [5], and given the exposed in Sect. 2.1, we are able to write the predictor $\eta_{it}$ of the autoregressive in space log-Poisson model as:

$$\eta_{it} = \log(\theta_{it}) = \mathbf{X}_{it}^T\beta + \rho \sum_{j\neq i} w_{ij}\eta_{jt} + \delta_t + \gamma_{it}, \tag{9}$$

considering, without loss of generality, that $\delta_t$ represents a temporal effect and $\gamma_{it}$ a space-time interaction effect. For each time $t$ this can be expressed in matrix notation as:

$$\eta_t = \mathbf{X}_t^T\beta + \rho W\eta_t + \delta_t 1_{n\times 1} + \gamma_t, \tag{10}$$

where $\eta_t$ denotes the log-risks $\eta_{it}$ for year $t$, $\mathbf{X}_t^T$ represents the observed covariates in year $t$ (including a first column of 1's for the intercept), $1_{n\times 1}$ is a column of $n$ 1's and $\gamma_t$ denotes the space-time interaction effects $\gamma_{it}$ for year $t$.

Equivalently this can be expressed as:

$$\eta_t = (I_n - \rho W)^{-1}\mathbf{X}_t^T\beta + (I_n - \rho W)^{-1}\delta_t 1_{n\times 1} + (I_n - \rho W)^{-1}\gamma_t \quad \Leftrightarrow$$

$$\eta_t = (I_n - \rho W)^{-1}\mathbf{X}_t^T\beta + \delta_t^* + \gamma_t^*, \tag{11}$$

where
$$\delta_t^* = (I_n - \rho W)^{-1}\delta_t 1_{n\times 1} \quad \Leftrightarrow \quad \delta_t 1_{n\times 1} = (I_n - \rho W)\delta_t^* \tag{12}$$
and
$$\gamma_t^* = (I_n - \rho W)^{-1}\gamma_t \quad \Leftrightarrow \quad \gamma_t = (I_n - \rho W)\gamma_t^* \tag{13}$$

Expression for $\eta_t$ in (11) is then given as a sum of three random effects, $x_1 = (I_n - \rho W)^{-1}\mathbf{X}_t^T\beta$, $x_2 = \delta_t^*$, and $x_3 = \gamma_t^*$, allowing its estimation through INLA methodology, which requires models to be written under such a formulation [5]. Temporal and spatio-temporal effects are considered in this transformed version ($\delta_t^*$ and $\gamma_{it}^*$), being related to the untransformed effects $\delta_t$ and $\gamma_{it}$, respectively, by a factor of $(1 - \rho)$. This relation can be used to recover the original effects.

When it is chosen a linear trend temporal component (4) the resulting model is the Bayesian Poisson spatio-temporal lag linear model (ST.splm.linear). A simple dynamic nonparametric formulation (6) corresponds to the Bayesian Poisson spatio-temporal lag dynamic model (ST.splm.dynamic).

# 3  Spatio-Temporal Modelling of S24 Data

The data considered in this study were provided by the Support Unit of the Call Center of the National Health Service of the Portuguese Directorate-General of Health. It is a comprehensive data set of the calls recorded by the S24 health line, over the period 2010–2016, and includes information such as user's gender, residence, age, call's day of the week and the health problem specification.

The S24 has two call centers and offers various services, such as Triage, Counseling and Routing in disease situations (TCR); Therapeutic counseling to clarify issues relating to medication; Assistance in Public Health in specific topics as flu, heat, poisoning, etc.; General Health Information such as the location of public health units, pharmacies, among others. The S24 service is provided by qualified nurses, trained to give the best advice or, when appropriate, to assist citizens in solving the situation by themselves, being available to the beneficiaries of all different kinds of health sub-systems.

The majority of the calls answered by S24, approximately 92%, are catalogued as TCR. For those, the description of the health problem and the original intention of the user about how to solve it (go to an urgency room, for example) are recorded, and then a decision algorithm follows. The final disposition is given by this algorithm jointly with the evaluation of the nurse.

## 3.1  Econometric Analysis of S24 Calls to Assess Hospital Savings

This work focuses on the number of TCR calls to S24 at a municipality level in Continental Portugal annually over the period 2010–2016. The interest is evaluating the economic impact of the use of this health line concerning the reached savings by avoid unnecessary urgent care in hospitals. For that what is relevant are the TCR calls whose initial intention of the user was to go to hospital urgency but, according with the final health line disposition, that is not necessary. These are the calls analyzed in this work, described as TCR savings calls.

Taking into account that the savings achieved with S24 are proportional to the number of savings calls, this work investigates and models spatial and temporal dependencies of the number of TCR savings calls in the Portuguese municipalities and for the time period from 2010 to 2016. Given this, the data considered in this study are the number of S24 savings calls that were registered in each of the 278 municipalities of Continental Portugal from 2010 to 2016 inclusive.

Within this context, the expected savings can be given by the following simple measure:

$$S_t = \sum_{i=1}^{278} y_{it} p_t - C_t,$$

where $y_{it}$ are the number of savings calls in each municipality $i = 1, \ldots, 278$ and year $t = 1, \ldots, 7$; $p_t$ corresponds to the price of a simple medical appointment in the urgency, which is set every year in a decree-law by the Ministry of Health; and $C_t$ are costs associated with annual health line maintenance, provided by Portuguese Directorate-General of Health.

It should be emphasized that this is a simplistic measure which does not consider collateral costs as, for example, those caused by unnecessary increased contagion risk or those caused by increasing the number of patients in the urgency, requiring more human and financial resources.

The results of this study will contribute to understand one of the major factors regarding hospital costs of the Portuguese health care system, the non-urgent emergency situations, responsible for the decrease of hospital system efficiency. At the same time it will help to realize if this phenomenon has been mitigated through the creation, promotion and use of Saude24, with the perception that presently there are still about 15% of non-urgent cases per year in Portuguese Hospital Care System.

### 3.2 Preliminary S24 Data Analysis

The number of TCR savings calls are registered in each of the 278 municipalities of Continental Portugal from 2010 to 2016 inclusive. Naturally these numbers depend on the size and demographic structure of the population, in terms of age and gender characteristics of the underlying population, which requires adjustment in terms of (indirect) standardization. The observed $(y_{it})$ and the resulting expected number $(e_{it})$ of savings calls in each municipality $i = 1, \ldots, 278$, and year $t = 1, .., 7$, can then be used to roughly estimate the relative call risk, $\theta_{it}$, through the Standard Call Rate (SCR) in municipality $i$ and year $t$, $\mathrm{SCR}_{it} = \frac{y_{it}}{e_{it}}$, mapped in Fig. 1. Several demographic, socio-economic, development and health indicators were investigated as possible covariates for modelling the TCR savings calls counts using a simple log-Poisson model.

Taking into account that the covariates are related in the model to the natural log of SCR, the relationships between the selected variables for all years

**SCR**

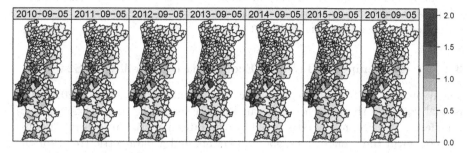

**Fig. 1.** SCR-2010 to 2016.

under analysis and the natural log of SCR were analysed. A positive relationship between the log of SCR and the average number of years of schooling was evident, suggesting that increased levels of schooling are connected to an increased risk of savings calls. It was also noted a slightly negative relationship between the log of SCR and the number of hospitals, suggesting that an increase in the number of hospitals have a decreasing impact on the savings calls risk.

The expected number of savings calls is included in the model as an offset. Bayesian covariable selection using indicator auxiliary variables under different scenarios [16] was performed. The most significant set of explanatory variables turned out to be the *average number of years of schooling* ($x_1$), the *proportion of active population* ($x_2$), the *rurality index* ($x_3$), the *number of hospitals* ($x_4$) and the *number of health centers per 1000 inhabitants* in each municipality ($x_5$). This was implemented in R-package "R2WinBUGS" [17] that run WinBugs [18].

It was further fitted a log-Poisson model with the covariates and unstructured random effects to account for possible over-dispersion, that is expected in these Poisson data. This confirmed the significance of some of the previous set of covariates, but two, the *number of hospitals* and the *number of health centers* revealed not to be significant. Nevertheless these covariates were kept in the model for their intrinsic econometric interest.

### 3.3   Spatial and Temporal Correlation

Preliminary analyses of these data included using Moran's I statistics [19] to look for spatial dependence of the number of TCR savings calls to S24 per 1000 inhabitants, by municipality and by year, and in the residuals of the log-Poisson model with covariates and unstructured random effects fitted before for each year, using a contiguity neighbourhood spatial structure (results were obtained with R-project package spdep). These resulted in clear rejection of the spatial independence hypothesis in both cases suggesting that there is positive spatial correlation among of the number of TCR savings calls, from 2010 to 2016, and also a strong evidence of unexplained spatial correlation in each year, after accounting for the covariate effects.

The residual temporal correlation could be assessed similarly considering a temporal neighbourhood structure but with only 7 time periods the resulting estimates would not be reliable [19,21].

### 3.4 Spatio-Temporal Bayesian Econometric Modelling of S24

The number of TCR savings calls in each municipality for the period 2010–2016 is analysed here through the Bayesian Poisson spatial lag model with temporal effects. The first model considered incorporates a spatial autocorrelation lag component in the econometric model of counts and a parametric trend for the temporal component (ST.splm.linear model). Then a nonparametric dynamic space-time model is also implemented within the spatial lag Bayesian Poisson model with temporally structured effects and allowing an unstructured interaction between space and time (ST.splm.dynamic model).

The estimates were obtained in R-INLA, using `slpmINLA` function, adapted for the spatio-temporal linear and dynamic cases. Main results are displayed in Table 1 and correspond to formulation (11). The estimated temporal and spatio-temporal effects of the original formulation were retrieved in an ad hoc manner by the existing relation between parameters $\delta_t$ and $\delta_t^*$, $\gamma_{ti}$ and $\gamma_{ti}^*$, being quite similar to each other.

**Table 1.** Parameter estimates (mean and 95% credible intervals) for the ST.splm.linear model and for ST.splm.dynamic model, for the S24 2010-2016 data. $\sigma^2$ is the estimated variance of the spatial effects for the autoregressive model.

| Variable | Id | ST.splm.linear Model | ST.splm.dynamic Model |
|---|---|---|---|
| | | Mean (CI) | Mean (CI) |
| Average number of years of **schooling** | $x_1$ | 0.41 (0.14; 0.62) | 0.14 (0.10; 0.19) |
| Proportion of **active population** | $x_2$ | $-3.89$ ($-7.66$; $-0.02$) | $-0.11$ ($-0.88$; 0.63) |
| **Rurality** index | $x_3$ | 0.17 ($-0.53$; 0.84) | 0.11 ($-0.05$, 0.26) |
| Number of **hospitals** | $x_4$ | 0.18 ($-4.01$; 4.33) | 0.54 ($-0.42$; 1.49) |
| Number of **health centers** | $x_5$ | 0.61 ($-2.31$; 1.00) | $-0.17$ ($-0.55$, 0.21) |
| Intercept | | $-1.11$ ($-3.95$; 1.68) | $-1.00$ ($-1.61$, $-0.39$) |
| $\alpha^*/\sigma_T^2$ | | 0.06 (0.05; 0.09) | 1.17e$-$04 (3.9e$-$05; 5.74e$-$04) |
| $\rho$ | | 0.56 (0.55; 0.56) | 0.56 (0.55; 0.57) |
| $\sigma^2$ | | 0.08 (0.07; 0.10) | 0.08 (0.07; 0.09) |
| $\sigma_{slo}^2/\sigma_I^2$ | | 0.04 (0.03; 0.05) | 0.005 (0.004; 0.006) |

In relation to the ST.splm.linear model only two of the initial covariates revealed to be significant, the average number of years of schooling and proportion of active population residents. This model has an estimated value of the spatial dependence parameter $\rho$ of 0.56. The main linear trend $\alpha$, which represents the global time effect, is estimated as 0.06, being significant, and the estimated value of $\sigma_{slo}^2$ is 0.04.

For the ST.splm.dynamic formulation only the average number of years of schooling is significant and the estimated values of $\sigma_I^2$ and $\sigma_T^2$ are 0.005 and 1.17e−04, respectively. It has an estimated value of the spatial dependence parameter $\rho$ of 0.56, similar to the value obtained for the linear case.

In order to compare models, the chosen measures were the WAIC (Watanabe-Akaike information criteria) and the DIC (Deviance information criteria), as DIC is the predictive measure most used in Bayesian applications [22] and WAIC revealed to be more stable and particularly helpful with mixture structures [23]. In terms of the different temporal structures, DIC and WAIC were concordant and smaller for the dynamic parametrization - see Table 2. In what concerns each of the different temporal structures considered, one can say that within the parametric trend formulation, similar estimates were obtained for the spatial effects; the main linear trend was significant and displays an estimated value of 0.06, although the significance of the initial set of covariates differed from the simple log-Poisson regression model.

**Table 2.** DIC and WAIC measured for the case of a linear and a dynamic trend.

| Model | DIC | pD | WAIC | pW |
|---|---|---|---|---|
| ST.splm.linear | 16997 | 463 | 17474 | 773 |
| ST.splm.dynamic | 16387 | 1007.9 | 16370 | 760 |

The dynamic parametrization improved the model fit (smaller DIC and WAIC) suggesting that this parametrization for time is more appropriate to S24 data. Under this formulation, only one of the initial set of covariates revealed to be significant, the average number of years of schooling.

The estimated posterior means of the spatial main effect, $\zeta_i = \exp(\varepsilon_i)$, and the estimated posterior temporal trend $\xi_t = \exp(\delta_t^*)$, for the ST.splm.dynamic formulation are depicted in Fig. 2, suggesting a soft increase in the time effect and mild spatial effect around the metropolitan area of Lisbon.

The estimated posterior mean for the space-time interaction for the ST.splm.dynamic model, for the years 2010, 2012, 2014 and 2016, are displayed in Fig. 3. The considered space-time interaction effects did not seem to be of added value in explaining the TCR savings calls risk.

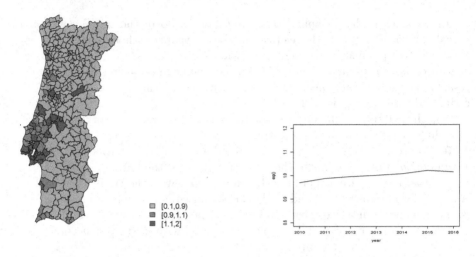

**Fig. 2.** Estimated spatial and temporal effects for the chosen model.

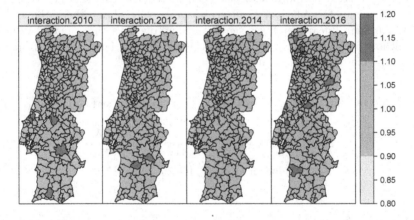

**Fig. 3.** Estimated spatio-temporal interaction effects for years of 2010, 2012, 2014 and 2016 for the chosen model.

### 3.5   The Savings Index

The S24 data analysis can be extended, exploring the econometric analysis of a Savings Index, obtained for each municipality $i = 1, \ldots, 278$ and year $t = 1, \ldots, 7$ as:

$$IS_{it} = \frac{(y_{it}p_t - C_{it})}{U_{it}}$$

where $y_{it}$ is the number of savings calls, $p_t$ corresponds to the price of a simple medical appointment in the urgency, $C_{it}$ are costs associated with annual health line maintenance attributable to municipality $i$ and is $U_{it}$ are the total number of calls whose initial intention is urgency. It is mapped in Fig. 4.

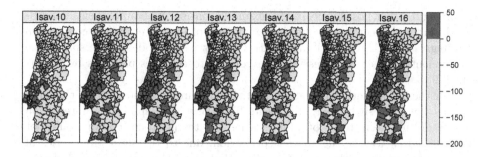

**Fig. 4.** The Savings Index from 2010 to 2016.

The municipalities of metropolitan area of Lisbon stand out as the ones corresponding to higher savings. On the other hand municipalities of northern interior should be considered for having implemented management policies in order to improve the impact of S24 in solving their non-urgent emerging situations.

## 4   Discussion

Induced by the application of modelling the number of savings calls to a national health line S24, this work proposes a Bayesian Poisson spatio-temporal lag approach for modelling lattice data. It comprehends different spatio-temporal models for Poisson count data which resorts to autocorrelated random effects to account for spatial and temporal correlation, here under Bayesian paradigm, extending a spatial autoregressive model for count data. Within this novel spatio-temporal modelling formulation, spatial dependencies are accounted in the observed responses. Including a spatial lag term on the log relative risks allows to accommodate the magnitude of the spatial influences while preserving other important factors, corresponding to the autoregressive lag Poisson model. The lag model with temporal effects had not yet been implemented in a Poisson response Bayesian setting.

The benefits of the autoregressive approach over other classical approaches for count data, as hierarchical models, are mainly concerned with econometric interpretation, since the response variable in a given area constitutes a good predictor of the response variable in its neighbourhood areas.

The models derived for count data were accommodated in the mathematical framework given by

$$
\begin{aligned}
y_{it}|\eta_{it} &\sim \text{Poisson}\left(e_{it}\theta_{it}\right), \\
\eta_{it} = \log(\theta_{it}) &= \mathbf{X}_{it}^{T}\beta + u_{it}, \quad i = 1, \ldots, n, \ t = 1, \ldots, T
\end{aligned}
\tag{14}
$$

with different representations of $u_{it}$ corresponding to different model specifications. Within this common frame other possibilities can also be investigated for spatio-temporal modelling. For example, time effects can be further explored resorting to other possibilities, as for example considering temporal effects a priori distributed according to the time analogous of Leroux et al. [20] conditional autoregressive (CAR) distribution [21]. Other ways of modeling the space-time component can be also investigated according to the ones proposes by Knorr-Held [9].

For the S24 savings calls data, a spatial structure was evident from the analysis as well as a slight temporal trend. The considered space-time interaction effects did not seem to be of added value. The temporal correlation could not be assessed as well as the spatial correlation, due to the short time series of seven time periods, although we consider that is was important to include the temporal component and allowing an interaction term between time and space. The small number of time periods was also the reason for not considering more complex structures for space-time interaction effects. An alternative would have been considering a different distribution [20] for the spatial effects for each year, resulting in differentiated autocorrelation parameter for each year, and evaluating afterwards the time evolution of these estimates [21].

In terms of the savings index, one can say that over the last seven years, there has been a more comprehensive effectiveness of the S24 line over space in solving the non-urgent emergency situations, that could be handled by primary health care services or in a self care basis. The savings index detected the municipalities of the metropolitan area of Lisbon as those that most contribute to the economic success of the S24 line. At the same time it identified the northern interior municipalities as those in which the use of the health line should be encouraged. This suggests that the S24 line is not equally well disseminated over the whole territory and, moreover, that this is not even associated with the available health services offer. Consequently, regional directed campaigns of the S24 line use should be considered as a priority.

The results of this study contribute to understand one of the major factors regarding hospital costs of Portuguese health care system, the non-urgent emergency situations, responsible for major efficacy losses of the hospital systems, and at the same time helps to realize if this phenomenon have been mitigated through the creation, promotion and use of S24, knowing that presently there are still about 15% of non-urgent cases per year in Portuguese Hospital Care System.

This study could now be extended in order to reach a more detailed health econometric analysis of the savings obtained by the use of S24, developing an economic understanding of the advantages for the health system and learning about the political and economic factors that influence health policies at a global, national, regional and local levels. The main reason for the support of public health research is the common understanding that new knowledge leads to more effective health care, expecting that the upper mentioned econometrics analysis contributes, in general, to an improvement by helping to reduce the per capita costs of the health care, through management policies [10].

**Acknowledgements.** This work is financed by national funds through FCT - Foundation for Science and Technology - under the projects UID/MAT/00297/2019 and UID/MAT/00006/2013.

# References

1. Hughes, D., McGuire, A.: Stochastic demand, production responses and hospital costs. J. Health Econ. **22**, 999–1010 (2003)
2. Portal of the National Portuguese Health Service. https://www.dgs.pt/paginas-de-sistema/saude-de-a-a-z/saude-24.aspx. Accessed 3 Sept 2015
3. Cressie, N., Wikle, C.: Statistics for Spatio-Temporal Data. Wiley, Hoboken (2011)
4. Cressie, N.: Statistics for Spatial Data. Wiley, Hoboken (1993)
5. Simões, P., Carvalho, M.L., Aleixo, S., Gomes, S., Natário, I.: A spatial econometric analysis of the calls to the portuguese national health line. Econometrics **5**(24), 24 (2017). MDPI Journals
6. Goméz-Rubio, V., Bivand, R., Rue, H.: A new latent class to fit spatial econometrics models with integrated nested laplace approximations. Spat. Stat.: Emerg. Patterns-Part 2 **27**, 116–118 (2015). Details of the implementation in http://www.math.ntnu.no/inla/r-inla.org/doc/latent/slm.pdf, downloaded in September of 2016
7. Blangiardo, M., Cameletti, M.: Spatial and Spatio-temporal Bayesian Models with R-INLA. Wiley, Hoboken (2015)
8. Bernardinelli, L., et al.: Bayesian analysis of space-time variation in disease risk. Stat. Med. **14**(21–22), 2433–2443 (1995)
9. Knorr-Held, L.: Bayesian modelling of inseparable space-time variation in disease risk. Stat. Med. **19**, 2555–2567 (2000)
10. Sobolev, B., Levy, A. (eds.): Comparative Effectiveness Research in Health Services. Springer, Boston (2016). https://doi.org/10.1007/978-1-4899-7600-0
11. Lesage, J., Pace, R.: Introduction to Spatial Econometrics. CRC Press, Boca Raton (2009)
12. Besag, J.: Spatial interaction and the statistical analysis of lattice systems (with discussion). J. R. Stat. Soc. B **36**, 192–236 (1974)
13. Rue, H., Martino, S., Chopin, N.: Approximate Bayesian inference for lattent Gaussian models by using integrated nested Laplace approximations. J. Roy Stat. Soc. B **71**(Part 2), 319–392 (2009)
14. Lambert, D., Brown, J., Florax, R.: A two-step estimator for a spatial lag model of counts: theory, small sample performance and an application. Reg. Sci. Urban Econ. **40**, 241–252 (2010)
15. Bivand, R., Goméz-Rubio, V., Rue, H.: Approximate Bayesian inference for spatial econometrics models. Spat. Stat. **9**, 146–165 (2014)
16. George, E., McCulloch, R.: Approaches for Bayesian variable selection. Stat. Sin. **7**, 339–373 (1997)
17. Gelman, A., Sturtz, S., Ligges, U., Gorjan, G., Kerman, J.: Package R2WinBUGS (2015)
18. Lunn, D., Spiegelhalter, D., Thomas, A., Best, N.: The BUGS project: evolution, critique and future directions. Stat. Med. **28**, 3049–3067 (2009)
19. Anselin, L., Bera, A.K.: Spatial dependence in linear regression models with an introduction to spatial econometrics. In: Statistics Textbooks and Monographs, vol. 155, pp. 237–290 (1998)

20. Leroux, B.G., Lei, X., Breslow, N.: Estimation of disease rates in small areas: a new mixed model for spatial dependence. In: Halloran, M.E., Berry, D. (eds.) Statistical Models in Epidemiology, the Environment, and Clinical Trials. IMA, vol. 116, pp. 179–191. Springer, New York (2000). https://doi.org/10.1007/978-1-4612-1284-3_4
21. Lee, D., Rushworth A., and Napier G.: CARBayesST: an R package for spatio-temporal areal unit modelling with conditional autoregressive priors. R Package Version 2.2 (2015). https://cran.r-project.org/web/packages/CARBayesST/. Accessed 25 Feb 2016
22. Spiegelhalter, D., Best, N., Carlin, B., Van der Linde, A.: Bayesian measures of model complexity and fit. J. R. Stat. Soc. B **64**(4), 583–639 (2002)
23. Gelman, A., Hwang, J., Vehtari, A.: Understanding predictive information criteria for Bayesian models. J. Stat Comput **24**, 997–1016 (2014)

# Knowledge of the Boarded Population About Zika Virus

João Faria[1,3], Rosa Teodósio[1,2]🆔, and M. Filomena Teodoro[3,4(✉)]🆔

[1] IHMT - Institute of Hygiene and Tropical Medicine,
UNL - New University of Lisbon, Lisbon, Portugal
paleta007@hotmail.com, rosaTeo@ihmt.unl.pt
[2] GHTM - Global Health and Tropical Medicine,
IHMT - Institute of Hygiene and Tropical Medicine,
UNL - Universidade Nova de Lisboa, Rua da Junqueira 100,
1349-008 Lisbon, Portugal
[3] CINAV - Center of Naval Research,
Portuguese Naval Academy, Portuguese Navy, Base Naval de Lisboa, Alfeite,
2810-001 Almada, Portugal
maria.alves.teodoro@marinha.pt
[4] CEMAT - Center for Computational and Stochastic Mathematics,
IST-Instituto Superior Técnico, Lisbon University,
Avenida Rovisco Pais, n. 1, 1048-001 Lisbon, Portugal

**Abstract.** The objective of this study is to describe the knowledge, attitudes and preventive practices regarding the infection by the Zika virus (ZIKV) among the population embarked on Portuguese Navy ships. We have performed a statistical analysis, a cross-sectional study that, besides allowing us to describe knowledge, attitudes and practices related to ZIKV infection, also let us to stratify the different groups under study: those who will navigate in endemic areas of Zika virus and navigators that have already traveled to endemic areas of ZIKV. The knowledge level about ZIKV reveals significant differences between the distinct questions and groups. The preliminary results obtained are in agreement with similar performed studies.

**Keywords:** Literacy · Questionnaire · Statistical approach · Factorial analysis · Zika virus

## 1 Introduction

During a study of yellow fever in the Zika Forest of Uganda, the Zika virus was detected in a rhesus monkey at 1947. Between 1960s and 1980s, few cases of human ZIKV infection were identified through serological methods, mostly benign. However, with the expansion of urban centers, transatlantic travel and increasing airflow, as well as the movement of asymptomatic carriers between countries and continents, have contributed with the dissemination of Zika, which have been showing a huge increase [1,2]. All of these have empowered an increase

© Springer Nature Switzerland AG 2019
S. Misra et al. (Eds.): ICCSA 2019, LNCS 11621, pp. 97–110, 2019.
https://doi.org/10.1007/978-3-030-24302-9_8

in the transmission of Zika, as well as a possibility of genetic mutations in certain pathogenic microorganisms, allowing the existence of more resistant virus and with greater epidemic potential. The rapid expansion of the disease and importation into several countries, on opposite sides of the globe, relates, in addition to the constant intercontinental migratory flows, the prolonged viraemia time and the persistence of the virus in certain body fluids, as well as to the high number of asymptomatic cases [3,5]. Knowing that military staff can visit ZIKV endemic sites where the exposure to the virus can occur, prevention of disease and promotion of the health of the staff is an important issue. It is pertinent to analyze the knowledge, attitudes and practices regarding this issue, in a way to develop intervention strategies, through health education actions. The objective of this study is to describe the knowledge, attitudes and preventive practices regarding infection by Zika virus, among the population embarked on ships of the Portuguese Navy. We are carrying out a statistical analysis (firstly applying some descriptive techniques [4], secondly applying some traditional comparison tests), a cross-sectional study that, in addition to allowing us to describe knowledge, attitudes and practices regarding ZIKV infection, will allow us to compare the different groups under study: those who will navigate in endemic areas of Zika and who have navigated to Zika endemic zones of Zika. A questionnaire was applied to these two groups. The preliminary results are in accordance with similar studies already performed. In the present work we apply an exploratory factorial analysis to identify which questions can do the major contribute to the individual knowledge about Zika infection.

The outline of this article is developed in four sections. In Sect. 2 is presented some background about Zika infection. The methodology is presented in Sect. 3. The questionnaire is detailed and it is made a brief summary about the Factorial Analysis approach. The Sect. 4 corresponds to the empirical application where are given more details about data, the data analysis and the exploratory Factorial Analysis results are partially described. It is presented a summary about exploratory analysis of the data set corresponding to pre-mission group. Finally in Sect. 5 are drawn some conclusions, some suggestions for future work are pointed.

## 2   Preliminaries

In the decades after the discovery of the Zika virus few were reported cases of human infection, being limited to equatorial Africa. In 1977 a geographical expansion occurred, with some cases being identified in equatorial Asia (India, Indonesia, Malaysia and Pakistan), but without the need for public health intervention. As in Africa, these cases demonstrated a rare periodicity and a mild clinical picture, very similar to that presented in dengue (DENV) and chikungunya (CHIKV) virus infections. This similarity may have been one of the reasons why ZIKV infection has been so rarely reported in Asia [6,7]. In 2007 the first report of an outbreak of Zika occurred in humans outside Africa and Asia. This occurred on the island of Yap (Micronesia), associated with a rash, conjunctivitis and arthralgia, but without hospitalization [8]. As reported by Kindhauser

[6], until this event, no human outbreaks were documented, with only 14 isolated cases. In 2008, the first documented case of sexual transmission of this disease appeared, which until then was known to be transmitted by mosquitoes [6]. Five years later, in 2013, a larger outbreak occurred in French Polynesia, with an estimated incidence of infection in about 70% of the population, with particular scientific interest, because in addition to the mild clinical picture, the first neurological manifestations happens[1] [7]. On May 7, 2015, the first Zika outbreak in Brazil was reported, with no associated complications. In July and October 2015, in this same country, new outbreaks of Zika are reported, however, associating cases of GBS and an increase in the number of births of children with microcephaly, respectively. On October 21, 2015, the first outbreak of Zika in Cape Verde began, with no reported neurological complications [2,6,7,9–11]. Thus, in view of the significant increase in the number of confirmed cases of Zika and the association of microcephaly and neurological disorders with infection, on 1 February 2016 the World Health Organization (WHO) declared Zika as a public health emergency of international importance ESPII) [12,13]. On 18 November of the same year, despite the fact that the virus was associated with these disorders, as well as the challenge posed to Public Health, WHO put an end to this alert. Nevertheless, as a precautionary measure, the Emergency Committee suggests four attitudes [12]:

- surveillance of Zika virus transmission;
- long-term measures;
- measures associated with intercontinental travel;
- sharing of information,

so it can be possible to verify that the rapid expansion of the disease and importation into several countries, on opposite sides of the globe, is related to the constant intercontinental migratory flows, the prolonged viraemia time, the persistence of the virus in certain body fluids, and, to the high number of asymptomatic cases [14].

## 3   Methodology

### 3.1   Questionnaire

Thus, in order to obtain answers to the objectives defined for this study, two self-filling questionnaires were developed, with questions of open response and closed response questions, elaborated with a simple and easily understood language for the participants. The questions elaborated were based on the pre-validated and tested questionnaire by Rosalino et al. in [15], contributions of various scientific articles consulted, related to knowledge, Attitude and Practice (KAP) studies and the resource kit of the WHO [16].

The questionnaire is divided into two parts, the first with the independent variables and a second part, with the dependent variables. The initial part concerns the socio-demographic variables of the participants and is composed of five

---

[1] Guillain-Barré syndrome (GBS) in adults and microcephaly appears in newborns.

questions (open or closed). The second part consists of 28 questions of open or closed response, with the possibility of choosing more than one answer in each question and also some questions in the form of Likert scale. This second part aimed at evaluating participants' knowledge, attitudes and practices regarding Zika virus infection, comprising 12 questions about knowledge issues, other 10 about attitudes and four that consider practices details. In question 2 of the second part, it was questioned if the participant had knowledge or had already read about the topic in question and, in the event of a negative answer, the participant should give his participation as finished and submit the questionnaire to the researcher.

The authors of [17] indicate that with these studies, it is possible to evaluate the extent of an already known situation, to confirm or refute a hypothesis, to provide new perspectives of the reality of a given situation; improve knowledge, attitudes and practices about specific subjects, even when applying the questionnaire itself, which can serve as an educational tool; may allow establishing baseline or benchmarks for use in future assessments and assist in assessing the effectiveness of activities and programs that aim to change health behaviors. These may also suggest intervention strategies based on specific local circumstances or factors, allowing the implementation of activities appropriate to that particular population [17]. The results obtained may reveal misconceptions or shortcomings, which may represent an obstacle to the activities that are intended to be implemented, as well as to highlight potential barriers to behavior change/adoption [17].

### 3.2 Factorial Analysis

Factor analysis (FA) is a technique often used to reduce data. The purpose is to get a reduced number of variables from an initial big set of variables and get easier interpretations [18]. The FA computes indexes with variables that measures similar things. There are two types of factor analysis: exploratory factorial analysis (EFA) and confirmatory factorial analysis (CFA) [19]. It is called EFA when there is no idea about the structure or the dimension of the set of variables. When we test some specific structure or dimension number of certain data set we name this technique the CFA. There are various extraction algorithms such as principal axis factors, principal components analysis or maximum likelihood (see [20] for example). There are numerous criteria to decide about the number of factors and theirs significance. For example, the Kaiser criterion proposes to keep the factors that correspond to eigenvalues greater or equal to one. In the classical model, the original set contains $p$ variables $(X_1, X_2, \ldots, X_p)$ and $m$ factors $(F_1, F_2, \ldots, F_m)$ are obtained. Each observable variable $X_j$, $j = 1, \ldots, p$ is a linear combination of these factors:

$$X_j = \alpha_{j1}F_1 + \alpha_{j2}F_2 + \cdots + \alpha_{jm}F_m + e_j, \qquad j = 1, \ldots, p, \qquad (1)$$

where $e_j$ is the residual. The factor loading $\alpha_{jk}$ provides an idea of the contribution of the variable $X_j$, $j = 1, \ldots, p$, contributes to the factor $F_k$, $k = 1, \ldots, m$.

The factor loadings represents the measure of association between the variable and the factor [18, 19].

FA uses variances to get the communalities between variables. Mainly, the extraction issue is to remove the largest possible amount of variance in the first factor. The variance in observed variables $X_j$ which contribute to a common factor is defined by communality $h_j^2$ and is given by

$$h_j^2 = \alpha_{j1}^2 + \alpha_{j2}^2 + \cdots + \alpha_{jm}^2, \qquad j = 1, \ldots, p. \tag{2}$$

According with the author of [21], the observable variables with low communalities are often dropped off once the basic idea of FA is to explain the variance by the common factors. The theoretical common factor model assumes that observables depend on the common factors and the unique factors being mandatory to determine the correlation patterns. With such objective the factors/components are successively extracted until a large quantity of variance is explained. After the extraction technique be applied, it is needed to proceed with the rotation of factors/components maximizing the number of high loadings on each observable variable and minimizing the number of factors. In this way, there is a bigger probability of an easier interpretation of factors 'meaning'.

## 4    Empirical Application

### 4.1    Data

The Naval Base of Lisbon, in Almada, is the geographical area chosen for the application of the questionnaire due the localization of some ships of Portuguese Navy. Actually, the Portuguese Navy has 17 vessels and 2 submarines, all with international operational capacity, able to "...*face the multiple challenges posed by a very dynamic and unpredictable international environment...*" [22], however, when traveling out of the national territory, the boarded staff are subject to the exposure of multiple infectious agents, harmful to their well-being, as well as to the effective fulfillment of the assigned missions.

Initially a pre-test was constructed and subsequently applied, which allowed us to determine if questionnaires 1 and 2 were properly understood by the potential participants, as well as to evaluate the pertinence, disposition and chaining of the questions. These were applied to the garrison of the Portuguese Republic Ship Corte-Real (in Portuguese, Navio da República Portuguesa (NRP)), a frigate of the Portuguese Navy, with characteristics similar to the target sample of the study. At the time of application of the pre-test, this ship was moored at the Lisbon Naval Base (BNL), however, with future possibility of projection to any area of the globe. After applying these questionnaires, 20 for each version, the necessary changes were made, in order to obtain the final version.

The target population selected to respond to the questionnaires is the staff of some selected ships described in them top of Table 1 to which was given the approval to apply the questionnaire. Some of these ships had returned from mission overseas, others were moored in preparation for departure on mission.

A questionnaire was applied to each element of ship staff. Data collection is still being organized and analyzed but some important results and a detailed discussion can be already found in [4].

We performed a statistical approach by factorial analysis using partial data concerning to pre-mission boarded staff relatively to knowledge questions so we could reduce the dimensionality, but firstly were applied some descriptive techniques, secondly were used some traditional comparison tests to al question from pre-mission data. By last was considered the general linear models to obtain some predictive models, but this step is not completed yet. The preliminary results evidences that distinct groups have a different level of Zika virus knowledge. This issue is in line with similar studies already conducted.

Summarizing the data, several groups of individuals were preliminary considered, 256 individuals answered to a questionnaire about Zika. The first step organizes the data and get some simple measures by descriptive statistic techniques and performs some intermediate level techniques (see [23]), e.g, proportion tests, independence tests, non parametric tests, etc. (Fig. 1).

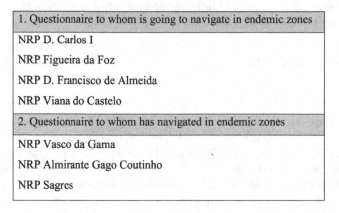

**Fig. 1.** Ships considered in the study. The questionnaire to the individuals of staff from each ship split into specific situations: the staff is going to an endemic zone of Zika (top) and the staff that already was in an endemic zone of Zika (bottom).

All groups present a minimum and maximum age of 20 and 49 years, with a mean age of $31 \pm 6.8$ years. The groups do not have identical distribution of ages. There exist $85, 5\%$ of individuals with age between 20 and 39 years.

The groups were composed of 84% men and 16% women. The distribution per gender is statistically different ($p\text{-}value = 0.025$). About educational level of participants (see Fig. 2), 63% of the individuals completed the high school and 22% have an university level degree (bachelor or master).

In Fig. 3 are displayed some of the countries visited by the ships considered in this work. A large number of the countries identified in the study as mooring points from our ships during their missions are on the CDC list (countries with a record of indigenous Zika cases), namely:

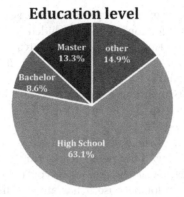

**Fig. 2.** Educational level of the participants considered in the study.

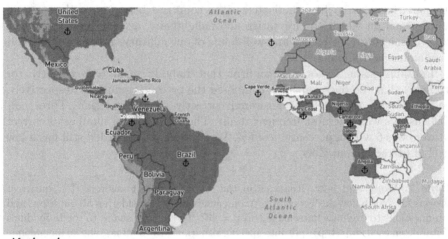

**Map legend**

⚓    Mooring Points

◼    Countries or territories with reported cases of Zika (past or present)**
◼    Zone  with low probability of infection with Zika by high elevation (>2000 meters)
◻    Countries with mosquito, but no cases of Zika registered **
◼    Countries or territories without mosquitoes that propagate Zika *

* *Aedes aegypti*
** Zika's autochthonous cases

**Fig. 3.** Mooring ports of the ships considered in the study  (adapted from [25]).

– Africa: Angola, Cameroon, Cape Verde, Gabon, Guinea-Bissau, Ivory Coast, Nigeria, Senegal;
– Asia: Indonesia, Thailand;
– The Caribbean: Curacao;
– North America: United States (Continental US);
– South America: Brazil, Colombia.

In 2015 the Pan American Health Organization issued the epidemiological alert entitled "Zika virus infection", which included details on laboratory, case management, disease prevention and control measures and more relevant to our study, recommendations for travelers [24], so the year 2015 was set as the lower limit for the date of the mission.

Also, some participants mentioned some visited ports as Indonesia and Thailand that are not included in Fig. 3, but also belong to the list of countries included in the "Area at Zika risk" [25].

Madeira Island was one of the points that the ships from Table 1 have visited during their mission in Navy. This point of mooring is frequently used in the return from trips from Africa or the American continent. This is identified by the CDC [26] with yellow color because it has an established population of Ae. aegypti in this territory, constituting a potential risk of introducing the disease on the island, similar to the Dengue outbreak in 2012. In addition, some of the participants who have indicated other countries bring us to the greatest concern and on which our formative and enlightening actions should focus, in order to safeguard the health and well-being of our military staff, as well as their companions and families.

Detailing some issues, we confirm that nobody answered correctly (or wrongly) all seven questions that composed the pre-questionnaire. Respectively, we have 10.9% of staff that answered correctly to one question. Three correct answers was the most frequent result. The maximum of number of correct answers was 6 with a percentage of 6%. We can infer the boarded still has a low level of literacy about Zika.

**Table 1.** Worst and best situations in the sense of correct answers (C), Incorrect answers (I), Not Know answers (nK), Wrong answers (W) considering all questions and sub-questions to evaluate knowledge (total = 43). The questionnaire to the individuals of staff from each ship (top) split into specific situations: the staff is going to an endemic zone of Zika (138 individuals) and the staff that already was in an endemic zone of Zika (120 individuals).

| | Pre mission | % | pos-mission | % |
|---|---|---|---|---|
| best | 36C+7I | 0,70% | 35C+8I | 0,80% |
| worst | 3W+40 miss | 2,90% | 3E+40 miss | 7,60% |
| not Know | 3 NK+40 Miss | 8,70% | 3NK+40 miss | 8,50% |
| Max Wrong | | 2,50% | | 2,50% |

In a preliminary data analysis of pre-mission questionnaires, and taking into account the non-quantitative nature of the involved variables, were calculated measures of association, nonparametric Spearman correlation coefficient, nonparametric test of Friedman for paired samples, etc.

We measure the homogeneity and internal consistence of questionnaire and respective validation. The alpha-Cronbach coefficient was adequate, giving the indication of a good internal consistency. This measure of questionnaire reliability is improved if some questions are not considered. The same issue is confirmed when were performed several tests to compare the answers of questions associated with knowledge issue. The paired T-test, McNemar's test for frequencies comparison, Crochan's Q test for binary variables comparison. Also were performed the Friedman test ($p$-$value$ < 0.001) and Kendalls coefficient of concordance test ($p$-$value$ < 0.001). All tests conduced to the same conclusion: the distributions of considered questions are not the same. Notice that the Spearman correlation coefficient conduces to significant relations between some questions, also Friedman's tests supports such association ($p$-$value$ < 0.001). Even this detail could be considered so we could let some questions, all questions were considered pertinent and important, so were included in study. Also was performed a runs test to each individual question from pre-mission data, were the null hypothesis confirms the value of the estimated median as the real values versus all other values. The runs tests are displayed in Table 2. The runs test valuates if the estimated median is an adequate descriptor of the analyzed answer. Very few questions had a significant test: We can say that only about the effects of Zika Infection on pregnants and/or fetus, the fetus malformation (me = 1; p-value = 0.05), fetus microcephaly (me = 1; p-value = 0.010), born dead (me = 2; p-value = 0.07) were significant. These means that the majority of participants achieved that the fetus microcephaly was not a possibility or did not know the fact, The same for fetus malformation. When the test is not significant (for a significance level less than 10%), it means that we can consider the estimated value of mean as the representative value. For example, the question about the consequences of Zika infection, we can consider for serious sequelae me = 2, meaning that the majority of participant did not know the answer; for GBS me = 2, the majority of participants did not Know the answer; the same for newborn with microcephaly. All answers from questionnaire can have a similar interpretation. We leave these details for another time.

We also evaluate association of the questionnaire answers with sociodemographic characteristics of participants. The Spearman coefficient and the Kruskal-Wallis test were used for such purpose. Given the extension of all issues, similarly to previous paragraph, the results will be described in the extended version of this manuscript.

The next step of process applies a FA so we can reduce the dimensionality. Under the aim of a preliminary and exploratory approach, we have considered the questions associated to knowledge from the pre-mission group. For such purpose we estimate the communality for the factors, analyzed the significance of R-matrix, test the multi-collinearity or singularity. The Bartlett's sphericity test provided a strongly significant level $p < 0.001$, so we confirmed the existence of patterned relationships. Also, the Kaiser-Meyer-Olkin measure (KMO) of sampling adequacy conduced to $KMO = 0.741$, so the data is appropriate to apply an EFA.

In Table 3 are presented the eigenvalues and total variance accounted by each factor by descendent order. The $i^{th}$ line corresponds to cumulative variance percentage explained by the first $i$ factors. Notice that Table 3 contains the information before extraction, after extraction and after rotation.

**Table 2.** Results of runs test applied to all questions individually. Partial output.

Row labels (repeated for each block of the partial output):

- Test Value[a]
- Cases < Test Value
- Cases >= Test Value
- Total Cases
- Number of Runs
- Z
- Asymp. Sig. (2-tailed)

a. Median
b. All values are greater than or less than the cutoff. Runs Test cannot be performed.
c. Only one run occurs. Runs Test cannot be performed.

**Table 3.** Total variance accounted for each factor.

| Total variance explained | | | | | |
|---|---|---|---|---|---|
| Factor | Initial eigenvalues | | | Rotation sums of squared loadings | | |
| | Total | % of variance | Cumulative % | Total | % of variance | Cumulative % |
| 1 | 11,217 | 23,866 | 23,866 | 6,218 | 13,299 | 13,299 |
| 2 | 3,470 | 7,383 | 31,249 | 5,130 | 10,914 | 24,143 |
| 3 | 3,111 | 6,619 | 37,869 | 3,583 | 7,623 | 31,766 |
| 4 | 2,398 | 5,102 | 42,970 | 2,870 | 6,106 | 37,873 |
| 5 | 2,234 | 4,752 | 47,723 | 1,962 | 4,175 | 42,048 |

If we consider the Kaiser criterion for simplicity, we retain the first 5 factors (eigenvalues great or equal to one). Other criteria may be applied, for example using the scree plot or using the average of extracted communalities to determine the eigenvalue cut-off. The varimax algorithm which produces orthogonal factors was applied after the extraction process. This technique is adequate when we want to identify variables to create indexes or new variables without inter-correlated components. In the present case, we could get the 'meaning' of each factor. To get such meaning we consider Table 4 analyzing the rotated factors scores. Namely each of first five factors factor are related with:

- **F1** - knowledge how to be infected by Zika virus and Which is the infection symptomatology;
- **F2** - Complications and consequences of Zika infection;
- **F3** - Measures to avoid Zika infection transmission and How can it be transmitted;
- **F4** - How to avoid the infection by Zika virus;
- **F5** - How took acknowledge about ZiKa.

The first 5 or 6 factors (about 50% of variance explication) can be used as independent variables in a predictive model. In [27] we can find a first propose for a very simple predictive model. The next step of our work: consider the factors as explanatory variables in a generalized linear models approach or a mixed linear models approach to get predictive models. Some simple mixed linear models including these factors were already obtained so we could identify some risk factors, but their validation is still ongoing.

## Table 4. Rotated factors scores.

Rotated Factor Matrix[a]

| | Factor 1 | 2 | 3 | 4 | 5 |
|---|---|---|---|---|---|
| 5 - Como ser infectado com Zika - Sexo com pessoa infectada, sem sintomas | ,863 | | ,239 | | |
| 5 - Como ser infectado com Zika - Sexo com pessoa infectada | ,856 | | ,260 | | |
| 5 - Como ser infectado com Zika - Beijar pessoa infectada | ,778 | ,111 | ,239 | | -,119 |
| 5 - Como ser infectado com Zika - Pelo ar (tosse, espirros) | ,757 | ,196 | ,152 | ,237 | |
| 5 - Como ser infectado com Zika - Transmissão vertical | ,669 | ,125 | | | |
| 5 - Como ser infectado com Zika - Transfusão sanguínea | ,622 | ,115 | | ,105 | |
| 6 - Como evitar infecção por Zika - Ar condicionado | ,531 | ,242 | | ,245 | |
| 7 - Sinais e sintomas de Zika - Manchas na pele | ,508 | ,392 | | ,123 | ,427 |
| 6 - Como evitar infecção por Zika - Relações sexuais | ,502 | ,154 | ,272 | ,160 | |
| 7 - Sinais e sintomas de Zika - Dor | ,457 | ,314 | | ,151 | ,328 |
| 7 - Sinais e sintomas de Zika - Conjuntivite | ,453 | ,425 | | ,126 | ,396 |
| 9 - Complicações de Zika - Síndrome Guillain-Barré | ,206 | ,706 | | ,106 | ,153 |
| 10 - Consequências para a grávida e/ou feto - Feto nascer morto | ,278 | ,677 | | | ,173 |
| 10 - Consequências para a grávida e/ou feto - Aborto | ,349 | ,657 | ,139 | | |
| 9 - Complicações de Zika - Sequelas cerebrais graves | | ,599 | | ,155 | |
| 10 - Consequências para a grávida e/ou feto - Outras malformações | ,324 | ,596 | ,185 | | ,205 |
| 9 - Complicações de Zika - Microcefalia | | ,594 | ,207 | | |
| 10 - Consequências para a grávida e/ou feto - Microcefalia | ,129 | ,588 | ,245 | -,106 | |
| 10 - Consequências para a grávida e/ou feto - Nenhuma | | ,571 | ,265 | ,134 | |
| 9 - Complicações de Zika - Nenhuma | -,130 | ,568 | ,199 | ,186 | |
| 9 - Complicações de Zika - Morte | | ,408 | ,157 | ,171 | -,183 |
| 8 - Todas as pessoas com Zika apresentam sintomas? | ,164 | ,366 | | | ,136 |
| 7 - Sinais e sintomas de Zika - Febre | ,228 | ,337 | | ,267 | |
| 17 - Medidas para evitar transmitir Zika - Preservativo | | ,188 | ,792 | | |
| 17 - Medidas para evitar transmitir Zika - Evitar relações sexuais | ,173 | ,241 | ,771 | ,135 | -,108 |
| 16 - Como Zika pode ser transmitido em PT - Relação sexual | ,278 | ,139 | ,695 | ,148 | |
| 16 - Como Zika pode ser transmitido em PT - Transmissão vertical | ,210 | ,254 | ,618 | | |
| 17 - Medidas para evitar transmitir Zika - Evitar engravidar | ,112 | ,177 | ,550 | ,142 | -,134 |
| 16 - Como Zika pode ser transmitido em PT - Picada mosquito | ,272 | ,111 | ,408 | ,213 | |
| 17 - Medidas para evitar transmitir Zika - Evitar ser picado | | | ,193 | | |
| 6 - Como evitar infecção por Zika - Inseticida | ,343 | ,220 | | ,610 | |
| 6 - Como evitar infecção por Zika - Rede mosquiteira | ,278 | ,263 | | ,591 | |
| 4 - Possibilidade infecção com Zika - Homens | | -,104 | ,223 | ,555 | ,136 |
| 6 - Como evitar infecção por Zika - Vestuário protector | ,458 | ,130 | | ,529 | |
| 4 - Possibilidade infecção com Zika - Mulheres | | | ,294 | ,449 | ,189 |
| 4 - Possibilidade infecção com Zika - Crianças | ,255 | | ,160 | ,425 | |
| 6 - Como evitar infecção por Zika - Repelente | ,371 | ,130 | | ,394 | -,169 |
| 1 - Causa de febre - Malária | ,100 | ,186 | ,183 | ,331 | ,252 |
| 1 - Causa de febre - Zika, Dengue, Chikungunya | | ,282 | ,103 | ,316 | ,166 |
| 3 - Conhecimento Zika - Enfermeiro, Médico, outro prof. saúde | -,130 | -,196 | | | -,657 |
| 3 - Conhecimento Zika - TV, rádio, jornais, pósters | ,156 | | | -,110 | ,394 |
| 25 - Existe tratamento para infecção por vírus Zika | | ,169 | -,121 | ,329 | ,385 |
| 5 - Como ser infectado com Zika - Picada mosquito | ,234 | ,189 | -,245 | ,156 | -,334 |
| 26 - Existe vacina contra o vírus Zika | | ,204 | ,161 | ,263 | ,321 |
| 1 - Causa de febre - Gripe | ,244 | ,121 | ,188 | ,146 | ,248 |
| 3 - Conhecimento Zika - Internet, facebook, twitter, instagram, outras redes | ,125 | | | | -,195 |
| 3 - Conhecimento Zika - Família, amigos, vizinhos | | | -,139 | -,101 | -,158 |

Extraction Method: Principal Axis Factoring.
Rotation Method: Varimax with Kaiser Normalization.
a. Rotation converged in 10 iterations.

# 5    Results and Conclusions

The objectives of this study are to determine the literacy of boarded staff about ZIKA, as well as to identify the best way of disclosure this infection. In this work was considered the data from pre-mission group and the subset of questions associated with knowledge. Almost 34% of staff did not know the existence of ZIKA virus. Between the individuals who knew the existence of ZIKA virus, the majority did not Known how could be infected. Also, between the individuals who knew the existence of ZIKA virus, the most part did not know how could make its prevention. An exploratory Factorial Analysis was applied to knowledge pre-mission data and some factors were selected and identified with a meaning. These factors can help to identify which are the themes that shall be focused in a disclosure issue. Some simple mixed linear models including these factors were already obtained so we could identify some factors that "'explain'" the individual literacy about Zika virus, but models analysis and their validation are still going on. A detailed analysis of these results will be described in an extended version of the present work.

**Acknowledgements.** M. Filomena Teodoro was supported by Portuguese funds through the *Center of Naval Research* (CINAV), Portuguese Naval Academy, Portugal and *The Portuguese Foundation for Science and Technology* (FCT), through the *Center for Computational and Stochastic Mathematics* (CEMAT), University of Lisbon, Portugal, project UID/Multi/04621/2019.

# References

1. Zanluca, C., et al.: First report of autochthonous transmission of Zika virus in Brazil. Mem. Inst. Oswaldo Cruz Rio de Janeiro **110**(4), 569–572 (2015)
2. Waldell, L., Greig, J.: Scoping review of the Zika virus literature. PLoS ONE **11**(5), e0156376 (2016)
3. European Centre for Disease Prevention and Control (ECDPC): Rapid risk assessment. Zika virus disease epidemic, Potential association with microcephaly and Guillain Barreé syndrome. 6th update, Stockholm. Accessed 20 May 2016
4. Faria, J.: Conhecimentos, atitudes e práticas de prevenção sobre Zika da população embarcada em navios da Marinha Portuguesa. Master thesis. Instituto de Higiene e Medicina Tropical, Universidade Nova de Lisboa, Lisboa (2019, under evaluation)
5. Cao-Lormeau, V.M., et al.: Guillain Barré Syndrome outbreak associated with Zika virus infection in French Polynesia: a case control study. Lancet **387**(10027), 1531–1539 (2016)
6. Kindhauser, A., et al.: Zika: the origin and spread of a mosquito-borne virus. Bull. World Health Organ. **94**(6), 675–686 (2016)
7. Olson, J., et al.: Zika virus, a cause of fever in Central Java, Indonesia. Trans. Roy. Soc. Trop. Med. Hyg. **75**(3), 389–393 (1981)
8. Paul, R.: The when and the where of Zika epidemic potential in Europe – an evidence base for public health preparedness. EBioMedicine **9**, 17–18 (2016)
9. WHO Europe: Zika virus. Technical report. Interim Risk Assessment - WHO European Region (2016). http://www.euro.who.int/__data/assets/pdf_file/0003/309981/Zika-Virus-Technical-report.pdf?ua=1. Accessed 10 Apr 2019
10. Sampathkumar, P., Sanchez, J.: Zika virus in the Americas: a review for clinicians. Mayo Clin. Proc. **91**(4), 514–521 (2016)
11. Rabaan, A., Bazzi, A., Al-Ahmed, S., Al-Ghaith, M., Al-Tawfiq, J.: Overview of Zika infection, epidemiology, transmission and control measures. J. Infect. Public Health **10**(2), 141–149 (2017)

12. WHO: WHO statement on the first meeting of the International Health Regulations (IHR 2005). Emergency Committee on Zika virus and observed increase in neurological disorders and neonatal malformations (2016). https://www.who.int/en/news-room/detail/01-02-2016-who-statement-on-the-first-meeting-of-the-international-health-regulations-(2005)-(ihr-2005)-emergency-committee-on-zika-virus-and-observed-increase-in-neurological-disorders-and-neonatal-malformations. Accessed 10 Apr 2019
13. Mlakar, J., Korva, M., Tul, N., Popovicć, M., et al.: Zika virus associated with microcephaly. N. Engl. J. Med. **374**, 951–958 (2016)
14. ECDC. Rapid Risk Assessment. Zika virus disease epidemic (2017). 10th update. https://ecdc.europa.eu/en/publications-data/rapid-risk-assessment-zika-virus-disease-epidemic-10th-update-4-april-2017. Accessed 10 Apr 2019
15. Rosalino, C., et al.: Conhecimentos, atitudes e práticas sobre Zika de viajantes visitando o Rio de Janeiro, Brasil, durante os Jogos Olímpicos e Paraolímpicos de 2016: Inquérito no Aeroporto Internacional António Carlos Jobim, Rio de Janeiro (2016)
16. WHO: Inquéritos sobre Conhecimentos, Atitudes e Práticas. Doenç do Vírus Zika e Potenciais Complicações - Pacote de recursos (2016). https://apps.who.int/iris/bitstream/handle/10665/204689/WHO_ZIKV_RCCE_16.2_por.pdf?sequence=5. Accessed 10 Apr 2019
17. Gumucio, S., et al.: The KAP survey model (Knowledge, Attitude & Practices) (2011). https://www.medecinsdumonde.org/en/actualites/publications/2012/02/20/kap-survey-model-knowledge-attitude-and-practices. Accessed 10 Apr 2019
18. Harman, H.H.: Modern Factor Analysis. University of Chicago Press, Chicago (1976)
19. Young, A.G., Pearce, S.: A beginner's guide to factor analysis: focusing on exploratory factor analysis. Tutor. Quant. Methods Psychol. **9**(2), 79–94 (2013)
20. Child, D.: The Essentials of Factor Analysis. Continuum International Publishing Group, New York (2006)
21. Marôco, J.: Análise Estatística com o SPSS Statistics. Report Number, ISBN 9789899676343 (2014)
22. Marinha Portuguesa: Os meios (2019). http://www.marinha.pt/pt/os_meios/Paginas/default.aspx. Accessed 10 Apr 2019
23. Tamhane, A.C., Dunlop, D.D.: Statistics and Data Analysis: From Elementary to Intermediate. Prentice Hall, Upper Saddle River (2000)
24. Ricamonte, B., et al.: Knowledge and attitude toward Zika virus disease among pregnant women in Iloilo City, Philippines. Public Health Res. **8**(5), 115–120 (2018)
25. PAHO/WHO: Timeline of Emergence of Zika virus in the Americas (2016). www.paho.org
26. Center for Disease Control and Prevention (CDC). https://wwwnc.cdc.gov/travel/files/zika-areas-of-risk.pdf. Accessed 10 Apr 2019
27. Faria, J., Teodósio, R., Teodoro, F.: Zika: literacy and behavior of individuals on board ships. A first approach. In: Simos, T., et al. (eds.) International Conference on Computational Methods in Science and Engineering (ICCMSE 2019). AIP proceedings (2019, submitted)

# Study About Pediatric Hypertension in
## *Lisboa and Vale do Tejo*

M. Filomena Teodoro[1,2(✉)] (ID) and Carla Simão[3,4]

[1] CINAV, Portuguese Naval Academy, Portuguese Navy, Base Naval de Lisboa,
Alfeite, 2810-001 Almada, Portugal
maria.alves.teodoro@marinha.pt
[2] CEMAT - Center for Computational and Stochastic Mathematics,
Instituto Superior Técnico, Lisbon University, Avenida Rovisco Pais, n. 1,
1048-001 Lisbon, Portugal
[3] Medicine Faculty, Lisbon University, Av. Professor Egas Moniz,
1600-190 Lisbon, Portugal
[4] Pediatric Department, Santa Maria's Hospital, Centro Hospitalar Lisboa Norte,
Av. Professor Egas Moniz, 1600-190 Lisbon, Portugal

**Abstract.** The pediatric high blood pressure has severe risk factors and
it's prevention is mandatory. To evaluate the pediatric arterial hypertension caregivers Knowledge, in [1,2] was done a preliminary study of
an experimental and simple questionnaire with 5 questions previously
introduced in [3]. The analysis of an improved questionnaire applied to
children caregivers and filled online was completed in [4,5]. In [6], was
performed an analysis of variance as a preliminary approach where the
authors obtain estimates about the childhood hypertension prevalence in
several regions of Portugal, using a sample collected during the hypertension day activities. The same study [6] evidences significant differences
on high blood pressure prevalence between girls and boys; also the children's age is a significant issue to take into consideration. Actually, in
present work we obtain similar results using ANOVA techniques and
more complex methods, for example general linear models and mixed
models between others, considering a sample from metropolitan zone of
*Lisboa and Vale do Tejo* (LVT).

**Keywords:** Pediatric hypertension · Caregiver · Questionnaire ·
Statistical approach · Analysis of variance · General linear models

## 1 Introduction

The high arterial blood pressure is a condition which, although traditionally
considered a disease of adults, may increase during the pediatric age and in
most cases, silently. The diagnostic criteria for Pediatric Hypertension (PH)
have as their main reference the normal distribution of blood pressure (BP) in
healthy children [7] and based on the concept that the pediatric BP increases
with age and with body mass [8]. Thus, taking into account that there is a

S. Misra et al. (Eds.): ICCSA 2019, LNCS 11621, pp. 111–121, 2019.
https://doi.org/10.1007/978-3-030-24302-9_9

strong correlation between body mass index (BMI) and BP levels [8], the PH has become highly prevalent among children and teens [9] due to a parallel growth with the epidemic of childhood obesity [10], the which suggests that obesity is a major risk factor in the development of pediatric hypertension [9,11].

Under the aim of a preliminary study about PH caregivers (parents or their legal representatives) acquaintance, a simpler questionnaire composed by five questions was introduced in [3]. To complete such work, different statistical techniques were performed in [1,2,12], namely logit modeling, exploratory factorial analysis and MANOVA, following e.g. [13,14]. In [15], a redesign of such questionnaire was built (including fifteen questions) and applied to a different target population. This work was continued in [4,5] using statistical multivariate techniques. In addition, in both questionnaires was included a question to check if the regular measurement of the BP, according to current European recommendations, was usually fulfilled.

A study about prevalence of pediatric hypertension at national level promoted by the Portuguese Society of Pediatrics (SPP) and Pediatric Hypertension Group (PHG) is ongoing. The medical individual characteristics of children and adolescents are observed by a medical team and a questionnaire was designed to be answered by caregivers of children and Portuguese teenagers where sociodemographic and familiar health history details are inquired. The data collection is still ongoing over several regions of Portugal (main land and islands). In present work we have considered a subset of such data set relatively to *Lisboa e Vale do Tejo* region.

In this article the objectives are to characterize the BP profile of a pediatric population with scholar age and to evaluate the prevalence of PH and normal-high BP and analyze the relation between PH/normal-high BP and age, sex, race and geographical origin. It was performed a preliminary approach in [6] using a sample non representative of Portuguese population evidences significant differences of high blood pressure prevalence between girls and boys; also the children's age is a significant issue. The work [6] is used as reference in the present work. We have obtained similar and confirmatory results in this manuscript.

This article is comprised of an introduction and results and final remarks Sections, Sect. 2 containing the description of data and methodology. The empirical application can be found in Sect. 3.

## 2    Data and Methodology

In [6] the authors have performed and observational, prospective, transverse pilot study (Tracking) in May 2017, in public and private schools from Northern to South of Portugal (Aveiro, Braga, Lisboa).

A sample, almost 5 hundred of observations, was collected by the PHG during the Hypertension Day activities, during an action of disclosure and tracking of PH. The target population was the set of students from first year until 12th year of schooling in three different groups of schools in Lisbon, Aveiro and Braga. These groups of schools have a population of students, aged between

5 of and 18 years old. The data collection occurred in May 2017, 25th, after adequate approval from Ministry of Education, General Direction of Health, Data Protection Committee and school Executive Committee. It was measured the blood pressure by oscillometric method (up to 3 measurements) and annotated some medical and socio-demographic characteristics for each student. The age was classified in three intervals: I (5–10 years); II (11–15 years); III (16–18 years). To characterize of the tensional profile was used the criteria defined SEH 2016. The classification of pediatric hypertension is presented in Table 1 (adapted from [10]).

**Table 1.** Classification of pediatric hypertension (adapted from [10]).

| Class | SBP and/or DBP Percentile |
|---|---|
| Normal | <90 |
| Normal-high | ≥90 until <95 mmHg |
| | Teenagers: AP > 120/80 mmHg, including percentile <90 |
| HBP - class 1 | $95 \leq$ Class $1 \leq 99 + 5$ mmHg |
| HBP - class 2 | >99 + 5 mmHg |

The blood pressure measurements and remaining information are analyzed statistically following [14]. This sample is not representative of the Portuguese population, but was considered to get some preliminary results that can be used as an alert to the PBP problem and also as an incitement to complete the sample collection stage of ongoing pediatric BP study. In the present work, we consider a partial data set which is still being collected in all regions of Portugal: *Madeira* (M), *Açores* (A), *Lisboa e Vale do Tejo* (LVT), *Norte* (N), *Centro* (C), *Sul* (S). It is still necessary to complete the data collection, in particular it is still missing the data from region *Sul*, so the prevalence of pediatric HTA in Portugal can be estimated correctly. The sample considers 962 individuals aged between 5 years and 18 years, and covers partially the region of *Lisboa e Vale do Tejo*.

## 3 Empirical Application

Matlab, R and SPSS software were used to organize and model the data. The first step organizes the data and get some simple measures by descriptive statistic techniques. There are the approximately the same number of girls and boys. In Fig. 1 we can find the characterization of students per race. The non-Caucasian students are few (11%) when compared with the number of remaining students, but race still was tested to be considered as explanatory variable. In a preliminary data analysis and taking into account the non-quantitative nature of some involved variables, were calculated some measures of association, nonparametric Spearman correlation coefficient, and performed several tests, namely nonparametric test of Friedman, median test, rank test, signal test so we could identify potential explanatory variables or compare distinct groups (age, gender).

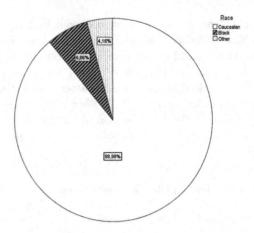

**Fig. 1.** Sample characterization (race).

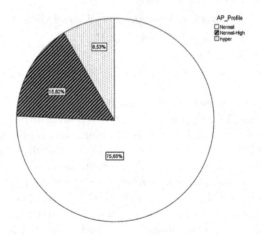

**Fig. 2.** AP distribution in sample (962 children).

In Fig. 2, we have the arterial pressure (AP) distribution in sample. We can observe that, in sample, 75.65% of child have normal level of BP; 15.82% of students have their AP profile classified has normal-high and 8.53% of students have pre-HBP. The blood pressure measurements and remaining information are analyzed statistically using a GLM approach. This sample, collected in LVT region, has a fewer percentage of children with normal AP profile than the case considered in [6] (less 10%).

The percentage of hypertensives by gender is different as we can see Fig. 3. 80% of the girls have a normal AP profile in opposite with 72% of boys. The distributions of AP profile per gender are statistically significant (means, medians, cdf). It means that there is statistical evidence that boys and girls have distinct AP profiles. The percentage of hypertension occurrence in boys is higher than

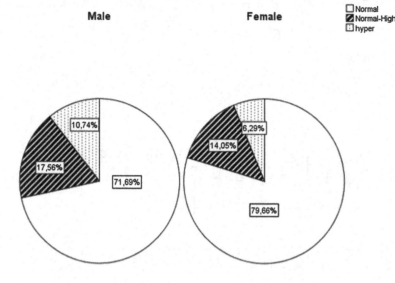

**Fig. 3.** Distribution of AP profile per gender.

in girls (10.74% versus 6.29%). More generally, there is a greater probability of an altered profile (normal-high BP or hypertension) for boys that for girls.

The box-plots of BP per age and per age group are represented in Fig. 4 (top and bottom respectively). It is visible that BP value tends to increase with the age.

Taking into consideration the age group defined previously, the differences between the 1st and 2nd groups, the 1st and 3rd groups and between the 2nd and 3rd groups gave conduced to distinct results. The tests were done separately for each situation. Testing the hypothesis that the older students have a higher HBP against the students of group 1 or group 2, the results provided that the groups 1 and 2 can be agglutinated, there is no significant difference; the group 3 presents higher and more significant values (difference of means parametric tests, difference of medians non-parametric test). In Fig. 4, we can observe that BP distribution per age and per age groups corroborates these results.

The sample distribution of weight (see Fig. 5) reveals that about 70% of young people have normal weight, being the remaining 30% weighted in excess[1]. Notice that the index of weight classification depends on gender and age and its construction depends on the BMI percentiles of young population for each age and gender (see Table 2).

---

[1] The index of weight classification (0-low; 1-normal; 2-Overweighted; 3-obesity type I, 4-obesity type II and III) is done acordingly with the rule established by National Helth service [16].

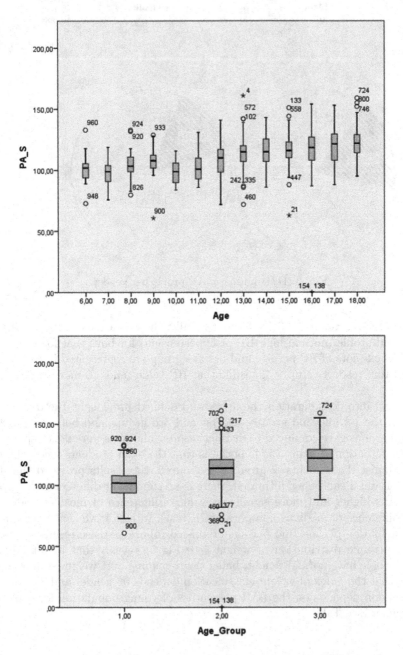

**Fig. 4.** Distribution of BP per age (top) and per age group (bottom).

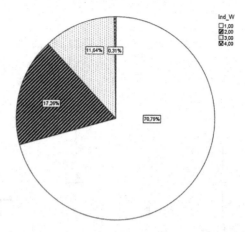

**Fig. 5.** Distribution of weight classification in sample.

**Table 2.** Weight classification for children and teenagers.

| Weight | Rule | Classification |
|---|---|---|
| Less than percentile 10% | Low | 0 |
| Between percentile 10% and 85% | Normal | 1 |
| Between percentile 85% and 95% | Overweighted | 2 |
| Above percentile 95% | Obesity level I/Obesity level II and III | 3/4 |

We have included the weight index (see Table 2) as an important information to include in our analysis. Figure 6 (top) evidences a positive relation between blood pressure and weight. The Spearman test is significant: there exists evidence of positive association between blood pressure and weight. At bottom of Fig. 6 we can see that the AP boxplots have a distinct behavior depending on the weight index.

Considering a multivariate regression test, we have performed an analysis of variance (ANOVA) with three factors, considering as main effects gender, age and weight index so we could analyze their influence on BP (see Table 3). The residual analysis was complete. The detailed results will be present in the extended version of this work. The heterogeneity of residual variance was taken into consideration.

The F test to evaluate the effect of gender, age group and weight index relatively to BP, can be found in Table 3. Notice that all factors have significant effects to BP when considered without interaction.

Other multivariate regression model was estimated, but including interaction between all factors (see Table 4).

In this case, and considering a significance level of 10%, the factor gender is not significant but its interaction with age Group is statistically important;

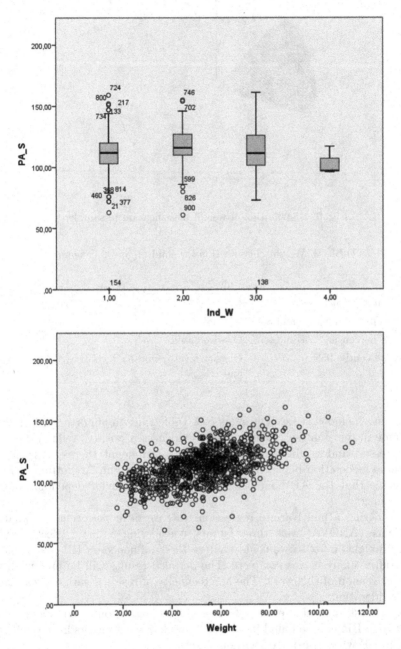

**Fig. 6.** Distribution of BP versus weight (top) and BP versus weight level (1-normal, 2, 3, 4-weight excess) (bottom).

**Table 3.** ANOVA results: F tests *p-value*. Design: Intercept + Gender + Age Group + Weight Index

Dependent Variable: AP_Profile

| Source | Type III Sum of Squares | df | Mean Square | F | Sig. |
|--------|-------------------------|-----|-------------|-----|------|
| Model | 1734,037ᵃ | 7 | 247,720 | 697,198 | ,000 |
| Gender | 5,159 | 1 | 5,159 | 14,521 | ,000 |
| Ind_W | 27,031 | 3 | 9,010 | 25,359 | ,000 |
| Age_G | 14,353 | 2 | 7,176 | 20,197 | ,000 |
| Error | 338,963 | 954 | ,355 | | |
| Total | 2073,000 | 961 | | | |

a. R Squared = .836 (Adjusted R Squared = .835)

**Table 4.** ANOVA results: F tests *p-value*. Design: Intercept + Gender + Age Group + Weight Index + interactions

**Tests of Between-Subjects Effects**

Dependent Variable: AP_Profile

| Source | Type III Sum of Squares | df | Mean Square | F | Sig. |
|--------|-------------------------|-----|-------------|-----|------|
| Model | 1748,583ᵃ | 20 | 87,429 | 253,596 | ,000 |
| Gender | ,876 | 1 | ,876 | 2,542 | ,111 |
| Ind_W | 15,680 | 3 | 5,227 | 15,161 | ,000 |
| Age_G | 12,825 | 2 | 6,412 | 18,600 | ,000 |
| Gender * Ind_W | 1,755 | 3 | ,585 | 1,697 | ,166 |
| Gender * Age_G | 1,899 | 2 | ,950 | 2,754 | ,064 |
| Ind_W * Age_G | 4,765 | 4 | 1,191 | 3,455 | ,008 |
| Gender * Ind_W * Age_G | 1,738 | 4 | ,435 | 1,260 | ,284 |
| Error | 324,417 | 941 | ,345 | | |
| Total | 2073,000 | 961 | | | |

a. R Squared = ,844 (Adjusted R Squared = ,840)

weight index and age group are statistically significant, also their interaction must be considered.

The pairwise comparison using the estimated marginal means, were studied in both models. This study concludes that, for a boy, BP has a mean greater than for a girl. An young individual with weight excess (not including level 4) has a BP mean greater than an young individual with normal weight. Identical conclusions are obtained by the model with interaction between factors. When we consider the model with interaction, the same is verified, for a boy the BP mean is greater than for a girl, when both have similar age. Also, for a boy the BP mean is greater than for a girl, when both have similar weight index. For the same gender, a boy hasWe can conclude that, considering the same weight index, older students have BP mean greater than younger students, for the same gender, an individual with weight excess as the BP mean is greater than for an individual with normal weight.

## 4    Results and Final Remarks

While the data collection at national level is not complete, we analyse statistically a subset of that collection: the Lisboa and Vale do Tejo region. It is performed a descriptive analysis and applied an analysis of variance. Relationships between individual characteristic variables and blood pressure are evaluated.

Some important issues about pediatric hypertension were obtained, e.g. gender age and weight are related with pediatric high blood pressure, reinforcing the importance and need of a caregiver's knowledge improvement and prevention measures implementation about pediatric high blood pressure.

**Acknowledgements.** This work was supported by Portuguese funds through the FCT, *Center for Computational and Stochastic Mathematics* (CEMAT), University of Lisbon, Portugal, project UID/Multi/04621/2019, and *Center of Naval Research* (CINAV), Naval Academy, Portuguese Navy, Portugal.

## References

1. Teodoro, M.F., Simão, C.: Perception about pediatric hypertension. J. Comput. Appl. Math. **312**, 209–215 (2017). https://doi.org/10.1016/j.cam.2016.03.016
2. Teodoro, M.F., Simão, C.: Completing the analysis of a questionnaire about pediatric blood pressure. Trans. Biol. Biomed. World Sci. Eng. Acad. Soc. **14**, 56–64 (2017)
3. Costa, J.R.B.: Hipertensão arterial em idade pediátrica: que conhecimento têm os prestadores de cuidados sobre esta patologia? Master thesis. Medical Faculty, Lisbon University (2015)
4. Teodoro, M.F., Romana, A., Simão, C.: An issue of literacy on pediatric hypertension. In: Simos, T., et al. (eds.) Computational Methods in Science and Engineering, vol. 1906, p. 110006. AIP, Melville, New York (2017)
5. Teodoro, M.F., Simão, C., Romana, A.: Questioning caregivers about pediatric high blood pressure. In: Gervasi, O., et al. (eds.) ICCSA 2017. LNCS, vol. 10408(V), pp. 44–53. Springer, Cham (2017). https://doi.org/10.1007/978-3-319-62404-4_4
6. Teodoro, M.F., Simão, C., Abranches, M., Deuchande, S., Teixeira, A.: Comparing childhood hypertension prevalence in several regions in Portugal. In: Machado, J., Soares, F., Veiga, G. (eds.) HELIX 2018. LNEE, vol. 505, pp. 206–213. Springer, Cham (2019). https://doi.org/10.1007/978-3-319-91334-6_29
7. Andrade, H., Antonio, N., Rodrigues, D.: Hipertensão arterial sistémica em idade pediátrica. Revista Portuguesa de Cardiologia **29**(3), 413–432 (2010)

8. Lurbe, E., Cifkovac, R.F.: Management of high blood pressure in children and adolescents: recommendations of the European Society oh Hypertension. J. Hypertens. **27**, 1719–1742 (2009)
9. Muntner, P., He, J.: Trends in blood pressure among children and adolescents. J. Am. Med. Assoc. **291**, 2107–2113 (2004)
10. National High Blood Pressure Education Program Working Group on High Blood Pressure in Children And Adolescents: The fourth report of the diagnosis, evaluation and treatment of high blood pressure in children and adolescents. Pediatrics **114**, 555–576 (2004)
11. Stabouli, S., Kotsis, V.: Adolescent obesity is associated with high ambulatory blood pressure and increased carotid intimal-medial thickness. J. Pediatr. **147**, 651–656 (2005)
12. Teodoro, M.F., Simão, C.: Notes about pediatrics hypertension literacy. Trans. Biol. Biomed. World Sci. Eng. Acad. Soc. **14**, 89–97 (2017)
13. Anderson, T.W.: An Introduction to Multivariate Analysis. Wiley, New York (2003)
14. Tamhane, A.C., Dunlop, D.D.: Statistics and Data Analysis: From Elementary to Intermediate. Prentice Hall, Upper Saddle River (2000)
15. Romana, A.: Hipertensão Arterial em Pediatria. Um estudo observacional sobre a literacia dos cuidadores. Master thesis. Medical Faculty, Lisbon University (2017)
16. https://www.mdsaude.com/obesidade/calcule-o-seu-peso-ideal-e-imc. Accessed 16 Apr 2019

# Some Issues About Iberian Energy Prices

M. Filomena Teodoro[1,2]([✉]) [iD] and Marina A. P. Andrade[3] [iD]

[1] CINAV, Center of Naval Research, Naval Academy, Portuguese Navy,
2810-001 Almada, Portugal
[2] CEMAT, Center for Computational and Stochastic Mathematics,
Instituto Superior Técnico, Lisbon University, 1048-001 Lisboa, Portugal
maria.alves.teodoro@marinha.pt
[3] ISTAR, ISCTE, Instituto Universitário de Lisboa, 1649-026 Lisboa, Portugal
marina.andrade@iscte.pt

**Abstract.** The work described in this article results from a problem proposed by the company EDP - Energy Solutions Operator, in the framework of ESGI 119*th*, European Study Group with Industry, during July 2016. Markets for electricity have two characteristics: the energy is mainly not storable and volatile prices at exchanges are issues to take into consideration. These two features, between others, contribute significantly to the risk of a planning process. The aim of the problem is the short term forecast of hourly energy prices. In present work, ARIMA modeling is considered to obtain a predictive model. The results show that in the time series traditional framework the season of the year, month or winter/summer period revealed significant explanatory variables in the different estimated models. The in-sample forecast is promising, conducting to adequate measures of performance.

**Keywords:** Electricity Price Forecasting · ARIMA models · MIBEL

## 1 Introduction

The study of the behavior of time series data is considered one of the current challenges in data mining [2,10]. A wide number of methods for Electricity Price Forecasting (EPF) can be found in literature, for example, in [9] we have a good description of such methods which are labeled in five categories. Data Mining refers the extraction of knowledge by analyzing the data from different perspectives and accumulates them to form useful information which could help the decision makers to take appropriate decisions. Due to the unique behavior of time series data, we can find several references about time series data mining in various application domains, namely survey articles [4,8], PhD thesis where detailed techniques and case studies are analyzed [11], private communications [3], which takes into consideration how Artificial Neural Networks may assist in formulating a GLM, chapters in books [5] where the authors define the major tasks considered by the time series data mining community. Besides that, the

© Springer Nature Switzerland AG 2019
S. Misra et al. (Eds.): ICCSA 2019, LNCS 11621, pp. 122–133, 2019.
https://doi.org/10.1007/978-3-030-24302-9_10

existing research is still considered not enough. In [10] time series data is considered one of the 10 challenges in data mining. In particular the discovery of an interesting pattern, also called motif discovery, is a non-trivial task which has become one of the most important data mining tasks. In fact motif discovery can be applied to many domains [2].

Under the 109th European Study Group with Industry, EDP - Energias de Portugal submitted the mathematical challenge simulating electricity prices not only for risk measures purposes but also for scenario analysis in terms of pricing and strategy. EDP Group is an Energy Solutions Operator which operates in the business areas of generation, supply and distribution of electricity and supply and distribution of gas. EDP with nearly 14 000 MW (2012 update and excluding wind power) of installed capacity in the Iberian Electricity Market – MIBEL[1], is the only company in the Iberian Peninsula with generation, distribution and supply (both electricity and gas) activities in Portugal and Spain.

The objective of the present work is the short term forecast of hourly energy prices. Electricity Price Forecasting (EPF) its a difficult purpose. A wide number of methods have been proposed to EFP. In [9] is described an almost complete review about the enormous quantity of available methods, analyzing their strengths and weaknesses. The author proposes the classification of such methods in four categories: multi-agent models, fundamental models, reduced-form models, statistical models and computational intelligence models.

In present work, usual techniques in time series modelling are used. The ARMA, ARIMA, ARIMAX, SARIMAX are considered useful techniques to obtain a predictive model where its predictive power is discussed.

The outline of this article is developed in four sections. Section 2 makes a brief summary about the time series modeling approach. The Sect. 3 are given more details on the challenge proposed by EDP and on the data provided. Will be presented a summary about exploratory analysis of the data sets provided by EDP and continues with the study on the co-variables that may predict the hourly prices pattern. Also are presented the results of our ARIMA approach. Finally in Sect. 4 conclusions are drawn and suggestions for future work are pointed.

## 2    ARIMA Approach

The identification of an ARIMA model to model the data can be considered one of the most critical phases when using ARIMA approach. For a stationary time series[2] the selection of the model to be used is mainly based on the estimated auto-correlations and partial auto-correlations, which we will use to compare with the theoretical quantities and identify a possible model for the data.

The auto-regressive models with order $p$ AR(p), the moving average with order $q$ MA(q) and their combination, ARMA(p, q) models have their

---

[1] http://www.mibel.com/.

[2] A time series is classified as stationary when it is developed in time around a constant mean.

auto-correlation functions (ACF) with a certain specific feature, similarly to a finger print:

The ACF of an autoregressive process with order $p$ is infinite in extent that decays according to a damped exponential/sinusoidal;

The ACF of a moving average with order $q$ process is finite, i.e. presents a cut after the lag q;

The ACP of ARMA process (p, q) is like a mixture of the processes described in previous items, the ACF has infinite that decays according to exponents/damped sinusoidals after the lag $q - p$.

The idea is to identify a pattern that behaves with the same profile that some theoretical model. In particular, the it is useful to identify MA models but it is not so simple to identify other kind of models. As a possible solution, we can compute the partial auto-correlation function (PACF). This function corresponds to the correlation of $X_t, X_{t-k+1}$ removing the effect of the observations $X_{t-1}, X_{t-2}, \ldots, X_{t-k-1}$ and is denoted by $\phi_{kk}$. In the case a stationary time series we can use the Yule-Walker equations to compute the PACF. Again, the PACF have a specific profile for each process like a proper finger print:

The PACF of a MA(d) is infinite in extent that decays according to a damped exponential/sinusoidal (similarly to the behaviour of an ACP from a AR(d) process;

The PACF of AR(p) the process is finite, i.e. presents a cut after the lag q, like the behaviour of an ACP from a MA(p) process;

The PACF of ARMA process (p, q) is similar to an ACF from a MA(q) process.

A general method for finding a.c. for a stationary process with f.a. is using the Yule-Walker equations.

This method seems to fail in the case of non-stationary time series (the irregular component is significant). To solve this issue we differentiate the non stationary series so many times ($d$ times) as necessary to get a stationary series. After these differences of successive terms of the chain, applied $d$ times, we can apply the same technique: identify which model(s) are identified from ACF and PACF. A model that represents a nonstationary series, differenciated d times, with an auto-regressive component with order p and a moving average component with order q is representes as an ARIMA (p, d, q).

To estimate the best models between several proposals, we usually apply the information criteria AIC, BIC: the best models have the lowest values of AIC and BIC. Also the log of likelihood function is a good statistic to evaluate the quality of the estimated models: the lowest value means a better model.

After selection, the models need to be validated. One of the rules is to analyze the residuals (the ith residual is the difference between the ith observation and its estimate). Residuals are supposed to be Gaussian and non-correlated. To verify this can be use several testes and other techniques (Llung-Box test, box-Pierce test, Kolmogorov-Smirnov test, Bera and Jarcke test, some graphics, e.g. boxplots, qq plots.

The estimates precision evaluation is another step to include in all process. For that we can compute the usual measures: MAPE, MADE, etc.

In general the procedure of all process is composed by the following iterates:

1. Models formulation: use of ACF and PACF;
2. Models adjustment: estimation of model parameters, application of suitability measures of estimates;
3. Validation of models: selection of variables, diagnostics, residual analysis and interpretation.
4. Analysis of precision and updating the models.

# 3   Empirical Application

## 3.1   Exploratory Analysis

Taking into consideration the challenge proposed by EDP, the available data consists in the daily market electricity prices as a strip of prices (one for each hour of the day), all simultaneously observed once at a given time of each day:

$$Y_t = [y_{1t}, y_{2t}, \ldots, y_{nt}], \quad n = 1, \ldots, 24 \text{ (or 23 or 25)}, \quad t = 1, 2, \ldots.$$

In the present work we consider the disaggregated data, i.e., hourly prices and average day price, from January 2008 to June 2016, in a total 3102 observations of the 24 (23 or 25) hours of the day.

In a preliminary exploratory analysis, the data originally provided consisted in a transformed ratio (in what follows named rescaled data) and revealed serious problems which can be visualized in the boxplot diagrams (Fig. 1). The rescaled data has different distributions and a great number of anomalies per hour. These details are also confirmed in Table 1 where some descriptive statistics and tests are summarized. The data detailed description follows what was presented in [7], since we have used the same database set.

From Table 1, we can see the different patterns of dispersion (observe the standard deviation and inter-quartile range columns respectively). Also we confirm that the data does not have normal distribution when we check the Kolmogorov-Smirnov and Jarcke and Bera normality tests.

Consequently, we consider a new data set with the real data. In a preliminary analysis, we have taken the period from $1^{st}$ January 2008 to $31^{st}$ December 2010, to exemplify some details and issues and to estimate the initial models considering several covariates of interest.

Since we have a huge dimensional data set, to compare graphically the rescaled data set and the real data set we restrict to the year 2010 the graphics in Fig. 2. We can conclude that rescaled data present a huge quantity of "uncommon" observations each hour of the day with exception of hours 4, 5 and 6. The rescaled data also presents different patterns of dispersion. By other hand, the real data displays unusual observations but in a fewer quantity than in rescaled data. The dispersion of real data presents more homogeneous patterns each hour.

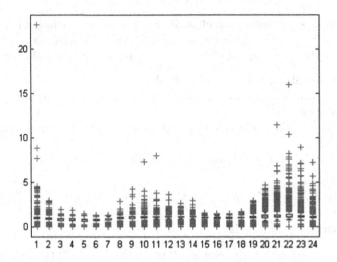

**Fig. 1.** Boxplot diagrams (rescaled data 01.01.2008–31.12.2016).

**Table 1.** Descriptive summary (rescaled data 01.01.2008–31.12.2016). Left: Mean, trimmean, media, standard deviation, inter-quartile range. Right: Skewness, kurtosis, Kolmogorov-Smirnov, and Jarcke and Bera normality tests.

| Hora | mean | trimmean | median | std | iqr | Hora | skewness | kurtosis | P-value (KS) | P-value (JB) |
|---|---|---|---|---|---|---|---|---|---|---|
| 1.0000 | 1.0212 | 0.9908 | 0.9900 | 0.5327 | 0.1800 | 1.0000 | 24.5154 | 927.2962 | 0 | 0.0010 |
| 2.0000 | 0.8695 | 0.8872 | 0.8900 | 0.2487 | 0.2000 | 2.0000 | -0.0747 | 12.7788 | 0 | 0.0010 |
| 3.0000 | 0.7531 | 0.7943 | 0.8100 | 0.2483 | 0.2100 | 3.0000 | -1.4003 | 5.3185 | 0 | 0.0010 |
| 4.0000 | 0.7114 | 0.7541 | 0.7800 | 0.2523 | 0.2300 | 4.0000 | -1.2967 | 4.6556 | 0 | 0.0010 |
| 5.0000 | 0.6802 | 0.7230 | 0.7500 | 0.2504 | 0.2400 | 5.0000 | -1.2724 | 4.2777 | 0 | 0.0010 |
| 6.0000 | 0.7107 | 0.7573 | 0.7800 | 0.2369 | 0.1900 | 6.0000 | -1.6251 | 5.3662 | 0 | 0.0010 |
| 7.0000 | 0.8111 | 0.8594 | 0.8700 | 0.2211 | 0.1600 | 7.0000 | -2.2851 | 8.3236 | 0 | 0.0010 |
| 8.0000 | 0.9488 | 0.9773 | 0.9900 | 0.2067 | 0.1600 | 8.0000 | -1.8786 | 12.7847 | 0 | 0.0010 |
| 9.0000 | 0.9911 | 1.0163 | 1.0300 | 0.2457 | 0.1900 | 9.0000 | 0.0254 | 24.4068 | 0 | 0.0010 |
| 10.0000 | 1.0582 | 1.0666 | 1.0700 | 0.2596 | 0.1500 | 10.0000 | 4.8500 | 122.5760 | 0 | 0.0010 |
| 11.0000 | 1.0975 | 1.0988 | 1.1000 | 0.2322 | 0.1200 | 11.0000 | 8.7122 | 269.0530 | 0 | 0.0010 |
| 12.0000 | 1.0823 | 1.0896 | 1.0900 | 0.1724 | 0.1100 | 12.0000 | -0.2557 | 39.8107 | 0 | 0.0010 |
| 13.0000 | 1.0955 | 1.0998 | 1.1000 | 0.1633 | 0.1200 | 13.0000 | -1.5259 | 24.3516 | 0 | 0.0010 |
| 14.0000 | 1.0709 | 1.0807 | 1.0800 | 0.1597 | 0.1100 | 14.0000 | -1.8895 | 28.5563 | 0 | 0.0010 |
| 15.0000 | 1.0096 | 1.0282 | 1.0300 | 0.1575 | 0.1000 | 15.0000 | -3.4210 | 21.3683 | 0 | 0.0010 |
| 16.0000 | 0.9690 | 0.9973 | 1.0000 | 0.1774 | 0.1300 | 16.0000 | -2.9380 | 15.0985 | 0 | 0.0010 |
| 17.0000 | 0.9547 | 0.9872 | 1.0000 | 0.1913 | 0.1500 | 17.0000 | -2.6087 | 12.1901 | 0 | 0.0010 |
| 18.0000 | 0.9987 | 1.0209 | 1.0300 | 0.1843 | 0.1400 | 18.0000 | -2.4575 | 13.7446 | 0 | 0.0010 |
| 19.0000 | 1.0861 | 1.0715 | 1.0600 | 0.2388 | 0.1700 | 19.0000 | 0.8480 | 13.3137 | 0 | 0.0010 |
| 20.0000 | 1.1944 | 1.1275 | 1.1000 | 0.3818 | 0.2500 | 20.0000 | 3.1875 | 20.0743 | 0 | 0.0010 |
| 21.0000 | 1.2651 | 1.1717 | 1.1500 | 0.4885 | 0.2575 | 21.0000 | 6.6494 | 88.1468 | 0 | 0.0010 |
| 22.0000 | 1.3302 | 1.2027 | 1.1700 | 0.6446 | 0.2400 | 22.0000 | 8.4558 | 126.6330 | 0 | 0.0010 |
| 23.0000 | 1.2139 | 1.1298 | 1.1100 | 0.4657 | 0.2000 | 23.0000 | 7.0455 | 75.4992 | 0 | 0.0010 |
| 24.0000 | 1.0760 | 1.0336 | 1.0200 | 0.3265 | 0.1700 | 24.0000 | 6.5014 | 82.1613 | 0 | 0.0010 |

It is possible to find different patterns per day and per hour (see Fig. 3), where, for example, we can see that 22 groups (hours) have mean ranks significantly different from group 1 (hour 1).

Electricity prices can be influenced by the present and past values of various exogenous factors, such as generation capacity, load profiles and meteorological conditions [9], in a preliminary stage we have selected defined and code the following candidates to co-variables: Day of the week – $C_1 = 0, 1, 2, 3, 4, 5, 6$ (Mon, ..., Sunday); Weekday/Saturday/Sunday – $C_2 = 0, 1, 2$;

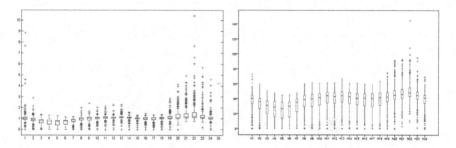

**Fig. 2.** Boxplot diagrams of rescaled (*left*) and real data (*right*). Time interval: 01.01.2010–31.01.2010.

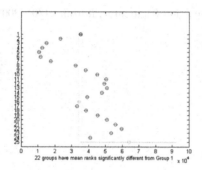

**Fig. 3.** Real data (01.01.2008–31.01.2008). Mean price per hour.

Weekday/Weekend – $C_3 = 0, 1$; Regular day/holiday – $C_4 = 0, 1$; Season – $C_5 = 0, 1, 2, 3$ (Winter, Spring, Summer, Autumn); Month – $C_6 = 0, \ldots, 11$ (Jan, $\ldots$, Dec); Summer/Winter Hour – $C_7 = 0, 1$.

## 3.2 The Model

Initially, to estimate the model as described before, we considered the time interval from 01/01/2008 to 31/12/2010. The first approach using IBM SPSS Statistics (version 22) was performed with difficulty due the high dimensionality of data. A question that arose was: "Can we reduce the number of components of $Y_t$?", e.g., are there significant differences between $Y_i$ and $Y_j$, for $i \neq j$? To solve partially such issue, we try to reduce the 24 h of a day to fewer reference hours. First of all, an analysis of data plot per hour was performed. The graphical representation of data (see Fig. 4) shows similar behavior in some distinct. Identified such similar hours we merge them into an unique interval of similarity. In this way the dimension of data can be reduced, by taking the mean or median or other measure of response variable.

We have selected and defined some time intervals which conduced to the best model performance. In this way, it was reduced the dimension defining the following time intervals: aurora, lunch time and dinner time. Aurora corresponds

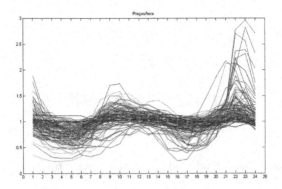

**Fig. 4.** Data representation (time interval from 01/01/2008 to 31/12/2010).

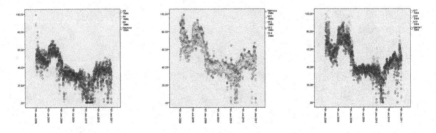

**Fig. 5.** Overlapped data: Aurora time (left), lunch time (center) and dinner time (right). Time interval from 01/01/2008 to 31/12/2010.

to the hours 3, 4 and 5 respectively. Lunch time merges the hours 11, 12, 13 and 14. Dinner time takes into account hours 17, 18 and 19. When the data is graphically overlapped for each hour in the defined time intervals (see Fig. 5) no significant differences were found.

We studied some possible explanatory variables which can contribute to explain the energy price per hour. In a preliminary stage of the study, using the initial explanatory variables proposed in Subsect. 3.1, an analysis of variance with second order interaction was performed. The best candidates to explanatory variables to include in a model were chosen: $C_1$, $C_4$, $C_5$, $C_6$, $C_7$.

It was also considered the fare defined by EDP as possible explanatory variable but it was not significant.

In GLM approach the significant explanatory variables were $C_4$, $C_6$, $C_7$, $H_2$, $H_7$, $H_8$ or $H_{16}$, $H_{20}$, $H_{22}$, $H_{23}$, $H_{24}$ and lunch time or $C_4$, $C_6$, $C_7$, $H_2$, $H_7$, $H_8$, $H_{16}$, $H_{20}$, $H_{22}$, $H_{23}$, $H_{24}$ in the several chosen models. In present work, in time series approach, the significant explanatory variables (an some lags) were $H_2$, $H_7$, $H_8$, $H_{16}$, $H_{20}$, $H_{22}$, $H_{24}$. The selected model has similar explanatory variables to some models obtained by GLM in [7].

Considering the obtained results as indicators, we can conclude that some of the explanatory variables proposed initially were not relevant for dependent variable, such as, EDP fares, Portuguese holidays (maybe the Iberian holidays can have some relevance, and not just the Portuguese ones). Also, some periods of time can be drop off as relevant explanatory variables, such as dinner time or some others. The season, month or winter/summer time period revealed significant explanatory variables in the different estimated models.

Using this preliminary model estimation as starting point, we repeated all estimation process considering a more recent sample so we could compare with the results published in [6,7]. The ARIMA model was estimated using hourly prices from 10/03/2014 to 29/5/2016. The remaining sample, from 30/05/2014 to 28/06/2016, was used to evaluate the forecasting performance of the selected model. To asses the in-sample prediction quality of the model, we use the Mean Absolute Percentage Error (MAPE) and the Root Mean Square Error (RMSE). The mean values of MAPE and RMSE are with accordance withe the results published in [6,7].

We have selected as preliminaries explanatory variables the same used earlier also considered in [6,7], where its done a VAR approach and a GLM approach respectively. There were estimated of model parameters and analyzed the suitability measures of estimates. The selection and validation of models such as selection of variables, diagnostics, residual analysis and interpretation was concluded. All models obtained good significant results. Here we present the model with similar performance (estimation and forecasting) and with best $R^2$.

In Fig. 6 we can find the details of the model selected by time series approach.

**ARIMA Model Parameters**

| | | | | | Estimate | SE | t | Sig. |
|---|---|---|---|---|---|---|---|---|
| DIF_1_Average-Model_1 | DIF_1_Average | No Transformation | AR | Lag 7 | .102 | .037 | 2.767 | .006 |
| | | | MA | Lag 1 | .888 | .017 | 51.352 | .000 |
| | H2 | No Transformation | Numerator | Lag 0 | .156 | .007 | 22.365 | .000 |
| | | | | Lag 1 | .156 | .007 | 23.078 | .000 |
| | H7 | No Transformation | Numerator | Lag 0 | .127 | .011 | 11.773 | .000 |
| | | | | Lag 1 | .129 | .011 | 12.175 | .000 |
| | H8 | No Transformation | Numerator | Lag 0 | .147 | .008 | 17.598 | .000 |
| | | | | Lag 2 | .141 | .008 | 16.703 | .000 |
| | | | Denominator | Lag 1 | -.928 | .023 | -40.121 | .000 |
| | H16 | No Transformation | Numerator | Lag 0 | .262 | .006 | 43.271 | .000 |
| | | | | Lag 1 | .263 | .006 | 44.348 | .000 |
| | H20 | No Transformation | Numerator | Lag 0 | .111 | .007 | 16.844 | .000 |
| | | | | Lag 1 | .112 | .007 | 17.142 | .000 |
| | H22 | No Transformation | Numerator | Lag 0 | .086 | .008 | 10.825 | .000 |
| | | | | Lag 2 | .090 | .008 | 11.538 | .000 |
| | | | Denominator | Lag 1 | -.654 | .057 | -11.393 | .000 |
| | | | | Lag 2 | .208 | .041 | 5.095 | .000 |
| | H24 | No Transformation | Numerator | Lag 0 | .056 | .007 | 8.495 | .000 |
| | | | | Lag 1 | .052 | .007 | 7.856 | .000 |

**Fig. 6.** Estimated ARIMAX model.

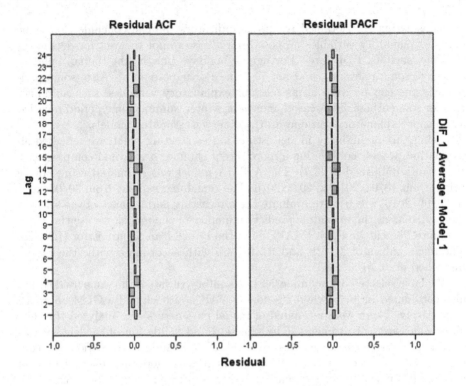

**Fig. 7.** Estimated ACP and PACF.

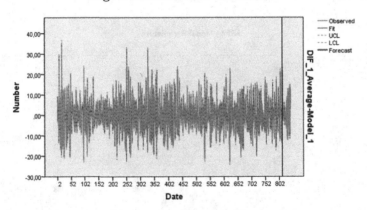

**Fig. 8.** Residuals representation. Estimation period: 10/03/2014 to 29/5/2016.

The diagnostic analysis and selection of the order of the models was done but we do not reproduce with detail such work. The ACF and PACF are displayed in Fig. 7. We can see that these functions are in agreement with the estimated model (ARIMA(7, 1, 1). It seems in disagreement with Fig. 6 where is displayed a model ARIMA(7, 0, 1), but the considered time series was differentiated previously (one time) to the model estimation.

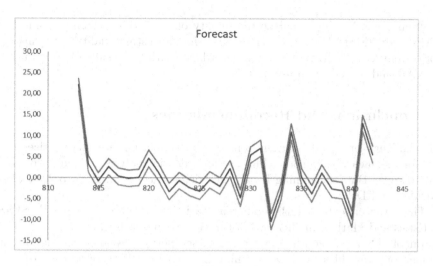

**Fig. 9.** Forecast (blue), UPL (orange), LPL (grey). Period: 30/05/2016 to 28/06/2016. (Color figure online)

**Table 2.** Forecast errors - MADE and RMSE. Period: 30/05/2016 to 28/06/2016.

| Date | MADE | RMSE | Date | MADE | RMSE |
|---|---|---|---|---|---|
| 30/05/2016 | 2,29 | 2,285 | 14/06/2016 | 5,36 | 5,362 |
| 31/05/2016 | 0,18 | 0,184 | 15/06/2016 | 4,74 | 4,735 |
| 01/06/2016 | 2,44 | 2,445 | 16/06/2016 | 7,72 | 7,720 |
| 02/06/2016 | 0,70 | 0,700 | 17/06/2016 | 8,72 | 8,718 |
| 03/06/2016 | 0,84 | 0,841 | 18/06/2016 | 5,15 | 5,154 |
| 04/06/2016 | 0,02 | 0,024 | 19/06/2016 | 11,05 | 11,047 |
| 05/06/2016 | 4,62 | 4,620 | 20/06/2016 | 0,72 | 0,722 |
| 06/06/2016 | 1,53 | 1,532 | 21/06/2016 | 3,50 | 3,499 |
| 07/06/2016 | 3,37 | 3,370 | 22/06/2016 | 0,34 | 0,335 |
| 08/06/2016 | 1,07 | 1,067 | 23/06/2016 | 0,96 | 0,958 |
| 09/06/2016 | 1,43 | 1,434 | 24/06/2016 | 2,98 | 2,980 |
| 10/06/2016 | 1,32 | 1,321 | 25/06/2016 | 10,03 | 10,035 |
| 11/06/2016 | 1,94 | 1,936 | 26/06/2016 | 12,83 | 12,828 |
| 12/06/2016 | 0,82 | 0,816 | 27/06/2016 | 5,50 | 5,496 |
| | | | | **2,366** | **2,365** |

When we analyze the graphics in Fig. 8, we can conclude that the residuals behavior is in accordance with the expected (null mean and constant variance). Also their Gaussian distribution was not rejected statistically. In Fig. 9 it is presented the forecast from 30/05/2016 to 28/06/2016. The model evidences adequate performance estimation. We almost cant distinguish the original series and the predicted series.

From Table 2 we can analyze the quality of prediction in-sample using the MAPE and RMSE. We can conclude that the forecasting quality is promising. Notice that the RMSE values are in accordance with the results obtained using the VAR and the GLM approach [6, 7].

## 4    Conclusions and Recommendations

The challenge proposed by EDP consisted in simulating electricity prices not only for risk measures purposes but also for scenario analysis in terms of pricing and strategy. Data concerning hourly electricity prices from 2008 to 2016 were provided by EDP.

The data were explored using different statistical software, namely IBM SPSS Statistics and Matlab. In this work a time series approach was considered. The season of the year, month or winter/summer period revealed not significant explanatory variables in the different estimated models in opposite to GLM approach [7]. Also, We have selected a model that not includes the reduced form of day hours (aurora time, lunch time, dinner time). From Table 2 we can analyze the quality of prediction in-sample by MADE and RMSE. We can conclude that the forecasting quality is promising. When compared with multivariate app-roach using the VAR approach and GLM approach [6, 7] for the same period (from 30/05/2016 to 28/06/2016) the RMSE values are in accordance with the RMSE computed using the VAR method. Although the forecast do not exactly replicate the real price the results are quite promising. The introduction of other co-variables, such as oil price, gas price, wind energy production, other meteoro-logical variables, would certainly improve the model and the forecast. Univariate time series approach still needs to be improved in the sense of comparison with other similar models. Others methods should be explored. It is still possible to explore another models in future work.

EPF literature has mainly concerned on models that use information at daily level, however this particularly problem proposed is interested in forecasting intra-day prices using hourly data (disaggregated data), maybe it is necessary to consider models that explore the complex dependence structure of the multi-variate price series. The problem of modeling distributional properties of energy prices can be classified in three main classes: reduced form models, forward price models and hybrid price models [1]. Temporal Distribution Extrapolation is another possible idea for our future work.

**Acknowledgements.** This work was supported by Portuguese funds through the *Center of Naval Research* (CINAV), Portuguese Naval Academy, Portugal and *The Portuguese Foundation for Science and Technology* (FCT), through the *Center for Computational and Stochastic Mathematics* (CEMAT), University of Lisbon, Portugal, project UID/Multi/04621/2019.

# References

1. Eydeland, A., Wolyniec, K.: Energy and Power Risk Management: New Developments in Modeling, Pricing, and Hedging. Wiley, Hoboken (2003)
2. Fu, T.: A review on time series data mining. Eng. Appl. Artif. Intell. **24**(1), 164–181 (2011)
3. Mulquiney, P.: Combining GLM and data-mining techniques for modelling accident compensation data (private communication)
4. Pal, S.H., Palet, J.N.: Time series data mining: a review. Bin. J. Data Min. Netw. **5**, 01–04 (2015)
5. Ratanamahatana, C.A., Lin, J., Gunopulos, D., Keogh, E., Vlachos, M., Das, G.: Mining time series data. In: Maimon, O., Rokach, L. (eds.) Data Mining and Knowledge Discovery Handbook, pp. 1049–1077. Springer, Boston (2010). https://doi.org/10.1007/978-0-387-09823-4_56
6. Costa e Silva, E., Borges, A., Teodoro, M.F., Andrade, M.A.P., Covas, R.: Time series data mining for energy prices forecasting: an application to real data. In: Madureira, A.M., Abraham, A., Gamboa, D., Novais, P. (eds.) ISDA 2016. AISC, vol. 557, pp. 649–658. Springer, Cham (2017). https://doi.org/10.1007/978-3-319-53480-0_64
7. Teodoro, M.F., Andrade, M.A.P., Silva, E.C., Borges, A., Covas, R.: Energy prices forecasting using GLM. In: Oliveira, T.A., Kitsos, C.P., Oliveira, A., Grilo, L. (eds.) Recent Studies on Risk Analysis and Statistical Modeling. CS, pp. 321–334. Springer, Cham (2018). https://doi.org/10.1007/978-3-319-76605-8_23
8. Vasimalla, K.: A survey on time series data mining. Int. J. Innov. Res. Comput. Commun. Eng. **2**(5), 170–179 (2014)
9. Weron, R.: Electricity price forecasting: a review of the state-of-the-art with a look into the future. Int. J. Forecast. **30**(4), 1030–1081 (2014)
10. Yang, Q., Wu, X.: 10 challenging problems in data mining research. Int. J. Inf. Technol. Decis. Mak. **5**(04), 597–604 (2006)
11. Zhu, Y.: High performance data mining in time series: techniques and case studies. Ph.D. thesis, Department of Computer Science, University of New York (2004)

# A Nonlinear Subgrid Stabilization Parameter-Free Method to Solve Incompressible Navier-Stokes Equations at High Reynolds Numbers

Riedson Baptista[1,2(✉)] [iD], Sérgio S. Bento[2(✉)] [iD], Leonardo M. Lima[3] [iD], Isaac P. Santos[1,2(✉)] [iD], Andrea M. P. Valli[1] [iD], and Lucia Catabriga[1] [iD]

[1] High Performance Computing Lab, Federal University of Espírito Santo, Vitória, ES, Brazil
{riedson.baptista,isaac.santos}@ufes.br,
{avalli,luciac}@inf.ufes.br
[2] Department of Applied Mathematics, Federal University of Espírito Santo, São Mateus, ES, Brazil
sergio.bento@ufes.br
[3] Department of Mechanical Engineering, Federal Institute of Espírito Santo, Aracruz, ES, Brazil
lmuniz@ifes.edu.br

**Abstract.** In this work we evaluate a Nonlinear Subgrid Stabilization parameter-free method to solve time-independent incompressible Navier-Stokes equations (NSGS-NS) at high Reynolds numbers, considering only the decomposition of the velocity field (not pressure) into coarse/resolved scales and fine/unresolved scales. In this formulation we use a dynamic damping factor which it is often essential for the nonlinear iterative process and for the reduction of the number of iterations. In order to reduce the computational costs typical of two-scale methods, the unresolved scale space is defined using bubble functions whose degrees of freedom are locally eliminated in favor of the degrees of freedom that live on the resolved scales. Accuracy comparisons with the streamline-upwind/Petrov-Galerkin (SUPG) formulation combined with the pressure stabilizing/Petrov-Galerkin (PSPG) are conducted based on 2D steady state benchmark problems with high Reynolds numbers, flow over a backward-facing step and lid-driven square cavity flow.

**Keywords:** Incompressible Navier-Stokes equation ·
Nonlinear Subgrid Stabilization · Variational multiscale method ·
Damping factor

## 1 Introduction

The Navier-Stokes equations are at the heart of fluid flow modeling, where many phenomena of scientific and engineering interest are modeled by them.

S. Misra et al. (Eds.): ICCSA 2019, LNCS 11621, pp. 134–148, 2019.
https://doi.org/10.1007/978-3-030-24302-9_11

The momentum and continuity equations, with velocity field and pressure as the unknowns, compose the Navier-Stokes equations. Regardless of the chosen discretization method, solving the Navier-Stokes causes many numerical and computational problems. In general, the numerical methods involve a significant time of calculations. Moreover, problems arise when the finite element method is used to solve the Navier-Stokes equations related, for example, if the velocity and pressure spaces do not fulfill the Ladyzhenskaya-Babuska-Brezzi (LBB) condition [6]. Another source of numerical difficulty is the presence of the nonlinear convective term. Because of that, most finite element techniques and computations reported in the past three decades are based on stabilized formulations. Furthermore, high Reynolds number flows are convection dominated and stabilization techniques with special nonlinear treatment must be used to avoid non-physical oscillation.

Many stabilized finite element formulations have been used to solve the Navier-Stokes equations. The streamline-upwind/Petrov-Galerkin (SUPG) [8] formulation combined with the pressure stabilizing/Petrov-Galerkin (PSPG) [24] was the precursor of the Galerkin/Least-Squares (GLS) stabilization methods [23], or its modification proposed in [15]. Another class of stabilized methods based on the idea of augmenting the Galerkin method with virtual bubble functions was introduced in [7]. All approaches try to reduce the numerical instabilities present at problems with high Reynolds or Mach numbers, shocks or thin boundary layers, and equal-order interpolation functions for velocity and pressure.

The variational multiscale (VMS) methodology was introduced by Hughes in [22] for the scalar convection-diffusion equation and extended for the Navier-Stokes equations by a set of researchers [4,10,11,19,27]. Recently, we present a nonlinear multiscale parameter-free method (NSGS-NS) to solve incompressible flow problems [3], consisting of a decomposition for both velocity and pressure fields into coarse/resolved and fine/unresolved scales, together with the addition of a residual-based nonlinear operator to the enriched Galerkin formulation. In this approach, the pressure fine-scale is approximated using a heuristic scaling of the continuity equation [9], based on the incompressibility constraint (LSIC) parameter [26]. We observed that the pressure solution did not present satisfactory results for the experiments performed there.

In this paper, we consider only the decomposition of the velocity field into resolved and unresolved scales, as it is considered in [19] – the pressure unknowns live onto the resolved scale. Since the subgrid scales are modeled by bubble functions, this approach leads to a numerical formulation satisfying the LBB condition, that can be considered an extension of the MINI element [2] to the Navier-Stokes equations. Besides of that, the artificial nonlinear viscosity operator described in [3] is added to the unresolved scales in order to stabilize the velocity field at high Reynolds number. Generally, the nonlinearity became more representative when the Reynolds numbers increase, needing a dynamic damping process to improve the convergence. Here, we use the dynamic dam-ping algorithm proposed in [25].

The remainder of this work is organized as follows. Section 2 briefly addresses the governing equations and the variational multiscale formulation. In the next section, we show the numerical formulation with the dynamic damping factor algorithm. Section 4 evaluates the numerical performance of two 2D benchmark problems for incompressible flow problems at high Reynolds numbers, and Sect. 5 concludes the paper.

## 2    The Incompressible Navier Stokes Equations

The incompressible Navier-Stokes equations result from the conservation principles of momentum and mass. Using primitive variables, the stationary case of these equations in two dimensions read

$$(\boldsymbol{u} \cdot \nabla)\boldsymbol{u} - 2\nu\nabla \cdot \varepsilon(\boldsymbol{u}) + \nabla p = \boldsymbol{f}, \text{ in } \Omega, \tag{1}$$

$$\nabla \cdot \boldsymbol{u} = 0, \text{ in } \Omega, \tag{2}$$

where $\boldsymbol{u} = (u, v)$ is the velocity field, $p$ is the kinematic pressure, $\nu$ is the kinematic viscosity, $\boldsymbol{f}$ is a body force, and $\varepsilon(\boldsymbol{u})$ is the strain rate tensor defined as

$$\varepsilon(\boldsymbol{u}) = \frac{1}{2}(\nabla \boldsymbol{u} + (\nabla \boldsymbol{u})^T).$$

These equations have to be solved in the domain $\Omega \subset \mathbb{R}^2$ with a smooth boundary $\Gamma$. Moreover, to provide a well-posed mathematical problem, a set of appropriate boundary conditions is added to equations system (1)–(2).

### 2.1    The Variational Formulation

The Galerkin finite element discretization of the Navier-Stokes equations (1)–(2) is based on its variational formulation. For simplicity, considering homogeneous Dirichlet boundary conditions for the velocity field, the variational formulation consists of finding $\boldsymbol{u} \in V$ and $p \in Q$ such that

$$\int_\Omega \boldsymbol{w} \cdot (\boldsymbol{u} \cdot \nabla \boldsymbol{u}) \, d\Omega + 2\nu \int_\Omega \varepsilon(\boldsymbol{w}) : \varepsilon(\boldsymbol{u}) \, d\Omega - \int_\Omega p\nabla \cdot \boldsymbol{w} \, d\Omega = \int_\Omega \boldsymbol{w} \cdot \boldsymbol{f} \, d\Omega;$$

$$\int_\Omega q\nabla \cdot \boldsymbol{u} \, d\Omega = 0,$$

for all $\boldsymbol{w} \in V$ and $q \in Q$, where

$$V = [H_0^1(\Omega)]^2, \quad Q = L_0^2(\Omega) = \left\{ p \in L^2(\Omega); \int_\Omega p \, d\Omega = 0 \right\}. \tag{3}$$

It is well known that the standard Galerkin finite element method is not suitable for solving the incompressible Navier-Stokes equations. The user has to choose functions spaces for velocity and pressure that satisfy the LBB condition

[6], for example, the Taylor-Hood and MINI elements [2,5,21]. Moreover, due to the presence of the nonlinear convective term, in the convection dominated regime (flows at high Reynolds number), stabilization techniques with special nonlinear treatment are required to provide stable numerical solutions. In the next section we present the Nonlinear Subgrid Stabilization method, presented in [3], for solving the problem (1)–(2).

## 3    The Numerical Formulation

The numerical formulation is constructed projecting the problem onto the finite-dimensional subspaces $V_h \subset V$ and $Q_h \subset Q$. To define the subspaces $V_h$ and $Q_h$, we consider a triangular partition $\mathcal{T}_h$ of the domain $\Omega$ into $n_{el}$ elements, where $\Omega = \bigcup_{e=1}^{n_{el}} \Omega_e$ and $\Omega_i \cap \Omega_j = \emptyset$, $i, j = 1, 2, \cdots, n_{el}$, $i \neq j$. Thus, the finite element subspaces $V_h$ and $Q_h$ are given by

$$V_h = \{u_h \in [H_0^1(\Omega)]^2; u_h|_{\Omega_e} \in [\mathbb{P}_1(\Omega_e)]^2\};$$

$$Q_h = \{p_h \in H^1(\Omega); p_h|_{\Omega_e} \in \mathbb{P}_1(\Omega_e), \int_\Omega p_h \, d\Omega = 0\},$$

where $\mathbb{P}_1(\Omega_e)$ is the set of first order polynomials in $\Omega_e$. Consider the enriched space

$$V_h^b = V_h \oplus V_b,$$

given by the direct sum of $V_h$, the standard finite element space, and of $V_b$, a space spanned by bubble functions (a polynomial function $\psi_b$ which takes the value 1 at the barycenter of the element $\Omega_e$, vanishes on its boundary $\partial\Omega_e$ and satisfies $0 \leq \psi_b \leq 1$), described as

$$V_b = \{u_b \in [H_0^1(\Omega)]^2; u_b|_{\Omega_e} \in [span(\psi_b)]^2, \forall \Omega_e \in \mathcal{T}_h\}.$$

The space $V_h$ is called resolved scale space, whereas $V_b$ is known as unresolved scale space. Solving the incompressible Navier-Stokes equation on spaces $V_h^b$ for velocity and $Q_h$ for pressure leads to a numerical formulation that can be considered an extension of the MINI element [2], a pair of elements satisfying the LBB condition, to the Navier-Stokes equations.

The Nonlinear Subgrid Stabilization (NSGS-NS) method for solving the incompressible Navier-Stokes equations consists of finding $u_h^b = u_h + u_b \in V_h^b$ and $p_h \in Q_h$, with $u_h \in V_h$ and $u_b \in V_b$, such that

$$\int_\Omega w_h^b \cdot (u_h^b \cdot \nabla u_h^b) \, d\Omega + 2\nu \int_\Omega \varepsilon(w_h^b) \colon \varepsilon(u_h^b) \, d\Omega \tag{4}$$

$$-\int_\Omega p_h \nabla \cdot w_h^b \, d\Omega + \sum_{e=1}^{nel} \int_{\Omega_e} \nabla w_b \colon (\delta_b \nabla u_b) \, d\Omega = \int_\Omega w_h^b \cdot f \, d\Omega; \tag{5}$$

$$\int_\Omega q_h \nabla \cdot u_h^b \, d\Omega = 0, \tag{6}$$

for all $\boldsymbol{w}_h^b \in V_h^b$ and $q_h \in Q_h$, with $\boldsymbol{w}_h \in V_h$ and $\boldsymbol{w}_b \in V_b$. To the Galerkin formulation is added the artificial nonlinear viscosity operator

$$\sum_{e=1}^{nel} \int_{\Omega_e} \nabla \boldsymbol{w}_b : (\delta_b \nabla \boldsymbol{u}_b) \, d\Omega,$$

acting only on the unresolved scales. The amount of artificial viscosity $\delta_b$ is calculated on the element-level according to

$$\delta_b = \delta_b(\boldsymbol{u}_h, p_h) = \begin{cases} \dfrac{h}{2} \dfrac{\|R(\boldsymbol{u}_h, p_h)\|}{\|\nabla(\boldsymbol{u}_h, p_h)\|}, & \text{if } \|\nabla(\boldsymbol{u}_h, p_h)\| > 0; \\ 0, & \text{otherwise,} \end{cases} \tag{7}$$

where $\| \cdot \|$ denotes the Euclidean norm and

$$R(\boldsymbol{u}_h, p_h) = \begin{cases} (\boldsymbol{u}_h \cdot \nabla)\boldsymbol{u}_h - 2\nu\nabla \cdot \boldsymbol{\varepsilon}(\boldsymbol{u}_h) + \nabla p_h - \boldsymbol{f} \\ \nabla \cdot \boldsymbol{u}_h \end{cases}$$

is the residue of the problem associated to the resolved scales on $\Omega_e$. The details of the construction of the matrices associated with the problem and the static condensation process are described in [3].

The linearization process of the resulting system – for example, by fixed point or Newton methods – aims to generate a monotonous decreasing sequence of residues. However, most nonlinear stabilization methods can present difficulties in the convergence process of the nonlinear iterations. There are some naivy strategies described in the literature to improve the convergence of these methods [28, 30]. Besides that, for more complex problems with large numbers of Reynolds, some nonlinear iterations may result in solutions that produce an increasing sequence of these residues, resulting in the divergence of the iterative process. Since we can not rule out such a solution and use it completely makes the process inefficient, we use only a small percentage of this solution. Thus we introduce a damping factor in the nonlinear iterative process, reducing the influence of such bad solutions. This damping factor can be a given value or generated dynamically. In our experiments, when the convergence of the nonlinear iterative method is not achieved, we use an adaptive process to choose this damping factor presented in [25] given by Algorithm 1.

We consider the damping factor $\omega \in [\omega_{min}, \omega_{max}]$, where $\omega_{min} = 0.05$ and $\omega_{max} = 1.0$. The actual solution $U_h^{k+1}$ is calculated in line 9 of the Algorithm. It is accepted if $\|R(U_h^{k+1})\| < \|R(U_h^k)\|$ or if the factor $\omega$ has reached the lower limit. If $\|R(U_h^{k+1})\| < \|R(U_h^k)\|$ and $\omega$ has not reached its maximum value, it is incremented and iterative process goes on. When $\|R(U_h^{k+1})\| > \|R(U_h^k)\|$, the solution $U_h^{k+1}$ is rejected and $\omega$ has its value reduced. In this case, a new value for $U_h^{k+1}$ is calculated and the residue is evaluated again.

---

**Algorithm 1.** Dynamic choice of the damping factor

---

1: $\omega_{min} := 0.05; \quad \omega_{max} := 1.0;$

2: $c_1 := 1.001; \quad c_2 := 1.1; \quad c_3 := 1.001; \quad c_4 := 0.9;$

3: initialize $\boldsymbol{U}_h^0 = \boldsymbol{0}$ and compute residual $\|R(\boldsymbol{U}_h^0)\|;$

4: $\omega := \omega_{max}; \quad k := 0; \quad switch := 1;$

5: **while** $\|R(\boldsymbol{U}_h^k)\| > tolerance$ **do**

6:     compute $\Delta\boldsymbol{U}_h^{k+1};$

7:     $first\text{-}damping := 1;$

8:     **while** $switch = 1$ **do**

9:         $\boldsymbol{U}_h^{k+1} := \boldsymbol{U}_h^k + \omega\Delta\boldsymbol{U}_h^{k+1};$

10:        compute residual $\|R(\boldsymbol{U}_h^{k+1})\|;$

11:        **if** $\|R(\boldsymbol{U}_h^{k+1})\| < \|R(\boldsymbol{U}_h^k)\|$ **or** $\omega \le c_1\omega_{min}$ **then**

12:           **if** $\|R(\boldsymbol{U}_h^{k+1})\| < \|R(\boldsymbol{U}_h^k)\|$ **and** $first\text{-}damping = 1$ **then**

13:              $\omega_{max} := min\{1, c_3\omega_{max}\};$

14:              $\omega := min\{\omega_{max}, c_2\omega\};$

15:           **end if**

16:           $switch := 0;$

17:        **else**

18:           $\omega := max\{\omega_{min}, \omega/2\}$

19:           **if** $first\text{-}damping = 1$ **then**

20:              $\omega_{max} := max\{\omega_{min}, \omega_{max}\};$

21:              $first\text{-}damping := 0;$

22:           **end if**

23:        **end if**

24:     **end while**

25:     $k := k + 1;$

26: **end while**

---

## 4 Numerical Experiments

In the experiments, we consider two well-known 2D benchmark problems for incompressible flows with high Reynolds numbers: the "backward-facing step" and the "lid-driven cavity". Our multiscale methodology is compared to the SUPG/PSPG presented in [12,29]. We evaluate the numerical solutions obtained by both methods with the results presented in [13] for the "backward-facing step" problem and with the high accuracy experiments presented in [14,20] for the "lid-driven cavity" problem.

The nonlinear system generated by the methods of this work is solved by the Picard iterative process with $tol_{nl} = 10^{-3}$ and maximum number of nonlinear steps equal to $itmax_{nl} = 10^3$. The resulting linear systems are solved by GMRES method with 45 vectors to restart, tolerance equals $10^{-12}$ with incomplete factorization ILU(10) preconditioners. The domains are discretized considering meshes generated by the Gmsh software [18] and the tests were performed on a machine with an Intel Core i5-6200U 2.3GHz×4 processor with 8GB of RAM and Ubuntu 18.04 operating system.

## 4.1    Flow over Backward-Facing Step

The backward-facing step problem is one of the most used and benchmarked geometry for computation fluid dynamic and experimental flow analysis. It consists of a fluid flowing into a straight channel which abruptly widens on one side, see Fig. 1(a) for the problem description. It produces a recirculation zone on the lower channel wall and a recirculation zone farther downstream on the upper wall, with high Reynolds numbers [1,13,17]. Here, the inlet velocity field is specified as a parallel flow with a parabolic horizontal component given by $u(y) = -32/3y^2 + 24y - 12$ for $0,75 \leq y \leq 1.5$, which produces a maximum inflow velocity of $u_{max} = 1.5$ and an average inflow velocity of $u_{avg} = 1.0$.

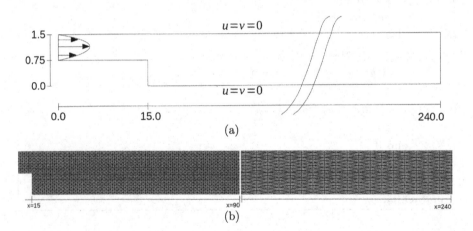

**Fig. 1.** Flow over a backward facing step: (a) problem description and (b) finite element mesh (43259 nodes and 83070 elements).

Figure 1(b) shows the triangular mesh used in all experiments, with a deeper refinement before $x = 90$. The total number of nodes and elements are 43259 and 83070, respectively. The stream function contours in Fig. 2 illustrate the main features of the separated flows with $Re = 500, Re = 800$ and $Re = 1000$. Our results show excellent agreement with the high accuracy experiments presented in [1,13]. In Fig. 3, we show the horizontal velocity profiles at $x = 25.5$ and 37.5 streamwise locations, and we compare them with the experiments in [13]. Our NSGS-NS solutions show very good agreement with them, at both $x = 25.5$ and 37.5 locations.

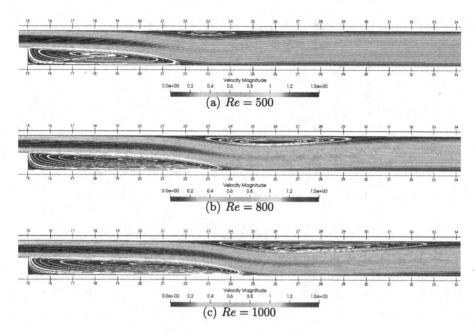

**Fig. 2.** Flow over a backward facing step: NSGS-NS solution with $Re = 500, 800, 1000$.

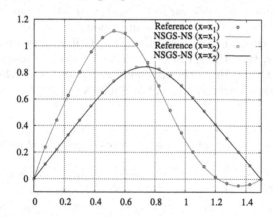

**Fig. 3.** Horizontal velocity profile for $Re = 800$ at two downstream locations, $x_1 = 25.5$ and $x_2 = 37.5$, with $0 \leq y \leq 1.5$.

In Table 1, we have tabulated our numerical results and reference values [13] for the dimensionless characteristic lengths $x_1, x_2$ and $x_3$, see Fig. 4, frequently used to characterize the simulation results of this problem. Those lengths are normalized by the channel step height $h$. As we can see, they are in an excellent agreement with the reference values observed in the reference. Moreover, the NSGS-NS method presents better solution for the characteristic lengths than the ones obtained by the SUPG/PSPG method.

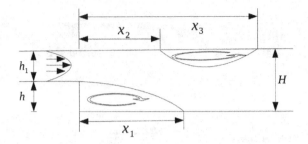

**Fig. 4.** Flow over a backward-facing step - characteristic lengths.

**Table 1.** Flow over a backward-facing step: characteristic lengths.

| | $Re = 500$ | | | $Re = 800$ | | | $Re = 1000$ | | |
|---|---|---|---|---|---|---|---|---|---|
| | $x_1/h$ | $x_2/h$ | $x_3/h$ | $x_1/h$ | $x_2/h$ | $x_3/h$ | $x_1/h$ | $x_2/h$ | $x_3/h$ |
| Reference [13] | 9.42 | 8.013 | 13.171 | 11.834 | 9.476 | 20.553 | 13.121 | 10.474 | 24.882 |
| NSGS-NS method | 9.41 | 8.01 | 13.17 | 11.83 | 9.47 | 20.55 | 13.12 | 10.47 | 24.88 |
| SUPG/PSGP method | 9.33 | 8.27 | 12.93 | 11.47 | 9.07 | 19.87 | 12.67 | 10.07 | 24.07 |

Computational performance of both methods are shown in the Table 2, where $(\#NLI)$ is the number of nonlinear iterations, $(\#LI)$ is the number of GMRES iterations and $(Time)$ is the CPU time in seconds. Note that NSGS-NS number of nonlinear iterations is greater SUPG/PSPG iterations with all Reynolds numbers. However, the SUPG/PSPG nonlinear iterations consume more linear iterations and CPU time than the corresponding NSGS-NS solutions. Therefore, in addition to present better solutions, the NSGS-NS method is computationally more efficient.

**Table 2.** Flow over a backward-facing step: computational performance.

| Methods | $Re = 500$ | | | $Re = 800$ | | | $Re = 1000$ | | |
|---|---|---|---|---|---|---|---|---|---|
| | $\#LI$ | $\#NLI$ | $Time(s)$ | $\#LI$ | $\#NLI$ | $Time(s)$ | $\#LI$ | $\#NLI$ | $Time(s)$ |
| NSGS-NS | 3972 | 52 | 245.32 | 6946 | 84 | 540.14 | 8719 | 101 | 734.31 |
| SUPG/PSPG | 22609 | 50 | 1247.06 | 47134 | 74 | 2257.29 | 63407 | 83 | 3271.85 |

### 4.2 The Lid-Driven Cavity Flow

The 2D lid-driven cavity flow problem has been widely used as a benchmark for numerical methods and has been analyzed by a number of authors [14,20]. The standard case is fluid contained in a square domain with Dirichlet boundary conditions on all sides, with three stationary sides and one moving side at the top, see Fig. 5. There are no body forces and the pressure is prescribed to be zero at the bottom left corner of the cavity. Here the domain is $\Omega = (0,1)^2$ and to avoid the irregularity of the solution at the upper corners [16], the horizontal velocity at the top side is given by

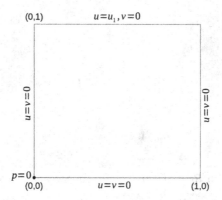

**Fig. 5.** The lid-driven cavity problem description.

$$
u_1(x) = \begin{cases} 1 - \frac{1}{4}\left(1 - \cos\left((0.1 - 1x)10\pi\right)\right)^2 & \text{for } x \in [0, 0.1], \\ 1 & \text{for } x \in (0.1, 0.9), \\ 1 - \frac{1}{4}\left(1 - \cos\left((x - 0.9)10\pi\right)\right)^2 & \text{for } x \in [0.9, 1]. \end{cases}
$$

As a result of the moving top side of the cavity, a recirculation region is developed that bears a primary vortex in the middle of the cavity and additional secondary vortices in the corners of the cavity. Figure 6 shows the streamlines and pressure isolines for the NSGS-NS method with $Re = 10000$ and $Re = 20000$, using a linear triangular finite element mesh with 14641 nodes. Our streamlines results show excellent agreement with the high accuracy experiments presented in [14, 20]. For $Re = 10000$, our pressure isolines are comparable with the ones presented in [20]. In Fig. 7, we present the horizontal velocity along the vertical line $x = 0.5$ and the vertical velocity along the horizontal line $y = 0.5$. Comparing the NSGS-NS solutions with the given reference solutions in [14] (black points), one can clearly see perfect agreement between the solutions. We can also observe in Fig. 7 that the SUPG/PSPG solutions do not present good agreement with the reference solutions.

Table 3 shows the computational performance of NSGS-NS and SUPG/PSPG methods in terms of nonlinear iterations ($\#NLI$), GMRES iterations ($\#LI$) and CPU time in seconds ($Time$). As we can see, the NSGS-NS nonlinear iterative process does not converge without the damping factor process with both Reynolds numbers. In the SUPG/PSPG method, the dynamic choice is not necessary for convergence of the iterative processes, but the algorithm significantly reduces the CPU time improving the computational performance of the method.

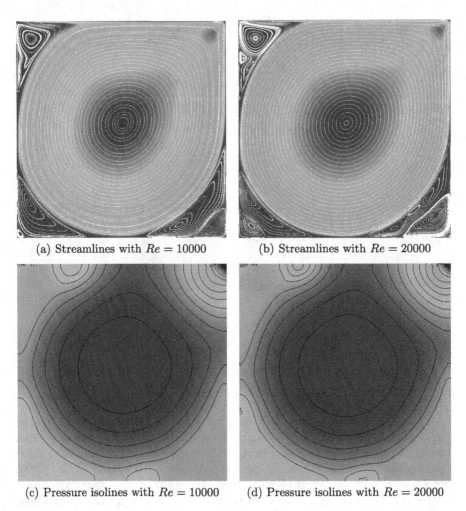

(a) Streamlines with $Re = 10000$    (b) Streamlines with $Re = 20000$

(c) Pressure isolines with $Re = 10000$    (d) Pressure isolines with $Re = 20000$

**Fig. 6.** The lid-driven cavity flow: streamlines and pressure isolines for the NSGS-NS method with $Re = 10000$ and $Re = 20000$.

Figure 8 shows the damping factor values required in each nonlinear iteration for both methods. In the SUPG/PSPG method, the damping factor increases in the course of the iterative process with only one rejection at the first iteration. Thus, the maximum possible number of iterations occurs in the beginning of the process improving the efficiency of the nonlinear iteration scheme. In the NSGS-NS method, there are some rejections but the dynamic process does not reduce the damping factor to the lower bound, $\omega_{min} = 0.05$. Observe also that, the strong damping necessary at the beginning of the iterative process slightly influences the damping at the end.

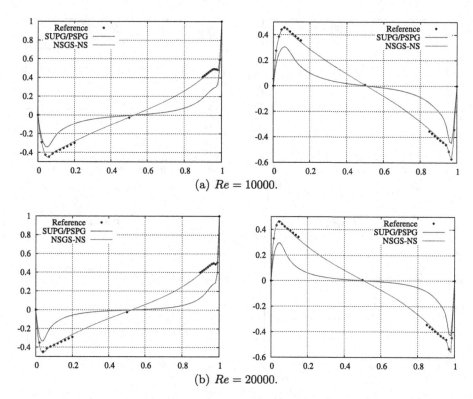

(a) $Re = 10000$.

(b) $Re = 20000$.

**Fig. 7.** The lid-driven cavity problem. Left: horizontal velocity along $x = 0.5, 0 \leq y \leq 1$, right: vertical velocity along $y = 0.5, 0 \leq x \leq 1$, (a) $Re = 10000$ and (b) $Re = 20000$.

**Table 3.** Performance computational. The lid-driven cavity flow.

| Methods | $Re = 10000$ | | | $Re = 20000$ | | |
|---|---|---|---|---|---|---|
| *With damping factor* | #LI | #NLI | Time(s) | #LI | #NLI | Time(s) |
| NSGS-NS | 6300 | 84 | 150.13 | 14898 | 205 | 360.09 |
| SUPG/PSPG | 858 | 21 | 27.07 | 1020 | 24 | 35.76 |
| *Without damping factor* | #LI | #NLI | Time(s) | #LI | #NLI | Time(s) |
| NSGS-NS | † | † | † | † | † | † |
| SUPG/PSPG | 1316 | 32 | 41.63 | 1820 | 42 | 61.19 |

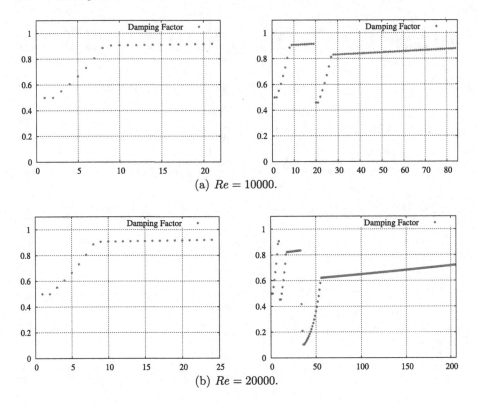

**Fig. 8.** The lid-driven cavity flow. Damping factor in each nonlinear iteration. Left: SUPG/PSPG method, right: NSGS-NS method, (a) $Re = 10000$ and (b) $Re = 20000$.

## 5    Conclusions

We evaluated the computational performance of the Nonlinear Subgrid Stabilization parameter-free method (NSGS-NS) [3] to solve the incompressible Navier-Stokes equations at high Reynolds numbers. The formulation considers a two-scale decomposition only of the velocity field, into coarse/resolved scales and fine/unresolved scales. Furthermore, we use a dynamic damping factor to improve the convergence of the nonlinear iterative process, in order to be able to solve flows at high Reynolds numbers.

With two 2D benchmark problems, we compare the proposed methodology with the SUPG/PSPG approach presented in [12,29]. In our studies, we investigate the backward facing step problem and the lid-driven cavity flow, at high Reynolds numbers. The solutions are compared with high accuracy experiments presented in the literature, the computational performance of both methods are presented and the efficiency of dynamic damping factor algorithm analyzed. We observed that, at all Reynolds numbers, our NSGS-NS solutions for both problems are in excellent agreement with the references. In particular, the SUPG/PSPG nonlinear iterations consume more linear iterations and

CPU time than the corresponding NSGS-NS solutions in the backward-facing problem. Therefore, the NSGS-NS method is computationally more efficient in this example. However, in the cavity problem, the NSGS-NS nonlinear iterative process does not converge without the damping factor process with both Reynolds numbers. In the SUPG/PSPG method, the damping algorithm significantly reduces the CPU time improving the computational performance of the method. Following the work presented here, we intend to extend the NSGS-NS method to transient problems and compressible flows given by the Navier-Stokes equations.

# References

1. Armaly, B.F., Durst, F., Pereira, J., Schönung, B.: Experimental and theoretical investigation of backward-facing step flow. J. Fluid Mech. **127**, 473–496 (1983)
2. Arnold, D.N., Brezzi, F., Fortin, M.: A stable finite element for the stokes equations. Calcolo **21**(4), 337–344 (1984)
3. Baptista, R., Bento, S.S., Santos, I.P., Lima, L.M., Valli, A.M.P., Catabriga, L.: A multiscale finite element formulation for the incompressible Navier-Stokes equations. In: Gervasi, O., et al. (eds.) ICCSA 2018. LNCS, vol. 10961, pp. 253–267. Springer, Cham (2018). https://doi.org/10.1007/978-3-319-95165-2_18
4. Bazilevs, Y., Calo, V., Cottrell, J., Hughes, T., Reali, A., Scovazzi, G.: Variational multiscale residual-based turbulence modeling for large eddy simulation of incompressible flows. Comput. Methods Appl. Mech. Eng. **197**(1–4), 173–201 (2007)
5. Brenner, S.C., Scott, L.R.: The Mathematical Theory of Finite Element Methods. Texts in Applied Mathematics. Springer, New York (2002)
6. Brezzi, F.: On the existence, uniqueness and approximation of saddle-point problems arising from lagrangian multipliers. ESAIM: Math. Model. Numer. Anal. - Modélisation Mathématique et Analyse Numérique **8**(R2), 129–151 (1974)
7. Brezzi, F., Bristeau, M., Franca, L., Mallet, M., Roge, G.: A relationship between stabilized finite element methods and the Galerkin method with bubble functions. Comput. Methods Appl. Mech. Eng. **96**(1), 117–129 (1992)
8. Brooks, A.N., Hughes, T.J.R.: Streamline Upwind/Petrov-Galerkin formulations for convection dominated flows with particular emphasis on the incompressible Navier-Stokes equations. Comput. Methods Appl. Mech. Eng. **32**, 199–259 (1982)
9. Calo, V.M.: Residual-based multiscale turbulence modeling: finite volume simulations of bypass transition. Ph.D. thesis, Stanford University (2005)
10. Codina, R., Blasco, J.: A stabilized finite element method for generalized stationary incompressible flows. Comput. Methods Appl. Mech. Eng. **190**, 2681–2706 (2001)
11. Codina, R., Badia, S., Baiges, J., Principe, J.: Variational Multiscale Methods in Computational Fluid Dynamics, pp. 1–28. American Cancer Society (2017)
12. Elias, R.N., Coutinho, A.L.G.A., Martins, M.A.D.: Inexact Newton-type methods for non-linear problems arising from the SUPG/PSPG solution of steady incompressible Navier-Stokes equations. J. Braz. Soc. Mech. Sci. Eng. **26**, 330–339 (2004)
13. Erturk, E.: Numerical solutions of 2-D steady incompressible flow over a backward-facing step, part i: high reynolds number solutions. Comput. Fluids **37**(6), 633–655 (2008)
14. Erturk, E., Corke, T.C., Gökçöl, C.: Numerical solutions of 2-D steady incompressible driven cavity flow at high reynolds numbers. Int. J. Numer. Methods Fluids **48**(7), 747–774 (2005)

15. Franca, L., Farhat, C.: Unusual stabilized finite element methods and residual free bubbles. Comput. Methods Appl. Mech. Eng. **123**(1–4), 299–308 (1995)
16. de Frutos, J., John, V., Novo, J.: Projection methods for incompressible flow problems with weno finite difference schemes. J. Comput. Phys. **309**, 368–386 (2016)
17. Gartling, D.K.: A test problem for outflow boundary conditions-flow over a backward-facing step. Int. J. Numer. Methods Fluids **11**(7), 953–967 (1990)
18. Geuzaine, C., Remacle, J.F.: Gmsh: a 3-D finite element mesh generator with built-in pre- and post-processing facilities. Int. J. Numer. Methods Eng. **79**(11), 1309–1331 (2009)
19. Gravemeier, V.: The variational multiscale method for laminar and turbulent flow. Arch. Comput. Methods Eng. **13**(2), 249 (2006)
20. Hachem, E., Rivaux, B., Kloczko, T., Digonnet, H., Coupez, T.: Stabilized finite element method for incompressible flows with high reynolds number. J. Comput. Phys. **229**(23), 8643–8665 (2010)
21. Hood, P., Taylor, C.: Navier-stokes equations using mixed interpolation. In: Finite Element Methods in Flow Problems, pp. 121–132 (1974)
22. Hughes, T.J.R.: Multiscale phenomena: green's functions, the Dirichlet-to-Neumann formulation, subgrid scale models, bubbles and the origins of stabilized methods. Comput. Methods Appl. Mech. Eng. **127**(1–4), 387–401 (1995)
23. Hughes, T.J., Franca, L.P., Balestra, M.: A new finite element formulation for computational fluid dynamics. v. circumventingthe Babuska-Brezzi condition: a stable Petrov-Galerkin formulation of the Stokes problem accommodating equal-order interpolations. Comput. Methods Appl. Mech. Eng. **59**, 85–99 (1986)
24. Hughes, T., Tezduyar, T.: Finite element methods for first-order hyperbolic systems with particular emphasis on the compressible Euler equations. Comput. Methods Appl. Mech. Eng. **45**, 217–284 (1984)
25. John, V., Knobloch, P.: On spurious oscillations at layers diminishing (SOLD) methods for convection-diffusion equations: part ii-analysis for P1 and Q1 finite elements. Comput. Methods Appl. Mech. Eng. **197**(21–24), 1997–2014 (2008)
26. Lins, E.F., Elias, R.N., Guerra, G.M., Rochinha, F.A., Coutinho, A.L.G.A.: Edge-based finite element implementation of the residual-based variational multiscale method. Int. J. Numer. Methods Fluids **61**(1), 1–22 (2009)
27. Masud, A., Khurram, R.: A multiscale finite element method for the incompressible Navier-Stokes equations. Comput. Methods Appl. Mech. Eng. **195**(13–16), 1750–1777 (2006)
28. Santos, I.P., Almeida, R.C.: A nonlinear subgrid method for advection-diffusion problems. Comput. Methods Appl. Mech. Eng. **196**, 4771–4778 (2007)
29. Tezduyar, T.E.: Adaptive determination of the finite element stabilization parameters. In: Proceedings of the ECCOMAS Computational Fluid Dynamics Conference, September 2001
30. Valli, A.M., Almeida, R.C., Santos, I.P., Catabriga, L., Malta, S.M., Coutinho, A.L.: A parameter-free dynamic diffusion method for advection-diffusion-reaction problems. Comput. Math. Appl. **75**(1), 307–321 (2018)

# Local Preconditioning Techniques Coupled with a Variational Multiscale Method to Solve Compressible Steady Flows at Low Mach Numbers

Sérgio Souza Bento[1]($\boxtimes$) , Leonardo Muniz de Lima[3] , Isaac P. Santos[1,2] , and Lucia Catabriga[2]

[1] Department of Applied Mathematics, Federal University of Espírito Santo, São Mateus, ES, Brazil
{sergio.bento,isaac.santos}@ufes.br
[2] High Performance Computing Lab, Federal University of Espírito Santo, Vitória, ES, Brazil
luciac@inf.ufes.br
[3] Department of Mechanical Engineering, Federal Institute of Espírito Santo, Aracruz, ES, Brazil
lmuniz@ifes.edu.br

**Abstract.** In this work we evaluate a combination of the Weiss-Smith and Choi-Merkle local preconditioners coupled with the density-based Nonlinear Multiscale Viscosity (NMV) finite element method for solving steady compressible flows at low Mach numbers. The multiscale formulation is based on the strategy of separating scales, in which the subgrid scale space is spanned by bubble functions, allowing to use a static condensation procedure in the local matrix system to define the resolved scale problem. Also, a residual-based nonlinear viscosity operator is added to the Galerkin formulation in order to obtain a stabilized formulation. As density-based methods do not work well in problems with Mach numbers tending to zero, resulting in a degradation of the solution accuracy, the resulting numerical method gathering those two approaches allows to solve compressible flows in the incompressible limit. We evaluate this methodology simulating a steady flow over the NACA 0012 airfoil under some regimes of inflow Mach numbers. The numerical result exhibits promising solutions to compressible flow problems in the incompressible limit.

**Keywords:** Local preconditioning · Compressible flows · Multiscale formulation

## 1 Introduction

It is well known that numerical formulations based on conservation variables for solving the compressible Euler equations are not suitable when the flow is

© Springer Nature Switzerland AG 2019
S. Misra et al. (Eds.): ICCSA 2019, LNCS 11621, pp. 149–164, 2019.
https://doi.org/10.1007/978-3-030-24302-9_12

in the incompressible limit, that is, when density variations are negligible [4,7]. This difficulty is caused by the very different magnitude of the wave speeds present in the system. Obviously, this problem can be overcome by writing the incompressible form of the governing equations. However, in some situation it is important to work with compressible flow solver since the numerical simulations should ideally cover a wider range of flow regime, for example, in wind turbine applications.

One way to overcome the difficulties of the numerical methods for flow at low Mach numbers is to use local preconditioning techniques, whose goal is the uniformization of the characteristic propagation speeds of the system [3,5,7]. Local preconditioning or preconditioning mass matrix scheme consists of premultiplying the time derivatives by a properly preconditioned matrix, modifying the time-marching behavior of the equations without altering the steady state solutions [3,7].

Besides the reduction of the stiffness of the system of equations, local preconditioning also improves accuracy at low speed and the convergence of the numerical formulation. However, the major drawback of these methodologies is their reduced capacity to perform robust computations in stagnation point regions difficulting their use in an industrial context [3]. To overcome these robustness issues, Colin et al. [3] have studied, in the context of finite volume method, a robust low speed preconditioning formulation for viscous flows, called WSCM (Weiss-Smith/Choi-Merkle) preconditioner. This preconditioner is based on the Weiss-Smith (WS) [9] and on the CM [2,4] preconditioners. The change of a parameter in the WSCM method allows to recover the methods WS and CM.

Bento et al. [1] proposed a nonlinear multiscale finite element method, called NMV (*Nonlinear Multiscale Viscosity*) method, for solving compressible flows. The method presents good results for flows in transonic and supersonic regimes, but suffers severe deficiencies when the flow is in the incompressible limit, since it is based on conservation variables.

In this work we combine the NMV method with the Weiss-Smith/Choi-Merkle (WSCM) local preconditioner, presented in [3], for solving compressible flows at low Mach numbers. The numerical experiments show that this numerical methodology yields good results.

The remainder of this work is organized as follows. In Sect. 2 we present the governing equations, whereas in Sect. 3 we describe the variational multiscale formulation. The local preconditioner WSCM is briefly addressed in Sect. 4 and the numerical experiments are presented in Sect. 5. Finally, the conclusions are presented in Sect. 6.

## 2  Governing Equations

We consider the two-dimensional compressible Euler equations for an ideal gas write in conservative variables without source terms as,

$$\frac{\partial \mathbf{U}}{\partial t} + \nabla \cdot \mathbf{F}(\mathbf{U}) = \mathbf{0}, \quad \text{in } \Omega \times (0, T_f], \tag{1}$$

where $T_f$ is a positive real number, representing the final time and $\Omega$ is a domain in $\mathbb{R}^2$, with boundary $\Gamma$, $\mathbf{U} \in \mathbb{R}^4$ is the vector of conservative variables, and $\mathbf{F}(\mathbf{U}) \in \mathbb{R}^{4 \times 2}$, is the Euler flux vector. Here,

$$\mathbf{U} = \begin{bmatrix} U_1 \\ U_2 \\ U_3 \\ U_4 \end{bmatrix} = \rho \begin{bmatrix} 1 \\ u \\ v \\ E \end{bmatrix}, \tag{2}$$

where $\rho$ is the fluid density, $\mathbf{u} = [u \; v]^T$ is the velocity vector, $\rho E$ is the total energy, $E$ is the total specific energy. Other important physical variables are the pressure $p$ and the Mach number $M = \frac{\|\mathbf{u}\|}{c}$, where $c = \sqrt{\gamma \frac{p}{\rho}}$ is the speed of sound, with $\gamma = \frac{c_p}{c_v}$ ($\gamma > 1$) being the ratio of specific heats, $c_p$ and $c_v$ are the coefficients of specific heat at constant pressure and volume, respectively, and $\| \cdot \|$ is the Euclidean norm. The system (1) is closed by the equation of state

$$p = (\gamma - 1)\left(\rho E - \frac{\rho}{2}\|\mathbf{u}\|^2\right). \tag{3}$$

Alternatively, Eq. (1) can be rewritten as in the quasi-linear form:

$$\frac{\partial \mathbf{U}}{\partial t} + \mathbf{A_x}\frac{\partial \mathbf{U}}{\partial x} + \mathbf{A_y}\frac{\partial \mathbf{U}}{\partial y} = \mathbf{0}, \quad \text{in } \Omega \times (0, T_f], \tag{4}$$

where $\mathbf{A}_x = \frac{\partial \mathbf{F}_x}{\partial \mathbf{U}}$ and $\mathbf{A}_y = \frac{\partial \mathbf{F}_y}{\partial \mathbf{U}}$ are the Jacobian matrices. Associated with Eq. (4) we have a proper set of boundary and initial conditions to complete the mathematical model,

$$\mathbf{BU} = \mathbf{Z}, \quad \text{on } \Gamma \times (0, T_f], \tag{5}$$
$$\mathbf{U}(\mathbf{x}, t) = \mathbf{U}_0, \tag{6}$$

where $\mathbf{B}$ denotes a general boundary operator, and $\mathbf{Z}$ and $\mathbf{U}_0$ are given functions.

## 3   The Variational Multiscale Formulation

To define the multiscale finite element method for Euler equations, we consider a triangular partition $\mathcal{T}_h$ of the domain $\Omega$ into $n_{el}$ elements, where $\Omega = \bigcup_{e=1}^{n_{el}} \Omega_e$ with $\Omega_i \cap \Omega_j = \emptyset$, for $i, j = 1, 2, \ldots, n_{el}$ and $i \neq j$. The function space $\mathcal{V}_{Zhb}$ is defined as the direct sum,

$$\mathcal{V}_{Zhb} = \mathcal{V}_{Zh} \oplus \mathcal{V}_b, \tag{7}$$

where the subspaces $\mathcal{V}_{Zh}$ and $\mathcal{V}_b$ are given by

$$\mathcal{V}_{Zh} = \{\mathbf{U}_h \in [H^1(\Omega)]^4; \quad \mathbf{U}_h|_{\Omega_e} \in [\mathbb{P}_1(\Omega_e)]^4, \mathbf{BU}_h = \mathbf{Z} \text{ on } \Gamma_D\}, \tag{8}$$
$$\mathcal{V}_b = \{\mathbf{U}_b \in [H_0^1(\Omega)]^4; \quad \mathbf{U}_b|_{\Omega_e} \in [span(\psi_b)]^4, \; \forall \; \Omega_e \in \mathcal{T}_h\}, \tag{9}$$

with $\mathbb{P}_1(\Omega_e)$ representing the set of first order polynomials in $\Omega_e$, $H^1(\Omega)$ denotes the Sobolev space of square-integrable functions whose first derivatives are also square-integrable, $H_0^1(\Omega)$ is a space of function in $H^1(\Omega)$ that vanish at the boundary of $\Omega$, and $\psi_b$ is a bubble function. The space $\mathcal{V}_{Zh}$ represents the resolved (coarse) scale space whereas $\mathcal{V}_b$ stands for the subgrid (fine) scale space.

The Nonlinear Multiscale Viscosity (NMV) method, presented in [1], adds a nonlinear artificial viscosity operator to the Galerkin formulation, acting isotropically in all scales of the discretization. The amount of artificial viscosity is given according to the YZ$\beta$ shock-capturing viscosity method [8]. The NMV method for the Euler equation consists of finding $\mathbf{U}_{hb} = \mathbf{U}_h + \mathbf{U}_b \in \mathcal{V}_{Zhb}$ with $\mathbf{U}_h \in \mathcal{V}_{Zh}$, $\mathbf{U}_b \in \mathcal{V}_b$ such that

$$
\int_\Omega \mathbf{W}_{hb} \cdot \left( \frac{\partial \mathbf{U}_{hb}}{\partial t} + \mathbf{A}_x^h \frac{\partial \mathbf{U}_{hb}}{\partial x} + \mathbf{A}_y^h \frac{\partial \mathbf{U}_{hb}}{\partial y} \right) d\Omega +
$$

$$
\sum_{e=1}^{n_{el}} \int_{\Omega_e} \delta_h(\mathbf{U}_h) \left( \frac{\partial \mathbf{W}_{hb}}{\partial x} \cdot \frac{\partial \mathbf{U}_{hb}}{\partial x} + \frac{\partial \mathbf{W}_{hb}}{\partial y} \cdot \frac{\partial \mathbf{U}_{hb}}{\partial y} \right) d\Omega = \mathbf{0}, \forall\, \mathbf{W}_{hb} \in \mathcal{V}_{0hb}, (10)
$$

where $\mathbf{W}_{hb} = \mathbf{W}_h + \mathbf{W}_b \in \mathcal{V}_{0hb}$ with $\mathbf{W}_h \in \mathcal{V}_{0h}$, $\mathbf{W}_b \in \mathcal{V}_b$ and the amount of artificial viscosity, $\delta_h(\mathbf{U}_h)$, is calculated on the element-level by using the YZ$\beta$ shock-capturing viscosity parameter [8],

$$
\delta_h(\mathbf{U}_h) = \| \mathbf{Y}^{-1} R(\mathbf{U}_h) \| \left( \sum_{i=1}^2 \left\| \mathbf{Y}^{-1} \frac{\partial \mathbf{U}_h}{\partial x_i} \right\|^2 \right)^{\frac{\beta}{2}-1} \| \mathbf{Y}^{-1} \mathbf{U}_h \|^{1-\beta} h^\beta, \quad (11)
$$

where

$$
R(\mathbf{U}_h) = \frac{\partial \mathbf{U}_h}{\partial t} + \mathbf{A}_x^h \frac{\partial \mathbf{U}_h}{\partial x} + \mathbf{A}_y^h \frac{\partial \mathbf{U}_h}{\partial y} \tag{12}
$$

is the residue of the problem on $\Omega_e$, $\mathbf{Y}$ is a diagonal matrix constructed from the reference values of the components of $\mathbf{U}$, $h$ is the local length scale defined as follow $h = \left( \sum_{a=1}^3 |\mathbf{j} \cdot \nabla N_a| \right)^{-1}$, $\mathbf{j}$ is a unit vector defined as $\mathbf{j} = \nabla\rho / \|\nabla\rho\|$ and $N_a$ is the interpolation function associated with node $a$. The local length $h$ is defined automatically taking into account the directions of high gradients and spatial discretization domain.

The numerical solution is defined considering iterative procedures for space and time. Given $\mathbf{U}_{hb}^i$ at iteration $i$, the nonlinear iterative procedure finds $\mathbf{U}_{hb}^{i+1}$ satisfying the formulation (10), where YZ$\beta$ shock-capturing viscosity parameter is function of the iteration $i$ $(\delta_h(\mathbf{U}_h^i))$. The numerical solution is advanced in time by the predictor-corrector algorithm given in [6] and adapted for the multiscale framework in [1] for the Euler equations.

## 4    Local Preconditioner for the Euler Equations

Local preconditioning or preconditioning mass matrix scheme consists of premultiplying the time derivatives by a properly matrix in order to uniform the eigenvalues, smoothing the discrepancy of the different time scales. It is applied to the set of continuous equations before any discretization is done. Denoting by **P** the (nonsingular) preconditioning matrix, then the system of Eq. (4) after the preconditioning process reads

$$\mathbf{P}^{-1}\frac{\partial \mathbf{U}}{\partial t} + \mathbf{A_x}\frac{\partial \mathbf{U}}{\partial x} + \mathbf{A_y}\frac{\partial \mathbf{U}}{\partial y} = 0$$

or

$$\frac{\partial \mathbf{U}}{\partial t} + \mathbf{PA_x}\frac{\partial \mathbf{U}}{\partial x} + \mathbf{PA_y}\frac{\partial \mathbf{U}}{\partial y} = 0, \quad \text{in } \Omega \times (0, t_f]. \tag{13}$$

The solutions of problems (4) and (13) evolve in time differently, but converge in time to the same steady-state solution, since the time derivatives go to zero.

In this work we study a combination of the Weiss-Smith (WS) [9] and Choi-Merkle (CM) [2,4] local preconditioners, presented in [3] with the name WSCM method. An explicit expression for the WSCM preconditioner in conservative variables [3] is

$$\mathbf{P} = \mathbf{I} + \alpha \begin{bmatrix} \theta & -u & -v & 1 \\ u\theta & -uu & -uv & u \\ v\theta & -uv & -vv & v \\ H\theta & -uH & -vH & H \end{bmatrix}, \tag{14}$$

where

$$\alpha = \frac{\gamma - 1}{c^2}\left[(1 - \delta)\epsilon - 1\right], \qquad \theta = \frac{1}{2}\|u\|^2 + \delta\frac{\epsilon c^2}{(\gamma - 1)[(1 - \delta)\epsilon - 1]} \tag{15}$$

and $H$ is the total enthalpy. For Euler equations, the preconditioning parameter $\epsilon$ is given by

$$\epsilon = \min\left\{1, \max\left\{M_{lim}^2, M^2, \sigma_{pgr}\frac{|\Delta p|}{\rho c^2}\right\}\right\},$$

where $M_{lim}^2 = 10^{-5}$, $\sigma_{pgr} = 2$. We define the maximum pressure variation ($\Delta p$) on the triangle as

$$|\Delta p| = \max\{|p_1 - p_2|, |p_1 - p_3|, |p_2 - p_3|\}, \tag{16}$$

where $p_i$ is the pressure on the node $i = 1, 2, 3$. The value of the parameter $\delta \in [0, 1]$ can define different preconditioners:

$$\delta = 0 \rightarrow \text{Weiss-Smith (WS) preconditioner;}$$
$$\delta = 1 \rightarrow \text{Choi-Merkle (CM) preconditioner;}$$
$$\delta \in (0, 1) \rightarrow \text{Weiss-Smith/Choi-Merkle (WSCM) preconditioner.}$$

## 5   Numerical Experiments

The flow over an airfoil is an attractive problem to analyze the numerical instability arising from low Mach number values, that occurs in several flow regimes modeled by Euler equations. This section shows the results of a flow passing through a NACA 0012 airfoil at an angle of attack of $0°$ and varying the inflow Mach number, $M = 0.001, 0.01, 0.1$, and $0.3$.

The experiment was executed taking into account an unstructured triangular mesh of 5,606 elements and 2,886 nodes, in the computational domain given by a circle centered at the $(0,0)$ with radius 15, as shown in Fig. 1. Aiming to avoid numerical instabilities of reflecting waves, we consider a prudent distance from the airfoil to the inflow and outflow boundaries [5]. The inflow data is set up by

$$
inflow \begin{cases} \rho & = 1.0; \\ u & = 1.0; \\ v & = 0.0; \\ \mathsf{T} & = 1.0, \end{cases} \tag{17}
$$

where $\mathsf{T}$ is the temperature.

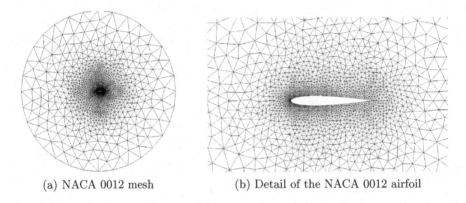

(a) NACA 0012 mesh                    (b) Detail of the NACA 0012 airfoil

**Fig. 1.** Unstructured triangular mesh of 5,606 elements and 2,886 nodes.

The numerical solution is advanced in time by the predictor-corrector algorithm adapted for the multiscale framework in [1] for the Euler equations. A restarted version of the GMRES solver is used to find the solution of the linearized system in each nonlinear and time iterations. We set 30 vectors to Krylov subspace base and $10^{-5}$ to solver tolerance. The time-step size is $10^{-3}$ and the simulation runs until $t_f = 20.0$ (20,000 steps), and 3 fixed nonlinear iterations. In this example, we evaluate the (density-based) NMV method [1] combined with the WSCM (Weiss-Smith/Choi-Merkle) local preconditioner for solving this benchmark problem. We vary the parameter $\delta \in \{0, 0.5, 1\}$ in order to recover the methods WS and CM. In the experiments we call NMV(WS), NMV(CM), and NMV(WSCM), for $\delta = 0$, $\delta = 1$ and $\delta = 0.5$, respectively, and by NMV(NP) the non-preconditioned case. The tests are carried out with the intention of analyzing accuracy issues, specially in the incompressibility limit. Since the flow at low speed presents an incompressible behavior, i.e., the density variation is almost negligible, we use the pressure contour to analyze this experiment.

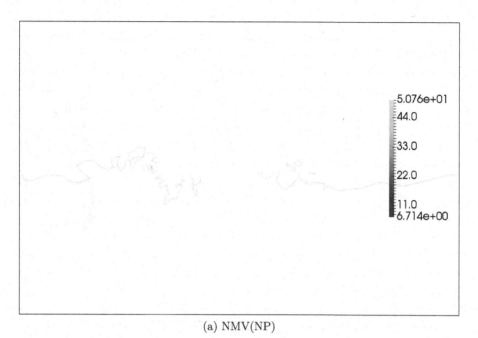

(a) NMV(NP)

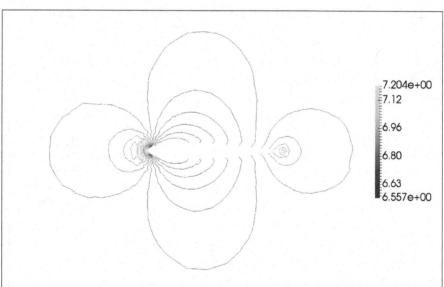

(b) NMV(WS)

**Fig. 2.** NACA 0012: Pressure contours for $M = 0.001$ at the inflow. In this experiment are plotted the contour of $p - p_{ref}$ with $p_{ref} = 714,279$, because the variation of pressure is very small.

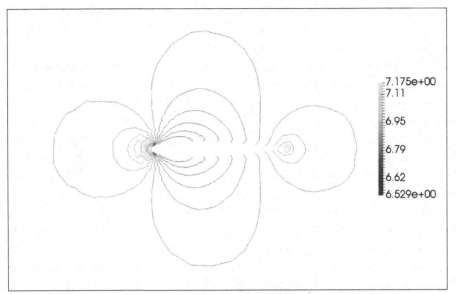

(c) NMV(CM)

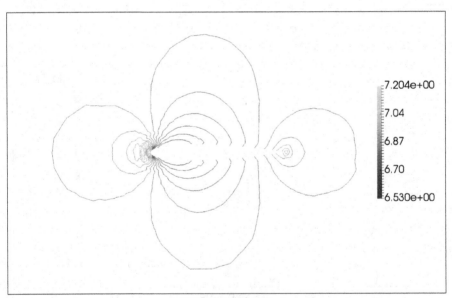

(d) NMV(WSCM)

**Fig. 2.** (*continued*)

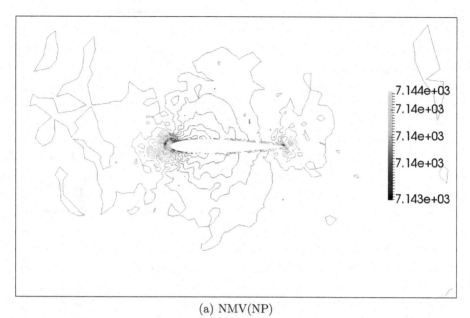

(a) NMV(NP)

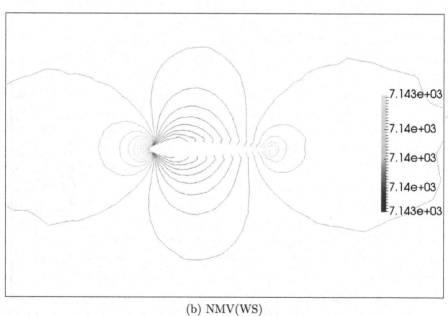

(b) NMV(WS)

**Fig. 3.** NACA 0012: Pressure contours for $M = 0.01$ at the inflow.

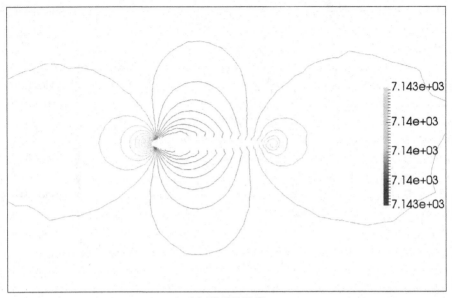

(c) NMV(CM)

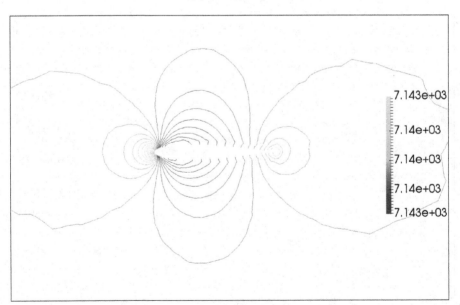

(d) NMV(WSCM)

**Fig. 3.** (*continued*)

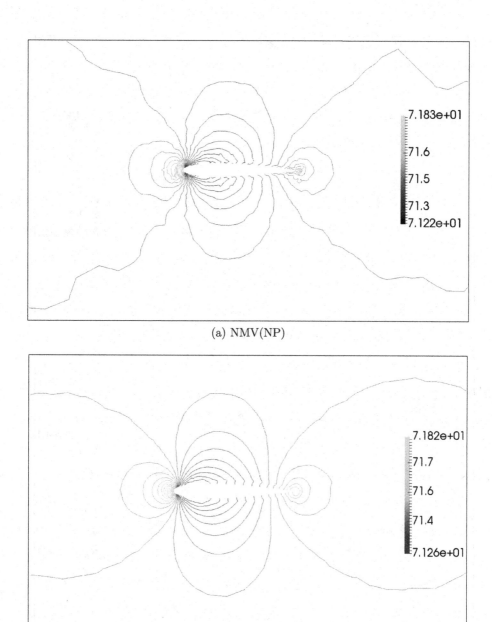

(a) NMV(NP)

(b) NMV(WS)

**Fig. 4.** NACA 0012: Pressure contours for $M = 0.1$ at the inflow.

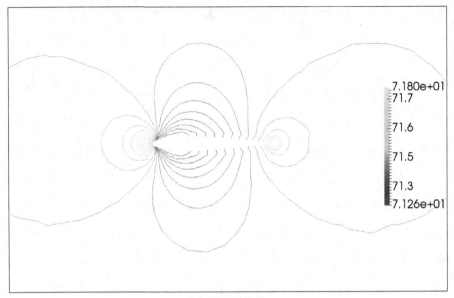

(c) NMV(CM)

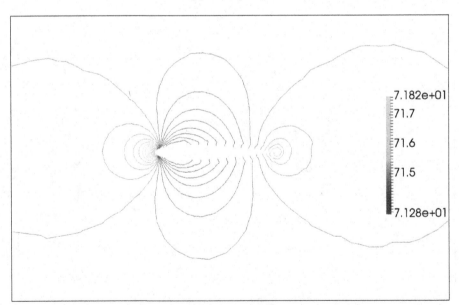

(d) NMV(WSCM)

**Fig. 4.** (*continued*)

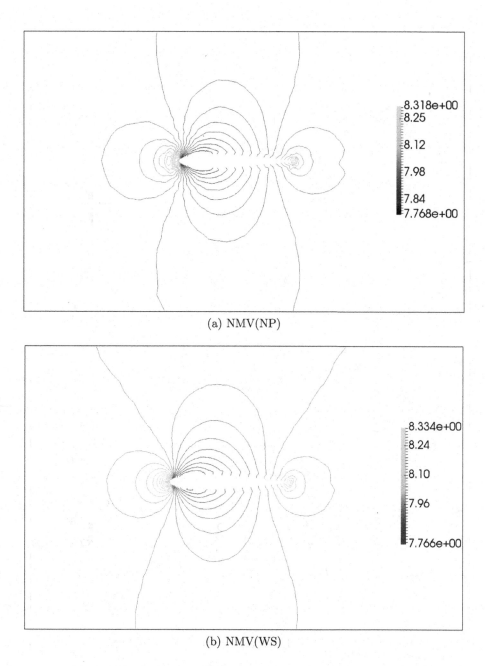

(a) NMV(NP)

(b) NMV(WS)

**Fig. 5.** NACA 0012: Pressure contours for $M = 0.3$ at the inflow.

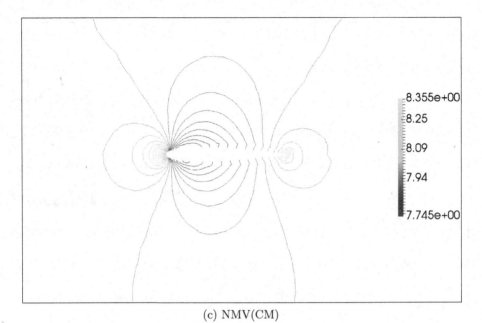

(c) NMV(CM)

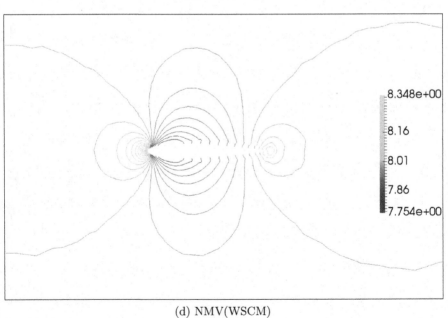

(d) NMV(WSCM)

**Fig. 5.** (*continued*)

Figures 2, 3, 4, and 5 show the pressure contours for inflow Mach numbers, $M = 0.001, 0.01, 0.1$, and $0.3$, respectively. As expected, the numerical solutions without local preconditioning, when the low Mach number approaches to zero, are completely oscillatory, as shown in Fig. 2(a) for $M = 0.001$, and Fig. 3(a) for $M = 0.01$.

On the other hand, the preconditioned formulation presents better results for this problem, as shown in Fig. 2(b)–(d), 3(b)–(d), 4(b)–(d), and 5(b)–(d). The three local preconditioners evaluated present good results for all inflow low Mach numbers simulated, but the WSCM preconditioner presented a slightly better solution in the transition regime, i.e., when $M = 0.3$, as we can see in Fig. 5(b)–(d).

## 6    Conclusions

We applied the NMV method coupled with the Weiss-Smith (WS), Choi-Merkle (CM), and Weiss-Smith/Choi-Merkle (WSCM) local preconditioners for solving the NACA 0012 airfoil problem at low Mach numbers. We simulated the flow over the NACA 0012 airfoil under the following regimes of inflow Mach numbers: 0.001; 0.01; 0.1; 0.3. The solutions obtained with the NMV without local preconditioning are completely oscillatory in the low Mach number limit (e.g. for $M = 0.001, 0.01$), since methods based on density variables fail in this case. On the other hand, our numerical methodology combined with local preconditioning exhibited promising results to this problem.

The study of other local preconditioning techniques and the extension of this methodology to compressible Navier-Stokes equations will be addressed in a further work.

**Acknowledgments.** The authors would like to thank the support through the Espírito Santo State Research Support Foundations (FAPES).

## References

1. Bento, S.S., de Lima, L.M., Sedano, R.Z., Catabriga, L., Santos, I.P.: A nonlinear multiscale viscosity method to solve compressible flow problems. In: Gervasi, O., et al. (eds.) ICCSA 2016. LNCS, vol. 9786, pp. 3–17. Springer, Cham (2016). https://doi.org/10.1007/978-3-319-42085-1_1

2. Choi, Y.H., Merkle, C.: The application of preconditioning in viscous flows. J. Comput. Phys. **105**(2), 207–223 (1993)

3. Colin, Y., Deniau, H., Boussuge, J.F.: A robust low speed preconditioning formulation for viscous flow computations. Comput. Fluids **47**(1), 1–15 (2011)

4. Ginard, M.M., Bernardino, G., Vázquez, M., Houzeaux, G.: Fourier stability analysis and local Courant number of the preconditioned variational multiscale stabilization (P-VMS) for Euler compressible flow. Comput. Methods Appl. Mech. Eng. **301**, 28–51 (2016)

5. Ginard, M.M., Vázquez, M., Houzeaux, G.: Local preconditioning and variational multiscale stabilization for Euler compressible steady flow. Comput. Methods Appl. Mech. Eng. **305**, 468–500 (2016)

6. Hughes, T.J.R., Tezduyar, T.E.: Finite element methods for first-order hyperbolic systems with particular emphasis on the compressible Euler equations. Comput. Methods Appl. Mech. Eng. **45**(1), 217–284 (1984)
7. Lopez, E.J., Nigro, N.M., Sarraf, S.S., Damián, S.M.: Stabilized finite element method based on local preconditioning for unsteady compressible flows in deformable domains with emphasis on the low Mach number limit application. Int. J. Numer. Methods Fluids **69**(1), 124–145 (2012)
8. Tezduyar, T.E., Senga, M.: Stabilization and shock-capturing parameters in SUPG formulation of compressible flows. Comput. Methods Appl. Mech. Eng. **195**(13–16), 1621–1632 (2006)
9. Weiss, J., Smith, W.: Preconditioning applied to variable and constant density flows. AIAA J. **33**(11), 2050–2057 (1995)

# Computational Optimization and Applications (COA 2019)

# Forecasting Wheat Prices Based on Past Behavior: Comparison of Different Modelling Approaches

Joana Dias[1,2(✉)] and Humberto Rocha[1,2]

[1] CeBER and Faculty of Economics, University of Coimbra, Coimbra, Portugal
joana@fe.uc.pt, hrocha@mat.uc.pt
[2] INESC-Coimbra, University of Coimbra, Coimbra, Portugal

**Abstract.** Being able to accurately forecast the evolution of wheat prices can be a valuable tool. Most of the published works apply classical forecasting models to wheat price time series, and they do not always perform out-of-sample testing. This work compares five modelling approaches for wheat price forecasts, using only past values of the time series. The models performance is assessed considering out-of-sample data only, by considering a sliding and growing time window that will define the data used to determine the models parameters, and the data used for out-of-sample forecasts.

**Keywords:** Agriculture · Machine learning · Price forecasting · Wheat

## 1 Introduction

According to the Food and Agriculture Organization of the United Nations (FAO), wheat is the most important grain source for humans, and it is grown in more land than any other commercial crop [1]. The demand has also increased due to its use as biofuels.

Wheat prices can be influenced by many different factors: competition in the main international wheat markets, existing regulations and policies, weather conditions, among other factors. Being able to develop models capable of accurately modelling and being able to explain wheat prices evolution is, thus, a difficult challenge. The United States (US) farm programs or the European Union Common Agricultural Policy are examples of policy factors influencing wheat production and price [2]. Brunner [3], examines the historical effects of El Niño on world primary commodity prices, reaching the conclusion that it has statistically significant economic effects. Hill et al. [4] evaluate the effect of using seasonal climate forecasts on international wheat economy. Ubilava [5] also follows this trend, reaching the conclusion that El Niño influences wheat prices.

In [6] the authors present an asymmetric-error generalized autoregressive conditional heteroscedasticity (GARCH) model, applying it to forecasts of U.S. soybean, sorghum and wheat prices. GARCH models can capture the phenomenon of volatility clustering, characterized by periods where the dependent variable presents high

© Springer Nature Switzerland AG 2019
S. Misra et al. (Eds.): ICCSA 2019, LNCS 11621, pp. 167–182, 2019.
https://doi.org/10.1007/978-3-030-24302-9_13

volatility, and others where the time series are almost constant. The authors use wheat prices from 1913 to 2000, adjusted for inflation.

Benavides [7] studies the volatility accuracy of volatility forecast models for wheat future prices returns, applying GARCH and ARCH models, and also an option implied and a composite forecast model. The authors recommend the use of the composite forecast model if both historical values and option implied volatility forecasts are available.

Yang et al. [2] study wheat future prices and volatility transmission for the United States, Canada and European Union in the period 1996 to 2002. They observe that Canadian prices are more influenced by the US prices than the other way around. Europe, on the other hand, appears to be self-dependent, having some influence on the US prices on the long run. The authors reach the conclusion that none of the three markets can be identified as being the international market leader.

In [8] the authors study the relationships among wheat prices from five different countries in the period 1981–1999. The objective is to discover dynamic causal relationships among these prices. Contradicting previous results, the authors reach the conclusion that US and Canada are leaders in these markets, with US having significant effects on the three markets other than Canada.

Roche and McQuinn [9] consider the Irish grain market and the influence of the British grain prices on Irish prices. The authors use a multivariate GARCH model, where relative effects of past variances and covariances are determined entirely by the data and are not decided by the user.

A season-average futures price forecasting model for corn, soybeans and wheat is presented in [10]. This model considers future prices, farm prices and marketing weights.

Jumah and Kunst [11] consider barley and wheat prices and study the use of seasonal models, since these grains are subject to seasonal variation due to the biological growth of the plant, related also to climatic factors. The authors observe that prices tend to increase in the first and fourth quarter of the year, and to fall in the third, although seasonal cycles are different for different countries.

Arshad and Hameed [12] investigate the relationships between cereal prices and petroleum prices. Data from 1980 to 2008 was considered, and the authors reached evidence of a long-run equilibrium relationship between the two product prices.

Algieri [13] develops a vector error correction model considering a broad range of explanatory variables: market-specific variables, macroeconomic variables, financial factors and weather conditions. The author considers data within the period 1980–2012. The author states that changes observed in wheat prices are like a roller coaster, and seem to be inconsistent with supply and demand fundamentals. Wheat price movements can be explained looking at speculation, global demand and real effective exchange rate. Speculation in the futures market is one of the reasons justifying wider price changes. Chen et al. [14] had already considered the effect of exchange rates in commodity prices. In [15] it is also possible to find the development of a structural vector autoregression model for wheat price variation, considering four structural factors: global real economic activity and commodity demand; wheat-specific supply and demand factors; speculative or precautionary demand; financial speculation, commodity index trading and comovement. The authors conclude that wheat price spikes can be mostly explained by shocks to current supply.

Ahumada and Cornejo [16] focus on three cereals: corn, soybeans and wheat. They try to improve the accuracy of price forecast models by explicitly using price cross-dependence among these products, considering equilibrium correction models.

There are not many examples in the literature of machine learning approaches applied to wheat price forecasting. Khamis and Abdullah [17] investigate the use of backpropagation neural networks and nonlinear autoregressive models with exogenous inputs networks to estimate the price of wheat using as inputs the prices of other three grains: oats, barley and soybeans. Historical values from 1978 to 2012 were used, and the authors concluded that the latter model performed better.

This paper presents a different approach for wheat price forecasting. The main goal is to be able to predict the monthly wheat prices for the next six months period using information on past prices only. A rolling window is considered, where prices that become known are incorporated into the training of the forecasting model, and new predictions are made for the next six months. Five different methods are tested: Autoregressive Integrated Moving Average (ARIMA) models, Classification and Regression Trees (CART), Random Forests (RF), Support Vector Machines (SVM) and Multivariate Adaptive Regression Splines (MARS). All the models are tested on out-of-sample data.

Section 2 describes the data used and an exploratory analysis is performed. The models that are used are also described. Section 3 presents the main computational results. Section 4 presents the main conclusions and paths for future research.

# 2  Materials and Methods

## 2.1  Data

According to the United States Wheat Associates, there are six classes of wheat grown in the United States that differ in color, hardness and growing season. In this work we consider the export prices of hard red winter wheat (accounting for about 40% of the total wheat production), delivered at the United States Gulf port for prompt or thirty days shipment. One of the decisions that has to be made is whether real prices or nominal prices should be modelled and predicted. Real prices (also known as constant prices) are indexed to a given year. All values are "deflated", meaning that the effect of the inflation with respect to that year is removed. Nominal prices (also known as current prices) include the effect of inflation. In this paper we choose to work with nominal prices. Monthly prices from February 1992 to February 2017 are considered. Figure 1 shows the price evolution during this time period. Looking at Fig. 1, it is not possible to clearly identify trends, cycles or seasonality. This is also the case looking at Fig. 2, where the three components of the time series are depicted: seasonal component, trend-cycle component, remainder component, considering an additive model based on [18] (STL decomposition). Figure 3 presents the same data but with all values of the same month plotted together. The horizontal lines indicate the mean value for each month. The plot is not particularly revealing, since there are not many differences for the different months.

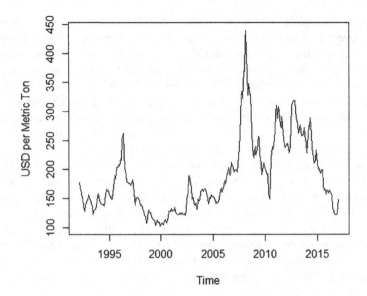

**Fig. 1.** Evolution of hard red winter wheat prices

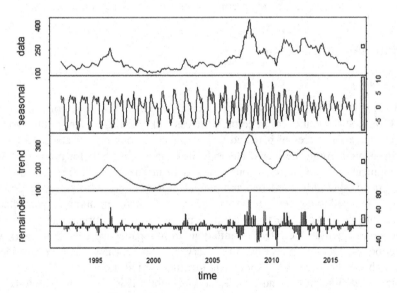

**Fig. 2.** STL decomposition

This work investigates the possibility of using forecasting models to predict monthly prices considering past information on prices only. It is thus important to understand whether there is a linear relationship between lagged values of this time series. One way of visually detecting autocorrelations is by looking at the Autocorrelation Function (ACF) and Partial Autocorrelation Function (PACF) plots. Defining as $y_t$ the value of the time series at time period $t$ and $y_{t-k}$ the value of the time series $k$ periods before, the ACF plot depicts the autocorrelations between $y_t$ and $y_{t-k}$ for different values for the lag $k$ (Fig. 4). As can be observed, the ACF declines very slowly. Up to 24 lags are statistically significantly different from zero.

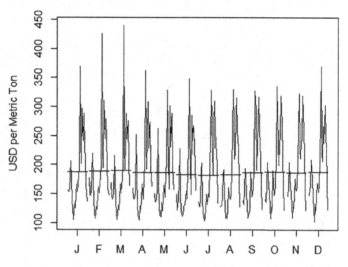

**Fig. 3.** Seasonal plot of monthly prices

The PACF measures the relationship between $y_t$ and $y_{t-k}$ after removing the effects of other time lags (from 1 to k $-$ 1). Figure 5 depicts the PACF plot. After the first lag, the PACF drops dramatically. Most PACFs after lag 2 are statistically insignificant. A stationary time series is such that its properties will not depend on the time of the observation. When a series is not stationary, it is possible to make it stationary by differencing. One way to determine if differencing can be beneficial is to use unit root tests. One of such tests is the Augmented Dickey-Fuller Test (ADF). The null-hypothesis for an ADF test is that the data are non-stationary. So large $p$-values are indicative of non-stationarity, and small $p$-values suggest stationarity. Using the usual 5% threshold, differencing is required if the $p$-value is greater than 0.05. Applying ADF test to this time series, the $p$-value is 0.14. Another popular unit root test is the Kwiatkowski-Phillips-Schmidt-Shin (KPSS) test. This reverses the hypotheses, so the null-hypothesis is that the data are stationary. In this case, small $p$-values (e.g., less than 0.05) suggest that differencing is required. In this case the $p$-value obtained is equal to 0.01. Figure 6 shows the series after first order differencing. This series is now stationary as can be concluded by looking at the ADF and KPSS tests, that present $p$ values equal to 0.01 and 0.10 respectively.

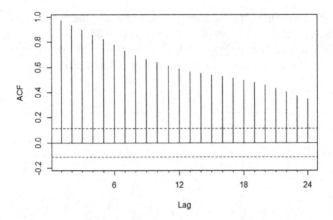

**Fig. 4.** ACF plot

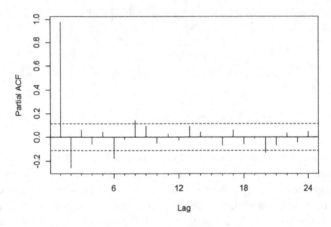

**Fig. 5.** PACF plot

## 2.2    Forecasting Models

In this paper five different forecasting models are used. All models were developed using $R$ language and libraries. The classical ARIMA model was applied to this time series. Four different machine learning models will also be applied, namely Classification and Regression Tree, Random Forests, Support Vector Machines and Multivariate Adaptive Regression Splines. Considering the machine learning frameworks, different models were developed for each of the forecasting horizons. This means that a model will be trained to forecast prices one month in advance, another model to forecast two months in advance, and so on. As most of these models have parameters that have to be fixed *a priori*, different parameters were tested and the model that presented the best cross validation (CV) error in the training set was chosen. The CV error is calculated by considering, within the training set, a sample set that is not used for training but only for testing the model. CV error was also used for deciding how

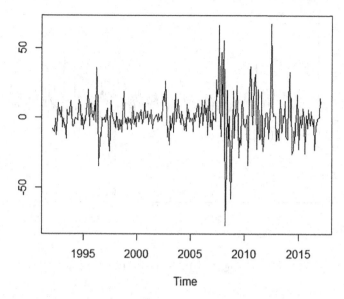

**Fig. 6.** First order differencing

many time lags should be considered in the input variables set. A short description of each of the models is presented next. It should be noticed that, unlike ARIMA models, machine learning models do not need to consider assumptions regarding the stationarity of the time series.

### ARIMA

An ARIMA($p$, $d$, $q$) is an autoregressive integrated moving average model where $p$ represents the number of autoregressive terms, $d$ represents the number of times the time series was differenced in order to become stationary and $q$ is the number of moving average terms. Different models are obtained with different values of $p$, $d$ and $q$. The model considered was the best one according to the Akaike Information Criteria (AIC), returned by using the function *auto.arima* from the $R$ forecast package. Both seasonal and non-seasonal models were tested. The best model was a non-seasonal ARIMA(0, 1, 1). The obtained residuals are depicted in Fig. 7. Figures 8 and 9 present the ACF and PACF plots for the residuals. None of the autocorrelations and partial autocorrelations is individually statistically significant. The Box-Pierce presents a $p$-value equal to 0.79. The Ljung-Box statistics present a $p$-value equal to 0.67. High $p$-values allow us to conclude that the residuals estimated are purely random.

### Classification and Regression Tree

CART models are represented by binary trees with different splitting rules in non-leaf nodes [19]. In each node, the algorithm will decide which variable gives the best split, by using a given criterion that corresponds to the minimization of a cost function (like the maximization of between-groups sum-of-squares error, for instance). The leaf nodes of the tree represent a given output variable that is used for making the prediction. After building the tree, it is usual to run a pruning algorithm, that will try to

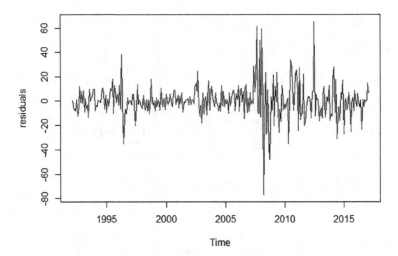

**Fig. 7.** ARIMA residuals

| February 1992 | ... | ... | ... | February 2012 | March 2012 | April 2012 | May 2012 | June 2012 | July 2012 | August 2012 | |
| February 1992 | ... | ... | ... | February 2012 | March 2012 | April 2012 | May 2012 | June 2012 | July 2012 | August 2012 | September 2012 |
| ... | | ... | ... | ... | ... | ... | ... | ... | ... | ... | ... |
| February 1992 | ... | ... | ... | ... | August 2016 | September 2016 | October 2016 | November 2016 | December 2016 | January 2017 | February 2017 |

**Fig. 8.** In–sample and out-of-sample data

| February 1992 | ... | August 2016 | September 2016 | | | | | |
| February 1992 | ... | August 2016 | prediction September 2016 | October 2016 | | | | |
| February 1992 | ... | August 2016 | prediction September 2016 | prediction October 2016 | November 2016 | | | |
| February 1992 | ... | August 2016 | prediction September 2016 | prediction October 2016 | prediction November 2016 | December 2016 | | |
| February 1992 | ... | August 2016 | prediction September 2016 | prediction October 2016 | prediction November 2016 | prediction December 2016 | January 2017 | |
| February 1992 | ... | August 2016 | prediction September 2016 | prediction October 2016 | prediction November 2016 | prediction December 2016 | prediction January 2017 | February 2017 |

**Fig. 9.** Incorporating previous predicted values in longer term forecasts: grey cells represent forecasted values

remove leaf nodes if they do not contribute to a decrease in the cost function, aiming at achieving a less complex model.

To make a forecast considering a vector of new and unseen input variables, it is only necessary to go from the top to the bottom of the tree, respecting the rules in each node. There is one and only one path from the root of the tree to each one of the leaves. Package *rpart* has been used in the computational tests performed.

### Random Forests

Random Forests can be interpreted as an ensemble of predictors. They are a combination of tree predictors such that each tree is constructed based on a sampling of the available training samples [20]. Each tree in the forest is also built considering a random selection of input variables that will determine the splitting rules in each node. Package *randomForest* for *R* has been used in the computational tests performed.

**Support Vector Machines**

Support Vector Machines are supervised learning models that were initially used as linear classifiers. They use kernels to extend data into a high dimensional feature space to improve the classification performance [21]. SVM can be applied to both classification problems and regression problems. SVM implementations require the user to define some parameters (the kernel function and a cost parameter that determines the trade off between model complexity and allowed deviations) [22]. Kernels usually considered are the linear kernel, the Gaussian basis function, the polynomial kernel, the Bessel function, the Laplace radial basis function. When there is no prior knowledge about the data, Gaussian, Laplace basis function and Bessel kernels are considered to be general-purpose kernels and thus an appropriate choice [23]. Package *Kernlab* was used in the computational tests performed.

**Multivariate Adaptive Regression Splines**

MARS has been first introduced by Friedman [24], and it is described by its author as a "flexible nonparametric regression modelling". The method produces continuous models with continuous derivatives, which is a differentiating aspect from the recursive partitioning approaches. MARS builds models that are weighted sums of basis functions, such that each basis function is either a constant, a function of the form max(0, $x$-constant) or max(0, constant-$x$), or a product of two or more of these functions. The algorithm begins by considering one single region. Then this region is recursively split, by defining a basis function, a predictor variable and a split point. The cost function to be minimized is the lack of fit of the model. Package *earth* has been used in the computational tests performed.

### 2.3 Methods

The forecasting models will be tested in out-of-sample data only. Prices from February 1992 to February 2012 will be used to estimate the models parameters. These models will then be used to forecast price values for the next six months (March 2012–August 2012). Then the in-sample time window will consider one more month (including March 2012). The models parameters are again estimated. New forecasts will be done for the next six months (April 2012–September 2012). The process will continue until the end of the available dataset. The last forecasting window will consider months from September 2016 to February 2017, being the models built with data until August 2016. This means that the models will be evaluated considering out-of-sample data, in a total of five years (60 months) predictions. Figure 8 illustrates the operation of the growing sliding window.

It is possible to calculate different forecasting metrics to assess the performance of the different models. Consider that $y_t$ is the observed value at period $t$, $\hat{y}_t$ is the forecasted value for that time period, made $k$ periods in advance, and that there are forecasts for periods $t \in T$. Mean relative absolute error (MAE) can be calculate as $\sum_{t \in T} \frac{|y_t - \hat{y}_t|}{y_t} / \#T$. Maximum relative absolute error (MaxAE) can be calculated as

$$max\left\{\frac{|y_t - \hat{y}_t|}{y_t}, \forall t \in T\right\}.$$ Root Mean Square Error (RMSE) is calculated as $\sqrt{\frac{\sum_{t \in T}(y_t - \hat{y}_t)^2}{\#T}}.$

These error metrics are calculated for all the forecasting futures considered (one to six months). The ability of correctly forecasting whether the price will increase or decrease in the future is also going to be considered.

## 3   Computational Results

Each of the models developed was tested in out-of-sample data, as explained in Sect. 2.3. The capability of predicting wheat prices one up to six months ahead is evaluated using different performance measures. All models were also compared with a naïve model that considers the prediction $\hat{y}_t = y_{t-k}$, meaning that the prediction made $k$ months ahead will simply be equal to the current price.

Table 1 presents the results considering MAE. Table 2 presents MaxAE results, and Table 3 RMSE results. The best value found is highlighted in each one of the tables.

**Table 1.**   Mean Absolute Error (MAE)

| | | | months ahead | | | |
|---|---|---|---|---|---|---|
| | 1 | 2 | 3 | 4 | 5 | 6 |
| ARIMA | 4,34% | 9,49% | 12,87% | 16,05% | 18,73% | 21,29% |
| CART | 5,43% | 9,06% | 13,54% | 16,17% | 16,86% | 18,95% |
| RF | 4,35% | 9,15% | 12,55% | 15,25% | 19,31% | 21,74% |
| SVM | 2,55% | 5,40% | 8,07% | 11,72% | 14,35% | 15,88% |
| MARS | 2,22% | 5,67% | 8,09% | 11,83% | 15,48% | 18,60% |
| Näive | 4,54% | 7,52% | 9,68% | 11,78% | 13,12% | 14,55% |

As expected, the models performance deteriorates as the forecasting horizon increases. No model is the "best" model under all the possible performance criteria. We can, however, conclude that SVM and MARS models present the best results for one to four months forecasts. It is interesting to note that the näive model achieves the best results for five and six months forecasts.

Models were also tested for the capacity of accurately forecasting if the future time series value would be greater or lower than the current one. Accuracy results are presented in Table 4. In this case, SVM presents the best results for all forecasting horizons. Results are very good in predicting the increase or decrease in future price compared with the current one for one and two months forecasts.

As it was possible to obtain very good results with MARS for one month forecasts, it makes sense to try to develop two to six months forecast models incorporating these predictions. This means that only one month prediction models are developed, since longer term predictions will consider as input variables the values already predicted for the shorter term forecasts. Figure 9 illustrates this situation. After having forecasts for the next month, it is possible to include these values as input data in longer term forecasts, so that two months forecasts still use the one month forecast model, and so on.

**Table 2.** Maximum Absolute Error (MaxAE)

| | months ahead | | | | | |
|---|---|---|---|---|---|---|
| | 1 | 2 | 3 | 4 | 5 | 6 |
| ARIMA | 21,58% | 27,85% | 37,66% | 35,29% | 45,21% | 50,73% |
| CART | 16,61% | 23,55% | 28,99% | 41,52% | 57,48% | 61,70% |
| RF | 15,79% | 25,40% | 27,22% | 31,05% | 46,23% | 71,73% |
| SVM | 8,89% | 14,37% | 24,76% | 30,71% | 35,04% | 36,33% |
| MARS | 6,77% | 16,77% | 23,10% | 32,09% | 39,05% | 38,79% |
| Näive | 21,90% | 25,37% | 27,15% | 36,32% | 35,28% | 33,33% |

**Table 3.** Root Mean Square Error

| | months ahead | | | | | |
|---|---|---|---|---|---|---|
| | 1 | 2 | 3 | 4 | 5 | 6 |
| ARIMA | 14,45 | 26,81 | 34,95 | 39,15 | 44,29 | 48,16 |
| CART | 15,57 | 21,97 | 32,71 | 39,10 | 41,05 | 43,92 |
| RF | 12,83 | 25,91 | 32,44 | 36,81 | 45,40 | 48,92 |
| SVM | 7,58 | 14,66 | 23,14 | 31,89 | 37,82 | 38,90 |
| MARS | 6,17 | 15,50 | 22,43 | 32,04 | 39,23 | 43,61 |
| Näive | 14,79 | 23,27 | 29,49 | 33,87 | 35,76 | 36,87 |

**Table 4.** Accuracy in Trend

| | months ahead | | | | | |
|---|---|---|---|---|---|---|
| | 1 | 2 | 3 | 4 | 5 | 6 |
| ARIMA | 55,93% | 54,39% | 50,91% | 45,28% | 50,98% | 55,10% |
| CART | 61,02% | 50,88% | 52,73% | 49,06% | 47,06% | 48,98% |
| RF | 69,49% | 49,12% | 58,18% | 50,94% | 47,06% | 42,86% |
| SVM | 86,44% | 75,44% | 69,09% | 56,60% | 58,82% | 61,22% |
| MARS | 84,75% | 75,44% | 65,45% | 56,60% | 47,06% | 40,82% |

Tables 5, 6, 7 and 8 show the performance metrics for this new approach, comparing with the initial MARS models and also with the best performance obtained earlier. It is possible to conclude that the performance for two to four months forecasts improves, since this methodology obtains the best results for MAE and RMSE.

**Table 5.** Mean Absolute Error (MAE)

|  | 2 | 3 | 4 | 5 | 6 |
|---|---|---|---|---|---|
| **Best previous result** | 5,40% | 8,07% | 11,72% | 13,12% | 14,55% |
| **MARS** | 5,67% | 8,09% | 11,83% | 15,48% | 18,60% |
| **MARS including previous forecasted values** | 3,52% | 7,58% | 10,79% | 13,24% | 14,55% |

**Table 6.** Maximum relative absolute error (MaxAE)

|  | 2 | 3 | 4 | 5 | 6 |
|---|---|---|---|---|---|
| **Best previous result** | 14,37% | 23,10% | 30,71% | 35,04% | 33,33% |
| **MARS** | 16,77% | 23,10% | 32,09% | 39,05% | 38,79% |
| **MARS including previous forecasted values** | 14,04% | 24,06% | 35,52% | 37,76% | 47,27% |

**Table 7.** Root Mean Square Error (RMSE)

|  | 2 | 3 | 4 | 5 | 6 |
|---|---|---|---|---|---|
| **Best previous result** | 14,66 | 22,43 | 31,89 | 35,76 | 36,87 |
| **MARS** | 15,50 | 22,43 | 32,04 | 39,23 | 43,61 |
| **MARS including previous forecasted values** | 10,69 | 21,53 | 30,00 | 35,49 | 37,99 |

**Table 8.** Accuracy in Trend

|  | 2 | 3 | 4 | 5 | 6 |
|---|---|---|---|---|---|
| **Best previous result** | 75,44% | 69,09% | 56,60% | 58,82% | 61,22% |
| **MARS** | 84,75% | 75,44% | 65,45% | 56,60% | 47,06% |
| **MARS including previous forecasted values** | 89,47% | 74,55% | 60,38% | 52,94% | 51,02% |

Figures 10a to f illustrate the forecasting values obtained by these models for $t + k$ time period, with $t$ the current time period and $k$ the future time horizon, $k = 1, ..., 6$.

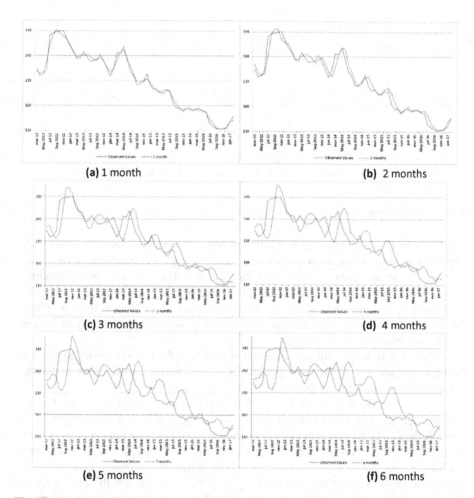

(a) 1 month

(b) 2 months

(c) 3 months

(d) 4 months

(e) 5 months

(f) 6 months

**Fig. 10.** Prediction based on one month forecast MARS models, incorporating previous predictions

Figure 11 illustrates the results obtained but from a different point of view: at time $t$ it is possible to predict prices for $t + k$, for $k = 1, ..., 6$. Figure 11 considers the prediction of prices between September 2016 and February 2016, using data available until August 2016. As can be seen in the figure, the forecasting value is capturing very well the trend of the price evolution.

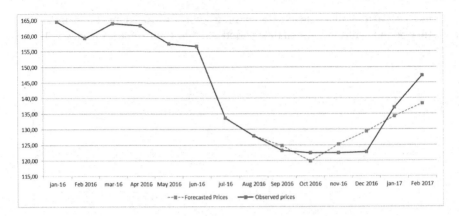

**Fig. 11.** Forecasts for the last six months of the available dataset

## 4 Conclusions

In this paper we have presented five different types of models to forecast wheat price one up to six months ahead, considering as predictor variables past time series values only. As far as the authors know, it is the first time that the investigated machine learning techniques are applied to this problem. The methodology used is different from other published works, since we aim at forecasting at the present time the prices for the next six months. All models were tested considering different performance criteria and using out-of-sample data.

Although it is not possible to select one approach as the best one under all criteria, the approach based on MARS that includes previous forecasted values seems to be the one with most consistent results.

As future work, it is possible to devise a forecasting model that considers an ensemble of different predictors. An ensemble can be understood as a collection of learning algorithms that are simultaneously used for making more reliable and accurate predictions than its individual components [25]. This collection can consider different machine learning based models, or the same type of models but trained using different sample sets or different input variables. It is also possible to consider the application of classification algorithms capable of accurately predicting the future increase or decrease in the price.

**Acknowledgements.** This work has been supported by the Fundação para a Ciência e a Tecnologia (FCT) under project grant UID/Multi/00308/2019.

# References

1. Curtis, B.C., Rajaram, S., Gómez, M.: Bread wheat: improvement and production: Food and Agriculture Organization of the United Nations (FAO) (2002)
2. Yang, J., Zhang, J., Leatham, D.J.: Price and volatility transmission in international wheat futures markets. Ann. Econ. Finan. **4**, 37–50 (2003)
3. Brunner, A.D.: El Nino and world primary commodity prices: warm water or hot air? Rev. Econ. Stat. **84**, 176–183 (2002)
4. Hill, H.S.J., et al.: Implications of seasonal climate forecasts on world wheat trade: a stochastic, dynamic analysis. Can. J. Agr. Econ./Revue canadienne d'agroeconomie **52**, 289–312 (2004)
5. Ubilava, D.: The ENSO effect and asymmetries in wheat price dynamics. World Dev. **96**, 490–502 (2017)
6. Ramirez, O.A., Fadiga, M.: Forecasting agricultural commodity prices with asymmetric-error GARCH models. J. Agr. Resource Econ. **28**(1), 71–85 (2003)
7. Benavides, G.: Price volatility forecasts for agricultural commodities: an application of historical volatility models, option implieds and composite approaches for futures prices of corn and wheat. SSRN (2004)
8. Bessler, D.A., Yang, J., Wongcharupan, M.: Price dynamics in the international wheat market: modeling with error correction and directed acyclic graphs. J. Reg. Sci. **43**, 1–33 (2003)
9. Roche, M.J., McQuinn, K.: Grain price volatility in a small open economy. Eur. Rev. Agr. Econ. **30**, 77–98 (2003)
10. Hoffman, L., Irwin, S.H., Toasa, J.: Forecast performance of futures price models for corn, soybeans, and wheat. Agricultural & Applied Economics Association, Milwaukee, WI (2007)
11. Jumah, A., Kunst, R.M.: Seasonal prediction of European cereal prices: good forecasts using bad models? J. Forecast. **27**, 391–406 (2008)
12. Arshad, F.M., Hameed, A.A.A.: The long run relationship between petroleum and cereals prices. Glob. Econ. Finan. J. **2**, 91–100 (2009)
13. Algieri, B.: A roller coaster ride: an empirical investigation of the main drivers of the international wheat price. Agr. Econ. **45**, 459–475 (2014)
14. Chen, Y.-C., Rogoff, K.S., Rossi, B.: Can exchange rates forecast commodity prices? Quart. J. Econ. **125**, 1145–1194 (2010)
15. Adjemian, M.K., Janzen, J., Carter, C.A., Smith, A.: Deconstructing Wheat Price Spikes: A Model of Supply and Demand, Financial Speculation, and Commodity Price Comovement. United States Department of Agriculture, Economic Research Service (2014)
16. Ahumada, H., Cornejo, M.: Forecasting food prices: the case of corn, soybeans and wheat. Int. J. Forecast. **32**, 838–848 (2016)
17. Khamis, A., Abdullah, S.: Forecasting wheat price using Backpropagation and NARX Neural Network. Int. J. Eng. Sci. **3**, 19–26 (2014)
18. Cleveland, R.B., Cleveland, W.S., McRae, J.E., Terpenning, I.: STL: a seasonal-trend decomposition procedure based on loess. J. Official Stat. **6**, 3–73 (1990)
19. Breiman, L., Friedman, J.H., Olshen, R.A., Stone, C.J.: Classification and Regression Trees. CRC Press, Boca Raton (1983)
20. Breiman, L.E.O.: Random forests. Mach. Learn. **45**, 5–32 (2001)
21. Li, D.-C., Liu, C.-W.: A class possibility based kernel to increase classification accuracy for small data sets using support vector machines. Expert Syst. Appl. **37**, 3104–3110 (2010)

22. Chapelle, O., Vapnik, V.: Model selection for support vector machines. In: Solla, S., Leen, T.K., Miller, K.-R. (eds.) Advances in Neural Information Processing Systems 12, pp. 230–236. MIP Press (2000)
23. Hornik, K., Meyer, D., Karatzoglou, A.: Support vector machines in R. J. Stat. Softw. **15**, 1–28 (2006)
24. Friedman, J.H.: Multivariate adaptive regression splines (with discussion). Ann. Stat. **19**, 79–141 (1991)
25. Re, M., Valentini, G.: Ensemble methods: a review. In: Srivastava, A.N., Scargle, J.D., Ali, K., Way, M.J. (eds) Data Mining and Machine Learning for Astronomical Applications, pp. 1–40. Chapman & Hall (2011)

# Dynamic Facility Location Problem with Stochastic Setup Times

Maria do Céu Marques[1,3](✉) and Joana Dias[2,3]

[1] Coimbra Polytechnic - ISEC, Rua Pedro Nunes, 3030-199 Coimbra, Portugal
cmarques@isec.pt
[2] Faculty of Economics and CeBer, University of Coimbra, Av. Dias da Silva,
165, 3004-512 Coimbra, Portugal
joana@fe.uc.pt
[3] Institute for Systems Engineering and Computers at Coimbra, Rua Sílvio Lima,
Pólo II, 3030-290 Coimbra, Portugal

**Abstract.** Dynamic facility location problems consider situations where it is important to decide not only where but also when to open (or close) facilities, given a planning time horizon. Considering explicitly multiple time periods is especially important if assignment costs are expected to change significantly in the future and relocating facilities is expensive. The majority of models presented in the literature considers binary decision variables that define whether facilities are open in a given time period. In addition, if a facility is first opened at some time period then clients can usually be assigned to it from that period forward, without any guarantee that the facility will be operational at the planned time period. In this paper, a new mathematical model is presented where uncertainty in the setup time of facilities is explicitly considered. This means that the decision maker is only capable of deciding where to locate facilities and when to begin all the necessary works to get the facilities operational, but the time elapsed until opening the facility is not known for sure. A primal-dual heuristic is also developed for this problem and its performance is compared with the performance of a commercial exact solver.

**Keywords:** Dynamic facility location · Primal-dual heuristics · Uncertainty

## 1 Introduction

Discrete location problems consider situations where there is a finite set of potential locations to install facilities, and there is a finite set of clients that have to be assigned to opened facilities. The objective is to decide what are the best locations to install facilities, and how to assign clients to these facilities, usually

---

Supported by the Fundação para a Ciência e a Tecnologia (FCT) under project grant UID/Multi/00308/2019.

S. Misra et al. (Eds.): ICCSA 2019, LNCS 11621, pp. 183–198, 2019.
https://doi.org/10.1007/978-3-030-24302-9_14

minimizing total cost (both location costs associated with opening facilities and also assignment costs), although many other objective functions might also be considered. Dynamic location problems consider that facilities can be opened at different time periods, during a given planning horizon. In a dynamic location problem the decisions have to consider not only where to open but also when to open the chosen facilities. These problems are most useful when there are significant expected changes in assignment costs, and relocating facilities to accommodate those changes is too expensive or even impossible. The explicit consideration of the time dimension increases the model relevance, comprehensiveness and connection to reality [11]. The data that are usually used to feed a dynamic location model are fixed location costs and assignments costs, both in the present and future time periods. It is also possible to consider maintenance costs and closing costs in cases where closing an existing facility is allowed. It is not realistic to assume that all these costs are known with certainty at the present time. Actually, even when considering location models where the time dimension is not explicitly included, an estimate of future costs has to be made in order to calculate meaningful present values for all the costs involved [9]. The uncertainty that is most of the times associated with location problems has been acknowledged by several authors, and there is a significant amount of published work in the area of location problems under uncertainty. An introduction to location problems under uncertainty can be found in [15], where the author addresses uncertainty in demands, variable production, transportation prices and selling prices. Snyder [19] provides a good literature review on stochastic location problems until 2006. The author distinguishes risk and uncertainty concepts, and considers approaches where the goal is the optimization of an expected value. Other objectives are also considered, representing robustness measures, like the minimization of the worst-case performance or the minimization of the maximum regret. There are not many works tackling dynamic location problems under uncertainty. A dynamic facility location problem under demand uncertainty is described by Baron et al. [5]. Uncertainty is represented by resorting to box and ellipsoidal uncertainty sets. Hernández et al. [14] consider a multiperiod stochastic model for the location of prison facilities in Chile, with demand uncertainty represented by scenarios. The decisions to consider are when and where to open facilities, with which capacity, and when and where to increase that capacity. The authors apply a branch-and-cluster coordination algorithm to calculate solutions to the model. Dynamic simple plant location problems under fixed and assignment costs uncertainty are tackled by Marques and Dias [17]. The authors consider uncertainty associated with the existence of customers in each time period, represented by scenarios. The model minimizes expected total cost, and a primal-dual heuristic is developed. In a posterior work, the authors introduce a measure of robustness by guaranteeing that the regret associated with each scenario is always upper bounded [18]. A multiobjective approach is also considered, where the authors develop relationships between non-dominated solutions and robust solutions [10]. Albareda-Sambola et al. [1] consider a multiperiod discrete facility location problem with demand and cost uncertainty represented by scenarios, describing two alternative formulations for the discrete equivalent model (two-stage and multi-stage models). A matheuristic approach is developed. De Rosa et al. [7] develop a model for capacitated facility location with uncertainty in demand, costs and revenues, represented by scenarios. Capacity adjustments during the planning horizon are allowed. The objective function is the minimization of the expected value of relative regret.

In this paper a dynamic facility location problem under uncertainty is studied, considering not only cost and demand uncertainty but also uncertainty related to the moment in which a facility is operational and clients can be assigned to it. Actually, the location decision variables are usually binary variables that define when each facility is opened. It is also assumed that clients can be assigned to a facility from that moment forward. In reality, there are many activities that have to be carried out from the moment a decision to open a facility is made until the moment that the facility is operational: property acquisition, infrastructure construction, preparation of human and material resources, and so on. These activities will consume resources (including time) and delays may occur. The existence of delays in projects is a matter of research by itself, especially in construction projects (see, for instance, [2–4]). Not having a facility ready when it was planned can have important impacts in the assignment of clients to existing facilities. As far as the authors know, this is the first time this issue is introduced in a dynamic location model. A latency period, defined as the number of periods elapsed from the moment it is decided that a facility will be opened until the moment it is really available, has been considered before [1]. However, this latency period was assumed to be known a priori, it was the same for all potential facilities and independent of the opening time period. If this preparation time is deterministic then deciding when to open a facility will immediately determine when the setup work needs to begin.

This paper is organized as follows: in Sect. 2 the developed mathematical model is presented. Then, the primal-dual heuristic developed to tackle the problem is described. Section 4 presents the computational experiments made. Section 5 presents the conclusions and paths for future research.

## 2    The Mathematical Model

The notation that will be used in this paper is as follows. The time horizon is represented by a finite set of time periods $T = \{1, ..., t, ..., T\}$. The set of possible future scenarios is denoted by $S = \{1, ..., s, ..., S\}$, where each scenario $s \in S$ will occur with probability $p^s$ such that $p^s > 0$ and $\sum_{s \in S} p^s = 1$. Let the set of potential facility sites be denoted by $J = \{1, ..., j, ..., M\}$ and the set of possible customer locations (or demand points) by $I = \{1, ..., i, ..., N\}$. For $(j, s) \in J \times S$, let $d_{js}$ be the number of time periods it takes to prepare facility $j$ under scenario $s$, i.e., the number of time periods required to set up facility $j$, for it to be ready and to be able to accept customers, under scenario $s$. Let us define $\delta_{it}^s$ as equal to 1 if customer $i$ has a demand that has to be fulfilled during period $t$ for scenario $s$, and 0 otherwise. Then we have to guarantee that all customers such that

$\delta_{it}^s = 1$ are assigned to an operational facility, for all $(t, s) \in \mathcal{T} \times \mathcal{S}$. In terms of costs: for $(j, t, s) \in J \times \mathcal{T} \times \mathcal{S}$, let $f_{jt}^s$ be the fixed cost associated with facility $j$, if this facility is opened in $t + d_{js}$, under scenario $s$, being the setup works initiated in $t$. This fixed cost considers both opening costs and operating costs in all the time periods during which the facility is operational, under scenario $s$; for $(i, j, t, s) \in I \times J \times \mathcal{T} \times \mathcal{S}$, $c_{ijt}^s$ represents the assignment cost of customer $i$ to facility $j$ in period $t$ and under scenario $s$. We assume that once it has been decided that a given facility will be opened, all the works necessary to have the facility operational will effectively take place, and once the facility is operational it will stay operational until the end of the planning horizon.

The decisions to be made are where and when to locate new facilities, and how to assign the existing customers to operational facilities over the whole planning horizon and under each scenario. Thus, the following binary decision variables are defined: $x_{jt}$ equals 1 if facility $j$ begins to be prepared at the beginning of period $t$, and 0 otherwise; $y_{ijt}^s$ equals 1 if customer $i$ is assigned to facility $j$ in period $t$ and under scenario $s$, and 0 otherwise. The objective is to minimize expected total cost including fixed and assignment costs over all scenarios. The dynamic facility location problem under uncertainty considering setup times can then be formulated as follows:

$$\min \quad \sum_{t \in \mathcal{T}} \sum_{j \in J} \sum_{s \in \mathcal{S}} p^s f_{jt}^s x_{jt} + \sum_{s \in \mathcal{S}} \sum_{t \in \mathcal{T}} \sum_{i \in I} \sum_{j \in J} p^s c_{ijt}^s y_{ijt}^s \tag{1}$$

subject to

$$\sum_{j \in J} y_{ijt}^s = \delta_{it}^s \qquad \forall i \in I, t \in \mathcal{T}, s \in \mathcal{S}, \tag{2}$$

$$\sum_{\tau \in \mathcal{T} : \tau + d_{js} \leq t} x_{j\tau} - y_{ijt}^s \geq 0 \qquad \forall i \in I, j \in J, t \in \mathcal{T}, s \in \mathcal{S}, \tag{3}$$

$$\sum_{t \in \mathcal{T}} x_{jt} \leq 1 \qquad \forall j \in J, \tag{4}$$

$$x_{jt} \in \{0, 1\} \qquad \forall j \in J, t \in \mathcal{T}, \tag{5}$$

$$y_{ijt}^s \in \{0, 1\} \qquad \forall i \in I, j \in J, t \in \mathcal{T}, s \in \mathcal{S}. \tag{6}$$

The objective function (1) minimizes expected total costs (fixed plus variable costs). Constraints (2) require that in every time period and under each scenario a customer with demand is assigned to exactly one operational facility. These constraints should be further analyzed. Actually, it is not possible to guarantee that these constraints are indeed all satisfied. The explicit consideration of uncertain setup times will possibly delay the opening of facilities in some scenarios. For instance, if all the potential facilities to be opened require setup times greater than zero, then there will be no operational facilities in the first time period of the planning horizon, nor possibly in other periods of time. Consequently, constraints (2) are not satisfied at least for $t = 1$. In order to ensure feasibility it is sufficient to consider that there is at least one facility $j \in J$ such that $d_{js} = 0, \forall s \in S$. This means that at least one facility will surely be opened and assignments will be guaranteed from period 1 forward. Another possibility is to consider the existence of at least one facility already operational at the beginning of the planning horizon.

Constraints (3) impose that a customer with demand can only be assigned to operational facilities. A customer can be assigned to different facilities at different time periods and different scenarios. However, a customer can only be assigned to a facility $j$ under scenario $s$ if $d_{js}$ time periods have already elapsed since the time the facility began to be prepared. Constraints (4) ensure that each facility begins to be built at most once during the time horizon (located at the same site in all scenarios, but with possible different building times). Finally, (5)–(6) restrict the decision variables to be binary.

This model is an extension of the model presented in [17]. The main difference is the consideration of uncertainty in setup times, represented in the present model by parameters $d_{js}, (j, s) \in J \times S$. As far as the authors know, it is the first time this feature is taken into account. Furthermore, in the above model the setup time of a given facility is only scenario dependent, but it could also depend on the initial building time of that facility. For this latter option, setup times would be defined as $d_{jt}^s, (j, t, s) \in J \times T \times S$, and in terms of problem formulation, constraints (3) have to be slightly changed to

$$\sum_{\tau \in T : \tau + d_{j\tau}^s \leq t} x_{j\tau} - y_{ijt}^s \geq 0 \qquad \forall i \in I, j \in J, t \in T, s \in S.$$

For ease in the exposition, we will assume the situation described earlier throughout this text.

## 3  Primal–Dual Heuristic

Primal–dual heuristics have proven their value when dealing with facility location problems [6,8,12,16,17,21]. One of the advantages of primal-dual heuristics relies on their capacity of providing both upper and lower bounds for the optimal solution. Even in cases where the heuristic is unable to find the optimal solution (or it is not possible to prove it is optimal), it still allows the obtained solution to be evaluated, and a maximum gap to be calculated. The dual problem and complementary slackness conditions used by the heuristic procedures are presented next.

### 3.1  Dual Problem and Complementary Slackness Conditions

Consider restrictions (4) rewritten as $\sum_{t \in T}(-x_{jt}) \geq -1, \forall j \in J$ and the linear programming relaxation of the primal problem defined by (1)–(4), where restrictions (5) and (6) are replaced by nonnegativity constraints. Let us define in (1) $\mathcal{F}_{jt}^s = p^s f_{jt}^s$ and $\mathcal{C}_{ijt}^s = p^s c_{ijt}^s$. Considering dual variables $v_{it}^s$, $w_{ijt}^s$ and $u_j$ associated with the restrictions (2), (3) and (4), respectively, the condensed dual problem can thus be formulated as follows (since it is possible to demonstrate that $w_{ijt}^s = \max\{0, v_{it}^s - C_{ijt}^s\}, \forall i, j, t, s$):

$$\max \quad \sum_{i \in I} \sum_{t \in T} \sum_{s \in S} \delta_{it}^s v_{it}^s - \sum_{j \in J} u_j \tag{7}$$

subject to

$$\sum_{i \in I} \sum_{s \in S} \sum_{\tau = t + d_{js}}^{T} \max\{0, v_{i\tau}^s - C_{ij\tau}^s\} - u_j \leq \sum_{s \in S} \mathcal{F}_{jt}^s \qquad \forall j, t, \tag{8}$$

$$u_j \geq 0 \qquad \forall j. \tag{9}$$

The corresponding slack variables $\pi_{jt}$ for constraints (8) are given by:

$$\pi_{jt} = \sum_{s \in S} \mathcal{F}_{jt}^s - \sum_{i \in I} \sum_{s \in S} \sum_{\tau = t + d_{js}}^{T} \max\{0, v_{i\tau}^s - C_{ij\tau}^s\} + u_j \qquad \forall j, t. \tag{10}$$

Then, the complementary slackness conditions are:

$$\pi_{jt} \, x_{jt} = 0 \qquad \forall j, t, \tag{11}$$

$$v_{it}^s \left( \sum_j y_{ijt}^s - \delta_{it}^s \right) = 0 \qquad \forall i, t, s, \tag{12}$$

$$w_{ijt}^s \left( \sum_{\tau \in T : \tau + d_{js} \leq t} x_{j\tau} - y_{ijt}^s \right) = 0 \qquad \forall i, j, s, t, \tag{13}$$

$$u_j \left( 1 - \sum_t x_{jt} \right) = 0 \qquad \forall j, \tag{14}$$

$$y_{ijt}^s \left( v_{it}^s - C_{ijt}^s - w_{ijt}^s \right) = 0 \qquad \forall i, j, t, s. \tag{15}$$

As it is well known from duality theory, if the dual and primal solutions satisfy all complementary slackness conditions, then the solutions are optimal. If not, the corresponding primal solution is said to have gap.

## 3.2   Algorithm

We reindex, for each scenario $s$, $C_{ijt}^s$ for each $(i, t)$ in nondecreasing order as $C_{it}^{s(k)}$, for $k = 1, 2, ..., k_{it}^s$, where $k_{it}^s$ denotes the number of facility-to-customer links for $(i, t)$ under scenario $s$. For instance, $C_{it}^{s(1)} = \min_{j \in J}\{C_{ijt}^s\}$. For convenience, we also include $C_{it}^{s(k_{it}^s+1)} = +\infty, \forall \, (i, t, s)$. Let $I^+$ be the set of pseudo customers

$(i, t, s)$ corresponding to the dual variables $v_{it}^s$ that the dual ascent procedure will try to increase. Initially, $I^+$ will be equal to all possible combinations $(i, t, s) \in I \times \mathcal{T} \times \mathcal{S}$, except those such that $\delta_{it}^s = 0$. Later, $I^+$ will be set within the respective procedures. The main steps of the heuristic are as follows:

1. Set $v_{it}^s = \min_{j \in J}\{C_{ijt}^s\}$, $\forall\ (i, t, s)$, and $u_j = 0, \forall\ j$.
   Set $I^+ = \{(i, t, s) \in I \times \mathcal{T} \times \mathcal{S} : \delta_{it}^s = 1\}$.
2. Execute the dual ascent procedure.
3. Execute the primal procedure. If an optimal solution is found, then stop.
4. Execute the primal–dual adjustment procedure. The heuristic stops when the optimal solution is found or when there are no primal or dual improvements after a given number of trials within the adjustment procedure.

**Dual Ascent Procedure.** In what follows, $(i, t, s)_q$, with $q \le |I \times \mathcal{T} \times \mathcal{S}|$, represents a given, but arbitrary, sequence of pseudo customers.

1. Consider any dual feasible solution $\{v_{it}^s\}$ such that $v_{it}^s \ge C_{it}^{s(1)}, \forall\ (i, t, s)$, and $\pi_{jt} \ge 0, \forall\ (j, t)$.
   For each $(i, t, s)$ define $k(i, t, s) = \min\{k : v_{it}^s \le C_{it}^{s(k)}\}$. If $v_{it}^s = C_{it}^{s(k(i,t,s))}$, then $k(i, t, s) \leftarrow k(i, t, s) + 1$.
2. $(i, t, s) \leftarrow (i, t, s)_1$ and $q \leftarrow 1$; $r = 0$.
3. If $(i, t, s) \notin I^+ \vee \delta_{it}^s = 0$, then go to step 7.
4. Set $\Delta_{it}^s = \min\left\{+\infty, \min_j\{\pi_{j\tau} : v_{it}^s - C_{ijt}^s \ge 0, \tau \le t - d_{js}, t \ge 1 + d_{js}\}\right\}$.
5. If $\Delta_{it}^s > C_{it}^{s(k(i,t,s))} - v_{it}^s$, then $\Delta_{it}^s = C_{it}^{s(k(i,t,s))} - v_{it}^s$; $r = 1$; $k(i, t, s) \leftarrow k(i, t, s) + 1$.
6. For all $j \in J$ with $v_{it}^s - C_{ijt}^s \ge 0$, set $\pi_{j\tau} = \pi_{j\tau} - \Delta_{it}^s, \tau \le t - d_{js}$; set $v_{it}^s = v_{it}^s + \Delta_{it}^s$.
7. If $q < |I^+|$, then $q \leftarrow q + 1$, $(i, t, s) \leftarrow (i, t, s)_q$, and return to step 3.
8. If $r = 1$, then return to step 2, otherwise stop.

The ascent procedure starts with a dual feasible solution and it tries to increase iteratively the values of dual variables $v_{it}^s$, increasing the dual objective function value. Some slacks have to be decreased namely those associated with facilities that can be operational (steps 4 and 6). Looking at step 4 it is possible to realize that, for a given $(i, t, s)$, $\Delta_{it}^s = +\infty$ if, and only if, there is no facility $j$ under the conditions stated in that step, meaning that those facilities can not be operational during that $t$ and $s$ due to the magnitude of the respective setup times. In such cases, the value $\Delta_{it}^s$ will be updated in the next step. This procedure stops when it is not possible to further improve the dual objective function value because all dual variables are blocked from increasing by at least one slack. The output of this procedure is a dual feasible solution $\{v_{it}^{s+}\}$, with an objective function value $v_D^+$, and an associated set of candidate facility locations $\{\pi_{jt}^+\}$, defined by the slacks that are equal to zero. This dual solution is the base for building a primal feasible solution using the procedure that is described next.

**Primal Procedure.** Let us first define the following sets and notation:

$J^* = \{(j,t) \in J \times T : \pi^+_{jt} = 0\};$

$J^{s*}_t = \{j \in J : (j,\tau) \in J^*, \tau \leq t - d_{js}\}, \forall t, s;$

$J^{s+}_t = \{j \in J : \text{facility } j \text{ is operational at time } t \text{ and scenario } s\}, \forall t, s.$

$t_1(j) = \min\{\gamma - d_{js} : j \in J^{s+}_\gamma, \gamma - d_{js} \geq 1\}$ and, if $t_1(j) \geq 1$,

$t_2(j) = \max\{\gamma \leq t_1(j) : (j,\gamma) \in J^*\}.$

$J^+ = \{(j, t_2(j)) \in J \times T : j \in J^{s+}_\tau \text{ for some } \tau \text{ and } s\}.$

Set $J^*$ represents all $(j,t)$ such that $j$ can begin to be prepared (built) at the beginning of $t$ without violating (11); set $J^{s*}_t$ includes all $j$ that can be operational in $t$ under scenario $s$; set $J^{s+}_t$ corresponds to all $j$ that are actually operational during $t$ and $s$; set $J^+ \subseteq J^*$ corresponds to all $j$ that start being prepared at the beginning of some $t$, i.e., $J^+$ dictates which facilities are actually built and when should the preparing works begin (location decisions). Notice that if $j \in J^+$, then $j$ starts to be prepared at the beginning of $t_2(j)$, a time period selected taking into account all the time period(s) and scenario(s) during which $j$ is operational and also the setup time(s) required in that scenario(s). The definition of $t_2(j)$ ensures that facility $j$ starts to be built such that it will be operational when needed, considering the primal assignment variables, since it is limited by time period $t_1(j)$. Furthermore, the slack (10) associated with time period $t_2(j)$ should also be zero. The steps of the primal procedure are as follows:

1. Set $J^+ = J^{s+}_t = \emptyset$, $\forall t, s$. Build $J^*$ and $J^{s*}_t$, $\forall t, s$.
2. For each $t \in T$, if $j \in J^{s*}_t$ such that $\exists (i,s) : v^{s+}_{it} \geq \mathcal{C}^s_{ijt}$ and $v^{s+}_{it} < \mathcal{C}^s_{ij't}, \forall j' \in J^{s*}_t \backslash \{j\}$, then: $J^{s+}_\tau = J^{s+}_\tau \cup \{j\}$, $\forall \tau \geq t$; if $j \in J^{s'*}_t$, then $J^{s'+}_\tau = J^{s'+}_\tau \cup \{j\}$, $\forall \tau \geq t$.
3. For each $(i,t,s)$, if $\nexists j \in J^{s+}_t$ with $v^{s+}_{it} \geq \mathcal{C}^s_{ijt}$, select $j \in J^{s*}_t : \mathcal{C}^s_{ijt} = \min\{\mathcal{C}^s_{ij't} : v^s_{it} \geq \mathcal{C}^s_{ij't}\}$. Then: $J^{s+}_\tau = J^{s+}_\tau \cup \{j\}$, $\forall \tau \geq t$; if $j \in J^{s'*}_t$, then $J^{s'+}_\tau = J^{s'+}_\tau \cup \{j\}$, $\forall \tau \geq t$.
4. Build $J^+$.
5. Update $J^{s+}_t$, $\forall t, s$. Assign each $(i,t,s)$ to facility $j \in J^{s+}_t$ with lowest $\mathcal{C}^s_{ijt}$.

The facilities that are considered first (step 2) are the ones that at a given time $t$ should be assigned to a given customer $(i,s)$, according to conditions (13), called *essential* facilities. Other facilities are only opened if strictly necessary, that is, if there is a customer that cannot be assigned to an *essential* facility (step 3). At the end, for each scenario $s$ and period $t$, each customer $i$ will be assigned to the facility operating in $t$ and $s$ with the lowest assignment cost.

Notice that the decision of where and when to locate facilities will not immediately determine in which time periods the facilities can be assigned to customers, since these time periods will not be the same under all scenarios. It is necessary to take into account the uncertainty in setup times, meaning that the same facility can be operational in a given time period under a given scenario but not prepared to be assigned to clients in the same time period under other scenario (setup times are scenario dependent). The assignment of customers to facilities has to take into consideration that a facility $j$ that has began to be prepared at period $t$ will only be operational under scenario $s$ from $t + d_{js}$ forward.

**Primal–Dual Adjustment Procedure.** This procedure tries to change the current dual solution, by decreasing the value of at least one variable $v_{it}^s$ (and thus possibly decreasing the value of some variables $w_{ijt}^s$), such that at least two slacks will be increased. The changes in the slacks' values may lead to the increase of other dual variables increasing the dual objective function value. Let us first consider the additional sets:

$$J_{it}^{s*} = \{j : \exists \tau \le t - d_{js} \mid (j, \tau) \in J^* \text{ and } v_{it}^s \ge C_{ijt}^s\}, \forall (i, t, s);$$
$$J_{it}^{s+} = \{j : \exists \tau \le t - d_{js} \mid (j, \tau) \in J^+ \text{ and } v_{it}^s > C_{ijt}^s\}, \forall (i, t, s);$$
$$I_{jt}^+ = \{(i, \tau, s) : J_{i\tau}^{s*} = \{j\} \text{ for } \tau \ge t\}, \forall (j, t).$$

The best source and the second-best source for $(i, t, s)$ in $J_{it}^{s+}$ will be represented by $j(i, t, s)$ and $j'(i, t, s)$, respectively, and such that $C_{ij(i,t,s)t}^s = \min_{j \in J_t^{s+}}\{C_{ijt}^s\}$, $\forall (i, t, s)$, and $C_{ij'(i,t,s)t}^s = \min_{j \in J_t^{s+}, j \ne j(i,t,s)}\{C_{ijt}^s\}, \forall (i, t, s)$ for $|J_{it}^{s+}| > 1$. We also define $C_{it}^{s-} = \max_j\{C_{ijt}^s : v_{it}^s > C_{ijt}^s\}$. For a given $(i, t, s)$, set $J_{it}^{s*}$ represents all facilities $j$ that can be open at period $t$ (because a slack $\pi_{j\tau}$ is equal to zero for some $\tau \le t - d_{js}$) and such that if $j$ is open then customer $i$ can be assigned to $j$ at period $t$ under scenario $s$. Similarly, for a given $(i, t, s)$, the set $J_{it}^{s+}$ considers all facilities that are in operation during period $t$ in the current primal solution, and such that customer $i$ would have to be assigned to $j$ in period $t$ under scenario $s$ to guarantee the satisfaction of (13). If $|J_{it}^{s+}| > 1$, for some $(i, t, s)$, then a complementary slackness condition (13) is violated. In such case, the decrease of the variable $v_{it}^s$ causes the increase of at least two slacks $\pi_{j\tau}$, associated with distinct facilities (step 4). Set $I_{jt}^+$ corresponds to all variables $v_{i\tau}^s$ whose value can be increased with the increase of slacks $\pi_{j\tau}, \tau \le t - d_{js}$. This set is then used in the dual ascent procedure (step 5). As stated above, the heuristic stops when the optimal solution is found or when there are no primal or dual improvements after a given number of trials within the adjustment procedure. The steps of the primal-dual adjustment are:

1. $(i, t, s) \leftarrow (i, t, s)_1, q \leftarrow 1$; set $v_D = v_D^+$ and $v_P = v_P^+$; set $r = 0$.
2. If $|J_{it}^{s+}| \le 1$, then go to step 9.
3. If $I_{j(i,t,s)t}^+ = \emptyset$ and $I_{j'(i,t,s)t}^+ = \emptyset$, then go to step 9.
4. For each $(j, \tau)$, with $\tau \le t - d_{js}$ and $v_{it}^s > C_{ijt}^s$, set $\pi_{j\tau} = \pi_{j\tau} + v_{it}^s - C_{it}^{s-}$; set $v_{it}^s = C_{it}^{s-}$.
5. (a) Set $I^+ = I_{j(i,t,s)t}^+ \cup I_{j'(i,t,s)t}^+$ and execute the dual ascent procedure.
   (b) Set $I^+ = I^+ \cup \{(i, t, s)\}$ and execute the dual ascent procedure.
   (c) Set $I^+ = I \times T \times S$ and execute the dual ascent procedure.
6. If $v_{it}^s$ is changed, then return to step 2.
7. Execute the primal procedure.
8. If neither $v_D^+ > v_D$ nor $v_P^+ < v_P$, then $r \leftarrow r + 1$; otherwise $r \leftarrow 0$ and update $v_D$ and $v_P$.
9. If $v_D \ge v_P$, or $r = r_{max}$ or $q = |I \times T \times S|$, then stop; otherwise $q \leftarrow q + 1, (i, t, s) \leftarrow (i, t, s)_q$, and return to step 2.

## 4   Computational Experiments

Let us consider that there are only 4 scenarios, equally likely, 5 time periods, 4 possible facility locations and 10 possible customers. Facility 1 has no setup time under all scenarios ($d_{1s} = 0, \forall s \in \mathcal{S}$). Facility 2 has a setup time that is equal to 1 ($d_{2s} = 1, \forall s \in \mathcal{S}$). Facility 3 has a setup time equal to 1 under scenarios 1 and 2, and equal to 3 under scenarios 3 and 4. Facility 4 has a setup time that is equal to 1 in all scenarios but scenario 4 where it is equal to 2. Setup times for facilities 2, 3 and 4 were generated by using a PERT distribution with a most probable time ($d_{mode}$) equal to 1, 3 and 1 respectively. All the needed data were randomly generated. The optimal solution for this instance is given in the first line of Table 1, called stochastic solution (SS). We report the location decisions, total fixed costs, total assignment costs for each scenario and expected total assignment costs, and also the optimal objective function value $f$. To illustrate the impact of ignoring the uncertainty associated with setup times, we have also searched for the optimal solution of the problem where a deterministic setup time is used. First, the dynamic location problem under uncertainty with setup times fixed to $d_{mod}$ has been solved. This problem is equivalent to problem (1)–(6) with $d_{js}$ replaced by $d_{mode}$. The optimal location decisions obtained from this problem were recorded. Then, with the location decisions fixed to the values previously found, the assignment costs for each scenario were calculated (it is equivalent to solve problem (1)–(6) with fixed location decisions). The optimal solution is reported in the last line of Table 1, called deterministic solution (DS).

**Table 1.** Illustrative example: stochastic and deterministic solutions.

|     | $(j,t) : x_{jt} = 1$ | Fixed costs | Assignment costs | | | | | o.f |
|-----|------|------|------|------|------|------|------|------|
|     |      |      | $s=1$ | $s=2$ | $s=3$ | $s=4$ | Total | $f$ |
| SS  | (1,1); (3,1) | 4017 | 3056,5 | 2671,3 | 2858,8 | 2373,0 | 10959,5 | 14976,5 |
| DS  | (1,1); (2,2) | 4144 | 3477,0 | 2958,3 | 2806,3 | 2294,8 | 11536,3 | 15680,3 |

The optimal solutions provided by the two approaches differ on the location decisions: the deterministic approach chooses to build facility 2, whilst the stochastic approach chooses facility 3. Facility 3 would hardly be a choice for the deterministic approach, given the *more pessimistic* $d_{mod}$. The option of ignoring uncertainty leads to a cost that is 4.49% higher than the stochastic solution $((f_{DS} - f_{SS})/f_{DS})$. If, for instance, both $d_{33}$ and $d_{34}$ increase one time period to 4, the optimal SS found also dictates $x_{22} = 1$, in addition to $x_{11} = 1$ and $x_{13} = 1$. Consequently, the fixed costs increase to 5298, but the assignment costs decrease to 10074, leading to $(f_{DS} - f_{SS})/f_{DS} = 1.97\%$. The value of using the stochastic approach instead of considering deterministic setup times will be highly dependent of the problem data, namely costs, variability and magnitude of setup times.

In order to analyze the proposed model and to assess the efficiency of the proposed heuristic, several test problems were randomly generated, with $S \in \{10, 20\}$ (number of scenarios), $T \in \{10, 15\}$ (number of time periods), $M \in \{10, 20, 50\}$ (number of possible facility locations) and $N \in \{100, 200\}$ (number of possible customers). For each combination of $(S, T, M, N)$, five instances were randomly generated. Two classes of test problems were generated considering different magnitudes in terms of setup times: shorter and longer setup times. The approach used in the generation of all test problems can be summarized as follows. First the networks (nodes and costs) were randomly generated using the algorithm described in [17]. Afterwards, setup times were also randomly generated. For each instance, we have selected one facility $j$ such that $d_{js} = 0, \forall s \in \mathcal{S}$, ensuring that there is at least one operating facility in $t = 1$ (feasible problems). For each potential facility site $j$ setup times were randomly generated from a PERT distribution (see, for instance, [13]). Although the use of this distribution is not exempted from criticism [20], we considered it as a good alternative for the stochastic generation of setup times. The PERT distribution requires three parameters: optimistic, $d_{min}$, most likely, $d_{mode}$, and pessimistic, $d_{max}$, setup times for the present case. These have been randomly generated from Uniform distributions $\mathcal{U}[l, u]$, with parameters $l$ and $u$ given in Table 2 dependent on the given time horizon $T$.

**Table 2.** Parameters used in the random generation of setup times.

|          | $d_{mode}$ | $d_{min}$ | $d_{max}$ |
|----------|------------|-----------|-----------|
| Shorter  | $[1, \frac{T}{4}]$ | $[1, d_{mode}]$ | $[d_{mode}, 3\frac{T}{4}]$ |
| Longer   | $[\frac{T}{4}, 3\frac{T}{4}]$ | $[\frac{T}{4}, d_{mode}]$ | $[d_{mode}, T]$ |

A total of 240 instances were generated (120 in each class) that were solved by the heuristic and by an exact algorithm, CPLEX MIP optimizer, v12.4. After some preliminary tests, we have established as stopping criterium the quality of the best solution achieved by the algorithms (2% for all test problems). This is a fairer criteria to compare a heuristic with a general solver, since many times the general solver will spend much time slightly improving an already very good solution or trying to prove the optimality of the optimal solution already found. The algorithm was coded in C–language and the computational experiments were carried out on a Intel(R) Core(TM)2 Duo CPU T9400 2.53 GHz with 4.00 GB of RAM. Codes and all instances are available from the authors upon request.

Tables 3, 4, 5 and 6 summarize the computational results obtained in terms of solution quality and computational time. Each table corresponds to a given class of setup times and a number $S$ of scenarios. We report the minimum, average and maximum gap on the five instances solved for each combination of $(S, T, M, N)$, as well as the minimum, average and maximum time (in seconds) spent by the algorithms to solve those instances (not including the time required to read the problems' data). Gap is given, in percentage, by the difference between the

**Table 3.** Computational results (shorter setup times and 10 scenarios).

| T | M | N | Gap (%) Heur | | | Cplex | | | Time (sec) Heur | | | Cplex | | |
|---|---|---|---|---|---|---|---|---|---|---|---|---|---|---|
| | | | Min | Aver | Max | Min | Aver | Max | Min | Aver | Max | Min | Aver | Max |
| 10 | 10 | 100 | 0,00 | 0,03 | 0,15 | 0,00 | 0,00 | 0,00 | 0,02 | 0,03 | 0,05 | 3,57 | 4,13 | 5,04 |
| | 10 | 200 | 0,00 | 0,03 | 0,12 | 0,00 | 0,31 | 1,07 | 0,06 | 0,07 | 0,09 | 8,71 | 9,75 | 10,87 |
| | 20 | 100 | 0,00 | 0,24 | 0,51 | 0,00 | 0,04 | 0,20 | 0,04 | 0,05 | 0,05 | 6,77 | 8,89 | 14,01 |
| | 20 | 200 | 0,00 | 0,04 | 0,07 | 0,00 | 0,00 | 0,00 | 0,10 | 0,11 | 0,12 | 18,95 | 20,23 | 21,72 |
| | 50 | 100 | 0,13 | 0,51 | 0,92 | 0,19 | 0,88 | 1,59 | 0,07 | 29,4 | 86,7 | 31,87 | 42,17 | 51,18 |
| | 50 | 200 | 0,38 | 0,71 | 1,01 | 0,22 | 1,41 | 2,55 | 0,17 | 0,19 | 0,21 | 84,1 | 145,2 | 246,1 |
| **Aver** | | | **0,08** | **0,26** | **0,46** | **0,07** | **0,44** | **0,90** | **0,08** | **4,9** | **14,5** | **25,6** | **38,4** | **58,2** |
| 15 | 10 | 100 | 0,00 | 0,04 | 0,15 | 0,00 | 0,00 | 0,00 | 0,04 | 0,06 | 0,08 | 5,49 | 6,22 | 6,80 |
| | 10 | 200 | 0,00 | 0,00 | 0,00 | 0,00 | 0,00 | 0,00 | 0,11 | 0,12 | 0,14 | 15,94 | 18,13 | 19,06 |
| | 20 | 100 | 0,00 | 0,05 | 0,18 | 0,00 | 0,07 | 0,34 | 0,09 | 0,09 | 0,09 | 11,83 | 14,11 | 18,83 |
| | 20 | 200 | 0,00 | 0,01 | 0,04 | 0,00 | 0,00 | 0,00 | 0,19 | 0,20 | 0,22 | 31,28 | 33,88 | 39,48 |
| | 50 | 100 | 0,44 | 0,95 | 1,59 | 0,00 | 1,62 | 3,32 | 0,14 | 50,8 | 113,1 | 40,9 | 85,8 | 127,4 |
| | 50 | 200 | 0,07 | 0,34 | 0,59 | 0,00 | 11,00 | 43,53 | 0,30 | 0,33 | 0,37 | 80,97 | 212,4 | 501,6 |
| **Aver** | | | **0,09** | **0,23** | **0,42** | **0,00** | **2,11** | **7,87** | **0,14** | **8,6** | **19,0** | **31,1** | **61,8** | **118,9** |
| | | | **0,09** | **0,25** | **0,44** | **0,03** | **1,28** | **4,38** | **0,11** | **6,79** | **16,8** | **28,4** | **50,08** | **88,5** |

Solver was unable to solve one of the instances with $(T, M, N) = (15, 50, 200)$.

**Table 4.** Computational results (shorter setup times and 20 scenarios).

| T | M | N | Gap (%) Heur | | | Cplex | | | Time (sec) Heur | | | Cplex | | |
|---|---|---|---|---|---|---|---|---|---|---|---|---|---|---|
| | | | Min | Aver | Max | Min | Aver | Max | Min | Aver | Max | Min | Aver | Max |
| 10 | 10 | 100 | 0,00 | 0,00 | 0,02 | 0,00 | 0,00 | 0,00 | 0,10 | 0,12 | 0,16 | 8,25 | 9,34 | 10,23 |
| | 10 | 200 | 0,00 | 0,00 | 0,00 | 0,00 | 0,00 | 0,00 | 0,20 | 0,23 | 0,26 | 23,1 | 26,25 | 30,65 |
| | 20 | 100 | 0,18 | 0,27 | 0,46 | 0,00 | 0,16 | 0,79 | 0,15 | 0,16 | 0,17 | 16,8 | 20,1 | 22,4 |
| | 20 | 200 | 0,00 | 0,01 | 0,02 | 0,00 | 0,18 | 0,91 | 0,31 | 0,33 | 0,35 | 44,8 | 49,7 | 65,2 |
| | 50 | 100 | 0,18 | 0,80 | 1,37 | 0,00 | 0,53 | 1,88 | 0,26 | 160,9 | 450,1 | 90,4 | 145,4 | 190,8 |
| | 50 | 200 | 0,33 | 1,13 | 1,97 | 0,00 | 19,10 | 38,20 | 0,57 | 32,24 | 158,8 | 291,7 | 467,2 | 643,2 |
| **Aver** | | | **0,12** | **0,37** | **0,64** | **0,00** | **3,33** | **6,96** | **0,27** | **32,3** | **101,7** | **79,1** | **119,7** | **160,4** |
| 15 | 10 | 100 | 0,00 | 0,02 | 0,11 | 0,00 | 0,00 | 0,00 | 0,17 | 0,24 | 0,29 | 16,16 | 18,81 | 23,35 |
| | 10 | 200 | 0,00 | 0,00 | 0,00 | 0,00 | 0,00 | 0,00 | 0,42 | 0,49 | 0,56 | 37,00 | 41,95 | 49,22 |
| | 20 | 100 | 0,00 | 0,06 | 0,20 | 0,00 | 0,00 | 0,00 | 0,30 | 0,31 | 0,32 | 28,42 | 35,14 | 43,48 |
| | 20 | 200 | 0,00 | 0,05 | 0,20 | 0,00 | 0,00 | 0,00 | 0,60 | 0,67 | 0,80 | 74,88 | 81,74 | 87,88 |
| | 50 | 100 | 0,70 | 1,35 | 2,69 | 0,00 | 10,79 | 41,53 | 42,49 | 371,88 | 754,31 | 159,73 | 282,60 | 352,50 |
| | 50 | 200 | 0,52 | 0,71 | 1,06 | – | – | – | 0,98 | 1,10 | 1,21 | – | – | – |
| **Aver** | | | **0,20** | **0,37** | **0,71** | **0,00** | **2,16** | **8,31** | **7,49** | **62,45** | **126,3** | **63,24** | **92,05** | **111,29** |
| | | | **0,16** | **0,37** | **0,68** | **0,00** | **2,80** | **7,57** | **3,88** | **47,39** | **113,9** | **71,88** | **107,11** | **138,08** |

Solver was unable to solve: three of the instances with $(T, M, N) = (10, 50, 200)$; one of the instances with $(T, M, N) = (15, 50, 100)$; any with $(T, M, N) = (15, 50, 200)$.

best objective function value found by the algorithm and the best known lower bound on the optimal value divided by this best known lower bound. The average

**Table 5.** Computational results (longer setup times and 10 scenarios).

| T | M | N | Gap (%) | | | | | | Time (sec) | | | | | |
|---|---|---|---|---|---|---|---|---|---|---|---|---|---|---|
| | | | Heur | | | Cplex | | | Heur | | | Cplex | | |
| | | | Min | Aver | Max | Min | Aver | Max | Min | Aver | Max | Min | Aver | Max |
| 10 | 10 | 100 | 0,00 | 0,11 | 0,26 | 0,00 | 0,00 | 0,00 | 0,03 | 0,04 | 0,04 | 2,23 | 2,46 | 2,76 |
| | 10 | 200 | 0,00 | 0,02 | 0,05 | 0,00 | 0,00 | 0,00 | 0,08 | 0,08 | 0,08 | 5,10 | 6,26 | 7,16 |
| | 20 | 100 | 0,00 | 0,09 | 0,22 | 0,00 | 0,05 | 0,27 | 0,04 | 0,06 | 0,08 | 4,74 | 5,45 | 6,46 |
| | 20 | 200 | 0,00 | 0,10 | 0,36 | 0,00 | 0,16 | 0,78 | 0,11 | 0,12 | 0,13 | 12,04 | 14,44 | 18,13 |
| | 50 | 100 | 0,80 | 1,13 | 1,75 | 0,00 | 0,85 | 1,83 | 14,54 | 37,28 | 94,65 | 14,06 | 20,38 | 25,76 |
| | 50 | 200 | 0,39 | 0,63 | 0,94 | 0,00 | 0,37 | 1,46 | 0,19 | 0,20 | 0,22 | 42,74 | 60,95 | 84,74 |
| **Aver** | | | **0,20** | **0,35** | **0,60** | **0,00** | **0,24** | **0,72** | **2,50** | **6,30** | **15,9** | **13,5** | **18,3** | **24,17** |
| 15 | 10 | 100 | 0,00 | 0,00 | 0,00 | 0,00 | 0,00 | 0,00 | 0,06 | 0,07 | 0,11 | 3,70 | 4,03 | 4,66 |
| | 10 | 200 | 0,00 | 0,00 | 0,00 | 0,00 | 0,00 | 0,00 | 0,13 | 0,15 | 0,17 | 9,53 | 10,75 | 12,01 |
| | 20 | 100 | 0,00 | 0,06 | 0,11 | 0,00 | 0,00 | 0,00 | 0,09 | 0,10 | 0,12 | 7,96 | 9,00 | 11,58 |
| | 20 | 200 | 0,00 | 0,02 | 0,10 | 0,00 | 0,00 | 0,00 | 0,20 | 0,22 | 0,26 | 20,67 | 22,21 | 23,62 |
| | 50 | 100 | 0,01 | 0,56 | 1,51 | 0,00 | 0,70 | 1,87 | 0,15 | 32,5 | 161,8 | 20,3 | 30,2 | 47,5 |
| | 50 | 200 | 0,15 | 0,46 | 0,99 | 0,00 | 0,09 | 0,26 | 0,31 | 0,37 | 0,42 | 51,64 | 85,40 | 125,05 |
| **Aver** | | | **0,03** | **0,18** | **0,45** | **0,00** | **0,13** | **0,36** | **0,16** | **5,6** | **27,1** | **18,9** | **26,9** | **37,4** |
| | | | **0,11** | **0,26** | **0,52** | **0,00** | **0,19** | **0,54** | **1,33** | **5,9** | **21,5** | **16,2** | **22,6** | **30,8** |

results for gap and computational time are also reported for each $T$, as well as for each $S$, in the last row of the corresponding table. Statistics refer only to those instances that were solved. The heuristic was able to solve all the instances whereas the solver could not solve some problems due to lack of memory. We report these cases at the bottom of each table. Both algorithms present gaps higher than 2% for some instances, which is justified as follows: for the general solver, this happens due to lack of memory to proceed with the calculations; for the heuristic this happens when the maximum number of trials to improve a solution within the adjustment procedure was reached. The computational results show that the heuristic is capable of finding very good quality solutions in reasonable computational times. The worst gap equals 2.69% and was observed in instances with shorter setup times and $(S, T, M, N) = (20, 15, 50, 100)$, the same set where the maximum computational time was also reached, 754,3 s. The larger gaps and computational times were observed in instances with largest $M$, 50 potential facility sites. Within these sets of instances, gap increases as the number of scenarios increases for shorter setup times. On the other hand, for longer setup times, gap decreases in some problems as the number of scenarios increases. The heuristic's performance was better in large sized problems with longer setup times than with shorter ones.

In terms of solution quality, the average minimum gap achieved by CPLEX is better than the average minimum gap obtained by the heuristic, although for many instance sets the minimum gap achieved is the same. However, less instances were solved by the solver, in particular large sized problems. The execution times required by the solver are clearly higher than those required by the heuristic. In the majority of problems, except instances with $(M, N) = (50, 100)$,

**Table 6.** Computational results (longer setup times and 20 scenarios).

| T | M | N | Gap (%) | | | | | | Time (sec) | | | | | |
|---|---|---|---------|---|---|---|---|---|-----------|---|---|---|---|---|
| | | | Heur | | | Cplex | | | Heur | | | Cplex | | |
| | | | Min | Aver | Max | Min | Aver | Max | Min | Aver | Max | Min | Aver | Max |
| 10 | 10 | 100 | 0,00 | 0,00 | 0,01 | 0,00 | 0,00 | 0,00 | 0,11 | 0,13 | 0,16 | 5,04 | 6,18 | 7,60 |
| | 10 | 200 | 0,00 | 0,00 | 0,00 | 0,00 | 0,00 | 0,00 | 0,25 | 0,28 | 0,31 | 16,19 | 18,59 | 20,20 |
| | 20 | 100 | 0,00 | 0,28 | 0,92 | 0,00 | 0,22 | 1,12 | 0,14 | 0,17 | 0,21 | 12,62 | 14,24 | 17,16 |
| | 20 | 200 | 0,01 | 0,04 | 0,06 | 0,00 | 0,00 | 0,00 | 0,29 | 0,36 | 0,40 | 27,22 | 32,54 | 35,12 |
| | 50 | 100 | 0,14 | 0,72 | 1,33 | 0,00 | 0,63 | 1,72 | 0,25 | 100,9 | 418,8 | 43,3 | 70,5 | 103,4 |
| | 50 | 200 | 0,17 | 0,55 | 1,01 | 0,00 | 9,54 | 24,22 | 0,56 | 0,63 | 0,72 | 139,9 | 209,1 | 343,3 |
| Aver | | | **0,05** | **0,27** | **0,55** | **0,00** | **1,73** | **4,51** | **0,27** | **17,1** | **70,1** | **40,7** | **58,5** | **87,8** |
| 15 | 10 | 100 | 0,00 | 0,01 | 0,05 | 0,00 | 0,00 | 0,00 | 0,23 | 0,28 | 0,36 | 8,91 | 10,59 | 12,98 |
| | 10 | 200 | 0,00 | 0,00 | 0,00 | 0,00 | 0,00 | 0,00 | 0,50 | 0,60 | 0,77 | 26,69 | 29,08 | 32,12 |
| | 20 | 100 | 0,00 | 0,13 | 0,37 | 0,00 | 0,00 | 0,00 | 0,34 | 0,38 | 0,44 | 18,41 | 24,08 | 28,30 |
| | 20 | 200 | 0,00 | 0,02 | 0,08 | 0,00 | 0,00 | 0,00 | 0,81 | 0,86 | 0,93 | 50,61 | 54,73 | 64,01 |
| | 50 | 100 | 0,03 | 0,43 | 0,85 | 0,00 | 0,18 | 0,59 | 0,50 | 31,82 | 156,9 | 52,1 | 110,7 | 187,9 |
| | 50 | 200 | 0,49 | 0,88 | 1,08 | – | – | – | 1,09 | 1,34 | 1,64 | – | – | – |
| Aver | | | **0,09** | **0,25** | **0,41** | **0,00** | **0,04** | **0,12** | **0,58** | **5,9** | **26,8** | **31,4** | **45,8** | **65,1** |
| | | | **0,07** | **0,26** | **0,48** | **0,00** | **0,96** | **2,51** | **0,42** | **11,5** | **48,5** | **36,5** | **52,8** | **77,5** |

Solver was unable to solve any of the instances with $(T, M, N) = (15, 50, 200)$.

the maximum computational time of the heuristic is smaller than the minimum time of CPLEX. On average, the heuristic presents better mean and maximum times. On average, the gap is also better for the heuristic than for CPLEX in the majority of problems, except for longer setup times and larger horizons. CPLEX presents a better behavior for instances with longer setup times than with shorter, and is also able of solving more problems.

It is possible to observe that, as expected, the objective function value is always higher when longer setup times are considered. Table 7 reports the average relative increase (in percentage) of the (Best) objective function values for longer setup times, considering the average over the five instances. In the majority of instances, this increase in total cost corresponds to an increase of assignment costs and a decrease of fixed facility costs. However, there are also instances where both fixed facility and assignment costs increase. Table 7 also reports the minimum and maximum number of operational facilities for each combination of $(S, T, M, N)$. Instances with longer setup times have less operational facilities. It should be noted that not only the number of operational facilities can change, but also the period of time when facilities become operational. This may have to do with the fact that with shorter setup times it is possible to take better advantage of the compromises between total fixed and assignment costs, since facilities can be operational during a longer period of time within the planning horizon.

**Table 7.** Relative increase of objective function values (RIof, in (%)) and number of operational facilities with shorter (♯ Sh) versus longer (♯ Lo) setup times.

| $T$ | $M$ | $N$ | RIof (%) | | $S = 10$ | | $S = 20$ | |
|---|---|---|---|---|---|---|---|---|
| | | | $S = 10$ | $S = 20$ | ♯ Sh | ♯ Lo | ♯ Sh | ♯ Lo |
| 10 | 10 | 100 | 11,2 | 10,4 | 7–9 | 5–7 | 8–9 | 5–8 |
| | 10 | 200 | 9,9 | 10,1 | 9–10 | 6–8 | 9–10 | 7–9 |
| | 20 | 100 | 9,0 | 10,7 | 10–13 | 8–12 | 11–13 | 8–11 |
| | 20 | 200 | 11,5 | 10,2 | 15–19 | 11–14 | 15–17 | 10–15 |
| | 50 | 100 | 12,1 | 11,1 | 15–21 | 14–19 | 17–20 | 13–15 |
| | 50 | 200 | 10,1 | 10,5 | 25–28 | 20–25 | 26–29 | 15–24 |
| **Aver** | | | **10,7** | **10,5** | | | | |
| 15 | 10 | 100 | 9,1 | 12,4 | 8–9 | 7–8 | 8–10 | 7–8 |
| | 10 | 200 | 9,6 | 9,0 | 10–10 | 9–10 | 10–10 | 8–9 |
| | 20 | 100 | 13,3 | 12,2 | 14–17 | 11–14 | 14–15 | 11–12 |
| | 20 | 200 | 12,7 | 12,8 | 18–19 | 14–14 | 15–18 | 12–15 |
| | 50 | 100 | 11,5 | 12,7 | 21–26 | 16–21 | 19–24 | 14–19 |
| | 50 | 200 | 14,4 | 13,7 | 28–35 | 23–28 | 27–33 | 22–25 |
| **Aver** | | | **11,8** | **12,1** | | | | |

## 5   Conclusions

A dynamic facility location problem incorporating setup time uncertainty has been introduced. As far as the authors know, it is the first time this problem is addressed, and it represents a situation that often happens in practice: projects due get delayed, and opening a facility implies, most of the times, a set of different and interrelated tasks that have to be executed. A primal–dual heuristic has been developed, and computational results reported. The heuristic is capable of calculating optimal or near-optimal solutions in much shorter computational times than the general solver. Future work will explicitly consider compromises between investment cost and setup time uncertainty.

## References

1. Albareda-Sambola, M., Alonso-Ayuso, A., Escudero, L.F., Fernández, E., Pizarro, C.: Fix-and-relax-coordination for a multi-period location-allocation problem under uncertainty. Comput. Oper. Res. **40**, 2878–2892 (2013)
2. Al-Momani, A.H.: Construction delay: a quantitative analysis. Int. J. Proj. Manag. **18**(1), 51–59 (2000)
3. Arantes, A., da Silva, P.F., Ferreira, L.M. D.: Delays in construction projects-causes and impacts. In: 2015 International Conference on Industrial Engineering and Systems Management (IESM), pp. 1105–1110. IEEE (2015)
4. Assaf, S.A., Al-Hejji, S.: Causes of delay in large construction projects. Int. J. Proj. Manag. **24**(4), 349–357 (2006)

5. Baron, O., Milner, J., Naseraldin, H.: Facility location: a robust optimization approach. Prod. Oper. Manag. **20**(5), 772–785 (2011)
6. Bilde, O., Krarup, J.: Sharp lower bounds and efficient algorithms for the simple plant location problem. Ann. Discret. Math. **1**, 79–97 (1977)
7. De Rosa, V., Hartmann, E., Gebhard, M., Wollenweber, J.: Robust capacitated facility location model for acquisitions under uncertainty. Comput. Ind. Eng. **72**, 206–216 (2014)
8. Dias, J., Captivo, M.E., Clímaco, J.: Efficient primal-dual heuristic for a dynamic location problem. Comput. Oper. Res. **34**(6), 1800–1823 (2007)
9. Dias, J.: Can we really ignore time in Simple Plant Location Problems? (No. 7/2015), Inesc-Coimbra (2015)
10. Dias, J.M., Marques, M.d.C.: A multiobjective approach for a dynamic simple plant location problem under uncertainty. In: Murgante, B., Misra, S., Rocha, A.M.A.C., Torre, C., Rocha, J.G., Falcão, M.I., Taniar, D., Apduhan, B.O., Gervasi, O. (eds.) ICCSA 2014. LNCS, vol. 8580, pp. 60–75. Springer, Cham (2014). https://doi.org/10.1007/978-3-319-09129-7_5
11. Dunke, F., Heckmann, I., Nickel, S., Saldanha-da-Gama, F.: Time traps in supply chains: is optimal still good enough? Eur. J. Oper. Res. **264**(3), 813–829 (2018)
12. Erlenkotter, D.: A dual-based procedure for uncapacitated facility location. Oper. Res. **26**(6), 992–1009 (1978)
13. Golenko-Ginzburg, D.: On the distribution of activity time in PERT. J. Oper. Res. Soc. **39**(8), 767–771 (1988)
14. Hernández, P., et al.: A branch-and-cluster coordination scheme for selecting prison facility sites under uncertainty. Comput. Oper. Res. **39**, 2232–2241 (2012)
15. Louveaux, F.V.: Discrete stochastic location models. Ann. Oper. Res. **6**(2), 21–34 (1986)
16. Louveaux, F.V., Peeters, D.: A dual-based procedure for stochastic facility location. Oper. Res. **40**(3), 564–573 (1992)
17. Marques, M.d.C., Dias, J.: Simple dynamic location problem with uncertainty: a primal-dual heuristic approach. Optimization **62**(10), 1379–1397 (2013)
18. Marques, M.d.C, Dias, J.: Dynamic location problem under uncertainty with a regret-based measure of robustness. Int. Trans. Oper. Res. (2015). https://doi.org/10.1111/itor.12183
19. Snyder, L.V.: Facility location under uncertainty: a review. IIE Trans. **38**, 537–554 (2006)
20. Trietsch, D., Baker, K.R.: PERT 21: fitting PERT/CPM for use in the 21st century. Int. J. Proj. Manag. **30**(4), 490–502 (2012)
21. Van Roy, T.J., Erlenkotter, D.: A dual-based procedure for dynamic facility location. Manag. Sci. **28**(10), 1091–1105 (1982)

# An Optimization Approach for Noncoplanar Intensity-Modulated Arc Therapy Trajectories

Humberto Rocha[1,2]([✉]) [ID], Joana Dias[1,2] [ID], Tiago Ventura[2,3] [ID],
Brígida Ferreira[2,4] [ID], and Maria do Carmo Lopes[2,3] [ID]

[1] CeBER and Faculdade de Economia, Universidade de Coimbra,
3004-512 Coimbra, Portugal
hrocha@mat.uc.pt, joana@fe.uc.pt
[2] INESC-Coimbra, 3030-290 Coimbra, Portugal
[3] Serviço de Física Médica, IPOC-FG, EPE, 3000-075 Coimbra, Portugal
{tiagoventura,mclopes}@ipocoimbra.min-saude.pt
[4] Escola Superior de Saúde, Politécnico do Porto, 4200-072 Porto, Portugal
bcf@ess.ipp.pt

**Abstract.** The latest generation of linear accelerators allows the simultaneous motion of gantry and couch leading to highly noncoplanar arc trajectories. The use of noncoplanar trajectories in arc radiotherapy was recently proposed to combine the benefits of arc treatment plans, such as short treatment times, with the benefits of step-and-shoot noncoplanar intensity-modulated radiation therapy (IMRT) treatment plans, such as improved organ sparing. In this paper, a two-step approach for the optimization of highly noncoplanar arc trajectories is presented and tested using a complex nasopharyngeal tumor case already treated at the Portuguese Institute of Oncology of Coimbra. In the first step, a set of noncoplanar beam directions is calculated resorting to one of the beam angle optimization (BAO) algorithms proposed in our previous works for step-and-shoot IMRT. In the second step, anchored in the points (beam directions) calculated in the first step, the proposed optimization strategy determines iteratively more anchor points that will define the noncoplanar arc trajectory, considering the dosimetric criteria used for the noncoplanar BAO search rather than geometric or time criteria commonly used. For the patient tested, the resulting noncoplanar arc therapy plan has undoubtedly greater overall quality compared to both the coplanar arc therapy plan and the typically used coplanar equispaced step-and-shoot IMRT plan.

**Keywords:** Noncoplanar radiotherapy · Arc therapy · Optimization · Treatment planning

## 1 Introduction

In classic step-and-shoot IMRT, a linear accelerator mounted on a gantry rotates around the patient delivering non-uniform radiation fields from a set of fixed

© Springer Nature Switzerland AG 2019
S. Misra et al. (Eds.): ICCSA 2019, LNCS 11621, pp. 199–214, 2019.
https://doi.org/10.1007/978-3-030-24302-9_15

coplanar beams. Allowing the rotation of the couch where the patient is laid results in noncoplanar beam irradiation which may improve treatment plan quality, particularly for complex intra-cranial tumors [1]. In arc therapy, irradiation is done continuously while the gantry rotates around the patient with the treatment beam always on. Nowadays, volumetric modulated arc therapy (VMAT) [2–4] is considered one of the most efficient IMRT arc techniques, in particular regarding dose delivery time. VMAT treatment plans typically use coplanar beam trajectories, performed for a fixed couch angle (usually 0°), where irradiation of the patient is modulated by a multileaf collimator (MLC), determining the gantry speed.

The use of noncoplanar trajectories in VMAT was recently proposed to combine the benefits of arc therapy treatment plans, such as short treatment times, with the benefits of noncoplanar IMRT treatment plans, such as improved organ sparing. Yang et al. [5] used principal component analysis to optimize the collimator angle dynamically and considered a hierarchical clustering algorithm to calculate noncoplanar arc trajectories. MacDonald and Thomas [6] embedded beams-eye-view (BEV) dose metrics in their arc trajectory optimization. Smyth et al. considered a fluence based local search algorithm [7] and also embedded geometrical metrics in their arc trajectory optimization [8]. Papp et al. [9] and Wild et al. [10] considered the travel salesman problem to find the best arc trajectories between fixed angles. A similar approach aiming to improve computational time and plan quality was recently proposed by Langhans et al. [11].

In this paper, we propose a two-step approach for optimizing noncoplanar arc trajectories. In the first step, a set of noncoplanar beam directions is calculated resorting to one of the BAO algorithms proposed in our previous works for step-and-shoot IMRT [12]. In the second step, anchored in the points (beam directions) calculated in the first step, the proposed optimization strategy determines iteratively more anchor points that will define the noncoplanar arc trajectory, considering the same dosimetric criteria used for the noncoplanar BAO rather than geometric or time criteria commonly used. A nasopharyngeal tumor case, corresponding to a complex intra-cranial tumor treated at the Portuguese Institute of Oncology of Coimbra (IPOC), is used to illustrate and test the proposed optimization strategy. The remainder of the paper is organized as follows. The nasopharyngeal tumor case is described in the next Section. In Section three we present the strategy proposed for noncoplanar arc trajectory optimization. Computational results are presented in Section four followed by the conclusions and future work in the last Section.

## 2    Nasopharyngeal Tumor Case

A clinical nasopharyngeal tumor case treated at IPOC was used to illustrate and test our approach. Nasopharyngeal tumors are intra-cranial tumor cases requiring treatments that are particularly difficult to plan given the large number of organs that surround the tumor. The brainstem, the spinal cord, the parotids (the larger salivary glands) and the oral cavity (that contains the remaining

**Table 1.** Prescribed doses for the planning target volumes and tolerance doses for the organs considered.

| Structure | Tolerance dose | | Prescribed dose |
|---|---|---|---|
| | Mean | Max | |
| $PTV_{70}$ | – | – | 70.0 Gy |
| $PTV_{59.4}$ | – | – | 59.4 Gy |
| Spinal cord | – | 45 Gy | – |
| Brainstem | – | 54 Gy | – |
| Left parotid | 26 Gy | – | – |
| Right parotid | 26 Gy | – | – |
| Oral cavity | 45 Gy | – | – |
| Body | – | 80 Gy | – |

salivary glands) are the organs-at-risk (OARs) considered. For safety purposes, the tumor volume is enlarged by adding a margin originating a structure called planning target volume (PTV). Two levels of radiation dose are prescribed: a higher radiation dose of 70 Gy is prescribed to the tumor (called $PTV_{70}$) and a lower radiation dose of 59.4 Gy is prescribed to the lymph nodes (called $PTV_{59.4}$).

Prescribed doses for the planning target volumes and tolerance doses for the organs considered are displayed in Table 1. The spinal cord and the brainstem are serial organs. Serial organs are compromised even if only a small part is damaged and therefore maximum-dose constraints are considered for such type of organs. On the other hand, parallel organs functioning is not much affected if a small part of the organ is damaged and thus mean-dose objectives are considered for such type of organs. The oral cavity and the parotids are parallel organs. A structure, called Body, that corresponds to the remaining organs and tissues is also considered to prevent the deposition of high radiation doses elsewhere.

## 3    Highly Noncoplanar Arc Trajectory Optimization

The latest generation of linear accelerators allows the simultaneous motion of gantry and couch. A treatment plan that uses simultaneous gantry and couch rotation while the treatment beam is on will be considered, leading to a highly noncoplanar arc trajectory. In this study, we provide an optimization approach for the noncoplanar arc trajectory of a VMAT plan, called $4\pi$ VMAT, and compare it with the coplanar arc trajectory of a VMAT plan, called $2\pi$ VMAT, and with the typically used equispaced step-and-shoot IMRT plan, called *Equi*. Previous works on noncoplanar VMAT start by calculating a noncoplanar trajectory of the incident beam and then a fully VMAT plan is optimized along the calculated trajectory. The main goal of this study is to present our optimization strategy for the noncoplanar arc trajectory. Instead of obtaining fully VMAT plans, the different plans will be compared considering unsequenced IMRT treatment plans.

The two-step approach that we propose for optimizing noncoplanar arc trajectories combines two optimization problems, the BAO problem and the arc trajectory optimization, that are quite challenging just by themselves. Furthermore, as a dosimetric criteria is used to guide these two optimization problems, the fluence map optimization (FMO) problem needs to be addressed as well. Formulation and resolution approaches used to address FMO and BAO problems are succinctly presented in the next two sub-sections, followed by the description of the proposed strategy for noncoplanar arc trajectory optimization.

### 3.1   Fluence Map Optimization

There are many different formulations for the FMO problem, some of them assuring an automated optimization procedure [13]. Some of the most used formulations consider a weighted sum of objectives and most of the times constraints are implemented as objectives as well. The objectives defined for target and organs are naturally conflicting, and it is difficult to define what is the best trade-off between them. Therefore, a multicriteria formulation for the FMO problem is the most appropriate formulation. A multicriteria approach based on a wish-list defined *a priori* is considered as proposed by Breedveld *et al.* [14–16].

The wish-list constructed for the nasopharyngeal tumor case in study is displayed in Table 2. Due to the complexity of the clinical case, it was necessary to computationally define a set of additional structures other than PTVs and OARs. $PTV_{59.4}$ shell is obtained by removing a 10 mm margin of $PTV_{70}$ to $PTV_{59.4}$ and its purpose is to prevent high doses in the lymph nodes. Ring $PTV_{59.4}$ and Ring $PTV_{70}$ are obtained by creating ring structures with 10 mm of thickness at 10 mm distance from $PTV_{59.4}$ and $PTV_{70}$, respectively. These two auxiliary structures aim at improving target coverage and conformity. Finally, External Ring is obtained by creating a ring of 10 mm thickness next to the patient outer contour. This auxiliary structure is used to prevent possible high entrance doses.

Following the prescribed and tolerance doses displayed in Table 1, a wish-list containing 9 hard constraints and 10 prioritized objectives was constructed. Constraints must be strictly fulfilled as all are maximum-dose type constraints. Following the order in the wish-list, defined *a priori*, objectives are sequentially optimized. For tumors, the logarithmic tumor control probability ($LTCP$) was considered for dose optimization [16],

$$LTCP = \frac{1}{N_T} \sum_{l=1}^{N_T} e^{-\alpha(D_i - T_i)},$$

where $T_i$ is the dose prescribed to the tumor, $D_i$ is the dose in voxel $i$, $N_T$ is the number of PTV voxels, and $\alpha$ is a parameter assessing cell sensitivity. Doses that are lower than the prescribed ones are penalized by $LTCP$, whilst doses $D_i$ higher than the prescribed ones will make $LTCP$ tend to zero. The objective is

**Table 2.** Wish-list constructed for the nasopharyngeal tumor case.

|  | Structure | Type | Limit | | |
|---|---|---|---|---|---|
| | $PTV_{70}$ | maximum | 74.9 Gy (=107% of prescribed dose) | | |
| | $PTV_{59.4}$ | maximum | 63.6 Gy (=107% of prescribed dose) | | |
| | $PTV_{59.4}$ shell | maximum | 63.6 Gy (=107% of prescribed dose) | | |
| | Spinal cord | maximum | 45 Gy | | |
| **Constraints** | Brainstem | maximum | 54 Gy | | |
| | Ring $PTV_{70}$ | maximum | 59.5 Gy (=85% of prescribed dose) | | |
| | Ring $PTV_{59.4}$ | maximum | 50.5 Gy (=85% of prescribed dose) | | |
| | External Ring | maximum | 45 Gy | | |
| | Body | maximum | 70 Gy | | |

|  | Structure | Type | Priority | Goal | Parameters | Sufficient |
|---|---|---|---|---|---|---|
| | $PTV_{70}$ | LTCP | 2 | 1 | $T_i = 70$ Gy; $\alpha = 0.75$ | 0.5 |
| | $PTV_{59.4}$ | LTCP | 1 | 1 | $T_i = 59.4$ Gy; $\alpha = 0.75$ | 0.5 |
| | $PTV_{59.4}$ shell | LTCP | 3 | 1 | $T_i = 59.4$ Gy; $\alpha = 0.75$ | 0.5 |
| | External ring | maximum | 4 | 42.75 Gy | – | – |
| **Objectives** | Spinal cord | maximum | 5 | 42.75 Gy | – | – |
| | Brainstem | maximum | 6 | 51.3 Gy | – | – |
| | Parotids | mean | 7 | 50 Gy | – | – |
| | Oral cavity | mean | 8 | 45 Gy | – | – |
| | Parotids | mean | 9 | 26 Gy | – | – |
| | Oral cavity | mean | 10 | 35 Gy | – | – |

to obtain an $LTCP$ of one, which corresponds to a homogeneous dose equal to the prescribed dose $T_i$.

This formulation of the FMO problem is addressed by $2p\epsilon c$, a primal-dual interior-point algorithm tailored for multicriteria IMRT treatment planning [14]. For more details on $2p\epsilon c$ interior-point algorithm see Breedveld *et al.* [14].

## 3.2   Noncoplanar Beam Angle Optimization

The BAO problem is most of the times formulated as a combinatorial optimization problem, considering a discrete sample of all continuous beam angle directions. Computational time constraints make exhaustive search-like approaches prohibitive. A number of different approaches have been proposed to reduce the computational time, including simulated annealing [17], neighborhood search [18], gradient search [19], branch-and-prune [20], genetic algorithms [21], or hybrid approaches [22]. None of these approaches is able to calculate, in a polynomial run time, the optimal solution of the combinatorial BAO problem (NP hard problem) [23]. An alternative formulation of the BAO problem has been considered in our works. All possible continuous beam angle directions around the tumor have been considered instead of a discretized set of beam directions, leading to a continuous global optimization problem [24–28]. The continuous formulation of the noncoplanar BAO problem is briefly described next.

Let $n$ be defined *a priori* as the number of noncoplanar beam irradiation directions and denote the couch angle as $\phi$ and the gantry angle as $\theta$. As gantry angles 370° and 10° are the same irradiation directions (for a fixed couch angle), we consider an unbounded formulation. The continuous formulation of the noncoplanar BAO problem considers an objective function for which the best beam irradiation set corresponds to the function's minimum:

$$\min f\Big((\theta_1, \phi_1), \ldots, (\theta_n, \phi_n)\Big)$$

$$s.t. \ \Big(\theta_1, \ldots, \theta_n, \phi_1, \ldots, \phi_n\Big) \in \mathbb{R}^{2n}. \tag{1}$$

The optimal value of the FMO problem has been used by us as the objective function, $f$, that guides the BAO search. In a noncoplanar beam irradiation setting, not all possible combinations of couch and gantry angles are feasible due to possible collision between the patient and the gantry. In order to maintain an unbounded formulation, noncoplanar irradiation directions that would cause collisions are penalized in the objective function as follows:

$$f\Big((\theta_1, \phi_1), \ldots, (\theta_n, \phi_n)\Big) = \begin{cases} +\infty & \text{if collisions occur} \\ \text{optimal FMO value} & \text{otherwise.} \end{cases}$$

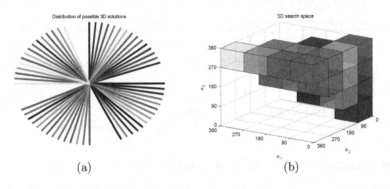

(a)                                    (b)

**Fig. 1.** All possible sorted combinations of three-beam angle sets divided by the four quadrants – (a) and the corresponding painted cubes in the reduced BAO search space $[0, 360]^3$ – (b).

The continuous BAO search space has a symmetric property explained by the simple fact that the order of irradiation directions is irrelevant in terms of optimization. By sorting the irradiation directions for each beam angle set, a large reduction of the BAO search space is obtained [12]. In previous works, we propose a multistart strategy that takes advantage of the symmetric feature of the continuous BAO search space. For an efficient sampling of the reduced BAO search space, the strategy sketched consists in considering all possible sorted combinations of beam angle sets divided by the four quadrants, as illustrated in Fig. 1(a) for a continuous three-dimensional BAO search space. Each of the represented three-beam angle set will define a starting point located in the different painted cubes illustrated in Fig. 1(b).

The two main aspects of the proposed multistart approach, after the definition of the initial starting points, are the local procedure considered to explore each of the cubes of the reduced search space, and the definition of each cube as a region of attraction to avoid overlapping of different local search procedures. For the local search procedure, pattern search methods (PSM) as described in Rocha et al. [29] are used for their ability to avoid local entrapment. Algorithms 1 and 2 display the PSM algorithm and the multistart algorithm, respectively. For further details on the parallel implementation of the multistart approach see Rocha et al. [29].

---

**Algorithm 1.** Parallel multistart PSM algorithm

**Initialization:**

- Set $k \leftarrow 0$;
- Choose the initial points $\mathbf{x}_i^0 \in [0, 360]^n, i = 1, \dots, N$, one for each of the $N$ cubes of the reduced search space;
- Compute $f(\mathbf{x}_i^0), i = 1, \dots, N$ in parallel;
- Set the best points in each cube, $\mathbf{x}^*$, as $\mathbf{x}_i^* \leftarrow \mathbf{x}_i^0, i = 1, \dots, N$ and the best function value in each cube, $f^*$, as $f_i^* \leftarrow f(\mathbf{x}_i^0), i = 1, \dots, N$;
- Set all the cubes as regions of attraction having active local searches, $\textbf{Active}_i \leftarrow 1, i = 1, \dots, N$;
- Choose PSM initial step-size, $\alpha_i^0 > 0, i = 1, \dots, N$, and minimal step-size $\alpha_{min}$;

**Iteration:**

1. Use PSM (algorithm 2) to locally explore the cubes with active local search;
2. For cubes $i$ with active local search do
   If $f(\mathbf{x}_i^k) < f(\mathbf{x}_i^*)$ then
       If $\mathbf{x}_i^k$ is in cube $i$ then
           $\mathbf{x}_i^* \leftarrow \mathbf{x}_i^k$;
           $f_i^* \leftarrow f(\mathbf{x}_i^k)$;
       Else
           $\textbf{Active}_i \leftarrow 0$;
           Determine cube $j \neq i$ where $\mathbf{x}_i^k$ is;
           If $f(\mathbf{x}_i^k) < f(\mathbf{x}_j^*)$ then
               $\mathbf{x}_j^* \leftarrow \mathbf{x}_i^k$;
               $f_j^* \leftarrow f(\mathbf{x}_i^k)$;
               $\textbf{Active}_j \leftarrow 1$;
   Else
       $\alpha_i^{k+1} \leftarrow \frac{\alpha_i^k}{2}$;
       If $\alpha_i^{k+1} < \alpha_{min}$ then
           $\textbf{Active}_i \leftarrow 0$;
3. If there exists active cubes go to first step and set $k \leftarrow k + 1$.

---

### 3.3  Noncoplanar Arc Trajectory Optimization

The optimization approach proposed for calculating noncoplanar arc trajectories is divided into two steps. In the first step, using the BAO algorithm described in Sect. 3.2, a set of noncoplanar beam directions is calculated. Then, in the

---

**Algorithm 2.** Parallel PSM algorithm

**Initialization:**

- Set $k \leftarrow 0$;
- Set $\mathbf{x}^0$ as the current best point $\mathbf{x}_i^*$ of a given cube;
- Set $\alpha_0$ as the current step-size parameter $\alpha$ for the corresponding cube;
- Set $\alpha_{min}$ to the same value defined in algorithm 1;

**Iteration:**

1. Compute in parallel $f(\mathbf{x}), \forall \mathbf{x} \in \mathcal{N}(\mathbf{x}^k) = \{\mathbf{x}^k \pm \alpha_k v_j, v_j \in [I - I]\}$, where $I = [e_1 \ldots e_n]$ is the identity matrix.
2. If search is successful, i.e. $\min_{\mathcal{N}(\mathbf{x}^k)} f(\mathbf{x}) < f(\mathbf{x}^k)$ then
   $$\mathbf{x}^{k+1} \leftarrow \operatorname{argmin}_{\mathcal{N}(\mathbf{x}^k)} \mathbf{f}(\mathbf{x});$$
   $$\alpha_{k+1} \leftarrow \alpha_k;$$
   Else
   $$\mathbf{x}^{k+1} \leftarrow \mathbf{x}^k;$$
   $$\alpha_{k+1} \leftarrow \frac{\alpha_k}{2};$$

3. If $\alpha_{k+1} \geq \alpha_{min}$ return to step 1 for a new iteration and set $k \leftarrow k + 1$.

---

second step, anchored in the points obtained by the BAO algorithm, novel anchor points are added iteratively considering only optimal FMO values. This iterative procedure ends when 20 anchor points are obtained, which is the typical number of anchor points considered in the literature (see, e.g., [9,11]). This second step is now described considering the nasopharyngeal tumor case to illustrate the optimization strategy sketched.

Although the BAO optimization procedure described in Sect. 3.2 explores the search space in a continuous manner, by defining appropriately the step-size parameter, $\alpha$, we end up with integer solutions. If the initial step-size parameter, $\alpha_0$, is a power of 2, and the initial point is a vector of integers, by halving the step-size parameter in unsuccessful iterations we obtain integer iterates until the step-size parameter becomes inferior to 1. This possibility is rather interesting for the BAO problem and was adopted in our PSM implementation.

For this second step, instead of considering the fine discretization of the BAO search space ($1°$), resulting from the outcome of integer solutions, we consider an equispaced beam grid separated by $10°$ for both the gantry and the couch. Note that finer beam grids separated by $5°$, $2°$ or $1°$ can be considered at a cost of larger computational times. After exclusion of infeasible couch-gantry angle pairs due to possible collisions of patient and gantry for a nasopharyngeal tumor case, we end up with 472 candidate beams homogeneously distributed as illustrated in Fig. 2. The coplanar (couch fixed at $0°$) $2\pi$VMAT and the 7-beam coplanar equispaced solution commonly used in clinical practice for step-and-shoot IMRT, are also displayed in Fig. 2, corresponding to the black and red points, respectively.

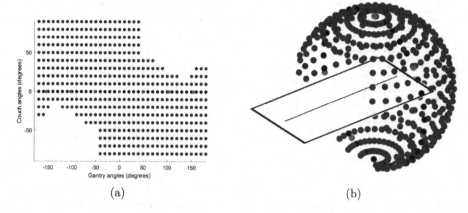

(a)                                                    (b)

**Fig. 2.** Candidate beams homogeneously distributed represented in 2D – (a) and the corresponding 3D representation – (b). Black beams correspond to the coplanar (couch fixed at $0°$) $2\pi$VMAT while red beams correspond to the 7-beam coplanar equispaced solution, commonly used in clinical practice for step-and-shot IMRT. (Color figure online)

The initial anchor points corresponding to the 7-beam noncoplanar BAO solution for the nasopharyngeal tumor case at hand are displayed in red in Fig. 3. For simplicity, the anchor points displayed correspond to the closest points in the equispaced beam grid. Some of the criteria commonly used for calculating noncoplanar arc trajectories include geometrical and time considerations. Our approach, similarly to the BAO approach, is based on dosimetric considerations, and will be guided by the optimal values of the FMO problem. Nevertheless, aiming to enhance one of the main features of VMAT, short treatment times, the following constraints are considered for the movement of the gantry/couch:

- The initial gantry/couch position is the beam of the 7-beam noncoplanar BAO solution with lower gantry angle value, corresponding to the leftmost anchor point in Fig. 3(a);
- The next anchor point to visit is the anchor point with lower gantry angle value among the ones that have not yet been visited;
- The final gantry/couch position is the beam of the 7-beam noncoplanar BAO solution with higher gantry angle value, corresponding to the rightmost anchor point in Fig. 3(a);
- When moving from one anchor point to the next one, the gantry must move towards the next anchor point while the couch must move towards the next anchor point or be halted.

The main goal of these movement restrictions is to define a trajectory from the leftmost anchor point to the rightmost anchor point of Fig. 3(a) as fast as possible, i. e., with the gantry always rotating towards the next anchor point and the couch always moving (when this is the case) towards the next anchor point. Defining in this way the possible gantry and couch movements, the feasible

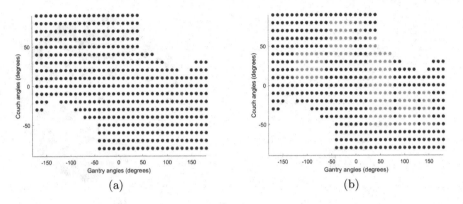

**Fig. 3.** The 7-beam noncoplanar BAO solution is displayed in red – (a) and the feasible points to consider when calculating a new anchor point are displayed in green – (b). (Color figure online)

points to consider when calculating a new anchor point are shown in green in Fig. 3(b).

There are different ways of considering the optimal value of the FMO problem to iteratively add novel anchor points, one by one. The most expensive, in terms of computational time, is to add each one of the green points, one at a time, to the existing set of anchor points and then compute the corresponding optimal FMO value considering these beams. The candidate beam that leads to the minimum optimal FMO value when added to the existing anchor beams will be selected as the next anchor point. Aiming to reduce the computational time we will only consider, at each iteration, the candidate beams that belong to the largest set of green beams between anchor points. The rationale of this idea is to add an anchor point where more degrees of freedom exist and, simultaneously, possibly reduce as much as possible the overall number of green points. For the nasopharyngeal tumor case used to illustrate our approach, the largest set of green beams is between the 4th and the 5th anchor point (54 candidate beams). By adding each of these green beams, one at a time, to the current set of anchor points we can compute the beam that leads to the best optimal FMO value and thus it is selected as new anchor point. In Fig. 4(a) the novel anchor point is displayed. This recently added red point leads to the infeasibility of some green beams due to the gantry/couch movement constraints here defined. At the end of each iteration, green candidate beams that became infeasible are removed as illustrated in Fig. 4(b). We are now in conditions to describe the algorithm for optimizing the noncoplanar arc trajectory.

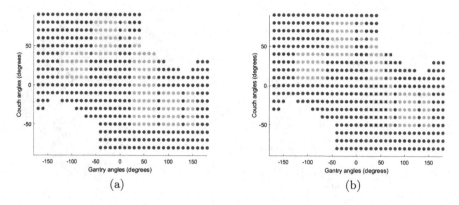

**Fig. 4.** Novel anchor point belonging to the largest set of green candidate beams is added – (a) and green candidate beams that became infeasible are removed – (b). (Color figure online)

---

**Algorithm 3.** Noncoplanar arc trajectory algorithm

**Initialization:**

- Use the noncoplanar BAO algorithm to compute the initial anchor points;
- Define the initial candidate beams to possibly be added as novel anchor points;

**Iteration:**

**While** candidate beams exist **and** number of anchor points is less than 20 **do**

1. Identify the largest set of candidate green beams between two anchor points;
2. Compute the optimal FMO value considering the set of beams composed of the anchor beams and each candidate beam identified in the previous step;
3. Add a novel anchor beam corresponding to the candidate beam that leads to the best optimal FMO value in the previous step;
4. Remove the green candidate beams that became infeasible.

---

## 4  Computational Results

Computational tests were conducted on a Dell Precision T5600 with Intel Xeon processor 64 GB 1600 MHz. An in-house MATLAB optimization suite, called YARTOS, developed at Erasmus MC Cancer Institute in Rotterdam, was used to compute dose distributions. YARTOS fluence optimizer, $2p\epsilon c$, was used to calculate the optimal FMO value for a given set of beams. For the noncoplanar BAO problem, the initial step-size considered by the PSM algorithm was $\alpha_0 = 2^5 = 32$ while the minimal value allowed was one, leading to integer values of the beams.

For the nasopharyngeal tumor case used in our computational tests, three treatment plans were compared in this study: $4\pi VMAT$, $2\pi VMAT$, and $Equi$, the typical seven-beam equispaced coplanar treatment plan used in step-and

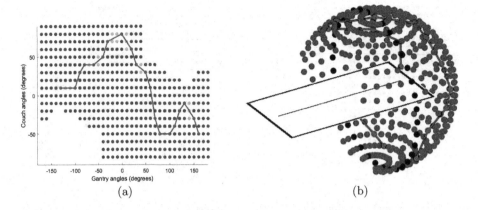

**Fig. 5.** Trajectory obtained by our noncoplanar arc trajectory optimization approach in 2D – (a) and in 3D – (b).

**Table 3.** Results in terms of FMO objective function value.

| Equi | $2\pi\,VMAT$ | | $4\pi\,VMAT$ | |
|------|-----------|------------|-----------|------------|
| FMO value | FMO value | % decrease | FMO value | % decrease |
| 560.33 | 522.19 | 6.8 | 473.92 | 15.4 |

shoot IMRT. The final trajectory obtained by our noncoplanar arc trajectory optimization approach is displayed in Fig. 5.

Table 3 depicts the results, in terms of optimal FMO value, for the three treatment plans compared in this study. $4\pi\,VMAT$ clearly outperforms the other treatment plans in terms of optimal FMO value, improving 15.4% the value obtained by *Equi* plan while the improvement of $2\pi\,VMAT$ was 6.8%.

The quality of the treatment plans is also acknowledged by a set of dose metrics. One of the metrics used for the tumors is coverage, the volume of PTV that receives 95% of the prescribed dose. At least 95% of the PTV volume is required. Other metrics typically screened for tumors are conformity and homogeneity that are output values of the YARTOS optimizer. Table 4 reports these tumor volume metrics. We can observe that slightly better target coverage, conformity and homogeneity numbers are obtained by $4\pi\,VMAT$ treatment plan. For the OARs, depending on the type of organ, serial or parallel, maximum and/or mean doses are typically used to acknowledge organ sparing. Table 5 displays the organ sparing results. As expected the difference between plans is more visible for organ sparing. By simple inspection of Table 5 it is clear that $4\pi\,VMAT$ treatment plan obtained by far the best organ sparing results.

**Table 4.** Target coverage, conformity and homogeneity obtained by treatment plans.

| Target parameters | $Equi$ | $2\pi\,VMAT$ | $4\pi\,VMAT$ |
|---|---|---|---|
| $PTV_{70}$ Coverage | 0.863 | 0.849 | 0.919 |
| $PTV_{70}$ Conformity | 0.505 | 0.466 | 0.555 |
| $PTV_{70}$ Homogeneity | 0.880 | 0.873 | 0.892 |
| $PTV_{59.4}$ Coverage | 0.930 | 0.928 | 0.937 |
| $PTV_{59.4}$ Conformity | 0.554 | 0.551 | 0.562 |
| $PTV_{59.4}$ Homogeneity | 0.856 | 0.857 | 0.867 |

**Table 5.** OARs sparing obtained by treatment plans.

| OAR | Mean dose (Gy) | | | Max dose (Gy) | | |
|---|---|---|---|---|---|---|
| | $Equi$ | $2\pi\,VMAT$ | $4\pi\,VMAT$ | $Equi$ | $2\pi\,VMAT$ | $4\pi\,VMAT$ |
| Spinal cord | – | – | – | 34.9 | 33.6 | 30.8 |
| Brainstem | – | – | – | 44.8 | 42.3 | 33.9 |
| Right parotid | 23.0 | 22.9 | 21.6 | – | – | – |
| Left parotid | 24.4 | 19.3 | 15.4 | – | – | – |
| Oral cavity | 17.5 | 12.9 | 10.9 | – | – | – |

# 5    Conclusions and Future Work

A novel approach for the optimization of highly noncoplanar arc trajectories was described and tested using a complex nasopharyngeal tumor case already treated at IPOC. For the patient tested, the resulting noncoplanar arc plan, $4\pi\,VMAT$, clearly outperforms both the coplanar arc plan, $2\pi\,VMAT$, and the typically used coplanar equispaced step-and-shoot IMRT plan. Our approach gathers two extremely challenging problems: the noncoplanar BAO problem, a continuous global highly non-convex optimization problem, and the noncoplanar arc trajectory problem, a combinatorial problem yet to be solved satisfactorily. In this approach, we take advantage of all the quality work already produced for the noncoplanar BAO problem and propose an optimization strategy, anchored on the solution calculated by the BAO problem, that also considers dose metrics to guide the optimization procedure but simultaneously embeds the goal of obtaining an efficient dose delivery time, which is one of the main features of rotational treatments.

Although, for the patient at hand, the overall quality of the treatment is undoubtedly greater considering the noncoplanar arc plan, $4\pi\,VMAT$, it comes with a cost. In terms of planning time, determining the optimal path of a highly noncoplanar arc plan following our optimization strategy is much more costly than simply using equispaced coplanar beams or using a coplanar arc (for a fixed couch angle of $0°$). That was already the case for noncoplanar BAO in step-and-shoot IMRT which is the main reason for the lack of BAO solutions in most of the treatment planning systems. Actually, angles are chosen manually, relying only on the experience of the planner, even in very challenging clinical cases. For this particular nasopharyngeal tumor case, the noncoplanar BAO procedure required the calculation of 2776 optimal FMO values (which consumes most of the computational time) while the optimization of the noncoplanar arc trajectory required the computation of 193 optimal FMO values. The number of function evaluations required in the second step of this two-step approach is 10% less than the number of function evaluations required for the first step, the noncoplanar BAO. Even knowing that the number of beams is increasing and thus the time required for each function evaluation also increases, in terms of computational time the second step is still 10% less than the noncoplanar BAO procedure (one hour against more than 10 h). One way of speeding the overall optimization process is to consider less beams in the first step and that was precisely the reason for choosing 7 beams instead of 9 or more beams. In future work, the trade-off between the time required for noncoplanar BAO procedures – fastest if less beams (e.g., 5 beams) are considered or slowest BAO with more beams – and the final quality of the corresponding treatment plans should be investigated. Moreover, other strategies to accelerate both the noncoplanar BAO procedure and the second step that determines the remaining anchor points should be investigated. Fully VMAT treatment plans should be compared as well in future work. Finally, it is worth to note that this two-step optimization approach is completely automated which makes computational time somehow less important.

**Acknowledgments.** This work has been supported by project grant POCI-01-0145-FEDER-028030 and by the Fundação para a Ciência e a Tecnologia (FCT) under project grant UID/Multi/00308/2019. The authors show gratitude to Ben Heijmen and Sebastiaan Breedveld for giving permission and helping them to install Erasmus-iCycle.

# References

1. Bangert, M., Ziegenhein, P., Oelfke, U.: Comparison of beam angle selection strategies for intracranial IMRT. Med. Phys. **40**, 011716 (2013)
2. Bedford, J.L.: Treatment planning for volumetric modulated arc therapy. Med. Phys. **36**, 5128–5138 (2009)
3. Otto, K.: Volumetric modulated arc therapy: IMRT in a single gantry arc. Med. Phys. **35**, 310–317 (2008)
4. Yu, C.X.: Intensity-modulated arc therapy with dynamic multileaf collimation: an alternative to tomotherapy. Phys. Med. Biol. **40**, 1435–1449 (1995)
5. Yang, Y., et al.: Choreographing couch and collimator in volumetric modulated arc therapy. Int. J. Radiat. Oncol. Biol. Phys. **80**, 1238–1247 (2011)
6. MacDonald, R.L., Thomas, C.G.: Dynamic trajectory-based couch motion for improvement of radiation therapy trajectories in cranial SRT. Med. Phys. **42**, 2317–2325 (2015)
7. Smyth, G., et al.: Non-coplanar trajectories to improve organ at risk sparing in volumetric modulated arc therapy for primary brain tumors. Radiother. Oncol. **121**, 124–131 (2016)

8. Smyth, G., Bamber, J.C., Evans, P.M., Bedford, J.L.: Trajectory optimisation for dynamic couch rotation during volumetric modulated arc radiotherapy. Phys. Med. Biol. **58**, 8163–8177 (2013)
9. Papp, D., Bortfeld, T., Unkelbach, J.: A modular approach to intensity-modulated arc therapy optimization with noncoplanar trajectories. Phys. Med. Biol. **60**, 5179–5198 (2015)
10. Wild, E., Bangert, M., Nill, S., Oelfke, U.: Noncoplanar VMAT for nasopharyngeal tumors: plan quality versus treatment time. Med. Phys. **42**, 2157–2168 (2015)
11. Langhans, M., Unkelbach, J., Bortfeld, T., Craft, D.: Optimizing highly noncoplanar VMAT trajectories: the NoVo method. Phys. Med. Biol. **63**, 025023 (2018)
12. Rocha, H., Dias, J., Ventura, T., Ferreira, B.C., Lopes, M.C.: A derivative-free multistart framework for an automated noncoplanar beam angle optimization in IMRT. Med. Phys. **43**, 5514–5526 (2016)
13. Dias, J., Rocha, H., Ventura, T., Ferreira, B.C., Lopes, M.C.: Automated fluence map optimization based on fuzzy inference systems. Med. Phys. **43**, 1083–1095 (2016)
14. Breedveld, S., Storchi, P., Keijzer, M., Heemink, A.W., Heijmen, B.: A novel approach to multi-criteria inverse planning for IMRT. Phys. Med. Biol. **52**, 6339–6353 (2007)
15. Breedveld, S., Storchi, P., Heijmen, B.: The equivalence of multicriteria methods for radiotherapy plan optimization. Phys. Med. Biol. **54**, 7199–7209 (2009)
16. Breedveld, S., Storchi, P., Voet, P., Heijmen, B.: iCycle: integrated, multicriterial beam angle, and profile optimization for generation of coplanar and noncoplanar IMRT plans. Med. Phys. **39**, 951–963 (2012)
17. Dias, J., Rocha, H., Ferreira, B.C., Lopes, M.C.: Simulated annealing applied to IMRT beam angle optimization: a computational study. Phys. Med. **31**, 747–756 (2015)
18. Aleman, D.M., Kumar, A., Ahuja, R.K., Romeijn, H.E., Dempsey, J.F.: Neighborhood search approaches to beam orientation optimization in intensity modulated radiation therapy treatment planning. J. Global Optim. **42**, 587–607 (2008)
19. Craft, D.: Local beam angle optimization with linear programming and gradient search. Phys. Med. Biol. **52**, 127–135 (2007)
20. Lim, G.J., Cao, W.: A two-phase method for selecting IMRT treatment beam angles: Branch-and-Prune and local neighborhood search. Eur. J. Oper. Res. **217**, 609–618 (2012)
21. Dias, J., Rocha, H., Ferreira, B.C., Lopes, M.C.: A genetic algorithm with neural network fitness function evaluation for IMRT beam angle optimization. Cent. Eur. J. Oper. Res. **22**, 431–455 (2014)
22. Bertsimas, D., Cacchiani, V., Craft, D., Nohadani, O.: A hybrid approach to beam angle optimization in intensity-modulated radiation therapy. Comput. Oper. Res. **40**, 2187–2197 (2013)
23. Bangert, M., Ziegenhein, P., Oelfke, U.: Characterizing the combinatorial beam angle selection problem. Phys. Med. Biol. **57**, 6707–6723 (2012)
24. Rocha, H., Dias, J., Ferreira, B.C., Lopes, M.C.: Selection of intensity modulated radiation therapy treatment beam directions using radial basis functions within a pattern search methods framework. J. Global Optim. **57**, 1065–1089 (2013)
25. Rocha, H., Dias, J., Ferreira, B.C., Lopes, M.C.: Beam angle optimization for intensity-modulated radiation therapy using a guided pattern search method. Phys. Med. Biol. **58**, 2939–2953 (2013)

26. Rocha, H., Dias, J., Ferreira, B.C., Lopes, M.C.: Pattern search methods framework for beam angle optimization in radiotherapy design. Appl. Math. Comput. **219**, 10853–10865 (2013)
27. Rocha, H., Dias, J., Ferreira, B.C., Lopes, M.C.: Noncoplanar beam angle optimization in IMRT treatment planning using pattern search methods. J. Phys.: Conf. Ser. **616**, 012014 (2015)
28. Rocha, H., Dias, J., Ventura, T., Ferreira, B.C., Lopes, M.C.: Beam angle optimization in IMRT: are we really optimizing what matters? Int. Trans. Oper. Res. **26**, 908–928 (2019)
29. Rocha, H., Dias, J., Ventura, T., Ferreira, B., do Carmo Lopes, M.: Comparison of combinatorial and continuous frameworks for the beam angle optimization problem in IMRT. In: Gervasi, O., et al. (eds.) ICCSA 2018. LNCS, vol. 10961, pp. 593–606. Springer, Cham (2018). https://doi.org/10.1007/978-3-319-95165-2_42

# A Network Flow Based Construction for a GRASP+SA Algorithm to Solve the University Timetabling Problem

Edmar Hell Kampke$^{(\boxtimes)}$ (iD), Leonardo Moreli Scheideger$^{(\boxtimes)}$ (iD),
Geraldo Regis Mauri$^{(\boxtimes)}$ (iD), and Maria Claudia Silva Boeres$^{(\boxtimes)}$ (iD)

Optimization Lab, Federal University of Espírito Santo, Vitória, ES, Brazil
edmar.kampke@ufes.br, leonardo.scheideger@aluno.ufes.br,
geraldo.mauri@ufes.br, boeres@inf.ufes.br

**Abstract.** Educational timetabling is one of the most researched topics in the field of timetabling. This problem consists of allocating a set of lectures to available rooms and periods, considering students and teachers requests and constraints. Several mathematical models for this problem can be found in the literature. The model considered in this paper is based on courses curricula of a university, proposed in the second International Timetabling Competition (ITC-2007). A maximum flow partial solution is used together with the GRASP constructive algorithm to generate a local solution improved by Simulated Annealing. Computational experiments were performed in ITC-2007 instances, and the results were compared to the best solutions of ITC-2007 and to the literature.

**Keywords:** University timetabling problem · Hybrid algorithm · Network flow

## 1 Introduction

The timetabling problem consists of allocating activities in a timetable in order to address the constraints of the stakeholders as best as possible. This problem can be found in several areas such as organization of sporting events, transportation, work schedules of employees, and others. Specifically, educational timetabling problems allocate a sequence of lectures involving students and teachers in a fixed period of time, satisfying specific restrictions [9].

The University Timetabling Problem (UTP) has many variations. According to Burke et al. [1], timetables generation vary considerably between universities, since each of them has specific requirements. In many of them, the high number of events associated with teachers and resources, combined with a wide variety of requirements, makes the generation of timetables a difficult task.

Supported by CNPq (process 301725/2016-0) and FAPES (process 73290475/2016).

UTP is classified as NP-complete for most formulations [13]. In this way, the optimal solution can only be guaranteed for small instances, which is not the case of most universities.

In order to encourage the study of different approaches to timetabling problems, *The International Series of Conferences on the Practice and Theory of Automated Timetabling* (PATAT) promoted three competitions (2002, 2007 and 2011) of educational timetabling, called *International Timetabling Competition* (ITC). The first two competitions are dedicated to universities and the last, to high school timetabling. These competitions encouraged the research community to promote a broader debate in timetabling problems and also made novel instances close to the reality of universities.

The ITC-2007 addressed the UTP in three different formulations, and the competitors could participate independently in each one of them. Each formulation has its own set of instances. The first formulation is specific for the application of final term exams. The second and third formulations deal with the weekly allocation of lectures at a university. The difference between them is that the second formulation (called *post-enrollment*) addresses the problem by considering student enrollment data, while the third (called *curriculum-based*) takes into account the groups of courses with a common set of students and therefore the lectures can not be allocated at the same time.

Since many resolution techniques have been implemented and/or improved after ITC-2007, in this work we adopt the third formulation established by ITC-2007, the Curriculum-Based Course Timetabling (CB-CTT) [12], in order to facilitate the comparison with the results obtained by other algorithms from the literature.

First place of ITC-2007 went to Müller [11] that solved the CB-CTT formulation using *Conflict-based Statistics* to generate the initial solution and *Hill Climbing* combined with *Great Deluge* and *Simulated Annealing* for refinement of the solution. The second place was given to Lü and Hao [10] with an Adaptive Tabu Search that has been applied successfully at the same formulation.

A recent work (Kiefer et al. [7]) applies the metaheuristic *Adaptive Large Neighborhood Search*, obtaining the best results known so far for 5 of the 21 instances of the competition.

A prior work of Kampke et al. [6] includes the proposal of a GRASP algorithm with *Hill Climbing* and *Simulated Annealing* as local search methods and a *Path-Relinking* procedure to intensify the search for good solutions of the CB-CTT addressed problem. The authors also applied new movements for generating neighbors in the local search phase. They analyzed the movements in order to choose that generate the best results such as *Kempe Chain, Move* and *Swap* [5].

Several approaches to solve timetabling problems are presented in [13], among which we highlight the use of network flow to model the problem combined with algorithms, such as Ford and Fulkerson algorithm [4], to find a solution.

In this work, the CB-CTT formulation is modeled as a maximum network flow problem and two algorithms are employed to solve it during the construction of an initial solution for the GRASP proposed by Kampke et al. [6]. To the best of our knowledge it is the first time that CB-CTT formulation for UTP is modeled as a network flow. This new proposal is the basis of an alternative GRASP constructive algorithm proposed in this work. The GRASP used here is the same of [6], except for the replacement of the constructive algorithm by that described in Sect. 4.2.

This paper is organized as follows. In Sect. 2 we describe the CB-CTT formulation for the university timetabling problem, adopted in ITC-2007. Sections 3 and 4 outlines, respectively, the modeling using network flow and the algorithms that we have implemented. Computational experiments results are reported in Sect. 5 and conclusions are drawn in Sect. 6.

## 2  Problem Description

The CB-CTT formulation for UTP considers a set of courses $C$ where each course $c$ have a number of lectures $l_c$ to be taught by a teacher. This formulation handles the weekly assignment of all lectures at a university according to a timetable $T$ divided into $|P|$ periods, where $P$ is a set of periods and $|P| = d \times q$. $d$ and $q$ are respectively the number of weekly school days and the fixed number of periods each day is divided.

It is worth noting that for each course, a set of unavailable periods is given. In addition, each course is associated to a minimum number of days, among which its lectures should be spread and attended by a fixed number of students. As previously stated in this work, a course can belong to some university curricula and courses on the same curriculum have students in common. A set $R$ of rooms is also given with each room characterized by its capacity.

Therefore, a solution of this problem represents the assignment of a pair period/room (timeslot) to all lectures of courses for a set of curricula so as to satisfy a set of *hard* constraints and to minimize the violations of *soft* constraints. The *hard* (denoted by **H1** to **H4**) and *soft* (denoted by **S1** to **S4**) constraints are summarized as follows:

- **H1.** *Lectures:* All lectures of a course must be assigned to distinct periods and rooms.
- **H2.** *Room Occupancy:* Two lectures cannot be assigned in the same period and in the same room.
- **H3.** *Conflicts:* Lectures of courses in the same curriculum or taught by the same teacher cannot be assigned in the same period, i.e., periods cannot have an overlapping of students or teachers.
- **H4.** *Availability:* If the teacher of a course is not available at a given period, then no lectures of the course can be assigned to that period.

- **S1.** *Room Capacity:* For each lecture, the number of students attending the course should not be greater than the capacity of the room hosting the lecture. Each surplus student is counted as a violation.
- **S2.** *Room Stability:* All lectures of a course should be scheduled at the same room. If this is impossible, the number of occupied rooms for these lectures should be as few as possible. Each distinct room is counted as a violation.

- **S3.** *Minimum Working Days:* The lectures of a course should be spread over a minimum number of days. Each day below the minimum is counted as a violation.
- **S4.** *Curriculum Compactness:* For a given curriculum, a violation is counted if there is one lecture not adjacent to any other lecture belonging to the same curriculum within the same day, which means that the weekly schedule of students should be as compact as possible.

The objective function $f(s)$ defines the quality of a feasible solution $s$ and is given by $f(s) = \sum_{i=1}^{4} \alpha_i \cdot |S_i|$, where $\alpha_i$ and $|S_i|$ are respectively the penalty and total number of violations of each soft constraint $i$. The CB-CTT formulation for UTP, adopted in ITC-2007, defines the values of $\alpha_i$: $\alpha_1 = 1$, $\alpha_2 = 1$, $\alpha_3 = 5$ and $\alpha_4 = 2$. We recall that in a feasible solution, the number of conflicts of hard constraints is zero, in other words, $\sum_{j=1}^{4} |H_j| = 0$, where $|H_j|$ are the total number of violations of each hard constraint $j$.

We briefly described some elements of the CB-CTT formulation for UTP. The whole formulation description can be found in [2].

## 3    A CB-CTT Network Flow Formulation

In this section we present a CB-CTT reformulation we proposed as a network flow model.

Maximum flow is a widely known problem in the field of Combinatorial Optimization, appearing in several important applications. This problem involves finding a maximum feasible flow through a single-source to a single-sink node of a flow network without exceeding the capacity of its arcs.

Therefore, let $G$ be a flow network represented by the digraph $G = (V, A, \Phi)$ where $V$ and $A$ are respectively the set of vertices and arcs and $\Phi = \{\Phi_{ij}\}$ is a vector, with $|\Phi| = |A| + 1$. The arc arrows indicate the flow direction and the $\Phi$ flow vector terms $\Phi_{ij}$, $\forall (i, j) \in A + (\tau, \mu)$, are the flow passing in the arc from vertice $i$ to vertice $j$. The maximum flow passing over the network $G$ is computed as the capacity $\Phi_{\tau\mu}$ of a dummy arc which links the network sink $\tau$ to its source $\mu$. Thus, the flow crosses the network passing by transshipment nodes between $\mu$ and $\tau$ in such a way that it should be possible to reach every vertice of $G$ from $\mu$ and each vertice of $G$ reach $\tau$.

In this work, we propose the CB-CTT reformulation as a maximum flow problem. In this case, the network $G$ is composed of a source $\mu$ and a sink $\tau$ that link two layers of transshipment nodes. The first layer consists of $|C|$ vertices representing the courses of set $C$ and the second represent the timeslots listed in the $P \times R$ set. A mathematical programming model for the CB-CTT reformulation is based on the classical model of the maximum flow problem and is given in Eqs. (1)–(6).

Maximize   $\Phi_{\tau\mu}$ $\qquad\qquad\qquad\qquad\qquad\qquad\qquad\qquad\qquad\qquad\qquad$ (1)

subject to:

$$0 \leq \Phi_{\mu c} \leq l_c \qquad \forall c \in C, \tag{2}$$

$$0 \leq \Phi_{cj} \leq 1 \qquad \forall c \in C, j \in P \times R, \tag{3}$$

$$0 \leq \Phi_{j\tau} \leq 1 \qquad \forall j \in P \times R, \tag{4}$$

$$\sum_{\{r|(k,r)\in A\}} \Phi_{kr} - \sum_{\{r|(r,k)\in A\}} \Phi_{kr} = \left\{ \begin{array}{ll} \Phi_{\tau\mu}, & if \ k = \mu \\ 0, & \forall k \in V - \{\mu, \tau\} \\ -\Phi_{\tau\mu}, & if \ k = \tau \end{array} \right., \tag{5}$$

$$\Phi_{ij} \in \mathbb{Z}^+, \quad \forall (i,j) \in A, \tag{6}$$

This model seeks to assign flows on the $|A|$ arcs of $G$ such that its whole flow ($\Phi_{\tau\mu}$) is maximized (objective function (1)), satisfying the set of constraints (2) to (6).

Constraints (2) to (4) limit the minimum and maximum capacities for each arc of $G$, while constraints (5) impose flow conservation. The constraints (6) define the domain of the variables.

It is worth highlighting that the maximum capacities of the arcs mentioned in constraints (2), which emanate from source $\mu$ to the set of vertices representing $C$, refer to the number of lectures of each course $c \in C$. The remaining sets of capacity constraints (Eqs. (3) and (4)), related to the set of arcs between the intermediate network vertices layers (representing $C$ and $P \times R$ of timeslots sets) and those linking the last layer to the sink $\tau$, must be at most 1. These capacities limits occur since a course must have at most one lecture allocated in a timeslot, which can in turn, be only occupied by a single lecture.

Figure 1 shows an input file pattern defined by ITC-2007 for a toy instance and its corresponding representation as a network flow is presented in Fig. 2. This file pattern can be divided into five parts in this order: header, information of courses, rooms, curricula and unavailability constraints. The header consists of seven lines, each containing, respectively, the instance name and number of courses, rooms, days, periods per day, curricula and unavailability constraints. The courses section shows, by line, the information for each course: its and the teacher names, number of lectures per week, minimum number of lecture days and number of students. Next, a sequence of $|R|$ lines with all rooms names and capacities. On the way of the list of rooms, the curricula are organized by their names followed by the number and names of the courses attached to each of them. The last file pattern section contains the unavailability constraints, each represented by the name of a course followed by the day and period in which it can not be allocated.

Figure 2 illustrates the corresponding network flow representation. Besides its source and destination nodes, the network consists of two further layers of vertices, one representing the set of courses $C$ and the other, the set $P \times R$ of timeslots. The network arcs labels indicate their capacity. Arcs linking the source $\mu$ to the first layer of nodes (set $C$) represent the number of lectures that should be allocated for each course. In this example, this value is two. The capacities of the set of arcs between the intermediate vertices layers are at most 1. At last, all the arcs linking the $P \times R$ layer to $\tau$ have unitary capacities.

```
Name: Toy3
Courses: 3
Rooms: 2
Days: 2
Periods_per_day: 2
Curricula: 2
Constraints: 2

COURSES:
DiscMath Edmar 2 2 40
CompProg Geraldo 2 2 35
GraphThe Edmar 2 3 20

ROOMS:
rA 38
rB 32

CURRICULA:
Cur1 2 DiscMath CompProg
Cur2 1 GraphThe

UNAVAILABILITY_CONSTRAINTS:
CompProg 0 0
CompProg 1 1
END.
```

**Fig. 1.** An input file pattern for a toy example.

In all cases, a flow equal to one indicates the allocation of a lecture of a course to a timeslot. For instance, the arc linking the vertice $DiscMath$ to $R_0 Q_1 D_0$ with capacity 1 means the allocation of a lecture of the $DiscMath$ course to the timeslot representing the period 1 of day 0 in room 0. Null flow indicates that no lecture of $DiscMath$ is allocated in this timeslot.

Therefore, this formulation ensures that the hard constraints **H2** (*Room Occupancy*) and **H4** (*Availability*) are satisfied but does not guarantee the same for **H1** (*Lectures*) and **H3** (*Conflicts*).

This formulation has no control over the soft constraints. The adopted strategy is the application of the maximum flow algorithm in order to allocate the lectures in different days and in the same room, assisting **S2** (*Room Stability*) and **S3** (*Minimum Working Days*), which are almost always not violated.

The order of courses in the network flow is defined randomly, whereas the order of timeslots is fixed, starting from room 0 at period 0 of day 0 and then varying the days, periods and rooms, in this order.

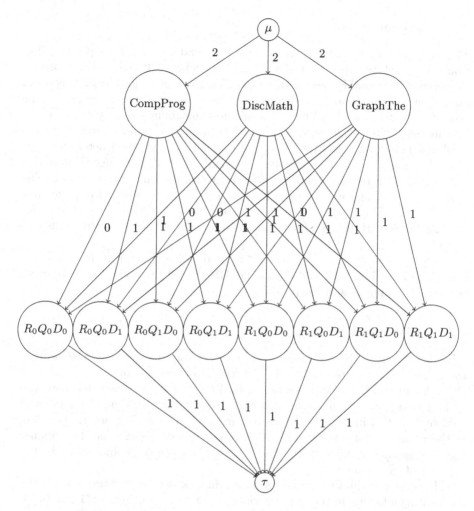

**Fig. 2.** Toy instance network flow representation.

## 4  Algorithms

In this work we used the CB-CTT reformulation as a network flow model (see Sect. 3) to apply maximum flow algorithms and thus to construct a partial solution, since there is no guarantee that all lectures will be allocated.

The GRASP algorithm proposed by Kampke et al. [6] is an iterative method in which two phases are applied in each iteration: construction of a complete initial solution ($IS_{CBCTT}$ method) and local search (Simulated Annealing metaheuristic). In this work, we propose an adaptation in this GRASP algorithm, specifically in the construction of an initial solution phase. Here, we construct a partial solution by maximum flow algorithms that will then be completed by $IS_{CBCTT}$ method. The implemented algorithms are presented below.

## 4.1  Maximum Flow

The Maximum Flow (MF) problem consists of finding the largest possible flow from one point (source) to another (sink) in a network flow. The algorithm proposed by Ford and Fulkerson [4] was the first to solve the problem and is based on finding, at each iteration, a flow path between source and sink, increasing the flow of the path arcs according to the smallest remaining capacity of them.

Finding paths which a flow can be sent through is the main routine of the Ford and Fulkerson algorithm. The way this path is computed determines the algorithm computational complexity. The Ford and Fulkerson algorithm implements a Depth-First Search (DFS) of the source to the sink in the network. The efficiency of the algorithm can be improved if DFS is replaced by a Breadth-First Search (BFS), trying firstly the paths with the least number of arcs. The algorithm with this modification was originally proposed by Edmonds and Karp [3].

Two versions of the MF algorithm are used and compared in this work, the original proposed by Ford and Fulkerson (MF-D) and the revised and improved version, by Edmonds and Karp (MF-B).

## 4.2  Initial Solution

In both versions of the MF algorithm, two modifications were made to improve the quality of the initial solution. The first modification consists in changing the order in which timeslots vertices (third level of the network flow) are visited: given a course $c$, timeslots with room capacity greater than the number of students enrolled in $c$ should be visited first and in ascending order, according to the room capacity. In the following, timeslots with room capacities smaller than the number of students enrolled in $c$ are visited in descending order by the capacity of the rooms.

The second modification consists of checking, for each visited timeslot vertice, if allocating a lecture in the timeslot violates the hard constraints **H1** (*Lectures*) and **H3** (*Conflicts*). This check prevents invalid allocations, but still does not guarantee the feasibility of initial solution as, in some cases, there will be no longer valid timeslots for the allocation. If this is the case, the lecture will not be allocated but will be added to the set of unallocated lectures $\overline{L}$, which is initially empty.

Both the MF algorithm versions implemented in this work visit the vertices of courses in sequential order, that is, the courses that are to the left (second level of the network flow) will be visited before those to the right. Thus, depending on the order in which courses are in network flow, eventually some lectures do not have more timeslots available and also are added in $\overline{L}$.

Even if, at the end of execution, the MF algorithm versions fail to obtain a solution using all lectures ($\overline{L} \neq \emptyset$), the partial solution and $\overline{L}$ are then sent to the GRASP constructive method $IS_{CBCTT}$ of Kampke et al. [6].

Therefore, in this work both versions of the MF algorithm try to construct a solution with all available lectures. If it is not possible, $IS_{CBCTT}$ is executed to allocate the remaining lectures and obtain a complete solution, which is then sent to local search method of GRASP.

### 4.3   Local Search

As the GRASP proposed by Kampke et al. [6] is used in this work with an alternative constructive method, we remember its local search procedure is the Simulated Annealing (SA) [8] algorithm that evolves over a neighborhood of a solution $s$. Let $N_m(s)$ be a neighborhood of $s$ defined by a given movement $m$.

To generate a neighbor solution $s' = s \oplus m$, $s' \in N_m(s)$, a movement $m$ is applied in the current solution $s$. The symbol $\oplus$ represents the transformation imposed over $s$ by the movement $m$.

In this work we consider $m$ the *Lecture Move* movement proposed by Müller [11] and selected as the best among nine tested in Kampke et al. [5]. For this movement, a lecture $l_1$ allocated in timeslot $t_1$ is randomly selected. Then a timeslot $t_2$ is also randomly selected. If $t_2$ is an empty timeslot, $l_1$ is moved to $t_2$. Otherwise, the movement consists of exchanging the lecture $l_1$ from timeslot $t_1$ to timeslot $t_2$, and the lecture $l_2$ from timeslot $t_2$ to timeslot $t_1$.

The SA algorithm has five main parameters: the initial solution $s$, the initial temperature $T_i$, the final temperature $T_f$, the cooling rate $\beta$ and $|N(s)|$, where $N(s)$ is a subset of $N_m(s)$ defined at each temperature $T_j$, $j = i, \dots, f$.

The algorithm starts from $T_i$ which is continuously cooled to $T_f$. At each temperature $T_j$, $j = i, \dots, f$, $|N(s)|$ neighbors are generated. For a given temperature $T_j$, if one of the neighbors generated is better than the incumbent solution, it is updated, otherwise, the neighbor solution can be accepted with probability equal to $e^{-\Delta f/T_j}$, where $\Delta f$ is the difference in the objective functions values $f$ of neighbor and current solutions.

### 4.4   GMF Proposed Algorithm

This section presents the hybrid algorithm GRASP+MF (MF-D or MF-B) + $IS_{CBCTT}$, denoted GMF-D and GMF-B respectively for MF-D and MF-B versions, proposed to solve the CB-CTT reformulation as a network flow.

The pseudocode of the whole method proposed in this work is presented in Algorithm 1.

---

**Algorithm 1.** GRASP with Maximum Flow algorithm and $IS_{CBCTT}$

---

**Input:** Maximum number of iterations $maxIter$
**Output:** Best solution found $s^*$

1  $f^* \leftarrow \infty$
2  $i \leftarrow 0$
3  **while** $i < maxIter$ **do**
4      $s_1 \leftarrow GMF()$
5      $\overline{L} \leftarrow LecturesNotAlocated(s_1)$
6      $s_2 \leftarrow IS_{CBCTT}(s_1, \overline{L})$
7      $s \leftarrow SA(s_2)$
8      **if** $f(s) < f^*$ **then**
9          $s^* \leftarrow s$
10         $f^* \leftarrow f(s)$
11     **end**
12     $i \leftarrow$ i+1
13 **end**

---

Note in Algorithm 1 that GMF as long as it does not satisfy the stop condition (line 3), repeatedly (lines 4–12) construct a solution (lines 4–6) and performs a local search phase (line 7). In construction phase, line 4 represents the construction of a partial solution $s_1$ by one of MF algorithm versions, line 5 presents the definition of set $\overline{L}$ of lectures not allocated in $s_1$ and line 6 refers to the execution of $IS_{CBCTT}$ which is responsible for allocating the lectures of $\overline{L}$ in $s_1$ obtaining a complete solution $s_2$. Finally, lines 8–11 ensure that the best solution found by the GMF algorithm is stored, while line 12 ensures that the proposed algorithm ends.

## 5    Computational Experiments

The methods GMF-D and GMF-B described in the last section were submitted, as an alternative constructive algorithm for GRASP+SA, to computational experiments performed on the ITC-2007 instances *comp01–comp21*. The obtained results are presented, analysed and also compared with those found on Kampke et al. [6], Kiefer et al. [7] and ITC-2007 winners.

The code was written in C++ language, compiled using *g*++ version 4.8.4 with the -O3 optimization flag and executed on a computer with Intel Core i5-3570 CPU 3.40 GHz × 4, 8 GB memory and Ubuntu 14.04 64 bit.

The next subsections present the parameters required for the GRASP+SA algorithm (Sect. 5.1) and discuss the results achieved (Sect. 5.2).

### 5.1    Parameters

GRASP has only two parameters to adjust: the *threshold* $\alpha$, which is used in $IS_{CBCTT}$ method to determine the size of the Restricted Candidates List (RCL), and the maximum number of iterations *maxIter*. The SA metaheuristic, used as the GRASP+SA local search method, has four parameters: the initial temperature $t_i$, the final temperature $t_f$, the cooling rate $\beta$ and the number of neighbors $|N(s)|$ generated in each temperature $T_j$, $j = i, \ldots, f$.

In this work, the *maxIter* parameter was replaced by unit of time (*timeout*), in order to be faithful to the rules imposed by the ITC-2007, that provided an executable tool, available in [12], for benchmarking all competitors machines. For the same reasons, Kampke et al. [6] and Kiefer et al. [7] also used this tool to define the execution time limits for their algorithms. In order to enable a fair comparison among all algorithms tested, the tool stipulated a timeout of 220 s for the machine used in this work for the computational tests.

The GRASP and SA parameter set is based on Kampke et al. [6] and afterwards empirically calibrated. Table 1 shows all parameters values used.

Table 1. GRASP+SA parameters values.

| Parameter | Value |
|---|---|
| $t_i$ | 17.3 |
| $t_f$ | 0.003 |
| $\beta$ | 0.9999 |
| $|N(s)|$ | 500 |
| $\alpha$ | 0.1 |
| *Timeout* | 220 s |

## 5.2 Discussion

Computational tests were performed, for each instance and algorithm version, considering 10 runs with different seeds for generating random numbers. The results analysis is carried out into three main steps: (i) the solutions obtained by the algorithms GMF-D and GMF-B, together with their respective versions without **H1** (*Lectures*) and **H3** (*Conflicts*) hard constraints inspection (see Sect. 4.2), denoted as GMF-D$^H$ and GMF-B$^H$, are all confronted with each other; (ii) from the conclusions of (i), we observed GMF-D outperformed the other algorithms. For this reason, the goal of this second step is to determine the number of times over all executions (success rate) that GMF-D succeed in achieving a complete solution of good quality, without using $IS_{CBCTT}$. The results of the runs considering or not the $IS_{CBCTT}$ to construct a solution are respectively denoted as GMF-D$^+$ and GMF-D$^-$ in Table 3; and (iii) results comparison with those of the aforementioned literature works. In the following, these three steps are detailed.

Table 2 presents the results obtained for GMF-D, GMF-B, GMF-D$^H$ and GMF-B$^H$. The first column of this table indicates the instance names. From the second to the fifth column, the $f$ average value from all GRASP+SA executions, using each of the proposed algorithms, are presented. The remaining columns

**Table 2.** Results of GRASP with proposed algorithms to construct a partial solution.

| Instances | $f$ average | | | | Time average ($\times 10^{-3}$) | | | |
|-----------|-------|-------|----------|----------|-------|-------|----------|----------|
| | GMF-D | GMF-B | GMF-D$^H$ | GMF-B$^H$ | GMF-D | GMF-B | GMF-D$^H$ | GMF-B$^H$ |
| comp01 | **5.0** | **5.0** | **5.0** | **5.0** | 0.012 | 0.105 | **0.004** | 0.007 |
| comp02 | 61.5 | 60.3 | 62.9 | **59.8** | 0.685 | 2.235 | **0.014** | 0.037 |
| comp03 | 85.2 | **83.2** | 86.0 | 86.7 | 0.363 | 1.359 | **0.013** | 0.033 |
| comp04 | **39.5** | 39.7 | 39.7 | 39.9 | 0.066 | 1.025 | **0.013** | 0.035 |
| comp05 | **342.5** | 344.9 | 347.7 | 351.1 | 12.365 | 20.125 | **0.026** | 0.050 |
| comp06 | **58.8** | 59.5 | 59.8 | 61.1 | 0.166 | 1.523 | **0.019** | 0.052 |
| comp07 | 28.8 | **27.5** | 28.4 | 31.0 | 0.323 | 2.390 | **0.023** | 0.064 |
| comp08 | 44.6 | 45.5 | **44.5** | 45.4 | 0.065 | 1.252 | **0.014** | 0.040 |
| comp09 | **106.6** | 109.8 | 106.8 | 108.9 | 0.109 | 1.101 | **0.014** | 0.039 |
| comp10 | 25.1 | 25.5 | **24.6** | 28.0 | 0.237 | 1.607 | **0.019** | 0.052 |
| comp11 | **0.0** | **0.0** | **0.0** | **0.0** | 0.009 | 0.162 | **0.005** | 0.010 |
| comp12 | **350.9** | 354.2 | 360.0 | 355.1 | 0.828 | 1.468 | **0.029** | 0.059 |
| comp13 | 75.6 | 76.2 | 76.1 | **75.5** | 0.079 | 1.206 | **0.014** | 0.041 |
| comp14 | **60.4** | 61.4 | 60.9 | 61.5 | 0.085 | 0.793 | **0.013** | 0.036 |
| comp15 | 86.2 | 84.8 | **82.8** | 84.7 | 0.352 | 0.965 | **0.013** | 0.033 |
| comp16 | 44.1 | 45.3 | 44.2 | **42.8** | 0.371 | 2.024 | **0.020** | 0.056 |
| comp17 | 85.3 | 85.8 | **82.2** | 84.7 | 0.143 | 1.272 | **0.017** | 0.045 |
| comp18 | 86.0 | **85.4** | 87.7 | 86.7 | 0.016 | 0.192 | **0.009** | 0.019 |
| comp19 | 72.3 | **69.4** | 69.6 | 70.1 | 0.706 | 1.298 | **0.012** | 0.031 |
| comp20 | 43.5 | **41.1** | 44.3 | 44.1 | 0.325 | 1.941 | **0.021** | 0.058 |
| comp21 | 111.3 | 111.2 | **110.0** | 113.2 | 0.690 | 2.178 | **0.017** | 0.045 |
| Average | **86.34** | 86.46 | 86.82 | 87.40 | 0.857 | 2.201 | **0.016** | 0.040 |

depict the respective average times. We can observe that GMF-D presents the best results on average. Nevertheless, the GMF-D mean was only 0.14% higher than that of GMF-B, even if, for 8 instances, the latter performed better than the former. Similar behaviour happens with GMF-D$^H$ and GMF-B$^H$. In this case, the first algorithm mean was only 0.66% better than the second and it occurs just the opposite for 6 instances. In general, DFS-based algorithms presented better results, once this kind of search seems to facilitate the allocation of lectures of the same course into consecutive timeslots of the flow graph. Thus, the way these timeslots are organized in the flow graph promote the allocation of the lectures on different days in the same room, avoiding the violation of soft constraints **S2** (*Room Stability*) and **S3** (*Minimum Working Days*).

It is possible to notice that the algorithms with feasibility checking perform better. These results indicate that feasible solutions as input for SA favored the achievement of slightly better results, once the differences on GMF-D and GMF-B average results are respectively 0.55% and 1.08%. Therefore we can conclude that SA performed satisfactorily, since it was able to find feasible and quality solutions eventually from infeasible solutions.

**Table 3.** Analysis of GMF-D algorithm in construction of a partial solution.

| Instances | % Sucess | $f$ average | | Time average ($\times 10^{-3}$) | |
|---|---|---|---|---|---|
| | | GMF-D$^-$ | GMF-D$^+$ | GMF-D$^-$ | GMF-D$^+$ |
| comp01 | 54.55 | 298.32 | 357.46 | 0.101 | 0.195 |
| comp02 | 0.00 | - | 716.71 | - | 6.328 |
| comp03 | 0.00 | - | 667.05 | - | 3.702 |
| comp04 | 22.22 | 565.55 | 540.93 | 0.277 | 0.594 |
| comp05 | 0.00 | - | 1615.88 | - | 72.026 |
| comp06 | 2.50 | 798.00 | 754.50 | 0.440 | 1.307 |
| comp07 | 0.00 | - | 828.00 | - | 2.646 |
| comp08 | 3.33 | 604.67 | 594.51 | 0.312 | 0.787 |
| comp09 | 2.50 | 683.50 | 676.42 | 0.276 | 1.031 |
| comp10 | 0.00 | - | 707.40 | - | 1.874 |
| comp11 | 100.00 | 144.10 | - | 0.090 | - |
| comp12 | 0.00 | - | 1545.90 | - | 5.753 |
| comp13 | 36.67 | 582.39 | 592.26 | 0.362 | 0.727 |
| comp14 | 6.67 | 621.17 | 607.13 | 0.280 | 0.760 |
| comp15 | 0.00 | - | 677.66 | - | 3.369 |
| comp16 | 0.00 | - | 713.79 | - | 2.554 |
| comp17 | 0.00 | - | 734.65 | - | 1.924 |
| comp18 | 83.75 | 531.93 | 540.38 | 0.123 | 0.181 |
| comp19 | 0.00 | - | 603.25 | - | 5.009 |
| comp20 | 0.00 | - | 931.00 | - | 2.176 |
| comp21 | 0.00 | - | 790.88 | - | 4.146 |

Considering the CPU time required to construct a solution, we can observe in Table 2 that GMF-B and GMF-B$^H$ run approximately 2.5 times, on average, slower than their corresponding GMF-D and GMF-D$^H$ versions. The difference in performance can be explained by the structure of the network flow. In this network, the distance between the source $\mu$ and the sink $\tau$ is fixed and equal to exactly four levels, driving the network growth only in breadth, thus the number of vertices DFS needs to visit is much smaller than BFS.

Since the overall results of GMF-D were better, the second results analysis step is focused in the information pointed out in Table 3. According to the Table 3, the first columns is for the instances denomination and the second column shows the percentage of times that GMF-D method has built a complete solution, that is, without using $IS_{CBCTT}$. In the third and fourth columns are presented the $f$ average of the solutions constructed respectively without or with $IS_{CBCTT}$. The respective CPU times are presented in the fifth and last columns.

**Table 4.** Comparison between GMF-D results and Kampke et al. [6] previous work.

| Instances | Kampke[a] | GMF-D | Instances | Kampke[a] | GMF-D |
|---|---|---|---|---|---|
| comp01 | 5 | 5 | comp12 | 375 | 341 |
| comp02 | 73 | 54 | comp13 | 97 | 71 |
| comp03 | 98 | 76 | comp14 | 72 | 58 |
| comp04 | 48 | 35 | comp15 | 101 | 80 |
| comp05 | 409 | 326 | comp16 | 69 | 41 |
| comp06 | 75 | 52 | comp17 | 105 | 80 |
| comp07 | 36 | 25 | comp18 | 102 | 82 |
| comp08 | 58 | 42 | comp19 | 87 | 68 |
| comp09 | 119 | 103 | comp20 | 88 | 38 |
| comp10 | 41 | 20 | comp21 | 136 | 100 |
| comp11 | 0 | 0 | Average | 104.48 | 80.81 |

[a] $GRASP+SA+Path\text{-}Relinking$, [6]

We observed that the $IS_{CBCTT}$ procedure run for instance *comp11* was not really necessary since GMF-D succeeded in generating a complete solution on all GRASP+SA executions. However, in the 12 other instances, the opposite occurred, that is, GMF-D algorithm was not able to construct a complete solution. In the remaining 8 instances, GMF-D achieved this result only a few times and in these cases, the quality of the solution constructed was, on average, 0.47% worse than those obtained combining GMF-D with $IS_{CBCTT}$. Nevertheless, the GMF-D algorithm, when constructing a complete solution, is on average 61.11% faster than when it needs $IS_{CBCTT}$ to complete the solution.

The last analysis step is related to Tables 4 and 5. These tables compare the GMF-D results with those of Kampke et al. [6], Müller [11], Lü & Hao [10], and Kiefer et al. [7]. In the work of Kampke et al. [6], only the best results obtained from the 10 runs of its GRASP+SA+Path-Relinking algorithm are presented. In order to promote a fair comparison, the best solutions achieved in all executions of GMF-D are also presented in Table 4. However, in the works of Müller [11], Lü and Hao [10] and Kiefer et al. [7] are reported the $f$ average over the 10 runs performed and consequently, in Table 5, these values are compared with the correspondent GMF-D results.

From Table 4 we can see that the results of the proposed algorithm improved on average 22.66% the results of Kampke et al. [6]. It is also noted that the GMF-D algorithm outperform results in all instances. The quality of results of GMF-D algorithm are already expected, since the proposed method constructs a partial solution without violations of hard constraints and also avoiding the violation of soft constraints **S2** and **S3**, since the algorithm proposed by Kampke et al. [6] uses the $IS_{CBCTT}$ method to construct a complete solution also without violations of hard constraints, but does not verify the violation of soft constraints in a specific way.

**Table 5.** Comparison between GMF-D and some of the best results in the literature.

| Instances | Müller[a] | Lü& Hao[a] | Kiefer[b] | GMF-D |
|-----------|-----------|------------|-----------|-------|
| comp01 | **5.0** | **5.0** | **5.0** | **5.0** |
| comp02 | 61.3 | 60.6 | **41.5** | 61.5 |
| comp03 | 94.8 | 86.6 | **71.7** | 85.2 |
| comp04 | 42.8 | 47.9 | **35.1** | 39.5 |
| comp05 | 343.5 | 328.5 | **305.2** | 342.5 |
| comp06 | 56.8 | 69.9 | **47.8** | 58.8 |
| comp07 | 33.9 | 28.2 | **14.5** | 28.8 |
| comp08 | 46.5 | 51.4 | **41.0** | 44.6 |
| comp09 | 113.1 | 113.2 | **102.8** | 106.6 |
| comp10 | 21.3 | 38.0 | **14.3** | 25.1 |
| comp11 | **0.0** | **0.0** | **0.0** | **0.0** |
| comp12 | 351.6 | 365.0 | **319.4** | 350.9 |
| comp13 | 73.9 | 76.2 | **60.7** | 75.6 |
| comp14 | 61.8 | 62.9 | **54.1** | 60.4 |
| comp15 | 94.8 | 87.8 | **72.1** | 86.2 |
| comp16 | 41.2 | 53.7 | **33.8** | 44.1 |
| comp17 | 86.6 | 100.5 | **75.7** | 85.3 |
| comp18 | 91.7 | 82.6 | **66.9** | 86.0 |
| comp19 | 68.8 | 75.0 | **62.6** | 72.3 |
| comp20 | 34.3 | 58.2 | **27.2** | 43.5 |
| comp21 | 108.0 | 125.3 | **97.0** | 111.3 |
| Average | 87.22 | 91.26 | **73.73** | 86.34 |

[a]http://www.cs.qub.ac.uk/itc2007/winner/finalorder.htm
[b]*Adaptive Large Neighborhood Search* (ALNS), [7]

In addition, the metaheuristic SA used as local search method in this work employs the *Lecture Move* movement to generate neighbor solutions, while only the classical *Move* and *Swap* movements are used in [6]. As reported by Kampke et al. [5], the *Lecture Move* is the best movement to be applied to CB-CTT formulation for UTP.

Observing the results presented in Table 5 and comparing them to each other, it can be concluded that the results presented by GMF-D algorithm surpassed on average the algorithms proposed by Müller [11] and Lü and Hao [10], respectively presented in the second and third columns, which are the winners of the ITC-2007. Specifically in comparison to Müller results, the GMF-D algorithm outperformed the results in 11 instances, in addition to the two instances (*comp01* and *comp11*) which the average are identical. In summary, the GMF-D algorithm found results with average improvements of 1.01% and 5.39% when compared to those found by Müller and Lü & Hao, respectively.

Finally, the results obtained by the ALNS [7] were 14.61% better than those from the GMF-D, on average. The ALNS algorithm proposed by Kiefer et al. [7] employs operators to destroy and reconstruct solutions allowing a greater diversification than that provided by the algorithm proposed in this work.

## 6   Conclusions

In this work, we presented a CB-CTT reformulation as a network flow model and the application of GMF-D and GMF-B algorithms to find the maximum flow which represents a partial solution in the original CB-CTT formulation. Then, we incorporated this algorithm to $IS_{CBCTT}$ procedure, previously proposed by Kampke et al. [6], in order to conclude the construction of a solution, submitted to a SA metaheuristic, which performs the GRASP local search phase.

Considering the official results from ITC-2007 we observed that the proposed GRASP+SA combined with the maximum network flow algorithm was able to present very competitive solutions, and it could be ranked in the first place when compared to the results obtained by the other competitors. On average, the GMF-D results were equal or better than those found by Müller and Lü & Hao in 13 and 17 of the 21 instances, respectively.

The input data and the source codes implemented in this work are available in https://bitbucket.org/Moreli04/timetabling-moreli.

## References

1. Burke, E., Jackson, K., Kingston, J.H., Weare, R.: Automated university timetabling: the state of the art. Comput. J. **40**(9), 565–571 (1997)
2. Di Gaspero, L., Schaerf, A., McCollum, B.: The second international timetabling competition (ITC-2007): curriculum-based course timetabling (track 3). Technical report (2007)
3. Edmonds, J., Karp, R.M.: Theoretical improvements in algorithmic efficiency for network flow problems. J. ACM **19**(2), 248–264 (1972)
4. Ford Jr., L.R., Fulkerson, D.R.: Flows in Networks. Princeton University Press, Princeton (1962)
5. Kampke, E.H., Segatto, E.A., Boeres, M.C.S., Rangel, M.C., Mauri, G.R.: Neighborhood analysis on the university timetabling problem. In: Gervasi, O., et al. (eds.) ICCSA 2017. LNCS, vol. 10406, pp. 148–164. Springer, Cham (2017). https://doi.org/10.1007/978-3-319-62398-6_11
6. Kampke, E.H., de Souza Rocha, W., Boeres, M.C.S., Rangel, M.C.: A GRASP algorithm with path relinking for the university courses timetabling problem. In: Proceeding Series of the Brazilian Society of Computational and Applied Mathematics, vol. 3, pp. 1081–1087 (2015)
7. Kiefer, A., Hartl, R.F., Schnell, A.: Adaptive large neighborhood search for the curriculum-based course timetabling problem. Ann. Oper. Res. **252**(2), 255–282 (2017)
8. Kirkpatrick, S., Gelatt, C.D., Vecchi, M.P.: Optimization by simulated annealing. Science **220**(4598), 671–680 (1983)

9. Lewis, R.: A survey of metaheuristic-based techniques for university timetabling problems. OR Spectrum **30**(1), 167–190 (2008)
10. Lü, Z., Hao, J.K.: Adaptive tabu search for course timetabling. Eur. J. Oper. Res. **200**(1), 235–244 (2010)
11. Müller, T.: ITC2007 solver description: a hybrid approach. Ann. Oper. Res. **172**(1), 429 (2009)
12. PATAT: International timetabling competition (2008). http://www.cs.qub.ac.uk/itc2007
13. Schaerf, A.: A survey of automated timetabling. Artif. Intell. Rev. **13**(2), 87–127 (1999)

# Orthogonal Bandit Learning for Portfolio Selection Under Cardinality Constraint

Mahdi Moeini[✉][iD]

Chair of Business Information Systems and Operations Research (BISOR),
Technische Universität Kaiserslautern, 67663 Kaiserslautern, Germany
mahdi.moeini@wiwi.uni-kl.de

**Abstract.** In this paper, we address the portfolio selection problem and solve it by means of a machine learning approach. More precisely, we study portfolio optimization under *cardinality constraint*, which limits the number of assets in a portfolio. This problem is known to be NP-hard and, consequently, difficult to solve for some settings of the cardinality parameter. In order to solve the problem, we introduce a hybrid approach that combines effectively an existing *bandit learning algorithm* with a *kernel search* heuristic. The bandit learning algorithm is used for conducting online portfolio selections and the kernel search manages the cardinality constraint. In order to investigate the performance of our algorithm, we carried out computational experiments on real-world market data sets. According to the numerical results, we observe that, despite the presence of cardinality constraint, our hybrid algorithm shows good performance in solving the test instances in reasonable computation time and, in many cases, the algorithm provides portfolios with higher cumulative wealth than those obtained through the existing bandit learning algorithm, which is applied on classical portfolio selection problem.

**Keywords:** Portfolio selection problem · Machine learning ·
Multi-armed bandit · Bandit learning · Cardinality constraint ·
Kernel search

## 1 Introduction

The portfolio selection is one of the classical optimization problems which arise in financial industry. By definition, the objective of the portfolio selection problem consists in finding an optimal way of diversifying a given amount of money among a set of available assets, while each combination of these assets defines a *portfolio* [5,21]. The seminal work of Nobel prize laureate Markowitz [16] provides a model for finding optimal portfolios. In the Mean-Variance (MV) model of Markowitz [16,17], each portfolio is assigned to an amount of return and a level of risk, which is defined by variance of the asset returns [1,5,12]. However, despite its simplicity, the MV model suffers from different aspects, e.g., poor performance in

© Springer Nature Switzerland AG 2019
S. Misra et al. (Eds.): ICCSA 2019, LNCS 11621, pp. 232–248, 2019.
https://doi.org/10.1007/978-3-030-24302-9_17

out-of-sample settings and lack of real-world constraints. Hence, several research papers have focused on bridging the gap between the classical model and the real-world situations such as including *buy-in threshold* [1,12,15,19] or *cardinality constraint* [5–7,9,13,15]. Similarly, alternative optimization models have been introduced to address other shortcomings of the MV model [1,10].

Furthermore, in the age of globalization, the financial industry faces the challenge of processing massive amount of data in order to make the best decisions. To this end, machine learning is an effective tool that might be used and, in particular, the *multi-armed bandit learning* methods have already been applied for portfolio optimization. The bandit learning strategies can fit well in the context of portfolio selection as they use existing knowledge and exploitation-exploration policy to catch new information, to optimize the reward, and to select the most beneficial arms, where each arm is assigned to an asset [3,8]. In the same stream of research, *orthogonal bandit learning algorithm* has been developed, by Shen et al., as an effective tool for finding optimal portfolios [21]. In this approach, *orthogonal portfolios* are constructed, the *Sharp ratio* and reward of each arm is computed, and then the optimal arms are selected to compose the optimal portfolio. However, the orthogonal bandit learning is used for solving a very basic portfolio selection model, which permits also short selling of assets. Hence, in order to handle more practical restrictions, i.e., portfolio selection under cardinality constraint, we extend the orthogonal bandit learning by combining it with a *Kernel Search* (KS) method [6]. The KS is a heuristic framework that starts with an initial set of assets, as the kernel, and then, by solving a sequence of problems, identifies further assets to add them into the kernel. This approach is suitable for handling cardinality constraint. In order to evaluate the performance of our hybrid algorithm, we carried out computational experiments on several real-world test instances and report the numerical results, which confirm the ability of our approach in providing high-quality solutions within reasonable computation time. Furthermore, despite limits imposed by the cardinality constraint, on many instances, our approach provides better portfolio compositions than those obtained through the basic orthogonal bandit learning algorithm.

We organize the remainder of this paper as follows: In Sect. 2, we present the basic concepts that we are going to use throughout this paper. Then, Sect. 3 is devoted to the notation, the description of the portfolio optimization problem, and the bandit learning approach, which we call *basic bandit*, for the portfolio selection. In Sect. 4, we modify and extend the basic bandit to handle cardinality constraint in a portfolio selection problem. Section 5 reports the test settings of our computational experiments and their numerical results. Finally, some conclusions are drawn in Sect. 6.

## 2    Preliminaries

In this section, we present the basic concepts that the contributions of this article are based on.

## 2.1  Bandits

The Multi-Armed Bandit (MAB) problem was first stated by Thompson in 1933 [2,22], although in a more specific form. His motivation for studying the bandit problem were clinical trials, where different treatments should be allocated to patients. Later Robbins [20] was one of the first researchers who picked up and studied the model.

By definition, the bandit problem generally describes the situation of a gambler, who must decide which arm of a K-slot machine to pull in order to maximize his total rewards within a fixed number of trials. In order to present a formal description, we follow the notation of [21]. Assume that $n$ arms representing $n$ actions and time steps $t_k$, where $k = 1, \ldots, m$ are given such that if an arm $i$ is pulled at time $t_k$, then we earn a bounded reward $r_i(t_k) \in \mathbb{R}$, where $i = 1, \ldots, n$. The objective of bandit learning consists in sequential (and one at a time) selection of suitable arms in order to maximize the total reward, earned by pulling arms, or to minimize the regret. In a stochastic context, where $\nu_i$ denotes the expected reward of arm $i$, the largest expected reward would be $\nu* := max_{1 \leq i \leq n}\nu_i$. If this expected reward takes place in $m$ plays, then the maximum expected reward will be $m\nu^*$ and the *pseudo regret* after playing $m$ times is computed as follows:

$$m\nu^* - \sum_{k=1}^{m} \mathbb{E}[r_{ik}(t_k)], \tag{1}$$

where $i_k$ is used to indicate the index of the arm selected at time $t_k$ and $r_{ik}(t_k)$ defines the corresponding reward (see [21] and references therein).

There are several approaches for solving the MAB problem. An easy and classical method is called the $\epsilon$-greedy strategy: at a given time $t$, with a probability of $1 - \epsilon$, the arm with the best (highest) reward is pulled; otherwise, a random arm is played with a probability of $\epsilon$. This two sided approach makes a trade-off between *exploitation* versus *exploration*. Another commonly accepted and utilized policy is called the *upper confidence bounds* (UCB) strategy [11,21]. The UCB algorithms establish guided exploration in contrast to simpler strategies like the $\epsilon$-greedy method, which randomly choose the target of exploration. In the UCB, as soon as each arm is played once, the following function is used to select the best arm $i^*$, at time $t_k$:

$$i^*(t_k) := \arg \max_{1 \leq i \leq n} \left( \overline{r}_i(t_k) + \sqrt{\frac{2 \, ln(k)}{k_i}} \right), \tag{2}$$

where, $\overline{r}_i(t_k)$ and $k_i$ denote the mean reward and the played number of the arm $i$ up to the time $t_k$ [21].

The typical and classical assumptions in bandit learning consists in considering rewards as independent and identically distributed (i.i.d.) for each arm, selecting the best arms at each play, defining the reward mean as the objective, and finally ignoring presence of historical data. These hypotheses are not respected in financial markets. In fact, if we assume each (financial) asset as an arm, it is well-known that assets are correlated, diversification is a priority in portfolio selection (to reduce risk of investment), the objective of portfolio optimization is minimizing risk as well as maximizing return, and the historical data are available and used. In order to bridge this gap, Shen et al. [21] developed a new bandit learning algorithm that we will discuss and extend in Sects. 3 and 4, respectively.

## 2.2 Portfolio Selection

Assume that we would like to invest a given capital, among a set of available assets, and in a discrete-time and finite horizon environment. The time horizon consists of time-steps $t_k = k \, \Delta t$, where $k$ stands for the time-step index and $\Delta t$ represents the duration between two time-steps. There is no specification with regard to which duration a time-step has to represent, i.e., it can be one day, one week, one month, or even one year, which basically depends on the underlying data. Given $n$ risky assets, the prices of $i$-th asset at time $t_k$ is $S_{k,i}$ (to simplify the notation, we might represent $t_k$ by $k$, whenever it causes no ambiguity) and $R_{k,i}$ defines the return of asset $i$ from time $t_{k-1}$ to $t_k$, and computed by $R_{k,i} := S_{k,i}/S_{k-1,i}$. In the following, the whole set of assets is referred to as asset pool $A$, consisting of all $n$ risky assets.

Let us denote the investment decision by a column vector $\omega_k = (\omega_{k1}, \ldots, \omega_{kn})^\top$ with the respective weight $\omega_{ki}$ (in percentage) of the $i$-th asset at time-step $k$. The sum over all weights must be equal to 1, which corresponds to the usage of the whole budget. Shen et al. [21] assume that *short selling* is permitted. Short selling means that the investor borrows the asset for sale as he presumes falling prices. If his prediction becomes true and the value decreases, he buys the same asset for a cheaper price and makes profit. In the opposite case, the investor will have loss. Therefore, $\omega_{ki} > 0$ refers to long- whereas $\omega_{ki} < 0$ indicates short-positions [21].

## 3 Bandit Learning with Orthogonal Portfolio

In this section, we present the algorithm of Shen et al. [21] that we call *Basic Bandit* (BB). It might be used for portfolio selection without cardinality constraint. Then, in Sect. 4, we will explain how we extend BB to take into account cardinality constraint.

Using return $R_{ik}$ of each asset $i$ at time $t_k$, we can compute the covariance matrix, denoted by $\mathbf{\Sigma_k}$, of the $n$ assets. For this purpose, we might use a factor model as described in [4], which is suitable for computing large-scale covariance matrices. Then, we can decompose $\mathbf{\Sigma_k}$ into its principal components:

$$\mathbf{\Sigma_k} = \mathbf{H_k}\mathbf{\Lambda_k}\mathbf{H_k}^\top, \tag{3}$$

where $\mathbf{\Lambda_k}$ is a diagonal matrix containing the eigenvalues $(\lambda_{k,1}, \ldots, \lambda_{k,n})$ of the matrix $\mathbf{\Sigma_k}$, sorted in decreasing order. Furthermore, the columns of the matrix $\mathbf{H_k}$ are actually the eigenvectors of the corresponding eigenvalues of $\mathbf{\Sigma_k}$.

The basic bandit finds a portfolio allocation based on the asset pool $A$ and provides the weights for the assets. However, in order to satisfy the condition of using the whole budget in percentage, the eigenvectors need to be normalized by their sum according to

$$\tilde{H}_{k,i} = \frac{\boldsymbol{H}_{k,i}}{\boldsymbol{H}_{k,i}^{\top}\boldsymbol{1}}, \tag{4}$$

where $\boldsymbol{1}$ is a vector with all entries equal to 1. In this way, we obtain $n$ uncorrelated portfolios with the return of $\tilde{H}_{k,i}R_k$, and the covariance matrix of these returns is computed as follows:

$$\tilde{\boldsymbol{\Sigma}}_{\mathbf{k}} = \tilde{\mathbf{H}}_{\mathbf{k}}\boldsymbol{\Sigma}_{\mathbf{k}}\tilde{\mathbf{H}}_{\mathbf{k}}^{\top} = \tilde{\boldsymbol{\Lambda}}_{\mathbf{k}}. \tag{5}$$

The entries on the diagonal of $\tilde{\boldsymbol{\Lambda}}_{\mathbf{k}}$ represent the respective variances of the portfolio $i$ at time-step $k$ as $\tilde{\lambda}_{k,i} = \lambda_{k,i}/(\boldsymbol{H}_{k,i}^{\top}\boldsymbol{1})^2$. The new portfolios are called *orthogonal portfolios* [21]. According to [18], the orthogonal portfolios represent the risk factors in the market and we can use eigenvector directions to characterize market fluctuations [21].

Additionally, some empirical studies revealed that the covariance matrix can be decomposed into two groups of factors as follows:

$$\tilde{\boldsymbol{\Sigma}}_{\mathbf{k}} = \sum_{i=1}^{l} \tilde{\lambda}_{k,i}\tilde{H}_{k,i}\tilde{H}_{k,i}^{\top} + \sum_{i=l+1}^{n} \tilde{\lambda}_{k,i}\tilde{H}_{k,i}\tilde{H}_{k,i}^{\top}, \tag{6}$$

where the first summation is characterized as the *systematic* movement of the market and the second one represents the *idiosyncratic* risks [21]. While the first one should be followed (passive investment), the second one contains a potential, which can be exploited by the investor (active investment).

After dividing the arms into two groups, we need to determine the best arm out of each group. A way to define an order is to compute the Sharpe ratio $\bar{r}_{k,i}$ as it takes directly into account the return per risk unit. At time-step $k$, the Sharpe ratio of the $i$-th orthogonal portfolio, which is represented by the $i$-th column vector, is computed by

$$\bar{r}_{k,i} = \frac{\boldsymbol{H}_{k,i}\mathbb{E}[R_{k,i}]}{\sqrt{\lambda_{k,i}}}, \tag{7}$$

where $\mathbb{E}[R_{k,i}]$ can be estimated by the James-Stein Shrinkage Estimator [18].

After retrieving the order, based on the Sharpe ratio of each arm, the optimal arm of each subset is computed by taking the one-sided confidence bound into the reward function:

$$i_k^* = \arg\max_{i=1,\ldots,l} \bar{r}_{k,i} + \sqrt{\frac{2\ln(k+\tau)}{\tau + k_i}},$$

$$j_k^* = \arg\max_{i=l+1,\ldots,n} \bar{r}_{k,i} + \sqrt{\frac{2\ln(k+\tau)}{\tau + k_i}}, \tag{8}$$

where $k_i$ is the number of times the $i$-th arm has been selected and $\tau$ stands for the length of the sliding time window. At this point, the arms of the bandit have been divided into two subsets and from each group, the best arms $i_k^*$ and $j_k^*$, according to the Sharpe ratio, have been determined. Then, we compute a weighted average of the selected two best arms in order to minimize the total variance of the selected portfolio. More precisely, assume that $\tilde{H}_{k,i_k^*}$ and $\tilde{H}_{k,j_k^*}$ are the uncorrelated portfolios corresponding to the best selected arms $i_k^*$ and $j_k^*$. Then, we minimize the total variance $\lambda_{k,p} = \theta_k^2 \tilde{\lambda}_{k,j_k^*} + (1 - \theta_k)^2 \tilde{\lambda}_{k,i_k^*}$ to obtain the portfolio mixture weight $\theta_k^*$ as follows

$$\theta_k^* = \arg \min_{\theta_k} \lambda_{k,p} = \frac{\tilde{\lambda}_{k,i_k^*}}{\tilde{\lambda}_{k,j_k^*} + \tilde{\lambda}_{k,i_k^*}}. \tag{9}$$

The value of $\theta_k^*$ is then used to obtain the portfolio mixture through

$$\omega_k = (1 - \theta_k^*)\tilde{H}_{k,i_k^*} + \theta_k^* \tilde{H}_{k,j_k^*}. \tag{10}$$

The output of each iteration through the algorithm is the weights vector $\omega_k$ which contains the weights for each asset from the asset pool. In order to investigate the forecast quality of the algorithm, we compute the net return of the portfolio $\mu_k$, from time $t_{k-1}$ to $t_k$, by using the return $R_{k+1}$ of the next time-step, i.e., $t_{k+1}$:

$$\mu_k = \omega_k^\top R_{k+1} - 1. \tag{11}$$

As a performance metric, we might use the achieved return to compute the *cumulative wealth* (CW), denoted by $\gamma_k$, as follows:

$$\gamma_k = \sum_{j=k-t_{tf}}^{k} \gamma_{j-1}(1 + \mu_j), \tag{12}$$

in which, for the very first iteration, $\gamma_{k-t_{tf}-1}$ is set to 1, representing a normalized initial investment of 1\$, and the subscript $tf$ stands for *time-frame* in the rolling horizon of the algorithm.

The above-described algorithm is summarized in Algorithm 1.

## 4    Extended Bandit Learning for Cardinality Constraint

We present *Extended Bandit* (ExtB) learning algorithm that is a modified and extended variant of the basic bandit with the objective of taking into account cardinality constraint, in absence of short selling possibility. The pseudo code of the ExtB is presented in Algorithm 2, which includes three parts: *basic bandit learning, asset limitation,* and *time restriction.* Since both the cardinality constraint and time limitation only reduce the selection and amount of assets, the other parts of the algorithm remain unaffected. Indeed, the basic bandit calculates the estimated covariance matrix, normalizes eigenvectors and eigenvalues,

---

**Algorithm 1.** Basic Bandit Learning Algorithm

---

1: **Inputs:** $m$,n, $l, \Delta t, \tau, \mathbf{R_k}$
2: **for** $k := \tau$ to $m$ **do**
3:     Calculate/estimate the returns $\mathbb{E}[\mathbf{R_k}]$ (James-Stein Shrinkage Estimator)
4:     Calculate/estimate the covariance matrix $\mathbf{\Sigma_k}$
5:     Perform principal component decomposition as in (3)
6:     Normalize eigenvector and eigenvalues as shown in (4) and (5)
7:     Compute sharpe ratio of each arm
8:     Compute adjusted reward function according to (8)
9:     Compute cutoff number $l$ and select best arm from each subset
10:     Compute optimal mixture weight $\theta_k^*$
11:     Compute optimal portfolio weight $\omega_k$
12:     Compute overall return and cumulative wealth $\gamma_k$
13: **end for**
14: **Outputs:** Portfolio weights and cumulative wealth for each time-step $k$

---

and computes an optimal portfolio weight vector. Then, asset limitation and time restriction parts, which are integrated into the basic bandit through the lines between 12 and 32, start handling cardinality constraint. Finally, prior to the last step, in order to evaluate the forecast quality and determine the cumulative value, we manipulate the weights to fit the cardinality constraint and replace the former weight vector.

In the following, we describe the two main complementary parts of the extended bandit learning algorithm, i.e., *asset limitation* and *time restriction*.

## 4.1    Asset Limitation with Kernel Search

The output of the basic bandit is a solution vector, which is computed by using orthogonal portfolios. More precisely, the solution vector, obtained through the basic bandit, shows the weight of each asset, i.e., the share that an asset receives from the total investment. This vector may contain a *large number* of assets with non-zero weights, which might be undesirable; in particular, if each asset from the former asset pool $A$ is part of the final portfolio and every redistribution of the asset allocation requires transaction costs. Furthermore, a typical investor might be interested in having a given number $C$, named *cardinality parameter*, of assets in his/her portfolio just for the sake of having a better control on his/her portfolio. Therefore, a limitation in form of a *cardinality constraint* appears to be appropriate. This constraint is a mean to impose a limit on the number of assets composing the portfolio and is a well-studied topic in the financial literature [5–7, 9, 13, 15].

Introduction of cardinality constraint adds a combinatorial aspect to the portfolio selection problem. In order to handle the situation of the new problem with the extended bandit approach, we need to make some additional assumptions. First, while the basic bandit allows short selling, assets may not be sold

---

**Algorithm 2.** Extended Bandit Learning Algorithm

---
1: **Inputs:** $m$,n, $l$, $\Delta t, \tau, \mathbf{R_k}, C, t_{ld}$
2: **for** $k = \tau$ to $m$ **do**
3:     Calculate/estimate the returns $\mathbb{E}[\mathbf{R_k}]$ (using James-Stein Shrinkage Estimator)
4:     Calculate/estimate the covariance matrix $\mathbf{\Sigma_k}$(French and Fama 3-Factor Model)
5:     Perform principal component decomposition as in (3)
6:     Normalize eigenvector and eigenvalues as shown in (4) and (5)
7:     Compute Sharpe ratio of each arm
8:     Compute adjusted reward function according to (8)
9:     Compute cutoff number $l$ and select best arm from each subset
10:     Compute optimal mixture weight $\theta_k^*$
11:     Compute optimal portfolio weight $\omega_k$
12:     **if** Cardinality Constraint selected **then**
13:         Determine adjusted asset pool $\hat{\mathbf{A}}$ with short positions removed
14:         Determine in decreasing order sorted $\bar{\mathbf{A}}$ based on their sharpe ratio $r_{k,i}$
15:         Set size of kernel $K$ as $C$ and fill with the $\lfloor C/2 \rfloor$ best assets from $\bar{\mathbf{A}}$
16:         Remove assets in $K$ from $\bar{\mathbf{A}}$ and set basket size
17:         **while** size($K$) < $C$ **do**
18:             Divide $\bar{\mathbf{A}}$ into baskets with the size from step 16
19:             **for** each basket $b_i$ **do**
20:                 Add temporarily $b_i$ to $K$ and calculate the expected return
21:                 Calculate needed time $\Delta \hat{t}$
22:                 **if** $t_{ld} < \Delta \hat{t}$ & timeRestriction.selected **then**
23:                     **break;**
24:                 **end if**
25:             **end for**
26:             Select the best basket $b_i^*$ and add its assets to the kernel $K$
27:             Remove the assets from the best basket $b_i^*$ from $\bar{\mathbf{A}}$
28:         **end while**
29:         For each asset that is not part of the selection: Set its weight to 0
30:         Adjust weights such that $\sum \omega_{k,i}^* = 1$
31:         $\omega_k = \omega_k^*$
32:     **end if**
33:     Compute the overall return and the cumulative wealth $\gamma_k$
34: **end for**
35: **Outputs:** Portfolio weights and cumulative wealth for each time-step $k$

---

short within the extended bandit. Furthermore, in order to have the most promising assets in the portfolio, we sort them through the combinatorial process of the extended bandit learning. For this purpose, we use the Sharpe ratio, which uses the simple mean of the $i$-th asset at time-step $k$:

$$\mu_{k,i} = \frac{1}{t_{tf}} \sum_{j=k-t_{tf}}^{k} R_{i,j},$$

and takes the last $t_{tf}$ return data depending on the size of the preceding horizon.

We summarize the asset limitation process, which uses *kernel search heuristic* [6], in Algorithm 3. In the following, we describe different steps of this algorithm.

---

**Algorithm 3.** Asset Limitation Procedure for Handling Cardinality Constraint

---
1: **Inputs:** $w_k, C$
2: Remove the short soled assets to determine adjusted asset pool $\hat{A}$
3: Use the Sharpe ratio to sort asset pool $\bar{A}$ in decreasing order of ratios
4: Set size of kernel $K$ as $C$ and fill with the $\lfloor C/2 \rfloor$ best assets from $\bar{A}$
5: Remove assets in $K$ from $\bar{A}$
6: Set basket size
7: **while** size($K$) < C **do**
8:     Divide $\bar{A}$ into baskets with the size from step 6
9:     **for** each basket $b_i$ **do**
10:         Unit $K$ with $b_i$ temporary and calculate the expected return
11:     **end for**
12:     Select the best basket $b_i^*$ and add its assets to the kernel $K$
13:     Remove the assets from the best basket $b_i^*$ from $\bar{A}$
14: **end while**
15: Set each asset's weight to 0, that is not part of the selection
16: Adjust weights such that $\sum \omega_{k,i}^* = 1$
17: $\omega_k = \omega_k^*$
18: **Output:** Adjusted weights vector $\omega_k$

---

The process starts with the adjustment of the asset pool $A$ by removing all short positions. Then, we compute the Sharpe ratio for the remaining assets and sort them in decreasing order to obtain the sorted asset pool $\bar{A}$.

The investor may set the value of the cardinality parameter $C$. Then, we define a set so-called *kernel* $K$ that has the same size as $C$. At the beginning of the combinatorial process, the kernel $K$ is filled to the half with the best assets from $\bar{A}$. Then, these specific assets are removed from $\bar{A}$.

Another concept in the kernel search heuristic is called *basket*, which is a set used to fill out the remaining parts of the kernel. The initial basket size is defined as $s_b = \lfloor C/4 \rfloor$. The basic idea of the kernel search is as follows: The available assets are divided into baskets of the same size. At each iteration of the heuristic, the value of the objective function is calculated, which is (in our case) the expected return, for the combination of the kernel and the respective basket. After evaluating each combination, we select the basket that leads to the best result and insert its assets into $K$. At the same time, we update the current asset pool by removing these assets from $\bar{A}$. We repeat these steps until the kernel is filled with the same amount of assets as the cardinality constraint. It might happen that for the last iteration the basket size is too big. Hence, the new basket size $\hat{s}_b$ equals the remaining free spots inside the kernel $K$ (for more details on the kernel search heuristic, see [6]).

As soon as the best assets have been found, the weights of the other positions are set to zero. The sum of all selected weights should be equal to 1; otherwise, parts of the budget remain unused. This adjustment is achieved by normalizing each weight by the sum of the weights of all remaining assets.

At a time step $t_k$, after finishing the process, the outcome is an weight-adjusted vector $\omega_k$ containing exactly $C$ assets with $\omega_{k,i} > 0$ for $i \in \{1, \ldots, n\}$.

## 4.2   Optional Time Restriction

The performance of the extended bandit primarily depends on the size of the problem. While the calculation process takes about 3 s for 48 assets with historical data from the last 120 months, it might take about 15 min for almost 500 assets with equal historical information. Consequently, larger data sets result in higher computation times. Hence, in order to have a time management in the combinatorial process, we restrict it by means of a *time restriction* procedure (See lines 21–24 of Algorithm 2).

Let a maximum duration $t_{max}$ be given, e.g., 15 min, which is 900 s. If we assume that the data set contains information for $t_h$ time-steps, the overall recurrence number of the calculation process is given by the difference $t_h - t_{tf}$. For example, let us assume that the data set consists of 48 assets and $t_h = 500$, the cardinality parameter is equal to 10, and the selected time-frame (sliding window horizon) $t_{tf}$ is 120. Then, the optimization process will be repeated 380 times.

Usually, the algorithm would just stop after a certain duration (set by the user), taking the solution, which has been found at that point in time. However, this approach might lead to a problem as the process might have to be aborted in the middle of the computation. This situation might be an issue; in particular, in case of the extended bandit as, due to the combinatorial process, the solution procedure might require long processing time. In order to handle this situation, we introduce the following mechanism. The maximum duration $t_{max}$ is divided into equal parts for each calculation point, which is called *cycle duration* $t_{cd}$, incorporating the basic bandit part as well as the kernel search part of the extended bandit. The cycle duration $t_{cd}$ is computed as follows:

$$t_{cd} := \frac{t_{max}}{t_h - t_{tf}}. \tag{13}$$

Additionally, the kernel search itself iterates through every possible basket to find the best combination. Because the number of iterations is known (which depends on the value of $C$ and the basket size), the cycle duration can be divided by the number of iterations to obtain the *loop duration* $t_{ld}$ for the kernel search:

$$t_{ld} = \frac{t_{cd}}{\left\lceil \frac{C/2}{s_b} \right\rceil}. \tag{14}$$

To continue the example from above, the respective cycle and loop duration are:

$$t_{cd} = \frac{t_{max}}{t_h - t_{tf}} = \frac{900\,\text{s}}{500 - 120} = 2.368\,\text{s}, \tag{15}$$

$$t_{ld} = \frac{t_{cd}}{\left\lceil \frac{C/2}{s_b} \right\rceil} = \frac{2.368\,\text{s}}{\left\lceil \frac{5}{2} \right\rceil} = 0.789\,\text{s}. \tag{16}$$

Using these values, we can have a better time management throughout the extended bandit learning algorithm. In fact, after each iteration, the algorithm checks whether the allowed duration is exceeded (see lines 21–24 of Algorithm 2). The query appears after the first iteration. This guarantees that the combinatorial process takes place at least once, which means that the best basket taken is naturally the first one. Basically, the final kernel $K$ would consist of the best $C$ assets from $\bar{\mathbf{A}}$. In case of a big data set or a very small time limit, $t_{cd}$ and $t_{ld}$ might be too small even for a single iteration and, consequently, the time limit will not be sufficient to find a solution.

## 5    Computational Experiments and Numerical Results

In order to investigate the performance of the algorithms in solving the portfolio selection problem (under cardinality constraint), we carried out a set of computational experiments and report the results in this section.

### 5.1    Data and Test Settings

For the computational experiments, we used six real-world data sets, selected from the finance page of *Yahoo!* as well as the financial literature [6,7,21]. Table 1 sums up the main information regarding these data sets. In particular, test instances FF48 and S&P500, which are daily information of assets, have already been used in the literature, but the other ones have been collected from monthly prices on the finance page of *Yahoo!* In Table 1, the column of time-steps gives the length of the total horizon covered by the corresponding data set.

**Table 1.** Data sets.

| Data set | Period | Time-steps |
|---|---|---|
| FF48 | Daily | 498 |
| 100 Assets | Monthly | 119 |
| 200 Assets | Monthly | 119 |
| 300 Assets | Monthly | 119 |
| 400 Assets | Monthly | 119 |
| S&P500 | Daily | 1258 |

The basic bandit as well as the extended bandit learning algorithms require setting values to some parameters, which are given in Table 2. More precisely, in this table, we provide the different combinations for the parameters of the tested algorithms. In particular, at each experiment using the extended bandit, the value of the cardinality parameter $C$ is selected from $\{5, 10, 15, 20\}$. These are selected values for which the portfolio optimization problem under cardinality constraint is known to be challenging and attract particular attention in the financial literature [5–7,9,13,15].

**Table 2.** Parameter settings for the experiments.

| Parameter | Tested values |
|---|---|
| Sliding window time-frame | 50% & 25% of respective time-steps |
| Asset limit (cardinality parameter $C$) | 5, 10, 15, 20 |
| Time limit | 20 min |

We implemented the algorithms in Java and ran the experiments on a computer with the following specifics: Windows 10 Professional, Intel i5-6600 CPU 3.30 GHz, 16 GB RAM.

## 5.2 Numerical Results

Shen et al. suggest in their paper to compute the cumulative wealth based on the returns of the last regarded time-step [21]. Basically, they take the return data for each asset from time-step $(k - t_{tf})$ until $k$, and calculate the realized return based on the same last returns at time-step $k$, which have already been taken into account to compute the asset allocation. Consequently, the *forecast* quality and potential of the algorithm is not considered. Therefore, in order to investigate whether the allocation leads to a yield, we suggest to compute the realized return or rather the cumulative wealth based on the return data at time-step $(k + 1)$. In order to verify the differences between these two separate cases, we tested the basic bandit and computed the cumulative wealth (CW) of the resulting portfolios at time-steps $k$ and $k + 1$, i.e., for return vectors $R_k$ and $R_{k+1}$, and report them in Table 3. This table contains also the computation time (CPU Time in seconds) of each experiment.

It can be seen that the settings with a smaller time-frame perform better, in terms of higher CW, except for the cases of $R_{k+1}$ of 200 Assets, $R_k$ of 300 Assets, and $R_k$ of 400 Assets. This might be explained by the fact that, in every time-step, a new asset allocation is computed and the portfolio converted appropriately. Therefore, the information and also the potential in the long-term development of the allocation will not be used, since the investor only holds the portfolio for one period. A smaller time-frame, on the other hand, makes a better use of the short-term development of the assets and the algorithm applies the market fluctuations into the asset allocation.

Further, the increase of computation time depends on the number of assets (in the instances) and their available time horizon. For example, while the algorithm takes only 0.88 s to run through a small data set consisting of 48 assets with available data for 498 time-steps and a time-frame of 125, it nearly takes 16 min to compute the overall cumulative wealth for the S&P500 data set, consisting of 500 assets, 1258 time-steps and a time-frame of 315. Finally, the differences between CW values for $R_k$ versus $R_{k+1}$ reveal the forecast errors that we might run in an investment.

Table 3. Results for basic bandit

| Data set | Time-frame | CPU time (s.) | CW $R_k$ | CW $R_{k+1}$ |
|---|---|---|---|---|
| FF48 | 125 | 0.90 | 65.03 | 67.18 |
| | 249 | 1.08 | 7.44 | 30.73 |
| 100 Assets | 30 | 1.02 | 5.67 | 10.99 |
| | 60 | 1.00 | 4.24 | 3.17 |
| 200 Assets | 30 | 6.70 | 3.67 | 1.86 |
| | 60 | 5.14 | 3.11 | 7.10 |
| 300 Assets | 30 | 21.59 | 0.17 | 6.43 |
| | 60 | 15.73 | 4.17 | 2.73 |
| 400 Assets | 30 | 51.81 | 0.50 | 2.39 |
| | 60 | 34.92 | 2.48 | 1.68 |
| S&P500 | 315 | 965.29 | 1.89 | 1.55 |
| | 629 | 695.66 | 1.29 | 1.11 |

In addition, we tested the extended bandit learning algorithm with 50% as well as 25% time-frames, and for different values of the cardinailty parameter $C$. The results are reported in Tables 4 and 5. In these tables, we present the cumulative wealth (CW) of the solutions provided by the basic bandit (BB) and extended bandit (ExtB) for vectors $R_{k+1}$. It is important to note that the cardinality constraint is taken into account only by the ExtB and the results of the BB ignores the presence of this constraint (hence, the results of the BB are repeated in all sections of Tables 4 and 5). However, the BB permits short selling, whereas this is not the case of the ExtB. Hence, the ExtB solves a more restricted version of the portfolio selection problem. Nevertheless, according to the results shown in Tables 4 and 5, we observe that the quality of CW for the solutions provided by the ExtB are quite competitive to those obtained through the BB. In many cases, the ExtB provides better performance, in terms of CW, than the basic bandit.

Regarding the influence of the cardinality constraint, we observe, from Tables 4 and 5, that the presence of this constraint does not have big impact either on the quality of the solutions or on the computation time of the extended bandit learning algorithm. This might mean that our ExtB learning algorithm has a good performance in handling the cardinality constraint. In addition, we see that a higher value of $C$ comes along with a reduction in the CW, which might be explained as follows: a higher value of $C$ permits presence of a larger number of assets in the portfolio. Since additional assets have lower quality than the firstly added ones (e.g., in the case of $C = 5$); hence, their imposed presence will have a negative impact on the whole portfolio. Consequently, a wise selection of a suitable value for the cardinality parameter $C$ is a matter of importance.

Comparing the results shown in Tables 4 versus 5, we observe that both algorithms, overall, provide solutions with higher CW-values when a smaller sliding horizon is used. However, using a smaller sliding horizon comes along with a higher computation effort. In fact, although the used data for each time-step becomes smaller, there are more time-steps for which an allocation has to be computed. Consequently, the whole computation process takes a bit longer.

**Table 4.** Results for extended bandit and basic bandit learning algorithms with $R_{k+1}$ and 50% as time-frame.

| Data set | Time-frame | Cardinality parameter $C$ | Computation time in s | CW ExtB $R_{k+1}$ | CW BB $R_{k+1}$ |
|---|---|---|---|---|---|
| FF48 | 249 | 5 | 1.16 | 22.90 | **30.73** |
| 100 Assets | 60 | 5 | 1.04 | **8.01** | 3.17 |
| 200 Assets | 60 | 5 | 5.05 | 2.65 | **7.10** |
| 300 Assets | 60 | 5 | 16.01 | 1.30 | **2.73** |
| 400 Assets | 60 | 5 | 37.48 | 0.82 | **1.68** |
| S&P500 | 629 | 5 | 705.89 | **1.69** | 1.11 |
| FF48 | 249 | 10 | 0.73 | 16.41 | **30.73** |
| 100 Assets | 60 | 10 | 4.31 | **4.31** | 3.17 |
| 200 Assets | 60 | 10 | 4.46 | 5.31 | **7.10** |
| 300 Assets | 60 | 10 | 14.63 | **3.39** | 2.73 |
| 400 Assets | 60 | 10 | 35.35 | 1.50 | **1.68** |
| S&P500 | 629 | 10 | 701.82 | **1.56** | 1.11 |
| FF48 | 249 | 15 | 0.71 | 13.70 | **30.73** |
| 100 Assets | 60 | 15 | 0.71 | 2.77 | **3.17** |
| 200 Assets | 60 | 15 | 4.31 | 5.68 | **7.10** |
| 300 Assets | 60 | 15 | 14.45 | 2.58 | **2.73** |
| 400 Assets | 60 | 15 | 35.00 | **3.25** | 1.68 |
| S&P500 | 629 | 15 | 691.10 | **1.22** | 1.11 |
| FF48 | 249 | 20 | 0.67 | 17.18 | **30.73** |
| 100 Assets | 60 | 20 | 0.67 | 1.96 | **3.17** |
| 200 Assets | 60 | 20 | 4.35 | 5.70 | **7.10** |
| 300 Assets | 60 | 20 | 14.36 | **5.02** | 2.73 |
| 400 Assets | 60 | 20 | 35.29 | **3.87** | 1.68 |
| S&P500 | 629 | 20 | 698.24 | **1.14** | 1.11 |

**Table 5.** Results for extended bandit and basic bandit learning algorithms with $R_{k+1}$ and 25% as time-frame

| Data set | Time-frame | Cardinality parameter $C$ | Computation time in s | CW ExtB $R_{k+1}$ | CW BB $R_{k+1}$ |
|---|---|---|---|---|---|
| FF48 | 125 | 5 | 1.36 | **88.06** | 67.18 |
| 100 Assets | 30 | 5 | 1.50 | 4.38 | **10.99** |
| 200 Assets | 30 | 5 | 7.18 | **2.38** | 1.86 |
| 300 Assets | 30 | 5 | 23.31 | 0.73 | **6.43** |
| 400 Assets | 30 | 5 | 53.44 | 0.14 | **2.39** |
| S&P500 | 315 | 5 | 984.32 | **2.4** | 1.55 |
| FF48 | 125 | 10 | 0.95 | 57.95 | **67.18** |
| 100 Assets | 30 | 10 | 1.15 | 9.05 | **10.99** |
| 200 Assets | 30 | 10 | 6.47 | **6.66** | 1.86 |
| 300 Assets | 30 | 10 | 22.24 | 1.82 | **6.43** |
| 400 Assets | 30 | 10 | 52.02 | 1.05 | **2.39** |
| S&P500 | 315 | 10 | 965.05 | **2.09** | 1.55 |
| FF48 | 125 | 15 | 0.86 | 57.94 | **67.18** |
| 100 Assets | 30 | 15 | 1.06 | 6.78 | **10.99** |
| 200 Assets | 30 | 15 | 6.31 | **9.22** | 1.86 |
| 300 Assets | 30 | 15 | 21.96 | **9.90** | 6.43 |
| 400 Assets | 30 | 15 | 52.14 | 1.53 | **2.39** |
| S&P500 | 315 | 15 | 953.74 | **1.89** | 1.55 |
| FF48 | 125 | 20 | 0.85 | 54.265 | **67.18** |
| 100 Assets | 30 | 20 | 1.03 | 8.72 | **10.99** |
| 200 Assets | 30 | 20 | 6.29 | **7.92** | 1.86 |
| 300 Assets | 30 | 20 | 22.03 | 5.14 | **6.43** |
| 400 Assets | 30 | 20 | 52.73 | 2.17 | **2.39** |
| S&P500 | 315 | 20 | 953.83 | 1.55 | 1.55 |

## 6    Conclusion

In this paper, we investigated a bandit learning algorithm introduced by Shen et al. [21] for solving basic portfolio selection problems. Further, we modified and extended this algorithm and combined it with the kernel search heuristic in order to handle cardinality constraint in a portfolio selection problem. To evaluate the algorithm, we conducted computational experiments on real-world instances and reported the results. According to the numerical results, our extended bandit learning algorithm can perform well in handling combinatorial aspect of the portfolio optimization under cardinality constraint and provides portfolios with a competitive quality to those obtained by the basic bandit learning algorithm.

An interesting future research direction might consist in enhancing our algorithm to take into account different kinds of transaction cost functions [10,14].

**Acknowledgments.** The author wishes to thank the Chair of Business Information Systems and Operations Research (BISOR) at the Technische Universität Kaiserslautern (Germany), where the paper was written, for the financial support.

# References

1. Bartholomew-Biggs, M.C.: Nonlinear Optimization with Financial Applications, 1st edn. Kluwer Academic Publishers, Dordrecht (2005)
2. Berry, D.A., Fristedt, B.: Bandit Problems: Sequential Allocaton of Experiments. University of Minnesota: Chapman and Hall Ltd., London (1985)
3. Chen, W., Wang, Y., Yuan, Y.: Combinatorial multi-armed bandit: general framework and applications. In: Proceedings of the 30th International Conference on Machine Learning, pp. 151–159 (2013)
4. Fan, J., Fan, Y., Lv, J.: High dimensional covariance matrix estimation using a factor model (2007). http://arxiv.org/pdf/math/0701124v1
5. Fernández, A., Gómez, S.: Portfolio selection using neural networks. Comput. Oper. Res. **34**, 1177–1191 (2007)
6. Guastaroba, G., Speranza, M.G.: Kernel search: an application to the index tracking problem. Eur. J. Oper. Res. **217**(1), 54–68 (2012)
7. Gulpinar, N., Le Thi, H.A., Moeini, M.: Robust investment strategies with discrete asset choice constraints using DC programming. Optimization **59**(1), 45–62 (2010)
8. Hoffman, M.D., Brochu, E., de Freitas, N.: Portfolio allocation for bayesian optimization. In: The Conference on Uncertainty in Artificial Intelligence, pp. 327–336 (2011)
9. Jobst, N., Horniman, M., Lucas, C., Mitra, G.: Computational aspects of alternative portfolio selection models in the presence of discrete asset choice constraints. Quant. Finance **1**, 1–13 (2001)
10. Konno, H., Yamamoto, R.: Global optimization versus integer programming in portfolio optimization under nonconvex transaction costs. J. Glob. Optim. **32**, 207–219 (2005)
11. Lai, T.L., Robbins, H.: Asymptotically efficient adaptive allocation rules. Adv. Appl. Math. **6**(1), 4–22 (1985)
12. Le Thi, H.A., Moeini, M.: Portfolio selection under buy-in threshold constraints using DC programming and DCA. In: International Conference on Service Systems and Service Management (IEEE/SSSM 2006), pp. 296–300 (2006)
13. Le Thi, H.A., Moeini, M., Pham Dinh, T.: Portfolio selection under downside risk measures and cardinality constraints based on DC programming and DCA. Comput. Manag. Sci. **6**(4), 477–501 (2009)
14. Le Thi, H.A., Moeini, M., Pham Dinh, T.: DC programming approach for portfolio optimization under step increasing transaction costs. Optimization **58**(3), 267–289 (2009)
15. Le Thi, H.A., Moeini, M.: Long-short portfolio optimization under cardinality constraints by difference of convex functions algorithm. J. Optim. Theory Appl. **161**(1), 199–224 (2014)
16. Markowitz, H.M.: Portfolio selection. J. Finance **7**(1), 77–91 (1952)
17. Markowitz, H.M.: Portfolio Selection. Wiley, New York (1959)

18. Meucci, A.: Risk and Asset Allocation. Springer, Dordrecht (2009)
19. Moeini, M., Wendt, O., Krumrey, L.: Portfolio optimization by means of a $\chi$-armed bandit algorithm. In: Nguyen, N.T., Trawiński, B., Fujita, H., Hong, T.-P. (eds.) ACIIDS 2016. LNCS (LNAI), vol. 9622, pp. 620–629. Springer, Heidelberg (2016). https://doi.org/10.1007/978-3-662-49390-8_60
20. Robbins, H.: Some aspects of the sequential design of experiments. Bull. Am. Math. Soc. **58**, 527–535 (1952)
21. Shen, W., Wang, J., Jiang, Y.-G., Zha, H.: Portfolio choices with orthogonal bandit learning. In: Proceedings of the Twenty-Fourth International Joint Conference on Artificial Intelligence (IJCAI 2015), pp. 974–980 (2015)
22. Thompson, W.R.: On the likelihood that one unknown probability exceeds another in view of the evidence of two samples. Biometrika **25**, 275–294 (1933)

# On Trajectory Optimization
# of an Electric Vehicle

Eligius M. T. Hendrix[1] , Ana Maria A. C. Rocha[2(✉)] ,
and Inmaculada García[1]

[1] Computer Architecture, Universidad de Málaga, 29080 Málaga, Spain
{eligius,igarciaf}@uma.es
[2] ALGORITMI Center, University of Minho, 4710-057 Braga, Portugal
arocha@dps.uminho.pt

**Abstract.** The efficient control of electrical vehicles may contribute to sustainable use of energy. In recent studies, a model has been analyzed and several algorithms based on branch and bound have been presented. In this work, we discuss a reformulated model on the control of an electric vehicle based on the minimization of the energy consumption during an imposed displacement. We will show that similar results can be obtained by applying standard software. Moreover, this paper shows that the specified control problem can be handled from a dynamic programming perspective.

**Keywords:** Electric vehicle · Energy optimization ·
Dynamic programming · Nonlinear optimization · Optimal control ·
Real-time control

## 1 Introduction

Efficient use of energy for transportation is of utmost importance. Efficient control of electric vehicles may lead to a more sustainable world. The literature on control of hybrid and electric vehicles has increased considerably over the last decade [6,10,11,14]. Literature on control typically focuses on continuous control using theory on the use of the Hamiltonian and co-states.

A simplified electric vehicle energy consumption model is presented in [7] and evaluated on standard driving cycles, whereas [15] presents a method to evaluate the real driving energy consumptions of electric vehicles. A simple electric vehicle energy consumption model that captures instantaneous braking energy regeneration as a function of the vehicle deceleration level can be found in [3]. A computationally efficient simulation model for estimating the energy consumption of electric vehicles is developed in [4]. In [13], a general formulation of energy-efficient driving of electric vehicles is presented, that covers several distinct scenarios and the most-adopted solution techniques.

In [8,9], a model for the control of a trajectory of a completely electric vehicle has been described. The final methodology suggested in those papers is a branch

© Springer Nature Switzerland AG 2019
S. Misra et al. (Eds.): ICCSA 2019, LNCS 11621, pp. 249–260, 2019.
https://doi.org/10.1007/978-3-030-24302-9_18

and bound (B&B) approach. This approach is counter-intuitive, as it does not make use of the dynamic characteristic of the problem. Similarly, a Mixed Integer Nonlinear Programming (MINLP) approach has been investigated in [12]. A more thorough mathematical analysis of the model can be found in [2]. As it does not feel that the problem has a multi-extremal character, the use of branch and bound does not seem appropriate. Our research question is whether standard software of implemented nonlinear optimization routines can reach a similar result.

To investigate the question, we first rewrite the model as an optimization problem in Sect. 2. From there we will investigate two possible approaches. A nonlinear optimization approach on a continuous relaxation of the problem in Sect. 3 and a state variable trajectory optimization as suggested in [9] is investigated in Sect. 4. Section 5 discusses a dynamic programming approach of the problem. Section 6 summarizes our findings.

## 2    Model

In the literature around this topic, the model to be studied is encapsulated in the convention of technical literature where subscripts are used for as well indices as indicators and small caps and capitals are mixed with greek letters. From the context, we first distinguish the technical data from the state and control variables. Therefore, we apply a notation following the convention of mathematical programming trying to distinguish between parameters and variables. Moreover, for the dynamics of the model, we will apply difference equations rather than differential equations based on a step size of $\delta$ seconds.

Indices
$t$ Moment in time with $\delta$ second slots, $t = 0, \ldots, T$

Parameters
$H$    Final control horizon in seconds
$\delta$    Time discretization slot, e.g. $\delta = 0.001$ s.
$T$    Number of periods (slots) in the horizon $T = \frac{H}{\delta}$
$P$    Target position to be reached in control horizon
$R$    Radius of the wheels, $R = 0.33$ m.
$B$    Resistance of the battery, $B = 0.05\,\Omega$
$S$    Voltage of power supply, $S = 150$ v
$Tr$    Transmission coefficient motor to wheels, $Tr = 10$
$C$    Resistance depending on air density, surface car and aerodynamics, $C = 0.517$ N
$L$    Inductance rotor, $L = 0.05$ H
$I$    Inductor resistance, $I = 0.03\,\Omega$
$Q$    Coefficient motor torque, $Q = 0.27$ Nm/A (Newton-Meters per Ampere)
$M$    Mass vehicle, $M = 250$ kg
$G$    Gravity constant, $G = 9.81$ m/s$^2$
$F$    Friction coefficient of the wheels, $F = 0.03$

Variables
$i_t \in [-150, 150]$    Induction (current) of the engine
$\omega_t$    Angular velocity in radians per second. So velocity $s_t = \frac{R}{Tr}\omega_t$ meter per second
$p_t \in [0, P]$    Position of the vehicle at time $t$
$u_t \in \{-1, 1\}$    Control, switch.

The control is of interest. One can switch very frequently, so one of the approaches is to consider a relaxation where $u_t \in [-1, 1]$. However, the most important in our approach is that we limit the real value of the current in simulating the dynamic system such that we keep the current $i_t \in [-150, 150]$.

The objective is given by the energy consumption $E$ in Joules

$$E = \delta \sum_{t=0}^{T-1} (S \cdot u_t \cdot i_t + B \cdot u_t^2 \cdot i_t^2). \tag{1}$$

The dynamics is given by difference equations taking the time step size $\delta$ into account. The position of the vehicle at time $t$ is given by

$$p_t = p_{t-1} + \delta s_t \tag{2}$$

and the induction of the engine at time $t$ is modelled as

$$i_t = i_{t-1} + \delta \frac{S u_t - I i_{t-1} - Q \omega_{t-1}}{L}. \tag{3}$$

The dynamics of the angular velocity at time $t$ is given by

$$\omega_t = \omega_{t-1} + \delta \frac{Tr}{R} \left( \frac{QTr}{RM} i_{t-1} - GF - \frac{C}{M} v_{t-1}^2 \right). \tag{4}$$

Based on this model, we can build a simulation program, which evaluates the energy consumption of a certain control rule to determine $u_t$. To keep the induction into boundaries, one can limit the actual control using bounds. Rewriting (3) and limiting $i_t \in [-150, 150]$ one can determine the limit parameter

$$\Delta_t = \frac{150L + (\delta I - L)i_{t-1} + \delta Q \omega_{t-1}}{\delta S}$$

and limit the values of the control to

$$u_t \in min\{-1, \text{sgn}(\Delta_t) \min\{|\Delta_t|, 1\}, \max\{1, \text{sgn}(\Delta_t) \min\{|\Delta_t|, 1\}$$

with $\text{sgn}(x)$ being the sign of real number $x$. This means we can send a larger control to the engine, but the reaction is limited such that the induction is not too high in absolute value preventing the engine to be destroyed.

## 3    Nonlinear Optimization on Continuous Control

Our first approach discretizes the horizon $H$ in a finite number of $n < T$ control slots with a global control continuous variable $v_k, k = 1, \ldots, n$ such that $u_t = v_k$ if moment $t$ falls into control slot $k$. In this way, we can apply simulation based optimization, where the optimizing routine sends trials of vector $v = (v_1, \ldots, v_n)$

and the simulation program returns the energy $E(v)$ and the deviation from the target $g(v) = P - p_T$. Following the convention of mathematical programming, the constraint is written as $g(v) \leq 0$, so the function $g$ tells us how far we are off target.

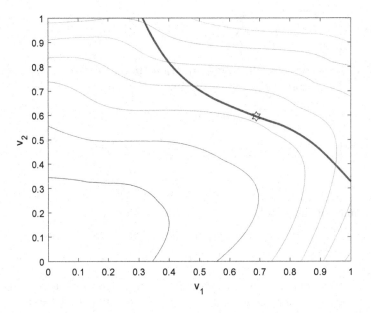

**Fig. 1.** Energy contours of $E(v_1, v_2)$ and the location constraint $g(v_1, v_2) \leq 0$ in red when optimizing over two slots. Using less energy in the left-down direction and feasible area in the right upper corner; the star gives the optimum found by NLP. (Color figure online)

Figure 1 provides a picture of the optimization problem considering only $n = 2$ slots. The contours of the total energy used $E(v)$ are given and the restriction on reaching the target position of $P = 100\,\text{m}$ is depicted in red. The functions expose a smooth behavior despite the evaluation is based on a finite step size simulation model. The value of the time step (time discretization slot) used in the simulation is $\delta = 0.001$ and the time horizon is $H = 10\,\text{s}$. The optimum is determined running the `fmincon` routine in Matlab version 2016b. The best point found is indicated for the two dimensional example. Of course, using only two slots is not energy friendly although the final target is reached. In the end the energy consumption reaches 31,589 J and the final speed is more than 10 m/s.

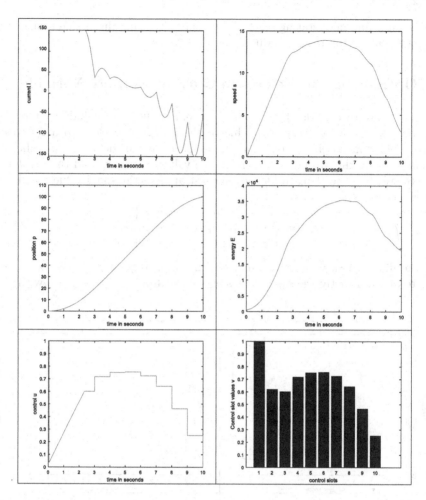

**Fig. 2.** Simulation result after optimizing $v$ (result in bar graph) over 10 slots. The graphs give the development in time up to the horizon of the control $u$, speed $s$, position $p$, energy use and actual current $i$.

The optimum solution can be used as starting value for finding the optimum trajectory when using more slots. Actually, we run the optimization for $n = 5, 10, 20$ control slots which reduces the energy use $E(v)$ to 24,094, 19,476 and 19,322 J respectively.

Figure 2 shows the result for $n = 10$ control slots. The optimum trajectory is found within 13 s using as starting value the optimum from the $n = 2$ case and the resulting control vector $v$ can be observed in the bar-graph at the right down corner. As said, the energy consumption went down to 19,476 J. One can observe that the internal control $u$ follows the external control $v$ most of the time apart from the first slot where the accelerator is pressed completely. The vehicle after first accelerating regenerates energy by using the engine brake with a negative induction reaching a final speed of 3 m/s.

## 4   Optimizing the Reference Current as State Variable

A second way to consider the control problem in [9] is to include an internal regulator that tries to keep the value of the induction $i$ close to a reference value $r$. This means if we follow a similar procedure of defining a number of $n$ control slots, the procedure sets reference values $r_1, \ldots, r_n$ and the regulator tries to stay close to that. In [9] they suggest apply a threshold value $\varepsilon$ and use as regulator

$$u_t = \begin{cases} 1 & \text{if} \quad i_{t-1} < r_t - \varepsilon \\ -1 & \text{if} \quad i_{t-1} > r_t + \varepsilon \\ u_{t-1} & \text{else} \end{cases}. \tag{5}$$

For the illustration, we built a simulator including regulator (5). We were not able to obtain exactly the same values as [9], but feeding the program with the

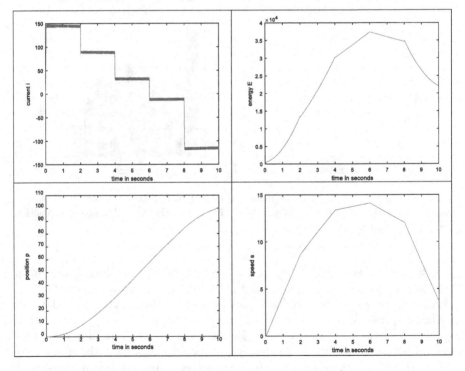

**Fig. 3.** Simulating current reference vector $r = (145, 90, 34, -10, -115)$ of 5 control slots during 10 s with time steps of $\delta = 0.0001$ s.

$n = 5$ slot reference value $r = (145, 90, 34, -10, -115)$ reaches the 100 m with an energy consumption of 22,039 J. The resulting speed, energy consumption and position are sketched in Fig. 3. One can observe the current fluctuating around the reference values $r_1, \ldots, r_n$ due to regulator (5).

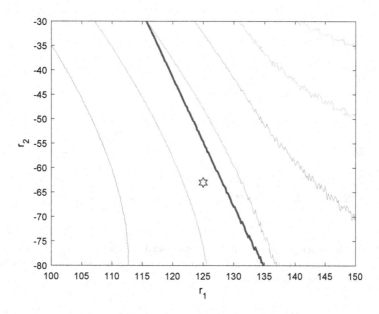

**Fig. 4.** Energy contours of $E(r_1, r_2)$ and location constraint $g(r_1, r_2) \leq 0$ in red optimizing over two slots. The star gives the "optimum" found by a genetic algorithm. Less energy use in the left-down direction and feasible area in the right upper corner. (Color figure online)

Optimizing the reference values for a finite number of slots becomes a challenge. Considering a continuous optimization approach for $n = 2$ slots provides us the energy contours in Fig. 4. At the left of the figure, the contours seem smooth, but at the right we observe strange behaviour. This phenomenon has been described in [5] and is due to simulation based optimization where `if..then..else` structures are included. This means that changing one coordinate of a coordinate $r_k$ of reference value vector $r$ a small step, does not change the control behaviour and the simulation returns more or less the same value for the energy used and position, i.e. the simulation does not change. We focus on this phenomenon by changing in the $n = 5$ dimensional reference vector $r$ only the value of $r_3$ observing the development of the energy consumption $E(r)$ and the deviation $g(r) = P - p_T$ from the target of $P = 100$ m in Fig. 5.

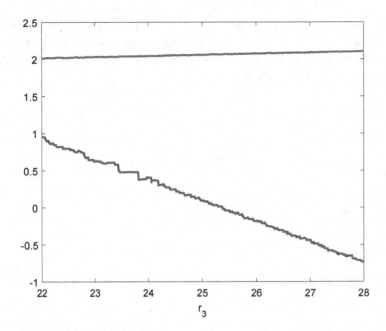

**Fig. 5.** Simulated energy use $E(r)$ in blue and deviation $g(r) = P - p_T$ in orange using regulator (5) as function of reference current $r_3$ of slot 3 keeping the other reference values constant. (Color figure online)

One can observe that the objective $E(r)$ and constraint function $g(r)$ are typically non-continuous. This means that software on nonlinear optimization including pattern search methods have a difficulty to find the optimum. [5] also provide a smoothing method to make the function continuous, although computationally this may lead to bad conditioned problems with high and low derivatives. [9] discretized the $n$ dimensional search space and looked for methods to reduce (bound) the feasible area. Such a method is highly non-attractive, as the number of combinations to consider increases exponentially with the number of slots $n$.

Although the problem from a smoothed view does not have local non-global optima, one can run population based algorithms. The optimization toolbox of Matlab has several variants of genetic algorithms and particle swarm algorithms available. As the optimum is also relatively flat in terms of objective and constraint (see Fig. 4), in our experience, the algorithms take a lot of time (hours) to get close to the optimum. For dimension $n = 2$ both standard algorithms take minutes. Moreover, the best point found as depicted in Fig. 4, seems far off of the optimum in the space of the reference value.

We have seen so far, that a continuous relaxation of the control can be handled by standard software even when the number of control slots grows. For the second method, where one optimizes reference values of the induction, the discrete control rule for $u$ turns the problem in a non-continuous optimization problem creating a hard to optimize problem. However, if we are able to create a method that is linear in the slots, perhaps the optimization can be handled in reasonable time.

## 5   A DP Procedure to Derive an Optimal Control Rule

In their findings, [9] report that for this system, the change in reference value $r_k - r_{k-1}$ does not influence the search for the best solution. This finding creates the possibility to consider dynamic programming (DP) with only two state variables, i.e. the speed $s_k$ and position $p_k$ at the beginning of a control slot. Enumerating the possibilities for the induction reference value $r_k$ over a discrete grid leads to a procedure which is linear in the number of control slots. We will illustrate that.

The dynamic programming procedure determines in fact the optimal trajectories for a complete grid of state values $(k, s, p)$, i.e. the slot number, speed and current position. In fact, the procedure also provides an answer to the control when we deviate from the optimal trajectory. Following the DP principle of Bellman [1] for a finite horizon dynamic system we can build a valuation of the state space according to the relation

$$V_{k-1}(s, p) = min_r[E(r, s, p, \frac{H}{n}) + V_k(\Phi(r, s, p, \frac{H}{n}))], \qquad (6)$$

where in our system we should define $E(r, s, p, \tau)$ as the energy use when using reference value $r$ from starting position $s$ and $p$ during a period of $\tau$ seconds. Similarly, function $\Phi(r, s, p, \tau) : \mathbb{R}^4 \to \mathbb{R}^2$ describes the transition function providing the state (speed and position) we arrive at using the same arguments $(r, s, p)$ during $\tau$ seconds.

If one is able to compute the so-called value function $V$ for all possible state values, one can also retrieve the optimal control value for the reference induction $r_k(s, p)$ from any state according to

$$r_k(s, p) = argmin_r[E(r, s, p, \frac{H}{n}) + V_k(\Phi(r, s, p, \frac{H}{n}))]. \qquad (7)$$

In theory, starting from $r_1(0, 0)$ we can find the optimal trajectory for the reference control $r$ following (7). For a practical implementation, we have to define a grid in the state space $(s, p)$ for each control slot $k$ and follow the recursion (6). One of the challenges to get this working is that the transformation (motion) function $\Phi$ will not take us to another grid point, such that interpolation or extrapolation is required. Another challenge is that in fact, we are only interested in those state values where we can still reach the target distance $P$. This can be formalised by identifying those values $(s, p)$ at the beginning of control slot $k$ for which

$$\Phi_2(150, s, p, \frac{n-k}{n}H) \geq P, \qquad (8)$$

i.e. a maximum reference current $r = 150$ from the current speed $s$ and position $p$ can still lead us to the target $P$ (second element of $\Phi$) given the rest of the time

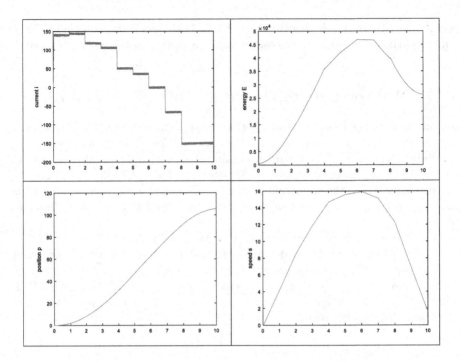

**Fig. 6.** Simulation result from DP reference induction values.

left. The state space can be bound on that providing lower and upper bounds $[\underline{s}_k, \overline{s}_k]$ and $[\underline{p}_k, \overline{p}_k]$. Basically, we cannot avoid infeasible combinations, as (8) is in fact a two-dimensional surface. However, maximum values $(\overline{s}_k, \overline{p}_k)$ can be generated by providing the maximum reference induction $r = 150$ from the start, i.e.

$$(\overline{s}_k, \overline{p}_k) = \Phi(150, 0, 0, \frac{k}{n}H). \tag{9}$$

In the implementation we used a grid of 15 equally distributed points over the ranges $[\underline{s}_k, \overline{s}_k]$ and $[\underline{p}_k, \overline{p}_k]$ for each control slot $k$. For the control variable $r_k$ we used a grid of 301 points within $[-150, 150]$, such that the mesh size between two trials is 1, as suggested in [9], i.e. $r_k$ has an integer value. Notice that for the evaluation of values for $r$, we can also find lower bounds $\underline{r}_k(s, p)$ using the monotonicity in the reference value $r$ of the transition function $\Phi$. For this, we run the possibilities from high to low and create a `while` construction such that as soon as a reference value provides infeasible positions, we reached a minimum reference value $\underline{r}_k(s, p)$ for the corresponding grid point.

We implemented the procedure in Matlab 2016b and run the dynamic programming recursion for $n = 10$ control slots. The computational time was 4 min and 11 s to reach a grid $r_k(s, p)$ of $10 \times 15^2$ control values. Starting from initial state $(s, p) = (0, 0)$, a simulation was run for the 10 control slots using small time steps of $\delta = 0.0001$. The result can be observed in Fig. 6 in terms of energy use, speed, induction and position. The final energy use is estimated on 26,299 J and strange enough the reference trajectory reaches a position of 105.7 m.

It may be clear that in contrast to the suggested enumeration and bounding method in [9], the computation is not exponential but linear in the number of time slots $n$. However, the final implementation requires further fine-tuning to reach a more exact target value.

# 6    Conclusions

This paper reformulated a model in literature on the control of an electric vehicle as an optimization problem. Relaxing the integrality of the control, provides an optimization problem which can be handled by standard nonlinear optimization software following an optimization-simulation approach. The optimization of reference values for one of the state variables (induction) provides a non-continuous optimization problem where bounding can be used to reduce the effect of the exponential enumeration in number of control slots. We have shown that the same control vision can be handled by a dynamic programming approach. The challenge for that method is to deal with the feasibility of candidate solutions. However, the computational time is linear in the number of time slots.

**Acknowledgments.** This paper has been supported by The Spanish Ministry (RTI2018-095993) in part financed by the European Regional Development Fund (ERDF) and by FCT – Fundação para a Ciência e Tecnologia within the Project Scope: UID/CEC/00319/2019.

# References

1. Bellman, R.: Dynamic Programming. Princeton University Press, Princeton (1957)
2. Cots, O.: Geometric and numerical methods for a state constrained minimum time control problem of an electric vehicle. ESAIM: COCV **23**(4), 1715–1749 (2017)
3. Fiori, C., Ahn, K., Rakha, H.A.: Power-based electric vehicle energy consumption model: model development and validation. Appl. Energy **168**, 257–268 (2016)
4. Genikomsakis, K.N., Mitrentsis, G.: A computationally efficient simulation model for estimating energy consumption of electric vehicles in the context of route planning applications. Transp. Res. Part D Transport Environ. **50**, 98–118 (2017)
5. Hendrix, E.M.T., Olieman, N.J.: The smoothed Monte Carlo method in robustness optimization. Optim. Methods Softw. **23**(5), 717–729 (2008)
6. Lei, F., Bai, Y., Zhu, W., Liu, J.: A novel approach for electric powertrain optimization considering vehicle power performance, energy consumption and ride comfort. Energy **167**, 1040–1050 (2019)
7. Luin, B., Petelin, S., Al-Mansour, F.: Microsimulation of electric vehicle energy consumption. Energy **174**, 24–32 (2019)
8. Merakeb, A., Messine, F.: Toward global minimum solutions for the problem of the energy consumption of an electrical vehicle. In: Cafiery, S., et al. (eds.) Proceedings of the Toulouse Global Optimization Workshop, pp. 85–88. ENSEEIHT (2010)
9. Merakeb, A., Messine, F., Aidéne, M.: A branch and bound algorithm for minimizing the energy consumption of an electrical vehicle. 4OR **12**(3), 261–283 (2014)

10. Onori, S., Serrao, L., Rizzoni, G.: Hybrid Electric Vehicles: Energy Management Strategies. Springer, London (2016). https://doi.org/10.1007/978-1-4471-6781-5
11. Sabri, M., Danapalasingam, K., Rahmat, M.: A review on hybrid electric vehicles architecture and energy management strategies. Renew. Sustain. Energy Rev. **53**, 1433–1442 (2016)
12. Sager, S., Claeys, M., Messine, F.: Efficient upper and lower bounds for global mixed-integer optimal control. J. Glob. Optim. **61**(4), 721–743 (2015)
13. Sciarretta, A., De Nunzio, G., Ojeda, L.L.: Optimal ecodriving control: energy-efficient driving of road vehicles as an optimal control problem. IEEE Control Syst. Mag. **35**(5), 71–90 (2015)
14. Sciarretta, A., Guzzella, L.: Control of hybrid electric vehicles. IEEE Control Syst. Mag. **27**(2), 60–70 (2007)
15. Yuan, X., Zhang, C., Hong, G., Huang, X., Li, L.: Method for evaluating the real-world driving energy consumptions of electric vehicles. Energy **141**, 1955–1968 (2017)

# A Multi-objective Approach to Solve the Build Orientation Problem in Additive Manufacturing

Marina A. Matos[1], Ana Maria A. C. Rocha[1] (ID), Lino A. Costa[1] (ID),
and Ana I. Pereira[2]([envelope]) (ID)

[1] ALGORITMI Center, University of Minho, 4710-057 Braga, Portugal
aniram@live.com.pt, {arocha,lac}@dps.uminho.pt
[2] Research Centre in Digitalization and Intelligent Robotics (CeDRI),
Polytechnic Institute of Bragança, 5300-253 Bragança, Portugal
apereira@ipb.pt

**Abstract.** Additive manufacturing (AM) has been increasingly used in the creation of three-dimensional objects, layer-by-layer, from three-dimensional (3D) computer-aided design (CAD) models. The problem of determining the 3D model printing orientation can lead to reduced amount of supporting material, build time, costs associated with the deposited material, labor costs, and other factors. This problem has been formulated and studied as a single-objective optimization problem. More recently, due to the existence and relevance of considering multiple criteria, multi-objective approaches have been developed.

In this paper, a multi-objective optimization approach is proposed to solve the part build orientation problem taking into account the support area characteristics and the build time. Therefore, the weighted Tchebycheff scalarization method embedded in the Electromagnetism-like Algorithm will be used to solve the part build orientation bi-objective problem of four 3D CAD models. The preliminary results seem promising when analyzing the Pareto fronts obtained for the 3D CAD models considered. Concluding, the multi-objective approach effectively solved the build orientation problem in AM, finding several compromise solutions.

**Keywords:** Additive manufacturing · 3D printing ·
Multi-objective optimization · Build orientation

## 1 Introduction

Additive manufacturing (AM) processes involve the use of three-dimensional (3D) computer-aided design (CAD) data to create physical models. Typically, AM is characterized by four processing stages: model orientation, creation of supports, slicing, and path planning [17]. AM allows the production of a wide range of shapes, with very complex geometries and not requiring many post-processing

© Springer Nature Switzerland AG 2019
S. Misra et al. (Eds.): ICCSA 2019, LNCS 11621, pp. 261–276, 2019.
https://doi.org/10.1007/978-3-030-24302-9_19

actions. The layered manufacturing processes apply physical or chemical phenomena to construct parts, adding layer-by-layer material. This type of manufacture began in the years 80 by Kruth [10]. Currently, layered manufacturing processes are used in several areas such as medical sciences (e.g. dental restorations and medical implants), jewelry, footwear industry, automotive industry and aircraft industry [16].

Over the years, the adoption of Rapid Prototyping (RP) technologies to fabricate a prototype model from a CAD file has grown and has been implemented in many model manufacturing companies due to its effectiveness in the prototype model development at a reduced time [2]. The performance of an RP depends on the orientation of the parts on the printer platform, that is, each piece must have the correct orientation in order to improve the surface quality, minimize the number of support structures and minimize the manufacturing time [19].

The automatic selection of the best orientation manages to reduce or eliminate errors involved throughout the model construction process [22]. The selection of the best orientation is a very important factor because affects the time and print quality, amount of supporting material, shrinkage, distortion, resin flow, material cost, volume and support area and has a better precision of the model [16,23]. Several approaches have been carried out to determine the orientation of a model based on single-objective optimization. Usually the objective functions used for optimal build orientation were the build height, staircase effect, volumetric error, volume of support structures and part area in contact with support structures, surface quality, surface roughness and build deposition time [2,3,11,14,18,19,22].

Recently, multi-objective approaches have been developed to determine the optimal object building orientation, essentially by reducing the multi-objective problem to a single-objective one using classical scalarization methods such as the weighted sum method. Cheng et al. [4] formulated a multi-objective optimization problem focused on the surface quality and production cost of the parts, obtaining solutions for all types of surfaces, whether with complex geometries or not, or even for curved surfaces. The Particle Swarm Optimization (PSO) algorithm was used in [12] to solve a multi-objective optimization problem in order to get the desired orientations for the support area, build time and surface roughness. A multi-objective optimization approach considering as objective functions the surface roughness and the build time, for different models, was developed by Padhye and Deb in [15]. They used the NSGA-II (Non-dominated Sorting Genetic Algorithm) and MOPSO (Multi-Objective Particle Swarm Optimization) algorithms to obtain the Pareto front. Gurrala and Regalla [7] applied the NSGA-II algorithm to optimize the strength of the model and its volumetric shrinkage as objective functions. They concluded, through the Pareto front, that with the shrinkage of the part its strength increases in the horizontal and vertical directions. A genetic algorithm was used in [1] for solving a multi-objective build orientation problem. They optimized several variables, yield and tensile strength, elongation and vickers hardness, for material properties used, surface roughness, support structure and build time and cost.

In this paper, we propose a multi-objective optimization approach to optimize the support area and the build time in order to get the best orientation of 3D CAD models using the Electromagnetism-like algorithm combined with weighted Tchebycheff scalarization method is proposed. The weighted Tchebycheff method was selected since it can be used to solve problems with nonconvex Pareto fronts and can find non-extreme solutions (trade-offs) in the presence of multiple conflicting criteria. Four models previously used in a single-objective context will be used [19].

This paper is organized as follows. Section 2 introduces the build orientation optimization problem and the multi-objective optimization approach used in this study. The description of the models used in the numerical experiments, the Pareto fronts obtained for each model as well as an appropriate discussion for each one is presented in Sect. 3. Finally, Sect. 4 presents the conclusions of this study and the future work.

# 2   Optimization Problem

## 2.1   Part Orientation

The surface finish of an object obtained through additive manufacturing process is highly important. A good surface finish can decrease or even eliminate time spent in subsequent post-processing (finishing). Part orientation can affect the surface finish due to the slicing process and the support material usage in the build of the part. Rotating a part to a different orientation can decrease the support usage and build time of a part.

One of the problems affecting the surface finish of the part is the staircase effect. The layer thickness have an impact on the staircase effect, since the smaller the thickness of the model layer the staircase effect will also be smaller, resulting in a better surface finish. This effect is related to the cusp height (CH) that is based on the maximum distance between the part surface and the model surface [13] (see Fig. 1). The CH is given by $CH = t\cos(\theta)$, where $t$ is the layer thickness and $\theta$ is the angle between the part surface and the CH.

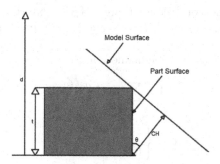

**Fig. 1.** Cusp height

In addition, the CAD model area is also very important for the construction of the part. For some functions, a direction vector $d$ is required and is calculated by $x^2 + y^2 + z^2 = 1$, where the variables $x$, $y$, and $z$ are given by (1):

$$d = \begin{cases} x = \sin\beta \times \cos\alpha \\ y = \sin\beta \times \sin\alpha \\ z = \cos\beta \end{cases} \tag{1}$$

Figure 2 shows the unit direction vector $d$ with the variables represented.

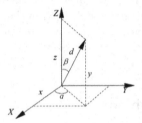

**Fig. 2.** Unit direction vector of build orientation [9].

## 2.2 Objective Functions

There are different measures that can be considered to determine the best build orientation for an improvement of the surface finish. Some of them take into account factors as the part accuracy, building time, structure support and part stability. The build orientation of a model can improve the accuracy of the part and reduce the number of generated supports, and consequently decrease the final building costs. At the same time, the construction/build time should be reduced in order to decrease the final building costs too. Thus, in this study a multi-objective optimization to determine the build orientation of a 3D CAD model according to two factors: the support area and the build time will be used.

The support area is defined as the total area of the downward-facing facets, that is, the quantity of supports to be used in the construction of the part, measured through the total contact area of the external supports with the object. In fact, the support area mostly affects post-processing and superficial finish [9,19].

The support area (SA) can be defined by

$$SA = \sum_i A_i \left| d^T n_i \right| \delta \tag{2}$$

$$\delta = \begin{cases} 1, & \text{if } d^T n_i < 0 \\ 0, & \text{if } d^T n_i > 0 \end{cases}$$

where $A_i$ is the area of the triangular face $i$, $d$ is the unit vector of the direction of construction of the triangular face $i$, $n_i$ is the normal unit vector of the triangular face $i$ and $\delta$ is the initial function [9]. In this study, it was considered the vector $d = (0, 0, 1)^T$ to be the direction of slicing after a rotation along the angles $(x, y)$, taking into account that each angle is between 0 and $180°$.

The build time includes the scanning time of the solid, the scanning time of the solid contours and the scanning time of the support needed for the part, where the scanning times of the solid and its contours are independent of the construction direction, and the scanning time of the support depends on your volume.

The preparation time of the piece encompasses the precise time for the platform to move downwards during the construction of each layer, the scraping time of this and other times of preparation of the part. This time depends on the total number of slices of the solid, the number of slices dependent on the height of the construction direction of a particular part of the piece. Therefore, minimizing this height and the number of layers, can decrease the construction time of the part [9,19].

The build time (BT) is given by (3):

$$BT = \max(d^T v_1, d^T v_2, d^T v_3) - \min(d^T v_1, d^T v_2, d^T v_3) \tag{3}$$

where $d$ is the direction vector and $v_1, v_2, v_3$ are the vertex triangle facets.

### 2.3   Multi-objective Approach

Based on the part build orientation problem, the multi-objective optimization intends to simultaneously minimize the support area and the build time, defined in Eqs. (2) and (3). The general multi-objective optimization problem is formulated as

$$\begin{aligned} \min \ &f(\theta_x, \theta_y) = \{f_1(\theta_x, \theta_y), f_2(\theta_x, \theta_y)\} \\ \text{s.t.} \ \ &0 \le \theta_x \le 180 \\ &0 \le \theta_y \le 180 \end{aligned} \tag{4}$$

where the objective functions $f_1(\theta_x, \theta_y)$ and $f_2(\theta_x, \theta_y)$ are, respectively, the support area, SA in (2), and the part building time, BT in (3). In this problem, the $\theta_x$ and $\theta_y$ are the rotation along the $x$-axis and the $y$-axis, respectively.

Approximating the Pareto optimal set is the main goal of a multi-objective optimization algorithm. A first attempt to solve this problem is to reformulate the multi-objective optimization problem to a single-objective one using a scalarization method in order to obtain different trade-offs between the objectives [8]. In scalarization methods, weights and/or goals are introduced. The simplicity is the main advantage of the weighted sum method based on the linear combination of the objectives. However, in the case of problems with nonconvex fronts, it is not possible to find non-supported solutions since there is no weights yielding these elements of the Pareto set.

In this paper, the weighted Tchebycheff scalarization method will be applied since it is suitable to tackle nonconvex problems. In this method, introduced by Steuer and Choo [21], the $L_\infty$ norm is minimized, i.e., the maximum distance to a reference point (or aspiration levels) is minimized. This method can be used as an a posteriori approach in which the decision making process takes place after the search. In this case, the reference point is defined as the *ideal vector* and the weights are uniformly varied to obtain different trade-offs. The ideal vector can be computed by determining the optimum of each objective. In this manner, after the search, a set of Pareto optimal solutions is presented as alternatives and the decision maker can identify the compromises and choose according to his/her preferences. A disadvantage of the weighted Tchebycheff method is, however, that in addition to the non-dominated points also weakly non-dominated points can be found [5].

The weighted Tchebycheff method is defined by:

$$\begin{aligned} \min \max_{i=1,\ldots,k} \left[ w_i(f_i(x) - z_i^\star) \right] \\ \text{s.t. } x \in \chi, \end{aligned} \tag{5}$$

where $k$ is the number of objective functions, $w_i$ are the components of the weights vector, $f_i$ is the $i$−th objective function, $z_i^\star$ are the components of the ideal vector and $\chi$ is the feasible set of the decision vectors.

Finally, the single-objective optimization problem to be solved, that resulted from a transformation of the multi-objective problem (4) through the weighted Tchebycheff scalarization method, is given by

$$\begin{aligned} \min \max \left\{ w_1(f_1(x) - z_1^\star), w_2(f_2(x) - z_2^\star) \right\} \\ \text{s.t. } 0 \leq \theta_x \leq 180 \\ 0 \leq \theta_y \leq 180. \end{aligned} \tag{6}$$

In this study, we are interested in the Electromagnetism-like (EM) algorithm, proposed in [6] and specifically designed for solving bound constrained optimization problems, to solve the problem (6). The EM algorithm is a population-based stochastic search method for global optimization that mimics the behavior of electrically charged particles. EM algorithm simulates the electromagnetism theory of physics by considering each point in the population as an electrical charge. The EM uses an attraction-repulsion mechanism to move a population of points towards optimality. The steps of the EM algorithm for bound constrained optimization are described in Algorithm 1 as shown below.

---

Randomly generate the population
Evaluate the population and select the best point
**while** *maximum number of function evaluations is not reached* **do**
    Compute the charges
    Compute the total forces
    Move the points except the best point
    Evaluate the new population and select the best point
**end**

---

**Algorithm 1.** EM algorithm

The EM algorithm starts with a population of randomly generated points from the feasible region. All points are evaluated (the corresponding objective function values are computed) and compared in order to identify the best point. Analogous to electromagnetism, each point in the space is considered as a charged particle. The charge of each point is related to the objective function value and determines the magnitude of attraction or repulsion of the point over the others in the population. Points with lower objective function values attract others while those with higher function values repel. The charges are used to find the total force exerted on each point as well as a direction for each point to move the points in the subsequent iterations. The total force vector exerted on each point by the other points is the sum of individual component forces, each depending on the charges. According to the electromagnetism theory, each individual force is inversely proportional to the square of the distance between the two points and directly proportional to the product of their charges. Then, the normalized total force vector exerted on the point is used to move the point in the direction of the force by a random step size. The best point is not moved and is carried out to the subsequent iteration. This process is repeated at least for a maximum number of objective function evaluations and the best point is identified as the output of the algorithm. A fully description of the EM algorithm can be found in [20].

## 3   Numerical Experiments

### 3.1   Models Description

In this section, we present the 3D CAD models that will be used. First, the CAD models should be converted into an STL (STereoLithography) format that is the standard file type used by most common 3D printing file formats. The STL files describe only the surface geometry of a 3D object, not presenting color, texture, or other common attributes of the CAD model. This represents a 3D solid object using triangular faces. The more complex the models are, the greater their number of triangular faces.

Figure 3 shows the STL files of the models that will be used in the present study, already used in a single-objective optimization study in [19]: Air Duct, Rear Panel Fixed, Rocket Shot and 45 Degree Short. Table 1 presents the data of the models studied in this work, namely the Size (*width* × *height* × *depth*), the volume (*Vol.*), the number of triangles (*Triangles*) and the number of slices (*Slices*) of each model. A slicing along the $z$-axis of 0.2 mm height was considered.

Table 1. Data of the models.

|  | Size (mm) | Vol. ($cm^3$) | Triangles | Slices |
|---|---|---|---|---|
| Air Duct | 52 × 109.9 × 102.5 | 30.6 | 6024 | 529 |
| Rear Panel Fixed | 142.5 × 142.5 × 113 | 46.2 | 3008 | 676 |
| Rocket Shot | 61.4 × 66.9 × 61.37 | 20.8 | 10616 | 324 |
| 45 Degree Short | 157.5 × 125 × 157.5 | 80.8 | 66888 | 625 |

Rear panel fixed          Air duct          Rocket shot          45 degree short

**Fig. 3.** STL representation of the models.

The numerical experiments were carried out on a PC Intel(R) Core(TM)i7-7500U CPU with 2.9 GHz and 12.0 GB of memory RAM. The EM algorithm was coded in MATLAB Version 9.2 (R2017a) as well as all the optimization code developed to solve the problem (6).

### 3.2  Results

In order to compute the solutions of the problem (6), we used the objective functions SA in (2) and BT in (3), that were normalized using the ideal and nadir vectors. The ideal vector $z^\star$ is constructed with the individual optimal objective values, corresponding to the lower bound of each objective in the entire feasible space. The nadir vector $z^{\mathrm{nad}}$ represents the upper bound of each objective in the entire Pareto optimal set. Normalized values of the $i$-th objective function can be computed by

$$f_i^{\mathrm{norm}}(x) = \frac{f_i(x) - z_i^\star}{z_i^{\mathrm{nad}} - z_i^\star}.$$

The weights were uniformly varied, i.e., $(w_1, w_2) \in \{(0,1), (0.1, 0.9), \ldots, (1,0)\}$. A population size of 20 and a maximum number of function evaluations of 2000 were considered for the EM algorithm. For each combination of weights, 30 independent runs were performed. In addition, the software *Simplify 3D* was used, which is a 3D model printing simulator, to show the solutions found for each model.

The Pareto fronts for the different models will be displayed. In all graphs, the solutions obtained are plotted with a blue dot and the non-dominated ones are marked with a red circle. Representative solutions will be selected to discuss the trade-offs between the objectives and identify the features associated to these solutions.

Figure 4 plots the solutions obtained in the objective space for the Rear Panel Fixed model. The table next to the Pareto front chart presents the angles and objective function values for the four representative non-dominated solutions of the Pareto front (solutions A to D). The Pareto front is nonconvex for this problem. Solutions A and D are the optimal solutions in terms of SA and BT, respectively. Solutions B and C are different trade-offs between the objectives. It is observed that solution B is little more advantageous in terms of BT in relation

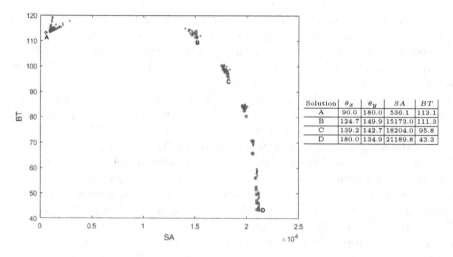

| Solution | $\theta_x$ | $\theta_y$ | $SA$ | $BT$ |
|---|---|---|---|---|
| A | 90.0 | 180.0 | 536.1 | 113.1 |
| B | 124.7 | 149.9 | 15173.0 | 111.3 |
| C | 139.2 | 142.7 | 18204.0 | 95.8 |
| D | 180.0 | 134.9 | 21189.8 | 43.3 |

**Fig. 4.** Pareto front and representative solutions for the Rear Panel Fixed model.

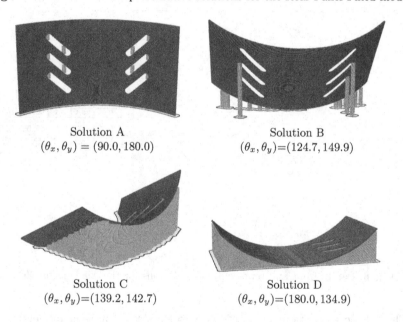

Solution A
$(\theta_x, \theta_y) = (90.0, 180.0)$

Solution B
$(\theta_x, \theta_y)=(124.7, 149.9)$

Solution C
$(\theta_x, \theta_y)=(139.2, 142.7)$

Solution D
$(\theta_x, \theta_y)=(180.0, 134.9)$

**Fig. 5.** Representation of the solutions A, B, C and D of Rear Panel Fixed model.

to solution A, but it is quite worse in terms of SA. When comparing solution C with solution D, a large decrease in the BT value and a small degradation in the SA value can be observed.

The 3D representations of solutions A to D can be seen in Fig. 5. Solution A, with the best value of SA and the worst value of BT, corresponds to the angles (90.0, 180.0). Conversely, solution D in the other extreme of the Pareto front has the angles (180.0, 134.9). There are other solutions that represent different compromises between the two objectives. Solution B with angles (124.7, 149.9) does not require many supports, but in terms of BT spends more time. Solution C with angles (139.2, 142.7) has a lower height (better in terms of BT), but requires many supports, as can be viewed in Fig. 5.

Figure 6 shows the Pareto front obtained for the Air Duct model and the table indicates the angles and objective function values for the six representative non-dominated solutions selected (solutions A to F). In this problem, the Pareto front is also nonconvex. Solutions A and B have similar values of BT, but solution B is significantly worse than solution A with respect to SA. This stresses the importance of identifying the compromises between the objectives. The gain in BT achieved by solution B when compared to solution A is negligible and the loss in terms of SA is large. Therefore, solution A is clearly preferable than solution B. When comparing the other compromise solutions between C and F, it is observed an improvement in terms of BT, but a degradation in the value of SA.

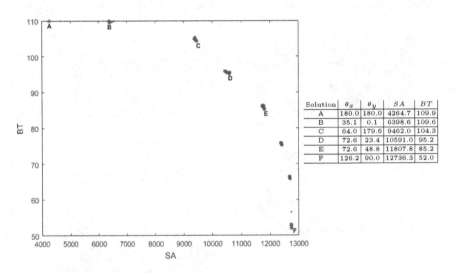

| Solution | $\theta_x$ | $\theta_y$ | $SA$ | $BT$ |
|---|---|---|---|---|
| A | 180.0 | 180.0 | 4264.7 | 109.9 |
| B | 35.1 | 0.1 | 6398.6 | 109.6 |
| C | 64.0 | 179.6 | 9462.0 | 104.3 |
| D | 72.6 | 23.4 | 10591.0 | 95.2 |
| E | 72.6 | 48.8 | 11807.8 | 85.2 |
| F | 126.2 | 90.0 | 12736.3 | 52.0 |

**Fig. 6.** Pareto front and representative solutions for the Air Duct model.

The 3D representations of solutions A to F for the Air Duct model are presented in Fig. 7. The best solution in terms of SA is the solution A with orientation (180.0, 180.0). The minimum value of BT is obtained with orientation (126.2, 90.0) corresponding to solution F. The remaining solutions are compromise solutions between the two objectives. In particular, solutions D and E have a similar $\theta_x$ value and a different $\theta_y$ value, where a rotation in $y$-axis is observed. This means that an improvement was obtained in terms of BT, since the orientation of the object to be printed led to a smaller height, but at the expense of an increase in the number of supports as can be seen in Fig. 7. The variation of $\theta_y$ allows to reduce BT from solution D to solution E (but SA increases).

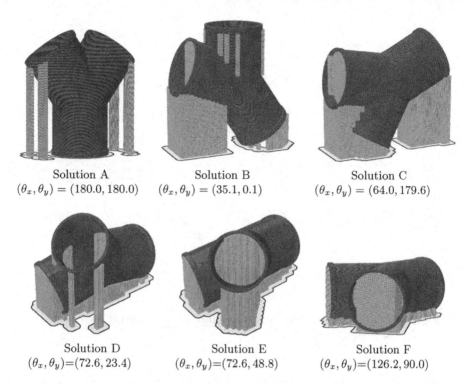

Solution A
$(\theta_x, \theta_y) = (180.0, 180.0)$

Solution B
$(\theta_x, \theta_y) = (35.1, 0.1)$

Solution C
$(\theta_x, \theta_y) = (64.0, 179.6)$

Solution D
$(\theta_x, \theta_y) = (72.6, 23.4)$

Solution E
$(\theta_x, \theta_y) = (72.6, 48.8)$

Solution F
$(\theta_x, \theta_y) = (126.2, 90.0)$

**Fig. 7.** Representation of the solutions A, B, C, D, E and F of Air Duct model.

Figure 8 shows the Pareto front obtained for the Rocket Shot model and the table indicates the angles and objective function values for five representative solutions (solutions A to E). Again, a nonconvex Pareto front was obtained. From the figure and the table, it turns out that solutions A and B have the same BT value. Therefore, solution A is preferable to solution B since has a better value of SA. Looking at solutions from C to E, it can be observed that, along the Pareto front, they constitute improvements in terms of BT, but worsening the values of SA. The 3D representations of solutions A to E are presented in Fig. 9. Solution A with orientation (180.0, 180.0) is the best in terms of SA and has fewer brackets. Conversely, the solution E with the angles (90.1, 135.0) minimizes BT but has the worst SA value. The remaining solutions are trade-offs between the two objectives. It should be noted that solution B with orientation (180.0, 0.0) is similar to solution A in terms of BT, but it is worse in terms of SA. This is due to the fact that rotating the solution A by 180° in the $y$-axis corresponds to a solution with the same height. The solution D with orientation (104.6, 135.0) when compared to solution C with orientation (97.9, 90.0) improves significantly in terms of BT with a small degradation of the value of SA, as it can be seen in Fig. 9.

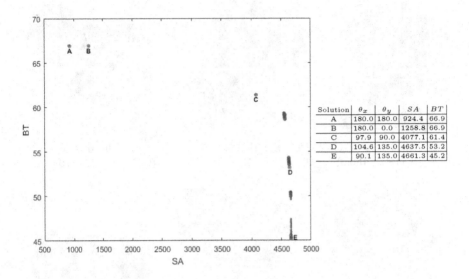

| Solution | $\theta_x$ | $\theta_y$ | $SA$ | $BT$ |
|----------|------|------|--------|------|
| A | 180.0 | 180.0 | 924.4 | 66.9 |
| B | 180.0 | 0.0 | 1258.8 | 66.9 |
| C | 97.9 | 90.0 | 4077.1 | 61.4 |
| D | 104.6 | 135.0 | 4637.5 | 53.2 |
| E | 90.1 | 135.0 | 4661.3 | 45.2 |

**Fig. 8.** Pareto front and representative solutions for the Rocket Shot model.

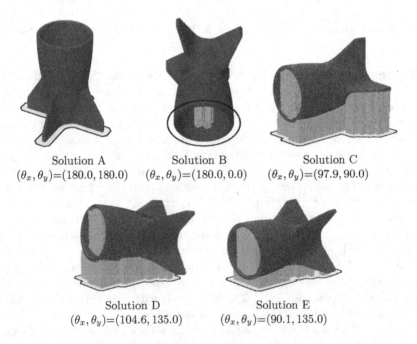

Solution A
$(\theta_x, \theta_y)=(180.0, 180.0)$

Solution B
$(\theta_x, \theta_y)=(180.0, 0.0)$

Solution C
$(\theta_x, \theta_y)=(97.9, 90.0)$

Solution D
$(\theta_x, \theta_y)=(104.6, 135.0)$

Solution E
$(\theta_x, \theta_y)=(90.1, 135.0)$

**Fig. 9.** Representation of the solutions A, B, C, D and E of Rocket Shot model.

In Fig. 10, it is presented the Pareto front obtained for the 45 Degree Short model as well as the corresponding angles and objective function values for the four representative non-dominated solutions (solutions A to D). As it can be seen, the Pareto front has some nonconvex regions. Solution A is the solution with the best SA value. Solution B represents a large improvement of the value of BT when compared to solution A. However, this implies some degradation of the SA value. Between solutions B and D there is a significant increase in SA and a slight reduction in the value of BT. Thus, solution B seems to be a good compromise between SA and BT. Solution D is the solution with the best BT value but with a large value of SA.

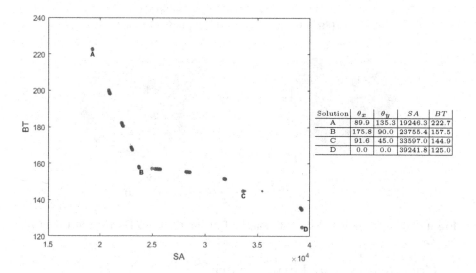

| Solution | $\theta_x$ | $\theta_y$ | $SA$ | $BT$ |
|---|---|---|---|---|
| A | 89.9 | 135.3 | 19246.3 | 222.7 |
| B | 175.8 | 90.0 | 23755.4 | 157.5 |
| C | 91.6 | 45.0 | 33597.0 | 144.9 |
| D | 0.0 | 0.0 | 39241.8 | 125.0 |

**Fig. 10.** Pareto front and representative solutions for the 45 Degree Short model.

The 3D representations of solutions A to D are presented in Fig. 11. Solution A with the angles (89.9, 135.3) has the best SA value, but the worst BT value. On the other extreme of the Pareto front, solution D with orientation (0.0, 0.0) has the best value of BT, since its orientation reduces the height of the model. However, this solution has the worst SA value since many supports are required. Solutions B and C with the angles (175.8, 90.0) and (91.6, 45.0), respectively, are compromise solutions between BT and SA. Solution C is better in BT and worse in SA when compared to solution B.

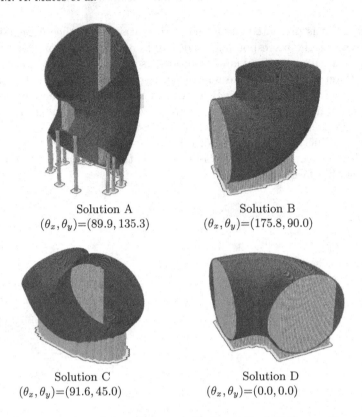

Solution A
$(\theta_x, \theta_y){=}(89.9, 135.3)$

Solution B
$(\theta_x, \theta_y){=}(175.8, 90.0)$

Solution C
$(\theta_x, \theta_y){=}(91.6, 45.0)$

Solution D
$(\theta_x, \theta_y){=}(0.0, 0.0)$

**Fig. 11.** Representation of the solutions A, B, C and D of 45 Degree Short model.

## 4    Conclusions and Future Work

In this paper, it is proposed a multi-objective approach to the build orientation optimization problem. The support area and the build time of 3D models are optimized simultaneously. Four building 3D CAD models are studied.

The weighted Tchebycheff scalarization method was used to transform the multi-objective problem into a single-objective one and embedded in the Electromagnetism-like algorithm to solve this multi-objective optimization problem. It is observed that the convexity of Pareto fronts depends on the 3D CAD models being optimized. All Pareto fronts obtained for the 3D models considered have nonconvex regions. This highlights the importance of using a scalarization method that can achieve nonsupported solutions. These results allow us to perceive the relationship between the objectives for each of the models. Moreover, it is possible to identify the trade-offs between the objectives and select the most appropriate solution. Therefore, it is clear the advantage of using a multi-objective approach that considers different criteria to find the best orientation of building 3D CAD models.

For future work, it is intended to apply this approach to multi-objective orientation problems with other criteria and with other more complex models.

**Acknowledgments.** This work has been supported and developed under the FIBR3D project - Hybrid processes based on additive manufacturing of composites with long or short fibers reinforced thermoplastic matrix (POCI-01-0145-FEDER-016414), supported by the Lisbon Regional Operational Programme 2020, under the PORTUGAL 2020 Partnership Agreement, through the European Regional Development Fund (ERDF). This work was also supported by FCT - Fundação para a Ciência e Tecnologia within the Project Scope: UID/CEC/00319/2019.

# References

1. Brika, S.E., Zhao, Y.F., Brochu, M., Mezzetta, J.: Multi-objective build orientation optimization for powder bed fusion by laser. J. Manufact. Sci. Eng. **139**(11), 111011 (2017)
2. Canellidis, V., Dedoussis, V., Mantzouratos, N., Sofianopoulou, S.: Pre-processing methodology for optimizing stereolithography apparatus build performance. Comput. Ind. **57**(5), 424–436 (2006)
3. Canellidis, V., Giannatsis, J., Dedoussis, V.: Genetic-algorithm-based multi-objective optimization of the build orientation in stereolithography. Int. J. Adv. Manufact. Technol. **45**(7–8), 714–730 (2009)
4. Cheng, W., Fuh, J., Nee, A., Wong, Y., Loh, H., Miyazawa, T.: Multi-objective optimization of part-building orientation in stereolithography. Rapid Prototyping J. **1**(4), 12–23 (1995)
5. Dächert, K., Gorski, J., Klamroth, K.: An augmented weighted tchebycheff method with adaptively chosen parameters for discrete bicriteria optimization problems. Comput. Oper. Res. **39**(12), 2929–2943 (2012)
6. Birbil, S.I., Fang, S.-C.: An electromagnetism-like mechanism for global optimization. J. Glob. Optim. **25**, 263–282 (2003)
7. Gurrala, P.K., Regalla, S.P.: Multi-objective optimisation of strength and volumetric shrinkage of fdm parts: a multi-objective optimization scheme is used to optimize the strength and volumetric shrinkage of FDM parts considering different process parameters. Virtual Phys. Prototyping **9**(2), 127–138 (2014)
8. Jaimes, A.L., Martınez, S.Z., Coello, C.A.C.: An introduction to multiobjective optimization techniques. Optim. Polym. Process. 29–57 (2009)
9. Jibin, Z.: Determination of optimal build orientation based on satisfactory degree theory for RPT. In: Ninth International Conference on Computer Aided Design and Computer Graphics, pp. 6–pp. IEEE (2005)
10. Kruth, J.P.: Material incress manufacturing by rapid prototyping techniques. CIRP Ann.-Manufact. Technol. **40**(2), 603–614 (1991)
11. Lan, P.T., Chou, S.Y., Chen, L.L., Gemmill, D.: Determining fabrication orientations for rapid prototyping with stereolithography apparatus. Comput.-Aided Des. **29**(1), 53–62 (1997)
12. Li, A., Zhang, Z., Wang, D., Yang, J.: Optimization method to fabrication orientation of parts in fused deposition modeling rapid prototyping. In: 2010 International Conference on Mechanic Automation and Control Engineering, pp. 416–419. IEEE (2010)

13. Livesu, M., Ellero, S., Martínez, J., Lefebvre, S., Attene, M.: From 3D models to 3D prints: an overview of the processing pipeline. In: Computer Graphics Forum, vol. 36, pp. 537–564. Wiley Online Library (2017)
14. Masood, S., Rattanawong, W., Iovenitti, P.: A generic algorithm for a best part orientation system for complex parts in rapid prototyping. J. Mat. Process. Technol. **139**(1–3), 110–116 (2003)
15. Padhye, N., Deb, K.: Multi-objective optimisation and multi-criteria decision making in SLS using evolutionary approaches. Rapid Prototyping J. **17**(6), 458–478 (2011)
16. Pandey, P., Reddy, N.V., Dhande, S.: Part deposition orientation studies in layered manufacturing. J. Mater. Process. Technol. **185**(1–3), 125–131 (2007)
17. Pereira, S., Vaz, A., Vicente, L.: On the optimal object orientation in additive manufacturing. Int. J. Adv. Manufact. Technol. **98**, 1–10 (2018)
18. Phatak, A.M., Pande, S.: Optimum part orientation in rapid prototyping using genetic algorithm. J. Manufact. Syst. **31**(4), 395–402 (2012)
19. Rocha, A.M.A.C., Pereira, A.I., Vaz, A.I.F.: Build orientation optimization problem in additive manufacturing. In: Gervasi, O., et al. (eds.) ICCSA 2018. LNCS, vol. 10961, pp. 669–682. Springer, Cham (2018). https://doi.org/10.1007/978-3-319-95165-2_47
20. Rocha, A.M.A.C., Silva, A., Rocha, J.G.: A new competitive implementation of the electromagnetism-like algorithm for global optimization. In: Gervasi, O., et al. (eds.) ICCSA 2015. LNCS, vol. 9156, pp. 506–521. Springer, Cham (2015). https://doi.org/10.1007/978-3-319-21407-8_36
21. Steuer, R.E., Choo, E.U.: An interactive weighted tchebycheff procedure for multiple objective programming. Math. Program. **26**(3), 326–344 (1983)
22. Thrimurthulu, K., Pandey, P.M., Reddy, N.V.: Optimum part deposition orientation in fused deposition modeling. Int. J. Mach. Tools Manuf. **44**(6), 585–594 (2004)
23. Wang, W.M., Zanni, C., Kobbelt, L.: Improved surface quality in 3D printing by optimizing the printing direction. In: Computer Graphics Forum, vol. 35, pp. 59–70. Wiley Online Library (2016)

# Optimizing the Kidney Exchange Problem with a Budget for Simultaneous Crossmatch Tests

Valeria Romanciuc[1] and Filipe Alvelos[2(✉)]

[1] Centro Algoritmi, Universidade do Minho, 4710-057 Braga, Portugal
pg33724@uminho.pt
[2] Centro Algoritmi/Departamento de Produção e Sistemas,
Universidade do Minho, 4710-057 Braga, Portugal
falvelos@dps.uminho.pt

**Abstract.** Many people in the world suffer from end stage renal disease, which has transplantation as the most effective form of treatment. However, kidneys obtained from deceased donors are not nearly enough to meet demand and willing living donors may display incompatibilities with their intended recipient. Kidney Exchange Programs have emerged as an attempt to answer the transplant shortage and bypass these incompatibility issues between donor-patient pairs. The process of selecting the pairs participating in the transplantation plan requires optimization models, one of which is presented in the current paper. We focus on maximizing the expected number of transplants taking into account that only a given number of actual incompatibility (crossmatch) tests can be made. We present an integer programming model to address this problem when recourse is feasible and we compare computationally its outcomes with other two approaches in 150 instances.

**Keywords:** Kidney exchange program · Integer programming · Optimization

## 1 Introduction

End stage renal disease (ESRD) affects about one in a thousand people in Europe [5]. Two options are available for treatment: dialysis and transplantation [4]. The latter has proved to be the preferred alternative, as it usually provides higher quality of life and higher chances of patient survival, while also being less costly than the former [14,19].

Kidneys for a transplant may be obtained both from deceased and living donors. In the first case, patients are placed on a waiting list, hoping to find a compatible donor. Despite being the standard practice for a long time, it failed to keep up with the fast growth of the number of patients suffering from ESRD, which significantly increased waiting times for transplantation [19]. As such, in order to bridge the gap between this shortage of kidneys and their ever-growing

© Springer Nature Switzerland AG 2019
S. Misra et al. (Eds.): ICCSA 2019, LNCS 11621, pp. 277–288, 2019.
https://doi.org/10.1007/978-3-030-24302-9_20

demand, new transplantation strategies emerged, one of them being the inclusion of living donors in the donor pool [7,8]. This not only increased the number of transplants taking place, but also improved the outcomes of transplantation when compared to using deceased-donor kidneys [8]. However, in order for transplantation to be carried out, the willing donor must be physiologically compatible with their intended recipient, which fails to happen in over 30% of the cases [18].

Evidence has shown very similar results in graft survival considering transplants conducted with kidneys obtained from genetically unrelated donors when compared to kidneys transplanted from siblings or other histocompatible donors [8,10]. As a result, alternative approaches have been adopted, including kidney exchange programs (KEPs).

KEPs provide an alternative solution for patients with willing yet incompatible donors. First proposed by Rapaport in 1986 [16], their simplest form consists in the following: given a patient $P_1$ with a willing but incompatible donor $D_1$, and another such donor-patient pair, $D_2$ and $P_2$, respectively, let us suppose that $D_1$ is compatible with $P_2$ and $D_2$ is compatible with $P_1$ (Fig. 1a). Therefore, by swapping donors, we could proceed with both transplants, as opposed to conducting none in the original scenario. This exchange can be generalized to include $k$ incompatible pairs, as depicted in Fig. 1b. For logistic reasons, since the transplants in an exchange must be done simultaneously, usually a certain limit is imposed on the number of pairs taking part in an exchange.

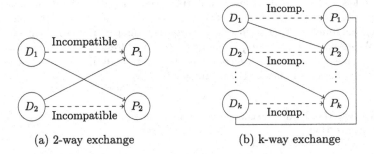

(a) 2-way exchange          (b) k-way exchange

**Fig. 1.** Representation of a 2-way kidney exchange and a k-way kidney exchange. The dashed arrows represent incompatibility and the full arrows represent compatibility between donor $(D_i)$ and patient $(P_i)$.

Additional variations were studied, including the non-directed donors (people willing to donate a kidney without having an associated recipient) as well as patient desensitization [12]. However, we will be focusing only on 2-way and 3-way exchanges within a network.

Compatibility between pairs is determined based on blood type and human leukocyte antigen (HLAs) matching. In the latter case, a preliminary test is performed (called "virtual" crossmatch): the pair is considered to be compatible if the virtual crossmatch is negative and incompatible otherwise [5]. Based on this information, a transplantation plan is defined. Afterwards, a more accurate test is applied (the "actual" crossmatch, henceforth referred to as crossmatch), possibly revealing new incompatibilities between pairs and thus cancelling programmed exchanges. Given the number of combinations, testing every two pairs for compatibility is only feasible in very small pools.

As for the definition of transplantation plans, KEPs have been addressed mostly with integer programming based approaches [1,7,13]. Different criteria can be maximized in order to determine the best transplantation plan, such as the number of transplants, the number of 2-way exchanges [6] or the expected number of transplants [13]. In order to take into account the uncertainty of the results of the crossmatch tests, we assume the probability of match failure for each transplant is known.

We address the problem of selecting which possible transplants should be tested, taking into account that each test has a cost, there is a budget, and all tests must be conducted simultaneously. A potential reason for simultaneity comes from the lack of time to wait for the result of a (set of) crossmatch test(s) to decide the next (ones) to conduct. The budget constraint allows modelling the case where there is a limit on the number of tests that can be performed. In this case, each arc has a unitary cost and the budget corresponds to the maximum number of tests. The budget constraint is also relevant in multi-agent (i.e., when several agents participate in a joint donor pool) kidney exchange programs, where tests may have different costs as a consequence, for example, of different logistic costs, as it happens in multi-country KEPs.

We will study two approaches. In the first, we do not consider the possibility of recourse once a certain solution is determined, so it is final and can not be modified. In the second approach, we consider the possibility of rearranging the transplants in a transplantation plan in case new incompatibilities arise and part of the exchange is cancelled. Such recourse approaches have been considered in [13,15].

As the tests are conducted simultaneously, the decision on which tests to conduct must be made before any results are known. We derive an integer programming model that takes into account this uncertainty and the budget constraint and perform a computational study.

Related work on deciding which arcs to test assume several runs of the KEP. In that case, after knowing the results of a set of tests, a new set of tests to conduct is decided. Different policies and approaches for that problem were proposed in [2,3,9].

The paper is structured as follows. In Sect. 2, we present the problem without recourse and an integer programming model. In Sect. 3, we extend the model for when recourse is allowed. In Sect. 4, results from computational tests are presented and compared for each approach. Finally, in Sect. 5 we provide some conclusions.

## 2   Problem Description and Model

KEPs are typically represented via graph theory. Let us consider a directed graph $G = (N, A)$, where $N$ is the set of nodes representing incompatible pairs of donor-patient, and $A$ is the set of arcs representing compatibility between pairs. Thus, given two pairs $i, j \in N$, the arc $(i, j)$ is in $A$ if the donor in pair $i$ is compatible with the patient in pair $j$. Furthermore, associated to each arc is a weight $p_{ij}$, which represents the probability of match failure of arc $(i, j)$.

Each feasible exchange between two or more pairs will be represented by a cycle in the aforementioned graph and we will only consider cycles of lengths 2 and 3 (2-cycles and 3-cycles, respectively), as they are the most common in actual KEPs.

In this section, we consider the problem of deciding which arcs to select such that they form a set of disjoint cycles corresponding to a maximum value of the expected number of transplants. The main difference to the well-known cycle formulation is the additional budget constraint. Transplants will be conducted only with tested arcs.

Let $C$ be the set of all cycles in $G$ (with at most 3 arcs). Given a 2-cycle $c \in C$ with arcs $(i, j)$, $(j, i) \in A$, the expected number of transplants is given by

$$E(c) = 2(1 - p_{ij})(1 - p_{ji}), \tag{1}$$

where $p_{ij}$ is the probability of failure associated with arc $(i, j) \in A$. Similarly for a 3-cycle $c \in C$ with arcs $(i, j)$, $(j, k)$, $(k, i) \in A$, the expected number of transplants is given by

$$E(c) = 3(1 - p_{ij})(1 - p_{jk})(1 - p_{ki}), \tag{2}$$

where $p_{ij}, p_{jk}$ and $p_{ki}$ are the probabilities of failure associated with arcs $(i, j), (j, k)$, and $(k, i)$, respectively.

The following parameters are defined.

$$a_{ij}^c = \begin{cases} 1, & \text{if arc } (i, j) \in A \text{ is in cycle } c \\ 0, & \text{otherwise} \end{cases} \quad \forall c \in C$$

$p_{ij}$ − probability of match failure of arc $(i, j) \in A$,   $\forall (i, j) \in A$
$b_{ij}$ − cost of a test conducted on arc $(i, j) \in A$,   $\forall (i, j) \in A$
$B$ − total budget available

The decision variables are defined as follows

$$w_c = \begin{cases} 1, & \text{if cycle } c \in C \text{ is selected for the plan} \\ 0, & \text{otherwise} \end{cases} \quad \forall c \in C$$

$$y_{ij} = \begin{cases} 1, & \text{if arc } (i, j) \in A \text{ is tested} \\ 0, & \text{otherwise} \end{cases} \quad \forall (i, j) \in A$$

The integer programming model is

$$\text{Maximize} \quad z = \sum_{c \in C} E(c) w_c \tag{3}$$

$$\text{Subject to:} \quad \sum_{c \in C} \sum_{(i,j) \in A} a_{ij}^c w_c \leq 1, \quad \forall i \in N \tag{4}$$

$$w_c - a_{ij}^c y_{ij} \leq 0, \quad \forall (i,j) \in A, \forall c \in C \tag{5}$$

$$\sum_{(i,j)\in A} b_{ij}y_{ij} \leq B \tag{6}$$

$$w_c, y_{ij} \in \{0,1\}, \forall c \in C, \forall (i,j) \in A \tag{7}$$

The objective function (3) maximizes the expected number of transplants. Constraints (4) ensure that each node (that is, each pair donor-patient) is in at most one selected cycle for the exchange. This is necessary because each pair can only donate (and consequently receive) one kidney. Constraints (5) make sure only cycles where every arc is tested are selected. Finally, constraints (6) ensure that the total available budget is not exceeded.

To illustrate this model, let us consider an example of a KEP network, which can be seen in Fig. 2.

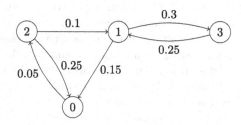

**Fig. 2.** Example of a KEP instance with four incompatible pairs and probabilities of failure.

In this instance we have four incompatible donor-patient pairs, represented by the nodes 0, 1, 2 and 3. We assume performing a test on each arc costs 1. The cycles in this network are $c_0 = \{02, 20\}$, $c_1 = \{13, 31\}$ and $c_2 = \{02, 21, 10\}$, with expected values of 1.425, 1.05 (both calculated with the formula in (1)) and 2.180 (calculated with the formula in (2)), respectively.

Assuming we only have two available crossmatch tests, the optimal solution would be to test the arcs of cycle $c_0$. If the number of tests increases by one, the optimal solution would be the cycle $c_2$, as it has the highest expected number of transplants and all its arcs can be tested.

However, if the number of available crossmatch tests is four, the optimal solution is no longer $c_2$ but rather the cycles $c_0$ and $c_1$ combined, as the expected number of transplants is equal to 2.475, which is higher than the expected value of cycle $c_2$.

We may also consider a particular case of the above model, when $p_{ij} = 0$, for every $(i,j) \in A$. In this situation, the expected value for each cycle is simply its length, which means we are maximizing the number of transplants. We have mentioned previously that it is the most studied variant (neglecting uncertainty), so in Sect. 4 we will also compare the expected value approach with the deterministic approach.

## 3   Dealing with Recourse

In this section, we will address the problem from the perspective where recourse is allowed. As mentioned, crossmatch tests may reveal new incompatibilities, cancelling some of the planned transplants. In such cases, we may try to rearrange the remaining arcs so that the rest of the planned transplants are salvaged and the crossmatch tests performed on them are not wasted. This is achieved by making use of backarcs in 3-cycles: arcs that form 2-cycles with other arcs in the current 3-cycle.

Let us consider again the example in Fig. 2. For two and three crossmatch tests, we would obtain the same solution as with the previous model. However, assuming we have available four tests, cycle $c_2$ with one backarc has an expected number of transplants of 2.515 (calculated with the expressions given in [15]), which is the maximum expected number of transplants for this number of tests (higher than cycles $c_0$ and $c_1$ combined). This illustrates how recourse may provide better results for a determined number of crossmatch tests.

The main difference in the recourse integer programming model with respect to the model (3–7) is the definition of the decision variables. In the recourse approach, these are associated not only with 2- and 3-cycles, but also sets of arcs made of 3-cycles and additional arcs (backarcs). In order to achieve this, we use the concept of "configurations": a set of arcs forming a 2-cycle, a 3-cycle or a 3-cycle with up to three backarcs (including none). A more detailed explanation of configurations of 3-cycles can be found in the appendix.

This allows us to define the following sets: $C_3^0$ as the set of all 3-cycle configurations with no backarcs, $C_3^1$ as the set of all configurations with one backarc, $C_3^2$ as the set of all configurations with two backarcs and finally $C_3^3$ as the set of all configurations with three backarcs. In this approach, by defining $C$ as the union of these four sets along with the set of 2-cycles ($C_2$), $C = C_2 \cup C_3^0 \cup C_3^1 \cup C_3^2 \cup C_3^3$, the model (3–7) applies to the recourse approach.

## 4   Computational Tests

Computational tests were conducted in order to evaluate the variation of the expected number of transplants, given an increase in the number of possible crossmatch tests. This model was implemented in C++ and CPLEX. Tests were carried out with 50 instances of 30, 40 and 50 pairs generated by the instances' generator described in [17] which takes into account the probabilities of blood type and tissue incompatibility. The probabilities of a positive crossmatch were obtained according to [11].

We assume conducting a test on each arc costs 1, with the total budget being equal to the number of nodes of a given instance. We defined this as such since, for an instance of $n$ nodes, the maximum possible number of transplants in a solution is precisely $n$ (that is, at most $n$ transplants are planned), which also means that no more than $n$ tests are needed.

In Table 1 some averages are presented, where we consider the three models previously discussed: optimization of the expected number of transplants with no recourse, optimization of the expected number of transplants with recourse and optimization of the number of transplants assuming no failures. It is important to note that the latter must be seen as an *upper bound* to the actual number of transplants and not an *expected* value as in the other two approaches. We name the approaches "No recourse", "Recourse", "Upper bound".

We consider the following for each set of instances with the same size (30, 40 and 50) and each approach:

- Average number of arcs;
- Average expected number of transplants for an unlimited number of tests;
- Average number of tests needed to achieve the maximum expected number of transplants;
- Convergence: the number of tests necessary so that all instances converge to their respective maximum expected number of transplants;
- Average execution time.

**Table 1.** Average results for 50 instances of 30, 40 and 50 nodes each.

| Number of pairs | 30 | 40 | 50 |
|---|---|---|---|
| Avg. no. of arcs | 217 | 377 | 594 |
| No recourse | | | |
| Avg. expected no. transplants | 8.244 | 10.996 | 14.940 |
| Avg. no. tests | 11.7 | 16.2 | 21.8 |
| Convergence | 17 | 25 | 34 |
| Avg. time (sec) | 0.939 | 1.5264 | 2.801 |
| Recourse | | | |
| Avg. expected no. transplants | 9.024 | 12.184 | 16.56 |
| Avg. no. tests | 14.796 | 20.94 | 28.531 |
| Convergence | 24 | 33 | 48 |
| Avg. time (sec) | 1.188 | 2.2554 | 4.4386 |
| Upper bound | | | |
| Avg. no. of transplants | 12.27 | 17.3 | 23.4 |
| Avg. no. tests | 12.27 | 17.3 | 23.4 |
| Convergence | 19 | 27 | 36 |
| Avg. time (sec) | 0.808 | 1.516 | 2.712 |

Instances of 30 pairs registered, on average, 217 arcs and 8.244 expected transplants. An average of 11.7 tests were necessary for each instance, but convergence was attained in all instances after 17 tests. Comparing to the recourse results, we have an average of 9.024 expected transplants, which is equal to an increase of about 10% of transplants. However, more tests are needed on average. If we consider the third model where an upper bound for the number of transplants is obtained, we obtain 12.3 transplants on average, which means an increase of about 49% when considering the "best case scenario". In this case, all instances converge after 19 tests.

A similar analysis can be done for instances of 40 nodes, where we registered an average of 377 arcs per instance. The average expected number of transplants with no recourse is 10.996, compared to 12.184 average expected transplants when allowing recourse, which is an increase of about 11%. As for the third model, we have an average for the upper bound on the number of transplants of 17.3.

Finally, for instances of 50 pairs, we have an average of 594 arcs per instance. On average, the first model has 14.94 expected transplants whereas the second model has 16.56, representing again an increase of approximately 11%. The final model gives us about 23.4 transplants, which is about 57% higher than the first approach considered.

A couple of conclusions can be drawn from these results. The expected number of transplants with recourse is around 10% higher than the expected number of transplants without recourse, regardless of the pool size, but requires more tests. The expected number of transplants with recourse is between 25% and 30% less than the upper bound given by neglecting potential failures. This is an optimistic empirical estimate on the proportion of cancelled transplants due to not taking into account the uncertainty associated with the crossmatch tests after the transplantation plan is set.

Computational times are negligible, as usually decisions must be taken in much more than a few seconds. Being fast allows models to be incorporated as submodels in other problems that address larger instances.

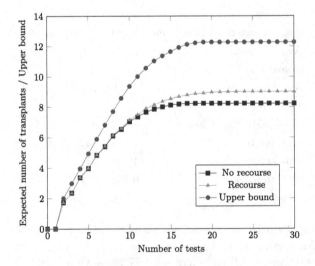

**Fig. 3.** Comparison of three approaches for instances of 30 pairs: expected number of transplants without recourse vs. expected number of transplants with recourse vs. upper bound on the number of transplants.

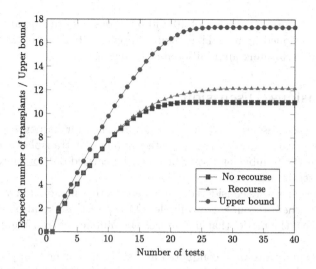

**Fig. 4.** Comparison of three approaches for instances of 40 pairs: expected number of transplants without recourse vs. expected number of transplants with internal recourse vs. upper bound on the number of transplants.

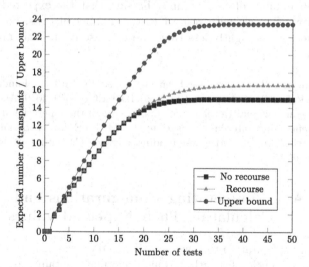

**Fig. 5.** Comparison of three models for instances of 50 pairs: expected number of transplants without recourse vs. expected number of transplants with internal recourse vs. upper bound on the number of transplants.

In addition, from Figs. 3, 4 and 5, we were able to not only take the same conclusions, but we can also observe that the expected number of transplants displays approximate linear growth until close to the convergence value. For instances of 30 pairs and considering the first 10 crossmatch tests, we see an average increase of around 0.7 expected transplants per test with no recourse and 0.8 with recourse. Instances of 40 and 50 nodes behave similarly, as can be seen in the mentioned figures. These slopes represent how many transplants we can expect by performing an additional crossmatch test.

## 5    Conclusions/Discussion

In this paper we presented optimization approaches for kidney exchange programs that aim to maximize the expected number of transplants considering constraints on the number of tests which can be carried out, or more generally, a budget constraint.

Two approaches were considered: one where there is no possibility of recourse, and the other where recourse is available. On top of this, we also established a comparison with the model that maximizes the number of transplants assuming no failures.

Computational tests were conducted and showed that both approaches have similar results when the number of tests is small, but a turning point is reached where recourse provides a significant higher expected number of transplants (around 10%).

For a small number of tests, it may be said that the expected number of transplants grows linearly with respect to the number of tests. For each additional test, there is an slightly less than one increase in the maximum number of transplants.

**Acknowledgments.** This work has been supported by FCT — Fundação para a Ciência e Tecnologia within the project Scope: UID/CEC/00319/2019. And also by the ERDF – European Regional Development Fund through the Operational Programme for Competitiveness and Internationalisation - COMPETE 2020 Programme, and by National Funds through the Portuguese funding agency, FCT within project POCI-01-0145-FEDER-016677.

## Appendix A    Enumerating Configurations and Calculating Their Expected Values

The concept of configuration that we used is based on the definition in [13]. Let us then consider a cycle of length 3. This cycle may contain zero, one, two or three backarcs. In the first case, it has one possible configuration (itself). In the second case, the backarc can be associated to three different arcs (Fig. 6), but all these graphs are isomorphic, belonging to the same equivalence class. In the third case, we also have three different combinations of each two backarcs, but again, they are isomorphic to one another (Fig. 7). In the last case, there is one possible configuration of three backarcs. This gives us four equivalence classes total, which can be observed in Fig. 8.

In order to use the formulas for the expected number of transplants in [15], we must then rearrange each configuration into what we may call "standard form". This means we will identify which equivalence class this configuration belongs to

**Fig. 6.** The three possible configurations of a 3-cycle with one backarc (one equivalence class) and the representative on the left.

**Fig. 7.** The three possible configurations of a 3-cycle with two backarcs (one equivalence class) and the representative on the left.

**Fig. 8.** All four possible configurations (representatives of each equivalence class) of a 3-cycle.

and consider its representative, calculating the expected number of transplants for this object. Considering the representative of the class each time means the disposition of the arcs in the configuration is always the same, which allows us to use the mentioned formulas regardless of the position of the backarcs (as we can always reduce them to the same four cases).

# References

1. Abraham, D.J., Blum, A., Sandholm, T.: Clearing algorithms for barter exchange markets: enabling nationwide kidney exchanges. In: Proceedings of the 8th ACM conference on Electronic commerce, pp. 295–304. ACM (2007). https://doi.org/10.1145/1250910.1250954
2. Alvelos, F., Viana, A.: Kidney exchange programs with a priori crossmatch probing. In: Kliewer, N., Ehmke, J.F., Borndörfer, R. (eds.) Operations Research Proceedings 2017. ORP, pp. 363–368. Springer, Cham (2018). https://doi.org/10.1007/978-3-319-89920-6_49
3. Alvelos, F., Viana, A., Klimentova, X.: Probing for maximizing the expected number of transplants. In: XIX CLAIO, Latin-Iberoamerican Conference on Operations Research Proceedings, 24–27 September, Lima, Perú (2018)
4. American Kidney Fund: Kidney Disease: Kidney Failure/ESRD. http://www.kidneyfund.org/kidney-disease/#kidney_failure_esrd. Accessed 14 Mar 2019
5. Biró, P., et al.: Kidney Exchange Practices in Europe: First Handbook of the Cost Action CA15210: European Network for Collaboration on Kidney Exchange Programmes (ENCKEP) (2017)

6. Bofill, M., et al.: The Spanish kidney exchange model: study of computation-based alternatives to the current procedure. In: ten Teije, A., Popow, C., Holmes, J.H., Sacchi, L. (eds.) AIME 2017. LNCS (LNAI), vol. 10259, pp. 272–277. Springer, Cham (2017). https://doi.org/10.1007/978-3-319-59758-4_31
7. Constantino, M., Klimentova, X., Viana, A., Rais, A.: New insights on integer-programming models for the kidney exchange problem. Eur. J. Oper. Res. **231**(1), 57–68 (2013). https://doi.org/10.1016/j.ejor.2013.05.025
8. Davis, C.L., Delmonico, F.L.: Living-donor kidney transplantation: a review of the current practices for the live donor. J. Am. Soc. Nephrol. **16**(7), 2098–2110 (2005). https://doi.org/10.1681/ASN.2004100824
9. Dücső, M.: Testing re-optimisation strategies in kidney exchange programmes (2018, unpublished)
10. Gjertson, D.W., Cecka, J.M.: Living unrelated donor kidney transplantation. Kidney Int. **58**(2), 491–499 (2000). https://doi.org/10.1046/j.1523-1755.2000.00195.x
11. Glorie, K.: Estimating the probability of positive crossmatch after negative virtual crossmatch. Technical report, Econometric Institute, Erasmus University Rotterdam (2012)
12. Glorie, K.: Clearing barter exchange markets: kidney exchange and beyond. Ph.D. thesis, Erasmus Research Institute of Management, Erasmus University Rotterdam (2014). http://hdl.handle.net/1765/77183
13. Klimentova, X., Pedroso, J.P., Viana, A.: Maximising expectation of the number of transplants in kidney exchange programmes. Comput. Oper. Res. **73**, 1–11 (2016). https://doi.org/10.1016/j.cor.2016.03.004
14. Laupacis, A., et al.: A study of the quality of life and cost-utility of renal transplantation. Kidney Int. **50**(1), 235–242 (1996)
15. Pedroso, J.P.: Maximizing expectation on vertex-disjoint cycle packing. In: Murgante, B., et al. (eds.) ICCSA 2014. LNCS, vol. 8580, pp. 32–46. Springer, Cham (2014). https://doi.org/10.1007/978-3-319-09129-7_3
16. Rapaport, F.: The case for a living emotionally related international kidney donor exchange registry. In: Transplantation Proceedings, vol. 18 (1986)
17. Saidman, S.L., Roth, A.E., Sönmez, T., Ünver, M.U., Delmonico, F.L.: Increasing the opportunity of live kidney donation by matching for two-and three-way exchanges. Transplantation **81**(5), 773–782 (2006). https://doi.org/10.1097/01.tp.0000195775.77081.25
18. Segev, D.L., Gentry, S.E., Warren, D.S., Reeb, B., Montgomery, R.A.: Kidney paired donation and optimizing the use of live donor organs. JAMA **293**(15), 1883–1890 (2005). https://doi.org/10.1001/jama.293.15.1883
19. Wolfe, R.A., et al.: Comparison of mortality in all patients on dialysis, patients on dialysis awaiting transplantation, and recipients of a first cadaveric transplant. New Engl. J. Med. **341**(23), 1725–1730 (1999). https://doi.org/10.1056/NEJM199912023412303

# Computational Astrochemistry
# (CompAstro 2019)

# Analytical Potential Energy Formulation for a New Theoretical Approach in Penning Ionization

Stefano Falcinelli[1]([⊠]) [iD], Marzio Rosi[1,2], Franco Vecchiocattivi[1],
and Fernando Pirani[3]

[1] Department of Civil and Environmental Engineering, University of Perugia,
Via G. Duranti 93, 06125 Perugia, Italy
{stefano.falcinelli,marzio.rosi}@unipg.it,
franco@vecchio.it
[2] ISTM-CNR, 06123 Perugia, Italy
[3] Department of Chemistry, Biology and Biotechnologies, University of Perugia,
Via Elce di Sotto 8, 06100 Perugia, Italy
fernando.pirani@unipg.it

**Abstract.** The analysis of recent Penning ionization electron spectra as a function of the collision energy for both $Ne^*$-Kr and $Ne^*$-Xe autoionizing reactions allowed the development of a new general theoretical approach able to fully describe the stereodynamics of the Penning ionization reactions at a state to state level. Details on such a general and original approach based on the dependence of the reaction probability on the relative orientation of the atomic and molecular orbitals of reagents and products, are given. The mutual orientation of the collisional partners with respect to the intermolecular axis of the intermediate $[Ne\text{---}Rg]^*$ (with Rg = Kr or Xe) excited collision complex (i.e. the transition state of studied reactions) controls the characteristics of the intermolecular potential, which is formulated in a new analytical form whose details are presented and discussed. Obtained results refer to a statistical/random orientation of the open shell ionic core of $Ne^*$, and in the two cases of $Ne^*$-Kr and $Ne^*$-Xe autoionizing collisions, we were able to reproduce and characterize the dependence on the collision energy of the experimental branching ratio between probabilities of spin-orbit resolved elementary processes already published. Such findings result from anisotropy effects connected to atomic orbital orientation/alignment, and their full understanding is a crucial point to describe the dependence of the stereo-dynamics on the electronic structure of the $[Ne\text{---}Rg]^*$ transition state. In this way, we are able to fully characterize the state to state reaction probability for the Penning ionization reactions involving Kr and Xe atoms with ionizing $Ne^*$ atoms in either $^3P_2$ and $^3P_0$ sublevels. This original methodology can be applied also to Penning ionization processes involving molecular targets, and in principle is able to point out the basic role of electronic rearrangements inside the transition state of various types of chemical reactions at thermal and sub-thermal collision energies which are of interest in astrochemical environments, being a much more arduous problem in order to be completely characterized.

© Springer Nature Switzerland AG 2019
S. Misra et al. (Eds.): ICCSA 2019, LNCS 11621, pp. 291–305, 2019.
https://doi.org/10.1007/978-3-030-24302-9_21

**Keywords:** Penning ionization · State to state · Transition state · Electron spectroscopy · Stereodynamics · Metastable atoms

# 1  Introduction

Penning ionization reactions are elementary processes involving metastable excited species $M^*$ able to ionize atomic or molecular collisional targets X. They can be schematized as it follows:

$$M^* + X \rightarrow [M\text{---}X]^* \rightarrow [M\text{---}X]^+ + e^- \rightarrow final \ ionic \ products \qquad (1)$$

where $[M\text{---}X]^*$ and $[M\text{-}'\text{-}X]^+$ are the intermediate neutral and ionic collisional complexes, respectively, being the first the transition state of the reaction [1, 2]. Excited atomic species able to produce Penning ionization are the rare gas atoms excited to their first electronic level as it can be seen from data of Table 1 [3].

**Table 1.** Main characteristics of the metastable noble-gas atoms.

| Atom | Electron configuration | Excitation energy (eV) | Lifetime (s) |
|---|---|---|---|
| $He^*(2^1S_0)$ | $1s\ 2s$ | 20.6158 | 0.0196 |
| $He^*(2^3S_1)$ | $"\ "$ | 19.8196 | 9000 |
| $Ne^*(^3P_0)$ | $2p^5\ 3s$ | 16.7154 | 430 |
| $Ne^*(^3P_2)$ | $"\ "$ | 16.6191 | 24.4 |
| $Ar^*(^3P_0)$ | $3p^5\ 4s$ | 11.7232 | 44.9 |
| $Ar^*(^3P_2)$ | $"\ "$ | 11.5484 | 55.9 |
| $Kr^*(^3P_0)$ | $4p^5\ 5s$ | 10.5624 | 0.49 |
| $Kr^*(^3P_2)$ | $"\ "$ | 9.9152 | 85.1 |
| $Xe^*(^3P_0)$ | $5p^5\ 6s$ | 9.4472 | 0.078 |
| $Xe^*(^3P_2)$ | $"\ "$ | 8.3153 | 150 |

In fact, metastable rare gas atoms are characterized: (i) by a high energy content ranging from $\sim 8.3$ eV for $Xe^*(^3P_2)$ up to $\sim 20.6$ (eV) for $He^*(2^1S_0)$ and able to ionize almost all atomic and molecular targets; (ii) by a long lifetime of several seconds allowing them to survive along the typical beam path in the crossed molecular beam experiments (see data of Table 1).

It has to be mentioned that Penning ionization reactions have been widely studied since they are relevant in radiation and plasma chemistry [4, 5], in the laser sources development as well as in combustion [6–9], atmospheric and astrochemistry [10–14] with a particular attention to processes occurring in planetary ionospheres [15–17]. In particular, the relevant role of ionic species in energy generation [18–20] and in space has been pointed out extensively by several review papers to which the interested reader can refer [21–24].

From an experimental point of view, Penning ionization processes are usually studied by crossed molecular beam technique coupled by either mass spectrometry or electron spectroscopy, the first being used to detect the final ions produced by reaction (1), while the latter is applied in order to detect the kinetic energy of emitted electron from the $[M\text{---}X]^*$ autoionizing transition state of such reactions (see Eq. (1)). The cross section for each ionization channel produced by the dynamical evolution of the intermediate $[M\text{---}X]^+$ ionic complex can be measured by mass spectrometry determinations [25, 26], where recently both ion-imaging [27–29] and coincidence techniques [30, 31] have been applied. A real spectroscopy of the transition state can be carried out by analyzing the energy of emitted electrons performing the so called Penning ionization electron spectroscopy (PIES) [32, 33]. A general scheme of a crossed molecular beam experimental apparatus is shown in Fig. 1.

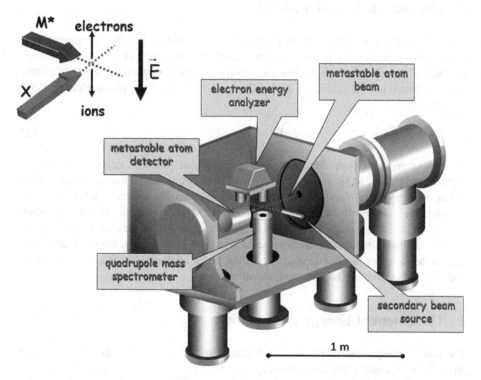

**Fig. 1.** The general scheme of a crossed molecular beam apparatus for the study of Penning ionization reactions.

From a theoretical point of view, the typical used approach in Penning ionization is based on the so called "Optical Potential Model", first introduced by Bethe for the description of nuclear reacting collisions [34]. It is based on the assumption that the interaction between the colliding partners can be described by a complex potential, and is widely discussed in the next section.

In this paper we report in detail analytical potential energy formulations recently adopted in a new theoretical model describing the microscopic dynamics of simple Penning ionization processes involving $Ne^*$-Kr and $Ne^*$-Xe atoms [35–37]. Such a model, thanks to the used Optical Potential Model in which the real part of the potential has been expressed by adopting an Improved Lennard Jones analytical function (see Sect. 3), was able to fully characterize the electron couplings inside the $[Ne\text{---}X]^*$ (where X = Kr or Xe) transition state of autoionizing reaction, reproducing the PIES spectra for both systems and the related branching ratios for the production of final ions in their specific spin-orbit states as a function of the collision energy [35, 36]. In such a way, we were able to formulate a complete description of the stereodynamics of the processes in a state to state picture in terms of adiabatic and non-adiabatic effects [35, 36].

## 2  The Optical Potential Model

As it is well known, the optical potential W, describing Penning ionization (i.e. autoionization processes), is expressed by a combination of a real part V (depicting the interaction between the two neutral incoming collisional partners) and an imaginary part $\Gamma$ (quantifying the ionization probability as a function of the internuclear distance R) [38–40]:

$$W = V - i/2\,\Gamma \tag{2}$$

The intensity of both these portions of the global potential depends on: (i) the separation distance, R; (ii) the relative orientation of two involved partners; (iii) and the characteristics of the manifold of quantum states attainable for the system along the collision. As discussed in details in next Sect. 3, such features, by configuration interaction, audit the mix among entrance and exit channels. In the case of $Ne^*$-Kr and $Ne^*$-Xe, the two simple atom-atom systems presented in this study, the used radial and angular terms point out the dependence of the potential energy on R and on the half-filled orbital orientation of $Ne^*$, respectively.

## 3  The Potential Energy Formulation

The real V component of the optical potential model of Eq. (2) can be formulated phenomenologically using the following Eq. (3):

$$V_t(R) = S(R)V(R)^{neut.-neut.} + (1 - S(R))V(R)^{ion-neut.} \tag{3}$$

where $V(R)^{neut.-neut.}$ and $V(R)^{ion-neut.}$ represents the interaction between the incoming neutral collision partners $[Ne\text{---}Rg]^*$ (where Rg = Kr or Xe) before the ionization and that between outcoming ionic states $[[Ne\text{---}Rg]^+$ after the autoionization, respectively. Either potential energy formulations have been depicted using the Improved Lennard Jones function widely applied in a number of cases [41–45], whose general form is the following:

$$V_{ILJ}(R) = \varepsilon \left[ \frac{m}{n(R) - m} \left( \frac{R_m}{R} \right)^{n(R)} - \frac{n(R)}{n(R) - m} \left( \frac{R_m}{R} \right)^{m} \right] \tag{4}$$

where

$$n(R) = \beta + 4 \left( \frac{R}{R_m} \right)^2 \tag{5}$$

In Eq. (4), $\varepsilon$ stands for the potential well depth whereas $R_m$ quantify its location in Å; $n(R)$ fixes the repulsive wall with its hardness, and the radial modulation of the attractive interaction. $S(R)$ in Eq. (3) is a switching function accounting for the transition between the neutral-neutral and the ion-neutral formulation, as previously adopted to describe the collisional interaction for other systems [39, 46–51]. Such a switching function has been defined by Eq. (6) below:

$$S(R) = \frac{1}{1 + e^{\left( \frac{R_0 - R}{d} \right)}} \tag{6}$$

In this formulation, the internuclear distance where the two combined limiting potential forms have the same weight is indicated as $R_o$, and the $d$ parameter accounts for the rapidity of the transition. It has to be noted that, in general, in order to carry out a complete representation of the real V component of Eq. (2) it is required to consider two additional features:

(i)  At large internuclear distance R, the ILJ formulation of the interaction potential appears to be complete; in fact, where R is large, the neutral-neutral interaction is prevailing and the collisional system is characterized by a substantial isotropic behavior which is typical of the interaction between an alkaline atom and a noble gas partner.

(ii) At short R distances, it is required to consider anisotropic contributions due to the open shell nature of the metastable atom because the role of its ionic core is coming out [52].

In our laboratory where developed guidelines to model such interactions [53, 54], giving us a powerful and reliable means to describe the interaction energy when an open "P" shell atom approaches a closed shell species. This can be done employing effective adiabatic potential energy curves, including contributions associated to pure $\Sigma$ and $\Pi$ molecular states: they are defined by the $\Lambda = 0$ and $\Lambda = 1$ electronic quantum number and are picked out as $V_\Sigma$ and $V_\Pi$, mixed by spin-orbit effects. A weighted sum of $V_0$ an $V_2$ Legendre radial terms, defined as $V_0 = (V_\Sigma + 2V_\Pi)/3$ and $V_2 = 5(V_\Sigma - V_\Pi)/3$ has been properly adopted for such a description. We can also formulate the related inverse relations as $V_\Sigma = V_0 + 2/5V_2$ and $V_\Pi = V_0 - 1/5V_2$. By this procedure, the $V_0$ term accounts for the spherical average of the interaction component, while all anisotropic contributions, which derive from quantized spatial orientations of the valence orbitals of the open shell atom within the interacting collisional complex, are evaluated by the $V_2$ anisotropic term employment. When we consider the case of collisions involving $^2P_J$ (or $^3P_J$) open shell atoms, as is the case of $Ne^+$ (or $Ne^*$) and $Kr^+$, $Xe^+$ ions with a inverted sequence of spin-orbit sublevels, it is possible to formulate the effective adiabatic potential energy curves $V_{|J,\Omega>}$ (where $\Omega$ is the quantum number fixing the absolute projection of $J$ along R) by the following Eqs. (7)–(9):

$$V_{|3/2,3/2>} = V_0 - \frac{1}{5} V_2 \tag{7}$$

$$V_{|3/2,1/2>} = V_0 + \frac{1}{10} V_2 + \frac{1}{2}\Delta - \frac{1}{2}\left(\frac{9}{25}V_2^2 + \Delta^2 - \frac{2}{5}V_2\Delta\right)^{1/2} \tag{8}$$

$$V_{|1/2,1/2>} = V_0 + \frac{1}{10} V_2 + \frac{1}{2}\Delta + \frac{1}{2}\left(\frac{9}{25}V_2^2 + \Delta^2 - \frac{2}{5}V_2\Delta\right)^{1/2} \tag{9}$$

In Eqs. (8) and (9) above, the $\Delta$ parameter represents the energy splitting between $J = 1/2$ and $J = 3/2$ atomic sublevels. In the case of $Ne^+$, we have $\Delta = 0.097$ eV; when we consider $Kr^+$, we have $\Delta = 0.665$ eV; and for $Xe^+$, results $\Delta = 1.306$ eV. Furthermore, in all three Eqs. (7)–(9) the $V_0$ term (both in the entrance and exit channel cases) has been formulated adopting the ILJ function defined by Eqs. (3)–(5) above. On the other hand, the use of an exponential decreasing function (determined by a pre-exponential factor A, and by a proper $\alpha$ exponent) allowed us to obtain a reliable representation of the $V_2$ term. All the used parameters for the accurate potential energy description of the two $Ne^*$-Kr and $Ne^*$-Xe autoionizing systems are given in Table 2 below.

**Table 2.** The Potential parameters of the real part of the formulated Optical Potential Model, V (see Eq. (2) and text) adopted in the description of the two investigated $Ne^*$-Kr and $Ne^*$-Xe autoionizing systems.

| System | Isotropic component | | | | | Anisotropic component | |
|--------|---------------------|--------------|------|-------------|------------|----------------------|------------------|
|        | $\varepsilon$ (meV) | $R_m$ (Å) | $\beta$ | $R_0$ (Å) | $d$ (Å) | A (meV) | $\alpha$ (Å$^{-1}$) |
| $Ne^*$-Kr | 9.0 | 5.18 | 6.7 | 3.85 | 0.55 | | |
| $Ne^+$-Kr | 209.0 | 2.86 | 8.0 | | | $1.674 \times 10^7$ | 4.32 |
| Ne-Kr$^+$ | 33.7 | 3.08 | 9.0 | | | | |
| $Ne^*$-Xe | 13.8 | 5.22 | 6.7 | 3.85 | 0.55 | | |
| $Ne^+$-Xe | 268.6 | 3.02 | 8.0 | | | $2.511 \times 10^7$ | 4.32 |
| Ne-Xe$^+$ | 28.4 | 3.27 | 8.0 | | | | |

It has to be noted that in the $Ne^*$-Rg (where Rg = Kr and Xe) autoionizing collisional systems, all involved potential energy curves are affected by a bond stabilization by Charge Transfer $V_x$, whose strength is depending by the coupling of the configuration interaction between quantum states having the same symmetry and differing for one electron exchange. This is a consequence of the fact that internal quantum states in both (Ne-Kr)$^+$ and (Ne-Xe)$^+$ ionic adducts should be the same of noble gas-halide systems. Furthermore, it has been also established [53, 54] that the term $V_2$ for such systems must be fixed equal to $\frac{5}{2} V_x$. Consequently, it happens that $V_2 < 0$, for the lower Ne-Kr$^+$ and Ne-Xe$^+$ quantum states, whereas $V_2 > 0$ for the upper Ne$^+$-Kr, and Ne$^+$-Xe states. This status is due to *bonding and antibonding* effects which appears between states of the same symmetry, even in the perturbation limit. Besides, such a kind of interaction potential analytical expression leads to a diverse correlation between atomic states, which represent the collisional system at a long range of internuclear separation distances R, where $|V_2| \ll \Delta$, and molecular states of the same system arising at short R range, where $|V_2| \gg \Delta$. Furthermore, it has been also pointed out that both $\Sigma$ and $\Pi$ characters of implicated potential energy curves $V_{|J,\Omega>}$ at all R values, can be formulated by the following Eqs. (10)–(12) [55, 56]:

$$V_{|3/2,1/2>} = cos^2\alpha V_\Sigma + sin^2\alpha V_\Pi \tag{10}$$

$$V_{|1/2,1/2>} = sin^2\alpha V_\Sigma + cos^2\alpha V_\Pi \tag{11}$$

where

$$cos^2\alpha = \frac{1}{2} + \frac{\left(1 - \frac{9V_2}{5\Delta}\right)}{4\sqrt{2}\sqrt{1 + \left[\left(\frac{1 - \frac{9V_2}{5\Delta}}{2\sqrt{2}}\right)\right]^2}} \tag{12}$$

Such equations are in agreement with the following asymptotic conditions: (i) at short R internuclear distances, all potential energy curves should account for quantum states having a pure $\Sigma$ or $\Pi$ character; (ii) at large R distances, where is prevailing the spin-orbit coupling, a mixing of the two characters occurs. Furthermore, it has to be noted that the different behavior of Ne$^+$-Kr and Ne$^+$-Xe with respect to Ne-Kr$^+$ and Ne-Xe$^+$, respectively, results from the opposite sign of $V_2$ potential term and from the different role played by the spin-orbit mixing, fixed by different $\Delta$ values. Since the character of $V_{|3/2,3/2>}$ term shows a pure $\Pi$ character at all internuclear distances R, the behavior of its related curves is not discussed in detail. It must be considered that has been already proved [57] that non adiabatic effects (which are promoted by changes in the electronic angular coupling schemes describing the transition from atom-atom to molecular states) play their crucial role with the highest probability at a R distance where $|V_2|$ is comparable with $\Delta$.

In the data analysis of PIES spectra recorded as a function of the collision energy for the two autoionizing Ne$^*$-Kr and Ne$^*$-Xe systems, already published [35, 36], it has been assumed that the population of the Ne$^*$ reagent atoms in their $^3P_2$ fine spin-orbit level is 5 times higher than $^3P_0$ (see also next section). Furthermore, we defined as x the $\Sigma$ character degree in the entrance channels, while in the exit ones it is indicated as y, and consequently the $\Pi$ character degree of each state has indirectly obtained from the $\Sigma$ one. After that, we determined the $A_{\Pi-\Pi}/A_{\Sigma-\Sigma}$ and $A_{\Pi-\Sigma}/A_{\Sigma-\Pi}$ ratios adopted to fix the relative role of the two proposed microscopic mechanisms of investigated autoionization reactions in terms of adiabatic and non-adiabatic effects. These data have been recently published [35, 36], has been fixed to the same value of $f = 0.2$, following the proper suggestion by Krauss [58]. All such assumptions drove us to the formulation of eight coefficients, expressed by Eqs. (13)–(20) below, which account for both the character of symmetry and the degeneracy of all allowed quantum states, as well as for the value of $f$. Their analytical definition is the following:

$$A = [(1 - x)y + f(1 + x)(2 - y)] \tag{13}$$

$$B = [xy + f(1 - x)(2 - y)] \tag{14}$$

$$C = [(1 - x)(2 - y) + f(1 + x)y] \tag{15}$$

$$D = [x(2 - y) + f(1 - x)y] \tag{16}$$

$$E = [x(1 - y) + f(1 - x)y] \tag{17}$$

$$F = [xy + f(1 - x)(1 - y)] \tag{18}$$

$$G = [(1 - x)(1 - y) + f(1 + x)y] \tag{19}$$

$$H = [(1 - x)y + f(1 + x)(1 - y)] \tag{20}$$

A, B, C, D, E, F, G, and H coefficients enable us to quantify the relative height $H_i$ of the peaks in the PIES, measured in $Ne^*$-Kr and $Ne^*$-Xe autoionizing collisions at the same collision energy for each channel $i = a, b, c$ respect to the reference one, that in the present cases corresponds to the $^3P_0$-$^2P_{3/2}$ reactive channel, with the relative value of $A_{\Sigma-\Sigma}$ and $A_{\Sigma-\Pi}$ probability terms (see next section). In particular, the performed analysis has been done adopting the following Eq. (21):

$$A_{\Sigma-\Pi} = \frac{H_a - \frac{5}{2}\frac{A}{B}}{\frac{1}{2}\{-\frac{DA}{B} + C\}} \quad \text{and} \quad A_{\Sigma-\Sigma} = \frac{1 - \frac{1}{5}DA_{\Sigma-\Pi}}{\frac{1}{5}B} \tag{21}$$

where $H_a$ represents the relative height of the $^3P_2$-$^2P_{3/2}$ PIES peak. In a consistent way, the relative heights of other $Ne^*$-Kr and $Ne^*$-Xe PIES peaks have been formulated by Eq. (22) below:

$$H_b = (A_{\Sigma-\Sigma}E + A_{\Sigma-\Pi}F)\frac{1}{5} \quad \text{and} \quad H_c = (A_{\Sigma-\Sigma}G + A_{\Sigma-\Pi}H)\frac{1}{2} \tag{22}$$

where $b$ and $c$ are related to the $^3P_0$-$^2P_{1/2}$ and $^3P_2$-$^2P_{1/2}$ reactive channels, respectively.

Different collision energies, representative of low, intermediate and high values in the ranges probed by the experiments, have been investigated in detail reproducing and fully describing in a consistent way the obtained experimental results for both studied $Ne^*$-Kr and $Ne^*$-Xe autoionizing atom-atom systems, as it is summarized in next section. This demonstrated that the proposed analytical formulation of the Optical Potential Model proposed in this paper, and discussed in detail above, is a new and original theoretical approach to give a reliable general description of the interaction between the autoionizing collisional partners in Penning ionization reactions. The reader interested to a complete description of the analysis applied to PIES spectra recorded in $Ne^*$-Kr and $Ne^*$-Xe experiments, and based on the potential energy formulation here presented, can refer to two recent publications by our group [35, 36]. In next section, only a brief description of such an analysis is given just to provide, for completeness of exposition, some proof of the reliability of the analytical method used to describe the interaction in collisional autoionization processes.

# 4    The $Ne^*$-Kr and $Ne^*$-Xe PIES Spectra

As already mentioned, recent PIES experiments performed for both $Ne^*$-Kr and $Ne^*$-Xe autoionizing systems [35, 36, 54] are consistent each other and confirm the suitability of the original methodology in the formulation of the Optical Potential Model of Eq. (2), fully described in detail in Sect. 3. In this section we recall only the main steps of the adopted methodology used in the analysis of PIES spectra, as an example of the reliability of our proposed theoretical model, whose complete analytical formulation has been given in Sect. 3. The interested reader to a complete overview of recent applications of our theoretical approach in modeling the interaction potential for Penning ionization can found details in the literature [35, 36].

The recorded PIES spectra in $Ne^*$-Kr and $Ne^*$-Xe as a function of the collision energy, and used to test the reliability of the analytical potential energy formulation here presented, are shown in Fig. 2. They demonstrate that electron spectra are composed by four contributions arising from four different channels associated with the two different spin-orbit states of the $Ne^*(^3P_{2,0})$ reactant and to the two spin-orbit states of $Kr^+$ and $Xe^+$ ($^2P_{3/2,1/2}$) products (see panels reported in Fig. 2).

In order to obtain the relative probability of the four channels, we have fitted the $Ne^*$-Kr PIES at the lowest investigated collision energy (where the recorded signal to noise ratio was the best, minimizing the experimental error [35, 59]) using four Gaussian functions, whose general analytical expression is the following:

$$y(x) = H exp^{\left(\frac{B-x}{C}\right)^2} \tag{23}$$

By imposing to the four used Gaussian functions the same width (expressed by the coefficient C) and the same relative peak position (i.e. the B change, defined according to the spin-orbit separation of $Ne^*$) we carried out the fitting of PIES spectra recorded at

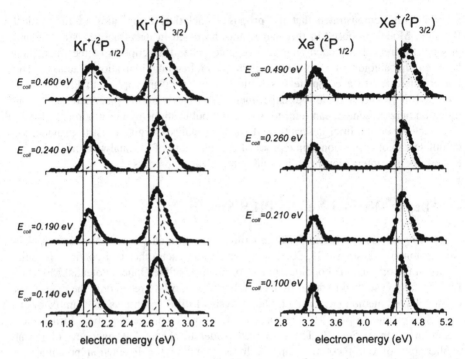

**Fig. 2.** The PIES spectra for the ionization of Kr and Xe by Ne* atoms measured as a function of the collision energy and for resolution conditions of about 80 meV. Their comparison emphasizes the dependence of the relative role of the four channels (see text), obtained by the variation of the relative height of the four Gaussian functions, and of the peak positions with the collision energy.

each investigated collision energy. By such a procedure we were able to refer the relative probability of the four different reactive channels to the relative height of the four PIES peaks, obtainable from the ratio of H parameter values. Although the Gaussian functions are symmetric, their combination supplied an asymmetric frame of the simulated global peak. This accounted for the shoulders observed in the right hand of each peak position (see Fig. 2). The parameters of the Gaussian functions used in the best-fitting procedure have been reported in Table 3. As a deeper test and further generalization of such a methodology, the same group of four Gaussian functions has been employed in the description of all PIES reported in Fig. 2, and recorded at higher collision energies: only their width has been adjusted (increased) to take into account for the reduced electron energy resolution conditions used in such measurements at higher collision energies (see the variation of the C parameter in Table 3 below).

**Table 3.** The parameters of Gaussian functions $f(x) = H exp\left[\left(\frac{B-x}{C}\right)^2\right]$ exploited for describing the Penning ionization electron energy spectra of the state to state ionization reactions, $Ne^*(^3P_{Ji}) + Kr(^1S_0) \rightarrow Ne(^1S_0) + Kr^+(^2P_{Jf}) + e^-$ (see text).

| Collision energy (eV) | $J_i \rightarrow J_f$ transition | $H$ (arb. units) | $B$ (eV) | $C$ (eV) | $H_{J_i \rightarrow J_f}/H_{0 \rightarrow 3/2}$ |
|---|---|---|---|---|---|
| 0.140 | $2 \rightarrow 1/2$ | 0.500 | 2.020 | 0.092 | 1.43 |
|  | $0 \rightarrow 1/2$ | 0.155 | 2.120 | 0.092 | 0.44 |
|  | $2 \rightarrow 3/2$ | 0.780 | 2.685 | 0.092 | 2.23 |
|  | $0 \rightarrow 3/2$ | 0.350 | 2.785 | 0.092 | 1.00 |
| 0.190 | $2 \rightarrow 1/2$ | 0.450 | 2.020 | 0.088 | 1.27 |
|  | $0 \rightarrow 1/2$ | 0.170 | 2.120 | 0.088 | 0.48 |
|  | $2 \rightarrow 3/2$ | 0.750 | 2.675 | 0.088 | 2.11 |
|  | $0 \rightarrow 3/2$ | 0.355 | 2.775 | 0.088 | 1.00 |
| 0.240 | $2 \rightarrow 1/2$ | 0.420 | 2.035 | 0.110 | 1.17 |
|  | $0 \rightarrow 1/2$ | 0.190 | 2.135 | 0.110 | 0.53 |
|  | $2 \rightarrow 3/2$ | 0.730 | 2.705 | 0.110 | 2.03 |
|  | $0 \rightarrow 3/2$ | 0.360 | 2.805 | 0.110 | 1.00 |
| 0.460 | $2 \rightarrow 1/2$ | 0.410 | 2.055 | 0.139 | 1.13 |
|  | $0 \rightarrow 1/2$ | 0.180 | 2.155 | 0.139 | 0.50 |
|  | $2 \rightarrow 3/2$ | 0.670 | 2.720 | 0.139 | 1.85 |
|  | $0 \rightarrow 3/2$ | 0.362 | 2.820 | 0.139 | 1.00 |

In this latter case the shoulders in the PIES peaks are less evident. Furthermore, the relative probability of the four state to state $Ne^*$-Kr and $Ne^*$-Xe reactions where determined from the data analysis, adopting the same methodology presented above to reproduce measured PIES peaks with their asymmetry. The left panel of Fig. 2 shows the PIES measured for $Ne^*$-Kr at different collision energies, and with their fit performed by the use of four Gaussian functions, always imposing the same boundary conditions as stressed above. As an example, the related used fit parameters only for the case of $Ne^*$-Kr autoionizing collisions are reported in Table 3. As indicated above, an internally consistent procedure applied at each collision energy allowed to obtain the ratio of the H parameter values of Table 3, providing the relative probability of the four reactive channels. In particular, in our procedure the $^3P_0$-$^2P_{3/2}$ reactive channel was chosen as the reference one, and values of the relative probability for the other channels, given in Table 3, have been so extracted. Their dependence on the collision energy has been determined also in the case of $Ne^*$-Xe system (whose PIES spectra are shown in the right panel of Fig. 2) adopting the same procedure described for $Ne^*$-Kr, and demonstrating the existence of an internally consistent behavior between the two autoionizing systems. The reader can found details on both the used best-fitting procedure and the related fit parameters also for the case of $Ne^*$-Xe system in recent publications [35, 36]. By this adopted model the dependence of the peak height ratio on the collision energy allowed us to extract information on the relative role of the two mechanisms for Penning ionization reactions that we have recently classified as

**Table 4.** Two different sequences of the $\Sigma$ character, whose values, defined as x in the entrance channels and y in the exit channels. The $\Pi$ character of each state has indirectly obtained from the $\Sigma$ one. The error in the $P_2/P_0$ ratio has been estimated by the uncertainty in the measured peak height.

| Energy range | $P_2/P_0$ ratio | Sequence 1 | | Sequence 2 | |
|---|---|---|---|---|---|
| | | x | y | x | y |
| High | 1.85 ± 0.09 | 0.85 | 0.73 | 0.90 | 0.74 |
| Intermediate | 2.12 ± 0.11 | 0.75 | 0.70 | 0.80 | 0.71 |
| Low | 2.82 ± 0.15 | 0.60 | 0.67 | 0.60 | 0.67 |

"indirect" or "direct" mechanism in terms of adiabatic and non-adiabatic effects, respectively [35]. The relative role of such two mechanisms is defined as $A_{\Sigma\text{-}\Pi}/A_{\Sigma\text{-}\Sigma}$ ratio, by taking into account: (i) the radial dependence of both $\Sigma$ and $\Pi$ characters, associated to the entrance and exit channels; (ii) the relative population $^3P_0/^3P_2$ of Ne$^*$ amounting to a 1/5 ratio, according to a statistical distribution of fine structure sublevels. As already mentioned above, all the explicit equations used to achieve this purpose are those already reported and discussed in Sect. 3 (see, in particular, Eqs. (21) and (22)) and constitute a new and original theoretical method for modeling the Optical Potential (see Eq. (2)) in a general and analytical form. In our procedure, we have also applied the same methodology assuming two different sequences of $\Sigma$ and $\Pi$ character (see Table 4), having all values confined within the estimated uncertainty band, in order to characterize the relative role of the two adiabatic and non-adiabatic mechanisms (see above) with its collision energy dependence.

# 5    Conclusions

In this paper, we presented a new analytical formulation for the potential energy describing the interaction in typical atom-atom autoionizing systems, as Ne$^*$-Kr and Ne$^*$-Xe. Obtained results refer to a statistical/random orientation of the open shell ionic core of Ne$^*$($^3P_{2,0}$) and in the two investigated cases (the Ne$^*$-Kr and Ne$^*$-Xe autoionizing collisions) we were able to characterize the dependence on the collision energy of the PIES spectra and of the relative experimental branching ratio between probabilities of spin-orbit resolved elementary processes already published.

This new and original methodology can be applied also to Penning ionization processes involving molecular targets already studied experimentally in our laboratory [60, 61], and in principle is able to point out the basic role of electronic rearrangements inside the transition state of various types of reactions at thermal [62–65] and subthermal collision energies which are of interest also in astrochemical environments [66–69], being a much more arduous problem in order to be completely characterized.

**Acknowledgments.** This work is dedicated to our colleague and friend Jaime De Andres whose memory and love for science will inspire our future research. Financial support from MIUR, "Ministero dell'Istruzione, dell'Università e della Ricerca", PRIN 2015 (STARS in the CAOS-Simulation Tools for Astrochemical Reactivity and Spectroscopy in the Cyberinfrastructure for Astrochemical Organic Species, 2015F59J3R). Support from Italian MIUR and University of Perugia (Italy) is acknowledged within the program "Dipartimenti di Eccellenza 2018-2022".

# References

1. Benz, A., Morgner, H.: Mol. Phys. **57**, 319–336 (1986)
2. Falcinelli, S., Bartocci, A., Cavalli, S., Pirani, F., Vecchiocattivi, F.: Chem. Eur. J. **22**(2), 764–771 (2016)
3. Falcinelli, S., et al.: Modeling the intermolecular interactions and characterization of the dynamics of collisional autoionization processes. In: Murgante, B., et al. (eds.) ICCSA 2013. LNCS, vol. 7971, pp. 69–83. Springer, Heidelberg (2013). https://doi.org/10.1007/978-3-642-39637-3_6
4. Falcinelli, S., Capriccioli, A., Pirani, F., Vecchiocattivi, F., Stranges, S., Martì, C., et al.: Fuel **209**, 802–811 (2017)
5. Falcinelli, S., Rosi, M., Cavalli, S., Pirani, F., Vecchiocattivi, F.: Chem. Eur. J. **22**(35), 12518–12526 (2016)
6. Cavallotti, C., Leonori, F., Balucani, N., Nevrly, V., Bergeat, A., et al.: J. Phys. Chem. Lett. **5**, 4213–4218 (2014)
7. Leonori, F., Balucani, N., Nevrly, V., Bergeat, A., et al.: J. Phys. Chem. C **119**(26), 14632–14652 (2015)
8. Leonori, F., Petrucci, R., Balucani, N., Casavecchia, P., Rosi, M., Berteloite, C., et al.: Phys. Chem. Chem. Phis. **11**, 4701–4706 (2009)
9. Leonori, F., Petrucci, R., Balucani, N., Hickson, K.M., Hamberg, M., Geppert, W.D., et al.: J. Phys. Chem. A **113**, 4330–4339 (2009)
10. Rosi, M., Falcinelli, S., Balucani, N., Casavecchia, P., Leonori, F., Skouteris, D.: Theoretical study of reactions relevant for atmospheric models of titan: interaction of excited nitrogen atoms with small hydrocarbons. In: Murgante, B., et al. (eds.) ICCSA 2012. LNCS, vol. 7333, pp. 331–344. Springer, Heidelberg (2012). https://doi.org/10.1007/978-3-642-31125-3_26
11. Alagia, M., et al.: Chem. Phys. Lett. **432**, 398–402 (2006)
12. Alagia, M., et al.: J. Phys. Chem. A **113**, 14755–14759 (2009)
13. Alagia, M., et al.: Phys. Chem. Chem. Phys. **12**, 5389–5395 (2010)
14. Falcinelli, S., Pirani, F., Alagia, M., Schio, L., Richter, R., et al.: Chem. Phys. Lett. **666**, 1–6 (2016)
15. Falcinelli, S., Pirani, F., Vecchiocattivi, F.: Atmosphere **6**(3), 299–317 (2015)
16. Biondini, F., Brunetti, B.G., Candori, P., De Angelis, F., et al.: J. Chem. Phys. **122**(16), 164307 (2005)
17. Biondini, F., Brunetti, B.G., Candori, P., De Angelis, F., et al.: J. Chem. Phys. **122**(16), 164308 (2005)
18. Nicolaides, C.A.: Chem. Phys. Lett. **161**(6), 547–553 (1989)
19. Falcinelli, S., Fernandez-Alonso, F., Kalogerakis, K., Zare, R.N.: Mol. Phys. **88**(3), 663–672 (1996)
20. Tosi, P., Correale, R., Lu, W., Falcinelli, S., Bassi, D.: Phys. Rev. Lett. **82**(2), 450–452 (1999)

21. Thissen, R., Witasse, O., Dutuit, O., Wedlund, C.S., et al.: Phys. Chem. Chem. Phys. **13**, 18264–18287 (2011)
22. Alagia, M., Balucani, N., Candori, P., Falcinelli, S., Richter, R., et al.: Rendiconti Lincei Scienze Fisiche e Naturali **24**, 53–65 (2013)
23. Falcinelli, S., Rosi, M., Candori, P., Farrar, J.M., Vecchiocattivi, F., et al.: Planet. Space Sci. **99**, 149–157 (2014)
24. Falcinelli, S.: Acta Phys. Pol., A **131**(1), 112–116 (2017)
25. Ben Arfa, M., Lescop, B., Cherid, M., Brunetti, B., Candori, P., et al.: Chem. Phys. Lett. **308**, 71–77 (1999)
26. Brunetti, B.G., Candori, P., Ferramosche, R., Falcinelli, S., et al.: Chem. Phys. Lett. **294**, 584–592 (1998)
27. Pei, L., Carrascosa, E., Yang, N., Falcinelli, S., Farrar, J.M.: J. Phys. Chem. Lett. **6**(9), 1684–1689 (2015)
28. Falcinelli, S.: AIP Conference Proceedings, vol. 2075, p. 050003 (2019)
29. Bettoni, M., Candori, P., Falcinelli, S., Marmottini, F., Meniconi, S., Rol, C., Sebastiani, G. V.: J. Photochem. Photobiol., A **268**, 1–6 (2013)
30. Alagia, M., Candori, P., Falcinelli, S., Pirani, F., et al.: Phys. Chem. Chem. Phys. **13**(18), 8245–8250 (2011)
31. Alagia, M., Candori, P., Falcinelli, S., Lavollée, M., et al.: J. Chem. Phys. **126**(20), 201101 (2007)
32. Hotop, H., Illenberger, E., Morgner, H., Niehaus, A.: Chem. Phys. Lett. **10**(5), 493–497 (1971)
33. Brunetti, B.G., Candori, P., Cappelletti, D., Falcinelli, S., et al.: Chem. Phys. Lett. **539–540**, 19–23 (2012)
34. Bethe, H.A.: Phys. Rev. **57**, 1125–1144 (1940)
35. Falcinelli, S., Vecchiocattivi, F., Pirani, F.: Phys. Rev. Lett. **121**(16), 163403 (2018)
36. Falcinelli, S., Vecchiocattivi, F., Pirani, F.: J. Chem. Phys. **150**(4), 044305 (2019)
37. Balucani, N., Bartocci, A., Brunetti, B., Candori, P., et al.: Chem. Phys. Lett. **546**, 34–39 (2012)
38. Miller, W.H., Morgner, H.: J. Chem. Phys. **67**, 4923–4930 (1977)
39. Brunetti, B., Candori, P., Falcinelli, S., Pirani, F., Vecchiocattivi, F.: J. Chem. Phys. **139**(16), 164305 (2013)
40. Falcinelli, S., Candori, P., Pirani, F., Vecchiocattivi, F.: Phys. Chem. Chem. Phys. **19**(10), 6933–6944 (2017)
41. Alagia, M., Brunetti, B.G., Candori, P., Falcinelli, S., et al.: J. Chem. Phys. **120**(15), 6980–6984 (2004)
42. Alagia, M., Biondini, F., Brunetti, B.G., Candori, P., et al.: J. Chem. Phys. **121**(21), 10508–10512 (2004)
43. Candori, P., Falcinelli, S., Pirani, F., Tarantelli, F., Vecchiocattivi, F.: Chem. Phys. Lett. **436**, 322–326 (2007)
44. Lombardi, A., Lago, N.F., Laganà, A., Pirani, F., Falcinelli, S.: A bond-bond portable approach to intermolecular interactions: simulations for N-methylacetamide and carbon dioxide dimers. In: Murgante, B., et al. (eds.) ICCSA 2012. LNCS, vol. 7333, pp. 387–400. Springer, Heidelberg (2012). https://doi.org/10.1007/978-3-642-31125-3_30
45. Cappelletti, D., Bartocci, A., Grandinetti, F., Falcinelli, S., et al.: Chem. Eur. J. **21**(16), 6234–6240 (2015)
46. Alagia, M., Brunetti, B.G., Candori, P., Falcinelli, S., et al.: J. Chem. Phys. **120**(15), 6985–6991 (2004)
47. Alagia, M., et al.: J. Chem. Phys. **136**, 204302 (2012)

48. Teixidor, M.M., Pirani, F., Candori, P., Falcinelli, S., Vecchiocattivi, F.: Chem. Phys. Lett. **379**, 139–146 (2003)
49. Alagia, M., Brunetti, B.G., Candori, P., et al.: J. Chem. Phys. **124**(20), 204318 (2006)
50. Alagia, M., Candori, P., Falcinelli, S., Mundim, K.C., Mundim, M.S.P., Pirani, F., et al.: Chem. Phys. **398**, 134–141 (2012)
51. Cappelletti, D., Candori, P., Falcinelli, S., Albertì, M., Pirani, F.: Chem. Phys. Lett. **545**, 14–20 (2012)
52. Pirani, F., Maciel, G.S., Cappelletti, D., Aquilanti, V.: Int. Rev. Phys. Chem. **25**, 165–199 (2006)
53. Aquilanti, V., Luzzatti, E., Pirani, F., Volpi, G.G.: J. Chem. Phys. **89**(10), 6165–6175 (1988)
54. Aquilanti, V., Liuti, G., Pirani, F., Vecchiocattivi, F.: J. Chem. Soc., Faraday Trans. **85**(8), 955–964 (1989)
55. Tosi, P., et al.: J. Chem. Phys. **99**(2), 985–1003 (1993)
56. Bartocci, A., Belpassi, L., Cappelletti, D., Falcinelli, S., et al.: J. Chem. Phys. **142**(18), 184304 (2015)
57. Aquilanti, V., Cappelletti, D., Lorent, V., Pirani, F.: J. Phys. Chem. **97**, 2063–2071 (1993)
58. Krauss, M.: J. Chem. Phys. **67**(4), 1712–1719 (1977)
59. Brunetti, B., Candori, P., Falcinelli, S., Lescop, B., et al.: Eur. Phys. J. D **38**, 21–27 (2006)
60. Brunetti, B., Candori, P., De Andres, J., Pirani, F., Rosi, M., et al.: J. Phys. Chem. A **101**(41), 7505–7512 (1997)
61. Alagia, M., Boustimi, M., Brunetti, B.G., Candori, P., et al.: J. Chem. Phys. **117**(3), 1098–1102 (2002)
62. Alagia, M., Candori, P., Falcinelli, S., Mundim, M.S.P., Pirani, F., et al.: J. Chem. Phys. **135**(14), 144304 (2011)
63. Alagia, M., Bodo, E., Decleva, P., Falcinelli, S., et al.: Phys. Chem. Chem. Phys. **15**(4), 1310–1318 (2013)
64. Troiani, A., Rosi, M., Garzoli, S., Salvitti, C., de Petris, G.: Chem. Eur. J. **23**, 11752–11756 (2017)
65. Pirani, F., et al.: Angew. Chem. Int. Ed. **58**(13), 4195–4199 (2019)
66. Gordon, S.D.S., Omiste, J.J., Zou, J., Tanteri, S., Brumer, P., Osterwalder, A.: Nat. Chem. **10**, 1190–1195 (2018)
67. Gordon, S.D.S., Zou, J., Tanteri, S., Jankunas, J., Osterwalder, A.: Phys. Rev. Lett. **119**, 053001 (2017)
68. Skouteris, D., Balucani, N., Faginas-Lago, N., et al.: A&A **584**, A76 (2015)
69. Skouteris, D., Balucani, N., Ceccarelli, C., Faginas Lago, N., et al.: MNRAS **482**, 3567–3575 (2019)

# Electronic Structure and Kinetics Calculations for the Si+SH Reaction, a Possible Route of SiS Formation in Star-Forming Regions

Marzio Rosi[1,2(✉)], Dimitrios Skouteris[3,4], Nadia Balucani[5,6,7],
Luca Mancini[5], Noelia Faginas Lago[5], Linda Podio[6],
Claudio Codella[6], Bertrand Lefloch[7], and Cecilia Ceccarelli[7]

[1] Dipartimento di Ingegneria Civile e Ambientale,
Università degli Studi di Perugia, 06125 Perugia, Italy
marzio.rosi@unipg.it
[2] CNR-ISTM, 06123 Perugia, Italy
[3] Scuola Normale Superiore, 56126 Pisa, Italy
dimitrios.skouteris@sns.it
[4] Master-Up, Strada Vicinale Sperandio 15, 06125 Perugia, Italy
d.skouteris@master-up.it
[5] Dipartimento di Chimica, Biologia e Biotecnologie,
Università degli Studi di Perugia, 06123 Perugia, Italy
{nadia.balucani,noelia.faginaslago}@unipg.it,
manciniluca00@gmail.com
[6] INAF, Osservatorio Astrofisico di Arcetri, 50125 Florence, Italy
{lpodio,codella}@arcetri.inaf.it
[7] Université Grenoble Alpes, IPAG, 38000 Grenoble, France
{bertrand.lefloch,
cecilia.ceccarelli}@univ-grenoble-alpes.fr

**Abstract.** The reaction between atomic silicon and the mercapto radical has been computationally investigated by means of electronic structure and kinetics calculations to establish its possible role in the formation of interstellar SiS. According to our kinetics estimates based on the electronic structure calculations of the Si+SH potential energy surface, the reaction is very fast reaching the gas-kinetics limit. Therefore, the title reaction is an efficient formation route of interstellar SiS provided that silicon atoms and mercapto radicals are present. Implications for the observation of an anomalously high abundance of SiS in the shocked region around a Sun-like protostar (L1157-B1) are also presented.

**Keywords:** Electronic structure calculations · Kinetics calculations · Astrochemistry · Silicon chemistry

## 1 Introduction

Since its first detection in 1975 by Morris et al. [1] towards the molecular envelope of the carbon-rich AGB star IRC+ 10216, silicon monosulfide (SiS) has been the object of sporadic detections, mostly in circumstellar envelopes around evolved stars [2, 3]. In

© Springer Nature Switzerland AG 2019
S. Misra et al. (Eds.): ICCSA 2019, LNCS 11621, pp. 306–315, 2019.
https://doi.org/10.1007/978-3-030-24302-9_22

addition to that, SiS detection has been achieved towards high mass star-forming regions with shocks (such as Sgr B2 and Orion KL [4–8]) and, more recently, in a shocked region, L1157-B1, around a low mass protostar [9]. The elements silicon and sulfur are relatively abundant in the universe with an atomic fraction of 30 and 16 ppm, respectively, and several species holding either a Si or an S atom have been detected so far [10]. Both Si and S are also expected to be depleted from the gas-phase on interstellar dust grains. For instance, most of interstellar silicon is retained in the silicates of interstellar dust particles and can only return to the gas phase after violent events, such as high intensity shocks that are able to sputter the refractory core of dust grains and release gaseous silicon. The most abundant interstellar silicon compound in the gas-phase is SiO, while SiS is much less abundant. In the case of L1157-B1, a shocked region driven by a fast jet ejected from a Sun-like protostar, a surprisingly high abundance of SiS has been observed in a delimited region around the protostar [9]. In that specific region, the relative abundance of SiS with respect to SiO is of the order of 0.04, that is much higher than the typical values (*ca.* $5 \times 10^{-3}$) for regions where SiS has been observed. The reasons for such a peculiar ratio remains a mistery and only a thourough comprehension of both silicon and sulphur interstellar chemistry can help us to understand the cause of this anomaly.

Until recently, very little was known about the SiS formation mechanisms. In an attempt to explain the L1157-B1 anomaly, recent theoretical work has been devoted to characterize the combined silicon/sulphur chemistry [11–13]. For instance, some of the present authors have characterized the potential energy surface of the reactions SiH+S and SiH+S$_2$ [11]. In addition, for the reaction H+SiS$_2$ we have performed kinetics calculations based on the capture theory and Rice-Ramsperger-Kassel-Marcus calculations [12]. In addition, Zanchet et al. [13] have suggested that the reactions Si+SO and Si+SO$_2$ can be responsible for SiS formation in the ouflows of star-forming regions like Sgr B2, Orion KL, and L1157-B1.

In this contribution we add another piece to the puzzle by reporting on a theoretical characterization of the potential energy surface (PES) and kinetics properties of the reaction Si+SH. As already mentioned, atomic silicon can be formed by the sputtering of the refractory silicates core in shocked regions like those of interest here. In addition, H$_2$S (the parent species of the SH radical) has been observed in L1157-B1 [14]. H$_2$S is easily converted into the SH radicals by chemical reactions or photodissociation [15]. In other words, Si and HS are plausible precursors of SiS if we can prove that the title reaction is efficient.

## 2  Computational Details

The Potential Energy Surface (PES) of the Si+SH was calculated employing a computational strategy which has been utilized with success in the past [16–19]. In this scheme the lowest stationary points, minima and transistion states, were optimized at the B3LYP level [20, 21] in conjunction with the aug-cc-pVTZ basis set [22, 23], augmented for S and Si with a tight d finction [24]. This basis set will be denoted aug-cc-pV(T + *d*)Z. At the same level of theory we have computed the harmonic vibrational frequencies in order to check the nature of the stationary points, i.e. minimum if all the frequencies are real, saddle point if there is one, and only one, imaginary frequency. The assignment of the saddle points was performed using intrinsic reaction coordinate (IRC) calculations [25, 26]. The energy of the main stationary points was computed also at the more accurate coupled cluster theory with the inclusion of single and double excitations and a perturbative estimate of connected triples (CCSD(T)) [27–29] using the same basis set aug-cc-pV(T + d)Z. Both the B3LYP and the CCSD(T) energies were corrected to 0 K by adding the zero point energy correction; therefore all the energetic values are enthalpies at 0 K. The accuracy of the employed approach, in particular as far as basis set completeness is concerned, has been recently investigated [30]. For comparison purposes since the systems investigated are relatively small, we reoptimized the geometry of all the stationary points also at the CCSD(T)/aug-cc-pV (T + d)Z level. All calculations were performed using Gaussian 09 [31], while the analysis of the geometries and the vibrational frequencies was performed using Molekel [32, 33]. It is assumed that the reaction takes place on the ground electronic state but, otherwise, all possible paths have been taken into account.

Having determined the characteristics of the stationary points, we have performed kinetics calculations on the calculated PES, as done in previous work by some of the present authors for similar reactive systems [12, 16, 34–37]. Initially, the capture (Langevin) model is used to calculate the rate coefficient for the initial association of Si and SH. The long-range interaction potential (determined as a series of points through quantum calculations) was fitted to a $V(r) = -C/r^6$ equation (the typical interaction equation for two neutral species). Having obtained an association rate constant, we have calculated the corresponding dissociation rate coefficient through the detailed balance principle

$$k_{diss}(E) = k_{ass}(E) \times \rho_{reac}(E)/\rho_{comp}(E)$$

where $k_{ass}(E)$ is the association rate coefficient (as a function of energy), $\rho_{reac}(E)$ is the density of states per unit volume of the associating reactants at energy E and $\rho_{comp}(E)$ is the density of states of the initial complex at energy E. Through this scheme, we have seen that the dissociation rate coefficient is essentially negligible (the large depth of the potential energy well raises the density of states of the complex). From this, we can deduce that the initial association rate coefficient equals the sum of all rate coefficients leading to specific products, i.e. the total reaction rate constant.

The microcanonical reaction rate coefficient for each subsequent unimolecular step is calculated using the Rice-Ramsperger-Kassel-Marcus (RRKM) scheme (see, for instance, [38–42], whereby the rate coefficient is given by the expression

$$k(E) = \frac{N(E)}{h\rho(E)}$$

where $N(E)$ is the number of microstates available in the transition state, $\rho(E)$ is the density of states per unit volume of the reactants and $h$ is Planck's constant. Subsequently, the rate constants are Boltzmann averaged to yield temperature-dependent ones. Tunnelling is taken account of by simulating each transition state by an Eckart barrier of the same energy and imaginary frequency.

# 3   Results

According to the present electronic structure calculations, the addition of the Si atom to the SH radical is a favored, barrierless process leading to the formation of a bound Si-S-H intermediate. The situation is rather similar to that observed in the isovalent reactions Si+OH [43, 44]. The optimized geometries of the stationary points located in the PES of the system Si+SH are reported in Fig. 1, while the energetics of the main processes involved in the Si+SH reaction is shown in Table 1. A schematic representation of the PES of the system Si+SH is presented in Fig. 2, where we have reported also the relative energies computed at B3LYP/aug-cc-pV(T + $d$)Z level and CCSD(T)/aug-cc-pV(T + $d$)Z level (in parentheses) at the B3LYP/aug-cc-pV(T + $d$)Z optimized geometries. When an Si atom approaches a SH radical, there is formation of a SiSH species in a very exothermic process, without any entrance barrier. SiSH, overcoming an energy barrier of almost 15 kcal/mol, can isomerize to the slightly more stable SSiH species or can dissociate into SiS+H, with a barrier which is very close to the endothermicity of the process. This is not surprising since this transition state is very late, showing an S—H distance very long (2.557 Å, see Fig. 1). SSiH can dissociate into SiS+H or S+SiH. Both reactions are endothermic, with an exit energy barrier which is equal to the endothermicity. The products S+SiH, moreover, lie above the reactants. From Fig. 2 and Table 1, we can see that the relative energies computed at B3LYP and CCSD(T) level (with the same geometries) differ by less than 3 kcal/mol. This is an expected result due to the different accuracy of the two methods. Since the investigated systems are relatively small, however, we decided to optimize the geometry of all the stationary points at CCSD(T)/aug-cc-pV(T + $d$)Z level.

**Table 1.** Enthalpy changes (kcal/mol, 0 K) computed at the B3LYP/aug-cc-pV(T + $d$)Z and CCSD(T)/aug-cc-pV(T + $d$)Z levels of theory for selected steps in the Si+SH reaction. Values in parentheses are computed at the optimized CCSD(T) geometries.

|  | $\Delta H_0^0$ | | Barrier height | |
|---|---|---|---|---|
|  | B3LYP | CCSD(T) | B3LYP | CCSD(T) |
| Si ($^3$P) + S ($^3$P) → SiS (($^1\Sigma^+$) | −139.2 | −138.6 (−138.7) | | |
| Si ($^3$P) + SH ($^2\Pi$) → SiSH | −83.2 | −81.8 (−81.7) | | |
| SiSH → SiS(($^1\Sigma^+$) + H ($^2$S) | 26.8 | 24.8 (24.7) | 27.0 | 25.7 (27.0) |
| SiSH → SSiH | −5.0 | −3.6 (−3.7) | 14.4 | 14.9 (14.9) |
| SSiH → SiS ($^1\Sigma^+$) + H ($^2$S) | 31.8 | 28.4 (28.4) | | |
| SSiH → S ($^3$P) + SiH ($^2\Pi$) | 100.7 | 97.7 (97.7) | | |

From Fig. 1 we can notice that there is a very good agreement between the B3LYP and CCSD(T) geometries, with the only exception of the S—H distance in the transition state of the dissociation reaction of SiSH into SiS+H. From Fig. 3, where we have reported the relative energies computed at CCSD(T)/aug-cc-pV(T + $d$)Z level at the geometries optimized at the same level, we can notice that the barrier height for the reaction SiSH → SiS + H is slightly higher than before, confirming that B3LYP sometimes tends to underestimate energy barriers.

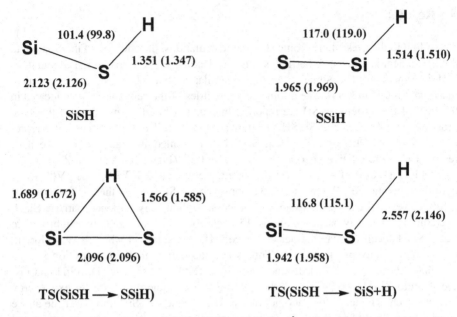

**Fig. 1.** B3LYP/aug-cc-pV(T + d)Z optimized geometries (Å and °) of minima and transition states for the SiSH system. Values in parentheses are optimized at CCSD(T)/aug-cc-pV(T + d)Z level.

The calculated rate coefficient as a function of temperature is shown in Fig. 4. As well visible, the rate coefficient is very high for the whole temperature range explored (from 0 to 500 K). The numerical value increases from $5.3 \times 10^{-10}$ at 10 K to $8.6 \times 10^{-10}$ at 100 K (a temperature typical of shocked regions) reaching a plateau at 300 K of ca. $1.0 \times 10^{-9}$ cm$^3$ s$^{-1}$. The trend of the rate constant with temperature follows the capture rate constants calculated using a Langevin-like model. In particular, the capture rate constant, as a function of energy, reaches a plateau at high energies and this is reflected in the canonical rate constant after Boltzmann averaging.

The two factors that influence the value of the rate constant are the long-range attractive potential of the two reactant molecules and their reduced mass. The long-range potential tail has been fitted to an appropriate inverse power law and it has been found to be singularly high in this case. Moreover, the relatively high reduced mass of the reactants (roughly equal to the mass of the silicon atom) further contributes to enhance the corresponding cross section and rate coefficient.

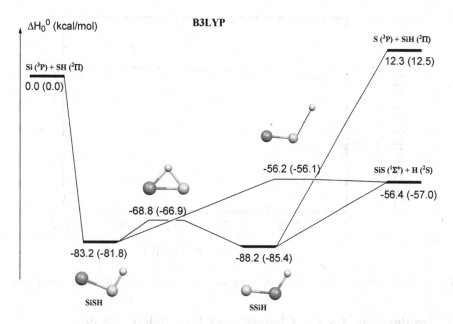

**Fig. 2.** Schematic representation of the Si+SH PES computed at B3LYP/aug-cc-pV(T + *d*)Z. Values in parentheses are CCSD(T)/aug-cc-pV(T + *d*)Z energies computed at the B3LYP optimized geometries.

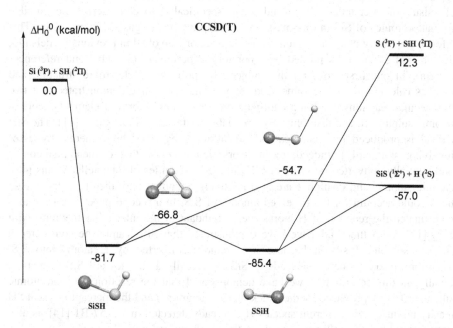

**Fig. 3.** Schematic representation of the Si+SH PES computed at CCSD(T)/aug-cc-pV(T + *d*)Z level.

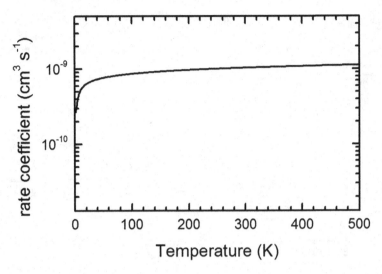

**Fig. 4.** Rate coefficients as a function of temperature for the title reaction (see text for details).

## 4 Implications for the Chemistry of Interstellar Silicon

As anticipated in the Introduction, the theoretical investigation on the reaction Si+SH reported here belongs to a systematic study that we have undertaken to understand the chemistry of interstellar silicon and, more specifically, to characterize the possible formation routes of SiS in low-mass star forming regions in gas-phase processes. This effort is necessary because the ion-molecule reactions invoked in previous models [45, 46] are not efficient, as proved by laboratory experiments (see [10] and references therein). In our first work on this subject, by performing electronic structure and kinetics calculations of the same kind reported here we have demonstrated that two bimolecular reactions involving the SiH radical and simple form of elemental sulphur (atomic sulphur, S, and disulphur, $S_2$) are viable routes of SiS formation [11]. The SiH radical is produced by silane photodissociation or by other high energy processes involving silane [47]. Indeed, recent work demonstrated that elemental silicon is preferentially converted into SiO or $SiH_4$ in the icy mantles of interstellar grains [48]. Atomic sulphur and disulphur are also relatively abundant and, therefore, their reactions could account for the observed amount of SiS. In a second paper, we have also investigated the reaction of H atoms (very abundant in the interstellar medium) with $SiS_2$ [12]. With that study, we have demonstrated that $SiS_2$ cannot be considered a stable reservoir of silicon because it is rapidly converted by H atoms into SiS. Therefore, every process that leads to $SiS_2$ is actually a step toward SiS formation. Finally, in this contribution we have demonstrated that the reaction between atomic silicon (possibly produced by the shock on silicate grains) and the mercapto radical SH (easily produced by its parent species $H_2S$ already detected in L1157-B1 [14]) is also very fast, with rate coefficients reaching the gas kinetics limit.

We plan to use the derived rate coefficients in astrochemical models, as recently done for other cases [34–36, 49–51], to verify whether these processes are at work in the ISM and can account for the observed overabundance of SiS in L1157-B1. Since silicon chemistry is mainly associated with shocked regions where elemental silicon is liberated in the gas phase, if we demonstrate that SiS is totally formed by neutral-neutral gas phase reactions, its presence and distribution in interstellar objects could become a kind of signpost for that type of chemistry being dominant in the above mentioned regions.

**Acknowledgments.** This work has been supported by MIUR "PRIN 2015" funds, project "STARS in the CAOS (Simulation Tools for Astrochemical Reactivity and Spectroscopy in the Cyberinfrastructure for Astrochemical Organic Species)", Grant Number 2015F59J3R and by the project PRIN-INAF 2016 The Cradle of Life - GENESIS-SKA (General Conditions in Early Planetary Systems for the rise of life with SKA). This project has received funding from the European Research Council (ERC) under the European Union's Horizon 2020 research and innovation programme, for the Project "The Dawn of Organic Chemistry" (DOC), grant agreement No 741002.

# References

1. Morris, M., Gilmore, W., Palmer, P., Turner, B.E., Zuckerman, B.: Detection of interstellar SiS and a study of IRC+ 10216 molecular envelope. Astrophys. J. **199**, L47–L51 (1975)
2. Cernicharo, J., Guélin, M., Kahane, C.: A $\lambda 2$ mm molecular line survey of the C-star envelope IRC+ 10216. Astron. Astrophys., Suppl. Ser. **142**, 181 (2000)
3. Prieto, L.V., et al.: Si-bearing molecules toward IRC+ 10216: ALMA unveils the molecular envelope of CWLeo. Astrophys. J. **805**, L13 (2015)
4. Dickinson, D.F., Kuiper, E.N.R.: Interstellar silicon sulfide. Astrophys. J. **247**, 112 (1981)
5. Ziurys, L.M.: SiS in Orion KL – Evidence for outflow chemistry. Astrophys. J. **324**, 544–552 (1988)
6. Ziurys, L.M.: SiS in outflow regions – more high-temperature silicon chemistry. Astrophys. J. **379**, 260–266 (1991)
7. Tercero, B., Vincent, L., Cernicharo, J., Viti, S., Marcelino, N.: A line-confusion limited millimeter survey of Orion KL II. Silicon-bearing species. Astron. Astrophys. **528**, A26 (2011)
8. MacKay, D.D.S.: The chemistry of silicon in hot molecular cores. Mon. Not. R. Astron. Soc. **274**, 694–700 (1995)
9. Podio, L., et al.: Silicon-bearing molecules in the shock L1157-B1: first detection of SiS around a Sun-like protostar. Mon. Not. R. Astron. Soc. Lett. **470**(1), L16–L20 (2017)
10. McGuire, B.A.: 2018 census of interstellar, circumstellar, extragalactic, protoplanetary disk, and exoplanetary molecules. Astrophys. J. Suppl. Ser. **239**, 17 (2018)
11. Rosi, M., et al.: Possible scenarios for SiS formation in the interstellar medium: electronic structure calculations of the potential energy surfaces for the reactions of the SiH radical with atomic sulphur and $S_2$. Chem. Phys. Lett. **695**, 87–93 (2018)
12. Skouteris, D., et al.: A theoretical investigation of the reaction H + $SiS_2$ and implications for the chemistry of silicon in the interstellar medium. In: Gervasi, O., et al. (eds.) ICCSA 2018. LNCS, vol. 10961, pp. 719–729. Springer, Cham (2018). https://doi.org/10.1007/978-3-319-95165-2_50
13. Zanchet, A., Roncero, O., Agúndez, M., Cernicharo, J.: Formation and destruction of SiS in space. Astrophys. J. **862**, 38 (2018)

14. Holdship, K., et al.: H2S in the L1157-B1 bow shock. Mon. Not. R. Astron. Soc. **463**, 802 (2016)

15. Neufeld, D.A., et al.: Discovery of interstellar mercapto radicals (SH) with the GREAT instrument on SOFIA. Astron. Astrophys. **542**, L6 (2012)

16. Skouteris, D., Balucani, N., Faginas-Lago, N., Falcinelli, S., Rosi, M.: Dimerization of methanimine and its charged species in the atmosphere of Titan and interstellar/cometary ice analogs. Astron. Astrophys. **584**, A76 (2015)

17. Leonori, F., et al.: Crossed-beam and theoretical studies of the S($^1$D) + C$_2$H$_2$ Reaction. J. Phys. Chem. A **113**, 4330–4339 (2009)

18. Troiani, A., Rosi, M., Garzoli, S., Salvitti, C., de Petris, G.: Vanadium hydroxide cluster ions in the gas phase: bond-forming reactions of doubly-charged negative ions by SO$_2$-promoted V-O activation. Chem. Eur. J. **23**, 11752–11756 (2017)

19. Berteloite, C., et al.: Low temperature kinetics, crossed beam dynamics and theoretical studies of the reaction S($^1$D) + CH$_4$ and low temperature kinetics of S($^1$D) + C$_2$H$_2$. Phys. Chem. Chem. Phys. **13**, 8485 (2011)

20. Becke, A.D.: Density functional thermochemistry. III. The role of exact exchange. J. Chem. Phys. **98**, 5648–5652 (1993)

21. Stephens, P.J., Devlin, F.J., Chablowski, C.F., Frisch, M.J.: Ab initio calculation of vibrational absorption and circular dichroism spectra using density functional force fields. J. Phys. Chem. **98**, 11623–11627 (1994)

22. Dunning Jr., T.H.: Gaussian basis sets for use in correlated molecular calculations. I. The atoms boron through neon and hydrogen. J. Chem. Phys. **90**, 1007–1023 (1989)

23. Woon, D.E., Dunning Jr., T.H.: Gaussian basis sets for use in correlated molecular calculations. III. The atoms aluminum through argon. J. Chem. Phys. **98**, 1358–1371 (1983)

24. Dunning Jr., T.H., Peterson, K.A., Wilson, A.K.: Gaussian basis sets for use in correlated molecular calculations. X. The atoms aluminum through argon revisited. J. Chem. Phys. **114**, 9244–9253 (2001)

25. Gonzalez, C., Schlegel, H.B.: An improved algorithm for reaction path following. J. Chem. Phys. **90**, 2154–2161 (1989)

26. Gonzalez, C., Schlegel, H.B.: Reaction path following in mass-weighted internal coordinates. J. Phys. Chem. **94**, 5523–5527 (1990)

27. Bartlett, R.J.: Many-body perturbation theory and coupled cluster theory for electron correlation in molecules. Annu. Rev. Phys. Chem. **32**, 359–401 (1981)

28. Raghavachari, K., Trucks, G.W., Pople, J.A., Head-Gordon, M.: Quadratic configuration interaction. A general technique for determining electron correlation energies. Chem. Phys. Lett. **157**, 479–483 (1989)

29. Olsen, J., Jorgensen, P., Koch, H., Balkova, A., Bartlett, R.J.: Full configuration–interaction and state of the art correlation calculations on water in a valence double-zeta basis with polarization functions. J. Chem. Phys. **104**, 8007–8015 (1996)

30. Rosi, M., et al.: An experimental and theoretical investigation of 1-butanol pyrolysis. Front. Chem. **7**, 326 (2019). https://doi.org/10.3389/fchem.2019.00326

31. Frisch, M.J., et al.: Gaussian 09, Revision A. 02. Gaussian, Inc., Wallingford (2009)

32. Flükiger, P., Lüthi, H.P., Portmann, S., Weber, J.: MOLEKEL 4.3. Swiss Center for Scientific Computing, Manno (2000–2002)

33. Portmann, S., Lüthi, H.P.: MOLEKEL: an interactive molecular graphics tool. Chimia **54**, 766–769 (2000)

34. Barone, V., et al.: Gas-phase formation of the prebiotic molecule formamide: insights from new quantum computations. Mon. Not. R. Astron. Soc. Lett. **453**, L31–L35 (2015)

35. Skouteris, D., Vazart, F., Ceccarelli, C., Balucani, N., Puzzarini, C., Barone, V.: New quantum chemical computations of formamide deuteration support gas-phase formation of this prebiotic molecule. Mon. Not. R. Astron. Soc. Lett. **468**, L1–L5 (2017)
36. Skouteris, D., et al.: The genealogical tree of ethanol: gas-phase formation of glycolalde-hyde, acetic acid and formic acid. Astrophys. J. **854**, 135 (2018)
37. Vazart, F., Latouche, C., Skouteris, D., Balucani, N., Barone, V.: Cyanomethanimine isomers in cold interstellar clouds: insights from electronic structure and kinetic calculations. Astrophys. J. **810**, 111 (2015)
38. Leonori, F., et al.: Crossed-beam dynamics, low-temperature kinetics, and theoretical studies of the reaction $S(^1D) + C_2H_4$. J. Phys. Chem. A **113**, 15328–15345 (2009)
39. Balucani, N., et al.: Combined crossed beam and theoretical studies of the $N(^2D) + C_2H_4$ reaction and implications for atmospheric models of Titan. J. Phys. Chem. A **116**, 10467–10479 (2012)
40. Leonori, F., Skouteris, D., Petrucci, R., Casavecchia, P., Rosi, M., Balucani, N.: Combined crossed beam and theoretical studies of the $C(^1D) + CH_4$ reaction. J. Chem. Phys. **138**(2), 024311 (2013)
41. Balucani, N., et al.: Formation of nitriles and imines in the atmosphere of Titan: combined crossed-beam and theoretical studies on the reaction dynamics of excited nitrogen atoms N $(^2D)$ with ethane. Faraday Discuss. **147**, 189–216 (2010)
42. Balucani, N., et al.: Combined crossed molecular beam and theoretical studies of the N $(^2D) + CH_4$ reaction and implications for atmospheric models of Titan. J. Phys. Chem. A **113**, 11138–11152 (2009)
43. Dayou, D., Duflot, D., Rivero-Santamaría, A., Monnerville, M.: A global ab initio potential energy surface for the $X^2A'$ ground state of the $Si + OH \rightarrow SiO + H$ reaction. J. Chem. Phys. **139**, 204305 (2013)
44. Rivero-Santamaría, A., Dayou, D., Rubayo-Soneirac, J., Monnerville, M.: Quasi-classical trajectory calculations of cross sections and rateconstants for the $Si + OH \rightarrow SiO + H$ reaction. Chem. Phys. Lett. **610–611**, 335–340 (2014)
45. Wakelam, V., et al.: The 2014 KIDA network for interstellar chemistry. Astrophys. J. Suppl. Ser. **217**(2), 20 (2015)
46. McElroy, D., Walsh, C., Markwick, A.J., Cordiner, M.A., Smith, K., Millar, T.J.: The UMIST database for astrochemistry 2012. Astron. Astrophys. **550**, A36 (2013)
47. Yang, T., Thomas, A.M., Dangi, B.B., Kaiser, R.I., Mebel, A.M., Millar, T.J.: Directed gas phase formation of silicon dioxide and implications for the formation of interstellar silicates. Nat. Commun. **9**, 774 (2018)
48. Ceccarelli, C., Viti, S., Balucani, N., Taquet, V.: The evolution of grain mantles and silicate dust growth at high redshift. Mon. Not. R. Astron. Soc. **476**, 1371–1383 (2018)
49. Balucani, N., Ceccarelli, C., Taquet, V.: Formation of complex organic molecules in cold objects: the role of gas-phase reactions. Mon. Not. R. Astron. Soc. **449**, L16–L20 (2015)
50. Skouteris, D., et al.: Interstellar dimethyl ether gas-phase formation: a quantum chemistry and kinetics study. Mon. Not. R. Astron. Soc. **482**, 3567–3575 (2019)
51. Ascenzi, D., Cernuto, A., Balucani, N., Tosi, P., Ceccarelli, C., Martini, L. M., Pirani, F.: Destruction of dimethyl ether and methyl formate by collisions with $He^+$. Astronom. Astrophys. (2019, in press). https://doi.org/10.1051/0004-6361/201834585

# A Computational Study of the Reaction N($^2$D) + C$_6$H$_6$ Leading to Pyridine and Phenylnitrene

Nadia Balucani[1], Leonardo Pacifici[1], Dimitrios Skouteris[2],
Adriana Caracciolo[1], Piergiorgio Casavecchia[1], Stefano Falcinelli[3],
and Marzio Rosi[3,4(✉)]

[1] Dipartimento di Chimica, Biologia e Biotecnologie,
Università degli Studi di Perugia, 06123 Perugia, Italy
{nadia.balucani,piergiorgio.casavecchia}@unipg.it,
leo.pacifici1@gmail.com,
adriana.caracciolo@studenti.unipg.it
[2] Master-Up, Strada Vicinale Sperandio 15, 06125 Perugia, Italy
d_skouteris@hotmail.it
[3] Dipartimento di Ingegneria Civile e Ambientale,
Università degli Studi di Perugia, 06125 Perugia, Italy
{stefano.falcinelli,marzio.rosi}@unipg.it
[4] CNR-ISTM, 06123 Perugia, Italy

**Abstract.** The reaction between nitrogen atoms in their first electronically excited state $^2$D with benzene has been characterized by electronic structure calculations of the stationary points along the minimum energy path. We focused our attention, in particular, to the two channels leading to C$_6$H$_5$N (phenylnitrene) + H and C$_5$H$_5$N (pyridine) + CH, due to the relevance of these products. The minima along these reaction paths have been characterized using different ab initio methods in order to find a reasonable compromise between chemical accuracy and computational costs. Our results suggest that, while for geometry optimizations even relatively low level calculations are adequate, for energies higher level calculations are necessary in order to obtain accurate quantitative results.

**Keywords:** Ab initio calculations · Titan atmosphere ·
Chemistry of planetary atmospheres · Prebiotic chemistry · Astrochemistry

## 1 Introduction

The atmosphere of Titan, the largest moon of Saturn [1], is believed to be in some way reminiscent of the primordial atmosphere of Earth [2, 3], being composed mainly by dinitrogen, methane, simple nitriles like HCN and HCCCN, simple hydrocarbons like C$_2$H$_6$, C$_2$H$_4$ and C$_2$H$_2$, H$_2$ and Ar. Dinitrogen is the prevalent species, being the 97% of the atmosphere and the second relevant constituent is CH$_4$ which represents an average amount of 2.7%. All the other species are present only in trace amounts, but their reactivity is very important as suggested by the plethora of information provided

© Springer Nature Switzerland AG 2019
S. Misra et al. (Eds.): ICCSA 2019, LNCS 11621, pp. 316–324, 2019.
https://doi.org/10.1007/978-3-030-24302-9_23

by the NASA/ESA/ASI Cassini-Huygens mission [4]. Recent investigations suggested also the presence of positive ions [1, 5, 6] and negatively charged ions [7] in Titan's ionosphere. More recent information were provided by the observations performed with the ALMA interferometer [8]. Among the species identified by Cassini Ion Neutral Spectrometer (INMS), benzene shows a relatively important mole fraction, being $1.3 \times 10^{-6}$ at 950 km [9]. However, the low number density and low temperature conditions (94 K at the surface and up to 200 K in the upper atmosphere of Titan [2, 4]) do not allow reactivity among neutral closed shell molecules because of the presence of relatively high activation energy barriers. In the range of altitude where benzene is present, however, molecular dinitrogen is converted into atomic nitrogen or ions by energetic processes [10] or by the interaction with Extreme Ultra-Violet (EUV) radiation. The dissociation of molecular dinitrogen induced by dissociative photoionization, galactic cosmic ray absorption, N$_2^+$ dissociative recombination, or dissociation induced by EUV photons produces atomic nitrogen in its electronic ground state $^4$S and in the first excited $^2$D state in similar amounts [10]. Atomic nitrogen in its $^4$S ground state exhibits very low reactivity with closed shell molecules. On the contrary, atomic nitrogen in its first electronically excited $^2$D state shows a significant reactivity with several molecules identified in the atmosphere of Titan. Atomic nitrogen in its excited $^2$D state is metastable but it shows a radiative lifetime long enough to react in binary collisions with other constituents of the upper atmosphere of Titan [11–19]. We have already investigated the reactions of atomic nitrogen in its excited $^2$D state with various hydrocarbons, like CH$_4$, C$_2$H$_2$, C$_2$H$_4$, C$_2$H$_6$, in laboratory experiments by the crossed molecular beam technique with mass spectrometric detection and time-of-flight analysis at different collision energies complemented by ab initio and kinetics calculations [20–25]. More recently, with the same approach, we have investigated the reaction between N($^2$D) and benzene [26] which is supposed to be very relevant in the upper atmosphere of Titan, from the stratosphere up to the thermosphere where the first haze layer is located.

The study of the potential energy surface of the system N($^2$D) + C$_6$H$_6$ [26] showed the presence of many exit reactive channels as well as many isomeric species with seven atoms of the second period and 6 hydrogen atoms and a total of 49 electrons. The ab initio study of these systems is computationally very challenging and a compromise between chemical accuracy and computational resources is necessary. In this manuscript we focus our attention on two of the main exit channels of the reaction between N($^2$D) and benzene, *i.e.* the formation of pyridine and phenylnitrene. We used different computational approaches in order to check if relatively simple calculations are sufficiently reliable.

## 2  Computational Details

The reactive channels of the N($^2$D) + C$_6$H$_6$ system leading to phenylnitrene and pyridine were investigated by locating the lowest stationary points at the B3LYP level of theory [27, 28], in conjunction with the 6-311+G** basis set [29, 30], on the doublet ground state potential energy surface. At the same level of theory we have computed the harmonic vibrational frequencies in order to check the nature of the stationary points, *i.e.* minimum if all the frequencies are real, saddle point if there is only one imaginary frequency. The assignment of the saddle points was performed using intrinsic reaction coordinate (IRC) calculations [31, 32] The geometry of all the species was optimized without any symmetry constraints considering for all the investigated species the electronic ground state. In order to check the accuracy of the computed geometries, we have optimized all the minima using a more extended basis set. We have optimized all the minima at the B3LYP level [27, 28] with the correlation consistent aug-cc-pVTZ basis set [33]. For selected systems, the energy was computed also at the higher level of calculation CCSD(T) [34–36] using the same correlation consistent aug-cc-pVTZ basis set [33] and the B3LYP/aug-cc-pVTZ optimized geometries, following a well established computational scheme [37–41]. The accuracy of the employed approach, in particular as far as basis set completeness is concerned, has been recently investigated [42]. Both the B3LYP and the CCSD(T) energies were corrected to 0 K by adding the zero point energy correction computed using the scaled harmonic vibrational frequencies evaluated at B3LYP/aug-cc-pVTZ level. The energy of $N(^2D)$ was estimated by adding the experimental [43] separation $N(^4S) - N(^2D)$ of 55 kcal mol$^{-1}$ to the energy of $N(^4S)$ at all levels of calculation. All calculations were done using Gaussian 09 [44] while the analysis of the vibrational frequencies was performed using Molekel [45, 46].

# 3    Results and Discussion

Figure 1 reports the main steps along the minimum energy paths leading to pyridine and phenylnitrene starting from the $N(^2D) + C_6H_6$ reactants, computed at the B3LYP/6-311+G** level. Table 1 reports the energy changes and barrier heights computed at the same level of theory for the processes leading to pyridine and phenylnitrene. We can notice that, while we have only one path leading to pyridine, we have three different paths leading to phenylnitrene. All the reported energies are relative to $N(^2D) + C_6H_6$. We can notice that all the minima, as well as the transition states, lie under the energy of the reactants. The interaction of $N(^2D)$ with $C_6H_6$ gives rise to the van der Waals adduct $C_6H_6N$ (1) more stable than the reactants by 30.1 kcal/mol, which evolves, through a barrier of only 2.5 kcal/mol, to minimum $C_6H_6N$ (2) more stable than the reactants by 52.1 kcal/mol. $C_6H_6N$ (2) can dissociate an hydrogen atom giving rise to phenylnitrene $C_6H_5N$ (10) in its triplet ground state, through a barrier of 25.9 kcal/mol, or isomerizes to the more stable species $C_6H_6N$ (3) in a process which shows almost no barrier (0.1 kcal/mol). $C_6H_6N$ (3) can isomerize to $C_6H_6N$ (4) through a barrier of 17.3 kcal/mol. $C_6H_6N$ (4) isomerizes to $C_5H_5NCH$ (5) through a barrier of 20.1 kcal/mol, which isomerizes to $C_5H_5NCH$ (6) through a barrier of 22.8 kcal/mol. $C_5H_5NCH$ (6) dissociates into pyridine (7) and CH, in a process endothermic by 56.4 kcal/mol. Alternatively $C_6H_6N$ (3) can isomerize to $C_6H_5NH$ (9) through a relatively high barrier of 48.4 kcal/mol. $C_6H_5NH$ (9) then dissociates into phenylnitrene and hydrogen in an endothermic process (85.8 kcal/mol) without any barrier. Phenylnitrene can be formed also through species $C_6H_6N$ (8) which can be formed from species $C_6H_6N$ (2).

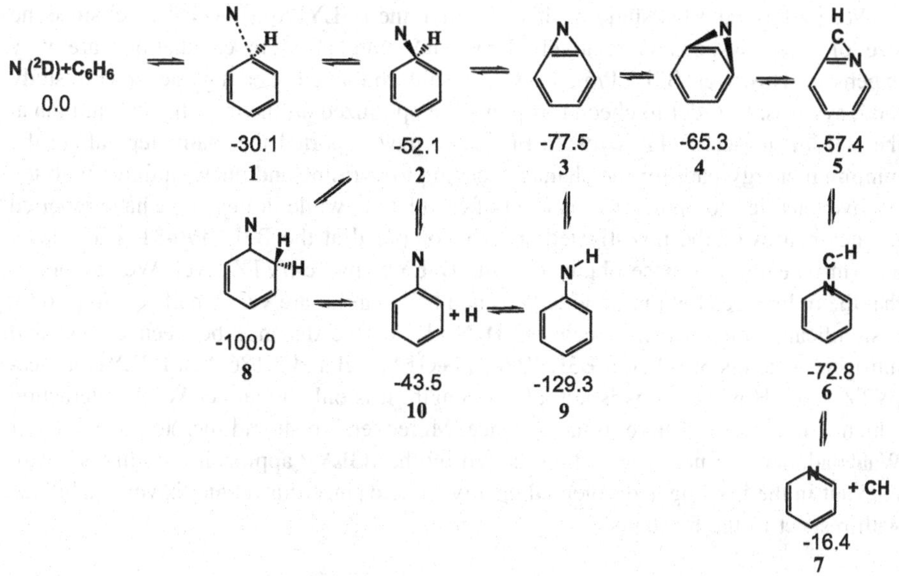

**Fig. 1.** Main steps along the minimum energy path for the channels leading to phenylnitrene and pyridine. Relative energies (kcal/mol, 0 K) with respect to the reactants N+C$_6$H$_6$ computed at B3LYP/6-311+G** level.

The species reported in Fig. 1 are only some of the possible isomers that can be formed starting from N($^2$D) and C$_6$H$_6$ [26]. The chemistry of this reaction indeed is very complex.

**Table 1.** Enthalpy changes and barrier heights (kcal/mol, 0 K) computed at the B3LYP/ 6-311+G** level of theory for selected dissociation and isomerization processes for the system N ($^2$D) + C$_6$H$_6$. When indicated, the superscript represents the spin multiplicity.

| | $\Delta H_0^0$ | Barrier height |
|---|---|---|
| N($^2$D) + C$_6$H$_6$ → C$_6$H$_6$N (1) | −30.1 | |
| C$_6$H$_6$N (1) → C$_6$H$_6$N (2) | −22.0 | 2.5 |
| C$_6$H$_6$N (2) → C$_6$H$_6$N (3) | −25.4 | 0.1 |
| C$_6$H$_6$N (3) → C$_6$H$_6$N (4) | 12.2 | 17.3 |
| C$_6$H$_6$N (4) → C$_5$H$_5$NCH (5) | 7.9 | 20.1 |
| C$_5$H$_5$NCH (5) → C$_5$H$_5$NCH (6) | −15.4 | 22.8 |
| C$_5$H$_5$NCH (6) → C$_5$H$_5$N (7) + CH | 56.4 | |
| C$_6$H$_6$N (2) → C$_6$H$_6$N (8) | −47.9 | 11.4 |
| C$_6$H$_6$N (8) → $^3$C$_6$H$_5$N (10) + H | 56.5 | |
| C$_6$H$_6$N (3) → C$_6$H$_5$NH (9) | −51.8 | 48.4 |
| C$_6$H$_5$N (9) → $^3$C$_6$H$_5$N (10) + H | 85.8 | |
| C$_6$H$_6$N (2) → $^3$C$_6$H$_5$N (10) + H | 8.6 | 25.9 |

We performed a fist study of this system at the B3LYP/6-311+G** level since the size of these systems is relatively large and more accurate calculations are very expensive. However, B3LYP/6-311+G** results could be not enough accurate to study these systems. In order to check this point, we optimized all the investigated minima at the B3LYP/aug-cc-pVTZ level. In Fig. 2 we have reported the main steps along the minimum energy path for the channels leading to pyridine and phenylnitrene, with the relative energies computed at this level of calculation, while in Fig. 3 we have reported the geometries of the investigated species computed at the B3LYP/6-311+G** level and (in parentheses) those obtained at the B3LYP/aug-cc-pVTZ level. We can notice that the differences both in bond lengths and bond angles are very small. We have only a significant difference in species $C_6H_6N$ (1) for the distance between carbon and nitrogen, which is 3.044 Å at B3LYP/6-311+G** level and 3.186 Å at B3LYP/aug-cc-pVTZ level. However, this is not a bond length. It is only a van der Waals interaction which is not very sensitive to the distance. Moreover, we should mention that van der Waals adducts are not very well described by the B3LYP approach, but this is not so relevant in the investigated potential energy surface since this adduct is very stabilized with respect to the reactants.

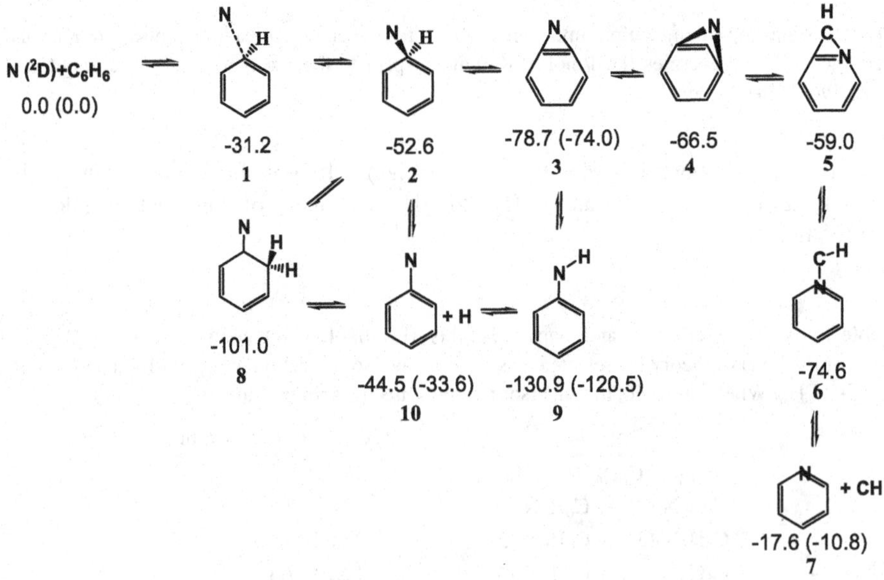

**Fig. 2.** Main steps along the minimum energy path for the channels leading to phenylnitrene and pyridine. Relative energies (kcal/mol, 0 K) with respect to the reactants $N+C_6H_6$ computed at B3LYP/aug-cc-pVTZ level. Values in parentheses are computed at CCSD(T)/aug-cc-pVTZ level

Since the geometries computed at B3LYP/6-311+G** and B3LYP/aug-cc-pVTZ level are very similar, we expect to have also similar energies with the two approaches. Comparing the results reported in Fig. 2 with those reported in Fig. 1, we can notice that the energy values differ by less than 2 kcal/mol. We can conclude that, as far as geometries are concerned, also the less expensive B3LYP/6-311+G** approach can be accepted.

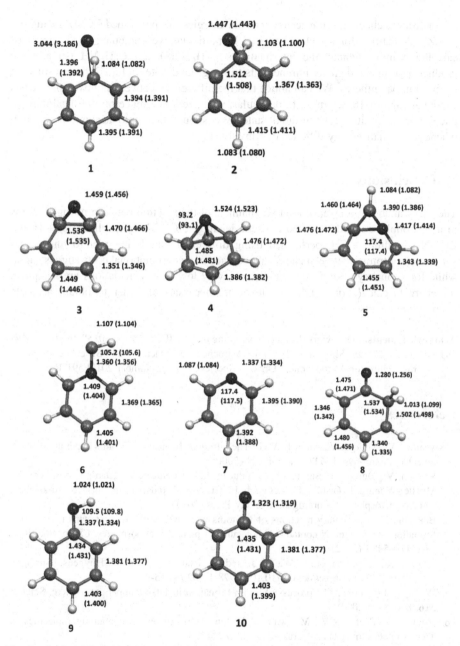

**Fig. 3.** Optimized geometries at B3LYP/6-311+G** level of the stationary points considered along the minimum energy paths leading from N($^2$D) + C$_6$H$_6$ to pyridine and phenylnitrene. Bond lengths in Å, angles in degrees. Values in parentheses are computed at B3LYP/aug-cc-pVTZ level.

In order to check also the accuracy of the energies, we performed CCSD(T)/aug-cc-pVTZ calculations for selected systems. In particular we computed at this level of calculation the reactants, the intermediates $C_6H_6N$ **(3)** and $C_6H_5NH$ **(9)** and the products pyridine and phenylnitrene in its triplet ground state. In Fig. 2 these results are reported in parentheses. We can notice that the differences between the two approaches can be as high as 10 kcal/mol. In particular, we have a difference of 10.9 kcal/mol for phenylnitrene in its triplet ground state. We should take into account this point, whenever a small energy difference is involved.

# 4  Conclusions

The study at ab initio level of the two channels of the reaction between nitrogen atoms in their doublet excited state and benzene leading to $C_6H_5N$ (phenylnitrene) + H and $C_5H_5N$ (pyridine) + CH, performed using different methods in order to find a reasonable compromise between chemical accuracy and computational costs suggests that, while for geometry optimizations even relatively low level calculations are adequate, for energies calculations of higher level are necessary in order to obtain accurate quantitative results.

**Acknowledgments.** This work has been supported by MIUR "PRIN 2015" funds, project "STARS in the CAOS (Simulation Tools for Astrochemical Reactivity and Spectroscopy in the Cyberinfrastructure for Astrochemical Organic Species)", Grant Number 2015F59J3R.

# References

1. Vuitton, V., Yelle, R.V., Anicich, V.G.: The nitrogen chemistry of Titan's upper atmosphere revealed. Astrophys. J. **647**, L175–L178 (2006)
2. Vuitton, V., Dutuit, O., Smith, M.A., Balucan, I.N.: Chemistry of Titan's atmosphere. In: Mueller-Wodarg, I., Griffith, C., Lellouch, E., Cravens, T. (eds.) Titan: Surface, Atmosphere and Magnetosphere. Cambridge University Press (2013)
3. Balucani, N.: Elementary reactions of N atoms with hydrocarbons: first steps towards the formation of prebiotic N-containing molecules in planetary atmospheres. Chem. Soc. Rev. **41**, 5473–5483 (2012)
4. Brown, R., Lebreton, J.P., Waite, J. (eds.): Titan from Cassini-Huygens. Springer, Heidelberg (2010). https://doi.org/10.1007/978-1-4020-9215-2
5. Waite Jr., J.H., et al.: The process of tholin formation in Titan's upper atmosphere. Science **316**, 870–875 (2007)
6. Vuitton, V., Yelle, R.V., McEwan, M.J.: Ion chemistry and N-containing molecules in Titan's upper atmosphere. Icarus **191**, 722–742 (2007)
7. Coates, A.J., et al.: Negative ions at Titan and Enceladus: recent results. Faraday Discuss. **147**, 293–305 (2010)
8. Lai, J.C.-Y., et al.: Mapping vinyl cyanide and other nitriles in Titan's atmosphere using ALMA. Astron. J. **154**(206), 1–10 (2017)
9. Vuitton, V., Yelle, R.V., Cui, J.: Formation and distribution of benzene on Titan. J. Geophys. Res. **113**, E05007 (2008)

10. Lavvas, P., et al.: Energy deposition and primary chemical products in Titan's upper atmosphere. Icarus **213**, 233–251 (2011)
11. Dutuit, O., et al.: Critical review of N, N$^+$, N$_2$$^+$, N$^{++}$ and N$_2$$^{++}$ main production processes and reactions of relevance to Titan's atmosphere. Astrophys. J. Suppl. Ser. **204**, 20 (2013)
12. Balucani, N.: Nitrogen fixation by photochemistry in the atmosphere of Titan and implications for prebiotic chemistry. In: Trigo-Rodriguez, J., Raulin, F., Muller, C., Nixon, C. (eds.) The Early Evolution of the Atmospheres of Terrestrial Planets. ASSSP, vol. 35, pp. 155–164. Springer, New York (2013). https://doi.org/10.1007/978-1-4614-5191-4_12
13. Balucani, N.: Elementary reactions and their role in gas-phase prebiotic chemistry. Int. J. Mol. Sci. **10**, 2304–2335 (2009)
14. Imanaka, H., Smith, M.A.: Formation of nitrogenated organic aerosols in the Titan upper atmosphere. PNAS **107**, 12423–12428 (2010)
15. Balucani, N., et al.: Dynamics of the N($^2$D) + D$_2$ reaction from crossed-beam and quasiclassical trajectory studies. J. Phys. Chem. A **105**, 2414–2422 (2001)
16. Balucani, N., et al.: Experimental and theoretical differential cross sections for the N ($^2$D) + H$_2$ reaction. J. Phys. Chem. A **110**, 817–829 (2006)
17. Homayoon, Z., Bowman, J.M., Balucani, N., Casavecchia, P.: Quasiclassical trajectory calculations of the N($^2$D) + H$_2$O reaction elucidating the formation mechanism of HNO and HON seen in molecular beam experiments. J. Phys. Chem. Lett. **5**, 3508–3513 (2014)
18. Balucani, N., Cartechini, L., Casavecchia, P., Homayoon, Z., Bowman, J.M.: A combined crossed molecular beam and quasiclassical trajectory study of the Titan-relevant N ($^2$D) + D$_2$O reaction. Mol. Phys. **113**, 2296–2301 (2015)
19. Israel, G., et al.: Complex organic matter in Titan's atmospheric aerosols from in situ pyrolysis and analysis. Nature **438**, 796 (2005)
20. Balucani, N., et al.: Combined crossed molecular beam and theoretical studies of the N ($^2$D) + CH$_4$ reaction and implications for atmospheric models of Titan. J. Phys. Chem. A **113**, 11138–11152 (2009)
21. Balucani, N., et al.: Cyanomethylene formation from the reaction of excited nitrogen atoms with acetylene: a crossed beam and ab initio study. J. Am. Chem. Soc. **122**, 4443–4450 (2000)
22. Balucani, N., Cartechini, L., Alagia, M., Casavecchia, P., Volpi, G.G.: Observation of nitrogen-bearing organic molecules from reactions of nitrogen atoms with hydrocarbons: A crossed beam study of N($^2$D) + ethylene. J. Phys. Chem. A **104**, 5655–5659 (2000)
23. Balucani, N., et al.: Formation of nitriles and imines in the atmosphere of Titan: combined crossed-beam and theoretical studies on the reaction dynamics of excited nitrogen atoms N ($^2$D) with ethane. Faraday Discuss. **147**, 189–216 (2010)
24. Balucani, N., et al.: Combined crossed beam and theoretical studies of the N($^2$D) + C$_2$H$_4$ reaction and implications for atmospheric models of Titan. J. Phys. Chem. A **116**, 10467–10479 (2012)
25. Rosi, M., Falcinelli, S., Balucani, N., Casavecchia, P., Skouteris, D.: A theoretical study of formation routes and dimerization of methanimine and implications for the aerosols formation in the upper atmosphere of Titan. In: Murgante, B., et al. (eds.) ICCSA 2013. LNCS, vol. 7971, pp. 47–56. Springer, Heidelberg (2013). https://doi.org/10.1007/978-3-642-39637-3_4
26. Balucani, N., Pacifici, L., Skouteris, D., Caracciolo, A., Casavecchia, P., Rosi, M.: A theoretical investigation of the reaction N($^2$D) + C$_6$H$_6$ and implications for the upper atmosphere of Titan. In: Gervasi, O., et al. (eds.) ICCSA 2018. LNCS, vol. 10961, pp. 763–772. Springer, Cham (2018). https://doi.org/10.1007/978-3-319-95165-2_53
27. Becke, A.D.: Density functional thermochemistry. III. The role of exact exchange. J. Chem. Phys. **98**, 5648–5652 (1993)

28. Stephens, P.J., Devlin, F.J., Chablowski, C.F., Frisch, M.J.: Ab initio calculation of vibrational absorption and circular dichroism spectra using density functional force fields. J. Phys. Chem. **98**, 11623–11627 (1994)
29. Krishnan, R., Binkley, J.S., Seeger, R., Pople, J.A.: Self-consistent molecular orbital methods. XX. A basis set for correlated wave functions. J. Chem. Phys. **72**, 650–654 (1980)
30. Frisch, M.J., Pople, J.A., Binkley, J.S.: Self-consistent molecular orbital methods 25. Supplementary functions for Gaussian basis sets. J. Chem. Phys. **80**, 3265–3269 (1984)
31. Gonzalez, C., Schlegel, H.B.: An improved algorithm for reaction path following. J. Chem. Phys. **90**, 2154–2161 (1989)
32. Gonzalez, C., Schlegel, H.B.: Reaction path following in mass-weighted internal coordinates. J. Phys. Chem. **94**, 5523–5527 (1990)
33. Dunning Jr., T.H.: Gaussian basis sets for use in correlated molecular calculations. I. The atoms boron through neon and hydrogen. J. Chem. Phys. **90**, 1007–1023 (1989)
34. Bartlett, R.J.: Many-body perturbation theory and coupled cluster theory for electron correlation in molecules. Annu. Rev. Phys. Chem. **32**, 359–401 (1981)
35. Raghavachari, K., Trucks, G.W., Pople, J.A., Head-Gordon, M.: Quadratic configuration interaction. A general technique for determining electron correlation energies. Chem. Phys Lett. **157**, 479–483 (1989)
36. Olsen, J., Jorgensen, P., Koch, H., Balkova, A., Bartlett, R.J.: Full configuration–interaction and state of the art correlation calculations on water in a valence double-zeta basis with polarization functions. J. Chem. Phys. **104**, 8007–8015 (1996)
37. Skouteris, D., Balucani, N., Faginas-Lago, N., Falcinelli, S., Rosi, M.: Dimerization of methanimine and its charged species in the atmosphere of Titan and interstellar/cometary ice analogs. Astron. Astrophys. **584**, A76 (2015)
38. Leonori, F., et al.: Crossed-beam and theoretical studies of the $S(^1D) + C_2H_2$ reaction. J. Phys. Chem. A **113**, 4330–4339 (2009)
39. Troiani, A., Rosi, M., Garzoli, S., Salvitti, C., de Petris, G.: Vanadium hydroxide cluster ions in the gas phase: bond-forming reactions of doubly-charged negative ions by $SO_2$-promoted V-O activation. Chem. Eur. J. **23**, 11752–11756 (2017)
40. Berteloite, C., et al.: Low temperature kinetics, crossed beam dynamics and theoretical studies of the reaction $S(^1D) + CH_4$ and low temperature kinetics of $S(^1D) + C_2H_2$. Phys. Chem. Chem. Phys. **13**, 8485 (2011)
41. de Petris, G., Cacace, F., Cipollini, R., Cartoni, A., Rosi, M., Troiani, A.: Experimental detection of theoretically predicted $N_2CO$. Angew. Chem. **117**, 466–469 (2005)
42. Rosi, M., et al.: An experimental and theoretical investigation of 1-butanol pyrolysis. Front. Chem. **7**, 326 (2019). https://doi.org/10.3389/fchem.2019.00326
43. Moore, C.E.: Atomic Energy Levels, Natl. Bur. Stand. (U.S.) Circ. N. 467. U.S., GPO, Washington, DC (1949)
44. Frisch, M.J., et al.: Gaussian 09, Revision A.02. Gaussian, Inc., Wallingford CT (2009)
45. Flükiger, P., Lüthi, H.P., Portmann, S., Weber, J.: MOLEKEL 4.3, Swiss Center for Scientific Computing, Manno (Switzerland) (2000–2002)
46. Portmann, S., Lüthi, H.P.: MOLEKEL: an interactive molecular graphics tool. CHIMIA **54**, 766–769 (2000)

# Cities, Technologies and Planning (CTP 2019)

# A Simulation Model Perspective on Social Capital

Andreas Koch[(✉)]

University of Salzburg, Salzburg, Austria
andreas.koch@sbg.ac.at

**Abstract.** This paper proposes an agent-based simulation model approach as one theoretical and methodological approach which helps derive knowledge that refers to the mechanisms and functions of social networks as a means of social capital production and dissemination. The approach is embedded in an empirical case study of two Austrian regions where a social project on enhancing well-being has been conducted. The data obtained from the simulation models are thus semi-empirical and semi-simulated. The primary aim of the paper is to investigate the selection processes of agents of different types and the linkage processes between them.

**Keywords:** Quantification of social capital ·
Mechanisms of social capital creation · Social network simulation

## 1 Introduction

The idea to conceptualise social relations also, if not primarily, in economic terms has, among others, been elaborated by Pierre Bourdieu and rests upon the empirical observation that economic principles such as competition, access to scarce resources and positions have been permeated into the social domain. For example, the valuation of scientific work has been expanded from the work's findings to scientific capital like reputation and prestige of scientists. Meanwhile, this successive inclusion of economic parameters into social relations is profound and comprehensive which justifies a Bourdieuian approach to extend the properties of economic capital towards the social relationships in general [26].

However, the idea of capitalising social relations is challenging, because it requires the ascription of numbers to them, which (shall) represent social values that are exchanged within and between communities, and which enable the mapping of differences discriminatorily, e.g., as rankings, ratings, and distinct positions. One difficulty of quantifying social-relational values such as trust, solidarity, or reciprocity, however, is given with their normative grounding which prohibits a direct translation of their qualities into quantities. Furthermore, it is questionable whether an approach that associates social actions with capitalistic characteristics is wishful since we often are reluctant to consider our social behaviour as prevailing rational or profit-oriented. Therefore, efforts to operationalise social capital are difficult to achieve by making a too strong analogy with economic capital. As [4, p. 241] claims: "The social world is accumulated history". The challenge is to adequately translate the definition of capital

© Springer Nature Switzerland AG 2019
S. Misra et al. (Eds.): ICCSA 2019, LNCS 11621, pp. 327–342, 2019.
https://doi.org/10.1007/978-3-030-24302-9_24

as "accumulated time" and, derived from this, "accumulated labour" into the realm of social interactions (see also [2], p. 211).

A core issue that frames the argumentation of this paper is the interrelationship between all sorts of capital. While economic markets rely strongly on the characteristics that are associated with social capital (trust and reciprocity), social capital, in turn, does so on economic capital's properties (efficiency and effectivity, benefit, or profit). However, these interrelations can be thought of as asymmetric, i.e., for every sort of capital there remains a nucleus which cannot be dissolved and represented by the others sorts. A complete translation and transformation of, for example, social capital's currencies (trust, solidarity, and reciprocity) are not feasible. The places where all these different currencies will be exchanged and valued are, in Bourdieu's terminology, the "social fields", which have multiple organisational functions without determining the structure of the superior "social spaces". In fact, the differentiation of the social fields will be regulated and organised by the social spaces [16].

This paper connects to this idea. The creation, growth and decline, and change of social capital depend on social networks. The availability of positions that are intrinsically tied to the distribution of resources which are capitalised through trust, reciprocity, solidarity (and many more) results from social network mechanisms. Network mechanisms' dynamics are, in turn, partially determined by temporal dynamics (from processes to evolution) and spatial dynamics (from local to global). The amalgamation of social networks, distribution of resources, temporal and spatial dynamics take place in social spaces which are composed of different and multiple communities on the one hand and different and multiple geographical places on the other. In other words, social spaces with their concrete geographical places influence the creation and distribution of social resources. Referring to Bourdieu on this line of arguments is still helpful: "[B]ourdieu's entire sociological work is steeped in the idea of a radical bondage of any social praxis to its social place [...]" [26, p. 10; translation A.K.].

The paper does not intend to deal with social spaces in a comprehensive manner but will focus on their meaning as a co-determinant in the production of social capital. With this focus, we attempt to approach social capital in a way that helps bypass an immediate capitalisation of social relations' currencies by emphasising a social-spatial dummy variable – the number of face-to-face meeting opportunities – that can be used to account for a quantitative representation of social capital *as a precondition*.

In doing so, this paper proposes an agent-based simulation model approach as one theoretical and methodological approach which helps derive knowledge that refers to the mechanisms and functions of social networks as a means of social capital production and dissemination. The approach is embedded in an empirical case study of two Austrian regions where a social project on enhancing well-being has been conducted. The data obtained from the simulation models are thus semi-empirical and semi-simulated. The primary aim of the paper is to investigate the selection processes of agents of different types and the linkage processes between them. In the context of selection, it is assumed that the number of face-to-face meeting opportunities plays a central role.

The agents represent people in different positions, in teams of up to approx. eight members, collaborating together in order to implement projects that are dedicated to enhancing local wellbeing. Characteristics of within-team collaboration (density, intensity, etc.) and between-team collaboration (new network connections) are used to compute network structure parameters (closeness and betweenness centrality) which serve as a quantitative proxy for social interactions and thus social capital.

## 2  Social Capital as a Source and Resource of/in Social Networks

The enabling meaning of versatile social interactions in collective human relations is commonly understood as a *conditio sine qua non* for human beings to live a decent life [9, 15]. To establish personal identity and autonomy, or the possibility to live one's life according to one's own capabilities and aspirations, requires a continuous exchange with other members of the communities and societies one is embedded into. While the nature of social interactions is seen as an unquestioned fact [22, 24], their valuation in operational terms is much harder to achieve because it inevitably relates to norms, expectations, and attitudes: "Each social relation stipulates norms and expectations about my behavior and the behavior of others" [30, p. 40]. According to Sack [29, p. 28], social relations are interrelated with (subjective) meaning and nature (space), and all three forces interdependently influence the relationship between self and place.

One generally accepted approach to quantify the value of social interactions is given by the theory of social capital. A huge body of theoretical reflections as well as empirical studies are available that considers the idea of transferring the concept of economic capital into the social realm as a suitable methodology in order to cope with social relations (see, for example, [10, 14]). The intention of this contribution is not, principally, to criticise this epistemological transfer, but to highlight some problematic implications of this approach that can be – at least partly – surmounted by a computational and generative simulation approach.

Social capital as a resource for knitting social ties between persons (we do not consider here non-human nodes as part of social networks, though these are important, see [19]) is theoretically addressed to different functions on different scales. Coleman [5, p. 302], for example, advocates a functional and meso-scaled approach: "Social capital is defined by its function. It is not a single entity, but a variety of different entities having two characteristics in common: They all consist of some aspect of a social structure, and they facilitate certain actions of individuals who are within the structure". Bourdieu [4, p. 248], in contrast, prefers a structural and micro-scaled definition of social capital as "the aggregate of the actual or potential resources which are linked to possession of a durable network of more or less institutionalized relationships of mutual acquaintance and recognition". By referring to different forms of social capital – bonding and bridging social capital – Putnam [28, p. 18ff; 27], in turn, directs his attention primarily to the societal benefits and challenges and thus the macro-scale perspective.

A common tendency can be seen in attempts that conceptualise social capital in the most comprehensive way possible; as basic ingredients of social networks. Such all-encompassing definitions, however, provide no concise understanding of the subject matter. Dill [7, p. 85], for example, offers such a broad definition and claims for his own approach that a definition should be a clear and simple one: "Social capital is the sum of intangible merits and goods within a community" (translation A.K.). His definition, for example, is anything but clear and simple. What can be accepted as "intangible merits" in communities and by whom? Who or what defines communities, and why are we dealing now with communities instead of networks? Are they identical? Who is producing and who is consuming intangible goods, based on which distribution rules? How does one sum up intangible goods? This definition is different from the accumulation and the "unit of calculation" concepts of social capital, because it provides no clues about distributional rules (it is a simple sum), the nature of intangible goods, and the nature of communities which is much harder to specify than talking about social networks [19]. Hence, such attempts are less suitable when attempting to grasp the very nature of social capital in qualitative as well as quantitative ways.

Bourdieu's approach, with its tighter and thus more appropriate relationship between the different sorts of capital, rests on the idea that the creation, consolidation, and transformation of social relations take time to evolve. "The social world is accumulated history, and if it is not to be reduced to a discontinuous series of instantaneous mechanical equilibria between agents who are treated as interchangeable particles, one must reintroduce into it the notion of capital and with it, accumulation and all its effects" [4, p. 241]. Availability and utilisation of social relations, of interacting with other individuals, are not realised in an environment that provides instantaneous linkages without any reference or framing, because social networks cannot emerge out of nothing. Social spaces with their material, relational and symbolic dimensions are one of the core presumptions to serve as a reference or frame. Capital, understood as 'accumulated labour', takes time to be recognised as trust, solidarity, or empathy. This perspective nurtures the idea of utilising a computational simulation approach in order to incorporate time and dynamics explicitly.

The actor-centred and utilitarian perspective of Bourdieu's approach – in the sense that the holder of a position in the network is the addressee and beneficiary of resources and not the individual person [16, p. 48] – not only presupposes an affiliation to one or many social networks, but also assumes knowledge about the structure and function(s) therewithin. Networks vary significantly in size and complexity; they can be concrete and manageable as, for instance, families and cliques, as well as abstract and opaque, as is the case for associations, organisations, labour markets, or electoral rolls. Furthermore it is remarkable that the unit of value, the currency, is implicitly given by solidarity, reciprocity, and trust, expressed explicitly as network connections, however (there are, obviously, more currency units than these three, but we focus here on these because they are in the core focus of our studies). "The volume of the social capital possessed by a given agent thus depends on the size of the network of connections he can effectively mobilize and on the volume of the capital (economic, cultural or symbolic) possessed in his own right by each of those to whom he is connected" (ibid.). This quantitative relation – the more connections one has the higher his/her social capital is – sounds odd, because it makes no qualitative difference in terms of network structure (intensity of relations), or the nature and value of relations (positions and roles of agents, weights of directions). "Resources" within the social capital context are understood as the availability of network relationships, which are, however, not specified – neither quantitatively nor qualitatively.

Capital can be assigned to three functions: (i) a means of exchange, (ii) a means of value hedge and preservation, and (iii) a unit of calculation. Accumulation may play a major role in all of these functions, but is not restricted to them. The worth of capital also stretches to the functions of distribution and circulation within a commodity and service economy. In addition, economic capital accumulation implies accumulation of both surplus and debt. The execution of all these functions requires not only a general usability of capital but also a (statistical) scale of measurement that enables comparisons and evaluations across a diverse field of objectives, and of spatial and temporal scales. All this is not given – or not sufficiently so – with social capital. It is possible to weigh and to qualify the direction of network relations as well as to explore network-related measures such as centralities, cliques, and positions; but still no adequate measures are available which account for the latent variables associated with social capital in an explicit and direct way. This statement does not negate approaches to social capital like, for example, "a network theory of social capital" [23] or empirical studies about "solidarity and mutual support" [3]. The approach that will be presented here belongs to the same category of approaches. They all, however, do not provide an immediate translation. In other words, it makes no sense to say "we must double solidarity or trust by doubling X".

One approach to investigate the creation and variation of social capital as mechanisms in social networks in order to derive quantitative measure is given with simulation modelling which will be presented in the next chapters.

## 3   The Empirical Case Studies to Investigate Social Capital

As a conclusion of Sect. 2, it would be a scientifically fruitful endeavour to develop indexes of social capital – based on trust, solidarity, network relations, etc. – to investigate social networks comparatively [19]. One way to follow this endeavour is to use a computational agent-based modelling approach since this approach allows for the qualification of network mechanisms, network structures, and network functions in quantitative measures [the generative methodology is delineated in 8]. In addition to the theoretical argumentation, it is also methodologically reasonable to apply a computational approach, because the development of network-analytical techniques and methods has been rapidly increased [2, 6, 25].

The following model approach can be characterised as semi-empirical as the initialisation of the simulation runs has been realised with data we collected as part of a project that has been conducted in four Austrian regions between 2011 and 2017. Semi-standardised questionnaires have been used as a first step to gain knowledge about the team networks, their sizes and compositions involved in the overall social project. Based on the results of the questionnaires, we selected actors for interviews who represented particular topological node properties. The models presented here refer to two of the four regions, one in Styria and the other in Upper Austria. The empirical networks of the Styrian region comprise of 79 team leaders with 396 team members and 441 connections, while the ones of the Upper Austrian region comprise of 59 team leaders and 418 team members with 655 connections. A detailed description of the project background together with the model approach that has been used in another context is given in [11, 12, 20].

## 4   The Agent-Based Model Design

In order to explore social network mechanisms as an indicator to derive knowledge about processes of social capital creation and variation, an agent-based simulation model has been developed whose origin grounds on ideas about team assembly mechanisms [13]. The NetLogo library includes this original model which has been implemented by [1]. The team assembly mechanisms' approach has been modified by the author in several ways to study different topics of social networks, among which the relationship between social and spatial topologies is one of them [18, 20, 21]. This approach provides a well justified methodological starting point as its central idea is to investigate processes of network growth due to new ties between existing and/or new actors of the network.

To analyse the issue of social capital metrics by incorporating empirical data, we modified the original model in a couple of ways concerning, for example, the initial-isation of the model, the size and network structure of initial teams, the merging procedure, and the qualification of network ties. Since there is a comprehensive description in [18, 20, 21], we only briefly delineate the basic model design charac-teristics here. Figure 1 illustrates the selection process of agents as a flow diagram.

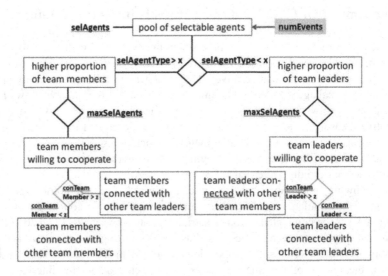

**Fig. 1.** The selection of agents within the simulation process. Source: [18]

As stated in Sect. 1, the central 'medium' to select agents as potential collaborators across the initial project-related networks is given with the number of opportunities to meet face-to-face during the project period (and thereafter). 'Meeting opportunities' can, for example, take the form of formal stakeholder meetings, announced workshops or informal meetings. The model-theoretical number of meetings varies from 1 to 160, representing the range of having at least one meeting to a situation of a weekly meeting rhythm (the project period comprises of 160 weeks, with 80 weeks of project implementation and another 80 weeks of post-project evaluation). Based on the empirical situation, however, there are three formal meetings (jury meetings with project presentations) to be included in any case. Virtual meetings had taken place for sure, but we have no valid information about these.

After the pool of selectable agents has been created, the model distinguishes the likelihood of selecting actors according to their function – team leaders and team members. The last step in the selection procedure takes the four principal types of ties into account by explicitly considering the initiator of a new cooperation. All steps represented in Fig. 1 will be repeated with reference to the simulated number of meetings. In order to simulate the modelled topology of the network empirically more realistic, we introduced a varying probability of dissolving ties between agents from time to time. The variation correlates inversely with the assigned intensity. The social network simulation models have been created with NetLogo 6.0 [30]; the Styrian case study model is available at OpenABM (https://www.openabm.org/model/5583/vers-ion/1).

## 5   Some Selected Model Results

Before discussing some relevant results of the simulation model presented here, we briefly summarise the outcomes of the statistical analysis conducted by the predecessor model [18, 20, 21]. Table 1 illustrates that the variable 'number of meetings' is statistically the most relevant in both regions in terms of explaining the statistical bivariate correlations of the number of connections among and between team leaders and team members against the independent variables described above. The correlations of the other independent variables with the dependent variables differ, however. The number of selectable agents and the composition of the pool with team leaders and team members are relevant explanatory measurements to explain the number of connections among team leaders, while the actual realisation of ties between team members is the second most important measurement to explain the number of connections among team members. Connections between all involved agents, again, depend on the size of the pool of agents. Furthermore, it is worth noting that the final modelled networks do not differ significantly between the two regions when comparing the types of connections (among team leaders, among team members, and between team leaders and team members).

In addition to the bivariate correlation analysis, multiple regression analyses of the two regions highlight the isolated influence of the independent variables in explaining the variation of the quantitative dimension of the connection types (see Tables 2 and 3). Isolated influence refers to as the exclusion of multicollinearity, i.e., interdependencies between the independent variables. This has been achieved by applying the 'stepwise selection' function.

**Table 1.** Bivariate correlation (Pearson) between the independent variables which determine the structure of the networks in the study regions of Steirische Eisenstrasse (Styria, S) and the Mühlviertler Alm (Upper Austria, UA). All variables do have a metrical or interval scale. *statistically significant for the 95% confidence interval; n = 3,888. Source: own data 1 = number of connections among team leaders, 1a for S, 1b for UA; 2 = number of connections among team members, 2a for S, 2b for UA; 3 = number of connections among all actors, 3a for S, 3b for UA

| Dependent variable | Independent variables | | | | | |
|---|---|---|---|---|---|---|
| | Num of meetings | Sel. of agents | Sel. of agent types | Max. num of agents selected | Ties of team leaders | Ties of team members |
| 1a | 0.785* | 0.234* | 0.235* | 0.169* | 0.065* | 0.002 |
| 1b | 0.779* | 0.238* | 0.236* | 0.168* | 0.068* | −0.005 |
| 2a | 0.633* | 0.185* | −0.188* | 0.130* | −0.001 | 0.194* |
| 2b | 0.623* | 0.176* | −0.181* | 0.124* | 0.003 | 0.194* |
| 3a | 0.756* | 0.267* | −0.084* | 0.194* | −0.004 | −0.001 |
| 3b | 0.735* | 0.259* | −0.097* | 0.189* | −0.001 | −0.005 |

All multiple regression models start with the number of events, but differ then according to the type of connections. While connections among team leaders and connections of all agents are then dependent on the number of selectable agents, it is the realised connections between team members that affect the connections among team members second most. This pattern can be detected in both regions though there are some (empirical) differences at the beginning of the simulation runs.

One conclusion drawn from the results presented in Tables 1, 2 and 3 is that although the 'number of events' parameter is most significant for all network compositions, the other independent variables also contribute to explain the variation of the size and composition of the networks though to a lesser extent and in different ways. Thus, measuring social capital implies a multi-dimensional consideration of determinants even though the number of meeting opportunities appears to be highly relevant.

A further conclusion is that team leaders, on average, benefit more from an increase of workshops and meetings than team members do. This is partially due to an implicit bias, occurring because there are fewer team leaders than team members, which leads more quickly to a higher number of linkages. In fact, considering the results of the cluster analyses (achieved through the Ward method, which yields more or less evenly distributed clusters), it can be concluded that team members also benefit significantly from an increase of events.

The relativity of benefit refers to the situation that there are five times more team members than team leaders in the Styrian region and even seven times more in the Upper Austrian region. According to the results for the Styrian region, team members increased their connectivity by a factor of 2.6 and team leaders by a factor of 1.5. Therefore, we can conclude that team leaders, on average, benefit more but team members also benefit from an increase in the number of events (for more cluster analysis details, see [20].

**Table 2.** Multiple regression analysis of the dependent variable 'number of meeting opportunities' and the independent variables (Upper Austria); Source: own data

| Models | R | R$^2$ |
|---|---|---|
| *Connections among team leaders* | | |
| Number of meeting opportunities | 0.779 | 0.606 |
| + number of selectable agents | 0.814 | 0.662 |
| + number of team leaders or team members | 0.847 | 0.718 |
| + maximum number of selectable agents | 0.864 | 0.746 |
| + realised ties of team leaders | 0.867 | 0.751 |
| *Connections among team members* | | |
| Number of meeting opportunities | 0.623 | 0.388 |
| + realised ties of team members | 0.653 | 0.426 |
| + number of team leaders or team members | 0.677 | 0.459 |
| + number of selectable agents | 0.700 | 0.489 |
| + maximum number of selectable agents | 0.711 | 0.505 |
| *Connections of all agents* | | |
| Number of meeting opportunities | 0.735 | 0.540 |
| + number of selectable agents | 0.779 | 0.607 |
| + maximum number of selectable agents | 0.802 | 0.643 |
| + number of team leaders or team members | 0.808 | 0.652 |

**Table 3.** Multiple regression analysis of the dependent variable 'number of meeting opportunities' and the independent variables (Styria); Source: own data.

| Models | R | R$^2$ |
|---|---|---|
| *Connections among team leaders* | | |
| Number of meeting opportunities | 0.785 | 0.617 |
| + number of selectable agents | 0.820 | 0.672 |
| + number of team leaders or team members | 0.852 | 0.726 |
| + maximum number of selectable agents | 0.869 | 0.755 |
| + realised ties of team leaders | 0.872 | 0.759 |
| *Connections among team members* | | |
| Number of meeting opportunities | 0.633 | 0.401 |
| + realised ties of team members | 0.662 | 0.438 |
| + number of team leaders or team members | 0.689 | 0.474 |
| + number of selectable agents | 0.713 | 0.508 |
| + maximum number of selectable agents | 0.725 | 0.525 |
| *Connections of all agents* | | |
| Number of meeting opportunities | 0.756 | 0.572 |
| + number of selectable agents | 0.802 | 0.643 |
| + maximum number of selectable agents | 0.825 | 0.681 |
| + number of team leaders or team members | 0.829 | 0.687 |

*Descriptive Statistics of Centrality Measures in the Styrian Study Region*

In order to investigate the course of the network creation, two common centrality measures have been used namely the closeness centrality and the betweenness centrality. Both centrality measures characterise an agent's position or role in the entire network. Commonly, closeness centrality (more precisely, actor closeness centrality) "[…] was developed to reflect how near a node is to the other nodes in a social network […]. Closeness and distance refer to how quickly an actor can interact with others, for example, by communicating directly or through very few intermediaries" [17, p. 65]. One index of (actor) closeness centrality is given with "[…] the inverse of the sum of the geodesic distances [topological shortest distances, A.K.] between actor $i$ and the $g - 1$ other actors" (ibid.). In NetLogo closeness centrality is defined slightly different "[…] as the inverse of the average of an [agent's] distances to all other [agents]" [30, n. p.]. Distances are also defined as the shortest paths. Betweenness centrality (again, in the sense of an actor betweenness centrality) in contrast refers to the mediator function of an agent (for example, mediating communication flows). This measure calculates "[…] the extent to which other actors lie on the geodesic path (shortest distance) between pairs of actors in the network. Betweenness centrality is an important indicator of control over information exchange or resource flows within a network" [17, p. 67]. The calculation of betweenness centrality in NetLogo refers to this approach: To calculate the betweenness centrality of an agent "[…] you take every other possible pairs of [agents] and, for each pair, you calculate the proportion of shortest paths between members of the pair that passes through the current [agent]. The betweenness centrality of an [agent] is the sum of these" [30, n.p.]. For the establishment of agents that possess a high closeness *and* betweenness centrality, it is remarkable that the range of involved team leaders (between 9% and 76%) and team members (between 3% and 58%) is very large. An attempt to explain this follows below. "High" closeness and betweenness centrality is defined as equal to, or larger than, two standard deviations from a standardised mean value.

*Descriptive Statistics of Centrality Measures in the Upper Austrian Study Region*

The networking processes in the Upper Austrian study region shows some similarities with the Styrian region, but also some distinct differences. The correlation pattern of variables is similar as a low number of events is given. What is different is the actual linkage process. While in the Styrian network (henceforth referred to as S-network) only 1% of all cases have at least 10% new relations with team leaders being created, it is 11% of all cases in the Upper Austrian-network (henceforth referred to as UA-network). With respect to all new relations, however, it is 2% in the UA-network but 4% in the S-network. Notwithstanding, the simulated UA-networks produce a higher number of highly centralised agents: there is a maximum of eight agents with high betweenness and closeness centrality compared with only four in the S-network.

As the number of meeting opportunities increases to 32, a high probability of selectable agents in general and of selectable team leaders, in particular, is less important for the emergence of cooperative team leaders. For the actual creation of ties, it remains crucial to have a high likelihood of repeated linkages. Furthermore, with 13% of all cases, there are many more cases given that create agents with a significantly high betweenness and closeness centrality (with at least six agents). With the lower number of events (4) there are only 4% of all cases available that help establish outstanding network agents. Thus, the UA-network not only supports the creation of a higher number of highly centralised agents (up to eight) than the S-network (up to four), but also promotes more chances for the emergence of these agents (13% compared with 4%).

A biweekly frequency of events, in turn, has more similarities with the low frequency of only four meetings in the course of 160 simulation steps. The number of cases with half of all team leaders involved in the simulated network decreases to 10%, and team leader involvement again depends more on the passive selection by team members. Knitting ties also requires a high linkage probability again. More meeting events, however, enable up to 95% of team leaders and 34% of team members to share new relations with other members of the network – a share that has not been reached with less frequent meeting opportunities.

*Centrality Measures as a Means to Understand the Dissemination of Social Capital*

The analysis of simulation results, as has been conducted so far, aimed to detect some patterns of correlations between relevant node- and edge-based parameters of the two social networks. The number of meeting events as a precondition (or framing condition) for the transformation of more or less fragmented, small, and project-related networks towards a large(r) connected collaborative network served as a reference point and guideline throughout the analysis.

A measure of a computationally derived sustainable network structure which promotes a proper generation and distribution of social capital should incorporate the following two criteria [31]:

- A good mix of ties of different strengths. Neither a network with a high proportion of strong (intense) ties, which would potentially imply lock-in effects of elite agents nor with a high proportion of weak ties, which would potentially imply fragmentation effects of non-committed agents, seem appropriate to maintain stable social networks.

- A good mix of agents with high betweenness and/or closeness centralities as well as low(er) betweenness and/or closeness centralities. This assumption refers to the thesis that a balanced structure of a network in terms of centralisation and decentralisation is beneficial for task allocation and communication.

The results of the semi-empirical network analyses can help us to approach to these two topics of suitable social network structures. In addition to the results presented above, we now briefly review the correlative significance – the strength of relationships between centralised agents and network characteristics – of the two networks. Besides the 'ordinary' agents (henceforth referred to as o-agents) in the networks whose relevance in transmitting and controlling communication processes is below the fixed threshold, we distinguish agents with a high betweenness *and* closeness centrality (bc-agents), those with a high closeness centrality (c-agents), and those with a high betweenness centrality (b-agents). Table 4 lists mean values and standard deviations of these agents and of relevant influential variables.

The values of Table 4 reveal that the initial network structures differ between the two regions since all simulation runs are designed in the same way in terms of

**Table 4.** Descriptive statistics of the central agents and of independent variables explaining their centralities for the Styrian network (left) and the Upper Austrian network (right). n = 243

| Variables | Styrian network | | Upper Austrian network | |
|---|---|---|---|---|
| | Mean | Standard deviation | Mean | Standard deviation |
| bc-agents | 1.41 | 0.682 | 5.01 | 1.126 |
| b-agents | 1.44 | 0.895 | 1.34 | 0.687 |
| c-agents | 2.88 | 1.536 | 4.49 | 1.826 |
| o-agents | 469.27 | 0.999 | 466.16 | 2.034 |
| New team leaders | 2.49 | 3.078 | 10.35 | 6.928 |
| New team members | 2.24 | 2.747 | 8.37 | 10.847 |
| New ties among team leaders | 26.91 | 3.210 | 19.72 | 7.788 |
| New ties among team members | 1.21 | 1.659 | 11.14 | 11.591 |
| New ties in total | 107.67 | 8.292 | 166.81 | 5.370 |

parameter values and temporal structure. The simulation runs used here excluded extreme values of meeting opportunities because they are empirically unrealistic: the range covers values from four events up to 80 events. On average, considerably more team leaders and team members with new connections are involved in the Upper Austrian networks, but these new connections are – for both agent types – relatively more often created with other team members (by comparing the means and standard deviations of 'new team leaders' and 'new team members' with 'new ties among team leaders', 'new ties among team members' and 'new ties in total'). Furthermore, the variation of the network structures is significantly higher in the Upper Austrian case than in the Styrian (considering the larger standard deviations). Also, there is a higher chance for agents to achieve a high betweenness *and* closeness centrality (bc-agents) or a high closeness centrality (c-agents) in the Upper Austrian networks. This will be briefly discussed here by including Pearson's correlation coefficients.

A closer look at the correlations between the three centrality types reveals a different structural pattern in the empirical networks of the two study regions (see Tables 5 and 6). Correlations here refer to the bivariate strength of the relationship between the three agent types of particular centrality and the influencing variables of new (cooperative) agents and new ties.

**Table 5.** Correlation coefficients between the highly centralised agents and the outcome of node and edge characteristics of the Styrian network. \*\*correlations are significant at the 99% level.

| | Cooperative team leaders | Cooperative team members | New ties among team leaders | New ties among team members | New ties in total |
|---|---|---|---|---|---|
| bc-agents | 0.637\*\* | 0.580\*\* | 0.593\*\* | 0.567\*\* | 0.477\*\* |
| b-agents | 0.386\*\* | 0.420\*\* | 0.348\*\* | 0.369\*\* | 0.317\*\* |
| c-agents | −0.667\*\* | −0.695\*\* | −0.473\*\* | −0.612\*\* | −0.321\*\* |

**Table 6.** Correlation coefficients between the highly centralised agents and the outcome of node and edge characteristics of the Upper Austrian network. [**]correlations are significant at the 99% level.

|            | Cooperative team leaders | Cooperative team members | New ties among team leaders | New ties among team members | New ties in total |
|------------|--------------------------|--------------------------|-----------------------------|-----------------------------|-------------------|
| bc-agents  | 0.474[**]                | 0.077                    | 0.458[**]                   | 0.168[**]                   | 0.188[**]         |
| b-agents   | 0.073                    | 0.274[**]                | 0.126                       | 0.237[**]                   | 0.340[**]         |
| c-agents   | 0.223[**]                | −0.156[*]                | 0.099                       | −0.107                      | 0.075             |

The fact that correlation values and correlation directions of the newly established nodes and links in both networks differ in a noticeable way must be caused by different initial conditions of the network structures. Not only do correlations of bc-agents, b-agents, and c-agents differ in terms of their strengths and statistical significance, but also in terms of the direction of correlations. While in the UA-network c-agents have both no significant correlation with new ties and a highly significant but weak positive correlation with cooperative team leaders and a significant but weak negative correlation with cooperative team members, the S-network represents a homogenous pattern with highly significant and strong positive correlations in all respects.

There are two issues that may help explain these results: first, c-agents and b-agents can be seen as residuals of centralised agents, because bc-agents already incorporate both centrality qualities. Second, the empirical S-network is less fragmented than the UA-network. As mentioned above, the S-network has 79 team leaders, of which 18% act simultaneously as team members in other project teams. The UA-network has only 59 team leaders, of which only 11% are in this double function and this by almost 50% more connections in total than compared with the S-network. New ties and the inclusion of additional cooperative agents may have the potential to decrease network fragmentation, but with the effect of a lower share of centralised agents as is the case in the S-network. In this respect, the S-network seems to be in a more balanced situation (across all value combinations of the involved variables).

This conclusion can claim some modest validity when taking distributional statistics into account. The mean value of the new cooperative team leaders in the UA-network is four times higher than it is in the S-network (Table 4). However, the standard deviation is also more than twice as high in the UA-network as it is in the S-network. A comparable situation is given with the new cooperative team members: on average, they are four times more often involved in the simulated UA-networks than in the S-networks, but, again, with a (here) four times higher standard deviation.

Finally, new connections among team leaders vary between 4% and 17% across all parameter value combinations in the UA-network while in the S-network they vary only between 5% and 7%. All these values indicate that the S-network is far less fragmented in the beginning (the empirical network) and hence depends less on the number of events than the UA-network. In other words: the number of events can be supportive for networks that are fairly fragmented, i.e. in our case they represent a network structure that is based on many unconnected small project-related networks with one centre each and a couple of team members tied to this centre.

# 6  Conclusion

The simulation models of the two Austrian regions were built to serve as a kind of missing link. Our empirical investigations of the emerging social networks as part of the empirical project focused primarily on an inquiry of the team leaders and their individual projects as well as the representatives of social institutions involved in the general project environment. Due to budgetary and temporal restrictions, we were not able to extend the inquiry to the team members and their network ties. This lack of data can be surmounted to a certain degree by utilising a model that simulates possible and probable linkage strategies of all participating agents based on knowledge we partly found through workshops and stakeholder meetings and through the literature. Based on these linkage strategies we obtain an idea of how mechanisms of social capital creation, variation, and dissemination may vary according to the parameters that have been investigated by social simulation techniques.

Relating the number of face-to-face meeting opportunities as one potential supportive determinant to enhance trust and solidarity in the creation and development of central positions or functions in social networks can be seen as a strategy to approach to social capital through the application of computational simulation techniques. It is, in other words, an attempt to explicitly translate Bourdieu's statement of "a radical bondage of any social praxis to its social place" and Sack's statement that "social relations, subjective meaning and space influence the relationship between self and place" into concrete situations of collaboration at local and regional levels.

With respect to the two criteria mentioned above we tried to detect some structural characteristics of the two regional social networks that help to better understand what is meant by social capital as a resource in social interactions. Referring to the "mix of ties" criterion we can conclude that both networks are equipped with a sustainable sample of ties of different intensity that would allow for both a sufficient strength to survive as a huge connected network and a sufficient flexibility to grow or shrink without losing fundamental bridging qualities.

Referring to the "mix of highly centralised agents" the network structures are less balanced, because in both cases the team leaders do play a crucial role as glue to preserve the networks as large connected graphs. One reason for this asymmetry can be explained by the initial structure of the networks which is characterised by the central team leaders surrounded by team members who are not connected with one another. The growth of the final network does not completely separate itself from this initial configuration (due to a lack of empirical data). In order to generate and disseminate social capital more equally within the whole network, it would be suggestive to strengthen the position and role of the team members.

With a small modification of Putnam's [28, p. 23] statement: "It would obviously be valuable to have distinct measures [of the evolution] of these various forms of social capital [over time]" (original quote includes the phrases within the brackets), we can conclude that a computational simulation approach can contribute to enrich the understanding of social capital from a generative, mechanism-sensitive, and quantitative point of view.

# References

1. Bakshy, E., Wilensky, U.: NetLogo Team Assembly model. Center for Connected Learning and Computer-Based Modeling. Northwestern University, Evanston, IL (2007). http://ccl.northwestern.edu/netlogo/models/TeamAssembly

2. Batagelj, V., Doreian, P., Ferligoj, A., Kejžar, N.: Understanding Large Temporal Networks and Spatial Networks. Wiley, Chichester (2014)

3. Bianchi, F., Casnici, N., Squazzoni, F.: Solidarity as a byproduct of professional collaboration: Social support and trust in a coworking space. Soc. Netw. **54**(2018), 61–72 (2018)

4. Bourdieu, P.: The forms of capital. In: Richardson J. (ed.) Handbook of Theory and Research for the Sociology of Education, New York, pp. 241–258 (1986)

5. Coleman, J.S.: Foundations of Social Theory. Harvard University Press, Cambridge (1990)

6. De Nooy, W., Mrvar, A., Batagelj, V.: Exploratory Social Network Analysis with Pajek. Cambridge University Press, Cambridge (2005)

7. Dill, A.: Gemeinsam sind wir reich. Wie Gemeinschaften ohne Geld Werte schaffen. Oekom Verlag, München (2012)

8. Epstein, J.: Generative Social Science. Studies in Agent-Based Computational Modeling. Princeton University Press, Princeton and Oxford (2006)

9. Eribon, D.: Rückkehr nach Reims. Suhrkamp, Berlin (2016)

10. Field, J.: Social Capital, 3rd edn. Routledge, New York (2016)

11. Gstach, I., Kapferer, E., Koch, A., Sedmak, C. (eds.): Sozialatlas Mühlviertler Alm. Mandelbaum Verlag, Wien (2015)

12. Gstach, I., Kapferer, E., Koch, A., Sedmak, C. (eds.): Sozialatlas Steirische Eisenstraße. Mandelbaum Verlag, Wien (2013)

13. Guimera, R., Uzzi, B., Spiro, J., Amaral, L.A.N.: Team assembly mechanisms determine collaboration network structure and team performance. Science **308**, 697–702 (2005)

14. Halpern, D.: Social Capital. Polity Press, Cambridge (2005)

15. Kaufmann, J.-C.: Die Erfindung des Ich: Eine Theorie der Identität. UVK, Konstanz (2005)

16. Kneer, G.: Differenzierung bei Luhmann und Bourdieu. Ein Theorievergleich. In: Nassehi, A., Nollmann, G. (eds.) Bourdieu und Luhmann. Ein Theorievergleich, pp. 25–56. Suhrkamp, Frankfurt a.M. (2004)

17. Knoke, D., Yang, S.: Social Network Analysis. Quantitative Applications in the Social Sciences, vol. 154, 2nd edn. SAGE Publications, London (2008)

18. Koch, A.: Determinants of social networking mechanisms and their potential effects on a place-based geography – an agent-based simulation approach. GI_Forum **1**, 369–382 (2017). https://doi.org/10.1553/giscience2017_01_s369

19. Koch, A.: Capital, the social, and the institution – Bourdieu's theory of social capital revisited. In: Kapferer, E., Koch, A., Sedmak, C. (eds.) Rethinking Social Capital, pp. 3–17. Cambridge Scholar Publishing, Newcastle upon Tyne (2017)

20. Koch, A.: Investigation of social networking mechanisms and their geospatial allocation effects – an agent-based simulation approach. In: Gervasi, O., et al. (eds.) ICCSA 2017. LNCS, vol. 10407, pp. 335–349. Springer, Cham (2017). https://doi.org/10.1007/978-3-319-62401-3_25

21. Koch, A.: The impact of event determinants on team assembly mechanisms of social networks. In: ESSA Proceedings, Rome (2016)

22. Latour, B.: Reassembling the Social. An Introduction to Actor-Network-Theory. Oxford University Press, Oxford (2005)

23. Lin, N.: Building a network theory of social capital. Connections **22**(1), 28–51 (1999)

24. Luhmann, N.: Soziale Systeme. Suhrkamp, Frankfurt a.M. (1984)
25. Namatame, A., Chen, S.-H.: Agent-Based Modeling and Network Dynamics. Oxford University Press, Oxford (2014)
26. Nassehi, A., Nollmann, G.: Einleitung: Wozu ein Theorievergleich? In: Nassehi, A., Nollmann, G. (eds.) Bourdieu und Luhmann. Ein Theorievergleich, pp. 7–22. Suhrkamp, Frankfurt a.M. (2004)
27. Putnam, R. (ed.): Gesellschaft und Gemeinsinn. Sozialkapital im internationalen Vergleich. Verlag Bertelsmann Stiftung, Gütersloh (2001)
28. Putnam, R.: Bowling Alone. Simon & Schuster Paperbacks, New York (2000)
29. Sack, R.D.: Homo Geographicus. The John Hopkins University Press, Baltimore (1997)
30. Wilensky, U.: NetLogo. Center for Connected Learning and Computer-Based Modeling. Northwestern University, Evanston, IL (1999). http://ccl.northwestern.edu/netlogo/
31. Woolcock, M.: The Place of Social Capital in Understanding Social and Economic Outcomes (2000). http://www.oecd.org/innovation/research/1824913.pdf

# Informal Settlements Spatial Analysis Using Space Syntax and Geographic Information Systems

Valerio Cutini[1], Valerio Di Pinto[2], Antonio M. Rinaldi[3,4(✉)], and Francesco Rossini[5]

[1] Dipartimento di Ingegneria dell'Energia, dei Sistemi, del Territorio e delle Costruzioni, Universitá di Pisa, Via Diotisalvi, 2, 56122 Pisa, Italy
valerio.cutini@unipi.it
[2] Dipartimento di Ingegneria Civile, Edile e Ambientale, Universitá di Napoli Federico II, Via Claudio, 21, 80125 Naples, Italy
valerio.dipinto@unina.it
[3] Dipartimento di Ingegneria Elettrica e delle Tecnologie dell'Informazione, Universitá di Napoli Federico II, Via Claudio, 21, 80125 Naples, Italy
antoniomaria.rinaldi@unina.it
[4] IKNOS-LAB - Intelligent and Knowledge Systems - LUPT, Universitá di Napoli Federico II, Via Toledo, 402, 80134 Naples, Italy
[5] School of Architecture, The Chinese University of Hong Kong (CUHK), AIT Building, Sha Tin, Hong Kong
rossini@cuhk.edu.hk

**Abstract.** This paper focuses on the use of quantitative and qualitative spatial analysis to infer the distinctive attributes of informal settlements. All over the world many cities are forced to face a tumultuous process of growth that is placing more than a quarter of the planet's urban population at the margins of society, relegating them to settlements where people have no security of tenure dwellings they inhabit, the neighbourhoods usually lack basic services as well as city infrastructure, and the housing do not comply with current planning rules and building regulations. The Habitat agency of United Nations defines them *informal settlements*. The intrinsic features of these settlements, where there seems to exist an hidden order and a delicate balance between social structure, relational spatial structure and spatial forms, remain, however, not yet fully understood. This paper aims to point out some key-features of informal settlements, recurring to the use of configurational analysis of urban network and of qualitative analysis of urban environment, through a comparative analysis. In the ArcGIS environment a case study is developed and evaluated, also recurring to a dedicated software plug-in able to implement Space Syntax analysis techniques in GIS workspace. It is hoped that this paper will draw attention to the hidden, distinctive features of informal settlements in order to make rehabilitation programmes more effective and sustainable.

© Springer Nature Switzerland AG 2019
S. Misra et al. (Eds.): ICCSA 2019, LNCS 11621, pp. 343–356, 2019.
https://doi.org/10.1007/978-3-030-24302-9_25

# 1    Introduction

Informal settlements are one the most critical issue of the present debate on urban regeneration strategies, involving urban planners as well as policy makers at any level. Although there is not an unambiguous definition of what an informal settlement is, they are commonly considered as residential areas where land use is mainly unregulated, allowing inhabitants to live in precarious dwelling lying in neighbourhoods usually lacking of basic services and infrastructure. Furthermore, informal settlements are often exposed to natural hazards and catastrophic events, like their inhabitants are constantly exposed to eviction, disease and violence [33], as a consequence of their socio-economic life's condition.

Such a definition currently includes more than 25% of the world population, with an impressive growing trend in the last 25 years [32], mainly located in a large part of Africa, Asia, and Latin America, but also including developed countries [9].

It is not easy to ascribe urban layout of informal settlements to design patterns, as it is hard to understand rules governing life within them. An informal settlement, in fact, consists not only of the urban space, but also and mainly of the local community living there; what we properly call the *informal society*. Recent researches have shown that these social groups occupy urban space in an entirely atypical way compared to what happens in formal settlements, trying to accommodate the need for social cooperation, which today has almost completely disappeared in the most advanced countries [10].

Such a new category of common spaces are hanging between public and private domain. There the main social functions take place, both of the public (trade, services, recreation) and of the strictly private (relationship activities, personal and domestic hygiene, cooking) life. We call them *space-in-between*. They are part of the idea that there is a community beyond the family characterizing the birth and development of informal settlements, often following temporal trajectories inconceivable for contemporary formal city. Spaces-in-between, although evident to a qualitative analysis of any informal settlement, are not yet sufficiently investigated [12].

The lack of patterns, the intrinsic incoherence of spatial forms, the dearth of infrastructures, the uncertain definition of public and private spaces, the precariousness of the located activities, the vagueness in land use and the complex functioning of informal society make the analysis tools blunt instruments, which can hardly be used in a labile field, where housing and urban activities have been increasing in a total absence of rules. This paper argues that addressing the specificities of informal settlements with an approach that places the spatial layer - in terms of the form of the settlement *(what you see)*, and the operational layer - in terms of how the same settlement works *(what is not seen)* on the same level is mandatory.

The configurational analysis of urban space has proved to be a useful analysis tool in this domain, able to provide relevant information both to make physical characteristics of the urban space to arise and to unveil the latent mechanisms that dominate the functioning of informal settlements. Moreover, this understanding of how informal settlements work is key in developing more effective on site upgrading strategies with the aim of addressing the community's needs [26].

The configurational approach, which is pivoted on the primary role of the urban grid at influencing and determining urban phenomena occurring within its paths, is able not only to provide new knowledge, but also to support other quantitative and qualitative spatial analysis techniques [6], in order to recognize and fully understand the intrinsic order of informal settlements, hidden behind the casual arrangement of their buildings and the chaotic pattern they define. The present work is focused on the comparative use of configurational analysis, analysis of urban forms and qualitative analysis of informal society to highlight the level of understanding that we currently have of some of the key features of informal settlements. The case study on the informal settlement of Baseco in Manila (Philippines) have been implemented to highlight the operational capabilities of the developed approach.

The paper is organized as follows: in Sect. 2 we present a theoretical background about the main aspects of our research; Sect. 3 presents the research methodology; a case study example is presented and discussed in Sect. 4. Eventually, conclusions are in Sect. 5.

## 2  Backgrounds

In this section we give a comprehensive overview of existing literature in our domain of interest, focusing on informal settlements and configurational analysis.

### 2.1  Informal Settlements

Informal settlements transcend the question of the physical adequacy of the architectural and urban spaces and the lack of services, strongly shifting the attention on what can almost be defined as a *philosophy of life in the city*. At the border of the city, or hermetically closed in enclaves, these settlement propose a set of relationships - natural, spatial and anthropic - that subvert that what is considered *normal* in the urban environment. In this sense, we need to look at informal settlements in their proper dimension, which is socio-cultural above all. The chaotic organization of its spaces could be seen as specific expression of this cultural ecosystem. Informal economies, promiscuous social relations and a limited stock of resources, in fact, certainly need a specific spatial organization, in which the functional hierarchies differ from those of a *formal* settlement. They have to presumably comply the ambiguous and little known social hierarchy also.

One of the typical characteristics of informal settlements is the existence of a category of spaces hanging in the balance between public and private domain that is completely unknown to the contemporary city, but which was well known in the most ancient past, where socio-spatial sharing it was much more pronounced than today. In these *spaces-in-between* there is a substantial part of public and private life of informal communities. They appear to be one of the main urban resources of informal settlements and certainly those that appear most useful to make them to renovate, especially in the perspective of on-site upgrading, which is a set of urban rebirth strategies that provide for a physical, social, economic and environmental revival excluding both the gutting of the built spaces and the removal of the settled populations.

Informal settlements are therefore something more complex than marginal degraded areas, which need deep knowledge and novel approaches, primarily aimed at understand their features and then to develop appropriate renovation strategies.

## 2.2   Configurational Analysis of Urban Environment

Cities are complex entities that are difficult to describe, moreover in formal or in disciplinarily terms. Hierarchies, geometries and the emphasis on parts rather then wholes are the common ideas and notions that planners and urban thinkers have used to simplify the city. Assessing complexity in urban environment fostered the development of models and approaches so as to get new meaning to the "urban science". In this broad framework, the configurational approach, as developed under the notion of Space Syntax [20] by Bill Hillier between the late 70' and the early 80', make the application of the science of sociological complex networks to cities and open spaces to flourish, providing new and deeper knowledge on the city and its functioning. The social-oriented approach to the city stimulated the debate on what a city is, or rather on whether the city is one thing or two. A city is certainly a set of buildings and blocks connected by streets and squares - or more generally of *open spaces* -, constituting its physical layer, but it is also a large set of activities linked by interaction, which is the social layer of the city [36]. The configurational approach of Space Syntax is pivoted on a novel idea about the relationship between these two dimensions of the city, since the link between physical and social layer stay for the link between structural and operational features of urban environment [17]. Space Syntax theorises that the urban space is "the common ground for physical and societal cities" [36], so as to develop a "unique" theory assuming the city as one thing. The open space of the city - the whole set of spaces that are freely accessible and so completely permeable -, which are the places where urban phenomena occur, is described as a spatial *configuration*, which is the set of "relations between all various spaces of a system" [36]. The urban layout could be hence represented as a network of connected open spaces, so as to create a graph expressing its topological structure. It is what we call an urban grid, whose elements affect the functioning of the city, generating and influencing movement rates and so steering the so-called theory of *movement economy* [18]. It is based on the idea that natural movement - that is the portion of movement that does not depend on the located activities, but only on the grid configuration [18] - is completely induced by spatial configuration. It implies that urban space has a generative role on urban phenomena, while activities can amplify the movement rate, acting as movement's multipliers, in terms of configurational attractors. As opposite, non-configurational attractors generate movement rates regardless of the grid, as it is the case of monopolistic urban activities. Configurational and non-configurational attractors, by generating the movement rates, define the way the city operates, and so they define human interaction that brings social and cultural pattern into the layout of the city. Urban layout has a strong influence on space potential that relates form and function in the city by a non-casual connection [19,36]. Space Syntax is pivoted on the idea that the so-called *dual graph*, obtained switching edges for nodes of the urban network, fully express the spatial configuration of the city, which lay on the topological structure of the urban grid. By applying Space Syntax techniques, each node of the urban graph is provided with a set of quantitative and non-discursive measures of centrality that root in structural sociology. The main centrality indices, known as *integration* and *choice*, are respectively related to the well-known concept of closeness [28] and betweenness [14]. The first one (integration) expresses how close in average a node is to all the others on the urban graph; the second one (choice) quantify the chance a node has to intercept and influence flows on the urban graph.

### 2.3 Space Syntax and Informality

Configurational approach is widely used to analyze unplanned city, in terms of autopoietic urban settlements also [9,16,19,22]. The aim of these studies is to highlight the latent order of the settlement, hidden by its chaotic physical structure and by the lack of archetypal forms in its design (i.e. the Hippodamian grid or the radial structure). Research in this field has shown that unplanned settlements often work better than those that respect plan directions, adapting better to the needs of its inhabitants and, for this reason, being more successful and less exposed to misuse of the urban space: what we call *urban pathologies*.

Despite the undeniable similarities between informal and autopoietic use of urban space, the use of configurational analysis for the study of informal settlements is largely underdeveloped [12]. There are few studies aimed at understanding the functioning of these settlements within the framework of the contemporary city, though interesting results have been obtained by applying Space Syntax techniques [11,21], since they allow to perform topological, topo-geometrical and statistical analysis at different scales, making complex relationship among urban patterns to arise [1]. Many of them have been applied to the case of informal settlements with preliminary but promising results [10].

## 3 Methodology

In this section we describe the proposed framework to analyze informal settlements. We first present the Space Syntax configurational techniques that could be used to analyze informal settlements, then we discuss on the comparison between structure and form in those urban areas. Eventually, a comprehensive approach is proposed.

In the frame of configurational analysis, Space Syntax represents the most important general theory that provides users with a largely tested set of techniques. At urban scale, the so-called *Axial Analysis* [19,20] and the strictly related *Angular Segment Analysis* [29,30] widely proved to be a reliable tool focused on spatial permeability, able to define a spatial hierarchy representative of urban functioning, able to proxy urban phenomena. As it is the case, those techniques will be applied as the basis of configurational analysis of informal settlement in this paper.

Axial Analysis and Angular Segment Analysis share a large part of the operative work-flow, firstly based on the split of urban space into two main components: the subset of open space - that are urban areas freely accessible with no restrictions - and the complementary subset of closed space.

On the open space map a *dual* network-making process [24] could be performed, recurring to a combination of algorithms simulating the fragmentation of open spaces into the minimal set of maximum size convex spaces [31]. Angular Segment Analysis needs of an additional algorithmic process aimed at spitting lines into segments [30]. Entire the process could be performed using *DepthmapX*, a software by University College of London [34].

The obtained network could be analyzed as a purely topological graph with spatial meaning. Many approaches could be implemented at the aim, but latest research trend is to integrate the analysis into GIS environment, in order to take advantage of its capabilities to post process configurational data and to collect and harmonize external data. This work recurs to a tailor-made add-in, developed to integrate Space Syntax techniques into ArcGIS software [13] stressing the remote communication interface of DepthmapXnet [35]. As a result, configurational data are stored as numerical attributes of a geographical database.

The distribution of Centrality indexes could be analyzed and visualized in GIS software. The same indexes could be used for post-processing analysis such as Background Patchwork Analysis [1] and statistics.

The same GIS environment could collect qualitative data analysis. They are based on the recognition of homogeneous urban patterns in terms of pace, arrangement, density, and types of buildings. Results could be stored as areal features provided of additional attributes.

Configurational and qualitative data are therefore spatially coherent and could be investigated to find their mutual relationship. Further qualitative data could be used to verify assertions.

This paper proposes an evolution of the traditional approach to the study of complex urban areas. More specifically, the founding idea of treating the settlement as a unitary "urban phenomenon in itself", characterized by complementary mechanisms, both physical and visual, as well as social and functional, ensures that there are no privileged components in reading and understanding urban dynamics. Developing rehabilitation strategies would take advantages by its implementation in terms of their sustainability and likelihood of success. Likewise, the recourse to GIS environment is innovative in a sector where qualitative and quantitative analysis are integrated. Using GIS at any stage of the process, since information acquisition to analysis and diagnosis, make it possible to increase result reliability if compared to the use of many specific tools, primarily due to a simpler data harmonization and a better control of single analysis sub-processes.

# 4    Case Study and Evaluation

In this section we show a case study about the comparative analysis of structure and form in an informal settlement. At the purpose, the BaSECo compound in Manila have been selected, due to its main feature that make it one of the most critical and complex to approach informal settlement of the world.

## 4.1    Bataan Shipyard and Engineering Corporation. BaSECo

The Baatan Shipyard and Engineering Corporation compound, well known as BaSECo, lies on the edge of the port of Manila, by the banks of Pasig river. Manila is the political and economic center of the Philippines with a metropolitan area that is the 18th largest urban agglomeration in the world. Unfortunately, about 35% of its 14 million population actually live in slums and informal settlements (Fig. 1). BaSECo has an extension of about 0,6 Km. sq. and an official population of 70.000 and more inhabitants [23]. Probably it is an underestimation due to the lack of a reliable registry. Unofficial reconstructions, in fact, consider exceeding one hundred thousand inhabitants. Literally arose in the late 1950s as a service area for the Bataan Shipyard and Engineering Company, Baseco has been structured in the same decade as a marine floods protection barrier and as Manila port waste disposal site. This makes it a real "floating waste heap", grown over time according to the needs of the city. In the last twenty years Baseco has almost doubled in surface (Fig. 2). Thanks to constant media sensitization, in 2002 Baseco was officially recognized as an urban settlement of the city of Manila, corresponding to the Baranggay (local government unit of the Philippines) n. 649. As a result, Baseco has been included in public renovation programs and a growing local and international debate is taking place on the most appropriate strategies [15,27].

## 4.2    Structure and Form in BaSECo

BaSECo compound has a very labile territorial and urban morphology, radically changing year by year. As a result of such a transformation process, by now its urban area results extremely fragmented, with few well-structured public spaces and many common space where the boundary of private property is not clearly recognizable.

This state reverberates on the urban network describing the topological structure of the settlement. The main mechanism of land creation by throwing and accumulating waste, and the subsequent uncontrolled occupation of the areas made useful up to their complete saturation, de facto makes open spaces to be residual implying an extremely high average density of lines (more than $48,000/Km^2$), much higher than western cities, due to the lack in main streets and squares.

The configurational analysis of the settlement highlights a strong polarization of the higher values of global integration and choice indexes, with peaks on

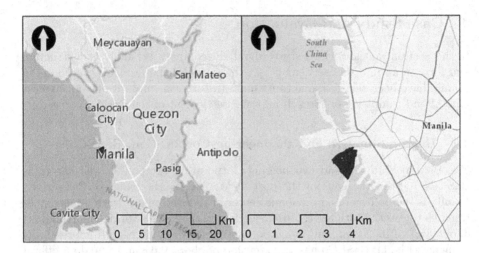

**Fig. 1.** The BaSECo compound in the frame of Metro Manila

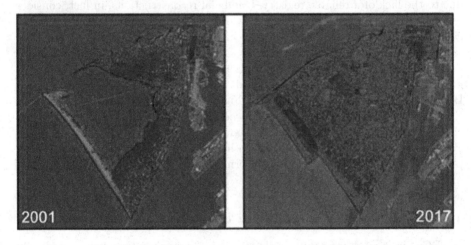

**Fig. 2.** BaSECo surface growing over last two decades

the few existing paved roads. It is the main configurational structure, or the *foreground* structure, of the settlement (Fig. 3).

Such a topo-geometrical state indicates the lacking of a real urban center, in favour of the uncertain infrastructural framework, mainly used as a set of paths for pedestrian and vehicular movement, as well for the activities directly connected (shops and the few services above all). They holds together and connects a large array of highly autonomous local centralities. It is confirmed by the so-called local analysis, obtained limiting the configurational indexes calculation at defined metric and topological radii, in order to make the patchwork of local places composing the city as a whole to arise. Since local analysis metric radius are selected by means of their capability to express the parts from the whole,

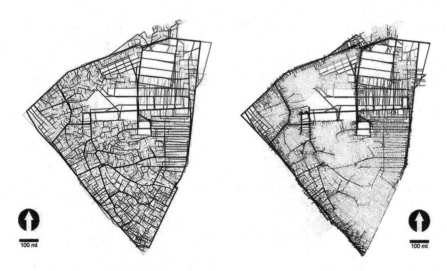

**Fig. 3.** BaSECo configurational analysis. Global choice (left) and global integration (right). Darker the line, higher the index.

the 200 m radius, which proved to be the most suitable for the case, reflects the high fragmentation of BaSECo consistently with the topological radius 3, which is widely used to predict pedestrian movement in the city (Fig. 4).

Therefore, Baseco is constituted by many groups of highly autonomous lines (high index of local integration) and small magnitude (less than 200 m). Such result is clearly shown in the so-called *background patchwork analysis* (BPA) also [1]. It is a bi-dimensional graph whose lower peaks on the y-axis indicate how many local centralities there are, and the distance of the same peaks along the x-axis stands for their mean topo-geometrical mutual distance (Fig. 5).

BPA allows to have a clear overview of the relationship between local centralities in the frame of the topological structure of the city as a whole, depicting the background of the urban environment held together by the main configurational structure.

Configurational structure of BaSECo reflects in its urban morphology. Mainly consisting of squatters, the settlement is characterized by large chaotic urban patterns, where one or two floors small buildings, often built with recycled materials, are organized according to non-geometric or pseudo-geometrical schemes. They literally fill up almost the 40% of BaSECo. There are, however, other patterns organized in linear or orthogonal schemes. These are the few areas where urban planning has actually been implemented and those that directly overlook the paved roads. They are mostly conventional buildings, often made of bricks, concrete and steel, although almost never exceeding the two floors and provided with minimal equipments. In the compound there are some infrastructures, mostly concentrated in the northern part of the settlement. They represent almost the only real building stock of BaSECo.

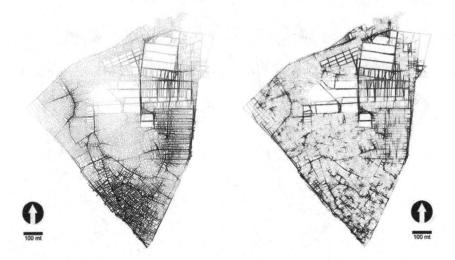

**Fig. 4.** BaSECo configurational analysis. Local integration at metric radius 200 (left) and local integration at topological radius 3 (right). Darker the line, higher the index.

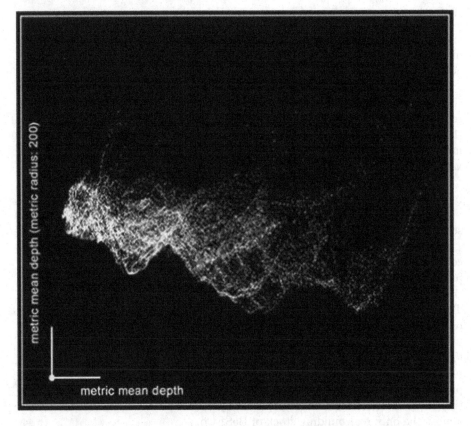

**Fig. 5.** Background patchwork analysis of BaSECo compound

The limit between the different urban forms, as clearly arguable by a qualitative analysis, is represented by the system of main roads, already highlighted
by global configurational analysis. Basing on such a set of borders, 14 pseudo-
homogeneous urban districts are discernible (Fig. 6).

Summarizing, Baseco's housing stock complies very low standards. Almost
completely deprived even of sanitary services, it respects a strict localization
hierarchy: along the main roads and in the few other structured contexts, buildings appear to be more refined, in order to exploit the positional advantage with
commercial activities. The remaining building stock is on the limit of permanent construction definition. There, dwelling constitutes only a part of families'
private domain, which is completed by common spaces facing their home, which
really seems to act as a balancing element for the ultra-local communities in
BaSECo.

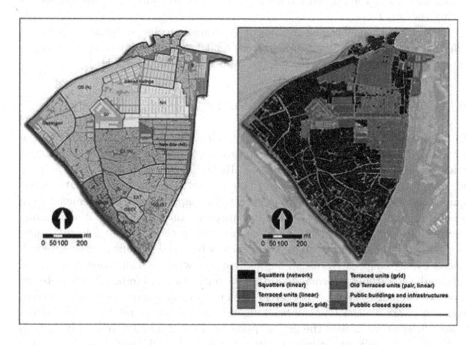

**Fig. 6.** Urban districts and urban morphology in BaSECo

The configurational structure and the form of BaSECo - that is the way
the settlement *operates* and the set of forms through it *appears* - are congruent
and strictly connected. The functional hierarchy and the location attractiveness faithfully the follows the distribution of global centrality indexes. They are
also the main factor affecting morphology, build quality, and aesthetics of built
environment.

Analysing the relationship between configurational centrality and urban
forms, features and phenomena by means of visual comparison, a real gradient of

quality is clearly recognizable: the more we move away from the lines with higher centrality values, the more the characteristics of informality are manifested, as long as we reach the most extreme conditions. This is confirmed by the distribution of local indexes, with peaks of greater magnitude in the most segregated areas (lower values of global integration), corresponding to the hyper-fragmented pattern dominated by the spaces-in-between at promiscuous common use. An exceptions to this trend are the global peak lines, due to the large number of their connections.

The existence of completely distinct hierarchical levels appears therefore a distinguishing feature of informal settlements. On a higher level, there are the urban supporting structures, which the need for minimal services and vital activities turns into privileged areas at higher quality. On the lower level, there are real informal patterns, where all the worst qualities of precariousness are manifested and where the population is organized in small community sharing spaces facing the squatters.

It is also confirmed by the analysis of the annual incomes of settled population [25], which follows a similar gradient from relative wealth (global topo-geometric integration) to relative poverty (global topo-geometric segregation).

## 5   Conclusions and Future Works

In this paper a comparative analysis between form and functional structure in unplanned urban environment has been proposed, in order to deeply understand what an informal settlement actually is. Recurring to Space Syntax techniques we give a comprehensive overview of how the settlements operates. Otherwise, qualitative urban analysis allows us to clearly shape the same settlements from spatial organization to construction features and materials. Comparison among them confirmed the research hypothesis pivoted on the idea that informal space is the mainly the output of an informal society based on specific relationship balanced by the cooperative use of common space: what we call space-in-between, although yet without a formal definition in configurational terms. A complete use case has been discussed to show a real implementation of our framework. Current research effort is regarding the reaching of a formal configurational definition of space-in-between, as well the use of quantitative and qualitative urban analysis techniques to make other key-features of informal settlements to arise, giving useful information to planners and policy makers aimed at developing sustainable regeneration programmes. Moreover, we are looking for implementing our approach to establish an alternative upgrading strategy which is socially, economically and environmentally sustainable, offering a model for other informal settlements in the Philippines.

As a mid-term goal, we are working on the full integration of qualitative and quantitative information on urban environment using techniques to represent [2] and integrate domain ontologies [3,4] in the frame of an extended knowledge base [5], under the notion of *Configurational Ontology* [7]. Our aim is to model a domain of knowledge on the city where measurable and unmeasurable features of the urban environment are joined by an appropriate set of relationships [8]. As a result, a new way to think at the city as a complex phenomenon is expected.

# References

1. Al Sayed, K., Turner, A., Hillier, B., Iida, S., Penn, A.: Space Syntax Methodology, 4th edn. Bartlett School of Architecture UCL, London (2014)
2. Albanese, M., Maresca, P., Picariello, A., Rinaldi, A.: Towards a multimedia ontology system: an approach using TAO_XML, pp. 52–57 (2005)
3. Caldarola, E., Rinaldi, A.: An approach to ontology integration for ontology reuse, pp. 384–393 (2016)
4. Caldarola, E., Rinaldi, A.: A multi-strategy approach for ontology reuse through matching and integration techniques. Adv. Intell. Syst. Comput. **561**, 63–90 (2018)
5. Cataldo, A., Rinaldi, A.: An ontological approach to represent knowledge in territorial planning science. Comput. Environ. Urban Syst. **34**(2), 117–132 (2010)
6. Cataldo, A., Cutini, V., Di Pinto, V., Rinaldi, A.M.: Subjectivity and objectivity in urban knowledge representation. In: KDIR, pp. 411–417 (2014)
7. Cataldo, A., Di Pinto, V., Rinaldi, A.M.: A methodological approach to integrate ontology and configurational analysis. In: Murgante, B., et al. (eds.) ICCSA 2014. LNCS, vol. 8580, pp. 693–708. Springer, Cham (2014). https://doi.org/10.1007/978-3-319-09129-7_50
8. Cataldo, A., Pinto, V.D., Rinaldi, A.M.: Representing and sharing spatial knowledge using configurational ontology. Int. J. Bus. Intell. Data Min. **10**(2), 123–151 (2015)
9. Cutini, V., Di Pinto, V.: Informal settlements, complexity and urban models: is there any order in autopoietic urban systems? In: 10th International Conference on Innovation in Urban and Regional Planning (INPUT) (2018)
10. Cutini, V., Di Pinto, V.: Space-in-between. Assetto configurazionale e sostenibilità urbana degli insediamenti informali. In: XXI Conferenza Società Italiana degli Urbanisti (2018)
11. Cutini, V., Di Pinto, V.: Urbanistica ed architettura nei paesi in via di sviluppo: quale forma per la città informale? Urbanistica Informazioni (278), 79–83 (2018)
12. Cutini, V., Di Pinto, V., Rossini, F.: At the border of the city. a preliminary study to an evidence-based approach to informal settlements. Urbanistica Informazioni (272), 31–35 (2017)
13. ESRI: Arcgis desktop - version 10.3.1 (2015)
14. Freeman, L.: Centrality in social networks conceptual clarification. Soc. Netw. **1**, 215–239 (1978)
15. Galuszka, J.: Community-based approaches to settlement upgrading as manifested through the big ACCA projects in Metro Manila, Philippines. Environ. Urban. **1**(26), 276–296 (2014)
16. Hillier, B.: Spatial sustainability in cities: organic patterns and sustainable forms. In: Proceedings of the 7th International Space Syntax Symposium (2009)
17. Hillier, B.: The genetic code for cities: is it simpler than we think? In: Portugali, J., Meyer, H., Stolk, E., Tan, E. (eds.) Complexity Theories of Cities Have Come of Age, pp. 129–152. Springer, Berlin (2012). https://doi.org/10.1007/978-3-642-24544-2_8
18. Hillier, B., Penn, A., Hanson, J., Grajewski, T., Xu, J.: Natural movement: or, configuration and attraction in urban pedestrian movement. Environ. Plann. B Plann. Des. **20**(1), 29–66 (1993). https://doi.org/10.1068/b200029

19. Hillier, B.: Space is the Machine. Cambridge University Press, Cambridge (1996)
20. Hillier, B., Hanson, J.: The Social Logic of Space. Cambridge University Press, Cambridge (1984)
21. Karimi, K., Parham, E.: An evidence informed approach to developing an adaptable regeneration programme for declining informal settlements. In: Proceedings of the 8th International Space Syntax Symposium (2012)
22. Mohamed, A., Mohareb, N.: Social networks in space of unplanned settlements in Cairo metropolitan area. In: Proceedings of the 10th International Space Syntax Symposium (2015)
23. Philippine Statistic Authority: Highlights of the Philippine population 2015 census of population (2018)
24. Porta, S., Crucitti, P., Latora, V.: The network analysis of urban streets: a dual approach. Phys. A Stat. Mech. Appl. **369**(2), 853–866 (2006)
25. Rossini, F.: Students workshop on Baseco compound draft booklets. Technical report (2018)
26. Rossini, F., Rinaldi, A., Di Pinto, V.: Public spaces and critical density, a preliminary study proposal for Baseco informal settlement in manila. In: XXIV International Conference: City and Territory in the Globalization Age. ISUF, Valencia (2017)
27. Rubin, D., Oman, R., Videcnik, S.: Manila: Future Habitations. Harvard University Graduate School of Design, Cambridge (2018)
28. Sabidussi, G.: The centrality index of a graph. Psychometrika **31**, 581–603 (1966). https://doi.org/10.1007/BF02289527
29. Turner, A.: Angular analysis: a method for the qualtification of space. Technical report (2000)
30. Turner, A.: Angular analysis. In: Proceedings of the 3rd International Space Syntax Symposium (2001)
31. Turner, A.: An algorithmic definition of the axial map. Environ. Plann. B Plann. Des. 425–444 (2005). https://doi.org/10.1068/b31097
32. UN-Habitat: The State of the World Cities Report 2012/13. Routledge, New York (2013)
33. UN-Habitat: Habitat III Issue Papers 22 Informal Settlements. UN-Habitat, New York (2015)
34. Varoudis, T.: Depthmapx - multi-platform spatial network analyses software - version 0.50 (2015). http://archtech.gr/varoudis/depthmapX/
35. Varoudis, T.: Depthmapxnet - version 0.35 (2017). http://archtech.gr/varoudis/depthmapX/?dir=depthmapXnet
36. Vaughan, L.: The spatial syntax of urban segregation. Prog. Plann. **67**, 205–294 (2007)

# The Electronic Government of St.-Petersburg as Relevant Experience of Construction of Digital Economy

Galina S. Tibilova[1(✉)], Andrey V. Ovcharenko[1], Elena N. Stankova[2], and Natalya V. Dyachenko[3]

[1] St. Petersburg State Unitary Firm "St. Petersburg Information and Analytical Centre", 59, Chernyakhovsky ul., St. Petersburg 191040, Russia
tibilova.galina@yandex.ru
[2] Saint Petersburg State University, 7-9 Universitetskaya nab., St. Petersburg 199034, Russia
e.stankova@spbu.ru
[3] Russian State Hydrometeorological University, 79 Voronezhsky ul., St. Petersburg 192007, Russia
nat230209@yandex.ru

**Abstract.** In given article it is shown how in the Russian Federation in whole and in St.-Petersburg in particular there was an environment for digital transformation of sphere of allocation of the state services and a technological platform and how now on the basis of this platform interaction of subjects (executive powers of the government of St.-Petersburg (further – EPG) and receivers of the state services) is carried out.

**Keywords:** Computer technologies · Digital economy · The state services · The electronic government

## 1 Introduction

According to United Nations research «the Electronic government 2018» the Russian Federation (further – the RF) is included into number of the countries with very high EGDI (an index of development of the electronic government (the metric includes development of online transactions, tendencies in sphere of the open government and transportable services, and also involvement of the public in rendering of innovative state services), including:

- Very high OSI (the online service index, represents a composite metric of usage of informational-communication technologies the states at rendering of the public services (further – PS));
- Very high EPI (an index of electronic involvement on the basis: electronic informing or availability of the information online; electronic listenings or public listenings online and electronic decision-making or direct implicating of citizens in decision-making processes).

© Springer Nature Switzerland AG 2019
S. Misra et al. (Eds.): ICCSA 2019, LNCS 11621, pp. 357–371, 2019.
https://doi.org/10.1007/978-3-030-24302-9_26

Since 2016 of the RF has risen on three positions in a rating of the countries on development of the electronic government, having passed from group with high EGDI in group with very high EGDI. St.-Petersburg in turn traditionally is included into number of leaders on development of the electronic government in the country according to various federal ratings.

It is important to mark that the digital government is included in the program «Digital economy» as one of federal projects, thus, the experience stored in this sphere is to relevant tasks of construction of digital economy as a whole. Uniqueness of the Russian experience in this sphere is caused by the big territorial remoteness, high autonomy of locales and presence of serious regional specificity at saving of control action of the federal authority. Locales essentially differ each other not only a degree of development of an informational-technical infrastructure, but also the legislation, structure PS, powers of authorities and their allocation between departments.

## 2 The Main Problems of Construction of the Electronic Government and Digital Economy as a Whole

Construction of the electronic government, as well as construction of digital economy, represents the multifactor, many-dimensional task. At its solution it is possible to select two main groups of problems:

- Scientifically-methodical problems;
- technical and technological problems.

In sort of the extremely extensive subject domain of one of the main scientifically-methodical problems at construction of the electronic government is its formalization, structurization, framing of criteria of the estimation of its components and, on their basis, methods of planning, an estimation and rise of efficiency of actions. It is necessary to carry out on the basis of the common theoretical approaches ranking of directions, actions, projects, up to separate administrative processes taking into account their social, economic, organizational, legal and other characteristics.

Besides, in practice chances when resource allocation on those or other actions is carried out by advanced rates, and before performers there is an atypical task of as much as possible effective mastering of the selected resources, that is a choice of projects and separate processes which will provide the greatest social and economic effect not at the least expenses, but at the fixed.

Separately it is necessary to mark that such tasks as the electronic government and digital economy are cross-industry, system and demand the comprehensive approach, unlike tasks of local automation of activity of those or other structures, however at their solution it is impossible to neglect branch interests because of risks to paralyse the smoothly running departmental business processes.

In the present article it is shown, how research and formalization of a subject domain and ranking of its components at the initial stages of construction of the electronic government in St.-Petersburg with usage of following methods were carried out:

- The system-target approach, methods of definition of the purposes, estimations of their significance, decomposition, and also definition of their interrelations;
- Multicriteria optimization;
- The process oriented approach, application of quantitative measures of the information.

In group of technical and technological problems the problems of identification of the person in digital space and creations under tasks of the electronic government of a necessary informational-technical infrastructure have the greatest value. In the present article experience of solution of the given tasks in St.-Petersburg is briefly reflected.

## 3  The Purposes of Construction of the Electronic Government

The purposes of construction of the electronic government are:

- Support of allocation to applicants PS in electronic form, improvement of quality of service of applicants;
- Support of implementation of a principle of one window in territory of St.-Petersburg, that is a principle, at which:
  - Interdepartmental informational interaction is hidden from the applicant, all necessary actions carry out authorities independently;
  - For the applicant there is one entry point where he accesses behind allocation of service and where receives result;
- Support of interaction of multifunctional centre and executive powers of the government of St.-Petersburg, the organizations subordinated to them, federal public authorities, local governments;
- Reduction of paper document flow;
- Minimization of expenses of resources of the budget of St.-Petersburg;
- Rise of a transparency of activity of executive powers of the government of St.-Petersburg and local governments, the organizations.

## 4  Overcoming Departmental (Branch) Isolation of Informational Resources at Construction of the Electronic Government in St.-Petersburg

At the moment of the beginning of construction of the electronic government many departmental informational resources existed only on a paper, departmental intelligence systems were absent. Existing systems thus formed and developed absolutely independently from each other both with legal, and with technical the points of view. It has led to departmental (branch) isolation of informational resources.

Thus PS (function) being fixed to certain department represents cross-industry process of acceptance of solution on the basis of a collection of data bases, collection, actualization and which storage in one departmental (branch) system are inexpedient, and in certain cases – are impossible. For support of solution of these tasks the information from various external in relation to departmental (branch) system of the sources distributed territorially is required. The given information belongs to the various organizations and departments, can be stored in the intelligence systems which in any way have been not integrated with each other, or in general to be absent in electronic form.

Thus, for support of process of decision-making call to external sources of the information behind necessary data according to certain algorithm which depends on concrete process of decision-making should be carried out.

After decision-making, the sequence of reception of data bases from the external sources, derived at realization of the given algorithm, ceases to exist as sequence, преобразуясь in the distributed collection of the data bases which have been not linked among themselves.

For overcoming of departmental isolation the interdepartmental automated information system of electronic public services of allocation in St.-Petersburg the state and municipal services in electronic form (IAIS EPS) which realises reception of data bases from independent departments and departmental intelligence systems in electronic form has been created.

Cross-industry systems such, namely functioning in the conditions of the distributed data bases, are not selected in a separate class owing to what practical and theoretical questions of their designing are poorly taken up. Development of such systems is carried out in the conditions of absence of the common bases and theoretical approaches to creation of their supply with information [1–3].

In this connection theoretical and practical aspects of designing of system were formed in a parallel way. For framing of design solutions of system it was necessary to select at once "pilot" package PS, and also to work out the common approaches to their choice further, to define criteria of selection. In spite of the fact that "the pilot" project has been initially limited only by services in the social policy sphere, all set of processes of rendering of services could not be captured at once, without preliminary structurization which has allowed to lower uncertainty and to make over processes various operations (for example, an expert estimation on various characteristic).

For structurization of social PS, given to the population of St.-Petersburg, following tags of structurization have been used:

- Result of allocation of service, namely:
    - Monetary payment (single monetary payment (the manual, compensation), regular monetary payment (the manual, compensation);
    - Document output (the document of disposable usage (help, other documents), the document of reusable usage (help, the certificate and the permission);
- Sort of the legislation regulating allocation of service (the regional legislation, the federal legislation);
- The organization, making solution on service allocation (department of social protection of the population of administration of area (DSPP), other organization).

According to these tags of structurization 54 social PS have been divided into 20 classes. Further expert estimations of the specified classes of services in following groups of criteria have been spent:

- The significance of group PS for citizens (a demand, requirement for automation from the point of view of convenience of citizens, etc.);
- The significance of group of services for the organizations, rendering the given services (labour input of allocation PS, requirement for optimization, etc.).

By results of expert estimations for the further analysis 2 groups PS have been selected:

- The single allowances assigned in DSPP (5 pieces);
- The regular allowances assigned in DSPP under the regional legislation (7 pieces).

Thus, it was possible to lower uncertainty with 54 PS to 12, necessity of further ranking of processes was thus obvious. Solution on what processes is necessary for researching first of all, should be accepted not only taking into account opinions of experts which can be contradictory, but also on the basis of the certain quantity indicators which values can be installed without engaging of experts.

For the specified purposes the mathematical model including of some criteria on which basis solution on can be accepted what decision-making processes from those classes which have been selected at the previous stage on the basis of expert estimations has been generated, are priority for further research. The criteria included in model, and their interpretation are presented in Table 1.

**Table 1.** Characteristics of decision-making processes

| The characteristic name | Semantic interpretation |
|---|---|
| Quantity of the standard documents regulating performing of process of decision-making | Characterises the significance of the given process for higher instances |
| Quantity of changes of the standard documents regulating performing of given process, for the certain period | Characterises "modifiability" of processes. Their is more often the standard base varies, the it is necessary to finish subsequently an intelligence system for automation of a supply with information of process of decision-making is more often |
| Quantity of the organizations involved in decision-making process | Characterises requirement for automation of collection of the information for consumers of result of decision-making. The more the organizations represent the documents necessary for decision-making, the more desirably for the consumer of result automation of process of collection of the given information for it. Besides, that above an organizational fragmentation, that the costs above linked to it |
| Relative period of decision-making (the ratio of the minimum period of decision-making, namely time necessary on decision-making, to maximum period of decision-making, that is by time which has been taken away on decision-making) | Characterises requirement for automation of collection of the information for the persons, making solution. The more the given ratio, there are more risks to delay decision-making. Thus, automation of collection of the information, accelerating this process, reduces the minimum time necessary on decision-making, and "liberates" an extra time |

The given criteria have been formalized and presented in the form of relative characteristics of decision-making processes. As decision-making process cannot be a part of a finite package partially or more once, the given multicriteria task represented the task of integer programming with booleans. The task consisted in finding solution (schedule), that is collection N of decision-making processes values of the specified criteria for which are maximum (are minimum) taking into account limitations. The criteria, maximised (minimised) in a task in view, are relative, dimensionless, therefore their rationing for convolution of criteria is not required. Convolution of criteria has been applied to task solution.

Following the results of ranking from 12 SS have been selected 5.

Depending on a reality situation each service could have some variants of implementation.

The choice of variants of implementation in the conditions of limitations was the following task of designing. Informational processes have been presented in the form of the digraphs which tops were data bases, and each path represented a variant of implementation of service. Everyone PS included following steps:

- Identification of the applicant;
- Identification of the object of the statement;
- Confirmation of a category of the applicant;
- Side conditions of allocation PS.

The example of the count for PS «the Lump sum at a birth of the child» is presented on Fig. 1.

The data bases entering into informational process possess two main characteristics: a demand and availability.

Availability of those or other data bases is defined by presence or possibility of support of reception of the array in electronic form. It depends on a degree of automation of a source of the information. Following degrees of automation of a source of the information have been selected:

- Absence of an intelligence system for an information source. Necessary data bases are presented for an information source only on paper carriers;
- Presence of an intelligence system for an information source, however the intelligence system has no web tools on allocation of a necessary data base;
- Presence of an intelligence system for an information source. The source intelligence system has web tools on allocation of a necessary data base.

Each degree of automation assumed requirement for performance of certain operations that has allowed to calculate the resources necessary on support of availability of a data base, and to consider their limitations.

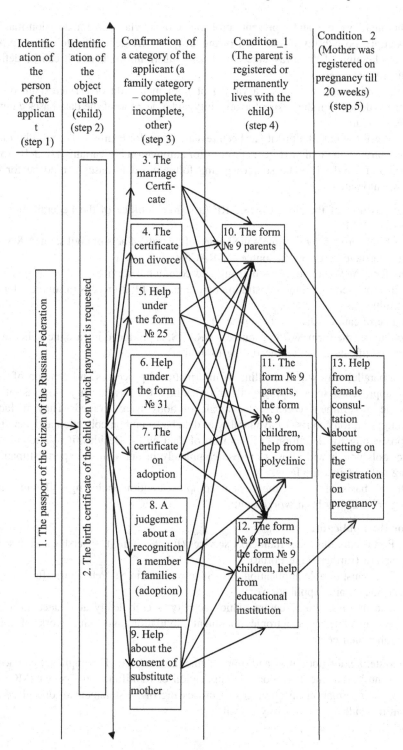

**Fig. 1** Informational process at decision-making on the state service «the Lump sum at a birth of the child»

The data base demand represents probability of its claiming for decision-making. For example, probability of claiming of the array "Marriage certificate" above probability of claiming of the array «the Consent of substitute mother» . It can be defined statistically or expertly.

Availability and demand of a variant of implementation of service (path on the column) is defined on the basis of availability and a demand of the data bases entering into its structure.

As a result of calculations it has been revealed that, for example, for SS «the Lump sum at a birth of the child» (Fig. 1) priority for automation are variants 1-2-3-10-13, 1-2-4-10-13, 1-2-5-10-13. The sources giving following data bases should be for this purpose automated:

- The passport of the citizen of the RF (a source – office of the Federal migration service OFMS);
- The birth certificate (a source – the bodies of records of acts of civil status BRACS);
- The marriage certficate (a source – BRACS);
- The form № 9 – (a source – housing and communal services);
- Help about setting on the registration on pregnancy till 20 weeks (a source – female consultations);
- The certificate on divorce (a source –);
- Help under the form № 25 (a source – BRACS, is produced in case the father in the birth certificate is written according to mother).

In a parallel way with modelling of informational processes and creation of theoretical approaches to a supply with information of cross-industry systems of the electronic government concrete technical solutions were formed. They included, including, solutions on rise of availability of data bases and on collection and analytical data processing for definition of a demand of data bases. Besides, it was required to realise tools which will allow to refuse completely in due course expert estimations, leaning only against the facts.

On the basis of "pilot" the current complex solution including following main making (Fig. 2) has been worked out:

- **For the applicant:**
  - Portal «the State and municipal services (function) in St.-Petersburg» https://gu.spb.ru (further – the Portal);
  - The transportable application «the State services in St.-Petersburg (further – the Transportable application);
  - The multifunctional centre, which activity is completely automated in a subsystem «Internal electronic document circulation and office-work of multifunctional centre».

In system exterritorialities and omnichannel are realised. The applicant can access through the Portal, the Transportable application or multifunctional center (MC) and receive the information on all stages of processing of its statement in one place and without dependence from a way of call.

- **For Executive bodies of the state (EBS):**
  - Electronic office of the official – the unified solution intended for reception and processing of electronic statements, arrived through the Portal, the Transportable application or MC, and also for involvement support in the electronic interdepartmental interaction EBS, not having own departmental intelligence systems or not having possibility to realise in the systems of necessary electronic tools. It provides an availability of data bases;
  - Office of approvals – the solution intended for automation of difficult processes of interdepartmental negotiation during rendering of services in which the considerable quantity of participants (for example, warrants on production earthen, building and repair work is involved);
- **For handle of informational processes:**
  - Creation and performing of regulations of electronic interaction – a subsystem providing routing of data bases and performing of electronic regulations of allocation of service (business logician), including internal link between subsystems;
- **For heads and controllers:**
  - The register of the state and municipal services (functions) of St.-Petersburg (the Register of credentials) – the tool of the registration which contains detailed descriptions of all powers EBS, all state functions and services, allows to carry out their analytics. Provides refusal of expert estimations and an objective estimation of a demand of data bases;
  - Statistics – the analytics and registration tool intended for centralised collection, the analysis and storage of the statistical data about allocation of the state services without dependence from a way of their allocation. Provides refusal of expert estimations and an objective estimation of a demand of data bases;
- **For interdepartmental interaction:**
  - System of interdepartmental electronic interaction of St.-Petersburg (SIE SPb) – the unified complex solution intended for integration of departmental (branch) intelligence systems of regional and federal levels on a basis tools-oriented of the architecture and the concept of the uniform integration bus. It provides an availability of data bases.

At program level the main mechanism of interaction is the web tools (web services) providing an informational exchange by XML-messages. At interaction with external IS by means of web tools the tools-adapters – the special Javas-units intended for support of necessary transformation of transferred informational objects can be used in a format corresponding IS.

- **For safety:**
  - The information security system – complex solution on protection of the personal data, protection against unauthorized access etc. Distinctive feature of the given solution is usage of means and the software of domestic developers.

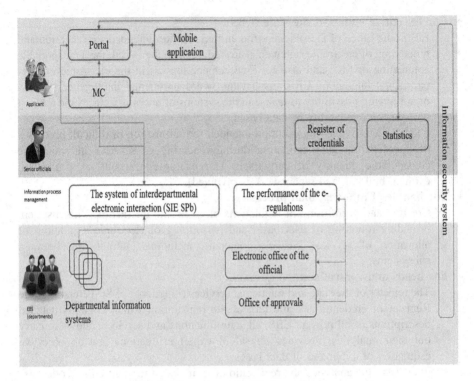

**Fig. 2** The common architecture of system

## 5   Authentification of the Applicant

Authentification of the applicant – one of key tasks of construction of the electronic government as the electronic government assumes performing of legally significant operations in electronic form.

At the moment of the beginning of construction of the electronic government in St.-Petersburg the problem of authentification of officials has been solved. In 2005 has started operation Certifying centre of executive powers of the government of St.-Petersburg successfully functioning till now (certifying center EBS). Certifying center EBS provides representatives of persons EBS and the subordinated organizations with keys of the electronic digital signature under which certificates, including, identification and authentification of the authorised persons is carried out. Domestic algorithms of enciphering (now – State Standart P 34.10-2012 «Information technology are thus used. Cryptography protection of the information. Processes of creation and check of the electronic digital signature») and the domestic software of company KriptoPro.

However usage of mechanisms of a digital signature by the citizens who are not employees EBS and the subordinated organizations, is inexpedient. For this purpose it is required to equip a workstation of the user with resources of reading of carrier EP and to instal specialised program supports that demanded, first, special skills, secondly, essential financial expenses (about 5000 rbl.).

Nevertheless, in 2010 at federal level it has been declared the project beginning the Universal electronic card (UEC) in this connection all regional initiatives have been prohibited. Idea UEC has been borrowed, including, from foreign experience, for example, experience of an ID-card of Estonia, however such features of the RF, as huge territory and a considerable quantity of subjects thus have not been considered. UEC contained, including, the qualified digital signature, however the project has not been claimed (all in St.-Petersburg it is produced less than 3000 cards) and has stopped the existence since January, 1st, 2017. The project failure is linked by that specificity of locales has not been considered, thus financing of output of cards should be carried out at the expense of resources of the budget of subjects.

During existence UEC card technologies of identification and authentification have become outdated, having given way to transportable and biometric technologies.

Successful alternative became created with 2011 Uniform system of identification and authentification (USIA). Usage USIA does not demand from citizens presence of the additional equipment and the software, skills of their usage.

The main functionality USIA:

- Identification and authentification of users, including:
- Support of various methods of authentification: under the password, on a digital signature, and also two-factor authentification (under the constant password and the disposable password sent in the form of a sms);
- Support of levels of reliability of identification of the user (the simplified account, the standard account, the confirmed account).
- Conducting the identification data, namely – conducting registers physical, legal bodies, bodies and the organizations, officials of bodies, the organizations and intelligence systems;
- Authorization of authorized persons BS at access to the following functions USIA.

Call of participants of informational interaction to USIA should occur only on HTTPS protocol (to use HTTP protocol it is forbidden).

Developers of the state sites, portals and other web applications can give to the users possibility to enter into system, using account USIA. It saves developers of necessity to do own storage of accounts, to provide safety of storage of passwords, to develop mechanisms of registration, authentification of users, to support them in working order.

USIA uses standard SAML of version 2.0. SAML is based on language XML and defines ways of information interchange about authentification of users, their powers and the identification data. According to the terminology accepted in this standard, USIA appears in a role of the entrusted supplier of identification (Identity Provider), and the system appears in a role of the service provider (Service Provider). In ЕСИА the mechanism of authentification of the users, grounded on specifications OAuth 2.0 and OpenID Connect 1.0 extension is created.

For authorisation support in any intelligence system through USIA it is necessary:

- To register an intelligence system in the register of intelligence systems USIA and in the test environment;

- To fulfil finishings of integrated system for the purpose of support of support of the selected mechanism of identification and authentification;
- To connect the productive version of integrated system to productive USIA environment.

In open access on a site of the Ministry of communications and link all necessary regulations and methodical guidelines are placed. Now USIA is the main tool of identification and authentification of applicants at reception of the state services. One of foreign clones USIA is SingPass Singapore. IAIS EPS uses USIA for identification and authentification since 2013.

For today on change to card technologies transportable technologies and technologies of operation with biometric given (fingerprints, retinas of an eye, the person) come. Projects on application of these technologies already are spent today MasterCard, by the Savings Bank, Aeroflot, the World food programme of the United Nations and many other things.

In Russia since July, 1st, 2018 the Uniform intelligence system of the personal data has earned. The system provides processing, including collection and storage, the biometric personal data, their check and an information transfer about a degree of their correspondence to the given biometric personal data of the citizen of the Russian Federation. From the end of 2017 possibility to use for identification of the client the data of uniform system of identification and authentification (USIA), and also the data of the above-stated Uniform intelligence system of the personal data is given banks.

## 6 The Common Software and Development Tools

At the moment of the beginning of creation of the electronic government the domestic software market was слаборазвит. At creation of the state intelligence systems it was widely applied proprietary the software of the western production, mainly Oracle and IBM. Besides, resources of business modelling and software engineering of production of IBM were applied, however practice has shown inexpediency of their usage which demanded too big financial, time and human resources.

However in 2014, in connection with a new wave of the antirussian sanctions, in the country the course on import substitution has been taken that has caused necessity of intensive refusal from proprietary the western software.

By the current moment the domestic software market is in a creation stage is one of priority directions of Digital economy, the market of the domestic software and means of protection of the information is thus most developed. As intermediate solution in all other directions the domestic electronic government has been translated to the software with an open initial code. Translation was carried out without lowering of rates of the extension and functional development of systems, without the termination of their commercial operation. Operating systems of Linux set, database management system PostgreSQL, mySQL, MongoDB, a server of Apache applications, development language – Java are widely used.

# 7  Means

In sort of the big territorial remoteness of locales and separate objects in the locales sometimes remote, the problem of creation of an informational-technical infrastructure in the Russian Federation is actual to this day. The important feature of an infrastructure of the electronic government is necessity to provide high level of informational safety as electronic the governments assumes processing of the personal data.

Since 2002 in St.-Petersburg successfully develops and the Uniform multiservice telecommunication network of executive powers of the government (further – UMTNEBS), serviced by subordinated establishment of Committee on information and link by the St.-Petersburg state unitary firm "automatic telephone exchange Smolnogo" functions. By means of UMTNEBS the uniform protected telecommunication space which allows to provide safe access to the state intelligence systems is created and to connect city objects to the Internet.

Besides, in St.-Petersburg the Regional distributed data-processing centre (DDPC) – a technological platform for allocation of informational resources of St.-Petersburg functions. On powers DDPC, since 2012, expansion of the state intelligence systems is made. Now in DDPC 47 state intelligence systems are placed and the archive of city system of the video observation, 28000 observation cameras covering more with depth of archive of 7 days is stored.

IAIS EPS it is placed in DDPC. For its functioning it is selected over 50 virtual servers from 2 to 16 kernels and from 2 to 128 Gb of the RAM on the basis of Linux set operating systems. The system functions daily and round the clock.

# 8  The Reached Practical Results

For today the electronic government of St.-Petersburg unites more than 3 million users and represents a uniform platform of interaction of citizens, MC and authorities. Allocation more than 200 regional electronic services, more than 60 online payments and 18 online tools of transportable applications is realised. For representatives of business in building sphere for today on the Portal well already 63 services given in the electronic form.

In the Private office access to which is carried out through USIA, besides feed of electronic statements on the state services following possibilities are given to the user:

- Monitoring of the status of the put in statement without dependence from a way of feed;
- The information on the calculated penalties and payments;
- Subscriptions on notices on the various events linked to reception of the state services, for example, about possibility to pass prophylactic medical examination or approach of record to the doctor.

For today it is fixed an order of 100 million visitings of the Portal. The share of electronic calls from a total number of the statements submitted citizens has made 81,36%.

For today network MC, 350 services giving more, includes 57 stationary MC, 6 centres «My business» and 4 transportable MC. In 2018 development of network MC for business is started.

By means of a subsystem «Office of approvals» in 2018 it is spent more than 424 thousand negotiations.

By means of a subsystem «Electronic office of the official» in 2018 it has been handled more than 292 thousand interdepartmental inquiries.

By means of the automated system «the Register of the state and municipal services (functions)» (Register of credentials) and subsystems of Statistics the analysis of activity EBS is carried out. For today in the Register it is presented more than 3000 powers of authorities of St.-Petersburg, more than 300 types of data, 455 state services. 163 authorities in St.-Petersburg quarterly give statistics on the state and municipal services. Thanks to integration with state automated system data "Handle" are automatically transferred to federal level.

Users of SIE SPb are 83 regional enforcement authorities, 19 agencies of employment, 46 federal enforcement authorities and 111 local governments. The integration service bus of St.-Petersburg handles 130000 inquiries in day.

For metrics of success and efficiency of the electronic government are including results of annual monitoring of quality of the services, from year to year satisfactions of citizens showing high common level quality of rendering of services – in 2015 it made 89,2%, in 2016–90,9%, in 2017–91%, in 2018–92,41%.

## 9  Prospects for the Development of E-Government

Currently, a large-scale digital transformation of the interaction of the state with citizens and business is being carried out.

Digital transformation is based on the following basic principles:

1. Proactivity

Currently, the process of providing public services begins at the moment when a citizen applies to the EPG with an application and a package of documents.

In the proactive provision of public services, the initiator of the process is the state, which, on the basis of an analysis of the data known to it about the citizen, itself offers him to receive the services due to him.

The concept of "proactivity" is closely related to the concept of superservice. Superservice is a set of public services provided to a citizen upon the occurrence of a particular life situation (birth of a child, moving to another region, etc.). In the future, all public services included in the superservice should be provided on the basis of one application, formed proactively.

2. Expanding the boundaries of interaction with public services to public services and other commercial and non-commercial electronic services

The interaction of the state with citizens and business needs to be understood more broadly than regulatory public services. It is necessary to create and develop social electronic services that citizens can use in their daily activities, as well as to enable businesses to promote their services in a trusted, state-guaranteed digital environment.

It is obvious that other services in addition to public services should also be provided to citizens proactively.

3. Direct participation of citizens and business in solving city-wide problems

Must be created by tools of direct participation of citizens and businesses in solving city problems, to create new projects, the development of "smart" cities and the solution to any problems of improvement, including needs to be implemented integration with social networks.

Currently, the development of a methodological framework for the introduction of a proactive approach, which will require the introduction of self-learning system and elements of artificial intelligence in the process of providing services. The final implementation of proactivity is planned to be completed by 2024.

# References

1. Stankova, E.N., Barmasov, A.V., Dyachenko, N.V., Bukina, M.N., Barmasova, A.M., Yakovleva, T.Y.: The use of computer technology as a way to increase efficiency of teaching physics and other natural sciences. In: Gervasi, O., et al. (eds.) ICCSA 2016. LNCS, vol. 9789, pp. 581–594. Springer, Cham (2016). https://doi.org/10.1007/978-3-319-42089-9_41
2. Dyachenko, N.V., Barmasov, A.V., Stankova, E.N., Struts, A.V., Barmasova, A.M., Yakovleva, T.Y.: Prototype of informational infrastructure of a program instrumentation complex for carrying out a laboratory practicum on physics in a university. In: Gervasi, O., et al. (eds.) ICCSA 2017. LNCS, vol. 10408, pp. 412–427. Springer, Cham (2017). https://doi.org/10.1007/978-3-319-62404-4_30
3. Stankova, E.N., Dyachenko, N.V., Tibilova, G.S.: Virtual laboratories: prospects for the development of techniques and methods of work. In: Gervasi, O., et al. (eds.) ICCSA 2018. LNCS, vol. 10963, pp. 3–11. Springer, Cham (2018). https://doi.org/10.1007/978-3-319-95171-3_1

# CO-TAMP: Transnational Platform for Territorial Attractiveness Monitoring in the Danube Region

Ljiljana Živković[1(✉)] and Blaž Barborič[2]

[1] Ministry of Construction, Transport and Infrastructure, Belgrade, Serbia
liliana.zivkovic@gmail.com
[2] Geodetic Institute of Slovenia, Ljubljana, Slovenia
blaz.barboric@gis.si

**Abstract.** Besides the carefully selected set of indicators, geographical visualization or geovisualization is also one of the success factors of any territorial monitoring system. Utilizing the latest GIS-based applications, geovisualization is today more than a plain – static – visual presentation of the territorial structures and dynamics using the maps and different computer graphics; it's about a set of tools, methods and techniques that enables interactivity and exploration capabilities over the monitoring system content, which includes different geospatial data. Deployment of these capabilities results in the various interactive visual analyses, leading to the recognition and presentation of the previously invisible spatial relations and data patterns, which are of shared importance for the spatial planning stakeholders and territorial development policy decision-makers, on all levels. Relaying on the rapidly developing interactivity feature, which is being fed by the increasing number of geospatial data from various sources, there is a growing number and variety of the monitoring systems in Europe, from local via national and transnational to European level. One of those transnational monitoring systems, namely Common Territorial Attractiveness Monitoring Platform (CO-TAMP), has been developed as a part of the Danube Transnational Programme's project Attractive Danube, which aimed to provide support to the territorial attractiveness policy priorities identification, decision-making and implementation throughout the Danube region. The aim of this paper is to research geovisualization feature and its advantages on the transnational level, and to present them in case of the CO-TAMP platform.

**Keywords:** Geovisualization · Transnational monitoring system ·
Common Territorial Attractiveness Monitoring Platform (CO-TAMP) ·
Attractive Danube project · Danube region

## 1 Introduction

The potential of spatial planning for the coordination of territorial impacts of sectoral policies in Europe has been increasingly recognized since the introduction of European Spatial Development Perspectives (ESDP), as Dühr confirmed [3]. Also, connected to

© Springer Nature Switzerland AG 2019
S. Misra et al. (Eds.): ICCSA 2019, LNCS 11621, pp. 372–387, 2019.
https://doi.org/10.1007/978-3-030-24302-9_27

the success and continuous development of the European Observation Network for Territorial Development and Cohesion (ESPON) since 2002, his claim that cartographic presentations can be powerful instruments for communicating the objectives of territorial development strategy or policy has been confirmed by the growing number and variety of territorial monitoring system initiatives on the different levels within European area [15]. However, due to the many factors, especially a difference between spatial planning systems – or traditions – among the European countries, and thus their different expectations from the cartographic presentation for spatial planning and territorial governance, geovisualization has been a particularly challenging within a transnational spatial planning context, where examples of the transnational territorial development visioning have been scarce until these days [3, 4].

Thus, in recent years of the ESPON Programme [7], which has been established as the main knowledge platform for monitoring the Cohesion Policy [14] and other related – thematic – policies and development priorities implementation on the different territorial levels, there were notable improvements also in domain of the transnational spatial planning and monitoring system development, as well as within the macroregional strategies geovisualization field [3].

Additionally, in the recently published Final report of the ESPON project COMPASS [10], territorial development stakeholders have been encourage to use more the tool kits developed by the ESPON projects for strategic visioning and dimensioning of spatial planning, where the monitoring of territorial development and its relation to the other strategies and narratives should get critical role at all levels, especially transnational [10]. The main aim of these COMPASS project's conclusions and recommendations is to strengthen the role of spatial planning in shaping the future territorial development policy in Europe, as well as to support national spatial planning and territorial development policy priorities to be more reflected in the next Cohesion Policy 2021–2027, and vice versa [17].

Therefore, the aim of this paper is to research ESPON-promoted geovisualization feature as well as its components and advantages using the transnational CO-TAMP platform as an example. This platform is developed as a result of the Interreg Danube Transnational Programme (DTP) project "Improving Capacities for Enhancing Territorial Attractiveness of the Danube Region" or Attractive Danube [13, 16].

After the Introduction chapter, the paper structure continues with definition and description of the geovisualization elements and advantages, in general and within transnational monitoring system context in Europe. Afterwards, relevant information about the Attractive Danube project (aim, objectives, concept, CO-TAMP application) are provided, followed by the description of methodology and steps performed for the CO-TAMP platform establishment. Paper is closing with the chapter discussing current platform advantages and disadvantages, as well as proposals for the potential future directions of CO-TAMP development and/or improvement, after paper finishes with concluding remarks.

Innovative aspect of the here presented research refers to (1) methodology of the transnational monitoring system development that combines existing knowledge and results produced by the other European initiatives, like ESPON, INSPIRE, etc., and (2) the Attractive Danube project's practical approach to the building of CO-TAMP application.

CO-TAMP platform has been chosen as the example for the transnational monitoring system geovisualization research because the authors were involved in the Attractive Danube project implementation.

## 2  Geovisualization and Territorial Monitoring Systems

Supported by the technological possibilities of nowadays computers and GIS-based applications, geovisualization assumes by definition the ability of maps, graphics and images to make existing spatial relationships and underlying spatial data patterns visible and understandable to the territorial development decision-makers and other stakeholders [3]. However, geovisualization is more than cartographic presentation or communication of the results by maps, since the same includes also capabilities of an interactive mapping application (that is, interactive user interfaces), like adding and removing data layers during the visual exploration, interactive map or spatial queries, etc. According to MacEachren "interaction is a key factor distinguishing geovisualization from traditional cartography", where geovisualization "is an active process in which an individual engages in sorting, highlighting, filtering, and otherwise transforming data in a search for patterns and relationships" [1]. On one side, these additional qualities of geovisualization indicate shift in the spatial planning and territorial development domain: from map as a product for communication, to the map as basis for visual thinking. On the other side, geovisualization initiates also general move from rational comprehensive planning tradition with rigid structures for responding to the spatial dynamics, to the communicative spatial planning system led by the development principles and goals as an implementation lead [5], especially for the territorial development planning and visioning on transnational level [4].

This change in usage of the maps and mapping in general is best described by 'cartography cube', as a new geovisualization model (Fig. 1). Following this model, the usage of maps and mapping tools for the visualization in domain of spatial planning and territorial development is increasingly shifting towards the need for higher human-map interaction, as well as revealing the unknown by exploration, analysis and synthesis during the customized visual thinking phase. Thus, the main goal of territorial monitoring systems development today is to become the advanced user-driven interactive map tools for better decision-making.

Identified shift in geovisualization feature supports findings of Soria-Lara et al. [5] that evaluation of the maps within territorial monitoring systems or spatial planning observatories should be based on their performance; for example, in what degree maps (1) facilitate decision-making process, and (2) allow stakeholder groups (decision-makers, planners and public) to learn and understand the existing development problems.

Finally, although there is no generally accepted definition of the territorial monitoring systems, it could be said that objectives of transnational monitoring systems in Europe today are [7, 15]:

– To enable collection, storage, processing, dissemination and geovisualization of the territorial development indicators in consistent and reproducible way;

- To provide information for the territorial development indicators' usability assessment and their values interpretation;
- To provide possibilities for connecting to the other relevant policy monitoring systems on different European level, and thus improve coordination among policies from the same and different domains as well as their integrated delivery; and
- To be reliable – evidence-based – platform with relevant and updated indicators for the territorial development and spatial planning decision-making, as well as policies management in general; etc.

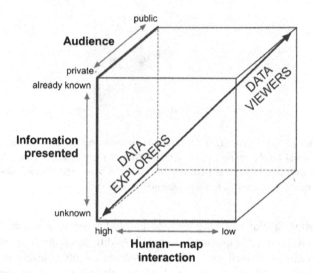

**Fig. 1.** MacEachren's graphic characterization of visualization through the use of maps [3]

### 2.1 Monitoring Territorial Dynamics and Policy Implementation in Europe

After the introduction of common main principles and long-term objectives for the territorial development and spatial planning in Europe by the ESDP document, and launching of the ESPON Programme for knowledge and information creation for the EU policies spatial impacts assessment, a number of territorial monitoring initiatives for the policies implementation support have emerged in Europe [15]. And, while these initiatives are differing by their specific objectives, territorial scopes as well as the other functional and thematic elements, just some of them have geovisualization capabilities, in sense of interactivity needed for the data exploration and user-driven customization of maps necessary for the visual thinking and communication of its results (Fig. 2).

So, as Soria-Lara et al. research also confirmed [5], maps are excellent tools for the territorial development and spatial planning, since they can improve the process of learning and understanding on the present and future territorial development problems, on all governance levels. Also, as Lindberg and Dubois concluded [4], comparing to the traditional cartography and its methods of presentation, geovisualization is "a key

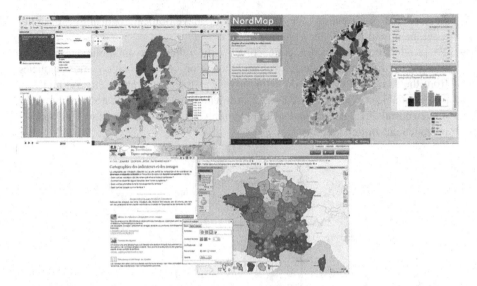

**Fig. 2.** Examples of geovisualization for territorial monitoring systems on European, macro-regional and national levels (respectively): RIMAP (http://rimap.espon.eu/) (top left), NordMap (http://nordmap.org/) (top right) and l'Observatoire des territoires (http://www.observatoire-des-territoires.gouv.fr/observatoire-des-territoires/en/node) (bottom)

feature supporting spatial visioning and the co-production of a shared transnational understanding of the spatial planning in Europe". Additionally, these authors also stress that the transnational as well as monitoring systems on other levels in order to be successful should: (a) address specific and relevant themes of strategic importance for the current political ambitions using the selected indicators, and (b) provide continuously updated information.

This means that, besides the limited set of right indicators as well as their appropriate geovisualization, relevance and usability of territorial monitoring systems also demand their thematic durability. In other words, territorial monitoring systems should have well prepared documentation and traceable information on the selected territorial development indicators, like a fact sheet, which would ensure reproducibility and consistency of the performed analyses over time, and thus secure comparability of the spatial development indicators' values across time and space [4, 16, 17].

Therefore, appropriate presentation of the territorial dynamics by the territorial development indicators within the transnational monitoring system should include [15, 16, 18]: (1) the fact sheet for each territorial development indicator with its definition and core metadata, needed for the indicator usability assessment, analysis and values interpretation, and (2) the set of tools, methods and techniques that support interactive visualization of indicators' values. Hence, these elements needed for the description, interpretation and presentation of the transnational development dynamics were also critical for the concept and design methodology of here presented transnational monitoring system – CO-TAMP.

## 3   Attractive Danube Project

### 3.1   Project Aim and Objectives

Within the 1st Call of DTP [13], under the priority "Well-governed Danube Region" and targeting the specific objective "Improve institutional capacities to tackle major societal challenges", 12 financing project partners from 11 Danube countries[1] implemented the Attractive Danube project [11].

The aim of this project was to strengthen multilevel, cross-sectoral and transnational governance and institutional capacities of the policy planners involved in territorial development within the Danube region. Also, recognizing the lack of good quality data as one of the common challenges and obstacle of partner-countries for efficient and effective territorial attractiveness policy priorities management, next project objectives were specified [16]:

– To make quality territorial attractiveness-related data available to the policy planning stakeholders;
– To improve and strengthen multilevel and cross-sector territorial attractiveness development planning; and
– To increase the skills, knowledge and capacities of territorial attractiveness policy planning stakeholders.

In next lines, territorial attractiveness concept and related indicators along the Common territorial monitoring framework are presented first, while the CO-TAMP development methodology and platform features are described in the following Chaps. 4 and 5.

### 3.2   Territorial Attractiveness: Concept and Indicators

The definition of territorial attractiveness adopted by the Attractive Danube project combines the ESPON's ATTREG [12] and SEE Programme's Attract-SEE projects' results [18], as well as Europe 2020 [6] and TA 2020 goals [2], and it describes territorial attractiveness quality as "capacity of certain Territorial Capitals and Assets to attract and retain target groups (tourists, residents, migrants and companies/investments) by already existing or developed advantages (environmental, economic and human, anthropic, socio-cultural, and institutional), imposed by relevant policies and their goals."

In order for the above identified definition and concept in general to be measurable and manageable, each territorial advantage – i.e. capital – is described with the several territorial attractiveness relevant indicators (Table 1) needed for the regular territorial monitoring, both on national and transnational levels.

---

[1] Slovenia (Geodetic Institute of Slovenia - Lead partner), Hungary (Lechner Ltd., EMFIE), Czech Republic (CENIA), Slovakia (TUKE), Germany (aifora GmbH), Bulgaria (BIFORUM), Romania (URBASOFIA), Serbia (IAUS), Croatia (KCKZZ), Montenegro (ISSP), and Bosnia and Herzegovina (FMPU).

**Table 1.** List of transnational territorial attractiveness relevant indicators compiled by the Attract-SEE project partners from different sources/databases, like EUROSTAT, OECD, EC, EEA, UN, UNESCO, WB, ESPON projects [18]

| No. | Indicator | No. | Indicator |
|-----|-----------|-----|-----------|
| 1 | Air pollution: Ozone concentration | 12 | Research & Experimental Development expenditure as % of GDP |
| 2 | Population connected to urban waste water treatment with at least secondary treatment | 13 | Employment rate 20–64 years by sex [%] (regional) |
| 3 | Electricity generated from renewable sources | 14 | Youth unemployment rate |
| 4 | Consumption of water per capita | 15 | Share of employment by sector |
| 5 | % of terrestrial area protected (total and by ecological region) | 16 | Number of overnight stays of tourists per capita per year |
| 6 | Population (or households) with accessibility to high-speed broadband (1 Mbit/second up and down) | 17 | Share of tourism related employment in total employment |
| 7 | European cultural sites on the UNESCO World Heritage List, 2010 | 18 | % of GDP of foreign direct investment |
| 8 | Life expectancy at birth by sex | 19 | Population growth rate (%) |
| 9 | Gross disposable household income | 20 | % of population in age 20–64 years |
| 10 | People at risk of poverty or social exclusion, or % in risk of poverty | 21 | Ageing index |
| 11 | Population aged 25–64 with tertiary education | 22 | Number of foreign students and/or professors |

In the course of the Attractive Danube project implementation, here identified 22 quantitative indicators were planned to be collected and used for the standardized and consistent monitoring and coordination of the transnational – or macro-regional – advantages and protection of diversities in the Danube region, through the selective social, economic, cultural and environmental development goals identification and territorial attractiveness relevant policies integration [17].

In order for the Attractive Danube project results to be sustained and CO-TAMP platform to be durable, data for those 22 indicators were planned to be collected by the project partners up to 2021, i.e. 3 years after the project ends.

### 3.3   Common Territorial Monitoring Framework

Aiming for the CO-TAMP platform to be designed and built as durable interactive visualization platform, which could support the informed and timely territorial attractiveness-related decision-making and policy management in the each partner-country as well as on the Danube region level, project partners have established comprehensive framework for territorial monitoring, so-called Common territorial monitoring framework [18]. This framework includes elements that would provide underlying context for the CO-TAMP platform sustainability and relevance in the long run. These elements include variety of 'soft' and 'hard' tasks, which regularly performed would support the emergence of specific co-creation process needed for keeping the social and technical components of CO-TAMP platform integrated.

Thus, after identifying main elements for the transnational monitoring system during the Attract-SEE project[2], and their reconsideration and minor adjustments against the DTP goals as well as the contexts of Danube region countries at the beginning of Attractive Danube project, stakeholders along the focus groups were invited – as part of participatory approach – to join the activities for building requirements-driven interactive Web mapping application named CO-TAMP.

In next lines, development methodology for the establishment of CO-TAMP platform would be described, and afterwards resulting Web mapping application features would be presented.

# 4 Methodology

During the initiation phase, the Attractive Danube project partners have upgraded those 22 transnational indicators selected during the previous Attract-SEE project, as well as relevant national databases. Also, relying on the previously defined Common territorial monitoring framework and its elements, they agreed on the methodology consisting of a 3-step approach for CO-TAMP platform development.

## 4.1 Data Sources Identification, Their Analysis and Data Collection

In this first step, following those 22 indicator definitions, all project partners had first to identify the available data sources or datasets on national level for those indicators calculation. Then, project partners performed detailed analysis of identified data sources, in sense of their reliability, conditions of availability, existing data formats, data access methods, data collection frequency, standards, coverage, etc. After extensive analysis of the data sources for indicators, project partners had to determine the collection and calculation methods for every indicator. The main challenge in this first step was to find the national data source for each indicator with the same measurement method and unit as well as specified period of time (from 2008 to 2021 as planned) for all project partners, in order for the indicators' values to be standardize and, thus, mutually comparable.

## 4.2 Indicators Definition, Values Storage and Quality Assessment

In order for the Attractive Danube project results to be sustainable and developed CO-TAMP platform to be durable, appropriate documentation had to be prepared for keeping the analytical work results consistent, reproducible and traceable. In

---

[2] Common territorial monitoring framework includes CO-TAMP goals, institutional, legal and financial frameworks (except technological one), its content and users.

accordance with the good practice, this documentation was planned to consist of the fact sheet – or indicator methodological sheet – and metadata information for each indicator and its source.

Further, using the collected and processed datasets from identified data sources, the indicators' values were calculated, input and stored within the CO-TAMP platform database by using one of the two methods (depended on the project partner capacities): (1) by keying-in indicator values directly to the Web mapping application as attributes of the spatial units (NUTS regions), and (2) by filling indicator values into the Excel table and their later migration to the database.

Finally, calculated and input indicators' values had been subject to the data quality assessment procedure, conducted in a view of achieving one of the main project objectives, that is, to make quality territorial attractiveness-related data available for the Danube region. This data quality assessment procedure included the indicators' values verification against the four standard quality criteria: completeness, consistency, accuracy and logical sense of the calculated values.

### 4.3    Geovisualization Tool for Territorial Monitoring

CO-TAMP as transnational monitoring system was planned to support the collection, storage, analysis and management in general of the standardized, reliable, updated and relevant indicators data, on one side; and to provide diversified model of tools, methods and techniques for the geographical visualization through the interactive user inter-faces, on the other side. Required interactivity of the CO-TAMP platform was found necessary for appropriate informing territorial attractiveness policy process in each partner-country[3], as well as to support coordination of the national policies and EU priorities within the Danube region.

Relying on the results of previous EU-funded project, and aiming to efficiency and effectiveness in general, the Attractive Danube project partners have decided to adapt the already developed STAGE II Web mapping application as a basis for the CO-TAMP platform development.

#### STAGE II Web Mapping Application
STAtistics&GEography or STAGE II solution (http://gis.stat.si/index.php) is an inte-grated platform and a freely accessible interactive cartographic application for the analysis, display, evaluation and dissemination of the geospatial statistics and usage of data (like images, charts, files) on a mobile phone, tablet and desktop computer. This user-friendly application is developed[4] and maintained by the Geodetic Institute of Slovenia, the Lead partner of the Attractive Danube project, in association with the Statistical Office of the Republic of Slovenia [9].

For purpose of the Attractive Danube project, existing STAGE II registry with the four types of aggregating spatial units for Slovenia was extended with the spatial units for project partner countries (from NUTS0 to NUTS3), which are stored within the

---

[3] http://www.interreg-danube.eu/approved-projects/attractive-danube/section/attractiveness-indicators.

[4] Project was funded by the EUROSTAT.

EuroGeographics[5] database. For CO-TAMP application, national and federal state[6] boundary data were used for the indicators' values aggregation, management and geovisualization.

# 5   CO-Tamp

Based on the STAGE II solution, CO-TAMP platform[7] was developed as an interactive cartographic solution for collecting, processing, archiving and visualizing the territorial attractiveness relevant indicators for the Danube region. This transnational monitoring system consists of the two closely linked parts, Web map viewer and the powerful analytical tools for geovisualization, which would be described in more details in the next three chapters.

## 5.1   Architecture Framework

The CO-TAMP user interface is a Web application, which central part consists of the interactive map with alternative cartographic background (MapBox, OpenStreetMap, White background; see Fig. 7) and the overlay layer in form of an interactive mapping tool, showing the indicators' values by the national and federal spatial units. The menu placed on the left side of Web map viewer allows user the selection of indicator for presentation as well as dynamic time and space variations of the indicator values. Besides mentioned variables, user can change through the menu existing color scheme, transparency and distribution of the selected indicator's values by grade.

The system has modular design and it is hierarchically arranged in the six structurally connected sets (Fig. 3). The bottom OS layer is a platform independent, which means that CO-TAMP application can be installed in any environment that supports Java 8. The servers' layer consists of the open source PostgreSQL database with PostGIS add-on. Also, GEO network is used as a tool for handling mandatory INSPIRE [8] regulations. However, besides installed INSPIRE Network Services (CSW, WMS and WFS), this solution allows any Web mapping service to be included without modifying the program code.

An important feature of the CO-TAMP application is that the spatial units and indicators' values are stored independently within the database, and their dependence is only reflected within the distribution environment, that is, in display. This enables quick and easy – independent – updating of these two datasets.

The language of CO-TAMP application is (only) English for the moment. So, when user opens application, first obligatory step is the selection of a variable, that is, indicator which would be displayed and/or analyzed (Fig. 4). By default, the choropleth map containing the latest available indicator values for selected variables is rendered.

---

[5] https://eurogeographics.org/.

[6] Only for Germany.

[7] http://cotamp.gis.si/attractive_danube/.

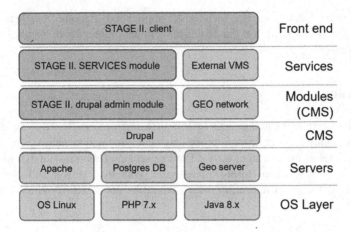

**Fig. 3.** CO-TAMP web mapping application: architecture framework

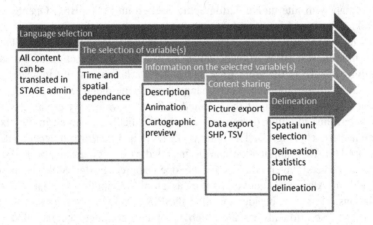

**Fig. 4.** CO-TAMP web mapping application: client work-flow diagram

The CO-TAMP application offers various operations that can be performed on the choropleth maps, like data export, picture export and spatial querying.

However, since CO-TAMP application is implemented as the centralized database, i.e. as client-server model, requirements in the sense of hardware and software may vary depending on the expected number of users. Also, on the client side, CO-TAMP application was tested within Chrome, Mozilla and Edge browsers for the desktop users, and within Chrome and Safari browsers for the mobile users.

Finally, CO-TAMP application is the highly scalable solution, and it can be used even globally since it is coordinate system independent.

## 5.2    Documentation

The CO-TAMP platform is designed around those 22 indicators (Table 1.), which values are derived from the various data sources. These data sources are, in most of the cases, databases on national or EU level that have data needed for the calculation of indicators' values. Majority of these sources are managed by the state authorities in partner countries, so these databases have already metadata (data update frequency, quality, etc.) and, thus, it is relatively easily to incorporate them (data) into the CO-TAMP database. By storing and archiving of data into the CO-TAMP application database users can recreate indicators values and visualize them even in the case when methodology of indicator calculation is changed, and original data source doesn't store that data anymore.

Anyway, in order for the analytical work performed by using CO-TAMP application to be traceable and reproducible, and obtained results to have consistency and relevance, project partners have created relevant documentation. Thus, besides the fact sheet for each indicator in the Territorial Attractiveness Atlas of the Danube Region, metadata accessible within the CO-TAMP application complement those fact sheets information by providing the basic information about data sources for indicators – that is, used databases – for all partner countries (Fig. 5).

Additionally, due to its modular design, the CO-TAMP application is extendable and upgradable, and it's relatively easy to update its content and information, which is important for this transnational monitoring system durability.

| Type of indicator | Transnational (CO-TAMP), collection at national level |
|---|---|
| Annual range | 2008/2021 |
| Data source for indicator | Statistical office of the Republic of Slovenia (SURS) http://pxweb.stat.si/pxweb/Dialog/varval.asp?lang=2&ma=0867325S&path=../Database /Dem_soc/08_zivljenjska_raven/08_silc_kazalniki_revsc/15_08673_porazdel_dohodka/& ti= |
| Key statistical data used | / |
| Spatial level | National, Regional, County |
| Data completeness | Data available for the period 2008-2016 (by 09.01.2018), annual periodicity. |
| Policy/goals | This indicator measures the disposable income of the households and by extension, individuals; it is an indicator with a high degree of comparability which provides relevant information on the welfare of the citizens over a certain period, as well as the level of poverty. |
| Contact person if available | On behalf of the ATTRACTIVE DANUBE partner: Blaž Barborič, e-mail: blaz.barboric@gis.si |
| Conditions of use | Indicators available for download |

**Fig. 5.** Indicator metadata (Example indicator: Gross disposable household income)

## 5.3    Geovisualization Features

Besides core functionalities available on the administrator side, which are used for the general – that is, default – adjustment of variable parameters and geospatial layers, CO-TAMP application offers the three groups of functionalities on the client – user – side (Fig. 6). All user functionalities are designed to be intuitive, and could be approached from the single point – menu – making thus CO-TAMP application highly user-friendly.

**Fig. 6.** CO-TAMP application: menu with the three groups of user functionalities (Example indicator: Population growth rate (%) in the Danube region in 2014)

The first group of user functionalities is activated by selecting one of those 22 indicators from the menu on the left side, which is the main place for interacting with the indicators data stored in the CO-TAMP database. After selecting indicator, short description and link to the metadata information for that indicator become available, both necessary for its usability evaluation and values interpretation. Besides this information, dynamic time and space variations fields become also accessible for the selected indicator values, where value domain for time ranges from 2008 to 2017 year and space field has default value "Danube region". Also, part of this first group of the CO-TAMP user functionalities includes Download, Share and Animate options.

The second group of the user functionalities, gathered under the Legend Settings option in the CO-TAMP application, provides tools for customization of the selected indicator's values display in the map view by making available: (1) list of different types of classification, (2) several color palettes, (3) distinct color for the unclassified, and (4) color transparency possibility.

Finally, option Spatial Query presents third group of the CO-TAMP user functionalities, where delineation function is used for getting the insights into relations between data stored in the CO-TAMP application database, thus providing better understanding of the territorial attractiveness status and issues in the Danube region. Selected indicators' values are here displayed using the method of a bar chart, which combined with the available filtering methods (by point, circle, rectangle or other polygon) allows indicators' values and their relations to be further analyzed, specified and compared.

On the other side, in the CO-TAMP map view (Fig. 7), choropleth map is rendered according to the various options set for the selected indicator's values through the menu, which are limited by the general settings made within the administrator module. Also, at the moment, the choropleth mapping technique is the only method for thematic mapping and spatial presentation of indicators' values within the CO-TAMP application. Therefore, display in the CO-TAMP map view depends mainly on the classification method chosen from Legend Settings, where available options for data optimization correspond to those in the other GIS applications, like Jenks, Manual, Quantiles, Equal intervals and Categorized.

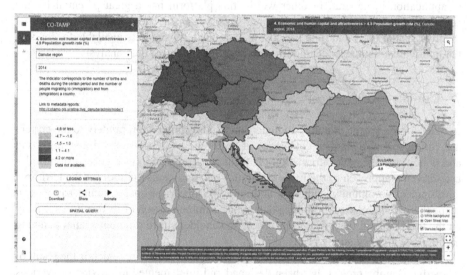

**Fig. 7.** CO-TAMP application: map view (Example indicator: Population growth rate (%) in the Danube region in 2014)

## 6  Discussion

Here developed and implemented solution – CO-TAMP – for the transnational monitoring and dissemination of the Attractive Danube project's results, provides advantages of the interactive geovisualization needed for better analysis, visualization and understanding of the territorial attractiveness quality and spatial dynamics in the Danube region. Moreover, this Web mapping application contains the components necessary for its analytical procedures consistency and reproducibility that would secure the CO-TAMP durability, mandatory for this platform to be successful in supporting efficient and effective decision-making and policy management in the Danube region.

On technology side, the open source CO-TAMP application with its modular design and scalability feature, provides easily accessible and flexible solution. These capabilities open possibilities for its future simple adjustments to the new user requirements, as well as additional or changed content handling; furthermore, these capabilities make feasible simple upgrading and/or combining of CO-TAMP application with the new technologies and data management concepts.

On the user side, related to the CO-TAMP content and geovisualization feature, this platform's structure and tools create user-friendly and intuitive environment that lead the user actions logically towards discovering and displaying known as well as new insights of the relations between spatial phenomena and their dynamics within the Danube region.

In future, research and development of the CO-TAMP platform should generally be focused on the introduction of advanced data analysis, as well as further development of application in general. In other words, this platform has a great potential for the advanced data analysis and data mining, since it transparently organizes data across different spatial units and time periods, making them thus readily available for input to the multivariate analysis techniques and other geostatistical data analysis.

# 7 Conclusions

In order for the spatial planning to understand and respond appropriately to the current and future spatial dynamics challenges, it needs the evidence-based decision-making and policy management information platform that could support highly customized – user-driven – approach to the maps creation. Proved to be useful tool for the territorial development community gathering and empowering, these maps should trigger and shape the individual visual thinking and public communication of its results, especially on the transnational level in Europe where stakeholders have different spatial planning traditions and expectations in this domain.

In this paper presented the transnational CO-TAMP platform, which is the result of Attractive Danube project, has been designed and implemented to provide the various geovisualization features in order for the territorial attractiveness policies and priorities to be monitored and evaluated by the Danube countries against the national, EUSDR as well as the other EU and regional policies and initiatives goals. Also, here introduced transnational monitoring system solution is based on the knowledge created by the ESPON and other EU-related initiatives and projects, producing thus new knowledge and lessons learnt that could be applied in the other projects, but also serve as input for the new development programming round in Europe (2021–2027).

Finally, with emergence of new technologies and the growing complexity of spatial relations and development challenges, it could be expected that number of transnational and territorial monitoring systems in general would increase in future, and that geovisualization for spatial planning and territorial development purposes is going to see rapid development in the coming years.

# References

1. Nöllenburg, M.: Geographic visualization. Human-Centered Visualization Environments: GI-Dagstuhl Research Seminar, Dagstuhl Castle, Germany, Revised Lectures, pp. 257–294 (2006). https://doi.org/10.1007/978-3-540-71949-6_6
2. EU: Territorial Agenda of the European Union 2020 (2011). http://ec.europa.eu/regional_policy/en/information/publications/communications/2011/territorial-agenda-of-the-european-union-2020S
3. Dühr, S.: The Visual Language of Spatial Planning: Exploring Cartographic Representation for Spatial Planning in Europe. Routledge, New York (2007)
4. Lindberg, G., Dubois, A.: How to monitor territorial dynamics. Nordregio News Publication Issue    (2014).    http://www.nordregio.se/Publications/Publications-2014/Monitoring-Territorial-Dynamics/
5. Soria-Lara, J.A., Zúñiga-Antón, M., Pérez-Campaña, R.: European spatial planning observatories and maps: merely spatial databases or also effective tools for planning? Environ. Plan. B: Plan. Des. **42**(5), 904–929 (2015). http://journals.sagepub.com/doi/abs/10.1068/b130200p
6. EUROPE 2020 a strategy for smart, sustainable and inclusive growth. http://ec.europa.eu/eu2020/pdf/COMPLET%20EN%20BARROSO%20%20%20007%20-%20Europe%202020%20-%20EN%20version.pdf
7. ESPON Inspire Policy Making by Territorial Evidence. https://www.espon.eu/main/
8. INSPIRE Infrastructure for spatial information in Europe. http://inspire.ec.europa.eu/
9. Geodetic Institute of Slovenia (2018). STAGE 2.0 Technical report
10. ESPON: COMPASS – comparative analysis of territorial governance and spatial planning systems in Europe. Final Report (2018). https://www.espon.eu/planning-systems
11. Attractive Danube. http://www.interreg-danube.eu/approved-projects/attractive-danube
12. ESPON: ATTREG - The Attractiveness of European regions and cities for residents and visitors – Final Report (2013). http://www.espon.eu/main/Menu_Projects/Menu_ESPON2013Projects/Menu_AppliedResearch/attreg.html
13. Danube Transnational Programme. http://www.interreg-danube.eu/
14. EU Regional or Cohesion Policy. http://ec.europa.eu/regional_policy/en/
15. Živković, L.: A proposal for the spatial planning monitoring system in Serbia. In: Gervasi, O., et al. (eds.) ICCSA 2017. LNCS, vol. 10407, pp. 555–570. Springer, Cham (2017). https://doi.org/10.1007/978-3-319-62401-3_40
16. Živković, L., Barborič, B.: "Attractive Danube" – improving capacities for enhancing territorial attractiveness of the Danube region. In: REAL CORP Conference, Vienna, Austria (2017). http://programm.corp.at/cdrom2017/papers2017/CORP2017_17.pdf
17. Živković, L., Barborič, B.: "ATTRACTIVE DANUBE project – territorial attractiveness analysis of the Danube Region. In: REAL CORP Conference, Vienna, Austria (2018). http://programm.corp.at/cdrom2018/papers2018/CORP2018_7.pdf
18. Živković, L., et al.: Towards a monitoring information system for territorial attractiveness policy management in South East Europe. Geodetski vestnik **59**(4), 752–766 (2015). https://doi.org/10.15292/geodetski-vestnik.2015.04.752-766

# An Agent-Based Model (ABM) for the Evaluation of Energy Redevelopment Interventions at District Scale: An Application for the San Salvario Neighborhood in Turin (Italy)

Caterina Caprioli[✉] , Marta Bottero , and Marialisa Pellegrini

Interuniversity Department of Regional and Urban Studies and Planning (DIST),
Politecnico di Torino, Castello del Valentino: Viale Pier Andrea Mattioli, 39,
10125 Turin, TO, Italy
{caterina.caprioli,marta.bottero,
marialisa.pellegrini}@polito.it

**Abstract.** The optimization of mobility connections, the use of renewable energy resources and the retrofit of buildings are only some of the aspects that affect urban transformations and planning. Decision maker and urban planners must be faced with multi-dimensional aspects and objectives in a long-term vision. In that context, different methods have been developed in order to consider these multi-dimensional perspectives. However, only a few approaches try to simulate the effects in a multi-temporal way. Agent-based model (ABM) try to do exactly this, considering, in particular, the interactions among agents through a bottom-up approach. Aim of this research is to apply an ABM to a real case study in the San Salvario neighborhood in Turin (Italy), simulating a complex socio-economic-architectural adaptive system to study the temporal diffusion of energy requalification operations and the willingness of inhabitants to adopt different retrofit actions. The two applications were, firstly, built on a computer grid environment and, then, integrated with GIS maps, in order to analyse the effects in the real distribution of buildings of San Salvario. Agents are designed to choose which system adopt, based on different theories of human behaviors. We discuss limitations of the current models and we suggest future directions of this research.

**Keywords:** Agent-based model · Energy ·
Geographic Information System (GIS)

## 1 Introduction

Nowadays, urban regeneration is a "universal question", a current problem and a crucial factor in new planning trends and it has become an integral part of new urban and housing policies [1]. Problems in the field of urban regeneration and planning concern normally multiple conflicting aspects and incommensurable elements, this requiring specific approaches for the analysis. In particular, sustainable neighbourhood

© Springer Nature Switzerland AG 2019
S. Misra et al. (Eds.): ICCSA 2019, LNCS 11621, pp. 388–403, 2019.
https://doi.org/10.1007/978-3-030-24302-9_28

policies require a territorial approach, the analysis of a large stock of buildings and the development of scenarios, that need a very large amount of data, of information and of a wide range of criteria. In this context, decision makers held appropriate tools to structure problems, to plan and evaluate alternatives in a multi-temporal, multi-objective and long-term perspective. The present paper investigates the use of integrated evaluation tools for supporting decision problems in the context of urban regeneration operations, focusing in particular on the application of Agent-based model and GIS tools. Geographical Information System (GIS) plays a key role here, because it is able to support decision-making processes by integrating different geospatial data and by producing results that simulate well the real spatial environment with their dynamics.

A real case study, the district of San Salvario in the city of Turin (Italy), is considered in the development of the evaluation.

## 2 Dynamic Models: A Brief Overview

About 30 years ago, new modelling approaches from different sources come onto the horizon, in order to integrate dynamic to the traditional model [2]. In particular, Cellular Automata (CA), Agent-Based Models (ABM), Systems Dynamics Models (SDM), Spatial Econometric Models (SEM) and Microsimulation Models (MM) all informed the debate [2]. Heppenstal et al. [2] provide a useful overview of the origin and development of this dynamic models, in particular, in their connection in the evolution of spatial models. Starting from this study, in this paper, we briefly describe in Table 1, the most used dynamic models, in order to underline strengths and weakness and to highlight the reasons why we adopted ABM for our simulations. In particular, we focus on the differences in their scale of using, in the construction of population and environment and in their execution and definition of time.

For the dynamic models' comparison, the parameters were defined based on our research question, i.e. the study of the diffusion of more sustainable energy production technologies and retrofit systems at district-scale. So, first of all, the scale and the time were relevant, since the aim was to test in a long-term perspective the effects emerging from the simulation at a specific level of detail, i.e. the district scale. Secondly, the environment parameter was investigated as our objective was to integrate the spatial dimension, in order to represent buildings, their characteristics and the population in a real geographic distribution. Furthermore, the analysis of technology diffusion and retrofit actions adoption in a real-environment requires a population characterized not by homogeneous groups, but by single agents with their own decision rules and specific characteristics distributed in a real space.

Based on this comparison, it is quite clear as agent-based model was chosen for our application. It represents a powerful methodology in decision making thanks to its ability to consider qualitative and subjective aspects together with real data in a multi-temporal and spatial dimension.

**Table 1.** Comparison between dynamic models in spatial context

| Model | Scale | Environment | Population | Time |
|---|---|---|---|---|
| Agent-Based Models (ABM) (Multi Agent Systems (MAS)) [2] | Small scale (but large scale for land cover) | Environment contains agents (often more passive than population) | Hundreds of autonomous agents (detailed) | Flexible (both short and long intervals) |
| Cellular Automata (CA) [3] | Quite flexible (often small) | Two-dimensional mesh of finite cells Homogeneus | (environment replaces population) | Flexible |
| Land Use Transportation Interaction Models (LUTI) [2] | Large scale (aggregate and cross-sectional models) | (population replaces environment) | Location of activities and their interactions | Usually no temporal effects, only spatial (in general short-term dynamics) |
| Microsimulation Models (MM) [2] | Any scale (composed by individuals) | Large scale population | Population as distribution of characteristics (of a sample) | Flexible (both short and long intervals) |
| Systems Dynamic Models (SDM) [4] | Quite flexible | Entity flow and resource sharing, it is represented by "processes" | Equations capture decision rules. The focus is on "processes" not on "agents" | Flexible (both short and long intervals) |
| Spatial Econometric Models (SEM) [5] | Spatial scale varies with the time-scale | Spatial autoregressive structure | Population groups with dynamic relationships | Flexible (in general short-interval time) |

## 2.1   Agent-Based Models (ABM)

Agent-based modeling (ABM) has become a widely used approach in many disciplines in the last 15 years [2], spanning physic, biology, ecology, social sciences, economy and geography [6, 7]. The increasing development of ABM goes in parallel with the study of complex systems, characterized by non-linear relationships between constantly changing entities [8]. These models seem to be particularly successful in these studies, mainly because they rely on the idea of effects and synergetic characteristics emerging from the analysis of subcomponent relationships [8]. In fact, ABM allows to study and verify the influence of decisions at the micro level which effects emerging at macro level [9].

Agents are the crucial component in this model. About them, there is no universal agreement among researchers about the precise definition of agent [6], beyond the essential property of autonomy [8]. The autonomy characteristic means that agents have control over their actions and internal state in order to achieve goals. Certainly, agents are individual objective-oriented entities, which interact with the others inside of a shared environment. This environment can provide only information about the spatial location of each agent, but also a rich set of information and data, which are available for the agent through a GIS integration [8].

The model is often described using the standard ODD protocol (Overview, Design Concepts and Details) [10] to facilitate the readability of the structure and to ensure the replicability of the model. The steps of this approach are the following: formulation of the question, formulation of the hypothesis, definition of the model structure, implementation of the model through software, analysis and revision [10].

Their "exploratory simulation" capability is fundamental in studying complex system. In fact, ABM can be used as a sort of virtual laboratory, where multiple simulation sessions occur varying inputs and changing parameters [11].

## 3 Materials and Method

### 3.1 Study Area Presentation and Objective

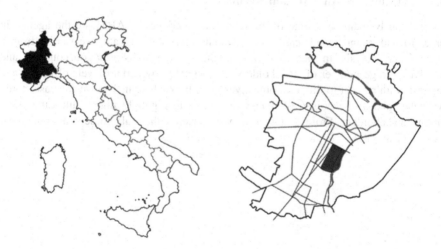

**Fig. 1.** Location of the area under investigation (San Salvario, Turin, Italy)

San Salvario is one of the 34 districts of the city of Turin (Italy) (Fig. 1). Not far from the city centre and the Porta Nuova railway station, this neighborhood is characterized by a multi-ethnical population, many leisure places and some relevant historical buildings, such as Castello del Valentino [12]. With a surface of about 2.2 km$^2$ and a diversified population of about 35.400 inhabitants (4% of the total population of the city) [13], it represents an interesting place to test ABM. In addition, the presence of not homogeneous building stock is an occasion to verify different energy savings actions of retrofitting and the diffusion of energy generation systems, in particular, PVs. In fact, ambitious objective, in the Energy Center mind [14], is to transform the San Salvario neighborhood in an exemplary eco-district for the city of Turin, in which experiment different policies and actions, that could be extended to the overall city.

Starting from this context, our research takes place. Through the development of an ABM, the model investigates the choices of individual agents with respect to an architectural and energy requalification at the district scale, considering social and economic aspects. These choices reflect rules and opinions that vary over time. People change their mind when faced with persuasive arguments and influenced by other agents' decisions [15]. The model tries to observe the dynamic trends and behaviors of the agent inhabitants by varying the attributes of agents and considering external factors, such as economic incentives. This happens in an environment in which agents' choices and actions influence the decisions of others after communication and interaction among them.

### 3.2 Stakeholders Analysis and Agents

As previously mentioned, one of the main characteristics of ABM are the agents. In order to understand in our case study, which actors are relevant, we started from a stakeholder analysis. In fact, as it is well know, urban transformation concerns and involves a large number of stakeholders, characterized by certain levels of power and interest, with respect to different objectives [16]. In our first analysis of the case study, we developed a power interest matrix (see [17]) to highlight mainly the differences among stakeholders. From that matrix, we clustered the stakeholders in four agent classes (Table 2).

**Table 2.** List of the San Salvario neighborhood stakeholders clustered in four agent classes

| INHABITANTS | | PUBLIC ADIMISTRATION | |
| --- | --- | --- | --- |
| | Homeowners | | Municipality of Turin |
| | Tenants | | Metropolitan city of Turin |
| | Surrounding inhabitants | | Transport agency (GTT) |
| | Future inhabitants | | Politecnico di Torino and Università degli studi di Torino |
| | Young people and students | | Government department responsible for the environment and historical building |
| | Neighborhood community | | Environmental associations |
| | Multi-etnical community | | Water provider (SMAT) |
| | Religious community | | Municipal waste management company (AMIAT) |
| **WORKERS AND ACTIVITIES** | | **PROVIDERS** | |
| | Owners of commercial activities | | Photovoltaic panels providers |
| | Owners of sports facilities | | Energy provider (ENEL/IREN) |
| | Restaurants owners | | |
| | Potential entrepreneurs | | |

The agents, as required by ABM, are heterogeneous autonomous entities [6] characterized by their own attributes and behaviors. They can interact with all the elements in the model, but, the real-world social networks tend to have non-random network structure with properties such as short average path length, excess clustering, and skewed degree distributions [18].

In these first applications, the most relevant agents are the neighborhood inhabitants, because they are directly involved in the transformation. In fact, based on their socio-economic status, they have the final say in the setting of retrofitting systems or the adoption of PVs. They are entities without specialised knowledge, with high interests and expectations, with limited economic resources and with low power to contrast a major intervention, but they are fundamental because without them the realization of the project is not feasible.

In the definition of the agents' objectives, economic and technical aspects were considered (such as investment costs, energy consumption, efficiency and reliability of installed systems, market price, lifetime of each technology, architectural quality).

However, also the municipality has a key role. It cannot act actively in the model, but through different incentives and policies can change the inhabitants' opinions, in particular, with respect to their economic possibilities.

### 3.3  Simulation Experiments

This section presents different simulation experiments. The first one investigates on the temporal diffusion of the photovoltaic system in the San Salvario neighborhood, whereas the second one tests the adoption of different retrofit systems. Both applications were implemented in NetLogo 6.0.4 [19], a free software based on an evolution of the programming language Logo [20]. It is a powerful data processing system with an intuitive interface, an effective graphic support and an ease of use, also in the code writing [19].

**Application 1.** The first experiment explores the temporal diffusion of PV microgeneration systems in the San Salvario district, simulating households' choices during a period of 50 years. Many factors influence these choices, such as households age and skills, family income, neighbourhood influence, incentives. The initial state of the model simulates the characteristics of the inhabitants and the environment of the San Salvario neighborhood, based on data obtained from Turin census (2011) [21], information provided by the municipality in their GIS maps [13] (see [17]) and different data from the literature [22–24].

Important parameters considered in the experiment are the percentage of San Salvario buildings equipped with a photovoltaic system and the percentage of homes connected to the national grid. Furthermore, the income is fundamental to identify if a household can or cannot install the PV.

At the beginning of the experiment, the households start to take their decisions. Those who have already had a PV, but its service life is over, can decide to buy another one or to connect to the national grid. On the contrary, those connected to the national grid can choose to install a PV, influenced by the neighbours' choices or by their eager to innovate.

The steps for the construction of this model are the following:

1. replication of the state of art, defining the characteristics of the agents and of the environment. We assumed that 80% of households are connected to the national grid;
2. definition of the current cost of PV and its variation over time (cost reduction trend);
3. consideration of the lifetime of PV. Every 20 years the PV must be substituted, and the households can decide to install another PV or not.

The conditions to install the PV are expressed by Eq. (1):

$$C_{PV} < C_{kWh} \tag{1}$$

where $C_{kWh}$ is the cost of connection to the national electric grid and it is equal to 0.087 €/kWh according to the current Italian charges [25] and $C_{PV}$ is the cost of the photovoltaic system, that considers also the amount of energy produced by the national grid and necessary to cover the total consumption of each households. This cost is given by Eq. (2):

$$C_{PV} = CC_{PV} + \%C_{kWh} \tag{2}$$

where $CC_{PV}$ is the cost of all components of the PV (including operating and maintenance costs) and $\%C_{kWh}$ is a percentage of the costs to be paid to the national grid when the kWh produced by the PVs do not cover the total kWh used by each agent; $kW_P$ (kilowatt-peak) takes into account the family's activity profile, energy demand and usage factor (including non-use rates and system losses) [26].

Many studies show as incentives and subsidies are largely responsible for the rapid growth of photovoltaic installations, emphasizing the importance of public administration in the diffusion of new technologies [27]. For that reason, we subtracted the value of the incentive from the total cost of the PV ($C_{PV-Total}$), as follow:

$$C_{PV-Total} = (CC_{PV} - S_{kWP}) * kW_P + \%C_{kWh} \tag{3}$$

where $kW_P$ (kilowatt-peak) takes into account the available coverage area of the roof for the installation, the efficiency and the losses due to inclination and the environmental factors (at 0.8) and $S_{kWP}$ is the value of incentive that increases, based on the annual $kW_P$ produced for the lifetime of the PV. The diffusion of a new technology depends on its real advantages, its easiness of use and social acceptance. The latter is crucial for the diffusion of new technology and, in particular, for photovoltaic systems characterized by a visual impact. Neighbourhood influence by "early" adopters plays an important role in increasing future adoptions. Visibility (the photovoltaic installed on the roofs) and word of mouth lead to an increase of consumers in a certain radius. These parameters can be measured through two aspects: the detection radius (space of interaction) and the neighbourhood threshold (minimum percentage of neighbours within a detection radius that have already adopted the technology).

Househoulds without PV develop firstly the idea of installing. In the application it has been assumed that this idea depends on the age and the skills of each household, on the level of innovation and on the influence of their neighbourhood. The idea of installing is verified by the following formula (4):

$$(F_{PV/RR} / F_{Total/RR}) * 100 > V_{RR} \tag{4}$$

where $F_{PV/RR}$ is the number of households with PVs in a certain radius RR, and $F_{Total/RR}$ is the total number of households within the same detection radius and $V_{RR}$ it is the proximity threshold.

All the variables used in the aforementioned experiment and their relative numerical values are summarized in Table 3.

**Table 3.** Variables of Application 1

| Variables name | Value | Unit of measure |
|---|---|---|
| $CC_{PV}$ | 2000 | €/kW$_P$ |
| PV lifetime | 20 | years |
| Coefficient of reduction | 0.80 | – |
| Energy cost | 0.087 | €/kWh |
| Discount rate | 0.82 | % |
| Incentives for kW$_P$ | 500 | €/kW$_P$ |
| RR | 30 | buildings |
| VRR | 0.05 | – |
| Energy requirements | 30 | kWh/m$^2$ |
| PV production | 1250 | kWh/kW$_P$ |

The initial detection radius is based on the population distribution. Once the idea of installing is verified, the agent checks the economic availability and evaluates all the other economic parameters as explained before.

In order to simulate the behavior of agents, we applied two of the most widespread behavioral theories presented in literature: the theory of planned behavior (TPB) and the Belief-Desire-Intention (BDI) model. The first, proposed by Ajzen [28], states that three aspects (attitude toward behavior, subjective norms and perceived control) shape an individual's behavioral intentions and behaviors. This theory has recently been used in agent-based model to predict diffusions of innovation and adoption of solar plants [29]. The second model (BDI) combines a philosophical model on human practical reasoning, originally developed by Bratman [30], with an abstract logical semantic. The model has been very successful, despite the criticism regarding the low adaptability in describing some behaviors. Based on this model, every agent considers the advantages and disadvantages of alternative options, balancing beliefs, desires and intentions. Beliefs are the set of agent's information. These beliefs need not necessarily be true, they are just the agent's perception of the world with respect to their local view. Desires represent the agent's objectives, that can be multiple and conflicting. Intentions are the agent's commitment to achieving these goals [29].

Starting from these assumptions, two different behavioral models have been built in the present simulation.

**Application 2.** The second application concerns the temporal diffusion of different types of retrofit: double glazing, envelop insulation and HVAC (heating, ventilation, and air conditioning). As the previous application, also this one takes into account the complexity of a decision in which human actors interact with other ones in an environment with different information and external aspects, as policies and incentives. This model is more complicated than the previous one because the number of parameters and choices are higher. Also in this case, the initial state of the model simulates the characteristics of the state of art of the San Salvario neighborhood, based on data obtained from Turin census (2011) [21], information provided by the municipality in their GIS maps [13] (see [17]) and different data from the literature [23, 24, 31, 32].

In the first simulation, we investigated essentially on the diffusion of a single technology. Otherwise, here, the agents choose among different options. However, as the previous application, the diffusion of a specific technology is based on the social acceptance of the agents (i.e. on the influence of neighbours) and the agents' behaviors follow the Theory of Planned Behavior (TPB) and the Belief-Desire-Intention model (BDI). The aspects that influence agents' choices are both internal, as technical (e.g. energy consumption), economic (e.g. family income), social (e.g. neighbourhood influence, agents own characteristics) and external (municipal policies and incentives).

The first four parameters that affect the simulation are:

- the percentage of San Salvario inhabitants who have already carried out small retrofit operations in order to improve the performance of their dwellings;
- the percentage of inhabitants who did not carry out any intervention;
- the percentage of historic buildings protected by the government department responsible for the environment and historical buildings;
- the energy consumption of each dwelling.

Retrofit technologies are installed only if the family income is sufficient and if:

$$C_{glass/ins/sys} < C_{kWh} \tag{5}$$

where $C_{kWh}$ is the cost of energy consumption per kWh at the initial state and $C_{glass/ins/sys}$ is the cost of the system adopted, given by:

$$C_{glass/ins/sys} = CC_{glass/ins/sys} + \%C_{kWh} \tag{6}$$

where $CC_{glass/ins/sys}$ is the cost of the raw material, the operating and maintenance costs and where $\%C_{kWh}$ is the cost referred to the energy consumption, reduced by a certain percentage based on the different technologies applied. The percentage of cost savings for the energy consumption of each technology results from the values of the Tabula project [33]. In this model, the $S_\%$ incentives are calculated in % of the total cost, they are equal to 65% or 50% [23, 34]. The total cost of the $C_{glass/ins/sys-Total}$ system is given by:

$$C_{glass/ins/sys-Total} = \left(CC_{glass/ins/sys} - S_\%\right) + \%C_{kWh} \tag{7}$$

The all variables and their relative values are summarized in Table 4.

**Table 4.** Variables of Application 2

| Variables name | Value | Unit of measure |
|---|---|---|
| $CC_{glass}$ | 150 | €/m$^2$ |
| $CC_{ins}$ | 20 | €/m$^2$ |
| $CC_{sys}$ | 1.500 | €/m$^2$ |
| Glass lifetime | 25 | years |
| Insulating lifetime | 25 | years |
| HVAC lifetime | 20 | years |
| Energy cost | 0.087 | €/kWh |
| Discount rate | 0.82 | – |
| Incentives | 50 | % |
| RR | 30 | buildings |

# 4   Results and Discussion

## 4.1   Application 1: Temporal Diffusion of PV Systems

*1. The first model* (Fig. 2) was developed without any integration with GIS environment. Consequently, the distribution of buildings and agents is based only on a regular grid without a real representation of the district.

In this model, a few semplifications have been assumed. Despite the simplifications, the model seems to be useful as it provides verifications on the possible trends emerging from different economic variations.

The agents (inhabitants of the San Salvario neighbourhood) are represented through a "home" shape, that highlight their fixed position, as they decide only for their property. In this experiment, the difference between turtles and patches are totally lost. In addition, the interactions among households of the same apartment buildings do not exist. The properties of each "home" are the result of an average of the attributes of each household that is part of the same apartment building.

This theoretical model shows the variation of trends caused by changes in economic variables, such as reduction of PV cost or increasing of incentives. In fact, after 50 years, the percentage of households that decide to install the photovoltaic (coloured in white) is 37,5% and those who already had a PV (coloured in yellow) are 18,5%. This growth is due to the continuous reduction in PV costs, the increase of neighbours with a PV and of awareness of the socio-economic benefits of PV.

As mentioned before, some parameters were defined *a priori* in the model. Therefore, particularly important is to test how the model changes based on the variations of these elements. By means of a sensitivity analysis, we varied the value of the neighborhood threshold (minimum percentage of neighbours within a detection radius that have already adopted the technology). Maintaining the same detection radius but increasing the number of households with a PV on their roofs (from 5% to 10%), the number of households that adopt a PV decrease. On the contrary, if the detection radius increases the new adopters of PV systems increase. Beyond the final results, these considerations highlight that the definition of these parameters are very important and can change significantly the results of the experiment. At the same time, the development of this model can be very useful in order to test the effects of different types or levels of incentives (in this specific case, for the diffusion of PV systems).

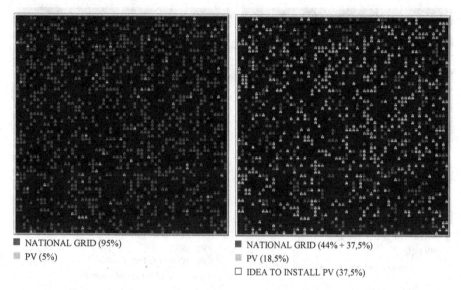

■ NATIONAL GRID (95%)
▩ PV (5%)

■ NATIONAL GRID (44% + 37,5%)
▩ PV (18,5%)
☐ IDEA TO INSTALL PV (37,5%)

**Fig. 2.** Initial setting of the model (Application 1), in the year zero (left), and the situation after fifty years (right). (Color figure online)

*2. The second model* (Fig. 3) was developed in a more realistic environment, through the integration of GIS, with the location of the real shape of the buildings of the San Salvario neighborhood. The parameters (Table 3) and the influence model are the same described in Application 1. Compared to the first model, this experiment allows defining clearly and separately patches (buildings) and turtles (households) with their specific characteristics (year of construction, roof dimension, architectural quality, age, skills, number of households and so on). In fact, with respect to the previous simulation, the data and the characteristics are not defined random, but specific for each element of the system.

In addition, the dynamics of interactions among households of the same apartment buildings are presented here. In fact, the PVs can be applied only if a certain percentage of households of the same apartment building agrees in the PV installation. The results of the simulation are shown in Fig. 3 where the buildings with a grey contour are those in which the PV has been applied. In the other buildings, the percentage of households agree are not sufficient for the adoption of this technology.

In this integrated model, different changes in the parameters' values were also tested to verify the possible variations of the results. The most interesting one for this application is related to the minimum percentage of households who must agree on the installation of PV.

Due to the difficulties in the integration of GIS data at this scale of representation, we developed the model in a very small portion of the San Salvario neighborhood. Future applications will go deep on this investigation.

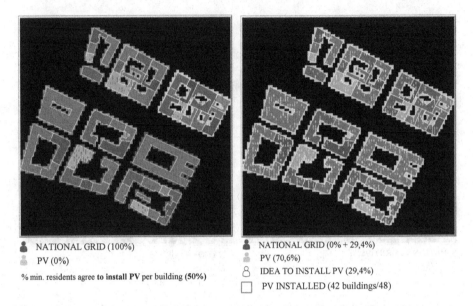

👤 NATIONAL GRID (100%)

👤 PV (0%)

% min. residents agree **to install PV** per building **(50%)**

👤 NATIONAL GRID (0% + 29,4%)

👤 PV (70,6%)

👤 IDEA TO INSTALL PV (29,4%)

☐ PV INSTALLED (42 buildings/48)

**Fig. 3.** Initial setting of the model (Application 1_with GIS), in the year zero (left), and the situation after fifty years (right).

### 4.2 Application 2: Temporal Diffusion of Retrofit Technologies

For this application, only one model was developed (Fig. 4) without any integration of GIS.

The strong increase of retrofit actions from year 0 to 50 is due to many factors, including the decline in the costs of the systems, but, in particular, for the neighbours' influence and for the increasing awareness on the socio-economic benefits of these actions.

As, the previous application, the advantages and disadvantages are quite the same. Certainly, the most relevant aspect of this model is its ability to highlight the reasons that affect mostly the agents' choices, in particular, with respect to the diffusion of information and incentives. However, the quite limited data and the lack of integration with GIS give us only a partial view of the real dynamics of these choices.

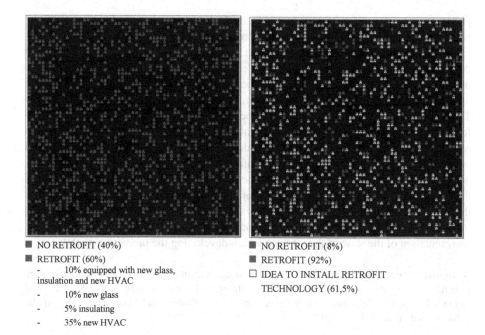

NO RETROFIT (40%)
RETROFIT (60%)
-        10% equipped with new glass,
insulation and new HVAC
-        10% new glass
-        5% insulating
-        35% new HVAC

NO RETROFIT (8%)
RETROFIT (92%)
☐ IDEA TO INSTALL RETROFIT
TECHNOLOGY (61,5%)

**Fig. 4.** Initial setting of the model (Application 2), in the year zero (left), and the situation after fifty years (right).

## 5   Conclusion and Future Insights

Agent-based model is an alternative approach to design heterogeneous agents with different behaviors and to simulate complex interactions among them (non-linear, discontinuous and discrete) [35]. ABM leaves the static nature of most evaluation approaches, in order to analyse different outcomes and effects emerging at different times (hours, days, months, years) [2]. In this way, the model can realistically simulate urban developments or geographical phenomena [2]. The approach offers an opportunity to study and test social theories which can not be easily described using mathematical formulas and this in a well-defined environment, from buildings to entire cities [2].

This paper explores the choices of individual agents with respect to an architectural and energy requalification at the district scale, in particular, investigating on the temporal diffusion of the photovoltaic system (PV) and the willingness of inhabitants to adopt different retrofit actions.

These experiments demonstrate how ABM can serve as a virtual laboratory that contributes to scientific and policy debates on energy requalification of buildings at urban scale. However, as any other approach that tries to analyse a complex system has some limits and their outputs must be interpreted with caution. In fact, the aim of these first applications is not to give quantitative and accurate forecastings of these phenomena or a solution for policies. Instead, these experiments let to understand which factors affect these energetic and retrofit actions.

The own nature of the modelling system, based on human agents with different and contrasting behaviors and aims, subjective choices and specific characteristics, is very promising, but also not easy to build. Some aspects are difficult to quantify, calibrate and the quality of the inputs data determine significantly the outputs obtained. Therefore, the way of using the results can be also different, as to formulate quantitative forecasts or only qualitative trends. For that reason, it becomes necessary to develop robustness and sensitivity analysis in order to verify the accuracy of the model developed and the elements that vary significantly the outputs.

Future implementations of these experiments will concern exactly the development of these robustness analyses and the collection of more structured data and information about the San Salvario inhabitants through surveys and workshops. This latter is particularly important in order to reduce uncertainties and hypotheses and to recreate a more precise representation of the state of the art from which developing the predictive model.

**Acknowledgment.** Part of the work illustrated in the present paper has been developed in the research project titled VALIUM (Valuation for Integrated Urban Management) that has been supported from the Department of Regional and Urban Studies and Planning - DIST of the Politecnico di Torino (I call 2017).

# References

1. Andersen, H.T., van Kempen, R.: New trends in urban policies in Europe: evidence from the Netherlands and Denmark. Cities (2003). https://doi.org/10.1016/s0264-2751(02)00116-6
2. Heppenstall, A.J.J., Crooks, A.T., See, L.M., Batty, M.: Agent-based models of geographical systems (2012)
3. Kari, J.: Theory of cellular automata: a survey. Theor. Comput. Sci. (2005). https://doi.org/10.1016/j.tcs.2004.11.021
4. Sterman, J.: Business Dynamics—Systems Thinking and Modeling for a Complex World (2000)
5. LeSage, J.P.: An Introduction to Spatial Econometrics. Rev. d'économie Ind. (2013). https://doi.org/10.4000/rei.3887
6. Macal, C.M., North, M.J.: Tutorial on agent-based modelling and simulation. J. Simul. (2010). https://doi.org/10.1057/jos.2010.3
7. Grimm, V., et al.: A standard protocol for describing individual-based and agent-based models. Ecol. Modell. (2006). https://doi.org/10.1016/j.ecolmodel.2006.04.023
8. Parker, D.C., Manson, S.M., Janssen, M.A., Hoffmann, M.J., Deadman, P.: Multi-agent systems for the simulation of land-use and land-cover change: a review (2003)
9. Crooks, A., Castle, C., Batty, M.: Key challenges in agent-based modelling for geo-spatial simulation. Comput. Environ. Urban Syst. (2008). https://doi.org/10.1016/j.compenvurbsys.2008.09.004
10. Polhill, J.G., Parker, D., Brown, D., Grimm, V.: Using the ODD protocol for describing three agent-based social simulation models of land-use change. JASSS (2008)
11. Railsback, S.F., Grimm, V.: Agent-Based and Individual-Based Modeling: A Practical Introduction (2011)
12. Mela, A.: La città con-divisa. Lo spazio pubblico a Torino. Franco Angeli, Milano (2014)

13. http://www.geoportale.cittametropolitana.torino.it
14. http://www.energycenter.polito.it/en/
15. Deakin, M., Allwinkle, S.: Urban regeneration and sustainable communities: the role of networks, innovation, and creativity in building successful partnerships. J. Urban Technol. (2007). https://doi.org/10.1080/10630730701260118
16. Dente, B.: Understanding policy decisions. In: Dente, B. (ed.) Understanding Policy Decisions. SAST, pp. 1–27. Springer, Cham (2014). https://doi.org/10.1007/978-3-319-02520-9_1
17. Caprioli, C., Bottero, M.C.: Agent-based modelling and Geographic Information System for the evaluation of eco-district's scenarios. In: Leone, A., Gargiulo, C. (eds.) Environmental and Territorial Modelling for Planning and Design, pp. 35–45. FedOAPress, Naples (2018)
18. Gaston, M.E.: Social network structures and their impact on multi-agent system dynamics. Appl. Artif. Intell. (2005)
19. Tisue, S., Wilensky, U.: NetLogo: design and implementation of a multi-agent modeling environment. SwarmFest (2004)
20. Harvey, B.: Computer Science LOGO Style (1997)
21. https://www.istat.it/
22. Bertolini, M., D'Alpaos, C., Moretto, M.: Do smart grids boost investments in domestic PV plants? Evidence from the Italian electricity market. Energy **149**, 890–902 (2018). https://doi.org/10.1016/j.energy.2018.02.038
23. Bottero, M., Bravi, M., Dell'Anna, F., Mondini, G.: Valuing buildings energy efficiency through Hedonic Prices Method: are spatial effects relevant? Valori e Valutazioni **21**, 27–39 (2018)
24. D'Alpaos, C., Bragolusi, P.: Buildings energy retrofit valuation approaches: state of the art and future perspectives. Valori e Valutazioni **20**, 79–94 (2018)
25. www.luce-gas.it
26. Stefanutti, L. (ed): Manuale degli Impianti di Climatizzazione. Tecniche Nuove Edizioni (2008)
27. Robinson, S.A., Stringer, M., Rai, V., Tondon, A.: GIS-integrated agent-based model of residential solar PV diffusion. In: 32nd USAEE/IAEE North American Conference (2013)
28. Ajzen, I.: From intentions to actions: a theory of planned behavior. In: Kuhl, J., Beckmann, J. (eds.) Action Control. SSSSP, pp. 11–39. Springer, Heidelberg (1985). https://doi.org/10.1007/978-3-642-69746-3_2
29. Namazi-Rad, M.-R., Padgham, L., Perez, P., Nagel, K., Bazzan, A. (eds.): Agent Based Modelling of Urban Systems. Springer, Cham (2017). https://doi.org/10.1007/978-3-319-51957-9
30. Bratman, M.: Intentions, Plans, and Practical Reason (1987)
31. Canesi, R., D'Alpaos, C., Marella, G.: Forced sale values vs. market values in Italy. J. Real Estate Lit. **24**, 377–401 (2016)
32. D'Alpaos, C.: Methodological approaches to the valuation of investments in biogas production plants: incentives vs. market prices in Italy. Valori e Valutazioni **19**, 53–64 (2017)
33. https://areeweb.polito.it/ricerca/episcope/tabula/
34. www.agenziaentrate.gov.it
35. Bonabeau, E.: Agent-based modeling: methods and techniques for simulating human systems. Proc. Natl. Acad. Sci. (2002). https://doi.org/10.1073/pnas.082080899

# Future Computing System Technologies and Applications (FISTA 2019)

# Hardware Acceleration of Language Processing in Scripting Programming Languages

Hiroyuki Maeda[✉] and Kazuaki Tanaka

Kyushu Institute of Technology, Kitakyushu, Japan
maeda@sein.mse.kyutech.ac.jp, kazuaki@mse.kyutech.ac.jp

**Abstract.** This paper describes a hardware acceleration of language processing system in scripting programming languages. Scripting programming languages are high development efficiency since which is easy to write and high source code readability. On the other hand, embedded software developments take a lot of time and the difficulty level is high. We think that it is good to use scripting programming languages in embedded software developments for the improvement of development efficiency.

However, scripting programming languages require many hardware resource such memory and their execution speeds are slower than procedural languages such as C language. Therefore, we propose a hardware acceleration of language processing in scripting programming languages. Hardware acceleration technology can improve the processing performance of scripting programming languages by a pipeline processing.

We focus on a scripting programming language 'mruby/c' for embedded software developments. We implemented the hardware which performs the memory management and the instruction decoder in mruby/c. In this paper describes results of implementation of the hardware acceleration and the performance evaluation.

**Keywords:** Scripting language · FPGA · Hardware acceleration

## 1 Introduction

Embedded systems are advancing high functionality and complication. Embedded system developments take a lot of time and the difficulty level of developments are high since embedded system developments require the both of hardware and software development. Generally, the cost of software developments take rather than the hardware. Embedded software developments require to control the hardware such as some sensors and output devices.

In addition, IoT (Internet of Things) which various devices are connected to the internet and are controlled and observed through the communication is

S. Misra et al. (Eds.): ICCSA 2019, LNCS 11621, pp. 407–416, 2019.
https://doi.org/10.1007/978-3-030-24302-9_29

used in many industrial areas. It is increasing the additional value of embedded system by IoT appearance. IoT developments require the developments of wireless communication techniques in addition to both of hardware and software developments. Embedded software developments including IoT take a long time and costs.

Therefore, we think that it is good to use a scripting programming language in embedded software developments to improve software developments efficiency. Many script programming languages enable easy programming. The number of codes of script programming languages are shorter than the procedural language such as C language and also superior in readability. It is possible to improve the productivity of software developments using script programming languages. It is also easy to learn scripting programming languages for programming beginners.

However, scripting programming languages require many memory for the execution but hardware resources in embedded system are limited. In addition, the execution speed of scripting programming languages are slower than the procedural language such as C language.

In this paper, we propose the hardware acceleration of language processing system in scripting programming languages. The execution speed of hardware processing by the pipeline processing is faster than software processing. The hardware acceleration is possible to reduce the memory footprint of scripting programming languages. We improved the processing performance of scripting programming languages by using hardware acceleration.

## 2   Scripting Programming Languages

Scripting programming languages are a programming language that makes it easy to write codes because it is a simple syntax and is superior in readability. Currently, many scripting programming languages have appeared and are used in some system developments. This section describes the features of scripting programming languages.

### 2.1   Scripting Programming Languages for Web Application Developments

Many scripting languages are mainly used in Web application developments. The programming language Ruby is one of scripting programming languages and used widely in Web application developments.

#### – Ruby

The scripting programming language 'Ruby' is popular in developing Web applications. Ruby is an object-oriented scripting programming language. Ruby is developed in JAPAN and released as an open source software. The Web application framework Ruby on Rails for Ruby is provided and is popular in many enterprises.

Ruby is a programming language with high development efficiency since it is easy to write programs and has high readability. Ruby is a simply syntax and the code of Ruby can be written shortly.

Ruby is an interpreter language and a dynamic programming language. The types of variable and functions are interpreted in execution. Thus, programmers need not to write types and Ruby can extend programs flexibly.

Ruby performs a dynamic memory allocation in the same as many scripting programming languages. Programmers are not required to consider the memory management since the memory allocation and free in execution are performed the garbage collection in Ruby's language processing system. Programmers are not required to consider the memory management since the memory management in execution are performed by the garbage collection in Ruby's language processing system.

Ruby is difficult to use in embedded software developments with a little hardware resources. Ruby assumes the execution environment which has many hardware resources such as a server machine. The Ruby interpreter needs a lot of hardware resources to execute syntax and semantic analysis process. In addition, execution speeds become slow by Ruby interpreter and dynamic memory allocation.

## 2.2 Scripting Programming Languages for Embedded Software Developments

Ruby has another implementation for embedded software developments.

### – mruby

mruby is the lightweight implementation of Ruby for embedded software developments. It is published as an open source software [1]. mruby is enabled to execute on embedded devices while maintaining Ruby's high developments efficiency. Ruby is an interpreter language and is not suitable for embedded software developments. Therefore, mruby is a complier language and is executed by the mruby virtual machine (mruby VM). The construction of mruby program execution is shown in Fig. 1.

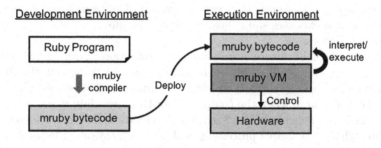

**Fig. 1.** mruby program execution

mruby is a compiler language and the dedicated mruby compiler generates from Ruby program to the mruby bytecode in the development environment. The mruby bytecode is a hardware independent format. The mruby VM interprets the mruby bytecode and executes in the execution environment. The mruby VM is consisted a part that executes mruby bytecode according to Ruby syntax and a part that controls hardware. Developer can rewrite a hardware dependent part in mruby VM and mruby can deploy in various embedded devices.

– **mruby/c**

mruby/c is the another implementation of mruby. mruby/c is published as an open source software [2]. mruby/c is the further lightweight implementation than mruby.

In the execution mechanism of mruby/c, the mruby compiler and the mruby bytecode is used same as mruby, but mruby/c is different the virtual machine. The mruby/c VM is a small implementation than the mruby VM. The mruby/c VM restricts some functions and reduces the memory size than mruby VM.

mruby and mruby/c are different the required memory size and target devices are different each. mruby requires less 400 KBytes memory and mainly targets embedded devices with OS (Operation System). On the other hand, mruby/c requires only 50 KBytes memory and mainly targets small embedded devices such as one-chip microcomputer, especially small IoT devices.

mruby/c supports concurrent execution functions without OS [3]. In IoT developments, it requires to control many sensors and communication technologies. By using multiprogramming, an algorithm in main and a program to control sensors can be developed independently and be improved the development efficiency.

In this study attempted to implement the hardware acceleration of mruby/c.

## 3   Hardware Acceleration

This section describes the difference between software and hardware processing.

– Software Processing
  The merit of software processing is to change a processing flexibly by rewriting the source code. However, the execution speed of software is slow because it interprets and executes single instruction one by one.
– Hardware Processing
  In the merit of hardware processing, the execution speed is fast because it can be pipeline processing by implementing the dedicated circuit. The hardware processing is good at simple arithmetic processing. The circuit scale becomes large when the complex algorithm including many conditional branches is implemented. The hardware acceleration should be implemented circuits which is a simple processing such as less conditional branches.

The hardware acceleration is expected to improve the performance by implementing the software processing which has become the overhead in systems [4]. In addition, Cooperating between hardware and software is can be maintained the flexibility of rewriting the processing [5].

We analyzed the mruby/c VM for efficiency implementation of hardware acceleration. The hardware implementation of all language processing in mruby/c VM takes a lot of costs. Therefore, we thought that it is good to implement hardware of only processing that is expected the improvement of processing by hardware acceleration.

mruby/c VM firstly loads the mruby bytecode and repeatedly performs instruction decode and instruction execution. In addition, mruby/c VM performs the dynamic memory allocation and memory free in execution. The following processing is performed in each phase.

1. Loading the mruby bytecode and Instruction Decode
   mruby bytecode is consisted of header information and several machine language instructions. mruby/c VM fetches and decodes one machine language instructions from the mruby bytecode.
2. Instruction execution
   mruby/c VM executes the instruction according to the instruction types.
3. Memory Management
   mruby/c VM performs the dynamic memory allocation in execution. mruby/c VM dynamically allocates the memory when the instruction execution requires the memory. mruby/c frequently occurs the dynamic memory allocation in execution.

We focus on the instruction decoder of the mruby bytecode. The instruction decoder repeatedly performs simple bit operations. We implemented the hardware acceleration of instruction decoder of mruby/c.

We also focus on the dynamic memory allocation. We think that it becomes the bottleneck in processing since mruby/c frequently occurs the dynamic memory allocation in execution. In the dynamic memory allocation, it determines memory to allocate by calculating from the requested size and state of free memory. We implemented the hardware acceleration of calculation the free memory area to allocate.

## 4   Hardware Acceleration Implementation

In this study used a FPGA (Field Programmable Gate Array) for the implementation of hardware acceleration. The FPGA is a rewritable integrated circuit and can flexibly configure system by rewriting its internal logic circuit. We used Terasic's DE0-Nano board with Intel's Cyclone IV (EP4CE22) FPGA chip. This FPGA chip has 22,320 logic elements and 594 Kbit SRAM.

For the implementation of hardware acceleration, we used Nios II system that is a soft-core processor for an Intel FPGA. The Nios II system can be constructed embedded processors in FPGA. The Nios II system is also provided many peripheral circuits for configuration of embedded systems. It is possible to develop original embedded systems in FPGA by using Nios II embedded processor and peripheral circuits. Since the Nios II can be reconfigured the system flexibility, it is suitable for research and development of embedded systems [6].

The circuit configuration of the implemented Nios II system is shown in Fig. 2.

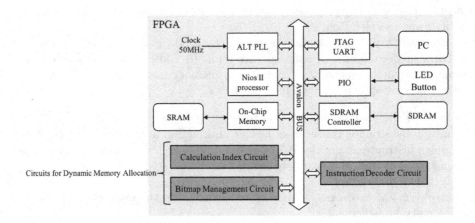

**Fig. 2.** Configuration of Nios II system

This system is constructed by Nios II processor, some peripheral circuits and custom component circuits. Their circuits are connected by the Avalon-Bus that is dedicated bus line. The details of each circuits are shown next.

- Nios II Processor : Nios II/f
  Nios II/f is a "fast" version designed for superior performance, which is the highest performance in the Nios II processor family. The wordlengh of Nios II processor is 32 bits. Nios II processor provides the software development environment based on GNU C/C++ tool chain.
- On Chip Memory (SRAM)
  The On Chip Memory is SRAM and an internal memory of the FPGA. The SRAM achieves a high speed access, but memory size is small capacity. The SRAM is stored the configuration information of circuit implemented in FPGA.
- SDRAM/SDRAM Controller
  The SDRAM is an external memory on FPGA board. The SDRAM is a large capacity but, a low access speed. The SDRAM is used as main memory and the mruby/c is written to it.
- ALT PLL
  The ALT PLL (Altera Phase-Locked Loop) multiples the input 50 MHz clock which is supplied from board to 100 MHz.

- JTAG UART

    The JTAG UART is the interface core that provides a serial communication between FPGA board and Nios II development environment on host PC.
- PIO

    The PIO (Parallel I/O) is the interface core that provides input/output access to user logic or external devices such as LEDs and switches.
- Instruction Decoder Circuit

    The Instruction Decoder Circuit is the custom component circuit which we implemented for the instruction decoder. The Instruction Decoder Circuit decodes instructions required mruby/c execution. These details describe in next section.
- Circuits for Dynamic Memory Allocation

    Circuits for Dynamic Memory Allocation are custom component circuits for dynamic memory allocation. Circuits for Dynamic Memory Allocation are configured the Index Calculation Circuit and the Bitmap Management Circuit in Fig. 2. These details describe in next section.

### 4.1   Custom Component Circuit of Instruction Decoder

We implemented the instruction decoder circuit that is a custom component circuit. The instruction decoder circuit can decode the mruby bytecode that mruby/c VM performs conventionally. The instruction decoder circuit is used the bit operations such as bit shift.

The wordlength of one instruction is 32 bits, which is consisted the operation code part and data part. Conventional, mruby/c VM decodes one instruction to the operation code and some data part one by one. The instruction decoder circuit decodes operation code part and some data part by pipeline processing.

### 4.2   Custom Component Circuits for Dynamic Memory Allocation

Custom component circuits for dynamic memory allocation are implemented the memory allocation function of mruby/c. mruby/c is implemented the TLSF (Two-Level Segregated Fit) memory allocator algorithm for dynamic memory allocation.

- TLSF Allocator

    TLSF allocator can be dynamic memory allocation that is fast that does not depend on data size and inhibits the fragmentation of memory [7]. TLSF is especially suitable to embedded systems that is time restriction such as real-time requirements. TLSF finely segregates and manages free memory blocks for each size by two-level. When TLSF allocates a memory block, it uses the index to each free blocks. TLSF manages free memory blocks of first and second level segregations by two bitmaps. TLSF calculates the index from required size and first and second level bitmaps. TLSF determines the allocation memory block from the index.

We implemented custom component circuits for the dynamic memory allocation. Custom component circuits for the dynamic memory allocation is consisted the Index Calculation Circuit and the Bitmap Management Circuit. The feature of custom component circuits for the dynamic memory allocation is shown in Fig. 3.

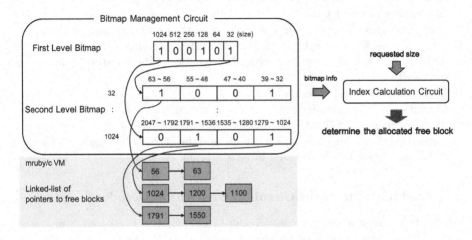

**Fig. 3.** Custom component circuits for dynamic memory allocation

The Bitmap Management Circuit manages bitmaps information of each size free memory blocks by two level. In first-level bitmap is segregated free blocks by a power of 2 size and set the corresponding bitmap to "1". In second-level is segregated the each size in first level more finely. When it determines the free memory block to allocate, it refers the bitmap information in Bitmap Management Circuit.

The Index Calculation Circuit is the circuit that calculates the index of free memory block to allocate. The Index Calculation Circuit calculates the index of free memory block to allocate from then requested size and the bitmap information.

mruby/c VM manages the pointer to the memory by the linked-list for each size. mruby/c VM cooperates the linked-list of free block and bitmap information in the Bitmap Management Circuit.

## 5    Evaluation

In this section describes implementation costs and the effect of the hardware acceleration of language processing in scripting programming language. The circuit scale of instruction decoder circuit and circuits for dynamic memory allocation are shown in Table 1.

The total circuit scale including NIos II system and custom component circuits is required 6,488 logic elements. Logic elements in DE0-Nano board is

**Table 1.** The number of logic elements

| Total | Nios II system | Decoder circuit | Circuits for memory allocator |
|-------|----------------|-----------------|-------------------------------|
| 6,488 | 2,183          | 1,273           | 3,032                         |

22,320, total scale of our configuration circuits is about 14%. The Nios II system without custom component circuits are required 2,183 logic elements. Instruction decoder circuits is required 1,273 logic elements. Custom component circuits for dynamic memory allocation is required 3,032 logic elements. Circuits for dynamic memory allocation are consisted index calculation circuit and the bitmap management circuit. The index calculation circuit is required 1,421 logic elements and the bitmap management circuit is required 1,611 logic elements. They are small implementation.

In their memory usage, mruby/c without custom component circuits is 151 KBytes. When we replaces memory allocation and instruction decoder with custom component circuits, its memory usage is 149 KBytes.

To confirm the effectiveness of hardware acceleration, we measured the execution speed of the only software processing and processing combining custom component circuits. In this study used program which combines calculating fibonacci numbers by recursion and calculating four arithmetic operations by while-loop as a benchmark program for measurements. Execution speeds are shown in Table 2.

**Table 2.** Execution speeds

| Only software | With custom component circuits |
|---------------|--------------------------------|
| 1289 [ms]     | 1157 [ms]                      |

In results of measurement, mruby/c that is only software processing takes time of 1289 ms. On the other hand, it takes time of 1175 ms using Custom Component Circuits for instruction decoder and memory allocation. Therefore, it was able to short 132 ms. It has been able to execute more fast by hardware acceleration.

## 6   Conclusion

The paper describes the hardware acceleration of a scripting programming language for embedded software developments. We analyzed the language processing of a scripting programming language and implemented hardware of language processing that it becomes the bottleneck in processing. In this study focused on a scripting language 'mruby/c' for small embedded system. For implementation of hardware acceleration, we used the Intel FPGA and the soft-core Nios II system. We implemented the instruction decoder circuit and circuits for dynamic memory allocation. The circuit scale of the instruction decoder circuit and circuits for dynamic memory allocation are a small implementation. Results of investigation, we confirmed the effectiveness of hardware acceleration. mrubyhas been able to execute more fast by hardware acceleration.

Im future works, we will improve the execution speed of scripting programming languages by hardware acceleration. We think that the effect of hardware acceleration for scripting programming languages is low in current research results since execution speeds are slightly speedup by hardware acceleration. We will analyze the language system of scripting programming language and implement for more efficient hardware acceleration.

# References

1. https://github.com/mruby/mruby
2. https://github.com/mrubyc/mrubyc
3. Tanaka, K., Maeda, H., Higashi, H.: Concurrent execution in scripting programming language 'mruby'. In: Gervasi, O., et al. (eds.) ICCSA 2018. LNCS, vol. 10962, pp. 136–146. Springer, Cham (2018). https://doi.org/10.1007/978-3-319-95168-3_9
4. Jasrotia, K., Zhu, J.: Hardware implementation of a memory allocator. In: Proceedings Euromicro Symposium on Digital System Design. Architectures, Methods and Tools, pp. 355–358 (2002)
5. Joao, J.A., Mutlu, O., Patt, Y.N.: Flexible reference-counting-based hardware acceleration for garbage collection. In: ISCA 2009 Proceedings of the 36th Annual International Symposium on Computer Architecture, pp. 418–428 (2009)
6. Salunke, P.G., Sayyed, A.M.: Design of embedded web server based on NIOS-II soft core processor. In: International Conference on Electrical Electronics and Optimization Techniques (ICEEOT), pp. 488–492 (2016)
7. Masmano, M., Ripoll, I., Crespo, A., Real, J.: TLSF: a new dynamic memory allocator for real-time systems. In: Proceeding ECRTS 2004 Proceedings of the 16th Euromicro Conference on Real-Time Systems, pp. 79–86 (2004)

# A Machine Learning Framework for Edge Computing to Improve Prediction Accuracy in Mobile Health Monitoring

Sigdel Shree Ram[1(✉)], Bernady Apduhan[1(✉)],
and Norio Shiratori[2(✉)]

[1] Graduate School of Information Science, Kyushu Sangyo University,
Fukuoka 813-8503, Japan
k18gjk01@st.kyusan-u.ac.jp, bob@is.kyusan-u.ac.jp
[2] Research and Development Initiative, Chuo University,
Tokyo 112-8551, Japan
norio@riec.tohoku.ac.jp

**Abstract.** The great challenges in the aging society and the lack of human resources, especially in health care, remains a formidable task. The cloud centric computing paradigm offers a solution in processing IoT applications in health care. However, due to the large computing and communication overheads, an alternative solution is sought. Here, we consider machine learning in edge computing to detect and improve the predictability accuracy in mobile health monitoring of human activity. With multi-modal sensor data, we conducted pre-processing to sanitize the data and classify the activities in the dataset. We used and compare the processing performance using random forests and SVM machine learning algorithms to identify and classify the activities in the dataset. We achieved approximately 99% accuracy with random forest which was better than SVM, at 98%. We used confusion matrix to identify the majority of mismatched data belonging to initial value of sensors while recording a particular activity, and also used visual representation of the data for better understanding. We extract the activity's ECG data and classify into four categories to provide more specific information from the person's activity data. The aforementioned experiments provided promising results and insights on the implementation to improve the prediction accuracy on the health status of people undergoing some activity.

**Keywords:** Edge computing/intelligence · Mobile health · Machine learning

## 1 Introduction

The popularity of IoT (Internet of Things) applications is gaining much interests in various fields in industry, manufacturing, agriculture, medical, and other sectors of society. The deployment of IoT devices (sensors, actuators, etc.) to detect and acquire data will generate a large volume of data which creates great challenges on how to store and process this large amount of collected data, as well as how to unleash and harness the wealth of knowledge hidden in the data.

© Springer Nature Switzerland AG 2019
S. Misra et al. (Eds.): ICCSA 2019, LNCS 11621, pp. 417–431, 2019.
https://doi.org/10.1007/978-3-030-24302-9_30

The data center in a cloud computing environment offers a cost-effective means of storing and processing the huge data collected by IoT devices. However, the large communication overhead incurred to transfer data from the IoT devices to/from the data center has raised crucial issues especially for applications which requires near-real time responses. Specifically, the problems of cloud centric computing, i.e., narrow bandwidth, long latency, intermittent connection, delay in decision making, etc., paves the way of edge computing as a new revolutionary way of correcting the aforementioned deficiencies. Edge computing is not a replacement of cloud computing, but rather as a supplement. That is, much of the processing maybe be done at the edge nodes which are in close proximity to the edge devices or sources. However, whenever the processing capacity of edge nodes is not sufficient at certain times, some part(s) of the application processing can be offloaded to the data center. The short data transfer time between the source (IoT devices) and edge node, can be considered as part of the solution to IoT applications requiring near-real time responses. However, the limited processing and storage capacities of edge nodes are seen as another hindrances to the processing requirements.

In this paper, considering the above-mentioned processing and storage limitations of edge nodes, we study the use and performance of machine learning techniques to augment the data classification accuracy, in an effort to establish our platform to develop a semantic-based mobile health monitoring system.

The rest of the paper is organized as follows. Section 2 described our research objectives, and Sect. 3 cites some related researches. In Sect. 4, we described our experiment environment and the datasets, whereas Sect. 5 described our system architecture. The experiment methods are explained in Sects. 6 and 7 describe the experiment results and observations. Section 8 describe the ECG classification prediction, whereas Sect. 9 discuss the activity data classification and ECG data categorization. Section 10 gives the summary and concluding remarks of the study. Last but not the least, Sect. 11 cites some of our future work.

## 2  Research Objective

The first objective of this research is to study and identify the most viable supervised machine learning algorithm [7] (Random Forests (RF), Support Vector Machines (SVM)) which will suit to our proposed semantic-based mobile health monitoring system. We will use datasets and conduct experiments to quantify the data classification accuracy of the activity sets using RF and SVM algorithms. Confusion matrix and graphs will be used for visual analysis of the results. To determine more specific conditions of the subject (patient), we extract the ECG values of the activity sets and categorize it accordingly. These experiments will provide us better understanding of machine learning algorithms and to gain insights to realize intelligent analytics in edge computing for personalized mobile health monitoring system. After comparing and contrasting between experiments expected outcome was positive.

## 3   Related Research

In Mahmut Taha Yazici et al. [1], their research used Random Forest, Support Vector Machine (SVM) and Multi-Layer Perceptron for testing data sets on Raspberry pi. They have compared accuracy, processing capacity, power consumption between three algorithms in Raspberry pi. They have concluded that when the size of dataset is small, SVM is slightly faster than Random Forest; but when the size of data is large, Random Forest was faster with higher accuracy. While we share similar objectives, our tests were conducted on a PC which provides more processing power and generate our envisioned model.

Whereas, Calvier et al. [2], proposed a method to bridge existing knowledge models with ad hoc taxonomies to address the problem of textual documents classification. This method allows the expert user to match their needs by optimizing text document classification. This technique is used on web based textual documents. In contrast, in our study, we have implemented the basic concept of semantization to improve the data pre-processing and in identifying the critical cases.

Furthermore, in Andreotti, Carr et al. [8], has classified the short segments of ECG into 4 groups using convolutional neural networks. The objective of this research was to detect arrhythmia. We used similar dataset in identifying the ECG status and comparing ECG status with the activity classifier's result.

## 4   Experiment Environment and Dataset

In our experiments, we used a Mac PC (macOS High Sierra version 10.13.6, 3.1 GHz Intel Core i5 CPU, and 8 GB RAM), Python 3.7 programming language and Anaconda navigator as the programming platform with Spyder 3.3.1 IDE.

### 4.1   Dataset

In this research two datasets are used. One dataset [10] consist of data of ECG value with four different classifications which is further more explained in Sect. 8 and another dataset [4–6] consist of data generated from multi-modal sensors placed on the subject's chest, right wrist, and left ankle. These three sensors record the body movement and turns of different human activity. In this experiment, 1,200,000 raw data were filtered down to 350,000 by removing null labeled data so that there will be less confusion while training the model. The activity and attribute are displayed in Tables 1 and 2, respectively.

**Table 1.** Activity labels and data size in terms of time and intervals

| S.N. | Activity | S.N. | Activity |
|------|----------|------|----------|
| 1 | Standing still (1 min) | 7 | Frontal elevation of arms (20x) |
| 2 | Sitting and relaxing (1 min) | 8 | Knees bending (crouching) (20x) |
| 3 | Lying down (1 min) | 9 | Cycling (1 min) |
| 4 | Walking (1 min) | 10 | Jogging (1 min) |
| 5 | Climbing stairs (1 min) | 11 | Running (1 min) |
| 6 | Waist bends forward (20x) | 12 | Jump front & back (20x) |

*In brackets are the number of repetitions (Nx) or the duration of the activity (min)

**Table 2.** Attribute information which was recorded from 3 sensors.

| Column | Attribute | Positional notation |
|--------|-----------|---------------------|
| 1 | Acceleration from the chest sensor | X axis |
| 2 | Acceleration from the chest sensor | Y axis |
| 3 | Acceleration from the chest sensor | Z axis |
| 4 | Electrocardiogram signal | Lead I |
| 5 | Electrocardiogram signal | Lead II |
| 6 | Acceleration from the left-ankle sensor | X axis |
| 7 | Acceleration from the left-ankle sensor | Y axis |
| 8 | Acceleration from the left-ankle sensor | Z axis |
| 9 | Gyro from the left-ankle sensor | X axis |
| 10 | Gyro from the left-ankle sensor | Y axis |
| 11 | Gyro from the left-ankle sensor | Z axis |
| 12 | Magnetometer from the left-ankle sensor | X axis |
| 13 | Magnetometer from the left-ankle sensor | Y axis |
| 14 | Magnetometer from the left-ankle sensor | Z axis |
| 15 | Acceleration from the right-lower arm sensor | X axis |
| 16 | Acceleration from the right-lower arm sensor | Y axis |
| 17 | Acceleration from the right-lower arm sensor | Z axis |
| 18 | Gyro from the right-lower-arm sensor | X axis |
| 19 | Gyro from the right-lower-arm sensor | Y axis |
| 20 | Gyro from the right-lower-arm sensor | Z axis |
| 21 | Magnetometer from the right-lower-arm sensor | X axis |
| 22 | Magnetometer from the right-lower-arm sensor | Y axis |
| 23 | Magnetometer from the right-lower-arm sensor | Z axis |
| 24 | Classification label | Activity |

*Units: Acceleration (m/s$^2$), gyroscope (deg/s), magnetic field (local), ecg (mV)

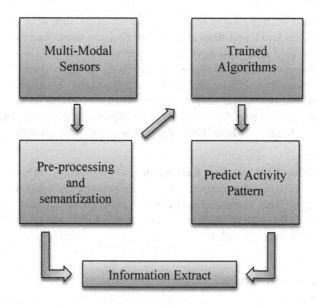

**Fig. 1.** Block diagram of a personalized health monitoring system

## 5 System Architecture

Our proposed personalized health monitoring system consist of multi-modal sensors to record the human body activities and vital signs of the body, i.e. Electrocardiogram values, motions, etc., as shown in Fig. 1. To outline the scope of semantization, we conducted preliminary experiments to find out the critical values. By extracting such information, we can be more accurate to predict as well as to react immediately on critical situations. The sensors data is pre-processed and the output data is passed to the trained models to predict the activity. Furthermore, after the prediction, semantization can be applied to augment the prediction accuracy of the subject's activity.

**Multi-modal Sensors**
Multi- modal sensors are such sensors which can record multiple instances at a same time. The data used in this experiments are recorded from 3 sensors which has 23 attributes.

**Pre-processing and Semantization**
Those data are pre-processed to maximize the prediction accuracy and narrow down the data composition. The detailed pre-processing is mentioned in Sect. 6.1. Semantization of data like labeling or extracting information took place. In Sect. 9, the basic concept of semantization (extracting information/giving meaning) is explained.

**Trained Algorithms**
Generally, in this experiment the choice of algorithms has been narrow down to two algorithms, i.e., the support vector machine and random forest after reviewing some related articles and considering the platform, i.e. edge computing.

Random forest (RF) algorithm was used because of its simplicity and high accuracy. RF creates random forest from assembly of decision trees. And the classification is achieved by having most votes overall in the forest.

Whereas, Support Vector Machine (SVM) looks at the extreme value of the datasets and creates the decision line, known as hyperplane. Although this algorithm takes a bit more time during the training process when the training dataset is huge. But one of the major advantage of SVM is it provides higher precision and very good with large number of features. These both algorithms were used to train and test the experiments.

**Predict Activity and Information Extraction**

The model predicts the activity according the algorithm used and the nature of the input data. Those output were compared and contrast between two models output which provides a generic level of semantization. This flow of data and output is explained with experiment in Sects. 8 and 9.

## 6   Experiment Methods

### 6.1   Data Pre-processing

To make the input data easier to work with machine learning algorithms, data preprocessing was conducted, as follows:

- **Importing Libraries and datasets**—Also includes adding labels and additional information as well as finding out the boundary of the datasets and removing the unnecessary data which leads to confusion while training the model. (Null class data were removed)
- **Missing data**—Although the missing value were very few in numbers, to get a better quality output, mean value calculation was used. Missing value was replaced by calculating the mean of the existing observation for that variable.
- **Splitting datasets**—We have implemented a 70:30, i.e., 70% of datasets is used for training purposes and the rest of the data for testing purposes.
- **Scaling data**—Dataset consists of different kinds of data with huge differences. So to optimize, we need to do the scaling of the data. Here, we used standardization to scale the data which converts the different variety of data into the same type considering the same basic features for SVM whereas for random forest scaling was not necessary because of the tree based features.

### 6.2   Training and Testing

After pre-processing the data, we train and test the algorithms one at time. In the experiments, we used Support Vector Machines and Random Forest supervised machine learning algorithms.

## 6.3  Data Analysis

During the analysis process, we concentrate on the accuracy check with respect to the processing speed. Accuracy check between real output of the testing data and output of predicted data. Furthermore, to understand the concentration of the predicted data and real data we have used confusion matrix.

# 7  Experiments and Observations

Experiments were conducted to understand the implementation of machine learning intelligence on edge devices while considering the data classification accuracy as the major measuring component. We calculate and compare the outcomes of RF and SVM ML-algorithms, to find out the best algorithm for this kind of datasets. The following measures were performed to analyze the outcome.

## 7.1  Data Classification Accuracy

The observation results were different with various parameters of machine learning algorithms. The maximum accuracy that was achieved with Random Forest was approximately 99%, whereas with SVM, it was approximately 98%. The result was highly influenced by the size of dataset. While considering larger dataset, the processing speed of Random Forest was faster than SVM.

## 7.2  Confusion Matrix

Confusion Matrix is a matrix which compares the real output and output obtained using an algorithm on a test dataset. In other words, a confusion matrix is a technique for summarizing the performance of a classification algorithm. Although we were able to achieve 99% accuracy, but classification accuracy alone can be a misleading metric for accuracy. Classification accuracy only provides a numerical value of whole datasets. To carefully analyze and understand every activity and its accuracy, confusion matrix is necessary.

The label and datasets are organized into a tabular form, or as a matrix, as shown in Figs. 2 and 3. Each row on the table corresponds to a predicted activity, whereas each column of the table corresponds to an actual activity. The diagonal concentrated values are the correctly predicted values. But if we compare the data between random forest and SVM in activity 2 (sit n relax), 3 (Lying Down) and 4 (walking), random forest is able to classify the data properly than support vector machine.

## 7.3  Visual Analysis

To perform visual analysis, we plotted the data of one particular data attributes of the predicted and actual data values, i.e., X-axis Acceleration from chest sensor. First, we plot the test results and then the predicted results, and later on combined them both to visualize the difference. There is not much difference between the graphs as shown in Figs. 2 and 3.

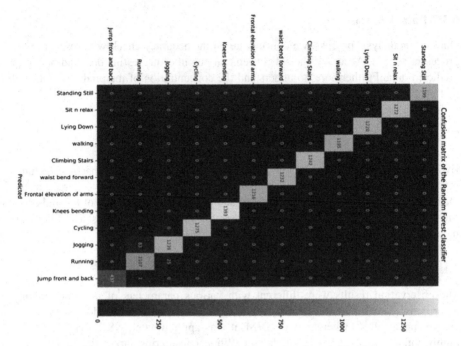

**Fig. 2.** Confusion matrix after using random forest algorithm

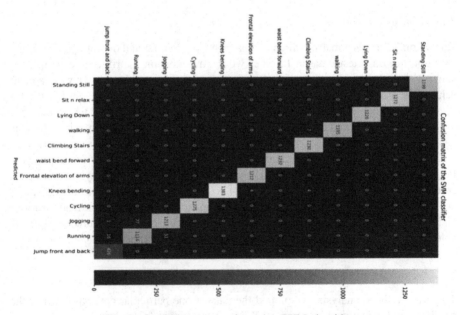

**Fig. 3.** Confusion matrix after using SVM algorithm

Testing data of acceleration recorded from chest as X-axis

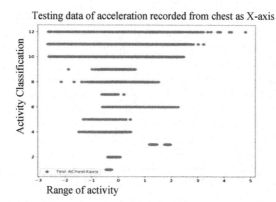

**Fig. 4.** Visual representation of testing data: X-axis acceleration recorded from chest sensors data using RF algorithm

Testing data of acceleration recorded from chest as X-axis

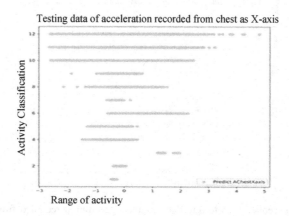

**Fig. 5.** Visual representation of predicted data: X-axis acceleration recorded from chest sensors data using RF algorithm

Figures 4 and 7 represents the testing data activity set of random forest and SVM. In both algorithms, the same data set was used, so there is not much difference. But in Figs. 5 and 8, we see the changes occurred on testing data result while using support vector machine and random forest. Then we combined both the visual representation of the activity sets and observed the differences between the real activity and predicted activity (Fig. 6 and 9).

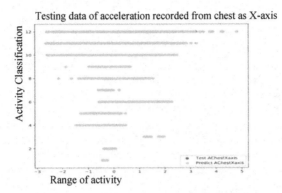

**Fig. 6.** Visual representation of testing and predicted data combined: X-axis acceleration recorded from chest sensors data using RF algorithm

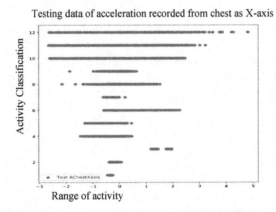

**Fig. 7.** Visual representation of testing data: X-axis acceleration recorded from chest sensors data using SVM algorithm

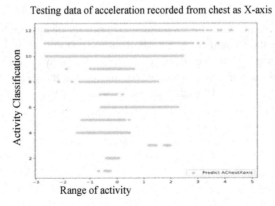

**Fig. 8.** Visual representation of predicted data: X-axis acceleration recorded from chest sensors data using SVM algorithm

Testing data of acceleration recorded from chest as X-axis

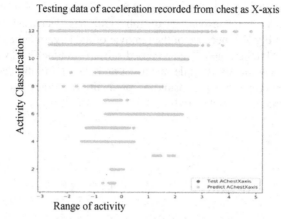

**Fig. 9.** Visual representation of testing and predicted data combined: X-axis acceleration recorded from chest sensors data using SVM algorithm

## 7.4    ECG Values Analysis with Respect to Different Activity Sets

In Fig. 10, the Y-axis represents the scaled ECG value, whereas the X-axis represents the number of recordings. Blue line represents the ECG notation whereas orange line represents the activity label. To understand the characteristic of the datasets and data concentrations, we have sorted the data values with respect to activity sets. Which can be observed in following diagram.

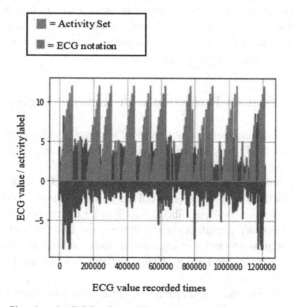

**Fig. 10.** Showing the ECG value with respect to activity sets before sorting.

In the above graph (Fig. 11), we compared the ECG values with respect to activity sets. We can observe that the datasets overall value has decreased drastically than previous graph, i.e. Fig. 10, because of the removal of the large number of ECG values with no activities. Although there is no recorded activity, but the ECG value fluctuates. Therefore, we can say that even while recording and classifying the data, we can still make a huge improvement on increasing the prediction accuracy and consistency of data by acquiring the activity data only.

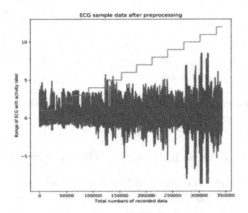

**Fig. 11.** Showing the ECG value with respect to activity sets after sorting.

From this ECG value, we identify the category classification so that we can implement the semantization to identify the critical situation. With semantization, a lot of information can be extracted from these data, which will further help to be more specific and accurate on analysis. For example, if the ECG value and activity value evaluation is on same track then the classification accuracy can be higher (more explanation on experiment results are given in Sect. 9).

## 8   ECG Classification Prediction with Random Forest

Having known that random forest provides more accurate activity classification on the used dataset, we studied the four categories of ECG data so that it can provide more specific information on the patient's status.

To make the model more informative and descriptive, ECG data is treated as an important data which outlines the objects vital signs in four categories (0- Classification Not Available, 1- Normal, 2- Atrial Fibrillation, 3- other Rhythm). To understand ECG classification and activity classification simultaneously, first ECG classification prediction model is trained and tested using random forest algorithm, as below (Fig. 13) The approach for training and testing of ECG datasets is same as of activity classification (Fig. 12).

*Note: Atrial Fibrillation – is an irregular, rapid heart rate which can increase the risk of heart stroke, heart failures or other heart related issues.

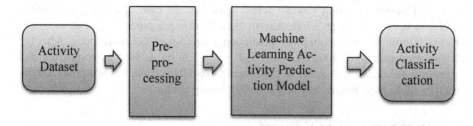

**Fig. 12.** Block diagram of training and testing of activity classification model

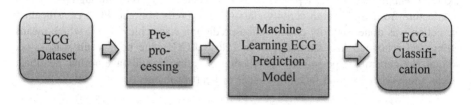

**Fig. 13.** Block diagram of training and testing of ECG classification model.

## 9  Activity Data Classification and ECG Data Categorization

After the training and testing of the models. Both models are used for same activity dataset which performs two task: activity classification and ECG classification, as in Fig. 14. Activity classification processes the whole activity datasets to predict the

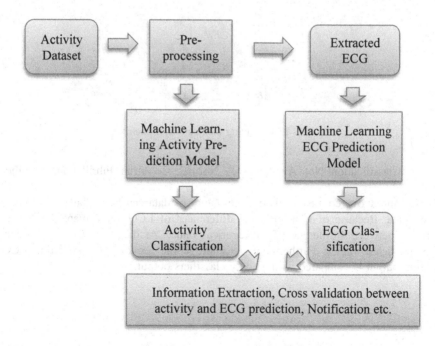

**Fig. 14.** Block diagram of activity classification and ECG classification simultaneously.

activity classification using random forest algorithm. In case of ECG classification, ECG data is extracted from whole activity dataset after pre-processing of datasets and processed through the random forest prediction model for ECG classification. After the classification process is finished, individual classification as well as comparing and contrasting the classification can be performed as required. By this approach the output becomes more meaningful than just activity classification.

### 9.1    Experiments with ECG Dataset

In this experiment, first of all, we extract the value from activity dataset. This data was a kind of relaxing and sitting represented as 2. This data was passed through the system architecture from which both activity classification prediction and ECG classification prediction was done. Activity classification prediction was achieved as 2 which means sitting and relaxing. And similarly, from 2 lead ECG value both result was 1, i.e. normal. So, generally a person who is relaxing or sitting should have normal heartbeat unless some other external factors like fear or heart problems.

### 9.2    Experiment Results and Observations

Highest training and testing accuracy achieved with random forest is 37.93%. The major reason behind low accuracy is because of similar kind of datasets which can be seen in Fig. 15. From the following confusion matrix grid we can observe the classification of dataset with higher confusion.

|   | 0 | 1 | 2 | 3 |
|---|---|---|---|---|
| 0 | 185 | 874 | 85 | 615 |
| 1 | 136 | 2019 | 117 | 1312 |
| 2 | 55 | 775 | 133 | 812 |
| 3 | 149 | 1642 | 131 | 1760 |

**Fig. 15.**   ECG training data confusion matrix.

*(0- Classification Not Available, 1- Normal, 2- Atrial Fibrillation, 3- other Rhythm)

From the above confusion matrix, the nature of data can be explained as highly related data. Because of very marginal differences of ECG value there is a lot of confusion between 4 different ECG categorical values. As diagonal values being correctly predicted values. Furthermore, to improve the accuracy of prediction ECG classifier output is compared with activity classifiers output.

# 10 Summary and Concluding Remarks

In this paper, we conducted experiments with mobile health data to determine which particular machine learning algorithm is best suited to our proposed personalized mobile health monitoring system. Experiment results depicts the characteristics of Support Vector Machines (SVM) and Random Forests (RF) machine learning algorithms with respect to our test dataset. The RF achieved a 99% data classification accuracy compared to 98% using SVM. Moreover, the RF exhibited faster processing speed with larger datasets. Confusion matrix was used to determine the behavior of the dataset with respect to the algorithm used. Furthermore, we classify and categorize the activity ECG datasets to derive more specific conditions of the subject. The aforementioned results provided us with clearer understanding of the algorithms and insights on realizing an intelligent edge analytics for mobile health monitoring.

## 10.1 Future Work

This study is still in its preliminary stage and much work has still to be done. We plan to study deeper on the algorithms while developing the framework on the data semantization for intelligent edge analytics.

# References

1. Rodriguez, N.D., Cuellar, M.P., Lilius, J., Calvo-Flores, M.D.: A survey on ontologies for human behaviour recognition. ACM Comput. Surv. **46**(4), 33 (2014). https://doi.org/10.1145/2523819. Article 43
2. Calvier, F.-É., Plantie, M., Dray, G., Ranwez, S.: Ontology based machine learning for semantic multiclass classification. In: TOTH: Terminologie Ontologie: Théories et Applications, Chambery, France, p. 100 (2013)
3. Bajaj, G., Agarwal, R., Singh, P., Georgantas, N., Issarny, V.: A study of existing ontologies in the IoT-domain. In: Elsevier JWS SI on Web Semantics for the Internet/Web of Things (2017)
4. Banos, O., et al.: Design, implementation and validation of a novel open framework for agile development of mobile health applications. BioMed. Eng. OnLine **14**(S2:S6), 1–20 (2015)
5. Banos, O., et al.: mHealthDroid: a novel framework for agile development of mobile health applications. In: Pecchia, L., Chen, L.L., Nugent, C., Bravo, J. (eds.) IWAAL 2014. LNCS, vol. 8868, pp. 91–98. Springer, Cham (2014). https://doi.org/10.1007/978-3-319-13105-4_14
6. Dua, D., Taniskidou, E.K.: UCI machine learning repository. University of California, School of Information and Computer Science, Irvine (2017). http://archive.ics.uci.edu/ml
7. Machine learning. https://machinelearningmastery.com/. Accessed 07 May 2019
8. Andreotti, F., Carr, O., Pimentel, M.A.F., Mahdi, A., De Vos, M.: Comparing feature-based classifiers and convolutional neural networks to detect arrhythmia from short segments of ECG. In: Computing in Cardiology, vol. 44, pp. 1–4 (2017)
9. Goldberger, A.L., et al.: PhysioBank, PhysioToolkit, and PhysioNet: components of a new research resource for complex physiologic signals. Circulation **101**(23): e215–e220
10. Physionet. https://www.physionet.org/. Accessed 07 May 2019

# Geographical Analysis, Urban Modeling, Spatial Statistics (GEO-AND-MOD 2019)

# An Unsupervised Machine Learning Approach in Remote Sensing Data

Mauro Mazzei[(✉)]

National Research Council, Istituto di Analisi dei Sistemi ed Informatica
"Antonio Ruberti", via di Taurini, 19, 00185 Rome, Italy
mauro.mazzei@iasi.cnr.it

**Abstract.** The analysis, image recognition, the classification in remote sensing data always up to date is for the insiders a very useful system for the management, planning, protection of our territory. Technological evolution the succession of applications and tools in GIS environment, have refined more and more techniques allowing us to computerize much of the territory bringing an enrichment of geographical data distributed more or less updated, remote sensing, digital orthoimage help us in the areas where the local computerization is not always updated. In this paper I want to demonstrate that an approach based on machine learning applied to territorial analysis using dynamic matrices, provides for the definition of numerical indices assigned to each recognized pattern. The numerical indices will be the elements of recognition where the territorial computerization is insufficient. The data from remote sensing or digital orthoimage are variable matrices where the numerical indices have to express their potential. The goal is to educate the recognition in matrix form to obtain a dynamic topology where the computerization has not been updated.

**Keywords:** Data mining · Spatial data mining · Spatial data analysis · Spatial statistical model

## 1 Introduction

The method of territorial analysis using dynamic matrices involves the definition and processing of the numerical indices assigned to the information layer (remote sensing images) examined. The numerical indices will be the elements of recognition where the territorial computerization is insufficient. The data from remote sensing or from digital orthoimage are the variable matrices where the numerical indices must express their potential.

The aim is to create a self-learning system to obtain a dynamic topology able to learn the evolutionary changes of territorial contexts and/or landscapes. Some of the most common numerical, spatial and connectivity indexes for territorial analysis can be summarized in these types.

- An index or numerical indicator is a mathematical expression (sometimes an algorithm) capable of transforming a set of data into a synthetic numerical value (in a given scale) attributable to an emergent property of a landscape.

© Springer Nature Switzerland AG 2019
S. Misra et al. (Eds.): ICCSA 2019, LNCS 11621, pp. 435–447, 2019.
https://doi.org/10.1007/978-3-030-24302-9_31

- The distance indices express in terms of space or time the distance between two or more objects within a n-dimensional space.
- The connectivity indices express the degree of geographical relationship between the different objects placed in a geographical or process dimension. In particular the graphs are able to express in numerical form the relationships between the different objects and at the same time to characterize the spatial patterns.
- Spatial indexes are able to describe the shape of patches, evaluate their individual and collective complexity expressed in an environmental mosaic. Border irregularities, area width, concentration and interspersion are fundamental parameters for the characterization of a landscape.
- The spatial arrangement of the patches is measured through irregularity indices, while the tissue structure of the mosaic requires indices based on adjacency ratios.

The methods of landscape analysis can be summarized in some types:

- Numerical, spatial, multiscale analysis and modeling are the main approaches used in landscape analysis.
- The landscape analysis can be conducted on an organism, patch, mosaic or entire landscape scale.
- Shape, size, irregularity, spatial arrangement, morphological diversity and typological diversity are some of the characteristics of the objects identified in a landscape that are analyzed with the use of numerical indices and spatial indices.
- Spatial statistics, fractal mathematics, neutral models are some of the approaches in the study of the complexity of landscapes.

In this work a method of landscape analysis is presented with the aim of instructing the system to automatically recognize the emerging characteristics of the territory or landscape, through the self-learning of the elements that compose it. The elements used for the analysis are the data obtained from the satellite images that make up the variety of elements to be analyzed.

## 1.1  Numerical Indices

By numerical indexes i mean mathematical expressions able to capture the information emitted by the emergent properties of a system, or in this case, of a landscape. These indices actually measure the variety of objects, their abundance and their spatio-temporal dynamics. Where Ai is the abundance of the object I [22];

$$A = \sum A_i \tag{1.1}$$

The Geographical Distance Index represents a fundamental element of the landscape. The distance in a Euclidean space is given by the application of the Pythagorean theorem, given two points $X'Y'$ and $X''Y''$ their distance is given by the following:

$$d = \sqrt{(X' - X'')^2 + (Y' - Y'')^2} \tag{1.2}$$

the distance between two points is generally calculated as the shortest spatial interval, but while this is true for isotropic surfaces, in the presence of anisotropic surfaces such as environmental mosaics the minimum distance between two points is generally not a straight line.

When we are in the presence of a group of points in a Euclidean space, for example a group of trees or other objects that are scattered, the distance between the points is not the measure of each but the standard distance that represents the dispersion of the whole. This distance can be calculated with a quadratic average of the distance from the center of gravity;

$$d_1 = \sqrt{\left( \sum^{n/i=1} \left( d_{ic}^{2/n} \right) \right)} \tag{1.3}$$

$d_{ic}$ is the distance between each observation $i$ is the middle center of all points $c$, $n$ the number of points.

## 1.2  Spatial Indices

By spatial indexes i mean those indexes that describe the spatial characteristics of the objects i encounter in an environmental mosaic. These characteristics are both topological (size, shape) and chorological (position with respect to other objects of the same type or different). Spatial indexes are able to describe the shape of the patches, evaluate their individual complexity and that expressed collectively in an environmental mosaic. Irregularity of the edges, width of the area, interdispersion and contagion are fundamental parameters for the characterization of a landscape.

The shape indices are based on the difference between a geometric figure giving (circles, square) and the patch inscribed within this figure, assuming the maximum regularity for geometric figures and whose ratios between appropriately treated area and the respective perimeter is about 1.

$$Y^1 = \left( 2\sqrt{\pi A} \right) \big/ P \tag{1.4}$$

Where A is the area and P the perimeter of the patch with g 1 $\simeq$ 1 for circular patches and g1 < 1 for shapes other than circle or based on polygons. Or simplified area perimeter report for forms represented in raster format we have:

$$Y^3 = A/p^3 \tag{1.5}$$

The perimeter is calculated in raster data through the Sobel operator which is an algorithm used to process digital images in particular to perform contour recognition (edge detection).

The operator applies two 3 × 3 kernels, i.e. two convolution matrices to the original image to calculate approximate values of the derivatives - one in the horizontal direction, and one in the vertical direction. If we call A the source image, and Gx and

Gy the two images whose points represent respectively the approximate values of the horizontal and vertical derivatives, the operation is described by:

$$G_x = \begin{bmatrix} +1 & 0 & -1 \\ +2 & 0 & -2 \\ +1 & 0 & -1 \end{bmatrix} * A \; e \; G_y \begin{bmatrix} +1 & +2 & +1 \\ 0 & 0 & 0 \\ -1 & -2 & -1 \end{bmatrix} * A \qquad (1.6)$$

## 1.3   Connectivity Indices

The connectivity indices express the degree of "geographical relationship" between the different objects placed in a geographical or process dimension. In particular, the graphs are able to express in numerical form the chorological relations between the different objects and at the same time to characterize their spatial patterns.

The connectivity indices express the maximum of the distances between the node i from each of the other nodes j. Each graph can be converted by a matrix where $d_{ij} = 1$ if it exists;

$$K_i = \max d_{ij} \qquad (1.7)$$

Accessibility index is given by the following:

$$A_1 = \sum^{n/i=1} d_{ij} \qquad (1.8)$$

Where $d_{ij}$ is the number of nodes encountered to arrive at the chosen node. The value of the accessibility index is inversely proportional to the accessibility of the network node.

## 2   Data Organization

The starting data are remote sensing images obtained from sensors with high spatial and radiometric resolutions (QuickBird). The radiometric resolution therefore expresses the number of gray levels (dynamic range) used to represent the data collected by the sensor. In general, the detection systems are designed to record the greatest possible number of signal levels to minimize the loss of information relative to the observed scene, but the upper limit of the instrument's dynamic range is defined by the signal-to-noise ratio. The acquired QuickBird image was provided in 16-bit mode, so the intensity of the energy arriving at the detector is divided into discrete brightness ranges that are converted to $2^{16}$ (= 65536) gray levels. The acquired QuickBird satellite image is provided in two modes: multispectral and panchromatic. The multispectral image is recorded in four bands, partly overlapping, in the blue, green, red and near infrared channels, and therefore allows to trace the spectral response of the elements present on the ground, while the panchromatic integrates the signal received in a single wide band of 140 nm. The spectral resolution in this case is therefore rather low, but this allows to optimize the spatial resolution of the sensor, which is able to detect the signal coming from a surface on the ground of only 70 cm per side [6, 7] (Fig. 1).

**Fig. 1.** Input remote sensing image.

The image in the preprocessing phase is corrected radiometrically and geometrically, after which we pass to the data insertion phase through a reading function of each individual pixel within the database. This phase allows data to be stored in an RDBMS for direct access without having to store a huge amount of data. The process used starting from the input data to get to the final output is shown (Fig. 2).

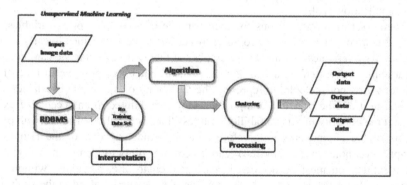

**Fig. 2.** The process unsupervised machine learning.

## 2.1 Data Analysis

Digital images are two-dimensional arrays, each element of which contains the pixel value to be displayed. To calculate the partial derivatives of this discrete representation, discrete operators will be required. This technique consists in scrolling on the original image a square matrix containing elements. For each position the scalar product is calculated between the covering matrix and the covered area and then all the elements of the result are added. The value obtained will constitute the value to replace the pixel located in the middle of the examined area.

For each image, the mosaic thus obtained, we proceeded with an automatic extraction of "object" with the criterion of "similarity" between tiles assigned to satisfying the criteria of closeness and proximity of the relative levels of radiometric value. The automatic extraction was performed through algorithms and techniques of image processing, smoothing operators, laplace operators, threshold operators, edge extraction, form extraction.

"Object" are the structural unit of an environmental system heterogeneous, identified on the basis on the differences that appear within the area itself.

Each image was converted into a set of "objects" each of which were calculated fifteen numeric attributes related to the geometric properties of the object (perimeter, delta-X and delta-Y, area, etc.) and others to its inertial properties (Jx, Jy, Rx, Ry, etc.).

The image, when converted into two distinct sets of objects, each characterized by fifteen attributes, were subjected to a factor analysis procedure with the method of principal components (Hotelling) [8, 9, 11].

The Principal Components Analysis (PCA) is a linear transformation that transforms the data into a new coordinate system; the new set of variables, the principal components, are linear functions of the original variables and are uncorrelated. The greatest variance by any projection of the data comes to lie on the first coordinate, the second greatest variance on the second coordinate, and so on. In practice, this is achieved by computing the covariance matrix for the full data set. Next, the eigenvectors and eigenvalues of the covariance matrix are computed, and sorted according to decreasing eigenvalue. One can see that the PCA's bias is not always appropriate; features with low variance might actually have high predictive relevance; this depends on the application [10].

Given a set of p observations for each variable of a complex of m variables, the principal component analysis is proposed to determine new variables linearly related with the given variables, but in a lesser number of these latter, so that we can represent the variability expressed by the original variables. If it is not possible to meet these conditions, it is not possible, to represent the variability of the original variables with less than m, t and he principal component analysis is limited to an acceptable extent represent the majority of this variability with less than m variables. The problem of the analysis of the components is therefore related to the reduction of the number of descriptive variables m of p objects, regardless of the ability to identify new variables; Such identification must be decided in each particular case, generally, without any reference to the statistics, and in the field of the phenomena involved in the study [12, 13, 17, 19, 20].

## 2.2   Statistical Analysis

The evaluation of the variance between the two aerial photos examined is based on the classification of objects extracted and subjected to statistical methodology of the analysis of the main components (Hotelling).

The principal component analysis is a multivariate statistical technique that explains the variability of a statistical variable in k dimensions $Z = (Z1, Z2, ..., Zk)$ in terms of k variables $Y1, Y2, ... Yk$, linear combinations of the $Zj$. It has:

$$Yi = \sum\nolimits_j bij\ Zj\ (i = 1, 2, ..., k) \tag{2.1}$$

where $bij$ are constants to be determined. $Yi$ are called the main components of the variable $Z$ and assuming they are not related to each other ordered by importance, in the explanation of the variability of $Z$ we have:

$$\text{cov}(Yi, Yj) = 0 (i \neq j) \tag{2.2}$$

$$V(Y1) \geq V(Y2) \geq ... \geq V(Yk) \tag{2.3}$$

where cov is covariance and V is variance. Without loss of generality we can assume that the variables $Zi$ are standardized, with mean equal to 0 and variance equal to 1, so as to eliminate the influence of the origin and the unit of measurement data, so that it results the following expression:

$$Zj = (Xj - \mu j)/\sigma j \tag{2.4}$$

Also, impose the condition that the overall variance of $Zj$ is equal to that of $Yi$, i.e.:

$$\Sigma i\ V(Yi) = \Sigma i\ V(Zi) = k \tag{2.5}$$

At last, suppose that the vectors

$$b\ i = (bi, 1,\ bi, 2, ..., bi, k) \tag{2.6}$$

have unit length, i.e., they fulfill the condition:

$$\Sigma j b2\ ij = 1 (i = 1, 2, ..., k) \tag{2.7}$$

On account of this, the vectors $bi$ that maximize the variance of $Y1$, of $Y2$, ..., to $Yk$ with the constraints (2.3) and (2.4), are the eigenvectors of the matrix $C$ of the coefficients of correlation between the variables $Zj$, which correspond to the eigenvalues $\lambda 1, \lambda 2, ..., \lambda k$ of $C$, sorted by non-increasing value. We then have:

$$|C - \lambda I| = 0 \tag{2.8}$$

$$b\ i(C - \lambda i\ I) = 0 \tag{2.9}$$

where I is the unit matrix. The matrix C is symmetric and positive definite for which the solutions $\lambda i$ of the (2.8) are non-negative and such that their sum (trace of the matrix C) is equal to k. We then have:

$$\Sigma i \lambda i = k(i = 1, 2, \ldots, k) \tag{2.10}$$

The variance of the i-th component is:

$$V(Yi) = \lambda i \tag{2.11}$$

And the contribution of Yi to the overall variance is:

$$Pi = V(Yi)/k = \lambda i/k \tag{2.12}$$

## 2.3  Spatial Statistical Models

This procedure allowed us to calculate the correlation coefficients between the 15 variables adopted to describe each object (See Table 1), with the aim of drastically reducing the number of variables, thereby explaining the overall variability of the system with a smaller number of attributes, each of which appears to be a linear combination of the attributes of departure [1–5].

**Table 1.**  Variable considered

| Variable | F1 | F2 | F3 | F4 | F5 | F6 |
|---|---|---|---|---|---|---|
| Nzm - F6 | 0.0424 | −0.0031 | 0.2495 | −0.1517 | 0.0175 | 0.9553 |
| Nt - F2 | 0.0951 | 0.9901 | −0.0063 | −0.0058 | 0.0255 | 0.0039 |
| Area - F2 | 0.0951 | 0.9901 | −0.0063 | −0.0058 | 0.0255 | 0.0039 |
| P - F2 | 0.071 | 0.9709 | 0.0264 | −0.0043 | −0.0024 | 0.0064 |
| DeltaX - F1 | 0.9736 | 0.0744 | 0.0292 | 0.0418 | 0.0453 | 0.016 |
| DeltaY - F1 | 0.9083 | 0.0265 | −0.02 | −0.1049 | 0.0885 | 0.0208 |
| ArIdl - F1 | 0.9388 | 0.1517 | −0.0109 | −0.0125 | −0.0368 | 0.0116 |
| Gx - F4 | −0.0147 | 0.0068 | 0.076 | −0.9825 | 0.115 | −0.1055 |
| Gy - F3 | 0.0294 | 0.005 | 0.9862 | 0.0612 | −0.0762 | −0.127 |
| Jx - F2 | 0.0428 | 0.9929 | −0.0022 | 0.0039 | −0.0139 | −0.0071 |
| Jy - F2 | 0.0499 | 0.9926 | −0.0027 | 0.003 | −0.0139 | −0.0071 |
| Rx - F1 | 0.9627 | 0.0388 | 0.0435 | 0.0674 | 0.1535 | 0.0096 |
| Ry - F1 | 0.9765 | 0.0216 | 0.0139 | −0.005 | 0.1021 | 0.0108 |
| ArRe - F1 | 0.9443 | 0.0876 | 0.0101 | 0.0459 | −0.0366 | 0.0068 |
| R/AAR - F5 | 0.1646 | 0.0115 | 0.0585 | 0.0961 | 0.9777 | 0.016 |

The Table 2 show the percentage of total explained variance that is derived from 6 components. The first extract component has eigenvalue 6.02, explained the 40% of the total variance. The second extract component has eigenvalue 4.43 explained a improve of 30% of the cumulative variance, they explained a total variance of the 70%. The sixth component explained the 96% of the cumulative total variance [19].

**Table 2.** Percentage of total explained variance

| Components | Eigenvalues | % Variance | % Cumulatative |
|---|---|---|---|
| 1 | 6.02 | 40 | 40 |
| 2 | 4.43 | 30 | 70 |
| 3 | 1.14 | 7 | 77 |
| 4 | 1.01 | 7 | 84 |
| 5 | 0.95 | 6 | 90 |
| 6 | 0.87 | 6 | 96 |

I have reduced the size of the area of the object definition, from 15 to 6, after which i have reconstructed the images with the new standardized object values greater than average and minor than average, that is greater than and lower than zero - based on each major component. These are illustrated in the Fig. 3 and in the Fig. 4 [14–16].

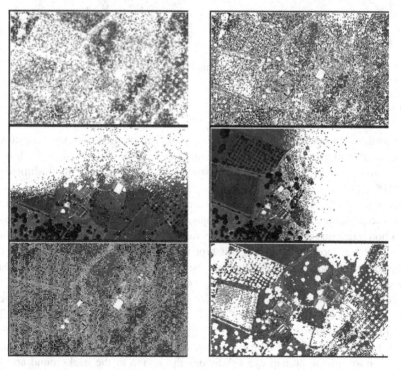

**Fig. 3.** Results of components from 1 to 6 greater than zero.

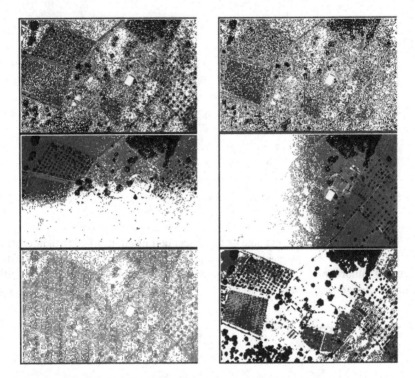

**Fig. 4.** Results of components from 1 to 6 lower than zero.

## 3 Conclusions

Factor analysis summarized very much the starting information without reconstructing a significant pattern normally used in supervised methods. The Fig. 5 show the correlations between factors and their spatial distribution in a multi-dimensional space [18, 21].

The distribution of the variables in a multi-dimensional space shows that in the sixth corresponding component in the graph Fig. 5, by identified with *S6* simbology, have a homogeneous distribution in all the variables analyzed with a preponderance in the variable that most characterizes this type of analysis, that is the depth of the pixel expressed by the radiance of the elements belonging to the territory and/or landscape analyzed.

I consider only the main components of the mosaic, belonging to the sixth component that has explained the 96% of the cumulative total variance (See Fig. 6). They highlight all the elements belonging to the analyzed mosaic. The results obtained are the exact perception that the human eye has when observing a landscape from above. The perception of the human eye subdivides the image in the background and foreground, highlighting the emerging texture. This is the same result that I obtained by training the system through machine learning techniques. In the two images below, the

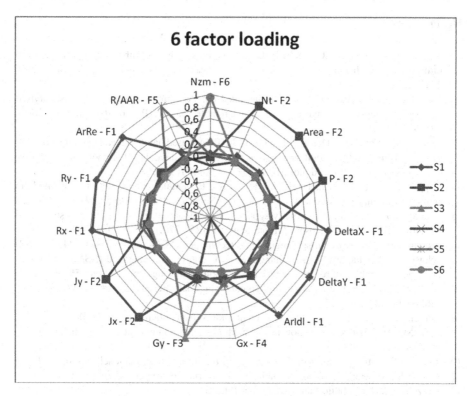

**Fig. 5.** Results of the distribution of the 6 factor loading.

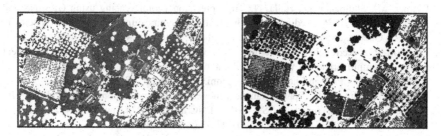

**Fig. 6.** Results only of component 6 greater and lower than zero.

background of the texture is highlighted in the image on the left with the links to the housing structures, while in the image on the right all the emerging of trees vegetation elements are represented with their respective connective systems.

In the future works it is foreseen to instruct the system to the perception of increasingly complex images such as urban and suburban territories where many discriminating elements insist.

# References

1. Niladri, S.M., Susmita, G., Ashish, G.: Fuzzy clustering algorithms incorporating local information for change detection in remotely sensed images Appl. Soft Comput. **12**(8), 2683–2692 (2012)
2. Castellana, L., D'Addabbo, A., Pasquariello, G.: A composed supervised/unsupervised approach to improve change detection from remote sensing. Pattern Recogn. Lett. **28**(4), 405–413 (2007)
3. Deng, J.S., Wang, K., Deng, Y.H., Qi, G.J.: PCA based land use change detection and analysis using multitemporal and multisensor satellite data. Int. J. remote Sens. **29**(16), 4823–4838 (2008). https://doi.org/10.1080/01431160801950162
4. Coppin, P., Jonckheere, I., Nackaerts, K., Muys, B.: Digital change detection methods in ecosystem monitoring: a review. Int. J. Remote Sens. **25**, 1565–1596 (2004)
5. Byeungwoo, J., David, A.: Partially supervised classification using weighted unsupervised clustering. IEEE Trans. Geosci. Remote Sens. (TGRS) **37**(2), 1073–1079 (1999)
6. Browna, L.G.: Survey of image registration techniques. ACM Comput. Surv. **24**(4) (1992)
7. Schwarz, K.P., Chapman, M.A., Cannon, M.E., Gong, P.: An integrated INS/GPS approach to the georeferencing of remotely sensed data. Photogram. Eng. Remote Sens. **59**(11), 1167–1674 (1993). https://www.asprs.org/wp-content/uploads/pers/1993journal/nov/1993_nov_1667-1674.pdf
8. Hotelling, H.: The generalization of student's ratio. Ann. Math. Statist. **2**, 30–378 (1931)
9. Zevi, M.: The matrix calculation in the method of the components princiapli. Faculty of Architecture, Rome (1977)
10. Ricci, F.: Statistics and Statistical Processing of the Information. Zanichelli, Bologna (1975)
11. Saddocchi, S.: Manuale di analisi statistica multivariata F. Angeli, Milano (1993)
12. Mezzetti, A.: Air pollution and vegetation, Edagricole (1987)
13. Fischler, M.A., Bolles, R.C.: Random sample consensus: a paradigm for mode l fitting with applications to image analysis and automated cartography. Comm. ACM **24**, 381–395 (1981)
14. Cramer, M., Stallmann, D., Halla, N.: High precision georeferencing using GPS/INS and image matching. In: Proceedings of the International Symposium on Kinematic Systems in Geodesy, Geomatics and Navigation, Banff, Alberta, Canada, 3–6 June, pp. 453–462 (1997)
15. Zuendorf, G., Kerrouche, N., Herholz, K., Baron, J.C.: Efficient principal component analysis for multivariate 3D voxel - based mapping of brain functional imaging data sets as applied to FDG - PET and normal aging. Hum. Brain Mapp. **18**, 13–21 (2003)
16. Mazzei, M., Palma, A.L.: Spatial statistical models for the evaluation of the landscape. In: Murgante, B., et al. (eds.) ICCSA 2013. LNCS, vol. 7974, pp. 419–432. Springer, Heidelberg (2013). https://doi.org/10.1007/978-3-642-39649-6_30
17. Mazzei, M., Palma, A.L.: Comparative analysis of models of location and spatial interaction. In: Murgante, B., et al. (eds.) ICCSA 2014. LNCS, vol. 8582, pp. 253–267. Springer, Cham (2014). https://doi.org/10.1007/978-3-319-09147-1_19
18. Mazzei, M., Palma, A.L.: Spatial multicriteria analysis approach for evaluation of mobility demand in urban areas. In: Gervasi, O., et al. (eds.) ICCSA 2017. LNCS, vol. 10407, pp. 451–468. Springer, Cham (2017). https://doi.org/10.1007/978-3-319-62401-3_33
19. Mazzei, M.: Software development for unsupervised approach to identification of a multi temporal spatial analysis model. In: Muller J. (ed.) Proceedings of the 2018 International Conference on Image Processing, Computer Vision, & Pattern Recognition 2018. Computer Science, Computer Engineering & Applied Computing

20. Amato, F., Tonini, M., Murgante, B., Kanevski, M.F.: Fuzzy definition of rural urban interface: an application based on land use change scenarios in Portugal. Environ. Model Softw. **104**, 171–187 (2018)
21. Ranjbar nia, B., Murgante, B., Molaei Qelichi, M., Rustaei, S.: A comparative study employing CIA methods in knowledge-based urban development with emphasis on affordable housing in Iranian cities (case: Tabriz). In: Gervasi, O., et al. (eds.) ICCSA 2017. LNCS, vol. 10407, pp. 485–501. Springer, Cham (2017). https://doi.org/10.1007/978-3-319-62401-3_35
22. Farina, A.: Ecologia del paesaggio. UTET, Torino (2004)

# Spatial Patterns of Development of Mobile Technologies for 5G Networks

Piotr A. Werner[(⊠)] and Mariusz Porczek[(⊠)]

Faculty of Geography and Regional Studies, University of Warsaw,
Krak. Przedm. 30, 00-927 Warsaw, Poland
{peter, mt.porczek}@uw.edu.pl

**Abstract.** The paper deals with spatial (geographical) conditions for forth-coming 5G Mobile Technologies, especially their infrastructure at a global scale. The main assumption presents the idea that all networks, which evolved to converge together into one: internet and wireless computer networks, cellular mobile communication, radio and TV diffusion networks, constituting the infrastructure of information society are developing in the similar manner and depend on similar factors. Thus the spatial processes of these technologies should present alike spatial patterns of development, especially for expected IoT and wireless services, which are perceived as pillars of new networks usability. The main processes which let to interconnect them are related to convergence of the signal through the main gateways and interaction between users. The recognized spatial factors influencing on these processes are: the population potential, hierarchy of the cities (metropolitan urbanization) and geographical distance. These qualities are recognized and quantified in a set of models of spatial pattern development using the dedicated spatial (geographical) measures. The empirical approach involves the use of location quotients of infrastructure networks confronted with evaluated level of interaction between populated urban places applied to previous generation of mobile networks (estimated using geographical - population potential), verified by countries' mobile penetration statistics.

**Keywords:** Spatial patterns · Mobile communication · Fifth generation

## 1 Introduction

Mobile technologies intertwined with information and communication technologies (ICT) have determined the development of nowadays economy gradually replacing personal computers. They spread themselves sector by sector and countries. They are carriers of disruptive innovations: widespread wireless internet technologies and strengthen interaction between densely and sparsely populated places. The main determinants of spatial extent of development of infrastructure of mobile technologies are: spatial distribution of urban areas as well as areas along main transport routes between them. But since the last decade of XXth century the mobile technologies have changed themselves also, from the carrier of voice and short messages to completely new spatial emergent phenomenon involving wide areas of economy and social aspects

© Springer Nature Switzerland AG 2019
S. Misra et al. (Eds.): ICCSA 2019, LNCS 11621, pp. 448–459, 2019.
https://doi.org/10.1007/978-3-030-24302-9_32

of life, including way of life, entertainment and tourism. However, dealing with the significance of information and communication technologies (ICT) in social development, one can stress the implementation and ICT projects have huge positive potential, but often have also negative consequences, sometimes expected, sometimes not expected. This observation have found confirmation in opinion stating: "Over the last twenty years, rather than reducing poverty, ICTs have actually increased inequality, and if 'development' is seen as being about the relative differences between people and between communities, than it has had an overwhelming negative impact on development." [1]. The subsequent generations of technologies with different mobile devices are strictly converge with ICT, replacing the common use of PCs (personal computers) in everyday life of people. On the other side, each generation needed the advancement of infrastructure of base transceiver stations facilitating wireless communication between user devices and network. The differentiation of the infrastructure base of mobile technologies can help infer about the differentiation of the progress of development of ICT mobile technologies. The main hypothesis to verify in the presented research states that, emergent processes of development of internet and ICT take place, at the global scale, in most populated and urbanized areas leveraged and based on adoption of the disruptive innovation of mobile technologies. The approach uses the well known, modified, population potential model [2–5], and operate on the set of global statistical input data variables by countries and cities (with population over 250 thousands inhabitants), as well crowdsourcing data concerning the infrastructure of the base transceiver stations. The results of the modelling are verified comparing the accessible volume of mobile subscriptions by countries. The analysis presents the spatial evolution of mobile technologies diffusion since 1990, but the final verification concerns the data collected at the 2015–2018. This is slightly different approach from classic analysis of diffusion innovation process, which usually focused on time and number of different adopters, because in this research the main determinant is friction of space – geographical distance.

## 2 Methodology

Spatial development of mobile technology generations has been evaluated using available ITU statistics data of overall penetration (%) by countries since 1990 using anamorphic cartograms. Scaling of area of countries is proportional to range of penetration in different years. Next the recent state and dominant generations of mobile technologies has been presented using location quotients (according the data in 2017). Data for the number and type of BTSs have been acquired from voluntary (crowdsourcing) data base. Source of presented data is complete database acquired from opencellid.org (accessed Feb. 2019), which counted over 40 million records identifying base transceiver stations (BTS) and their generations of mobile technology. In fact BTS information is derived from voluntary crowdsourcing reports and later verified. OpenCellID is actively updated crowdsourcing database collecting GPS location data for cell identifiers. It had already been previously used in scientific research and its advantages and disadvantages are recognized [6]. But the volume of stored data since

2009 lets assume, that is close to real current situation at the global scale. Location quotients have been calculated for each country based on the formula (Eq. 1):

$$lq_c = \frac{MG_c}{MG_w} / \frac{BTS_c}{BTS_w} \tag{1}$$

where: $lq_c$ – location quotient of certain mobile generation technology in defined country, $MG_c$ – number of base transceiver stations of certain generation in country, $MG_w$ – number of base transceiver stations of certain generation in the world, $BTS_c$ – total number of base transceiver stations in country, $BTS_w$ – total number of base transceiver stations in the world.

It shows regional specialization within spatial unit (in above described case: country specific) related to global values. Location quotient determines in which countries occurs concentration ($lq > 1$) or severance ($lq < 1$) of certain mobile cellular technologies. Interpretation of the estimated location quotients show to what degree recently there is the domination of the certain generation of mobile technology in each country. The value greater than 1 means greater domination of certain mobile cellular generation, less than 1 lets infer that this generation is being withdrawn or, in case of newest generations, is starting. Value close to 1 lets assume, that the whole country reached the mature state of certain generation. The whole procedure were repeated for each mobile technology generations separately. Some authors claim that location quotients sometimes fulfil the function similar to standardization measures. But in this research they simply measure the over- or under-concentration of the mobile technology location.

Considering the problem of interactions between people needs to apply the proper method to evaluate the overall volume of potential contacts. There are set of models in scientific, geographical and mathematical literature. But for the recent study the modified formula of classic population potential model has been applied. It also has been previously used for similar study concerning the spatial simulation of initial stage of cellular phone network development in Poland [2].

On the other side there are 1860 cities of the world with inhabitants over 250K as the input data into the model. Variables used were the following: their geolocation (longitude, latitude), population data and calculated distances between them, i.e. between each pair potentially interacted masses (populated places). The only modification introduced into the model was Zipf's rule of the order and magnitude of cites, i.e. the rank of city. The model incorporates the absolute difference of the ranks of cities during calculation of potential interaction between them for each pair separately. The formula of the model is the following (Eq. 2):

$$V_i = \sum_{i=1}^{n} \sum_{j=1}^{n} \frac{P_i P_j}{d_{ij} h_{ij}} \tag{2}$$

where: i, j – cities, $P_i, P_j$ – population of cities i and j (2015), $d_{ij}$ – calculated distance between cities i and j, $h_{ij}$ – absolute value of difference of the ranks of the cities i and j, n – total number of the cities (1860).

The distance between the cities has been calculated using Haversine formula (in km). In case of evaluation of sole inner city interaction (with itself i.e. for i = j) the denominator of the formula takes value equal 1. "Population potential is treated as an appropriate measure of accessibility, and a tool for an assessment of the volume of interaction involving alternative locations. The general potential model assumes that interactions pertaining to a given location decline proportionally to the distance from the origin. The larger the population potential in the target location, the greater its ability to generate spatial interactions. The population potential model encompasses both the population size of places (numerator) and the distance (denominator) involved; the latter expresses the friction of space. The numerator represents the total number of people able to overcome the resistance of geographical space." [2]. The friction of space involves also the difference of ranks of the cities. The choice of this model has been preceded the evaluation of others, in forms – without ranks or including the values of location quotients of newest generations of mobile technology – but the final results of verification were statistically weaker and they were dropped. The main axiom for adoption such formula of population potential was that Euclidean metrics exist in real world space.

Finally the results of the modeling of interactions between cities have been aggregated (dissolved) and correlated with volumes of mobile subscriptions by countries, and discussed.

## 3  Development of Mobile Cellular Technologies

Wireless telephony and Wi-Fi (802.11) protocol have been pointed as disruptive innovations which imprinted on track on the technological consciousness of society, economy and business [7]. Android OS and iOS (Apple) together have gained over 97% share of the mobile devices used in the world since 2009, when Open Handset Alliance, supported inter alia by Google, decided to use Linux 2.6 kernel of the projected mobile platform (Fig. 1). This decision made a convergence between two loosely coupled technologies (up to this moment): internet and mobile phones (smartphones), replacing the competition of several other market strong players offering their operation systems (Nokia/Symbian, Microsoft/Windows Mobile, RIM BlackBerry and others). This new process, co-played with the diffusion of mobile phones and internet (separately since 1980), created the emergent phenomena which in turn accelerated the development both of the set of internet tools and allowed mobile applications for access to internet services. Thus, within 10 years, the number of users of smartphones significantly exceeded the users using computers accessing the internet (see Fig. 2). The mobile devices with Android OS (or Apple iOS) became the easiest and quickest way to access the internet for the overwhelming majority of users. So the research concerning dissemination of mobile technologies (smartphones) in fact is related to diffusion of Android or iOS (Apple) devices and cellular infrastructure network. This is new dimension and element which should be taken into account in the discussion of digital divides. Digital divides is defined "as the affordability of the hardware, software and services that make up information and communication technologies (ICTs)" [8].

Figure 2 presents common trends of growth of number of mobile subscriptions, Android & iOS users, compared to numbers of internet users, total and urban population as well as global domestic products and revenues of computer, communications and other services sector at the global scale since 2000.

Two of phenomena presented on Fig. 2 are similar to well known recognized diffusion process in form of logistic curve, i.e. number of world mobile subscriptions and (both) Android and iOS users of mobile devices. It is well known fact, that Android is the main operating system of ¾ of mobile devices - increased of market share worldwide from 4% in 2011 up to 75% in 2019 (source: gs.statcounter.com). If one take a look on mobile cellular evolution timeline (Fig. 3), nowadays, the forthcoming, perceived and predicted as disruptive innovation, fifth generation of mobile communication needs a huge investment into the infrastructure of future 5th mobile network, much more densely concentrated than previous ones (1st AMPS/TACS, NMT, 2nd - GSM/GPRS/, 3rd - UMTS, CDMA, 4th - LTE/LTE Advanced, WiMAX/. "5G will be smarter technology with no limits and to interconnect the whole world without limits. The upcoming life style will be different with uninterrupted access of information and interconnection" [9].

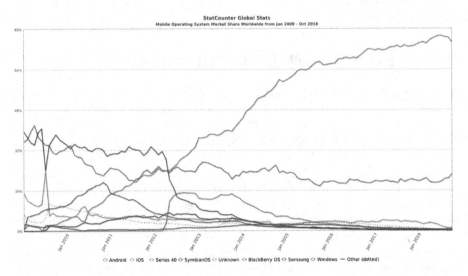

**Fig. 1.** Mobile operating system market share (source, http://gs.statcounter.com, access 11/21/18)

However, the spatial diffusion of mobile digital cellular generation was not so simple and in equal pace throughout the world (Fig. 4 a, b, c and d). The starting points of diffusion of cellular mobile telephony is pointed in USA (CDMA standard) and Finland (GSM standard). But in the last decade of XX century one can point also USA, Canada, Nordic (Scandinavian) countries in Europe, Australia and Japan. Initial differences in penetration have disappeared during the next 25 years, proving the

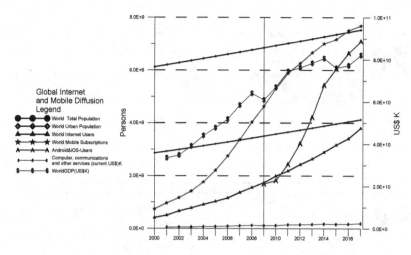

**Fig. 2.** Global internet and mobile diffusion (source, ITU, OECD, gs.statcounter.com, 2019)

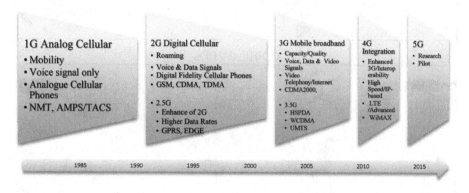

**Fig. 3.** Mobile cellular network evolution timeline [9]

significance of the masses of population as the target in marketing the use of mobile technologies. It took only twenty years to complete the dissemination of cellular phones since the introduction of second, digital GSM generation of mobile technologies.

On the other side, there are countries reached the high level of penetration but only with prevailed, certain generation of mobile technologies (Fig. 5 a, b, c and d).

LTE (Long Term Evolution) is recognized nowadays as the mature, modern, fast mobile technology and is dominating in most developed countries. But forecasts concerning forthcoming 5th generation anticipate evolution in multiplatform, hetero-geneous technological eco-system. Future applications would might support geonavi-gation, tele-medicine, crisis management, education, tourism, travelling and others with immediate service availability and on-demand adaptability [9]. However it is ques-tionable if this forthcoming intelligent technology is really capable of interconnecting

A.1990, 0-6%

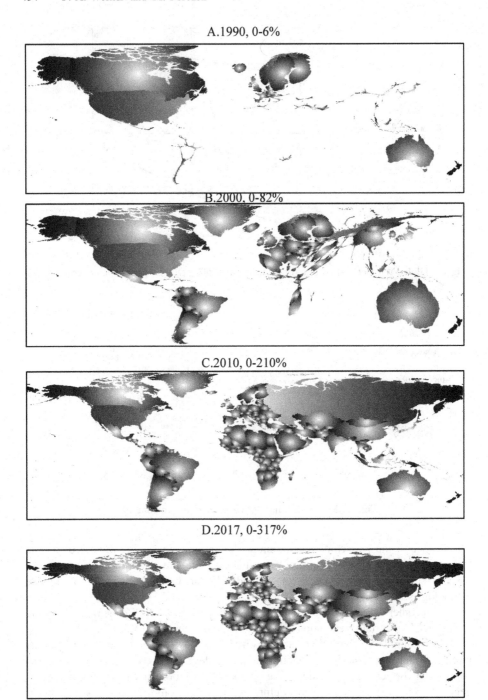

B.2000, 0-82%

C.2010, 0-210%

D.2017, 0-317%

**Fig. 4.** Global mobile penetration/anamorphic cartograms/. A. 1990, scaling size of countries (%): 0–6%, B. Scaling: 0–82%, C. Scaling: 0–210%, D. Scaling: 0–317%.

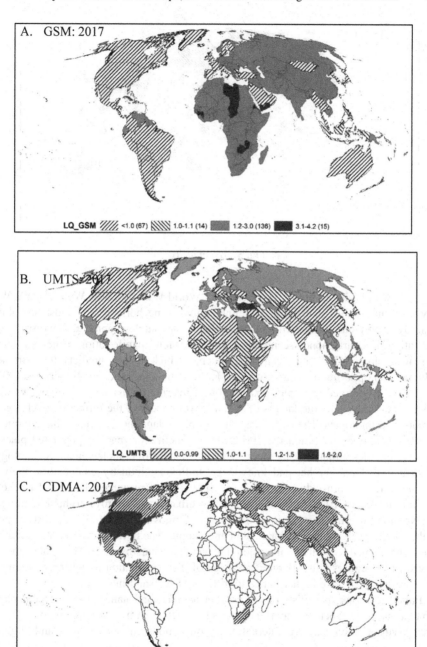

**Fig. 5.** Location quotients of mobile cellular BTSs by countries and technology (2017). A. GSM, B. CDMA, C. UMTS, D. LTE

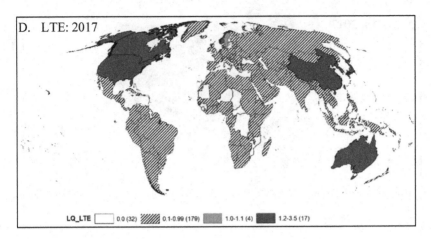

**Fig. 5.** (*continued*)

the entire world without limits. The vision of "World Wide Wireless Web" (WWWW) may gain the mature state in an undefined future time horizon, and most probably similarly to previous stages of mobile technologies spatial development. The disruptive innovation of smart phones seems the another version, manifestation of general purpose technology (GPT) emergent phenomena, which theory predicts that similar technological opportunities may not result in the same experience in all locations [10]. Some theories derived from past observation of internet diffusion and previous media may help to understand the factors of spatial development of the forthcoming changes in mobile technologies. There are inter alia: global village theory stating that adoption of such disruptive innovation may bring more benefits for sparsely populated places and smaller cities; urban density theory with advantages of complementary technology infrastructure, labor market and knowledge spillovers; industry composition theory with tendency to form advanced clusters, sharing local resources, labor and market. Last but not least GPT theory itself prove that urban areas improve co-habitation and co-invention lowering costs of implementation of innovation [ibid. 9]. All of them put on the forefront two factors: urbanization and people. The third, which is not explicitly listed and named is spatial dimension i.e. geographical distance. There have been proved that countries with a large percentage of their population living in urban areas are more likely to have higher penetration rates of ICT and internet [11].

Public relations specialists on the market adopted and named the emergent phenomena as Data Society (next to internet society) with main trends of hyperconnectivity involving more international connections, merge of real and digital worlds, huge consumption of info-data due to wide use fiber and wireless high bandwidth for 3D video on 4 K screens, cloud computing and software as a service (SaaS), augmented reality, smart city cameras monitoring, massive IoT (internet of things), industrial and commercial automation, mission critical broadband and self-driving (also electric) cars/vehicles.

## 4  Modeling the Global Interactions

The whole model of global interactions (Fig. 6) between global cities has been visualized as heat map with overlaid, scaled values of population potential of cities of logarithm at base 10. There revealed main global potential core areas of spatial diffusion of forthcoming 5th generation of mobile technology, which reflect the global distribution of world population.

The verification of main research hypothesis aimed correlation between aggregated values of modelled population potential by countries and available ITU data of volume of mobile subscriptions (Table 1). The procedure involved 150 countries of the world.

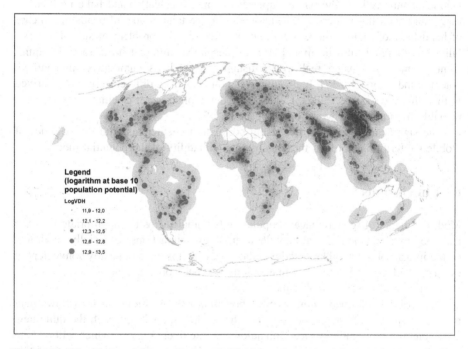

**Fig. 6.** Global volume of interactions – model of population potential of 1860 world cities overlaid on heat map (logarithm at base 10 values).

**Table 1.** Correlation and 2-tailed significance of coefficients between volumes of mobile subscriptions and global interactions (model of population potential) by countries: 2015, 2016, 2017.

| ** Correlation is significant at the 0.01 level (2-tailed) | Population potential/VDH/- Pearson correlation |
| --- | --- |
| Mobile subscription by countries (2015) | $0.874^{**}$ |
| Mobile subscription by countries (2016) | $0.871^{**}$ |
| Mobile subscription by countries (2017) | $0.876^{**}$ |

## 5   Discussion

Classic approach to spatial accessibility and use of population potential model is often considered in scientific, transport literature and also to solve the problem concerning mobility of people: migrations or commuting to work. The classic potential model can be treated as the tool for evaluation of accessibility involving the function of attractiveness of the places measured with the population number related to function of spatial resistance (or decay) [12, 13].

Spatial accessibility is treated as multidimensional phenomenon and reflects the complexity of methods and techniques of research. In case of mobile technology – this approach finds a little bit another, easier explanation. The classic approach of population potential reflects the whole superset of (mathematical) 'handshake problem' – how many handshakes there will be altogether for certain number of people, or in case of handshake of dial-up modem computers network. The problem of spatial accessibility incorporated into the model (Eq. 2), despite of different infrastructural equipment, is measured using real world distance, as well as cumulative, personified, potential indicators [14–17]. It also includes non-Euclidean difference of ranks derived from well known, statistical Zipf's law – model applied to set of cities, reflecting the invisible friction of real world urban space [2].

The significant results verified using correlation coefficients with the volumes of mobile subscriptions, proved the viability and suitability of the potential model.

## 6   Conclusions

Modified model of (geographical) population potential seems the appropriate measure and tool to estimation global mobile technology interactions, especially modified, taking into account the ranks of the populated places. It is the tool ideally convenient to evaluate the level and volume of interactions between populated places and proved its value in case of development of mobile technology.

Affordability of smart phones and exponential rise of volume of data flows may also occur in case of interconnection into the world wide wireless web the quite new active elements: wearable devices and automatic intelligent sensors, which will operate independently without the initial human action. There is also another aspect of this emergent phenomenon: the limited bandwidths range resources for use of 5$^{th}$ generation WWWW network. Hope, this is only engineering problem. The presented pilot study aimed only the verification of the usefulness of modified (geographic) population potential in spatial studies of dissemination of new generation of mobile technology. The model itself proved its value, however the trial to include location quotients into the model was unsuccessful. The current strategic aim is still open – to gain the model which can simulate the spatial spillover of such technological innovation (part of ICT). It also need to choose the proper places and initial conditions to start this kind simulation, and it also hooks on quite new set of determinant factors: social, economic and political.

# References

1. Unwin, P.T.H.: Reclaiming Information and Communication Technologies for Development. Oxford University Press, Oxford, New York (2017)
2. Werner, P.: Geograficzne uwarunkowania rozwoju infrastruktury społeczeństwa informacyjnego w Polsce. Uniwersytet Warszawski, Wydz. Geografii i Studiów Regionalnych, Warszawa (2003)
3. Werner, P.: Simulating of accessibility of ICT infrastructure in Poland using geographical potential models. In: Proceedings of the 16th International Conference on System Science, pp. 261–269. Wroclaw University of Technology (2007)
4. Werner, P.: Information society development level in carpathian regions. In: The World's Geo-Spatial Solutions. ICA, Santiago de Chile (2009). https://doi.org/10.13140/2.1.4741.7284
5. Werner, P., Korcelli, P., Kozubek, P.: Population potential as a modulator of land use changes in Poland's metropolitan areas. Quageo 33, 37–50 (2014). https://doi.org/10.2478/quageo-2014-0014
6. Ricciato, F., Widhalm, P., Craglia, M., Pantisano, F.: Estimating Population Density Distribution from Network-Based Mobile Phone Data. Publications Office of the European Union (2015)
7. King, A.A., Baatartogtokh, B.: How useful is the theory of disruptive innovation? MIT Sloan Manag. Rev. 57, 16 (2015)
8. Skaletsky, M., Pick, J.B., Sarkar, A., Yates, D.: Digital divides: past, present, and future (2017)
9. Sood, R., Garg, A.: Digital society from 1G to 5G: a comparative study. IJAIEM 3, 186–193 (2014)
10. Forman, C., Goldfarb, A., Greenstein, S.: Geographic location and the diffusion of internet technology. Electron. Commer. Res. Appl. 4, 1–13 (2005)
11. Wunnava, P.V., Leiter, D.B.: Determinants of intercountry internet diffusion rates. Am. J. Econ. Sociol. 68, 413–426 (2009)
12. Hansen, W.G.: How Accessibility Shapes Land-use. J. Am. Inst. Plan. 25, 73–76 (1959)
13. Harris, C.D.: The market as a factor in the localization of industry in the United States. Ann. Assoc. sAm. Geogr. 44, 315–348 (1954)
14. Geurs, K.T., van Eck, R.: Accessibility measures: review and applications. RIVM report 408505006. National Institute of Public Health and the Environment, Bilthoven (2001)
15. Geurs, K.T., van Wee, B.: Accessibility evaluation of land-use and transport strategies: review and research directions. J. Transp. Geogr. 12(2), 127–140 (2004)
16. Komornicki, T., Stępniak, M.: New investment projects in the road corridors and the improvement of the potential accessibility in Poland. Europa XXI 28, 33–52 (2015). https://doi.org/10.7163/eu21.2015.28.2
17. Pomianowski, W.: Transportation network structure and spatial accessibility. Dynamic graph approach. Ph.D. thesis. Stanislaw Leszczycki Institute of Geography and Spatial Organization, Polish Academy of Science, Warsaw (2018)

# Stochastic Blockmodeling for the Analysis of Big Data

Gabriella Schoier[✉] and Giuseppe Borruso

DEAMS – Department of Economic, Business, Mathematic and Statistical
Sciences "Bruno de Finetti", University of Trieste, Tigor 22, 34100 Trieste, Italy
{gabriella.schoier,giuseppe.borruso}@deams.units.it

**Abstract.** The aim of this paper is to consider the stochastic blockmodel to obtain clusters of units as regards patterns of similar relations; moreover we want to analyze the relations between clusters. Blockmodeling is a technique usually applied in social network analysis focussing on the relations between "actors" i.e. units. In our time people and devices constantly generate data. The network is generating location and other data that keeps services running and ready to use in every moment. This rapid development in the availability and access to data has induced the need for better analysis techniques to understand the various phenomena. Blockmodeling techniques and Clustering algorithms, can be used for this aim. In this paper application regards the Web.

**Keywords:** Blockmodeling · Gibbs sampling · Latent class model ·
Clustering algorithms · Big data

## 1 Introduction

Stochastic blockmodeling is a technique often used in social network analysis for studying the relationship between two factors. Its goal is to cluster objects with respect to some given observed variables using the existing relationships between actors.

The clustering problem has been considered in many contexts and by researchers in different disciplines. It is useful in several exploratory pattern-analysis, grouping, decision-making and machine-learning situations, including data mining web mining and spatial data mining.

Cluster analysis can be defined as the organization of a collection of patterns - usually represented as a vector of measurements, or a point in a multidimensional space - into clusters based on similarity [7, 11, 19, 25].

Unlike cluster analysis, which subdivides the elements of a network into groups based on the study of the properties and characteristics of the network units (actors in Social Analysis framework), blockmodel, allows the formation of homogeneous groups based on the study of the relationships existing between the actors of the network itself [1].

Different approaches have been developed in stochastic blockmodeling. In this paper we have applied the one proposed by Nowicki, Snijders and others [4, 9, 13–15, 17, 18] in order to study the navigational patterns through a website [11].

© Springer Nature Switzerland AG 2019
S. Misra et al. (Eds.): ICCSA 2019, LNCS 11621, pp. 460–472, 2019.
https://doi.org/10.1007/978-3-030-24302-9_33

In our analysis, the clusters, called colours, are formed by groups of units, which are the viewed web pages.

It is interesting to notice that other different applications in a big data and in a spatially big data context can be considered as the computational aspects and the visual representation are attractive tools.

Specifically, we have applied blockmodeling to establish three relationships between viewed web pages.

These relationships are: having common users, sharing the same (recoded) time in the pages and having same value as regards the impressions (that is the number of times the page has been viewed during the session divided by the number of viewed pages); they are induced directly by navigation itself, and they in turn reflect users browsing behaviour during the navigation.

Clustering the shared common web pages among users allows us to gather useful information different from, for instance, clustering of web users.

The advantage of blockmodeling is that a differentiated structure for the degree of similarity within and between clusters is allowed. To explain this an example on a web site of a portal for children is considered.

The paper aims to divide a set of Web pages into homogeneous groups on the base of three known relationships existing between the pages. The peculiarity of this application is the simultaneous study of several relationships and the fact that the input data are not of dichotomous type but can assume a wider range of values. As regards the study of the three relations, Ucinet [2, 3] and Stocknet (in particular the Block module [10, 16, 17] programs have been used.

## 2 The Methodology: Blockmodel and Stochastic Blockmodel

Graphs and oriented graphs have been used as mathematical models for social and physical phenomena where the relationships between the various units are known.

Two important types of graph models (oriented or not) are the blockmodel and the stochastic models. An integration of these two approaches has been proposed by Wassermann [22–24].

Blockmodels allow to elaborate the results of a positional analysis providing a simplified representation of the links and interactions present in a complex social network.

First it is necessary to briefly explain what a positional analysis means. Starting from a multirelational set, the final aim of a positional analysis is to group the "actors" in positions, so that individuals who can be considered similar, according to a strict definition, are inserted in the same block, obtaining a complete partition of all the actors belonging to the social network.

It is also necessary to give a definition of "role" and "position", keywords in a positional analysis. "Position" is a set of individuals that interact from and to other actors in the social network in the same way. "Role" is a system of associations between relations between individuals or between positions.

A blockmodel consists of a description of how the actors are assigned to the positions, *i.e.* a partition of the actors in a discrete number of subsets, the "positions", one or more image matrixes depending on the number of relations considered which indicate the presence or absence of a link for each pair of positions considered. The image matrix (one for every relation) is a square matrix whose size is the number of positions of the social network. It refers to positions and not to single individuals.

Let us consider a set of $R$ binary sub-matrices defined on $n$ actors belonging to $N$, which describe the relationships existing between individuals; there are as many submatrices as the considered relationships.

Consider $C_1, \ldots, C_c$, with $c < n$, an exclusive and exhaustive partition of $N$ in $c$ positions and consider the map function $\Phi(\cdot)$ such that $\Phi(i) = C_k$ indicates that the actor $i$ belongs to the class $C_k$.

Let us consider the relationships, no longer between the single actors (units), but between the positions through a matrix $C$ (image matrix) whose elements $c_{klr}$ can assume value 1 (oneblock) or 0 (zeroblock) depending if the relation $r$ between the positions $k$ and $l$ exists or not.

A blockmodel is therefore a matrix of size $(cxcxR)$ with values 1 and 0. It is the result of an empirical procedure based on the idea that units in a network can be grouped into equivalent sets, under a given definition of equivalence.

On the base on the type of the considered equivalence, a distinction is made between deterministic and stochastic blockmodel.

The deterministic blockmodel is based on the concept of structural equivalence: two actors are defined equivalent if they perfectly possess the same relational ties [11].

This approach has the disadvantage of not using statistical tests to determine how well the blockmodel adapts to real values. To overcome this problem, a stochastic approach has been developed, precisely what we will consider [1, 21].

In the stochastic blockmodel a stochastic equivalence is considered:

Two actors $i$ and $i'$ are stochastically equivalent if the probability that $i$ is in relation (to and from) with every other actor is the same also for the actor $i'$ i.e. if the probability of an event concerning X does not change by substituting $i$ with $i'$.

We have to notice that: structural equivalence $\Rightarrow$ stochastich equivalence (but *the vice versa* is not true).

As mentioned above a blockmodel is formed by a probability distribution $p(x)$ and a map function $\Phi$.

Depending on how the map function is found the stochastic blockmodel is distinguished between:

– *a priori blockmodel* where it is assumed that the map function is previously known and that it depends on exogenous characteristics of the actors in relation to the studied relations,
– *a posteriori blockmodel* where the map function is the result of the application of the data on the relations.

In general different approaches can be applied.

– Approach on the base of the *p1* model (Wassermann and Anderson [24] and Wasserman, Anderson and Faust [23]).

The stochastic blockmodel can be defined as a probability distribution (or a family of distributions) for graphs (oriented or not) in which the vertices set is divided into subset called blocks (or colors), which satisfy the property that the distribution of probability of the graph remains unchanged following permutations of the vertices within the block to which they belong. The probability that a bond is present between two vertices depends only on the color of the vertex, i.e. the block to which it belongs. Two vertices belonging to the same block are called stochastically equivalent.

Depending on whether the attributes of the vertices and therefore the blocks are known or not, we speak of a priori or a posterior stochastic blockmodel. The latter is much more complex than the former.

Wassermann and Anderson [24] and Wasserman, Anderson and Faust [23] have studied the a posterior blockmodel with respect to the *p1* family. This is a log-linear exponential family of probability distribution for graphs.

In a first phase the vertices are "blocked" through an ML estimation of the vertices parameters themselves, then they are grouped on the basis of multiple comparisons of the estimated parameters, i.e. the vertices that have approximately similar estimates of the two parameters considered (productivity parameter and popularity parameter) are put in the same group.

In general, the *p1* model in statistical inference has the problem that the number of parameters increases with the increase in the number of vertices; this problem is solved with the combination of p1 and blockmodel, since even if the number of vertices increases, the number of blocks remains unchanged, as instead of considering the single vertices we consider the blocks.

Another disadvantage of the posterior blockmodeling based on the p1 model derives from its too restrictive nature. In fact, in the p1 model the vertices having a high productivity parameter are relatively more likely to have outbound links, i.e. to other vertices ($\rightarrow$), while vertices with a high popularity have a high probability of having inbound links, *i.e.* from other vertices. This excludes the important case of oriented graphs with vertices classes where the density of relations is elevated within the class and low among different classes.

– Bayesian approach (Snjders and Nowicki [17]).

This is a more generic approach than the previous one, because it is not related to the *p1* function.

Each vertex of the observed graph belongs to a block, however the structure of the blocks is not observed. Moreover the relationships are independent, conditioned only by the block structure.

In particular, two methods are considered:

– in the case of a graph with few vertices (<20) we can use both the method of maximum likelihood (ML estimation) and the Bayesian estimates implemented using Gibbs sampling,
– in the case of a higher number of vertices, even if very high, the Bayes method can be used.

# 3  The Application

## 3.1  The Data and the Preliminary Phase

The objective of this application is to use the posteriori stochastic blockmodeling according to a Bayesian approach developed by Snijders and Nowicki adapting it to the case of an analysis based on the study of several relationships observed on the same set of actors.

The environment in which this analysis has been developed is the Web Mining [8, 20]. In particular, an analysis of three relationships between users and Web pages has been considered. The objective has been to divide the various pages into groups whose elements are considered stochastically equivalent [12].

The analysis regards the log files of the web site www.girotondo.com, a portal for children. In this site there are seven different sessions: *Bacheca, Corso, Favolando, Giochi, Links, News, Percome*, it has 362 jhtml pages.

The period of observation is from the 29/11/2000 to the 18/01/2001. The original file contained 3000,000 records. Record of log files containing information about any object (with .gif, .jpeg., etc. extension) that is not its Internet address are cancelled.

The log-file information taken into account in the analysis concerns:

- IP address and page visited, that is if the user having IP address i has visited or not the page j of the site (data expressed in a dichotomous form),
- time spent by user $i$ on page $j$,
- impressions, *i.e.* the ratio between the number of times a page has been viewed in a session and the total number of pages viewed within the session.

In this way we obtain a file indicating the Internet address for every visited page. We have proceeded into a recodification of the Web pages transforming their URL into a number in order to handle them easily, in so doing 117 pages have been considered. After the pre-processing of the data we have obtained a file with 10,000 records. The data considered consist of a finite set of vertices (visited pages) on which $R = 3$ relational variables (having more than one user in common, having users which stay the same interval of time, having users with the same value for the impression) are measured; this is a *network N* (set of units and relation(s) defined over it). These variables are collected into three sets of (10000 × 117) matrices $X_1, X_2, X_3$ called sociomatrices which represent three 2-mode networks (users x pages).

The first problem that had to be considered is related to the determination of the inputs required by Stocnet and in particular the applicative Block [17], *i.e.* a single network representing a matrix of adjacencies, therefore of one-mode type. For this purpose, the free Ucinet program has been used [2].

Once the three matrices have been obtained and precisely one matrix for visited pages, one for times and one for the impressions they have had to be re-coded.

At this point these three rectangular matrices which represent three 2-mode networks have been changed into three square matrices representing three 1-mode networks (pages x pages).

An 1-mode matrix is a matrix in which both the rows and the columns refer to the same set of objects (vertices), while in a 2-mode matrix the rows and columns refer to two sets of different objects, in our case respectively IP addresses and web pages.

Ucinet allows to pass from a 2-mode matrix to a 1-mode matrix, that is a matrix called *actor-by-actor* that counts the number of events that each pair of actors has in common, or an *event-by-event* matrix, as in our case, which counts the number of actors accessing both pages, or, in general, both event.

It has been decided to recode the matrices after each Ucinet application. So after transforming the 2-mode matrices into 1-mode matrices these have been made dichotomous; in particular, for the time and impression matrices, a value of 0 was assigned for the values included in the interval [0, 10] and value 1 for the elements > 10. As far as regards the third matrix a distinction between cases in which two pages have 0 or 1 users in common, to which the value 0 has been assigned, and those with more than one user in common recoded with the value 1 has been considered.

Ucinet allows to have multiple matrices within the same data-file. It is possible to insert each matrix in a different spreadsheet sheet. In our case we have got a spreadsheet with three sheets.

Finally the three matrices have been aggregated in one matrix. Aggregation means the transformation of more than one matrix into one that contains their characteristics.

Ucinet allows different aggregation methods. The one used in this case is the procedure that assigns a single value to each unique combination of values between the relations. A single network file has thus obtained to be used as input in the Stocnet application. To be able to use the matrix in Stocnet you have to delete the labels and transform the file into text format. From now on, therefore, the various pages will no longer be indicated by their name, but by numbers.

## 3.2 Stochastic Blockmodel Application

A stochastic blockmodeling technique has been applied using the free program Stocnet that gives a graphical interface for different modules (the one for stochastic block modeling is Block). In Block we have recodified the values of the input matrix so to have four values: 0, 1, 2, 3.

A Blockmodeling allows to describe and to interpret a dataset through a block structure so to give a simplified representation of the existing ties and relation(s).

The primary tool of this technique is the *blockmodel* which, in our case, consists of a mapping of approximately equivalent 117 units or vertices (in our analysis visited pages) into discrete subsets called blocks and a statement regarding the relations between the positions or clusters or colours (in our case the three relations).

This represents a partition of the vertices into blocks and a mapping function $\Phi(\cdot)$ which describes the subdivision of the vertices through the positions.

One of the main procedural goals of *blockmodeling* is to identify clusters of units that share structural characteristics defined in terms of the $R$ relations where the optimal value of a criterion function has to be found. The criterion function can be constructed indirectly as a function of compatible (dis)similarity measure between pairs of units (see e.g. for the case of Web data [11]), or directly as a function measuring the fit of a clustering to an ideal one with perfect relations within each cluster and between clusters. In this paper we will consider this second possibility, moreover the approach we will adopt is the stochastic.

Let us consider the matrix $X = \{X_1, X_2, X_3\}$, it is called super-sociomatrix. The probability distribution for $X$, gives the probability that various relational linkages between actors across all relations are equal to a value $x$.

A stochastic blockmodel is based either on the probability distribution for $X$ and on the mapping function $\Phi(\cdot)$. There are two categories of stochastic blockmodels: *a priori* and *a posteriori*.

In this paper we will consider the *a posteriori* stochastic blockmodeling structure proposed by Snijders and Nowicki, (see these article for a more detailed description).

Assume that a set of 117 vertices is given; this is divided in $B$ positions, classes or *colours*. The colours assumed by the vertices are described by the attribute vector: $s = (s_1, \ldots, s_{117})$, where $s_i$ is the attribute of the $i$-th vertex. Conditional on the vector $s$, $x$ is modelled. The model can be regarded as a mixture model.

The stochastic blockmodel is given by the joint distribution of $(X, S)$. In terms of cluster analysis the fact that the heterogeneity is modelled by stochastic membership of the classes makes it analogous to a mixture rather than a discrete classification model. In input there is the matrix of the relations, in output a partition of the vertices in classes such that all the vertices belong to a certain class have the same probability of having a certain relation with other vertices belonging to other classes.

The final conclusions consist on the probability for the vertices to belong to a certain group and in the probability distribution of the relation, these estimations have been obtained with the Gibbs sampling [5, 6]. A non informative prior has been chosen.

In order to assess the suitableness of the adopted model Snijders and Nowicki [16] present two indices $I_d$ $H_s$ (see [9] for the formulas).

After a preliminary analysis (based on 50,000 iterations) on the base of the results of the indices $I_d$ $H_s$ presented in Table 1 the analysis has been fixed on 5/6/7/8 classes; for each of them a Gibbs sampling of 10,000 iterations have been performed.

**Table 1.** Different partitions

| B = classes | Gibbs sequences | $I_d$ | $H_s$ |
|---|---|---|---|
| B = 5 | 1 | 0.2287 | 0.0438 |
| B = 6 | 1 | 0.2190 | 0.0379 |
| B = 7 | 1 | 0.1667 | 0.0277 |
| B = 8 | 1 | 0.1414 | 0.0166 |

The two indices, estimated by the posterior mean, may give different solutions, in this case Nowicki and Snijders suggest to give more importance to the conclusions derived by index $H_s$.

The result are reported in Table 1, on the base of these data a partition of eight colours has to be preferred.

In more detail we can see from Table 2 the pages belonging to different colours/blocks:

**Table 2.** Colours/blocks

| COLOUR 1 | COLOUR 2 | COLOUR 4 | COLOUR 6 |
|---|---|---|---|
| PERCHE' | AIUTO AIUTO | BAZAR\MYCOMPUTER\01 | FAVOLANDO\03_00\01 |
| PRESENTAZIONE | BACHECA\BACHECA | CORSO\FATTO\01 | FAVOLANDO\04_00\01 |
| SICURO | FAVOLANDO\07_00\02 | CORSO\FATTO\03 | FAVOLANDO\06_00\01 |
| FAVOLANDO\04_00\02 | FAVOLANDO\08_00\03 | CORSO\NAVIGA\01 | FAVOLANDO\06_00\02 |
| FAVOLANDO\06_00\03 | FAVOLANDO\09_00\02 | GIOCHI\GIOCHI\09_00\GIOCHI2 | FAVOLANDO\07_00\01 |
| GIOCHI\GIOCHI\08_00\GIOCHI2 | FAVOLANDO\11_00\02 | GIOCHI\GIOCHI\09_00\GIOCHI3 | FAVOLANDO\07_00\03 |
| GIOCHI\GIOCHI\09_00\GIOCHI4 | MAPPA\01 | GIOCHI\GIOCHI\09_00\SCARICA | FAVOLANDO\07_00\04 |
| LINKS\02 | | \REBUS\REBUS2 | FAVOLANDO\08_00\01 |
| LINKS\07_00\02 | | GIOCHI\GIOCHI\12_00\GIOCHI2 | FAVOLANDO\08_00\03 |
| LINKS\09_00\02 | **COLOUR 3** | LINKS\ARCHIVIO | FAVOLANDO\08_00\04 |
| LINKS\09_00\022 | | LINKS\LINKS | FAVOLANDO\09_00\01 |
| LINKS\11_00\011 | BAZAR\01 | LINKS\03_00\01 | FAVOLANDO\09_00\03 |
| LINKS\11_00\02 | GIOCHI\GIOCHI\08_01\GIOCHI1 | LINKS\06_00\011 | FAVOLANDO\09_00\04 |
| NEWS\03_00\011 | GIOCHI\GIOCHI\09_01\GIOCHI1 | LINKS\07_00\011 | FAVOLANDO\10_00\01 |
| NEWS\04_00\01 | LINKS\12_00\022 | LINKS\07_00\022 | FAVOLANDO\10_00\02 |
| NEWS\04_00\022 | | LINKS\12_00\011 | FAVOLANDO\10_00\03 |
| NEWS\07_00\02 | **COLOUR 5** | NEWS\02 | FAVOLANDO\11_00\01 |
| NEWS\08_00\011 | | NEWS\03_00\01 | FAVOLANDO\11_00\03 |
| NEWS\09_00\011 | FAVOLANDO\ARCHIVIO | NEWS\05_00\01 | FAVOLANDO\11_00\04 |
| NEWS\12_00\01 | FAVOLANDO\05_00\01 | PERCOME\02 | FAVOLANDO\11_00\05 |
| PERCOME\03_00\022 | FAVOLANDO\05_00\02 | PERCOME\03_00\01 | FAVOLANDO\11_00\06 |
| PERCOME\05_00\02 | FAVOLANDO\12_00\01 | PERCOME\03_00\02 | FAVOLANDO\12_00\04 |
| PERCOME\07_00\02 | FAVOLANDO\12_00\02 | PERCOME\LIBRINEWS\LIBRO | FAVOLANDO\12_00\08 |
| PERCOME\08_00\022 | FAVOLANDO\12_00\05 | PERCOME\LIBRINEWS\10_00\01 | **COLOUR 7** |
| PERCOME\09_00\02 | FAVOLANDO\12_00\06 | | |
| PERCOME\09_00\022 | FAVOLANDO\12_00\07 | **COLOUR 8** | FAVOLANDO\05_00\03 |
| PERCOME\10_00\02 | GIOCHI\GIOCHI\01_01\GIOCHI1 | | FAVOLANDO\05_00\05 |
| PERCOME\10_00\022 | | LINKS\01 | FAVOLANDO\10_00\04 |
| PERCOME\11_00\02 | | NEWS\01 | FAVOLANDO\10_00\06 |
| PERCOME\11_00\022 | | PERCOME\01 | FAVOLANDO\12_00\09 |
| PERCOME\LIBRINEWS\10_00\01 | | GIOCHI\GIOCHI\05_00\GIOCHI1 | GIOCHI\GIOCHI\04_00\GIOCHI1 |
| | | GIOCHI\GIOCHI\11_00\GIOCHI1 | GIOCHI\GIOCHI\06_00\GIOCHI1 |
| | | GIOCHI\GIOCHI\12_00\GIOCHI1 | GIOCHI\GIOCHI\07_00\GIOCHI1 |

As one can see from Table 2 we have obtained eight colours whose pages can be summarized in the following scheme:

(1) COLOUR 1/block1: in this cluster, the most numerous, the pages are obtained through a random navigation, it contains some pages of the sections *News*, *Links* and *Percome* and a few pages of the section *Links*,

(2) COLOUR 2/block2: in this cluster there are the initial pages of two sections: *Favolando* and *Bacheca* and the help,

(3) COLOUR 3/block3: in this cluster there are the other pages of the section *Links* it is not homogeneous,

(4) COLOUR 4/block4: in this cluster there are pages of the sections *Corso*, *Giochi* and *Links*,

(5)  COLOUR 5/block5: in this cluster there are the pages of the section *Favolando* and one page of *Giochi,*

(6)  COLOUR 6/block6: in this cluster there are pages of the sections *Favolando, Links* and *Percome,*

(7)  COLOUR7/block7: in this cluster there are the most recent Web pages of the site, the last published tale and the last game introduced,

(8)  COLOUR 8/block8: in this cluster there are a few pages of section *Giochi,* and only one pages of the sections *News, Links* and *Percome.*

The positions and the relational ties between positions for a stochastic blockmodel need to be represented in order to interpret the model; there are two common way of representation: *density tables* and *reduced graphs.*

Density tables contain the probabilities that vertices relate to and are related to by other vertices when the vertices are in the same or different positions, each row and column of these tables correspond to a position. Reduced graphs give a graphical representation of the situation.

In Table 3 the density table represents the final probabilities estimated for the case of the multiple relation 2 = (1,1) which can be summarized as: "the pages share a few users that stay a little on them and don't visit them a lot of times during the session".

These probabilities are high in the case in which both the pages belong to the same colour except for block (3), (4) and (7), the relation is sure when: one page has colour (1) and the other has colour (2), (3) or (8), one page has colour (2) and the other has colour (5), (6) or (8), one page has colour (5) and the other colour (6). Ambiguous situations regards one page belonging to colour (7) and the other to colour (8).

**Table 3.** Density table

|   | 1 | 2 | 3 | 4 | 5 | 6 | 7 | 8 |
|---|------|------|------|------|------|------|------|------|
| 1 | 0.99 | 0.96 | 0.95 | 0.02 | 0.02 | 0.00 | 0.01 | 0.98 |
| 2 | 0.96 | 0.76 | 0.60 | 0.10 | 0.93 | 0.98 | 0.13 | 0.91 |
| 3 | 0.95 | 0.60 | 0.17 | 0.14 | 0.14 | 0.02 | 0.09 | 0.83 |
| 4 | 0.02 | 0.10 | 0.14 | 0.06 | 0.04 | 0.00 | 0.06 | 0.18 |
| 5 | 0.02 | 0.93 | 0.14 | 0.04 | 0.88 | 0.98 | 0.85 | 0.85 |
| 6 | 0.00 | 0.98 | 0.02 | 0.00 | 0.98 | 0.99 | 0.13 | 0.05 |
| 7 | 0.01 | 0.13 | 0.09 | 0.06 | 0.85 | 0.13 | 0.38 | 0.50 |
| 8 | 0.98 | 0.91 | 0.83 | 0.18 | 0.85 | 0.05 | 0.50 | 0.85 |

The results may be viewed by the reduced graph in Fig. 1 which consists of nodes corresponding to the positions and lines or arcs corresponding to the relations.

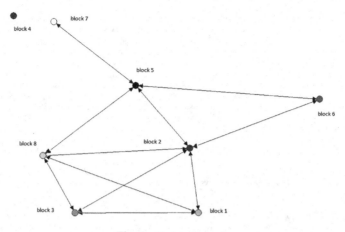

**Fig. 1.** Reduced graph

In Table 4 the density table represents the final probabilities estimated for the case of the multiple relation 1 = (0, 0) which can be summarized as: "the pages share no users that stay a little on them and don't visit them a lot of times during the session".

In this case we have found a certain ambiguity as regards the probability of relation between group 7 and group 8 (0, 46) and between group 3 and 5 (0, 76). As one can see from Table 4.

**Table 4.** Density table

|   | 1 | 2 | 3 | 4 | 5 | 6 | 7 | 8 |
|---|---|---|---|---|---|---|---|---|
| 1 | 0.00 | 0.01 | 0.01 | 0.98 | 0.97 | 0.99 | 0.98 | 0.01 |
| 2 | 0.01 | 0.04 | 0.03 | 0.88 | 0.01 | 0.01 | 0.84 | 0.02 |
| 3 | 0.01 | 0.03 | 0.09 | 0.83 | 0.76 | 0.96 | 0.84 | 0.03 |
| 4 | 0.98 | 0.88 | 0.83 | 0.93 | 0.95 | 0.99 | 0.93 | 0.80 |
| 5 | 0.97 | 0.01 | 0.76 | 0.95 | 0.02 | 0.00 | 0.13 | 0.12 |
| 6 | 0.99 | 0.01 | 0.96 | 0.99 | 0.00 | 0.00 | 0.86 | 0.94 |
| 7 | 0.98 | 0.84 | 0.84 | 0.93 | 0.13 | 0.86 | 0.57 | 0.46 |
| 8 | 0.01 | 0.02 | 0.03 | 0.80 | 0.12 | 0.94 | 0.46 | 0.05 |

The results may be viewed by the reduced graph in Fig. 2 which consist of the nodes corresponding to the positions and lines or arcs corresponding to the relations.

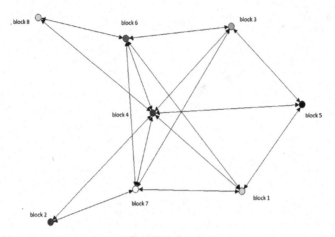

**Fig. 2.** Reduced graph

In Tables 5 and 6 the density table representing the final probabilities estimated for the case of the multiple relation $3 = (2, 2)$ which can summarise as: "the pages share enough users that stay a certain time on them and visit them enough times during the session" and for the multiple relation $4 = (6, 6)$ which can be summarized as: "the pages share many users that stay a lot on them and visit them a lot of times during the session".

As one can see from the density tables (Tables 5 and 6) these two relations do not present interesting relations among blocks.

**Table 5.** Density table

|   | 1 | 2 | 3 | 4 | 5 | 6 | 7 | 8 |
|---|---|---|---|---|---|---|---|---|
| 1 | 0.00 | 0.03 | 0.03 | 0.00 | 0.00 | 0.00 | 0.00 | 0.01 |
| 2 | 0.03 | 0.16 | 0.34 | 0.01 | 0.01 | 0.01 | 0.01 | 0.02 |
| 3 | 0.03 | 0.34 | 0.65 | 0.01 | 0.07 | 0.01 | 0.05 | 0.03 |
| 4 | 0.00 | 0.01 | 0.01 | 0.00 | 0.00 | 0.00 | 0.00 | 0.01 |
| 5 | 0.00 | 0.04 | 0.02 | 0.02 | 0.02 | 0.00 | 0.01 | 0.02 |
| 6 | 0.00 | 0.01 | 0.01 | 0.00 | 0.00 | 0.00 | 0.00 | 0.01 |
| 7 | 0.00 | 0.01 | 0.05 | 0.01 | 0.01 | 0.00 | 0.00 | 0.02 |
| 8 | 0.01 | 0.02 | 0.03 | 0.02 | 0.02 | 0.01 | 0.01 | 0.05 |

**Table 6.** Density table

|   | 1 | 2 | 3 | 4 | 5 | 6 | 7 | 8 |
|---|---|---|---|---|---|---|---|---|
| 1 | 0.00 | 0.00 | 0.01 | 0.00 | 0.00 | 0.00 | 0.00 | 0.01 |
| 2 | 0.00 | 0.04 | 0.03 | 0.01 | 0.01 | 0.01 | 0.01 | 0.02 |
| 3 | 0.01 | 0.03 | 0.09 | 0.02 | 0.07 | 0.01 | 0.05 | 0.03 |
| 4 | 0.00 | 0.01 | 0.02 | 0.00 | 0.00 | 0.00 | 0.00 | 0.01 |
| 5 | 0.00 | 0.01 | 0.07 | 0.00 | 0.02 | 0.00 | 0.01 | 0.02 |
| 6 | 0.00 | 0.01 | 0.01 | 0.00 | 0.00 | 0.00 | 0.00 | 0.01 |
| 7 | 0.00 | 0.01 | 0.05 | 0.00 | 0.01 | 0.00 | 0.03 | 0.02 |
| 8 | 0.01 | 0.02 | 0.03 | 0.01 | 0.02 | 0.01 | 0.02 | 0.05 |

The advantage of stochastic blockmodeling with respect to a classical cluster analysis is clear: a differentiated structure for the degree of similarity within and between the clusters is allowed. Different clusters present low internal similarity; moreover, the pattern between clusters similarities is interesting and varied; such results are more difficult to obtain with classical cluster analysis.

# 4 Conclusions

In this paper we present the Bayesian analysis based on the program Stocknet (module Block) and applied it in the case of Web Mining. We obtained an useful tool to understand how an user navigates through the site, which pages are more attractive and which are less interesting. For this reason it seems to be a potential tool especially if applied in the case of commercial sites.

The results presented in the previous section show that stochastic blockmodeling may be useful in order to improve the comprehension of different problems, for instance in this application we consider the type of behaviour of the users of a site.

It is interesting to notice that other different applications in a big data and in a spatially big data context can be considered as the computational aspects and the visual representation of this methodology are attractive tools.

# References

1. Anderson, C.J., Wasserman, S., Faust, K.: Building stochastic blockmodels. Soc. Netw. **14**, 137–161 (1992)
2. Borgatti, S.P., Everet, M.G.: Freeman: UCINET for windows software for social network analysis harvard: analytic technologies. http://www.analytictech.con/ucinet_5_description. htm
3. Borgatti, S.P., Foster, P.C.: The network paradigm in organizational research: a review and typology. J. Manag. **29**, 991–1013 (2003)
4. Burk, W.J., Steglich, C.E.G., Snijders, T.A.B.: Beyond dyadic interdependence: actor-oriented models for co-evolving social networks and individual behaviors. Int. J. Behav. Dev. **31**, 397–404 (2007)
5. Gelman, A., Carlin, J.B., Stern, H., Rubin, D.B.: Bayesian Data Analysis. Chapman and Hall, London (1995)
6. Gilks, W.R., Richardson, S., Spiegelhalter, D.: Markov Chain Monte Carlo in Practice. Chapman and Hall, London (1996)
7. Jan, A.K.: Data clustering. 50 years beyond K-means. Pattern Recogn. Lett. **31**, 651–666 (2010)
8. Mobasher, B., Doi, H., Luo, T., Nakagawa, M., Sung, Y., Wiltshire, Y.: Discovery of aggregate usage profiles for web personalization. Conference on Knowledge Discovery in Databases (2000). http://www.maya.cs.depaul.edu/ ~ mobasher/personalization
9. Nowicki, K., Snijders, T.A.: Estimation and prediction for stochastic blockstructures. J. Am. Stat. Assoc. **96**, 1077–1087 (2001)
10. Ripley R., Snijders T.A., Boda, Z., Vörös, A., Preciad, P.: Manual for SIENA version 4.0. Department of Statistics, University of Oxford, Oxford (2017). http://www.stats.ox.ac.uk/ ~ snijders/siena/

11. Schoier, G., Borruso, G.: A methodology for dealing with spatial big data. Int. J. Bus. Intell. Data Min. **12**(1), 1–13 (2017)
12. Schoier, G.: Blockmodeling techniques for web mining. In: Haerdle, W., Roenz, B. (eds.) Compstat. Springer, Berlin (2002). https://doi.org/10.1007/978-3-642-57489-4_26
13. Snijders, T.A.: Stochastic actor-oriented models for network dynamics. Annu. Rev. Stat. Appl. **4**, 343–363 (2017). https://doi.org/10.1146/annurev-statistics-060116-054035
14. Snijders, T.A., Lomi, A., Torló, V.: A model for the multiplex dynamics of two-mode and one-mode networks, with an application to employment preference, friendship, and advice. Soc. Netw. **35**, 265–276 (2013)
15. Snijders, T.A., van de Bunt, G.G., Steglich, C.E.G.: Introduction to stochastic actor-based models for network dynamics. Soc. Netw. **32**, 44–60 (2010)
16. Snijders, T.A., Nowicki, K.: Manual for blocks (2001)
17. Snijders, T.A., Boer, P., Huisman, M., Zeggelink, E.P.H.: StOCNET: an open software for the advanced statistical analysis of social networks (2001)
18. Snijders, T.A., Nowicki, K.: Estimation and prediction for stochastic blockmodels for graphs with latent block structure. J. Classif. **14**, 75–100 (1997)
19. Steinbach, M., Ertöz, L., Kumar, V.: The challenges of clustering high dimensional data (2003). http://www-users.cs.umn.edu/~kumar/papers/high_dim_clustering_19.pdf
20. Srivastava, J., Colley, R., Deshpande, M., Ton, P.: Web usage mining: discovery and applications of usage patterns from web data (2000). http://www.maya.cs.depaul.edu/~mobasher/personalization
21. Wang, Y.J., Wong, G.Y.: Stochastic blockmodels for directed graphs. J. Am. Stat. Assoc. **82**, 8–18 (1987)
22. Wasserman, S., Faust, K.: Social Network Analysis: Methods and Applications. Cambridge University Press, New York (1994)
23. Wasserman, S., Faust, K.: Blockmodels: interpretation and evaluation. Soc. Netw. **14**, 5–61 (1992)
24. Wasserman, S., Anderson, C.: Stochastic a posteriori blockmodels: construction and assessment. Soc. Netw. **9**, 1–36 (1987)
25. Xu, R., Wunsch II, D.: Survey of clustering algorithms (2005) http://ieeexplore.ieee.org/iel5/72/30822/01427769.pdf

# Workflow Discovery Through Semantic Constraints: A Geovisualization Case Study

Vedran Kasalica[✉] and Anna-Lena Lamprecht[✉]

Department of Information and Computing Sciences, Utrecht University,
3584 CC Utrecht, Netherlands
{v.kasalica,a.l.lamprecht}@uu.nl

**Abstract.** The construction of computational pipelines, for example automated cartographic workflows for the construction of thematic maps, typically requires detailed knowledge about the available tools for the individual steps and the technicalities of their composition. It is a time-consuming process and comes with the risk of missing meaningful workflows because many possible pipelines are never taken into account. Automated workflow composition techniques can facilitate comprehensive workflow discovery based on semantic constraints: The users express their intention about the workflows by means of high-level constraints, and receive possible workflows that meet their request. The successful application of such methods essentially depends on the availability and quality of semantic domain models that describe the tools and data types in the domain. In this paper, we present an exemplary domain model for a geovisualization use case, and show how it enables the abstract specification and automated composition of a complex cartographic workflow.

**Keywords:** Scientific workflows · Automated workflow composition · Workflow discovery · Workflow synthesis · Semantic domain modeling · Geoscience · Geovisualization

## 1 Introduction

The combination of diverse computational tools into purpose-specific pipelines is a frequent challenge for 21st century scientists. One example from the field of geovisualization is the creation of automated cartographic workflows for the construction of thematic maps, which usually comprise several computational steps [6,35]. Whether the workflows are implemented in a conventional scripting or programming language or with a dedicated scientific workflow management system [3,7,28], their construction typically requires the users to know which components to connect, and which connections are possible with regard to the compatibility of input and output data types and formats. The idea of semantics-based automated component discovery and composition is to assist the user

---

The original version of this chapter was revised: The presentation of Figures 4 and 5 was corrected. The correction to this chapter is available at https://doi.org/10.1007/978-3-030-24302-9_53

© Springer Nature Switzerland AG 2019
S. Misra et al. (Eds.): ICCSA 2019, LNCS 11621, pp. 473–488, 2019.
https://doi.org/10.1007/978-3-030-24302-9_34

in this aspect of workflow development [9,20,24,30]. Ideally, users would only need to state their intents about the workflow at an abstract, conceptual level, and the system would automatically translate this specification into a concrete executable workflow. The PROPHETS [31] and WINGS [15] frameworks are recent exemplary implementations of such approaches.

In practice the success of semantics-based automated workflow composition depends on the availability of rich tool annotations and controlled vocabularies formalizing the domain's specific terminology. However, this information is usually not available in the required form. The EDAM ontology [16] is a prominent example of a controlled vocabulary for describing operations, data types and formats in the bioinformatics domain, which is used for the comprehensive annotation of tools in the bio.tools [17] registry and thus facilitates semantics-based workflow discovery [32]. To the best of our knowledge, none of the existing ontologies and tool repositories in the geospatial domain are comparable to EDAM and bio.tools regarding scope and comprehensiveness. There has been considerable progress in the last years regarding the development of ontologies for the formalization of geospatial knowledge (e.g. [5,10,26,33]), but these are mostly focused on the classification of data, observation and measurements, rather than on technical entities of workflows (like operations, data types and formats) as in EDAM. Similarly, community standards like the Geospatial Data Abstraction Library (GDAL) [14] and the Open Geospatial Consortium (OGC) [1] aim to provide detailed classifications of the entities from the domain in order to facilitate the smooth interoperability of systems. Hence, classification and annotation endeavors such as those described in [13,27], are a crucial step towards a general and uniform classification and annotation of the technical entities of the domain.

In this paper, we show for a geovisualization example (the automated creation of a topographic map of the Netherlands that depicts waterbird movements) what automated workflow composition can accomplish once suitable technical vocabularies and tool annotations are available. We define taxonomies that provide the terminology for referring to operations and data types in the example domain. Then we add semantic annotations using the terms from these taxonomies to selected tools from the GMT (Generic Mapping Tools) [38]. Finally, we show how a workflow synthesis[1] framework can be used for the high-level specification, automated composition and refinement of executable workflows.

We use our new implementation of a scientific workflow discovery framework (provisionally called APE, for Automatic Pipeline Explorer) that aims to provide a flexible, practical and intuitive tool for automated workflow composition. It has been inspired by the PROPHETS [23,25,31] loose programming framework and uses the same Semantic Linear-Time Logic (SLTL) synthesis method [36]. The new implementation is however independent from a concrete workflow environment, and uses standard formats for the representation of ontologies and tool annotations as well as for the created workflows, in order to ease the integration with existing software environments.

---

[1] In this context, synthesis refers to the automatic creation of a concrete sequence of semantically described components according to an abstract specification [8].

The paper is structured as follows. Section 2 describes the application example (creation of a map that presents animal tracking data and topographical features of the area) that we address in this paper. Then, Sect. 3 describes the domain model that we set up for the use case, before Sect. 4 goes through an exemplary incremental synthesis process. Section 5 discusses achievements and limitations of the current approach, and concludes the paper with a summary and outline of future work.

## 2 Use Case: Creation of a Topographic Map with Depiction of Animal Movement Patterns

Cartographic workflows are implemented by sequences of tools that perform the individual elementary operations of the map creation process. There are many different Geographic Information System (GIS) tools available that can be used for map creation, such as the tools provided within ArcGIS [18], the Geospatial Data Abstraction Library (GDAL) [14], the CSISS Geospatial Web Services [2] or the already mentioned Generic Mapping Tools (GMT). For the purpose of this paper, we focus on the GMT, but the same approach can in principle be applied to any other of the aforementioned tools. One of the main reasons for choosing the GMT for this case study are its support for different data input formats and the concise and well-structured documentation of the tools, which provides a rich source of information as basis for the semantic domain modeling. In addition, the modularity of the GMT makes it highly suitable for workflow composition, as the individually accessible elementary operations allow firm control over the entire plotting process.

Our workflow use case is about discovering a computational pipeline that creates a topographic map depicting waterbird movement patterns in the Netherlands (see Fig. 1). Wildlife tracking is an important process for biologists and environmental scientists to improve their understanding of animal behavior. Movement behavior gives insight to the ecology of animals, their interaction with other organisms and effect on the ecosystem dynamics. It can help to predict how environmental changes can affect their role in the ecosystem. The use case combines tools from the GMT collection with data from the Movebank [21] online database of animal tracking data. It is used to help animal tracking researchers to manage, share, protect, analyze, and archive their data. The database supports multiple sources of data, among others, integration with the Argos system (http://www.argos-system.org/), which is probably the largest source of wildlife tracking data worldwide. This type of sources provide diverse, robust and high-quality data, which is however often difficult to exploit and plot on a map, especially for ornithologists and other field researchers who are not very familiar with GIS tools (cf. [11, 12]). The data we focus on in our example was used to find correspondences between movement patterns of a keystone waterbird species and the landscape configuration [19]. The data represents mallard movement patterns in the Netherlands [4].

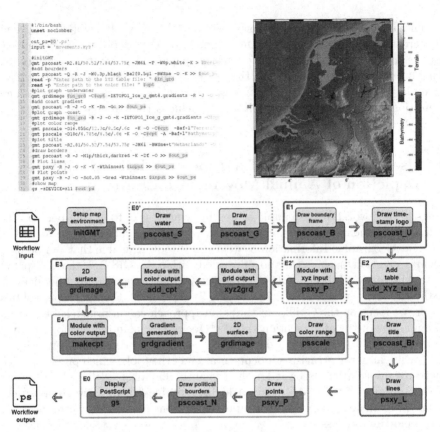

**Fig. 1.** Incremental development of the workflow (extension steps E0-E4), the corresponding generated GMT script, and the map created by its execution.

# 3   Domain Modeling

In this section we describe the domain model that we set up for the use case scenario. It comprises a tool and a type taxonomy for defining a controlled vocabulary for the operations and data types in the domain. In addition, it incorporates tool definitions using the terms provided by the taxonomies and a set of so-called domain constraints that express additional relevant knowledge. Overall, the GMT comprises over 100 different tools that can be parameterized on an elementary level, resulting in even more possible operations that would have to be defined as tools. For simplicity and conciseness, we have hence limited the domain model to the GMT tools relevant to the example scenario.

Figures 2 and 3 show the type and the tool taxonomy, respectively. The classification of tools and types in these taxonomies is essential for the effective usage of the synthesis algorithm. It provides the domain-specific, abstract terminology that the workflow developer can use to specify workflows without needing to have knowledge about the concrete tools and data types available (demonstrated in

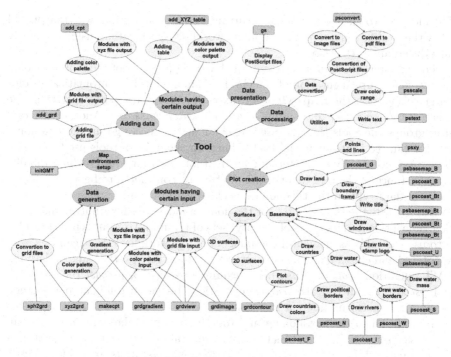

**Fig. 2.** Tool taxonomy

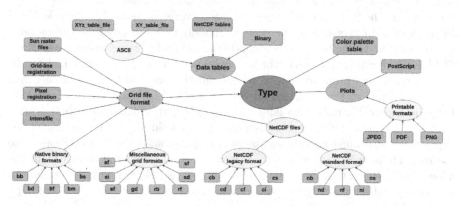

**Fig. 3.** Type taxonomy

the next section). To the best of our knowledge, there is no similarly structured classification model available for the GMT (or any other GIS tool set), so we defined new taxonomies for this purpose. The data types used by the GMT tools are well documented [39] and at the same time not overly comprehensive, hence the type taxonomy follows straightforward from the documentation and covers all of the data types mentioned in the documentation. The tool taxonomy, on the other hand, focuses on classifying just a part of the GMT in a detailed manner.

The idea was to classify the tools occurring in our scenario in a way that would allow the workflow developer a simplified workflow specification, using the newly introduced abstract classes.

For example, the tool *pscoast_s* in the lower right corner of the tool taxonomy (Fig. 2) is an implementation of the GMT command used to automatically color water surfaces on the map. The tool taxonomy allows us to abstract from the concrete tool and refer to it simply as a *Draw water mass* tool. Another abstract class groups the tools that are used to *Draw water*. As we go up the taxonomy tree we can see that our initial tool belongs to the class of tools used to create *Basemaps*, eventually characterizing all the tools used for *Plot creation*. Finally, every instance of the tool taxonomy is, naturally, considered to be a *Tool*. Every tool and data type in the taxonomies is classified in a similar manner.

Table 1 lists the tools defined for the domain model, each with its name, function description and its (possibly empty) sets of input and output types. The idea is to use the tools as elemental components of our workflows, that can be easily annotated and classified. In some cases, several tools refer to the same underlying GMT operation (*polymorphism*). For example *pscoast_B*, *pscoast_Bt*, *pscoast_U* and *pscoast_Td* all call the *pscoast* operation, but with different parameters, causing it to perform different functions.

In addition to the taxonomies and tool annotations, the domain model can comprise a set of SLTL formulas to express general knowledge that the synthesis algorithm also takes into account. These *domain constraints* are typically used to avoid obtaining workflows that are ambiguous, redundant, or not relevant to the domain. The SLTL formulas are evaluated over sequences of states (identified by a set of data types from the domain model) that are connected by actions (corresponding to the tools in the domain model) and thus represent a workflow. SLTL is a semantic extension of the widely known Linear-Time Logic (LTL). Like LTL, it comprises propositional variables and the classical Boolean connectives ($|$, $\&$ and $\neg$), and temporal modal operators $G$, $F$, $U$ and $X$. In a nutshell, $G\phi$ requires the formula $\phi$ to hold *globally* (always), $F\phi$ specifies that $\phi$ must hold *finally* (eventually), $\phi_1 U \phi_2$ requires $\phi_1$ to hold *until* $\phi_2$ holds, and $X\phi$ expresses that $\phi$ must be valid in the *next state*. In addition, SLTL allows us to use concrete as well as abstract tools from the tool taxonomy to constrain the allowed transitions to a state, expressed as $\langle tool_c \rangle \phi$ (which requires $\phi$ to hold in a state reachable by $tool_c$), and concrete as well as abstract types from the type taxonomy for the propositions characterizing the states. For a full definition, please refer to [36].

For the formulation of the domain constraints, knowledge of the SLTL syntax is not required, as our framework provides natural-language templates for several common workflow constraints, which can simply be instantiated by selecting the relevant terms from the taxonomies. Table 1 (**G1-G19**) lists the original SLTL and the natural-language representations of the domain constraints defined in this study. The constraints create a basic framework for map generation, thus simplifying the specification for the process developer. For example, constraints **G1**, **G2** and **G3** guarantee that generating/importing a certain file

**Table 1.** Tool annotations and domain constraints

| Name | Description | Data type in | Data type out |
|------|-------------|--------------|---------------|
| add_cpt | Provide a color palette (.cpt) file | | cpt_file |
| add_XYZ_table | Provide an xyz table file | | XYZ_table_file |
| add_grd | Provide a grid file | | NetCDF |
| grdgradient | Compute directional gradient | NetCDF | Intensfile |
| makecpt | Make color palette tables | cpt_file | cpt_file |
| xyz2grd | Convert an xyz table file to a 2-D grid file | XYZ_table_file | NetCDF |
| psconvert | Crop and convert PostScript files to PDF | PostScript | PDF |
| psconvert | Crop and convert PostScript files to PNG | PostScript | PNG |
| psconvert | Crop and convert PostScript files to JPEG | PostScript | JPEG |
| grdcontour | Contouring of 2-D gridded data sets | NetCDF | PostScript |
| grdview | 3-D perspective imaging of 2-D gridded data | NetCDF, cpt_file | PostScript |
| grdview | 3-D perspective imaging of 2-D gridded data | NetCDF, cpt_file, Intensfile | PostScript |
| grdimage | Produce color images from 2-D gridded data | NetCDF, cpt_file | PostScript |
| grdimage | Produce color images from 2-D gridded data | NetCDF, cpt_file, Intensfile | PostScript |
| psxy_L | Plot lines | XYZ_table_file | PostScript |
| psxy_P | Plot location points | XYZ_table_file | PostScript |
| pstext | Plot text strings on maps | XYZ_table_file | PostScript |
| psscale | Plot gray scale or color scale on maps | cpt_file | PostScript |
| pscoast_B | Drawing the map boundaries and grid | | PostScript |
| psbasemap_B | Drawing the map boundaries and grid | | PostScript |
| pscoast_Bt | Write the title of the map | | PostScript |
| psbasemap_Bt | Write the title of the map | | PostScript |
| pscoast_U | Draw the GMT logo and the time stamp | | PostScript |
| psbasemap_U | Draw the GMT logo and the time stamp | | PostScript |
| pscoast_Td | Draw the windrose | | PostScript |
| psbasemap_Td | Draw the windrose | | PostScript |
| pscoast_G | Coloring land surfaces | | PostScript |
| pscoast_S | Coloring water mass | | PostScript |
| pscoast_I | Draw rivers | | PostScript |
| pscoast_N | Draw political borders | | PostScript |
| pscoast_W | Draw water borders | | PostScript |
| pscoast_F | Coloring countries for which the country codes were provided | | PostScript |
| initGMT | Setup the GMT map environment | | |
| gs | Tool used to display PostScript files | PostScript | |

| ID | Constraints in natural-language | Constraints in SLTL |
|----|--------------------------------|---------------------|
| G1 | If **Tools with xyz output** is used, tool **Tools with xyz input** has to be used subsequently | G(¬<**Tools with xyz output**> true \| X F <**Tools with xyz input**> true |
| G2 | If **Tools with grid output** is used, tool **Tools with grid input** has to be used subsequently | G(¬<**Tools with grid output** true \| X F <**Tools with grid input**> true |
| G3 | If tool **Tools with color palette output** is used, tool **Tools with color palette input** has to be used subsequently | G(¬<**Tools with color palette output**> true \| X F <**Tools with color palette input**> true |
| G4 | If **Data processing** is used, tool **Data generation** cannot be used subsequently | G(¬<**Data processing**> true \| X G ¬<**Data generation**> true |
| ... | | |
| G16 | If **Data presentation** is used, tool **Plot creation** cannot be used subsequently | G(¬<**Data presentation**> true \| X G ¬<**Plot creation**> true |
| G17 | Do not use tool **3D surfaces** | G ¬ <**3D surfaces**> true |
| G18 | Use the data type **Plots** | F **Plots** |
| G19 | Use tool **Map environment setup** | F <**Map environment setup**> true |

format requires a subsequent usage of that particular file. In other words, we made sure that the synthesis will not construct a program that loads or generates files that are not being used in the process. Similarly, using constraints **G5 - G16** we ensure proper ordering of the tools, to avoid overriding important annotation data and to prevent unnecessary permutations in the solutions. Furthermore, we target 2D and not 3D map representations and use the constraint **G17** to exclude the tools used for 3D plotting, which are represented by an abstract class *3D_surfaces* in the tool taxonomy. Finally, we want to use GMT tools and have a map as a product of each of our programs. This requirement can be fulfilled by using an abstract class from the type taxonomy, more specifically, by enforcing the usage of a data type *Plots* and the tool setup *initGMT*, as displayed in **G18** and **G19**. These 19 general constraints will be used in all synthesis runs.

## 4   Workflow Synthesis

In this section we focus on the workflow specification and synthesis phase and show how our framework can be applied to discover and compose a complex workflow without having to identify and connect the individual required tools manually. Our concrete case example is the creation of an executable workflow that annotates animal movement patterns on a topographic map of the Netherlands. Concretely, Sect. 4.1 explains the initial first synthesis step, and the following Sects. 4.2 to 4.5 discuss the increments that finally lead to the intended map creation workflow.

### 4.1   Initial Workflow

Synthesis in our framework starts with two sets of data types (possibly empty), that correspond to the input and output of the workflow. In addition, SLTL constraints can be added to express further intents of the user. In our scenario the initial data type is the table format provided by the use case, while the output data type corresponds to the common map representation format - PostScript. This would already provide enough specification to get a transition from our initial data into a PostScript file. However, we would like to add some context to the plotted locations, such as distinguishing land from water surface. Thus, we add constraints to express the first, trivial requirements that need to be fulfilled (see Table 2): Constraint **E0.1** ensures that a tool for drawing the sea will be used. *Draw_water* contains three subclasses (see Fig. 2), where each of them contains a different tool that can be used to satisfy the constraint. Moreover, constraints **E0.2** and **E0.3** follow the same logic for the drawing of the land and the political borders, respectively. Finally, constraint **E0.4** ensures that the workflow displays the generated map to the user (handy for immediate verification). These constraints are combined with the general constraints (**G1-G19**) to form the initial workflow specification.

With this specification as input, we start the actual workflow synthesis. Note that in this study, we perform the search for possible workflows until the first

**Table 2.** Initial workflow constraints

| ID | Constraints |
|------|-------------|
| E0.1 | Use tool **Draw_water** |
|      | F <Draw_water> true |
| E0.2 | Use tool **Draw_land** |
|      | F <Draw_land> true |
| E0.3 | Use tool **Draw_political_bourders** |
|      | F <Draw_political_bourders> true |
| E0.4 | Use **Display_PostScript** as last tool in the solution |
|      | F(<Display_PostScript> true |
|      | G(¬<Display_PostScript> true \| ¬ X X true) |

**Fig. 4.** Initial workflow output

depths where solutions are found (the search depth is the same as the length of the solutions). Usually, the shortest solutions are also the most relevant with respect to the specification, as they present the smallest number of steps necessary to satisfy the workflow specification, so this is a workable heuristic. For the initial loose specification, our synthesis tool finds 32 solutions of length 6. That is, even though only five constraints (*G19* and *E0.1 - E0.4*) were used that enforce the use of certain tools, each solution contained at least one additional step. The reason for this lies in the general constraint in the domain model: the existence of the input data type *XYZ_table* requires subsequent usage of a tool that would implement the XYZ table (see **G1** in Table 1). Thus, the domain model ensures the usage of a tool that is required, but not explicitly requested by the process developer.

From the possible workflows suggested by the synthesis framework for our specification, we chose to use the workflow shown in Fig. 1 under labels **E0** and **E0'**, as it uses proper tools for coloring the land and the sea, draws the political borders and uses point locations to depict the animal movement patterns. The framework provides the workflow and its implementation as a shell script, which upon execution produces the map presented in Fig. 4.

The presented map is not yet the intended result. To add more information to the map, more steps need to be included into the workflow. One possibility is to also consider synthesis solutions of lengths greater than 6. For example, we might want to use both points and lines to depict mallard movement patterns. A workflow for that case would be found at depth 7, additionally including the tool *psxy_L*. If we expand our search correspondingly, we find that there are 2100 possible workflows of this length, and their evaluation is required in order to find the suitable one. The evaluation of this amount of workflows is usually not feasible. An alternative approach is to reduce the size of the search space and thus the number of possible solutions found. This is accomplished by adding further constraints, describing the actually desired workflow as precisely as possible, and starting the synthesis process again.

**Table 3.** Extension 1 constraints

| ID | Constraints |
|----|-------------|
| E1.1 | Use tool **Draw_lines** |
| | F <**Draw_lines**> true |
| E1.2 | Use tool **Draw_points** |
| | F <**Draw_points**> true |
| E1.3 | Use tool **Draw_boundary_frame** |
| | F <**Draw_boundary_frame**> true |
| E1.4 | Use tool **Write_title** |
| | F <**Write_title**> true |
| E1.5 | Use tool **Draw_time_stamp_logo** |
| | F <**Draw_time_stamp_logo**> true |

**Fig. 5.** Extension 1 map

## 4.2  Extension 1: Annotations

As mentioned before, the first map clearly lacks further information, such as annotations (frame, grid, title etc.). In order to properly annotate the map, we have to define corresponding tool enforcement constraints. For example, we would like to have both annotations of the mallard locations as well as annotations of the path taken, in order to properly understand the movements patterns from the map (see **E1.1** and **E1.2** in Table 3). In addition, we would like the map to include, the coordinates and boarder frame of the map (see **E1.3**), the name of the area of interest (see **E1.4**), the time it was created, as well as the name of the tool set used in the process (see **E1.5**). Our goal is to enrich the annotation of the previously generated map, hence, extend the generated workflow with corresponding annotation tools.

Our new workflow specification consists of the constraints used before and the new set of constraints. For this specification, the synthesis returns over 8,000 (shortest) solutions of length 10. Although the number of candidate solutions is too big to evaluate, they were mostly different permutations of the tools, or they incorporated different versions of the same tools (e.g. some tools have *pscoast* and *psbasemap* version of it). Evaluation of the first 5 candidate solutions has shown that the optimal solution in this scenario corresponds to the workflow presented in Fig. 1 under labels **E0**, **E0'** and **E1**, where the label *E1* corresponds to the newly introduced annotation tools. The execution of the workflow produces a properly annotated version of the map (see Fig. 5).

## 4.3  Extension 2: Providing the Elevation Dataset

Even though the annotated map is self-explanatory and can be presented as such, there is still room for improvement. The figure lacks information on the characteristics of the area, as the land and the sea are depicted with simple plain colors. The study [19], that motivated us to choose the corresponding waterbird tracking data in our scenario, focuses on predicting animal movement based on the landscape configuration. Therefore, it is natural to assume that

**Table 4.** Extension 2 and 3 constraints

| ID | Constraints |
|------|---------------------------|
| E2.1 | Use tool **Add_table** |
|      | F <Add_table> true |
| E3.1 | Use tool **2D_surfaces** |
|      | F <2D_surfaces> true |

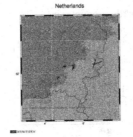

**Fig. 6.** Extension 2 map    **Fig. 7.** Extension 3 map

the map should depict some of the topographic and bathymetric features of the Netherlands and its surroundings.

One of the ways to solve this problem is to introduce a file that contains elevation data of the region. The data would be used to plot the relief of the land and the sea. Our initial workflow uses two plotting tools that are not required in this scenario, *pscoast_S* and *pscoast_G* (see **E0'** labeled elements in Fig. 1), as the plain coloring will be overwritten by the elevation data. Therefore, we will extend the workflow obtained in the previous extension step without the two mentioned tools. In order to allow for an easier evaluation of our candidate solutions, we will keep the desired parts of the previously generated workflow and separately synthesize the following sub-workflow.

In order to accurately extend the workflow, we require the usage of the elevation data table. This is accomplished by enforcing the usage of the appropriate abstraction class from our taxonomy (see **E2.1** in Table 4). The synthesis finds two possible workflows at depth 2 that are aimed to extend the previous workflow. Both of the candidate solutions use a system tool **add_XYZ_table** and a tool for plotting lines and points. Based on the generated output the workflows did not differ, and thus we have chosen an arbitrary candidate. Our extended graph corresponds to the tools labeled with **E0**, **E1**, **E2** and **E2'** in Fig. 1. The output of our workflow is presented in is Fig. 6.

### 4.4   Extension 3: Plotting the Elevation Dataset

We can observe that the current workflow does not properly utilize the provided elevation data (see Fig. 6). The reason for this is the plotting tool (*psxy_P*) used in the process. The idea of the specified workflow extension was to introduce detailed elevation data and to use a tool that can depict that elevation on the map (i.e. using a rich coloring scale). However, the extended workflow only distinguishes between positive and negative elevations, plotting them as black and blue tiles, respectively. In order to solve this issue and draw a proper relief map, the part of the workflow using the mentioned tool needs to be redefined. We expect the usage of a tool, tailored for plotting surfaces based on a elevation data, and thus, our synthesis requires a constraint enforcing it (see **E3.1** in Table 4).

**Table 5.** Final workflow constraints

| ID | Constraints |
|----|-------------|
| E4.1 | Use tool **2D_surfaces** |
|      | F <2D_surfaces> true |
| E4.2 | Use tool **Gradient_generation** |
|      | F <Gradient_generation> true |
| E4.3 | Use tool **Tools_with_color_palette_output** |
|      | F <Tools_with_color_palette_output> true |
| E4.4 | Use tool **Draw_color_range** |
|      | F <Draw_color_range> true |

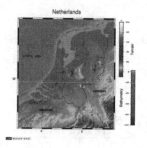

**Fig. 8.** Final map

The synthesis over the two constraints (see **E2.1** and **E3.1**) finds the two shortest solutions at depth 4. Note that similarly to the initial step, the synthesis extended our workflow with four new elements, even though we have introduced only two constraints. This time, however, the reason for it was the tool annotation part of the domain model, more specifically the dependency between input and output types of the workflow elements.

Considering that the first, out of the two solutions, requires a new grid file to be provided, whereas the second one uses the provided XYZ table to generate the required grid file, we chose the second for inclusion in the workflow (see **E3** labeled tools in Fig. 1). Our workflow has thus been extended to **E0**, **E1**, **E2** and **E3** labeled tools in Fig. 1. The generated map is presented in Fig. 7.

## 4.5   Final Extension: Topographical and Bathymetrical Features

The current map (Fig. 7) has some inconsistencies with the actual coastline of the Netherlands. We pinpointed Amsterdam's airport (Schiphol) on the map to illustrate the issue. The problem is the elevation of the country, as about one third of the Netherlands lies below sea level and our basic elevation color palette depicts all negative heights as blue. To solve this issue, we have to separate the plotting of the topographical and bathymetrical features, which requires a further extension of our workflow. The idea is to use the existing workflow for plotting the bathymetrical data and the annotations of the map, while a newly synthesized sub-workflow will be used to plot valid topographical features.

In order to ensure the desired behavior we have to specify the appropriate constraints. The proper plotting tool usage is covered by using the constraint used in the previous step (see **E4.1** in Table 5). Additionally, we would like to emphasize the topographical features of the Netherlands, by shading the generated map (see **E4.2**). However, these constraints do not guarantee the usage of a different color palette, which is crucial in order to distinguish negative sea and land elevations. As we need a new color palette, it is intuitive to use a constraint of the form **E4.3**. Finally we enforce drawing the elevation legend - color scale (see **E4.4**). Our goal is to extend the existing workflow with a new set of tools, and thus we perform the synthesis of the described sub-workflow.

The first two solutions are found at depth 4. Similar to the previous case, both of them are using the appropriate plotting tool, but the two solutions differ when it comes to the color palette data. The first solution requires the file to be imported from the system, while the second solution generates the color palette from a part of the already provided color palette file. As the second solution seems more intuitive and does not require us to manually generate another color palette file, we have selected it (see **E4** labeled sub-workflow in Fig. 1). The new extended workflow is presented in Fig. 1 with labels **E0**, **E1**, **E2**, **E3** and **E4**. The final product is the map in Fig. 8, created by a workflow that has been composed automatically based on a set of semantic constraints, which described the workflow developer's intentions free from the technicalities of the underlying GMT-based implementation.

## 5   Discussion and Conclusions

We demonstrated how workflow synthesis technology can simplify the discovery and creation of geographic data manipulation processes once an adequate domain model is available. A workflow developer, for example an ornithologist as in the applied scenario, can compose a purpose-specific workflow without having to be familiar with the concrete tools in the domain. Instead of trying to find out which tools can be combined and how, the they can use abstract terms from the domain ontology to describe the intended workflow in a declarative way. The synthesis algorithm translates the specification into concrete and executable candidate workflows, from which the developer can choose one, test it, and if required re-create or extend the pipeline under development.

We designed an exemplary workflow scenario along with the corresponding domain-specific vocabularies and formalized domain knowledge. To the best of our knowledge, no such taxonomies or ontologies and tool annotations are yet available in the domain of geographic information and data processing, thus we contribute an elemental example for the classification of tools and data types. Although it copes well with our use case, it is still not the ideal solution, in particular with regard to scalability to larger application scenarios. Ideally, such domain models would be standardized and defined by the corresponding scientific communities and provided in a structural way, analogously to the previously mentioned EDAM ontology and bio.tools registry in the bioinformatics domain. In the scope of future work we plan to explore if the core concepts for spatial information as proposed by Kuhn [22] can form the basis of an domain ontology that is more easily extensible to other use case scenarios.

The quality of the results obtained by any workflow discovery framework essentially depends on the quality of the domain model. Only an accurate and detailed formalization of the relevant technical domain knowledge enables the process developer to specify the intended workflow in a simple and precise manner, and the discovery framework to provide accurate and satisfying solutions. Furthermore, the domain model can provide the vocabulary for different levels of abstraction, allowing process developers with different levels of expertise to use the framework transparently. As we have shown in the previous section, workflows can be specified using only abstract terms from the domain model, with no knowledge about the GMT being required for that step. In principle, the concrete tools could be replaced with corresponding ones from, e.g., the CSISS services [2] or the GDAL tools [14], and without changing the specification the synthesis would return different, but semantically equivalent workflows.

The constraint-driven synthesis approach used in APE allows for a very fine-granular and explicit formulation of the workflow developers' intentions. This is not only useful to prune the search space in order to filter out irrelevant results, but a decrease of the size of the search space usually also means a speedup of the synthesis process. It lies in the nature of synthesis problems that they suffer from state explosion effects, that is, the combinatorial blowup of the search space causing exponential runtime complexity of the algorithms [29,37]. APE relies on the efficiency of state-of-the-art SAT solving techniques for the implementation of the synthesis algorithm, which has led to significant improvements of the runtime performance compared to earlier implementations.

The comparison and ranking of the synthesis candidate solutions is open issue. As mentioned before, the current approach implements a simple heuristics of ranking the solutions by their length. Although this is a workable evaluation in most cases, quite often it is not sufficient on its own to filter out less desired solutions. For example, in Sect. 4.2, the synthesis has returned over 8,000 different solutions of length 10, which is not manageable without further support. The synthesis research community regards in particular domain-specific search heuristics (exploiting e.g. non-functional properties or additional knowledge about e.g. the preferred ordering of tools) as a promising approach to solve this issue [8,34]. Such heuristics would allow rankings between simple tool permutations or comparison between similar tools in order to pre-select and provide better candidate solutions. This is an open problem in the field and a crucial step towards effective and efficient workflow synthesis in practice.

In summary, we believe that there lies a great and not yet exploited potential in the use of workflow synthesis technology to support the semantics-based discovery of domain-specific computational pipelines. Future research needs to address the challenges of large-scale semantic domain modeling and state-explosion effects. Furthermore, to be adopted by the scientific community, the workflow synthesis frameworks need to be integrated with the scientists' accustomed software ecosystems in order to support not only their construction, but also their systematic benchmarking with real input data. These are some of the challenges that we are going to address with the future development of our semantics-based workflow discovery framework.

## References

1. Abstract Specifications—OGC. https://www.opengeospatial.org/docs/as
2. CSISS/GMU Geospatial Web Services. http://cube.csiss.gmu.edu/grassweb/manuals/index.html. Accessed 14 Feb 2019

3. Scientific workflow system. https://en.wikipedia.org/w/index.php?title=Scientific_workflow_system&oldid=877419140. Accessed 14 Feb 2019
4. Movement patterns of a keystone waterbird species are highly predictable from landscape configuration (2017). http://hdl.handle.net/10255/move.644
5. Albrecht, J., Derman, B., Ramasubramanian, L.: Geo-ontology tools: the missing link, **12**, 409–424 (2008)
6. Asche, H.: Process-oriented geoinformation systems and applications. In: Margaria, T., Steffen, B. (eds.) ISoLA 2012. LNCS, vol. 7610, pp. 324–324. Springer, Heidelberg (2012). https://doi.org/10.1007/978-3-642-34032-1_31
7. Atkinson, M., Gesing, S., Montagnat, J., Taylor, I.: Scientific workflows: past, present and future. Futur. Gener. Comput. Syst. **75**, 216–227 (2017)
8. Bodik, R., Jobstmann, B.: Algorithmic program synthesis: introduction. Int. J. Softw. Tools Technol. Transf. **15**(5), 397–411 (2013)
9. Chen, L., et al.: Towards a knowledge-based approach to semantic service composition. In: Fensel, D., Sycara, K., Mylopoulos, J. (eds.) ISWC 2003. LNCS, vol. 2870, pp. 319–334. Springer, Heidelberg (2003). https://doi.org/10.1007/978-3-540-39718-2_21
10. Cox, S.J.D.: An explicit owl representation of ISO/OGC observations and measurements. In: Proceedings of SSN 13, SSN 2013, vol. 1063, pp. 1–18. CEUR-WS.org, Aachen (2013)
11. Coyne, M.S., Godley, B.J.: Satellite tracking and analysis tool (STAT): an integrated system for archiving, analyzing and mapping animal tracking data. Mar. Ecol. Prog. Ser. **301**, 1–7 (2005). https://doi.org/10.3354/meps301001
12. Dodge, K.L., Galuardi, B., Miller, T.J., et al.: Leatherback turtle movements, dive behavior, and habitat characteristics in ecoregions of the Northwest Atlantic Ocean. PLoS ONE **9**(3), e91726 (2014). https://doi.org/10.1371/journal.pone.0091726
13. García-Chapeton, G.A., Ostermann, F.O., de By, R.A., Kraak, M.J.: Enabling collaborative GeoVisual analytics: systems, techniques, and research challenges. Trans. GIS **22**(3), 640–663 (2018)
14. GDAL/OGR contributors: GDAL/OGR Geospatial Data Abstraction software Library. Open Source Geospatial Foundation (2018). Accessed 14 Feb 2019
15. Gil, Y., Ratnakar, V., Kim, J., et al.: Wings: intelligent workflow-based design of computational experiments. IEEE Intell. Syst. **26**(1), 62–72 (2011)
16. Ison, J., Kalaš, M., Jonassen, I., et al.: EDAM: an ontology of bioinformatics operations, types of data and identifiers, topics and formats. Bioinformatics **29**, 1325–1332 (2013)
17. Ison, J., Rapacki, K., Ménager, H., et al.: Tools and data services registry: a community effort to document bioinformatics resources. Nucleic Acids Res. **44**(D1), D38–D47 (2015)
18. Johnston, K., Ver Hoef, J.M., Krivoruchko, K., Lucas, N.: Using ArcGIS Geostatistical Analyst, vol. 380. Esri, Redlands (2001)
19. Kleyheeg, E., van Dijk, J.G.B., Tsopoglou-Gkina, D., et al.: Movement patterns of a keystone waterbird species are highly predictable from landscape configuration. Mov. Ecol. **5**(1), 2 (2017). https://doi.org/10.1186/s40462-016-0092-7
20. Kona, S., Bansal, A., Blake, M., Gupta, G.: Generalized semantics-based service composition. In: ICWS 2008, pp. 219–227. IEEE Computer Society (2008)
21. Kranstauber, B., et al.: The movebank data model for animal tracking. Environ. Model. Softw. **26**(6), 834–835 (2011)
22. Kuhn, W.: Core concepts of spatial information for transdisciplinary research. Int. J. Geogr. Inf. Sci. **26**(12), 2267–2276 (2012)

23. Lamprecht, A.L.: User-Level Workow Design - A Bioinformatics Perspective. Lecture Notes in Computer Science, vol. 8311. Springer, Heidelberg (2013). https://doi.org/10.1007/978-3-642-45389-2

24. Lamprecht, A.L., Margaria, T., Steffen, B.: Bio-jETI: a framework for semantics-based service composition. BMC Bioinform. **10 Suppl 10**, S8 (2009)

25. Lamprecht, A.L., Naujokat, S., Margaria, T., Steffen, B.: Synthesis-based loose programming. In: Proceedings of QUATIC 2010, Portugal, pp. 262–267. IEEE (2010)

26. Lehmann, J., Athanasiou, S., Both, A., et al.: The GeoKnow handbook. Technical report (2015). http://jens-lehmann.org/files/2015/geoknow_handbook.pdf

27. Lemmens, R., Wytzisk, A., de By, R., Granell, C., Gould, M., Van Oosterom, P.: Integrating semantic and syntactic descriptions to chain geographic services. IEEE Internet Comput. **10**(5), 42–52 (2006)

28. Liu, J., Pacitti, E., Valduriez, P., et al.: A survey of data-intensive scientific workflow management. J. Grid Comput. **13**(4), 457–493 (2015)

29. Lustig, Y., Vardi, M.Y.: Synthesis from component libraries. Int. J. Softw. Tools Technol. Transf. **15**(5), 603–618 (2013)

30. Martin, D., et al.: Bringing semantics to web services: the OWL-S approach. In: Cardoso, J., Sheth, A. (eds.) SWSWPC 2004. LNCS, vol. 3387, pp. 26–42. Springer, Heidelberg (2005). https://doi.org/10.1007/978-3-540-30581-1_4

31. Naujokat, S., Lamprecht, A.-L., Steffen, B.: Loose programming with PROPHETS. In: de Lara, J., Zisman, A. (eds.) FASE 2012. LNCS, vol. 7212, pp. 94–98. Springer, Heidelberg (2012). https://doi.org/10.1007/978-3-642-28872-2_7

32. Palmblad, M., Lamprecht, A.L., Ison, J., Schwämmle, V.: Automated workflow composition in mass spectrometry-based proteomics (2018)

33. Reza, K., Krzysztof, J., Femke, R., Luc, B., Ali, A.: Collaborative ontology development for the geosciences. Trans. GIS **18**(6), 834–851 (2014). https://doi.org/10.1111/tgis.12070

34. Schrijvers, T., Tack, G., Wuille, P., Samulowitz, H., Stuckey, P.J.: An introduction to search combinators. In: Albert, E. (ed.) LOPSTR 2012. LNCS, vol. 7844, pp. 2–16. Springer, Heidelberg (2013). https://doi.org/10.1007/978-3-642-38197-3_2

35. Simon, M., Asche, H.: Automated spatial data processing and refining. In: Lamprecht, A.-L. (ed.) ISoLA 2012/2014. CCIS, vol. 683, pp. 38–49. Springer, Cham (2016). https://doi.org/10.1007/978-3-319-51641-7_3

36. Steffen, B., Margaria, T., Freitag, B.: Module configuration by minimal model construction. Technical report, FMI, Universität Passau (1993)

37. Valmari, A.: The state explosion problem. In: Reisig, W., Rozenberg, G. (eds.) ACPN 1996. LNCS, vol. 1491, pp. 429–528. Springer, Heidelberg (1998). https://doi.org/10.1007/3-540-65306-6_21

38. Wessel, P., Smith, W.H.F.: Free software helps map and display data. EOS Trans. Am. Geophys. Union **72**(41), 441–446 (1991)

39. Wessel, P., Smith, W.H., Scharroo, R., et al.: Generic mapping tools: improved version released. EOS Trans. Am. Geophys. Union **94**(45), 409–410 (2013)

# A User-Centred Approach to Design Transport Interchange Hubs (TIH): A Discussion Illustrated by a Case Study in the Russian Arctic

Clarice Bleil de Souza[1]([⊠]) ⓘ, Ilya V. Dunichkin[2] ⓘ,
and Camilla Pezzica[1] ⓘ

[1] Welsh School of Architecture, Cardiff University, Bute Building,
King Edward VII Avenue CF10 3NB, Cardiff, UK
{Bleildesouzac,Pezzicac}@cardiff.ac.uk
[2] Moscow State University of Civil Engineering, Yaroslavskoye Sh. 26,
Moscow 129337, Russia
ecse@bk.ru

**Abstract.** This paper proposes a user-centred approach to design Transport Interchange Hubs (TIH). It is based on a literature review of existing information related to TIHs outside the domain of transport engineering, so the focus is on the building and the usage of it by its main customers: the travellers. A literature review is used to extract high level information on travellers' needs, technical and functional requirements of TIHs, constraints and design parameters. A product development approach is used to classify and combine this data so a proper set of design specifications to better address users' needs is proposed. A case study in the Russian Arctic is presented to illustrate the discussion due to the complexity of needs, requirements and parameters involved in designing TIHs in extreme climates. A proof of concept, using Axiomatic Design, to develop design specifications and manage constraints is applied and discussed considering how different types of simulation tools, essential to assess performance of complex buildings, can be integrated to the design process. Robust specifications, despite being part of parametric design methods, are underexplored in the architecture design domain. This work intends to provide a contribution to the body of knowledge in this area opening avenues for further research in how to define common design targets and objectives for different stakeholders as well as to manage the collaborative work of consultants involved in designing complex buildings.

**Keywords:** Decision-making in design · Transport Interchange Hubs (TIH) ·
Russian Arctic · Sustainable urban development

## 1 Introduction

Transport Interchange Hubs (TIH) are points of exchange for people and/or cargo between different modes of transport and/or different types of vehicles. They "play a key role as part of public transport networks, facilitating the links between public

© Springer Nature Switzerland AG 2019
S. Misra et al. (Eds.): ICCSA 2019, LNCS 11621, pp. 489–504, 2019.
https://doi.org/10.1007/978-3-030-24302-9_35

transportation modes" [1]. Efficient TIHs can promote urban integration, be time savers, improve operational business models, and reduce the use of cars therefore contributing to diminish carbon emission addressing issues related to climate change. They are strategically important to many countries. In the EU, they are part of a strategic agenda which includes "the integration of a European high-speed rail network, the shift of road to freight transport over 300 km to other modes (i.e. rail or waterborne) and the connection of all core airports to the rail network." [2]. In China, they form part of the government economic and social development plan [3–5]. In Russia, they form part of the Strategy of Development of the Arctic Zone (Northern Sea Route) focused on the exploitation of mineral resources and the development of infrastructure around them [6].

As part of countries strategic agendas, TIH has been the topic of many research projects. In the EU, one can find at least five recent projects involving TIHs: HERMES [7]; City HUB [8]; NODES [9]; Alliance (2018) [10] and the recent VitalNodes [11].

In Russia, the focus is on modernizing transport network and infra-structure in the Arctic zone through the design, development and refurbishment of various sizes of TIH accommodating the peculiarities of migration flow in the Northern area. The average mobility index for the population of the Arctic is 9.8%, meaning 1 in 10 people either move in or out of the region [12]. Mobility usually involves long distance flows, i.e. flows to long distant connections, normally to and from territories outside the Arctic. This has an impact in transport infra-structure, meaning TIH must be adaptable and flexible to cope with cities' 'pulsating' populations [12].

TIHs can be viewed as complex systems because of the demands related to function, cost, quality and sustainability involved in their designs. Beyond having to accommodate different transport functions, they are a technologically driven and market-oriented apparatus difficult to design, costly to build, operate and maintain. The problem gets even more complicated if flexibility and adaptability requirements are part of their design and operation agendas and they have to be built on harsh climatic zones as in the case of TIHs in the Russian Arctic.

Despite a significant recent number of EU projects related to TIHs as well as some major Chinese initiatives reported in the literature [4, 5 and 13, to cite a few], systematic knowledge related to the design of TIHs remains unaddressed. The literature seems vast on the domain of transport engineering, but it is scarcely populated with a set of frameworks, methods, models and criteria to analyse and evaluate performances of the terminals in relation to building functioning and their relationships with the city (especially at the neighbourhood scale), user satisfaction and environmental concerns. Despite the recent focus on TIH customers' (travellers') satisfaction found in the literature (see Sect. 2 below), to the best of the author's knowledge there are no clear and robust methodologies to develop design specifications to fulfil their needs.

This paper proposes a user-centred approach to develop a robust set of specifications for the design of TIH buildings. It uses Axiomatic Design (AD), a methodological approach from product design, to start listing and discussing travellers' needs, technical and functional requirements, constraints and design parameters involved in the design of TIHs. It also borrows AD assessment methods to address how different types of building performance simulations can be better integrated through the design process so design proposals can be assessed at different stages and design specifications amended and revisited if necessary. The user-centred approach is proposed as a proof of concept to illustrate the importance of developing a robust set of design specifications to attend the most important TIH user, its travel customer. Robust design specifications, despite being part of parametric design methods, are underexplored in the architecture design domain. The authors see them as a starting point to effectively reconcile design targets and objectives of different stakeholders as well as to manage the work of different consultants involved in designing these types of complex buildings.

## 2   Customers' Needs – The State of the Art

Most of the recent literature about TIH focuses on customer satisfaction and overall travel experience, possibly because studies of this type have been rare until around 2015. Hernandez et al. [14] conducted a survey to collect travellers' data about various aspects of TIH and run a classification and regression tree model together with an important-performance analysis model to identify strengths and weaknesses on travellers' perceptions of a TIH in Spain. A similar work is proposed by [15], who produce a decision tree and apply descriptive and inferential statistics to surveys with customers to investigate user perception and satisfaction with quality of service provided by a TIH in Riga. Monzon et al. [16] report, from surveys with different stakeholders including customers, the influence of nine basic parameters in the overall quality of five different terminals. Average scores for these parameters are calculated based on the findings so weaknesses and strengths of different terminals can be identified. Hickman et al. [13] compare and contrast customer's surveys from three different Chinese terminals with actually what they deliver in order to calculate a 'disgruntlement level' for these terminals based on a hierarchy of customers' dissatisfaction indicators. Bryniarska et al. [17] propose a set of generic criteria to assess the quality of TIH buildings and surveyed travellers' in relation to the importance of distance, quality of infra-structure and information also aiming to rank customers' needs to derive a weighting system to enable assessing the quality of interchanges using multi-criteria evaluation. Liu et al. [5] and Li et al. [4] use surveys with customers to set up models to investigate different accessibility scenarios to TIH generated through multi-criteria evaluation, focusing on reducing travelling time or gauging easiness of travelling, respectively.

Some important characteristics can be identified from these studies. The first one is the trend to focus on rankings and attributing scores to customers' needs so multi-criteria evaluation assessments can be undertaken with properly justifiable weighting. The second one is all studies display a set of overarching criteria behind travellers' needs and aspirations similarly to what is proposed by [18] and recommended by Netherlands, British and other EU railway bodies. Finally, the aim of these studies is centred in the assessment of customers' needs to gauge the quality of existing terminals rather than investigating how these needs can be translated into design specifications. As a result, the translation of these needs into design guidelines tend to be presented as gigantic and unstructured lists of requirements with mixed information. These lists are not easily manageable nor suitable to be readily used by building designers, i.e. they need to be translated into a set of useful design specifications with appropriate hierarchies and relationships to be directly applied in project work. This work illustrates a proof of concept about how information from the literature can be translated into a set of useful design specifications for TIH buildings by adopting an AD approach.

## 3 Methodology: Adopting a Product Design Approach

The idea of using product design methods in architecture is not new. Marchesi and Matt [19] present a literature review on transferring product design methods, specifically Axiomatic Design (AD) to building design on the basis that AD would provide a more comprehensive analytical framework to problem specification which is extremely valuable in the design of complex buildings used by the general public as well as in projects in which many different types of consultants are involved. Besides that, a product design approach also has formal ways to assess project outcomes through targets, evaluation and assessment methods and procedures which can potentially contribute to 'extend' the assessment of architectural design solutions, facilitating the integration of simulation tools through the design process.

Developed by Nam and Suh at the MIT, AD provides a design specification model based on "principles of functional independence and complexity minimization [in which] problem and solutions are systematically specified in parallel, moving down along the hierarchy and design decisions are made in an explicit way maintaining data." [19]. The specification model is based on four different domains: the Customer domain in which customers' needs and aspirations are specified; the functional domain in which functional design requirements are specified; the Physical domain in which design parameters to meet requirements are specified and the Process domain which is concerned with the manufacturing of the parameters specified in the Physical domain [20]. During this mapping or translation process the designer needs to follow two Axioms: the 'Independence Axiom' and the 'Information Axiom'. The first is related to the independence of functional requirements, i.e. each functional requirement needs to be fulfilled independently of each other. The second is related to level of information of the design content, which must be kept to a minimum. This suggests "that physical integration is desirable to reduce the information content if the functional independence can be maintained" [20].

To the best of the authors' knowledge, there is no example of applying AD to the design of TIHs. The closest reference is [21], which applies AD to the design of an airport passenger's terminal. This paper borrows the structure of AD, to translate Customers' needs into Functional Requirements and subsequently Design Parameters, to develop a set of design specifications to better accommodate TIH travellers' needs since the early design stages (Fig. 1). Travellers' needs affect the perceived quality of the terminal and the transport services provided by it as well as the ability of this building to act as an economic hub for urban sustainable development. All these have an impact in the design of the building and its insertion into a given neighbourhood or city. Other stakeholders involved in the design and use of TIH, for instance business managers, transport operators, public authorities etc. are not part of this study. However, important information referring to terminal capacity and operation as well as building standards and regulations are used as boundary conditions to this design problem and expressed as Input Constraints.

Input Constraints (ICs) are an imposed part of design specifications [20] and in this paper will be treated constraints related to: the existing infra-structure affecting the placement of the terminal in a given neighbourhood (IC1); the health and safety and fire safety regulations, transport safety standards, etc. (IC2); the extreme climatic conditions and restrictions in building on the permafrost (IC3) defined by (REF). IC1 and IC2 will not be explored in detail in this paper, as IC1 is site dependent and IC2 would mainly involve complying with regulations to whatever design specification is proposed. It would vary country by country and make the whole paper extremely long and prescriptive, diverging attention from the discussion on functional requirements and design parameters.

Besides the aforementioned constraints, the work addresses and discusses: (i) Travellers' Needs and Aspirations (TNAs), mainly using the Customers' Pyramid proposed by [18] together with further relevant information from the literature [13–17]; (ii) Functional Requirements (FRs), by translating Travellers' Needs and Aspirations into a set of functional specifications considering a 'solution neutral' environment and; (iii) Design Parameters (DPs) discussing and defining the physical variables to satisfy each FR individually listed. The work does not go beyond two levels of specification in terms of most of the FRs as it is the intention it remains solution neutral (unbiased) and can be used as a starting point to rethink the design of terminal buildings adopting a customer/traveller perspective (Fig. 1).

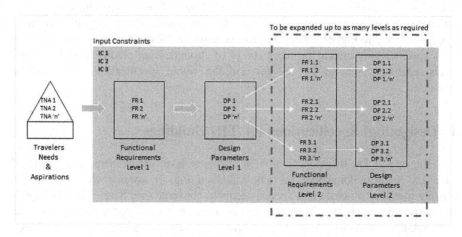

**Fig. 1.** Applying the Axiomatic Design structure to the design of TIH

Section 4 illustrates how the design problem decomposition is structured and how the first Axiom is applied. It starts by proposing how customers' needs can be translated into FRs and DPs as well as how ICs are imposed. An illustration of applying Axiom 1 is displayed in the second level of design specifications through three design matrices. These matrices are mathematical expressions of how FRs and DPs are related to each other. Design goals are defined as an FR vector whereas "the set of design parameters in the physical domain that has been chosen to satisfy the FRs constitutes the DP vector." [20]. If functional requirements are independent from each other, the matrix is diagonal and the design is called uncoupled. This is an ideal situation because it means each FR can be independently satisfied by a single DP enabling the design process to be fully controlled, facilitating manufacturing, maintenance and replacement of parts. If the matrix is triangular, "the independence of FRs can be guaranteed if and only if the DPs are determined in a proper sequence" [20]. This situation is called decoupled design and is also considered an acceptable solution because the clear hierarchy of FRs still enables the design process to be fully controlled as well as its manufacturing and maintenance. When the matrix has any other shape, either the design is redundant (having more parts then needed) or is out of control, meaning every time a parameter is changed the propagation of changes reaches different FRs and therefore different DPs.

Section 5 focuses on proposing how to meet the second Axiom in building design as well as how to trigger the zigzag process. The Second Axiom relates design success with complexity of information. The latter is defined in relation to the tolerance provided by each DP to fulfil required tolerances for each FR. This "probability of success can be computed by specifying the design range for the FR and by determining the system range that the proposed design can provide to satisfy the FR" [20]. The authors believe that assessing compatibility between probability ranges of FRs and DPs in building design calls for the use of building performance simulation. This part of the paper therefore discusses how different types of simulations can be better integrated throughout the design process from the early stages of design specifications. Since simulation results have an impact in gauging how proposed DPs affect each other, these can also be used to trigger the zigzag process in which FRs and DPs assessed at lower level specifications inform the correctness of dependencies predicted at the upper levels, enabling them to be changes and the whole specification process to be reassessed.

## 4 Design(ing) Specifications for TIH Buildings

Van Hagen and De Bruyn [18] provide an upper level comprehensive pyramid of travellers' needs and/or aspirations to be addressed (Fig. 2), towards which most of the existing literature on customers' needs seems to converge (see Sect. 2 of this paper). Needs and aspirations at each level of this pyramid are related to: the transport service provided, the staff, as well as the place where the service is provided – i.e. the building. In general, as one goes down in the pyramid the weighting of the services in fulfilling needs and aspirations of travellers increases and the building mainly acts as a 'background' to enable services and people to properly operate in the fulfilment of these needs.

Fulfilling needs at the bottom of the pyramid mean the building mainly needs to comply with a set of regulations which impose conditions for transport service operation to happen in a safe and secure way. These conditions are expressed as a set of building design constraints (health and safety, fire safety, transport operation, etc.)

defined in this paper as IC2, which would be imposed at different levels of specification for FRs and DPs. However, when considering building TIHs in the Arctic, 'Safety and Security' needs must be extended to include constraints related to building in extreme climatic conditions. These constraints have clear implications in building layout and building envelope design (IC3) and can potentially affect the design specification from its very beginning.

Major constraints related to extreme climatic conditions and restrictions in building on the permafrost (IC3) include requirements for almost all spaces to be enclosed. As part of this constraint indoor air temperatures need to be controlled at different ranges according to the following types of space usage: spaces of permanence such as sitting area, between 18 °C and 24 °C; circulation spaces, between 0 °C and 5 °C and platform areas between −15 °C to 0 °C [22]. Besides that, building on the permafrost implies having compact and large footprint buildings with prohibitive costs of using underground spaces, deep pile foundations and concentrated building utility entry points [23].

The second layer of the pyramid, 'Reliability' is again very dependent on transport service provision. However, the role of the building changes to the one of an 'enabler', meaning it has to provide adequate capacity, and potentially flexibility and adaptability, to hold and deliver the different types of transport services assigned to it. Transport and traffic recommendation values and variables are applied as a set of design constraints to guarantee adequate service availability, therefore fulfilling travellers' reliability needs. These constraints are also part of IC2 as they are defined by transport operation guidelines which include a series of safety parameters.

The remaining layers of the pyramid have large implications on the design of the terminal building, particularly in decisions related to its layout and enclosure, both defined mainly at the early design stages. Figure 2 relates travellers' needs and aspirations with the ICs discussed above and shows the proposed set of FRs to fulfil needs at the middle and top of the pyramid. These FRs are a translation of requirements fulfilled by high level DPs specified by the TFL Interchange [24]. Contrarily to what is found in the literature [3, 25, 26, to cite a few] which tends to show high level DPs biased by the zoning system of: 'Access & Interchange zone', 'Facilities or Concourse zone' and 'Platform zone', the TFL Interchange [24] presents what are the primary spaces directly related to travellers' needs. The authors connect these DPs to travellers' needs by proposing the set of FRs listed in Fig. 2.

'Speed' is a need directly related to travellers' routes; *how fast* to move as well as *how far* to move from any pair of origin – destination. As noted in [5, 13–18, 26] speed is related to total traveling time which includes not only transportation time, waiting time and time required to walk from a specific point of the city to the terminal but also walking time inside the terminal building itself. Since there is no prescribed quantity associated to this portion of the total traveling time, the provision of short unobstructed traveller routes inside the building becomes an essential functional requirement (FR3).

'Easiness' is a need related to way-finding [13–18, 26–28], first in terms of efficiently assisting travellers in deciding where to go inside the terminal building (FR2). Second, it involves not only the provision of appropriate information but mainly how easy it is to make decisions related to travelling in general, such as buying ticket, passing control points, gathering information, etc. Specific types of spaces need to be provided for these decisions to take place and the shape, combination and location of these spaces are also an essential part of the building layout.

'Comfort' and 'Experiences' are needs related to opportunities the building can offer to compensate for waiting time (FR1). These can be translated into, for instance, offering convenience shopping, food and refreshments, 'workstations', etc. [13–18, 26] Opportunities can also be exploited by non-travellers and business managers if terminals are configured as city hubs, neighbourhood 'hot spots', social and leisure places, etc. [26–28]. They are a FR in which multiple stakeholders' requirements need to be reconciled as, despite them being a place to enhance travellers' experience, terminals should also benefit citizens of the city and TIH neighbourhood, attract business investors, etc. to become sustainable.

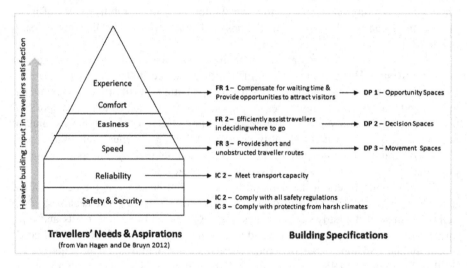

**Fig. 2.** Travellers' needs and aspirations with corresponding upper level building specification expressed as ICs, FRs and DPs.

High level DPs presented by the TFL Interchange [24] comprise the following three types of spaces to be managed inside TIH buildings: Movement Spaces (DP3), where travellers move from A to B within the terminal, Decision Spaces (DP2) where travellers' decisions take priority and Opportunity Spaces (DP1), which are actually all other spaces within the building which do not include movement or decision making and can therefore be used to enhance traveling experience as well as provide economic benefits to become sustainable. The TFL Interchange [24] affirms these are main spatial management principles to be used in the design of TIH buildings and "should be applied at brief development stage, and then considered throughout design development to evaluate design concepts against anticipated needs; and subsequently written into interchange facility management agreements to ensure design integrity is retained post-implementation" [24]. These high level FRs and their corresponding DPs seem to satisfy the First Axiom as the FRs are independent of each other and in principle could be independently distributed in space. The amount of content of the design at this stage is logical and minimal potentially satisfying also the Second Axiom. More importantly, these high-level DPs are abstract enough to promote layout diversity as they enable multiple combinations and can be adapted to multiple scale terminals, fulfilling well the different sizes of TIH building required by the Russian Arctic.

The multiplicity of combination enabled by these DPs can be better understood once they are decomposed into a set of subsequent FRs with their corresponding second level DPs as displayed in Fig. 3.

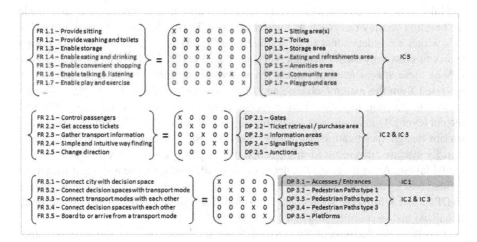

**Fig. 3.** Second level FRs and DPs with their corresponding design matrixes and constraints

Figure 3 specifies second level FRs and DPs for the three different types of spaces, which need to be accommodated by a terminal building with their corresponding matrixes to study levels of independence among them. The very basic functions of Opportunity Spaces (DP 1) to compensate for travellers waiting time are expressed in black and include: an area to sit, washing and toilets and an area to store luggage. The additional functions represented in red show examples of enhancing travel experience during waiting times as well as providing opportunities to attract visitors and can include areas to eat and drink, shop, meet people, interact with the community, entertain children, etc. The list of FRs in this case will be context specific, i.e. it will depend on the scale and role the TIH will have in the urban environment, both locally and globally, which will establish its hierarchical importance in relation to the surrounding neighbourhood and/or city. NODES [27], provides a set of 5 different typologies of TIHs considering the presence of commercial areas within or around the terminals as well as the density of residential and mixed-use areas in the surroundings of the TIH and their respective impact on vehicular and pedestrian traffic congestion as well as parking needs. As this paper attempts to be generic enough to be adapted to different contexts, it leaves this matrix open for new FRs and DPs to be included accommodating different sizes of terminals. In theory, FRs related to Opportunity Spaces (DP 1) are considered independent from each other and will have to fulfil constraints related to regulatory frameworks for building in extreme climates (IC 3), if located within the building.

However, their size might have an impact in FR 3.1 and will be constrained by the insertion of the terminal in the city (IC 1). Further impact of FRs from DP1 and FRs from DP3 would need to be explored at a lower level and results from these explorations should be used to revisit level 2 FRs again, until a full set of independent FRs can be effectively reached in practice.

Functions of Decision Spaces (DP2) include: passing control lines to reach different types of transport modes, getting access to tickets, gathering information about transport operations as well as about where to go inside the terminal, and provide opportunities and information for passengers to change and find appropriate directions to take inside the building so they can reach its different spaces. These FRs are expressed as a set of DPs which are independent of each other (see Fig. 3) with the corresponding design matrix to show they satisfy the first AD axiom. IC 3 and IC2 need to be applied to these DPs as these spaces need to respect strict thermal comfort constraints in order to be protected from the extreme climate and fulfil transport regulations and standards with regards to meeting capacity. Further decomposition of these second level DPs into second level FRs at an abstract level are still possible but they will be mainly related to interior design specifications (finishing) and the design of signalling, information and security systems, diverging from the scope of this paper which focuses mainly on TIH spatial layout. As in the case with decomposing DP1, there will be a stage in which the number and location of DPs 2.1, 2.2 and 2.5 will be affected and potentially dependent on DPs 1 and 3, however further decomposition is also necessary for these to be properly visualized and decoupling strategies to be applied.

Functions of Movement Spaces (DP3) include: entering the terminal building, walking from one decision space to another or to a transport mode, move between two different types of transport modes and boarding to or arriving from a transport mode. Three different types of constraints apply to these DPs: IC 1 which imposes restrictions in terms of how the building is inserted in the neighbourhood, IC 3 which imposes these spaces should all be protected from the harsh climate and IC 2 which establishes these spaces need to have adequate capacity to meet demand as imposed by the transport and traffic regulations. Note the separation between arrival and departure is not explicitly stated yet because these can be accommodated via specifying origin – destination for each type of pedestrian path. The level of independence between these FRs is expressed by the design matrix displayed in Fig. 3. However, further decomposition of these DPs is needed to verify if assumed independence of FRs in level 2 holds true.

Figure 4, provides a level 3 set of FRs for DP 1.1, DP 3.1 and DP 3.2 to 3.4. FRs for sitting area (DP 1.1) have to provide enough capacity to accommodate a certain number of people waiting, including the elderly and those with disabilities which are mainly defined by constraints imposed by transport regulations (IC 2), and provide appropriate furniture for them. They need to be secure and 'naturally' surveyed by design (i.e. inhibit crime by allowing sufficient flow of people around them) and then meet a series of environmental quality criteria such as being well lit and ventilated, appropriately shaded and guaranteeing air temperatures within the comfort zone (from 18 °C to 24 °C) as defined by the set of constraints referring to building in an extreme climate such as the Arctic (IC 3). Exploring subsequent DPs for these FRs involves assessing the number and positioning of these DPs in space, information which is context specific.

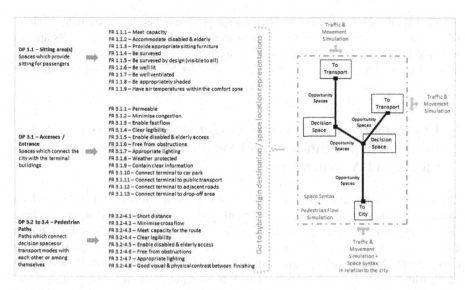

**Fig. 4.** Zooming into a set of DPs to illustrate the exploration of third level FRs in combination with a generic hybrid origin destination/space location representation.

Accesses/Entrances (DP 3.1) are the main points of connection between the terminal building and the city. Their positioning will determine how well the terminal integrates with the city at a neighbourhood scale and therefore should take into consideration local patterns of pedestrian movement, easy way finding for pedestrians and different types of vehicles as well as to and from movement routes for all transport modes reaching the building [26–28]. Thus, FRs for positioning Accesses/Entrances can be specified in terms of the quality of connections from terminal to: car park, public transport stops, drop-off area and points and areas characterized by high flows in adjacent open public spaces and roads. Beyond connections, FRs for DP 3.1 also need to: be permeable (i.e. integrating the surroundings and terminal as if they are a single space) and cognitively legible, minimize mobility congestion, enable fast flow of pedestrians to the terminal and circulation of vehicles around the terminal, be free from obstructions and universally accessible (disabled and elderly), have appropriate lighting and be weather protected (as imposed by IC 3). All these FRs will lead to context specific level 3 DPs as well as context specific constraints (IC 1).

DPs 3.2 to 3.4 need to be carefully examined so an adequate number of them is provided to meet the different terminal demands. This calls for diagrams to be produced so all potential origin – destination pairs of pedestrian movement within the terminal building are mapped to assess what needs to be given priority and therefore made shortest and with minimum crossing, what can be grouped or integrated with other path, what can be grouped and integrated with other type of space (e.g. be together with siting area, be together with eating and drinking area etc.). FRs at this level, include important requirements to satisfy travellers needs in relation to speed such as: short distance, minimum cross flow, segregation arrival/departure, adequate capacity, guaranteed disable access, lack of obstruction and clear spatial legibility. Again, exploring subsequent DPs for these FRs involves assessing the number and positioning of these DPs in space, information which is context specific. This is why in Fig. 4 FRs are not followed by a set of third level DPs but by an abstract origin destination/space location diagram to represent context and be able to discuss how it can affect DPs and the construction of design matrices from this level down.

## 5   Exploring the Use of Hybrid Origin Destination/Space Location Representations and Simulations to Meet the Second Axiom, a Discussion

The aforementioned set of specifications suggest TIHs can be seen as buildings which basically host pedestrian flows with different types of origin-destination pairs. These origin-destination pairs are represented in a generic graph (Fig. 4) as lines which connect different types of decisions spaces, access/entrance and transport boarding arrival points, surrounded by opportunity spaces, a combination of origin-destination graph with a space location diagram. This type of representation is essential to assess dependences at lower levels as it enables the visualization and exploration of different combinations of pedestrian flows and space distributions in site prior to their sizing and shaping. Hybrid representations are important to extract hierarchies of routes and spaces therefore providing important information for dependencies between FRs to be reassessed. In combination with matrices, they empower designers to make decisions in relation to moving towards a decoupled design and therefore in fulfilling the First Axiom, opening the possibility for matrices to be revisited at higher levels, corrected at this level and continued at lower levels, so the coherence of design specifications can be controlled. This process is not linear, it triggers a zigzag in the workflow through several iterations.

Besides that, hybrid representations are essential to aid in fulfilling the Second Axiom, as they provide information to simulate the performance of the overall design solution so probability ranges required by FRs and probability ranges provided by DPs can be adjusted to become compatible. They connect the design specification to simulation tools, in particular to those related to space connections, visual navigation, and pedestrian flow. Starting from the assumption that 'space is the machine' [29], there is a mutual dependency between built form and spatial navigation patterns, which could be explored both ways. The relation between the two is not one to one, meaning that the same flow pattern can be generated through different building layouts. In this sense the hybrid representation is a means to explore spatial configurations, without being tied to any given design outcome.

The fulfilling of many of the FRs related to positioning entrances/accesses and visual navigation inside the building can be investigated through the use of Space Syntax Theory [31], using combinations of Axial or Segment Analysis models, which translate mobility/street networks and internal building layouts in corresponding graph representations made of nodes (representing analysed elements) and connected edges (representing their topological links). Segment Analysis models can be complemented by fine-tuned Visibility Graph Analysis (VGA) models to explore the configurational qualities of the entrance spaces of a terminal building and how the TIH is connected with other public spaces and locations within a neighbourhood and a city; including the complexities implied in improving way-finding and increase cognitive ease in visually locating both the terminal and its accesses. Space Syntax models can also help clarifying the overlaps and dynamics between to-movement (i.e. movement to the TIH as a destination from all other points in the city), and through-movement flows (i.e. movement passing through on shortest routes from every origin to every destination). To this end, a multidimensional study of street networks must be conducted both at a local (the immediate surroundings) and at a global level (the city as a whole) as the "urban space is locally metric but globally topo-geometric" [32]. As suggested by [27–31], when properly deployed Space Syntax offers useful guidance for integrating the design of TIH and surrounding public open spaces while increasing travellers' safety though natural surveillance and co-awareness.

The success of fulfilling FRs related to the positioning of entrances/accesses as well as the positioning of platforms to different transport modes, should also be investigated through Traffic and Movement simulations. Micro-simulations, which include car – following models, can be used, for instance, to examine points of congestions around the terminal building and assess delays and their potential impact in overall travel time. They can also be used to study lanes and intersection geometry assisting in assessing how well integrated the terminal is with the city's infrastructure system as well as how good is its accessibility.

Besides that, the different types of pedestrian paths inside the building connecting decision spaces with transport modes, different types of transport modes with each other and different types of decision spaces with each other can also be assessed using pedestrian flow simulations in combination with Space Syntax. The domain of pedestrian modelling is widely explored to assess station performance in relation to a series of parameters which impact on health and safety as well as in total travel time. They are used to size paths, test how their length, positioning and connections affect total travel time, test the impact of obstructions in disrupting pedestrian flow, test and size control gates and platform area, etc. They enable density maps to be generated showing waiting times, emergency evacuation routes, clearing times, journey times in different routes, etc. [34]. The authors discuss in more detail the issue of pedestrian flow in the design of TIH in another paper also submitted to this conference [35].

Space Syntax can contribute to assess TIHs' interior spatial intelligibility, visual relationships and visual-control among spaces or spatial enclosure, signals positioning as well as the perceived socio-spatial qualities of opportunity spaces. Given that past research has found a correlation between the Integration index and density of economic activities in cities [33], the retrieval of Space Syntax metrics could in fact effectively inform the location\organisation of opportunity spaces within terminal buildings.

Since results from simulation related to traffic and movement as well as pedestrian flow are expressed as probabilities, they can be used to test if design specifications meet the Second Axiom which states that in order to minimize information, "the design must be able to accommodate large variations in design parameters (...) and yet still satisfy the functional requirements" [20]. This association of probability ranges with design specifications and simulations moves the problem away from analysis multi-criteria and establishes a different design paradigm.

# 6 Conclusions and Future Work

The way terminals are operated, the differences in preferences among its users and the way they should respond to the environment and the different functions they host go beyond 'design by drawing'. The fact that the context chosen for this discussion was the Russian Arctic also introduced extra challenges to the design problem. Main challenges involved: (i) the need for space enclosures and temperature controls in almost all types of spaces, (ii) the need for design specifications which can cope with a high variety in building size (from a couple of platforms to large multimodal terminals), and (iii) a design system which opens the possibility of properly taking into account the impact of variations in population fluctuations and the consequences of these on requiring reducing or expanding terminal capacity.

Instead of opting for analysis multi-criteria which is always controversial in terms of justifying the different weights attributed to each different objective to be met, the authors proposed the use of AD to organize information from the literature in relation to designing the layout of TIH. The AD structure helps to map design specifications, control them through the application of the First Axiom, and assess them using the Second Axiom. It is therefore considered a robust method to reduce gaps between what a designer knows about a problem, what is the proposal to solve it and what solution is actually delivered.

Going deep into design specifications and applying the First Axiom reduced the amount of complexity initially associated with layout design by simplifying its rationale to three different types of spaces: control spaces, movement spaces and opportunity spaces. This rationale is adaptable to different building sizes which not only fits into the Arctic context but can also be transferred to many other places. The use of AD also changed the approach to design priorities, from the simple fulfilling multiple assessment criteria to the search for a clear hierarchy of pedestrian flows to be evaluated using different types of computer simulation tools. Beyond that, the idea of using the Second Axiom to coordinate this group of simulation tools and relate them to design specifications, opens the possibility for uncertainty to be inserted into the design problem from its very beginning. It also changes the way designers are supposed to deal with uncertainty by not having it exclusively in the solution domain anymore but also bringing it to the design specification domain. If, on one hand, this can break designers free from the paradigm of 'classic' design optimization, it brings, on the other hand, a series of new challenges to the design process such as for instance how can probability ranges (tolerance values) be assigned to DPs which are mainly defined as spaces or spatial properties (either at a building level of neighbourhood scale level)?

The implementation of AD in writing design specification for TIHs is not supposed to end with this paper. Beyond, future work on fully exploring the Second Axiom, should also include developing and overlaying design specifications for different stakeholders and dealing with potential conflicts arising from it. Furthermore, it should be tested in different contexts and in practice.

# References

1. Monzon, A.: Innovative design and operation of new or upgraded efficient urban transport interchanges. In: Monzon, A. (ed.) City-HUB. Project Report. European Commission, Seventh Framework Cooperation Work Programme (2015)
2. Yatskiv, I., Nathaniel, E., Richter, K.: Special issue introduction: research in sustainable transport interchanges. Transp. Telecommun. **9**(3), 179–182 (2018)
3. Jia, J., Fang, Y.: Underground space development in comprehensive transport hubs in China. Proc. Eng. **165**, 404–417 (2016)
4. Li, L., Ren, H., Zhao, S., Duan, Z., Zhang, Y., Zhang, A.: Two dimensional accessibility analysis of metro stations in Xi'an, China. Transp. Res. Part A **106**, 414–426 (2017)
5. Liu, R., Chen, Y., Wu, J., Xu, T., Gao, L., Zhao, X.: Mapping spatial accessibility of public transportation network in an urban area – a case study on Shanghai Hongqiao Transportation. Transp. Res. Part D **59**, 478–495 (2018)
6. Dunichkin, I.: Transport interchange hubs under the conditions of the far North. In: Murgul, V., Popovic, Z. (eds.) EMMFT 2017. AISC, vol. 692, pp. 446–452. Springer, Cham (2018). https://doi.org/10.1007/978-3-319-70987-1_47
7. HERMES – High efficient and reliable arrangements for crossmodal transport. https://cordis. europa.eu/project/rcn/93149/reporting/en. Accessed 10 Feb 2019
8. City-HUB. http://www.cityhub.imet.gr/. Accessed 10 Feb 2019
9. NODES Interchanges - New tools for designing and operation of urban transport interchanges. http://www.nodes-interchanges.eu/. Accessed 10 Feb 2019
10. Alliance – Enhancing excellence and innovation capacity in sustainable transport interchanges. http://alliance-project.eu/. Accessed 10 Feb 2019
11. VitalNodes - Building a lasting expert network that delivers evidence-based recommendations for Vital Urban Nodes along TEN-T Corridors. https://cordis.europa.eu/project/rcn/212872/factsheet/en. Accessed 10 Feb 2019
12. Zamyatina, N., Goncharov, R.: Population mobility and the contrasts between cities in the Russian Arctic and their southern Russian counterparts. Area Dev. Policy **3**(3), 293–308 (2018)
13. Hickman, R., Chen, C.L., Chow, A., Saxena, S.: Improving interchanges in China: the experiential phenomenon. J. Transp. Geogr. **42**, 175–186 (2015)
14. Hernandez, S., Monzon, A., Ona, R.: Urban transport interchanges: a methodology for evaluating perceived quality. Transp. Res. Part A **84**, 31–43 (2016)
15. Tsami, M., Adamos, G., Natrhanail, E., Budilovich, E., Yatskiv, I., Magginas, V.: A decision tree approach for achieving high customer satisfaction at urban interchanges. Transp. Telecommun. **19**(3), 194–202 (2018)
16. Monzon, A., Alonso, A., Lopez-Lambas, M.: Joint analysis of intermodal long distance-last mile trips using urban interchanges in EU cities. Transp. Res. Proc. **27**, 1074–1079 (2017)
17. Bryniarska, S., Zakowska, L.: Multi-Criteria evaluation of public transport interchanges. Transp. Res. Proc. **24**, 25–32 (2017)
18. Van Hagen, M., de Bruyn, M.: The ten commandments of how to become a customer-driven railway operator. In: European Transport Conference, pp. 1–19. Association for European Transport AET, Glasgow (2012)
19. Marchesi, M., Matt, D.T.: Application of axiomatic design to the design of the built environment: a literature review. In: Farid, A., Suh, N. (eds.) Axiomatic Design in Large Systems, pp. 151–174. Springer, Cham (2016). https://doi.org/10.1007/978-3-319-32388-6_6
20. Suh, N.P.: Axiomatic Design: Advances and Applications. Oxford University Press, New York (2001)

21. Pastor, J. B. R., Benavides, E. M.: Axiomatic design of an airport passenger terminal. In: Thompson, M. K. (ed.) Proceedings of the 6th International Conference on Axiomatic Design, ICAD, pp. 95–102. Korean Advanced Institute of Science and Technology (KAIST), Daejon (2011)

22. Shiklomanov, N.I., Streletskiy, D.A., Grebenets, V.I., Suter, L.: Conquering the permafrost: urban infrastructure development in Norilsk, Russia. Polar Geogr. **40**(4), 273–290 (2017)

23. Russian Transport Regulations SNIP 2.07.01-89

24. Transport for London (TfL) Interchange: Interchange best practice guidelines 2009. Quick reference guide. http://www.tfl.gov.uk/interchange. Accessed 28 Jan 2019

25. Monzon, A., Hernandez, S., Di Ciommo, F.: Efficient urban interchanges: the city-HUB model. Transp. Res. Proc. **14**, 1124–1133 (2016)

26. Booth, R.: D3.3.1 identification and specification of the key areas of interchange design. In: Hoogendoom, C. (ed.) NODES 'New Tools for Design and Operation of Urban Transport Interchanges'. Project Report. European Commission, DG Research and Innovation (2015)

27. Aldecoa, J.: D3.2.1 mobility analysis and urban planning for interchanges. In: Hoogendoom, C. (ed.) NODES 'New Tools for Design and Operation of Urban Transport Interchanges'. Project Report. European Commission, DG Research and Innovation (2015)

28. Pastor, A.G., Pinedo, J.C.: D3.2.2 urban planning and development at a close-up level. In: Hoogendoom, C. (ed.) NODES 'New tools for Design and Operation of Urban Transport Interchanges'. Project Report. European Commission, DG Research and Innovation (2015)

29. Hillier, B.: Space is the Machine: A Configurational Theory of Architecture. Cambridge University Press, Cambridge (1996)

30. Dauden, F.J.L., Carpio-Pinedo, J., Garcia-Pastor, A.: Transport interchange and local urban environment integration. Proc. - Soc. Behav. Sci. **160**, 215–223 (2014)

31. Hillier, B., Hanson, J.: The Social Logic of Space by Bill Hillier [WWW Document]. Cambridge Core (1984). https://doi.org/10.1017/CBO9780511597237

32. Hillier, B., Turner, A., Yang, T., Park, H.-T.: Metric and topo-geometric properties of urban street networks: some convergences, divergences and new results. J. Space Syntax **1**, 279 (2010)

33. Hillier, B.: Cities as movement economies. Urban Des. Int. **1**, 49–60 (1996)

34. Brookes, I, Greenwood, R., Wilson, T., Yariv, B.: Station Design Principles for Network Rail. Safety Technical & Engineering Guidance. Document no. BLDG-SP80-002. Network Rail, UK (2015)

35. Dunichkin, I.V., Bleil de Souza, C., Bogachev, K., Pezzica, C.: Exploring specific features of Transport Interchange Hubs (TIH) design, taking into account the climatic conditions of the Russian Arctic. In: International Conference on Computational Science and its Applications. Under Review (2019)

# A Methodology for Defining Smart Camera Surveillance Locations in Urban Settings

Rodrigo Tapia-McClung[✉][iD] and Tania Gómez-Fernández

Centro de Investigación en Ciencias de Información Geoespacial,
Contoy 137, Col. Lomas de Padierna, Tlalpan, 14240 Mexico City, Mexico
rtapia@centrogeo.edu.mx, gfe.tania@gmail.com

**Abstract.** In this paper we propose a methodology to solve the problem of locating a set of cameras in an uncontrolled open space, such as a city. For this purpose, the geometric approach of the problem is transformed towards the optimization of a surveillance service system in which a metaheuristic model is used to maximize the service capabilities of the set of cameras.

**Keywords:** Differential evolution · Surveillance · Crime prevention

## 1 Introduction

Insecurity situations in many cities have forced the authorities to find a way to bring harmonious coexistence and lead ideal behavior on citizens in such a way that everyone can feel their integrity and possessions are protected. In this continuous search to guarantee the population's well-being, it is valuable to incorporate the use of technology to facilitate the work of people assigned to public surveillance tasks. Among the most popular tools are video surveillance technologies such as closed circuit television (CCTV). Despite the opinions against video surveillance systems related to privacy issues [1], there is proof that CCTV can serve as a tool to prevent or reduce incidents related to criminal behavior [2].

The implementation of video surveillance systems in public spaces has many faces opened for discussion. In recent years, society has questioned the use of cameras as a tool to guarantee safety, although there are obvious advantages, it is often ethical and moral issues that generate acceptance or rejection of this method of surveillance, particularly when economic investment does not necessarily translate into greater security for society [3]. In relation to this problem, Scotland Yard promoted initiatives with the intention of improving the use of CCTV, which affected the way of how public surveillance cameras had been exploited until then, as the legal system vaguely allowed the images captured with this tool to be used as evidence in court [4]. Despite the disapproval, many authorities are still betting on this surveillance method and continuously assign a good part of the security budget to these projects [5], recognizing to a large

© Springer Nature Switzerland AG 2019
S. Misra et al. (Eds.): ICCSA 2019, LNCS 11621, pp. 505–520, 2019.
https://doi.org/10.1007/978-3-030-24302-9_36

extent that cameras are a very useful technology but are not the absolute solution to society's problems. The cost of these security alternatives is considerable for all the infrastructure and maintenance they require, so it is convenient to obtain the maximum benefit and optimize the use of this resource. In the end, CCTV is perceived as a necessary evil [6].

There are a number of applications that exploit CCTV capabilities for specific surveillance tasks [7–10]. Most of these applications require that the cameras are previously placed in the area that wants to be observed. This means that camera placement must be carefully studied.

An important part of the assembly of the surveillance is to determine the camera locations. Particularly when dealing with observing public space, the system could have many elements that can be scattered in very large and irregular areas. Camera placement becomes a critical step when their locations have a great influence on the performance and cost of the system, therefore a strategic positioning is preferred over an arbitrary one.

Location problems are studied extensively in combinatorial optimization [11] and use enumeration and search techniques to find the solution, but there exist $NP$-hard complexity problems where enumeration and search techniques have difficulties in recognizing optimal configurations when the worst case of the problem occurs. It is common that location models are subject to multiple conditions that compete with each other, so it becomes more difficult to find an exact solution to the problem. Although there are models that can find exact solutions, they are limited and not necessarily easy to implement [12]. Exhaustive methods are designed so that they guarantee finding an optimal solution in a finite amount of time. This "finite amount of time" increases exponentially respect to complexity and dimension of the problem. Heuristics do not guarantee this, and sometimes return solutions that are sub-optimal. But they usually find "good" solutions in a "reasonable" amount of time. Many heuristic algorithms are specific and very problem-dependent. In contrast, metaheuristics is a more sophisticated method and a problem-independent algorithmic framework that uses strategies to lead the search of the solution. For this reason, the use of a heuristic or metaheuristic model can be a more feasible approach. A heuristic solution can be developed specifically for the conditions of the problem, while a metaheuristic solution has a more independent structure and can be adapted for other instances of the same problem [13,14]. Since the cost and maintenance of CCTV systems is substantial, it is convenient to study the placement from an optimization perspective because it can suppose an improvement in the way the available resources are destined for the installation. CCTV is recognized as a useful tool that serves multiple purposes to meet the operational needs of a city and also reinforces the sense of security. The implementation of a methodology based on the analysis of spatial data and optimization by heuristic models can help establish the placement of the cameras of a CCTV network, which meet the specific surveillance needs to record significant activities in a given time and space. Even more, we want to incorporate the use of heuristic models as a tool geared towards obtaining a robust and acceptable solution for camera placement that is used specifically for urban street observation.

# 2    Background and Related Work

Nowadays the complexity involved in video surveillance systems applications demands for pretty fussy planning for camera locations, particularly when there are multiple cameras to be placed that must also be coordinated in order to accomplish a given task without compromising performance [8,15]. Planning becomes complex when multiple factors present in the space to be monitored and the capabilities of the devices that make up the system are taken into consideration.

We started by looking at surveillance systems applications, focusing on how the camera placement was solved before assigning tasks for the system. However, sometimes the placement depends on the space and the assigned task. For example, the placement will be different if the scene corresponds to a closed, open, private or public space, because it depends on many factors that may constrain or relax the placement conditions for the devices. Also, in the reviewed articles on the topic [9,16,17], the requirements of the devices are taken into account so they can perform the assigned task keeping continuity, accuracy, and quality on the records.

Initially, the *Art Gallery* problem [18] we consider as the first approach because it focuses on coverage and visibility analysis using space triangulations to find the minimum number of guards that keep watch over a full or specific objective. This problem considers the demand of surveillance to be uniform, unlike outdoors public surveillance systems that attend specific points while simultaneously try to watch all the space. With this in mind, we decided to look into covering models since they consider measures of spatial availability of services as a parameter to quantify the effectiveness of a location configuration. One definition of a measure of effectiveness in [19] is "how well a particular location configuration performs with respect to the overall purpose facilities are intended to serve".

The *Location Set-Covering Problem* (LSCP) [19] proposes to identify the location of the minimum set of facilities that satisfy all the demand points within a maximal service distance of a facility. Some authors consider the maximal service distance is not good for the performance of the system because eventually it will be economically unfeasible to satisfy all the demands with a limited set of facilities [11,19]. However, it may be impossible for a surveillance system to achieve a complete coverage of all the demand points because the devices' sensor distance is too short and this implies the need of a lot of facilities to cover all the objectives that require video surveillance. In the *Maximal Covering Location Problem* (MCLP) [11], the full coverage restriction of the LSCP is relieved. This model determines the locations that maximize the portion of demand served within a standard distance with a given number of facilities. Instead of maximal service distance, this model proposes a standard distance to satisfy the maximum request of service, which is similar to what surveillance cameras have to do. With the cameras capabilities we expect to cover the maximum proportion of the space or at least as many objectives as possible [20]. Even if the cameras have the best zooming capabilities and widest field of view, maximizing the surveillance service does not depend on these characteristics, but rather in the location of the facilities.

Analyzing criminal spatial displacement may offer relevant information that could be added to planning the location for surveillance facilities. If we were to consider predicting the occurrence of a crime, we would likely rely on statistical reports, but in fact it would be very difficult to actually get the right position and time of occurrence. In this sense, criminal incidence has a stochastic nature. Waples *et al.* [2] refer six types of displacements and conclude that spatial displacement of crime is a complex subject to explore, especially since no standardized method has been yet specified. Furthermore, CCTV by itself cannot displace crime frequently or uniformly across offence types or space, but careful management with realistic objectives could be an effective crime prevention measure. Bearing on the complexity of the criminal spatial displacement, we may consider investigations that incorporate stochastic nature of the demand-to-location modelling.

According to Hogan and ReVelle [11], coverage models which include stochastic demands and spatial availability are likely to be multi-objective. They may be viewed on a hierarchical or true multi-objective sense. We consider our location problem with a multi-objective hierarchical approach. Because we are focused on using a limited number of cameras, we try to maximize the coverage of the observed space together with the proportion of previously recorded crimes, as well as optimize the overlap between the observed spaces of different cameras. It is realized that in applications of surveillance systems target coverage must satisfy certain conditions of continuity on the camera records to reconstruct the displacement or recognition of an object between several cameras. This feature implies that overlap between camera records and the maximization of the observed space are opposed objectives, so a maximum threshold must be defined for the overlap and try not to exceed it.

As an extension of the MCLP, the *Backup Coverage Model* [11] suggests that "providing secondary, or backup coverage, to as much of the population as possible is an appealing method by which to protect coverage from varying with time or with unit availability". Criminal displacement may vary from time and location [2], taking advantage of the blind spots and spaces without surveillance facilities. It would be helpful to have a principal coverage to maximize the observed surface and a secondary coverage to control the blind spots. Particularly, the *Backup Coverage Model 2* (BACOP2) [11] suggests the need of backup coverage to deal with areas of high demand where the probability of nearly simultaneous demand points is large. This problem allocates different levels of coverage with a fixed number of facilities. Also, the backup coverage will be provided when the principal coverage is already set.

Despite the existence of exhaustive methods to solve the problem, we will use a metaheuristic approach to solve it. A number of problems have incorporated metaheuristic approaches to solve spatial optimization problems [21,22]. Unlike exhaustive methods, metaheuristics may balance exploration and exploitation of the solutions space. This approach is fairly useful when resources are limited, so it is possible to get a robust solution that can be improved with additional field validation [14].

Differential evolution (DE) is a search method based on the global evolution of populations [23]. The DE method is similar to a Genetic Algorithm (GA) in that it allows each generation of solutions to evolve from the best qualities of the previous one. The differential evolution algorithm (DEA), derived from the concept of DE, is a bio-inspired algorithm that simulates the mechanism of natural evolution and can be used to solve real-valued problems, although good results have also been obtained in combinatorial problems [23]. Like the genetic algorithm, it uses crossing and mutation operators and the best solution must be chosen in each generation. In addition, it has few but high-impact parameters that control the convergence and quality of the solutions, takes less time, and is relatively easy to customize, unlike GA.

# 3  Proposed Approach

A method based on a differential evolution algorithm (DEA) to generate a robust solution to locate a set of cameras designed for street surveillance is presented. For this, a hierarchical approach will be used because we choose to maximize the proportion of recorded crimes over the other objectives to discriminate between alternate locations. Figure 1 shows the pseudo-code of the DEA used to develop the camera location methodology in this research. Figure 2 shows a schematic flow diagram of the methodology that was developed to solve the problem of locating cameras in urban settings with the restrictions that subject the fitness function.

The first two steps correspond to data preparation while the rest correspond to the algorithm implementation itself. On Step 1, raw crime incidence data are cleaned and layers for the study area are adjusted. In this work, city blocks are considered to be obstacles. Next, on Step 2, a spatially enabled data base (DB) is created and the adjusted layers are loaded. These layers serve as default inputs and auxiliary information during algorithm execution. In Step 3, `psycogp2` is used to connect Python and the DB so transactions can be executed and committed by the algorithm.

Before running the DEA, the parameters must be configured to our specific needs in Step 4. Parameters are separated into three groups: The first contains camera features, like field of view partition and sensor distance. The second contains differential evolution parameters like the stop criteria, size of population, cross rate and crossing factor. The third are the weights for the objective criteria. One needs to previously choose some criteria that are to be used as objectives to help evaluate the quality of the solutions. These criteria are quantified in the fitness function, so different weights are assigned depending on the properties of these criteria. Next, the DEA optimization method on Step 5 is executed. Figure 3 shows this execution in more detail and is explained below. As a result of this step, a list with the best solutions of the optimization process is obtained. Lastly, by using the `seaborn` and `folium` libraries, it is possible to create a chart of the performance and an interactive map that shows the evolution process of assigning locations together with the best solution obtained from the process.

Algorithm description for DE

1. **begin**
2. Set the generation counter $G = 0$. Randomly initialize a population of $NP$ individuals $X_i$, with $D$ attributes each. Initialize $F$ and $CR$ parameters.
3. Evaluate the fitness for each individual in $P$.
4.     **while** stopping criteria not satisfied **do**
5.     **for** $i = 1$ to $NP$ **do**
6.         randomly select $a \neq b \neq c \neq d \neq i$
7.         **for** $j = 1$ to $D$ **do**
8.             $j_{rand} = \lfloor rand(0, 1) * D \rfloor$
9.             **if** $rand(0, 1) \leq CR$ or $j = j_{rand}$ **then**
10.                 $u_{i,j} = x_{a,j} + F \times (x_{b,j} - x_{c,j})$
11.                 /* five mutation strategies */
12.             **else**
13.                 $u_{i,j} = x_{i,j}$
14.             **end if**
15.         **end for**
16.     **end for**
17.     **for** $i = 1$ to $NP$ **do**
18.         Evaluate offspring $u_i$
19.         **if** $u_i$ is better than $X_i$ **then**
20.             $X_i = u_i$
21.         **end if**
22.     **end for**
23.     Memorize best solution achieved so far
24.     **end while**
25. **end**

**Fig. 1.** Pseudo-code for DEA. Adapted from [24]

As mentioned before, Fig. 3 stems from Step 5 of Fig. 2 and helps understand the proposed adaptation of the original DEA.

**Step A.** Sampling strategy. First, we need to identify the solution space. In order to position the cameras, all available public roads area considered as feasible candidates for installing devices. Then, a sampling strategy is used to generate initial random solutions that will serve as a starting point in the algorithm. When implementing a sampling strategy, it is possible to privilege certain zones in the street network that should have more devices due to the higher known criminal incidence in that area. At the same time, the solution space is reduced for exploration, leaving more chances for improving the final solution. For instance, by using random sampling, the initial solution has an equal chance of choosing locations inside all the street surface. In a stratified sampling, however, it is possible to partition the surface according to the density of incidents per square kilometer. The partition is then used to choose a different proportion of random positions in each fraction of the partition.

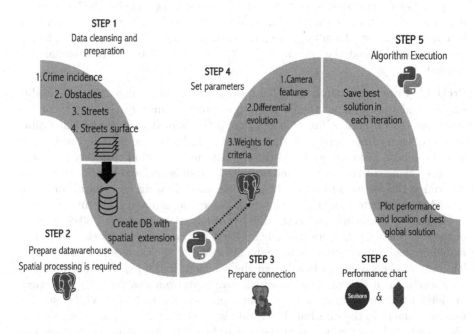

**Fig. 2.** Schematic flow diagram of the methodology that was developed to solve the problem of locating cameras in urban settings

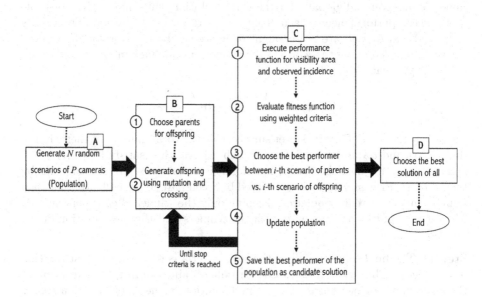

**Fig. 3.** Schematic diagram explaining the execution of the DEA

**Step B.** Generating solutions. New scenarios are generated using the DEA crossing and mutation rules. Also, a function that randomly chooses three different scenarios $(x_a, x_b, x_c)$ from the population and recombines them according to the DEA conditions and the rule $x_a + F \times (x_b - x_c)$ to obtain a new scenario is defined.

**Step C.** Fitness function. Because the goal is to maximize both the visible surface and the observed thefts, it is important to quantify the quality of the solutions. To do this, a function $v(x, y, d, g)$ is defined to measure the visible surface of each camera in each scenario. Here, $x$ and $y$ are the camera coordinates, $d$ is the sensor distance, and $g$ is the field of view partition. Another function, $c(x, y, v)$, is used to count the thefts inside the visible surface of each camera. To determine the visible surface of the solution, the following procedure to find an *isovist* is constructed (see Fig. 4): For each camera location in the solution, $k$ rays of length $d$ are built, where $k$ is the number of partitions from 0 to 360 degrees by $g$ degrees. Each ray is truncated when it first intersects a city block, a vertex is added at the intersection and the segment closest to the camera location is kept. The rest of the ray is discarded from the solution. If the ray does not intersect with anything, it is kept as is. When all rays have been analyzed, the $k$ vertices are joined to form a closed polygon that represents the estimated visible surface for each camera in the solution. The total visible surface $V(\bar{x}, \bar{y})$ of the scenario is obtained by joining the polygons $v(x, y, d, g)$ for all the cameras in each scenario. The global surface is the union of all the polygons in the solution. The theft count $C(\bar{x}, \bar{y})$ is obtained by taking into account all thefts contained in the polygon of the visible surface of the solution $V(\bar{x}, \bar{y})$. This is carried out locally for each camera's polygon and globally for the whole solution, thus making it is possible to know the performance of each element and the overall solution. The results of $V(\bar{x}, \bar{y})$ and $C(\bar{x}, \bar{y})$ are not enough to choose the best option for the camera locations. Therefore, a fitness or objective function is defined in order to measure the quality of each scenario:

$$f(\bar{x}, \bar{y}) = \alpha_1 \frac{V(\bar{x}, \bar{y})}{\mathcal{V}} + \alpha_2 \frac{C(\bar{x}, \bar{y})}{\mathcal{C}},$$

where $\mathcal{V}$ is the area of all the street surface, $\mathcal{C}$ is the total number of thefts in the surface, $\alpha_1$ and $\alpha_2$ are the weights for each criteria that satisfy $0 \leq \alpha_1, \alpha_2 \leq 1$ and $\alpha_1 + \alpha_2 = 1$. Using the $f(\bar{x}, \bar{y})$ function it is possible to rank the solutions by their quality. Fitness values are compared between parents and offspring for each element in the current population, keeping only the winner of each comparison. Then, the population is updated with the winners and the best solution of the iteration is kept.

**Step D.** The final solution. When the stop criteria is reached, the best solution of all is kept. This scenario is the best result obtained during the execution of the algorithm, not necessarily the optimal solution of the whole solution space.

**Model Constraints.** There are some restrictions and limitations to our problem and approach. First, we assume there are no cameras installed on the surface

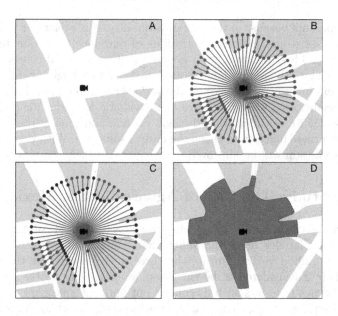

**Fig. 4.** Construction of isovists for individual cameras

we want to monitor. Second, that it is possible to place surveillance cameras anywhere on the perimeter or inside the surface. In addition, the number of available cameras is fixed and all have the same operating properties. In particular, and for the sake of simplicity, it is assumed they all have a viewing angle of $\theta = 360°$ and the maximum distance of the sensor $d$ is the same for all devices. At this stage, we do not account for overlaps between the visibility polygons of each camera.

**Algorithm Tuning.** To improve the obtained results, some parameters can be modified depending on what wants to be attained. The DEA parameters can be tuned when some problems are identified during the algorithm execution. However, before modifying the parameters, some patterns must be recognized. For example, if the crossing factor is very large, cameras accumulate in the outer limits of the valid surface. This means that cameras were located outside the valid surface, but the algorithm relocates them in a position closest to the valid surface. To correct this, the crossing factor is reduced and one must recall that camera displacement depends on the measurement reference system. Displacement is different for geometries and geographies (degrees vs. meters). On the other hand, if the performance for scenarios is seen to be stuck from the beginning, then the crossing rate is modified. This parameter controls the number of cameras reassigned by each scenario. When the crossing rate is low, few cameras will be reassigned; if it is high, then almost all cameras will be reassigned and the algorithm behaves as the random search case. It is important to consider that population size also influences the obtained results. For example, if a small population is generated (*e.g.* 4 scenarios), each offspring will be a redundant case of the parents because of the lack of variability. It is preferable to use larger population sizes to get more configurations of parents. If we want to improve the choice of the best scenario, then we can modify the initial conditions of the general algorithm. By adding more camera features like height or different camera types, and including obstacles on the surface like threes, lighting structures, buildings height, etc., we will achieve more realistic locations for the cameras. Furthermore, if we consider other decision criteria and modify the weights, we upgrade the fitness function to choose an elite of solutions. With this, the quality of the final solution will be improved.

## 4   Case Study: The City of Aguascalientes, Mexico

As a case study, the Mexican city of Aguascalientes in the state of Aguascalientes is considered. The city hosts the annual San Marcos Fair, which attracts an average of 8 million visitors during the three-week period that the Fair lasts [25]. The Fair is considered to be the most important one in the country and has several types of events such as concerts of both international and national artists, bullfighting events, charrería, and the largest livestock exhibition in Latin America [26].

The state of Aguascalientes is located in the central-northern region of the country, 480 km northwest of Mexico City. It is a very small state, covering an area of approximately 5,470 km$^2$ (about 0.03% of the country), and is subdivided into 11 municipalities. The central municipality of the state of Aguascalientes, also called Aguascalientes, contains about 76% of the state population and accounts for around 85% of the criminal incidence in the state. Furthermore, because there is a large number of incoming visitors during the Fair, it makes sense to focus on criminal incidence around it. In order to study what happens in and around the Fair grounds, this research methodology only focuses on the first ring of the city. Figure 5 shows the location of the state and city of Aguascalientes together with the limit of the first ring that is used in this study.

The first ring is bounded by the road circuit named "Aguascalientes Convention of 1914", also known as "Primer Anillo". This ring-shaped road structure contains the downtown area and distributes transport services from north to south and from west to east using only this road.

The San Marcos Fair has been held annually during April and May since 1828 and lasts for about of 24 days [26]. During the festivities, various fairgrounds located to the southwest of the city are used to distribute all scheduled events. Due to this organizational structure, it is possible to recognize the increase in the number of visitors in that part of the city and, consequently, the demand for other tourist services such as lodging, food, transportation, and banking services also increase. For this case study, we use official data from the National Institute of Statistics and Geography (Instituto Nacional de Estadística y Geografía - INEGI) of city blocks and streets of the state of Aguascalientes. Geo-referenced crime data records were obtained from the state's General Attorney's office for thefts between January 2011 and May 2018 in the whole state. Because some

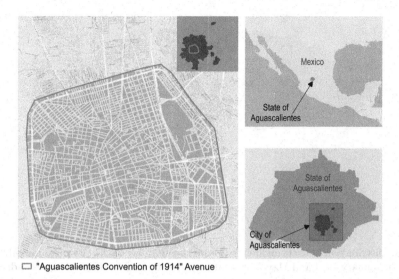

☐ "Aguascalientes Convention of 1914" Avenue

**Fig. 5.** The location of the state and city of Aguascalientes together with the boundary of the first ring

crime incidents are reported to occur on parks and inside buildings, for the purpose of this methodology, such crime locations were modified so they are accounted for on the street network and in the visible surface of the solution described above. We also consider 10 scenarios of 50 cameras that have a sensor distance of 100 m and partition the field of view with a 1° resolution. For this case, the stop criteria is the number of iterations set to 30.

According to official records, the first ring experiences three main types of theft: pedestrian, vehicle, and auto parts. Together, these three types of crime represent 67% of the recorded incidence between January 2011 and May 2018 (24%, 24%, and 19%, respectively). The temporal change of these crime types inside the first ring also shows that during the Fair the number of visitors concentrated in and around the fairgrounds create conditions ripe for theft exposure. Figure 6 shows the distribution of theft incidences during the Fair and their temporal behavior. Even though the city of Aguascalientes has low theft counts compared to other cities in the country, this distribution shows a significant increase during the Fair. By considering the spatial distribution of the three most common types of thefts together with the city infrastructure and services, it is found that pedestrian incidence is more pervasive around certain facilities, such as banks and, particularly, the fairgrounds. Figure 7 shows the spatial distribution of these incidences. The fairgrounds are located just to the left of the map center and to the southwest. When the temporal nature of the data is taken into consideration, it is found that 33% of the crime incidence corresponds to pedestrian thefts that took place in April, 30% in May, and then drops to the monthly average of 23%.

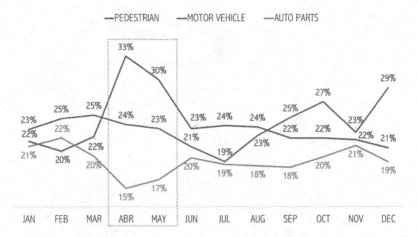

**Fig. 6.** Distribution of theft incidences inside the first ring of the city of Aguascalientes between January 2011 and May 2018. Dates spanning the San Marcos Fair are indicated

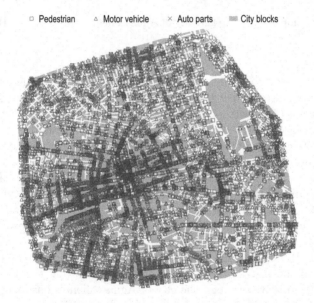

**Fig. 7.** Spatial distribution of the three main types of theft inside the first ring of the city of Aguascalientes

## 5    Results and Discussion

The cross and mutation parameters, $CR$ and $F$, have a significant impact on the obtained solution and should be consider as a threshold. The use of high values for these two parameters results in the case of a random search. Conversely, low values produce a stagnation for the obtained solutions. For the specific case studied here, the effect that $F$ has on the displacement of camera locations needs to be taken into account due to the measurement units for the cartographic representation. As such, an $F$ value of 0.5 (that corresponds to an approximate shifting distance of $\sim$50 km) produces unacceptable camera locations as it places them beyond the observable surface of road networks under consideration and a reassigning process needs to be triggered. For the case study presented here, $F$ has a value of 0.001, which roughly represents a shifting distance of 100 m.

The parameters $\alpha_1$ and $\alpha_2$ also have an influence on the obtained solution. Depending on their value, they can make one criterion be preferred over the other. That is, either the number of observed incidences or the observed area is preferred. For this case study, both of the proposed criteria for the objective function are opposed: forcing the system to obtain the maximum amount of observed incidences can compact camera locations to specific points, thus leaving areas of the city unprotected without surveillance. On the other hand, if the system must maximize the observed area, then camera locations would be selected on broad streets and street corners that may not necessarily have high criminal incidence. Likewise, the algorithm is adaptable and could incorporate a way for the values of both $\alpha_1$ and $\alpha_2$ to be optimized.

The inclusion of the performance function that considers obstacles or intersections, such as city blocks, allows for a better understanding and exploitation of camera locations. The performance function could be further improved by adding more contextual information about the area under study coupled with camera characteristics. Thus, the performance function would provide results that would be a better match to reality and would therefore improve the quality of the solution.

An improvement is observed from the starting solution by shifting from a uniform to a stratified sampling scheme. Incidence saturation on the surface indicates that there are areas more prone to theft than others. With this idea in mind, the street surface was fragmented into five categories according to the amount of criminal incidence. With this, the stratified sampling is used to proportionately distribute the number of cameras between the strata.

The final solution for this case study is shown in Fig. 8. The graphs on the right show the performance of the solution for different iterations. In the performance graphs, the variations in each decision criterion show they are competing while searching for the solution. Then, the algorithm should find a solution that maximizes both criteria simultaneously. For this case, in order to maximize both criteria, the DEA results in a decrease of the percentage of observed crimes in favor of an increase of the visible surface. By the end of the simulation, it can be seen that the percentage of observed crimes has decreased about 0.5%, while the visible surface increases approximately 0.8% from their initial values. The map shows the distribution of cameras and their isovists that represent the observable area for each camera. Upon visual inspection, a good match is observed on many locations when comparing the incidence map (Fig. 7) and the density of crimes added to the final solution. Regarding Fig. 7, there are some regions that seem to have high incidence and very few cameras. This apparent discrepancy can be explained because the incidence map only shows three types of crimes, while the final solution uses all crime types on the study area. Also, even though the observed area drops, after inspecting the map it is found that cameras are located in small but conflicting streets.

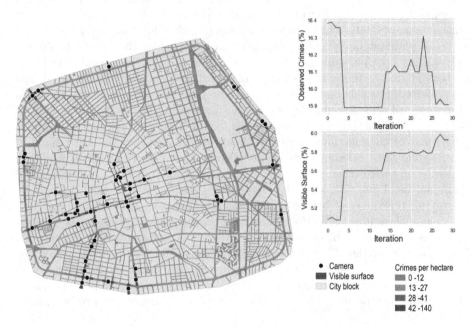

**Fig. 8.** Map depicting the proposed solution for camera locations on top of the spatial density of all crime types per hectare and graphs that show the performance of the algorithm

## 6    Conclusions and Future Work

A methodology to locate a set of surveillance cameras in an urban setting by using a metaheuristic model was proposed. This methodology improves the surveillance coverage thanks to the competition and selection structures in the DE algorithm. The case study proved it is possible to automate the location selection for surveillance cameras with very few available inputs. Furthermore, by simulating possible solutions it is possible to cut down costs for decision-makers and they have a flexible tool that can be adapted for specific needs.

With the existence of detailed information such as protruding facades, trees, lamp posts, or other types of obstacles, the obtained solutions would be far more realistic since there would be precise knowledge of the environment under study. If camera attributes such as field of view or detection and zoom capabilities are considered, together with the tasks the system would have to work on such as object recognition or tracking, it would be possible to have more control over the solution space and obtained results would be more attached to what the system would do in reality. Additionally, the stop criteria was set to an upper limit to the number of allowable iterations but could include a tolerance threshold for the dissimilarity of the fitness function for the latest solutions from the best generations, stopping the execution when there are no significant changes between the performance of the best scenarios. For the tolerance threshold to work, however, it is required that decision criteria are good enough to rank the solutions and prevent ties.

This research used a DE algorithm based on the intuitive idea of natural evolution. However, there are other metaheuristic models that could be included, like Genetic Algorithm, Particle Swarm Optimization or Ant Colony Optimization, which have also been used with good results in finding camera locations [9,13,16,17]. It could even be possible to consider an adaptive model that uses previous knowledge to spawn the new solution. Future work includes further tuning the algorithm and evaluating the inclusion of other stop criteria to have a better final solution. Additionally, it will be interesting to adapt the algorithm so it works with an existing network of surveillance cameras already in place. Also an overlap threshold for the camera visibility polygons can be implemented by using Jaccard's similarity coefficient to reduce the redundancy of information captured by the solution and maximize the observed surface.

# References

1. Bennett, T., Gelsthorpe, L.: Public attitudes towards CCTV in public places. Stud. Crime Crime Prev. 5(1), 72–90 (1996)
2. Waples, S., Gill, M., Fisher, P.: Does CCTV displace crime? Criminol. Crim. Justice 9(2), 207–224 (2009)
3. Li, A.: Pros and Cons of Surveillance Cameras in Public Places (2017). https://reolink.com/pros-cons-of-surveillance-cameras-in-public-places
4. Bowcott, O.: CCTV boom has failed to slash crime, say police (2008). https://www.theguardian.com/uk/2008/may/06/ukcrime1
5. Norris, C., McCahill, M., Wood, D.: The growth of CCTV: a global perspective on the international diffusion of video surveillance in publicly accessible space. Surveill. Soc. 2(2–3), 110–135 (2004). Editorial
6. Kelly, H.: After Boston: The pros and cons of surveillance cameras (2013). https://edition.cnn.com/2013/04/26/tech/innovation/security-cameras-boston-bombings/index.html
7. Bodor, R., Schrater, P., Papanikolopoulos, N.: Multi-camera positioning to optimize task observability. In: IEEE International Conference on Advanced Video And Signal Based Surveillance - Proceedings of AVSS 2005 (2005). https://doi.org/10.1109/AVSS.2005.1577328
8. Hu, W., Tan, T., Wang, L., Maybank, S.: A survey on visual surveillance of object motion and behaviors. IEEE Trans. Syst. Man Cybern. Part C 34(3), 334–352 (2004). https://doi.org/10.1016/j.artint.2008.12.005
9. Jun, S., Chang, T., Yoon, H.: Placing visual sensors using heuristic algorithms for bridge surveillance. Appl. Sci. 8(1) (2018). https://doi.org/10.3390/app8010070
10. Morris, B.T., Trivedi, M.M.: A survey of vision-based trajectory learning and analysis for surveillance. IEEE Trans. Circ. Syst. Video Technol. 18(8), 1114–1127 (2008). https://doi.org/10.1109/TCSVT.2008.927109

11. Hogan, K., ReVelle, C.: Concepts and applications of backup coverage. Manag. Sci. **32**(11), 1290–1306 (2012)
12. Rana, S.: Isovist Analyst - An Arcview extension for planning visual surveillance. ESRI International User Conference. ESRI (on CD-ROM), 1(Chvátal), 9 (2006). http://eprints.ucl.ac.uk/2104
13. Basu, S., Sharma, M., Ghosh, P.S.: Metaheuristic applications on discrete facility location problems: a survey. OPSEARCH **52**, 530 (2015). https://doi.org/10.1007/s12597-014-0190-5
14. Jordanski, M.: Metaheuristic approaches for solving facility location and scale decision problem with customer preference. IPSI BgD Trans. (Two Res. Oriented J.) **13**(1) (2017). http://ipsitransactions.org/journals/papers/tir/2017jan/p2.pdf
15. Xie, Y., Wang, M., Liu, X., Wu, Y.: Surveillance video synopsis in GIS. ISPRS Int. J. Geo-Inf. (2017). https://doi.org/10.3390/ijgi6110333
16. Konda, K.R., Conci, N.: Global and local coverage maximization in multi-camera networks by stochastic optimization. Infocommun. J. (2013). https://doi.org/10.1200/jco.2011.35.9182
17. Xu, Y.C., Lei, B., Hendriks, E.A.: Camera network coverage improving by particle swarm optimization. EURASIP J. Image Video Process. (2011). https://doi.org/10.1155/2011/458283
18. O'Rourke, J.: Art Gallery Theorems and Algorithms. Oxford University Press, Oxford (1987)
19. Church, R., Meadows, M.: Location modeling utilizing maximum service distance criteria. Geogr. Anal. **11**(4), 358–373 (1979)
20. Murray, A., Kim, K., Davis, J., Machiraju, R., Parent, R.: Coverage optimization to support security monitoring. Comput. Environ. Urban Syst. (2007). https://doi.org/10.1016/j.compenvurbsys.2006.06.002
21. Giagkiozis, I., Purshouse, R., Fleming, P.: An overview of population-based algorithms for multi-objective optimization. Int. J. Syst. Sci. **46**(9), 1572–1599 (2015). https://doi.org/10.1080/00207721.2013.823526
22. Tong, D., Murray, A.: Spatial optimization in geography. Ann. Assoc. Am. Geogr. **102**(6), 1434–1444 (1986)
23. Storn, R., Price, K.: Differential evolution - a simple and efficient heuristic for global optimization over continuous spaces. J. Glob. Optim. **11**, 341 (1997). https://doi.org/10.1023/A:1008202821328
24. Li, X., Yin, M.: Application of differential evolution algorithm on self-potential data. PLoS ONE **7**(12), e51199 (2012). https://doi.org/10.1371/journal.pone.0051199
25. Datos de Afluencia. Patronato de la Feria Nacional de San Marcos - Coordinación Estatal de Planeación y Proyectos. http://www.aguascalientes.gob.mx/ceplap/datos/default.aspx
26. Historia de la Feria Nacional de San Marcos en Aguascalientes: México Desconocido, 31 March 2016. https://www.mexicodesconocido.com.mx/feria-san-marcos-aguascalientes.html

# Exploring Specific Features of Transport Interchange Hubs (TIH) Design, Taking into Account the Climatic Conditions of the Russian Arctic

Ilya V. Dunichkin[1]($\boxtimes$) (ID), Clarice Bleil de Souza[2] (ID),
Konstantin Bogachev[1] (ID), and Camilla Pezzica[2] (ID)

[1] Moscow State University of Civil Engineering,
Yaroslavskoye Sh. 26, 129337 Moscow, Russia
ecse@bk.ru, t9645750303@gmail.com
[2] Welsh School of Architecture, Cardiff University, Bute building, King
Edward VII Avenue, Cardiff CF10 3NB, UK
{Bleildesouzac, Pezzicac}@cardiff.ac.uk

**Abstract.** This paper provides a more detailed analysis of the context of designing Transport Interchange Hubs (TIHs) in the Arctic Zone of the Russian Federation (AZRF). It uses a design framework proposed by another paper also submitted to his conference by the same authors [1] to discuss how green spaces can be integrated to TIHs in extreme climates to enhance the qualities of different types of spaces inside terminals considering implications of these in the overall assessment of building performance. It also discusses, the way pedestrian flow and movement is assessed and used in the design of TIH in the AZRF through advanced analysis techniques and how these could potentially be integrated with parametric design tools, finishing by considering the complexities involved in designing compact buildings, a necessary requirement to reduce heat losses and the impact of building footprint on the permafrost.

**Keywords:** Transport interchange hubs (TIH) · Arctic ·
Arctic Zone of the Russian Federation · Sustainable urban development ·
Pedestrian flow · Indoor landscaping · Simulations

## 1 Introduction

The Russian Arctic hosts cities since the 16th century and have been sustained by intensive investments from the Soviet times to date, including the revival of the Northern Sea Route which is expected to foster and increase economic development in the region [2]. Within this vast territory and extreme climate, with temperatures reaching an average of −30 °C in winter, cities tend to be generally small in size and isolated from one another. Their survival and economic viability is dependent upon the exploitation of mineral resources and, due to their peculiar functioning mechanism, they host populations with a high turn-over, with an average migration index of 9.8% [2]. However, despite these parallel and dynamic population expansion and contraction

© Springer Nature Switzerland AG 2019
S. Misra et al. (Eds.): ICCSA 2019, LNCS 11621, pp. 521–534, 2019.
https://doi.org/10.1007/978-3-030-24302-9_37

phenomena, cities in the Arctic Zone of the Russian Federation (AZRF) are in a state of (instable) equilibrium that makes them generally resilient to fluctuations in economic development, i.e. when development goes negative, people can easily leave whereas when conditions improve, people tend to come back. Long-term resilience is hence perhaps explained by seasonal migration. People in the Arctic undertake regular trips to Southern Russia due to fix-term business contracts; since the Soviet times they are granted governmental subsidies to travel to the South to maintain family and business ties, meaning they have a 'double-territorial identity' divided between the Arctic itself and the different parts of the country they also feel they belong to. These unique characteristics of migration in the AZRF mean that mobility needs to be preserved as a 'safety valve' to cope with economic dynamic fluctuations and to connect the North and South of the country [2]. Supporting mobility means investing in building and refurbishing transport networks, infrastructure and related facilities.

Transport is a serious issue in the Russian Arctic. It has implications in urban and social sustainable development as well as economic growth. Despite technological improvements in design and operation of passenger transport systems, total travelling time, in the AZRF remains significant; varying within 40–100 min (for short distances), depending on the size of the settlement, weather conditions and the number of available modes of transport. This time is directly affected by the necessity to travel long distances within a vast territory as well as a lack of coordination among different modes of transport reaching interchange terminals. The combination of these two factors can result in, on average, 12 h waiting time within terminal buildings, meaning that any improvement targeted at reducing total travelling time by increasing the speed of vehicles along the journey, may be ultimately ineffective, due to the significant amount of time spent by passengers in TIHs during transfers. As a result, passengers' experience is strongly influenced not only by the time spent on the trip, but also by the quality and length of waiting time during their travel across extreme climate zones.

Compensating for waiting time, is a critical design requirement in TIHs around the world and has been in the agenda of several European projects in the recent years such as for instance: HERMES [3]; City HUB [4]; NODES [5]; Alliance [6]. Addressing this requirement normally involves providing several facilities and amenities to travellers such as offering convenience shopping, food and refreshments, 'workstations', etc. [7–12]. These opportunities can be exploited by non-travellers and business managers through the design of more 'interesting' terminals, which can fulfil travellers' needs as well as act as community hubs, benefiting its customers (the travellers), and the city as a whole. In this context, TIH are seen not only as a host of pedestrian flow while people move from one mode of transport to another but also as a community centre for intercity passengers [13].

However, to date, implemented projects of terminals and stations in AZRF settlements have not taken into account the specifics of a market economy. They have not exploited fully opportunities which terminals could provide to introduce retail spaces, domestic hotels, 'interesting' waiting rooms, etc. while fulfilling the requirements and related design parameters for guaranteeing comfortable and functional human flows through universal design. Contrarily to the literature on TIHs in the European continent, Midland of Russia and Japan, which lately has seen more research in the area of customer satisfaction, TIH design strategies adopted in the AZRF have not yet properly integrated passengers' flow inside terminals with opportunity spaces to improve the quality of their waiting time. They also do not take properly into account the movement of people with limited mobility (PLM) inside terminals. To the best of the authors' knowledge there are no reports on customer satisfaction surveys among users of TIHs in the AZRF targeting terminals' design nor quantitative methods and models to predict and assess the integration of pedestrian flows within terminals with interior opportunity spaces.

This paper uses the methodology proposed by another paper submitted to this conference [1], to analyse in more detail passengers' movement within terminals as well as potential ways to explore design opportunities that would enhance the quality of passengers' waiting time. Movement is discussed in terms of how passengers' flow is currently simulated in the design of TIH in the AZRF [14] in contrast with how it could potentially be enhanced by borrowing some complementary analysis methods from Western Europe and Japan, whereas waiting time is exploited in terms of leisure opportunities potentially provided by TIHs once designed as community hubs suitable to operate in a harsh climate environment.

## 2  Methodology

In the paper [1] also submitted to this conference, the authors proposed a framework to address travellers' needs in the design of TIH using the Axiomatic Design (AD) method [15]. In this method, travellers' needs are translated into TIH functional requirements and subsequently into design parameters, to structure the development of a set of design specifications which can be used to more holistically take into account the integration of passenger flows and leisure opportunities provided to compensate for waiting times within TIH.

When applying this method, terminal buildings are understood as buildings, which provide shelter to mainly three different types of spaces:

(i)   Decision spaces, comprising places within the terminal in which decisions take priority (e.g. buying a ticket, gathering information about transfer, passing a control point, etc.);

(ii)  Movement spaces, in which passengers flow from one decision space to another, between different transport modes, or from a decision space to a transport mode;

(iii) Opportunity spaces, in which neither movement nor decision-making take priority and can be used to compensate for travellers' waiting time.

Under this framework, TIH become buildings, hosting passenger flows from different set of origin-destination pairs surrounded by opportunity spaces compensating for waiting time. The breaking of internal spaces into three different components is adaptable to different building scales, enabling the design of simple stations up to the design of complex buildings. This type of adaptability is important in designing TIHs in the AZRF as cities vary in size and terminals need to accommodate for fluctuations in population. Having TIHs as buildings which mainly host passenger flows also aid in focusing of safety and planning efficiency, two important design considerations in extreme climates which should take into account low temperatures and the risk of frostbite during emergency evacuation of passengers [16].

Section 3 focuses on discussing how green community areas can be designed as part of opportunity spaces in harsh climate zones, as in the case of AZRF. It is anticipated that this would improve the (costumer) experience associated to long waiting times by offering a positive opportunity for people to gather around and interact with nature. Sections 4 and 5 of this paper, will explore in more detail how movement spaces are currently embedded in the design of terminals in the AZRF and how simulation methods more commonly used in Western Europe could potentially add to the design of these spaces, from improving visual communication and information effectiveness up to the development of more compact layouts.

## 3  Indoor Gardening: An Extra Attraction to Compensate for Waiting Time and Organize Human Flow

A characteristic feature of cities in the AZRF is their targeted provision of gathering spaces. These spaces were considered strategic in the development of Arctic cities in Russia as they contribute to maintain population's mental well-being under extreme climatic conditions of low temperature, snowdrifts, strong winds and stand long periods of darkness during the winter [17]. Community spaces in the AZRF are normally provided as theatres, libraries, clubs and sport facilities (mainly in large cities), indoor activities which can function throughout the long and extreme periods in which going outdoors is inhospitable or unsafe. The use of indoor landscaping as a core for community gathering is underexplored. However, once considered too expensive indoor green spaces are now more affordable through new technologies [18]. This opens an interesting opportunity for the design of TIH in which compensating for waiting time by enabling/promoting the distribution and use of green spaces can also aid in creating community hubs.

Green elements can be central in promoting well-being and community integration, even more so in extreme climates such as the one of the AZRF where they are quite rare. They can "overcompensate or generate artificial interiors that normalize conditions, reverting them to familiar temperature latitudes where most people live" [17] thus enabling a smoother transition from one condition to another during seasonal migrations. Their viability can be justified by the need to enhance travellers' experience, qualitatively improving several types of opportunity spaces and by aiding in temperature and moisture regulation of indoor environments that they would produce in return. Landscaping features can be adequately disposed alongside movement spaces and/or combined with amenities (such as cafes, restaurants, etc.) as well as waiting rooms and hotels, promoting sustainable architecture and developing TIH as multifunctional public spaces [19]. Besides that, they can be deployed as specific attractions in atriums acting as internal gardening and supporting social interactions.

Gardening inside and outside TIH can help to make the public space more sustainable, safe and educational [20]. However, considering landscaping as a key component of opportunity spaces alongside movement spaces implies assessing their influence in design decisions related to location and direction of pedestrian flows.

Additionally, one of the first design decisions to make concerns if these spaces will be disconnected from the climate, i.e. operated and controlled artificially, or if they will be climate adaptive and therefore potentially have seasonal use only. This suggests that, functional requirements of these spaces should be carefully crafted in relation to how they can potentially contribute to improve the experience of travellers passing through movement spaces and/or be used as opportunity spaces themselves by fulfilling specific community needs and/or hosting specific types of social activities.

From these set of functional requirements, design parameters such as the following can then be defined, to support these spaces' distribution, shape and sizing:

- Linear landscaping for pedestrian malls, aboveground crossings and concourses;
- Group landscaping of recreation areas, halls, atriums, foyers, lobbies;
- Solitary-dot landscaping of recreations, halls, atriums, foyers, lobbies;
- Systematic landscaping of recreations, halls, atriums, indoor areas for baggage claim;
- Vertical landscaping in separately standing vertical gardening modules and pots on walls, pillars and columns.

Related maintenance considerations need to be factored in the design specification as design constraints to allow irrigation, sanitation, replacement, and pruning. These constraints cannot interfere with movement spaces as this could disrupt pedestrian flow by creating risks for travellers' safety, obstructing visibility and hindering internal way-finding. BIM can provide an initial environment for safety analysis and the detection of functional clashes [21] and once connected to dynamic thermal simulations (to verify the potential for these spaces to provide thermal comfort), space syntax, and pedestrian flow simulations aid in improving the quality of design specifications. The design of green spaces and of the surrounding areas has hence to be perfectly integrated as to satisfy their programmatic use.

Different types of physical and cognitive interactions between green spaces and pedestrian flows can be assessed through pedestrian flow simulations and Space Syntax analysis as part of Environmental Psychology studies. Space syntax can help in creating enclosed green spaces that trigger small or larger groups' social interaction (e.g. by using the Clustering index), promote safety through co-awareness (Connectivity index), invite people to stay in a place where they can look at others' (Integration index); which means that it could help quantifying the 'Interaction' qualities of green pockets [22]. Also, Space Syntax can be used to explore space configurations in 3D, therefore accounting for the visual integration of vertical landscaping in the design and its influence on the visibility of vertical signalling [23].

To the best of the authors' knowledge, there is no simulation tool comprehensive enough to deal simultaneously with these different simulation domains, meaning the effective deployment and distribution of green spaces inside TIHs calls for more research related to integrated software development. Current parametric design environments (e.g. Dynamo for Revit or Grasshopper for Rhyno) tend to integrate different types of building performance assessment methods (airflow, thermal, daylight, spatial etc.) but are not sufficiently well connected to pedestrian flow simulations or Space Syntax.

## 4  Pedestrian Flow in TIHs to Assess and Inform Design

Quantitative methods and simulation tools in general are not sufficiently used to predict and simulate the dynamics and interactions of passengers' flows in TIHs in the AZRF and, in the Western Europe, they started being used quite recently [5]. If added to that, one considers there is insufficient unified automated control system of the transport complex and a lack of electronic data available for passengers about the network in general, improvements in relation to total travel time in AZRF become limited [24]. In most cases, the focus tends to be on design parameters related to transport network demands, mainly to rationalize infrastructure costs and reduce vehicle travel time. However, 'soft' design parameters such as those listed in Table 1 should be used for specific tasks such as to configure key connections within terminal spaces as well as the links between terminals and the city.

**Table 1.** Design parameters for movement spaces within TIH buildings.

| Type of connection | Design parameters for access/entry points to terminal | Design parameter for movement spaces inside the terminal |
|---|---|---|
| Pedestrian | Sidewalks, pedestrian areas and squares, alleys, landscaping areas, entrance and exit from the open parking lot, etc. | Horizontal – paths, corridors, pedestrian malls<br>Vertical - Escalators, lifts, stairs, ramps |
| Vehicles | Open Parking, drop-off area, bus stops, private hired vehicles area, etc. | Underground and surface parking, entrance groups, ramps, car lifts |

Connections are central in the design of TIH buildings and can be initially analysed in terms of hybrid origin-destination/space representations as proposed in [1]. However, connections should be designed not only according to transport safety and efficiency but also with regards to enabling cognitive ease during spatial navigation, effortless movement and environmental comfort, which can be seen as a holistic requirement including adequate temperatures up to a pleasant journey [25]. Besides that, connections should be adequate to effectively accommodate elderly and people with disabilities, promoting social inclusion and well-being through movement without borders for all.

The final shape and size of the aforementioned design parameters should primarily account for the density, speed and direction of flows considering a wide range of special cases. A commonly employed method prescribed by statutory authorities and building regulations in Russia is the empirical formula, based on a gas/hydrodynamic analogy, proposed by Predtechesky and Milinskii [26] which relates speed, density of flow and path capacity with each other and therefore is able to predict how flow characteristics change in relation to different widths and route types, how crowding and bottlenecking happen in a path with insufficient capacity as well as how convergence and divergence, merging and branching of flows can be determined. Despite being easy to use and requiring very simple computation, the method does not take into account the non-homogeneity of flow speeds, which means for instance it cannot account for the needs of people with limited mobility (PLM), nor "special cases of pedestrian flow (e.g. movement at high density conditions, crossing flows and contra-flows, etc.)" [26]. A more advanced method is proposed by Kholshevnikov [26, 27] who investigates the effect of emotional state and nature of pathway in travel speed stating that once a threshold density is exceeded, flow speed will change. Proposals for connecting travel speed with people's physical ability and density of crowd enabling a series of considerations on how these affect cross flows, contra-flows, movement in routes with unlimited width and movement through openings are outlined. More advanced and stochastic model are developed to relate travel speed with inter-person distance and density of flow.

Gas-hydrodynamic analogy models are good for assessing high density crowd behaviour, such as in emergency situations. They are also suitable to cope with situations in which pedestrians respond to group forces rather than individual needs. However, they are not really suitable to cope with pedestrian undertaking random decisions, e.g. adopting alternative routes within the building by going shopping instead of going to the platform, etc. Thus, for instance a massive outflow of visitors to the TIH shopping areas would load pedestrian mobility interchanges to the utmost and creates traffic jams already at the exit from the parking lot, significantly overloading those located around the street. The flow of people in such a situation would provoke a discomfort for those reaching the terminal because the sizing of pathways was based on regulations and standards for building evacuation which do not consider the fact that people can go to the TIH for shopping. Essentially, pathways will be geometrically sized and shaped based on the former rather than also taking the latter into consideration.

The gas-hydrodynamic analogy is a basic tool in aiding design assessment and analysis of pedestrian flow in large buildings [27] meaning the method can be used to suitably size both peak and average flows within TIHs. With insufficient substantiation of the design solution, design proposals do not withstand the extreme load of human flow and consequently density thresholds are rapidly exceeded and crowding or queuing conditions occur. This, instantly reduces the perceived comfort of the TIH space for travellers, increasing total travelling time, and furthermore, creates a threat to the safety of children and people with limited mobility. Therefore, permissible density should be determined for both peak and average flows, so the pathway with lowest carrying capacity among the following can be adequately sized considering:

- Flow from local transportation to the TIH;
- Flow from long-distance routes to the TIH;
- Flow within the TIH (from decision space to transport, between transport modes and between decision spaces);
- Flow from targeted visits to TIH related functions (commercial premises).

However, the estimation of pedestrian flow density is a non-trivial issue because empirical flow density estimations show large variations and lack consistency [26]. An acceptable approximation for flow density estimation is obtained when using the G.F. Voronoi algorithm [28] due to their capacity of generating an optimised subdivision of spaces into sub-regions whose boundaries are organically defined depending on the distribution of seeds points. The algorithm can be applied at any scale, meaning Voronoi diagrams could also be used to optimize the configuration of existing TIH plans having irregular morphologies [29]. Overall, using a Voronoi diagram could be a reasonable strategy to address problems related to facility location and zoning of elements within buildings as well as in cities as this method works with geometric proximity to trace regions of influence in space. Using simulations to aid space distribution with shortest connections can be extremely effective especially when the aim is to minimize the total length of movement spaces inside the building. This can be achieved either through simulations (e.g. via using Voronoi algorithms as described above) or through physical models such as those used by for instance Frei Otto to find minimal surface, following a well-known form-finding optimisation method [30].

Connecting the previously mentioned Voronoi algorithm, Voronoi diagrams or even more complex form finding principles with the results of the gas-hydrodynamic analogy to calculate and then appropriately accommodate pedestrian flows in TIH buildings suggests a clear route to use parametric analysis and parametric/generative design tools to find original and more effective design solutions for TIHs.

Gas-hydrodynamic analogy models are considered macroscopic flow models as in these models "individuals have no autonomy neither to change their kinematic state nor to control their interactions" [34]. They are appropriate to size occupancy and capacity in relation to maximum flow and speed, meaning they can be easily applied to building design and assessment and also connected to parametric design tools as suggested in the aforementioned paragraph. On the other side of the spectrum, microscopic models "consider that each individual can control her own dynamics and can recreate with accuracy specific local interactions (collision, overtaking) or model individual interest or preferences" [31], yielding potentially different design solutions. For instance, original results were obtained in a study considering a system of "agents" moving according to an algorithm that models the behaviour of birds, which in nature move in group following approximately one unique direction. This "swarm urbanism" approach was tested in a parametric design experiment to revamp the city of Melbourne in 2009 (see Fig. 1a) [32]. Furthermore, for the parametric design of the Taipei street network, Chan and Lin from the University of Southern California [33] have proposed the use of Ants colonies' movement in a modified "swarm logic" approach (see Fig. 1b). Both methods are transferable to the design of TIHs to investigate 'logical' and preferred paths informing the internal layout of movement spaces and commercial software based on microsimulations are already available and being used in TIH refurbishment across Western Europe [5, 11].

Grounding TIH Planning decisions on the results of such simulation has the potential to deliver optimal performance and provide control to designers in relation to how design decisions affect pedestrian flow [34], empowering design experiments and aiding in the search for evidence-based design solutions. This is particularly important in the case of designing TIHs in the Arctic in which further constraints in relation to building compacity and safety need to be applied.

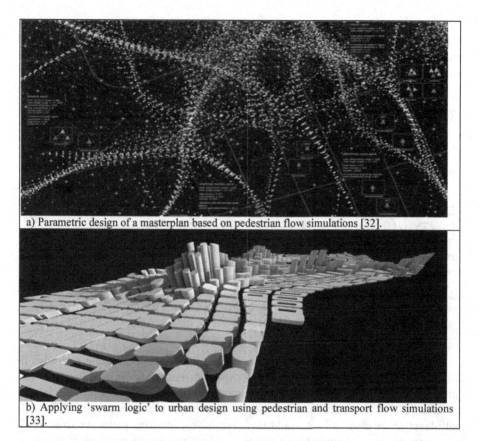

a) Parametric design of a masterplan based on pedestrian flow simulations [32].

b) Applying 'swarm logic' to urban design using pedestrian and transport flow simulations [33].

**Fig. 1.** Using agent based simulations in pedestrian movement and road network

## 5 The Impact of Compactness in Pedestrian Flow

The analysis of pedestrian flow becomes particularly complex once compactness is stated as an essential functional requirement of TIHs in harsh climates to reduce heat losses and minimize impact on the permafrost through a contained and optimized building footprint [35]. Contrarily to western Europe and Japan in which waiting areas are controlled within the comfort zone (18°C to 24°C), circulation spaces are controlled around up to 15°C and platforms are left uncontrolled, in the AZRF all spaces need to be controlled. Spaces of permanence such as sitting area should be kept within the comfort zone (between 18°C and 24°C); circulation spaces need to be controlled between 0°C and 5°C and platform areas conditioned between −15°C to 0°C to guarantee passengers safety. Once constraints related to building on the permafrost are added to that, such as compact and large building footprints with concentrated utility point built on pile foundations, considerations related to space distribution will forcefully need to be examined three dimensionally, i.e. by exploring multi-level space distributions.

Examples of multi-level space distributions include for instance the one presented in Fig. 2, with parking area, roads and bus lines, trolleybuses, trams, recreational spaces with indoor landscaping in the lower tier and shopping and leisure areas in the middle tier, and train station, railways in the upper tier.

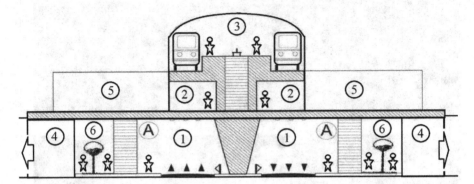

**Fig. 2.** Theoretical model of TIH: (1) Stopping points of urban ground-based passenger transport; (2) Vestibules station; (3) Railway station; (4) Car parking; (5) Distributive pedestrian level. (6) Green Vestibules for human flows.

The gas hydrodynamic analogy model is particularly useful in sizing pathways in this case because it does take into consideration different scenarios including not only different types of horizontal routes but also non-planar ones such as staircases, ramps, etc. under different circumstances of use (peak, average, emergency, etc.). TIHs with multi-level space distributions would therefore have pedestrian pathways sized similarly to entertainment complexes or stadiums, which require attention when assessing pedestrian flows in emergency situations and when restrictions are imposed on entrances for screening passengers and visitors due to different types of security requirements. In this type of space distribution, not only the sizing needs to happen in relation to full building evacuation but also the positioning of non-planar pathways and entrances. This means, for instance, entrances in the first level, stairs, escalators etc. need not only to be sized based on full building evacuation but also strategically positioned in relation to fastest exit routes, adding complexity to the layout of movement spaces calling for safety constraints and requirements related to different pairs of origin-destination to be considered together.

Particularly in multi-level space distributions, pedestrian flows become stable if enough space is given to entrances and if there is at least a duplication of vertical pathways between different levels (typically stairs plus elevators or similar automated systems). Despite more complex in terms of the sizing and layout of movement spaces, multilevel TIHs enable an efficient reallocation of pedestrian flows and better possibilities of exploring building centrality, i.e. developing key nodal spaces, potentially aiding the distribution of opportunity spaces provided with catering, trade, places for quiet rest, etc. (Figure 2). Pedestrian and transport areas with parking lots are at different levels and do not intersect, resulting in a barrier-free and more protected environment all. In addition, a rational distribution of movement spaces towards key nodal spaces are easier to be conditioned at separate temperatures, enabling the latter to be more comfortable environments for social interaction. Multi-level systems are also an interesting option in refurbishment of existing facilities as they enable incremental upgrading through the creation of multilevel platforms staging construction, which in the Arctic can only happen during the brief warm season, and facilitating internal conditioning.

# 6 Conclusions

This paper aimed to explore specific requirements and related features of TIH design in the AZRF. Fitting within a design method developed in another paper [1] by the same authors, it explored in more detail the use of green spaces as an extra-attraction on compensating for waiting time as well as methods to simulate human flow within terminals to improve travelers' comfort and speed, thus aiding in reducing total travelling time. It also discussed the complexities involved in the adoption of a multi-level schematic layout which on the one hand increases building compactness but on the other hand affects flow density and increases the complexity of design assessment.

The study suggests the use of green spaces inside TIH not only improves comfort and well-being promoting the creation of pleasant community spaces, but can also positively contribute to directing pedestrian flow. When designed together with movement spaces, they can aid in the organization and distribution of pedestrians and, if carefully crafted, influence flow density and speed as well as support the organization of movement for people with limited mobility. Further studies are needed to better address cognitive interactions between green spaces and pedestrian flow. Space Syntax can aid to that and would need to be integrated to pedestrian flow simulations together with dynamic thermal modelling to properly assess holistic performance of green spaces and their contribution in overall building performance.

The study also shows that rationalizing the distribution of movement spaces based on origin-destination alone is far from sufficient to design safe, functional and effective TIH as these paths need to be carefully set up and sized with support of pedestrian flow simulations. Different models were discussed in Sect. 4, from macroscopic models, based on the gas-hydrodynamic analogy, as recommended by Russian regulations and standards up to microscopic models such as agent based simulations which recently started being adopted to assess station refurbishment in Western Europe. Particular emphasis was given to the impact of compact layouts in pedestrian flow in which greater attention should be paid to the sizing of entrances and exits' points as well as sizing and positioning of vertical pathways. However, multi-level spatial layouts are highlighted as beneficial not only in terms of diminishing heat losses and minimizing impact on the permafrost but also for facilitating vehicles and vehicle/pedestrian segregation, and concentrating the distribution of opportunity spaces in key nodal points favoring indoor environmental control.

Further studies are necessary to better clarify which models are appropriate to be used in aiding design decisions and design assessment of different types of TIHs, considering not only building size and capacity but also its function in relation to the city. As pedestrian flows goes beyond simple internal origin-destination movement, a suitable choice for sizing and optimizing layout in TIHs designed to respond to neighborhood needs might be different than the ones used to size and design TIHs which act like city hubs. In addition, modelling of pedestrian flows still seems limited in accounting for the needs of people with limited mobility with regards to how they affect and are affected by flow density and speed. The same can be said in relation to accounting for movement of people in winter clothes, typical in AZRF, preventing functional requirements to be appropriately defined in relation to how these groups of people should be taken into account in design solutions (e.g. wider pathways, segregated routes, etc.).

Besides modelling choices, fine-tuning is still necessary to better integrate pedestrian flow models to the design process considering not only their use in parametric design but also their integration with other models such as for instance thermal simulations and space syntax so more integrated design solutions can be proposed beyond the context of the Russian Arctic.

# References

1. Bleil de Souza, C., Dunichkin, I.V., Pezzica, C.: A user-centred approach to design Transport Interchange Hus (TIH): a discussion illustrated by a case study in the Russian Arctic. In: International Conference on Computational Science and Its Applications. Under review (2019)
2. Zamyatina, N., Goncharov, R.: Population mobility and the contrasts between cities in the Russian Arctic and their southern Russian counterparts. Area Dev. Policy 3(3), 293–308 (2018)
3. HERMES – High efficient and reliable arrangements for crossmodal transport. https://cordis.europa.eu/project/rcn/93149/reporting/en. Accessed 10 Feb 2019
4. City-HUB. http://www.cityhub.imet.gr/. Accessed 10 Feb 2019
5. NODES Interchanges - New tools for designing and operation of urban transport interchanges. http://www.nodes-interchanges.eu/. Accessed 10 Feb 2019
6. Alliance – Enhancing excellence and innovation capacity in sustainable transport interchanges. http://alliance-project.eu/. Accessed 10 Feb 2019
7. Hickman, R., Chen, C.L., Chow, A., Saxena, S.: Improving interchanges in China: the experiential phenomenon. J. Transp. Geopgr. 42, 175–186 (2015)
8. Hernandez, S., Monzon, A., Ona, R.: Urban transport interchanges: a methodology for evaluating perceived quality. Transp. Res. Part A 84, 31–43 (2016)
9. Tsami, M., Adamos, G., Natrhanail, E., Budilovich, E., Yatskiv, I., Magginas, V.: A decision tree approach for achieving high customer satisfaction at urban interchanges. Transp. Telecommun. 19(3), 194–202 (2018)
10. Monzon, A., Alonso, A., Lopez-Lambas, M.: Joint analysis of intermodal long distance-last mile trips using urban interchanges in EU cities. Transp. Res. Proc. 27, 1074–1079 (2017)
11. Booth, R.: D3.3.1 Identification and specification of the key areas of interchange design. In: Hoogendoom, C. (eds.) NODES 'New tools for Design and Operation of Urban Transport InterchangeS'. Project Report. European Commission, DG Research and Innovation (2015)
12. Danilina, N., Vlasov, D.: Aspects of transport transit hubs construction management in coordination with object lifecycle projecting. In: MATEC Web of Conferences, vol. 86, p. 05017. EDP Sciences (2016)

13. Vlasov, D., Danilina, N., Shagimuratova, A.: The priority directions of public transport transit hubs development on commuter railways. In: Murgul, V., Popovic, Z. (eds.) Energy Management of Municipal Transportation Facilities and Transport, EMMFT 2017. Advances in Intelligent Systems and Computing, vol. 692, pp. 299–309. Springer, Cham (2017). https://doi.org/10.1007/978-3-319-70987-1_32

14. Dunichkin, I.: Transport interchange hubs under the conditions of the Far North. In: Murgul, V., Popovic, Z. (eds.) EMMFT 2017. AISC, vol. 692, pp. 446–452. Springer, Cham (2018). https://doi.org/10.1007/978-3-319-70987-1_47

15. Suh, N.P.: Axiomatic Design: Advances and Applications. Oxford University Press, New York (2001)

16. Kholshchevnikov, V., Korolchenko, D., Zosimova, O.: Efficiency evaluation criteria of communication paths structure in a complex of buildings of maternity and child-care institutions. In: MATEC Web of Conferences, vol. 106, p. 01037. EDP Sciences (2017)

17. Jull, M.: Toward a Northern architecture: the microrayon Arctic urban prototype. J. Archit. Educ. 70(2), 214–222 (2016)

18. Korol, O., Shushunova, N., Lopatkin, D., Zanin, A., Shushunova, T.: Application of high-tech solutions in ecodevelopment. In: MATEC Web of Conferences, vol. 251, p. 06002. EDP Sciences (2018)

19. Esaulov, G.V.: Sustainable architecture: from approaches to strategy of development. Vestnik of Tomsk State University of Architecture and Building. English version appendix (2014). No. 4

20. Krasheninnikov, A.: Structure of social space in pedestrian realm. Archit. Mod. Inf. Technol. 4(21), 1–7 (2012)

21. Cherkina, V., Shushunova, N., Zubkova, J.: Application of BIM-technologies in tasks of quality management and labour safety. In: MATEC Web of Conferences, vol. 251, p. 06004. EDP Sciences (2018)

22. Cutini, V.: Lines and squares: towards a configurational approach to the morphology of open spaces. In: Proceedings of the 4th International Space Syntax Symposium, London (2003)

23. Varoudis, T., Psarra, S.: Beyond two dimensions: architecture through three-dimensional visibility graph analysis. J. Space Syntax 5(1), 90–108 (2014)

24. Kagan, P.: Monitoring of the development of urban areas with the use of information technology. In: MATEC Web of Conferences, vol. 193, p. 05031. EDP Sciences (2018)

25. Vigier, T., Siret, D., Moreau, G., Lescop, L.: Sensitive suggestion and perception of climatic effects in virtual urban environments. In: Proceedings of the ACM Symposium on Applied Perception, p. 139. ACM (2013)

26. Kholshchevnikov, V.V., Samoshin, D.A.: Parameters of pedestrian flow for modeling purposes. In: Klingsch, W., Rogsch, C., Schadschneider, A., Schreckenberg, M. (eds.) Pedestrian and Evacuation Dynamics 2008, pp. 157–170. Springer, Heidelberg (2010). https://doi.org/10.1007/978-3-642-04504-2_12

27. Kholshchevnikov, V.V.: Experimental researches of human flow in staircases of high-rise buildings. Int. J. Appl. Eng. Res. 10(21), 42549–42552 (2015)

28. Nikolic, M., Bierlaire, M.: Pedestrian flow characterisation based on spatio-temporal Voronoi tessellations. In: 15th Swiss Transport Research Conference STRC – Ascona, 15–17 April 2015

29. Chatzikonstantinou, I.: A 3-dimensional architectural layout generation procedure for optimization applications: DC-RVD. In: Proceedings of the 32nd International Conference on Education and Research in Computer Aided Architectural Design in Europe, eCAADe: Conferences 1, vol. 1, pp. 287–296. Northumbria University, Newcastle upon Tyne (2014)

30. Goldsmith, N.: The physical modeling legacy of Frei Otto. Int. J. Space Struct. 31(1), 25–30 (2016)

31. Martinez-Gil, F., Lozano, M., Garcia-Fernandez, I., Fernandez, F.: Modeling, evaluation, and scale on artificial pedestrians: a literature review. ACM Comput. Surv. **50**(5), 72 (2017)
32. Leach, N.: Swarm urbanism. Archit. Des. **79**(4), 56–63 (2009)
33. Chan, A., Lin, Y.: Taipei. Ant Urbanism. In: Leach, N. (ed.) Digital Cities. Wiley, London (2009)
34. Vlasov, D., Shirokaya, N.: Development of a polyfunctional structure of transport hubs in Smart City. In: IOP Conference Series: Materials Science and Engineering, vol. 365, no. 2, p. 022022. IOP Publishing (2018)
35. Evreenova, N.Yu.: The choice of parameters of transport hubs, formed with the participation of rail transport. Thesis Ph.D. (technical). Moscow State University of Railway Engineering - MIIT, Moscow (2014)

# Location Theory and Circular Economy. Demolition, Constructions and Spatial Organization of Firms – An Applied Model to Sardinia Region. The Case Study of the New Cagliari Stadium

Ginevra Balletto[1(✉)], Giuseppe Borruso[2(✉)], and Giovanni Mei[1]

[1] DICAAR – Department of Civil and Environmental Engineering
and Architecture, University of Cagliari, Via Marengo, 2, Cagliari, Italy
balletto@unica.it, ing.gmei@gmail.com
[2] DEAMS –Department of Economics, Business, Mathematics and Statistical
Sciences "Bruno de Finetti", University of Trieste, Trieste, Italy
giuseppe.borruso@deams.units.it

**Abstract.** The paper tackles a classical topic of location theory, as the Weber theory of industrial location within a modern framework of building construction and its consideration into the circular economy debate. Starting from a research project involving universities, construction and recycling enterprises and public bodies in Sardinia Island (Italy), the authors propose a model of industrial location that, starting from the assumption of the classical Weberian model, consider it both in a theoretical fashion and applying it to a real-world case study. The project of the new football stadium of Cagliari involves the demolition of the existing stadium, which will represent a source of 'secondary' raw materials for the realization of the new sport facility. The authors discuss about the 'best' locations for concrete factories, according to different scenarios, considering the insertion of a new 'material source' in the circular economy concept.

**Keywords:** Location theory · Industrial symbiosis · MEISAR ·
Circular economy · Recycled aggregates

## 1 Introduction

The paper starts from a set of considerations about circular economy in the field of constructions, with particular reference to the recycled aggregate concrete [1, 2]. Sardinia represents a closed market for Natural aggregate materials and Recycled

This study is supported by MEISAR (https://meisar.org/en/) Building materials and sustainable infrastructure - recycled aggregates - POR Sardinia FESR 2014/2020 - Priority axis I - "Scientific Research, Technological Development and Innovation" Action 1.1.4 Top-Down and RE-MINE - Restoration and rehabilitation of abandoned mining sites, funded by the Foundation of Sardinia (Grant CUP F72F16003160002).
    The paper derives from the joint reflections of the three authors. However, Ginevra Balletto realized Sects. 1, 3.1, 4.2, 4.4 and 5. Giovanni Mei wrote Sects. 2 and 4.1. Giuseppe Borruso wrote Sects. 3.2 and 4.3.

S. Misra et al. (Eds.): ICCSA 2019, LNCS 11621, pp. 535–550, 2019.
https://doi.org/10.1007/978-3-030-24302-9_38

Aggregate (RA) materials [3]. It is not possible, in fact, to interchange those materials with other Italian regions or send waste from demolitions towards these same destinations. Building constructions and demolition need proximal locations of prime (and secondary) sources as well as for waste disposal [4]. Extraction of prime materials (resources), processing, waste disposal, processing of recycled (second) materials, re-inserting them into the production process must happen within the regional territory [5]. Also, concrete batching products must reach their destination from the processing plants within a range of 30 km [6]. Over such distance the products are degraded and their quality is reduced [7]. This needs to be coupled with the analysis of characters and quality of materials, as in the framework of MEISAR project [8, 9].

The general Italian economic situation of (private in particular) building constructions [10], is stagnating [11], with mainly public local authorities - municipalities, regions, etc. - having developed construction plans of public buildings and infrastructure. The potential markets both for Natural and Recycled Aggregates are therefore related to this kind of economic decision makers [12]. We developed a model of optimal location of industrial activities related to resources extraction, manipulation of natural aggregates, treatment of waste from demolition, production of recycled aggregates and, finally, residual waste treatment and disposal, by means of the elaboration of a geographical model of industrial location and its consideration within a circular economy framework [13]. The remaining part of the paper is organized as follows. Section 2 concerns the data collection process, at Region Sardinia level to estimate the quantities of materials computed over the different territories. A map has been realized with the data described in the first section, georeferenced, visualized and shared to provide a working instrument for sharing information and an analytical tool for the location of the different actors involved. In Sect. 3 we propose the adaptation of a classical model of industrial location to consider a circular economical approach, considering putting into the market part of the waste deriving from demolition, hypothesising a set of localization scenarios for the treatment plants (batching plants). In Sect. 4 the case study is described, that of the demolition of the Sant'Elia football stadium and the construction of the new facility. We estimate its potential of waste production that - after a proper treatment - can be put into the circle of recycling and allow a network integration among the different actors - including companies belonging to the cluster MEISAR with positive consequences on the building construction sector in the Metropolitan Area of Cagliari and Southern Sardinia. Concluding remarks highlight major results and future developments of the research.

## 2  Data Collection and Mapping

### 2.1  Data Collection

The data collection phase aims to provide a framework on the production and management of construction and demolition waste (CDW), with particular attention to those CER codes actually destined for the production of RA for the packaging of concrete, the firm whose property is the subject of the MEISAR research project. Data collection but sought to extend attention to other products and sectors, directly or indirectly connected, in the production of aggregates for concrete, i.e., the natural aggregate quarries and concrete mixing centers. However, the "raw material" for the production of RA is constituted by the aggregates coming from the construction and demolition activities, the CDWs, which can be cataloged as code CER 17 of the European Waste Catalog. Table 1 shows CER 17 classification.

**Table 1.** CER 17 - Construction and demolition wastes (including excavated soil from contaminated sites)

| CER 17 | Construction and demolition wastes |
|--------|-------------------------------------|
| 17 01 | Concrete, bricks, tiles and ceramics |
| 17 02 | Wood, glass and plastic |
| 17 03 | Bituminous mixtures, coal tar and tarred product |
| 17 04 | Metals (including their alloys) |
| 17 05 | Soil (including excavated soil from contaminated sites, stones and dredging spoil) |
| 17 06 | Insulation materials and asbestos-containing construction materials |
| 17 08 | Gypsum-based construction material |
| 17 09 | Other construction and demolition waste |

In general, the typical CDW composition is shown in Table 2.

**Table 2.** Typical CDW composition - % by weight (Fonte ARPA Regione Veneto, 2018)

| Typical CDW composition | % by weight |
|--------------------------|-------------|
| Concrete | 10% |
| Reinforced concrete | 20% |
| Brick | 50% |
| Asphalt | 5% |
| Excavated soil | 6% |
| Wood, paper and | 2% |
| Plastic | 5% |
| Steel | 3% |

Not all the fractions of the CDW are destined for the production of RA, but only concrete, armed and not, which constitute 30% by weight of the total of the CDW and which can be cataloged in the sub-category CER 17.01.

The CDW, like all waste, must be managed in accordance with what is defined as the Waste Hierarchy (Article 179 of Legislative Decree 152/2006 - Environmental Consolidation Act). The law establishes the hierarchy on waste management: 1. Prevention; 2. Reuse and preparation for reuse; 3. Recycle; 4. Recovery; 5. Disposal. Once the Prevention that is preparatory to the production of the waste has been removed, the other operations can be summarized in Recovery and Disposal. Typical recovery operations on CDW Management are classified in the environmental regulation (D.lgs 152/2006) with the code R5 (Inorganic substance recycling reclamation) and R13 (Storage of waste pending any of the operations numbered R1 to R12 - excluding temporary storage, pending collection, on the site where the waste is produced). Typical Disposal operation on CDW management are classified in the same environmental regulation with the code D1 (Landfill).

The data collection phase aimed to investigate what were the productions of CDWs in Sardinia with particular reference to the CER 17 code and what were the operating methods for managing them on the island. The first source for the study of production and management of CDWs in Sardinia was the Special Waste Report 2017 (ISPRA 2018) which provides data on the production of CDW at national and regional level. The first step was to find a data source that was not limited to the provision of data at the regional level but provided greater territorial detail. This data source was extrapolated from ENVIRONMENTAL AREA, portal on environmental compliance to be borne by companies, service offered by the Italian Chambers of Commerce handicraft agriculture (CCIAA) and managed by Ecocerved (https://www.ecocamere.it/), company consortium of the Italian system of Chambers of Commerce operating in the field of environmental information systems. In Sardinia there are 4 CCIAAs (Cagliari, Oristano, Nuoro and Sassari), whose territorial competences correspond to the borders of the old four provinces before the 2001 reform that brought them to eight. As of today, only the Cagliari and Sassari Chamber of Commerce have adhered to the Environment Area portal and provide annual statistical data on waste referring to MUD data (Single Environmental Declaration Model), which producers and waste managers must complete annually with reference to the year previous one.

The same data were obtained, upon request to the missing Chamber of Commerce and Ecocerved, also for the Chamber of Commerce of Nuoro and Oristano. The available data have been studied and analyzed in order to obtain the necessary information, useful for determining the productions and the management activities of the CDW that can be used for the production of RA (Fig. 1).

The Table 3 shows the type of waste management (CER 17) in Sardinia, and underlines the singularity of each area about CER 17 management.

The research focused on identifying companies operating in the field of inert construction and demolition waste, starting from the 4 companies participating in the project[1]. All the companies authorized to operate in the inert waste sector have been identified in the available and mapped databases, with the criterion expressed in the following sections. Companies adhering to the Cluster were asked for more informative detail on the MUD declarations presented, while the other companies identified are administering a form that will be integrated into the geographical data. Finally, natural aggregates, inert waste landfills - the last step in the waste hierarchy - and concrete plants were searched through specialized websites or public databases.

---

[1] The companies are the Recycle by Quartucciu, the SMT of Sarroch, the Ecofrantumazioni of Olbia and the Ecoinerti of Iglesias

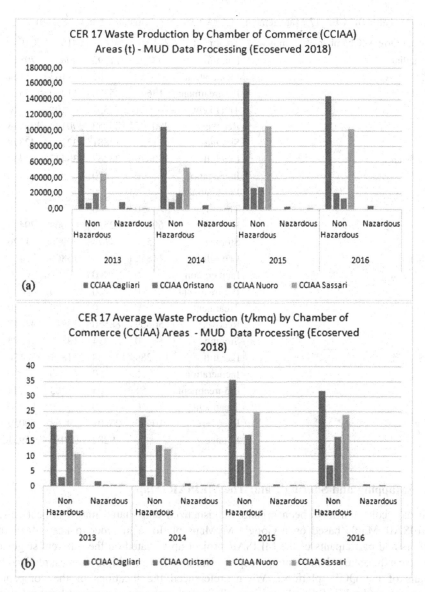

**Fig. 1.** Declared production of CDW - CER 17 by Chamber of Commerce (CCIAA) areas - Sardinia (a); Average declared production (t/km²) of CDW - CER 17 by Chamber of Commerce (CCIAA) areas - Sardinia (b)

**Table 3.** CER 17 Management - CCIAA Cagliari, Oristano, Nuoro, Sassari

| Data Origin (Chamber of Commerce) | Treatment | 2013 | 2014 | 2015 | 2016 |
|---|---|---|---|---|---|
| Cagliari | Landfill | 93702 | 71692 | 90880 | 79817 |
| | Incineration | 50 | 81 | 103 | 124 |
| | Pre-treatment | 13639 | 5370 | 11200 | 5564 |
| | Treatment | 171 | 352 | 198 | 16 |
| | Recovery | 200295 | 184052 | 290122 | 429543 |
| | Storage | 11527 | 34881 | 32140 | 42378 |
| Oristano | Landfill | 30879 | 26267 | 38433 | 53738 |
| | Incineration | 0 | 0 | 0 | 0 |
| | Pre-treatment | 0 | 0 | 0 | 0 |
| | Treatment | 0 | 0 | 0 | 0 |
| | Recovery | 69603 | 82530 | 97068 | 79449 |
| | Storage | 577 | 4174 | 5990 | 1726 |
| Nuoro | Landfill | 11852 | 355 | 15806 | 6461 |
| | Incineration | 0 | 0 | 0 | 0 |
| | Pre-treatment | 0 | 0 | 0 | 0 |
| | Treatment | 0 | 0 | 0 | 0 |
| | Recovery | 56669 | 88550 | 83914 | 44417 |
| | Storage | 0 | 27634 | 18858 | 16583 |
| Sassari | Landfill | 148289 | 143748 | 191851 | 134186 |
| | Incineration | 0 | 0 | 0 | 0 |
| | Pre-treatment | 51 | 105 | 103 | 144 |
| | Treatment | 0 | 0 | 0 | 0 |
| | Recovery | 10490 | 23504 | 29065 | 50059 |
| | Storage | 0 | 9282 | 23980 | 5931 |

## 2.2  Mapping and Sharing Data: The MEISAR_Map

The data collected have been organized, visualized and shared into a project called "MEISAR_Map", based on a Google MyMaps platform in order to keep all of the authors and participants of the MEISAR project up-to-dated on the different stages of the research, obtained elaborating geographical data from multiple sources, realized by means of the QGIS platform. We georeferenced the locations of the companies belonging to the MEISAR cluster, as well as all the players at regional level involved into the different processes of production, use and disposal of natural and recycled aggregates: quarry concessions, aggregate treatment and recycling plants, batching plants, worksites, landfills, MEISAR cluster firms (Fig. 2).

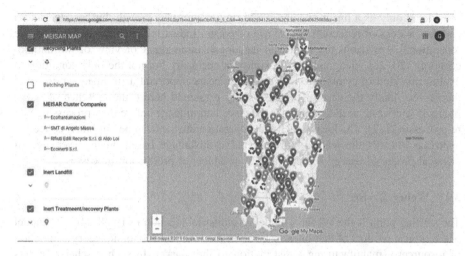

**Fig. 2.** The MEISAR_MAP and a sample of the data realized. http://bit.ly/MEISAR_MAP

Geo-referencing was performed using the geocoding service provided by the Google platform was used, while data coming from official sources as RAS - Sardinia Region authority held plane coordinates in national geodetic systems and were loaded without further corrections. The data have been integrated and controlled by means of the direct observation and check on different sources[2].

## 3    The Model – Circular Economy and Industrial Location à la Weber Revised

### 3.1    Circular Economy and Industrial Symbiosis

The research carried is interesting within a theoretical framework of a circular economy of recycled aggregates [14, 15], revising a classical model of industrial location adapted to the current situation. That has been done both analysing the theoretical foundations but also trying to hypothesize practical effects and evidences, to benefit the MEISAR clusters both in terms of the academics and of the industries involved (n 5 companies of aggregate recovery).

The circular economy concept within the classical industrial localization models is consistent with the industrial symbiosis, in considering to-date challenges of re-using par of waste of a production - or demolition - process again into the production process [16].

Such concept is associated with the theories carried on by authors like Georgescu-Roegen, Ayres, Kuznets, et al. [17–19], in which the economical process must not be

---

[2] I.e. in the case of data on quarries and their licenses the 'Quarries Cadaster', although quite outdated, dating back to 2007, has been checked and data crossed with existing licenses, verifying their locations by observing the regional orthoimages and satellites maps in Google Maps.

considered only as a linear one and based on a continuous growth, but inserted into a circular process of reduction and re-use of waste. Industrial symbiosis appears as the 'operational arm' from the industrial and localization point of view of the circular economy [20, 21]. Geographical proximity is necessary but not the only condition to exploit this kind of symbiosis. However, it appears important as in many cases – and this is very likely the case of the case study presented here – the presence of bulky products and waste need to minimize the costs and mileage before their processing and re-processing [22]. The idea is such that separate industries can be put into a collective approach towards the reach of a competitive advantage based on the exchange of physical products, energy sources, and by-products of production processes [23].

## 3.2  Weber Revised

The starting point is the Weber's model of industrial location in 1909 [24]. The model was a typical product of that linear scheme of the classical economic theory: extraction of resources - manufacturing - distribution to the market. In such a scheme, enters space: namely as an origin of resources and as place of disposal of waste, without caring about their destiny. In the present case, the production is characterized by the presence of two different kinds of materials, as raw materials - extracted from quarries - and 'second' raw materials - as those coming from recycling. In doing this, the model become a 'circular one', as waste - or part of waste - is reused. A spatial consequence is that destinations of final products become also locations of origin of new materials.

Going to the roots of the model, Alfred Weber in his essay on the "Theory of Industrial Location" set some simplifying assumptions, as the fixed locations of all inputs and market, and the fact that the manufacturing firm chooses the best location where the sum of the total transport costs, incoming and outgoing, is minimized. In the most basic version of the model, the industry uses only one input material localized at a given location of a homogeneous plane and sells its output in a unique market localized in the same plane. Technology is allowing constant returns of scale and not allowing input substitution.

In Weber's hypotheses it is important the classification of resources. Weber talks about localized materials (inputs), as those having a fixed location in space, furtherly organized in "pure" - they are completely used into the production process and therefore in the final product - and "gross" - the lose some weight during the production process, and therefore having only a part into the final product. Other resources are defined as ubiquitous or non-localized, being fairly uniformly distributed and accessible in space.

The target is a localization leading to minimizing transport costs, with transport considered as relying on a unique mode. That happens, in Weber's simplified model, where there is only one site for materials and one for the market, by means of minimizing the following formula:

$$T = t w_r * d(R) + t w_m * d(M)$$

With:

T = Total Transport Cost (in ton-km)
$w_r$ = weight per unit of input
$t$ = Transport Cost in € per ton-km
$w_m$ = weight per unit of output
d(R) = Distance RF (resource site - production site)
d(M) = Distance FM (production site – market)

The manufacturing firm F will locate in a point between the resource site R and the market place M. Such location will depend on the weight of the materials compared to the final product. Weber introduced an indicator called MI = Material index: MI = weight of the localized resources/weight of the final product; Pure Resources: MI = 1; Gross Resources: MI > 1

In the case of pure resources entering completely into the final product, no waste will be available, and therefore the location will happen at an intermediate point between R and M (first case, Fig. 4). In the case in which gross resources prevail, (IM > 1), localization will occur at a close proximity of the resources site R, to minimize transport costs of waste (third case, Fig. 3).

An extreme case is given by the localization in the market-place M, (second case, Fig. 4) in the case in which the final product is mainly realized using perishable resources available at the same market location - as water, for instance, considered as ubiquitous.

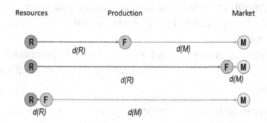

**Fig. 3.** Location à la Weber in the simplified model (along a line)

## 4   The Case Study

The opportunity to insert the proposed model into a real case is given by the Sant'Elia Stadium, which is scheduled to be demolished together with the realization of a new facility for the Cagliari Football Team. The following actions - and related sections - have been performed: Sect. 4.1 Quantification of concrete in present Stadium and quantification of the extractable concrete (main material) of the current stadium (Sant'Elia); Sect. 4.2 Policy considerations.

## 4.1    Recycled Aggregates (RA) from Sant'Elia Stadium

The characterization of the concrete of the Sant'Elia Stadium refers to the beams of the second ring and the foundation blocks. Before performing the demolition of part of these structures, tests were carried out to evaluate the mechanical performance of concrete. The obtained debris, divided by source, were crushed to obtain two types of coarse RA, both with grain size 4–16 mm. The demolition materials of the beam and foundation have been kept separate for the subsequent characterization tests according to the tests foreseen in the UNI EN 12620: 2008 standard for CE marking level 2+ [25]. Six concrete mixes, with 30%, 50% and 80% of total mass of coarse RA, were produced in order to obtain a description of physical and mechanical properties. An additional mix of ordinary concrete with only natural aggregates was produced for comparison. Tests on recycled concrete (workability values at 14 and 28 days, compression) gave the following encouraging results:

- Recycled concrete produced with coarse recycled aggregates, even when the natural aggregates replacement percentages reaches 80%, as shown equivalent mechanical performances then those of ordinary concrete.
- The performance of recycled concrete is not related to the parent concrete mechanical characteristics.
- The results showed that the care in the study of the design of the mixture is fundamental for competitive recycled concretes.
- The durability tests on recycled concrete are in progress, the first results obtained show optimal performance of concretes even in the long term.
- The selective demolition of the structures is fundamental to obtain concrete recycled aggregates immediately marketable, with size distribution similar to those required by the concrete plants.
- Following the results presented and the extensive international literature on the topic, Public Administrations must produce specifications that provide the use of recycled concretes.

After these interesting results, volumetric quantification was carried out instead of the concrete of the Sant'Elia stadium.

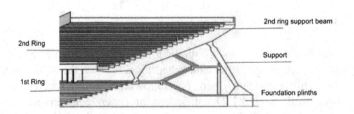

**Fig. 4.** Section and detail of the Sant'Elia stadium - Cagliari

From the design drawings (Fig. 4) and site inspections, together with the characterization of the materials, it was possible to make a preliminary estimate of the potential reusable material. The total volume of recoverable concrete is therefore equal to approximately 8.880 m³. These 8,800 m³ in place are destined to grow if in pile; the literature confirmed also by the information received from the cluster companies has faced a growth coefficient of 2.5–3, or m³ of RA in a heap equal to 22,000–26,400 m³

## 4.2 Policy Considerations

The case is an interesting one as the new facility will be realized in close proximity to the existing one and the process of demolition/construction will occur in a condition of spatial and temporal closeness. This is interesting in terms of production of waste, their treatment and reuse in recycled aggregates, as they have important implications from the urbanistic and planning point of view, given the effects generated by such activities in the area of Cagliari and South Sardinia.

With reference the volumes of materials estimated in the previous section, that for the considerations described above must be packaged and placed in the concrete packaging process within a distance not exceeding 30 km from the stadium. Therefore all the companies potentially interested in the circular economy process - recycling plants and concrete mixing centers - will be those included within this range in response to the demand for concrete for the new stadium, using the ARs from the current stadium.

To activate this process, which is moreover desirable, it is necessary in the tender to provide for the use of the RAs at least in the percentage of 30% to be sent in the packaging of the concrete on the aggregates, thus falling under the ordinary regime envisaged by the legislation in line with the guidelines of the Plan for Ecological Public Procurement in Sardinia Region [26].

## 4.3 Contextualization of Weber Model

The case study presented here can be inserted into the Weberian localization theory in a linear context, with two fixed locations, one of extraction of resources and one of market (M), together with a production site in site between them (F).

With reference to the original model - represented by Scenario 0 in Fig. 5 - the proposal here foresees a set of basic hypotheses.

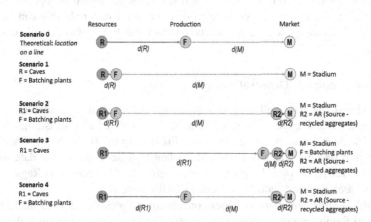

**Fig. 5.** The Weberian localization model of batching plants in a circular economy

The point R indicates to a generic extraction site - a quarry - from where Natural aggregates are taken as raw materials. M is the market site, or the area of Sant'Elia Stadium where the new facility will be realized. F indicates the place of production of aggregates, the batching plants.

In its more simplified version the model foresees four scenarios (Fig. 7), although in more realistic simulations considering also real quantities of materials and products, waste and capacity of production and processing plants, it will be possible to evaluate further scenarios with multiple locations - of extraction and production - as well as to hypothesize more efficient allocations.

– Scenario 1 is the classical case. The batching plant, F is localized in close proximity of resources. Waste recycling from demolition is not considered.
– From Scenario 2 on, the market site M is considered as a second site of resources (R2), together with quarries (R1). The localization of the batching plant F remains in proximity of raw materials but R2 becomes important for extracting 'second' raw materials. In this case, however, as these latter need a further processing, a transport of second raw materials from the extraction site to processing site (F), still localized in R1, and again to the market M.
– In Scenario 3, the production plant F is localized in close proximity of the market (M) and second raw materials (R2). Such scenario is an optimal one when the share of second raw materials (Recycled Aggregates) is prevalent and the recourse to standard raw materials is scarce. In any case the cost of transport of raw materials to the processing plant and location is considered.
   Scenarios 2 and 3 are extreme cases as they are based on the hypotheses that foresee, respectively that standard raw materials (NA - Natural Aggregates) are dominant - in the first case - and second raw materials (RA - Recycled Aggregates) are - in the second one.
– Scenario 4 identifies cases à la Weber where a batching plant could be localized in a point F in an intermediate position in which the cost function of transport of raw materials - first or second; NA or RA - is minimized, not necessarily therefore foreseen a location of a batching plant is in proximity of a resources' site.

A part from the theoretical aspects, such scenarios are linked by operational considerations, among theme, the percentage of demolition materials that can be transformed into RA, that in the specific case could reach the 100% of structural concrete of the stadium.

## 4.4 Some Empirical Observations

We considered the data collected and organized referring them particularly to the Cagliari area – Municipality – Metropolitan area. We created a set of isolines from the Sant'Elia Stadium location, spaced by 5 km distance up to 30 km, being this distance the maximum one drivable from a batching plant to a destination. The data used are those above described, plus the graphical road network of the Sardegna Region, where the service areas/shortest path algorithms in QGIS were run.

In Table 4 some summary statistics concerning the presence of dedicated plants in the Cagliari Region are presented. A first general observation we can do is that a wide percentage of plants and disposal sites are actually located very close to the urban area of Cagliari, in an area of intermediate dimension between the Municipality of Cagliari and its Metropolitan area.

**Table 4.** Summary statistics of plants in the area

| Plants | Plants within 30 km from Sant'Elia stadium | Total Plants in Sardinia | % Plants 30 km from Sant'Elia over total |
|---|---|---|---|
| Batching plants | 9 | 61 | 14.75 |
| MEISAR cluster | 1 | 4 | 25.00 |
| Quarries | 15 | 91 | 16.48 |
| Waste disposal | 12 | 61 | 19.67 |
| Treatment plants | 20 | 101 | 19.80 |
| Total | 57 | 318 | 17.92 |

A further visual analysis (Fig. 6) can help also in deriving some extra information on the spatial distribution and concentration of the plants. We can notice how batching plants are furtherly concentrated and in close proximity of the Cagliari urban area, with 7 plants within 15 km of the Sant'Elia area. Another consideration is that all the other three categories considered (quarries, waste disposal and treatment plants) are generally located at close proximity to each other, forming in many cases some real clusters in

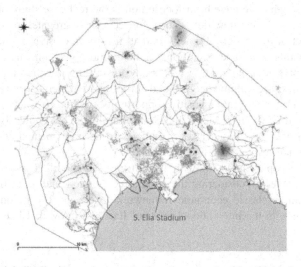

**Fig. 6.** The spatial distribution and concentration (heat map) of batching plants (grey dots), quarries, waste disposal, treatment plants (lighter dots) within 30 km from the Sant'Elia Stadium (orange and red area). Highlighted: The Donori Cluster (North) and the Quartu Sant'Elena (East) Cluster. (Color figure online)

the area. We can particularly notice two clusters in the Eastern part of the area considered (Eastern part of Quartu Municipality) and North-eastern of the urban area (Donori).

These clusters confirm the co-existence in space of plants whose activity is strictly related and follow principle of geographical industrial location theory. Also, batching plants tend to be 'attracted' by the areas of extraction/processing – here also confirming partly the theory and the Scenario 1 case.

As a general remark, we can notice that batching plants are located at intermediate locations between the built-up urban area and the extraction/disposal sites, and very rarely located in proximity to them. The presence of the two clusters confirm that the metropolitan city of Cagliari is the most suitable territorial dimension for developing governance policies for the re-use of RA [12].

## 5   Conclusions

The present research represents an intermediate point within a wider research project that is mainly based on the analysis of concrete and natural aggregates used in the construction sector and its usability in a circular economy system. What we carried on so far represents both a conceptual and an operational framework for modeling the circular economical concept among an industrial localization model and to understand what could be the real and actual implications of implementing, in Sardinia, a system of reusing waste from construction into the production process as recycled aggregates.

The case study appeared interesting as Sardinia appears as a closed market for both natural and recycled aggregates, being it quite difficult - if not impossible - to set flows with the continents of this kind of products and by-products.

In particular what we have been focused on is the real case study of the Sant'Elia old football stadium as an important source for recycled aggregates, particularly in line with the project of realization of a new football facility in close proximity to the, now dismissed, existing one. The operations of demolition and construction of the new facility will represent an interesting case study for putting in action a plan for a local circular economy: the volumes considered, in terms of materials, are such that their optimal use can transform into a positive opportunity for the construction system of the entire sub-region of Cagliari Metro and South Sardinia. That could also represent an interesting test-bed for a broader set of policies to be implemented at regional and - possibly - national level.

The present paper ended up with the set-up of a modified model of industrial localization capable of considering the circular economic - and industrial symbiosis - principles within a classic economic framework to develop operational governance policies, in line with the international trend of Itaca, BREAM and Leed agreements.

# References

1. de Larrard, F., Colina, H. (eds.): Concrete Recycling: Research and Practice. CRC Press, Boca Raton (2019)
2. Rodríguez-Robles, D., Van den Heede, P., De Belie, N.: Life cycle assessment applied to recycled aggregate concrete. In: de Brito, J., Agrelo, F. (eds.) New Trends in Eco-efficient and Recycled Concrete, pp. 207–256. Woodhead Publishing (2019)
3. Delvoie, S., Zhao, Z., Michel, F., Courard, L.: Market analysis of recycled sands and aggregates in NorthWest Europe: drivers and barriers. In: IOP Conference Series: Earth and Environmental Science, vol. 225, no. 1, p. 012055. IOP Publishing, January 2019
4. Balletto, G., Pani, L., Mei, G., Borruso, G.: Approcci economia circolare applicati agli stadi: dalle antiche campagne di spoglio alla demolizione con recupero di frazioni. Il caso dello stadio di Cagliari. In: Cuboni, F., Desogus, G., Quaquero, E. (eds.) Edilizia Circolare, pp. 1161–1180. Edicom Edizioni, Monfalcone (Gorizia) (2018)
5. Balletto, G. et al.: La pianificazione sostenibile delle risorse. Analisi e proposte per il dimensionamento del fabbisogno minerario di seconda categoria ad uso civile. La Sardegna come caso di studio. Franco Angeli, Milano (2005)
6. Renner, G.T.: Geography of industrial localization. Econ. Geogr. **23**(3), 167–189 (1947)
7. Pasini, C.S.: Economia industriale. Economia dei mercati imperfetti. LUISS University Press-Po, Roma (2013)
8. Materiali per l'Edilizia e le Infrastrutture Sostenibili: gli Aggregati Riciclati (MEISAR) cluster Top-Down finanziato dalla Regione Autonoma della Sardegna attraverso: POR Sardegna FESR 2014/2020 - Asse Prioritario I "Ricerca Scientifica, Sviluppo Tecnologico e Innovazione" Azione 1.1.4
9. Pani, L., Francesconi, L., Lopez Gayarre, F.: Properties of precast hollow concrete blocks using recycled concrete aggregates. In: Sardinia 2015 15th International waste management and Landfill Symposium, pp. 1–10. CISA, Coop. Libraria Editrice (2015)
10. De Angelis, G.: Il Mercato del Lavoro in Italia: una lettura a partire dal caso dell'Edilizia. Argomenti **10**, 65–82 (2018)
11. Il Mercato Delle Costruzioni in Sardegna Rapporto annuale 2016 e stime previsionali 2017. http://www.cnasarda.it/media/Estratto%20Rapporto%20Costruzioni%20marzo%202017.pdf
12. Balletto, G., Garau, C., Desogus, G., Mei, G.: Urban redevelopment and energy saving. The case of the incentives in Italy, between risks and opportunities. In: Third International Conference on Advances in Information Processing and Communication Technology-IPCT, pp. 110–114. Institute of Research Engineers and Doctors, USA (2015)
13. Lloyd, P.E., Dicken, P.: Location in Space: A Theoretical Approach to Economic Geography. Harper & Row, New York (1972)
14. Sferra, A.S.: I rifiuti in edilizia: Riuso e riciclo nell'industria 4.0. FrancoAngeli (2019)
15. Kamino, G., Gomes, S., Bragança, L.: Improving the sustainability assessment method SBTool Urban–a critical review of construction and demolition waste (CDW) indicator. In: IOP Conference Series: Earth and Environmental Science, vol. 225, no. 1, p. 012004. IOP Publishing, January 2019
16. Baldassarre, B., Schepers, M., Bocken, N., Cuppen, E., Korevaar, G., Calabretta, G.: Industrial symbiosis: towards a design process for eco-industrial clusters by integrating circular economy and industrial ecology perspectives. J. Clean. Prod. **216**, 446–460 (2019)
17. Arrow, K.J.: The economic implications of learning by doing. Rev. Econ. Stud. **29**(3), 155–173 (1962)

18. Ayres, R.U.: Industrial metabolism: theory and policy. In: Ayres, R.U., Simonis, U.E. (eds.) Industrial Metabolism: Restructuring for Sustainable Development, pp. 23–37. United Nations University Press, Tokyo (1994)
19. Kuznets, S.: Modern Economic Growth. Rate, Structure and Spread. Yale University Press, New Haven (1966)
20. Domenech, T., Bleischwitz, R., Doranova, A., Panayotopoulos, D., Roman, L.: Mapping industrial symbiosis development in europe_ typologies of networks, characteristics, performance and contribution to the circular economy. Resour. Conserv. Recycl. **141**, 76–98 (2019)
21. Lamonica, B., Lacy, P.: Circular Economy: Dallo spreco al valore. EGEA, Milano (2016)
22. Oliveira Neto, G.C., Correia, J.M.: Environmental and economic advantages of adopting reverse logistics for recycling construction and demolition waste: a case study of Brazilian construction and recycling companies. Waste Manag. Res. **37**, 176–185 (2019)
23. Lucia, M.G., Duglio, S., Lazzarini, P. (eds.): Verso un'economia della sostenibilità: Lo scenario e le sfide. FrancoAngeli, Milan (2018)
24. Weber, A.: Über des Standort der Industrien. Part. I. Reine Theorie des Standorts, Tübingen (English Trans. by C.J. Friedrich (1929) Alfred Weber's Theory of Location of industries). The University of Chicago Press (1909)
25. Tam, V.W., Soomro, M., Evangelista, A.C.J.: A review of recycled aggregate in concrete applications (2000–2017). Constr. Build. Mater. **172**, 272–292 (2018)
26. Official website. https://www.gppbest.eu/?page_id=41&lang=en

# Modeling the Epidemiological Processes of Economically Significant Infections of Animals

Sarsenbay Abdrakhmanov[1] , Ersyn Mukhanbetkalyev[1] ,
Altay Ussenbayev[1] , Dina Satybaldina[2(✉)] ,
Ablaikhan Kadyrov[2] , and Nurlan Tashatov[2]

[1] S. Seifullin Kazakh Agrotechnical University, 010011 Nur-Sultan, Kazakhstan
[2] L.N. Gumilyov Eurasian National University, 010008 Nur-Sultan, Kazakhstan
satybaldina_dzh@enu.kz

**Abstract.** Analysis of the retrospective and current states of the epidemiological situation on economically significant zoonoses (rabies, anthrax, and animal foot and mouth disease) in Kazakhstan over the past eight decades is considered. A reliable factual data for computer simulations and modern quantitative epidemiology methods were provided by the state veterinary and public health services. Historical and modern trends of the spatial and geographical distribution, the presence of cluster foci and the potential occurrence of infections outbreaks by country regions were assessed by mapping the incidence of diseases among animals and humans and using an environmental niche modeling, a space-time cube technology, as well as a negative binomial nesting density model, a linear regression and a generalized linear models. As a research result the statistically reliable visualization of the cluster zoning of Kazakhstan territory by risk emergent outbreaks categories of animals' and humans' infectious diseases was obtained. It allows predicting the likelihood of zoonoses outbreaks in the country regions.

**Keywords:** Computer modeling · Epidemiology ·
Geographical information systems

## 1 Introduction

In connection with the entry of Kazakhstan into the World Trade Organization, the need for socio-economic stability, including animal epidemics that can spread to humans, is becoming increasingly important for each administrative unit of the country [1–3].

The list of the most economically significant diseases of the World Organization for Animal Health (OIE) includes animal infections such as rabies, anthrax and foot and mouth disease (FMD), and global control of their outbreaks is a new challenge for modern human and animal medicine because of rabies and anthrax are dangerous zoonoses and can cause human deaths. FMD has an economic perspective because of a decrease in productivity in food-producing animals, trade restrictions imposed on the countries in which the disease is present [1–4].

© Springer Nature Switzerland AG 2019
S. Misra et al. (Eds.): ICCSA 2019, LNCS 11621, pp. 551–560, 2019.
https://doi.org/10.1007/978-3-030-24302-9_39

A retrospective spatiotemporal analysis of outbreaks of foot and mouth disease among livestock in Kazakhstan from 1955 to 2013 showed that during this period several strategies for foot and mouth disease controlling were implemented in the country, which led to the recognition of Kazakhstan by the OIE as a foot and mouth disease-free country with partial vaccination (2015) [4].

As in many endemic countries, animal rabies is recorded annually in Kazakhstan. There is also a vaccination program for domestic dogs, cats, farm animals and a limited fox vaccination program by distributing vaccines-soaked baits. However, a decrease in the incidence in animals was not observed [1, 2].

The first reliable information about anthrax in Kazakhstan was provided at the end of the 19th century, while anthrax foci began to be officially registered since the early 1930s. Stationary foci of natural infection were formed and maintained their activity over a long period of time in a significant part of the territory of Kazakhstan [3].

Currently, the prevention strategy for the above diseases is provided by their constant monitoring in all territorial units of the country. In today's world, the decision to control of these diseases is only possible by analyzing the epidemiological behavior of these dangerous zoonoses using computer technologies to simulate the spatial distribution and population dynamics of infectious agents among animals and humans.

The goal of this article is to review our latest research results on analysis the epidemiological situation for economically significant zoonoses - rabies, anthrax, and FMD - in the RK performed by computer simulation using modern quantitative epidemiology methods.

## 2    Materials and Methods

### 2.1    Studies Area

The epidemics of infections in the territory of Kazakhstan covering 2,724,900 km$^2$ were analyzed, including 14 oblasts (oblasts) and 179 districts; average population density here is 6.58 individuals/km$^2$.

### 2.2    Data

To analyze the epidemic situation of infections in Kazakhstan, we used the data of registered anthrax outbreaks in the period 1933–2014, outbreaks of foot and mouth disease from 1955 to 2013, and outbreaks of rabies in 2010–2013 in animals and people. The database was provided by official veterinary statistics and public health statistics of the country and the OIE, as well as data from veterinary research institutions and laboratories, supplemented by their own data collected during the expedition visits to assess preserved infection foci throughout the country. Recorded for each outbreak information included geographical coordinates, the date of confirmation of the disease, the name and administrative affiliation of the settlement, infected species, the number of infected and susceptible animals in infected herds.

## 2.3   Methods

**Rabies.** Spatio-temporal clusters of rabies outbreaks were identified using Kuldorf scan statistics. Preliminary data analysis using the Multi-distance Spatial Cluster Analysis software tool (Ripley K-function) was performed to determine the maximum distance of spatial outbreak clustering. The curves were plotted for the selected clusters based on the available data on the dynamics of cases of rabies in the second stage analysis. The time step of the epidemic curve implies a period equal to the average incubation period of rabies for the respective animal category, the duration of the infectious periods were modelled using the Pert distribution. In order to simulate the possible number of new outbreaks of rabies in the event of an epidemic in a new territory, a technique based on the concept of basic reproductive ratio was used [1]. The geographical distribution of rabies cases was also analyzed by mapping the cases of the disease in animals according to the corresponding coordinates. The distribution and density of common rabies cases were analyzed using the kernel density function smooth Scatter. Economic losses and disease burden were estimated using Monte Carlo simulations. They were summed up for Disability Adjusted Life Years (DALY) or for cost estimation and repeated 10,000 times. The total number of cases in farm animals and people by regions was also analyzed in a generalized linear model (GLM) with the number of confirmed cases in foxes and dogs as independent variables. The negative binomial regression model was used as a statistical model [2].

**Anthrax.** For assessment the risk of anthrax in each area, the maximum entropy technique (Maxent) was used. Using this approach, the values of the assumed risk factors represented by geospatial variables are determined at the locations of the recorded outbreaks. A regression equation was compiled for each location based on the Gibbs distribution. It was described the likelihood of observing a disease outbreak in each location. The values of the constants were selected using several iterations applying the Monte-Carlo method, which ensured the maximum probability distribution corresponding to the observed distribution of the disease outbreaks.

Then there was developed a risk map based on the distribution of infection obtained throughout the study area. The following factors were chosen as the proposed explanatory variables: a set of 19 climate variables included in BIOCLIM (the altitude above sea level in m; the maximum green vegetation fraction, reflecting the presence and intensity of vegetation cover; the land cover type, reflecting the category of land use; the soil type) (FAO 2016).

All geospatial variables were obtained in raster format, cropped along the border of Kazakhstan, processed with a resolution of $1 \times 1$ km$^2$, and converted to ASCII format, according to the requirements of Maxent software. The output of the Maxent model was a solid surface, which was the most appropriate distribution of areal suitability for the appearance of anthrax.

After developing a continuous risk surface, which is characterized by the distribution of suitability to anthrax outbreaks throughout the study area, a generalization was applied to compare risk categories in accordance with administrative divisions of the second level (districts). The results of this rating were presented in the form of a risk map, which was the main result of research.

**Foot and Mouth Disease.** There was used Kuldorf space-time scan statistics to detect the statistically significant groups of foot and mouth disease outbreaks, called a space-time clusters, for each of the three lines. A group of infected farms located close to each other was interpreted as the cluster, it was suggested that the farms were epidemiologically linked either to local transmission processes or to common risk factors. The resulting p-values of the scan statistic, adjusted for multiple hypotheses testing, denote the probability that the observed space–time cluster resulted from a random spatiotemporal distribution of outbreaks. The space–time density of outbreaks (STDO) was used to define the speed of the outbreak's spread within space–time clusters. At last, values of the STDO were compared using ANOVA to know whether STDOs were influenced by serotype.

## 2.4   Software

Geospatial analysis, processing the raster and vector data, converting the data into different formats and visualizing the results were carried out using the ArcGIS 10.4 and 10.5 geographical information system (ESRI, Redlands, CA, USA), Global Position System receivers (eTrex Legend, Global Sat GH-801 and Shturman SVG-40). Identification of space-time clusters was performed by means of SatScan 9.1 software package.

The distribution and density of rabies cases was analyzed in R using the function smooth Scatter; calculations of economic losses and disease burden from rabies were undertaken with glm.nb function from the MASS package. Statistical analysis was performed by Monte Carlo simulation method with @Risk 6.2 software (http://www.palisade.com/risk/) based on a standard Microsoft Excel package (Microsoft, USA).

Modelling by maximum entropy method was performed with the Maxent software [1–4].

## 3   Results

### 3.1   Rabies

Analysis of cases of rabies in 2010–2013 showed that clusters were mainly found among cattle in the category of farm animals, dogs – in domestic animals, and foxes – in wild animals. The initial segments of the epidemic curves were constructed for the three identified clusters, they included the fitted exponential curves.

The calculation of the main reproductive ratio confirms the hypothesis about the secondary nature of epidemics in domestic animals, since it appears that epidemics in these animal populations do not develop independently, but epidemics are supported by contact with wild world animals [1].

Mapping the official data of the public health and veterinary surveillance in 2003–2015 showed that rabies in farm animals have been occurred over most of Kazakhstan, but in its distribution regional variations were revealed. There were two distinct districts (Zhambyl and Kostanay Oblasts) where large clustering of outbreaks was observed (Fig. 1).

**Fig. 1.** Rabies in Kazakhstan (2003–2013): kernel density assessment in animals. A higher density of rabies cases is defined with darker shading. There are no outbreaks in white parts of the map [2].

There were treated an average 64,289 individuals with per annum underwent post exposure prophylaxis (PEP). Annually, it might result in 1140 DALYs. Every year PEP is protected 118 cases of human rabies or possibly 1184 at an estimated cost of $1193 or $119 averted respectively per DALY. It was estimated that in Kazakhstan an economic impact of rabies per annum is $20.9 million, with approximately half of it being attributed to the PEP and the income loss whilst persons were treated. There were annually assessed $5.4 million to be the life time income loss in lethal cases. An animal vaccination and control programs also particularly contributed to the economic losses [2].

## 3.2 Anthrax

A model was developed, the resulting predictive ability of which was rated as "good". To anthrax outbreak distribution existing most significantly contributed such variables as the maximum green vegetation fraction, the precipitation level of the most humid month, the precipitation level of the most humid quarter and the soil type. Regarding moisture and vegetation, an increase in variables had led to a corresponding monotonic increase in fitness, what was illustrated by response curves.

The continuous surface, showing the distribution of suitability to the outbreak of anthrax and taking into account considered geospatial factors, was converted into a grid format and superimposed on the map of Kazakhstan.

Averaged over the districts values of the risk had constructed the last map of risk, what reflected the influence of districts of country on the appearance of anthrax and accompanied by the map demonstrated the 95<sup>th</sup> percentile of risk (Fig. 2).

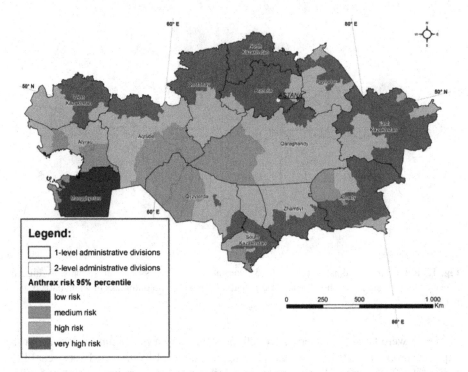

**Fig. 2.** Values of the 95th percentile in zoning of Kazakhstan by the risk of re-occurrence of anthrax (Maxent modelling) [3].

According to mapping the lowest risk of anthrax was indicated in western and central areas, and higher risk – in other geographical regions of the country [3].

### 3.3   Foot and Mouth Disease

In the study period there were revealed 35 statistically significant clusters for serotype A lineages, 41 clusters for serotype O and 13 clusters for lineage A22 by the spatiotemporal cluster analysis (Fig. 3).

In the late 1960s, there was a significant cessation of outbreaks of serotypes O and A clusters, which coincided with the onset of mass prophylactic livestock vaccination in 1970s.

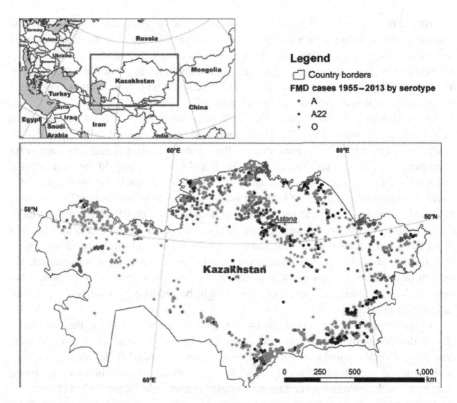

**Fig. 3.** Map of recorded foot and mouth disease outbreaks' location in 1950–2013 with serotypes [4].

ANOVA analysis of STDOs did not reveal significant differences between the lineages, and therefore, STDOs could be combined between lineages. The value could be used as an indicator of the possible development of the epidemic situation in the event of a new outbreak, especially in the absence of prophylactic vaccinations. Analysis of the seasonality showed that two seasonal peaks of the incidence were observed: in spring and autumn. There was no clear seasonality evident at the location of the clusters [4].

## 4  Discussion

Rabies is one of the dangerous lethal viral zoonotic diseases what transmitted to humans through bites of infected animals. Now the infection registered in more than 100 countries. The disease caused neurological clinics and had 100% fatality ratio if clinical signs present. Annually in the world 55,000 people and average a million animals die from this viral infection. Economical losses from rabies each year achieve more than EURO 4 billion [5].

According to the WHO the rabies problem must be researched by medical and veterinary professionals together. The epidemic curves developed in these studies were constructed for the three identified clusters, and the fitted exponential curves support the hypothesis about the secondary nature of the epidemics in domestic animals, since it is believed that these animals were infected by contact with wild animals. The found results agree well with the data of other authors [6, 7].

The reviewed research showed that 36% of animals should be vaccinated in the farm animals' category, while the figure increased to 41% for the wild animals' category. The obtaining vaccinations' ratio of the productive animals and wild carnivores corresponds to the current vaccination in Kazakhstan. It should be denoted the closeness of two clusters to the country's border, for it could be interpreted as a possible cross-border transfer of rabies in wildlife populations and the further spread in farm and pet animals' populations. Obtained data indicate that PEP was prophylactic for 713 rabies deaths in a 6 year period or an average of 119 annually deaths. The financial sums expended to control and destruction of stray and infected animals were $3.4 million annually. It was established that in spite of using the vaccination, the amount of areas with rabies cases in livestock or in the total numbers of cases was not reduced. The economic influence of rabies might be reduced by modifications of the vaccination program [1, 2].

It was known that for period 1961–2016 annual morbidity from anthrax in Kazakhstan decreased by more than 100 times [8]. But in the last decade there were described several endemic cases of disease among people [9]. In modern science environmental modelling is widely used for simulation the probability of a disease emergence with reference to certain territorially limited risk factors [10, 11].

In this research interpretive representation and statistical significant assessment of results was obtained with convenient maximum entropy method, applied in the anthrax research. The model's results approved the strong dependence of anthrax outbreaks locations from environmental conditions. Simulations showed a growth of local applicability to anthrax connected with an increase in the territorial ecological variables. Results were fitted to the foci in pastures and other places for animal feeding where anthrax was identified historically. Taking into account the range of relative pH values, it can be assumed to be associated with slightly acidic soils. The continuous probability surface was aggregated by averaging the values of risk by districts.

Research results produces more illustrative material in view of practical applicability and gives possibilities for official Kazakhstan veterinary service to make right decisions on planning of control measures against anthrax. So it gives an opportunity to identify districts where maximum plausible risk raises against a mean level, and decision-makers may refer to a continuous risk surface to reveal districts with significantly exposure to anthrax [3].

The present analysis has shown that the efficacy of the foot and mouth disease's outbreaks controlling strategy in Kazakhstan was clearly evidenced through the interruption of spatiotemporal clustering. There was suggested that immunity after vaccination developed decreasing the susceptibility of neighbour population and stopped the virus local spreading. After implementation the vaccination strategy clusters of A and O serotype strains of the foot and mouth disease no longer distributed in the country.

The space-time patterns of A22 lineage outbreaks allowed suggesting that trade relations of Kazakhstan with neighbour countries and transboundary movements of wild animals could be a cause of A22 lineage importation into Kazakhstan. Seasonality patterns described with peaks of infection prevalence in spring could be referable to productive animal farming practices in Kazakhstan where livestock is moved from winter location to pastures in the spring.

Applied in the research parameter STDO shows the amount of new outbreaks per unit area in a certain time interval. This parameter is very important for practical goals to compare the local epidemics intensity and to prognosis the expected number of outbreaks in bigger areas. It may be served to predict the expected amount of foot and mouth disease outbreaks within a particular area, and thus easily applicable to decision makers [4].

## 5   Conclusion

The reviewed studies give a detailed overview of the distribution and burden of infections as rabies, anthrax and foot and mouth disease in Kazakhstan. The results are largely based on detailed surveillance and budgetary data provided by the veterinary and public health services and demonstrate that in Kazakhstan there is a substantial economic cost and health impact of such diseases of animals and humans.

The widespread use of post exposure prophylaxis (PEP) prevents annually at least 118 and up to 1184 fatalities of humans bitten by rabid animals. The annually economic costs of this disease are exceeding $20 million.

In studies employed a data-driven approach to quantify suitability of Kazakhstan districts to anthrax re-emergence with relation to environmental conditions. The research allowed illustrating the niche nature of anthrax and strong dependence of its historical outbreak locations in the country on a combination of environmental factors. There was creating a map of anthrax re-emergence risk categories that could be applied by the veterinary service to plan a vaccination and surveillance activity. The availability of this map also enables consideration of risks of preserved soil foci re-activation when developing projects of construction works that impact historically formed landscapes.

Using historical data on foot and mouse disease incidence in Kazakhstan, there was demonstrated that quantitative methods for analysis of spatiotemporal data can effectively evaluate the trends of local epidemic formation and illustrate the impact of different disease control strategies. In addition, estimated values of within-herd prevalence by species, size and duration of space–time clusters by serotype, and seasonal patterns of incidence contribute to our epidemiological understanding of foot and mouse disease distribution in endemic regions attempting eradication.

**Acknowledgements.** This work has been accomplished under the National Budgetary Program # 249 "Providing conditions for the development manufacturing, processing and sale of livestock production".

# References

1. Abdrakhmanov, S.K., Beisembayev, K.K., Korennoy, F.I., Yessembekova, G.N., Kushubaev, D.B., Kadyrov, A.S.: Revealing spatio-temporal patterns of rabies spread among various categories of animals in the Republic of Kazakhstan, 2010–2013. Geospat. Health 11 (455), 199–205 (2016)
2. Sultanov, A.A., Abdrakhmanov, S.K., Abdybekova, A.M., Karatayev, B.S., Torgerson, P.R.: Rabies in Kazakhstan. PLOS Negl. Trop. Dis. 10(8), 1–15 (2016)
3. Abdrakhmanov, S.K., et al.: Maximum entropy modeling risk of anthrax in the Republic of Kazakhstan. Prev. Vet. Med. 144, 149–157 (2017)
4. Abdrakhmanov, S.K., et al.: Spatiotemporal analysis of foot-and-mouth disease outbreaks in the Republic of Kazakhstan, 1955–2013. Transbound Emerg. Dis. 65(5), 1235–1245 (2018)
5. Botvinkin, A.D., Otgonbaatar, D., Tsoodol, S., Kuzmin, I.V.: Rabies in the Mongolian steppes. Dev. Biol. 131, 199–205 (2008)
6. Aikimbayev, A., Briggs, D., Coltan, G., et al.: Fighting rabies in Eastern Europe, the Middle East and Central Asia—experts call for a regional initiative for rabies elimination. Zoonoses Public Health 61, 219–226 (2014). https://doi.org/10.1111/zph.12060. PMID: 23782901
7. Fooks, A.R., Banyard, A.C., Horton, D.L., Johnson, N., McElhinney, L.M., Jackson, A.C.: Current status of rabies and prospects for elimination. Lancet 384, 1389–1399 (2014). https://doi.org/10.1016/S0140-6736(13)62707-5. PMID: 24828901
8. Lukhnova, L. Yu., Aikimbayev, A.M., Pazylov, E.K.: Epidemic process of anthrax in Kazakhstan. Bull. Agric. Sci. Kazakhstan 'Bastau' 7, 44 (2004)
9. Abdrakhmanov, S.K., Mukhanbetkaliyev, Y.Y., Beysembayev, K.K., Kushubayev, D.B., Kadyrov, A.S.: Spatio-temporal analysis of the epidemiological situation on anthrax in Kazakhstan. In: Proceedings of 4th Conference of ISOCARD «Silk Road Camel: The Camelids, Main Stakes For Sustainable Development», 8–12 June, Almaty, Kazakhstan, pp. 222–224 (2015)
10. Stevens, K.B., Pfeiffer, D.U.: Spatial modelling of disease using data - and knowledge-driven approaches. Spat. Spatiotemporal Epidemiol. 2, 125–133 (2011)
11. Korennoy, F.I., Gulenkin, V.M., Malone, J.B., Mores, C.N., Dudnikov, S.A., Stevenson, M.A.: Spatio-temporal modeling of the African swine fever epidemic in the Russian Federation, 2007–2012. Spat. Spatiotemporal Epidemiol. 11, 135–141 (2014)

# Ecosystem Indicators and Landscape Ecology Metrics as a Tool to Evaluate Sustainable Land Planning in ICZM

Andrea Fiduccia[1]([⊠]) [iD], Luisa Cattozzo[2] [iD], Leonardo Marotta[3] [iD],
Leonardo Filesi[2] [iD], and Luca Gugliermetti[1] [iD]

[1] Department of Astronautical Electrical and Energy Engineering (DIAEE),
Sapienza University of Rome, Via Eudossiana 18, 00184 Rome, Italy
andrea.fiduccia@uniroma1.it
[2] Department of Architecture and Arts, IUAV University,
Santa Croce 1957 Ca' Tron, 30135 Venice, Italy
[3] Studio Associato Entropia, Via F. Corridoni 3, 62019 Recanati, Italy

**Abstract.** In the frame of Integrated Coastal Zone Management (ICZM) planners need tools to design and assess a sustainable state for the coast. Sustainability and progress indicator have to be integrated to identify improvements in the state of coastal zones as a result of ICZM implementation [1].

There are two useful approaches in order to take into account, system property, complexity and evolution, and integrating humans and bio-geospheres: system ecology (and ecosystem health concepts, as defined in [2]) and landscape science and ecology (as defined for example in [3–7]). The holistic approach in the context of human-nature relations is the real challenge of modern landscape ecology. It regards the background of increasing environmental problems and the discussion about sustainability [4] and for sustainability planning [8].

In the paper, it is proposed a brand new synthetic ecosystem indicator suited to monitoring regeneration plans of coastal zones: the Land Eco-Biodiversity. In order to have more benchmarks in assessing the state of implementation of a strategy, the plan, as well as from an ecosystemic point of view, is measured from a landscape point of view through Landscape Ecology indexes. In fact, the fragmentation of the landscape is part of the resource efficiency indicators defined by Eurostat in the context of monitoring the main objectives defined in the Europe 2020 strategy in the Category: "Nature and ecosystems | Biodiversity".

The study area is the Delta of Po River (Italy).

**Keywords:** ICZM · Landscape ecology metrics · Ecosystem indicators

## 1 Landscape Ecology: A Paradigm for ICZM

The 2007 Integrated Maritime Policy for the European Union [9] acted as an important factor in stimulating the consolidation of coastal and marine information to support policy implementation. This approach includes the development of coastal and marine Decision-Support Systems (DSS) [10, 11]. In order to create a coastal information

© Springer Nature Switzerland AG 2019
S. Misra et al. (Eds.): ICCSA 2019, LNCS 11621, pp. 561–576, 2019.
https://doi.org/10.1007/978-3-030-24302-9_40

system it is needed a large amount of data and of high quality structured information. High quality coastal information systems can be organized as a set of indices and indicators. An indicator is a measured or observed parameter that provides information about a system. An index is a more elaborated and organized information that provides as a coherent view of the reality and an integration information of one (or more) qualities. It is supposed an indicator or index (or a set of them) is a model of reality [12–16] and it has a significance extending beyond what is directly obtained from observations [17].

Indices and indicators, as the system models, simplify systems, functions, forms and processes. A set of meaningful and representative indicators, however, would facilitate knowledge, decision-making, monitoring and assessment of planned interventions in terms of policy and management objectives [17, 18]. As such, they have to provide a concrete contribution to a difficult communication among stakeholders in the rationalization of multi-purpose decision-making processes. In general, sharing coastal knowledge and offering organized information (such as indicators and indices) once it is built requires also the development of useful comprehensive tools to disseminate that information, taking advantage of technologies such as models and earth observing systems to do so [19].

The development and use of indicators and indices for coastal areas and coastal zone management and planning is already worldwide done (e.g. [17]), and it is more and more comprehensive of coastal system, with increasing consideration for the geo-ecological, economic and social aspects (e.g. [20]).

The *working group on indicators and data* of the European ICZM expert group proposed two set of indicators to be used by member states and candidate countries [18, 21–23]:

- Progress indicators;
- Indicators of sustainable development.

In 2010, Marotta et al. [24] proposed a complementary set of indicators in order to integrate the Habitat Directive and to define a sustainability state for the coast using a framework based on a landscape approach.

Landscape ecology has two different approaches, both very powerful in integration of Coastal Zone Management. The two different views are rooted in the European versus North American traditions [7, 25, 26]. Both perspectives can be derived from Troll original definition of landscape ecology as "the study of the main complex causal relationships between the life communities and their environment" [27], which "are expressed regionally in a definite distribution pattern (landscape mosaic, landscape pattern)" [28].

Wu [29] describes the difference as follows: "It is true that the two traditions differ in some significant ways: the former has been characterized by a society-centered holistic view that focuses on solution-driven research, whereas the latter is dominated by a bioecology-centred spatial view that focuses on question-driven studies". He outlines "the differences hinge mainly on the ways these anthropogenic influences are incorporated in research, ranging from treating humans as one of the factors creating and responding to spatial heterogeneity" [30] considering the landscape as a "total human ecosystem" [31]. Following the concept of landscape as total human ecosystem,

Barrett and Farina [32] presented a landscape paradigm able to integrate in landscape ecology and economy both assessment and planning. Desaigues [33] presented the socio-economic value of the ecotone also with a planning focus.

The environmental factors can be natural or cultural (anthropic). If the control is "mostly natural" it is called "Natural Ecosystem", while if it is "mostly human" controlled it is called "Cultural Ecosystem" [34]. Some of the environmental factors are Natural, others are Cultural. The majority is a mix between them. We can measure the degree of cultural control with the quantity of subsidiary energy supplied to the system [35].

The methodology for ICZM of Marotta et al. [24] is fully based on paradigm of landscape ecology. It follows several steps:

1. *Definition of homogeneous environmental management units, and analysis of spatial and temporal structure, hierarchy and dynamics over multiple scales.* This step requires the production of a habitat map based on landscape ecology.
2. *Analysis of land-use changes in the coastal system.*
3. *Implementation of spatial indices* characterizing each patch type and state.
4. *Conservation-gaps analysis.* The step is focused in the assessment of ecosystem health, cumulative impacts and habitat loss in coastal ecotones [36]. An urban and infrastructure index has been used as evaluation tool [37, 38].
5. *Assessment of coastal conflicts* using a coastal conflict index following the work of Vallega [39].
6. *Multi Criteria Analysis (MCA) in order to minimize conflicts over a set of values and constraints.*

Such a methodology is very reliable from a scientific point of view, but it has a drawback in its complexity. The framework uses maps and dashboards to share the results with decision makers and stakeholders, but indices and indicators are hard to understand for non-technicians people and harder to implement and update.

Therefore, in the paper we present a "lean" version of the methodology taking also in account the new Analytical Assessment Framework for Land System of EU [40].

## 2 Steps Towards a "Lean" Methodology for ICZM

### 2.1 Soil Consumption

Soil consumption is a phenomenon associated with the loss of a fundamental environmental resource, due to the occupation of an originally agricultural, natural or semi-natural surface. The phenomenon refers to an increase in artificial ground cover, linked to settlement and infrastructure dynamics.

It is a process mainly due to the construction of new buildings and settlements, to the expansion of cities, to the densification or conversion of land within an urban area, to the development of new infrastructures.

Therefore, soil consumption is defined as a variation from a non-artificial land (unused soil) to an artificial ground cover (soil consumed).

Land Cover refers to the biophysical coverage of the earth's surface, including artificial surfaces, agricultural areas, woods and forests, semi-natural areas, wetlands, water bodies, as defined by Directive 2007/2/EC [41].

The soil sealing, the permanent covering of part of the land and its soil with artificial materials (such as asphalt or concrete) for the construction, for example, of buildings and roads, is the most obvious and most widespread form of artificial transformation of the land. Soil sealing is the main cause of soil degradation in Europe, entails an increased risk of flooding, contributes to climate change, threatens biodiversity, causing the loss of fertile agricultural lands and natural and semi-natural areas: it contributes together with the urban sprawl to the progressive and systematic destruction of the landscape, mainly rural one [42].

## 2.2    Land System

According to EEA [40] "Land *systems are the terrestrial component of the Earth system, encompassing all processes and activities related to the human use of land. These include socio-economic, technological and organisational inputs and arrangements, as well as the benefits gained from land and the unintended social and ecological outcomes of societal activities. The land systems concept combines land use (the activities, arrangements and inputs associated with land use) with land cover (the ensemble of physical characteristics of land discernible by Earth Observation)".*

## 2.3    The Land System Assessment

In the Briefing no. 10/2018 of EEA [40] is proposed an approach for the assessment of Land Systems based on DPSIR framework:

1. Formulation of a policy-relevant question. The assessment has to be related with priorities of decision-makers.
2. Mapping pressures (land processes). The processes are *"physical, biological or chemical processes that directly influence changes in ecosystem functions and services"* [40]. In this category are included extreme weather events and biological dispersal. Data sources are products of Earth Observation (e.g. Copernicus land monitoring products) and spatially distributed statistical data on socio-economic activities.
3. Territorial assessment. *"The territorial assessment describes land systems as a state of natural capital and a socio-economic purpose of natural resources. This includes land management practices, such as the arrangements, activities and inputs people undertake across regions. From a practical perspective, this includes analysis of the spatial distribution of land use and land cover (LU/LC) patterns, the local and regional variances of land management practices, the degree of imperviousness and soil sealing and the existence of conservation and non-conservation areas. A territorial analysis results in map categories, which represent specific characteristics of land processes e.g. intensity levels of agricultural land use, forest management practices or peri-urban land take at a given time"* [40].

4. Dynamic assessment. *"Changes in the state of land systems can be measured from land cover flows from one broad LU/LC category to another. (...) However, both types of land process result in changes in the services and goods provided by land systems"* [40]. Kuemmerle et al. [43] mapped spatial patterns of changes in the extent and management intensity in Europe's agriculture, forestry and urban areas for the period 1990–2006.

5. Functional assessment. This is the step of measurement of the effects (impacts) generated by land process on the delivery of environmental functions. The *"analytical framework compares the provision of functions and services across geographical regions, taking into account that they occur within different land use types and are subject to contrasting management activities evaluated in steps 3 and 4"* [40]. Stavi et al. [44] proposed a conceptual model suited to score soil functions and ecosystem services and compare them across broad types of conventional, conservation and integrated agricultural systems.

6. Key policy message. The results of the assessment steps should provide an answer to the policy question of Step 1 and could help to formulating scenarios and policies.

# 3   The Land Eco-Biodiversity Index

## 3.1   Vegetation Series Map

The study of land use shows how the anthropic practices of recent years led the territory far away from the natural vocation of soils developing productive activities that most of the time do not respect the cycles of nature. In particular, the spread of agricultural practices in recent years, sometimes justified by the need for forms of economic incentive, has led to an excessive simplification of both the landscape and the variety of products.

In the paper, it is proposed to adopt for the territorial regeneration projects a methodology based on the recovery of the health status of the landscape. The "healthy" state of a landscape is that in which the places are in the natural vegetational state. It can be identified following the Hierarchical Classification of the Land approach [45]. The distribution models of spontaneous plant communities can be constructed using biogeography and plant ecology, i.e. the area distribution of species and the ecological factors determining their presence or absence, in particular the climate, the soil (chemism and morphology) and the availability of water. Given a biogeographic context it is possible to hypothesize what should be the potential vegetation (the one that would exist in the absence of anthropic disturbance) based on the aforementioned ecological factors.

Starting from the main ecological factors in conditioning the distribution of vegetation, the one that determines the differentiation between the large biomes, i.e. the climatic region, leads to the definition of homogeneous areas for lithological, bioclimatic and geomorphological features to the point of being able to hypothesize (and possibly verify) a certain potential vegetation for each of them.

The science of vegetation is not limited to describing the spontaneous vegetation by proposing the models of plant communities known as plant associations (fulcrum of that discipline called Phytosociology). Perhaps the most interesting viewpoint is that which leads us to investigate the successional relationships between grasslands, bushes and woods, the definition of the so-called "vegetation series" [46]. Therefore, for a given biogeographic context and an ecologically homogeneous environment (identified with the criteria dictated by the hierarchical classification of the land) it is possible to establish which is the series of reference vegetation, i.e. the potential vegetation (generally of forest type) and the communities plants dynamically linked to it based on successional relationships (grasslands and bushes) determined by recovery processes after ailments such as fires, deforestation and cultivation of the land.

From an operative point of view, in order to produce a Vegetation Series Map (only for the stage of maturity in a successional key) at the regional scale (1: 250,000) and at provincial scale (1: 50,000) it is possible to proceed by interpreting the Map of Systems of Soils. The information contained in it represents a synthesis of the pedological survey and allows recognizing in the territory of the areas (the cartographic units) homogeneous for the soils present within them, grouped in hierarchically organized containers, which describe the growth environment. In order not to create discontinuity, it is proposed not to separate urban areas.

The described methodology has been applied to the area of the delta of Po River in Veneto Region (Italy). From a climatic point of view, the Veneto region, although presenting a remarkable articulation, is entirely located in the temperate climatic region. This has determined the remarkable peculiarity of the north Adriatic coastal vegetation that is in the only strip of Mediterranean coast not having a Mediterranean climate. In the coastal sector there are soils with well-defined characteristics, consistent with a clearly differentiated potential vegetation. The area investigated consists of floodplain in which the differences in substrate, morphology and water availability are articulated on non-net gradients [47].

According to the method already described combinations of tree species have been identified according to the prevailing potential vegetation. The combinations of the tree species are representative of ecological variants with respect to the reference plant associations and the prevalent communities in the mosaics which, on the regional detail scale, are not allowed to be resolved in a single type. The elaboration led to individuation of 7 classes of potential vegetation at the 1: 250,000 scale on the north Adriatic coast which includes the coastal territories of Venice, Rovigo and Ferrara, and of 6 different classes of potential vegetation at the most detailed 1: 50,000 scale for the only area of the Po River delta. Since the soil maps produced by the Veneto and Emilia-Romagna regions are not based on a common survey and cartographic methodology, the interpretation of the information contained in them resulted in an evaluation in terms of homogenization of the classes. They have been assigned on the basis of vegetation potential for types of soil. This interpretative process has led to the identification of 7 homogeneous areas for potential vegetation.

The identification of potential vegetation makes it possible to identify the Habitats according to Directive 92/43/EEC [48], which represents one of the main regulatory instruments aimed at the conservation of biodiversity in Europe. This regulatory reference, which is the basis for identifying the sites of the Natura 2000 network, in particular lists and codifies species of community importance, some of which are classified as priorities.

Finally, the presence of certain species corresponds to a specific code and typological description in terms of land use, according to the European standard legend Corine Land Cover. Based on these two references, it was possible to identify the theoretically corresponding Habitat and Corine Land Cover codes for each potential vegetation class.

## 3.2    The Land Eco-Biodiversity Index

In order to characterize the biodiversity rate of the study area, it was decided to take into consideration the species of fauna and flora of the Annexes of the two Community Directives "Birds" (79/409/CEE) [49] and "Habitat" (92/43/CEE) [48], selecting only those present in the environments that characterize the study area. For the floristic component only, the species defined as "important" by the Standard form of the ZPS (Special Protected Zone) I3270023 "Po Delta" were also considered.

Data on these species are obtained as an analytical result of the bibliography available.

Each habitat of a regeneration plan can be used by a single fauna or botanical species in a marginal or temporary way (weighted value = 1), or permanently, especially from a reproductive point of view (weighted value = 2). The presence of each species was therefore analyzed according to the concept of "species habitat", proper to the monitoring plans and to the environmental incidence assessments.

Multiplying these values by the extension of the area of each habitat according to the regeneration scenario, it is thus possible to obtain a Land EcoBiodiversity Index (LEBI) referring to the entire study area comparable with the current one [50].

We have a land divided in n Habitat H1, H2, ..., Hn

The areas (in hectares) of the habitats are A1, A2, ..., An

We have m indicator species S1, S2, ..., Sm

We have the following matrix of the presence of the indicator species in the habitats:

| | | Habitat | | | |
|---|---|---|---|---|---|
| | | H1 | H2 | | Hn |
| Indicator | S1 | $P_{S1H1}$ | $P_{S1H2}$ | | $P_{S1Hn}$ |
| Species | S2 | $P_{S2H1}$ | $P_{S2H2}$ | | $P_{S2Hn}$ |
| | | | | | |
| | Sm | $P_{SmH1}$ | $P_{SmH2}$ | | $P_{SmHn}$ |

Where

$P_{SjHi}$ = 0 absence of the species in the habitat

      1 presence of the species in the habitat

      2 breeding site of the species in the habitat

$$\text{LEBI} = \sum\nolimits_{i=1}^{n} TP_{Hi} * \frac{Ai}{\sum_{i=1}^{n} Ai} \qquad (1)$$

Where

$$TP_{Hi} = \sum\nolimits_{j=1}^{m} P_{SjHi} \qquad (2)$$

In the following Figs. 1 and 2, Tables 1, and 2 there is the synthesis of the experimentation of LEBI in the delta of Po River (Italy) [50].

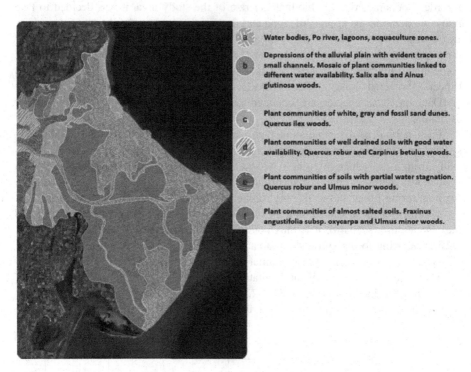

**Fig. 1.** Potential vegetation map (scale 1:50.000) [50]

## 4   Discussion

### 4.1   Issues Regarding Data About Indicator Species

The data on the presence of indicator species in habitats are the result of a survey conducted on several sources: the current situation does not allow access to a single national-level data source on standard bases. In fact, each Region and each Province operate with different methods: therefore, the output data is also not easily comparable. Within the Veneto Region itself, which includes the study area, there are substantial

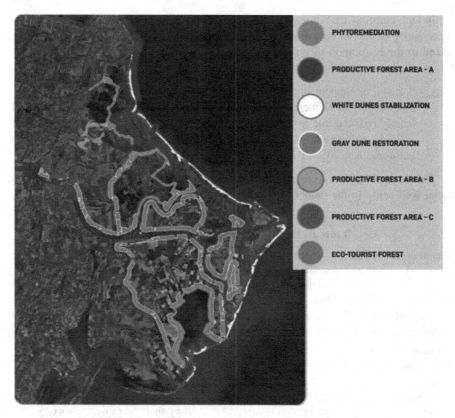

**Fig. 2.** Map of places eligible for regeneration projects [50]

differences between the modus operandi in the Province of Rovigo and in the Province of Venice.

However, since numerous data are available for the study area, some of which are in the national ISPRA database, others are available by periodical publications relating to the different species, it was decided to exploit the information in order also to test the potential of the proposed Indicator. However, a standardization of the monitoring of the species should be implemented at least for a regional level.

Finally, a way to improve LEBI could be a better modelization of vegetational indicator species considering quality and conservation status and using a more detailed scale according to [51].

## 4.2  Landscape Value

A second point of attention is the opportunity to extend the number of indicators, in order to have more benchmarks to assess the planning scenarios and then the status of the implementation of the chosen strategy.

A first option is to use a multiplying weighing factor depending, for example, on the landscape value added to the areas subject to intervention.

In fact, current LEBI limits itself to identifying the level of general regeneration of the territory subject to interventions. By way of example only, we could use as weight linked to the restoration of typical elements of the delta landscape according to their historical presence on the territory:

$LII_{Hi}$ = 1 (low: an element introduced by man in recent times);
  2 (medium: an element present in the past and recently disappeared or significantly reduced due to the anthropic action);
  3 (high: an element of the past completely or almost disappeared due to the anthropic action).

This factor (Landscape Intervention Index) would allow introducing a measure of social well-being in the model (Table 2).

**Table 1.** LEBI implementation in study area [50]

| Environment | Indicator TP | Current scenario (surface in ha) | Potential regeneration surface (ha) | Scenario 1 (surface in ha) | Scenario 2 (surface in ha) | Scenario 3 (surface in ha) |
|---|---|---|---|---|---|---|
| Arable land | 16 | 20690,02 | – | 20616,98 | 20324,8 | 19959,97 |
| Wetlands | 91 | 19820,06 | 13,49 | 19820,19 | 19820,73 | 19821,41 |
| White & Grey dunes | 90 | 202,58 | 6546,83 | 266,02 | 519,79 | 837 |
| Forests | 18 | 481,75 | 946,84 | 491,22 | 529,09 | 576,03 |
| Total surface | – | 41194,41 | 7507,16 | 41194,41 | 41194,41 | 41194,41 |
| **LEBI** | – | **52,47** | – | **52,59** | **53,05** | **53,62** |

### 4.3  Indicators of Landscape Ecology: Composition and Configuration

A second option is to evaluate the scenarios, as well as from an ecosystemic point of view, also from a landscape point of view, using indices of Landscape Ecology. It would be possible, for example, to evaluate the connectivity of a territory before and after certain interventions, thus extending the sphere of monitoring to a system of indices and indicators more complex than the LEBI alone.

Using some metrics of Landscape Ecology, we can analyze two of the main features of a landscape: composition and configuration. The composition of a landscape refers to the richness and abundance of the different elements that are part of it, without however considering their spatial distribution; even if the composition metrics are not explicitly spatial, they also have important consequences in terms of spatial effects. The landscape configuration, instead, applies to the spatial properties of the elements, such as their distribution, position, orientation and shape.

According to a methodology of ISPRA [52], we propose to adopt the following indicators:

**Table 2.** Weighted LEBI implementation in study area [50]

| Environment | Indicator TP | Landscape Intervention Index | Weighted TP | Current Scenario | | | Potential Regeneration Surface (ha) | Scenario 1 | | |
|---|---|---|---|---|---|---|---|---|---|---|
| | | | | Surface (ha) | LEBI | Weighted LEBI | | Surface (ha) | LEBI | Weighted LEBI |
| Arable land | 16 | 1 | 16 | 20690,02 | 8,04 | 8,04 | - | 20616,98 | 8,01 | 8,01 |
| Wetlands | 91 | 2 | 182 | 19820,06 | 43,78 | 87,57 | 13,49 | 19820,19 | 43,78 | 87,57 |
| W&G dunes | 90 | 3 | 270 | 202,58 | 0,44 | 1,33 | 6546,83 | 266,02 | 0,58 | 1,74 |
| Forests | 18 | 3 | 54 | 481,75 | 0,21 | 0,63 | 946,84 | 491,22 | 0,21 | 0,64 |
| Total surface | - | - | - | 41194,41 | - | - | 7507,16 | 41194,41 | - | - |
| LEBI | - | - | - | - | 52,47 | 97,56 | - | - | 52,59 | 97,96 |

| Environment | Indicator TP | Landscape Intervention Index | Weighted TP | Current Scenario | | | Potential Regeneration Surface (ha) | Scenario 2 | | |
|---|---|---|---|---|---|---|---|---|---|---|
| | | | | Surface (ha) | LEBI | Weighted LEBI | | Surface (ha) | LEBI | Weighted LEBI |
| Arable land | 16 | 1 | 16 | 20690,02 | 8,04 | 8,04 | - | 20324,8 | 7,89 | 7,89 |
| Wetlands | 91 | 2 | 182 | 19820,06 | 43,78 | 87,57 | 13,49 | 19820,73 | 43,78 | 87,57 |
| W&G dunes | 90 | 3 | 270 | 202,58 | 0,44 | 1,33 | 6546,83 | 519,79 | 1,14 | 3,41 |
| Forests | 18 | 3 | 54 | 481,75 | 0,21 | 0,63 | 946,84 | 529,09 | 0,23 | 0,69 |
| Total surface | - | - | - | 41194,41 | - | - | 7507,16 | 41194,41 | - | - |
| LEBI | - | - | - | - | 52,47 | 97,56 | - | - | 53,05 | 99.56 |

| Environment | Indicator TP | Landscape Intervention Index | Weighted TP | Current Scenario | | | Potential Regeneration Surface (ha) | Scenario 3 | | |
|---|---|---|---|---|---|---|---|---|---|---|
| | | | | Surface (ha) | LEBI | Weighted LEBI | | Surface (ha) | LEBI | Weighted LEBI |
| Arable land | 16 | 1 | 16 | 20690,02 | 8,04 | 8,04 | - | 19959,97 | 7,75 | 7,75 |
| Wetlands | 91 | 2 | 182 | 19820,06 | 43,78 | 87,57 | 13,49 | 19821,41 | 43,79 | 87,57 |
| W&G dunes | 90 | 3 | 270 | 202,58 | 0,44 | 1,33 | 6546,83 | 837 | 1,83 | 5,49 |
| Forests | 18 | 3 | 54 | 481,75 | 0,21 | 0,63 | 946,84 | 576,03 | 0,25 | 0,76 |
| Total surface | - | - | - | 41194,41 | - | - | 7507,16 | 41194,41 | - | - |
| LEBI | - | - | - | - | 52,47 | 97,56 | - | - | 53,62 | 101,57 |

- Composition:
  - Patch Richness (PR) describes the number of different types of land cover in the land unit of analysis;
  - Percentage of Landscape (PLAND), describes in percentage terms the composition of a given landscape;
- Configuration:
  - Patch Density (PD) indicates the degree of subdivision of a specific class of land cover typology, related to the entire extent of the landscape;
  - Mean Patch Size index (AREA_AM) expresses the average size of the elements of a given type of land cover in terms of weighted average;
  - Shape (SHAPE_AM) is a measure of the geometric complexity of the landscape elements of a given land cover category;
  - Edge Contrast (ECON_AM) measures the length of the edge shared between two types of land cover in a given landscape;

- Patch Compaction (GYRATE_AM), expresses the average distance between the various cells of a single spatial unit of the same class of land cover, reported in the total area of the land cover class;
- Contagion (CONTAG) measures the level of aggregation of the land cover classes and it is calculated at the landscape level;
- Cohesion (COHESION) indicates the tendency of land cover types to aggregate;
- Aggregation index (AI), as the previous one indicates the tendency of the types of coverage to aggregate;
- Simpson Diversity Index (SIDI) is a measure of the diversity of homogeneous spatial units.

In ISPRA methodology [52] indicators have been calculated for EU NUTS 3 administrative area units. We propose to measure indicators for the areal units of Vegetation Series Map more consistent from and ecological point of view than an administrative unit.

### 4.4   Indicators of Landscape Ecology: Fragmentation and Connectivity

EUROSTAT [53] considers the fragmentation of the landscape as a national level indicator in the context of monitoring the main objectives defined in the Europe 2020 strategy.

The Effective Mesh Size Index [54, 55] can be used to measure fragmentation considering the fragmenting role of the soil consumption. The index can be interpreted as the area of accessible land (without encountering physical barriers) starting from any point within the reference territorial unit.

In ISPRA methodology [52], the effective mesh size was calculated using a regular grid with the resolution of one kilometer for the whole Italy. The fragmenting element is the artificial coverage of the soil obtained from the National Soil Consumption Map [54], integrated with OpenStreetMap vector data to improve the identification of linear infrastructures (roads and railways). The level of fragmentation (effective mesh density) was assessed by 5 classes consistent with the definition of the European Environment Agency for the Landscape fragmentation indicator Effective Mesh Density (Seff).

Another way to assess the fragmentation of a territory is to analyze it in terms of connectivity. The Percolation Index [7] is capable to study whether a territory is traversable (or not) by a theoretical animal that must reach two points moving through the landscape patches. The analysis of percolation capacity, therefore, allows us to understand whether and how a landscape is connected. In other words, whether it is able to percolate, that is to allow the flow of a factor, such as the movement of animals, from one side to the other of a territorial unit of reference. This index measures, therefore, the intensity of the barrier action of highly artificialized and urbanized areas. Using some "penalty rules" we can model also the effect of soil consumption and of natural risks (landslide, flooding and seismic).

# 5  Conclusions

In this work, a set of indices and a methodology in the frame of Integrated Coastal Zone Management (ICZM) have been presented.

Comparing the Marotta et al. [24] methodology with the EU DPSIR approach [40] we can observe (Table 3):

**Table 3.** Comparison between ICZM methodologies

| | Methodology for ICZM by Marotta et al. [24] | EEA DPSIR framework [40] |
|---|---|---|
| A | | *1. Formulation of a policy-relevant question* |
| B | *1. Definition of homogeneous environmental management units, and analysis of spatial and temporal structure, hierarchy and dynamics over multiple scales* <br> *2. Analysis of land-use changes in the coastal system* <br> *3. Implementation of spatial indices* characterizing each patch type and state <br> *4. Conservation-gaps analysis* | *2. Mapping pressures (land processes)* <br> *3. Territorial assessment* <br> *4. Dynamic assessment* <br> *5. Functional assessment* |
| C | *5. Assessment of coastal conflicts* using a coastal conflict index following the work of Vallega [39] <br> *6. Multi Criteria Analysis (MCA) in order to minimize conflicts over a set of values and constraints* | |
| D | | *6. Key policy message* |

1. The two approaches can be integrated in a very comprehensive workflow (A + B + C + D) or in a simpler way for local plans (A + B + D).
2. The indices and the methodology we presented can be used to implement a "lean" version of the block B of the integrated workflow.

It is a lean methodology, but focused to face the core of the contemporary dynamics of coastal systems: anthropic actions are producing soil consumption with reduction of sustainability and environmental quality and improvement of risks due to climate change. The "backbone" datasets, Land Use/Land Cover, are systematically updated using Earth Observation products and other data are coming from public bodies (thanks to INSPIRE [41] and other EU's Directives, Eurostat, etc.). Therefore ecosystemic and landscape ecology indices and indicators can be "easily" calculated (even if there are some issues regarding the data standards for indicator species in habitats) and mapped. This kind of maps and indicators and methodology are the foundation of Coastal DSS needed by decision makers and stakeholders for ICMZ. A further step in the methodology will be the exploitation of bottom-up, open and crowdsourced geo-information coming from the so-called Neo-Geography and the real-time/near real-time information of social networks in order to integrate official datasets and to collect feedbacks in a participatory ICZM process.

# References

1. Meiner, A.: Integrated maritime policy for the European Union—consolidating coastal and marine information to support maritime spatial planning. J. Coast. Conserv. **14**, 1–11 (2010)
2. Jørgensen, S.E., Xu, F.L., Salas, F., Marques, J.: Application of indicators for assessment of ecosystem health. In: Jørgensen, S.E., Costanza, R., Xu, F.L. (eds.) Handbook of Ecological Indicators for Assessment of Ecosystem Health, pp. 5–104. CRC Press, Boca Raton (2005)
3. Naveh, Z.: From biodiversity to ecodiversity—holistic conservation of the biological and cultural diversity of Mediterranean landscapes. In: Rundel, P.W., Montenegro, G., Jaksic, F. M. (eds.) Landscape Disturbance and Biodiversity in Mediterranean-Type Ecosystems, pp. 23–53. Springer, Berlin (1998). https://doi.org/10.1007/978-3-662-03543-6_2
4. Naveh, Z.: The total human ecosystem: integrating ecology and economics. Bioscience **50** (4), 357–361 (2000)
5. Buttschardt, T.: Wofür steht Geoökologie? Forum der Geoökologie **12**(1), 38–41 (2001)
6. Bastian, O.: Landscape Ecology – towards a unified discipline? Landscape Ecol. **16**, 757–766 (2001)
7. Farina, A.: Principles and Methods in Landscape Ecology: Towards a Science of Landscape, 412 p. Springer, Dordrecht (2006)
8. Botequilla Leitão, A., Miller, J., Ahern, J., McGarigal, K.: Measuring Landscapes. A Professional Planner's Manual, 246 p. Island Press, Washington D.C. (2006)
9. European Commission: Communication from the Commission to the European parliament, the Council, the European economic and social committee and the Committee of the Regions —An Integrated Maritime Policy for the European Union. Brussels COM(2007)575 Final (2007)
10. Van Kouwen, F., Dieperink, C., Schot, P., Wassen, M.: Applicability of decision support systems for integrated coastal zone management. Coast. Manag. **36**(1), 19–34 (2008)
11. Fabbri, K.P.: A strategic decision support framework for integrated coastal zone management. Int. J. Environ. Technol. Manag. **6**, 206–217 (2006)
12. Jørgensen, S.E., Nielsen, S.N.: Thermodynamic orientors: exergy as a goal function in ecological modeling and as an ecological indicator for the description of ecosystem development. In: Müller, F., Leupelt, M. (eds.) Eco Targets, Goal Function and Orientors, pp. 64–86. Springer, Heidelberg (1998). https://doi.org/10.1007/978-3-642-58769-6_5
13. Jørgensen, S.E.: Application of exergy and specific exergy as ecological indicators of coastal areas. Aquat. Ecosyst. Health Manag. **3**, 419–430 (2000)
14. Jørgensen, S.E.: Parameters, ecological constraints and exergy. Ecol. Model. **62**, 163–170 (2002)
15. Jørgensen, S.E.: Eco-Exergy as Sustainability, 220 p. WIT, Southampton (2006)
16. Jørgensen, S.E.: Application of holistic thermodynamic indicators. Ecol. Ind. **6**, 24–29 (2006)
17. IOC (Intergovernmental Oceanographic Commission): A Handbook for Measuring the Progress and Outcomes of Integrated Coastal and Ocean Management, (Prepared by Belfiore, S., Barbiere, J., Bowen, R., Cicin-Sain, B., Ehler, C., Mageau, C., McDougall, D., Siron, R.). IOC Manuals and Guides, 46, ICAM Dossier, 2, 217 p. UNESCO, Paris (2006)
18. EEA (European Environment Agency): The changing faces of Europe's coastal areas. Report n. 6/2006, 107 p. (2006). http://reports.eea.europa.eu/eea_report_2006_6/en. Accessed 23 May 2008
19. Vallega, A.: From Rio to Johannesburg: the role of coastal GIS. Ocean Coast. Manag. **48**(7–8), 588–618 (2005)

20. Maelfait, H., Belpaeme, K. (eds.): The Coastal Compass, Key Indicators as Guidelines for ICZM. Ostend, Belgium, 63 p. Coordination Centre for Integrated Coastal Zone Management (2007)

21. EEA (European Environment Agency): Urban sprawl in Europe The ignored challenge, EEA Report n. 10/2006, Office for Official Publications of the European Communities, Luxembourg, 56 p. (2006)

22. EEA (European Environment Agency): The continuous degradation of Europe's coasts threatens European living standards. EEA Briefing 2006(3), (TH-AM-06-003-EN-C). Office for Official Publications of the European Communities, Luxembourg (2006)

23. DEDUCE. Indicators Guidelines to adopt an indicators-based approach to evaluate coastal sustainable development. (Prepared by Martí, X., Lescrauwaet, A.K., Borg, M., Valls, M.), 97 p. DEDUCE Consortium, Government of Catalonia, Barcelona (2007)

24. Marotta, L., Ceccaroni, L., Matteucci, G., Rossini, P., Guerzoni, S.: A decision-support system in ICZM for protecting the ecosystems: integration with the habitat directive. J. Coast. Conserv. **15**, 393–415 (2010)

25. Wiens, J.A.: Toward a unified landscape ecology Issues in Landscape Ecology. In: Wiens, J. A., Moss, M.R. (eds.) International Association for Landscape Ecology. Snowmass Village, USA, pp. 148–151 (1999)

26. Wu, J., Hobbs, R.: Key issues and research priorities in landscape ecology: an idiosyncratic synthesis. Landscape Ecol. **17**, 355–365 (2002)

27. Troll, C.: Luftbildplan and ökologische Bodenforschung. Zeitschrift der Gesellschaft für Erdkunde Zu Berlin, pp. 241–298 (1939)

28. Troll, C.: Landscape ecology (geoecology) and biogeocenology: a terminological study. Geoforum **8**, 43–46 (1971)

29. Wu, J.: Landscape ecology, cross-disciplinarity, and sustainability science. Landscape Ecol. **21**, 1–4 (2006)

30. Turner, R.K., Burgess, D., Hadley, D., Coombes, E., Jackson, N.: Coastal Management in the 21st Century: Coping Strategies For Vulnerability Reduction, CSERGE Working Paper ECM 06–04, 21 p. (2006). http://www.uea.ac.uk/env/cserge/pub/wp/ecm/ecm_2006_04.pdf. Accessed 4 Dec 2008

31. Naveh, Z., Lieberman, A.S.: Landscape Ecology - Theory and Applications, 2nd edn, 360 p. Springer, New York (1994)

32. Barrett, G.W., Farina, A.: Integrating ecology and economics. Bioscience **50**(4), 311–312 (2000)

33. Desaigues, B.: The socio-economic value of ecotones. In: Naiman, R.J., Decamps, H. (eds) The Ecology and Management of Aquatic-Terrestrial Ecotones, MAB, UNESCO, Paris, pp. 263–293 (1990)

34. De Marchi, A.: Ecologia funzionale, 316 p. Garzanti, Milano (1992)

35. Odum, H.T.: Environmental Accounting: Emergy and Environmental Decision Making, 370 p. Wiley, New York (1996)

36. Thrush, S.F., Halliday, J., Hevit, J.E., Lohrer, A.M.: The effects of habitat loss, fragmentation, and community homogenization on resilience, in estuaries. Ecol. Appl. **18**(1), 12–21 (2008)

37. Marotta, L.: Ecologia Urbana e sistemi costieri. In: Bettini, V. (ed.) Ecologia Urbana. UTET, Torino, pp. 419–454 (2004)

38. Marotta, L., Cecchi, A., Ridolfi, E., Breton, F., Ceccaroni, L.: Downscaling indicators of integrated coastal zone management in the Mediterranean Sea. In: Proceedings of the Littoral (2008) CORILA/EUCC, Venice (2008)

39. Vallega, A.: Fundamental of coastal zone management, 263 p. Kluwer, Dordrecht (1999)

40. EEA (European Environment Agency): Land systems at European level – analytical assessment framework. EEA Briefing no. 10/2018 (2018). ISBN 978-92-9213-988-9. ISSN 2467-3196. https://doi.org/10.2800/141532

41. EU: Directive 2007/2/EC of the European Parliament and of the Council of 14 March 2007 establishing an Infrastructure for Spatial Information in the European Community (INSPIRE). OJ L 108, 25.4.2007, pp. 1–14 (2007)

42. European Commission: Guidelines on best practice to limit, mitigate or compensate soil sealing. Bruxelles, 15.5.2012, SWD 101 (2012)

43. Kuemmerle, T., et al.: Hotspots of land use change in Europe. Environ. Res. Lett. **11**, 064020 (2016)

44. Stavi, I., Bel, G., Zaady, E.: Soil functions and ecosystem services in conventional, conservation, and integrated agricultural systems. A review. Agron. Sustain. Dev. **36**, 32 (2016)

45. Blasi, C., Carranza, M.L., Frondoni, R., Rosati, L.: Ecosystem classification and mapping: a proposal for Italian landscapes. Appl. Veg. Sci. **3**(2), 233–242 (2000)

46. Géhu, J.M., Rivas Martínez, S.: Notions fondamentales de phytosociologie. Ber Int Symp Int Vereinigung Vegetationsk **1980**, 5–30 (1981)

47. Filesi, L., Lapenna, M.R.: La vegetazione potenziale (con cartografia). In: Vittadini, M.R., Bolla, D., Barp, A. (eds.) Spazi verdi da vivere. ULSS 20 Verona, Regione del Veneto, Università IUAV di Venezia (printed by il Prato), Venezia- Saonara (PD) (2015)

48. EU: Council Directive 92/43/EEC of 21 May 1992 on the conservation of natural habitats and of wild fauna and flora. Off. J. L 206, 0007–0050 (1992)

49. EU: Council Directive 79/409/EEC of 2 April 1979 on the conservation of wild birds. OJ L 103, 25.4.1979, pp. 1–18 (1979)

50. Cattozzo, L.: From linearity to circularity. A regenerative model applied to a coastal landscape. Ph.D. thesis. IUAV, School of Doctorate "Architecture, City and Design", Track "New technologies and information for the region and environment", Venice (2019)

51. Buffa, G., Filesi, L., Gamper, U., Sburlino, G.: Qualità e grado di conservazione del paesaggio vegetale del litorale sabbioso del Veneto (Italia settentrionale). Fitosociologia **44**(1), 49–58 (2007)

52. ISPRA (Istituto Superiore per la Protezione e la Ricerca Ambientale): TERRITORIO. Processi e trasformazioni in Italia. ISPRA. Rapporti 296/2018 (2018)

53. Eurostat's online database. Data table t2020_rn110. https://ec.europa.eu/eurostat/tgm/table.do?tab=table&plugin=1&language=en&pcode=t2020_rn110. Accessed 18 Apr 2019

54. Jaeger, J.A.G.: Landscape division, splitting index, and effective mesh size: new measures of landscape fragmentation. Landscape Ecol. **15**, 115–130 (2000)

55. ISPRA-SNPA: Consumo di suolo, dinamiche territoriali e servizi ecosistemici - Edizione 2018. ISPRA. Rapporti 288/2018 (2018)

# Cumulative Impact of Societal Activities on Marine Ecosystems and Their Services

Henning Sten Hansen(✉)

Aalborg University Copenhagen, A.C Meyers Vaenge 15,
2450 Copenhagen, Denmark
hsh@plan.aau.dk

**Abstract.** Marine space is overall under increasing pressure from human activities and in the way harming the marine ecosystems. Maritime spatial planning is one of the governance elements in the EU Integrated Maritime Policy (2007) that aims to maximise the sustainable use of the seas and oceans. Maritime spatial planning aims to ensure that the increased use of the marine space takes place in a way that are consistent with the sustainable development in the seas and oceans. According to the MSP Directive it is required to follow an ecosystem-based and thus holistic approach. For this to happen, tools are needed, and some tools are available but with various advantages and disadvantages. The aim of the current research has been to develop a comprehensive package of tools to assess the environmental impacts of societal activities under different maritime spatial planning proposals.

**Keywords:** Maritime spatial planning · Marine environment ·
Cumulative impact · Decision-support tools · Agenda 2030

## 1 Introduction

The sea is a scene of a wide range of activities. From nature's own use to human activities like oil exploration, offshore wind farms, shipping, fishery, aquaculture, and recreation. In the recently launched Blue Growth initiative, the European Commission (EC) identifies a potential for further job-creation and innovative technology development in the sea area, like new offshore renewable energy technologies, sustainable aquaculture, maritime coastal and cruise tourism, marine mineral resources, and biotechnology utilising marine organisms. Human activities are not always compatible with the need of nature, and may lead to several threats like eutrophication, habitat damage, and proliferation of invasive species [1].

In 2015, the United Nations adopted the 2030 Agenda for Sustainable Development and its 17 Sustainable Development Goals (SDG), and they entered into force by 1st January 2016[1]. Number 14 of the 17 SDG's concerns the *conservation and sustainable use of the oceans, seas and maritime resources*. Careful management and regulation of the global marine resources is a key element in obtaining a sustainable future, and to

---

[1] https://www.un.org/sustainabledevelopment/development-agenda/.

© Springer Nature Switzerland AG 2019
S. Misra et al. (Eds.): ICCSA 2019, LNCS 11621, pp. 577–590, 2019.
https://doi.org/10.1007/978-3-030-24302-9_41

make this operational a set of ten Goal 14 targets with deadlines are defined. Thus, it is expected according to target 14.2 already by 2020 to sustainably manage and protect marine and coastal ecosystems to avoid significant adverse impacts, strengthening their resilience, and act for their restoration in order to achieve healthy and productive oceans.

In the sea, everything is connected. Fish, nutrients, and hazardous substances move from one location to another without barriers. The marine space is characterised not only by a three-dimensional water column supporting multi-functional use (different uses at the same location but at different depths) but is actually strongly four-dimensional (seasonal and diurnal cycles appears in many forms in the marine environment). Hence, Maritime Spatial Planning (MSP) needs to be based on this context different from terrestrial planning which traditionally only needs to address two dimensions – the earth surface. Accordingly, the EC launched a new directive on maritime spatial planning and this directive entered into force in 2014 and required its member states to establish maritime spatial plans by 2021 [2]. According to the MSP Directive it is required to follow an ecosystem-based and thus holistic approach. For this to happen, tools are needed, and some tools are available but with various advantages and disadvantages.

Therefore, the aim of the current research has been to develop a comprehensive package of tools to assess the environmental impacts of societal activities under different maritime spatial planning proposals. After this introduction follows a description of the background and theory behind cumulative impact assessment. Next, follows the design and implementation of the new toolbox, and some examples of its use. The paper ends with a discussion of the proposed approach to tools target towards cumulative impacts assessment on marine ecosystems from anthropogenic activities.

## 2  Theory

Development of ecosystem-based maritime spatial planning (MSP) comprises a number of tasks including identification of the planning needs, pre-planning and stakeholder engagement, defining and analysing existing and future conditions, preparing and approving the spatial management plan, implementation of the plan, and finally, monitoring and evaluating the performance [3].

Maritime spatial planning is characterised by being a continuing and iterative process adapting over time, and therefore unsuitable to be expressed as a static plan. Practical tools supporting maritime spatial planning and supporting cross-border coordination and participation are still limited.

### 2.1  Protecting the Marine Environment

The Marine Strategy Framework Directive (MSFD) [4] marks an important step forward in the EU marine environmental policy being the first legal framework specifically aimed at protecting and preserving the marine environment. In addition, it aims at preventing the deterioration of the marine environment and, where feasible, restoring marine ecosystems in areas where they have been adversely affected.

The MSFD requires that the EU member states, that share the same marine region (i.e., Baltic Sea, the Mediterranean Sea, and the Black Sea) should collaborate to develop marine strategies in order to ensure coherence in the assessment, setting environmental targets and monitoring efforts. The regional platforms for developing coherent marine strategies are the Regional Sea Conventions, which are the required regional coordination structures. Furthermore, the MSFD states that the marine strategies shall apply an ecosystem - based approach to the management of human activities.

Achieving a Good Environmental Status in the European marine regions require appropriate planning decisions which furthermore requires the comprehensive knowledge of the impacts induced by different anthropogenic activities and natural changes. Therefore, methods and techniques are required in to efficiently estimate the cumulative impacts from multiple and interactive human activities and their pressures enabling planners and decision makers to apply science-based information to assess different efforts in marine management by using scenarios.

An ecosystem oriented maritime planning support tool needs to respond to a number of challenges to integrated planning and management, including to consider effects of various and/or alternative economic and other activities in the maritime space – and to communicate benefits and trade-offs of different alternatives with stakeholders in the planning phases. This requires a framework for assessment of effects that can: (a) integrate effects of multiple human activities, (b) integrate the impacts of spatially explicit maritime human activities on multiple ecosystem services related to the sea and coastal ecosystems, (c) address ecosystem services related to waters, sea bed, sub sea bed, as well as to coastal ecosystem services, (d) economic and social impacts related to involved and affected stakeholders, (e) ensure conservation of biologically and eco-logically sensitive marine areas, (f) support governance of maritime activities at various governance levels and between horizontal authorities and stakeholders. A large number of impact assessment frameworks for terrestrial activities exist along lines of EIA, SEA or sustainable development criteria [5].

The DPSIR (Drivers-Pressures-States-Impacts-Responses) framework from the European Environment Agency is used to act as an integrated approach to their State of the Environment Reporting and is the basic concept behind the many tools for cumulative impact on ecosystems from anthropogenic activities and pressures. The MYTILUS toolbox, which is the aim of this research is such a tool.

At the top level of the framework you find the Driving forces representing different kind of needs for humans [6]. Examples are need for food, water, shelter, transport, culture, etc. In addition, the number of people including their age structure, and edu-cation levels is an important driver, affecting the strength of the other drivers.

The driving forces lead to human activities like transportation (e.g. sailing) or food production (e.g. fishery). These human activities exert pressures on the environment – often trough emission of substances, noise, radiation, etc. The pressures subsequently change the State of the environment – e.g. reduced biodiversity in the seas and oceans, or fewer fish due to overfishing.

If the impact on the ecosystem goes beyond what is acceptable by the societies, some response is required in order reduce the pressure on the ecosystems. This may be done by regulation – e.g. through higher taxation of the human activities being the reason to the adverse effects, or by maritime spatial planning dictation what is allowed and what is forbidden in specific sea areas.

To take the right decisions, knowledge about cause-effect links must be provided, but most often the impact on marine ecosystems is not only the result of a single human activity but cumulative effects of several human activities.

## 2.2   Cumulative Impact Assessment

The concept of cumulative impact assessment (CIA) on the marine environments originally defined by Halpern et al. [7] was the first effort in this direction and has served as inspiration for further research into that direction. He developed an index to assess the cumulative impact on the marine environment at a rather high spatial resolution in a global perspective.

According to Halpern [7] the cumulative impact is determined from three components: maps of pressures from different human activities; maps over different ecosystems, and a matrix describing the sensitivity of each ecosystem to each pressure. Thus, the cumulative impact ($I_a$) on the environment within a square pixel can be estimated by multiplying the values for each pressure ($P$) with the values for each ecosystem component ($E$) and its specific sensitivity $\mu$. Finally, these impacts are summarised over all pressures and ecosystems:

$$I_a = \sum_{i=1}^{n} \sum_{j=1}^{m} P_i \times E_j \times \mu_{i,j} \tag{1}$$

Here $n$ is the number of pressure layers and $m$ is the number of ecosystems. The sensitivity variable $\mu$ represents the sensitivity of ecosystem $j$ to pressure $i$ and are most often derived by expert judgment in a rather complicated process – see for example the way this is done in the assessment of the cumulative impact in the Baltic Sea [8].

Equation (1) has led to other indices describing the impact on the environment but underlining different aspects. The subscript $a$ in $I_a$ refers to the calculation principle of just adding the impact on all ecosystems for all pressure layers.

Closely related to the two equations above is the so-called cumulative pressure index ($PI$), which form the dynamic part of Eq. (1), and is calculated similarly but without considering the ecosystem component:

$$PI = \sum_{i=1}^{n} \left( P_i \frac{1}{m} \sum_{j=1}^{m} \mu_{i,j} \right) \tag{2}$$

Focusing on the ecosystems part of Eq. (1) will provide an index of the ecological diversity/complexity $E_{Div}$ ending up with an expression like:

$$E_{Div} = \sum_{j=1}^{m} E_j \tag{3}$$

It has been argued that the additive principle in Eq. (1) is too simple, and can be improved by averaging over the ecosystems to estimate the so-called $I_{Mean}$ index:

$$I_{Mean} = \sum_{i=1}^{n} \sum_{j=1}^{m} \frac{1}{E_{Div}} 1P_i \times E_j \times \mu_{i,j} \tag{4}$$

This set of equations build the foundation for cumulative impact assessment on marine ecosystems from human activities and pressures.

## 2.3    Tools for Cumulative Impact Assessment

Based on the original ideas by Halpern et al. [7] several tools have been developed to calculate the cumulative impact on ecosystems and their services. Generally, all the data layers are created in "standard" GIS software like ArcGIS or QGIS. Therefore, the most straight forward approach to calculate cumulative impact is to apply the selected GIS tool. This can be done, but the calculations will take rather long time, which is often the case using general purpose tools compared to dedicated tools. For stakeholder meetings this is not appropriate, if the calculations have to be repeated several times with different options. In addition, the learning curves for ArcGIS or QGIS are rather steep putting emphasis among the users on learning a GIS tool instead of focusing on the actual topic – estimating the cumulative impact on the ecosystems from various anthropogenic activities and pressures. Therefore, several efforts to develop dedicated tools for cumulative impact assessments have been done.

The EcoImpactMapper tool developed by Stock [9] is probably the most well-known approach and has been used in many contexts [10, 11]). The EcoImpactMapper is a stand-alone desktop tool with a simple user interface which is straight to use. It applies CSV files to represent the pressure and ecosystem layers. This is one of the main challenges using EcoImpactMapper, that it cannot use 'standard' raster and shape files, but data needs to be transformed to and from CSV files when moving between GIS software packages and EcoImpactMapper. This, is perhaps the main disadvantage using EcoImpactMapper.

Tools4MSP is a set of tools aiming to support ecosystem-based maritime spatial planning [12]. The software package consists of three parts: Maritime Use Conflict Analysis, Cumulative Effects Assessments, and Marine Ecosystem Services Threat Assessment. Focusing on the tool for Cumulative Effects Assessments it is based on an open source geo-python library. It is very flexible but not straightforward to use.

Finally, Symphony is developed as a dedicated tool to the Swedish Agency for Marine and Water Management [13] and it is based on SeaSketch, which is commercial product with a starting price of 3000$ per year for the simplest version. It is web based and more a collaborative planning system supporting stakeholder involvement than just a tool for cumulative impact assessment. Thus, the system is comprehensive, but the licensing price is an important obstacle for its wider use.

Altogether, the existing tools for cumulative impact assessment have various challenges of being used in practical maritime spatial planning – and particularly during stakeholder involvements, where all the calculation processes need to be carried out fast and smoothly.

## 2.4    Marine Spatial Data Infrastructure

One of the main challenges regarding decision support systems for maritime spatial planning hereunder assessing the cumulative impact on the marine ecosystems is the accessibility to up-to-data good quality data covering the whole study area. A Spatial Data Infrastructure is about facilitation and coordination of the exchange and sharing of spatial data. It is described as the underlying infrastructure, often in the form of policies, standards and access networks that allows data to be shared between people within organisations, states or countries. The fundamental interaction between people and data is governed by the technological components of SDI represented by the access network, policies and standards [14]. The INSPIRE Directive which was adopted by the European Council and Parliament in spring 2007 and entered into force May 2007 [15] aims to make more and better spatial information available for Community policy-making and implementation in a wide range of sectors – including the marine environment. Considering the large number of data sets, they prioritised and put into three annexes with different time frames. Unfortunately for maritime spatial planning, the data sets connected to this topic is allocated to annex three of the INSPIRE Directive with a rather long time horizon.

Kocur-Bera and Dudzińska [16] examine geoportals of interest for the Baltic Sea region, and they similarly conclude that current environmental data unfortunately are not available from one single entry and that the resolution of the data is sometimes inadequate for marine planning. Two of their examples are INSPIRE geoportal, which links the user to terrestrial and marine environmental data at various European institutions' homepages, and HELCOM Data & Map Service, which hosts many marine datasets from the Baltic Sea region that can be viewed, and some of them downloaded through ArcGIS rest service or WMS [16]. The main advantage of the data at the HELCOM data portal is, that the data are coherent and harmonised, and available for the whole Baltic Sea from just one data portal. The main challenge concerning the HELCOM data concerns the temporal dimension, where data are of different age and sometimes not even the newest available data. This is clearly a major challenge if data are being used in real decision making on maritime spatial plans. During the last three years, the Baltic Lines project has developed a new data portal BASEMAPS (Baltic Sea Map Service) based on a modern distributes architecture, where data are retrieved from the original sources among associated data providers but identified from the BASEMAPS data portal [17]. However, although the data represents the most recent edition, they are not harmonised across national borders and represent challenges concerning the different languages present in the Baltic Sea Region. Thus, there is at the moment no straight forward solution easily to feed data into different tools for cumulative impact assessment.

Moving the study area outside the Baltic Sea makes the data challenges even bigger although the North Sea Commission (OSPAR) has a data service called ODIMS (OSPAR's Data and Information Management System)[2], which contain 45 pre-processed maps and 233 Data Layers. Other important sources of marine data are the

---

[2] https://odims.ospar.org.

European Marine Observation and Data Network (EMODnet)[3] and the International Council for the Exploration of the Sea (ICES)[4] with access to huge amount of marine data. However, although the availability of data seems overwhelming, you are not sure, that the *right* data are available. To estimate the cumulative impact on ecosystems from anthropogenic activities requires many data layers for a specific area, and quite often you cannot find the same data for even two neighbouring seas making comparisons difficult.

# 3   Implementation

The overall aim of developing the MYTILUS toolbox is first of all to avoid some of the main challenges of the tools described above.

The MYTILUS Toolbox contains several building blocks and the overall structure is presented in Fig. 1. The core part is the cumulative impact assessment tool, which calculates the cumulative impact on different ecosystems from a range of human activities and their pressures.

## 3.1   Systems Design

The modelling system applies native ESRI ASCII raster data. This facilitates an easier exchange of data between MYTILUS and GIS software like ArcGIS and QGIS. In this way, MYTILUS can be used as a decision-support tool while doing data preparation and advanced visualisation in general purpose GIS- packages (Fig. 1).

The design of MYTILUS has focus on three aspects: (a) user friendliness, (b) analytical capacity, and (c) processing speed:

(a)  Generally, large GIS software systems like ArcGIS and QGIS are rather complicated systems with a steep learning curve, and potential users working with maritime spatial planning are not necessarily GIS experts. Therefore, building a stand-alone application focusing on a logical and easy to learn user interface has been given high priority. Everything is organised into projects – typically representing different geographical areas (sea basins). Under each project the user can define various scenarios – typically as baseline scenario describing the impact on the environment today followed by a set of alternative scenarios describing various spatial planning options as well as changing human activities. The user can visualise the different pressure and ecosystem layers and edit the values in the sensitivity matrix if needed. All calculations are carried out using dedicated easy-to-use dialog boxes, and results are shown within a short time frame.

(b)  The main aim of MYTILUS toolbox is to provide knowledge about the expected impact on the marine environment from various human activities under various maritime spatial planning proposals. This requires a flexible approach in the calculation process, where all combinations of pressures and ecosystems can by

---

[3] http://www.emodnet.eu.

[4] https://www.ices.dk/Pages/default.aspx.

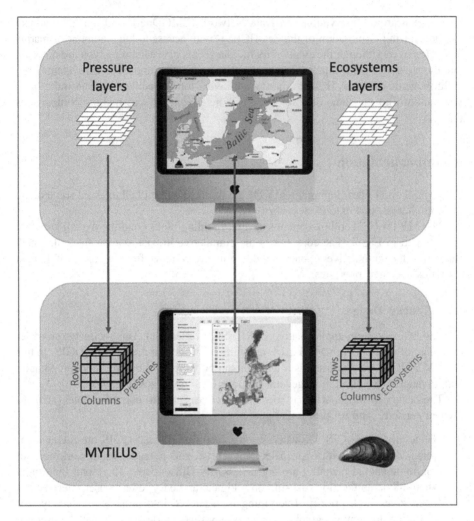

**Fig. 1.** MYTILUS systems architecture.

analysed numerically and visually based on Eqs. (1)–(4). Also, a direct comparison of the results from two scenarios can be made to identify interesting spatial patterns and differences. Finally, the out from the calculations can be imported directly into ArcGIS or QGIS if more analysis or professional map production is required.

(c) The calculations can be time consuming for large data sets, and this has been an issue in some existing tools. Therefore, there has been put a lot of efforts in the design and implementation of MYTILUS to support very fast calculations. This is done in several ways. First, the input data are preferably using integer values, which are generally faster than floating points. Second, the input data layers are organised in two data cubes – one for each of the two groups of layers representing pressures, and ecosystems (Fig. 1). This is for efficiency in data retrieval by substantially reduction in reading data files from the disk. Finally, the calculations are carried out with extensive use of parallel processing, utilising the full power of today's computers with at least four CPU cores – but even with 6, 8, 10 and more cores. In practice the calculations on the raster cells are done row by row in traditional serial processing but using parallel processing the calculations can be done for several rows of cells simultaneously dependant on the number of CPU cores – but speeding up the processing time significantly.

The MYTILUS software is developed using the Delphi 10.1 Integrated Development Environment from Embarcadero[5], without using software libraries requiring royalties. Accordingly, the software is freeware with full accessibility to the source code. The software is easy to install on every computer running Windows 10 – also Mac computer under BootCamp or with virtualisation software.

The next paragraph demonstrates the use of MYTILUS with some examples from the Baltic Sea. The examples are by no means exhaustive but provides an idea of the possibilities with the MYTILUS toolbox.

## 4  Examples

Currently, the MYTILUS toolbox is being tested in the Baltic Sea, where HELCOM[6] provides freely available Baltic Sea wide data on human activities, pressures, and ecosystems. The pressure layers available from HELCOM's data portal are used for their own assessment of the Baltic Sea Environment [18] and follows the pressure layers mentioned in the Marine Strategy Framework Directive (MSFD) (European Commission, 2008).

The data used for testing the MYTILUS software comes from the HELCOM data portal mentioned earlier. Originally, Halpern et al. [7] recommended to $\log(x + 1)$ transform the pressure data in order to reduce the extreme outliers. Afterwards the pressure data are re-scaled to values between 0 and 100 in opposite to Halpern et al. [7] rescaling into the interval 0–1. As mentioned above, MYTILUS primarily makes use of integer values of performance reasons. Most of the data on ecosystems are binary (1 or 0) meaning that an ecosystem can exists in a particular raster cell or not. If this is not the case, they ecosystem layers are $\log(1 + x)$ transformed and rescaled similar to the pressure layers. All data on pressures and ecosystems from HELCOMS data portal are in raster format with 1 km cell size and using the INSPIRE EEA Reference Grid using ETRS89/LAEA Europe as projected reference system [15].

Figure 2 illustrate the flexibility and analytical capacity of cumulative impact assessment toolbox in MYTILUS. The user has the flexibility to calculate the so-called additive cumulative impact index $I_a$ on the environment according to Eq. (1) as well as the $I_{Mean}$ index according to Eq. (2). The map in Fig. 2 shows the spatial distribution of

---

[5] https://www.embarcadero.com/products/delphi.

[6] HELCOM (Helsinki Convention).

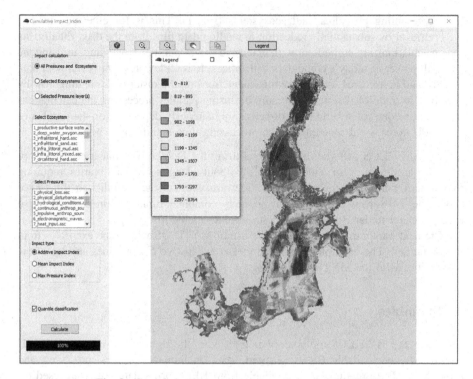

**Fig. 2.** Cumulative impact assessment dialog in MYTILUS

index $I_a$, with a strong impact on the environment in the South-western Baltic Sea and along the coast around Stockholm and Helsinki.

In addition, the user can also select a single or groups of pressure layers and combine with a single or groups of ecosystems thus getting possibilities for better understanding of cause-effect relationships. In order to enhance the visual analytical capacity, the user can choose between the traditional equal interval in the definition of class intervals, and the equal-area classification enhancing the visual differences.

Finally, the user can calculate the max-pressure index – i.e. the pressure in each grid cell providing the highest impact. This is important in identifying needed actions regarding reducing pressures from human activities in certain areas – and this has to be reflected in maritime spatial plan. The user can also identify the second highest and third highest important pressure in each cell – again to assess the

For Cumulative Impact Assessment to support environmental management in an area it is necessary to establish a fixed baseline against which to evaluate the effects of new spatial planning options, new technological development trends, or future changes due to for example climate changes. Establishing such a baseline for the cumulative impact assessment can be developed from historical conditions or from the present conditions. Alternative spatial scenarios are important steps for analysing and visualizing how specifics goals and objectives may result in re-location of human activities within the planning area.

The figure below shows an example, where the left map illustrates the impact on the ecosystems according to the baseline scenario, while the right-side map shows the impact for the same area but for an alternative scenario after adding 8 new fish farms (Fig. 3). The adverse effect on the environment from fish farms is related to the emission of primarily nitrogen but also phosphorous leading to eutrophication and later on oxygen depletion in the water. The spreading of nitrogen kernel is off-course dependent on many several physical characteristics not at least sea currents, but currently the contribution of additional nitrogen from fish farms is modelled isotopically applying a kernel density function. The impact from the enhanced nitrogen emission is a little higher around the new fish farms compared to the baseline scenario, but not significant higher (both maps is based on an equal interval classification). Thus, it may be appropriate to allocate space to new fish farms in the proposed area unless other challenges – like the general high pressure from nitrogen emissions in the whole Baltic Sea Basin.

The user can test different effects of new human activities compared the current situation illustrated by the baseline scenario, and in this way facilitate an optimum location of new activities, or identifying areas, where existing activities needs to be reduced or even closed down in order to requirements of a good ecological status of the marine waters according the EU Marine Strategy Framework Directive.

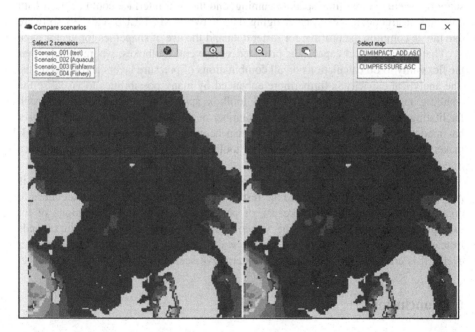

**Fig. 3.** Comparison of two different scenarios demonstrating the effect on the cumulative impact from new fish farms (right map)

## 5    Discussion

Since the approval of the Maritime Spatial Planning Directive by the European Union in 2014 [2] with a strong encouragement to adopting an ecosystem-based approach, the interests for cumulative impact assessment of marine ecosystems due to pressures from human activities has increased heavily. Particularly, the assessment of cumulative effect on global marine waters by Halpern et al. [7] has provided interest in developing tools to carry out the assessments. The tools being developed like EcoImpactMapper [9], Tools4MSP [12] and Symphony [13] are all fine examples on tools to support the ecological assessment in the MSP process. However, they all have their advantages and disadvantages, and that was the main reason behind developing the MYTILUS toolbox for cumulative assessment of the impact on marine ecosystems from human activities and pressures. Additionally, the advantage of having our own system with easy possibility to further development was a second reason.

Working with CSV files were not found appropriate when exchanging data with 'standard' GIS software like ArcGIS and QGIS, and the costs of using the Seasketch-based Symphony was out of scope for our financial capabilities.

As stated in Sect. 3.1 the ambition was to build a new cumulative impact tool with three priorities: user friendliness, high analytical capacity, and high-performance calculations. The MYTILUS toolbox was tested during a recent PhD course on decision support systems in maritime spatial planning, and the user interface could be used with only few instructions – even exchanging data between MYTILUS and GIS software due the de common data format for raster data and the use of shapefiles for vector data.

The high analytical capacity is provided via several toolboxes, where the user has the flexibility to do calculations on all combinations of pressure layers and ecosystems. The analytical capacity is furthermore enhanced by many possibilities to visualise the resulting maps. Finally, the MYTILUS toolbox applies a scenario-based approach facilitating the inclusion of an unlimited number of different scenarios, where the user has made step-by-step changes in the human activities and pressures and afterwards make visual comparisons two-by-two. The toolbox can also calculate several statistics to compare scenarios.

The last point in the requirement list was the high-performance calculations. It is annoying the wait long time to see the results of a calculation. By using data cubes to organise the input data and make use of parallel-processing the calculations of for example cumulative impact for the whole Baltic Sea can be calculated in seconds instead of other systems where you have to wait in minutes. Especially, at stakeholder events it is critical to provide results of alternative scenarios quickly.

## 6    Conclusion

Marine space is increasingly used for many human activities, and the recently announced Blue Growth initiatives will contribute to a continuous growth of maritime activities. This will inevitably lead to enhanced – and perhaps even irreversible – pressure and impact on the marine ecosystems, which is a prerequisite for obtaining benefits like food, transport, energy, etc. by ecosystem services.

Therefore, there is a need for a well organised allocation of marine space, and that is the background for the EU Directive on Maritime Spatial Planning from 2014 [2]. This planning needs to be performed based on information and knowledge.

The so-called index on cumulative impact assessment originally developed by Halpern et al. [7] was pioneering for this work and inspired several researchers working with the impact on the ecosystems from human activities and pressures. The various tools like EcoImpactMapper, Tools4MSP, and Symphony are good examples on tools for cumulative impact assessments – but with their advantages and disadvantages.

The current paper has described the development of a new tool for cumulative impact aiming at user friendliness, high analytical capacity, and high-performance calculations. The success of the applied approach is demonstrated be a set of examples, and the current version is just a first version of the MYTILUS toolbox. It is expected that tools like MYTILUS can contribute to make more knowledge based maritime spatial plans among the EU Member States, as well as contributing to the process of reaching the targets set by the UN SDG goal 14 on the marine environment.

Currently, the next step in the development with focus on adding dynamics (time-series) into the impact calculations is under implementation and will be finished Autumn 2019. In addition, the calculation of conflict and synergy scores in connection with multi-use of marine space.

**Acknowledgement.** The current research has been supported by the NorthSEE project[7] funded by North Sea Programme of the European Regional Development Fund of the European Union, and the BONUS BASMATI project[8], which has received funding from BONUS (art. 185), funded jointly by the EU, Innovation Fund Denmark, Swedish Research Council Formas, Academy of Finland, Latvian Ministry of Education and Science, and Forschungszentrum Jülich GmbH (Germany).

# References

1. Blaesbjerg et al.: Marine Spatial Planning in the Nordic Region. TemaNord, 2009:525. Nordic Council of Ministers (2009)
2. European Commission. Directive 2014/89/EU of the European Parliament and of the Council of 23 July 2014 establishing a framework for maritime spatial planning. The Official Journal of the European Union, L 257/135 (2014)
3. Ehler, C., Douvere, F.: Marine Spatial Planning: a step-by-step approach toward ecosystem-based management. Intergovernmental Oceanographic Commission and Man and the Biosphere Programme. In: OC Manual and Guides No. 53 IDNPU, editor (2009)
4. European Commission. Directive 2008/56/EC of the European Parliament and of the Council of 17 June 2008 establishing a framework for community action in the field of marine environmental policy (Marine Strategy Framework Directive). The Official Journal of the European Union, L 164/19 (2008)
5. Hacking, T., Guthrie, P.: A framework for classifying the meaning of Triple Bottom-Line, Integrated, and Sustainability Assessment. Environ. Impact Assess. Rev. **28**, 73–89 (2008)

---

[7] https://northsearegion.eu/northsee/.

[8] https://bonusbasmati.eu.

6. Kristensen, P.: The DPSIR framework. Paper presented at the 27–29 September 2004 Workshop on a Comprehensive/Detailed Assessment of the Vulnerability of Water Resources to Environmental Change in Africa Using River Basin Approach. UNEP Headquarters, Nairobi, Kenya (2004)

7. Halpern, B.S., et al.: A global map of human impact on marine ecosystems. Science **319**, 948–952 (2008)

8. HELCOM: The assessment of cumulative impacts using the Baltic Sea Pressure Index and the Baltic Sea Impact Index - supplementary report to the first version of the HELCOM 'State of the Baltic Sea' report (2017). http://stateofthebalticsea.helcom.fi/about-helcom-and-the-assessment/downloads-and-data/

9. Stock, A.: Open source software for mapping human impacts on marine ecosystems with an additive model. J. Open Res. Softw. **4**, 1–7 (2016)

10. Korpinen, S., Meski, L., Andersen, J.H., Laamanen, M.: Human pressures and their potential impact on the Baltic Sea ecosystem. Ecol. Indic. **15**(1), 105–114 (2012)

11. Micheli, F., et al.: Cumulative human impacts on mediterranean and black sea marine ecosystems: assessing current pressures and opportunities. PLoS ONE **8**(12), e79889 (2013)

12. Menegon, S., Sarretta, A., Depellegrin, D., Farella, G., Venier, C., Barbante, A.: Tools4MSP: an open source software package to support Maritime Spatial Planning. PeerJ Computer Science (2018). https://doi.org/10.7717/peerj-cs.165

13. Swedish Agency for Marine and Water Management: Symphony - Integrated planning support for national maritime planning from an ecosystem approach. Gothenburg (2018). (in Swedish)

14. Rajabifard, A., Feeney, M.E.F., Williamson, I.: Spatial data infrastructures: concept, nature and SDI Hierarchi. In: Williamson, I.P., Rajabifard, A., Feeney, M.E.F. (eds.) Developing Spatial Data Infrastructures: From Concept to Reality, pp. 17–40. Taylor and Francis, London, New York (2003)

15. European Commission. Directive 2007/2/EC of the European Parliament and of the Council of 14 March 2007 establishing an Infrastructure for Spatial Information in the European Community (INSPIRE). Official Journal of the European Union (2007)

16. Kocur-Bera, K., Dudzińska, M.: Information and database range used for maritime spatial planning and for integrated management of the coastal zone – case study in Poland. Baltic Sea. Acta Adriatica **55**(2), 179–194 (2014)

17. Hansen, H.S., Reiter, I.M., Schrøder, L.: A system architecture for a transnational data infrastructure supporting maritime spatial planning. In: Kő, A., Francesconi, E. (eds.) EGOVIS 2017. LNCS, vol. 10441, pp. 158–172. Springer, Cham (2017). https://doi.org/10.1007/978-3-319-64248-2_12

18. HELCOM: First version of the 'State of the Baltic Sea' report – June 2017 – to be updated in 2018 (2017). http://stateofthebalticsea.helcom.fi

# Predicting Sediment Concentrations Using a Nonlinear Autoregressive Exogenous Neural Network

Vladimir J. Alarcon[(⊠)] [iD]

Civil Engineering Department, Universidad Diego Portales,
441 Ejercito Avenue, Santiago, Chile
vladimir.alarcon@udp.cl

**Abstract.** An application of a Nonlinear Autoregressive Exogenous Neural Network (NARX) to predict total suspended sediment concentrations (SST) for a water body located in central Chile (Francia Creek, Valparaiso) is presented. Input data consisting of precipitation and stream flow time-series were fed to the developed NARX, for prediction of daily SST concentrations for a whole year. Sensitivity analysis was used for achieving the best NARX configuration that provided the best fit of simulated vs. measured data for year 2014. Parameters varied during sensitivity analysis were: number of nodes, number of iterations, feedback and forward delays, years of daily data used as training dataset. The resulting NARX is an open-loop net, consisting of a 12-node hidden layer, 100-iterations, using the Bayesian regularization backpropagation algorithm. SST concentrations predicted by the NARX net agreed successfully with measured SST concentrations ($r = 0.73$, $r^2 = 0.53$, NSE = 0.18, PBIAS = $-13.6\%$, Index of Agreement = 0.87).

**Keywords:** NARX · Neural network · Sediment concentrations · Prediction

## 1 Introduction

Response variables in hydrology (streamflow, sediment and pollutant concentrations, etc.) strongly depend in antecedent and current conditions of processes that determine the status of the response variable under study. The magnitude and duration of state variables in previous days will determine the magnitude and duration of the response variable, during an individual event. Seasonality is also a factor: most hydrological variables vary drastically during the year with trends particular to dry or wet seasons. Hydrological and water quality models capture that dependence using mechanistic and empirical algorithms that represent the physical processes. In particular, response variables such as stream flow and contaminant concentrations in rivers are studied not only for scientific purposes but also for water quality management and restoration.

Total suspended sediment concentrations (SST) in water bodies are indicators of several hydrological processes taking place within a watershed. The presence of SST depends on intensity and duration of rainfall events, soil matrix and surface characteristics, hillslopes conditions, land cover, stream flow. Antecedent conditions of most

© Springer Nature Switzerland AG 2019
S. Misra et al. (Eds.): ICCSA 2019, LNCS 11621, pp. 591–601, 2019.
https://doi.org/10.1007/978-3-030-24302-9_42

of those hydrological variables are also determinant of the current SST status. Estimating or predicting SST in rivers, lakes or estuaries it is usually performed through hydrological and water quality modeling. The resulting hydrological and water quality models have been proven to be very useful for water quality management purposes. However, the models are user-specific because of their complexity and, hence, require skilled operator expertise. Options more amenable for use by non-experts requiring water quality predictions are badly needed.

Event-based models use simple formulations for rainfall-runoff generation [1] but are usually developed for short-term purposes such as flood/flow forecasting and/or infrastructure designing. Other approaches that do not require to know any information regarding the physical process (such as non-parametric algorithms) constitute an alternate method. Continuous non-parametric hydrological models were shown to be very useful for long-term water resources management (e.g., estimation of design flows, land-use change impacts, effects of climate change, etc.). Non-parametric models such as antecedent precipitation indices, regression, artificial neural networks, fuzzy logic, and frequency analysis were used extensively [1]. From those available options, artificial neural networks seem to provide opportunities for implementing a tool that do not require extensive input information regarding the physical process, is user-friendly, and provides reliable predictions.

The Artificial Neural Network (ANN) approach to time-series prediction is a non-parametric method. For simple non-linear functions of one or several independent variables ANN are universal interpolators, but simple ANN configurations have limitations modeling seasonal patterns. Special configurations of ANN have been used with success to predict flows and sediment concentrations for rivers around the world. For example, [2–5] report good predictions of streamflow under flood and drought conditions. Similarly, ANN was used extensively for estimating sediment concentrations (e.g., [6–9]). However, in most of those applications of ANN, the validation period of the model output corresponded to within-year events or seasons because the input data was partitioned following the seasonality dependence of the input time-series. Also, some of those researches scaled the input data for improving predictions. There are not ANN models' validations for a whole year where all seasonality dependence is captured that use raw (not scaled) input data.

In this research, an application of a Nonlinear Autoregressive Exogenous Neural Network (NARX) to predict total suspended sediment concentrations (SST) for a water body located in central Chile (Francia Creek, Valparaiso). The NARX application is used to predict daily SST concentrations for year 2014 without scaling the input data, neither partition the input data per season.

## 2   Methods

### 2.1   Data Used for the Development of the Neural Network

Francia Creek watershed is a 324-hectares catchment located in the city of Valparaiso, Chile (Fig. 1). Precipitation, stream flow, and sediment concentrations (SST) from 2006 through 2014 for the exit of the catchment are reported in [10].

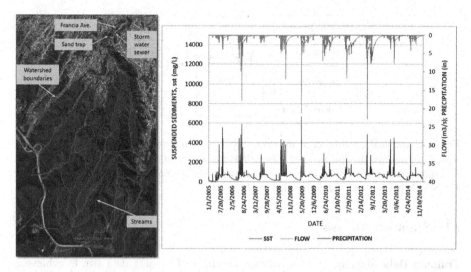

**Fig. 1.** Study area and data used for building the NARX net. The left-hand side of the figure shows Francia Creek watershed. The catchments exit is located at a sand trap at the outskirts of Valparaiso city. Time series of SST, precipitation and stream flow are shown at the right-hand side of the figure. Daily data beginning 1/1/2005 through 12/31/2014 are shown.

As shown in Fig. 1, three time-series were used for the development of the neural network. Daily total suspended solids concentrations $SST(t)$, precipitation $p(t)$, and stream flow $q(t)$, where time $(t)$ spans from 2005 through 2014 at daily time step.

## 2.2 NARX Neural Network

An artificial neural network is composed by several processing elements (neurons) that interact between each other through weights and activation functions that are adjusted until a desired output is achieved. NARX neural networks are recurrent dynamic networks, provided with feedback connections which enclose at least two layers of the network, and can use past values of predicted or true (measured) time-series [11]. NARX nets are particularly applicable for prediction of time-series. There are two types of NARX architectures: the closed-loop NARX architecture in which prediction of total suspended solids, $SST(N + 1...N + K)$, is done from the present and past measured values of precipitation, $p(1, 2...N)$, and stream flow, $q(1, 2...N)$, and the past predicted values of total suspended solids $SST(N - 1), SST(N - 2)...SST(N - J)$.

In the open-loop architecture, the future value of total suspended solids, $SST(t + 1)$, is predicted from the measured present and past values of precipitation, $p(t)$, stream flow, $q(t)$, and the measured past values of total suspended solids, $SST(t)$. In this research, an open-loop NARX net was used. Figure 2 presents a conceptual description of the NARX net used in this research.

All computations were performed using MATLAB. The Bayesian regularization backpropagation algorithm was used.

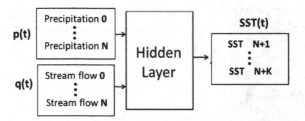

**Fig. 2.** Conceptual description of the open-loop NARX net used in this research. Input data consist of measured precipitation and stream flow time-series: $p(0, 1, 2..., N)$ and $q(0, 1, 2..., N)$, correspondingly. Training is performed using measured total suspended solids, $SST(0, 1, 2..., N)$. The NARX net predicts total suspended solids $SST(N + 1, N + 2, N + 3 ... N + K)$.

## 2.3    Sensitivity Analysis

**Training Data Size.** In order to explore the effect of training data size to achieve a successful prediction of SST, the number of years for training and prediction was varied. Table 1 details the process.

**Table 1.**  Training data size

| Model run | Number of years used for training | | | Number of years used for Prediction | | |
|---|---|---|---|---|---|---|
| | Precipitation $p(t)$ | Flow $q(t)$ | SST | Precipitation $p(t)$ | Flow $q(t)$ | SST |
| 1 | 9 | 9 | 9 | 10 | 10 | Predicted |
| 2 | 3 | 3 | 3 | 4 | 4 | Predicted |
| 3 | 2 | 2 | 2 | 3 | 3 | Predicted |

Initially, all data (9 years) previous to 2014 were used for training. For the prediction phase, precipitation ($p$) and flow data ($q$) from years 2005 through 2014 were used to predict total suspended solids, $SST$, for year 2014. Similarly, $p$ and $q$ data from years 2011–2013 were used for training and subsequently predictions for $SST$ for year 2014 was done using $p$ and $q$ data from 2011–2014. Finally, training was performed with data from 2 years previous to 2014, and predictions of $SST$ were done with $q$ and $p$ data from years 2012–2014.

**Number of Neurons in Hidden Layer.** In conjunction with the variation of other NARX net characteristics, the number of hidden layer nodes ranged from 5 to 50.

**Number of Iterations.** The variation of the number of iterations ranged from 50 to 1000. Its effects on SST predictions for year 2014 were explored.

# 3 Results

## 3.1 Effects of Number of Iterations

The effects on the prediction of daily SST concentrations for year 2014, when the number of iterations is varied during training of the NARX net, is shown in Fig. 3.

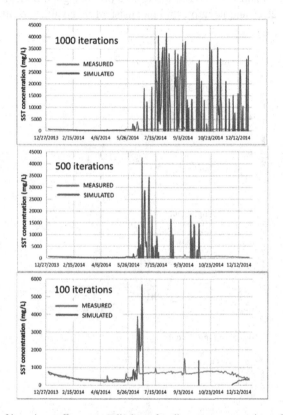

**Fig. 3.** Number of iterations effect on prediction of sediment concentrations, SST, for 2014. For simplicity only positive SST values are shown in the comparison charts.

Figure 3 shows that overtraining of the NARX net produce unstable results. For 1000 and 500 extreme (positive and negative) sediment concentrations SST values are estimated. For simplicity all charts show only positive value. Very high negative SST values were estimated. For 100 iterations, the NARX net produces SST values within the range of measured SST concentrations for the first half of year 2014. For the second half of the year extreme positive and negative SST are incorrectly estimated.

## 3.2 Input Data-Size Effects

Figure 4 clearly shows that there is a non-linear effect of the number of years used for NARX net training on estimation of SST values for year 2014. While using 9 years (2005–2013) of daily precipitation, flow and SST data for training the net produces SST estimations for 2014 within the range of measured SST values (although skewed to the right), using 3 and 2 years of training data produce good SST predictions for the firsts half of year 2014 and negative and inconsistent SST values for the second half of the year.

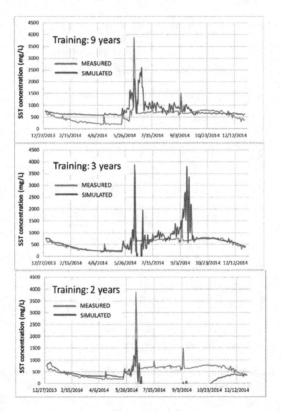

**Fig. 4.** Input data-size effect on prediction of sediment concentrations (SST) for 2014. For simplicity, only positive SST values are shown in the comparison charts.

## 3.3 Effects of Number of Hidden Layer Nodes

The previous sections showed that fewer number of iterations (100), and input-data size (3 and 2 years of training data), predicted SST values within the range of measured SST concentrations for year 2014. In both explorations 19 nodes in the hidden layer were implemented. In this section, the number of nodes were varied to test if better SST predictions were achieved. Figure 5 summarizes the effects of different number of nodes on SST predictions when an input-data size of 3 years of daily precipitation, flow and SST are used for the NARX net training.

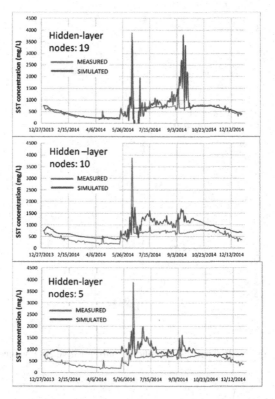

**Fig. 5.** Number of hidden-layer nodes effect on prediction of sediment concentrations (SST) for 2014. For simplicity, only positive SST values are shown in the comparison charts.

Figure 5 shows that keeping the number of iterations constant (100) and input-data size limited to 3 years while varying the number of nodes, better predicted values for SST concentrations are achieved. While using 19 nodes in the hidden layer still produces instability at mid-year (negative SST values), using 10 and 5 nodes produce SST predictions within the range of measured SST values and with similar temporal trends.

## 3.4   Fine-Tuning the NARX Net

The exploration of previous sections shows that using around 10 nodes in the hidden-layer, while using 100 iterations and three years of daily data for training the NARX net, SST predictions fit better with measured SST values. In this section, fine-tuning of the NARX net is performed further reducing the input-data size to 2 years, varying the number of nodes, and varying other NARX net parameters such as input and feedback delays, and train- value- and test- ratios. Figure 6 shows the results of the process.

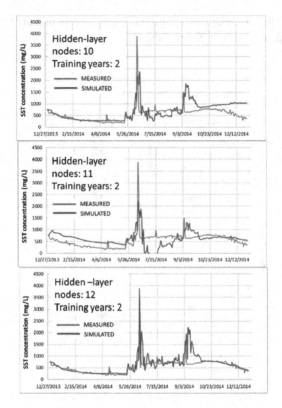

**Fig. 6.** Fine-tuning the NARX net. For simplicity, only positive SST values are shown in the comparison charts.

Other NARX net parameters were varied in the fine-tuning process. Input delays were varied from 1/15 to 1/60, feedback delays from 1/2 to 1/6, train ratios from 60 to 95, value ratios from 5 to 40, and test ratios from 1 to 10.

### 3.5    Goodness of Fit

Figure 6 shows that the best fit between simulated and measured SST values for year 2014 is achieved with a NARX net with a 12-node hidden layer, using 2 years of daily precipitation, flow and SST data for NARX net training, and 100 iterations. Figure 7 and Table 2 present goodness of fit indicators and their quality level.

Figure 7 shows that standard indicators of fit for predicted vs. measured SST concentrations for year 2014 are good. The Pearson correlation coefficient (R = 0.73) shows that measured and predicted SST values follow a linear trend. The $R^2$ value (0.53) shows that the fit of measured vs predicted SST is moderate, however, F-value and P-values show that the correlation is significant. Most important, P-values show that the regression line has an approximate slope of 1 (slope = 0.93), meaning that predicted and measured SST concentration values are not only linearly correlated but their magnitudes are similar.

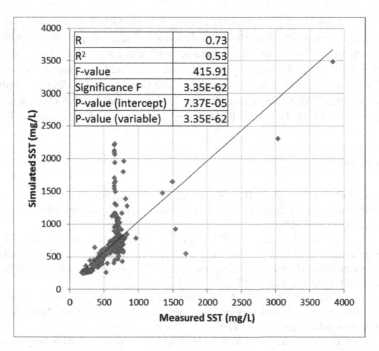

| R | 0.73 |
| R² | 0.53 |
| F-value | 415.91 |
| Significance F | 3.35E-62 |
| P-value (intercept) | 7.37E-05 |
| P-value (variable) | 3.35E-62 |

**Fig. 7.** Comparison of predicted vs. measured SST concentrations for year 2014. Statistical indicators of fit are shown to be good in the context of SST concentration prediction.

**Table 2.** Indicators of fit for the comparison of predicted SST vs. measured SST

| Indicator | Value | Recommended range | Goodness of fit | Source |
|---|---|---|---|---|
| NSE* | 0.18 | 0–1 | Acceptable | [12] |
| PBIAS** | −13.6% | ±15% | Very good | [12] |
| Index of agreement | 0.82 | >0.7 | Very good | [13] |

(*) NSE: Nash–Sutcliffe efficiency coefficient. (**) Percent bias.

Table 2 shows values of indicators of fit for the comparison of predicted SST vs. measured SST. All indicators rank the fit between acceptable (NSE = 0.18) to very good (PBIAS = −13.6%, Index of Agreement = 0.82).

## 4 Conclusions

This computational exploration shows that a NARX net can be used for predicting total suspended sediment concentrations for a complete calendar year (at daily time step) for the Francia Creek watershed (Valparaiso, Chile). Sensitivity analysis showed that the NARX parameters that are most influential on the generation of results consistent with measured data are: number of nodes in the hidden layer, number of iterations, and number years of daily precipitation, flow and sediment data (during network training).

The resulting NARX net configuration consisted of an open-loop network, with a 12-node hidden layer, using Bayesian regularization backpropagation algorithm. The number of iterations for achieving a trained network was 100, with 2-years of daily data (precipitation, flow, SST). Indicators of fit were calculated to compare how the predicted SST concentrations resemble measured data (for year 2014). SST concentrations predicted by the NARX net agreed successfully with measured SST concentrations ($r = 0.73$, $r^2 = 0.53$, NSE = 0.18, PBIAS = $-13.6\%$, Index of Agreement = 0.87).

# References

1. Xu, N., Saiers, J.E., Wilson, H.F., Raymond, P.A.: Simulating streamflow and dissolved organic matter export from a forested watershed. Water Resources Res. **48**(5), Article number W05519 (2012)
2. Xu, C.Y., Xiong, L., Singh, V.P.: Black-Box hydrological models. In: Duan, Q., Pappenberger, F., Thielen, J., Wood, A., Cloke, H., Schaake, J. (eds.) Handbook of Hydrometeorological Ensemble Forecasting, pp. 1–48. Springer, Heidelberg (2017). https://doi.org/10.1007/978-3-642-40457-3_21-1
3. Nacar, S., Hınıs, M.A., Kankal, M.: Forecasting daily streamflow discharges using various neural network models and training algorithms. KSCE J. Civil Eng. **22**(9), 3676–3685 (2018). https://doi.org/10.1007/s12205-017-1933-7
4. Dariane, A.B., Azimi, S.: Streamflow forecasting by combining neural networks and fuzzy models using advanced methods of input variable selection. J. Hydroinform. **20**(2), 520–532 (2018). https://doi.org/10.2166/hydro.2017.076
5. Daliakopoulos, I.N., Tsanis, I.K.: Comparison of an artificial neural network and a conceptual rainfall–runoff model in the simulation of ephemeral streamflow. Hydrol. Sci. J. **61**(15), 2763–2774 (2016). https://doi.org/10.1080/02626667.2016.1154151
6. Besaw, L.E., Rizzo, D.M., Bierman, P.R., Hackett, W.R.: Advances in ungauged streamflow prediction using artificial neural networks. J. Hydrol. **386**(1–4), 27–37 (2010). https://doi.org/10.1016/j.jhydrol.2010.02.037
7. Halecki, W., Kruk, E., Ryczek, M.: Estimations of nitrate nitrogen, total phosphorus flux and suspended sediment concentration (SSC) as indicators of surface-erosion processes using an ANN (Artificial Neural Network) based on geomorphological parameters in mountainous catchments. Ecol. Ind. **91**, 461–469 (2018). https://doi.org/10.1016/j.ecolind.2018.03.072
8. Meral, R., Dogan Demir, A., Cemek, B.: Analyses of turbidity and acoustic backscatter signal with artificial neural network for estimation of suspended sediment concentration. Appl. Ecol. Environ. Res. **16**(1), 697–708 (2018). https://doi.org/10.15666/aeer/1601_697708
9. Sari, V., dos Reis Castro, N.M., Pedrollo, O.C.: Estimate of suspended sediment concentration from monitored data of turbidity and water level using artificial neural networks. Water Resources Manag. **31**(15), 4909–4923 (2017). https://doi.org/10.1007/s11269-017-1785-4
10. Bhattacharya, B., Van Kessel, T., Solomatine, D.P.: Spatio-temporal prediction of suspended sediment concentration in the coastal zone using an artificial neural network and a numerical model. J. Hydroinform. **14**(3), 574–584 (2012). https://doi.org/10.2166/hydro.2012.123
11. Alarcon, V.J., Magrini, C.: Scenarios of sediment transport management in Francia Creek, Valparaiso, Chile. In: Gervasi, O., et al. (eds.) ICCSA 2018. LNCS, vol. 10962, pp. 205–218. Springer, Cham (2018). https://doi.org/10.1007/978-3-319-95168-3_14

12. Moriasi, D.N., Arnold, J.G., Van Liew, M.W., Bingner, R.L., Harmel, R.D., Veith, T.L.: Model evaluation guidelines for systematic quantification of accuracy in watershed simulations. Trans. ASABE **50**(3), 885–900 (2007)
13. Krause, P., Boyle, D.P., Bäse, F.: Comparison of different efficiency criteria for hydrological model assessment. Adv. Geosci. **5**, 89–97 (2005). https://doi.org/10.5194/adgeo-5-89-200

# Using Gridded Multi-mission Sea Surface Height Data to Estimate Tidal Heights at Columbia River Estuary

Vladimir J. Alarcon[(✉)] [iD]

Civil Engineering Department, Universidad Diego Portales,
441 Ejercito Ave., Santiago, Chile
vladimir.alarcon@udp.cl

**Abstract.** Measured tidal height time-series are critical for establishing initial and boundary conditions for hydrodynamic models of estuaries. The inexistence of tidal stations in the developing world is more evident than in other parts of the world. The lack of tidal height time-series data oftentimes forces modelers to interpolate or extrapolate these critical data, introducing important uncertainty bounds in the output of hydrodynamic models of estuaries. This paper assesses the feasibility of using gridded multi-mission sea surface height data for estimating tidal heights for the Columbia River estuary located in Northwestern USA. Ocean surface anomaly and geostrophic velocities gridded data, along with historical measured tidal heights are used for training and calibration of the ANN model. A nonlinear autoregressive exogenous neural network is used to predict tidal heights at a 14-min time step. Statistical comparison between measured and predicted data showed that the quality of predicted values was good. Regression analysis for goodness of fit showed the applicability of the proposed method: $R^2 = 0.93$, significance-F $= 4.57 * 10^{-18}$, F $= 370.80$, P-value for the intercept $= 0.13$, standard error $= 0.26$ m. Overall, the neural network provides good estimations of tidal heights, considering that it uses coarse-spatial-resolution ocean surface and water velocity data with daily temporal resolution.

**Keywords:** NARX · Neural network · Tidal heights · Prediction · Gridded multi-mission · Ocean surface topography

## 1 Introduction

Measured tide data are critical for establishing initial and boundary conditions for small-scale estuary hydrodynamic models. Although coastal waters (estuaries, bays) receive fresh water inputs from rivers draining to the water body, tidal effects are present kilometers upstream from the estuary along the incoming rivers. Hence, the water surface elevations and velocities calculated by hydrodynamic models for estuaries/bays and coastal rivers are also strongly dependent on boundary conditions provided at open-ocean boundaries. However, the lack of tidal stations throughout of the developing world precludes the correct characterization of the hydrodynamics of coastal water bodies. For example, when modelers are put to the task of developing an

© Springer Nature Switzerland AG 2019
S. Misra et al. (Eds.): ICCSA 2019, LNCS 11621, pp. 602–611, 2019.
https://doi.org/10.1007/978-3-030-24302-9_43

estuary or bay hydrodynamic model, interpolation or extrapolation of these critical data is performed, generating undesired uncertainty in the output of hydrodynamic models.

Several researches have explored the use of satellite altimeter data for hydrodynamic modeling. Le Provost et al. [1] assimilated satellite altimetry into a hydrodynamic model (FES94.1) assimilating empirical Topex/Poseidon (T/P) CSR2.0 tidal solution into the hydrodynamic model. Matsumoto et al. [2] assimilated T/P data into the hydrodynamic model NAO99.0 for modeling ocean tides around Japan. Egbert and Erofeeva [3] presented a computationally efficient relocatable system for generalized inverse modeling of barotropic ocean tides which required repeated solution of the forward and adjoint linearized shallow water equations (the same equations that are solved by hydrodynamic models). Foreman et al. [4] assimilated T/P and other satellite altimeter data into the FUNDY5 hydrodynamic code for removing tides from satellite altimeter observations. Han et al. [5] enriched a 3-D hydrodynamic model (Princeton Ocean Model, POM) with multi-mission satellite altimeter data. The abundant literature in this topic shows that assimilation OSTM data into ocean hydrodynamic models is feasible. However, using OSTM data for enriching estuary or bay hydrodynamic models is not as common.

This paper assesses the use of gridded multi-mission ocean surface topography data for estimating tidal heights for the Columbia River estuary located in Northwestern USA. Although the estuary tidal regime is fairly documented through several tidal stations in the area, this study area was chosen precisely because tidal gauge data was necessary to compare the estimations produced in this study. A range of algorithms exist for estimating tidal heights ranging from statistical methods to harmonic analysis. From those available options, artificial neural networks seem to provide opportunities for implementing a system that would combine spatial and temporal data. The novelty of this research is the use of a combination of tidal time-series data with gridded spatial data of ocean surface topography and water velocities.

# 2   Methods

## 2.1   Review on the Application of Artificial Neural Networks for Estimating Tidal Heights

The artificial neural network (ANN) approach to prediction of tidal heights is relatively widespread. Qiang et al. [6] developed a forecasting method for tidal heights from observed data and ANN. An artificial neural network was developed for estimating tidal heights from observed tide heights before their current time node. In this research, the neural network was optimized for one year and using multiple stations and artificial neural networks of each observation station is proposed. Wang and Deng [7], proposed a novel remote sensing algorithm for the retrieval of spatially distributed gage height data in nearshore waters using the Moderate Resolution Imaging Spectroradiometer (MODIS Aqua) satellite data and ground truth measurements collected daily from U.S. Geological Survey stations along the Louisiana Gulf Coast. The proposed methodology produced daily, spatially distributed gage height data. Ahn et al. [8] proposed a fuzzy neural network realizing Takagi-Sugeno-Kang inference mechanism employing meta-cognitive learning algorithm for wave prediction/forecasting in coastal regions. Kaveh et al. [9] used ANN for postprocessing of water level predictions (produced by a hydrodynamic model). A back-propagation artificial neural network technique was applied. The proposed method was used to improve surge predictions of the hydro-dynamic model in the region. López et al. [10] present an infra-gravity water wave hindcast methodology through using ANN to construct and analyze the single and the joint probability density functions of two characteristic wave-heights, highlighting the potential of the methodology to characterize the infra-gravity wave conditions inside a port basin and its suitability to study other coastal problems in which these waves are involved. Kim et al. [11] proposed a methodology to estimate damage of breakwater armor blocks incorporating a wave height prediction ANN into a Monte Carlo simu-lation. The waves predicted by the ANN were comparable to those from a wave transform analysis. Chen et al. [12] explored the use of an artificial neural network (back propagation neural network) and adaptive neuro-fuzzy inference system algo-rithms to improve incorrect calculations produced by a two-dimensional hydrodynamic model, in predicting storm surge height during typhoon events. Sertel et al. [13] compared five different methods to estimate daily mean sea level heights. These researchers compared: the least squares estimation of sea level model, the multilinear regression (MLR) model, feed forward back propagation ANN (FFBP), radial basis function ANN (RBF), and generalized regression ANN (GRNN). Results of the study illustrated that the ANN and MLR models provided comparatively better results than the conventional model used for estimating sea level, least squares estimation. FFBP, RBF, and MLR algorithms produced significantly better results than the GRNN method, and the best performance was obtained using the FFBP algorithm. El-Rabbany and El-Diasty [14] explored using a neural network-based model for sequentially predicting tidal heights using tide data series collected at various tide gauges. A mod-ular, three-layer feedforward neural network trained using the back-propagation algorithm is used for this purpose. The results of this research showed that the accuracy level of the tidal prediction has improved by a factor of 5 when using the neural network model.

However, in most of the above summarized applications of ANN to tidal heights estimations, the researchers either used data from multiple stations, or produced coarse averaged daily tidal heights, or combined ANN with hydrodynamic models, fuzzy sets, genetic algorithms, introducing complexity and uncertainty to the estimations. None of those researches produced tidal heights estimations at under-an-hour temporal resolution.

## 2.2    Study Area

The Columbia River Estuary is a water body located on Northwestern USA on the Oregon–Washington border. The Columbia River is the main river feeding the estuary; it is the largest river in the region (longitude: 2000 km approximately) draining a watershed of around 670000 $km^2$. The NOAA National Ocean Services provides data from several tidal stations in the area. In this research, tidal data from the Astoria station (Fig. 1) were used for comparison to simulated tidal heights.

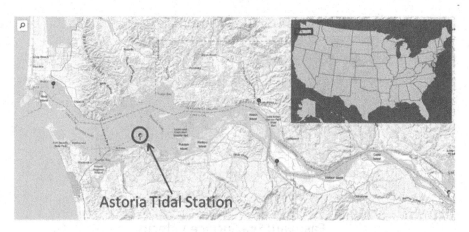

**Fig. 1.** Study area. Columbia River estuary and tidal stations in the area. Tidal time-series data from Astoria tidal gauge were used in this study.

Tidal time-series measured at Astoria tidal station for the period January 1 through January 31 were downloaded from NOAA data portals. The data provided by NOAA has a temporal resolution of 6 min. The original temporal time-step was resampled to 14 min to avoid long processing times. Results simulated by the model developed in this study were compared to tidal heights reported at Astoria Station during the calibration and validation processes.

## 2.3 Gridded Multi-mission Ocean Surface Topography Data

The multi-mission gridded altimeter fields with enhanced coastal coverage data product provided by NASA [15] consists of sea surface height anomalies and zonal and meridional geostrophic velocities for the US west coast. The geographical zone currently covered by this product goes from 35.25 to 48.5° latitude North, and from 227.75 to 248.5° longitude East [15]. Platforms and sensors used in the generation of the gridded data were: Jason-1/Poseidon-2, Topex/Poseidon/Poseidon-altimeter, OSTM/Jason-2/ Poseidon-3 [15]. In this research, daily data from January 1 through January 19, 2011, were downloaded from the Jet Propulsion Laboratory website [15]. Figure 2 shows the gridded sea surface height anomalies and water surface velocities for the study area for January 1, 2011. Data are provided as a 0.25-degrees spatial-resolution grid. For brevity, Fig. 2 shows the data in a 1-degree grid.

## 2.4 Artificial Neural Network

A nonlinear autoregressive exogenous neural network was used in this research. This type of neural network is provided with feedback connections and can use past values of predicted or true (measured) time-series (Boussaada et al. [16]). This key feature makes them applicable for time-series prediction and they are designed for using one or more time-series as input data as well. However, the data that are available for this research are incongruent in temporal resolution. While tidal time-series were resampled

## Mean Sea-level Anomaly

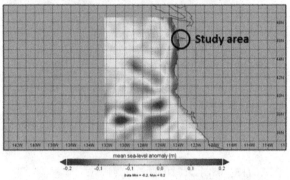

## Eastward Sea Surface Velocity

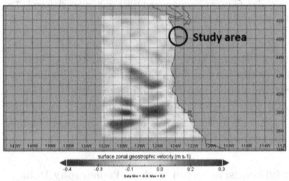

**Fig. 2.** Mean sea surface height anomaly and zonal and meridional geostrophic eastward velocities for the US west coast. Data are visualized for January 1, 2011. Daily data for the period 1/1/2011–1/19/2011, were downloaded from [15].

to a 14-min time step, multi-mission OST and geostrophic velocities have a 1-day temporal resolution. Clearly, daily gridded data would not be appropriate to model and simulate 14-min tidal time-series. To overcome this hurdle, spatial data in the east direction were used as time-series data. It is hypothesized that surface anomalies and geostrophic velocities far away from the coast are precursors of tides occurring at the estuary hours or days later.

An open-loop architecture is proposed in which the future value of tidal heights at cell $i$ occurring at time $t + n$, $TH_i^{t+n}$, is predicted from the measured value of ocean surface topography at cell $i - k$, at time $t$, $OST_{i-k}^t$, eastward geostrophic velocity, $v_{i-k}^t$ s, and the measured past values of tidal heights at cell $i$ occurring at time $t - m$, $TH_i^{t-m}$. Figure 3 presents a conceptual description of the neural network configuration used in this research.

All computations were performed using MATLAB. The Bayesian regularization backpropagation algorithm was used.

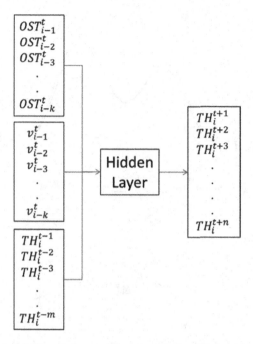

**Fig. 3.** Conceptual description of the open-loop neural network used in this research. Ocean surface topography (OST) spatial-series, eastward geostrophic water velocity (v) spatial-series, and past tidal height time-series (TH), were fed to the neural network to predict future TH values.

## 3  Results

### 3.1  Assessment of NOAA-Predicted Tidal Height Data at Astoria Station

An assessment of measured tidal heights at Astoria station was performed in relation to predicted NOAA-predicted tidal heights. The data provided by the station's website include predictions made with traditional harmonic analysis. Figure 4 shows results of the comparison. Regression analysis was performed to ascertain whether the predictions were statistically consistent with measured values. The analysis showed that the indicators: F (55798.84), significance-F ($2.87 * 10^{-284}$), and P-values for the intercept ($5.69 * 10^{-30}$) and the independent variable ($2.87 * 10^{-284}$) were well within the statistical requirements for goodness of fit. The standard error was 0.016 m (0.054 ft). As shown in the figure, although those indicators are very good, and the coefficient of determination is high ($R^2 > 0.9$), predicted values overestimate tidal heights consistently for all simulation times.

### 3.2  Tidal Heights Predicted Using the Neural Network

Sensitivity analysis using number of nodes, number of iterations, feedback delays, forward delays, size of training data (number of spatial grid cells and number of past tidal height values). The objective of the sensitivity analysis was to achieve the most

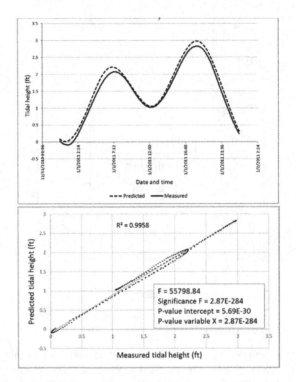

**Fig. 4.** Assessment of NOAA-predicted tidal height data at Astoria station. Tidal heights predictions through traditional harmonic analysis consistently overestimate measured tidal heights.

appropriate neural network configuration that provided the best fit of predicted tidal heights vs. measured tidal heights. The resulting neural network consisted in an open-loop non-linear autoregressive exogenous neural network, provided with a 2-node hidden layer. The number of iterations that provided good predicted results was 50, with fast input delay (1:1) and fast feedback delay (1:2). The network used Bayesian regularization backpropagation. The training size consisted in 33 spatial grid values for ocean surface topography (OST) and eastward geostrophic velocity (v). These spatial data were fed to the neural network in conjunction with a time-series of past tidal heights measured at Astoria Station, resampled every 14 min (raw data were provided with 6-min interval). Past tidal heights for one day (103 values) were used for training. The neural network was set up to predict 103 values for the next day. Figure 5 shows the results of this process.

Figure 5 shows a comparison of tidal heights predicted by the neural network for a daily event in which the maximum-height tide reached more than 2.7 m (9.2 ft). The neural network predicts tidal heights with a 14-min interval, generating 103 tidal height values per day. The comparison with measured data shows that the statistical fit between predicted and measured values is good. The regression analysis performed with predicted and measured values showed that: significance-F = $4.57 * 10^{-18}$,

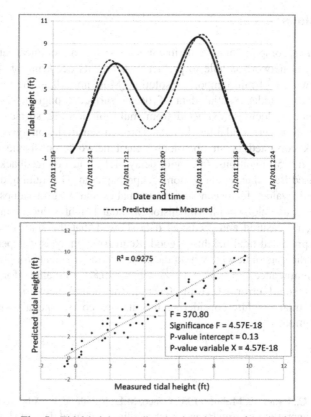

**Fig. 5.** Tidal heights predicted using the neural network.

F = 370.80, P-value for the intercept = 0.13, and P-value for the independent variable = $4.57 * 10^{-18}$. These indicators are within the statistical requirements for goodness of fit. As shown above, the P-value of the intercept is slightly higher than the P-value corresponding to the comparison of tidal heights calculated using harmonic analysis. The standard error calculated for the neural network predicted values was 0.26 m (0.88 ft). It is widely known that the standard error provides the absolute measure of the typical distance that the data points fall from the regression line; in the case of the tidal values calculated by the neural network, they fall 0.26 m (in average) from the line shown in Fig. 5. Tidal peaks and tidal minima are the regions in which the neural network predictions differs more noticeably and are responsible of the increase in the standard error. The predicted values are also slightly biased to the left for hours before noon, and to the right for tidal heights corresponding to times after noon. Overall, the neural network provides good estimations of tidal heights, considering that it uses coarse-spatial-resolution ocean surface topography and velocity data and daily temporal resolution.

## 4  Conclusions

This prospective computational experiment shows that a nonlinear autoregressive exogenous neural network is able to predict tidal heights occurring at the Columbia River estuary with a 14-min temporal resolution. Most important, the neural network successfully uses gridded spatial data of ocean surface topography and eastward geostrophic water velocities (extracted from multi-mission sea surface height data) along with past time-series tidal height data. Through sensitivity analysis the resulting neural network consisted in an open-loop neural network, consisting of a 2-node hidden layer, with 50 iterations, fast input delay (1:1), and fast feedback delay (1:2). The network used Bayesian regularization backpropagation. The training data consisted in 33 spatial grid-values for ocean surface anomalies and 33 grid-values of eastward geostrophic velocity, along with 103 historical tidal height values. Statistical comparison between measured and predicted data showed that the statistical fit between measured and predicted tidal heights is good. Regression analysis was performed, and the resulting indicators of fit were within the statistical requirements for goodness of fit: $R^2 = 0.93$, significance-F = $4.57 * 10^{-18} < F = 370.80$, P-value for the intercept = 0.13, standard error = 0.26 m. Overall, the neural network provides good estimations of tidal heights, considering that it uses coarse spatial data with daily temporal resolution.

## References

1. Le Provost, C., Lyard, F., Molines, J.M., Genco, M.L., Rabilloud, F.: A hydrodynamic ocean tide model improved by assimilating a satellite altimeter-derived data set. J. Geophys. Res. **103**, 5513–5529 (2018)
2. Matsumoto, K., Takanezawa, T., Ooe, M.: Ocean tide models developed by assimilating TOPEX/POSEIDON altimeter data into hydrodynamical model: a global model and a regional model around Japan. J. Oceanogr. **56**(5), 567–581 (2018). https://doi.org/10.1023/A:1011157212596
3. Egbert, G.D., Erofeeva, S.: Efficient inverse modelling of barotropic ocean tides. J. Atmos. Ocean. Technol. **19**, 183–204 (2002). http://volkov.oce.orst.edu/tides/
4. Foreman, M.G.G., Thomson, R.E., Smith, C.L.: Seasonal current simulations for the western continental margin of Vancouver Island. J. Geophys. Res. **105**(C8), 19665–19698 (2000)
5. Han, G., Paturi, S., de Young, B., Yi, Y., Shum, C.-K.: A 3-D data-assimilative tidal model of the Northwest Atlantic. Atmos. Ocean **48**(1), 39–57 (2010). https://doi.org/10.3137/OC303.2010
6. Qiang, L., Bing-Dong, Y., Bi-Guang, H.: Calculation and measurement of tide height for the navigation of ship at high tide using artificial neural network. Pol. Marit. Res. **25**(s3), 99–110 (2018). https://doi.org/10.2478/pomr-2018-0118
7. Wang, J., Deng, Z.: Development of a MODIS data-based algorithm for retrieving gage height in nearshore waters along the Louisiana Gulf Coast. J. Coast. Res. **34**(1), 220–228 (2018). https://doi.org/10.2112/jcoastres-d-16-00161.1
8. Anh, N., Prasad, M., Srikanth, N., Sundaram, S.: Wave forecasting using meta-cognitive interval type-2 fuzzy inference system. Procedia Comput. Sci. **144**, 33–41 (2018). https://doi.org/10.1016/j.procs.2018.10.502

9. Kaveh, N.A., Ghaheri, A., Chegini, V., Nazarali, M.: Application of a hybrid approach for tide-surge modeling in the Persian Gulf. J. Coast. Res. **32**(5), 1126–1134 (2016). https://doi.org/10.2112/JCOASTRES-D-15-00033.1

10. López, M., López, I., Iglesias, G.: Hindcasting long waves in a port: an ANN approach. Coast. Eng. J. **57**(4), Article no. 1550019 (2015). https://doi.org/10.1142/s0578563415500199

11. Kim, D.H., Kim, Y.J., Hur, D.S.: Artificial neural network based breakwater damage estimation considering tidal level variation. Ocean Eng. **87**, 185–190 (2014). https://doi.org/10.1016/j.oceaneng.2014.06.001

12. Chen, W.-B., Liu, W.-C., Hsu, M.-H.: Predicting typhoon-induced storm surge tide with a two-dimensional hydrodynamic model and artificial neural network model. Nat. Hazards Earth Syst. Sci. **12**(12), 3799–3809 (2012). https://doi.org/10.5194/nhess-12-3799-2012

13. Sertel, E., Cigizoglu, H.K., Sanli, D.U.: Estimating daily mean sea level heights using artificial neural networks. J. Coast. Res. **24**(3), 727–734 (2008). https://doi.org/10.2112/06-742.1

14. El-Rabbany, A., El-Diasty, M.: A new approach to sequential tidal prediction. J. Navig. **56**(2), 305–314 (2003). https://doi.org/10.1017/S0373463303002285

15. NASA Jet Propulsion Laboratory: Physical Oceanography Distributed Active Archive Center (PODAAC). NASA EOSDIS PO.DAAC, Pasadena, CA (2015). https://podaac.jpl.nasa.gov/

16. Boussaada, Z., Curea, O., Ahmed, R., Camblong, H., Najiba, M.B.: A nonlinear autoregressive exogenous (NARX) neural network model for the prediction of the daily direct solar radiation. Energies **11**, 620 (2018). https://doi.org/10.3390/en11030620

# Multi-criteria Evaluation vs Perceived Urban Quality: An Exploratory Comparison

Ivan Blečić[1]([envelope]), Alessandra G. Santos[2], Ana Clara Moura[3], and Giuseppe A. Trunfio[4]

[1] Department of Civil and Environmental Engineering and Architecture, University of Cagliari, Cagliari, Italy
ivanblecic@unica.it
[2] Geoprocessing Laboratory, Federal University of Minas Gerais (UFMG), Belo Horizonte, Brazil
alessandragtsantos@gmail.com
[3] Department of Urban Planning, Geoprocessing Laboratory, Federal University of Minas Gerais (UFMG), Belo Horizonte, Brazil
anaclara@ufmg.br
[4] Department of Architecture, Design and Urbanism, University of Sassari, Alghero, Italy
trunfio@uniss.it

**Abstract.** This study compares a service-based and environmental evaluation of an urban area with that of its perceived walkability. The Pampulha region in Belo Horizonte, Brazil was first put through a multi-criteria spatial evaluation with respect to a set of spatial data considered relevant for liveability and quality of life in cities, and was subsequently assessed in terms of perceived walkability (using a machine learning procedure of a training set provided by local auditors). The two types of analysis were compared and qualitatively aggregated to obtain a joint spatial score of the urban environment. The findings provide useful insights for planning and urban policy.

**Keywords:** Urban quality · Spatial multi-criteria analysis · Walkability assessment · Machine learning

## 1 Introduction

In this study we conduct an exploratory analysis of factors of quality and attractiveness of urban environments and cityscapes. There are in general two ways in which such "quality" may be framed and assessed. One is centred on observable features sourced from available spatial data, represented through a series of indicators, and then in some way aggregated through a multi-criteria analysis. This framing can be said to follow the logic of a capability approach [1–3] insomuch as it attempts to analytically describe what there is, what it is like, what are the observable features of the urban environment, considered as enablers for people having certain capabilities in cities.

© Springer Nature Switzerland AG 2019
S. Misra et al. (Eds.): ICCSA 2019, LNCS 11621, pp. 612–627, 2019.
https://doi.org/10.1007/978-3-030-24302-9_44

The second way to frame the "quality" is to rely on subjective perceptions people have of the urban environment. Here the point is to survey declared preferences, based on their direct, "synthetic" perception of places.

Of course, the two ways of framing the urban quality are in principle related. One would assume that an urban environment endowed with valuable features, services, facilities, attractive and safe places would come out favourably in declared subjective judgements. But there are, in principle, also reasons for divergence between the two. One such reason is possibly of technical nature, the fact that it may not be easy to construct the statistical model capable to reduce with sufficient fidelity the synthetic subjective judgements to the available data and observable features.

However, there is another, more fundamental reason why one should not expect the two approaches entirely to match. The general point is that capabilities, while relevant for a normative definition of well-being and quality of life [1], do not necessarily nor perfectly map onto individual preference structures (say, as represented by a utility function). That is to say, when defining well-being, the capability approach emphasizes functional capabilities (which is urban context may mean access to certain services, places, public spaces, "right to the city", participation, safety and so on) which are construed in terms of what people have reason to value, instead of utility (happiness, desire-fulfilment or choice) or individual resources (e.g. income, commodities, assets). In other words, the focus on capabilities enables to acknowledge the existence of claims, like rights, which may empirically diverge from, and normatively dominate over utility-based claims [4].

In this study we take both routes and then perform an exploratory comparison between the two sets of evaluative outcomes. With a dose of agnosticism, we hold that both are informative from the perspective of urban policy and planning. Both how we may assume and model what the well-being and urban quality of people *should be* given the observable features of the urban environment, and what people themselves *believe* it to be. With such an agnostic attitude, our point is not so much to straitjacket one set of evaluations into the other, but to compare them, to see when they line up or differ, and perhaps to hint at why that may be so.

The remainder of this paper is organised as follows. In the next section we briefly present our case-study urban area – the Pampulha region in Belo Horizonte, Brazil.

For the multi-criteria evaluation, we use and aggregate 19 variables describing urban environment and landscape characteristics. The methodology and the results of that analysis are presented in Sect. 3.

In Sect. 4 we describe the methodology employed to assess the perceived urban quality, for which as we have employed a machine-learning classifier trained on a dataset of evaluative judgments on the perceived walkability of streets from Google Street View photography.

Finally, to streamline the comparison between the two sets of results, we define three levels (ordinal classes "low", "medium" and "high") of quality for each, yielding $3 \times 3$ possible combinations of outcomes. The discussion of these results and their qualitative comparison is presented in the concluding section.

## 2  Case-Study Area

The case urban area for our study was Pampulha, an urban region of about 145.000 inhabitants in the northwest of the city of Belo Horizonte, Brazil. The area (Fig. 1) is famous for its main attraction, the Pampulha Lake, and for its icons of Brazilian modern architecture designed by Oscar Niemeyer, the landmarks for leisure and sports, but also for important structures as the Federal University of Minas Gerais, the stadium, the first airport of the city and the zoo. In 2016 Pampulha Modern Ensemble was recognized by UNESCO as a World Heritage site.

Pampulha Region presents large variability in land uses: low density residential areas, with high and low land costs, as well as shantytowns; besides institutional, industrial and services and commerce areas. In comparison to other regions of the city, Pampulha is characterised by relatively abundant vegetation cover, flat area with low slope of roads, low density housing and just a few high-rise developments, good road infrastructure even though often lacking diffused commercial activities. Its variable character was one of the factors that guided choosing this study area, described by some numbers and characteristics: density (4.859 hab/km$^2$, relatively low density if compared to other areas of the city); topography (mostly flat, distinctively from most other areas of the city and more favourable for active mobility (walking, biking, …)), traffic (relatively less intense, with fewer traffic jams); vegetation (expressive amount of remaining green areas in parks and in private lots units); leisure (among the main destinations for open-air activities within Belo Horizonte); and available data (large amount of data of this Region available under a research's agreement signed between Belo Horizonte Council (PBH) and the Laboratory of Geoprocessing (LabGeo); also, LabGeo has developed previous studies of Pampulha Region, saving time of literature review to characterize it.

## 3  Features of Urban Quality: A Multi-criteria Analysis

The first part of the study was based on the use of a multi-criteria analysis to define and combine variables, in order to evaluate the conditions of urban quality resulting from a set of territorial features [5]. For that, we begin with 19 spatial variables, reported in Table 1 which, on our preliminary assessment, are relevant for the urban quality. These variables were demonstrative of urban infrastructure and landscape characteristics, for example roads width, visibility of waterbodies, presence of vegetation, composition of buildings.

As the spatial unit of data, we used individual road tracks plus the frontal part of the lots (the first 15 m), representing the portion that a person captures with the observation while walking along the sidewalks.

All the variables were normalised in the range of values from 1 to 5, representing respectively the worst and best conditions. Examples of such evaluations on some variables are shown in Fig. 2.

Once all the variables were processed, we applied the aggregation procedure, the multi-criteria analysis based on weighted sum. In the first test, all the variables received the same weight. After that we applied the sensitivity analysis to suitability evaluation

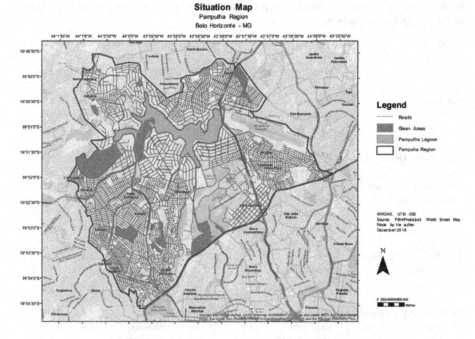

**Fig. 1.** The Pampulha Region (Color figure online)

(SASE) [6, 7], a method allowing a more robust analysis in comparison to the traditional multi-criteria analysis [8]. The method performs a Monte Carlo weighted sum simulation, using different weights delimited in a range from minimum to maximum values for each variable, and computes the degree of "doubt" on the performance of the variables. In our case, we can thus identify areas that are considered of high quality and without doubts (small uncertainty), areas of high quality but with doubts about the results (large uncertainty), areas of low quality and without doubts about that (small uncertainty), and areas of low quality but with doubts about the results (large uncertainty).

This analysis allowed to pinpoint the following three variables which were the greatest source of uncertainty:

- Residence's concentration: probably due to a specific characteristic of Pampulha Region that, for example, areas with low density have an ambiguous effect on walkability.
- Roads' Hierarchy: it is a technical nomenclature used by the City Hall that not necessarily express road's characteristics.
- Quantity of Bus Lines: Belo Horizonte's bus system (BRT/MOVE) works in a way not reflected by the values of the variable, generating an inconsistent data comparing main avenues (with few lines but regular services) and ordinary roads (with more lines but not so regular services).

**Table 1.** List of the starting variables used for in the MCA. In the first two columns the list of data and their spatialization in process maps.

| Urban data | MCA - Delphi Method | | | MCA - Monte Carlo Weighted Sum + Uncertainty – SASE | | |
|---|---|---|---|---|---|---|
| | Data | WT absolute | WT relative | Data | WT range | Variance |
| Bus stops | Bus stop concentration | 7,8 | 6,00% | Bus stop concentration | 4 to 8 | −0.001 |
| Cycle grid | Cycle grid | 8 | 6,10% | Cycle grid | 4,1 to 8,1 | 0.005 |
| Urban parks, Green areas | Permeability percentage | 9,1 | 6,90% | Permeability percentage | 4,9 to 8,9 | 0.421 |
| Land densification and buildings height | Building's height predominance | 7 | 5,40% | Building's height predominance | 3,4 to 7,4 | 0.003 |
| | Building's height variability | 5,1 | 4,00% | Building's height variability | 2 to 6 | 0.04 |
| Lots limits, block contours and land use | Commerce concentration | 7 | 5,40% | Commerce concentration | 3,4 to 7,4 | 0.002 |
| | Industry concentration | 8,7 | 6,70% | Industry concentration | 4,7 to 8,7 | 0.001 |
| Public and private equipment for leisure and tourism | Cultural attractions concentration | 8,4 | 6,40% | Cultural attractions concentration | 4,4 to 8,14 | 0.005 |
| Public and private urban equipment for health and education | Urban equipment concentration | 7,5 | 5,80% | Urban equipment concentration | 3,8 to 7,8 | 0.003 |
| Roads grid, hierarchy, type, width and pavement | Roads width | 9,3 | 7,10% | Roads width | 5,1 to 9,1 | 0.011 |
| | Roads type | 8,6 | 6,60% | Roads type | 4,6 to 8,6 | 0.004 |
| | Roads paving type | 8,4 | 6,40% | Roads paving type | 4,4 to 8,4 | 0.093 |
| Topography and roads grid | Roads slope | 8,7 | 6,70% | Roads slope | 4,7 to 8,7 | 0.054 |
| Trees along the roads and in the frontal part of the lots | Trees concentration | 9,4 | 7,20% | Trees concentration | 5,2 to 9,2 | 0.295 |
| Waterbodies | Waterbodies visibility | 8,5 | 6,50% | Waterbodies visibility | 4,5 to 8,5 | 0.005 |
| Roads connection and urban services or commerce | Potential interaction of urban nodes | 8,8 | 6,80% | Potential interaction of urban nodes | | 0.054 |
| Bus lines | x | x | x | x | x | x |
| Lots limits, block contours and land use | x | x | x | x | x | x |
| Roads grid, hierarchy, type, width and pavement | x | x | x | x | x | x |

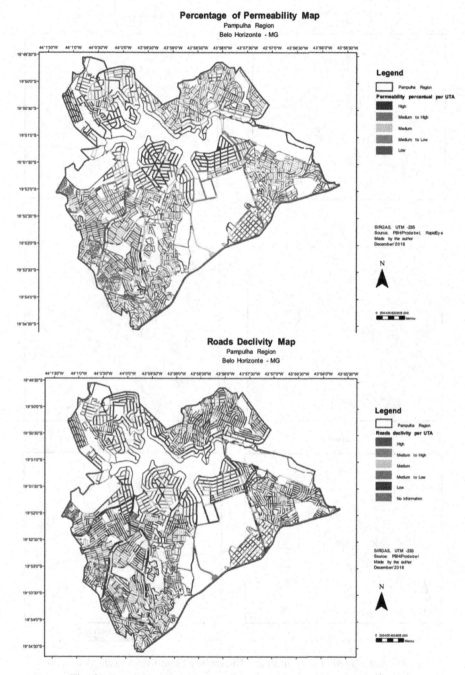

**Fig. 2.** Examples of evaluation maps for variables used in the MCA.

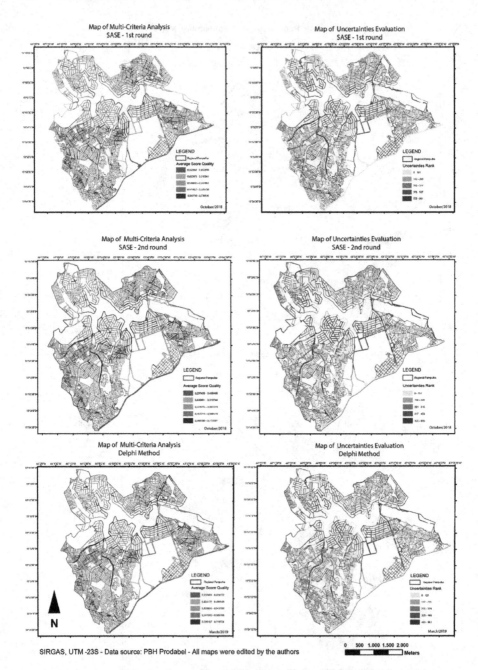

**Fig. 3.** Multi-Criteria (Suitability) and Uncertainty (Sensitivity) Evaluation Maps.

The Multi-Criteria Analysis Map and the Uncertainties Map generated with all the 19 variables are presented in Fig. 3, first row (maps *a* and *b*), applying the same weight to all variables. Uncertainty calculation demonstrated that 3 variables were quite irregular in their performance and were therefore excluded from the subsequent evaluation. Another round of analysis with the remaining 16 variables are presented in Fig. 3, second row (maps *c* and *d*).

To further improve the analysis, citizens' preferences were integrated through a Delphi Method [9, 10]. For that, 15 people we interviewed, presenting their opinion about the importance of the variables to their preferences to walk along a road, considering not only Pampulha, but a urban area in a general sense in Brazil. They composed a group including different ages, different social and economic conditions and different education level. After collecting these opinions, new variables weights were defined. Then, it was once more processed by the SASE Multi-Criteria evaluation tool because it was able to test a range of weights instead of just the final average value of voluntaries votes. The range was defined according to probability function, what means the value of the standard deviation of the votes to the lower and to the higher limit of the range. The results were presented in Fig. 3, third row (maps *e* and *f*), MCA (Suitability) and Uncertainty (Sensitivity).

Following the above described procedure, the multi-criteria analysis produced the evaluation maps with their "level of trust", presenting thus more robust results.

## 4 Perceived Urban Quality: Walkability Evaluation Based on Deep Learning

For the assessment of perceived urban quality through walkability evaluation, we used the machine learning technique presented in [11], based on a deep convolutional neural network (CNN) trained on a dataset of georeferenced street images from Google Street View. In brief, the adopted approach is based on the following two steps: first, the CNN is trained on a set of labelled images; then, the trained CNN can be used for predicting the perceived walkability on a different set of street-level images, so allowing a massive and fast evaluation of urban landscapes.

From the work described in [11], we had already trained a CNN on a dataset composed of images from some Italian cities. Nevertheless, to apply the CNN-based methodology to the Pampulha Region, and potentially to other areas with similar characteristics, we extended that pre-existent dataset with new training samples from the current area of study. In fact, as the result of the training phase, the CNN learns to classify effectively the specific types of urban landscapes that are included in the training set. However, cities in different parts of the world can be characterized by significantly different urban landscapes. For these reasons, adding new and different examples to the training set can be crucial to enhance the generalization ability of the CNN with the aim of classifying unseen street-level images belonging to different places of the world.

More in detail, the pre-existing dataset was built by downloading, at 5.300 different street points, four images with headings shifted by 90° so to roughly describe the 360-degree panorama (see Fig. 4). Each group of four images was classified by trained observers in terms of perceived quality of walkability on the relatively narrow rating scale of five values (from 1 → low walkability to 5 → high walkability).

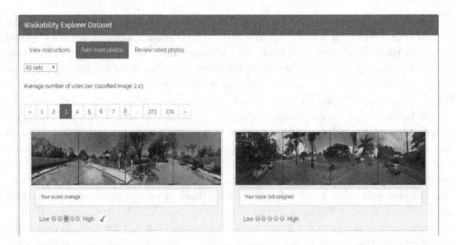

**Fig. 4.** Web user interface for the assessment of perceived walkability

Following the approach described in [11], we then performed an additional assessment of human-perceived walkability, specific for the Pampulha Region, through the web user interface represented in Fig. 4, on a random set of images downloaded

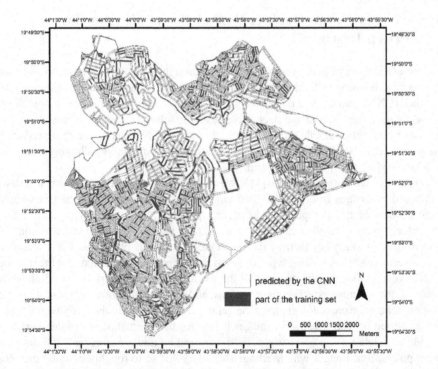

**Fig. 5.** Streets of the Pampulha Region used for the CNN training process (i.e. those evaluated by at least three people)

from Google Street View. At the end of the process, we extended the original dataset with the 1.757 photos that collected at least three votes, which were averaged. In Fig. 5 we show the map of Pampulha Region in which the highlighted streets used in the training process are highlighted.

As a result, the whole dataset of 7.057 images was partitioned into the adopted five classes as follows: 606 images in class 1, 2.331 in class 2, 2.706 in class 3, 1.048 in class 4 and the remaining 366 in class 5.

### 4.1   Adopted CNN Architecture and Implementation

As already done in [11], given the relatively small amount of data available for training, we use *transfer learning* in order to train a CNN capable to classify an input image from Google Street View into one of the five ordinal categories of perceived walkability mentioned above. In practice, such an approach consists of using a certain number of the first convolutional blocks of a deep CNN, pre-trained on a large dataset, to build a different neural network characterized by much less parameters to learn. In practice, the outputs of the pre-trained CNN layers can be considered as features extracted from the input image that are used to feed a relatively simpler neural network. Only the latter is actually trained with the available data. More in detail, also in the present study we adopted a feature extractor based on the VGG16 model pre-trained on the Places dataset with 365 scene categories (i.e. Places365), which is made available by the MIT Computer Vision Group [12].

The VGG16 model [13] is a deep neural network composed of 13 convolutional layers followed by 3 fully connected layers. In particular, the RGB image is used as input for a stack of convolutional layers endowed with small receptive fields based on $3 \times 3$ filters. Some of the convolutional layers are followed by a spatial max-pooling performed over a $2 \times 2$ pixel window. The CNN architecture adopted in the present work exploits the features extracted at the end of the thirteenth VGG16 layer, which corresponds to a $7 \times 7 \times 512$ tensor after max pooling. However, instead of flattening the 25088 features to connect the convolutional structure to a traditional neural network classifier, in order to minimise over-fitting by reducing the total number of parameters in the model we adopted the approach proposed in [14], which consists of using a global average pooling operator. The latter takes the tensor of dimension $7 \times 7 \times 512$ and gives a tensor of size $1 \times 1 \times 512$. In practice each $7 \times 7$ feature is reduced to a single scalar by simply taking the average of all $7 \times 7$ values. Therefore, for each input image we have 512 scalar features extracted and used as input for two fully-connected ReLU layers with 512 and 256 channels respectively. Finally, the last layer of our network is composed of four outputs, each in the interval [0, 1]. However, instead of using the classical softmax function for the output nodes, which would force the sum of outputs to be 1, we use a standard sigmoid function.

In order to classify each image into one of the five ordered categories, we use a generalisation of ordinal perceptron learning approach [15] proposed in [16]. In the adopted method, the class 1 correspond to the CNN output (0, 0, 0, 0), the class 2 is encoded as (1, 0, 0, 0), the class 3 as (1, 1, 0, 0) and so on. To convert an output vector to its category, the method scans the output nodes from left to right and stops when the output of a node is smaller than a predefined threshold $T$ (we use $T = 0.5$) or no nodes are left.

The implementation was carried out by using the Keras framework [17], with Tensorflow backend [18], and executed on a workstation equipped with a NVidia Quadro P6000 GPU.

### 4.2  CNN Training and Application

The 7.057 labelled images composing the dataset were randomly partitioned into a training set (70%), validation set (10%) and test set (20%). The training was performed using some standard data augmentation techniques to artificially enlarges the training and to prevent overfitting. In particular, for each original image in the training set we generated five new images by using a horizontal flip, a random zooming with scale in the range [0.6, 0.8], a shearing in counter-clockwise direction with a random angle up to 0.5° and a random rotation with angle up to 5°. Therefore, the training process of the CNN was carried out based on 24.700 images, while 706 images were used for controlling overfitting (validation set) and the remaining 1.411 images were used for testing the results after training.

The learning phase was performed using the mean squared error (MSE) as loss function and the *adadelta* [19] optimiser with its default parameters provided in Keras. Moreover, to prevent overfitting, the learning process was stopped after ten epochs without improvements of the loss function in the validation set. During the learning phase we stored the CNN weights corresponding to the minimum validation loss, which was 0.28.

The obtained CNN was evaluated on the 706 images included in the test set and the results are reported in the confusion matrix of Table 2. The overall accuracy (i.e. number of patterns correctly classified) was 71% while the achieved accuracy within one class was 98% (i.e. only 2% of the images were affected by an error greater than one class).

**Table 2.** Confusion matrix obtained on the test set

| Human perception | CNN classification | | | | |
|---|---|---|---|---|---|
| | 1 | 2 | 3 | 4 | 5 |
| 1 | **102** | 11 | 0 | 0 | 0 |
| 2 | 29 | **396** | 103 | 3 | 0 |
| 3 | 5 | 51 | **331** | 43 | 0 |
| 4 | 0 | 13 | 97 | **136** | 23 |
| 5 | 2 | 0 | 10 | 18 | **39** |

After the evaluation of accuracy described above, we retrained the CNN using 90% of the available data and leaving the remaining 10% for validation and overfitting control. Then, we applied the CNN to 7.662 Google Street View photos that covers the street network of the Pampulha Region. As explained above, each input image processed by the CNN is composed of four photos with headings differing by 90°, in such a way to describe the 360° view from the centre of the edge. After applying the CNN to each image, the classification of the streets is computed as the average score predicted by the CNN for each image belonging to that street. The results of this classification are shown in Fig. 6.

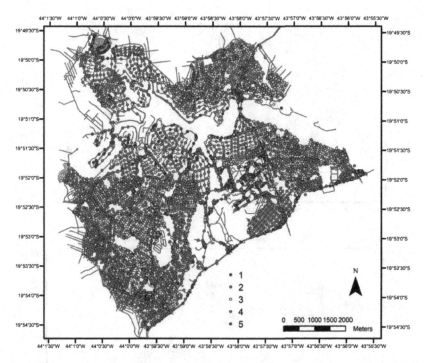

**Fig. 6.** CNN-classification of expected perceived walkability, with levels from 1 (low) to 5 (high).

## 5   Comparison and Discussion of Results

As anticipated in the introduction, to simplify and streamline the qualitative comparison between the two sets of results, we defined three levels ("low", "medium" and "high") of quality for each analysis, using uniform-interval thresholds values for the MCA values, and setting walkability levels 1 and 2 as "low", 3 as "medium", and 4 and 5 as "high". We report these classifications in Fig. 7.

Comparing the results of the two final maps, the first thing to observe is that both methods presented very few areas with "low" interest for walkability or quality of cityscape (roads in red). Probably this is because Pampulha is a relatively appreciated region of the city, in comparison to other areas. It has a large lake, expressive vegetation cover, not so dense housing areas, and roads with good conditions to walk. The

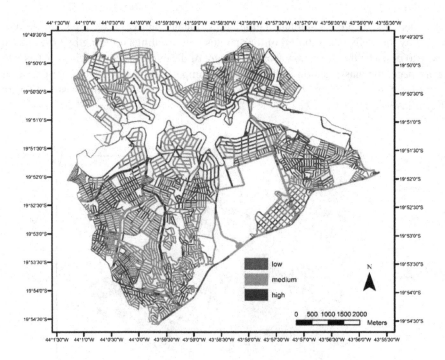

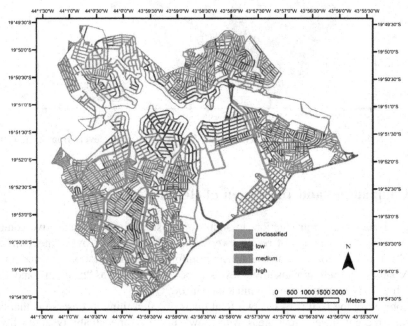

**Fig. 7.** MCA (above) vs. CNN classified perceived urban quality: three levels (Color figure online)

results confirm the anecdotal impression of the place as one of the more attractive areas of the city of Belo Horizonte. From both evaluative approaches, it is possible to conclude that the place is good for walking. However, previous studies and observations of peoples' behaviour showed that they are not too much walked, even having very good conditions for that. Besides perhaps being related to more general cultural attitudes, studies have shown that it may also be related to widespread caution and worry for the (perceived) lack of safety along the streets [20].

Looking at the "high" conditions, the technical approach provided by multi-criteria analysis, based on the selection of main variables according to a knowledge-driven suggestion by the expert opinions (the main variables were defined by the planning experts who know the area, while the importance of each variable, composing the weights to be used in weighted-sum MCA were defined by representatives of the local residents, consulted through a Delphi method) presented a larger number of roads with good conditions in comparison to CNN method. That may possibly be so because the MCA considered many variables, for many of which Pampulha presents relatively good scores. Comparing the two results, where the MCA tells there are the best conditions, CNN also recognises it, but in a smaller portion of the same area. To use Daniel Kahneman's distinction [21] we could say that MCA is based on a "slow thinking", more analytical and calculating, trying to integrate many variables in the evaluation, while CNN classification is driven by "fast thinking", guided by more intuitive, emotional reaction of people to places.

The parts in which the results were very different are explained by the variables chosen and the objectives of the analysis. In the centre part of the region, there is a neighbourhood in the shape of a star, to the south of the lake. This area is called "Bandeirantes" and it is characterised by large lots (around $1000 \text{ m}^2$), expressive vegetation, large roads of low slope, which makes it to be perceived as a very pleasant area, due to these spatial characteristics. But, considering the list of variables used in MCA (that also represents a "list of desires" to a Brazilian to feel secure to walk along the road), the area is very empty in terms of housing density, commerce, services and so one, which make the perception of those places not so interesting and secure as they are pleasant from the point of view of their visual values.

Further studies should be developed in other parts of the city with the same methods. A next step of the research can be the selection of the "high" values in CNN results, to be compared with the results of MCA, in order to identify with are the main variables that are present in those areas. This next step can be based on data-mining and the extraction of the variables that compose the best conditions in the territory, as the signature of the array of variables, what can be used as a guiding reference for urban planning and policy.

**Acknowledgments.** This study was supported by the research grants for the projects: "Healthy Cities and Smart Territories" (2016/17) funded by Fondazione di Sardegna and the Autonomous Region of Sardinia. We gratefully acknowledge the support of NVIDIA Corporation with the donation of the Quadro P6000 GPU used for this research. In Brazil, the study was supported by CNPq, Process 401066/2016-9, Edital Universal 01/2016.

# References

1. Sen, A.: The Idea of Justice. Harvard University Press, Cambridge (2009)
2. Blečić, I., Cecchini, A., Talu, V.: Capability approach and urban planning. Fertile urban capabilities and quality of urban life of the most disadvantaged inhabitants [Approccio delle capacità e pianificazione urbana. Capacità urbane feconde e qualità della vita urbana degli abitanti più svantaggiati]. Archivio di Studi Urbani e Regionali **48**, 34–52 (2018). https://doi.org/10.3280/ASUR2018-122003
3. Brighouse, H., Robeyns, I.: Measuring Justice: Primary Goods and Capabilities. Cambridge University Press, Cambridge (2010)
4. Sen, A.: Utilitarianism and welfarism. J. Philos. **76**, 463–489 (1979). https://doi.org/10.2307/2025934
5. Rocha, N.A., Moura, A.C.M., Casagrande, P.: Análise combinatória e pesos de evidência na produção de análise de multicritérios em modelos de avaliação. Geogr. y Sistemas de Información Geográfica (GEOSIG) **11**, 49–74 (2018). https://docs.wixstatic.com/ugd/79758e_4d6e3e3aa4394cb99da67962a23aa240.pdf
6. Ligmann-Zielinska, A., Jankowski, P.: Impact of proximity-adjusted preferences on rank-order stability in geographical multicriteria decision analysis. J. Geogr. Syst. **14**, 167–187 (2012). https://doi.org/10.1007/s10109-010-0140-6
7. Ligmann-Zielinska, A., Jankowski, P.: Spatially-explicit integrated uncertainty and sensitivity analysis of criteria weights in multicriteria land suitability evaluation. Environ. Model Softw. **57**, 235–247 (2014). https://doi.org/10.1016/j.envsoft.2014.03.007
8. Moura, A.C.M., Jankowski, P.L.: Contribuições aos estudos de análises de incertezas como complementação às análises multicritérios - "sensitivity analysis to suitability evaluation". Revista Brasileira de Cartografi **68**, 665–684 (2016). http://www.seer.ufu.br/index.php/revistabrasileiracartografia/article/view/44274
9. Dalkey, N., Helmer, O.: An experimental application of the DELPHI method to the use of experts. Manag. Sci. **9**, 458–467 (1963). https://doi.org/10.1287/mnsc.9.3.458
10. Moura, A.C.M.: Reflexões metodológicas como subsídio para estudos ambientais baseados em análise multicritérios. In: Anais XIII Simpósio Brasileiro de Sensoriamento Remoto, pp. 2899–2906. INPE, Florianópolis (2007). http://marte.sid.inpe.br/col/dpi.inpe.br/sbsr@80/2006/11.13.14.41/doc/2899-2906.pdf
11. Blečić, I., Cecchini, A., Trunfio, G.A.: Towards automatic assessment of perceived walkability. In: Gervasi, O., et al. (eds.) ICCSA 2018. LNCS, vol. 10962, pp. 351–365. Springer, Cham (2018). https://doi.org/10.1007/978-3-319-95168-3_24
12. Zhou, B., Lapedriza, A., Khosla, A., Oliva, A., Torralba, A.: Places: a 10 million image database for scene recognition. IEEE Trans. Pattern Anal. Mach. Intell. **40**, 1452–1464 (2018). https://doi.org/10.1109/TPAMI.2017.2723009
13. Simonyan, K., Zisserman, A.: Very deep convolutional networks for large-scale image recognition (2014)
14. Lin, M., Chen, Q., Yan, S.: Network in network (2013). https://arxiv.org/abs/1312.4400v3
15. Crammer, K., Singer, Y.: Pranking with ranking. In: Dietterich, T.G., Becker, S., Ghahramani, Z. (eds.) Advances in Neural Information Processing Systems, vol. 14, pp. 641–647. MIT Press (2002)
16. da Costa, J.P., Cardoso, J.S.: Classification of ordinal data using neural networks. In: Gama, J., Camacho, R., Brazdil, P.B., Jorge, A.M., Torgo, L. (eds.) ECML 2005. LNCS (LNAI), vol. 3720, pp. 690–697. Springer, Heidelberg (2005). https://doi.org/10.1007/11564096_70
17. Chollet, F., et. al.: Keras (2015). https://github.com/fchollet/keras

18. TensorFlow: Large-scale machine learning on heterogeneous systems. https://www.tensorflow.org/

19. Zeiler, M.D.: ADADELTA: an adaptive learning rate method (2012). https://arxiv.org/abs/1212.5701v1

20. Moura, A.C.M., Ramos, V., Faria, D., Freitas, V.: Geodesign no ensino de planejamento urbano em escala local: a construção compartilhada de ideias para projetos e políticas. Geogr. y Sistemas de Información Geográfica (GEOSIG) **11**, 127–152 (2018). https://docs.wixstatic.com/ugd/79758e_17fda28772a247458c4f086b58e33281.pdf

21. Kahneman, D.: Thinking, Fast and Slow. Farrar, Straus and Giroux, New York (2011)

# Situation Analysis of Cities in Ardabil Province in Terms of Health Indicators

Amin Safdari Molan[1]([⊠]), Keramatollah Ziari[1], Ahmad Pourahmad[1], Hossein Hataminejad[1], and Mehdi Parsa[2]

[1] Department of Geography, University of Tehran, Tehran, Iran
a_sfdari@ut.ac.ir
[2] Department of Geography, University of Mohaghegh Ardabili, Ardabil, Iran

**Abstract.** Regional planning's and development policy objectives seek to identify the disadvantaged and underdeveloped regions in order to obtain proper national and regional strategies for their development and consequently reduce inter-regional and intra-regional disparities between them; hence, this study aims at analyzing the improvement of the city of Ardabil province in the health sector so that it can be used for planning in the future. Because of the practical purposes and the nature of this study, the type of research that is used here is descriptive-analytic. The data were collected using documentary research and Statistical Yearbook. For organizing and analyzing the mathematics, Analytic Hierarchy Process (AHP) technique is used and the obtained rankings are all based on TOPSIS method. Moreover, using *Williamson's scattering coefficient, the unbalanced distribution of the services was identified and using cluster analysis,* the cities were clustered into three levels of developed, semi-developed, and non-developed with regards to the health care services available for them, and finally for a more efficient representation of them, some maps were drawn. Excel, SPSS, and ArcGIS software's were used in various stages of research. The outcomes illustrate that the city of Ardabil first class in terms of health indicators and Kosar city has ranked last. The results also demonstrate that more than half of the cities in Ardabil province are disadvantaged and in terms of health conditions, indexes are very instable. Finally, it is suggested that development plans based on these cities' level of developments should be executed and non-developed areas should be the first priority in development programs and projects as well.

**Keywords:** Development · Multiple attribute decision making · Ardabil province · Health indicators

## 1 Introduction

One of the main symptoms of underdevelopment is inequality in different aspects of a city. In fact, developed countries, in addition to the high economic and social indicators, have a relatively equitable distribution of income and opportunities [6]. In order to solve the problems of regional imbalance, the first step is to recognize and categorize areas in terms of how developed they are in social, cultural, and economic areas [8]. This gives the planners and policy makers a profound and better understanding of

© Springer Nature Switzerland AG 2019
S. Misra et al. (Eds.): ICCSA 2019, LNCS 11621, pp. 628–641, 2019.
https://doi.org/10.1007/978-3-030-24302-9_45

regional issues, and as a result can suggest policies and preparation of action plans, and thus accelerate the development of disadvantaged areas come into being [14]. Level of development is a way to measure regional development and it shows the difference in spatial, economic, social and cultural areas and distinguishes the status of each region in relation to the other in terms of the level of development measures. By using this, the formation of polar regions will be determined and finally in planning development areas, less developed regions need to be considered and the imbalance between areas will be prevented [3]. Among the different development indicators, health indicator is regarded as the most important indicator of progress in any country and the success of national development programs is largely tied on achieving fulfilling the objectives of this section. If the quality and quantity of health indicators in a society are high, and also they are distributed in a balanced way, there will be a relatively high amount of wealth and welfare in that society [18]. A glance at the country's health indicators over the past decade, on the one hand shows the rapid promotion and process of these indicators and on the other hand, it shows that in different regions and provinces, there are disparities among the indicators [12]. The health sector matters so much that the improvement of health indicators brings about the development of society and the promotion of human and social development in the country [17]. Multiple Attribute Decision Making (MCDM) is one of the most common methods of decision-making. These methods will ensure that the decision making process is a clean, rational and efficient process and improve the quality of decisions and evaluations. Multiple Attribute Decision Making refers to a process in which the evaluation or decision-making is performed based on different indices that might be even antithetic and since they can evaluate integrated index, is considered a useful tool at the disposal of the planners. By using this method, we can distinguish the cities of Ardabil province in terms of health indicators and point out to the differences in these cities and also we can determine each city's status in relation to the other in terms of their level of development. Consequently, in development planning areas, the poor and less developed areas, will receive more attention and it will also prevent the risk of regional imbalance. To this end, we used several methods to analyze the cities of Ardabil on the basis of eight health indicators so we can achieve a balance in the province in terms of health indicators and the areas are prioritized concerning the due attention that needs to be paid for them. In this study, we show that cities in Ardabil province can be ranked according to several health indicators. Besides, due to the geographical nature of these places, most of them are disadvantaged and in serious need of improvement. Using development plans and prioritizing these cities, we can help in the betterment of people's living conditions. It is of great importance in today's world because it addresses one of the major issues in environmental studies and urban planning.

## 1.1  Research Questions

According to the problem and the descriptive nature of this research, this study does not need any hypotheses and questions below make up the formation of this study.

- Concerning the health indicators, are the development of the cities in Ardabil province balanced?
- In relation to health indicators, which cities are developed and which cities are non-developed?

## 2  Literature Review

Many studies have been conducted throughout the world and in Iran to determine the levels of development of cities and the inequality between them. The most important ones are mentioned here:

Sayehmiri [9] in a study to rank the health situation of the city of Ilam, using numerical taxonomy and principal component analysis, have shown that concerning the health status in Ilam province, the cities of Ilam, Mehran, Darrehshahr and Dehloran are developed cities and Shirvan, Chardavol, Eivan and Abdanan are underdeveloped. Zangiabadi et al. [15] in a study entitled Analysis of the Degree Development of the Cities of East Azarbaijan Province, through TOPSIS and AHP models, have ranked the cities and finally presented strategies to achieve the desired balance. Tofighi et al. [13], in their study Ranking the Cities of West Azarbaijan province and How They Benefit from Structural Indicators of Health, applied Scalogram model in their research and have concluded that as far as the benefits from structural indicators of health are concerned, there is a large gap between the cities of West Azerbaijan province. Kalantari et al. [2] conducted a research study using TOPSIS technique titled Review and Assessment of the Health Care Services in Zabol and noted that the geographical distribution of health care centers in the city is imbalanced and is unable to meet the needs of people. Seydaei et al. [10], in their article The Analysis of Indicators of Health System in Kermanshah used TOPSIS, AHP, and cluster analysis for modeling and mentioned that none of the cities of Kermanshah are developed with regards to the health indicators. In their research to determine the degree of development of Yazd province cities with regards to their access to health care centers, Sarai et al. [19] applied Morris model and concluded that there is an unbalanced distribution in facilities and services in Yazd province. Tavakolinia et al. [20], analyzed the cities of Ardabil province in terms of regional development disparities in the health sector using VIKOR model and have reached the conclusion that concerning the level of development in health indicators these cities are not in a balanced state in such a way that the city of Khalkhal with a final score of 0.0924 (Greatly Developed) and Pars Abad with a final score of 0.9989 (Poorly Developed) ranked respectively the first and last in their study. Literature review shows that although extensive research has been done on the level of development of the cities in Iran including Ardabil province. The present study focuses on a different approach that can be utilized to differently analyze the cities in Ardabil province.

# 3   Research Method

The purpose of this study is practical and the purpose and method that is used here is descriptive-analytic. The data were collected by means of documentation, library method, officially released data and the press. To measure the development level of the cities in Ardebil province concerning health indicators, TOPSIS technique is used and AHP model is applied for weighting the indices. Moreover, for an uneven distribution of indicators in the cities, Williamson's scattering coefficient is employed and further took advantage of clustering analysis to categorize the cities with regards to their level of development. SPSS software is used to analyze the data and for graphical representation of the data ARC GIS is used. To learn more about the techniques and methods involved in this study, they are briefly introduced here.

**AHP Technique.** Analytic hierarchy process (AHP) is one of the most extensive multi-criteria decision aids [7]. It is a flexible, robust and simple approach to make decisions more easily in the absence of conflicting decision criteria where choosing between the available options are difficult [1]. This multi-criteria evaluation method was proposed for the first time by L. Saati in 1980 and has had many applications in science [16]. This technique allows us to compare our indices as a couple and measure each index's score in relation to the other [11]. The first step in AH is to create a hierarchy of the subject matter at hand in which the objectives, criteria, sub-criteria, options and the relationship between them is also demonstrated. The next Four steps in the AHP include: measurement of the criteria and sub-criteria, measurement of the options, calculating the final score and evaluating the logical inconsistency of judgments [2].

**TOPSIS Techniques.** TOPSIS model was introduced in 1981 by Huang and Yoon. This model is used to determine the rankings of one or more options over several criteria. Furthermore, the specified quality weights by the decision maker is normalized into a comparable scale. By defining a near zone coefficient, we can determine the rankings by calculating the distance from both *Positive (PIS)* and negative (NIS) ideal *solutions*. According to this method, the best and the worst condition may be determined for each indicator but we should bear in mind that the most appropriate option is the one with the shortest distance from the best condition and maximum distance from the worst condition. This way we can have the best solution for our problem [5]. The advantages of TOPSIS model include [22]:

1. The *simultaneous application* of *quantitative* and *quantitative criteria*;
2. It is a simple and fast method;
3. The *output* of the model *can determine the order of priority options*;
4. It has the criteria and indicators of the initial weighting coefficients;
5. The contrast and the match of the options are considered.

**Williamson's Dispersion Coefficient:** One of the basic methods to obtain local and regional disparities is the dispersion coefficient. Using this method, we can determine how far an indicator is imbalanced distributed among local and regional areas. In other words, to determine the spatial distribution of an index or inequality level of development between different regions, Williamson's dispersion coefficient method is used. We can calculate this coefficient with the following equation:

$$cv = \frac{\sqrt{\sum_{i=1}^{n} \frac{(X_i - \overline{X})^2}{N}}}{\frac{\sum_{i=1}^{n} X_i}{N}}$$

In that equation, $X_i$, is the value of a variable in a particular area or region (index value of the area); $\overline{\chi}$ is the average value of the variable (mean index value of the area) and N shows the number of areas and regions. High values of CV represents extreme inequality in the distribution of indicators throughout the areas and regions [24].

**Cluster Analysis:** It is one of the most widely used quantitative methods in studying an area, in fact clustering is a way of leveling the regions, towns, villages and so on in such a way that the regions at a particular level are very similar to each other and are significantly different from other levels [23].

### 3.1   Introduction of the Study Area

Ardabil province with an area equal to 17867 km$^2$ (1.1% of the total area of the country), is located between the northern latitude of 37 45 to 39 42 and eastern latitude of 47 30 to 48 55 of the Greenwich meridian in North West part of Iran. The average height of this province is more than 1400 m above sea level in which the lowest point is in the height of 100 m and is located at ParsAbad and Bilesavar and its highest peak is Sablan with a *height* of 4,811 m above sea level. Ardabil province borders Azerbaijan from north, Gilan province from east, and West Azerbaijan from south. Also, according to the latest national distribution, the province is divided into 10 cities: Ardabil, Bilesavar, Pars Abad, Khalkhal, Sareiyn, Kosar, Meshkinshar, Moghan, Namin and Nir. This province has 29 districts, 26 cities and 71 rural districts (Fig. 1).

### 3.2   Introducing Variables and Indicators

Variable and indicators are one of the major components of assessing progress towards development [4]. Because not only the development levels of residential areas need an extensive series of indicators but also they are necessary in any scientific study. It should be noted that considering all aspects of scientific research is neither possible nor desirable. Therefore, proper selection of a limited number of indicators could lead us to more actual results [12]. The present study analyzes and evaluates the development level of cities in Ardabil based on 8 health indicator and in 10 cities of the province. The variables that were used in this research, have been turned into indicators and analyzed include the number of: specialist doctors, general practitioners, medical institutions, hospital beds, laboratories, pharmacies, pharmacist, and nurses.

Since the collection of information and data for the analysis of the study should be both official and trustworthy, the indicators that are used here are all accessible through

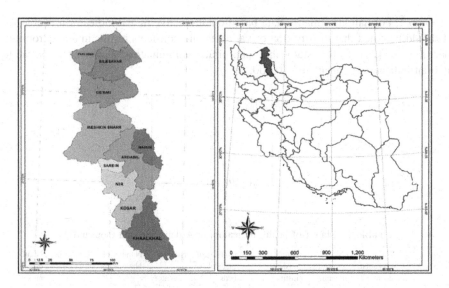

**Fig. 1.** Distribution of cities in Ardabil province

official statistical agencies. This way the accuracy of the information's presented in this paper is approved. Table 1 contains both the classification and the description of indicators used in this study:

**Table 1.** Raw data of health indicators for each city in Ardabil Province based on Statistics in 2017

| City | Population | No. of specialist doctors | No. of general doctors | Number of medical institutions | Number of medical beds | Number of laboratory | Number of pharmacies | Number of pharmacists | Number of nurses |
|---|---|---|---|---|---|---|---|---|---|
| Ardabil | 564365 | 269 | 100 | 174 | 1416 | 25 | 83 | 9 | 709 |
| Bilesavar | 53768 | 7 | 12 | 3 | 36 | 1 | 4 | 0 | 32 |
| Parsabad | 173182 | 41 | 14 | 12 | 224 | 6 | 16 | 1 | 117 |
| Khalkhal | 92332 | 17 | 33 | 9 | 113 | 3 | 7 | 1 | 145 |
| Sareyn | 18231 | 2 | 7 | 1 | 0 | 0 | 1 | 0 | 5 |
| Kosar | 26198 | 2 | 10 | 1 | 0 | 0 | 1 | 0 | 6 |
| Germi | 84267 | 12 | 12 | 5 | 96 | 2 | 6 | 1 | 82 |
| Meskinshahr | 151156 | 34 | 33 | 20 | 153 | 3 | 13 | 2 | 110 |
| Namin | 61333 | 3 | 29 | 4 | 50 | 1 | 3 | 1 | 22 |
| Nayyer | 33656 | 2 | 15 | 1 | 0 | 0 | 1 | 0 | 7 |
| Total | 1172647 | 385 | 265 | 230 | 2043 | 41 | 135 | 15 | 1136 |

Source: Statistics of Ardabil Province in 2017.

## 4 Findings

Given that the techniques and processes along with their data are not separately provided here, the steps of the proposed model are explained with the research data so that identifying the level of development and the areas in relation to health indicators will be easy to understand for the readers:

Step 1: Formation of matrix data based on alternative m and indicator n (Table 2). It should be noted that the division of variables and constants results in an appropriate denominator [21]. In this study the appropriate denominator for converting variable into an indicator is considered 10,000.

$$
A_{ij} = \begin{bmatrix} a_{11} & a_{12} & \cdots & a_{1n} \\ a_{21} & a_{22} & \cdots & a_{2n} \\ \cdot & & & \cdot \\ \cdot & & & \cdot \\ \cdot & & & \cdot \\ a_{m1} & a_{m2} & \cdots & a_{mn} \end{bmatrix}
$$

**Table 2.** Matrix of health indicators in Ardabil (per ten thousand)

| City | No. of specialist doctors | No. of general doctors | Number of medical institutions | Number of medical beds | Number of laboratory | Number of pharmacies | Number of pharmacists | Number of nurses |
|------|------|------|------|------|------|------|------|------|
| Ardabil | 4.77 | 1.8 | 3.08 | 25.1 | 0.44 | 1.47 | 0.16 | 12.56 |
| Bilesavar | 1.3 | 2.23 | 0.56 | 5.7 | 0.18 | 0.74 | 0 | 5.96 |
| Parsabad | 2.37 | 0.81 | 0.7 | 12.93 | 0.34 | 0.92 | 0.05 | 6.75 |
| Khalkhal | 1.84 | 3.57 | 0.97 | 12.24 | 0.32 | 0.75 | 0.1 | 15.7 |
| Sareyn | 1.1 | 3.84 | 0.55 | 0 | 0 | 0.55 | 0 | 2.74 |
| Kosar | 0.76 | 3.82 | 0.38 | 0 | 0 | 0.38 | 0 | 2.3 |
| Germi | 1.42 | 1.42 | 0.6 | 11.4 | 0.23 | 0.71 | 0.11 | 9.73 |
| Meskinshahr | 2.25 | 2.18 | 1.32 | 10.12 | 0.2 | 0.86 | 0.13 | 7.28 |
| Namin | 0.49 | 4.73 | 0.65 | 8.15 | 0.16 | 0.49 | 0.16 | 3.59 |
| Nayyer | 0.84 | 6.34 | 0.42 | 0 | 0 | 0.42 | 0 | 2.96 |

Source: Author's calculations for turning data into indicators

Step 2: Standard Matrix Formation Without Scale (Table 3).

$$
r_{ij} = \frac{a_{ij}}{\sqrt{\displaystyle\sum_{k=1}^{m} a_{kj}^2}} \quad R_{ij} \xrightarrow{\phantom{xx}} \begin{bmatrix} r_{11} & r_{12} & \cdots & r_{1n} \\ r_{21} & r_{22} & \cdots & r_{2n} \\ \cdot & & & \cdot \\ \cdot & & & \cdot \\ \cdot & & & \cdot \\ r_{m1} & r_{m2} & \cdots & r_{mn} \end{bmatrix}
$$

Step 3: Determining the weight of each indicator by the following equation:

$$
\sum_{i=1}^{n} W_i = 1 \rightarrow V_{ij} = \begin{bmatrix} W_1 r_{11} & \cdots & W_n r_{1n} \\ \vdots & \ddots & \vdots \\ W_1 r_{m1} & \cdots & W_n r_{mn} \end{bmatrix}
$$

**Table 3.** Standardized matrix of health indicators for cities in Ardabil

| City | No. of specialist doctors | No. of general doctors | Number of medical institutions | Number of medical beds | Number of laboratory | Number of pharmacies | Number of pharmacists | Number of nurses |
|------|------|------|------|------|------|------|------|------|
| Ardabil | 0.72 | 0.16 | 0.81 | 0.7 | 0.58 | 0.59 | 0.53 | 0.48 |
| Bilesavar | 0.19 | 0.2 | 0.14 | 0.18 | 0.24 | 0.29 | 0 | 0.23 |
| Parsabad | 0.35 | 0.7 | 0.18 | 0.35 | 0.45 | 0.36 | 0.16 | 0.26 |
| Khalkhal | 0.28 | 0.32 | 0.25 | 0.34 | 0.42 | 0.3 | 0.33 | 0.6 |
| Sareyn | 0.16 | 0.35 | 0.14 | 0 | 0 | 0.22 | 0 | 0.1 |
| Kosar | 0.11 | 0.34 | 0.1 | 0 | 0 | 0.15 | 0 | 0.08 |
| Germi | 0.21 | 0.12 | 0.15 | 0.31 | 0.3 | 0.28 | 0.4 | 0.37 |
| Meskinshahr | 0.34 | 0.2 | 0.34 | 0.28 | 0.26 | 0.34 | 0.43 | 0.28 |
| Namin | 0.07 | 0.43 | 0.17 | 0.22 | 0.21 | 0.19 | 0.53 | 0.13 |
| Nayyer | 0.12 | 0.57 | 0.11 | 0 | 0 | 0.16 | 0 | 0.11 |

Source: Author's Calculations

As mentioned earlier, in the present study AHP technique is used to calculate the weight of each indicator. Table 4 shows the obtained weights of the indicators.

**Table 4.** Indicators' weight investigated in this study

| Indicator | No. of specialist doctors | No. of general doctors | Number of medical institutions | Number of medical beds | Number of laboratory | Number of pharmacies | Number of pharmacists | Number of nurses |
|------|------|------|------|------|------|------|------|------|
| Weight | 0.089 | 0.061 | 0.111 | 0.194 | 0.182 | 0.35 | 0.25 | 0.08 |

Source: Research findings

After calculating the weight of each indicator, standard values are multiplied in their weight and weighted matrix is formed. (Table 5).

**Table 5.** Weighted matrix without scale

| City | No. of specialist doctors | No. of general doctors | Number of medical institutions | Number of medical beds | Number of laboratory | Number of pharmacies | Number of pharmacists | Number of nurses |
|------|------|------|------|------|------|------|------|------|
| Ardabil | 0.064 | 0.01 | 0.089 | 0.133 | 0.104 | 0.021 | 0.133 | 0.038 |
| Bilesavar | 0.017 | 0.012 | 0.015 | 0.034 | 0.43 | 0.01 | 0 | 0.018 |
| Parsabad | 0.031 | 0.043 | 0.02 | 0.066 | 0.081 | 0.013 | 0.04 | 0.021 |
| Khalkhal | 0.025 | 0.019 | 0.027 | 0.064 | 0.076 | 0.01 | 0.082 | 0.048 |
| Sareyn | 0.014 | 0.021 | 0.015 | 0 | 0 | 0.008 | 0 | 0.008 |
| Kosar | 0.01 | 0.021 | 0.011 | 0 | 0 | 0.005 | 0 | 0.08 |
| Germi | 0.019 | 0.007 | 0.016 | 0.059 | 0.054 | 0.01 | 0.1 | 0.03 |
| Meskinshahr | 0.03 | 0.12 | 0.037 | 0.053 | 0.047 | 0.012 | 0.107 | 0.022 |
| Namin | 0.006 | 0.026 | 0.019 | 0.042 | 0.038 | 0.007 | 0.132 | 0.01 |
| Nayyer | 0.011 | 0.035 | 0.012 | 0 | 0 | 0.006 | 0 | 0.009 |

Source: Research findings

Step 4: To determine distance i from the highest performance of any indicator which is shown by A is determined as follows (Table 6):

**Table 6.** Calculation of the highest and lowest performance of any indicator

| | Number of nurse | Number of pharmacists | Number of pharmacies | Number of laboratory | Number of medical beds | Number of medical institutions | General practitioner | Specialist doctors |
|---|---|---|---|---|---|---|---|---|
| $A^*$ | 0.048 | 0.132 | 0.021 | 0.104 | 0.133 | 0.089 | 0.043 | 0.064 |
| $A^-$ | 0.006 | 0 | 0.006 | 0 | 0 | 0.011 | 0.007 | 0.006 |

Source: Research findings

$$A^* = \{(\max v_{ij} \mid j \in J), (\min v_{ij} \mid j \in J') \mid i = 1, 2, \ldots m)\} = \{v_1^*, v_2^*, \ldots, v_j^*, \ldots, v_n^*\}$$

Step 5: To determine the lowest performance of any indicator which is shown by $(A^-)$ is determined as follows:

$$A^- = \{(\min v_{ij} \mid j \in J), (\max v_{ij} \mid j \in J') \mid i = 1, 2, \ldots m)\} = \{v_1^-, v_2^-, \ldots, v_j^-, \ldots, v_n^-\}$$

Step 6: To determine the criteria of distance for the minimum and maximum alternative, the following formula is used:

$$s_i^- = \sqrt{\sum_{j=1}^{n} \left(v_{ij} - v_j^-\right)^2} \qquad s_i^* = \sqrt{\sum_{j=1}^{n} \left(v_{ij} - v_j^*\right)^2}$$

For each of the cities in Ardabil, the distance criteria for the maximum and minimum alternatives were calculated (Table 7).

**Table 7.** The determined distances from the maximum and minimum alternatives and their difference from these alternatives

| City | $S_i^*$ | $S_i^-$ | City | $S_i^*$ | $S_i^-$ |
|---|---|---|---|---|---|
| Ardabil | 0.034 | 0.24 | Kosar | 0.239 | 0.014 |
| Bilesavar | 0.201 | 0.058 | Germi | 0.134 | 0.131 |
| Parsabad | 0.142 | 0.122 | Meskinshahr | 0.126 | 0.134 |
| Khalkhal | 0.119 | 0.138 | Namin | 0.151 | 0.145 |
| Sareyn | 0.237 | 0.017 | Nayyer | 0.214 | 0.029 |

Source: Research findings

Step 7 and 8: At this stage a coefficient which is equal with the division of minimum and maximum alternative is obtained. In other words, a relative vicinity of (Ai) to (A*) was calculated as follow: $C_i^* = \frac{S_i^-}{S_i^- + S_i^*}$

After calculating the distance criteria, priority coefficient ($C_i^*$) for each city were calculated (Table 8). The value of $C_i^*$ fluctuated between zero and one. In this regard $C_i^* = 1$ represents the maximum alternative and $C_i^- = 0$ represents the minimum alternative.

**Table 8.** Calculation and rankings of the cities based on the results from TOPSIS technique

| City | $c_i$ | Rank | City | $c_i$ | Rank |
|------|-------|------|------|-------|------|
| Ardabil | 0.876 | 1 | Parsabad | 0.462 | 6 |
| Khalkhal | 0.537 | 2 | Bilesavar | 0.224 | 7 |
| Meskinshahr | 0.504 | 3 | Nayyer | 0.119 | 8 |
| Germi | 0.494 | 4 | Sareyn | 0.067 | 9 |
| Namin | 0.49 | 5 | Kosar | 0.055 | 10 |

Source: Research findings

According to the final coefficient of each city concerning their level of development of health indicators, it is revealed that the cities of Ardabil, Khalkhal, Meshgin Shahr ranked respectively first to third and the cities of Nir, Sarein and Kosar had the lowest rankings. Figure 2 is a geographical demonstration of these information's.

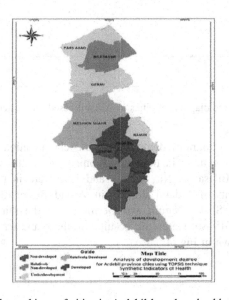

**Fig. 2.** The rankings of cities in Ardabil based on health indicators

Also, the output from Williamson's dispersion coefficient shows 0.159. As noted, this coefficient is an indicator that determines to what extent an indicator is imbalanced distributed between regions or areas. The indicators are between zero and one. If the obtained number tends to be closer to zero, it shows a reduction of regional disparities

[24] and in the case of our research it also shows the balance and relative equality of the cities in Ardabil concerning their development of health indicators.

Furthermore, the classification for the cities in terms of homogeneity in developed or non-developed health care services and standard score variables, cluster analysis was used. The results obtained from cluster analysis in SPSS software shows the cities in three separatecategories. These categories are shown in Fig. 3.

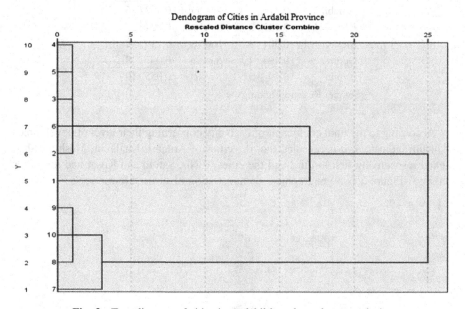

**Fig. 3.** Tree diagram of cities in Ardabil based on cluster analysis

Tree diagram (dendrogram) demonstrates the classification of cities in Ardabil concerning their homogeneity in their development of health indicators and in this regard the cities of Bilesavar, Nir, Sareyn and Kosar are in the first cluster (non-developed) and the city of Ardabil alone is in second cluster (developed). Khalkhal, Pars Abad, Meshgin Shahr, Namin and Germi are in the third cluster (relatively-developed). Using GIS software, the results of these clusters and their level of development are shown in Fig. 4.

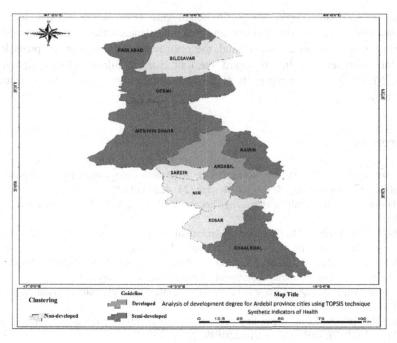

**Fig. 4.** City clustering in Ardabil

## 5 Conclusion

Scientific and efficient decision making with regard to prioritization of regional issues, increases the success rate of regional initiatives and policy development programs and using the multi-criteria decision-making models can facilitate the decision-making process.

Desirable access of people of different regions to the facilities and health services are considered important indicators in increasing the quality of life and sustainable development of human societies. Moreover, improving the health status of citizens in each city or region is one of the major reasons of human development. Hence, the present study aimed to assess the state of health indicators, analyzed 8 indicators in Ardabil province using AHP and TOPSIS model and then the inequality rate in the distribution of health services were determined through the dispersion coefficient and with the help of cluster analysis which is one of the methods for identifying homogeneous areas, the current situation of the cities was analyzed. The results (based on the dispersion coefficient analysis) indicates that in terms of the level of development of health indicators, the cities in Ardabil province are relatively balanced. In addition, the results from TOPSIS model shows that with regards to health indicators the city of Ardabil with a final score of 0.876 and the city of Kosar with a final score of 0.055 are respectively highly developed and non-developed areas in the province. Also, the results of cluster analysis showed that the cities of Bilesavar, Kosar, Sarein, as well as Nir are the most non-developed areas and all are placed in a homogeneous category.

Due to the dramatic improvements in health care services on the one hand and increased demand for health services and lack of balance between the needs and the provision of services on the other hand, the priority was to invest in the provision of essential health services. In this regard, the four cities of Bilesuar, Kosar, Sareyin, as well as Nir should be the top priority of developmental programs of health indicators in the province.

# References

1. Bertolini, M., Braglia, M.: Application of the AHP methodology in making a proposal for a public work contract. Int. J. Project Manage. **24**, 422–430 (2006)
2. Ghodousipour, H.: Analytic Hierarchy Process AHP. Amir Kabir University Press, Tehran (2009)
3. Jadidi Miyandashti, M.: Balanced distribution of financial resources to the level of development of regions. Econ. Res. J. (11 and 12), 17–41 (2004)
4. Molden, B., Bilhaz, S., Haddad Tehrani, N., Moharamnejad, N.: Sustainable Development Indicators. Published by the Department of Environment, Tehran (2002)
5. Momeni, M.: Principles of Regional Planning. Islamic Azad University of Najaf Abad, Najaf Abad (2008)
6. Mosallanejad, A.: Economic policy and social responsibility of government. Polit. Q. **42**(1), 311–331 (2012). https://doi.org/10.22059/jpq.2012.29942
7. Omkarprasad, V., Sushil, K.: Analytic hierarchy process: an overview of applications. Eur. J. Oper. Res. **16**, 1–29 (2006)
8. Rezvani, M.R., Sahnh, B.: Evaluation of rural development using fuzzy logic in the village of Aghghla and February Turkmen. J. Rural Dev. **8**(3), 2 (1994)
9. Shaye Miri, A., Shaye Miri, K.: Ranking of health status of Ilam city's using numerical taxonomy and main components analysis. J. Ilam Univ. Med. Sci. **9–8**(29–29), 30–35 (2001)
10. Sydaii, S., Jamini, D., Jamshidi, A.: An analysis on the status of health-therapeutic indexes in the provinces of Kermanshah using TOPSIS, AHP and cluster analysis models. Spat. Plann. **4**(1), 43–64 (2014)
11. Sharif Zadegan, M., Fathi, H.: Evaluation of environmental vulnerability for regional planning in Alborz environment triple areas by hierarchical method. J. Environ. Sci. **3**(3) (2005)
12. Taghvaei, M., Norouzi, Avargani A.: An analysis of spatial distribution of rural facilities and ser-vices and ranking of Chaharmahal Bakhtyari districts. J. Isfahan Univ. **3**, 59–74 (2007). (in Persian)
13. Hamouzadeh, P., Moradi Hovasin, N., Sadeghifar, J., Tofighi, S.: Ranking West Azerbaijan districts regarding utilization of structural indices of health care. J. Qazvin Univ. Med. Sci. **17**(2), 41–49 (2013)
14. Venkatesh B.S.: Problems and prospects of development of backward regions: a study of Karnataka State. Thesis of Doctor of Philosophy in Economics, under Supervision of Hemlata Rao, Bangalore University, Bangalore (2000)
15. Zangi Abadi, A., Alizadeh, J., Ahmadian, M.: An analysis on the degree of development in East Azarbaijan province (using AHP and TOPSIS techniques). New Attitudes Q. Hum. Geogr. **4**(1) (2011)
16. Zebardast, E.: The application of analytical hierarchy process in urban and regional planning. Fine Arts J. **10**, 13–21 (2001)

17. Hamouzadeh, P., Hovasin, N.M., Sadeghifar, J., Tofighi, S.R.: Ranking West Azerbaijan districts regarding utilization of structural indices of health care. J. Qazvin Univ. Med. Sci. **17**, 41–49 (2013)
18. Nastran, M.: Analysis and measuring degree of concentration and distribution of health indices in Isfahan. J. Fac. Lit. Humanities Isfahan **3**(27–26), 145–162 (2001)
19. Sarai, M.H., Kamalizadeh, Y.: Determining the degree of development of the city of Yazd in terms of access to health centers by using Morris. Pamaysh Environ. Mag. **6**(22), 63–80 (2013)
20. Tavakolinia, J., Kanooni, R., Khavariyan, A., Paseban, V.: The analysis of regional development disparities in the health sector Ardabil province. J. Reg. Plan. (18), 1–14 (2015)
21. Kalantari, K.: Processing and Analysis of Data on Socio-Economic Research Using the Software SPSS. Saba Cultural Publications, Tehran (2010)
22. Taghipour, A.: Places of employment with emphasis Brastqrar survey processing industries (CASE STUDY: Khanmyra district, city Lordegan). M.Sc. thesis, University of Sistan and Baluchestan, Zahedan (2009)
23. Hossinzadeh, D.K.: Pianificazione regionale, Sadeh Publishing, Prima stampa, Teheran (2001)
24. Hekmatniya, M., Mousavi, M.: Model in Geography with an Emphasis on Urban and Regional Planning. Modern Science Publishing, First Printing, Tehran (2006)

# Spatial Analysis of the Proximity Effects of Land Use Planning on Housing Prices (Case Study: Tehran, Iran)

Amin Safdari Molan[(✉)] and Ebrahim Farhadi

Tehran University, Tehran, Iran
{a_safdari, e.farhadi71}@ut.ac.ir

**Abstract.** The concept of housing in the urban planning and economy of countries is very important because the highest percentage of urban usage is residential use, which today accounts for about 40% of land use in residential areas, while the highest percentage of household cost in developing countries such as Iran is According to economic studies, housing accounts for over 50% of household income. According to the results of this study, the research is of the applied type, considering the nature of the main approach to the current paper, is descriptive-analytical. According to the study area and the nature of the subject of the research, Quantitative methods and techniques (Geographical Weighting Regression Model). Several factors affect the price of housing is one of the factors, proximity to a variety of land use, which plays Has a key impact on housing prices. In TehranCity, Because of the combination of land use and special features that user this city, we have evaluated the effects of each application on housing prices. By identifying the effects of each type of usage on housing prices, it would be possible to find a way to plan for housing and housing economics in the city and to draw on future studies on this issue. Given that the topic of housing economics is an inclusive and interdisciplinary topic (politics, economics, management, geography, etc.), so this article further discusses the influence of geographic factors (types of uses) on housing prices. It was found that: green land-use and parks with $R^2/87$, urban land-use services with $R^2/80$, access to gardens and farmland with $R^2/36$, and commercial and administrative Land-Use with $R^2/24$ respectively, have the highest impact on housing prices in level city.

**Keywords:** Spatial analysis · Housing economics · Land use ·
Geographic weight regression model · Tehran city

## 1 Introduction

Housing as an economic commodity has characteristics that differentiate it from other commodities and complicates supply and demand analysis and markets. On the one hand, housing is a commodity that after food and clothing is considered to be the most basic human need and the most expensive household commodity, and on the other hand, as a durable, durable immovable commodity, is the capital of investment in which is the largest portion of the household's assets. In addition to households, it is

© Springer Nature Switzerland AG 2019
S. Misra et al. (Eds.): ICCSA 2019, LNCS 11621, pp. 642–659, 2019.
https://doi.org/10.1007/978-3-030-24302-9_46

also a great attraction for businesses. In particular, in terms of inflation, which ensures lower investment returns in other sectors, buying and building housing is a safe and secure investment that is more cost-effective in the long run than other forms of investment. In addition, the uncertainty about the future and the lack of a proper social security system make housing a household income in old age and disability [25]. Housing and its issues today are a global issue and planners and policymakers in different countries are trying to solve their problems [6]. Lack of adequate resources, lack of economic management, lack of comprehensive housing planning and other shortcomings in the economic infrastructure on one hand, and rapid population growth on the other hand, has made it difficult and multifaceted to provide shelter in these countries [27]. Housing relative to other goods due to characteristics such as non-replaceable, capital-worthy, durable, cost-effective and immovable [12] can be a major factor in inequality and, at the same time, social solidarity. Housing ownership is a clear demonstration of the level of living. Hence, the rate of achieving desirable housing status is considered as one of the indicators of economic development in the world [4]. Housing therefore has a fundamental importance in human [20]. Housing satisfies the basic needs of the human being and It therefore affects the lives of citizens and can be easily linked to living conditions and cause them to rise. Economically, housing accounts for over 50% of household income. In addition to economic aspects, the socio-cultural aspect of housing is also very important [18]. The housing sector is a leading sector in the economy, which, in addition to its social and cultural effects, is also important economically. Housing is a durable and costly commodity (50% of the financial and income potential of each person is spent on housing during their lives), and it is considered an investment, saving, and source of income and increase in income in Iran (Currently, in Iran, one of the important indicators in identifying wealthy people is not the amount of income, but the amount of assets, possessions and capital). This sector greatly affects economic fluctuations by creating economic growth and creating employment in the construction sector and other parts of the building sector, through its impact on consumption and investment, changes in GDP and inflation. Regarding the economic conditions of Iran and inflation, there is no reasonable relationship between the annual salary of a person and the basic costs in Iranian society; therefore, reviewing the policies of housing and providing social welfare plays a major role in rewriting the type of cultural and economic look to housing in Iranian society, which shows that the inefficiencies that occurred in the housing planning system and the resulting results are the same. The issue of housing in urban economics and urban planning is important in several respects: first, in terms of urban land use, since the highest urban land use is the residential use, which today accounts for about 40% of land use, consisting of residential areas, on the other hand, because of this The highest percentage of household expenditure in third-world nation will be allocated to it. There is no doubt that the first and most important factor in the construction of housing is the "factor of the earth". In Iran, the price of land accounts for a large share of the price of housing. In most cases, the share of land prices exceeds 50% for the whole building, sometimes reaching 80 to 85%. There are several factors affecting housing prices, one of which is the types of land uses that play a key role in determining housing prices. In the city of Tehran, due to the combination of user and special features that govern the use of this city and the different prices of housing, we are investigating the effects of each usage on the price of housing, so that by identifying the effects of each type of usage on the price of housing, appropriate planning for housing and housing economy city. Given that the economy of housing is a comprehensive and interdisciplinary topic (politics, economics, management, geography, etc.), this article discusses the impact of geographic factors (types of uses) on housing prices.

## 2 Theoretical Foundations

### 2.1 Background of the Research

See Table 1

**Table 1.** The background to the economic issues of housing in Iran is given in the following table.

| Researchers | Title of research | Summary of results |
|---|---|---|
| Fardin Yazdani | An Introduction to Theoretical The Relationship between Macroeconomic Policies and Housing | The models presented show that the government, through financial and monetary policies, has significant effects on the supply and demand of housing, it seems that a significant part of the developments in recent years can be explained using these patterns |
| Mahmoud Jahani | Housing market stagnation and exit strategies | Following the unprecedented growth of investment in the housing sector, which reached about 60% in 2007 at constant prices, since August 2008, the declining trend of production and investment in housing has started to emerge in Tehran, and with its prolonged spread to the whole country, a comprehensive and complete recession on the housing sector prevailed |
| Mohsen Ebrahimi | The relationship between stock price fluctuations and housing prices | The relationship between the growth rate of housing prices and stock prices by seasonal data of 1997 shows that there is no strong relationship between the growth rates of these two markets, but more than anything else, the variance of these two variables, which has had a meaningful relationship |

(*continued*)

**Table 1.** (*continued*)

| Researchers | Title of research | Summary of results |
|---|---|---|
| Ali Akbar Gholizadeh | The bubble of housing prices and its determinants in Iran | The rapid growth of liquidity, if other factors are steady, causes the formation of a housing bubble. Therefore, in the absence of liquidity absorption in the capital market, the likelihood of its transfer to the housing market and the price shock in the housing market are high. In this situation, monetary authorities can prevent it by implementing prudent monetary policies |
| Saeed Abedin in Kush, Sarah Rahimian | Analysis of factors influencing housing prices in urban areas of Iran during the period (1991–2006) with emphasis on urban grouping | One of the most important results of this study is the point that the effect of economic variables on housing prices varies from city to city. For example, in Tehran, variables such as the volume of liquidity and household income have a greater impact on housing prices than other cities, and in contrast to the comparison of the elasticity of variables, it is likely that the manufacturing cost variable may have a greater role in housing prices in small and large urban areas than Tehran Plays |
| Reyhane Sadat Shojaee | Investigating the relationship between land prices and the use of urban land in Tehran's three Jamalabad, Yousefabad and Yakhche Abad neighborhoods | In statistical surveys between land prices and other variables, it was determined that land use price has the highest correlation coefficient. In the sample of this research, land prices are inversely related to diversity of use and the correlation coefficient between these two variables is negative |
| Younessalmani, Sarah Sadeghi | Investigating the effect of oil income shocks on housing prices in Iran through the Dutch disease mechanism of the SVAR model | Based on the results of the immediate response and analysis of variance, oil revenue shocks, along with its intrinsic shocks, are the most important determinant of the relative price of housing |
| Ali Chegani, Ali Ghaedi | Review the cycles of the boom and the recession in the housing sector | The results of this study show that despite the relative increase in the volume and real value of |

(*continued*)

**Table 1.** (*continued*)

| Researchers | Title of research | Summary of results |
| --- | --- | --- |
| | | transactions carried out in the housing market in 2014, the data on value added and investment in the housing sector, construction permits and housing prices indicate a stagnation in this sector in 2013 and Continue to 2014 |
| Bahram Sobhani, Mohsen Tartar | Factors affecting the price of residential land in Tehran | The results of the study show that liquidity, oil revenue, stock price index and inflation in short term have a significant effect on land prices, but the effect of exchange rate on land prices in the short run is not significant. The variables of liquidity and oil revenue in the long run also have a significant effect on land prices, but the effect of stock price index on land prices in the long run is not significant |
| Ali Ghaedi | Assessment of the relationship between investment in the housing sector and gross domestic product | The results indicate that there is a twofold causality between investment in the housing sector and the business cycle, and adopting policies that boost investment in the housing sector can create economic prosperity and vice versa |

Source: Research findings: 2019.

## 2.2    Satisfaction of Citizens from the Residential Environment

Concepts of residential satisfaction are closely related to concepts such as standard of living, well-being, livability, quality of place, quality of life associated with health and quality of life. In fact, these concepts are overlapping and sometimes synonymous [28]. Planning systems play an important role in increasing the supply of affordable housing through financing. The supply of land involves a large part of the cost of affordable housing. It is also one of the major challenges for countries. Recent research has shown that remote sites limit people's access to urban facilities and workplaces [29] and additional behavioral costs that are not feasible for low-income families.

Residential satisfaction is essentially the provision of the needs of residents in line with their aspirations (perceptions and mental aspirations and individual characteristics), taking into account the realities of society (the actual perception of the status quo). Important factors affecting residential satisfaction as a multifactor concept are definite. Therefore, in order to better assess residential accommodation and its influential factors, many modeling has been done so far. The results of the research show that the important factors affecting the level of housing satisfaction, including the characteristics of the inhabitants of the socio-cultural and economic factors of housing and society and, most importantly, the coherence of needs and aspirations. And many of these factors follow the cultural and social characteristics of the country and society under study. Therefore, residence satisfaction is a function of the characteristics of the individuals living in the objective and subjective features of the habitat of the needs and aspirations of individuals as socioeconomic, cultural and physical factors of housing and society [16]. The factors affecting the satisfaction of residential space can be summarized in the following graph (Fig. 1).

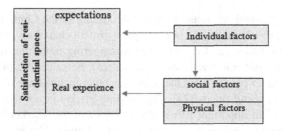

**Fig. 1.**  Source: Ghafourian and Hesari, 2016: 6

## 2.3   Housing Economy

Housing sector is one of the most important economic sectors in the country because, on the one hand, the market slump is bad for the negative impact on investment in this sector and the decline of economic growth for economic policymakers and statesmen, and on the other hand, rapid boom and rapid growth. The price is never desirable for politicians and policymakers because of their severe impact on increasing household expenses and social dissatisfaction [14]. Because housing accounted for a significant portion of the net wealth of the private sector, as well as housing costs, such as renting or mortgage lending, constitute the most important part of household expenses. Also, rent is the most important component and in the assessment of price risk and stability, the important factor (CPI) is the price index for goods and services. Meanwhile, the periodic fluctuations of the housing market are affecting the investment of the housing sector, the supply side of this commodity and the labor market, and the mobility and mobility of the workforce [27]. Finally, housing is a precious commodity whose purchase involves borrowing from the banking system of the country, and the main problem facing the banking system in providing housing loans is that the purchase of housing requires long-term credits, while housing loan sources in the banking system of Iran are short-lived. This problem has caused the mortgage coverage to be low [1]. Several basic features, the theory of demand, distinguishes housing from other economic markets. First, housing is completely non-homogeneous. The theoretical root of the non-homogeneity of the commodity is the difference in the service it provides to its holders. Second, housing is a durable commodity. Third, there are different motives for buying housing. Fourth, housing commodities, unlike many other commodities, can be provided in two types of property and leases, and ultimately the cost of housing finance among the essential commodities has the highest share of household income and it is inevitable for the household to provide. In general, housing demand can be subdivided into demand for housing and demand for housing. In housing demand, it is only household shelter, while in the demand for housing, investment returns and other factors such as bourgeoisie, lease and … are the main motivations of housing demand. Simply put, housing demand is the demand for housing as much as households need shelter [14].

### 2.4    The Structural Characteristics of the Housing Market

1. The staggering growth of housing prices: According to the Central Bank Statistics released between 69 and 85, the housing price growth chart does not fit entirely into the growth of inflation, and its curve has a staggering trend that fluctuates around the inflationary axis. On the basis of this, it can be said that, in addition to the general inflationary pressures on the economy, other factors have also contributed to the change in housing prices [23]. The housing market is not the only market for production, and an important part of the activities of this market is devoted to the transfer and redevelopment of existing residential units. The increase in prices in this part of the housing market leads to the diversion of capital from the manu-facturing sector to the service sector (buying and selling) of housing. Other factors also affect pricing. The way housing deals are conducted mainly by intermediaries (trading companies) and because these intermediaries can determine prices and prices in harmony with each other. Price levels affect the supply and demand mechanisms of the housing market [10].
2. The gap between supply and demand: According to economic laws, demand for more goods from each supply will increase the price of that commodity. One of the reasons for the crisis in housing prices in Iran is a large difference between the supply and demand in the housing market. The demand for housing can be divided into two parts: actual demand (demand) and capital demand. There are various reasons for the high demand in the Iranian housing market. One of these reasons is the demographic structure of the country. Placing a significant part of the age pyramid of the population at the age of matrimonial housing is facing a potential demand which, due to the periodic depreciations of the building sector and the lack of response to housing needs over the past years, has led to the accumulation of demand and its subsequent delivery. Is Undoubtedly, part of this demand can never become a reality due to the low purchasing power of families. However, the actual demand, given the supply of this section, can easily lead to a price crisis [19].
3. A high share in the household's household basket: One of the most important economic indicators used in assessing the housing situation in different countries is the share of housing costs in the household income basket, which can be the basis for policy-making in the housing sector. In countries that have a successful expe-rience in solving the housing problem of different classes of society, the share of housing costs in the household basket is less than 15%, while in our country this

share is 53% reported, reaching 63.8% for the lower deciles. In our country, a high percentage of household income is spent on paying rent or installments [23].

## 2.5 The Most Important Factors Affecting Housing Prices

The factors influencing housing prices are multiplicative in terms of micro factors and macro factors. The macroeconomic factors, such as monetary policy, have a huge impact on housing prices, which should be considered as important in changing housing prices. In general, factors affecting housing prices can be divided into two categories: first, the fundamental factors determined by the supply and demand forces of the market, and the second is the non-fundamental factors that are not related to the economic performance of the housing, but include those outside the function of the housing sector Affect housing prices. Fundamental factors on a macro scale may include factors such as monetary policy and interest rates on bank deposit yields. On a small scale, factors such as construction density affect the housing pattern [5]. In the neighborhoods, there is another factor that can be considered: the effect of the mixing of applications and its undeniable impact on housing prices. Thus, in residential neighborhoods, the proximity to retail outlets can add value to housing prices, which is why services are offered with better conditions. Also, in traditional housing price considerations, changing the distance from the city center and main access is considered to be a major factor in the difference in housing prices, and according to that distance from the city's commercial center, housing prices are subject to spatial changes [14]. Other important factors influencing housing prices are, of course, also referred to as housing production factors: land prices, construction materials, labor costs, and technology. In terms of physical indicators, these indicators are of economic, social, cultural and technical dimensions. Among the physical indicators that affect housing prices, we can point to the density of land and land area. The price of housing and land is usually directly related to congestion, both in construction and in demographic terms. In other words, the higher the price of housing and land, the greater the density of the city. The increase in land prices due to its constraints and unsustainability of supply against demand, as well as the necessity of its optimal use, leads to an increase in construction density followed by a demographic density (with a constant occupancy). Accordingly, due to the significant contribution of land prices to residential dwellings, fluctuations in land prices have a decisive impact on land area and housing infrastructure and, as a result of construction, density [5]. The variables that affect housing prices are as follows:

1. Physical or structural variables such as land area, number of rooms, old buildings and floor area.
2. Access variables such as access to the workplace, training centers, access to shopping malls, etc.
3. Economic and social variables such as income and.
4. Spatial variables [2].

The main macro and micro factors affecting housing prices are designed in the following graph (Fig. 2).

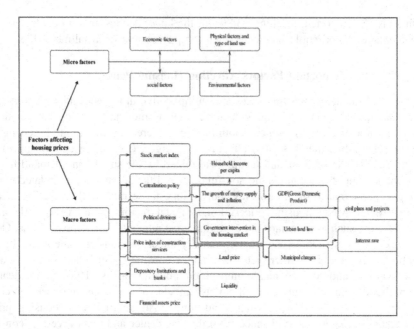

**Fig. 2.** Factors affecting housing prices. Source: Research findings, 2019

## 3 Study Area

Tehran is the capital of Iran with a geographical position of 51° 5 min to 51° and 36 min east and 35° 35 min to 35° and 50 min' north latitude and its elevation is from sea level between 1800 m in the north to 1200 The meter is in the center and 1050 m in the south. Tehran between the Alborz Mountains and the northern margin of Iran's

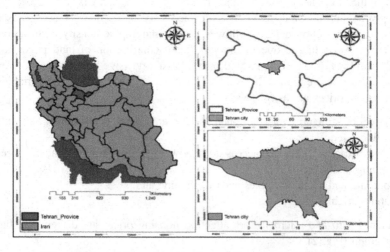

**Fig. 3.** Map of the study area. Source: Draw the authors, 2019

central desert is fairly flat in the plain. Its area is 594 km (22 districts) with an area of 2,000 km$^2$ and 8 million inhabitants (with its 12 million city-states) (Fig. 3).

# 4    Methodology of Research

The present research is objective, applied and developmental, and, as far as the method is concerned, is descriptive-analytical. In order to do this paper and determine the effects of each land use on housing price, the dependent variable of this study was the first phase of the GIS file for the price of residential in the summer of 1395 (2016) that taken from the Iranian Statistics Organization. Each type of the GIS land use files of the region, including green and parks land-uses, commercial and office land-uses, industrial and workshop land-uses, vacant and non-built-in land-uses, military uses, urban service utilities, gardens and farmland as variables Independent were considered. To obtain the relationship between the independent variable and the dependent variable, we obtained the ArcGIS software using the Geographically Weighted Regression model to the results of the study. The GWR model is described in detail below.

## 4.1    Geographic Weights Regression

Carlton, Brandson and Fudringham introduced the term geographic weight regression [8]. In linear regression, spatial data is assumed in a static process. The general linear regression is as follows [24]:

$$Y_i = \beta_0 + \sum_k \beta_k x_{ik} + \varepsilon_i \qquad i = 1, 2, \ldots, n \qquad (1)$$

Here $Y_i$ is the estimated value of the dependent variable for viewing i, $\beta_0$ is the constant coefficient, $\beta_k$ is the estimated parameter for k, $x_{ik}$ is the kthest variable for i and $\varepsilon_i$ is the error component that is assumed to be distributed normally. Estimates of the parameters in the measurement of these models in the space are constant.

$$\beta' = (X^T X)^{-1} X^T Y \qquad (2)$$

Extensive geographic weight regression model is a general regression framework. The main essence of this model is as follows.

$$y_i = \beta_0(u_i, v_i) + \sum \beta_k(u_i, v_i) X_{ik} + \varepsilon_i \qquad i = 1, 2, \ldots, n \qquad (3)$$

Where $u_i$, $v_i$ represents the coordinates of the i-th point in space, $k(u_i, v_i)$ $\beta$ is a continuous function of $k(u, v)$ $\beta$ at every point i, and $X_{i1}, \ldots, X_{ip}$ are the explanatory variables at point i and $\varepsilon_i$ is an error. For the given data set, the regional parameters $k(u, v)$ $\beta$ are estimated using the least squares weighting steps. $W_{ij}$ weights for $j = 1, 2, \ldots, n$. In each position $(u_i, v_i)$, the continuous function of the intervals between points i and other data points is obtained.

$$\beta = \begin{bmatrix} \beta_0(u_1, v_1) & \beta_1(u_1, v_1) & \cdots & \beta_p(u_1, v_1) \\ \vdots & \vdots & \ddots & \vdots \\ \beta_0(u_n, v_n) & \beta_1(u_n, v_n) & \cdots & \beta_p(u_n, v_n) \end{bmatrix}$$

This matrix is a regional parameter matrix. Each row is derived from the following equation.

$$\beta'(i) = \left(X^T W(i) X\right)^{-1} X^T W(i) Y \tag{4}$$

As $i = 1, 2, \ldots, p$ represents the matrix rows, X is the matrix of independent variables, Y is the dependent variable and W(i) is the space weight $n \times n$ matrix as follows:

$$W(i) = diag\lfloor W_{i1}, W_{i2}, \ldots, W_{in} \rfloor \tag{5}$$

$$W(i) = \begin{bmatrix} W_{i1} & 0 & \cdots & 0 \\ 0 & W_{i2} & \cdots & 0 \\ \vdots & & \ddots & \vdots \\ 0 & \cdots & \cdots & W_{in} \end{bmatrix}$$

Estimates in Eq. (4) are estimates of least squares, but the weight matrix is not constant. Therefore, W(i) must be calculated (mean Eq. 5) for each point i and $W_{ij}$ represents an approximate value from any point of data in position i. The data points near i have a higher weight in estimating the parameters $\beta(i)$ than the points farther away. Different weight functions are definitely defined. The most common is the Gaussian kernel function and the bi-square weight function.

Some of the advantages of geographic weight regression are [8]:

- Achieving precision and details (geographic weight regression allows a researcher to make a local analysis in front of an overview) [21].
- The coefficients of each of the predictors vary across space. An analysis of how different relationships across space and the spatial pattern recognition of local estimates are possible for a proper understanding of possible contributing factors [11].

The separation of the general coefficient of determination (R2) from local coefficients and their geographical distribution analysis allows for less or more independent variables to be able to detect explanatory power [11, 21]. In most cases, the estimated errors by geographical weight regression are smaller than the estimated errors by the regular regression and the spatial correlation problem is eliminated or reduced [15]. The implementation of this technique in the GIS facilitates the production of a wide range of maps (dependent and independent variables, local R2, local coefficients, t values and standard residual values) using generated results [24]. The production of interpolated surfaces is possible to identify the spatial contiguous distribution of parameters and to apply the principles of prediction to find the values of the missing observations [3]. Geographic weight regression facilitates identification of the spatial structure of the model, which measures the degree of spatial dependence in the model and the identification of data clusters. The results provided for each location are used as a criterion for local policies and decisions. This is why this technique is often based on location [30].

Although the geographic weight regression model is a relatively new method for analyzing spatial data, it has been used in many different subjects, including [8]:

- Foresters [1, 9, 26, 33]
- User and Ground Coverage [31, 32]
- Health [33]
- Crime [7]
- Urban space [13, 17, 22].

## 5  Findings of the Research

Euclidian Distance of Different Urban Land-Uses in Urban Space

In this section, we analyze the effects of land-use patterns on housing prices. For this purpose, the Euclidean distance of various urban land-use was presented in the form of the following maps as independent variables.

Euclidian Distance Map city of garden and farmland          Euclidian Distance Map city of vacant land-uses

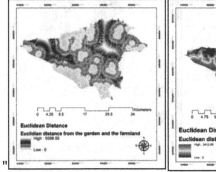

Source: Draw the authors, 2019                    Source: Draw the authors, 2019

Euclidean distance map city of commercial and office user          Euclidean distance map of service user

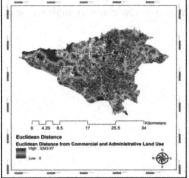
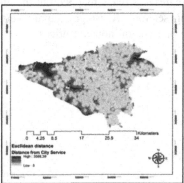

Source: Draw the authors, 2019                    Source: Draw the authors, 2019

Euclidean distance map of the city of industrial uses    Euclidean distance map of the military uses

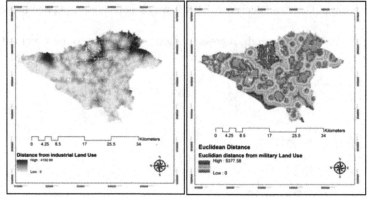

Source: Draw the authors, 2019            Source: Draw the authors, 2019

Map of Euclidian City Distance from Urban Green Utilities    Average housing prices in the neighborhoods

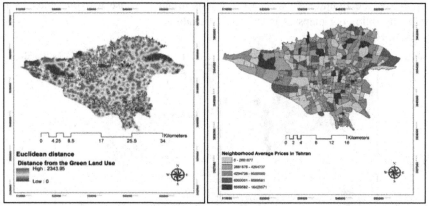

Source: Draw the authors, 2019            Source: Draw the authors, 2019

According to the following map, which is a dependent variable in this research, each of the effects of the use on the price of housing is determined. Finally, geographic weight regression maps mapped out the effects of each application on housing prices.

In this section, we use geographic weight regression maps to analyze the effects of land use patterns on housing prices.

## 5.1    The Impact Each of Land-Use on Housing Prices

Impact of Commercial land-use on Housing Prices.    Impact of green land-use and park on housing prices.

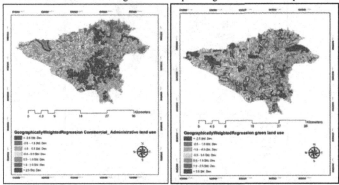

Source: Draw the authors, 2019                    Source: Draw the authors, 2019

Impact of industrial land uses on housing prices    Impact of vacant land uses on Housing Prices

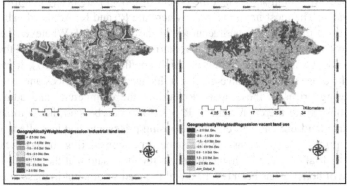

Source: Draw the authors, 2019                    Source: Draw the authors, 2019

Impact of city utilities on housing prices    Impact of access to gardens and farmland on housing prices

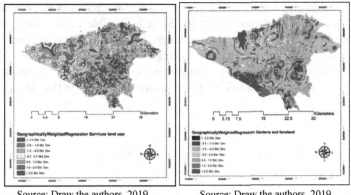

Source: Draw the authors, 2019                    Source: Draw the authors, 2019

The impact of military use on housing prices

Source: Draw the authors, 2019

The trend of regression model in determining land-use patterns and its effect on housing prices in Tehran shows that the output of model parameters confirms the high predicted value. The most important values here are $R^2$ and $R^2$ Adjusted values, which in fact represent the goodness and accuracy of the model used. Whatever these values are closer to 1, it means that the descriptive variables used can explain well the changes of the dependent variable. Regarding the high coefficient of $R^2$ (0.87), it can be said that green land-use and parks have greatly influenced housing prices and have led to a rise in housing prices in these areas. Regarding the commercial and administrative land-use, considering the coefficient of $R^2$ (0.24), it can be said that commercial and administrative land-use had less effect on housing prices and had less effect on the rise in housing prices in these areas. At the same time, considering the coefficient of $R^2$ (−0.21), industrial land-use on housing prices, it can be said that the effect of this user on the price of housing has been reversed and reduced its amount in these areas. vacant and not built land-use, in this regard, considering the coefficient $R^2$ (−0.28), the user has been negatively affected by the housing price and, like the industrial one, has reduced the price of housing in these areas. In this regard, the urban services land-use of the city, given the high coefficient of $R^2$ (0.80), can be said to have had a significant impact on housing prices and has led to a rise in housing prices in these areas. At the same time, given the coefficient of $R^2$ (0.36), it is possible to say that gardens and farmland have had less impact on housing prices and have had less effect on the rise in housing prices in these areas. Regarding the high and the reverse of $R^2$ (−0.72), it can be said that access to military user, terminals and storage facilities has had significant inverse on housing prices and has led to lower housing prices in the vicinity of these areas (Table 2).

**Table 2.** The effects of land use on housing prices in Tehran

| Band with | Residual squares | Effective number | Sigma | AICc | R2 | R2Adjusted | Dependent field | Explanatory field |
|---|---|---|---|---|---|---|---|---|
| 8456.66 | 6.76622 | 15.0350 | 1481216 | 96867.6 | 0.87 | 0.87 | Housing prices in Tehran | Green and parks |
| 1600.88 | 2.19610 | 214.189 | 3094196 | 82183.5 | 0.24 | 0.17 | | Commercial and administrative land-use |
| 1441.84 | 8.41138 | 232.583 | 2178467 | 64331.1 | −0.21 | −0.11 | | Industrial land use |
| 1107.34 | 8.77761 | 360.936 | 1734069 | 103727 | −0.28 | −0.20 | | Vacant land use |
| 1263.46 | 6.97 | 257.819 | 1407321 | 117812 | 0.36 | 0.36 | | Gardens and farm land |
| 3727.76 | 7.60733 | 54.1520 | 1666603 | 87977 | 0.80 | 0.79 | | Urban land use services |
| 12142.0 | 1.13841 | 7.73766 | 2817321 | 46929.1 | −0.72 | −0.72 | | Military land use |

Source: Research findings: 2019.

# 6  Conclusion

The factors affecting on housing price at the neighborhood level, in addition to macro factors, can be considered as another factor, and the effect of the mixing of uses and its undeniable effect as a factor on the price of housing. Thus, in residential neighborhoods, the proximity to retail outlets can add value to housing prices, which is why services are offered with better conditions. Also, in Traditional theories housing prices, changing the distance from the city center and main access is considered to be a major factor in the difference in housing prices, and based on that the distance from the city's commercial center Causes housing prices to spatial changes. Other important factors influencing housing prices are, of course, also referred to as housing production factors: land prices, construction materials, labor costs, and technology has been used. In terms of physical indicators, these indicators are of economic, social, cultural and technical dimensions. Among the physical indicators that affect housing prices, we can point to the density Floor area ratio and land area. The price of housing and land is usually directly related to congestion, both in construction and in demographic terms.

Given that the topic of the housing economy is a comprehensive and interdisciplinary topic (politics, economics, management, geography, etc.), this paper discusses the impact of geographical factors (types of uses) on housing prices, and thus it was found that in Tehran metropolis city that User mixing at its maximum, the following uses had the most impact on housing prices, respectively:

1. Green land-use and parks with $R^2/87$
2. urban services land-use with $R^2/80$
3. Access to gardens and farmlands with $R^2/36$
4. commercial and administrate land-use with $R^2/24$

In this regard, in order to prevent the stagnation of housing prices in Tehran and citizens' satisfaction and facilitate access to urban housing, the proposals are presented as follows:

1. Facilitate and discounted construction permits and give incentives to build
2. Discount on housing costs for real housing applicants
3. Managing the resources of all financial institutions, including pension funds, social security, insurance and investment in housing construction
4. Use of new financing tools
5. Strengthening effective demand through saving policy
6. Paying facilities for half-finished projects
7. Supporting Housing investment companies and developers to build housing through the assignment of land, company licensing and payment facilities.

**Acknowledgments.** Thanks to the organization from Iranian researchers and technicians for assistance and support in the preparation of this article: The Iranian National Science Foundation (INSF).

# References

1. Abedin Dercoosh, S., Rahimian, S.: Analysis of factors influencing housing prices in urban areas of Iran during the period (2006 -1991). Econ. Hous. Q. (46), 11 (2010). (In Persian)
2. Emadzadeh, A.N., Ali, M.V.R.: Factors affecting housing prices in Mashhad. Spatial econometric approach in Hadanik Method. Q. J. Econ. Res. **11 & 12**, 81–99 (2004)
3. Anselin, L.: Spatial Econometrics: Methods and Models. Kluwer Academic Publishers, Dordrecht (1988)
4. Arnott, R.: Housing policy in developing. Countries: the importance of the informal economy. World Bank Commission on Growth and Development (2008)
5. Azizi, M.M.: Position of housing indicators in the housing planning process. Beautiful Arts J. **17**(17), 31–42 (2004). (In Persian)
6. Buckley, R., Jerry, K.: Housing policy in developing countries: conjectures and refutations. World Bank Res. Obs. **20**, 233–257 (2005). Fall 2005
7. Cahill, M., Gordon, M.: Using geographically weighted regression to explore local crime patterns. Soc. Sci. Comput. Rev. **25**(2), 174–193 (2007)
8. Cardozo, O.D., García-Palomares, J.C., Gutiérrez, J.: Application of geographically weighted regression to the direct forecasting of transit ridership at station-level. Appl. Geogr. **34**, 548–558 (2012)
9. Clement, F., Orange, D., Williams, M., Mulley, C., Epprecht, M.: Drivers of afforestation in Northern Vietnam: assessing local variations using geographically weighted regression. Appl. Geogr. **29**(4), 561–576 (2009)
10. Daneshpour, A., Hosseini, S.: The place of physical factors in the reduction of housing prices. Arman. Shahr Arch. Urban Dev. Q. **5**(9), 61–71 (2012). Autumn and Winter 2012
11. Fotheringham, A.S., Brunsdon, C., Charlton, M.E.: Geographically Weighted Regression: The Analysis of Spatially Varying Relationships. Wiley, Chichester (2002)
12. Gallent, N., Robinson, S.: Local perspectives on rural housing affordability and implications for the localism agenda in England. J. Rural. Stud. **27**, 297–307 (2011)
13. Gao, J., Li, S.: Detecting spatially non-stationary and scale-dependent relationships between urban landscape fragmentation and related factors using geographically weighted regression. Appl. Geogr. **31**(1), 292–302 (2011)
14. Gholizadeh, A.A.: Theory of Housing Prices in Iran in Simple Language. Noor Alam Publications, Hamadan (2008). (In Persian)

15. Hadayeghi, A., Shalaby, A.S., Persaud, B.N.: Development of planning level transportation safety tools using geographically weighted poisson regression. Accid. Anal. Prev. **42**(2), 676–688 (2010)

16. Ali, H.N., Mojtaba, R., Hussein, Z.: Examination of individual variables affecting citizens' satisfaction with the quality of life environment (case study: comparison of old and new text in Shiraz city). Geogr. Dev. **8**(17), 63–82 (2010)

17. Hanham, R., Spiker, J.S.: Urban sprawl detection using satellite imagery and geographically weighted regression. In: Jensen, R.R., Gatrell, J.D., McLean, D.D. (eds.) Geo-Spatial Technologies in Urban Environments, pp. 137–151. Springer, Berlin (2005). https://doi.org/10.1007/3-540-26676-3_12

18. Hatami Nejhad, H., Seifadini Frank, M.M.: An investigation of indicators of informal housing in Iran (case study: Sheikh Abad Quarter of Qom). J. Geogr. Res. **38**(58), 129–145 (2006)

19. Karami, A.: Study of the Housing Market in Iran (with Emphasis on Government Policies). Tadbir Economics Research Institute (2007). Printing: 1

20. King, P., Aldershot, A.: A social philosophy of hosing. Habitat Int. **29**, 603–611 (2005)

21. Lloyd, C.D.: Local Models for Spatial Analysis. Taylor & Francis, Boca Raton (2010)

22. Luo, J., Wei, Y.H.D.: Modeling spatial variations of urban growth patterns in Chinese cities: the case of Nanjing. Landscape and Urban Planning **91**(2), 51–64 (2009)

23. Mashhad Municipality Economical Studies Group: Investigation of IRAN Housing Market and Influential Factors on it. Management of the Expansion and Researches of the Mashhad Municipality, Mashhad (2010)

24. Mennis, J.: Mapping the results of geographically weighted regression. Cartogr. J. **43**(2), 171–179 (2006)

25. NajiMeidani, A.A., Fallahi, M.A., Zabihi, M.: Investigating the dynamic effect of macroeconomic factors on housing price fluctuations in Iran during the period (1990 to 2007). Knowl. Dev. **17**(31), 158–184 (2010)

26. Pineda, N.B., Bosque-Sendra, J., Gómez-Delgado, M., Franco, R.: Exploring the driving forces behind deforestation in the state of Mexico (Mexico) using geographically weighted regression. Appl. Geogr. **30**(4), 576–591 (2010)

27. Pourmohammadi, M.R.: Housing Planning. Tehran University Press, Tehran (2008). (In Persian)

28. Rafieian, M., Asgari, A., Asgarizadeh, Z.: Assessment of citizens' satisfaction from urban habitat. Environ. Sci. **7**(1), 57–68 (2009)

29. Riazi, M., Emami, A.: Residential satisfaction in affordable housing: a mixed method study. Cities **82**, 1–9 (2018)

30. Smith, M.J., Goodchild, M.F., Longley, P.A.: Geospatial Analysis. A Comprehensive Guide to Principles, Techniques and Software Tools. Matador, Leicester (2009)

31. Tu, J.: Spatially varying relationships between land use and water quality across an urbanization gradient explored by geographically weighted regression. Appl. Geogr. **31**(1), 376–392 (2011)

32. Tu, J., Guo, X.: Examining spatially varying relationships between land use and water quality using geographically weighted regression I: model design and evaluation. Sci. Total Environ. **407**(1), 358–378 (2008)

33. Zhang, L., Shi, H.: Local modeling of tree growth by geographically weighted regression. For. Sci. **50**(2), 225–244 (2004)

# Providing a Livable Housing Development Model for Increasing Urban Livability (Case Study of Tehran)

Amin Safdari Molan, Keramatollah Ziari[✉], Ahmad Pourahmad, and Hossein Hataminejad

Department of Geography, University of Tehran, Tehran, Iran
{a_safdari,zayyari}@ut.ac.ir

**Abstract.** In the century 21 with the rapid rise of urbanization and the increase in urban populations its necessary to supplying and increasing good quality and conditions of the living in housing. One of the new ideas is urban planning for better housing and affordable transport access, with an emphasis on urban livability. Urban livability is a modern approach to urban planning that can respond to many urban problems. Any type of travel in the city is transferred from one housing to another land use and will end in housing. For that matter in the city's housing and neighborhoods and access to activities and housing must be combined with the indicators of livability, so in this article is present to create the best pattern or method of access to housing for all male groups, with emphasis on three elements of housing and transportation and urban livability. The method of this research descriptive-survey. Using previous studies and researches, a paired matrix questionnaire was designed that after confirming the validity of several experts, 50 questionnaires were sent to experts and experts, and 43 questionnaires were collected and after calculating the adaptive ratio, the analysis was carried out. Data were obtained. Library information (books, articles, archives, etc.) and field (distribution of questionnaires) have been used for data collection. Research results from the questionnaire indicate that most respondents have affordable housing in transport access and communication and urban transport network as the most important alternative to improving urban transport as well as housing livability. Urban transport, urban livability, and urban health, on the other hand, in the next step, have modern transportation, quality, and affordable transport and access to services with very little difference. The results indicate that they are in the third and fourth positions, and the rest in the next positions, they are effective in improving housing and urban transport livability.

**Keywords:** Livable housing · Transportation livable · Livable city · Tehran

---

This article is part of Ph.D. Dissertation Amin Safdari Molan at University of Tehran under the title "Pattern of housing development with urban livability approach in the city of Tehran".

S. Misra et al. (Eds.): ICCSA 2019, LNCS 11621, pp. 660–674, 2019.
https://doi.org/10.1007/978-3-030-24302-9_47

# 1  Introduction

Previously, most people lived in rural areas and only 30% lived in urban areas. Since 2014, More than 50% of the world's population is urbanized and is increasing day by day [21, 53]. According to statistics in 2017, more than 54% of the world's population is urban [53]. Increasing urban population and increasing demand for housing and urban services have caused problems in cities (Tehran's case) (including: lack of adequate land and housing, inappropriate housing, and access to appropriate transportation and environmental problems that are mutually exclusive Related) that will increase sustainable development attention. livability is one of the concepts of sustainable development that addresses social, economic, environmental, and also satisfaction. The definitions offered are livability, all referring to the quality of space, location, or city [8, 36, 48, 60] Or to create a livable place to live [49, 57]. The rise in the cost of buying or renting housing in cities has also been a problem for low-income groups (and female households) [22, 33, 59]. The country Iran in the form of five-year plans before the revolution and six developments after the revolution sought to resolve the issue of housing. Therefore, the challenges facing housing in Iran, including housing instability, lack of compliance with demand and housing patterns, the growing trend of informal settlements, inefficient and cross-sectoral policies, and project-driven housing policy, existence The widespread texture, the ineffectiveness of the manufacturing system in the construction industry, the inequality and the imbalance in the production and distribution of housing, and in recent years have changed the "deprivation" pattern into "bad housing" [7]. In recent years, issues such as improving quality of life through socio-economic justice [41, 58] and minimizing environmental problem [32] have been the most emphases of social and environmental researchers for increasing the livability and sustainability of cities in developing countries (for example, India can be mentioned: [16, 34, 41]. In this paper, I will discuss housing livability for the first time. Most previous studies in the field of housing have focused on physical discussion and economic and profit debate. The innovation of this article is a combination of physical, environmental and social and economic contexts in Iran and in the city Tehran, and paying attention to housing in terms of livability increases the access of all categories of society to adequate housing and all activities and high quality of life and good governance.

# 2  Literature Reviews

Livability is a concept that can have many meanings, it covers various aspects of urban quality of life, housing, transportation, the physical environment, and the socioeconomic, biological, security, cultural and educational environment, and leisure facilities, as other scholars point to these, refer to: [4, 12, 26, 27, 51]. Various researchers have defined the Livability of their different viewing angles. Lynch emphasizes the five dimensions of urban Livability, which are: vitality, sense, fit, access and control [28]. Douglas has five essential dimensions' livability i.e. direct investment in talent, access to work, safe environment and good governance [55]. Urbanization has positive and negative effects on the quality and quantity of citizens' lives. One of the most important parts of the city is the housing and transportation network. Which is linked to other sectors such as employment, access to various urban activities. the lack of access to housing livable and sustainable and affordable, especially for low-income and financially vulnerable groups, as well as for women without a job or income family head. In many cities, housing is not only affordable for low income groups and financially disadvantaged families and women, but also unlivability. Housing and living environments are important in achieving urban livability and sustainability. Because it has a significant impact on economic and social activities, and thus affects all issues relating to the urban environment and society. Previous research on housing and transportation has not paid attention to urban livability, and has focused on housing on the basis of economic considerations. In this paper, I will discuss housing livability and transportation for the first time.

## 2.1 Urban Livability Aspect

Urban livability is a multi-dimensional concept that enhances urban housing and transport sustainability. Its multidimensional nature makes it difficult to assess the components at a location [24]. The most important aspects of housing and transport livability are:

Housing: One of the main indicators of the livability of a city is housing, which is affordable and accessible to all different income groups. The quality of housing and the conditions of the residential environment and the manner of designing and communicating the neighborhood are effective in the health and well-being of the community [1, 17, 31, 42].

Transport: Transportation has a key role to play in urban and urban activities and has close ties with housing [2, 48]. Streets and alleys, sidewalks, transportation, congestion, User access, public transport with housing are connected and on the other hand affect the livability of housing and residential neighborhoods and the city. The city's communications network performs two important tasks: the access or creation of a road to the car for use, and the creation of a public place for people to participate in various economic, social and cultural activities [11, 48].

Urban amenity: a desirable or useful feature or facility of a building or place. comfort in access to housing and transportation, and jobs and various activities.

Access to commercial and social services: Easy and convenient access to work, home and near each other, as well as proximity to study centers and higher education centers and hospitals and medical centers, in addition to comfort and pleasure, increase the livability of that place to live or create a livability [19, 20]. Natural livable Environment: New research emphasizes the role of the natural environment in the vitality and health of people, for example, spending time in green spaces and walking in rural spaces [30, 45]. But due to the construction and urban development, the natural environment is further degrading, which requires attention in urban development planning.

The mental perception of livability is including the satisfaction of the inhabitants, the feeling of society and the safety, comfort and have a good feeling to a living environment in the neighborhoods and city. have a livable housing and city cause the good feeling of citizens and this feeling gives them satisfaction to their place of residence or living such as neighborhoods or cites environment and, consequently, have a housing livability and city with accessible facilities such as transport livability cause their participation in the built urban environment, and the sense of social and safety and as a result of all of this we have liveable city and reach a liveable housing and liveable environment for living [60]. The place and dwelling of life are very important in every field. In other words, housing has the greatest impact on socio-economic and cultural indicators. In fact, housing is a welfare, affordable and afford-able place for good transport and sustainability and urban livability. According to [54]. real estate decisions are a result of a "complex function of a wide range of housing and location attributes". Currently, some of these attributes are related to searching for livable and sustainable neighborhoods. People are looking for a place to live in communities and cities that offer both quality of life indicators and sustainability components [43]. The concept of viability in this study consists of objective and subjective aspects of the living environment. the objective which is related to the built environment and resources available to residents in their homes, neighborhoods, and communities and the subjective experience of livability in particular living environ-ments, which encompasses a sense of community, safety, and well-being. Both aspects are essential for establishing actual livability performance and are examined in this study [60].

## 3 Methodology Research

### 3.1 Study Area

The metropolis of Tehran has been the capital of Iran for over 200 years. The city of Tehran is 51.52° Longitude and 35.43° latitude. The average elevation of the city is 1100 m. Tehran has been the center of political administrative gravity of the country for 200 years (Tehran Municipality 2019). And now the old city of Tehran has grown and developed. And like other capitals in the advanced world, it wants to be the urban utopia.

The method of this research can be applied in terms of purpose and in terms of collecting data, descriptive-survey. In the first step, to identify and investigate the effective factors of housing and housing viability in access to appropriate transportation in Tehran, using previous studies, and the research done, the paired matrix question-naire was designed (Based on the Delphi method) [10, 29]. after verifying the validity and pre-test, and then examining and reviewing the professors of Tehran University, University of Tarbiat Modares and University of Shahid Beheshti, and some of the experts, 50 questionnaires in person and online for experts and experts in the field of housing and Urban transportation was sent and finally, 43 questionnaires were col-lected and the data were analyzed after calculating the compatibility ratio. To collect information, library methods (books, articles, archives, etc.) and field (questionnaire distribution) have been used. On the other hand, the AHP approach enables decision makers to define the criteria's trade-offs, thereby determining the weighting of the criteria. For these reasons, combining these approaches is essential to dealing with complex problems, integrating multiple criteria and efficiently weighting objective and subjective criteria [13, 14, 38, 39, 43].

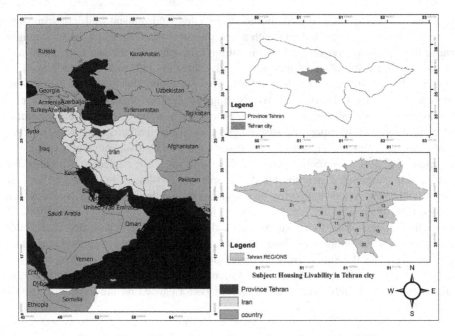

**Fig. 1.** Map of the study area. Source: Draw the authors, 2019

## 3.2 Fuzzy Logic

Logic, knowledge is the identification and presentation of the correct way of thinking, defining and reasoning. Fuzzy logic is a kind of logic that replaces the simpler machineries with a variety of conclusions in the human brain. As shown in Fig. 1, fuzzy logic consists a wide range of opinions and techniques that are basically firmly-fixed on four notions: fuzzy groups, verbal elements, diffusion possibility (membership function), and If- then Fuzzy's rules [25], the notion of fuzzy logic was first presented in the world by a prominent Iranian scholar, Lotfizadeh, in a 1965 monograph entitled "Fuzzy sets of information and control". A fuzzy set is a complex whose origins with membership (μ) belong to that collection. If x is a collection of elements that are represented with x, so the fuzzy set Ã in x is the set of tidy pairs as follows:

$$\tilde{A} = \{(x, \mu\tilde{A}(x)) | x \bullet \mathcal{X}\} \tag{1}$$

$\mu\tilde{A}(x)$ is the membership x in Ã. The membership function depicts the sum of *x* in the membership function space (M). In fuzzy sets, the membership function space (M) contains all real numbers between zero and one. The more μ (x) is closer to 1, the degree of belonging of the element x to the fuzzy set Ã is greater and if $\mu\tilde{A}(x) = 0$, then we say that the element x does not belong to the fuzzy set Ã [5].

$$\mu\tilde{A} : X \rightarrow [0, 1] \tag{2}$$

Multi-criteria Decision Making Techniques (MCDM)

Multi-criteria decision-making techniques are divided into two groups [52] of multi-objective models (MODMs) and multi-index models (MADMs). Multi-objective models are used to optimize multiple targets simultaneously, while multi-index models are used to select the preferred option [3]. Several indicators and group decision making in the subject literature have applications. It is extensive and allows managers and decision makers to evaluate options in a number of ways [5] (Table 1).

**Table 1.** Conversion of quantitative numbers to qualitative indicators [35].

| 1 | importance equal or not preferred [35]. |
|---|---|
| 3 | relatively more important [ 35, 15]. |
| 5 | more important [35 , 15]. |
| 7 | much more important [35 , 15]. |
| 9 | Infinitely more important [35, 15]. |
| 2,4,6, 8 | Intermediate Values Between Valuable Values [35, 15]. |

### 3.3    Method Fuzzy Topsis

The AHP hierarchical analysis process was developed by the hour in 1971 and aims to create a structure in decisions that are influenced by several independent factors [47]. Topsis (the prioritization method according to the similarity to the ideal positive solution) is known as one of the traditional methods of multi-criteria decision-making, which was proposed by Huang and Yun[1] in 1981 [23, 46]. to solve multi-criteria decision-making problems Which was based on the ideal determination. In fact, topsis is an applied method that compares alternatives with respect to their data values for each criterion and weight of the criteria[2] [57], and with respect to comparative simulation [44] among the eight methods of group models Compensatory Multi-Criteria Evaluation The TOPSIS method has the least defect in index ranking. In the following, we first consider the compatibility ratio [47]. and then the decision-making phases with the help of the Fuzzy Topsis technique [25]:

## 4    Discussions and Findings

**The First Stage of the Fuzzy Topsis Process**
The first step is to calculate the total weighted vector[3]

---

[1] Cheng et al. [46].

[2] Hadi-Vencheh and Mirjaberi [18], Cheng et al. [46].

[3] Weighted Sum Vector.

$$
WSV = \begin{bmatrix}
3/726 & 3/171 & 3/357 & 2/904 & 2/012 & 2/159 & 3/918 & 4/012 & 2/381 & 1 \\
0/971 & 2/101 & 2/106 & 0/651 & 0/971 & 1/322 & 1/524 & 2/173 & 1 & 0/419 \\
0/896 & 0/971 & 1/245 & 1/131 & 0/998 & 1/106 & 0/702 & 1 & 0/46 & 0/249 \\
2/345 & 0/871 & 1/126 & 0/872 & 0/894 & 0/974 & 1 & 1/424 & 0/656 & 0/255 \\
0/914 & 1/014 & 0/972 & 1/202 & 1/154 & 1 & 1/026 & 0/904 & 0/756 & 0/463 \\
1/231 & 2/957 & 1/452 & 1/019 & 1 & 0/866 & 1/118 & 1/002 & 1/029 & 0/497 \\
0/952 & 1/962 & 1/765 & 1 & 0/981 & 0/831 & 1/146 & 0/884 & 1/536 & 0/344 \\
1/521 & 1/572 & 1 & 0/556 & 0/668 & 1/028 & 0/888 & 0/803 & 0/474 & 0/297 \\
2/579 & 1 & 0/636 & 0/509 & 0/338 & 0/986 & 1/148 & 1/029 & 0/475 & 0/315 \\
1 & 0/387 & 0/657 & 1/05 & 0/812 & 1/094 & 0/426 & 1/116 & 1/029 & 0/268
\end{bmatrix} * \begin{bmatrix} ./235 \\ ./106 \\ ./072 \\ ./082 \\ ./082 \\ ./1 \\ ./094 \\ ./069 \\ ./071 \\ ./065 \end{bmatrix} = \begin{bmatrix} 2/64 \\ 1/08 \\ 0/79 \\ 1/004 \\ 0/83 \\ 1/13 \\ 0/99 \\ 0/83 \\ 0/901 \\ 0/721 \end{bmatrix}
$$

The second step is to calculate the compatibility vector[4]

$$
CV = \begin{bmatrix}
2/64 & \div & 0/235 \\
1/08 & \div & 0/106 \\
0/79 & \div & 0/072 \\
1/004 & \div & 0/082 \\
0/83 & \div & 0/082 \\
1/13 & \div & 0/1 \\
0/99 & \div & 0/94 \\
0/83 & \div & 0/069 \\
0/901 & \div & 0/071 \\
0/721 & \div & 0/065
\end{bmatrix} = \begin{bmatrix} 11/26 \\ 10/23 \\ 11/09 \\ 12/25 \\ 10/20 \\ 11/30 \\ 10/62 \\ 12/05 \\ 12/7 \\ 11/08 \end{bmatrix} \tag{3}
$$

Step three to obtain $\lambda_{max}$ (obtaining the mean of compatibility vector elements)

$$
\lambda_{max} = \frac{11/26 + 10/23 + 11/09 + 12/25 + 10/2 + 11/3 + 10/62 + 12/05 + 12/7 + 11/08}{10} = 11/278 \tag{4}
$$

Step four Calculate the compatibility index[5]

$$
CI = \frac{\lambda_{max-n}}{n-1} \qquad CI = \frac{11/278\_10}{10\_1} = 0/141 \tag{5}
$$

Step Five Calculate the compatibility ratio[6] (Table 2)

$$
CR = \frac{CI}{RI} \qquad CR = \frac{0/141}{1/51} = 0/093 \tag{6}
$$

---

[4] Consistency Vector.

[5] Consistency Index.

[6] Random Index.

**Table 2.** Random index

| n | 1 | 2 | 3 | 4 | 5 | 6 | 7 | 8 | 9 | 10 |
|---|---|---|---|---|---|---|---|---|---|----|
| C R | 0 | 0 | 0/58 | 0/9 | 1/12 | 1/24 | 1/32 | 1/41 | 1/45 | 1/51 |

## The Second Stage is the Fuzzy Topsis Process

The first step is to obtain vector weights w $\sim$ j (Table 3)

**Table 3.** Vector weights

| | Housing livability(Q1) | Transport livability(Q2) | Suitable Atmospheres and climatic(Q3) | Individual characters(Q4) | Housing prices(Q5) | costs of transport(Q6) | Convenience and comfort(Q7) | safety and security(Q8) | Private transport(Q9) | public transport(Q10) |
|---|---|---|---|---|---|---|---|---|---|---|
| Q1 | 1 | 2.381 | 4/012 | 3/918 | 2/159 | 2/012 | 2/904 | 3/357 | 3/171 | 3/726 |
| Q2 | 0/419 | 1 | 2/173 | 1/524 | 1/322 | 0/971 | 0/651 | 2/106 | 3/101 | 0/971 |
| Q3 | 0/249 | 0/46 | 1 | 0/702 | 1/106 | 0/998 | 1/131 | 1/245 | 0/971 | 0/896 |
| Q4 | 0/255 | 0/656 | 1/424 | 1 | 0/974 | 0/894 | 0/872 | 1/126 | 0/871 | 2/245 |
| Q5 | 0/463 | 0/756 | 0/904 | 1/026 | 1 | 1/154 | 1/202 | 0/972 | 1/014 | 0/914 |
| Q6 | 0/497 | 1/029 | 1/002 | 1/118 | 0/866 | 1 | 1/019 | 1/452 | 2/957 | 1/231 |
| Q7 | 0/344 | 1/536 | 0/884 | 1/146 | 0/831 | 0/981 | 1 | 1/765 | 1/962 | 0/952 |
| Q8 | 0/297 | 0/474 | 0/803 | 0/888 | 1/028 | 0/688 | 0/566 | 1 | 1/572 | 1/521 |
| Q9 | 0/315 | 0/475 | 1/029 | 1/148 | 0/986 | 0/338 | 0/509 | 0/636 | 1 | 2/579 |
| Q10 | 0/268 | 1/029 | 1/116 | 0/426 | 1/094 | 0/812 | 1/05 | 0/657 | 0/387 | 1 |
| | 4/10 | 9/79 | 14/34 | 12/87 | 11/35 | 9/84 | 10/89 | 14/43 | 17/006 | 16/1 |

The second step is to normalize the paired comparison matrix ($\tilde{v}_{ij}$) with new matrix options as follows (Table 4):

**Table 4.** Normalized matrix

| | Q1 | Q2 | Q3 | Q4 | Q5 | Q6 | Q7 | Q8 | Q9 | Q10 |
|---|---|---|---|---|---|---|---|---|---|---|
| Q1 | 1 | 2.381 | 4/012 | 3/918 | 2/159 | 2/012 | 2/904 | 3/357 | 3/171 | 3/726 |
| Q2 | 0/419 | 1 | 2/173 | 1/524 | 1/322 | 0/971 | 0/651 | 2/106 | 3/101 | 0/971 |
| Q3 | 0/249 | 0/46 | 1 | 0/702 | 1/106 | 0/998 | 1/131 | 1/245 | 0/971 | 0/896 |
| Q4 | 0/255 | 0/656 | 1/424 | 1 | 0/974 | 0/894 | 0/872 | 1/126 | 0/871 | 2/245 |
| Q5 | 0/463 | 0/756 | 0/904 | 1/026 | 1 | 1/154 | 1/202 | 0/972 | 1/014 | 0/914 |
| Q6 | 0/497 | 1/029 | 1/002 | 1/118 | 0/866 | 1 | 1/019 | 1/452 | 2/957 | 1/231 |
| Q7 | 0/344 | 1/536 | 0/884 | 1/146 | 0/831 | 0/981 | 1 | 1/765 | 1/962 | 0/952 |
| Q8 | 0/297 | 0/474 | 0/803 | 0/888 | 1/028 | 0/688 | 0/566 | 1 | 1/572 | 1/521 |
| Q9 | 0/315 | 0/475 | 1/029 | 1/148 | 0/986 | 0/338 | 0/509 | 0/636 | 1 | 2/579 |
| Q10 | 0/268 | 1/029 | 1/116 | 0/426 | 1/094 | 0/812 | 1/05 | 0/657 | 0/387 | 1 |
| | 4/10 | 9/79 | 14/34 | 12/87 | 11/35 | 9/84 | 10/89 | 14/43 | 17/006 | 16/1 |

$$r_{ij} = \frac{r_{ij}}{\left(\sum_{i=1}^{M} r_{ij}^2\right)^{\frac{1}{2}}} \tag{7}$$

Step 3: Calculate the meanings of the normalized matrix rows:

$$\frac{\sum_{i=1}^{n} xij}{n} \quad i = 1, 2. \ldots n, \; j = 1, 2. \ldots m \tag{8}$$

Step 4: Determine the Fuzzy Positive Ideal Solution (FPIS) and the Fuzzy Ideal Negative (FNIS) [6].

$$A^+ = \left[v_i^+, \ldots, v_j^+, \ldots, v_n^+\right]; v_j^+ = max_i\{v_{ij}\} \tag{9}$$

$$A^- = \left[v_i^-, \ldots, v_j^-, \ldots, v_n^-\right]; v_j^- = min_i\{v_{ij}\} \tag{10}$$

$$A^+ = \{0/231-0/186-0/216-0/26-0/2-0/19-0/304-0/27-0/24-0/24\}$$

$$A^- = \{0/055-0/022-0/041-0/046-0/034-0/073-0/003-0/05-0/03-0/06\}$$

The fifth step is to calculate distances sizes (Table 5)

**Table 5.** Calculate the distance measurements

| $d_1^+=$ | $d_2^+$ | $d_3^+=$ | $d_4^+$ | $d_5^+=$ | $d_6^+$ | $d_7^+=$ | $d_8^+$ | $d_9^+=$ | $d_{10}^+$ |
|---|---|---|---|---|---|---|---|---|---|
| 0/004 | = | 0/521 | = | 0/557 | = | 0/463 | = | 0/529 | = |
|  | 0/409 |  | 0/492 |  | 0/453 |  | 0/542 |  | 0/552 |
| $d_1^-=0/$ | $d_2^- =$ | $d_3^-$ | $d_4^- =$ | $d_5^-$ | $d_6^- =$ | $d_7^-$ | $d_8^- =$ | $d_9^- =$ | $d_{10}^-$ |
| 594 | 0/274 | = | 0/147 | = | 0/22 | = | 0/109 | 0/143 | = |
|  |  | 0/106 |  | 0/147 |  | 0/209 |  |  | 0/108 |

$$d_1^+ = \sqrt{\sum_{j=1}^{10} \left(v_{ij} - v_j^+\right)^2} \tag{11}$$

$$d_i^- = \sqrt{\sum_{j=1}^{10} \left(v_{ij} - v_j^+\right)^2} \tag{12}$$

$$d_2^+ = \sqrt{\begin{array}{c}(0/06 - 0/231)^2 + \\ (0/123 - 0/186)^2 + (0/216 - 0/216)^2 + (0/059 - 0/26)^2 + (0/098 - 0/2)^2 + (0/11 - 0/19)^2 + (0/118 - 0/304)^2 + \\ (0/15 - 0/27)^2 + (0/104 - 0/24)^2 + (0/102 - 0/24)^2=\end{array}}$$

It should be noted that $D_{ij}^+$ and $D_{ij}^-$ are definite numbers.

**Table 6.** Calculation of the effective indicators of livability on housing and transport urban

| $C_1 =$ 0/993 | $C_2 =$ 0/4 | $C_3 =$ 0/169 | $C_4 =$ 0/230 | $C_5 =$ 0/208 | $C_6=$ 0/326 | $C_7 =$ 0/311 | $C_8 =$ 0/167 | $C_9=$ 0/212 | $C_{10} =$ 0/164 |
|---|---|---|---|---|---|---|---|---|---|
| **Ra nk 1** | Ra nk 2 | Ran k 8 | Ran k 5 | Ran k 7 | Ran k 3 | Ran k 4 | Ran k 9 | Ran k 6 | Ran k 10 |

Step 6: Calculate the relative closeness of each option to the ideals and index rankings (Table 6)

$$C_i = \frac{d_i^-}{d_i^- + d_i^+} \qquad i = 1, 2, \dots, 10 \qquad (13)$$

The results from the questionnaire show that most respondents have a housing livability and affordability in an appropriate access to transportation and good communication networks and urban transport livability and sustainability as the most important alternative to housing livability and urban transport livability and Also, in terms of urban livability and urban health, in the next step, housing livability has access to a modern, high quality, livability and sustainable city transport system for increasing the housing livability and livability of the city, an appropriate price for housing and transportation, and With varied choices with very little difference, the results indicate, they are in the third and fourth positions. Other indicators and items are also in place at a later stage, each of which is effective in improving housing livability and urban transport livability. As a result, to reach a city livability, there should be a sustainable housing and transport (livability), followed by a residential neighborhood. The set of identified factors is presented as a model or for the livability of urban housing and transportation (Chart 1).

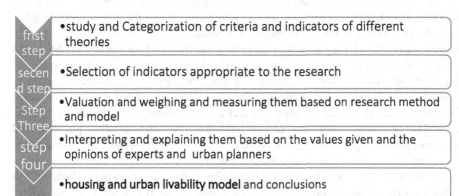

**Chart 1.** Conceptual research model design of the effective factors on Tehran metropolis livability. Source: Draw the authors, 2019.

# 5  Conclusions

Housing is one of the basic and essential needs of human life. Livable housing should be affordable, providing comfort and wellbeing for residents, as well as adequate access to daily activities and living needs. One of the indicators of housing livability is the availability of Livable and accessible transport for access to various activities in the city and the neighborhood. It is neighborhood livability that can be replied to the daily needs of life at the neighborhood level by foot. Accessible transportation is an important factor in accessing essential resources and services, including housing, employment, education and social welfare and recreation, these results are consistent with [49]. Attention to urban livability indicators can help housing and neighborhood and ultimately help the urban communication network to reach a Livable Community in Residential Environment for urban or neighborhoods in every place that people living. The importance of the needs of people with disabilities in the design of the environment, facilities and services of the city, increasing the quality of life for all, and supporting the integration of these results are consistent with [49]. In this study, the results of the respondents' expectations and the views of urban planning elites for having a housing and transportation Livable are important: Livable, sustainable and affordable housing, access to transportation facilities and access to equipment Transportation, components design including available routes, ramps, constraints, entrances, stairs, escalators, elevators, platforms and public transport, as well as safe and efficient transportation for people with different handicaps. Considered: including injuries, hearing loss and motility. The impact of design and planning of public transportation routes and pavements on the livability and affordability of housing and urban transport was also evaluated. The results showed that routes that were legible, obvious and accessible (such as metro stations, buses, bicycles and sidewalks) created a sense of comfort and well-being, as well as the availability of transportation services for people of all ages and ability to cause Increasing the housing and transport livability of the city.

The walking paths also affect the level of satisfaction and perceived safety and security, especially in people with mobility impairment and the elderly [19]. In addition, the general travel time for people with disabilities can be reduced and participation in travel and activity increases. It is suggested that the design is made available in the context of an integrated network approach and priority should be given to the points of focus of the passengers in the multimodal transport system. Given the advances in information technology, it is imperative that the availability of geographic information be available for pre-travel planning and real-time scheduling, in order to improve the reliability of travel. Awareness of the guidelines in urban strategic planning and transport should also be increased to achieve sustainable development of an accessible transportation system these results are consistent with.

In summary, we can say that to enhance the quality and livability of housing and urban transportation and neighborhoods livability, transport organizations, as well as private and public housing developers should be in the process of Urban construction will improve the development of urban housing and transport, and will consider the livability and integrity of the two structures that form the backbone of the city. It should also consider modern technology, quality, pricing and affordable urban transportation affordable for low-income groups, and the safety and security of an extensive range of communal and private and personal transport, that is, a spectrum of citizens with a spectrum There are different types of revenues, which should be planned for transportation on the basis of this spectrum, and more should be done on public transport and access to urban housing and public transport with an emphasis on the urban livability, construction And development. as well as in this research, the TOPSIS FUZZY Multiple Criteria Decision Making model has been used to rank alternative variables that affect the increase of housing livability, moreover the quality of urban transport and livability of settlements and the city from the point of view of housing and urban transport livability Approach.

**Acknowledgments.** Thanks to the organization from Iranian researchers and technicians for assistance and support in the preparation of this article: Iran National Science Foundation (INSF).

# References

1. Alnsour, J.A.: Illegal housing in Jordan. Jordan J. Soc. Sci. **166**(744), 1–32 (2011)
2. Armstrong, B., Davison, G., de Vos Malan, J., Gleeson, B., Godfrey, B.: Delivering sustainable urban mobility, report for the Australian Council of Learned Academies, Australian Council of Learned Academies, Melbourne (2015)
3. Azar, A., Rajabzadeh, A.: Applied Decision Making of MADM Approach, Tehran, Knowledge Perspective (2016)
4. Bardhan, R.H., Kurisu, K., Hanaki, K.: Linking urban form and quality of life in Kolkata, India. In: 47th ISOCARP Congress (2011)
5. Chen, C.-L., Hsieh, C.-T.: Vague controller: a generalization of fuzzy logic controller. Int. J. Syst. Sci. **30**, 1167–1186 (2010)
6. Chou, Y.C., Yen, H.Y., Dang, V.T., Sun, C.C.: Assessing the human resource in science and technology for Asian Countries: application of fuzzy AHP and Fuzzy TOPSIS. Symmetry **11**(2), 251 (2019)
7. Comprehensive Housing Plan: Summary of the Integrated Document (vision: 2016–2027), Ministry of Roads and Urban Development (2016)
8. Cutter, S.L.: Rating places: A Geographer's View on Quality of Life. Association of American Geographers, Washington, DC (1985)
9. Dempsey, N., Bramley, G., Power, S., Brown, C.: The social dimension of sustainable development: defining urban social sustainability. Sustain. Dev. **19**(5), 289–300 (2011)
10. Di Zio, S., Pacinelli, A.: Opinion convergence in location: a spatial version of the Delphi method. Technol. Forecast. Soc. Chang. **78**(9), 1565–1578 (2011)
11. Dumbaugh, E., Gattis, J.L.: Safe streets, livable streets. J. Am. Plann. Assoc. **71**(3), 283–300 (2005)
12. Farber, S., Neutens, T., Miller, H.J., Li, X.: The social interaction potential of metropolitan regions: a time-geographic measurement approach using joint accessibility. Ann. Assoc. Am. Geogr. **103**(3), 483–504 (2013)
13. Faria, P.A., Ferreira, F.A., Jalali, M.S., Bento, P., António, N.J.: Combining cognitive mapping and MCDA for improving quality of life in urban areas. Cities **78**, 116–127 (2018)

14. Fernandes, I.D., Ferreira, F.A., Bento, P., Jalali, M.S., António, N.J.: Assessing sustainable development in urban areas using cognitive mapping and MCDA. Int. J. Sustain. Dev. World Ecol. **25**(3), 216–226 (2018)
15. Yingyu, G., Chunping, L.: Study on eliminating the effect of external factors to the comprehensive evaluation based on PLS regression. In: 2009 IEEE International Conference on Grey Systems and Intelligent Services, GSIS 2009, Nanjing, pp. 835–838 (2009)
16. Giap, T.K., Thye, W.W., Aw, G.: A new approach to measuring the liveability of cities: the global liveable cities index. World Rev. Sci. Technol. Sustain. Dev. **11**(2), 176–196 (2014)
17. Gibson, M., Petticrew, M., Bambra, C., Sowden, A.J., Wright, K.E., Whitehead, M.: Housing and health inequalities: a synthesis of systematic reviews of interventions aimed at different pathways linking housing and health. Health Place **17**(1), 175–184 (2011)
18. Hadi-Vencheh, A., Mirjaberi, M.: Seclusion-factor method to solve fuzzy-multiple criteria decision-making problems. IEEE Trans. Fuzzy Syst. **19**, 201–209 (2011)
19. Hallgrimsdottir, B., Wennberg, H., Svensson, H., Ståhl, A.: Implementation of accessibility policy in municipal transport planning–progression and regression in Sweden between 2004 and 2014. Transp. Policy **49**, 196–205 (2016)
20. HIA (Housing Industry Association): The changing composition of Australia's new housing mix, Economics Research Note, HIA, Melbourne (2015)
21. https://www.un.org/development/desa/en/news/population/2018-revision-of-world-urbanization-prospects.html
22. Hui, E.C., Zhong, J., Yu, K.: Land use, housing preferences and income poverty: in the context of a fast rising market. Land Use Policy **58**, 289–301 (2016)
23. Hung, K.-C., Wou, Y.-W., Julian, P.: A fuzzy method for medical diagnosis of headache. IEICE Trans. Inf. Syst. **E93.D**(5), 1307–1308 (2010)
24. Hutton, T.A.: Thinking metropolis: from the 'livable region' to the 'sustainable metropolis' in Vancouver. Int. Plan. Stud. **16**(3), 237–255 (2011)
25. Yen, J., Langari, R.: Fuzzy Logic Intelligence, Control, and Information. Prentice Hall Publishing Company, Upper Saddle River (1999)
26. Jomehpour, M.: Assessing the livability of the new and old parts of Tehran, municipality districts 22 and 10 of Tehran (2015)
27. Kennedy, R.J., Buys, L.: Dimensions of liveability: a tool for sustainable cities. In: Proceedings of SB10mad Sustainable Building Conference (2010)
28. Knox, P., Pinch, S.: Urban Social Geography: An Introduction. Routledge, Abingdon (2014)
29. Koch, G., Prügl R.: The Parsimonious Delphi: theory-based development, empirical evaluation, and first application. In: Special Issue on "The Delphi technique: Current developments in theory and practice", Technological Forecasting & Social Change (2011)
30. Kondo, M.C., Jacoby, S.F., South, E.C.: Does spending time outdoors reduce stress? A review of real-time stress response to outdoor environments. Health Place **51**, 136–150 (2018)
31. Lawrence, R.J.: Housing and health: beyond disciplinary confinement. J. Urban Health **83** (3), 540–549 (2006)
32. Li, G., Weng, Q.: Measuring the quality of life in city of Indianapolis by integration of remote sensing and census data. Int. J. Remote Sens. **28**(2), 249–267 (2007)
33. Hu, L., et al.: Monitoring housing rental prices based on social media: an integrated approach of machine-learning algorithms and hedonic modeling to inform equitable housing policies. Land Use Policy **82**, 657–673 (2019)
34. Gough, M.: Three reasons to use livability as a vehicle for sustainability. (Planetizen) (2015)
35. Mehregan, M.R.: Advanced Operational Research. Academic Publishing, Tehran (2013)
36. Myers, D.: Building knowledge about quality of life for urban planning. J. Am. Plan. Assoc. **54**(3), 347–358 (1988)

37. Oberlink, M.R.: Opportunities for Creating Livable Communities. Public Policy Institute, AARP (2008)
38. Okulicz-Kozaryn, A.: City life: rankings (livability) versus perceptions (satisfaction). Soc. Ind. Res. **110**(2), 433–451 (2013)
39. Oliveira, I.A., Carayannis, E.G., Ferreira, F.A., Jalali, M.S., Carlucci, D., Ferreira, J.J.: Constructing home safety indices for strategic planning in residential real estate: a socio-technical approach. Technol. Forecast. Soc. Change **131**, 67–77 (2018)
40. Pandey, R.U., Garg, Y.G., Bharat, A.: A framework for evaluating residential built environment performance for livability. ITPI J. **7**(4), 12–20 (2010)
41. Paul, A., Sen, J.: Livability assessment within a metropolis based on the impact of integrated urban geographic factors (IUGFs) on clustering urban centers of Kolkata. Cities **74**, 142–150 (2018)
42. Rauh, V.A., Chew, G.R., Garfinkel, R.S.: Deteriorated housing contributes to high cockroach allergen levels in inner-city households. Environ. Health Perspect. **110**(Suppl. 2), 323–327 (2002)
43. Reis, I.F.C., Ferreira, F.A.F., Meidutė-Kavaliauskienė, I., Govindan, K., Fang, W., Falcão, P.F.: An evaluation thermometer for assessing city sustainability and livability. Sustain. Cities Soc. **47**, 101449 (2019)
44. Rivarda, S., Raymond, L., Verreault, D.: Resource-based view and competitive strategy: an integrated model of the contribution of information technology to firm performance. J. Strat. Inf. Syst. **15**, 29–50 (2006)
45. Roe, J., Aspinall, P.: The restorative benefits of walking in urban and rural settings in adults with good and poor mental health. Health Place **17**(1), 103–113 (2011)
46. Cheng, S., Chan, C.W., Huang, G.H.: Using multiple criteria decision analysis for supporting decision of solid waste management. J. Environ. Sci. Health Part A **37**(6), 975–990 (2002)
47. Saaty, T.L.: Fundamentals of the analytic network process, 12–14 August 1999. ISAHP, Kobe, Japan (1999)
48. Safdari Molan, Amin: Investigating the Effects of Urban Transportation System on Land Use System in metropolitan Tehran, Case Study of Tehran District 8, Master's Thesis, University of Tehran (2014)
49. Sze, N.N., Christensen, K.M.: Access to urban transportation system for individuals with disabilities. IATSS Res. **41**(2), 66–73 (2017)
50. Throsby, D.: Cultural heritage as financial asset in strategies for urban development and poverty alleviation (2005)
51. Tilaki, M.J.M., Abdullah, A., Bahauddin, A., Marzbali, M.H.: The necessity of increasing livability for George Town World Heritage Site: an analytical review. Mod. Appl. Sci. **8**(1), 123 (2014)
52. Triantaphyllou, E.: Multi-Criteria Decision Making: A Comparative Study, p. 320. Kluwer Academic Publishers, Springer, Dordrecht (2000). https://doi.org/10.1007/978-1-4757-3157-6_2. ISBN 0-7923-6607-7
53. United Nations World Urbanization Prospects: The 2014 Revision, Department of Economic and Social Affairs, Population Division, United Nations, New York, United States (2014)
54. Uysal, F., Tosun, Ö.: Multi criteria analysis of the residential properties in Antalya using TODIM method. Proc.-Soc. Behav. Sci. **109**, 322–326 (2014)
55. Uysal, M., Perdue, R., Sirgy, M.J. (eds.): Handbook of Tourism and Quality-of-Life Research: Enhancing the Lives of Tourists and Residents of Host Communities. Springer, Heidelberg (2012). https://doi.org/10.1007/978-94-007-2288-0

56. Van Kamp, I., Leidelmeijer, K., Marsman, G., De Hollander, A.: Urban environmental quality and human well-being: towards a conceptual framework and demarcation of concepts; a literature study. Landscape Urban Plan. **65**(1–2), 5–18 (2003)
57. Zanakis, S.H., Solomon, A., Wishart, N., Dublish, S.: Multi-attribute decision making: a simulation comparison of selection methods. Eur. J. Oper. Res. **107**(1998), 507–529 (1998)
58. Zanella, A., Camanho, A.S., Dias, T.G.: The assessment of cities' livability integrating human wellbeing and environmental impact. Ann. Oper. Res. **226**(1), 695–726 (2015)
59. Zhang, C., Jia, S., Yang, R.: Housing affordability and housing vacancy in China: the role of income inequality. J. Hous. Econ. **33**, 4–14 (2016)
60. Wei, Z., Chiu, R.L.H.: Livability of subsidized housing estates in marketized socialist China: an institutional interpretation. Cities **83**, 108–117 (2018)

# Evolution of Soil Consumption in the Municipality of Melfi (Southern Italy) in Relation to Renewable Energy

Valentina Santarsiero[1]([⊠]), Gabriele Nolè[1], Antonio Lanorte[1], Biagio Tucci[1], Pasquale Baldantoni[1], and Beniamino Murgante[2,3]

[1] IMAA-CNR, C.da Santa Loja, Zona Industriale,
Tito Scalo, 85050 Potenza, Italy
vsantarsiero87@gmail.com,
pasquale.baldantoni@gmail.com,
{gabriele.nole,alanorte,biagio.tucci}@imaa.cnr.it
[2] School of Engineering, University of Basilicata,
Viale dell'Ateneo Lucano 10, 85100 Potenza, Italy
[3] Environmental Observatory Foundation of Basilicata Region (FARBAS),
Corso Vittorio Emanuele II n. 3, 85052 Marsico Nuovo, PZ, Italy

**Abstract.** Soil consumption represent an important indicator of soil management, in last few years the European States have been promoted the use and installation of renewable energy sources, with a consequent soil consumption increase. The aim of this work is to implement a procedure that analyzes the change detection of the soil consumption and discriminate those related to soil consumption due to installation of renewable energy sources from that due to built-up areas. The select test site is the Municipality of Melfi (Southern Italy) because is highly significant because is characterized by fragmented and various environments. The increase of urbanization is due to the growth of built-up areas and the exponential development of renewable sources installation. The work herein presented concerns an application study on these processes with the images of Sentinel-2 satellite. In order to produce a synthetic map of soil consumption, the Sentinel-2 images were classified using a supervised classification. A first map of soil consumption was obtained divided the area characterized by urbanization from the area with the presence of the renewable energy sources. Eolic class have been subdivided and reclassified, divided the relevant street from the turbine pad. Eolic class have been reclassified discriminate the relevant street from the turbine pad and subdivided into other subclasses referred to the power wind turbines, in order to quantify the soil consumption related to each one. All processes have been processes developed integrating Remote Sensing and Geographic Information System (GIS), using open source software.

**Keywords:** Soil consumption · Renewable energy · Open source software

© Springer Nature Switzerland AG 2019
S. Misra et al. (Eds.): ICCSA 2019, LNCS 11621, pp. 675–682, 2019.
https://doi.org/10.1007/978-3-030-24302-9_48

# 1   Introduction

Soil consumption is a phenomenon associated with the loss of soil defined as a change from a non-artificial cover (soil not consumed) to an artificial ground cover (soil consumed). Land cover is defined as the biophysical coverage of the earth's surface, including artificial surfaces, agricultural areas, woods and forests, semi-natural areas, wetlands, bodies water, as defined by Directive 2007/2/CE.

In Italy the SNPA (National System of Environmental Protection) monitors soil consumption phenomenon and ISPRA (Superior Institute for the Protection and Environmental Research) every year elaborates a study of the state of art of the phenomenon. In Italy soil consumption continues to growth, though making an important slowdown in the last one years, probably due to the economic condition. Between 2016 and 2017 the new artificial roofs covered approximately 5400 hectares of territory, i.e. on average just over 14 hectares per day, about 2 $m^2$ of soil irreversibly lost every second. In absolute terms in Italy there are more than 23000 $km^2$ ($\sim 7.65\%$ of national territory) of soil lost. After having touched even the 8 $m^2$ at the second of the years 2000 and the slowdown started in 2008–2013 (between 6 and 7 $m^2$ per second), soil consumption is consolidated over the past three years, with reduced speed of soil consumption. There is always increased environmental sensitivity to problems of soil conservation and its functionality [9].

Soil consumption represents an important indicator of soil management and policies in reference with settlements processes and policies to protect and enhance the natural areas. Artificial land use trends could represent an effective indicator of the settlement process quality and could also provide information about the efficacy of protection and exploitation policies in natural and rural areas. Urban transformation has changed the concept of a city based on a center and suburbs surrounding it, with the space outside the urban area mostly characterized by rural landscapes [11]. The migration of the population from the countryside to the city involves an increasing demand of new buildings with consequent soil consumption. Moreover, in many territorial contexts, such as Basilicata, the phenomenon of urban sprawl is strongly present. The risk is that the application of urbanization policies without rules in the countryside, produce waterproofing of territory, wears out soils and distort landscapes [8]. Costs of urbanization grow, making increasingly difficult to sustain investment for public transport sector, construction and maintenance of road infrastructure and public services (public lighting, garbage collection, etc.). Other criticisms linked to urban sprawl are aesthetic pollution, noise and air pollution, environmental impact, and soil consumption. Urban sprawl and soil consumption generates a highly fragmented agricultural and natural landscape [7]. This phenomenon produces natural islands, defined by the boundaries of new urbanized areas, which are too small to accommodate the life of certain animal species; consequently soil consumption has also a negative impact on biodiversity [10].

In recent years the urban sprawl phenomenon is joined by an ever increasing consumption of land linked to renewable energy, which has so far been neglected.

In the last few years, in line with the European policies [1–3], which have targeted the increase of energy production from renewable sources in 2020, the European States have promoted and encouraged the use and installation of photovoltaic panels and wind turbines, with a consequent increase of soil consumption by these. The installation of renewable energy sources from environmental sustainability point of view cooperate to contributes to the decrease in the use of fossil energy sources, but introduce a new classes of soil consumption until now ignored, in disagreement with the goal of European Commission [4] that the expect to zeroing by 2050 the soil consumption.

The work herein presented concerns an application study on the process of soil consumption, carried out remote sensed information from Sentinel 2 satellite by Copernicus Mission. Copernicus is a European Mission with the aim to provide accurate information and plays an important role in data management for natural phenomenon monitoring and management. The mission is based on a series of 6 types of satellites, called Sentinels, specialized in precise applications. In particular Sentinel 2 is characterized by a multispectral sensor with mid high spatial and temporal resolution.

In order to produce a synthetic map of soil consumption, Sentinel 2 images were classified used an automatic classifier Support Vector Machine (SVM) based on machine learning theory [12]. All process steps have been developed integrating Geographical Information System and Remote Sensing, and adopting free and open source software QGIS (see: http://qgis.osgeo.org).

## 2  Material and Methods

### 2.1  Data

Multi-spectral and multi-temporal satellite data with medium and high spatial resolution are very appropriate in soil consumption phenomenon evaluation. Data used in present work is a satellite image Sentinel 2 (source: https://scihub.copernicus.eu/dhus/#/home) on 13 april 2018. Sentinel 2 satellite acquired images with 13 bands, from infrared to thermal infrared wavelengths (Table 1), characterized by a mid high spatial and temporal resolution. Sentinel 2 data have been processed with QGIS software.

**Table 1.** Sentinel 2 satellite feautures.

| Satellite | Bands | Range wavelength | Resolution (m) |
|---|---|---|---|
| Sentinel 2 | Band 1 – Coastal aereosol | 0.443 | 60 |
| | Band 2 – Blue | 0.490 | 10 |
| | Band 3 – Green | 0.560 | 10 |
| | Band 4 – Red | 0.665 | 10 |
| | Band 5 – Vegetation Red Edge | 0.705 | 20 |
| | Band 6 – Vegetation Red Edge | 0.740 | 20 |
| | Band 7 – Vegetation Red Edge | 0.783 | 20 |
| | Band 8 – NIR | 0.842 | 10 |
| | Band 8a –Vegetation Red Edge | 0.865 | 20 |
| | Band 9 – Water vapour | 0.945 | 60 |
| | Band 10 – SWIR – Cirrus | 1.375 | 60 |
| | Band 11 – SWIR | 1.610 | 20 |
| | Band 12 – SWIR | 2.190 | 20 |

## 2.2  Study Area

The study area is located in Basilicata Region, in the Municipality of Melfi (see Fig. 1), the third populous Municipality of the Region, with its 17878 habitants and 205.12 km$^2$ of extention. The settlement of the FCA Sata industrial center in the 1990s contributed to increase the population with consequent urban expansion linked to the construction of new buildings. Starting in the 2000s, the promotion of the installation of renewable energy sources (wind and photovoltaic) contributed to a substantial increase in soil consumption.

**Fig. 1.**  Study area (Basilicata Region and Melfi)

## 2.3  Methodologies

The methodology herein developed has been implemented in order to carry out an analysis to quantify the soil consumption due to renewable energy using Sentinel 2. Nowdays, satellite time series and ancillary data currently available, even free of charge (from national and international spatial agencies) and offer a great potential for a quantitative assessment of soil consumption. SVM models and algorithms are based on supervised learning approaches, also called machine learning, that are considered to be very powerful and widely used within both industry and academia [5]. During the last ten years, SVMs have been showing a great potential for data classification also in satellite data processing [6] and for these reasons has been adopted in this work.

The methodology developed to obtain a detailed map of soil consumption due to renewable energy sources, regard the use of SVM classifier, which is effective in recognizing and discriminating the spectral signatures of vegetation, water, buildings, roads, through remote sensing images. The used image of Sentinel 2 (level 2A[1])

---

[1] Level 2 https://earth.esa.int/web/sentinel/user-guides/sentinel-2-msi/product-types/level-2a.

acquired the 13 April 2018 was processed at 10 m of spatial resolution with the following bands 2, 3, 4, 5, 6, 7, 8, 8A, 11, 12. Following the SNPA reference, the soil consumption classes used to define the training areas are divided into two macro classes, ground consumed (level 1) and soil and not consumed (level 2). The first one can in turn be divided into reversible consumed soil and permanent consumed soil.

Many classes are not present in the Melfi area. Particular emphasis was placed on the identification and classification of renewable energies to quantify consumption of soil through the period 2010, 2014, 2018. For this reason, a new class of consumed soil coded with the value 119 absent in the reference SNPA (see Table 2) was added to the above legend.

**Table 2.** Legend of classification

| Code | Description | Code | Description |
|------|-------------|------|-------------|
| 1 | Soil consumed | 118 | Dump |
| 2 | Soil not consumed | 119 | Eolic pad |
| 11 | Soil permanent consumed | 121 | Dirt roads |
| 12 | Soil reversible consumed | 122 | Dirt areas and construction sites |
| 111 | Buildings | 123 | Mining areas |
| 112 | Streets (asphalt) | 124 | Quarry |
| 113 | Railway | 125 | Photovoltaic field |
| 114 | Airport | 126 | Other artificial covered areas |
| 115 | Port | 201 | Artificial water buildings |
| 116 | Other areas sealed unbuilt | 202 | Roundabouts and road junctions |
| 117 | Permanent greenhouses | 203 | Unpaved greenhouses |

The supervised classification process is an iterative process that ends with the choice of the output map after performing a photointerpretation check with orthophotos and data of the same period and with the evaluation of the accuracy matrix. At this point, considering that the map of soil consumption called bu_2017_utm33 N (SNPA) has a spatial detail that is not very high in some Italian territorial contexts, such as that of Melfi, some information layers of the Geo-Topographic Database have been exploited) of Basilicata Region - DBGT (source: https://rsdi.regione.basilicata.it/) (see Table 3).

Using Map Algebra, the 10-m rasterized information layers, or subsets thereof, were inserted on the previous classification map, replacing the corresponding pixels. This process was applied only on irreversible consumed soils since the DBGT update year is 2014.

**Table 3.** Legend of equivalence between DBGT and SNPA code.

| DBGT Classes | Type | SNPA code |
|---|---|---|
| Area attrezzata suolo | Not further qualified humanised area | 116,122 |
| el_stradale_grafo | Paved/Unpaved | 112,121 |
| Area a serv stradale | Roadside service area | 116 |
| Attrezzatura sportive | Sports fields, stairs, outdoor pool | 12,122,111 |
| Edifici_is | Built-up | 111 |
| Edifici_min_is | Built-up | 111 |
| El_copertura | | 11 |
| Rete_ferroviaria_grafo | | 113 |
| Manufatto_industriale | Silos container, tank, greenhouses | 12,11,0203 |

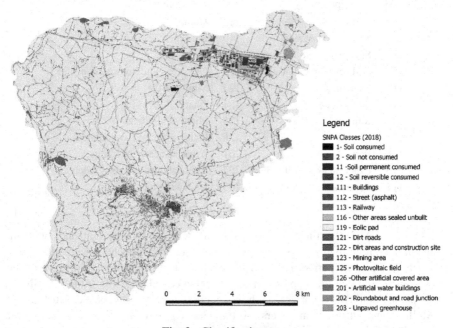

**Fig. 2.** Classification map

## 2.4 Results

The map thus obtained has indications on all the classes present in the Melfi area (see Fig. 2). Starting from this we proceeded to analyze in detail the pixels that can be associated with renewable energies regard the years 2010, 2014 and 2018.

Figure 3 represents a zoom of a small area (in yellow rectangle) characterized by the presence of installation of renewable energy (eolic installations and photovoltaic panels), in particular is evident the growth of soil consumption due to the expansion of wind turbines (blue circles) in the area. While is also evident the decrease of photovoltaic panel installation (red rectangular area).

Eolic class have been subdivided and reclassified, divided the relevant street from the wind turbine pad. In according with the goal of European Commission, that the expect to zeroing by 2050 the soil consumption, Eolic class have been subdivided into other subclasses referred to the power of wind turbines, in order to quantify the soil consumption related to each one. The pixels relative to the soil consumed by the wind turbines have been classified in the first category in the case of area pertaining to the single turbine (pitch) and as second category in the case of service street.

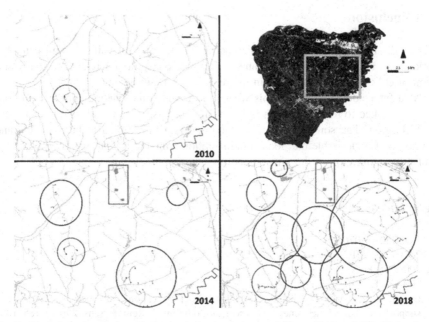

**Fig. 3.** Variation of eolic installation and photovoltaic panels from 2010 to 2018 (Color figure online)

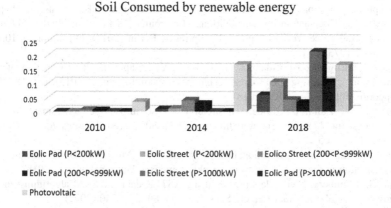

**Fig. 4.** Soil consumption due to renewable energy (2010–2018).

Figure 4 summarized and quantify the percentage and the area (km$^2$) of soil consumption in different classes: urbanization, eolic and photovoltaic sources.

Analyzed the soil consumption due to urban expantion and renewable energy is evident how in the first case the trend is constantly growing, while in the latter trend shows a strongly increment starting from 2014 caused by the development of small and large eolic stations because the economic policies have been promoted the installation of wind turbines.

# 3  Conclusion

This work shows that Melfi has an important and worrying soil consumption phenomenon in relation with the habitants. Infact soil consumption related to the installation of eolic turbines is more than the real energy requirement.

As a future development of this work is to monitor the phenomenon of soil consumption linked to renewable energy by expanding this type of analysis to other areas of the Region. The soil is a common good and is a finite good to be protected and monitored, it is desirable that local administrations implement intervention policies to limit the proliferation of the phenomenon.

# References

1. COM(2016) 0767
2. 2014/C 200/01
3. 2009/28/CE
4. 2007/2/CE
5. Dixon, B., Candade, N.: Multispectral landuse classification using neural networks and support vector machines: one or the other, or both? Int. J. Remote Sens. **29**(4), 1185–1206 (2008)
6. Mountrakis, G., Im, J., Ogole, C.: Support vector machines in remote sensing: a review. ISPRS J. Photogramm. **66**(3), 247–259 (2011)
7. Murgante, B., Borruso, G., Lapucci, A.: Sustainable development: concepts and methods for its application in urban and environmental planning. In: Murgante, B., Borruso, G., Lapucci, A. (eds.) Geocomputation, Sustainability and Environmental Planning. Studies in Computational Intelligence, vol. 348, pp. 1–15. Springer, Berlin (2011). https://doi.org/10.1007/978-3-642-19733-8_1
8. Nolè, G., Murgante, B., Calamita, G., Lanorte, A., Lasaponara, R.: Evaluation of urban sprawl from space using open sources technologies. Ecol. Inform. **26**(2015), 151–161 (2015)
9. Rapporto Ambiente – SNPA (2018)
10. Romano, B., Zullo, F.: Models of urban land use in Europe: assessment tools and criticalities. Int. J. Agric. Environ. Inf. Syst. **4**(3), 80–97 (2013). https://doi.org/10.4018/ijaeis.2013070105
11. Saganeiti, L., Favale, A., Pilogallo, A., Scorza, F., Murgante, B.: Assessing urban fragmentation at regional scale using sprinkling indexes. Sustainability, 4 (2018)
12. Zhu, G., Blumberg, D.G.: Classification using ASTER data and SVM algorithms; the case study of Beer Sheva. Israel Remote Sens. Environ. **80**, 233–240 (2002)

# Trend Definition of Soil Consumption in the Period 1994–2014 - Municipalities of Potenza, Matera and Melfi

Pasquale Baldantoni[1](✉), Gabriele Nolè[1], Antonio Lanorte[1], Biagio Tucci[1], Valentina Santarsiero[1], and Beniamino Murgante[2,3]

[1] IMAA-CNR, C.da Santa Loja, Zona Industriale Tito Scalo,
85050 Potenza, Italy
pasquale.baldantoni@gmail.com,
vsantarsiero87@gmail.com, {gabriele.nole,
antonio.lanorte,biagio.tucci}@imaa.cnr.it
[2] School of Engineering, University of Basilicata, Viale dell'Ateneo Lucano 10,
85100 Potenza, Italy
beniamino.murgante@unibas.it
[3] Farbas, Via Pretoria 277, 85100 Potenza, Italy

**Abstract.** Soil consumption often shows a temporal trend that seems to be disconnected from the real territory needs. In this study the phenomenon is analyzed in some areas of the Basilicata Region (South of Italy) that, on average, are characterized by a low increase in economic activities and a negative demographic trend. The implemented procedure aims to detect the land consumption within some of the most representative municipalities of the Basilicata region, in this case Potenza, Pignola, Melfi and Matera, in order to meet the ISPRA (The Italian Institute for Environmental Protection and Research, ISPRA - Istituto Superiore per la Protezione e la Ricerca Ambientale) guidelines, which provide for zeroing of land consumption by 2050. Also the Basilicata Region is affected by this phenomenon and it is fundamental to analyze the trend of variations and relate it to the economic activities and the demographic trend on the municipal territory, as each of these parameters can help to evaluate the state of art and improve the tools available to the planner with a view to current and future territory management. The analysis is performed by using Landsat images, that allow to access a historical database of over 30 years, thanks to which it was possible to obtain maps of land consumption for the years 1994, 2004 and 2014, using a supervised classification algorithm (SVM). The next step is to implement data obtained with other statistical information, available through ISTAT (National Italian Statistical Institute) censuses and other accredited sources.

**Keywords:** Soil consumption · SVM · Change detection

## 1 Introduzione

Il soil sealing, che si può tradurre, in modo non completamente proprio, con il termine di "impermeabilizzazione del suolo", è causato dalla copertura del suolo con materiali "impermeabili" o comunque dal cambiamento delle caratteristiche del suolo tanto da renderlo impermeabile in modo irreversibile o difficilmente reversibile [1].

© Springer Nature Switzerland AG 2019
S. Misra et al. (Eds.): ICCSA 2019, LNCS 11621, pp. 683–691, 2019.
https://doi.org/10.1007/978-3-030-24302-9_49

Questo lavoro ha l'obiettivo di analizzare la variazione del consumo di suolo sul territorio della Basilicata, in relazione all'andamento demografico, nel periodo fra il 1994 e il 2014; in particolare, sono stati presi in considerazione Comuni che, per diversi motivi, presentano un consumo di suolo significativo. Il DBGT[1] (Database Geo Topografico) della Regione Basilicata, completato nell'anno 2014, è costitutito da molteplici strati informativi che rappresentano, per le finalità dello studio, dati ancillari di notevole importanza per la definizione dell'impronta del consumo di suoloIl risultato dello studio rappresenta un'analisi di change detection, realativa agli anni 1994 e 2004 in confronto all'anno base 2014. Nel presente lavoro le mappe riferite agli anni citati sono state prodotte utilizzando immagini satellitari Landsat classificate utilizzando tecniche di remote sensing e map algebra con software opensource QGIS (source: http://qgis.osgeo.org).

## 2  Area Di Studio

La Basilicata è una Regione, situata nel sud Italia, con una popolazione di 564247 abitanti distribuiti su di un territorio di 10073,32 km$^2$ (fonte ISTAT, 2018). La geografia che la caratterizza è prevalentemente a carattere montuoso e collinare, con una sola piana, nella zona del Metapontino (litorale Jonico). Ai centri urbani, si alternano vaste zone disabitate o caratterizzate dalla presenza di case sparse o piccoli aggregati civili o industriali. Il 30% del territorio è interessato da zone sottoposte a vincoli ambientali [2], il che evidenzia ancor di più la necessità di un uso oculato e parsimonioso del suolo disponibile.

I comuni selezionati per lo studio in oggetto sono tre: Potenza (che è anche il capoluogo di Regione), Matera e Melfi. Il comune di Potenza è situato nella parte centro-ovest del territorio mentre Matera, l'altro capoluogo di provincia, si colloca nella parte ad est della Regione, al confine con la regione Puglia. Poichè investita del ruolo di Capitale Europea della Cultura 2019, risultano interessanti le valutazioni rispetto ad un aumento dei flussi turistici e ad un potenziale incremento delle strutture e infrastrutture legate alla ricettività, al fine di delineare un trend del consumo di suolo. L'ultimo comune oggetto di indagine è Melfi, situato ad est della regione, altro importante centro urbano, di grande interesse per l'evoluzione territoriale legata alla costruzione dell'indotto industriale FCA SATA, la cui costruzione è terminata nel 1993 e ha visto, nel 1994, l'avvio della produzione. Intorno allo stabilimento, si sono sviluppate una serie di attività di supporto, che hanno comportato un'importante variazione nel consumo di suolo (Fig. 1).

---

[1] Il database geotopografico della Regione Basilicata è disponibile al sito https://rsdi.regione.basilicata. it/dbgt-ctr/.

**Fig. 1.** Basilicata region and municipalities.

## 3 Analisi Dell'andamento Demografico

Dagli anni '50 ad oggi la popolazione della Basilicata evidenzia un trend di spopolamento importante [5]. Nel corso dell'ultimo ventennio è stata interessata da importanti variazioni (see Fig. 2) con una riduzione di circa il 2,6% nei decenni 1994–2004 e 2004–2014. Il consumo di suolo è stato valutato in relazione ai dati demografici.

## Inhabitants in Basilicata Region

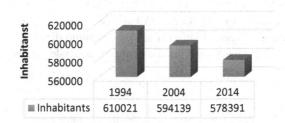

**Fig. 2.** Inhabitants in Basilicata region in 1994–2014 period.

### 3.1  Potenza

La Città di Potenza si estende per una superficie di circa 174 km$^2$, con 67211 abitanti al 1° gennaio 2019. The following Table 1 gives a summary dell'evoluzione demografica, dal 1994 al 2014.

**Table 1.** Inhabitants in Potenza municipality and inhabitants variation

| Year | Inhabitants | Period (variation) | Inhabitants ($\Delta$) |
|------|-------------|--------------------|------------------------|
| 1994 | 66419 | 1994–2004 | 2309 |
| 2004 | 68728 | 2004–2014 | −1325 |
| 2014 | 67403 | 1994–2014 | 984 |

Il saldo positivo nel ventennio è di 984 abitanti.

### 3.2  Matera

É il secondo capoluogo di provincia della Basilicata, con 60403 abitanti censiti al 1° gennaio 2019. La popolazione dal 1994 ad oggi è in crescita come si evince dalla Table 2. La sua estensione territoriale è più che doppia rispetto a Potenza, con circa 388 km$^2$; va evidenziato che tale superficie è in parte occupata dal Parco della Murgia Materana.

**Table 2.** Inhabitants in Matera municipality and inhabitants variation

| Year | Inhabitants | Period (variation) | Inhabitants ($\Delta$) |
|------|-------------|--------------------|------------------------|
| 1994 | 55468 | 1994–2004 | 1873 |
| 2004 | 58683 | 2004–2014 | 3215 |
| 2014 | 60556 | 1994–2014 | 5088 |

### 3.3  Melfi

La città di Melfi copre un territorio di 105 km$^2$, con una popolazione al 1° gennaio 2019 di 17878 persone. Negli ultimi vent'anni, il consumo di suolo ha subito un forte incremento anche a causa dell'insediamento industriale automobilistico della FCA SATA (Table 3).

**Table 3.** Inhabitants in Melfi municipality and inhabitants variation

| Year | Inhabitants | Period (variation) | Inhabitants ($\Delta$) |
|------|-------------|--------------------|------------------------|
| 1994 | 15943 | 1994–2004 | 961 |
| 2004 | 16756 | 2004–2014 | 813 |
| 2014 | 17717 | 1994–2014 | 1774 |

# 4 Dati e Metodologia

Le immagini satellitari utilizzate sono quelle delle missioni Landsat; tale scelta è stata fatta per la copertura trentennale dei dati, utili per realizzare un'accurata serie temporale. Le missioni Landsat-4 e Landsat-5 equipaggiano uno scanner multispettrale e un Thematic Mapper, con risoluzione spaziale a 30 metri, mentre il Landsat-8 monta un sensore OLI[2] ed un sensore termico, il primo con risoluzione a 30 metri, il secondo a 100 metri.

Il dato scaricato è il Level-2[3], corretto atmosfericamente rispetto alla radiazione solare riflessa. Nella seguente Table 4, sono riportate le bande utilizzate:

Table 4. Landsat 4–5 and Landsat 8 used bands

| Landsat 4–5 | Landsat 8 |
| --- | --- |
| Band 1 – Blue | Band 2 – Blue |
| Band 2 – Green | Band 3 – Green |
| Band 3 – Red | Band 4 – Red |
| Band 4 – Near Infrared (NIR) | Band 5 – Near Infrared |
| Band 5 – Shortwave infrared (SWIR) | Band 6 – Short-wave Infrared |
| Band 7 – Mid- Infrared (MIR) | Band 10 – Thermal Infrared |

Per l'elaborazione dei dati, viene utilizzato principalmente il plugin SCP – Semi-Automatic Classification Plugin (https://fromgistors.blogspot.com/) di QGIS, che consente operazioni di pre e post-processing del dato. Prima vengono definite le Region of Interest (ROI), con l'ausilio di immagini composte da bande in veri colori e falsi colori, dati ancillari del DBGT e firme spettrali. Le classi usate per la definizione delle ROI sono 4 categorie di Macroclassi (MC_ID) e 7 rispettive Classi (C_ID) associate alle stesse, come da Table 5:

L'algoritmo utilizzato per la classificazione supervisionata è la Support Vector Machine (SVM). SVMs are supervised automatic algorithms based on machine learning theory for data analysis [3] ed è presente in QGIS all'intenro del plugin DZETSAKA (https://github.com/lennepkade/dzetsaka). Uno dei punti di forza della SVM è quello di ottenere classificazioni accurate anche con un numero scarno di ROI.

---

[2] Operational Land Imager OLI captures data with improved radiometric precision over a 12-bit dynamic range, which improves overall signal to noise ratio. (source: https://www.usgs.gov/land-resources/nli/landsat/landsat-8?qt-science_support_page_related_con=0#qt-science_support_page_related_con).

[3] USGS and NASA released LANDSAT level 2A product (surface reflectances corrected for atmospheric effects with a cloud mask, a cloud shadow mask, and a water and snow mask). The thermal data are expressed as brightness temperatures at the top of atmosphere.

**Table 5.** Class definition for training areas

| MC_ID | C_ID | Definition | Description |
|---|---|---|---|
| 1 | 1 | Urban | Built-up, streets, industrial buildings |
| 2 | 2 | Veg_1 | Vegetation coverage – 100% |
| 2 | 3 | Veg_2 | Vegetation coverage – 75% |
| 2 | 4 | Veg_3 | Vegetation coverage – 50% |
| 2 | 5 | Veg_4 | Vegetation coverage – $\leq 25\%$ |
| 3 | 6 | Water | Lakes, basin, water sheet |
| 4 | 7 | Veget/Water | Moisture areas |

Una volta ottenuta la classificazione, per valutare la precisione dell'immagine e, quindi, l'affidabilità rispetto a quanto è stato classificato, viene effettuata una matrice di accuratezza [4]; la mappa così classificata viene analizzata e confrontata con i dati ancillari, ortofoto, etc., prestando particolare attenzione alla classe 1. Gli strati del DBGT del 2014 relativi alle aree urbane/impermeabili vengono rasterizzati in una mappa binaria 0-1 (1 suoli impermeabili, 0 resto del territorio). Questa mappa è fondamentale per poter individuare ed eliminare, mediante map algebra, eventuali pixel di classe 1 erroneamante classificati dalla SVM.

In questo modo la mappa del 2014 rappresenterà l'impronta del consumo di suolo che delimita la zona entro la quale sviluppare le analisi per gli anni precedenti (questo ridurrà notevolmente l'area da classificare). La modalità scelta si basa sulla assunzione che un suolo impermebilizzato non si trasformi in suolo permeabile nel corso degli anni. Questo concetto non è sempre vero (di seguito è riportato un caso di trasformazione inversa, see Fig. 3) ma essendo il dato aggregato a livello comunale, gli errori dovuti alla mancata quantificazione di questi rari casi possono essere trascurati.

**Fig. 3.** Contrada Bosco Piccolo – In purple, in 1994, is possible to see the urban agglomerate, which was destroyed, in 2014, due to a landslide. (Color figure online)

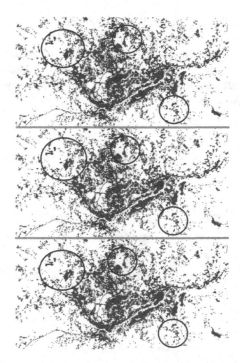

**Fig. 4.** Centro Urbano di Potenza. From upper to bottom: soil consumption evolution in 1994, 2004 and 2014. The most representative case are rounded in yellow. (Color figure online)

## 5   Risultati

Fino al 2004, nel comune di Potenza, il consumo di suolo è correlato positivamente al trend demografico. Successivamente, a fronte di un decremento della popolazione, si è registrata una correlazione negativa (see Fig. 5).

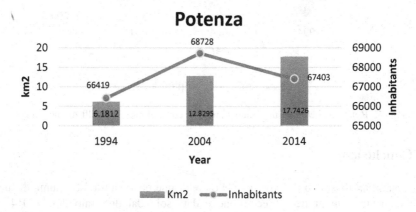

**Fig. 5.** Relations between inhabitants and soil consumption in Potenza municipality.

Il trend di crescita demografico nell'intero ventennio, per il comune di Matera, è positivamente correlato al consumo di suolo (see Fig. 4).

L'evoluzione del fenomeno nel territorio di Melfi è simile a quello di Matera (Fig. 6). E' però da considerare il ruolo importante dato dal comparto automobilistico della FCA che ha attratto nel tempo anche nuova popolazione trasferitasi nel Comune per questioni lavorative (see Fig. 7).

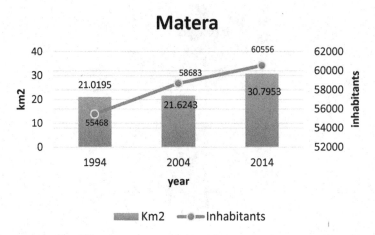

**Fig. 6.** Relations between inhabitants and soil consumption in Matera municipality.

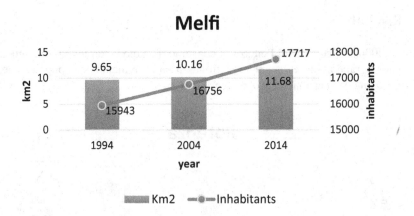

**Fig. 7.** Relations between inhabitants and soil consumption in Melfi municipality.

## 6   Conclusioni

I casi analizzati mostrano una sostanziale correlazione positiva tra il consumo di suolo e l'andamento demografico. L'eccezione è data solo dal decennio 2004–2014 nel Comune di Potenza. I Comuni studiati sono fra i più popolosi in Basilicata con un fermento socioeconomic e culturale di rilievo rispetto alla media. Tuttavia il Sistema insediativo Lucano è costituito da piccolo centri. Difatti circa il 96% Dei Comuni lucani si attestano sotto I 15000 abitanti e il 75% sotto I 5000. In questi contesti territoriali il fenomeno dello spopolamento è ancora più aggressivo e sono ancora più evidenti fenomeni di urban sprawl. Il prosieguo del presente lavoro prevedrà di applicare le analisi nel resto del territorio della Regione Basilicata.

# References

1. Barberis, R.: Consumo dei suoli e qualità dei suoli urbani, p. 703 (2005)
2. De Stefano, A.: Le aree protette e i parchi naturali. Regione Basilicata, p. 1 (2006)
3. Di Palma, F., Amato, F., Nolè, G., Martellozzo, F., Murgante, B.: A SMAP supervised classification of landsat images for urban sprawl evaluation. Int. J. Geo-Inf. 7 (2016)
4. Lanorte, A., et al.: Agricultural plastic waste spatial estimation by Landsat 8 satellite images. Comput. Electron. Agric. **141**, 35 (2017)
5. Saganeiti, L., Favale, A., Pilogallo, A., Scorza, F., Murgante, B.: Assessing urban fragmentation at regional scale using sprinkling indexes. Sustainability, 4 (2018)

# Energy Landscape Fragmentation: Basilicata Region (Italy) Study Case

Lucia Saganeiti[(⊠)], Angela Pilogallo, Giuseppe Faruolo,
Francesco Scorza, and Beniamino Murgante

Laboratory of Urban and Regional Systems Engineering (LISUT),
School of Engineering, University of Basilicata, Viale dell'ateneo Lucano 10,
85100 Potenza, Italy
{lucia.saganeiti,angela.pilogallo,francesco.scorza,
beniamino.murgante}@unibas.it

**Abstract.** All programs and policies that stimulated and continue to promote the construction of renewable energy production plants, pose a growing challenge to regional planners and administrators: how to manage the transformation of the landscape to find an effective sustainable arrangement for renewable energy technologies? In fact, while RES plants contribute to solve the global problem of climate change and to reduce emissions, at the local level they imply significant impacts on several components such as: land use, land take, diminishing aesthetic values, deterioration of habitat quality. The intensity of these effects depends on the location of the plants, the distance between the plants, the extension of the ancillary infrastructures and the technical characteristics. It is questionable whether the intensity of the negative impacts at the local level is more related to the technical characteristics of each installations or their dislocation on the territory. The present work is part of this debate, discussing fragmentation index resulted from the assessment of the current regional settlement structure of RES plants.

In facts, the case study concerns the territory of Basilicata region (Italy), which over the last years has seen an abundant increase in installation of renewable energy plants. The evolution of the regional energy system has been strongly influenced both by incentive policies and by (weak) urban and territorial planning policies. This approach could be a valuable contribution both in identifying a fragmentation threshold beyond which the expected negative impacts outweigh the benefits, and in providing useful procedure for managing future installations.

**Keywords:** RES · Fragmentation · Urban sprinkling · Urban sprawl

## 1 Introduction

The installation and operation of Renewable Energy Systems (RES) represents a significant land transformation. It produce effects on several territorial matrixes: land use change, land take, fragmentation of natural habitats with elimination of existing vegetation, visual impact on landscape components, change of micro-climate, glare from direct sunlight reflection (for photovoltaic fields) [1–5].

© Springer Nature Switzerland AG 2019
S. Misra et al. (Eds.): ICCSA 2019, LNCS 11621, pp. 692–700, 2019.
https://doi.org/10.1007/978-3-030-24302-9_50

A process by which ecosystems, habitats of vegetation and animal populations are divided into smaller and more isolated units (fragments) is defined as fragmentation. The main causes of habitat fragmentation are infrastructures, the growth of urban settlements and the development of rural settlements far from the existing ones [6–8] and, from the last decade also RES installations.

Renewable Energy Sources are in continuous evolution at world level [9]. If the incentive to exploit renewable sources is known to be one of the characteristics of the policy of conservation of the territory, including that of protected areas, at the same time the concerns of local communities and governments about the environmental, territorial and landscape impacts of this technology are rapidly increasing.

The case study regards the Basilicata region in south of Italy where the Regional Environmental Energy Plan (PIEAR) in force since 2010 encouraged the electricity production from renewable sources. Indeed according to energy services manager report, since 2000, there has been a very substantial development of wind farms in Italy. At the end of 2017, 5579 wind farms had been installed, most of which (93%) were small (with a capacity of less than 1 MW). Southern Italy has the highest number of wind farms installed at the end of 2017, Basilicata is the region with the highest percentage of farms in the country 25.1%, followed by Puglia 21.0%.

Since the expected impacts certainly depend on the location of RES plants, it is useful to investigate the energy landscape at regional level through sprinkling index (SPX) that has already returned good results in describing the settlement fragmentation [10]. The sprinkling phenomenon can be defined as, "a small quantity distributed in drops or scattered particles" [11–13].

SPX index, based on the extent and distance between RES plant aggregates, has been calculated for three time intervals (2008–2014, 2014–2017 and 2017–2018) dividing the regional territory with a grid of 1 $km^2$. The classification into six degrees of fragmentation has allowed us to see the evolution of the SPX index for each cell. In the majority of cases, the results show that the new installations took place following the sprinkling phenomenon.

## 2  Material and Methods

### 2.1  Study Area

Basilicata region in the south of Italy (Fig. 1), covers about 10.000 $km^2$ and has a population of 567.000 inhabitants (ISTAT [14], 2018). It is a mostly rural environment characterized by very low population and building density.

Despite this, according to ISPRA report 2018 [15], the percentage of land taken in Basilicata region was around 3.4%. Land take in Basilicata is due to the expansion of urban areas, the transformation of rural areas, and the use of agricultural land for renewable energy production through the construction of ground-mounted photovoltaic systems and numerous installation of wind turbine. Indeed, since 2010, a large part of the territory has been affected by the installation of RES plants. At the end of 2017, the number of RES plants was 2122, including wind turbines and photovoltaic fields with a total power output of about 1000 MW.

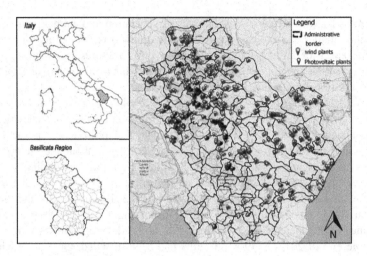

**Fig. 1.** Basilicata region study area.

## 2.2 Data Source and Processing

The basic geographical information structure is RES installations database derived from the combination of three official information sources: (1) TRC (Technical Regional Cartography produced by Basilicata Region and distributed through OGC standards in RSDI [16]), (2) GSE (National Energy Services Manager [17]) and (3) digitalization of plants from aerial photogrammetric survey at different dates: Ortophoto and Google Earth images.

Selected data sources allowed to evaluate not only the spatial dimension, but also the temporal one. Three temporal phases have been identified: (i) 2010–2014, (ii) 2014–2017, (iii) 2017–2018. The RES database includes, among other information, attributes concerning the installed generation capacity [Kw] or [Mw] of individual wind turbines. Three categories of wind energy plants have been defined on the basis of installed capacity. Table 1 shows the three categories considered (micro-mini, medium sized and big sized turbines) with wind turbines number for each temporal phase. For photovoltaic fields the power output data was not available.

For the assessment of land take related to wind turbines and photovoltaic field, the area around the RES installation was considered within an influence radius proportional to the power output (Table 1).

**Table 1.** Wind turbines classification and number for every temporal phase.

| Wind turbines | Power output (P) [Kw] | $N^{\circ}_{2010-2014}$ | $N^{\circ}_{2014-2017}$ | $N^{\circ}_{2017-2018}$ | Influence radius [m] |
|---|---|---|---|---|---|
| Micro-mini | P < 200 | 165 | 476 | 1132 | 15 |
| Medium | $200 \leq P < 1000$ | 32 | 95 | 75 | 25 |
| Big | $P \geq 1000$ | 21 | 65 | 61 | 35 |
| Photovoltaic fields | – | 241 | 241 | 241 | 25 |

Regards wind turbines, influence radius was calculated after detailed analysis of several case studies for each category. An example is shown in Fig. 2. As regards the photovoltaic fields, a pertinence belt of 25 m from the perimeter was considered, which generally corresponds to the border area that includes structures and modules, technical rooms, access areas and circulation areas within the plant. In the absence of up-to-date land use data, this approach allows to consider compromised areas (reversible or irreversible) occupied by auxiliary structures such as roads and technical annexes.

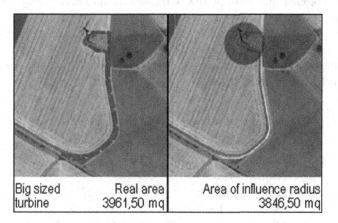

| Big sized turbine | Real area 3961,50 mq | Area of influence radius 3846,50 mq |

**Fig. 2.** Big size wind turbine, comparison between real area and calculated area with the radius of influence.

Since the expected effects' (e.g. loss of habitat quality) extend over an area larger than the sum of individual stands, wind turbines were aggregated with a maximum distance of 250 m [10, 18]. It is assumed, therefore, that this surface is definitively borrowed from previous land uses.

## 2.3    Methodology

The energy landscape fragmentation was spatially calculated using the sprinkling index (SPX) [7, 19]. The study area is divided by a 1 km² grid. SPX index assumes that the most compact form of agglomeration growth is the circular one and is based on the Euclidean distance between two or more geometries within each cell. In this case, geometries are represented by photovoltaic fields and wind turbines aggregates. It is expressed by the following formula:

$$SPX = \frac{\sum \sqrt{(x_i - x^*)^2 + (y_i - y^*)^2}}{R}$$

Where $x_i$ and $y_i$ are the centroid coordinates of each - photovoltaic fields and wind turbines aggregates – polygon present in each grid cell of 1 km²; $x^*$ and $y^*$ are the centroid coordinates of the major nucleus present in each cell. R is the radius of circular area of similar dimensions to those of the sum of the areas of the RES plants present for each cell.

SPX has a range of acceptable values from 0 to $+\infty$. As the index increases, the degree of fragmentation of a territory increases. The zero value can represent two situations: (i) "not fragmented" with the presence of a single aggregate with area much less than 1 km$^2$; (ii) "not fragmented", comparable to compaction phenomenon, with the presence of single aggregate with area of just 1 km$^2$. It is always advisable, therefore, to correlate the results of SPX index with the area occupied by the aggregate in each cell.

The SPX index produced a value for each grid cell that, through the subdivision into the six categories shown in Table 2, allowed us to identify the degree of energy landscape fragmentation. Null values of the index correspond to not urbanized cells, i.e. cells in which there is no aggregate.

**Table 2.** Fragmentation degree according to SPX index.

| Fragmentation degree | SPX |
|---|---|
| Not urbanized | Null |
| Not fragmented | SPX = 0 |
| Low fragmentation | 0 < SPX < 25 |
| Medium-low fragmentation | $25 \leq$ SPX < 50 |
| Medium fragmentation | $50 \leq$ SPX < 100 |
| Medium-high fragmentation | $100 \leq$ SPX < 200 |
| High fragmentation | $200 \leq$ SPX > 500 |

## 3 Results and Discussions

The classification of wind turbines based on power production gives a clear picture of the current state of study area over the three time intervals considered. First graph in Fig. 3 shows the number of RES installations plants that took place in the time intervals analysed. Number of photovoltaic fields remains stable from the first time interval, while wind turbines are growing rapidly, especially in the micro-mini class. Indeed, between the first and the last time, the percentage of micro-mini turbines, on the total of RES plants, increases from 36% to 75%.

In the same way, the area occupied by the RES plants was analysed. In the second graph (Fig. 3), the radius of influence was considered as an area of encumbrance for each plant. Excluding photovoltaic fields, the micro-mini class of wind turbines has occupied, an area of 125 hectares during the last year. Regards the power [MW] (third graph in Fig. 3), the largest percentage is represented by the big wind turbine class.

The Fig. 4 shows, in boxes *a, b* and *c*, SPX index distribution useful to assess energy landscape fragmentation over the time. The increase in number of cells affected by fragmentation from the first to the last interval is evident. In the box *d* is shown a

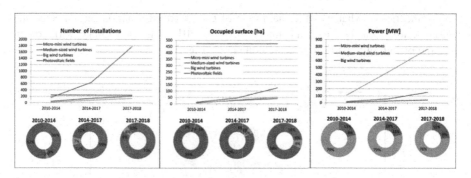

**Fig. 3.** Graphs representing the number, the area occupied [ha] and the power [MW] of RES plants in study area at three time intervals.

particular case of the phenomenon in which some cells vary their fragmentation degree between the first and the second interval and then return to the initial state.

Wind turbines installed far from the existing ones generate high degrees of fragmentation and therefore correspond to the sprinkling phenomenon. On the contrary, wind turbines installed near existing ones correspond to low degrees of fragmentation, i.e. to compaction phenomenon.

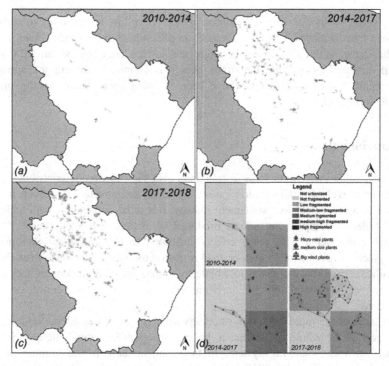

**Fig. 4.** Degree of energetic landscape fragmentation in boxes *a*, *b* and *c*; a detail a of phenomenon in box *d*.

To understand what was the main type of energy transformation that affected the region between the two extreme intervals (2010–2018), the percentage variation in SPX index and aggregates area were compared (Fig. 5).

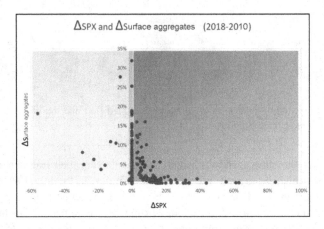

**Fig. 5.** Comparison of SPX and aggregates surface variation between 2010 and 2018. (Color figure online)

The graph is divided in three colored zones: (i) yellow corresponds to cells that have been transformed following a compaction phenomenon; (ii) green corresponds to cells that have suffered variation in aggregate surface area but not in SPX value; (iii) red corresponds to cells that have been transformed following the sprinkling phenomenon. Most wind turbines have been installed away from existing ones to generate sprinkling.

## 4   Conclusions

The considerable increase in RES installations over the last decade contributes to the already high level of fragmentation caused by urban settlements [10]. Such process, occurred in a context of low settlement density, has to be considered with additional care in order to compare the affects produced on natural and ecosystemic [20–24] territorial components with those effects attributed to the traditional antropization factors (such as residential growth or road infrastructures development). In such view the Basilicata case study allowed to isolate the impact of RES settlement and, potentially, to set up standards for environmental assessment procedure of future installations.

The issue of the rapid evolution of energy scenarios is of considerable importance at the level of the whole of Basilicata, having experienced a rapid increase in a de-regulated territorial planning system. In facts, the increase in the number of wind turbines in the decade 2008–2017 occurred in the absence of the Regional Landscape

Plan and industry standards such as those for noise reduction or protection from exposure to electric, magnetic and electromagnetic fields.

Those considerations highlight the conflicts between global objectives and local values. Even if an effective balance is far to be achievable, our effort is to enhance the role of integrate planning approach [25–27] in order to distribute benefits of Low Carbon Transition policies (see also [28, 29]) without losing competitive values on which the strategies of regional sustainable development are rooted.

Future developments of this study include integrating the data obtained with the data on fragmentation caused by urban aggregates and assessing the environmental fragmentation caused by infrastructure in the region.

**Acknowledgements.** This research has been developed within the MEVCSU and INDICARE projects supported by the Environmental Observatory Foundation of Basilicata Region (FARBAS).

# References

1. Chiabrando, R., Fabrizio, E., Garnero, G.: The territorial and landscape impacts of photovoltaic systems: definition of impacts and assessment of the glare risk. Renew. Sustain. Energy Rev. **13**, 2441–2451 (2009)
2. Opdam, P., Wascher, D.: Climate change meets habitat fragmentation: linking landscape and biogeographical scale levels in research and conservation. Biol. Conserv. **117**, 285–297 (2004)
3. Alsema, E., Nieuwlaar, E.: Energy viability of photovoltaic systems. Energy Policy **28**, 999–1010 (2000)
4. Broto, V.C.: Energy landscapes and urban trajectories towards sustainability. Energy Policy **108**, 755–764 (2017)
5. Zanon, B., Verones, S.: Climate change, urban energy and planning practices: Italian experiences of innovation in land management tools. Land Use Policy **32**, 343–355 (2013)
6. Van Bohemen, H.D.: Habitat fragmentation, infrastructure and ecological engineering. Ecol. Eng. **11**, 199–207 (1998)
7. Romano, B., Zullo, F., Fiorini, L., Ciabò, S., Marucci, A.: Sprinkling: an approach to describe urbanization dynamics in Italy. Sustainability **9**, 97 (2017)
8. De Montis, A., Martín, B., Ortega, E., Ledda, A., Serra, V.: Landscape fragmentation in Mediterranean Europe: a comparative approach. Land Use Policy **64**, 83–94 (2017)
9. McNew, L.B., Hunt, L.M., Gregory, A.J., Wisely, S.M., Sandercock, B.K.: Effects of wind energy development on nesting ecology of greater prairie-chickens in fragmented Grasslands. Conserv. Biol. **28**, 1089–1099 (2014)
10. Saganeiti, L., et al.: Assessing urban fragmentation at regional scale using sprinkling indexes. Sustainability **10**, 3274 (2018)
11. Romano, B., Zullo, F., Ciabò, S., Fiorini, L., Marucci, A.: Geografie e modelli di 50 anni di consumo di suolo in Italia. **5**, 17–28 (2015)
12. Romano, B., Zullo, F., Fiorini, L., Marucci, A., Ciabò, S.: Land transformation of Italy due to half a century of urbanization. Land Use Policy **67**, 387–400 (2017)
13. Zullo, F., Fazio, G., Romano, B., Marucci, A., Fiorini, L.: Science of the total environment effects of urban growth spatial pattern (UGSP) on the land surface temperature (LST): a study in the Po Valley (Italy). Sci. Total Environ. **650**, 1740–1751 (2019)

14. Istat.it. https://www.istat.it/
15. Marchetti, M., et al.: Consumo di suolo, dinamiche territoriali e servizi ecosistemici. Edizione 2018 (2018)
16. RSDI – Geoportale Basilicata. https://rsdi.regione.basilicata.it/
17. GSE. https://www.gse.it/
18. Saganeiti, L., Pilogallo, A., Scorza, F., Mussuto, G., Murgante, B.: Spatial indicators to evaluate urban fragmentation in basilicata region (2018)
19. Romano, B., Fiorini, L., Zullo, F., Marucci, A.: Urban growth control DSS techniques for de-sprinkling process in Italy. Sustainability **9**, 1852 (2017)
20. Scorza, F., Murgante, B., Las Casas, G., Fortino, Y., Pilogallo, A.: Investigating territorial specialization in tourism sector by ecosystem services approach. In: Stratigea, A., Kavroudakis, D. (eds.) Mediterranean Cities and Island Communities. PROIS, pp. 161–179. Springer, Cham (2019). https://doi.org/10.1007/978-3-319-99444-4_7
21. Pilogallo, A., Saganeiti, L., Scorza, F., Las Casas, G.: Tourism attractiveness: main components for a spacial appraisal of major destinations according with ecosystem services approach. In: Gervasi, O., et al. (eds.) ICCSA 2018. LNCS, vol. 10964, pp. 712–724. Springer, Cham (2018). https://doi.org/10.1007/978-3-319-95174-4_54
22. Leone, F., Zoppi, C., Leone, F., Zoppi, C.: Conservation measures and loss of ecosystem services: a study concerning the sardinian natura 2000 network. Sustainability **8**, 1061 (2016)
23. Cannas, I., Lai, S., Leone, F., Zoppi, C.: Green infrastructure and ecological corridors: a regional study concerning sardinia. Sustainability **10**, 1265 (2018)
24. Lai, S., Leone, F., Zoppi, C.: Implementing green infrastructures beyond protected areas. Sustainability **10**, 3544 (2018)
25. Las Casas, G., Scorza, F.: Sustainable planning: a methodological toolkit. In: Gervasi, O., et al. (eds.) ICCSA 2016. LNCS, vol. 9786, pp. 627–635. Springer, Cham (2016). https://doi.org/10.1007/978-3-319-42085-1_53
26. Las Casas, G., Scorza, F.: A renewed rational approach from liquid society towards anti-fragile planning. In: Gervasi, O., et al. (eds.) ICCSA 2017. LNCS, vol. 10409, pp. 517–526. Springer, Cham (2017). https://doi.org/10.1007/978-3-319-62407-5_36
27. Scorza, F., Santopietro, L., Giuzio, B., Amato, F., Murgante, B., Las Casas, G.: Conflicts between environmental protection and energy regeneration of the historic heritage in the case of the city of Matera: tools for assessing and dimensioning of sustainable energy action plans (SEAP). In: Gervasi, O., et al. (eds.) ICCSA 2017. LNCS, vol. 10409, pp. 527–539. Springer, Cham (2017). https://doi.org/10.1007/978-3-319-62407-5_37
28. Scorza, F., Attolico, A.: Innovations in promoting sustainable development: the local implementation plan designed by the province of Potenza. In: Gervasi, O., et al. (eds.) ICCSA 2015. LNCS, vol. 9156, pp. 756–766. Springer, Cham (2015). https://doi.org/10.1007/978-3-319-21407-8_54
29. Attolico, A., Scorza, F.: A transnational cooperation perspective for "low carbon economy". In: Gervasi, O., et al. (eds.) ICCSA 2016. LNCS, vol. 9786, pp. 636–641. Springer, Cham (2016). https://doi.org/10.1007/978-3-319-42085-1_54

# Investigating Urban Growth Dynamic – Land Surface Temperature Relationship

Angela Pilogallo[(⊠)], Lucia Saganeiti, Francesco Scorza,
and Beniamino Murgante

Laboratory of Urban and Regional Systems Engineering (LISUT),
School of Engineering, University of Basilicata, Viale dell'Ateneo Lucano 10,
85100 Potenza, Italy
{angela.pilogallo,lucia.saganeiti,francesco.scorza,
beniamino.murgante}@unibas.it

**Abstract.** According to the United Nations, 68% of the world's population is expected to live in urban areas by 2050. This makes urban growth one of the cornerstones of sustainable development policies that must be implemented from the outset. Well-managed urbanization is essential to minimize environmental degradation and land use, while maximizing the benefits of agglomeration and ensuring the expected well-being of all city dwellers. On the other hand, it is equally important that these growth dynamics interface systematically with ongoing climate change and its expected effects on the urban environment. Local climate regulation is a crucial urban ecosystem service as it directly affects the quality of urban life. Although its link with soil sealing and land-use change is theoretically known, it is worth explaining this relationship in terms of significant parameters of both altered surfaces and type of urban expansion.

This paper simultaneously analyzes the artificial soils dynamics transformation and land surface temperatures (LST) time series derived by MODIS satellites in a study area, the Basilicata region, widely affected by urban sprinkling and a marked depopulation.

Our results show a strong relationship between the increase in recorded minimum temperatures and the expansion of urban areas, especially where the main growth dynamic is compaction.

**Keywords:** Urban growth · Local worming area · LST · Urban dynamics

## 1 Introduction

The United Nations predicts that by 2050, 68% of the world's population will live in urban areas while the rural population is expected to decline to around 3.1 billion people [1]. This, together with expected climate change impacts, whose most considerable effects are likely to be experienced in urban areas [2], poses a challenge to urban and territorial planners: to develop effective tools capable of supporting sustainable development policies. Actually, the focus of the debate centres on the very concept of sustainable urban development because the question arises as to whether this should aim to increase population density or to allow urban expansion [3].

© Springer Nature Switzerland AG 2019
S. Misra et al. (Eds.): ICCSA 2019, LNCS 11621, pp. 701–710, 2019.
https://doi.org/10.1007/978-3-030-24302-9_51

Within the Italian context, further due consideration should be given to the modalities with which the growth of urban settlements has taken place in the last decades. In fact the globally widespread sprawl model is also flanked by sprinkling, technically defined as land take with a partially spontaneous development or subject to low controls and characterized by not homogeneous built-up areas and coexisting rural/residential/industrial/tertiary functions with very low building and population density [4].

The need to distinguish the evolutionary dynamics of settlements is due to the intensity of the ensuing effects. Damages due to urban sprinkling are much more serious than that caused by sprawl [5] and remedying in the long run is very difficult because it implies, for example, ecosystem fragmentation and thinning of biodiversity hotspots [6].

Assuming that urbanization is always matched by an increase in demand for ecosystem services (ES), what is needed for planning purposes is a deep understanding of ES spatial pattern and their trade-offs [7] resulting from land use/cover changes.

Increasingly within the scientific literature is the recourse to the ES methodological framework to analyse and evaluate change-related scenarios both in urban [3, 8–10] and regional context [11–14].

It is expected to be an useful tool to design land cover/land use change for the purpose of sustainably providing ecosystem services while recognizably meeting societal needs and respecting societal values [15] and therefore capable, when applied to the context under examination, of providing significant support during the policy definition processes that will then regulate urban expansion.

This work, in order to make a contribution to the study of local climate regulation ecosystem services, aims to investigate the relationship between temperature variations that occur between areas characterized by different levels of urbanization and the related development dynamics. It is deemed that climate regulation should be a key aspect of future planning activities because it produces a transversal impact with respect to the dimensions of well-being identified by the Millennium Ecosystem Assessment [16]: it influences the quality of life and the population health [17], effects ecological functions, such as air conditioning [18], and biodiversity [19, 20].

## 2  Materials and Methods

ES approach proves to be more and more promising both in assisting decision-making processes of local and regional environmental management [21] and in providing tools for the evaluation of all the connections between territory and human well-being [22]. The aim of this work is to investigate the relationship between urbanization and local climate regulation ecosystem service, whose importance within the urban context is shown to be growing globally.

Employed methodology is therefore structured into three macro-stages: i. Urbanization and temperatures data historical analysis; ii. Evaluation of the relationship between urban expansion phenomenon and land surface temperatures trend; iii. Discussion of results and conclusions.

In order to understand how the relationship between urbanization and temperature changes on the basis of different variables (e.g. fragmentation degree), the methodology was applied in the Basilicata region, interested by a marked sprinkling and a relevant depopulation [23, 24].

## 2.1 The Basilicata Case Study

Study area is located in Basilicata, a region in Southern Italy with an area of about 10,000 km$^2$ and a population of 567,118 inhabitants [25].

A constantly decreasing birth rate, a natural rate tending to zero and a large migration outflows have led to a constant decline in the population since the 80s.

Despite its population density as of 2014, equal to 57,2 inhabitants per km$^2$, is second only to that of Valle d'Aosta region, Basilicata is not exempt from land take phenomenon. Recent studies [26] confirm that it is among the regions of Southern Italy that show a greater correlation between the variation rates of urbanization and population trend and the highest urban development rates corresponding to the demographic variations.

From previous works [23, 24], it also appears that even urban development dynamics are not typical of the sprawl that characterizes most of the European continent, but attributable to the so called sprinkling [4], very common in the Iberian, Mediterranean and Balkan areas [5].

This expansion model is substantially characterized by very low population and building densities and a high degree of fragmentation with all that follows in terms of social, economic and environmental impacts [27–32].

## 2.2 Dataset

### Land Use Change/Urban Growth

All data on urban areas and aggregates number were calculated regarding a period ranging from 1998 to 2013 and on the basis of geo-topographic regional database (Regional Spatial Data Infrastructure – RSDI [33]) and satellite photos from the national geoportal of the Italian Ministry for the Environment, Land and Sea Protection.

Starting from the latest data on building stock taken from the Regional Technical Map and available at a scale 1:5000, photo-interpretation has been used to create the database for 1998. What is thus obtained is a shapefile of all the buildings featured in the two dates.

In order to identify areas where an increment in urban areas was matched by an increase in fragmentation or in compaction, buildings features have been aggregated.

Every aggregate corresponds to a complex polygon that includes at least two buildings at a relative maximum distance of 50 m. This distance-threshold was driven by the need to better represent the Basilicata settlement system.

### Land Surface Temperature (LST)

Apopular source of Earth's surface temperature estimates based on remote sensing are Moderate Resolution Imaging Spectroradiometer (MODIS) (LST) images, derived from the MODIS temperature bands [34]. MODIS data from the TERRA [35] and AQUA [36] sensors downloaded through the MODIStsp tool of R [37], a tool for automatic preprocessing of MODIS time series, available in open format. In particular, used images have a geometric resolution of 1 km per pixel and a temporal resolution of 8 days. Images of the LST temperature during daylight hours were used for a period between January 2001 and December 2017.

Previous studies [38, 39] have highlighted the variability of LST depending from air temperature and all the factors related to it: altitude, wind speed, surface emissivity, precipitation incidence, time of day, presence of clouds, characteristics of the satellite sensor and mathematical model for LST derivation. However, the purpose of this analysis is investigating the relationship between LST temperature and urban transformation so we considered not very significant this variability.

## 2.3    Methods

The study region has been discretized in a square mesh grid with a size of 1 km. This dimension corresponds to the maximum level of possible detail as it corresponds to the resolution of Modis LST.

Classification of all the cells by evolution dynamic was carried out by jointly considering the change both in artificial surface and in the number of aggregates.

Meshes with any urbanized surfaces in both time sections investigated were classified as "No urbanized" (NO URB); "Not transformed" (NO TRANSF) is instead referred to meshes that have not undergone any change in urbanized areas.

Areas that have been subjected to an increase in artificial surfaces have been further distinguished on the basis of expansion dynamics: "fragmented" (FRAGM) identifies all the areas in which anthropized surfaces increase corresponds to a growth in aggregates number; a reduction in aggregates number and therefore a densification of urban fabric occurred in meshes designated as "compacted" (COMP).

To these classes was added an additional one, named "Unchanged aggregation" (UN_AGGR), in which aggregates have grown in size but not in number. Designations and classification criteria are summarized in Table 1.

**Table 1.**  Criteria for classifying evolution dynamics

| Classification | Anthropized surface variation | Variation in aggregates number |
|---|---|---|
| NO URB | NULL | NULL |
| NO TRANSF | 0 | 0 |
| FRAGM | + | + |
| COMP | + | − |
| UN_AGGR | + | 0 |

For each mesh of this grid, resulting coverage percentage were also calculated.

As far as temperatures are concerned, all the series referring to daytime hours and acquired during the entire period from 2001 to 2017 have been analyzed.

Using GIS raster automated processes, for each cell and for every year considered, maximum daytime temperatures series were computed.

In order to identify the areas that show an aptitude to generate local warming areas, year by year were highlighted the cells in which the minimum temperature was higher than the average for the same year plus once the standard deviation.

Particular attention was therefore paid to the cells that show a change in this behavior as a result of a process of sealing and/or urban growth.

## 3   Results

First analysis aimed at comparing temperature trends and types of evolutionary dynamics. For each cell, classified on the basis of criteria described in Table 1, temperature trend has been then graphically displayed. Minimum, maximum and average values of the data set for the entire period have been graphed.

As it is possible to see on the graphs, a significant trend emerges especially with reference to minimums of maximum daytime temperature. In fact, it emerges that not only are the recorded temperatures higher in cells in which compaction occurred, but also the growth rate is higher than in the cells characterized by different evolution dynamics (Fig. 1).

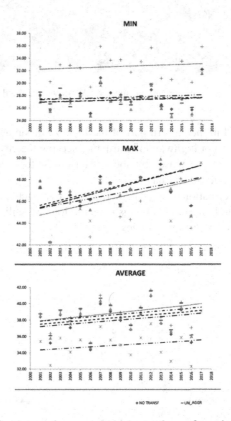

**Fig. 1.** Trend in minimum, maximum and average values of maximums daytime series in relation to evolution dynamics

On the basis of this dataset, local warming areas (LWA) defined on the following criterion have been searched:

$$LWA: \; Registered\,temp. \; > \; (\mathbf{mean\,temp.} + \mathbf{1} * \mathbf{st.\,dev.}) \qquad (1)$$

Analyzing the entire period, areas that show this behavior correspond for Basilicata region to the main industrial areas. Although they have not undergone large variations in anthropized surfaces, their coverage percentage is greater than those registered in correspondence of residential centers.

For the purposes of this work, however, analyses focused on those cells that showed abnormal temperature behavior as a result of artificial surfaces changing.

Within the Basilicata region, in one particular area (see Fig. 2) a considerable result is observed, since a significant increase in the artificial surface corresponds to an anomaly in the behavior of temperatures.

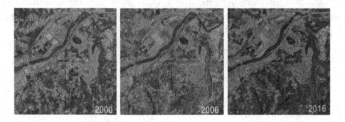

**Fig. 2.** Sealed surface increase in one the LWAs within Basilicata Region

This area is located in the eastern part of the Potenza urban aggregate and extends for 4 Km$^2$ around the major highway infrastructure serving the city. Between 2000 and 2016, artificial surface area increased by about 9% from 38 to 41 ha/km$^2$ resulting in a total sealing surface value of 165 ha.

The type of transformation was characterized by compaction with an increase in artificial surfaces due to both new buildings construction and sailing soil to be used for parking and storage of goods and vehicles.

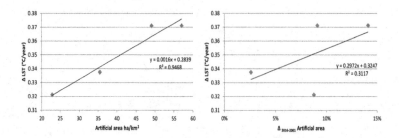

**Fig. 3.** Relationship between average annual LST variation and artificial surfaces increase in terms of final coverage degree (left) and percentage increase (right) in Basilicata case study

In the same period MODIS LST followed a growing trend showing from 2012 onwards a typical behavior of LWA growing at a higher speed than all the cells characterized by the same evolution dynamic.

The relationship between temperature variation and sealed surfaces increase was then analyzed by means of a regression analysis between the average annual increase in recorded temperatures and, respectively, the percentage variation in sealed soil and final coverage value expressed in ha/km$^2$.

As it is possible to see from Fig. 3, a relevant correlation ($R^2 = 0.95$) exists between temperature increase and final coverage degree.

## 4   Conclusions

City's population growth, and the consequent need to densify urban aggregates, is increasingly conflicting with the theme of livability of urban spaces and the services they provide for citizens' well-being.

The methodological framework of ecosystem services can be a support in developing an evaluation panel [40–42] of different transformation kind carried out in urban environment [43] as well at a regional scale.

This work was aimed at investigating the relationship between growth pattern (compaction or fragmentation) and recorded surface temperature, assumed significant for an ecosystem service regulating local climate of urban spaces.

Our results highlight that: 1. cells that have undergone compaction show simultaneously higher temperatures and a faster trend of growth over time; 2. within these areas, the strongest relationship occurs between recorded temperatures and artificial surface ratio.

Deepening this type of approach is considered to be useful in supporting the decision-making process underlying future urban policies and in assessing development scenarios in relation to both environmental sustainability and quality of life.

**Acknowledgements.** This research has been developed within the MEVCSU and INDICARE projects supported by the Environmental Observatory Foundation of Basilicata Region (FARBAS).

## References

1. United Nations: World Urbanization Prospects - Population Division - United Nations. https://population.un.org/wup/Publications/
2. Kabisch, N., et al.: Nature-based solutions to climate change mitigation and adaptation in urban areas: perspectives on indicators, knowledge gaps, barriers, and opportunities for action. Ecol. Soc. **21**, art39 (2016). https://doi.org/10.5751/ES-08373-210239
3. Bolund, P., Hunhammar, S.: Ecosystem services in urban areas (1999)
4. Romano, B., Zullo, F., Fiorini, L., Ciabò, S., Marucci, A.: Sprinkling: an approach to describe urbanization dynamics in Italy. https://doi.org/10.3390/su9010097
5. Romano, B., Zullo, F., Fiorini, L., Marucci, A., Ciabò, S.: Land transformation of Italy due to half a century of urbanization. Land Use Policy **67**, 387–400 (2017). https://doi.org/10.1016/J.LANDUSEPOL.2017.06.006

6. Fiorini, L., Marucci, A., Zullo, F., Romano, B.: Indicator engineering for land take control and settlement sustainability. WIT Trans. Ecol. Environ. **217**, 437–446 (2018). https://doi.org/10.2495/SDP180391

7. Haase, D., Schwarz, N., Strohbach, M., Kroll, F., Seppelt, R.: Synergies, trade-offs, and losses of ecosystem services in urban regions: an integrated multiscale framework applied to the Leipzig-Halle Region, Germany. Ecol. Soc. **17**, art22 (2012). https://doi.org/10.5751/ES-04853-170322

8. Hu, Y., Zhang, Y., Ke, X., Hu, Y., Zhang, Y., Ke, X.: Dynamics of tradeoffs between economic benefits and ecosystem services due to urban expansion. Sustainability **10**, 2306 (2018). https://doi.org/10.3390/su10072306

9. Tratalos, J., Fuller, R.A., Warren, P.H., Davies, R.G., Gaston, K.J.: Urban form, biodiversity potential and ecosystem services. Landsc. Urban Plan. **83**, 308–317 (2007). https://doi.org/10.1016/j.landurbplan.2007.05.003

10. Grafius, D.R., Corstanje, R., Harris, J.A.: Linking ecosystem services, urban form and green space configuration using multivariate landscape metric analysis. Landsc. Ecol. **33**, 557–573 (2018). https://doi.org/10.1007/s10980-018-0618-z

11. Burkhard, B., Kroll, F., Müller, F.: Landscapes' capacities to provide ecosystem services – a concept for land-cover based assessments. Landsc. Online **15**, 1–22 (2010). https://doi.org/10.3097/LO.200915

12. Sharma, R., et al.: Modeling land use and land cover changes and their effects on biodiversity in Central Kalimantan, Indonesia. Land **7**, 57 (2018). https://doi.org/10.3390/land7020057

13. Zhou, J., et al.: Effects of the land use change on ecosystem service value. Glob. J. Environ. Sci. Manag. **3**, 121–130 (2017). https://doi.org/10.22034/GJESM.2017.03.02.001

14. Polasky, S., Nelson, E., Pennington, D., Johnson, K.A.: The impact of land-use change on ecosystem services, biodiversity and returns to landowners: a case study in the State of Minnesota. Environ. Resour. Econ. **48**, 219–242 (2011). https://doi.org/10.1007/s10640-010-9407-0

15. Wu, J.: Landscape sustainability science: ecosystem services and human well-being in changing landscapes. Landsc. Ecol. **28**, 999–1023 (2013). https://doi.org/10.1007/s10980-013-9894-9

16. Alcamo, J., Bennett, E.M.: Millennium Ecosystem Assessment (Program): Ecosystems and Human Well-Being: A Framework for Assessment. Island Press, Washington, D.C. (2003)

17. Lafortezza, R., Carrus, G., Sanesi, G., Davies, C.: Benefits and well-being perceived by people visiting green spaces in periods of heat stress. Urban For. Urban Green. **8**, 97–108 (2009). https://doi.org/10.1016/j.ufug.2009.02.003

18. Grimm, N.B., et al.: Global change and the ecology of cities. Science **319**, 756–760 (2008). https://doi.org/10.1126/science.1150195

19. Čeplová, N., Kalusová, V., Lososová, Z.: Effects of settlement size, urban heat island and habitat type on urban plant biodiversity. Landsc. Urban Plan. **159**, 15–22 (2017). https://doi.org/10.1016/j.landurbplan.2016.11.004

20. Kaiser, A., Merckx, T., Van Dyck, H.: The Urban Heat Island and its spatial scale dependent impact on survival and development in butterflies of different thermal sensitivity. Ecol. Evol. **6**, 4129–4140 (2016). https://doi.org/10.1002/ece3.2166

21. Hou, Y., Müller, F., Li, B., Kroll, F.: Urban-rural gradients of ecosystem services and the linkages with socioeconomics. Landsc. Online **39**, 1–31 (2015). https://doi.org/10.3097/LO.201539

22. Haines-Young, R., Potschin, M.: The links between biodiversity, ecosystem services and human well-being. In: Raffaelli, D.G., Frid, C.L.J. (eds.) Ecosystem Ecology, pp. 110–139. Cambridge University Press, Cambridge (2010). https://doi.org/10.1017/CBO9780511 750458.007

23. Saganeiti, L., Favale, A., Pilogallo, A., Scorza, F., Murgante, B.: Assessing urban fragmentation at regional scale using sprinkling indexes. Sustainability **10**, 3274 (2018). https://doi.org/10.3390/su10093274

24. Saganeiti, L., Pilogallo, A., Scorza, F., Mussuto, G., Murgante, B.: Spatial indicators to evaluate urban fragmentation in Basilicata Region. In: Gervasi, O., et al. (eds.) ICCSA 2018. LNCS, vol. 10964, pp. 100–112. Springer, Cham (2018). https://doi.org/10.1007/978-3-319-95174-4_8

25. Istat. http://dati.istat.it/

26. Fiorini, L., Zullo, F., Marucci, A., Romano, B.: Land take and landscape loss: effect of uncontrolled urbanization in Southern Italy. J. Urban Manag. **8**, 42–56 (2019). https://doi.org/10.1016/J.JUM.2018.09.003

27. Larondelle, N., Haase, D., Kabisch, N.: Mapping the diversity of regulating ecosystem services in European Cities. Glob. Environ. Chang. **26**, 119–129 (2014)

28. Martellozzo, F., Amato, F., Murgante, B., Clarke, K.C.: Modelling the impact of urban growth on agriculture and natural land in Italy to 2030. Appl. Geogr. **91**, 156–167 (2018). https://doi.org/10.1016/j.apgeog.2017.12.004

29. Amato, F., Maimone, B.A., Martellozzo, F., Nolè, G., Murgante, B.: The effects of urban policies on the development of urban areas. Sustainability **8**, 297 (2016). https://doi.org/10.3390/su8040297

30. Amato, F., Martellozzo, F., Nolè, G., Murgante, B.: Preserving cultural heritage by supporting landscape planning with quantitative predictions of soil consumption. J. Cult. Herit. **23**, 44–54 (2017). https://doi.org/10.1016/j.culher.2015.12.009

31. Gomes, E.: Assessing the effect of spatial proximity on urban growth. Sustainability (2018). https://doi.org/10.3390/su10051308

32. Dupras, J., et al.: Environmental science and policy the impacts of urban sprawl on ecological connectivity in the Montreal Metropolitan Region. Environ. Sci. Policy **58**, 61–73 (2016). https://doi.org/10.1016/j.envsci.2016.01.005

33. RSDI – Geoportale Basilicata. https://rsdi.regione.basilicata.it/

34. Vaz, E., Nijkamp, P.: Gravitational forces in the spatial impacts of urban sprawl: an investigation of the region of Veneto, Italy. Habitat Int. **45**, 99–105 (2015). https://doi.org/10.1016/j.habitatint.2014.06.024

35. Hengl, T., Heuvelink, G.B.M., Perčec Tadić, M., Pebesma, E.J.: Spatio-temporal prediction of daily temperatures using time-series of MODIS LST images. Theor. Appl. Climatol. **107**, 265–277 (2012). https://doi.org/10.1007/s00704-011-0464-2

36. Wan, Z., Hook, S., Hulley, G.: MOD11A2 MODIS/Terra Land Surface Temperature/Emissivity 8-Day L3 Global 1 km SIN Grid V006 [Data set] (2015). https://doi.org/10.5067/MODIS/MOD11A2.006

37. Wan, Z., Hook, S., Hulley, G.: MYD11A2 MODIS/Aqua Land Surface Temperature/Emissivity 8-Day L3 Global 1 km SIN Grid V006 [Data set] (2015). https://doi.org/10.5067/MODIS/MYD11A2.006

38. Busetto, L., Ranghetti, L.: MODIStsp: an R package for automatic preprocessing of MODIS land products time series. Comput. Geosci. **97**, 40–48 (2016). https://doi.org/10.1016/J.CAGEO.2016.08.020

39. Arnfield, A.J.: Two decades of urban climate research: a review of turbulence, exchanges of energy and water, and the urban heat Island. Int. J. Climatol. **23**, 1–26 (2003). https://doi.org/10.1002/joc.859

40. Mazzariello, A., Pilogallo, A., Scorza, F., Murgante, B., Las Casas, G.: Carbon stock as an indicator for the estimation of anthropic pressure on territorial components. In: Gervasi, O., et al. (eds.) ICCSA 2018. LNCS, vol. 10964, pp. 697–711. Springer, Cham (2018). https://doi.org/10.1007/978-3-319-95174-4_53

41. Scorza, F., Pilogallo, A., Las Casas, G.: Investigating tourism attractiveness in inland areas: ecosystem services, open data and smart specializations. In: Calabrò, F., Della Spina, L., Bevilacqua, C. (eds.) ISHT 2018. SIST, vol. 100, pp. 30–38. Springer, Cham (2019). https://doi.org/10.1007/978-3-319-92099-3_4

42. Pilogallo, A., Saganeiti, L., Scorza, F., Las Casas, G.: Tourism attractiveness: main components for a spacial appraisal of major destinations according with ecosystem services approach. In: Gervasi, O., et al. (eds.) ICCSA 2018. LNCS, vol. 10964, pp. 712–724. Springer, Cham (2018). https://doi.org/10.1007/978-3-319-95174-4_54

43. Scorza, F.: Towards self energy-management and sustainable citizens' engagement in local energy efficiency agenda. Int. J. Agric. Environ. Inf. Syst. 7, 44–53 (2016). https://doi.org/10.4018/IJAEIS.2016010103

# Geospatial Database for the Generation of Multidimensional Virtual City Models Dedicated to Urban Analysis and Decision-Making

Andreas Fricke$^{(\boxtimes)}$ (iD) and Hartmut Asche

Hasso Plattner Institute, Digital Engineering Faculty, University of Potsdam,
Prof.-Dr.-Helmert-Str. 2-3, 14482 Potsdam, Germany
{andreas.fricke,hartmut.asche}@hpi.de

**Abstract.** The provision of a data base for the digital representation of a virtual spatial model is used as an example to demonstrate how a geographical problem solution can be achieved using modern service-based techniques and methods. Moreover it is explained which problems exist in the spectrum of digital twins and spatial databases with regard to the handling of ubiquitous geodata, which necessitate the conception of a new service-oriented approach. The database as the central medium towards a virtual representation of the urban environment is a particular focus. Ubiquitous geospatial data demand meaningful tools for integration and harmonisation, which are also included as part of a modular process chain. In this approach, procedures and workflow are designed on the basis of generic data models and standard schemes, with the aim of ensuring transparency and transferability, both methodologically and spatially. A workflow describing data acquisition, processing and utilisation is presented and exemplified by the Middle Eastern agglomeration region of East Jerusalem.

**Keywords:** Multidimensional virtual city model · Web-based platform ·
Database · Data model · Stereo imagery · Service-oriented computing ·
East Jerusalem

## 1 Introduction

Current geoinformation systems have not been designed to amalgamate and process heterogeneous, multidimensional geospatial data from different sources. It is hence not without limitations that this data can be used effectively and universally. What is lacking, in particular, is a geospatial processing and analysis environment including a harmonised, dynamic geospatial database continuous updating procedures as well as easy user access to elementary and specialist functionalities. The immense amount of unstructured, unfiltered data and a multitude of extensive software systems simply make it difficult for the non-professional user, in particular, to manage even simple problems with spatial data.

© Springer Nature Switzerland AG 2019
S. Misra et al. (Eds.): ICCSA 2019, LNCS 11621, pp. 711–726, 2019.
https://doi.org/10.1007/978-3-030-24302-9_52

## 2  Study Area

In order to make a comprehensive statement about the effectiveness of the approach, the special form of the Middle Eastern urban agglomeration area of East Jerusalem is chosen as the research area. In general, the form of connected human settlements is characterised as an urban agglomeration or extended urban space [1]. It consists of built-up areas of a central location and related suburbs linked by a corresponding contiguous urban area. According to INSEE [2], the concept of urban units is based on the continuity of buildings and the number of inhabitants. An urban unit is a municipality or a group of municipalities with a continuous building zone (not more than 200 m between two buildings) with at least 2,000 inhabitants. If the urban unit is located in a single municipality, it is an isolated city. If the urban unit extends over several communes and each of these communes concentrates more than half of its population in the contiguous construction zone, it is a multi-montane agglomeration. Rural municipalities are those that do not fit into the constitution of an urban unit. This means municipalities without a continuous construction zone of 2,000 inhabitants and those in which less than half of the urban population is located in a continuous construction zone [1]. Agglomeration regions with a strong urban character can also be described as metropolitan regions. The functional urban region and urban agglomerations are highly integrated functional areas - complementary functions of different levels at different locations to provide the population with all necessities - from housing function to jobs to education, shopping and use of various services; related to Christaller's theory of central places. Urban agglomerations allow for services of all hierarchies up to the highest to be offered efficiently, as the various hierarchical services are located in close distances and serve a large number of people living closely together or collaborating (Fig. 1).

**Fig. 1.**  Aerial view of a typical urban agglomeration in the Middle East. Source: wikimedia.org

The study area of a Middle Eastern urban agglomeration represents a peculiarity and adaptation of the classical concept of urban agglomeration in that it also takes up the fine granularity in the structure of vertical and horizontal building, distribution and diverse use. Both urban and rural units are interconnected and allow an almost complete geographical analysis and assessment of the contrasts. The area under study includes East Jerusalem – the Old Town, excluding the city of Jerusalem - which was a part of Jordan from the Palestinian War of 1948 until conquered by Israel in the Six-Day War of 1967. East Jerusalem is the urban type of a classical oriental city. This urban type is interesting as there have been only a few major urban transformations over time. What characterises the region in particular is a constant urban expansion following Western and European models, which is reflected in the heterogeneity of the urban region. Basically, this process, which took place in many oriental cities, is transferable. It is therefore of great interest to understand the structure and context of the urban agglomeration of East Jerusalem and also to generate the digital representation of this region. The digital representation can allow to obtain a clear insight into the difficult acquisition, modelling and processing of the geographical conditions, in also allowing a comparability of possible future changes.

# 3 Data Modelling, Acquisition, and Management

In order to maintain a complete database of the relevant spatial entities as up-to-date as possible, it is necessary to consider a variety of available data sources. Nowadays, the problem is usually not the availability of geodata, but its heterogeneous nature. It is not easily possible to utilise all available sources with and among each other, since there is a lack of data models and schemes that could guarantee a successful integration and harmonisation [3]. In order to check the usability of existing data, it is necessary to select the relevant objects and combine them in an object type catalogue. The object type catalogue provides the basis on which existing schemes can be selected, adapted or newly developed. The schemes represent the link between the object type catalogue as data modelling, and the technical implementation in as structure and mapping in a database. Schemes should be designed as generic as possible and as detailed as necessary. The result is an abstract model that organises and standardises elements of data and how they relate to each other and to the properties of the real world.

## 3.1 Data Model, Objects, and Schemes

Data modelling is a term used in methodologies for the formal representation of objects relevant in a defined context by means of their attributes and relationships at the conceptual level. The main goal of data modelling is the unambiguous definition and specification of objects and the assignment and management of their attributes required for information purposes and their relations and dependencies between objects in order to obtain an overview of the data view for an information system [4].

The result of modelling are data models which, after potentially recursive modelling steps, finally lead to usable data schemes or data bases (conceptual, logical, physical schemata). Databases are thus the technically enhanced conceptual data model and allow for its application with certain adaptations. As a rule, data models have a much longer lifespan and persistence than functions and processes (software systems), since they are detached from the technical level by the basic conceptual idea and thus are less susceptible to changes in a process [5]. It is true that data is more stable, but functions are not. Transferred to the use case, this means the identification of the relevant information requirement (attributes), whereby entity types and relationship types are identified and assigned. In addition, possible attribute values or proposals of attributes to be identified are determined. Finally, relationship cardinalities and the functional description of the entity and relationship types as well as the attributes are fixed. Under the premise of simplicity transferred to the application case of a Middle Eastern urban agglomeration, this means that an extremely generic basic data model can be derived: Each relevant object is unique and can be represented by multiple geometries and by multiple semantic attributes (rich information) as shown in Table 1.

**Table 1.** Comparison for the data model of relevant urban objects and rich information.

| Relevant urban objects | Rich information |
| --- | --- |
| Built environments (buildings, infrastructure) | Geometries or appearances |
| Natural features (terrain, vegetation, land use) | Semantics or attributes |
| Utility networks | Decompositions and relations |

Schemas are used to adapt the conceptual data models for application and transfer into a database and thus to coin them onto a database system. The INSPIRE schemes serve to ensure a long-term and as generic as possible technical convergence of the systematics, as the European Union has committed its member states to maintain all official geodata based on these schemes in the future. All functionalities and processes of integration and harmonisation, as already described in [8], take place via direct access in an INSPIRE compliant exchange scheme on the database. A feature catalogue provides an informative overview of the spatial object types and data types defined in the INSPIRE, providing implementers and decision makers with an easy introduction to the INSPIRE data models and data specifications. The INSPIRE Implementing Rules on Interoperability of Spatial Data Sets and Services and Technical Guidelines (Data Specifications) define common data models, code lists, map layers and additional metadata on interoperability to be used when exchanging spatial data sets [6].

### 3.2 Multi-dimensional Geodata

In many disciplines, two-dimensional data sets are the ones to choose. While two- and higher-dimensional data sets are multi-dimensional, the term multidimensional tends to be applied only to data sets with three or more dimensions. Normally, when thinking about multi-dimensional data, they are characterised by time or multiple phenomena obtained. Typically, the geographical dimension is limited to 3+1D (spatially and temporally). In fact, combining time series and cross-sectional data can be thought of as daily issues in the geospatial domain. But often these analyses or standard tasks are limited to one dimension only. As an example, weather forecast data sets provide forecasts for multiple target periods, conducted by multiple forecasters or automated models, and made at multiple horizons. Both semantic and numerical attributes help to generate an increased information space, which can be made addressable and usable. The multiple dimensions provide more information than can be gathered from two-dimensional data sets. Therefore, multi-dimensionality has two meanings which both are important but require different strategies [6]. The tricky task is to combine both in a flexible process chain to take advantage of different perspectives of one and the same object. The solution are partial reverse engineering techniques as a generalisation, where the most important facts are a multidimensional database based on different resources, while reverse engineering is used as a search for identical characteristics in different scales, harmonisation and homogenisation of geodata to enable geoprocessing at runtime.

### 3.3 Generalisation of Multi-dimensional Geodata as Data Integration

Generalisation is known and necessary for many different tasks, areas and applications. Nevertheless, their meaning could be described as simplification or abstraction, in order to ultimately obtain a more universal insight and evidence for a tested behaviour.

The process generally includes reducing complexity, emphasising the essential and suppressing the unimportant, maintaining the relationship between objects while maintaining a defined quality [7]. Last but not least, it is a process of semantic and numerical solution reduction. Quality is the selection and simplified representation of a detail, appropriate scope and/or purpose of an application, of various processes arising from the data source through the application of transformations, as derivation objectives are to reduce data in terms of quantity, type and cartographic representation, whilst maintaining consistency and clarity of representation. Thus, the term generalisation is divided into two main parts [7]. Model generalisation as new conceptualisation of phenomena (mostly qualitative extension) and visual generalisation as new structural representation of Phenomena (mostly quantitative). In either case, both types of generalisation aim at isolating the features that are independent of both feature and domain resolution. In addition, it also defines the capture in a software architecture. The proposed software architecture makes it possible to instantiate this method as a web-based service system. This means that users can adapt the system to their specific (micro-) task or workflow [8], regardless of their level of knowledge or professional affiliation. It is designed in such a way that it enables a complete division of the process chain as micro-tasks. The architecture is designed to meet two non-functional requirements: Scalability (vertical and horizontal) and adaptability (deployment and runtime). Included are experiments to evaluate these two requirements in terms of quality assurance and performance issues.

## 3.4   Data Acquisition

A problem with the use of existing data sources consists in the fact that these data sources are usually not available across the entire study area, be it in their extent, their characteristics or their quality [7]. In this approach, a basic data set is therefore derived from a uniform remote sensing data set, which is subsequently enriched and expanded with further existing data sources. This ensures that a basic level of comparability can be guaranteed as a reference in the study area.

Several methods exist which are appropriate to collect a comprehensive basic data set. Since the study area is characterised by a high heterogeneity and classical in-situ methods do not appear to be effective in terms of cost/benefit, a remote sensing campaign is used instead. For this purpose, high-resolution aerial imagery of the area is evaluated by methods of stereo photogrammetry. In the course of each photogram-metric analysis, pixels in at least two different images of the same spatial area are compared and three-dimensional coordinates are derived using compensation func-tions. This method is called matching in modern software systems. Influencing factors are primarily the visibility of two identical image-object points (image overlap) and the probability that the same image-object point is encountered. An increased resolution of the input data, however, only plays a subordinate role.

In sum, digital surface models can be derived for overlapping image areas. Nowadays, digital surface models are usually made available on a raster basis. A characteristic of raster data, however, is the basic regular generalisation through its cell-based data structure (Fig. 2).

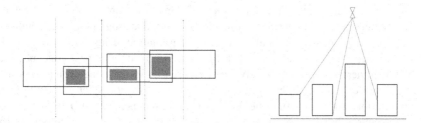

**Fig. 2.**  Schematic overview of different flight strips (rectangles) and overlapping areas in dark grey (left) and potential image-object rays with respect to visibility of buildings (right).

In order to process a surface model as objectively as possible, the result of the image matching is used for the further workflow instead. This result is characterised by irregular and inhomogeneously distributed points of the overlapping area of the pho-togrammetric analysis. This intermediate product is also called a point cloud. A dis-tinction is made between the sparse cloud and the dense cloud. Depending on the software system and implementation, the sparse cloud is the result of a pre-allocation of all images and overlapping areas in a bundle block (Fig. 3).

In a first iteration a mostly regular assignment of image-object points is made for each overlapping area, which is condensed in a second iteration, thus becoming a dense cloud until the squared resolution of the input data is reached at most; unless the subpixel area is used. This means that at an input resolution of 10 cm Ground Sampling Distance a theoretical dense cloud with a density of 10 * 10 points per square meter (100 points) can be derived.

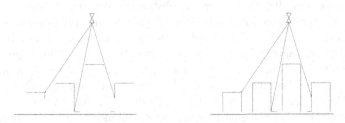

**Fig. 3.** Schematic overview of the visible image-object points of buildings and ground (left). The representation including building and ground points to be reconstructed (right).

### 3.5 Data Management

With the advent of digitalisation and the ever-growing volume of data, new disciplines (data science) have been opened up in information technology and related disciplines to address the scaling problem facing today's software systems and users. File sizes and file occurrences are multiplying in many domains, although this fact does not constitute the whole problem. Rather it is the awareness and the way in which data is stored, analysed and made usable [9]. Especially in the domain of geoinformatics, this functionality can be implemented with a database and database management system even with growing data and data volumes. In software development, working with databases is a must. But for people in other subdomains of computer science (e.g. with GIS) the advantages of a database may not always be so obvious. People tend to use the most familiar tools, such as classical monolithic GIS, although it is not the most efficient way to achieve goals. But abandoning the quasi-standards can provide great benefits. The data management is implemented as part of a modular process chain [8], which aims at realising the digital representation of the urban agglomeration of the East Jerusalem region in a web-based software environment on the basis of the derived area-wide basic data set [10].

## 4   Digital Twin vs Model

A digital twin is a digital replica of a physical object, device, system, place or person. Originally, digital twins were used in manufacturing to represent real devices, machines, factories and plants. For example, sensors attached to machines over an entire production line route data through an IoT network that can be accessed interactively.

The myth of the digital twin is based on ensuring a complete digital representation of a real object. This does not match the concept of model, since the fundamental principle is to abstract and generalise. Thus, it is the data of a digital twin as a visual model that assumes the form of representation and functions as an information medium. In contrast to geoinformatics, the digital twin is regarded in computer graphics as the most accurate image of a real object. In geoinformation science, however, the focus is always on the digital model, whose degree of abstraction serves as the basis for a variety of applications [9]. Models serve as abstraction of reality for better analysis in a wide range of applications. They differ in the degree of similarity defined and required by a particular application. Digital twins, on the other hand, are usually the most accurate image of reality, although they represent only one model due to possible fine-granular differences to the reference, reality. Therefore, digital twins are also called "Look-a-Like", "Feel-a-Like", "Work-a-Like", because the focus is often not on the solution of an application problem, but rather on the representation of reality in certain forms. The functions of a digital twin are usually limited to a few individuals. The spatial reference and the application context usually play a subordinate role. In contrast, digital twins as a model have a very low modelling depth with respect to classical spatial applications, since its degree of abstraction is very low. The degree of realisation is very high, therefore it is realistic, although the focus is still on technical processing and presentation. However, this is a limiting factor insofar as it falls below the limit of perception in terms of closeness to reality. For a large part of the applications, however, this is technically conceivable, but irrelevant, since it does not contribute to better presenting or solving a problem [6]. At this point, the different approaches of the aforementioned scientific disciplines become clear, although both use the example of the virtual city model to work on the same application. This corresponds to the observation of a continuum that reflects iconicity [11]. Both disciplines approach each other bipolarly, but always with different emphases on modelling and "look-a-like". However, there are points of contact that form the basis of this research. The application, which is based, among other things, on geodata, can certainly benefit from the complementary combination of different concepts, techniques and processes [6]. However, this offers the possibility to branch evaluations and analyses into specific assets for an improved root cause analysis and a multitude of new use cases for improved manufacturing processes. Digital twins help companies outperform previous performance levels in various aspects of manufacturing, from the product design phase to supply chain management. The main tasks and advantages of a digital twin are summarised:

- Monitoring (Unsurpassed level of monitoring)
- Maintenance (From reactive to predictive approach)
- Training (Education and guidance)
- Communication (Analytical information generation and accessibility)
- Strategy (Testing and improvements and traceability)

All different components of a physical object that are emulated, identified and described in a structured way with a digital twin are part of a multi-dimensional model. An accurate and comprehensive virtual model allows for visualising how the physical real object functions, behaves and changes at the moment. The biggest challenge for a digital twin of an urban city is that one model does not fit all. In other words, a model is needed that is as generic as possible and as domain-specific as necessary. Conversely, a digital twin would be needed for each individual image of an urban space. This is due to the fact that each urban or metropolitan region has functional spatial structures that can be expressed in socio-economic and socio-demographic differences. A generic digital twin is thus a modelled, abstract and generalised instance of the real world [12]. It is therefore a model of reality and no longer a digital twin, although the basic principles of the twin are maintained. However, the basic population of objects and data patterns that characterises an urban Middle Eastern agglomeration are the greatest common denominator and testify to the fact that a transparent transfer to different regions and spatial structures is at least possible.

## 5   Technical Objectives of a Geospatial Database

During the last decade of the century, database systems such as the open source PostGIS have developed into reasonably usable media that can be used effectively with the problems described in dealing with geodata. Today, however, most software developers assume, as they did ten years ago, that the design of scalable geodatabases is a simple task. As it turned out, at the beginning of 2000, there was not even the computer science necessary to design such things. Typical methods for representing dynamic geodata, from R trees or hyper dimensional hashing to space-filling curves, were all developed using techniques from the 1980s or earlier [13]. Geodatabases, at the level of the basics of computer science and implementations, are not linked to conventional databases at all. The superficial similarities hide countless design challenges that are specific to geodata models. All architectural differences must therefore be regarded as lessons to be mastered and manifested as critical faults in real applications. Predominant algorithms in the scientific discipline of computer science apply, with few exceptions, only those properties that are unique to one-dimensional scalar data models. This means that an abstraction to the integer already takes place in the data type definition. This circumstance is problematic, since multi-dimensional data are also represented reductively in this way in predominant database systems. A data model that is not scalar in its nature can only be represented with some difficulties using current methods. There are only a few operatively used systems that can handle non-scalar data types like paths, vectors, polygons and other elementary aggregations of scalar coordinates used in spatial analysis [13].

The reason for this is relatively profane: Computational relations today are always topological and not graphic. Geodata types include interval data types as well as some other common data types. An interval data type cannot be represented with less than two single values of any dimensionality, such as the boundary of a hyper rectangle. Interval data types differ from scalar types in two important aspects: Sets have no meaningful linearisation and intersection relationships are not synonymous with equality relationships. The algorithms that exist in the literature for interval data are simply not applicable for the use in the context of geographical issues due to the existing discrepancy. For example, there are no dynamic sharding algorithms that produce even distributions of interval data. Furthermore, there is no general partitioning function that distributes n-dimensional interval data evenly in n-dimensional space. Hash and range partitioning, which in this context is essentially just a distributed quad tree, have been shown to be wrong-headed decisions, but are still popular in naive ubiquitous implementations. Interval indexing algorithms in the literature are either not scalable or not general [13]. The R-Tree family of algorithms, the traditional choice for small datasets, cannot scale even in theory. The quad tree algorithm family is pathological to interval data. Since R-trees were invented to replace quad trees for this reason, the quad tree algorithm family is not suitable for interval data. Sophisticated variants of raster indexing (tiling) can be scaled for static interval data, but are unsuccessful for dynamic data, and most software engineers use variants that are even more naive in practice because they are quasi standard. The basic phenomenon and problem are that interval data sets do not have a usable order. The assumption that data is sortable is so widespread in computer science that many design patterns are either useless or simply wrong when applied to interval data, despite supposed results. For example, which is the best storage format for an analytical geodatabase is not obvious. Many storage formats, such as those used in columnar databases, make compromises that require the sortability of scalar data types [6].

### 5.1 Geospatial Databases in Times of Big Data

The problem described here increases in times of Big Data. The original use of most geographic databases was primarily to create maps, such as geospatial models, which can be displayed as image tiles or paper products. Mapping databases evolved in an environment where the data sets were small, rarely changed, the production of a finished edition could take days, and updating and continuation could be cyclical. However, modern spatial applications are increasingly based on real-time spatial analysis and contextualisation of data from the IoT, sensor networks and mobile platforms. These workloads have little in common with the original use cases. In fact, these workloads are different from all the workloads studied in database literature [14]. The basic problem is that there is no existing design that could be copied or that could support this use case.

For a modern spatial question and application, an optimised database engine must be designed and implemented according to the basic principles, which requires an increased level of capabilities and the lay user, who is mainly the user, faces unsolvable problems. Many geospatial data sources continuously generate data at extremely high rates. Not only are complex geospatial data analysed, indexed and stored, but low-latency queries against incoming and historical data that cannot be aggregated are also possible. Also much praised in-memory databases are useless here, since the volume of online data, for example, is quickly too large. Although technically feasible, virtually no databases have yet been developed for these applications. However, this again reflects the typical organisation of scalar data models and is therefore difficult to implement. Geographical applications are typically highly distorted and shift unpredictably across the data model [9]. Traditional skew and hotspot mitigation strategies, based on a priori assumptions about workload distribution and hard-coded in software such as those used for processing time series data, are largely useless in the geospatial domain. The adaptive reduction of severe and unpredictable hotspots is therefore a novel architectural requirement.

## 5.2    Database Engineering Missed Geospatial Requirements

Geospatial operators are inherently built around computer-aided geometry primitives. Looking up a description of the Vincenty algorithm, for example, is simple. The implementation of non-Euclidean operators, on the other hand, which are generally correct, precise and fast, exceeds the knowledge of most programmers. Implementations developed for cartographic and GIS application cases typically do not have the performance and precision required for analytics [9]. Analytics require the creation of responses in a time frame that counts with tiny and accurately characterised error limits. In practice, performance is often so miserable that commercial providers provide analytical results that are delivered in weeks for datasets that might not fit into memory. The reliable generation of correct and precise calculation results from complex geometry operations is known to be difficult to achieve, especially on a scale of urban agglomerations heterogeneity. This may be sufficient to produce maps, but it is almost useless for modern sensor analysis applications in times of digital twins [12]. The physical world is non-Euclidean. This creates horizon effects even within a single large building. The simplest geometric surface that still applies to most calculations is a geodetic ellipsoid. The computationally simpler approximations used by many common platforms under the hood work for maps, but not for spatial analysis. Geodata analysis requires the ability to perform polygon sections quickly. Polygon section algorithms, such as relational joins, are quadratic in nature. Naively intersecting polygons with thousands of nodes, as are common in some industries, can require millions of high-precision geodetic operations to evaluate a data set. This can be quickly multiplied by billions of data sets and the query cannot be completed in a month. The computational geometry must be precise when it comes to analysis. For trivial algebraic geometry, it is not difficult to guarantee error limits in floating-point calculations. However, most programmers do not realize that the transcendental functions implemented in their CPUs have significant precision losses in a variety of edge cases that need to be considered. On the scale of these data sets, edge cases are quickly and frequently tested [6].

It is clear that there are currently a large number of problems with the existence and use of databases in the context of spatial applications. However, these problems are not trivial and there is a small trend towards solving these problems that are not contained in public informatics literature. With the advent of mobile, IoT and sensor analytics as high-value markets, any database platform is in the process of at least enabling spatial analysis [15]. However, as described above, it is challenging to add adequate support for powerful spatial analysis to databases that have not been developed specifically for such use. There is ample evidence that many database companies have tried and failed, or that the products are being mistakenly presented as a geospatial database and as standard. From a database architecture perspective, the cause of the problem is that the internals of a database system that has been developed for traditional text and number data models are virtually everything but have a very limited link to a database system that is needed for spatial (real-time) data models. No amount of software duct tape bypasses this impedance mismatch, but most laymen try to build a geographic database. Geodatabases are difficult to create at best. They are almost impossible to build, as long as it is naively and predestined that they are essentially the same as traditional databases with a certain amount of geographical dispersion over them [8].

# 6  A Multi-usable Database for Virtual City Models

Addressing this issue, a comprehensive multi-usable database is built, embedded in a web-based, modular geospatial software environment that meets the requirements of seamless processing, analysis and visualisation of multidimensional geodata. Built to the principles of service-oriented computing, the geospatial database and the service platform is accessed via a string of web services targeted to non-expert users as well as experts of different application domains. By using the respective services, the lay audience will have restricted access to the system allowing them to select, process, analyse and visualise all data required for a particular application problem, such as location analysis of a community building. Experts will have full access to all system functionalities to perform more complex processing and analysis tasks, such as advanced network analysis of public transport. This geospatial service platform is designed for the use of stakeholders, both professional and non-professional, in urban agglomerations of the Middle East with particular attention to the communities of East Jerusalem. The desired modular components are shown in Fig. 4.

## 6.1  The Conceptualised Digital Twin of an Urban Environment

The first step in creating a digital representation (digital twin) is to characterise all components of an existing physical object in a virtual proxy. Given the complex nature of the Middle Eastern urban agglomeration that is digitally replicated, there are thousands of different components that represent the style and structure of the model. Therefore, a comprehensive basic data set is derived from stereophotogrammetric high-resolution image data for the entire study area. Using the intermediate product of point clouds, a first robust version of the digital twin sketches the objects of the building type exemplarily and stores these in a database. For example, a multi-dimensional model of a building in the study area can show how a Middle Eastern building is divided in its functional structure. Furthermore, on the basis of geostatical analyses, it can be recognised or deduced how certain facts affect the environment or whether improvements need to be made [15]. The digital representation therefore serves as a test medium for the real world, as long as the model is fed with up-to-date data. Due to the granular, highly varied nature of the objects constituting the urban fabric, processing needs to deal with different planimetric and vertical spatial as well as semantic dimensions and accuracies. This poses a major problem for precise photogrammetric image processing and subsequent construction of high-resolution 3D city models in oriental cities such as East Jerusalem.

The fundamental question that arises, however, is which form of representation (degree of iconicity) is sufficient to address a spatial question. In most cases, it is only a simplified geometry that offers an added value through semantic enrichment and can be used for decision support. Following this assumption, it is also sufficient to enrich a simple LOD1 geometry model with semantic data in order to add it to the database.

Any analysis that requires the spatial location as a base can be served in this way. The degree of detail, or conversely, the abstract level of the geometry has fewer effects. There are unique object primitives that are necessary. These object primitives are assigned geometries and semantics as characteristics, which form the basis for a digital representation. Different attribute classes, types and values can be added to the fundamental object of a building, for example the categories administration and public order, traffic and transport, service, business, residential, and culture and leisure. The first steps are therefore:

- Adding existing data to the database: geometries, reconstructed objects, integration of OpenStreetMap data
- Initiation of procedures for checking or securing data harmonisation, data fusion, data quality, data completeness, semantic enriching, plausibility of contained data
- Use of 2D/3D visualisation and geoanalysis for regularly update, monitor, process and disseminate relevant key indicators such as
  - Demographic trends: housing, and infrastructure
  - Socio-economic data: extent of poverty, unemployment, and food insecurity
  - Availability, accessibility and adequacy of health, training, transport and wastewater disposal (i.e. drinking water, wastewater and waste management)

## 6.2 Service-Based Process Chain with Encapsulated Modules

The geospatial software environment provides tools to define, compose, map, and execute workflows. Which allows for a cost-effective and easy to customise development, accessibility anywhere and to a range of devices. The web-based implementation also ensures increased interoperability, which is also reflected in simple commissioning and maintenance. The service-based approach is also characterised by increased security due to encapsulated components that can be flexibly composed and assembled [8].

One key component of the service platform is a powerful, eventually distributed database in which all geospatial data will be stored, harmonised, updated and managed. Along with the classical dimensions of space and time all available semantic attributes of the geospatial objects will be mapped. The basic data sets are acquired from high-resolution stereo aerial imagery and ancillary data from various sources. All data are collected and processed to the requirements of a data model specifically designed for that purpose and aligned to the EU INSPIRE conform schemes. An overview of the modular system component is given in Fig. 4.

For the generation of a virtual clone of an oriental city it is necessary to initially use a consistent reference data set. Since this is usually a problem, this approach also provides a stereophotogrammetric processing of aerial data sets. As an intermediate medium, a so-called point cloud is created, as described above, which is analysed using relatively simple algorithms in order to extract buildings in a first iteration. The parameters of area and angle are the most important in a neighbourhood environment. The point cloud is classified by spatial filter operations. In further steps, classified point clusters are simplified and aggregated. Finally, building outlines are reconstructed using polygon sections. Then building models are constructed according to the scheme of a Level-of-Detail 1 block. These raw buildings serve as a base geometry for a unique

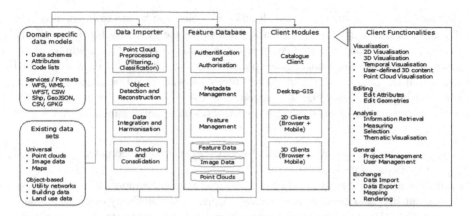

**Fig. 4.** Conceptual overview of relevant system components.

object, which can be semantically enriched in the following. The point cloud as such is also available as another highly accurate visual representation medium. The database act double as a central interface and anchor point for all project-relevant geodata. Robust and easy-to-use basic GIS functionalities are implemented for the provision, analysis and cartographic visualisation of this data. The modular encapsulated architectural and functional building blocks of the system are integrated into the geospatial software environment that support the decision-making-process. To be more precise: Standard interfaces are used to allow access to geodata from and within the spatial database and other tools operating on it that allow users to build 3D maps, e.g., for virtual reconstructions and future planning, to navigate the 3D environment, to access objects of interest and to request thematic data referenced by the objects. The system use means for the design, generation, and use of analytics maps, which represent thematic data such as urban functions, building and infrastructure conditions, where all is mapped to graphics attributes. Stakeholder-specific and application-specific map designs, including colour encodings and signatures, are implemented to allow users to produce their own maps according to their need and lastly to explore, compare, and assess large quantities of multi-dimensional geodata, its structures, and relations by projecting geospatial data to a non-geospatial reference frame using concepts of information cartography and advanced analytics functionalities such as functions to analyse demographic trends per community, ratios relating health services to number of people, housing scarcity, and plans for future housing development amongst other functions. An automated data processes can update the database content and trigger the generation and delivery of thematic maps as meaningful side-effect.

# 7  Conclusion

When fully operational, the web-based service platform allows for the guided composition and analysis of multidimensional, multifaceted virtual models of urban space by expert and non-specialist user groups. It will support both audiences to understand

and document the changing urban situation in East Jerusalem as well as to make informed decisions on urban planning and communal advocacy. It has been argued that the difficulties of a comprehensive database managing, and processing spatial data constitute a bottleneck in handling of spatial issues. This problem can be partially solved by elementarising several functions which are encapsulated in a modular way within a process chain embedded in a software environment. In an ongoing R&D project, the presented web-based approach will be further tested for its feasibility and advantages compared to previously applied limited methods.

Due to its historical development, East Jerusalem is facing dramatic development challenges that affect its urban fabric and community identifying a politically highly sensible environment. Urban agglomerations are evolving and abandoning early established urban concepts. As a result of inadequate urban planning with a strong focus on road infrastructure and housing, the study area also shows a weakly organised structure of neighbourhoods with different functions that lack meaningful distribution [1]. Urban development is poorly regulated as there are no development plans for the region. Some houses and buildings can be erected arbitrarily, which is observable. It is therefore extremely essential to establish a digital inventory of the region using modern technology and technical infrastructure. A first step has been taken with a modelled virtual representation of the study area in order to spatially assess and analyse future developments and to support the local society in their well-founded decision-making-process [8].

**Acknowledgements.** The work discussed here is part of a larger R+D project on East Jerusalem with Palestinian, East Jerusalem, and NGO partners funded by the European Union. Part of this research work is supported by a PhD grant from the HPI Research School for Service-Oriented Systems Engineering at the Hasso Plattner Institute for Digital Engineering, University of Potsdam. The funding of both institutions is gratefully acknowledged.

# References

1. Loibl, W., Etminan, G., Gebetsroither-Geringer, E., Neumann, H.M., Sanchez-Guzman, S.: Characteristics of urban agglomerations in different continents: history, patterns, dynamics, drivers and trends. In: Urban Agglomeration. IntechOpen (2018)
2. Insee (Institut national de la statistique et des études économiques). https://www.insee.fr/fr/metadonnees/definition/c1501. Accessed 03 Apr 2019
3. Miller, H.J., Goodchild, M.F.: Data-driven geography. GeoJournal **80**(4), 449–461 (2015)
4. Mucksch, H., Behme, W. (eds.): Das Data Warehouse-Konzept: Architektur-Datenmodelle-Anwendungen. Springer, Heidelberg (2013)
5. Hart, G., Dolbear, C.: Linked Data: A Geographic Perspective. CRC Press, Boca Raton (2016)
6. Tolpekin, V.A. Stein, A.: The core of GIScience: a systems - based approach. ITC Educational Textbook Series; no. 2012. University of Twente, Faculty of Geo-Information Science and Earth Observation (ITC), Enschede (2012)
7. Burrough, P.A., McDonnell, R., McDonnell, R.A., Lloyd, C.D.: Principles of Geographical Information Systems. Oxford University Press, Oxford (2015)

8. Fricke, A., Döllner, J., Asche, H.: Servicification – trend or paradigm shift in geospatial data processing? In: Gervasi, O., et al. (eds.) ICCSA 2018. LNCS, vol. 10962, pp. 339–350. Springer, Cham (2018). https://doi.org/10.1007/978-3-319-95168-3_23

9. Worboys, M.F.: A unified model for spatial and temporal information. Comput. J. **37**(1), 26–34 (1994)

10. Lü, G., et al.: Geographic scenario: a possible foundation for further development of virtual geographic environments. Int. J. Dig. Earth **11**(4), 356–368 (2018)

11. Galton, A.: Fields and objects in space, time and space-time. Spat. Cogn. Comput. J. **4**(1), 39–68 (2004)

12. Tao, F., Cheng, J., Qi, Q., Zhang, M., Zhang, H., Sui, F.: Digital twin-driven product design, manufacturing and service with big data. Int. J. Adv. Manuf. Technol. **94**(9–12), 3563–3576 (2018)

13. Rigaux, P., Scholl, M., Voisard, A.: Spatial Databases: With Application to GIS. Morgan Kaufmann, San Francisco (2002)

14. Milz, D., Zellner, M., Hoch, C., Radinsky, J., Pudlock, K., Lyons, L.: Reconsidering scale: using geographic information systems to support spatial planning conversations. Plan. Pract. Res. **33**(3), 291–308 (2018)

15. Nama, G.F., Ulvan, M., Ulvan, A., Hanafi, A.M.: Design and implementation web based geographic information system for public services in Bandar Lampung City—Indonesia. In: 2015 International Conference on Science in Information Technology (ICSITech), pp. 270–275. IEEE, October 2015

# Correction to: Workflow Discovery Through Semantic Constraints: A Geovisualization Case Study

Vedran Kasalica and Anna-Lena Lamprecht

**Correction to:**
**Chapter "Workflow Discovery Through Semantic Constraints: A Geovisualization Case Study"**
**in: S. Misra et al. (Eds.):** *Computational Science and Its Applications – ICCSA 2019*, **LNCS 11621,**
**https://doi.org/10.1007/978-3-030-24302-9_34**

The original version of the chapter starting on p. 473 unfortunately contained a mistake. The presentation of Figures 4 and 5 was incorrect. The figures have been corrected.

The updated version of this chapter can be found at
https://doi.org/10.1007/978-3-030-24302-9_34

© Springer Nature Switzerland AG 2019
S. Misra et al. (Eds.): ICCSA 2019, LNCS 11621, p. C1, 2019.
https://doi.org/10.1007/978-3-030-24302-9_53

# Author Index

Printed in the United States
By Bookmasters